Handbook of Interest and Annuity Tables

Contents

Preface vii
Explanation of Tables 1
Practice Problems and Solutions 15
Conversion Table 19

MONTHLY COMPOUNDING SECTION 23

Table 1—Future Worth of One Dollar with Interest 23
Table 2—Future Worth of One Dollar per Period with Interest 41
Table 3—Sinking Fund Factors 59
Table 4—Present Worth of One Dollar 77
Table 5—Present Worth of One Dollar per Period 95
Table 6—Partial Payment to Amortize 1 113

QUARTERLY COMPOUNDING SECTION 131

Table 1—Future Worth of One Dollar with Interest 131
Table 2—Future Worth of One Dollar per Period with Interest 149
Table 3—Sinking Fund Factors 167
Table 4—Present Worth of One Dollar 185
Table 5—Present Worth of One Dollar per Period 203
Table 6—Partial Payment to Amortize 1 221

SEMIANNUAL COMPOUNDING SECTION 239

Table 1—Future Worth of One Dollar with Interest 239
Table 2—Future Worth of One Dollar per Period with Interest 257
Table 3—Sinking Fund Factors 275
Table 4—Present Worth of One Dollar 293
Table 5—Present Worth of One Dollar per Period 311
Table 6—Partial Payment to Amortize 1 329

ANNUAL COMPOUNDING SECTION 347

Table 1—Future Worth of One Dollar with Interest 347
Table 2—Future Worth of One Dollar per Period with Interest 367
Table 3—Sinking Fund Factors 387
Table 4—Present Worth of One Dollar 407
Table 5—Present Worth of One Dollar per Period 427
Table 6—Partial Payment to Amortize 1 447

Preface

This book is concerned with the effects that compound interest and time have on money. It is intended primarily for people in real estate, banking, and finance who are involved in making investment decisions and need tools and methods to evaluate investment opportunities. It is also useful for students of business administration and those nonmathematically inclined members of the public who want to be able to easily measure or evaluate financial opportunities.

Although books similar to this one are on the market, most of them presuppose that the user is skilled in higher mathematics. Perhaps the most welcome feature of this book is that the tables are explained in such a way that anyone with the ability to add, subtract, multiply, and divide can understand their makeup and learn how to use them effectively. There are no complicated formulas—only straightforward, simple explanations.

After an easy-to-understand discussion of compound interest, each table is described and explained. Some typical problems and their solutions are given, which serve not only to illustrate how to use each table but also to introduce the techniques of problem solving.

The tables show the effect of compound interest and time on one monetary unit under six different situations. In the United States, the monetary unit is $1, but the tables can just as easily be used for any other monetary unit. The amounts given can be multiplied by any amount larger than $1 to assist in determining values. Tables such as these are nothing more than precomputed series of calculations set forth in an orderly manner for easy use. Each table is presented for monthly, quarterly, semiannual, and annual compounding periods, with the entire span of interest rates covered in each of the compounding periods.

The rate coverage for all compounding periods is from 5 through 22¾ percent in increments of ¼ percent, with additional coverage from 23 to 30 percent in increments of 1 percent in the annual tables.

The amounts are presented with ten decimal places for extreme accuracy when needed.

The key to using these tables successfully is in being able to select the proper table for the problem being solved. A short time spent with the instructions and practice problems should give you a clear understanding of the construction and use of each table and enable you to answer questions such as the following:

1. If your savings institution pays 6 percent interest, compounded annually, what will be the value at the end of 15 years of an initial deposit of $1,000 made today?

2. Your savings bank pays 6½ percent interest, compounded monthly. If you deposit $10 at the end of each month for the next 10 years, how much money will you have?

3. You will need $20,000 in 20 years, and you can get 7 percent interest, compounded quarterly. How much must you deposit at the end of each quarter to accumulate the required amount?

4. If you want 8 percent interest, compounded twice a year, what should you pay today so that 25 years from now you will receive $17,500?

5. If current interest rates are 8½ percent, compounded monthly, what should you pay today to receive $100 at the end of each month for the next 60 months?

6. If you borrow $25,000 for 30 years at 10 percent, compounded monthly, how much must you pay back at the end of each month to fully repay both the amount borrowed and the interest?

I wish to express may deep appreciation to Robert A. Arnold of Computer Sciences Corporation and to Sandor Rosenberg, a computer programmer, whose knowledge and dedication to precision and accuracy have made these tables possible. I would also like to express my indebtedness to W. Z. Smith, Jr., Director, Systems, Airline Tariff Publishing Company, for the use of unique printing equipment which made possible presentation of these tables in clear, easy-to-read type.

Jack C. Estes

Explanation of Tables

Tables such as the ones presented here are generally called compound interest and annuity tables. The names of the six tables vary from one text to another; we chose the name that seemed most descriptive of the function of each table. Regardless of the names used, the amounts shown are standard.

Before the individual tables are discussed, we present a review of compound interest and annuity and clarify a few terms.

An *annuity* is generally thought of as a regular series of payments, of equal amounts, made or received at regular intervals of time, such as monthly, quarterly, semiannually, or annually.

Simple interest is interest earned on the original principal only, during the entire life of the loan.

Compound interest is interest earned and then added to the original investment so that it, too, begins to earn interest. Simply stated, it is interest on interest.

The number of times per year that interest is earned and converted or added to the principal is called the *frequency of compounding*. The time span between compoundings is called the *interest period* (or the period). For instance, if interest is added only once a year, it is compounded annually. If interest is added twice a year, it is said to be compounded semiannually. Four interest additions per year would be quarterly compounding, and interest added once per month would be monthly compounding. The more times interest is compounded in a year, the greater will be the amount of interest earned in a year.

Interest rates are generally stated on an annual basis. If someone *simply* says "10 percent interest," 10 percent per annum is meant. This would mean that $1 deposited for one year would earn 10 cents interest. The interest rate shown at the top of each column in the tables in this book is the *annual rate* (also called the nominal rate or the nominal annual rate). The monthly, quarterly, and semiannual compounding tables have been computed using the rate per conversion period, which is the annual rate divided by the number of compoundings per year. For example, 12 percent interest compounded monthly would be 1 percent per compounding period, or 1 percent per month (.12 ÷ 12); quarterly compounding would be 3 percent (.12 ÷ 4); and semiannual compounding would be 6 percent (.12 ÷ 2). Refer to the conversion table, pages 19–22, which shows the annual percentage rate, as well as the fractional rate and its decimal equivalent per compounding period, for the monthly, quarterly, and semiannual tables.

Let's compare $1 deposited at 12 percent for one year under four different circumstances—at simple interest, annual compounding, semiannual compounding, and quarterly compounding.

Simple interest		
$1.00 × .12		.12
Annual compounding		
$1.00 × .12		.12
Semiannual compounding		
First period		
$1.00 × .06	.06	
Second period		
$1.00 + .06 = $1.06		
$1.06 × .06	.0636	
Total interest for year		.1236
Quarterly compounding		
First period		
$1.00 × .03	.03	
Second period		
$1.00 + .03 = $1.03		
$1.03 × .03	.0309	
Third period		
$1.03 + .0309 = $1.0609		
$1.0609 × .03	.031827	
Fourth period		
$1.0609 + .031827 = $1.092727		
$1.092727 × .03	.03278181	
Total interest for year		.12550881

As you can see, the amounts earned by simple interest and by annual compounding for one year are the same (but only for one year). In fact, until interest earned is added to the principal and begins to earn interest, it is simple interest. The only difference is in what happens to the 12 cents. Under simple interest, it would generally be paid to the investor. Under compound interest, it would be added to the original deposit and it, too, would earn interest for the second interest period. You will see how this takes place in the semiannual and quarterly compounding examples. You will also see that semiannual compounding results in more interest than annual compounding and that quarterly compounding results in more interest than semiannual compounding. Again, monthly compounding results in more total interest than quarterly compounding. In this example, the 12 percent interest compounded semiannually results in actual earnings of .1236, or an effective rate of 12.36 percent. Quarterly compounding results in an effective rate of 12.55 percent. Keep in mind that interest compounded more often than annually will actually earn more than the annual rate quoted. Always make certain you select the proper compounding period suitable for the problem you are solving.

The procedure used in the foregoing semiannual and quarterly compounding examples is the one that is used to make up Table 1—Future Worth of One Dollar with Interest. The other five tables are variations of Table 1. All tables are designed to assist you in calculating values under six different circumstances, which are described and illustrated in the instructions to follow. The compound interest and annuity tables provide answers related to the growth or the diminishment of an investment. In the final analysis, however, the user must rely on his or her judgment concerning selection of the rates to be used, depending on the risk of the particular investment being considered.

Each of these circumstances and its associated table, is concerned with the calculation of a value. There are two major categories of value: future value and present value. Tables 1, 2, and 3 are associated with the calculation of future value; Tables 4, 5, and 6 are concerned with the calculation of present value.

Future value pertains to the value that will exist at some time in the future. *Present value* is the value as of today of a sum or sums of money to be collected or paid in the future. In the example of quarterly compounding, an original deposit of $1 was shown to grow to $1.12550881. This is future value. Now the present value of $1.12550881 payable one year from now (and taken at 12 percent interest compounded quarterly) is $1.00.

A word here about rounding and accuracy is in order. The most frequently used rounding procedure is as follows:

1. Decide on the number of digits to be retained.
2. If the next digit to the right is above 5, add 1 to the last digit retained.
3. If the next digit to the right is below 5, leave the last digit as it is.
4. When the next digit to the right is 5 followed by zeros, if the preceding number is even, leave it as is. If the preceding number is odd, add 1 to it.

EXAMPLE: Round to six decimals:

5.1234 567 435	rounded to	5.123457
1.4364 534 628	rounded to	1.436453
3.2396 545 000	rounded to	3.239654
7.8943 635 000	rounded to	7.894364

The tables in the book are carried to ten decimals to provide extreme accuracy when desired. For most purposes, fewer decimals would be accurate enough. To save time, never use more decimals than needed. The ten decimals are arranged so that it is easy to use four decimals or seven, for example, 1.1234 567 890. Just round to the number of decimals you need and proceed. A general rule to follow is to use one more digit in the factor than the number of digits expected in the answer.

1. Estimate the number of digits expected in the answer.
2. Use one more digit than that expected in the answer.
3. Round as discussed above.

EXAMPLE: How many decimals should you use to multiply $1,000 by a factor of 2.1589 249 973? The factor is more than 2 and less than 3; therefore, the answer will be between $2,000 and $3,000. In any event, it will contain six digits, so round the factor to seven digits and proceed:

2.1589 249 973 rounded to 2.1589 250

$1,000 × 2.1589 250 = $2,158.9250 rounded to $2,158.92

If the amount to be multiplied by the factor had been $15.00, we would have needed only five digits; if it were $6.00, we would have used only four digits.

When computing long-term payments, it is desirable to deviate from normally mathematical correct rounding and round up *any* fractional portion of a cent. Perhaps the importance of this can best be explained by quoting from the preface of the *Handbook of Loan Payment Tables**:

> One deviation from absolute accuracy has been made in the rounding procedure. Normally, when computing payments or interest, any half cent or greater would be rounded up, and anything less than a half cent would be dropped. In these tables, any portion of a cent has been rounded up. This was done to ensure that any loan would be fully paid within the time periods specified, without a large lump sum payment at the end. With rounding up of any fraction of a cent, the user can be sure to repay fully the loan within the time period shown.

TABLE 1—FUTURE WORTH OF ONE DOLLAR WITH INTEREST

This table is also called "Amount of 1," "Amount of 1 at Compound Interest," and "Compound Amount of 1." It shows the future growth, with interest, of a *single* deposit of $1 made at the beginning of the first period. Note that, in this table, the deposit is made only once, at the *beginning* of the first period. For *all* other tables, the deposit or payment will be made periodically or repeatedly at the *end* of the period.

Let's work another example, but here we will multiply the principal amount at the beginning of each period by 1 plus the rate per period. The end result will be the same as multiplying the principal by the rate per period to get the interest and then adding it to the principal amount.

EXAMPLE: If $1.00 were to be deposited at the beginning of the first year at 6 percent interest compounded annually, what would be the value of the deposit at the end of the fifth year?

Beginning of first year—deposit	= $1.00
End of first year: $1.00 × 1.06	= $1.06
End of second year: $1.06 × 1.06	= $1.1236
End of third year: $1.1236 × 1.06	= $1.1910 160
End of fourth year: $1.1910 160 × 1.06	= $1.2624 769 600
End of fifth year: $1.2624 769 600 × 1.06	= $1.3382 255 776

*By Jack C. Estes, McGraw-Hill, New York, 1976.

Our original deposit has now grown to the figure above, which is the amount shown in the annual section, Table 1, at 6 percent for five years, page 348. If our deposit had been other than $1, we could have obtained the answer by multiplying the specific deposit by the amount shown above. For example, had our deposit been $500, we would have multiplied $500 × 1.3382 255 776, which comes to $669.1127, or $669.11.

Using the techniques shown above, we could if necessary devise a future worth table for as many time periods as we desired. However, even with an electronic calculator, this would require considerable time and effort. Instead, by referring to Table 1, we find that all the information we need is supplied.

Let's now do the previous example using the full 10 decimals, then seven decimals rounded, then four decimals:

$500 × 1.3382 255 776 = $669.11
$500 × 1.3382 256 = $669.11
$500 × 1.3382 = $669.10

As you can see, the variation is not great. Of course, working with larger sums would produce larger variations.

PROBLEM: If your savings institution pays 6 percent interest, compounded annually, what will be the value at the end of 15 years of an initial deposit of $1,000 made today?

SOLUTION: Referring to the annual compounding section, Future Worth of One Dollar with Interest, Table 1, under the 6 percent column, page 348 we find opposite 15 years the amount 2.3965 581 931. This amount multiplied by your original deposit of $1,000 equals $2,396.56, the future worth of your investment.

TABLE 2—FUTURE WORTH OF ONE DOLLAR PER PERIOD WITH INTEREST

This table is also called "Amount of 1 per Period," "Accumulation of 1 per Period," "Compound Amount of 1 per Period," and "Amount of Annuity of 1 per Period." It shows the future growth of a *series* of deposits of $1, made at the *end* of each period.

Remember that in Table 1 the deposit is made at the beginning of the period, whereas the other five tables are based on the deposit being made at the end of the period. The first figure shown in Table 2 is $1, which represents the deposit just made at the end of the first period and which, obviously, did not earn any interest.

The amounts to which a series of deposits will grow, as shown in Table 2, can be broken down into how much a deposit of $1 will grow in one period, how much a deposit of $1 will grow in two periods, how much in three periods, and so on, as shown in Table 1. Considered in this manner, then, Table 2 is nothing more than an addition of the amounts shown in Table 1. However, to compensate for the difference between the time of deposit of Table 1 and of Table 2, it is only necessary to add four time periods from Table 1 plus the deposit just made to construct Table 2 for five periods. For example, to obtain the amount to which $1, deposited at the end of each year for five years at 6 percent, compounded annually, will grow, add the first four years from Table 1, then add $1.

FROM TABLE 1:

First deposit: value at end of fourth year after deposit	=	$1.2624 769 600
Second deposit: value at end of third year after deposit	=	1.1910 160 000
Third deposit: value at end of second year after deposit	=	1.1236 000 000
Fourth deposit: value at end of first year after deposit	=	1.0600 000 000
Fifth deposit: value at time of deposit	=	1.0000 000 000
		$5.6370 929 600

which is the future worth of $1 deposited at the end of each year at 6 percent, compounded annually for five years, as shown in Table 2.

Perhaps this can be more clearly seen by the following table, which shows how $1 deposited at the end of each year will grow. Each periodic deposit is indicated by an asterisk, with its successive values shown to the right along the same horizontal line. The five-year column is then added to determine the amount to which the five separate deposits will grow by the end of the fifth year, which results in the same amount as the previous example.

First year	*Second year*	*Third year*	*Fourth year*	*Fifth year*
$1.00*	$1.06	$1.1236	$1.1910 160	$1.2624 769 600
	1.00*	1.0600	1.1236 000	1.1910 160 000
		1.00*	1.0600 000	1.1236 000 000
			1.00*	1.0600 000 000
				1.00*
				$5.6370 929 600

Note: In both examples, the final figure is the exact amount that is shown in the annual compounding section of Table 2 under 6 percent for five years, page 368. However, this will not always be the case. Each amount shown in the tables has been individually computed using 18 decimals before rounding to 10 places. This will often cause a variation in figures obtained by adding amounts from another table.

Had our annual deposit been $500 at 6 percent compounded annually for five years, we would have $500 × 5.6370 929 600 = $2,818.5464, or $2,818.55.

PROBLEM: Your savings bank pays 6½ percent interest, compounded monthly. If you deposit $10 at the end of each month for the next ten years, how much money will you have?

SOLUTION: Referring to the monthly compounding section, Future Worth of One Dollar per Period with Interest, Table 2, under the 6½ percent column, page 42, we find opposite 120 periods (10 years) the amount 168.4031 542 385. This multiplied by your regular deposit of $10 is $1,684.03, which is the amount you will have in 10 years.

TABLE 3—SINKING FUND FACTORS

This table is also called "Sinking Fund Payment," "Annuity Whose Accumulation at Compound Interest Is 1," and "Periodic Payment of Annuity Whose Amount Is 1." It shows the amount of regular deposits which must be made at the *end* of each period to accumulate $1 by some future date.

A sinking fund table is used when it is desired to accumulate a stipulated amount through regular deposits over a certain period of time. Some practical examples would be a person needing to accumulate money to pay off a note coming due; parents wishing to set up a college education fund; an apartment house owner desiring to put aside a sum each month for equipment replacement at some future date.

Without taking interest into consideration, if you needed $1 five years from now, you could divide $1 by five and determine that you would need to deposit 20 cents each year to accumulate the $1. For our purposes, however, we wish to determine the amount to be deposited each year, with interest, in order to accumulate $1. The amount we need then will be less than the 20 cents required when interest is not taken into account.

Table 2 shows the amount to which a series of deposits of $1, with interest, will grow in a certain period of time. We need to determine the amount of deposit necessary to accumulate $1, just the reciprocal of Table 2. Therefore, if we divide $1 by the amount shown in Table 2, we should have the periodic payment needed to accumulate $1 within a comparable period of time, as shown in Table 3.

Let's assume we wish to accumulate $500 in five years through regular payments annually. Also assume that we can get 6 percent compounded annually. If our reasoning is correct, we can divide $1 by the amount to which a series of annual deposits of $1 will grow at the above rates and time from Table 2, then multiply the result by $500 to determine the amount of the annual deposits required to accumulate the \$500: $\frac{1}{5.6370\ 929\ 600} = .1773\ 964\ 004$, which is the annual deposit needed to accumulate $1. This is the amount shown in the annual compounding section, Table 3, at 6 percent for five years, page 388. Thus, .1773 964 004 × \$500 = \$88.6982, rounded to $88.70. In this case, we would have rounded up any fractional part of a cent to assure accumulating the required amount within the time period.

Now, let's check to see if our procedure has been correct.

		Balance at end of each year
First year		
Initial deposit made at *end* of year		
		$ 88.70
Second year		
$88.70 × 1.06	$ 94.02	
Plus another deposit	88.70	
		$182.72
Third year		
$182.72 × 1.06	$193.69	
Plus another deposit	88.70	
		$282.39
Fourth year		
$282.39 × 1.06	$299.33	
Plus another deposit	88.70	
		$388.03
Fifth year		
$388.03 × 1.06	$411.31	
Plus another deposit	88.70	
		$500.01

We have accumulated the required amount; therefore, our procedure was correct. Note that we have actually accumulated 1 cent more than required. Some variation is to be expected because of rounding of the annual deposit and the interest.

PROBLEM: You will need $20,000 in 20 years, and you can get 7 percent interest, compounded quarterly. How much must you deposit at the end of each quarter to accumulate the required amount?

SOLUTION: Referring to the quarterly compounding section, Sinking Fund Factors, Table 3, under the 7 percent column, page 169, we find opposite 80 periods (20 years) the amount .0058 209 310. This multiplied by your future need of $20,000 is $116.42, which must be your regular quarterly deposit to accumulate the needed amount in 20 years.

TABLE 4—PRESENT WORTH OF ONE DOLLAR

This table is also called "Present Worth of 1," "Present Value Reversion of 1," "Present Value of 1," and "Present Value of 1 at Compound Interest." It shows the present worth of $1 which is to be collected in one lump sum at the *end* of a given time.

To determine the present value of a lump sum payment to be received in the future requires nothing more than a reversal of the compounding procedure. Instead of adding interest each conversion period, it is necessary to subtract or discount interest from the amount to be received in the future.

Table 1 shows how much a single deposit of $1 will grow, with interest. The present value of a single $1 future payment, as shown in Table 2, is just the reciprocal of Table 1. Therefore, if we divide $1 by the amount shown in Table 1, we should have the discounted amount for a comparable period and rate for Table 4.

Let's try another example to see if this reasoning is valid. Assume that a friend wants to borrow money to be repaid, with interest, in one lump sum of $500 at the end of five years. If you expect 6 percent, compounded annually, what amount would you be justified in lending your friend today?

Referring to the example in Table 1, we see that $1 deposited at the beginning of the first period will grow to 1.3382 255 776 in five years, when compounded annually at 6 percent. So, let's divide $1 by that amount: $\frac{1}{1.3382\ 255\ 776} = .7472\ 581\ 729$, which is the present worth of $1 to be received five years from now. This amount times $500 equals $373.6291, or $373.63, which is the amount you should lead your friend to achieve the return you want on your investment.

If our calculations are correct, we should be able to deposit the $373.63 in a bank at the rates and terms specified and have $500 at the end of the five years. Remember: in Table 1 the deposit is made at the beginning of the first period.

	Balance at end of each year
First year $373.63 × 1.06	$396.05
Second year $396.05 × 1.06	$419.81
Third year $419.91 × 1.06	$445.00
Fourth year $445.00 × 1.06	$471.70
Fifth year $471.70 × 1.06	$500.00

We have accumulated the required amount; therefore, our procedure must have been correct. In this example, we ended up with exactly the amount desired without variation, but, again, variation caused by rounding is not unusual.

PROBLEM: If you want 8 percent interest, compounded twice a year, what should you pay today so that 25 years from now you will receive $17,500?

SOLUTION: Referring to the semiannual compounding section, Present Worth of One Dollar, Table 4, under the 8 percent column, page 296, opposite 50 periods (25 years), we find .1407 126 153. This amount times the future receipt of $17,500 is $2,462.47, which is the present worth of that future payment.

TABLE 5—PRESENT WORTH OF ONE DOLLAR PER PERIOD

This table is also called "Present Worth of 1 per Period," "Present Value of Ordinary Annuity 1 per Period," and "Present Value of 1 per Period at Compound Interest." It shows the present worth of a *series* of receipts of $1 at the *end* of each period for a specified number of periods into the future. The most common use of this table is to measure the present worth of a specific number of future periodic payments, such as those from annuities and investment income.

You will recall that Table 2 was concerned with determining the total amount that would be accumulated at some time in the future by making a specific number of equal deposits. That amount to be collected in the future is the future worth. Now we want to determine the present value—or the value today—of the same series of future deposits. In other words, what should you be willing to pay in cash today for the right to receive a certain series of payments of $1 each? For example, the present worth of $1 to be received at the end of each of the next five years is equal to the present worth of $1 to be received one year from now, plus the sum of the present worths of $1 to be received two, three, four, and five years from now. Therefore, if we add the amounts shown in Table 4 for the first five years, we should obtain the desired amount for Table 5 for five years. Referring to the annual compounding section, Table 4 at 6 percent, page 408, we see:

FROM TABLE 4:		*For Table 5: cumulative total*
First year	.9433 962 264	.9433 962 264
Second year	.8899 964 400	1.8333 926 664
Third year	.8396 192 830	2.6730 119 495
Fourth year	.7920 936 632	3.4651 056 127
Fifth year	.7472 581 729	4.2123 637 856

which is a variation of 1 in the tenth decimal place from that amount shown for the comparable compounding period, rate and term, Table 5, page 428.

Accordingly, the right to receive $1 at the end of each year for five years is today worth $4.2123 637 855, or $4.21, if we are to obtain 6 percent, compounded annually on our investment. Stated another way, if we place $4.21 in the bank today under the above conditions, we would be able to withdraw $1 at the end of each of the next five years, at which time our funds would be exhausted. Let's use an example of 6 percent, annual compounding for five years, and $500 to see if we can verify our procedure.

The right to receive $500 at the end of each year for five years is worth $500 × 4.2123 637 856 (from previous example), which equals $2,106.18. Let's deposit this amount in the bank today and see if we can withdraw $500 at the end of each of the next five years.

Keep in mind that, in Table 5, payments (in this case, withdrawals) are made at the end of the year. However, the initial deposit would be in the bank at the beginning of the first year.

		Balance at end of each year
First year		
$2,106.18 × 1.06	$2,232.55	
Minus $500	500.00	
		$1,732.55
Second year		
$1,732.55 × 1.06	$1,836.50	
Minus $500	500.00	
		$1,336.50
Third year		
$1,336.50 × 1.06	$1,416.69	
Minus $500	500.00	
		$ 916.69
Fourth year		
$916.69 × 1.06	$ 971.69	
Minus $500	500.00	
		$ 471.69
Fifth year		
$471.69 × 1.06	$ 499.99	
	500.00	
		$ −.01

We have again determined that our construction of a table is valid, even though we are 1 cent short because of rounding.

PROBLEM: If current interest rates are 8½ percent, compounded monthly, what should you pay today to receive $100 at the end of each month for the next 60 months?

SOLUTION: Referring to the monthly compounding section, Present Worth of One Dollar per Period, Table 5, under the 8½ percent column, page 98, opposite 60 months, we find 48.7411 826 131. When this amount is multiplied by the regular payment to be received ($100), it is equal to $4,874.12, which is the present worth of such a series of payments.

TABLE 6—PARTIAL PAYMENT TO AMORTIZE 1

This table is also called "Periodic Payment to Amortize 1," "Investment to Amortize 1," "Annuity Whose Present Value at Compound Interest is 1," or just "Partial Payment." It shows the amount of the equal, regular payment required to repay both principal amount and the interest on a loan with payments made at the end of each period. Its most common use is to determine the amounts of regular payments necessary to repay a mortgage or other long-term loan.

Table 5 shows the amount you must deposit today to be able to withdraw a series of $1 amounts. Table 6 shows how much you can withdraw at the end of each time period in the future if you have $1 today. Therefore, Table 6 is just the reciprocal of Table 5. If we divide $1 by the amount shown in Table 5, we should obtain the corresponding entry for Table 6. Let's use another example and see.

If you borrow $500 at 6 percent compounded annually to be repaid in equal annual payments for five years, how much will your payments be? We saw in the example used in the discussion of Table 5 that the present worth of $1 per period for five years at 6 percent compounded annually was 4.2123 637 856. So, let's divide 1 by that amount: $\frac{1}{4.2123\ 637\ 856} = .2373\ 964\ 4004$, which is the annual payment required to repay $1 under the terms and conditions outlined. Thus, $500 × .2373 964 4004 = $118.6982 2002, or $118.70, per annum payment required to repay a $500 loan in five years at 6 percent, compounded annually. Let's see if this will fully repay both principal and interest.

		Balance at end of each year
First year		
$500 × 1.06	$530.00	
Less payment	118.70	
		$411.30
Second year		
$411.30 × 1.06	$435.98	
Less payment	118.70	
		$317.28
Third year		
$317.28 × 1.06	$336.31	
Less payment	118.70	
		$217.61
Fourth year		
$217.61 × 1.06	$230.67	
Less payment	118.70	
		$111.97
Fifth year		
$111.97 × 1.06	$118.69	
Less payment	118.70	
		$ −.01

Again our procedure is correct.

PROBLEM: If you borrow $25,000 for 30 years at 10 percent, compounded monthly, how much must you pay back at the end of each month to fully repay both the amount borrowed and interest?

SOLUTION: Referring to the monthly compounding section, Partial Payment to Amortize 1, Table 6, under the 10 percent column, page 118, opposite 360 periods (30 years), we find .0087 757 157. This is then multiplied by $25,000, and it equals $219.40, which is the monthly payment required.

Practice Problems and Solutions

One of the best ways to develop an understanding of these tables is to work some practice problems. The following problems, with suggested solutions, were developed for this purpose.

Many of the practice problems require the use of two or more tables, and these may seem unduly complicated. Just break the problem into individual steps and work on one at a time. That way, solving a complex problem becomes no more than solving a series of individual simple problems.

Another good way to become more familiar with these tables is to take an actual or simulated situation, develop a problem concerning it, work it out, then prove it in a way similar to that of some of the examples used in explaining the tables.

PROBLEM: You deposit $750 in a savings account at 6 percent compounded monthly. If the interest rate changes to 6½ percent at the end of the sixth year, how much will you have at the end of 10 years?

SOLUTION: Solving this type of problem requires nothing more than measuring the growth of the initial deposit for the first six years and then depositing that amount for an additional four-year period.

Refer to the monthly compounding section, Table 1, 6 percent opposite six years. The amount there, 1.4320 442 785, times $750 equals $1,074.03 as the amount to be deposited for an additional four years at 6½ percent. The total amount you have at the end of 10 years is 1.2960 204 354 × $1,074.03 = $1,391.96.

PROBLEM: You originate a $25,000, 30-year loan, to be repaid in equal monthly payments at 10 percent, compounded monthly. What is the unpaid balance at the end of the first five years?

SOLUTION: This problem requires the use of three separate tables.

First, you must determine the amount of the regular monthly payment required to amortize the loan. Refer to the monthly compounding section, Table 6, 10 percent column, 360 months, page 118. The amount there, .0087 757 157, times $25,000 equals $219.392892500, rounded up to $219.40, the monthly payment required to amortize the loan.

Second, consider how much the original loan would have grown if no payments had been made. Refer to the monthly compounding section, Table 1, 10 percent, 60 months, page 28. The amount there, 1.6453 089 348, times $25,000 equals $41,132.72, which is the amount now owed.

Third, assume that the regular monthly payments had been deposited into a savings account at 10 percent, compounded monthly for 60 months. Refer to Table 2, page 46. That amount, 77.4370 721 734, multiplied by $219.40 equals $16,989.69, the amount your regular monthly payments have accumulated.

Now, if you subtract the result obtained in the third step from that of the second step, you should have the unpaid balance at the end of the fifth year.

Result from second step	$41,132.72
Result from third step	16,989.69
Unpaid balance	$24,143.03

Note: Because of the variation caused by rounding, the actual balance could vary slightly.

ALTERNATIVE SOLUTION: First, compute the monthly payment as above.

Second, assume the principal reduction is deposited into a savings account at the same interest rate and compounding periods as those on the loan, and also assume that this same amount is deposited into a savings account each time period for the time span you are working with. $25,000 × 10 percent = $2500 per annum interest ÷ 12 months = 208.33333333 as the first month's interest.

Regular monthly payment	$219.40
First month's interest	208.33333333
Principal reduction	$ 11.06666667

Third, refer to the monthly compounding section, Table 2, 10 percent, for 60 months, page 46. That amount is 77.4370 721 734 times 11.0666 666 667 equals 856.97, the amount of principal reduction at the end of the first five years.

Original loan balance	$25,000.00
Principal reduction	856.97
Loan balance	$24,143.03

PROBLEM: If you expect 8½ percent, compounded annually, on your investments, what should you pay for the right to receive $1,600 at the beginning of each year for the next 15 years?

SOLUTION: This is a little different from any problems thus far. Table 5 is constructed with payments at the end of each period. In this problem you will, in effect, have $1,600 of your initial investment returned to you immediately. Then you will receive $1,600 at the end of each of the next 14 years. Refer to the annual compounding section, Table 5, 8½ percent, for 14 years. The amount is $1,600 × 8.0100 966 847 = $12,816.15. To this add the immediate return of $1,600 = $14,416.15 as the amount you should pay for the income.

Another, perhaps more direct, solution would be to add 1 to the 14-year amount: thus, 8.0100 966 847 + 1 = 9.0100 966 847 × $1,600 = $14,416.15.

PROBLEM: You have inherited a parcel of land containing a small store which is under lease for 18 more years at a monthly rental of $325. Because of the changing character of the area, you expect the property to be worth $65,000 when the lease expires. What is the value of your inheritance if current interest rates are 7½ percent compounded monthly?

SOLUTION: In this problem, there are two values: the rental income and the right to receive $65,000 at the end of the lease period.

Refer to the monthly compounding section, Table 5, 7½ percent opposite 18 years (216 months). The amount, 118.3469 302 617, times $325 equals $38,462.75, the present worth of the series of rent payments. Now refer to the monthly compounding section, Table 4, 7½ percent, opposite 18 years (216 months). The amount, .2603 316 859, multiplied by $65,000 equals $16,921.56, which is the present worth of $65,000 to be received 18 years from now. Add these two values together: $38,462.75 + $16,921.56 = $55,384.31. This is the total value of your inheritance.

PROBLEM: You will start receiving income from a trust fund starting five years from now. This income will be $4,150 every six months, and it will continue for 20 years from the time you start receiving it. If the current interest rates are 5½ percent compounded semiannually, what is the present worth of your future receipts?

SOLUTION: The easiest way to solve this problem is to consider the present worth of the future income as if it were to start today and rerun a full 25 years. Then subtract from that value the present worth of the receipts for the first five years which you will *not* receive. Refer to the semiannual compounding section, Table 5, 5½ percent column, opposite 25 years (50 periods). That amount is 26.9971 699 802. Subtract from this the amount shown in the same table opposite five years (10 periods): 8.6400 761 634. Then 26.9971 699 802 minus 8.6400 761 634 equals 18.3570 938 168. Multiplying by $4,150, we arrive at $76,181.94 as the present worth of $4,150 every six months for the next 20 years, but delayed five years in starting.

ALTERNATIVE SOLUTION: Another way to solve this problem is to estimate the present worth of the series of receipts for the 20-year period, then to discount the receipt of that worth because it will be delayed for five years. Refer to the semiannual compounding section, Table 5, 5½ percent, opposite 20 years (40 periods). That amount, 24.0781 010 600, times $4,150 equals $99,924.12. Now consider this as a lump sum payment you will receive five years (10 periods) from now. Refer to the semiannual compounding section, Table 4, 5½ percent, opposite 10 periods. The amount, .7623 979 055, times $99,924.12 equals $76,181.94, the present worth of your receipts.

PROBLEM: You plan to retire as soon as you can accumulate $80,000. You can get 7 percent, compounded annually. If you deposit $1,750 at the end of each year, how long will it be before you are able to retire?

SOLUTION: To solve this type of problem, you must first determine how much each $1 of your annual deposits will have to grow in order to reach your desired objective. You would therefore divide the $80,000 by the annual deposits of $1,750, making 45.7142 857 143 the amount that each $1 of the annual deposits will have to amount to.

Refer to the annual compounding section, Table 2, 7 percent column, and follow it down to the figure closest to 45.7142 857 143. The amount falls between 21 and 22 years and is closer to 21 years. For our purposes, let's use the 21-year amount of 44.8651 767 837. Multiplying that by $1,750, we obtain $78,514.06, the amount you will have at the end of 21 years.

ADDITIONAL PROBLEM: Suppose that you were not able to start your retirement plan for five years but had some money now, and that you still wanted to have approximately $80,000 by the end of the original 21-year period, and that after five years you could make the annual deposits of $1,750. How much would you have to deposit today to start your program?

SOLUTION: Consider how much you would now have if you had made the regular deposits each year for five years. Refer to the annual compounding section, Table 2, 7 percent, opposite five years. You will see that each $1 deposited would have amounted to $5.7507 390 100. This amount times $1,750 equals $10,063.79, the amount you would now have. If you deposit that amount now, then make your regular deposits of $1,750 each year for the next 16 years, you should accumulate $78,514.06 by the end of the original 21-year period.

You can test this by referring to the same table opposite 16 years. That amount, 27.8880 535 509, times $1,750 equals $48,804.09, which is the amount now accumulated from the annual deposits for 16 years. Now add the amount your $10,063.79 initial deposit would have grown by referring to Table 1, annual compounding, 7 percent. This amount, 2.9521 637 486, multiplied by $10,063.79, will equal $29,709.96. Thus, $29,709.96 + $48,804.09 = $78,514.05.

Conversion Table

Showing the Rate per Conversion Period and Its Decimal Equivalent

Annual	*Semiannual*	*Quarterly*	*Monthly*
5 .050000	2 1/2 .025000	1 1/4 .012500	5/12 .004167
5 1/4 .052500	2 5/8 .026250	1 5/16 .013125	7/16 .004375
5 1/2 .055000	2 3/4 .027500	1 3/8 .013750	11/24 .004583
5 3/4 .057500	2 7/8 .028750	1 7/16 .014375	23/48 .004792
6 .060000	3 .030000	1 1/2 .015000	1/2 .005000
6 1/4 .062500	3 1/8 .031250	1 9/16 .015625	25/48 .005208
6 1/2 .065000	3 1/4 .032500	1 5/8 .016250	13/24 .005417
6 3/4 .067500	3 3/8 .033750	1 11/16 .016875	9/16 .005625
7 .070000	3 1/2 .035000	1 3/4 .017500	7/12 .005833
7 1/4 .072500	3 5/8 .036250	1 13/16 .018125	29/48 .006042
7 1/2 .075000	3 3/4 .037500	1 7/8 .018750	5/8 .006250
7 3/4 .077500	3 7/8 .038750	1 15/16 .019375	31/48 .006458
8 .080000	4 .040000	2 .020000	2/3 .006667
8 1/4 .082500	4 1/8 .041250	2 1/16 .020625	11/16 .006875
8 1/2 .085000	4 1/4 .042500	2 1/8 .021250	17/24 .007083
8 3/4 .087500	4 3/8 .043750	2 3/16 .021875	35/48 .007292
9 .090000	4 1/2 .045000	2 1/4 .022500	3/4 .007500
9 1/4 .092500	4 5/8 .046250	2 5/16 .023125	37/48 .007708

Annual	*Semiannual*	*Quarterly*	*Monthly*
9 1/2	4 3/4	2 3/8	19/24
.095000	.047500	.023750	.007917
9 3/4	4 7/8	2 7/16	13/16
.097500	.048750	.024375	.008125
10	5	2 1/2	5/6
.100000	.050000	.025000	.008333
10 1/4	5 1/8	2 9/16	41/48
.102500	.051250	.025625	.008542
10 1/2	5 1/4	2 5/8	7/8
.105000	.052500	.026250	.008750
10 3/4	5 3/8	2 11/16	43/48
.107500	.053750	.026875	.008958
11	5 1/2	2 3/4	11/12
.110000	.055000	.027500	.009167
11 1/4	5 5/8	2 13/16	15/16
.112500	.056250	.028125	.009375
11 1/2	5 3/4	2 7/8	23/24
.115000	.057500	.028750	.009583
11 3/4	5 7/8	2 15/16	47/48
.117500	.058750	.029375	.009782
12	6	3	1
.120000	.060000	.030000	.010000
12 1/4	6 1/8	3 1/16	1 1/48
.122500	.051250	.030625	.010208
12 1/2	6 1/4	3 1/8	1 1/24
.125000	.062500	.031250	.010417
12 3/4	6 3/8	3 3/16	1 1/16
.127500	.063750	.031875	.010625
13	6 1/2	3 1/4	1 1/12
.130000	.065000	.032500	.010833
13 1/4	6 5/8	3 5/16	1 5/48
.132500	.066250	.033125	.011042
13 1/2	6 3/4	3 3/8	1 1/8
.135000	.067500	.033750	.011250
13 3/4	6 7/8	3 7/16	1 7/48
.137500	.068750	.034375	.011458
14	7	3 1/2	1 1/6
.140000	.070000	.035000	.011667
14 1/4	7 1/8	3 9/16	1 3/16
.142500	.071250	.035625	.011875
14 1/2	7 1/4	3 5/8	1 5/24
.145000	.072500	.036250	.012083

Annual	*Semiannual*	*Quarterly*	*Monthly*
14 3/4 .147500	7 3/8 .073750	3 11/16 .036875	1 11/48 .012292
15 .150000	7 1/2 .075000	3 3/4 .037500	1 1/4 .012500
15 1/4 .152500	7 5/8 .076250	3 13/16 .038125	1 13/48 .012708
15 1/2 .155000	7 3/4 .077500	3 7/8 .038750	1 7/24 .012917
15 3/4 .175700	7 7/8 .078750	3 15/16 .039375	1 5/16 .013125
16 .160000	8 .080000	4 .040000	1 1/3 .013333
16 1/4 .162500	8 1/8 .081250	4 1/16 .040625	1 17/48 .013542
16 1/2 .165000	8 1/4 .082500	4 1/8 .041250	1 3/8 .013750
16 3/4 .167500	8 3/8 .083750	4 3/16 .041875	1 19/48 .013958
17 .170000	8 1/2 .085000	4 1/4 .042500	1 5/12 .014167
17 1/4 .172500	8 5/8 .086250	4 5/16 .043125	1 7/16 .014375
17 1/2 .175000	8 3/4 .087500	4 3/8 .043750	1 11/24 .014583
17 3/4 .177500	8 7/8 .088750	4 7/16 .044375	1 23/48 .014792
18 .180000	9 .090000	4 1/2 .045000	1 1/2 .015000
18 1/4 .182500	9 1/8 .091250	4 9/16 .045625	1 25/48 .015208
18 1/2 .185000	9 1/4 .092500	4 5/8 .046250	1 13/24 .015417
18 3/4 .187500	9 3/8 .093750	4 11/16 .046875	1 9/16 .015625
19 .190000	9 1/2 .095000	4 3/4 .047500	1 7/12 .015833
19 1/4 .192500	9 5/8 .096250	4 13/16 .048125	1 29/48 .016042
19 1/2 .195000	9 3/4 .097500	4 7/8 .048750	1 5/8 .016250
19 3/4 .197500	9 7/8 .098750	4 15/16 .049375	1 31/48 .016458

Annual	*Semiannual*	*Quarterly*	*Monthly*
20 .200000	10 .100000	5 .050000	1 2/3 .016667
20 1/4 .202500	10 1/8 .101254	5 1/16 .050625	1 11/16 .016875
20 1/2 .705000	10 1/4 .102500	5 1/8 .051250	1 17/24 .017083
20 3/4 .207500	10 3/8 .103750	5 3/16 .051875	1 35/48 .017292
21 .210000	10 1/2 .105000	5 1/4 .052500	1 3/4 .017500
21 1/4 .212500	10 5/8 .106250	5 5/16 .053125	1 37/48 .017708
21 1/2 .215000	10 3/4 .107500	5 3/8 .053750	1 19/24 .017917
21 3/4 .217500	10 7/8 .108750	5 7/16 .054375	1 13/16 .018125
22 .220000	11 .110000	5 1/2 .055000	1 5/6 .018333
22 1/4 .222500	11 1/8 .111250	5 9/16 .055625	1 41/48 .018542
22 1/2 .225000	11 1/4 .112500	5 5/8 .056250	1 7/8 .018750
22 3/4 .227500	11 3/8 .113750	5 11/16 .056875	1 43/48 .018958
23 .230000			
24 .240000			
25 .250000			
26 .260000			
27 .270000			
28 .280000			
29 .290000			
30 .300000			

TABLE 1. FUTURE WORTH OF ONE DOLLAR WITH INTEREST
Payable at beginning of each period

SEMI ANNUAL Compounding

HALF YEARS	21% Nominal Annual Rate	21¼% Nominal Annual Rate	21½% Nominal Annual Rate	21¾% Nominal Annual Rate	HALF YEARS
1	1.1050 000 000	1.1062 500 000	1.1075 000 000	1.1087 500 000	1
YEARS					
1	1.2210 250 000	1.2237 890 625	1.2265 562 500	1.2293 265 625	2
2	1.4909 020 506	1.4976 596 695	1.5044 402 344	1.5112 437 973	4
3	1.8204 286 764	1.8328 195 229	1.8452 805 723	1.8578 121 424	6
4	2.2227 889 246	2.2429 844 856	2.2633 404 189	2.2838 578 148	8
5	2.7140 808 466	2.7449 398 809	2.7761 143 367	2.8076 070 767	10
6	3.3139 605 657	3.3592 274 034	3.4050 603 904	3.4514 659 564	12
7	4.0464 286 998	4.1109 857 548	4.1764 981 035	4.2429 787 798	14
8	4.9407 906 031	5.0309 794 028	5.1227 098 519	5.2160 065 181	16
9	6.0328 288 462	6.1568 575 668	6.2832 917 858	6.4121 753 629	18
10	7.3662 348 419	7.5346 949 496	7.7068 108 105	7.8826 574 970	20
11	8.9943 568 979	9.2208 772 686	9.4528 369 672	9.6903 602 442	22
12	10.9823 346 312	11.2844 087 480	11.5944 362 623	11.9126 172 484	24
13	13.4097 051 431	13.8097 360 025	14.2212 282 628	14.6444 968 124	26
14	16.3735 852 223	16.9002 038 759	17.4431 364 084	18.0028 689 259	28
15	19.9925 568 961	20.6822 846 574	21.3949 879 813	22.1314 049 718	30
16	24.4114 117 840	25.3107 537 512	26.2421 562 271	27.2067 239 972	32
17	29.8069 440 736	30.9750 236 043	32.1874 807 338	33.4459 484 884	34
18	36.3950 238 875	37.9068 950 977	39.4797 556 658	41.1159 928 848	36
19	44.4392 340 422	46.3900 436 139	48.4241 410 604	50.5449 821 969	38
20	54.2614 157 464	56.7716 279 836	59.3949 328 685	62.1362 892 157	40
21	66.2545 451 617	69.4764 973 866	72.8512 261 282	76.3857 908 281	42
22	80.8984 560 061	85.0245 776 025	89.3561 267 277	93.9030 816 625	44
23	98.7790 372 449	104.0521 481 137	109.6003 157 137	115.4375 525 883	46
24	120.6116 739 519	127.3378 807 911	134.4309 522 406	141.9104 497 068	48
25	147.2698 691 871	155.8347 057 541	164.8871 246 641	174.4542 853 209	50
26	179.8201 920 242	190.7088 084 598	202.2433 333 013	214.4612 868 869	52
27	219.5649 499 664	233.3873 539 155	248.0628 244 816	263.6429 565 981	54
28	268.0942 930 327	285.6168 910 476	304.2630 077 606	324.1032 895 620	56
29	327.3498 341 503	349.5348 273 293	373.1956 938 125	398.4287 828 522	58
30	399.7023 312 433	427.7568 986 484	457.7455 107 188	489.7990 860 248	60
31	488.0465 390 064	523.4842 139 749	561.4506 170 816	602.1230 267 385	62
32	595.9170 252 903	640.6342 554 539	688.6507 634 478	740.2058 306 625	64
33	727.6295 858 051	784.0011 948 873	844.6688 979 742	909.9546 893 508	66
34	888.4539 150 076	959.4520 872 900	1036.0339 159 908	1118.6314 702 904	68
35	1084.8244 415 722	1174.1669 704 183	1270.7538 748 705	1375.1633 800 764	70
36	1324.5977 637 707	1436.9326 959 466	1558.6511 074 342	1690.5248 709 052	72
37	1617.3669 845 081	1758.5025 168 481	1911.7732 573 928	2078.2071 283 706	74
38	1974.8455 222 590	2152.0361 464 974	2344.8974 374 380	2554.7952 252 829	76
39	2411.3357 538 163	2633.6382 981 882	2876.1486 074 985	3140.6776 321 884	78
40	2944.3012 388 035	3223.0177 439 039	3527.7580 504 561	3860.9184 374 988	80
41	3595.0654 201 101	3944.2938 632 330	4326.9936 852 748	4746.3295 908 633	82
42	4389.6647 545 899	4826.9836 891 104	5307.3011 483 843	5834.7890 404 280	84
43	5359.8904 069 732	5907.2098 435 992	6509.7033 941 829	7172.8611 539 820	86
44	6544.5601 841 744	7229.1787 964 890	7984.5173 837 813	8817.7887 457 145	88
45	7991.0715 988 816	8846.9899 420 002	9793.4597 003 106	10839.9419 276 204	90
46	9757.2981 990 244	10826.8495 270 673	12012.2292 045 391	13325.8285 475 812	92
47	11913.9050 334 637	13249.7800 325 583	14733.6748 072 599	16381.7950 008 624	94
48	14547.1758 934 851	16214.9358 843 757	18071.6809 203 122	20138.5757 359 898	96
49	17762.4654 453 426	19843.6611 844 378	22165.9331 808 147	24756.8860 831 703	98
50	21688.4143 703 994	24284.4555 174 707	27187.7638 800 107	30434.2976 668 278	100
51	26482.0961 566 170	29719.0510 510 484	33347.3217 105 513	37413.6905 328 632	102
52	32335.3014 596 332	36369.8496 241 522	40902.3658 648 374	45993.6435 732 035	104
53	39482.2114 647 487	44509.0241 748 072	50169.0524 913 030	56541.2077 506 965	106
54	48208.7672 537 448	54469.6569 676 772	61535.1648 897 858	69507.6085 637 621	108
55	58864.1100 360 037	66659.3704 351 702	75476.3410 903 473	85447.5495 032 852	110
56	71874.5499 567 114	81577.0084 516 972	92575.9778 914 973	105042.9423 049 222	112
57	87760.6223 608 935	99833.0506 946 571	113549.6442 826 778	129132.0791 785 958	114
58	107157.9139 182 100	122174.5955 161 294	139275.0258 801 953	158745.4950 051 011	116
59	130842.4918 419 824	149515.9337 080 007	170828.6534 622 652	195150.0536 869 818	118
60	159761.9536 013 566	182975.9643 413 263	209530.9525 832 256	239903.1446 707 078	120

TABLE 1. FUTURE WORTH OF ONE DOLLAR WITH INTEREST
Payable at beginning of each period

HALF YEARS	22% Nominal Annual Rate	22¼% Nominal Annual Rate	22½% Nominal Annual Rate	22¾% Nominal Annual Rate	HALF YEARS
1	1.1100 000 000	1.1112 500 000	1.1125 000 000	1.1137 500 000	1
YEARS					
1	1.2321 000 000	1.2348 765 625	1.2376 562 500	1.2404 390 625	2
2	1.5180 704 100	1.5249 201 246	1.5317 929 932	1.5386 890 678	4
3	1.8704 145 522	1.8830 881 216	1.8958 331 717	1.9086 500 247	6
4	2.3045 377 697	2.3253 813 864	2.3463 897 739	2.3675 640 473	8
5	2.8394 209 861	2.8715 589 730	2.9040 239 686	2.9368 189 272	10
6	3.4984 505 969	3.5460 208 736	3.5941 834 149	3.6429 449 168	12
7	4.3104 409 805	4.3788 980 669	4.4483 635 671	4.5188 511 774	14
8	5.3108 943 321	5.4073 985 924	5.5055 449 711	5.6053 595 180	16
9	6.5435 529 065	6.6774 697 859	6.8139 721 431	6.9531 069 055	18
10	8.0623 115 361	8.2458 509 354	8.4333 552 103	8.6249 054 114	20
11	9.9335 740 437	10.1826 080 580	10.4375 947 845	10.6986 695 826	22
12	12.2391 565 792	12.5742 640 359	12.9181 544 200	13.2710 476 670	24
13	15.0798 648 212	15.5276 639 487	15.9882 345 563	16.4619 259 265	26
14	18.5799 014 462	19.1747 482 806	19.7879 384 251	20.4200 159 632	28
15	22.8922 965 719	23.6784 472 435	24.4906 656 664	25.3297 854 577	30
16	28.2055 986 063	29.2399 595 374	30.3110 254 287	31.4200 553 264	32
17	34.7521 180 428	36.1077 407 212	37.5146 300 658	38.9746 639 728	34
18	42.8180 846 405	44.5886 027 414	46.4302 163 673	48.3456 956 397	36
19	52.7561 620 855	55.0614 204 800	57.4646 474 759	59.9698 893 752	38
20	65.0008 673 056	67.9940 576 487	71.1214 801 026	74.3889 933 548	40
21	80.0875 686 072	83.9642 681 797	88.0239 443 582	92.2750 131 773	42
22	98.6758 932 810	103.6855 068 626	108.9433 848 846	114.4615 308 379	44
23	121.5785 681 115	128.0388 022 955	134.8344 611 986	141.9825 540 048	46
24	149.7969 537 702	158.1121 160 453	166.8787 136 178	176.1207 061 811	48
25	184.5648 267 402	195.2489 463 517	206.5384 829 010	218.4670 036 621	50
26	227.4023 230 266	241.1083 477 025	255.6236 442 280	270.9950 052 098	52
27	280.1824 022 011	297.7390 476 009	316.3742 009 266	336.1527 902 047	54
28	345.2127 377 520	367.6709 716 234	391.5625 071 155	416.9770 519 383	56
29	425.3366 141 842	454.0282 655 694	484.6197 841 972	517.2346 233 903	58
30	524.0572 423 363	560.6688 638 641	599.7927 047 853	641.5980 313 308	60
31	645.6909 282 826	692.3568 393 093	742.3371 897 819	795.8632 604 858	62
32	795.5557 927 370	854.9752 337 496	918.7582 625 410	987.2198 767 152	64
33	980.2042 922 313	1055.7888 776 754	1137.1069 058 730	1224.5860 983 540	66
34	1207.7097 084 581	1303.7689 399 895	1407.3474 689 719	1519.0244 317 928	68
35	1488.0191 317 913	1609.9937 069 085	1741.8123 908 948	1884.2572 420 876	70
36	1833.3883 722 800	1988.1434 944 338	2155.7649 919 184	2337.3062 868 840	72
37	2258.9178 134 862	2455.1118 041 632	2668.0960 157 789	2899.2860 192 778	74
38	2783.2126 379 964	3031.7600 252 782	3302.1857 095 289	3596.3876 316 723	76
39	3429.1962 912 753	3743.8493 983 405	4086.9707 820 591	4461.0997 022 182	78
40	4225.1127 504 804	4623.1918 755 404	5058.2649 319 829	5533.7223 323 385	80
41	5205.7614 198 668	5709.0712 910 453	6260.3932 072 244	6864.2453 420 613	82
42	6414.0186 454 179	7049.9983 309 534	7748.2147 803 789	8514.6780 568 765	84
43	7902.7123 730 194	8705.8777 045 585	9589.6264 492 783	10561.9392 663 613	86
44	9736.9319 147 972	10750.6843 333 506	11868.6611 101 146	13101.4420 417 471	88
45	11996.8738 122 217	13275.7681 140 906	14689.3226 020 653	16251.5404 836 629	90
46	14781.3482 240 383	16393.9348 932 753	18180.3319 267 123	20159.0456 417 356	92
47	18212.0991 468 376	20244.4859 668 566	22501.0014 361 701	25006.0676 767 292	94
48	22439.1273 588 187	24999.4412 403 314	27848.5050 587 349	31018.5031 457 335	96
49	27647.2488 188 005	30871.2240 632 811	34466.8763 390 998	38476.5629 622 469	98
50	34064.1752 696 441	38122.1510 514 319	42658.1449 190 640	47727.8316 891 118	100
51	41970.4703 497 284	47076.1508 454 980	52796.1196 724 853	59203.4667 955 997	102
52	51711.8165 179 004	58133.2353 318 200	65343.4474 883 994	73438.2928 486 835	104
53	63714.1291 317 051	71787.3698 135 614	80872.7261 805 643	91095.7271 328 214	106
54	78502.1785 031 739	88648.5404 662 870	100092.6350 119 140	112998.6983 623 928	108
55	96722.5341 337 605	109470.0049 216 506	123880.2753 014 642	140167.9994 603 669	110
56	119171.8343 062 063	135181.9433 745 060	153321.1969 785 779	173869.8618 431 180	112
57	146831.6170 486 768	166933.0135 463 796	189758.9376 980 180	215674.9684 216 818	114
58	180911.2353 656 747	206141.6659 359 192	234856.3352 353 126	267531.6556 337 080	116
59	222900.7330 940 478	254559.5118 189 712	290671.4111 560 798	331856.7161 033 497	118
60	274635.9932 451 763	314349.5749 066 893	359751.2887 136 419	411648.0338 075 677	120

TABLE 2. FUTURE WORTH OF ONE DOLLAR PER PERIOD WITH INTEREST
Payable at end of each period

HALF YEARS	5% Nominal Annual Rate	5¼% Nominal Annual Rate	5½% Nominal Annual Rate	5¾% Nominal Annual Rate	HALF YEARS
1	1.0000 000 000	1.0000 000 000	1.0000 000 000	1.0000 000 000	1
YEARS					
1	2.0250 000 000	2.0262 500 000	2.0275 000 000	2.0287 500 000	2
2	4.1525 156 250	4.1602 743 379	4.1680 457 969	4.1758 300 137	4
3	6.3877 367 285	6.4078 054 297	6.4279 404 003	6.4481 418 240	6
4	8.7361 159 004	8.7748 805 932	8.8138 382 523	8.8529 897 711	8
5	11.2033 817 679	11.2678 582 655	11.3327 648 213	11.3981 042 323	10
6	13.7955 529 699	13.8934 350 830	13.9921 372 899	14.0916 664 711	12
7	16.5189 528 390	16.6586 638 699	16.7997 863 947	16.9423 349 363	14
8	19.3802 248 264	19.5709 725 837	19.7639 794 848	19.9592 730 939	16
9	22.3863 487 083	22.6381 842 676	22.8934 448 660	23.1521 788 834	18
10	25.5446 576 116	25.8685 380 655	26.1973 975 013	26.5313 158 921	20
11	28.8628 559 032	29.2707 113 535	29.6855 661 457	30.1075 463 467	22
12	32.3490 379 833	32.8538 430 491	33.3682 219 932	33.8923 660 304	24
13	36.0117 080 312	36.6275 581 604	37.2562 089 207	37.8979 412 359	26
14	39.8598 007 503	40.6019 936 406	41.3609 754 193	42.1371 478 740	28
15	43.9027 031 633	44.7878 256 180	45.6946 083 050	46.6236 128 631	30
16	48.1502 775 109	49.1962 980 740	50.2698 683 093	51.3717 579 327	32
17	52.6128 853 099	53.8392 530 470	55.1002 276 542	56.3968 459 825	34
18	57.3014 126 287	58.7291 624 423	60.1999 097 224	61.7150 301 445	36
19	62.2272 966 430	63.8791 615 340	65.5839 309 388	67.3434 057 074	38
20	67.4025 535 356	69.3030 842 493	71.2681 449 883	73.3000 650 694	40
21	72.8398 078 083	75.0155 003 289	77.2692 894 973	79.6041 558 959	42
22	78.5523 230 786	81.0317 544 643	83.6050 353 198	86.2759 426 700	44
23	84.5540 344 345	87.3680 075 170	90.2940 385 703	93.3368 718 324	46
24	90.8595 824 277	94.0412 799 293	97.3559 955 584	100.8096 407 209	48
25	97.4843 487 881	101.0694 974 451	104.8117 007 857	108.7182 705 310	50
26	104.4444 939 455	108.4715 392 615	112.6831 081 777	117.0881 835 320	52
27	111.7569 964 515	116.2672 887 428	120.9933 957 280	125.9462 847 868	54
28	119.4396 943 969	124.4776 868 304	129.7670 337 485	135.3210 486 381	56
29	127.5113 289 257	133.1247 882 951	139.0298 569 240	145.2426 102 390	58
30	135.9915 899 526	142.2318 209 800	148.8091 403 841	155.7428 624 228	60
31	144.9011 641 940	151.8232 481 956	159.1336 800 177	166.8555 582 218	62
32	154.2617 856 313	161.9248 344 329	170.0338 772 641	178.6164 193 669	64
33	164.0962 885 289	172.5637 145 718	181.5418 286 333	191.0632 511 147	66
34	174.4286 631 356	183.7684 667 714	193.6914 202 161	204.2360 637 722	68
35	185.2841 142 069	195.5691 892 360	206.5184 274 645	218.1772 013 106	70
36	196.6891 224 886	207.9975 810 654	220.0606 205 358	232.9314 774 789	72
37	208.6715 093 146	221.0870 274 045	234.3578 755 096	248.5463 198 583	74
38	221.2605 044 736	234.8726 891 231	249.4522 918 060	265.0719 223 177	76
39	234.4868 175 126	249.3915 972 644	265.3883 161 510	282.5614 063 617	78
40	248.3827 126 492	264.6827 525 183	282.2128 734 534	301.0709 918 900	80
41	262.9820 874 770	280.7872 299 846	299.9755 049 788	320.6601 779 154	82
42	278.3205 556 556	297.7482 895 095	318.7285 142 283	341.3919 338 238	84
43	294.4355 337 856	315.6114 918 895	338.5271 209 498	363.3329 017 890	86
44	311.3663 326 835	334.4248 212 573	359.4296 237 372	386.5536 109 935	88
45	329.1542 532 756	354.2388 139 767	381.4975 716 957	411.1287 043 447	90
46	347.8426 873 477	375.1066 943 932	404.7959 456 776	437.1371 784 142	92
47	367.4772 233 947	397.0845 178 055	429.3933 496 238	464.6626 373 721	94
48	388.1057 578 290	420.2313 210 408	455.3622 125 737	493.7935 617 322	96
49	409.7786 118 191	444.6092 810 401	482.7790 019 385	524.6235 927 727	98
50	432.5486 540 425	470.2838 818 775	511.7244 486 654	557.2518 335 455	100
51	456.4714 296 534	497.3240 906 634	542.2837 849 563	591.7831 674 430	102
52	481.6052 957 796	525.8025 428 044	574.5469 952 412	628.3285 953 453	104
53	508.0115 638 784	555.7957 371 163	608.6090 811 446	667.0055 924 323	106
54	535.7546 492 998	587.3842 413 150	644.5703 412 252	707.9384 858 071	108
55	564.9022 284 206	620.6529 084 379	682.5366 663 131	751.2588 541 457	110
56	595.5254 037 344	655.6911 047 756	722.6198 513 143	797.1059 506 557	112
57	627.6988 772 984	692.5929 499 282	764.9379 243 991	845.6271 507 058	114
58	661.5011 329 617	731.4575 696 289	809.6154 945 464	896.9784 255 631	116
59	697.0146 278 178	772.3893 620 160	856.7841 184 642	951.3248 437 629	118
60	734.3259 933 511	815.4982 780 666	906.5826 879 693	1008.8411 017 204	120

SEMI ANNUAL
Compounding

TABLE 2. FUTURE WORTH OF ONE DOLLAR PER PERIOD WITH INTEREST
Payable at end of each period

HALF YEARS	6% Nominal Annual Rate	6¼% Nominal Annual Rate	6½% Nominal Annual Rate	6¾% Nominal Annual Rate	HALF YEARS
1	1.0000 000 000	1.0000 000 000	1.0000 000 000	1.0000 000 000	1
YEARS					
1	2.0300 000 000	2.0312 500 000	2.0325 000 000	2.0337 500 000	2
2	4.1836 270 000	4.1914 367 676	4.1992 593 281	4.2070 946 934	4
3	6.4684 098 843	6.4887 447 655	6.5091 466 521	6.5296 157 290	6
4	8.8923 360 463	8.9318 779 782	8.9716 164 707	9.0115 524 311	8
5	11.4638 793 115	11.5300 928 889	11.5967 478 111	11.6638 469 416	10
6	14.1920 295 615	14.2932 335 508	14.3952 854 837	14.4981 924 608	12
7	17.0863 241 618	17.2317 688 836	17.3786 840 605	17.5270 847 993	14
8	20.1568 813 033	20.3568 323 381	20.5591 547 595	20.7638 774 683	16
9	23.4144 353 747	23.6802 640 783	23.9497 154 260	24.2228 405 516	18
10	26.8703 744 890	27.2146 558 411	27.5642 438 156	27.9192 236 181	20
11	30.5367 802 954	30.9733 986 435	31.4175 343 962	31.8693 229 530	22
12	34.4264 702 153	34.9707 335 184	35.5253 589 026	36.0905 534 030	24
13	38.5530 422 515	39.2218 054 702	39.9045 308 917	40.6015 251 537	26
14	42.9309 225 246	43.7427 208 565	44.5729 745 604	45.4221 257 763	28
15	47.5754 157 063	48.5506 084 109	49.5497 981 112	50.5736 079 063	30
16	52.5027 585 228	53.6636 841 401	54.8553 719 627	56.0786 829 403	32
17	57.7301 765 169	59.1013 203 404	60.5114 121 269	61.9616 211 635	34
18	63.2759 442 668	64.8841 189 948	66.5410 690 942	68.2483 587 512	36
19	69.1594 492 726	71.0339 898 295	72.9690 225 895	74.9666 121 130	38
20	75.4012 597 333	77.5742 333 245	79.8215 825 880	82.1460 000 872	40
21	82.0231 964 511	84.5296 289 945	87.1267 970 028	89.8181 745 214	42
22	89.0484 091 149	91.9265 292 725	94.9145 664 873	98.0169 598 160	44
23	96.5014 572 300	99.7929 593 532	103.2167 668 198	106.7785 020 468	46
24	104.4083 959 753	108.1587 233 747	112.0673 793 731	116.1414 283 225	48
25	112.7968 672 902	117.0555 173 389	121.5026 302 018	126.1470 170 800	50
26	121.6961 965 082	126.5170 492 012	131.5611 383 180	136.8393 800 695	52
27	131.1374 948 756	136.5791 665 822	142.2840 737 611	148.2656 568 305	54
28	141.1537 683 135	147.2799 925 859	153.7153 261 084	160.4762 225 163	56
29	151.7800 328 038	158.6600 702 403	165.9016 841 187	173.5249 099 834	58
30	163.0534 368 015	170.7625 161 052	178.8930 272 403	187.4692 471 251	60
31	175.0133 911 027	183.6331 836 314	192.7425 297 709	202.3707 104 953	62
32	187.7017 066 209	197.3208 368 892	207.5068 785 031	218.2949 963 412	64
33	201.1627 405 541	211.8773 353 246	223.2465 047 462	235.3123 102 385	66
34	215.4435 514 539	227.3578 302 426	240.0258 316 753	253.4976 766 079	68
35	230.5940 637 374	243.8209 737 639	257.9135 380 189	272.9312 694 762	70
36	246.6672 422 190	261.3291 410 438	276.9828 391 647	293.6987 659 400	72
37	263.7192 772 701	279.9486 665 984	297.3117 868 343	315.8917 238 915	74
38	281.8097 812 559	299.7500 956 305	318.9835 885 533	339.6079 856 710	76
39	301.0019 969 344	320.8084 513 102	342.0869 482 247	364.9521 094 249	78
40	321.3630 185 477	343.2035 190 203	366.7164 291 984	392.0358 300 733	80
41	342.9640 263 772	367.0201 486 456	392.9728 413 246	420.9785 519 159	82
42	365.8805 355 836	392.3485 760 499	420.9636 535 744	451.9078 750 520	84
43	390.1926 602 006	419.2847 649 593	450.8034 339 158	484.9601 579 319	86
44	415.9853 932 069	447.9307 705 475	482.6143 182 474	520.2811 185 222	88
45	443.3489 036 532	478.3951 260 998	516.5265 103 071	558.0264 767 341	90
46	472.3788 518 856	510.7932 542 214	552.6788 146 036	598.3626 409 473	92
47	503.1767 239 655	545.2479 041 476	591.2192 045 508	641.4674 416 569	94
48	535.8501 864 550	581.8896 168 132	632.3054 281 314	687.5309 154 765	96
49	570.5134 628 101	620.8572 194 429	676.1056 535 684	736.7561 429 546	98
50	607.2877 326 952	662.2983 515 365	722.7991 576 469	789.3601 438 981	100
51	646.3015 556 163	706.3700 242 414	772.5770 595 042	845.5748 341 501	102
52	687.6913 203 534	753.2392 152 333	825.6431 028 911	905.6480 480 398	104
53	731.6017 217 629	803.0835 013 565	882.2144 901 064	969.8446 310 122	106
54	778.1862 666 183	856.0917 314 231	942.5227 710 185	1038.4476 072 555	108
55	827.6078 102 553	912.4647 417 185	1006.8147 908 116	1111.7594 274 729	110
56	880.0391 258 999	972.4161 169 253	1075.3537 003 372	1190.1033 023 002	112
57	935.6635 086 672	1036.1729 993 473	1148.4200 332 051	1273.8246 272 483	114
58	994.6754 163 450	1103.9769 495 012	1226.3128 540 235	1363.2925 054 520	116
59	1057.2811 492 004	1176.0848 613 347	1309.3509 824 871	1458.9013 749 395	118
60	1123.6995 711 867	1252.7699 355 405	1397.8742 983 240	1561.0727 475 953	120

TABLE 1. FUTURE WORTH OF ONE DOLLAR WITH INTEREST
Payable at beginning of each period

MONTHLY Compounding

MONTHS	5% Nominal Annual Rate	5¼% Nominal Annual Rate	5½% Nominal Annual Rate	5¾% Nominal Annual Rate	MONTHS
1	1.0041 666 667	1.0043 750 000	1.0045 833 333	1.0047 916 667	1
2	1.0083 506 944	1.0087 691 406	1.0091 876 736	1.0096 062 934	2
3	1.0125 521 557	1.0131 825 056	1.0138 131 171	1.0144 439 902	3
4	1.0167 711 230	1.0176 151 791	1.0184 597 606	1.0193 048 677	4
5	1.0210 076 693	1.0220 672 455	1.0231 277 011	1.0241 890 368	5
6	1.0252 618 680	1.0265 387 897	1.0278 170 364	1.0290 966 093	6
7	1.0295 337 924	1.0310 298 969	1.0325 278 645	1.0340 276 972	7
8	1.0338 235 165	1.0355 406 527	1.0372 602 839	1.0389 824 133	8
9	1.0381 311 145	1.0400 711 430	1.0420 143 935	1.0439 608 707	9
10	1.0424 566 608	1.0446 214 543	1.0467 902 928	1.0489 631 832	10
11	1.0468 002 303	1.0491 916 732	1.0515 880 817	1.0539 894 651	11
YEARS					
1	1.0511 618 979	1.0537 818 867	1.0564 078 604	1.0590 398 313	12
2	1.1049 413 356	1.1104 562 648	1.1159 975 675	1.1215 653 642	24
3	1.1614 722 313	1.1701 786 978	1.1789 486 025	1.1877 823 941	36
4	1.2208 953 550	1.2331 131 160	1.2454 505 706	1.2579 088 663	48
5	1.2833 586 785	1.2994 322 660	1.3157 037 725	1.3321 755 935	60
6	1.3490 177 442	1.3693 181 849	1.3899 198 072	1.4108 270 158	72
7	1.4180 360 522	1.4429 627 004	1.4683 222 097	1.4941 220 048	84
8	1.4905 854 679	1.5205 679 569	1.5511 471 239	1.5823 347 158	96
9	1.5668 466 494	1.6023 469 705	1.6386 440 143	1.6757 554 905	108
10	1.6470 094 977	1.6885 242 138	1.7310 764 171	1.7746 918 119	120
11	1.7312 736 294	1.7793 362 318	1.8287 227 339	1.8794 693 171	132
12	1.8198 488 741	1.8750 322 915	1.9318 770 706	1.9904 328 684	144
13	1.9129 557 963	1.9758 750 658	2.0408 501 227	2.1079 476 892	156
14	2.0108 262 454	2.0821 413 547	2.1559 701 114	2.2324 005 651	168
15	2.1137 039 324	2.1941 228 452	2.2775 837 725	2.3642 011 178	180
16	2.2218 450 372	2.3121 269 116	2.4060 573 999	2.5037 831 529	192
17	2.3355 188 461	2.4364 774 592	2.5417 779 498	2.6516 060 878	204
18	2.4550 084 228	2.5675 158 140	2.6851 542 056	2.8081 564 639	216
19	2.5806 113 130	2.7056 016 586	2.8366 180 091	2.9739 495 477	228
20	2.7126 402 855	2.8511 140 206	2.9966 255 617	3.1495 310 273	240
21	2.8514 241 108	3.0044 523 119	3.1656 587 980	3.3354 788 077	252
22	2.9973 083 799	3.1660 374 258	3.3442 268 375	3.5324 049 138	264
23	3.1506 563 652	3.3363 128 920	3.5328 675 181	3.7409 575 039	276
24	3.3118 499 244	3.5157 460 940	3.7321 490 158	3.9618 230 038	288
25	3.4812 904 520	3.7048 295 522	3.9426 715 564	4.1957 283 655	300
26	3.6593 998 786	3.9040 822 755	4.1650 692 231	4.4434 434 603	312
27	3.8466 217 215	4.1140 511 863	4.4000 118 664	4.7057 836 125	324
28	4.0434 221 892	4.3353 126 212	4.6482 071 214	4.9836 122 830	336
29	4.2502 913 424	4.5684 739 135	4.9104 025 398	5.2778 439 114	348
30	4.4677 443 140	4.8141 750 600	5.1873 878 407	5.5894 469 254	360
31	4.6963 225 924	5.0730 904 778	5.4799 972 898	5.9194 469 289	372
32	4.9365 953 693	5.3459 308 552	5.7891 122 118	6.2689 300 768	384
33	5.1891 609 574	5.6334 451 029	6.1156 636 452	6.6390 466 509	396
34	5.4546 482 804	5.9364 224 093	6.4606 351 463	7.0310 148 450	408
35	5.7337 184 387	6.2556 944 069	6.8250 657 516	7.4461 247 752	420
36	6.0270 663 560	6.5921 374 549	7.2100 531 076	7.8857 427 256	432
37	6.3354 225 094	6.9466 750 448	7.6167 567 767	8.3513 156 457	444
38	6.6595 547 489	7.3202 803 352	8.0464 017 295	8.8443 759 124	456
39	7.0002 702 089	7.7139 788 230	8.5002 820 349	9.3665 463 740	468
40	7.3584 173 184	8.1288 511 583	8.9797 647 572	9.9195 456 916	480
41	7.7348 879 138	8.5660 361 105	9.4862 940 739	10.5051 939 957	492
42	8.1306 194 594	9.0267 336 943	10.0213 956 256	11.1254 188 768	504
43	8.5465 973 819	9.5122 084 633	10.5866 811 109	11.7822 617 302	516
44	8.9838 575 244	10.0237 929 814	11.1838 531 409	12.4778 844 748	528
45	9.4434 887 256	10.5628 914 801	11.8147 103 675	13.2145 766 690	540
46	9.9266 355 315	11.1309 837 132	12.4811 529 004	13.9947 630 460	552
47	10.4345 010 448	11.7296 290 185	13.1851 880 307	14.8210 114 950	564
48	10.9683 499 217	12.3604 705 977	13.9289 362 762	15.6960 415 131	576
49	11.5295 115 204	13.0252 400 273	14.7146 377 690	16.6227 331 559	588
50	12.1193 832 114	13.7257 620 110	15.5446 590 019	17.6041 365 168	600

MONTHLY
Compounding

TABLE 1. FUTURE WORTH OF ONE DOLLAR WITH INTEREST
Payable at beginning of each period

MONTHS	6% Nominal Annual Rate	6¼% Nominal Annual Rate	6½% Nominal Annual Rate	6¾% Nominal Annual Rate	MONTHS
1	1.0050 000 000	1.0052 083 333	1.0054 166 667	1.0056 250 000	1
2	1.0100 250 000	1.0104 437 934	1.0108 626 736	1.0112 816 406	2
3	1.0150 751 250	1.0157 065 215	1.0163 381 798	1.0169 700 999	3
4	1.0201 505 006	1.0209 966 596	1.0218 433 449	1.0226 905 567	4
5	1.0252 512 531	1.0263 143 506	1.0273 783 297	1.0284 431 910	5
6	1.0303 775 094	1.0316 597 378	1.0329 432 956	1.0342 281 840	6
7	1.0355 293 969	1.0370 329 656	1.0385 384 052	1.0400 457 175	7
8	1.0407 070 439	1.0424 341 790	1.0441 638 215	1.0458 959 747	8
9	1.0459 105 791	1.0478 635 236	1.0498 197 089	1.0517 791 395	9
10	1.0511 401 320	1.0533 211 462	1.0555 062 323	1.0576 953 972	10
11	1.0563 958 327	1.0588 071 938	1.0612 235 577	1.0636 449 338	11
YEARS					
1	1.0616 778 119	1.0643 218 146	1.0669 718 520	1.0696 279 366	12
2	1.1271 597 762	1.1327 809 250	1.1384 289 330	1.1441 039 227	24
3	1.1966 805 248	1.2056 434 497	1.2146 716 270	1.2237 655 181	36
4	1.2704 891 611	1.2831 926 242	1.2960 204 354	1.3089 737 859	48
5	1.3488 501 525	1.3657 299 022	1.3828 173 242	1.4001 149 297	60
6	1.4320 442 785	1.4535 761 278	1.4754 271 614	1.4976 020 432	72
7	1.5203 696 361	1.5470 727 820	1.5742 392 509	1.6018 769 833	84
8	1.6141 427 085	1.6465 833 107	1.6796 689 690	1.7134 123 722	96
9	1.7136 994 988	1.7524 945 371	1.7921 595 106	1.8327 137 402	108
10	1.8193 967 340	1.8652 181 658	1.9121 837 521	1.9603 218 163	120
11	1.9316 131 435	1.9851 923 829	2.0402 462 394	2.0968 149 794	132
12	2.0507 508 156	2.1128 835 593	2.1768 853 086	2.2428 118 797	144
13	2.1772 366 385	2.2487 880 639	2.3226 753 493	2.3989 742 430	156
14	2.3115 238 303	2.3934 341 928	2.4782 292 190	2.5660 098 695	168
15	2.4540 935 622	2.5473 842 232	2.6442 008 195	2.7446 758 419	180
16	2.6054 566 833	2.7112 365 990	2.8212 878 455	2.9357 819 573	192
17	2.7661 555 504	2.8856 282 569	3.0102 347 175	3.1401 943 973	204
18	2.9367 659 720	3.0712 371 026	3.2118 357 115	3.3588 396 536	216
19	3.1178 992 711	3.2687 846 462	3.4269 382 974	3.5927 087 279	228
20	3.3102 044 758	3.4790 388 061	3.6564 467 019	3.8428 616 234	240
21	3.5143 706 447	3.7028 168 952	3.9013 257 093	4.1104 321 487	252
22	3.7311 293 361	3.9409 887 971	4.1626 047 173	4.3966 330 577	264
23	3.9612 572 294	4.1944 803 479	4.4413 820 644	4.7027 615 453	276
24	4.2055 789 075	4.4642 769 352	4.7388 296 467	5.0302 051 279	288
25	4.4649 698 122	4.7514 273 286	5.0561 978 444	5.3804 479 315	300
26	4.7403 593 802	5.0570 477 563	5.3948 207 781	5.7550 774 188	312
27	5.0327 343 742	5.3823 262 445	5.7561 219 169	6.1557 915 843	324
28	5.3431 424 181	5.7285 272 354	6.1416 200 620	6.5844 066 503	336
29	5.6726 957 510	6.0969 965 022	6.5529 357 319	7.0428 652 989	348
30	6.0225 752 123	6.4891 663 809	6.9917 979 739	7.5332 454 772	360
31	6.3940 344 731	6.9065 613 378	7.4600 516 330	8.0577 698 155	372
32	6.7884 045 284	7.3508 038 957	7.9596 651 069	8.6188 157 011	384
33	7.2070 984 658	7.8236 209 411	8.4927 386 204	9.2189 260 540	396
34	7.6516 165 291	8.3268 504 368	9.0615 130 544	9.8608 208 526	408
35	8.1235 514 938	8.8624 485 669	9.6683 793 656	10.5474 094 615	420
36	8.6245 943 745	9.4324 973 405	10.3158 886 376	11.2818 038 185	432
37	9.1565 404 837	10.0392 126 857	11.0067 628 047	12.0673 325 391	444
38	9.7212 958 650	10.6849 530 629	11.7439 060 943	12.9075 560 038	456
39	10.3208 841 225	11.3722 286 329	12.5304 172 352	13.8062 824 945	468
40	10.9574 536 717	12.1037 110 147	13.3696 024 838	14.7675 854 563	480
41	11.6332 854 377	12.8822 436 706	14.2649 895 226	15.7958 219 598	492
42	12.3508 010 283	13.7108 529 597	15.2203 422 898	16.8956 524 493	504
43	13.1125 714 105	14.5927 599 019	16.2396 768 010	18.0720 618 664	516
44	13.9213 261 230	15.5313 926 989	17.3272 780 323	19.3303 822 437	528
45	14.7799 630 566	16.5304 000 606	18.4877 179 323	20.6763 168 725	540
46	15.6915 588 373	17.5936 653 887	19.7258 746 415	22.1159 661 522	552
47	16.6593 798 512	18.7253 218 721	21.0469 529 986	23.6558 552 407	564
48	17.6868 939 474	19.9297 685 540	22.4565 064 200	25.3029 636 290	576
49	18.7777 828 648	21.2116 874 321	23.9604 602 444	27.0647 567 756	588
50	19.9359 554 235	22.5760 616 586	25.5651 366 418	28.9492 199 437	600

TABLE 1. FUTURE WORTH OF ONE DOLLAR WITH INTEREST
Payable at beginning of each period

MONTHLY Compounding

	7% Nominal Annual Rate	7¼% Nominal Annual Rate	7½% Nominal Annual Rate	7¾% Nominal Annual Rate	
MONTHS					MONTHS
1	1.0058 333 333	1.0060 416 667	1.0062 500 000	1.0064 583 333	1
2	1.0117 006 944	1.0121 198 351	1.0125 390 625	1.0129 583 767	2
3	1.0176 022 818	1.0182 347 257	1.0188 674 316	1.0195 003 996	3
4	1.0235 382 951	1.0243 865 605	1.0252 353 531	1.0260 846 730	4
5	1.0295 089 352	1.0305 755 627	1.0316 430 740	1.0327 114 698	5
6	1.0355 144 040	1.0368 019 567	1.0380 908 433	1.0393 810 648	6
7	1.0415 549 047	1.0430 659 685	1.0445 789 110	1.0460 937 341	7
8	1.0476 306 416	1.0493 678 254	1.0511 075 292	1.0528 497 562	8
9	1.0537 418 204	1.0557 077 560	1.0576 769 513	1.0596 494 108	9
10	1.0598 886 476	1.0620 859 904	1.0642 874 322	1.0664 929 800	10
11	1.0660 713 314	1.0685 027 599	1.0709 392 287	1.0733 807 471	11
YEARS					
1	1.0722 900 809	1.0749 582 974	1.0776 325 989	1.0803 129 978	12
2	1.1498 060 175	1.1555 353 412	1.1612 920 181	1.1670 761 732	24
3	1.2329 255 875	1.2421 523 030	1.2514 461 355	1.2608 075 593	36
4	1.3220 538 779	1.3352 619 248	1.3485 991 513	1.3620 667 940	48
5	1.4176 252 596	1.4353 508 852	1.4532 944 083	1.4714 584 613	60
6	1.5201 055 043	1.5429 423 438	1.5661 174 301	1.5896 357 015	72
7	1.6299 940 541	1.6585 986 749	1.6876 991 963	1.7173 041 100	84
8	1.7478 264 560	1.7829 244 077	1.8187 196 710	1.8552 259 512	96
9	1.8741 769 719	1.9165 693 857	1.9599 116 057	2.0042 247 089	108
10	2.0096 613 767	2.0602 321 638	2.1120 646 371	2.1651 900 034	120
11	2.1549 399 601	2.2146 636 591	2.2760 297 039	2.3390 829 034	132
12	2.3107 207 441	2.3806 710 763	2.4527 238 048	2.5269 416 634	144
13	2.4777 629 335	2.5591 221 269	2.6431 351 281	2.7298 879 236	156
14	2.6568 806 163	2.7509 495 644	2.8483 285 772	2.9491 334 063	168
15	2.8489 467 309	2.9571 560 601	3.0694 517 271	3.1859 871 510	180
16	3.0548 973 204	3.1788 194 435	3.3077 412 417	3.4418 633 299	192
17	3.2757 360 947	3.4170 983 368	3.5645 297 906	3.7182 896 919	204
18	3.5125 393 219	3.6732 382 103	3.8412 535 020	4.0169 166 836	216
19	3.7664 610 734	3.9485 778 925	4.1394 599 942	4.3395 273 043	228
20	4.0387 388 490	4.2445 565 686	4.4608 170 314	4.6880 477 510	240
21	4.3306 996 069	4.5627 213 023	4.8071 218 506	5.0645 589 196	252
22	4.6437 662 317	4.9047 351 227	5.1803 112 129	5.4713 088 288	264
23	4.9794 644 680	5.2723 857 168	5.5824 722 352	5.9107 260 426	276
24	5.3394 303 571	5.6675 947 735	6.0158 540 628	6.3854 341 701	288
25	5.7254 182 093	6.0924 280 282	6.4828 804 481	6.8982 675 304	300
26	6.1393 091 546	6.5491 060 604	6.9861 633 053	7.4522 880 752	312
27	6.5831 203 098	7.0400 159 003	7.5285 173 188	8.0508 036 708	324
28	7.0590 146 093	7.5677 235 060	8.1129 756 838	8.6973 878 481	336
29	7.5693 113 461	8.1349 871 753	8.7428 070 705	9.3959 011 390	348
30	8.1164 974 754	8.7447 719 636	9.4215 339 047	10.1505 141 262	360
31	8.7032 397 341	9.4002 651 813	10.1529 520 670	10.9657 323 446	372
32	9.3323 976 382	10.1048 930 546	10.9411 521 220	11.8464 231 820	384
33	10.0070 374 181	10.8623 386 336	11.7905 421 957	12.7978 449 406	396
34	10.7304 469 621	11.6765 610 436	12.7058 726 283	13.8256 782 328	408
35	11.5061 518 407	12.5518 161 791	13.6922 625 411	14.9360 598 979	420
36	12.3379 324 876	13.4926 789 494	14.7552 284 664	16.1356 196 433	432
37	13.2298 426 247	14.5040 671 912	15.9007 151 990	17.4315 196 277	444
38	14.1862 290 177	15.5912 673 735	17.1351 290 435	18.8314 972 248	456
39	15.2117 526 605	16.7599 622 304	18.4653 736 429	20.3439 112 194	468
40	16.3114 114 903	18.0162 604 641	19.8988 885 877	21.9777 917 159	480
41	17.4905 647 458	19.3667 286 744	21.4436 910 231	23.7428 940 530	492
42	18.7549 590 855	20.8184 256 824	23.1084 204 863	25.6497 570 502	504
43	20.1107 565 942	22.3789 394 266	24.9023 872 241	27.7097 659 311	516
44	21.5645 648 145	24.0564 266 241	26.8356 242 620	29.9352 203 006	528
45	23.1234 689 486	25.8596 554 059	28.9189 435 154	32.3394 075 819	540
46	24.7950 663 885	27.7980 511 470	31.1639 962 567	34.9366 823 510	552
47	26.5875 037 426	29.8817 457 326	33.5833 382 768	37.7425 520 429	564
48	28.5095 165 379	32.1216 305 167	36.1905 001 055	40.7737 695 410	576
49	30.5704 717 936	34.5294 132 506	39.0000 626 826	44.0484 332 033	588
50	32.7804 136 714	37.1176 792 788	42.0277 389 042	47.5860 949 211	600

MONTHLY
Compounding

TABLE 1. FUTURE WORTH OF ONE DOLLAR WITH INTEREST
Payable at beginning of each period

	8% Nominal Annual Rate	8¼% Nominal Annual Rate	8½% Nominal Annual Rate	8¾% Nominal Annual Rate	
MONTHS					MONTHS
1	1.0066 666 667	1.0068 750 000	1.0070 833 333	1.0072 916 667	1
2	1.0133 777 778	1.0137 972 656	1.0142 168 403	1.0146 365 017	2
3	1.0201 336 296	1.0207 671 218	1.0214 008 762	1.0220 348 929	3
4	1.0269 345 205	1.0277 848 958	1.0286 357 991	1.0294 872 307	4
5	1.0337 807 506	1.0348 509 169	1.0359 219 693	1.0369 939 084	5
6	1.0406 726 223	1.0419 655 170	1.0432 597 500	1.0445 553 223	6
7	1.0476 104 398	1.0491 290 299	1.0506 495 065	1.0521 718 715	7
8	1.0545 945 094	1.0563 417 920	1.0580 916 072	1.0598 439 581	8
9	1.0616 251 394	1.0636 041 418	1.0655 864 227	1.0675 719 869	9
10	1.0687 026 404	1.0709 164 203	1.0731 343 266	1.0753 563 660	10
11	1.0758 273 246	1.0782 789 707	1.0807 356 947	1.0831 975 062	11
YEARS					
1	1.0829 995 068	1.0856 921 386	1.0883 909 059	1.0910 958 213	12
2	1.1728 879 317	1.1787 274 199	1.1845 947 640	1.1904 900 913	24
3	1.2702 370 516	1.2797 350 933	1.2893 021 683	1.2989 387 640	36
4	1.3756 661 004	1.3893 983 303	1.4032 647 550	1.4172 666 576	48
5	1.4898 457 083	1.5084 588 447	1.5273 005 979	1.5463 737 278	60
6	1.6135 021 673	1.6377 219 091	1.6623 000 813	1.6872 419 126	72
7	1.7474 220 514	1.7780 618 019	1.8092 322 913	1.8409 426 004	84
8	1.8924 572 199	1.9304 277 203	1.9691 519 725	2.0086 447 786	96
9	2.0495 302 358	2.0958 502 001	2.1432 070 992	2.1916 239 245	108
10	2.2196 402 345	2.2754 480 860	2.3326 471 162	2.3912 717 059	120
11	2.4038 692 793	2.4704 360 988	2.5388 319 080	2.6091 065 660	132
12	2.6033 892 439	2.6821 330 514	2.7632 415 602	2.8467 852 716	144
13	2.8194 692 672	2.9119 707 687	3.0074 869 849	3.1061 155 141	156
14	3.0534 838 258	3.1615 037 715	3.2733 214 840	3.3890 696 580	168
15	3.3069 214 774	3.4324 197 909	3.5626 533 352	3.6977 997 420	180
16	3.5813 943 291	3.7265 511 834	3.8775 594 909	4.0346 538 467	192
17	3.8786 482 921	4.0458 873 240	4.2203 004 870	4.4021 939 526	204
18	4.2005 741 874	4.3925 880 614	4.5933 366 702	4.8032 154 264	216
19	4.5492 197 733	4.7689 983 265	4.9993 458 595	5.2407 682 807	228
20	4.9268 027 708	5.1776 639 921	5.4412 425 689	5.7181 803 717	240
21	5.3357 249 709	5.6213 490 927	5.9221 989 288	6.2390 827 091	252
22	5.7785 875 120	6.1030 545 183	6.4456 674 569	6.8074 370 729	264
23	6.2582 074 255	6.6260 383 121	7.0154 058 425	7.4275 661 442	276
24	6.7776 355 553	7.1938 377 057	7.6355 039 202	8.1041 863 826	288
25	7.3401 759 637	7.8102 930 436	8.3104 130 286	8.8424 438 974	300
26	7.9494 069 486	8.4795 737 577	9.0449 779 646	9.6479 535 868	312
27	8.6092 038 048	9.2062 065 676	9.8444 717 606	10.5268 418 430	324
28	9.3237 634 746	9.9951 060 969	10.7146 335 376	11.4857 931 467	336
29	10.0976 312 445	10.8516 081 141	11.6617 097 023	12.5321 009 071	348
30	10.9357 296 578	11.7815 056 209	12.6924 987 871	13.6737 229 322	360
31	11.8433 898 259	12.7910 880 337	13.8144 002 530	14.9193 419 534	372
32	12.8263 853 404	13.8871 837 226	15.0354 676 057	16.2784 316 624	384
33	13.8909 689 978	15.0772 061 952	16.3644 662 079	17.7613 287 647	396
34	15.0439 125 737	16.3692 042 385	17.8109 362 004	19.3793 115 965	408
35	16.2925 498 978	17.7719 163 572	19.3852 609 860	21.1446 859 033	420
36	17.6448 235 039	19.2948 298 772	21.0987 417 655	23.0708 784 325	432
37	19.1093 351 524	20.9482 451 136	22.9636 786 633	25.1725 390 521	444
38	20.6954 005 455	22.7433 450 378	24.9934 590 230	27.4656 521 721	456
39	22.4131 085 840	24.6922 709 134	27.2026 535 075	29.9676 583 152	468
40	24.2733 855 425	26.8082 044 154	29.6071 206 937	32.6975 867 628	480
41	26.2880 645 710	29.1054 567 843	32.2241 209 126	35.6762 002 846	492
42	28.4699 609 654	31.5995 656 216	35.0724 401 517	38.9261 530 516	504
43	30.8329 536 843	34.3073 999 792	38.1725 249 086	42.4721 629 351	516
44	33.3920 736 335	37.2472 744 539	41.5466 289 655	46.3411 995 015	528
45	36.1635 992 764	40.4390 730 596	45.2189 731 365	50.5626 891 316	540
46	39.1651 601 807	43.9043 837 139	49.2159 191 356	55.1687 388 269	552
47	42.4158 491 597	47.6666 442 491	53.5661 588 123	60.1943 804 022	564
48	45.9363 437 208	51.7513 009 356	58.3009 201 149	65.6778 369 245	576
49	49.7490 375 942	56.1859 805 892	63.4541 912 582	71.6608 134 226	588
50	53.8781 831 787	61.0006 774 263	69.0629 647 062	78.1888 140 787	600

TABLE 1. FUTURE WORTH OF ONE DOLLAR WITH INTEREST
Payable at beginning of each period

MONTHS	9% Nominal Annual Rate	9¼% Nominal Annual Rate	9½% Nominal Annual Rate	9¾% Nominal Annual Rate	MONTHS
1	1.0075 000 000	1.0077 083 333	1.0079 166 667	1.0081 250 000	1
2	1.0150 562 500	1.0154 760 851	1.0158 960 069	1.0163 160 156	2
3	1.0226 691 719	1.0233 037 132	1.0239 385 170	1.0245 735 833	3
4	1.0303 391 907	1.0311 916 793	1.0320 446 969	1.0328 982 436	4
5	1.0380 667 346	1.0391 404 485	1.0402 150 508	1.0412 905 418	5
6	1.0458 522 351	1.0471 504 895	1.0484 500 866	1.0497 510 275	6
7	1.0536 961 269	1.0552 222 745	1.0567 503 164	1.0582 802 546	7
8	1.0615 988 478	1.0633 562 796	1.0651 162 565	1.0668 787 817	8
9	1.0695 608 392	1.0715 529 842	1.0735 484 268	1.0755 471 718	9
10	1.0775 825 455	1.0798 128 718	1.0820 473 519	1.0842 859 925	10
11	1.0856 644 146	1.0881 364 294	1.0906 135 601	1.0930 958 162	11
YEARS					
1	1.0938 068 977	1.0965 241 477	1.0992 475 841	1.1019 772 197	12
2	1.1964 135 294	1.2023 652 064	1.2083 452 511	1.2143 537 928	24
3	1.3086 453 709	1.3184 224 831	1.3282 705 980	1.3381 902 164	36
4	1.4314 053 333	1.4456 820 896	1.4600 982 459	1.4746 551 341	48
5	1.5656 810 269	1.5852 253 211	1.6050 094 693	1.6250 363 648	60
6	1.7125 527 068	1.7382 378 440	1.7643 027 816	1.7907 530 552	72
7	1.8732 019 633	1.9060 197 703	1.9394 055 702	1.9733 690 730	84
8	2.0489 212 282	2.0899 967 041	2.1318 868 876	2.1746 077 646	96
9	2.2411 241 722	2.2917 318 546	2.3434 715 107	2.3963 682 184	108
10	2.4513 570 781	2.5129 393 185	2.5760 553 965	2.6407 431 868	120
11	2.6813 112 807	2.7554 986 444	2.8317 226 711	2.9100 388 350	132
12	2.9328 367 736	3.0214 708 024	3.1127 643 050	3.2067 965 047	144
13	3.2079 570 928	3.3131 156 963	3.4216 986 421	3.5338 166 965	156
14	3.5088 855 955	3.6329 113 650	3.7612 939 658	3.8941 854 982	168
15	3.8380 432 675	3.9835 750 380	4.1345 933 049	4.2913 037 085	180
16	4.1980 781 995	4.3680 862 232	4.5449 417 016	4.7289 189 297	192
17	4.5918 868 916	4.7897 120 228	4.9960 161 852	5.2111 609 345	204
18	5.0226 375 554	5.2520 348 933	5.4918 587 216	5.7425 806 381	216
19	5.4937 956 026	5.7589 830 849	6.0369 124 319	6.3281 930 457	228
20	6.0091 515 245	6.3148 640 185	6.6360 614 060	6.9735 245 785	240
21	6.5728 513 866	6.9244 008 855	7.2946 744 684	7.6846 652 267	252
22	7.1894 301 840	7.5927 727 791	8.0186 532 861	8.4683 260 211	264
23	7.8638 483 256	8.3256 586 999	8.8144 852 523	9.3319 023 645	276
24	8.6015 315 408	9.1292 858 097	9.6893 016 185	10.2835 438 225	288
25	9.4084 145 299	10.0104 823 412	10.6509 413 955	11.3322 310 305	300
26	10.2909 887 089	10.9767 356 169	11.7080 215 972	12.4878 604 443	312
27	11.2563 544 337	12.0362 556 664	12.8700 144 551	13.7613 377 329	324
28	12.3122 781 222	13.1980 449 856	14.1473 322 969	15.1646 806 946	336
29	13.4672 547 361	14.4719 750 286	15.5514 208 486	16.7111 326 700	348
30	14.7305 761 230	15.8688 700 832	17.0948 617 968	18.4152 875 183	360
31	16.1124 057 700	17.4005 992 424	18.7914 855 303	20.2932 273 400	372
32	17.6238 605 694	19.0801 772 530	20.6564 950 705	22.3626 742 435	384
33	19.2771 002 544	20.9218 750 996	22.7066 023 018	24.6431 575 887	396
34	21.0854 252 253	22.9413 412 611	24.9601 777 230	27.1561 982 850	408
35	23.0633 835 518	25.1557 346 725	27.4374 150 602	29.9255 118 846	420
36	25.2268 880 125	27.5838 705 205	30.1605 122 184	32.9772 323 857	432
37	27.5933 441 149	30.2463 801 117	33.1538 701 907	36.3401 588 588	444
38	30.1817 901 227	33.1658 861 718	36.4443 117 101	40.0460 272 239	456
39	33.0130 502 203	36.3671 950 660	40.0613 216 008	44.1298 097 415	468
40	36.1099 020 441	39.8775 075 726	44.0373 109 848	48.6300 450 463	480
41	39.4972 599 300	43.7266 500 019	48.4079 077 094	53.5892 018 356	492
42	43.2023 753 506	47.9473 276 234	53.2122 756 000	59.0540 796 464	504
43	47.2550 561 542	52.5754 025 548	58.4934 653 968	65.0762 505 026	516
44	51.6879 063 713	57.6501 984 744	64.2988 005 219	71.7125 455 995	528
45	56.5365 885 151	63.2148 347 446	70.6803 011 330	79.0255 916 197	540
46	61.8401 104 886	69.3165 927 879	77.6951 502 626	87.0844 017 408	552
47	67.6411 394 052	76.0073 178 255	85.4062 062 210	95.9650 269 124	564
48	73.9863 448 477	83.3438 593 946	93.8825 658 539	105.7512 735 485	576
49	80.9267 743 279	91.3885 543 854	103.2001 837 022	116.5354 944 082	588
50	88.5182 639 661	100.2097 567 035	113.4425 526 114	128.4194 601 281	600

MONTHLY
Compounding

TABLE 1. FUTURE WORTH OF ONE DOLLAR WITH INTEREST
Payable at beginning of each period

MONTHS	10% Nominal Annual Rate	10¼% Nominal Annual Rate	10½% Nominal Annual Rate	10¾% Nominal Annual Rate	MONTHS
1	1.0083 333 333	1.0085 416 667	1.0087 500 000	1.0089 583 333	1
2	1.0167 361 111	1.0171 562 934	1.0175 765 625	1.0179 969 184	2
3	1.0252 089 120	1.0258 445 034	1.0264 803 574	1.0271 164 741	3
4	1.0337 523 196	1.0346 069 252	1.0354 620 605	1.0363 177 259	4
5	1.0423 669 223	1.0434 441 927	1.0445 223 536	1.0456 014 055	5
6	1.0510 533 133	1.0523 569 452	1.0536 619 242	1.0549 682 514	6
7	1.0598 120 909	1.0613 458 274	1.0628 814 660	1.0644 190 087	7
8	1.0686 438 584	1.0704 114 897	1.0721 816 788	1.0739 544 290	8
9	1.0775 492 238	1.0795 545 878	1.0815 632 685	1.0835 752 707	9
10	1.0865 288 007	1.0887 757 833	1.0910 269 471	1.0932 822 992	10
11	1.0955 832 074	1.0980 757 431	1.1005 734 329	1.1030 762 865	11
YEARS					
1	1.1047 130 674	1.1074 551 401	1.1102 034 505	1.1129 580 115	12
2	1.2203 909 614	1.2264 568 872	1.2325 517 014	1.2386 755 354	24
3	1.3481 818 424	1.3582 459 838	1.3683 831 517	1.3785 938 608	36
4	1.4893 540 986	1.5041 964 963	1.5191 836 966	1.5343 170 820	48
5	1.6453 089 348	1.6658 301 414	1.6866 029 818	1.7076 304 887	60
6	1.8175 942 802	1.8448 321 526	1.8724 724 500	1.9005 210 331	72
7	2.0079 201 527	2.0430 688 499	2.0788 253 749	2.1152 001 098	84
8	2.2181 756 310	2.2626 070 993	2.3079 191 041	2.3541 289 082	96
9	2.4504 476 055	2.5057 358 621	2.5622 597 527	2.6200 466 286	108
10	2.7070 414 909	2.7749 900 601	2.8446 296 184	2.9160 018 858	120
11	2.9905 041 091	3.0731 770 057	3.1581 176 176	3.2453 876 605	132
12	3.3036 489 675	3.4034 056 712	3.5061 530 760	3.6119 801 972	144
13	3.6495 841 847	3.7691 191 043	3.8925 432 428	4.0199 822 980	156
14	4.0317 433 395	4.1741 303 255	4.3215 149 391	4.4740 715 047	168
15	4.4539 195 517	4.6226 620 843	4.7977 607 966	4.9794 537 253	180
16	4.9203 031 301	5.1193 908 860	5.3264 905 908	5.5419 229 166	192
17	5.4355 231 636	5.6694 957 506	5.9134 882 328	6.1679 275 093	204
18	6.0046 934 672	6.2787 122 106	6.5651 750 402	6.8646 443 359	216
19	6.6334 633 392	6.9533 921 105	7.2886 799 825	7.6400 609 099	228
20	7.3280 736 332	7.7005 698 336	8.0919 176 658	8.5030 669 983	240
21	8.0954 187 018	8.5280 356 436	8.9836 749 133	9.4635 565 382	252
22	8.9431 148 263	9.4444 169 081	9.9737 068 865	10.5325 410 667	264
23	9.8795 758 123	10.4592 680 497	11.0728 437 992	11.7222 759 619	276
24	10.9140 965 006	11.5831 701 629	12.2931 093 922	13.0464 009 451	288
25	12.0569 450 235	12.8278 413 351	13.6478 524 640	14.5200 964 534	300
26	13.3194 647 209	14.2062 588 224	15.1518 928 968	16.1602 576 760	312
27	14.7141 867 285	15.7327 943 538	16.8216 837 749	17.9856 882 488	324
28	16.2549 543 557	17.4233 639 746	18.6754 913 693	20.0173 158 292	336
29	17.9570 604 874	19.2955 939 907	20.7335 949 570	22.2784 320 214	348
30	19.8373 993 733	21.3690 047 455	23.0185 086 616	24.7949 594 024	360
31	21.9146 343 117	23.6652 141 433	25.5552 277 403	27.5957 487 123	372
32	24.2093 828 924	26.2081 630 435	28.3715 020 144	30.7129 096 134	384
33	26.7444 216 359	29.0243 648 739	31.4981 394 309	34.1821 788 114	396
34	29.5449 120 623	32.1431 820 665	34.9693 430 790	38.0433 297 595	408
35	32.6386 504 317	35.5971 321 974	38.8230 853 463	42.3406 286 409	420
36	36.0563 436 355	39.4222 270 232	43.1015 233 086	47.1233 418 589	432
37	39.8319 139 783	43.6583 479 494	47.8514 598 970	52.4463 008 516	444
38	44.0028 358 730	48.3496 618 429	53.1248 558 868	58.3705 307 076	456
39	48.6105 077 934	53.5450 815 279	58.9793 983 103	64.9639 497 880	468
40	53.7006 631 743	59.2987 757 628	65.4791 315 096	72.3021 483 768	480
41	59.3238 243 389	65.6707 340 176	72.6951 577 346	80.4692 552 864	492
42	65.5358 039 578	72.7273 919 391	80.7064 149 481	89.5589 023 524	504
43	72.3982 590 175	80.5423 240 259	89.6005 403 490	99.6752 978 764	516
44	79.9793 027 966	89.1970 107 346	99.4748 290 578	110.9344 213 226	528
45	88.3541 809 243	98.7816 880 157	110.4372 984 530	123.4653 529 648	540
46	97.6060 182 301	109.3962 881 364	122.6078 698 011	137.4117 537 278	552
47	107.8266 437 997	121.1514 815 998	136.1196 801 058	152.9335 121 890	564
48	119.1175 024 239	134.1698 310 232	151.1205 385 278	170.2085 776 213	576
49	131.5906 614 886	148.5870 690 071	167.7745 433 077	189.4350 000 938	588
50	145.3699 232 997	164.5535 133 179	186.2638 768 782	210.8332 010 174	600

TABLE 1. FUTURE WORTH OF ONE DOLLAR WITH INTEREST
Payable at beginning of each period

MONTHLY Compounding

MONTHS	11% Nominal Annual Rate	11¼% Nominal Annual Rate	11½% Nominal Annual Rate	11¾% Nominal Annual Rate	MONTHS
1	1.0091 666 667	1.0093 750 000	1.0095 833 333	1.0097 916 667	1
2	1.0184 173 611	1.0188 378 906	1.0192 585 069	1.0196 792 101	2
3	1.0277 528 536	1.0283 894 958	1.0290 264 010	1.0296 635 690	3
4	1.0371 739 214	1.0380 306 474	1.0388 879 040	1.0397 456 914	4
5	1.0466 813 490	1.0477 621 847	1.0488 439 131	1.0499 265 347	5
6	1.0562 759 281	1.0575 849 552	1.0588 953 339	1.0602 070 653	6
7	1.0659 584 574	1.0674 998 141	1.0690 430 808	1.0705 882 595	7
8	1.0757 297 433	1.0775 076 249	1.0792 880 770	1.0810 711 029	8
9	1.0855 905 992	1.0876 092 589	1.0896 312 544	1.0916 565 908	9
10	1.0955 418 464	1.0978 055 957	1.1000 735 540	1.1023 457 282	10
11	1.1055 843 133	1.1080 975 231	1.1106 159 255	1.1131 395 301	11
YEARS					
1	1.1157 188 362	1.1184 859 374	1.1212 593 281	1.1240 390 214	12
2	1.2448 285 214	1.2510 107 922	1.2572 224 809	1.2634 637 216	24
3	1.3888 786 292	1.3992 379 786	1.4096 724 343	1.4201 825 251	36
4	1.5495 980 478	1.5650 280 022	1.5806 083 666	1.5963 405 757	48
5	1.7289 157 305	1.7504 618 121	1.7722 718 752	1.7943 490 985	60
6	1.9289 838 467	1.9578 669 208	1.9871 763 720	2.0169 184 047	72
7	2.1522 036 124	2.1898 466 182	2.2281 400 438	2.2670 949 898	84
8	2.4012 541 097	2.4493 126 475	2.4983 228 085	2.5483 032 337	96
9	2.6791 244 407	2.7395 217 526	2.8012 677 537	2.8643 922 730	108
10	2.9891 496 030	3.0641 165 555	3.1409 475 995	3.2196 886 873	120
11	3.3350 505 163	3.4271 712 779	3.5218 167 951	3.6190 557 212	132
12	3.7209 786 807	3.8332 428 795	3.9488 699 335	4.0679 598 512	144
13	4.1515 660 031	4.2874 282 553	4.4277 072 485	4.5725 456 101	156
14	4.6319 803 894	4.7954 282 113	4.9646 080 547	5.1397 196 928	168
15	5.1679 877 693	5.3636 190 182	5.5666 130 918	5.7772 454 936	180
16	5.7660 212 995	5.9991 324 454	6.2416 168 554	6.4938 493 708	192
17	6.4332 585 737	6.7099 452 769	6.9984 711 217	7.2993 400 917	204
18	7.1777 077 688	7.5049 794 330	7.8471 010 280	8.2047 430 934	216
19	8.0083 037 584	8.3942 139 563	8.7986 352 264	9.2224 513 973	228
20	8.9350 153 492	9.3888 102 658	9.8655 518 225	10.3663 952 433	240
21	9.9689 649 268	10.5012 522 513	11.0618 420 082	11.6522 327 644	252
22	11.1225 619 462	11.7455 029 683	12.4031 935 381	13.0975 643 133	264
23	12.4096 518 701	13.1371 798 978	13.9071 964 533	14.7221 733 731	276
24	13.8456 823 421	14.6937 509 729	15.5935 737 515	16.5482 973 508	288
25	15.4478 885 890	16.4347 538 310	17.4844 400 279	18.6009 319 596	300
26	17.2355 002 782	18.3820 410 448	19.6045 914 786	20.9081 733 565	312
27	19.2299 723 117	20.5600 544 095	21.9818 310 697	23.5016 027 183	324
28	21.4552 423 276	22.9961 317 294	24.6473 331 364	26.4167 185 202	336
29	23.9380 180 001	25.7208 499 541	27.6360 521 929	29.6934 224 333	348
30	26.7080 975 839	28.7684 089 719	30.9871 813 142	33.3765 654 931	360
31	29.7987 275 532	32.1770 608 768	34.7446 661 013	37.5165 620 137	372
32	33.2470 016 258	35.9895 900 979	38.9577 809 691	42.1700 796 511	384
33	37.0943 059 609	40.2538 504 176	43.6817 753 152	47.4008 150 623	396
34	41.3868 158 762	45.0233 656 187	48.9785 980 418	53.2803 657 749	408
35	46.1760 500 432	50.3580 012 994	54.9177 099 335	59.8892 102 040	420
36	51.5194 888 143	56.3247 162 894	61.5769 945 429	67.3178 092 285	432
37	57.4812 641 013	62.9984 030 983	69.0437 795 299	75.6678 444 061	444
38	64.1329 290 861	70.4628 279 448	77.4159 818 478	85.0536 097 756	456
39	71.5543 170 017	78.8116 821 664	86.8033 917 938	95.6035 762 964	468
40	79.8344 992 899	88.1497 582 067	97.3291 127 629	107.4621 503 400	480
41	89.0728 546 360	98.5942 649 403	109.1311 755 848	120.7916 503 028	492
42	99.3802 617 110	110.2762 988 450	122.3643 486 151	135.7745 283 963	504
43	110.8804 299 370	123.3424 894 877	137.2021 673 162	152.6158 680 260	516
44	123.7113 842 461	137.9568 399 772	153.8392 099 440	171.5461 909 419	528
45	138.0271 216 552	154.3027 854 840	172.4936 491 831	192.8246 125 865	540
46	153.9994 595 365	172.5854 956 670	193.4101 131 911	216.7423 888 283	552
47	171.8200 977 688	193.0344 499 045	216.8628 935 718	243.6269 026 286	564
48	191.7029 195 175	215.9063 176 539	243.1595 423 444	273.8461 452 108	576
49	213.8865 582 593	241.4881 800 938	272.6449 050 794	307.8137 530 694	588
50	238.6372 618 589	270.1011 334 857	305.7056 430 896	345.9946 697 652	600

MONTHLY
Compounding

TABLE 1. FUTURE WORTH OF ONE DOLLAR WITH INTEREST
Payable at beginning of each period

MONTHS	12% Nominal Annual Rate	12¼% Nominal Annual Rate	12½% Nominal Annual Rate	12¾% Nominal Annual Rate	MONTHS
1	1.0100 000 000	1.0102 083 333	1.0104 166 667	1.0106 250 000	1
2	1.0201 000 000	1.0205 208 767	1.0209 418 403	1.0213 628 906	2
3	1.0303 010 000	1.0309 386 940	1.0315 766 511	1.0322 148 713	3
4	1.0406 040 100	1.0414 628 599	1.0423 222 412	1.0431 821 543	4
5	1.0510 100 501	1.0520 944 599	1.0531 797 646	1.0542 659 647	5
6	1.0615 201 506	1.0628 345 908	1.0641 503 871	1.0654 675 406	6
7	1.0721 353 521	1.0736 843 606	1.0752 352 870	1.0767 881 332	7
8	1.0828 567 056	1.0846 448 885	1.0864 356 546	1.0882 290 071	8
9	1.0936 852 727	1.0957 173 050	1.0977 526 926	1.0997 914 403	9
10	1.1046 221 254	1.1069 027 525	1.1091 876 165	1.1114 767 244	10
11	1.1156 683 467	1.1182 023 848	1.1207 416 542	1.1232 861 646	11
YEARS					
1	1.1268 250 301	1.1296 173 675	1.1324 160 464	1.1352 210 801	12
2	1.2697 346 485	1.2760 353 969	1.2823 661 022	1.2887 269 007	24
3	1.4307 687 836	1.4414 317 458	1.4521 719 515	1.4629 899 442	36
4	1.6122 260 777	1.6282 663 340	1.6444 628 200	1.6608 170 246	48
5	1.8166 966 986	1.8393 179 298	1.8622 160 851	1.8853 944 965	60
6	2.0470 993 121	2.0777 254 778	2.1088 033 767	2.1403 395 767	72
7	2.3067 227 440	2.3470 347 845	2.3880 427 825	2.4297 586 060	84
8	2.5992 729 256	2.6512 512 546	2.7042 579 664	2.7583 131 891	96
9	2.9289 257 927	2.9948 994 627	3.0623 451 148	3.1312 952 778	108
10	3.3003 868 946	3.3830 904 468	3.4678 487 477	3.5547 124 073	120
11	3.7189 585 619	3.8215 977 244	3.9270 475 684	4.0353 844 585	132
12	4.1906 155 936	4.3169 431 609	4.4470 516 815	4.5810 535 036	144
13	4.7220 905 425	4.8764 939 689	5.0359 126 834	5.2005 085 063	156
14	5.3209 698 179	5.5085 722 796	5.7027 483 310	5.9037 268 836	168
15	5.9958 019 754	6.2225 789 169	6.4578 837 187	6.7020 352 094	180
16	6.7562 197 415	7.0291 332 149	7.3130 111 489	7.6082 916 492	192
17	7.6130 775 138	7.9402 309 577	8.2813 711 727	8.6370 930 637	204
18	8.5786 062 989	8.9694 227 915	9.3779 576 023	9.8050 101 167	216
19	9.6665 883 013	10.1320 157 613	10.6197 496 714	11.1308 541 750	228
20	10.8925 536 539	11.4453 009 713	12.0259 749 368	12.6359 802 989	240
21	12.2740 020 992	12.9288 107 530	13.6184 069 922	14.3446 312 030	252
22	13.8306 527 853	14.6046 091 672	15.4217 026 046	16.2843 277 279	264
23	15.5847 257 416	16.4976 201 602	17.4637 834 925	18.4863 121 119	276
24	17.5612 590 533	18.6359 982 546	19.7762 686 580	20.9860 512 026	288
25	19.7884 662 619	21.0515 472 883	22.3949 639 666	23.8238 077 132	300
26	22.2981 390 919	23.7801 934 288	25.3604 165 546	27.0452 887 242	312
27	25.1261 012 541	26.8625 194 986	28.7185 426 503	30.7023 818 769	324
28	28.3127 198 027	30.3443 685 593	32.5213 385 268	34.8539 911 159	336
29	31.9034 813 448	34.2775 257 291	36.8276 855 987	39.5669 854 402	348
30	35.9496 413 277	38.7204 883 771	41.7042 621 243	44.9172 759 476	360
31	40.5089 556 723	43.7393 361 472	47.2265 756 334	50.9910 385 162	372
32	45.6465 051 961	49.4087 137 529	53.4801 320 645	57.8861 018 195	384
33	51.4356 245 930	55.8129 411 590	60.5617 597 143	65.7135 230 301	396
34	57.9589 492 318	63.0472 676 621	68.5811 084 996	74.5993 765 911	408
35	65.3095 947 146	71.2192 885 219	77.6623 477 459	84.6867 848 683	420
36	73.5924 860 322	80.4505 452 123	87.9460 887 897	96.1382 233 880	432
37	82.9258 552 907	90.8783 330 932	99.5915 621 650	109.1381 377 930	444
38	93.4429 293 866	102.6577 433 876	112.7790 830 832	123.8959 146 650	456
39	105.2938 317 217	115.9639 698 347	127.7128 433 834	140.6492 540 655	468
40	118.6477 251 025	130.9949 143 246	144.6240 731 807	159.6679 981 149	480
41	133.6952 264 137	147.9741 302 696	163.7746 211 677	181.2584 772 768	492
42	150.6511 275 322	167.1541 474 870	185.4610 090 059	205.7684 443 507	504
43	169.7574 613 208	188.8202 280 438	210.0190 225 827	233.5926 756 454	516
44	191.2869 564 680	213.2946 089 256	237.8289 112 251	265.1793 295 487	528
45	215.5469 304 859	240.9412 946 274	269.3212 753 727	301.0371 649 093	540
46	242.8836 764 396	272.1714 709 488	304.9837 338 731	341.7437 354 974	552
47	273.6874 060 226	307.4496 205 101	345.3684 741 336	387.9546 925 273	564
48	308.3978 195 382	347.3004 309 465	391.1008 020 348	440.4143 450 791	576
49	347.5103 822 937	392.3165 985 226	442.8888 239 901	499.9676 485 104	588
50	391.5833 969 993	443.1676 432 329	501.5344 110 644	567.5738 139 550	600

TABLE 1. FUTURE WORTH OF ONE DOLLAR WITH INTEREST
Payable at beginning of each period

MONTHLY Compounding

MONTHS	13% Nominal Annual Rate	13¼% Nominal Annual Rate	13½% Nominal Annual Rate	13¾% Nominal Annual Rate	MONTHS
1	1.0108 333 333	1.0110 416 667	1.0112 500 000	1.0114 583 333	1
2	1.0217 840 278	1.0222 052 517	1.0226 265 625	1.0230 479 601	2
3	1.0328 533 547	1.0334 921 014	1.0341 311 113	1.0347 703 846	3
4	1.0440 425 994	1.0449 035 767	1.0457 650 863	1.0466 271 286	4
5	1.0553 530 609	1.0564 410 537	1.0575 299 436	1.0586 197 311	5
6	1.0667 860 524	1.0681 059 236	1.0694 271 554	1.0707 497 489	6
7	1.0783 429 013	1.0798 995 932	1.0814 582 109	1.0830 187 564	7
8	1.0900 249 494	1.0918 234 846	1.0936 246 158	1.0954 283 463	8
9	1.1018 335 530	1.1038 790 355	1.1059 278 927	1.1079 801 295	9
10	1.1137 700 832	1.1160 676 999	1.1183 695 815	1.1206 757 351	10
11	1.1258 359 258	1.1283 909 474	1.1309 512 393	1.1335 168 112	11
YEARS					
1	1.1380 324 816	1.1408 502 641	1.1436 744 407	1.1465 050 247	12
2	1.2951 179 292	1.3015 393 251	1.3079 912 264	1.3144 737 717	24
3	1.4738 862 710	1.4848 614 828	1.4959 161 344	1.5070 507 841	36
4	1.6773 304 506	1.6940 046 148	1.7108 410 484	1.7278 412 964	48
5	1.9088 565 351	1.9326 056 122	1.9566 451 792	1.9809 787 282	60
6	2.1723 407 397	2.2048 136 231	2.2377 650 810	2.2712 020 658	72
7	2.4721 943 229	2.5153 622 042	2.5592 747 276	2.6039 445 805	84
8	2.8134 374 404	2.8696 516 350	2.9269 770 928	2.9854 355 456	96
9	3.2017 831 921	3.2738 428 257	3.3475 088 896	3.4228 168 540	108
10	3.6437 332 717	3.7349 644 524	3.8284 603 572	3.9242 767 217	120
11	4.1466 868 176	4.2610 351 819	4.3785 122 580	4.4992 029 798	132
12	4.7190 642 895	4.8612 031 127	5.0075 925 579	5.1583 588 235	144
13	5.3704 484 442	5.5459 048 550	5.7270 556 181	5.9140 843 104	156
14	6.1117 447 704	6.3270 470 186	6.5498 871 312	6.7805 273 784	168
15	6.9553 640 680	7.2182 132 621	7.4909 385 017	7.7739 087 094	180
16	7.9154 302 308	8.2349 005 065	8.5671 949 015	8.9128 253 970	192
17	9.0080 167 087	9.3947 884 178	9.7980 818 377	10.2185 991 019	204
18	10.2514 156 094	10.7180 468 476	11.2058 157 661	11.7156 752 158	216
19	11.6664 439 460	12.2276 865 769	12.8158 050 794	13.4320 805 028	228
20	13.2767 921 555	13.9499 594 606	14.6571 087 068	15.3999 477 886	240
21	15.1094 207 245	15.9148 149 350	16.7629 606 032	17.6561 175 199	252
22	17.1950 115 629	18.1564 208 218	19.1713 695 930	20.2428 274 533	264
23	19.5684 816 803	20.7137 574 898	21.9258 053 976	23.2085 033 895	276
24	22.2695 677 681	23.6312 957 029	25.0759 832 259	26.6086 657 519	288
25	25.3434 914 715	26.9597 699 439	28.6787 610 920	30.5069 689 853	300
26	28.8417 164 921	30.7570 606 608	32.7991 660 531	34.9763 932 301	312
27	32.8228 101 935	35.0892 007 781	37.5115 678 926	40.1006 105 844	324
28	37.3534 241 381	40.0315 239 750	42.9010 214 309	45.9755 515 287	336
29	42.5094 099 686	45.6699 746 996	49.0648 016 923	52.7112 008 413	348
30	48.3770 893 186	52.1026 026 978	56.1141 596 356	60.4336 566 227	360
31	55.0546 990 105	59.4412 680 486	64.1763 301 390	69.2874 909 792	372
32	62.6540 357 394	67.8135 863 521	73.3968 284 807	79.4384 565 569	384
33	71.3023 277 756	77.3651 479 000	83.9420 767 649	91.0765 895 973	396
34	81.1443 650 233	88.2620 494 145	96.0024 076 989	104.4197 676 063	408
35	92.3449 230 965	100.6937 823 852	109.7954 999 350	119.7177 882 391	420
36	105.0915 219 959	114.8765 282 283	125.5703 069 842	137.2570 457 627	432
37	119.5975 655 736	131.0569 175 691	143.6115 506 141	157.3658 926 431	444
38	136.1059 143 447	149.5163 190 219	164.2448 598 328	180.4207 866 325	456
39	154.8929 514 640	170.5757 320 446	187.8426 482 141	206.8533 384 353	468
40	176.2732 099 391	194.6013 689 536	214.8308 356 439	237.1583 918 931	480
41	200.6046 385 490	222.0110 231 666	245.6965 358 093	271.9032 879 564	492
42	228.2945 946 312	253.2813 344 146	280.9968 481 842	311.7384 858 758	504
43	259.8066 640 672	288.9560 772 606	321.3689 131 975	357.4097 404 504	516
44	295.6684 226 482	329.6556 170 584	367.5414 120 733	409.7720 633 049	528
45	336.4802 687 612	376.0876 977 859	420.3477 189 027	469.8057 295 628	540
46	382.9254 752 724	429.0597 493 470	480.7409 423 335	538.6346 295 789	552
47	435.7816 288 975	489.4929 283 608	549.8111 283 655	617.5473 092 922	564
48	495.9336 485 759	558.4381 365 996	628.8049 347 475	708.0210 930 965	576
49	564.3886 008 047	637.0942 956 278	719.1481 320 836	811.7497 408 322	588
50	642.2925 599 683	726.8291 954 289	822.4713 377 719	930.6751 566 671	600

TABLE 1. FUTURE WORTH OF ONE DOLLAR WITH INTEREST
Payable at beginning of each period

MONTHS	14% Nominal Annual Rate	14¼% Nominal Annual Rate	14½% Nominal Annual Rate	14¾% Nominal Annual Rate	MONTHS
1	1.0116 666 667	1.0118 750 000	1.0120 833 333	1.0122 916 667	1
2	1.0234 694 444	1.0238 910 156	1.0243 126 736	1.0247 344 184	2
3	1.0354 099 213	1.0360 497 214	1.0366 897 851	1.0373 301 123	3
4	1.0474 897 037	1.0483 528 119	1.0492 164 533	1.0500 806 283	4
5	1.0597 104 169	1.0608 020 015	1.0618 944 855	1.0629 878 693	5
6	1.0720 737 051	1.0733 990 253	1.0747 257 105	1.0760 537 619	6
7	1.0845 812 317	1.0861 456 387	1.0877 119 795	1.0892 802 560	7
8	1.0972 346 794	1.0990 436 182	1.1008 551 659	1.1026 693 258	8
9	1.1100 357 506	1.1120 947 611	1.1141 571 658	1.1162 229 696	9
10	1.1229 861 677	1.1253 008 864	1.1276 198 983	1.1299 432 103	10
11	1.1360 876 730	1.1386 638 345	1.1412 453 054	1.1438 320 956	11
YEARS					
1	1.1493 420 292	1.1521 854 675	1.1550 353 528	1.1578 916 984	12
2	1.3209 871 001	1.3275 313 515	1.3341 066 662	1.3407 131 853	24
3	1.5182 659 942	1.5295 623 308	1.5409 403 639	1.5524 006 673	36
4	1.7450 069 186	1.7623 394 892	1.7798 405 969	1.7975 118 453	48
5	2.0056 097 928	2.0305 419 482	2.0557 788 117	2.0813 240 436	60
6	2.3051 316 291	2.3395 609 239	2.3744 972 051	2.4099 478 318	72
7	2.6493 846 642	2.6956 080 968	2.7426 282 170	2.7904 585 881	84
8	3.0450 491 461	3.1058 404 751	3.1678 325 503	3.2310 488 341	96
9	3.4998 029 646	3.5785 042 598	3.6589 585 873	3.7412 046 222	108
10	4.0224 706 412	4.1231 006 034	4.2262 265 228	4.3319 097 743	120
11	4.6231 945 691	4.7505 765 963	4.8814 410 428	5.0158 823 660	132
12	5.3136 318 275	5.4735 453 164	5.6382 369 771	5.8078 485 520	144
13	6.1071 803 871	6.3065 393 692	6.5123 630 360	6.7248 596 242	156
14	7.0192 390 988	7.2663 030 113	7.5220 095 369	7.7866 591 321	168
15	8.0675 065 093	8.3721 287 320	8.6881 869 392	9.0161 079 677	180
16	9.2723 243 021	9.6462 450 569	10.0351 630 666	10.4396 765 681	192
17	10.6570 720 288	11.1142 633 704	11.5909 681 130	12.0880 148 326	204
18	12.2486 207 910	12.8056 927 372	13.3879 779 438	13.9966 120 254	216
19	14.0778 546 749	14.7545 330 729	15.4635 878 276	16.2065 608 706	228
20	16.1802 700 590	16.9999 585 861	17.8609 906 221	18.7654 422 924	240
21	18.5966 644 227	19.5871 052 308	20.6300 756 046	21.7283 498 480	252
22	21.3739 280 241	22.5679 779 971	23.8284 666 543	25.1590 759 100	264
23	24.5659 538 073	26.0024 962 788	27.5227 213 889	29.1314 851 367	276
24	28.2346 831 983	29.9596 983 308	31.7897 162 095	33.7311 048 032	288
25	32.4513 080 812	34.5191 290 270	36.7182 460 776	39.0569 662 311	300
26	37.2976 522 804	39.7724 388 152	42.4108 723 126	45.2237 369 654	312
27	42.8677 593 567	45.8252 260 093	48.9860 568 643	52.3641 896 050	324
28	49.2697 175 266	52.7991 594 522	56.5806 274 727	60.6320 604 394	336
29	56.6277 571 204	60.8344 242 164	65.3526 250 149	70.2053 594 425	348
30	65.0846 612 783	70.0925 395 050	75.4845 922 907	81.2902 028 849	360
31	74.8045 366 638	80.7596 053 969	87.1873 726 877	94.1252 510 854	372
32	85.9759 979 631	93.0500 436 982	100.7044 977 724	108.9868 468 459	384
33	98.8158 279 620	107.2109 080 980	116.3172 551 135	126.1949 652 027	396
34	113.5731 842 276	123.5268 502 666	134.3505 417 973	146.1201 025 939	408
35	130.5344 340 237	142.3258 417 215	155.1796 254 442	169.1912 537 695	420
36	150.0287 112 822	163.9857 664 793	179.2379 534 229	195.9051 481 894	432
37	172.4343 034 644	188.9420 170 121	207.0261 727 677	226.8369 447 714	444
38	198.1859 922 487	217.6962 461 989	239.1225 485 024	262.6526 152 516	456
39	227.7834 904 916	250.8264 511 967	276.1949 971 729	304.1232 827 750	468
40	261.8011 391 815	288.9985 919 300	319.0149 860 023	352.1418 244 293	480
41	300.8990 525 556	332.9799 777 458	368.4735 869 069	407.7420 951 823	492
42	345.8359 276 508	383.6546 913 226	425.6000 194 520	472.1211 871 185	504
43	397.4837 668 589	442.0413 598 749	491.5830 686 211	546.6652 032 250	516
44	456.8447 991 785	509.3136 308 758	567.7958 230 973	632.9791 006 435	528
45	525.0709 285 205	586.8237 638 878	655.8242 488 518	732.9212 459 249	540
46	603.4860 864 635	676.1298 127 272	757.5001 926 499	848.6434 262 711	552
47	693.6119 232 142	779.0269 443 585	874.9395 022 665	982.6371 782 201	564
48	797.1973 353 093	897.5835 240 702	1010.5860 566 825	1137.7874 312 454	576
49	916.2524 030 429	1034.1826 922 889	1167.2626 225 191	1317.4346 212 352	588
50	1053.0873 961 793	1191.5702 687 812	1348.2295 950 162	1525.4466 111 736	600

TABLE 1. FUTURE WORTH OF ONE DOLLAR WITH INTEREST
Payable at beginning of each period

MONTHLY Compounding

MONTHS	15% Nominal Annual Rate	15¼% Nominal Annual Rate	15½% Nominal Annual Rate	15¾% Nominal Annual Rate	MONTHS
1	1.0125 000 000	1.0127 083 333	1.0129 166 667	1.0131 250 000	1
2	1.0251 562 500	1.0255 781 684	1.0260 001 736	1.0264 222 656	2
3	1.0379 707 031	1.0386 115 576	1.0392 526 759	1.0398 940 579	3
4	1.0509 453 369	1.0518 105 795	1.0526 763 563	1.0535 426 674	4
5	1.0640 821 536	1.0651 773 390	1.0662 734 259	1.0673 704 149	5
6	1.0773 831 805	1.0787 139 676	1.0800 461 243	1.0813 796 516	6
7	1.0908 504 703	1.0924 226 243	1.0939 967 200	1.0955 727 595	7
8	1.1044 861 012	1.1063 054 952	1.1081 275 110	1.1099 521 520	8
9	1.1182 921 774	1.1203 647 942	1.1224 408 247	1.1245 202 740	9
10	1.1322 708 297	1.1346 027 634	1.1369 390 187	1.1392 796 026	10
11	1.1464 242 150	1.1490 216 735	1.1516 244 810	1.1542 326 473	11
YEARS					
1	1.1607 545 177	1.1636 238 240	1.1664 996 305	1.1693 819 508	12
2	1.3473 510 504	1.3540 204 037	1.3607 213 881	1.3674 541 470	24
3	1.5639 438 187	1.5755 703 999	1.5872 809 965	1.5990 761 980	36
4	1.8153 548 531	1.8333 712 537	1.8515 626 959	1.8699 308 440	48
5	2.1071 813 470	2.1333 544 689	2.1598 472 008	2.1866 633 783	60
6	2.4459 202 681	2.4824 220 850	2.5194 609 617	2.5570 446 872	72
7	2.8391 130 012	2.8886 054 793	2.9389 502 810	2.9901 619 047	84
8	3.2955 132 425	3.3612 501 538	3.4282 844 170	3.4966 413 614	96
9	3.8252 818 844	3.9112 307 573	3.9990 925 059	4.0889 092 966	108
10	4.4402 132 289	4.5512 012 902	4.6649 399 306	4.7814 967 301	120
11	5.1539 975 651	5.2958 862 489	5.4416 507 056	5.5913 959 742	132
12	5.9825 259 581	6.1624 194 083	6.3476 835 377	6.5384 775 322	144
13	6.9442 440 332	7.1707 380 368	7.4045 705 015	7.6459 776 121	156
14	8.0605 626 337	8.3440 416 151	8.6374 287 544	8.9410 682 161	168
15	9.3563 344 925	9.7093 256 115	10.0755 574 509	10.4555 237 932	180
16	10.8604 075 315	11.2980 025 962	11.7531 340 440	12.2265 008 103	192
17	12.6062 671 065	13.1466 249 843	13.7100 265 201	14.2974 493 696	204
18	14.6327 814 955	15.2977 260 365	15.9927 408 706	16.7191 792 358	216
19	16.9850 672 278	17.8007 984 686	18.6555 263 170	19.5511 064 313	228
20	19.7154 935 184	20.7134 331 838	21.7616 645 564	22.8627 109 797	240
21	22.8848 481 707	24.1026 443 289	25.3849 736 652	26.7352 415 669	252
22	26.5636 909 015	28.0464 111 618	29.6115 624 019	31.2637 089 398	264
23	30.8339 242 213	32.6354 722 047	34.5418 766 018	36.5592 169 505	276
24	35.7906 168 390	37.9754 129 639	40.2930 862 944	42.7516 884 388	288
25	41.5441 201 880	44.1890 952 499	47.0018 702 761	49.9930 528 283	300
26	48.2225 251 931	51.4194 839 925	54.8276 643 121	58.4609 736 449	312
27	55.9745 139 739	59.8329 365 899	63.9564 501 639	68.3632 074 089	324
28	64.9726 699 725	69.6230 304 742	74.6051 754 873	79.9427 008 456	336
29	75.4173 201 991	81.0150 169 567	87.0269 096 429	93.4835 514 703	348
30	87.5409 951 357	94.2710 038 302	101.5168 579 462	109.3179 777 899	360
31	101.6136 055 897	109.6959 859 665	118.4193 772 887	127.8344 701 300	372
32	117.9484 517 504	127.6448 626 645	138.1361 598 570	149.4873 220 654	384
33	136.9091 982 277	148.5306 032 038	161.1357 794 385	174.8077 763 028	396
34	158.9179 703 606	172.8337 484 767	187.9648 271 832	204.4170 584 752	408
35	184.4647 520 434	201.1134 673 135	219.2609 014 652	239.0416 186 249	420
36	214.1182 942 951	234.0204 218 873	255.7677 605 528	279.5309 543 198	432
37	248.5387 774 302	272.3117 382 037	298.3529 981 910	326.8784 526 830	444
38	288.4925 087 314	316.8684 261 206	348.0286 621 627	382.2457 626 864	456
39	334.8689 828 392	368.7156 496 979	405.9753 058 330	446.9912 956 709	468
40	388.7006 846 759	429.0463 142 592	473.5700 442 658	522.7035 533 407	480
41	451.1860 757 796	499.2485 128 587	552.4192 816 748	611.2401 009 171	492
42	523.7162 757 949	580.9374 636 442	644.3968 879 813	714.7731 416 428	504
43	607.9060 331 340	675.9926 729 333	751.6887 317 565	835.8428 107 831	516
44	705.6296 743 113	786.6011 790 546	876.8446 278 812	977.4194 966 700	528
45	819.0628 322 963	915.3078 719 111	1022.8389 344 716	1142.9767 178 061	540
46	950.7308 828 869	1065.0740 460 234	1193.1412 391 713	1336.5763 440 341	552
47	1103.5651 674 498	1239.3455 342 454	1391.7988 146 851	1562.9682 526 347	564
48	1280.9682 537 191	1442.1319 897 792	1623.5328 031 275	1827.7068 643 687	576
49	1486.8896 875 641	1678.0991 406 169	1893.8504 150 311	2137.2874 186 212	588
50	1725.9139 221 958	1952.6761 390 060	2209.1758 094 472	2499.3053 310 954	600

MONTHLY
Compounding

TABLE 1. FUTURE WORTH OF ONE DOLLAR WITH INTEREST
Payable at beginning of each period

MONTHS	16% Nominal Annual Rate	16¼% Nominal Annual Rate	16½% Nominal Annual Rate	16¾% Nominal Annual Rate	MONTHS
1	1.0133 333 333	1.0135 416 667	1.0137 500 000	1.0139 583 333	1
2	1.0268 444 444	1.0272 667 101	1.0276 890 625	1.0281 115 017	2
3	1.0405 357 037	1.0411 776 134	1.0418 197 871	1.0424 622 248	3
4	1.0544 095 131	1.0552 768 936	1.0561 448 092	1.0570 132 600	4
5	1.0684 683 066	1.0695 671 016	1.0706 668 003	1.0717 674 034	5
6	1.0827 145 507	1.0840 508 227	1.0853 884 688	1.0867 274 901	6
7	1.0971 507 447	1.0987 306 776	1.1003 125 603	1.1018 963 946	7
8	1.1117 794 213	1.1136 093 222	1.1154 418 580	1.1172 770 318	8
9	1.1266 031 469	1.1286 894 484	1.1307 791 835	1.1328 723 571	9
10	1.1416 245 222	1.1439 737 847	1.1463 273 973	1.1486 853 670	10
11	1.1568 461 825	1.1594 650 964	1.1620 893 990	1.1647 191 003	11
YEARS					
1	1.1722 707 983	1.1751 661 862	1.1780 681 282	1.1809 766 377	12
2	1.3742 188 245	1.3810 155 653	1.3878 445 148	1.3947 058 189	24
3	1.6109 565 983	1.6229 227 950	1.6349 753 898	1.6471 149 886	36
4	1.8884 773 775	1.9072 039 915	1.9261 123 971	1.9452 043 212	48
5	2.2138 068 828	2.2412 816 411	2.2690 916 265	2.2972 408 589	60
6	2.5951 811 617	2.6338 783 984	2.6731 445 252	2.7129 877 856	72
7	3.0422 550 920	3.0952 448 325	3.1491 463 673	3.2039 751 933	84
8	3.5663 468 052	3.6374 270 653	3.7099 089 664	3.7838 198 511	96
9	4.1807 242 162	4.2745 812 920	4.3705 255 120	4.4686 028 455	108
10	4.9009 409 143	5.0233 433 947	5.1487 768 093	5.2773 155 639	120
11	5.7452 299 178	5.9032 632 993	6.0656 098 584	6.2323 863 909	132
12	6.7349 652 619	6.9373 154 178	7.1457 016 524	7.3603 027 249	144
13	7.8952 031 038	8.1524 985 022	8.4181 233 706	8.6923 455 647	156
14	9.2553 160 449	9.5805 405 732	9.9171 228 424	10.2654 570 390	168
15	10.8497 367 281	11.2587 273 274	11.6830 463 444	12.1232 649 387	180
16	12.7188 295 352	13.2308 756 553	13.7634 245 389	14.3172 926 656	192
17	14.9099 124 521	15.5484 776 844	16.2142 517 846	16.9083 881 536	204
18	17.4784 549 722	18.2720 452 221	19.1014 932 506	19.9684 113 911	216
19	20.4894 823 626	21.4726 896 984	22.5028 604 002	23.5822 273 455	228
20	24.0192 218 451	25.2339 788 611	26.5099 026 315	27.8500 595 606	240
21	28.1570 323 660	29.6541 187 017	31.2304 713 727	32.8902 697 005	252
22	33.0076 668 083	34.8485 175 809	36.7916 229 538	38.8426 401 249	264
23	38.6939 239 180	40.9527 995 015	43.3430 383 878	45.8722 505 353	276
24	45.3597 570 791	48.1263 452 059	51.0610 521 053	54.1740 562 022	288
25	53.1739 186 399	56.5564 535 531	60.1533 980 793	63.9782 947 459	300
26	62.3342 320 506	66.4632 318 290	70.8648 010 820	75.5568 714 167	312
27	73.0725 999 648	78.1053 426 734	83.4835 635 681	89.2308 999 630	324
28	85.6608 750 916	91.7867 576 741	98.3493 254 708	105.3796 082 200	336
29	100.4177 424 232	107.8646 939 629	115.8622 057 702	124.4508 554 009	348
30	117.7167 870 698	126.7589 410 338	136.4935 718 845	146.9735 527 739	360
31	137.9959 519 467	148.9628 213 060	160.7987 267 456	173.5723 321 902	372
32	161.7686 247 451	175.0560 706 051	189.4318 550 392	204.9848 692 728	384
33	189.6366 348 632	205.7199 748 705	223.1636 308 934	242.0823 416 993	396
34	222.3054 893 302	241.7551 583 011	262.9019 609 359	285.8935 899 538	408
35	260.6022 334 344	284.1024 873 835	309.7164 210 281	337.6336 506 121	420
36	305.4963 882 162	333.8676 365 986	364.8670 444 031	398.7374 534 843	432
37	358.1244 948 794	392.3499 572 092	429.8382 360 533	470.8996 171 528	444
38	419.8188 874 884	461.0764 028 834	506.3787 261 896	556.1214 465 734	456
39	492.1414 223 601	541.8413 979 398	596.5486 381 384	656.7664 361 436	468
40	576.9230 180 464	636.7536 891 616	702.7749 375 307	775.6258 175 307	480
41	676.3100 068 991	748.2914 044 637	827.9167 552 248	915.9959 701 237	492
42	792.8184 716 581	879.3667 559 766	975.3423 421 591	1081.7698 409 707	504
43	929.3979 426 450	1033.4020 769 237	1149.0197 274 122	1277.5449 095 871	516
44	1089.5060 681 247	1214.4191 775 866	1353.6235 195 735	1508.7506 918 729	528
45	1277.1961 481 884	1427.1443 534 162	1594.6607 260 339	1781.7993 192 605	540
46	1497.2197 481 700	1677.1317 870 121	1878.6189 766 829	2104.2633 691 694	552
47	1755.1469 893 562	1970.9085 659 580	2213.1411 415 208	2485.0858 786 195	564
48	2057.5075 622 742	2316.1451 028 765	2607.2310 421 034	2934.8283 654 018	576
49	2411.9560 324 509	2721.8554 073 162	3071.4957 936 376	3465.9637 352 861	588
50	2827.4656 235 265	3198.6324 385 013	3618.4313 004 813	4093.2221 985 914	600

TABLE 1. FUTURE WORTH OF ONE DOLLAR WITH INTEREST
Payable at beginning of each period

MONTHLY Compounding

	17% Nominal Annual Rate	17¼% Nominal Annual Rate	17½% Nominal Annual Rate	17¾% Nominal Annual Rate	
MONTHS					MONTHS
1	1.0141 666 667	1.0143 750 000	1.0145 833 333	1.0147 916 667	1
2	1.0285 340 278	1.0289 566 406	1.0293 793 403	1.0298 021 267	2
3	1.0431 049 265	1.0437 478 923	1.0443 911 223	1.0450 346 165	3
4	1.0578 822 463	1.0587 517 683	1.0596 218 262	1.0604 924 202	4
5	1.0728 689 115	1.0739 713 250	1.0750 746 445	1.0761 788 706	5
6	1.0880 678 877	1.0894 096 628	1.0907 528 164	1.0920 973 497	6
7	1.1034 821 828	1.1050 699 267	1.1066 596 283	1.1082 512 897	7
8	1.1191 148 470	1.1209 553 068	1.1227 984 145	1.1246 441 734	8
9	1.1349 689 740	1.1370 690 394	1.1391 725 581	1.1412 795 351	9
10	1.1510 477 012	1.1534 144 068	1.1557 854 912	1.1581 609 616	10
11	1.1673 542 103	1.1699 947 389	1.1726 406 963	1.1752 920 924	11
YEARS					
1	1.1838 917 282	1.1868 134 133	1.1897 417 065	1.1926 766 213	12
2	1.4015 996 242	1.4085 260 780	1.4154 853 281	1.4224 775 230	24
3	1.6593 422 014	1.6716 576 423	1.6840 619 297	1.6965 556 860	36
4	1.9644 815 065	1.9839 457 124	2.0035 987 140	2.0234 423 035	48
5	2.3257 334 059	2.3545 733 827	2.3837 649 531	2.4133 123 300	60
6	2.7534 165 413	2.7944 392 731	2.8360 645 831	2.8783 011 959	72
7	3.2597 470 677	3.3164 780 120	3.3741 843 167	3.4328 825 454	84
8	3.8591 875 896	3.9360 405 896	4.0144 078 069	4.0943 187 556	96
9	4.5688 602 650	4.6713 457 670	4.7761 083 946	4.8831 982 600	108
10	5.4090 358 752	5.5440 158 144	5.6823 353 516	5.8240 764 019	120
11	6.4037 128 304	6.5797 123 320	6.7605 113 578	6.9462 397 653	132
12	7.5813 026 500	7.8088 908 513	8.0432 623 194	8.2846 177 741	144
13	8.9754 414 966	9.2676 964 053	9.5694 046 374	9.8808 699 356	156
14	10.6259 509 451	10.9990 264 042	11.3851 198 031	11.7846 825 704	168
15	12.5799 754 286	13.0537 920 697	13.5453 518 628	14.0553 153 913	180
16	14.8933 288 514	15.4924 155 227	16.1154 700 398	16.7634 460 724	192
17	17.6320 888 331	18.3866 065 467	19.1732 468 255	19.9933 702 231	204
18	20.8744 841 211	21.8214 712 746	22.8112 113 966	23.8456 252 463	216
19	24.7131 290 823	25.8980 148 065	27.1394 495 733	28.4401 197 518	228
20	29.2576 690 994	30.7361 113 502	32.2889 350 477	33.9198 659 352	240
21	34.6379 124 344	36.4780 292 229	38.4154 926 834	40.4554 310 989	252
22	41.0075 380 146	43.2926 143 724	45.7045 138 196	48.2502 468 767	264
23	48.5484 850 509	51.3802 554 339	54.3765 662 646	57.5469 414 223	276
24	57.4761 498 704	60.9787 763 275	64.6940 687 390	68.6348 916 623	288
25	68.0455 384 026	72.3704 296 719	76.9692 317 393	81.8592 306 918	300
26	80.5585 500 585	85.8901 966 607	91.5735 051 143	97.6315 906 846	312
27	95.3726 010 533	101.9356 374 676	108.9488 182 411	116.4429 157 109	324
28	112.9108 334 877	120.9785 818 395	129.6209 529 308	138.8787 432 856	336
29	133.6742 017 948	143.5790 036 487	154.2154 537 327	165.6374 303 137	348
30	158.2557 817 840	170.4014 873 980	183.4765 570 863	197.5518 907 491	360
31	187.3577 110 003	202.2347 708 897	218.2897 121 230	235.6155 215 921	372
32	221.8112 442 752	240.0149 387 268	259.7083 746 036	281.0131 242 208	384
33	262.6004 973 280	284.8529 486 726	308.9858 847 824	335.1577 835 396	396
34	310.8905 566 184	338.0673 003 017	367.6133 938 327	399.7348 528 779	408
35	368.0607 583 685	401.2228 065 950	437.3649 864 956	476.7544 137 504	420
36	435.7440 873 222	476.1766 085 875	520.3513 653 785	568.6138 433 867	432
37	515.8738 206 103	565.1327 861 697	619.0837 214 035	678.1724 375 608	444
38	610.7387 490 361	670.7071 709 199	736.5497 231 434	808.8404 114 958	456
39	723.0485 530 996	796.0042 668 420	876.3039 245 042	964.6850 491 622	468
40	856.0112 011 306	944.7085 409 295	1042.5753 265 160	1150.5573 050 635	480
41	1013.4245 802 993	1121.1927 680 310	1240.3953 480 809	1372.2427 992 272	492
42	1199.7849 778 116	1330.6466 159 903	1475.7500 781 091	1636.6419 053 999	504
43	1420.4155 108 978	1579.2292 522 151	1755.7614 162 360	1951.9845 380 274	516
44	1681.6181 740 159	1874.2504 591 993	2088.9025 834 868	2328.0863 236 648	528
45	1990.8538 462 756	2224.3855 848 551	2485.2545 243 035	2776.6541 306 276	540
46	2356.9554 007 406	2639.9306 484 497	2956.8109 587 289	3311.6504 670 646	552
47	2790.3800 027 676	3133.1051 037 529	3517.8413 157 137	3949.7280 900 198	564
48	3303.5078 039 231	3718.4111 624 021	4185.3225 300 079	4710.7483 534 997	576
49	3910.9955 632 411	4413.0602 436 907	4979.4527 689 314	5618.3994 300 958	588
50	4630.1952 965 049	5237.4790 908 983	5924.2626 345 386	6700.9336 494 593	600

MONTHLY
Compounding

TABLE 1. FUTURE WORTH OF ONE DOLLAR WITH INTEREST
Payable at beginning of each period

MONTHS	18% Nominal Annual Rate	18¼% Nominal Annual Rate	18½% Nominal Annual Rate	18¾% Nominal Annual Rate	MONTHS
1	1.0150 000 000	1.0152 083 333	1.0154 166 667	1.0156 250 000	1
2	1.0302 250 000	1.0306 479 601	1.0310 710 069	1.0314 941 406	2
3	1.0456 783 750	1.0463 223 978	1.0469 666 850	1.0476 112 366	3
4	1.0613 635 506	1.0622 352 176	1.0631 074 214	1.0639 801 621	4
5	1.0772 840 039	1.0783 900 449	1.0794 969 941	1.0806 048 522	5
6	1.0934 432 639	1.0947 905 601	1.0961 392 394	1.0974 893 030	6
7	1.1098 449 129	1.1114 404 999	1.1130 380 527	1.1146 375 734	7
8	1.1264 925 866	1.1283 436 575	1.1301 973 894	1.1320 537 854	8
9	1.1433 899 754	1.1455 038 840	1.1476 212 658	1.1497 421 258	9
10	1.1605 408 250	1.1629 250 889	1.1653 137 603	1.1677 068 465	10
11	1.1779 489 374	1.1806 112 413	1.1832 790 141	1.1859 522 660	11
YEARS					
1	1.1956 181 715	1.1985 663 705	1.2015 212 322	1.2044 827 702	12
2	1.4295 028 119	1.4365 613 446	1.4436 532 715	1.4507 787 437	24
3	1.7091 395 381	1.7218 141 169	1.7345 800 577	1.7474 380 001	36
4	2.0434 782 893	2.0637 084 968	2.0841 347 683	2.1047 589 631	48
5	2.4432 197 757	2.4734 916 029	2.5041 321 749	2.5351 459 064	60
6	2.9211 579 607	2.9646 438 531	3.0087 679 764	3.0535 395 642	72
7	3.4925 895 395	3.5533 224 229	3.6150 986 065	3.6779 357 931	84
8	4.1758 035 189	4.2588 927 598	4.3436 177 323	4.4300 102 927	96
9	4.9926 665 676	5.1045 656 377	5.2189 489 301	5.3358 710 692	108
10	5.9693 228 723	6.1181 607 096	6.2706 779 494	6.4269 647 668	120
11	7.1370 308 975	7.3330 216 761	7.5343 526 966	7.7411 683 262	132
12	8.5331 638 313	8.7891 131 755	9.0526 847 361	9.3241 038 700	144
13	10.2024 057 368	10.5343 354 790	10.8769 929 191	11.2307 224 588	156
14	12.1981 816 915	12.6261 002 412	13.0689 379 350	13.5272 116 983	168
15	14.5843 676 891	15.1332 191 403	15.7026 064 116	16.2932 934 193	180
16	17.4373 350 284	18.1381 675 397	18.8670 150 048	19.6249 911 930	192
17	20.8483 946 218	21.7397 976 364	22.6691 191 169	23.6379 637 570	204
18	24.9267 194 557	26.0565 903 494	27.2374 279 348	28.4715 200 675	216
19	29.8028 387 361	31.2305 529 239	32.7263 479 749	34.2934 553 622	228
20	35.6328 155 540	37.4318 904 682	39.3214 019 451	41.3058 761 138	240
21	42.6032 417 767	44.8646 051 012	47.2454 993 178	49.7522 160 864	252
22	50.9372 100 314	53.7732 069 021	56.7664 705 575	59.9256 870 545	264
23	60.9014 539 171	64.4507 574 293	68.2061 196 533	72.1794 575 485	276
24	72.8148 849 717	77.2485 104 110	81.9511 009 311	86.9389 129 784	288
25	87.0587 996 251	92.5874 667 535	98.4659 877 730	104.7164 227 409	300
26	104.0890 828 174	110.9722 239 848	118.3089 749 613	126.1291 269 466	312
27	124.4507 988 672	133.0075 757 330	142.1507 453 788	151.9203 602 253	324
28	148.7956 365 786	159.4184 073 014	170.7971 387 493	182.9854 563 314	336
29	177.9027 669 275	191.0735 418 376	205.2163 886 106	220.4028 293 452	348
30	212.7037 808 918	229.0143 215 478	246.5718 481 162	265.4714 104 459	360
31	254.3125 055 728	274.4888 641 807	296.2613 107 807	319.7557 398 582	372
32	304.0606 528 928	328.9931 216 965	355.9642 551 899	385.1402 793 263	384
33	363.5404 418 251	394.3200 918 065	427.6986 105 239	463.8948 305 520	396
34	434.6555 583 072	472.6188 012 701	513.8889 615 377	558.7533 305 768	408
35	519.6820 838 389	566.4650 012 904	617.4484 982 938	673.0087 594 620	420
36	621.3413 428 208	678.9459 006 382	741.8774 805 056	810.6274 549 542	432
37	742.8870 001 568	813.7617 239 254	891.3815 445 373	976.3868 025 295	444
38	888.2091 967 300	975.3474 359 350	1071.0138 517 754	1176.0410 806 808	456
39	1061.9590 556 697	1169.0186 363 104	1286.8458 829 155	1416.5212 187 073	468
40	1269.6975 443 068	1401.1464 240 239	1546.1726 509 246	1706.1754 015 314	480
41	1518.0734 562 333	1679.3669 840 465	1857.7592 687 720	2055.0588 740 545	492
42	1815.0362 098 859	2012.8327 908 843	2232.1372 057 929	2475.2830 055 101	504
43	2170.0902 744 003	2412.5136 926 873	2681.9602 460 002	2981.4357 314 635	516
44	2594.5993 657 850	2891.5577 805 380	3222.4321 795 534	3591.0879 689 555	528
45	3102.1501 493 951	3465.7239 142 450	3871.8206 831 394	4325.4035 848 180	540
46	3708.9870 892 189	4153.9001 332 129	4652.0747 581 610	5209.8740 920 006	552
47	4434.5323 615 863	4978.7250 062 778	5589.5665 958 297	6275.2035 786 370	564
48	5302.0074 734 468	5967.3323 607 236	6715.9829 438 266	7558.3745 898 583	576
49	6339.1764 804 779	7152.2438 894 374	8069.3961 022 705	9103.9319 640 726	588
50	7579.2345 921 609	8572.4389 998 265	9695.5507 481 140	10965.5291 916 428	600

TABLE 1. FUTURE WORTH OF ONE DOLLAR WITH INTEREST
Payable at beginning of each period

MONTHLY Compounding

MONTHS	19% Nominal Annual Rate	19¼% Nominal Annual Rate	19½% Nominal Annual Rate	19¾% Nominal Annual Rate	MONTHS
1	1.0158 333 333	1.0160 416 667	1.0162 500 000	1.0164 583 333	1
2	1.0319 173 611	1.0323 406 684	1.0327 640 625	1.0331 875 434	2
3	1.0482 560 527	1.0489 011 333	1.0495 464 785	1.0501 920 884	3
4	1.0648 534 402	1.0657 272 556	1.0666 016 088	1.0674 764 998	4
5	1.0817 136 196	1.0828 232 970	1.0839 338 849	1.0850 453 839	5
6	1.0988 407 519	1.1001 935 874	1.1015 478 106	1.1029 034 225	6
7	1.1162 390 638	1.1178 425 262	1.1194 479 625	1.1210 553 747	7
8	1.1339 128 490	1.1357 745 834	1.1376 389 919	1.1395 060 777	8
9	1.1518 664 691	1.1539 943 007	1.1561 256 255	1.1582 604 486	9
10	1.1701 043 549	1.1725 062 926	1.1749 126 669	1.1773 234 851	10
11	1.1886 310 072	1.1913 152 477	1.1940 049 977	1.1967 002 675	11
YEARS					
1	1.2074 509 981	1.2104 259 298	1.2134 075 790	1.2163 959 594	12
2	1.4579 379 129	1.4651 309 315	1.4723 579 527	1.4796 191 300	24
3	1.7603 885 881	1.7734 324 701	1.7865 702 987	1.7998 027 312	36
4	2.1255 829 578	2.1466 086 465	2.1678 379 408	2.1892 727 699	48
5	2.5665 372 640	2.5983 107 669	2.6304 709 873	2.6630 225 513	60
6	3.0989 679 812	3.1450 627 260	3.1918 334 323	3.2392 898 712	72
7	3.7418 519 821	3.8068 654 743	3.8729 948 775	3.9402 591 106	84
8	4.5181 029 106	4.6079 286 814	4.6995 213 376	4.7929 152 611	96
9	5.4553 878 691	5.5775 563 587	5.7024 348 085	5.8300 827 573	108
10	6.5871 135 277	6.7512 188 415	6.9193 776 152	7.0916 891 089	120
11	7.9536 168 038	8.1718 503 435	8.3960 252 400	8.6263 019 774	132
12	9.6036 025 485	9.8914 195 502	10.1878 006 593	10.4929 988 697	144
13	11.5958 794 828	11.9728 307 061	12.3619 545 330	12.7636 414 270	156
14	14.0014 562 557	14.4922 247 398	15.0000 893 210	15.5256 418 589	168
15	16.9060 723 312	17.5417 646 055	18.2012 220 672	18.8853 280 241	180
16	20.4132 539 108	21.2330 067 330	22.0855 008 027	22.9720 367 003	192
17	24.6480 038 097	25.7009 819 173	26.7987 140 591	27.9430 926 212	204
18	29.7612 568 019	31.1091 349 341	32.5177 627 457	33.9898 649 573	216
19	35.9352 592 310	37.6553 035 779	39.4572 997 664	41.3451 343 943	228
20	43.3900 646 265	45.5789 558 452	47.8777 865 819	50.2920 544 177	240
21	52.3913 768 422	55.1699 500 084	58.0952 691 022	61.1750 517 831	252
22	63.2600 202 615	66.7791 380 360	70.4932 398 303	74.4130 858 045	264
23	76.3833 746 065	80.8312 002 485	85.5370 314 755	90.5157 768 983	276
24	92.2291 819 092	97.8401 807 178	103.7912 822 741	110.1030 252 801	288
25	111.3622 177 529	118.4282 917 173	125.9411 285 414	133.9288 750 674	300
26	134.4644 209 797	143.3486 751 168	152.8179 198 748	162.9105 424 776	312
27	162.3591 993 249	173.5129 533 640	185.4304 221 769	198.1637 256 118	324
28	196.0407 772 804	210.0245 779 083	225.0026 796 391	241.0455 551 319	336
29	236.7096 322 013	254.2191 949 958	273.0199 567 603	293.2068 392 914	348
30	285.8152 816 684	307.7135 054 763	331.2844 847 402	356.6556 145 796	360
31	345.1079 471 312	372.4644 059 786	401.9831 045 755	433.8344 484 684	372
32	416.7009 352 261	450.8405 749 247	487.7693 457 056	527.7144 701 612	384
33	503.1459 601 604	545.7091 220 955	591.8630 208 633	641.9097 492 158	396
34	607.5240 918 006	660.5404 715 136	718.1710 752 214	780.8164 252 392	408
35	733.5555 710 326	799.5353 144 035	871.4342 256 632	949.7819 446 864	420
36	885.7324 064 269	967.7782 763 461	1057.4048 939 845	1155.3109 198 182	432
37	1069.4784 782 161	1171.4239 199 880	1283.0631 123 897	1405.3155 347 061	444
38	1291.3428 560 003	1417.9218 875 434	1556.8785 048 570	1709.4201 380 847	456
39	1559.2332 204 053	1716.2894 191 157	1889.1281 773 127	2079.3317 488 662	468
40	1882.6977 082 955	2077.4412 159 418	2292.2824 479 773	2529.2907 375 524	480
41	2273.2652 270 580	2514.5887 154 146	2781.4728 954 916	3076.6190 332 816	492
42	2744.8563 674 249	3043.7233 839 244	3375.0602 920 601	3742.3869 606 664	504
43	3314.2795 605 700	3684.2017 070 456	4095.3237 378 312	4552.2243 774 288	516
44	4001.8301 634 914	4459.4532 768 273	4969.2968 617 774	5537.3073 389 414	528
45	4832.0138 252 535	5397.8378 790 106	6029.7824 741 806	6735.5582 729 895	540
46	5834.4199 162 791	6533.6829 336 198	7316.5837 536 482	8193.1058 675 010	552
47	7044.7761 514 194	7908.5392 399 557	8877.9981 787 690	9966.0608 720 835	564
48	8506.2219 956 322	9572.7009 628 960	10772.6302 761 074	12122.6761 758 380	576
49	10270.8462 389 395	11587.0454 637 262	13071.5912 223 579	14745.9743 172 840	588
50	12401.5435 428 448	14025.2602 790 844	15861.1678 582 702	17936.9435 768 144	600

MONTHLY
Compounding

TABLE 1. FUTURE WORTH OF ONE DOLLAR WITH INTEREST
Payable at beginning of each period

MONTHS	20% Nominal Annual Rate	20¼% Nominal Annual Rate	20½% Nominal Annual Rate	20¾% Nominal Annual Rate	MONTHS
1	1.0166 666 667	1.0168 750 000	1.0170 833 333	1.0172 916 667	1
2	1.0336 111 111	1.0340 347 656	1.0344 585 069	1.0348 823 351	2
3	1.0508 379 630	1.0514 841 023	1.0521 305 064	1.0527 771 754	3
4	1.0683 519 290	1.0692 278 965	1.0701 044 026	1.0709 814 474	4
5	1.0861 577 945	1.0872 711 173	1.0883 853 528	1.0895 005 016	5
6	1.1042 604 244	1.1056 188 174	1.1069 786 026	1.1083 397 811	6
7	1.1226 647 648	1.1242 761 349	1.1258 894 870	1.1275 048 232	7
8	1.1413 758 442	1.1432 482 947	1.1451 234 324	1.1470 012 608	8
9	1.1603 987 750	1.1625 406 097	1.1646 859 577	1.1668 348 242	9
10	1.1797 387 545	1.1821 584 825	1.1845 826 762	1.1870 113 431	10
11	1.1994 010 671	1.2021 074 069	1.2048 192 969	1.2075 367 475	11
YEARS					
1	1.2193 910 849	1.2223 929 693	1.2254 016 266	1.2284 170 705	12
2	1.4869 146 179	1.4942 445 715	1.5016 091 464	1.5090 084 990	24
3	1.8131 304 291	1.8265 540 587	1.8400 742 904	1.8536 917 996	36
4	2.2109 150 811	2.2327 668 395	2.2548 300 285	2.2771 066 501	48
5	2.6959 701 393	2.7293 184 867	2.7630 723 846	2.7972 366 802	60
6	3.2874 419 531	3.3362 997 293	3.3858 733 944	3.4361 732 881	72
7	4.0086 774 097	4.0782 693 327	4.1490 547 648	4.2210 539 241	84
8	4.8881 454 957	4.9852 477 594	5.0842 584 575	5.1852 146 957	96
9	5.9605 610 391	6.0939 318 115	6.2302 585 837	6.3696 062 462	108
10	7.2682 549 922	7.4491 794 020	7.6345 690 024	7.8245 330 450	120
11	8.8628 453 403	9.1058 245 284	9.3554 132 736	9.6117 899 608	132
12	10.8072 745 948	11.1308 958 835	11.4641 386 427	11.8072 868 656	144
13	13.1782 942 930	13.6063 288 705	14.0481 741 399	14.5042 727 415	156
14	16.0694 945 752	16.6322 807 499	17.2146 554 413	17.8172 962 303	168
15	19.5949 984 239	20.3311 830 528	21.0948 667 785	21.8870 708 387	180
16	23.8939 663 868	24.8526 952 221	25.8496 840 626	26.8864 514 407	192
17	29.1360 895 951	30.3797 599 087	31.6762 448 965	33.0277 759 138	204
18	35.5282 879 013	37.1360 049 227	38.8161 220 196	40.5718 837 319	216
19	43.3228 775 288	45.3947 913 270	47.5653 390 598	49.8391 945 570	228
20	52.8275 306 311	55.4902 737 629	58.2866 438 519	61.2233 173 718	240
21	64.4174 198 891	67.8309 205 147	71.4245 481 831	75.2077 681 698	252
22	78.5500 275 253	82.9160 403 412	87.5237 575 203	92.3865 062 510	264
23	95.7832 032 835	101.3559 847 587	107.2517 548 284	113.4891 613 590	276
24	116.7971 841 675	123.8968 431 699	131.4264 748 187	139.4120 231 257	288
25	142.4214 451 159	151.4506 300 146	161.0502 160 165	171.2561 090 350	300
26	173.6674 404 736	185.1321 853 323	197.3511 966 652	210.3739 277 593	312
27	211.7685 286 519	226.3042 817 492	241.8344 773 980	258.4269 240 395	324
28	258.2286 559 016	276.6327 629 423	296.3443 619 630	317.4560 449 568	336
29	314.8817 208 735	338.1539 445 105	363.1408 631 727	389.9684 247 458	348
30	383.9639 632 327	413.3570 043 250	444.9934 044 040	479.0438 698 985	360
31	468.2022 336 909	505.2846 959 154	545.2956 415 672	588.4656 672 829	372
32	570.9216 296 953	617.6564 598 033	668.2061 661 352	722.8812 710 704	384
33	696.1767 454 301	755.0189 139 325	818.8209 228 626	887.9996 932 993	396
34	848.9117 168 958	922.9298 121 116	1003.3844 907 411	1090.8339 818 128	408
35	1035.1553 794 543	1128.1829 135 218	1229.5489 870 240	1339.9990 842 976	420
36	1262.2592 411 983	1379.0828 616 213	1506.6913 286 403	1646.0777 495 530	432
37	1539.1876 655 564	1685.7811 941 865	1846.3020 048 468	2022.0700 068 566	444
38	1876.8717 173 756	2060.6870 796 233	2262.4614 798 691	2483.9453 140 895	456
39	2288.6406 396 785	2518.9693 981 464	2772.4239 774 717	3051.3208 259 186	468
40	2790.7479 925 758	3079.1704 822 829	3397.3328 515 210	3748.2945 900 110	480
41	3403.0132 223 641	3763.9563 489 494	4163.0972 022 357	4604.4690 594 854	492
42	4149.6039 851 654	4601.0337 778 676	5101.4660 831 669	5656.2083 930 804	504
43	5059.9901 053 980	5624.2713 417 725	6251.3448 361 776	6948.1829 441 436	516
44	6170.1068 242 310	6875.0697 458 569	7660.4081 304 693	8535.2665 372 705	528
45	7523.7732 543 802	8404.0369 210 744	9387.0765 832 270	10484.8671 153 159	540
46	9174.4220 312 396	10273.0356 464 157	11502.9389 137 744	12879.7897 459 672	552
47	11187.2084 340 517	12557.6865 479 828	14095.7200 552 142	15821.7535 878 920	564
48	13641.5822 294 593	15350.4277 474 604	17272.9182 832 610	19435.7121 919 909	576
49	16634.4237 546 043	18764.2549 548 948	21166.2621 598 283	23875.1606 332 047	588
50	20283.8680 289 003	22937.2933 318 125	25937.1720 789 498	29328.6548 818 222	600

TABLE 1. FUTURE WORTH OF ONE DOLLAR WITH INTEREST
Payable at beginning of each period

MONTHLY Compounding

MONTHS	21% Nominal Annual Rate	21¼% Nominal Annual Rate	21½% Nominal Annual Rate	21¾% Nominal Annual Rate	MONTHS
1	1.0175 000 000	1.0177 083 333	1.0179 166 667	1.0181 250 000	1
2	1.0353 062 500	1.0357 302 517	1.0361 543 403	1.0365 785 156	2
3	1.0534 241 094	1.0540 713 083	1.0547 187 722	1.0553 665 012	3
4	1.0718 590 313	1.0727 371 544	1.0736 158 169	1.0744 950 191	4
5	1.0906 165 643	1.0917 335 415	1.0928 514 336	1.0939 702 413	5
6	1.1097 023 542	1.1110 663 229	1.1124 316 884	1.1137 984 519	6
7	1.1291 221 454	1.1307 414 557	1.1323 627 562	1.1339 860 488	7
8	1.1488 817 830	1.1507 650 023	1.1526 509 222	1.1545 395 460	8
9	1.1689 872 142	1.1711 431 326	1.1733 025 846	1.1754 655 752	9
10	1.1894 444 904	1.1918 821 256	1.1943 242 559	1.1967 708 888	10
11	1.2102 597 690	1.2129 883 715	1.2157 225 655	1.2184 623 612	11
YEARS					
1	1.2314 393 149	1.2344 683 740	1.2375 042 615	1.2405 469 915	12
2	1.5164 427 864	1.5239 121 663	1.5314 167 971	1.5389 568 380	24
3	1.8674 072 660	1.8812 213 740	1.8951 348 125	1.9091 482 754	36
4	2.2995 987 244	2.3223 082 906	2.3452 374 066	2.3683 881 492	48
5	2.8318 162 778	2.8668 161 393	2.9022 412 847	2.9380 967 931	60
6	3.4872 098 972	3.5389 938 579	3.5915 359 577	3.6448 471 373	72
7	4.2942 873 669	4.3687 759 932	4.4445 410 528	4.5216 041 505	84
8	5.2881 542 933	5.3931 157 966	5.5001 384 931	5.6092 624 254	96
9	6.5120 411 002	6.6576 308 879	6.8064 448 238	6.9585 536 261	108
10	8.0191 834 313	8.2186 347 766	8.4230 044 749	8.6324 127 657	120
11	9.8751 377 511	10.1456 447 089	10.4235 039 320	10.7089 136 855	132
12	12.1606 328 672	12.5244 775 265	12.8991 305 352	13.2849 106 543	144
13	14.9750 814 073	15.4610 714 068	15.9627 290 065	16.4805 559 439	156
14	18.4409 039 894	19.0862 036 792	19.7539 451 701	20.4449 040 936	168
15	22.7088 541 757	23.5613 148 208	24.4455 913 287	25.3628 642 639	180
16	27.9645 758 293	29.0856 979 952	30.2515 234 432	31.4638 249 572	192
17	34.4366 781 020	35.9053 743 095	37.4363 891 767	39.0323 533 902	204
18	42.4066 792 909	44.3240 490 401	46.3276 911 399	48.4214 685 675	216
19	52.2212 520 950	54.7166 367 457	57.3307 152 093	60.0691 071 531	228
20	64.3073 029 055	67.5459 575 919	70.9470 043 842	74.5185 501 581	240
21	79.1905 410 359	83.3833 484 358	87.7972 202 634	92.4437 632 060	252
22	97.5183 456 033	102.9341 065 586	108.6494 342 204	114.6808 323 237	264
23	120.0879 247 043	127.0688 991 481	134.4541 378 532	142.2669 615 164	276
24	147.8809 917 310	156.8625 373 118	166.3875 685 646	176.4888 510 922	288
25	182.1064 671 506	193.6418 413 700	205.9053 251 529	218.9427 132 473	300
26	224.2530 631 549	239.0447 290 460	254.8087 173 345	271.6087 242 193	312
27	276.1540 384 657	295.0931 579 683	315.3268 735 591	336.9433 856 824	324
28	340.0669 399 475	364.2831 708 829	390.2183 497 829	417.9941 033 980	336
29	418.7717 995 643	449.6960 536 196	482.8968 707 570	518.5413 274 152	348
30	515.6920 579 737	555.1355 560 865	597.5869 354 084	643.2748 836 686	360
31	635.0434 745 936	685.2972 872 476	739.5163 791 619	798.0127 216 118	372
32	782.0175 013 137	845.9778 278 654	915.1546 706 338	989.9722 809 361	384
33	963.0070 960 925	1044.3328 735 684	1132.5078 048 062	1228.1071 347 364	396
34	1185.8847 986 992	1289.1959 043 035	1401.4832 345 867	1523.5246 111 783	408
35	1460.3451 641 136	1591.4715 716 971	1734.3414 751 686	1890.0038 728 006	420
36	1798.3264 484 789	1964.6213 233 112	2146.2549 663 514	2344.6386 182 359	432
37	2214.5298 897 620	2425.2628 904 286	2655.9996 670 439	2908.6343 838 952	444
38	2727.0591 703 733	2993.9103 367 648	3286.8109 064 085	3608.2976 341 758	456
39	3358.2078 765 784	3695.8876 251 980	4067.4425 033 003	4476.2627 743 409	468
40	4135.4292 069 759	4562.4563 870 047	5033.4774 310 859	5553.0143 176 582	480
41	5092.5301 096 411	5632.2081 173 138	6228.9497 709 416	6888.7752 052 620	492
42	6271.1417 895 521	6952.7827 963 659	7708.3518 859 730	8545.8493 556 785	504
43	7722.5305 492 477	8582.9904 731 036	9539.1183 077 403	10601.5277 075 909	516
44	9509.8277 292 059	10595.4302 930 177	11804.6995 564 189	13151.6933 024 494	528
45	11710.7757 440 962	13079.7236 051 926	14608.3660 063 471	16315.2935 588 560	540
46	14421.1096 597 820	16146.5051 307 046	18077.9151 858 512	20239.8883 390 987	552
47	17758.7214 001 856	19932.3499 337 836	22371.4970 808 396	25108.5325 863 978	564
48	21868.7877 153 400	24605.8556 118 929	27684.8229 728 239	31148.3145 598 360	576
49	26930.0849 628 513	30375.1505 670 257	34260.0864 066 909	38640.9479 160 122	588
50	33162.7653 780 587	37497.1627 291 647	42397.0029 263 365	47935.9116 840 711	600

MONTHLY Compounding

TABLE 1. FUTURE WORTH OF ONE DOLLAR WITH INTEREST
Payable at beginning of each period

MONTHS	22% Nominal Annual Rate	22¼% Nominal Annual Rate	22½% Nominal Annual Rate	22¾% Nominal Annual Rate	MONTHS
1	1.0183 333 333	1.0185 416 667	1.0187 500 000	1.0189 583 333	1
2	1.0370 027 778	1.0374 271 267	1.0378 515 625	1.0382 760 851	2
3	1.0560 144 954	1.0566 627 547	1.0573 112 793	1.0579 600 692	3
4	1.0753 747 611	1.0762 550 433	1.0771 358 658	1.0780 172 288	4
5	1.0950 899 651	1.0962 106 055	1.0973 321 633	1.0984 546 388	5
6	1.1151 666 144	1.1165 361 772	1.1179 071 413	1.1192 795 080	6
7	1.1356 113 357	1.1372 386 188	1.1388 679 002	1.1404 991 820	7
8	1.1564 308 769	1.1583 249 182	1.1602 216 734	1.1621 211 456	8
9	1.1776 321 096	1.1798 021 927	1.1819 758 297	1.1841 530 257	9
10	1.1992 220 316	1.2016 776 917	1.2041 378 765	1.2066 025 935	10
11	1.2212 077 688	1.2239 587 989	1.2267 154 617	1.2294 777 676	11
YEARS					
1	1.2435 965 779	1.2466 530 350	1.2497 163 766	1.2527 866 170	12
2	1.5465 324 487	1.5541 437 896	1.5617 910 220	1.5694 743 077	24
3	1.9232 624 609	1.9374 780 721	1.9517 958 171	1.9662 164 084	36
4	2.3917 626 148	2.4153 629 188	2.4391 911 965	2.4632 496 026	48
5	2.9743 878 030	3.0111 195 134	3.0482 971 840	3.0859 261 364	60
6	3.6989 384 933	3.7538 212 800	3.8095 069 117	3.8660 069 647	72
7	4.5999 872 523	4.6797 126 915	4.7608 031 744	4.8432 817 866	84
8	5.7205 284 056	5.8339 780 297	5.9496 536 930	6.0675 986 046	96
9	7.1140 295 492	7.2729 464 168	7.4353 796 554	7.6014 063 292	108
10	8.8469 828 028	9.0668 407 237	9.2921 157 218	9.5229 401 195	120
11	11.0020 775 387	11.3032 045 059	11.6125 091 912	11.9302 119 361	132
12	13.6821 459 774	14.0911 742 023	14.5123 429 100	14.9460 098 515	144
13	17.0150 699 164	17.5668 050 858	18.1363 125 979	18.7241 611 194	156
14	21.1598 827 216	21.8997 108 752	22.6652 468 654	23.4573 784 648	168
15	26.3143 577 422	27.3013 410 277	28.3251 301 881	29.3870 898 104	180
16	32.7244 452 391	34.0352 996 513	35.3983 790 663	36.8157 528 269	192
17	40.6960 081 144	42.4302 096 068	44.2379 340 254	46.1222 824 360	204
18	50.6094 164 271	52.8957 495 812	55.2848 706 200	57.7813 781 810	216
19	62.9376 970 805	65.9426 467 531	69.0904 081 938	72.3877 372 966	228
20	78.2691 047 130	82.2076 007 095	86.3434 145 881	90.6863 885 196	240
21	97.3351 907 799	102.4843 549 230	107.9047 792 251	113.6106 938 807	252
22	121.0457 101 674	127.7624 321 029	134.8503 697 146	142.3299 568 411	264
23	150.5320 309 391	159.2754 237 378	168.5247 154 274	178.3090 651 277	276
24	187.2011 185 469	198.5611 904 007	210.6080 967 370	223.3832 104 805	288
25	232.8026 704 123	247.5369 106 426	263.2003 875 437	279.8514 965 509	300
26	289.5126 042 611	308.5926 409 226	328.9258 346 495	350.5942 096 244	312
27	360.0368 839 309	384.7079 523 793	411.0640 022 592	439.2197 338 127	324
28	447.7406 367 902	479.5973 364 152	513.7134 154 677	550.2486 044 398	336
29	556.8087 237 190	597.8914 750 112	641.9960 682 060	689.3440 876 612	348
30	692.4454 233 866	745.3632 219 125	802.3130 001 711	863.6010 475 252	360
31	861.1227 589 369	929.2093 227 610	1002.6636 954 994	1081.9078 347 608	372
32	1070.8893 162 040	1158.4016 223 534	1253.0452 405 209	1355.3996 562 082	384
33	1331.7542 889 886	1444.1248 982 346	1565.9511 577 411	1698.0265 499 745	396
34	1656.1650 764 491	1800.3226 872 770	1956.9948 068 365	2127.2649 371 069	408
35	2059.6012 215 833	2244.3777 420 404	2445.6884 590 893	2665.0090 440 060	420
36	2561.3130 310 912	2797.9603 237 602	3056.4169 194 663	3338.6876 644 961	432
37	3185.2401 205 096	3488.0857 293 743	3819.6542 780 753	4182.6632 244 003	444
38	3961.1537 137 973	4348.4326 608 011	4773.4845 043 871	5239.9845 109 175	456
39	4926.0772 031 904	5420.9867 740 016	5965.5017 587 365	6564.5824 685 281	468
40	6126.0527 525 779	6758.0896 144 053	7455.1852 427 262	8224.0210 627 190	480
41	7618.3382 394 132	8424.9929 284 772	9316.8670 886 677	10302.9435 252 430	492
42	9474.1393 641 579	10503.0430 039 862	11643.4413 796 213	12907.3897 640 591	504
43	11782.0072 922 358	13093.6504 374 636	14550.9993 724 793	16170.2051 567 258	516
44	14652.0639 499 414	16323.2390 568 545	18184.6222 121 642	20257.8166 143 775	528
45	18221.2565 879 709	20349.4155 109 609	22725.6201 814 263	25378.7215 439 907	540
46	22659.8923 386 489	25368.6606 068 448	28400.5797 098 703	31794.1227 067 037	552
47	28179.7645 689 342	31625.9177 389 459	35492.6695 692 965	39831.2514 259 920	564
48	35044.2587 852 078	39426.5463 333 412	44355.7704 111 744	49900.0587 245 664	576
49	43580.9203 018 852	49151.2236 453 098	55432.1326 810 191	62514.1257 573 021	588
50	54197.0833 510 957	61274.5221 304 939	69274.4440 031 641	78316.8601 217 660	600

TABLE 2. FUTURE WORTH OF ONE DOLLAR PER PERIOD WITH INTEREST
Payable at end of each period

MONTHLY Compounding

MONTHS	5% Nominal Annual Rate	5¼% Nominal Annual Rate	5½% Nominal Annual Rate	5¾% Nominal Annual Rate	MONTHS
1	1.0000 000 000	1.0000 000 000	1.0000 000 000	1.0000 000 000	1
2	2.0041 666 667	2.0043 750 000	2.0045 833 333	2.0047 916 667	2
3	3.0125 173 611	3.0131 441 406	3.0137 710 069	3.0143 979 601	3
4	4.0250 695 168	4.0263 266 462	4.0275 841 241	4.0288 419 503	4
5	5.0418 406 398	5.0439 418 253	5.0460 438 846	5.0481 468 180	5
6	6.0628 483 091	6.0660 090 708	6.0691 715 858	6.0723 358 548	6
7	7.0881 101 771	7.0925 478 605	7.0969 886 222	7.1014 324 641	7
8	8.1176 439 695	8.1235 777 574	8.1295 164 867	8.1354 601 613	8
9	9.1514 674 860	9.1591 184 101	9.1667 767 706	9.1744 425 746	9
10	10.1895 986 005	10.1991 895 531	10.2087 911 641	10.2184 034 453	10
11	11.2320 552 614	11.2438 110 074	11.2555 814 570	11.2673 666 285	11
YEARS					
1	12.2788 554 916	12.2930 026 806	12.3071 695 387	12.3213 560 936	12
2	25.1859 205 340	25.2471 462 388	25.3085 601 784	25.3701 629 720	24
3	38.7533 355 200	38.8979 880 786	39.0433 314 462	39.1893 692 070	36
4	53.0148 852 061	53.2829 979 479	53.5528 517 740	53.8244 590 466	48
5	68.0060 828 408	68.4416 607 886	68.8808 230 988	69.3236 021 211	60
6	83.7642 585 981	84.4155 851 172	85.0734 124 901	85.7378 119 877	72
7	100.3286 525 342	101.2486 172 345	102.1793 912 030	103.1211 140 355	84
8	117.7405 123 014	118.9869 615 785	120.2502 815 749	121.5307 233 032	96
9	136.0431 958 600	137.6793 075 487	139.3405 122 080	141.0272 327 961	108
10	155.2822 794 457	157.3769 631 526	159.5075 819 053	161.6748 129 201	120
11	175.5056 710 611	178.1339 958 390	180.8122 328 545	183.5414 226 909	132
12	196.7637 297 732	200.0073 809 060	203.3186 335 800	206.6990 334 133	144
13	219.1093 911 143	223.0571 578 911	227.0945 722 155	231.2238 655 657	156
14	242.5982 988 991	247.3465 953 712	252.2116 606 780	257.1966 396 705	168
15	267.2889 437 852	272.9423 646 264	278.7455 503 598	284.7028 419 764	180
16	293.2428 089 237	299.9147 226 444	306.7761 599 862	313.8330 058 256	192
17	320.5245 230 600	328.3377 049 661	336.3879 163 270	344.6830 096 337	204
18	349.2020 214 691	358.2893 289 035	367.6700 084 852	377.3543 924 616	216
19	379.3467 151 232	389.8518 076 869	400.7166 565 304	411.9546 882 195	228
20	411.0336 685 157	423.1117 761 289	435.6273 952 848	448.5977 796 012	240
21	444.3417 865 818	458.1605 284 263	472.5073 741 168	487.4042 729 157	252
22	479.3540 111 832	495.0942 687 497	511.4676 736 458	528.5018 950 481	264
23	516.1575 276 441	534.0143 753 116	552.6256 403 112	572.0259 138 573	276
24	554.8439 818 560	575.0276 786 360	596.1052 398 140	618.1195 833 937	288
25	595.5097 084 876	618.2467 547 941	642.0374 304 952	666.9346 154 027	300
26	638.2559 708 724	663.7902 344 106	690.5605 577 755	718.6316 786 654	312
27	683.1892 131 682	711.7831 282 890	741.8207 708 449	773.3809 278 210	324
28	730.4213 254 178	762.3571 705 498	795.9724 628 565	831.3625 634 095	336
29	780.0699 221 711	815.6511 802 227	853.1787 359 507	892.7674 249 806	348
30	832.2586 353 615	871.8114 422 871	913.6118 925 108	957.7976 192 187	360
31	887.1174 221 666	930.9921 092 045	977.4539 541 288	1026.6671 851 529	372
32	944.7828 886 203	993.3556 240 464	1044.8972 098 452	1099.6027 986 402	384
33	1005.3986 297 799	1059.0731 663 795	1116.1447 953 140	1176.8445 184 422	396
34	1069.1155 872 987	1128.3251 221 304	1191.4113 046 368	1258.6465 763 493	408
35	1136.0924 252 915	1201.3015 787 211	1270.9234 367 092	1345.2782 139 537	420
36	1206.4959 254 301	1278.2028 468 340	1354.9206 780 264	1437.0245 688 258	432
37	1280.5014 022 533	1359.2400 102 377	1443.6560 240 047	1534.1876 130 104	444
38	1358.2931 397 244	1444.6355 051 843	1537.3967 409 902	1637.0871 469 304	456
39	1440.0648 501 240	1534.6237 309 672	1636.4251 712 518	1746.0618 519 720	468
40	1526.0201 564 208	1629.4516 933 159	1741.0395 833 818	1861.4704 052 132	480
41	1616.3730 993 206	1729.3796 823 942	1851.5550 706 655	1983.6926 599 662	492
42	1711.3486 702 585	1834.6819 872 621	1968.3045 001 264	2113.1308 960 187	504
43	1811.1833 716 579	1945.6476 487 625	2091.6395 151 044	2250.2111 436 891	516
44	1916.1258 058 554	2062.5812 529 004	2221.9315 943 880	2395.3845 860 540	528
45	2026.4372 941 547	2185.8037 668 906	2359.5731 710 891	2549.1290 439 628	540
46	2142.3925 275 536	2315.6534 201 705	2504.9788 146 320	2711.9505 487 269	552
47	2264.2802 507 625	2452.4866 327 947	2658.5864 794 151	2884.3850 076 613	564
48	2392.4039 812 193	2596.6789 937 609	2820.8588 239 075	3066.9999 679 583	576
49	2527.0827 648 899	2748.6262 919 515	2992.2846 041 525	3260.3964 847 008	588
50	2668.6519 707 375	2908.7456 025 219	3173.3801 458 759	3465.2110 991 622	600

MONTHLY Compounding

TABLE 2. FUTURE WORTH OF ONE DOLLAR PER PERIOD WITH INTEREST
Payable at end of each period

MONTHS	6% Nominal Annual Rate	6¼% Nominal Annual Rate	6½% Nominal Annual Rate	6¾% Nominal Annual Rate	MONTHS
1	1.0000 000 000	1.0000 000 000	1.0000 000 000	1.0000 000 000	1
2	2.0050 000 000	2.0052 083 333	2.0054 166 667	2.0056 250 000	2
3	3.0150 250 000	3.0156 521 267	3.0162 793 403	3.0169 066 406	3
4	4.0301 001 250	4.0313 586 482	4.0326 175 200	4.0338 767 405	4
5	5.0502 506 256	5.0523 553 079	5.0544 608 649	5.0565 672 971	5
6	6.0755 018 788	6.0786 696 584	6.0818 391 946	6.0850 104 882	6
7	7.1058 793 881	7.1103 293 962	7.1147 824 903	7.1192 386 722	7
8	8.1414 087 851	8.1473 623 618	8.1533 208 954	8.1592 843 897	8
9	9.1821 158 290	9.1897 965 408	9.1974 847 169	9.2051 803 644	9
10	10.2280 264 082	10.2376 600 644	10.2473 044 258	10.2569 595 040	10
11	11.2791 665 402	11.2909 812 106	11.3028 106 581	11.3146 549 012	11
YEARS					
1	12.3355 623 729	12.3497 884 044	12.3640 342 159	12.3782 998 350	12
2	25.4319 552 411	25.4939 376 090	25.5561 107 014	25.6184 751 458	24
3	39.3361 049 647	39.4835 423 419	39.6316 849 809	39.7805 365 433	36
4	54.0978 322 191	54.3729 838 368	54.6499 265 379	54.9286 730 535	48
5	69.7700 305 099	70.2201 412 272	70.6739 675 458	71.1315 430 518	60
6	86.4088 556 983	87.0866 165 373	87.7711 682 565	88.4625 854 547	72
7	104.0739 272 164	105.0379 741 453	106.0134 001 630	107.0003 525 787	84
8	122.8285 416 922	124.1439 956 493	125.4773 481 248	126.8288 661 762	96
9	142.7398 997 512	144.4789 511 264	146.2448 327 290	148.0379 982 607	108
10	163.8793 468 065	166.1218 878 397	168.4031 542 385	170.7238 784 488	120
11	186.3226 287 002	189.1569 375 158	192.0454 595 767	194.9893 296 637	132
12	210.1501 631 121	213.6736 433 866	217.2711 338 891	220.9443 341 767	144
13	235.4473 277 088	239.7673 082 672	244.1862 183 282	248.7065 320 977	156
14	262.3047 660 641	267.5393 650 226	272.9038 558 190	278.4017 545 746	168
15	290.8187 124 494	297.0977 708 639	303.5447 666 777	310.1645 941 186	180
16	321.0913 366 555	328.5574 270 058	336.2377 560 837	344.1390 146 396	192
17	353.2311 100 819	362.0406 253 177	371.1202 555 376	380.4790 039 579	204
18	387.3531 944 072	397.6775 237 037	408.3389 005 825	419.3492 717 473	216
19	423.5798 542 298	435.6066 520 609	448.0501 472 150	460.9259 960 770	228
20	462.0408 951 615	475.9754 507 805	490.4209 295 799	505.3976 219 311	240
21	502.8741 289 399	518.9408 438 872	535.6293 617 105	552.9657 153 294	252
22	546.2258 672 290	564.6698 490 438	583.8654 862 671	603.8458 769 178	264
23	592.2514 458 764	613.3402 267 922	635.3320 734 186	658.2687 191 699	276
24	641.1157 815 046	665.1411 715 550	690.2454 732 279	716.4809 116 305	288
25	692.9939 624 325	720.2740 470 832	748.8365 251 222	778.7462 989 354	300
26	748.0718 760 435	778.9531 692 099	811.3515 282 726	845.3470 966 782	312
27	806.5468 748 481	841.4066 389 512	878.0532 769 620	916.5851 705 419	324
28	868.6284 836 278	907.8772 291 948	949.2221 652 929	992.7834 044 940	336
29	934.5391 501 941	978.6233 284 208	1025.1573 658 803	1074.2871 642 466	348
30	1004.5150 424 526	1053.9199 451 254	1106.1780 874 832	1161.4658 626 137	360
31	1078.8068 946 290	1134.0597 768 501	1192.6249 168 624	1254.7146 338 611	372
32	1157.6809 056 869	1219.3543 479 736	1284.8612 505 050	1354.4561 246 383	384
33	1241.4196 931 599	1310.1352 206 878	1383.2748 222 334	1461.1424 096 089	396
34	1330.3233 058 124	1406.7552 838 665	1488.2793 331 227	1575.2570 404 625	408
35	1424.7102 987 602	1509.5901 248 363	1600.3161 905 749	1697.3172 375 951	420
36	1524.9188 749 014	1619.0394 893 821	1719.8563 638 633	1827.8762 343 916	432
37	1631.3080 967 491	1735.5288 356 629	1847.4023 639 454	1967.5257 847 359	444
38	1744.2591 730 064	1859.5109 880 788	1983.4903 558 685	2116.8988 451 139	456
39	1864.1768 244 949	1991.4678 975 169	2128.6924 126 461	2276.6724 434 654	468
40	1991.4907 343 311	2131.9125 148 199	2283.6189 200 806	2447.5707 477 888	480
41	2126.6570 875 460	2281.3907 847 595	2448.9211 426 423	2630.3683 484 058	492
42	2270.1602 056 649	2440.4837 682 658	2625.2939 611 891	2825.8937 687 641	504
43	2422.5142 821 050	2609.8099 011 624	2813.4787 940 369	3035.0332 206 892	516
44	2584.2652 246 087	2790.0273 981 872	3014.2667 136 593	3258.7346 211 077	528
45	2755.9926 113 130	2981.8368 116 445	3228.5017 721 185	3498.0118 884 455	540
46	2938.3117 674 664	3185.9837 546 339	3457.0845 492 067	3753.9495 381 766	552
47	3131.8759 702 323	3403.2617 994 427	3700.9759 382 123	4027.7075 983 495	564
48	3337.3787 894 801	3634.5155 623 678	3961.2011 852 270	4320.5268 673 722	576
49	3555.5565 729 512	3880.6439 869 587	4238.8541 989 722	4633.7345 378 854	588
50	3787.1910 847 041	4142.6038 384 455	4535.1021 492 620	4968.7502 122 148	600

TABLE 2. FUTURE WORTH OF ONE DOLLAR PER PERIOD WITH INTEREST
Payable at end of each period

MONTHLY Compounding

MONTHS	7% Nominal Annual Rate	7¼% Nominal Annual Rate	7½% Nominal Annual Rate	7¾% Nominal Annual Rate	MONTHS
1	1.0000 000 000	1.0000 000 000	1.0000 000 000	1.0000 000 000	1
2	2.0058 333 333	2.0060 416 667	2.0062 500 000	2.0064 583 333	2
3	3.0175 340 278	3.0181 615 017	3.0187 890 625	3.0194 167 101	3
4	4.0351 363 096	4.0363 962 275	4.0376 564 941	4.0389 171 097	4
5	5.0586 746 047	5.0607 827 880	5.0628 918 472	5.0650 017 827	5
6	6.0881 835 399	6.0913 583 507	6.0945 349 213	6.0977 132 525	6
7	7.1236 979 439	7.1281 603 074	7.1326 257 645	7.1370 943 173	7
8	8.1652 528 486	8.1712 262 759	8.1772 046 756	8.1831 880 514	8
9	9.2128 834 902	9.2205 941 013	9.2283 122 048	9.2360 378 076	9
10	10.2666 253 106	10.2763 018 574	10.2859 891 561	10.2956 872 184	10
11	11.3265 139 582	11.3383 878 478	11.3502 765 883	11.3621 801 983	11
YEARS					
1	12.3925 852 896	12.4068 906 077	12.4212 158 170	12.4355 609 455	12
2	25.6810 315 719	25.7437 806 116	25.8067 228 988	25.8698 590 694	24
3	39.9301 007 103	40.0803 811 831	40.2313 816 823	40.3831 059 487	36
4	55.2092 362 089	55.4916 289 242	55.7758 642 148	56.0619 551 923	48
5	71.5929 016 481	72.0580 775 572	72.5271 053 242	73.0000 198 203	60
6	89.1609 435 866	89.8663 189 740	90.5787 888 150	91.2984 311 950	72
7	107.9989 806 974	109.0094 358 475	110.0318 714 089	111.0664 428 416	84
8	128.1988 210 340	129.5874 881 691	130.9951 473 604	132.4220 827 637	96
9	149.8589 094 619	151.7080 362 571	153.5858 569 044	155.4928 581 472	108
10	173.0848 074 335	175.4867 029 677	177.9303 419 404	180.4165 166 627	120
11	197.9897 074 475	201.0477 780 499	204.1647 526 176	207.3418 689 091	132
12	224.6949 846 973	228.5248 678 005	232.4358 087 750	236.4296 769 105	144
13	253.3307 885 987	258.0615 934 170	262.9016 204 944	267.8536 139 710	156
14	284.0366 770 795	289.8123 416 970	295.7325 723 538	301.8013 016 188	168
15	316.9622 967 213	323.9430 720 100	331.1122 763 290	338.4754 298 290	180
16	352.2681 120 693	360.6321 837 569	369.2385 986 705	378.0949 672 164	192
17	390.1261 876 635	400.0714 488 544	410.3247 665 002	420.8964 684 218	204
18	430.7210 266 035	442.4670 141 150	454.6005 603 156	467.1354 864 982	216
19	474.2504 697 328	488.0404 787 659	502.3135 990 713	517.0880 987 304	228
20	520.9266 598 255	537.0300 527 345	553.7307 250 249	571.0525 549 975	240
21	570.9770 754 741	589.6918 017 593	609.1394 960 920	629.3510 585 207	252
22	624.6456 397 168	646.3009 858 301	668.8497 940 564	692.3316 896 274	264
23	682.1939 088 081	707.1534 979 573	733.1955 576 303	760.3704 840 199	276
24	743.9023 469 251	772.5674 107 874	802.5366 500 558	833.8736 779 549	288
25	810.0716 930 231	842.8846 391 509	877.2608 716 938	913.2801 337 408	300
26	881.0244 265 007	918.4727 272 319	957.7861 288 550	999.0639 600 333	312
27	957.1063 388 184	999.7267 697 008	1044.5627 710 033	1091.7373 425 757	324
28	1038.6882 187 293	1087.0714 768 518	1138.0761 094 015	1191.8536 022 839	336
29	1126.1676 593 353	1180.9633 945 396	1238.8491 312 872	1300.0104 989 351	348
30	1219.9709 957 759	1281.8932 905 188	1347.4454 247 566	1416.8538 001 861	360
31	1320.5553 829 925	1390.3887 196 596	1464.4723 307 141	1543.0811 372 303	372
32	1428.4110 236 938	1507.0167 814 468	1590.5843 395 171	1679.4461 701 133	384
33	1544.0635 573 822	1632.3870 841 771	1726.4867 513 105	1826.7630 875 786	396
34	1668.0766 220 821	1767.1549 313 472	1872.9396 205 222	1985.9114 683 081	408
35	1801.0546 012 565	1912.0247 468 884	2030.7620 065 807	2157.8415 325 848	420
36	1943.6455 692 975	2067.7537 571 502	2200.8365 546 266	2343.5798 157 307	432
37	2096.5444 499 475	2235.1559 488 804	2384.1144 318 366	2544.2352 971 972	444
38	2260.4964 030 425	2415.1063 238 873	2581.6206 469 672	2761.0060 218 999	456
39	2436.3004 560 833	2608.5454 726 251	2794.4597 828 686	2995.1862 533 328	468
40	2624.8133 983 333	2816.4844 906 068	3023.8221 740 283	3248.1742 011 713	480
41	2826.9539 564 210	3040.0102 633 440	3270.9905 636 936	3521.4803 695 010	492
42	3043.7072 717 972	3280.2911 474 353	3537.3472 778 037	3816.7365 755 190	504
43	3276.1297 018 678	3538.5830 775 009	3824.3819 558 528	4135.7056 925 534	516
44	3525.3539 682 009	3816.2361 308 820	4133.6998 819 208	4480.2921 755 738	528
45	3792.5946 768 987	4114.7015 844 183	4467.0309 624 621	4852.5534 320 375	540
46	4079.1542 380 362	4435.5395 001 908	4826.2394 010 654	5254.7121 059 624	552
47	4386.4292 130 186	4780.4268 798 779	5213.3341 242 884	5689.1693 485 706	564
48	4715.9171 207 875	5151.1664 303 483	5630.4800 168 787	6158.5191 547 367	576
49	5069.2237 360 502	5549.6959 863 088	6080.0100 292 129	6665.5638 508 401	588
50	5448.0709 150 972	5978.0986 392 562	6564.4382 246 684	7213.3308 264 924	600

MONTHLY Compounding

TABLE 2. FUTURE WORTH OF ONE DOLLAR PER PERIOD WITH INTEREST

Payable at end of each period

MONTHS	8% Nominal Annual Rate	8¼% Nominal Annual Rate	8½% Nominal Annual Rate	8¾% Nominal Annual Rate	MONTHS
1	1.0000 000 000	1.0000 000 000	1.0000 000 000	1.0000 000 000	1
2	2.0066 666 667	2.0068 750 000	2.0070 833 333	2.0072 916 667	2
3	3.0200 444 444	3.0206 722 656	3.0213 001 736	3.0219 281 684	3
4	4.0401 780 741	4.0414 393 875	4.0427 010 498	4.0439 630 613	4
5	5.0671 125 946	5.0692 242 832	5.0713 368 489	5.0734 502 920	5
6	6.1008 933 452	6.1040 752 002	6.1072 588 183	6.1104 442 003	6
7	7.1415 659 675	7.1460 407 172	7.1505 185 683	7.1549 995 226	7
8	8.1891 764 073	8.1951 697 471	8.2011 680 748	8.2071 713 941	8
9	9.2437 709 167	9.2515 115 391	9.2592 596 820	9.2670 153 522	9
10	10.3053 960 561	10.3151 156 810	10.3248 461 047	10.3345 873 392	10
11	11.3740 986 965	11.3860 321 013	11.3979 804 313	11.4099 437 052	11
YEARS 1	12.4499 260 211	12.4643 110 720	12.4787 161 260	12.4931 412 114	12
2	25.9331 897 618	25.9967 156 161	26.0604 372 748	26.1243 553 824	24
3	40.5355 577 431	40.6887 408 463	40.8426 590 595	40.9973 162 041	36
4	56.3499 150 651	56.6397 571 391	56.9314 948 188	57.2251 416 076	48
5	73.4768 562 452	73.9576 501 313	74.4424 373 457	74.9312 540 946	60
6	92.0253 250 965	92.7595 504 103	93.5011 879 456	94.2503 194 412	72
7	112.1133 077 144	113.1726 257 343	114.2445 587 761	115.3292 709 129	84
8	133.8685 829 824	135.3349 411 386	136.8214 549 457	138.3284 267 818	96
9	157.4295 353 681	159.3963 927 468	161.3939 434 199	163.4227 096 446	108
10	182.9460 351 817	185.5197 216 015	188.1384 164 104	190.8029 768 155	120
11	210.5803 918 953	213.8816 143 736	217.2468 575 961	220.6774 719 126	132
12	240.5083 865 871	244.6738 983 927	248.9282 202 674	253.2734 086 775	144
13	272.9203 900 780	278.1048 390 824	283.4099 272 851	288.8386 990 742	156
14	308.0225 738 733	314.4005 485 758	320.9395 036 228	327.6438 388 104	168
15	346.0382 216 115	353.8065 150 384	361.7863 532 108	369.9839 646 229	180
16	387.2091 493 629	396.5892 630 417	406.2436 928 367	416.1810 989 716	192
17	431.7972 438 125	443.0381 562 173	454.6306 569 857	466.5865 992 170	204
18	480.0861 281 110	493.4673 543 857	507.2945 887 293	521.5838 299 070	216
19	532.3829 659 904	548.2179 383 940	564.6135 331 075	581.5910 784 977	228
20	589.0204 156 215	607.6602 170 366	626.9989 509 042	647.0647 366 847	240
21	650.3587 456 387	672.1962 316 606	694.8986 722 943	718.5027 715 399	252
22	716.7881 267 958	742.2624 753 957	768.8001 115 680	796.4485 128 546	264
23	788.7311 138 265	818.3328 454 015	849.2337 660 059	881.4947 854 939	276
24	866.6453 332 989	900.9218 480 988	936.7770 240 238	974.2884 181 905	288
25	951.0263 945 609	990.5880 790 636	1032.0583 099 227	1075.5351 630 720	300
26	1042.4110 422 915	1087.9380 011 217	1135.7615 949 968	1186.0050 633 358	312
27	1141.3805 707 135	1193.6300 461 955	1248.6313 073 827	1306.5383 098 968	324
28	1248.5645 211 836	1308.3790 686 468	1371.4776 758 941	1438.0516 315 511	336
29	1364.6446 866 803	1432.9611 802 364	1505.1825 462 040	1581.5452 672 577	348
30	1490.3594 486 634	1568.2189 994 019	1650.7057 111 227	1738.1105 735 651	360
31	1626.5084 738 895	1715.0673 503 568	1809.0918 004 170	1908.9383 250 427	372
32	1773.9578 010 617	1874.4994 505 578	1981.4777 796 249	2095.3277 708 477	384
33	1933.6453 496 682	2047.5936 283 896	2169.1011 116 981	2298.6965 163 061	396
34	2106.5868 860 525	2235.5206 165 024	2373.3086 400 598	2520.5913 046 654	408
35	2293.8824 846 631	2439.5514 701 311	2595.5662 568 435	2762.6997 810 199	420
36	2496.7235 255 857	2661.0661 639 515	2837.4694 257 163	3026.8633 278 794	432
37	2716.4002 728 651	2901.5629 256 212	3100.7546 348 240	3315.0910 700 064	444
38	2954.3100 818 258	3162.6683 691 294	3387.3118 620 729	3629.5751 550 334	456
39	3211.9662 875 950	3446.1484 964 972	3699.1981 422 284	3972.7074 260 820	468
40	3491.0078 313 688	3753.9206 422 353	4038.6523 332 224	4347.0976 131 876	480
41	3793.2096 856 547	4088.0664 413 492	4408.1111 876 673	4755.5931 818 866	492
42	4120.4941 448 027	4450.8459 086 001	4810.2268 449 467	5201.3009 899 270	504
43	4474.9430 526 457	4844.7127 242 470	5247.8858 694 467	5687.6109 168 154	516
44	4858.8110 450 281	5272.3308 296 580	5724.2299 715 942	6218.2216 459 160	528
45	5274.5398 914 574	5736.5924 450 343	6242.6785 604 472	6797.1687 951 921	540
46	5724.7740 271 061	6240.6376 311 112	6806.9532 897 277	7428.8556 105 398	552
47	6212.3773 739 614	6787.8755 271 440	7421.1047 735 016	8118.0864 551 568	564
48	6740.4515 581 235	7382.0074 088 217	8089.5416 632 816	8870.1033 496 522	576
49	7312.3556 391 288	8027.0517 220 624	8817.0622 952 813	9690.6258 408 078	588
50	7931.7274 767 987	8727.3712 620 094	9608.8891 349 990	10585.8945 022 173	600

TABLE 2. FUTURE WORTH OF ONE DOLLAR PER PERIOD WITH INTEREST
Payable at end of each period

MONTHLY Compounding

MONTHS	9% Nominal Annual Rate	9¼% Nominal Annual Rate	9½% Nominal Annual Rate	9¾% Nominal Annual Rate	MONTHS
1	1.0000 000 000	1.0000 000 000	1.0000 000 000	1.0000 000 000	1
2	2.0075 000 000	2.0077 083 333	2.0079 166 667	2.0081 250 000	2
3	3.0225 562 500	3.0231 844 184	3.0238 126 736	3.0244 410 156	3
4	4.0452 254 219	4.0464 881 316	4.0477 511 906	4.0490 145 989	4
5	5.0755 646 125	5.0776 798 110	5.0797 958 875	5.0819 128 425	5
6	6.1136 313 471	6.1168 202 595	6.1200 109 383	6.1232 033 843	6
7	7.1594 835 822	7.1639 707 490	7.1684 610 249	7.1729 544 118	7
8	8.2131 797 091	8.2191 930 235	8.2252 113 414	8.2312 346 664	8
9	9.2747 785 569	9.2825 493 031	9.2903 275 978	9.2981 134 481	9
10	10.3443 393 961	10.3541 022 873	10.3638 760 246	10.3736 606 199	10
11	11.4219 219 416	11.4339 151 591	11.4459 233 765	11.4579 466 124	11
YEARS					
1	12.5075 863 561	12.5220 515 885	12.5365 369 365	12.5510 424 286	12
2	26.1884 705 857	26.2527 835 335	26.3172 948 768	26.3820 052 689	24
3	41.1527 161 222	41.3088 626 762	41.4657 597 494	41.6234 112 458	36
4	57.5207 111 085	57.8182 170 254	58.1176 731 632	58.4190 934 290	48
5	75.4241 369 255	75.9211 227 315	76.4222 487 536	76.9275 525 848	60
6	95.0070 275 762	95.7713 959 811	96.5435 092 490	97.3234 529 469	72
7	116.4269 284 462	117.5376 999 369	118.6617 562 372	119.7992 705 218	84
8	139.8561 637 652	141.4049 778 298	142.9751 858 031	144.5671 094 843	96
9	165.4832 229 643	167.5760 243 783	169.7016 645 141	171.8607 038 029	108
10	193.5142 770 833	196.2732 088 883	199.0806 816 682	201.9376 229 866	120
11	224.1748 374 277	227.7403 646 734	231.3754 952 975	235.0817 027 668	132
12	257.7115 698 188	262.2448 608 500	266.8754 911 579	271.6057 236 536	144
13	294.3942 790 335	300.0798 741 105	305.8987 758 423	311.8543 626 439	156
14	334.5180 793 979	341.5668 797 777	348.7950 272 545	356.2074 459 364	168
15	378.4057 689 972	387.0583 833 060	395.9486 279 855	405.0835 333 496	180
16	426.4104 266 037	436.9409 154 381	447.7821 096 698	458.9438 682 687	192
17	478.9182 522 141	491.6383 164 674	504.7599 391 858	518.2967 303 967	204
18	536.3516 740 485	551.6153 375 104	567.3926 806 274	583.7022 323 876	216
19	599.1727 470 077	617.3815 893 889	636.2415 703 415	655.7776 056 269	228
20	667.8868 699 297	689.4958 726 747	711.9235 460 264	735.2030 250 402	240
21	743.0468 515 491	768.5709 256 889	795.1167 749 564	822.7280 279 014	252
22	825.2573 578 732	855.2786 307 965	886.5667 308 697	919.1785 872 115	264
23	915.1797 767 516	950.3557 232 353	987.0928 739 716	1025.4649 064 016	276
24	1013.5375 387 760	1054.6100 509 839	1097.5959 939 134	1142.5900 089 184	288
25	1121.1219 373 178	1168.9274 388 584	1219.0662 815 429	1271.6592 037 508	300
26	1238.7984 945 246	1294.2792 151 602	1352.5922 017 572	1413.8905 162 252	312
27	1367.5139 244 916	1431.7304 648 274	1499.3702 469 650	1570.6261 825 048	324
28	1508.3037 496 261	1582.4490 792 137	1660.7156 585 557	1743.3453 162 644	336
29	1662.3006 314 802	1747.7156 793 903	1838.0742 124 494	1933.6778 670 795	348
30	1830.7434 830 720	1928.9344 972 858	2033.0351 743 332	2143.4200 022 513	360
31	2014.9874 360 065	2127.6453 071 187	2247.3455 406 740	2374.5510 572 287	372
32	2216.5147 425 804	2345.5365 085 019	2482.9256 931 177	2629.2522 145 865	384
33	2436.9467 005 800	2584.4594 723 813	2741.8866 065 488	2909.9270 878 344	396
34	2678.0566 967 071	2846.4442 717 059	3026.5487 650 094	3219.2244 043 049	408
35	2941.7844 735 683	3133.7169 304 855	3339.4629 549 765	3560.0630 011 798	420
36	3230.2517 350 066	3448.7183 378 000	3683.4331 223 225	3935.6593 705 416	432
37	3545.7792 153 200	3794.1249 874 677	4061.5414 977 735	4349.5580 133 925	444
38	3890.9053 496 915	4172.8717 195 909	4477.1762 160 089	4805.6648 890 924	456
39	4268.4066 960 336	4588.1766 572 118	4934.0616 758 893	5308.2842 758 771	468
40	4681.3202 725 427	5043.5685 499 560	5436.2919 138 645	5862.1593 903 098	480
41	5132.9679 906 704	5542.9167 569 990	5988.3672 896 112	6472.5171 489 915	492
42	5626.9833 800 757	6090.4641 241 129	6595.2348 126 314	7145.1174 949 457	504
43	6167.3408 205 630	6690.8630 341 416	7262.3324 711 686	7886.3077 541 714	516
44	6758.3875 161 757	7349.2149 372 174	7995.6379 606 617	8703.0825 353 259	528
45	7404.8784 686 826	8071.1136 965 986	8801.7222 483 803	9603.1497 378 102	540
46	8112.0147 318 165	8862.6931 184 266	9687.8084 542 207	10595.0032 911 763	552
47	8885.4852 540 257	9730.6790 692 527	10661.8365 752 782	11688.0033 122 966	564
48	9731.5126 463 632	10682.4466 241 639	11732.5346 341 777	12892.4644 367 383	576
49	10656.9032 437 206	11726.0827 310 845	12909.4968 887 031	14219.7531 579 266	588
50	11669.1018 621 500	12870.4549 236 938	14203.2698 035 448	15682.3950 926 841	600

MONTHLY
Compounding

TABLE 2. FUTURE WORTH OF ONE DOLLAR PER PERIOD WITH INTEREST
Payable at end of each period

	10% Nominal Annual Rate	10¼% Nominal Annual Rate	10½% Nominal Annual Rate	10¾% Nominal Annual Rate	
MONTHS					MONTHS
1	1.0000 000 000	1.0000 000 000	1.0000 000 000	1.0000 000 000	1
2	2.0083 333 333	2.0085 416 667	2.0087 500 000	2.0089 583 333	2
3	3.0250 694 444	3.0256 979 601	3.0263 265 625	3.0269 552 517	3
4	4.0502 783 565	4.0515 424 635	4.0528 069 199	4.0540 717 259	4
5	5.0840 306 761	5.0861 493 887	5.0882 689 805	5.0903 894 517	5
6	6.1263 975 984	6.1295 935 814	6.1327 913 341	6.1359 908 572	6
7	7.1774 509 117	7.1819 505 266	7.1864 532 582	7.1909 591 087	7
8	8.2372 630 027	8.2432 963 540	8.2493 347 242	8.2553 781 174	8
9	9.3059 068 610	9.3137 078 437	9.3215 164 031	9.3293 325 463	9
10	10.3834 560 849	10.3932 624 315	10.4030 796 716	10.4129 078 171	10
11	11.4699 848 856	11.4820 382 148	11.4941 066 187	11.5061 901 163	11
YEARS					
1	12.5655 680 930	12.5801 139 578	12.5946 800 516	12.6092 664 027	12
2	26.4469 153 651	26.5120 258 230	26.5773 373 023	26.6428 504 650	24
3	41.7818 210 903	41.9409 932 288	42.1009 316 285	42.2616 402 776	36
4	58.7224 918 329	59.0278 824 882	59.3352 796 128	59.6446 975 298	48
5	77.4370 721 734	77.9508 458 260	78.4689 122 113	78.9913 103 635	60
6	98.1113 136 273	98.9071 788 396	99.7111 371 418	100.5232 781 126	72
7	120.9504 183 209	122.1153 775 523	123.2943 285 550	124.4874 541 228	84
8	146.1810 757 246	147.8174 165 081	149.4764 690 345	151.1585 758 029	96
9	174.0537 126 585	176.2812 716 596	178.5439 717 351	180.8424 143 531	108
10	204.8449 789 035	207.8037 143 530	210.8148 135 293	213.8792 802 804	120
11	238.8604 930 874	242.7134 055 409	246.6420 134 382	250.6479 248 899	132
12	276.4378 761 020	281.3743 224 848	286.4174 943 971	291.5698 824 808	144
13	317.9501 021 586	324.1895 536 735	330.5763 706 011	337.1143 030 289	156
14	363.8092 007 418	371.6055 015 263	379.6017 073 308	387.8033 307 581	168
15	414.4703 462 078	424.1165 366 964	434.0298 053 277	444.2180 902 658	180
16	470.4363 756 157	482.2701 525 053	494.4560 675 254	507.0053 488 280	192
17	532.2627 796 353	546.6726 732 457	561.5415 123 152	576.8849 312 665	204
18	600.5632 160 687	617.9955 758 723	636.0200 045 959	654.6579 723 834	216
19	676.0156 007 086	696.9824 909 899	718.7062 837 104	741.2161 015 750	228
20	759.3688 359 900	784.4569 561 340	810.5048 760 883	837.5516 649 214	240
21	851.4502 442 188	881.3310 021 816	912.4199 900 929	944.7691 019 425	252
22	953.1737 791 575	988.6146 624 151	1025.5665 013 140	1064.0976 074 502	264
23	1065.5490 974 707	1107.4265 033 848	1151.1821 484 782	1196.9052 236 582	276
24	1189.6915 800 691	1239.0052 873 662	1290.6410 733 907	1344.7145 241 083	288
25	1326.8334 028 201	1384.7228 880 089	1445.4688 530 249	1509.2200 692 221	300
26	1478.3357 665 060	1546.0985 938 373	1617.3591 882 005	1692.3078 335 967	312
27	1645.7024 074 179	1724.8149 487 372	1808.1924 314 118	1896.0768 277 694	324
28	1830.5945 226 872	1922.7352 945 834	2020.0561 564 858	2122.8631 623 342	336
29	2034.8472 584 919	2141.9231 989 124	2255.2679 950 887	2375.2668 302 923	348
30	2260.4879 247 961	2384.6639 701 999	2516.4009 898 926	2656.1815 146 843	360
31	2509.7561 174 085	2653.4884 850 635	2806.3117 417 508	2968.8277 632 333	372
32	2785.1259 470 848	2951.1995 758 224	3128.1716 587 869	3316.7899 103 289	384
33	3089.3305 963 074	3280.9012 535 352	3485.5016 492 424	3704.0571 696 460	396
34	3425.3894 474 799	3646.0310 712 036	3882.2106 375 961	4135.0693 685 042	408
35	3796.6380 517 995	4050.3959 645 683	4322.6383 252 916	4614.7678 482 880	420
36	4206.7612 362 608	4498.2119 441 835	4811.6026 638 457	5148.6521 144 794	432
37	4659.8296 773 957	4994.1480 526 079	5354.4525 596 563	5742.8428 857 639	444
38	5160.3403 047 628	5543.3750 450 221	5957.1263 870 626	6404.1522 650 388	456
39	5713.2609 352 084	6151.6193 008 291	6626.2169 497 462	7140.1618 367 989	468
40	6324.0795 809 196	6825.2225 283 324	7369.0436 011 022	7959.3095 862 478	480
41	6998.8589 206 735	7571.2078 849 896	8193.7323 125 252	8870.9866 366 191	492
42	7744.2964 749 391	8397.3532 026 267	9109.3045 654 957	9885.6449 137 526	504
43	8567.7910 820 977	9312.2720 810 775	10125.7760 398 815	11014.9169 722 478	516
44	9477.5163 355 933	10325.5036 957 527	11254.2661 780 305	12271.7493 569 405	528
45	10482.5017 109 113	11447.6122 554 926	12507.1198 232 043	13670.5510 286 273	540
46	11592.7221 876 124	12690.2971 476 780	13898.0422 629 875	15227.3585 556 648	552
47	12819.1972 559 650	14066.5149 189 995	15442.2491 549 456	16960.0199 652 824	564
48	14174.1002 908 651	15590.6143 636 867	17156.6329 746 090	18888.3993 623 752	576
49	15670.8793 786 351	17278.4861 276 629	19059.9478 065 981	21034.6046 616 280	588
50	17324.3907 959 676	19147.7283 884 348	21173.0145 003 684	23423.2410 438 072	600

TABLE 2. FUTURE WORTH OF ONE DOLLAR PER PERIOD WITH INTEREST
Payable at end of each period

MONTHLY Compounding

MONTHS	11% Nominal Annual Rate	11¼% Nominal Annual Rate	11½% Nominal Annual Rate	11¾% Nominal Annual Rate	MONTHS
1	1.0000 000 000	1.0000 000 000	1.0000 000 000	1.0000 000 000	1
2	2.0091 666 667	2.0093 750 000	2.0095 833 333	2.0097 916 667	2
3	3.0275 840 278	3.0282 128 906	3.0288 418 403	3.0294 708 767	3
4	4.0553 368 814	4.0566 023 865	4.0578 682 412	4.0591 344 457	4
5	5.0925 108 028	5.0946 330 338	5.0967 561 452	5.0988 801 372	5
6	6.1391 921 518	6.1423 952 185	6.1456 000 583	6.1488 066 719	6
7	7.1954 680 799	7.1999 801 737	7.2044 953 922	7.2090 137 372	7
8	8.2614 265 373	8.2674 799 878	8.2735 384 730	8.2796 019 967	8
9	9.3371 562 805	9.3449 876 127	9.3528 265 501	9.3606 730 996	9
10	10.4227 468 798	10.4325 968 716	10.4424 578 045	10.4523 296 904	10
11	11.5182 887 262	11.5304 024 673	11.5425 313 584	11.5546 754 186	11
YEARS					
1	12.6238 730 395	12.6384 999 904	12.6531 472 840	12.6678 149 487	12
2	26.7085 659 754	26.7744 844 996	26.8406 067 064	26.9069 332 666	24
3	42.4231 231 859	42.5853 843 846	42.7484 279 264	42.9122 578 858	36
4	59.9561 506 683	60.2696 535 638	60.5852 208 597	60.9028 673 076	48
5	79.5180 796 858	80.0492 599 541	80.5848 913 202	81.1250 143 159	60
6	101.3436 923 630	102.1724 715 491	103.0097 083 837	103.8554 966 492	72
7	125.6949 395 385	126.9169 726 085	128.1537 436 980	129.4054 457 665	84
8	152.8640 846 970	154.5933 490 717	156.3467 278 412	158.1245 855 684	96
9	183.1772 117 136	185.5489 869 442	187.9583 742 997	190.4060 193 660	108
10	216.9981 385 101	220.1724 325 881	223.4032 277 692	226.6916 106 204	120
11	254.7327 835 945	258.8982 696 456	263.1461 003 563	267.4780 311 038	132
12	296.8340 378 923	302.2125 738 088	307.7081 669 716	313.3235 592 694	144
13	343.8072 003 398	350.6590 139 040	357.6737 998 452	364.8557 218 829	156
14	396.2160 424 781	404.8456 758 681	413.6982 317 909	422.7798 835 162	168
15	454.6895 748 350	465.4526 952 701	476.5161 487 138	487.8889 014 724	180
16	519.9295 963 045	533.2407 941 796	546.9513 240 377	561.0739 782 984	192
17	592.7191 171 318	609.0608 295 336	625.9274 213 987	643.3368 604 330	204
18	673.9317 565 964	693.8644 728 510	714.4801 072 646	735.8035 499 628	216
19	764.5422 281 843	788.7161 553 426	813.7706 323 234	839.7397 171 715	228
20	865.6380 380 913	894.8064 283 492	925.1010 597 414	956.5680 248 461	240
21	978.4325 374 650	1013.4669 068 030	1049.9313 399 894	1087.8876 014 732	252
22	1104.2794 850 355	1146.1869 832 800	1189.8984 561 515	1235.4959 298 722	264
23	1244.6892 949 175	1294.6325 224 315	1346.8378 907 808	1401.4134 508 723	276
24	1401.3471 645 895	1460.6667 704 436	1522.8076 958 117	1587.9112 188 059	288
25	1576.1333 006 207	1646.3737 419 737	1720.1154 811 732	1797.5419 873 622	300
26	1771.1454 848 966	1854.0843 781 090	1941.3486 760 240	2033.1751 512 998	312
27	1988.7242 521 807	2086.4058 036 769	2189.4084 594 443	2298.0360 222 952	324
28	2231.4809 811 957	2346.2540 511 336	2467.5478 055 402	2595.7499 765 288	336
29	2502.3292 363 709	2636.8906 617 746	2779.4141 418 724	2930.3920 782 945	348
30	2804.5197 364 205	2961.9636 236 730	3129.0971 806 171	3306.5428 588 734	360
31	3141.6793 694 450	3325.5531 601 887	3521.1825 497 013	3729.3510 141 640	372
32	3517.8547 228 152	3732.2229 437 708	3960.8119 272 133	4204.6038 792 652	384
33	3937.5606 502 827	4187.0773 778 770	4453.7504 676 722	4738.8066 446 582	396
34	4405.8344 592 210	4695.8256 659 933	5006.4624 043 605	5339.2713 982 851	408
35	4928.2963 683 503	5264.8534 719 329	5626.1958 191 455	6014.2172 123 208	420
36	5511.2169 615 603	5901.3030 708 715	6321.0776 914 319	6772.8826 446 092	432
37	6161.5924 474 109	6613.1629 971 546	7100.2204 726 871	7625.6521 946 679	444
38	6887.2286 275 740	7409.3683 141 080	7973.8415 841 209	8584.1984 451 725	456
39	7696.8345 820 067	8299.9127 644 114	8953.3974 045 744	9661.6418 345 302	468
40	8600.1271 952 630	9295.9742 087 143	10051.7335 056 897	10872.7302 474 883	480
41	9607.9477 784 692	10410.0549 269 634	11283.2531 044 960	12234.0408 819 858	492
42	10732.3921 866 575	11656.1385 434 646	12664.1059 424 423	13764.2071 553 706	504
43	11986.9559 931 275	13049.8655 453 582	14212.4000 677 755	15484.1737 558 438	516
44	13386.6964 632 150	14608.7295 975 648	15948.4392 985 066	17417.4833 302 335	528
45	14948.4132 714 763	16352.2971 182 918	17894.9894 799 774	19590.5987 322 412	540
46	16690.8501 312 561	18302.4528 711 498	20077.5770 286 403	22033.2652 420 440	552
47	18634.9197 565 932	20483.6746 564 807	22524.8236 770 565	24778.9177 152 628	564
48	20803.9548 564 569	22923.3405 497 457	25268.8218 098 476	27865.1382 342 895	576
49	23223.9881 737 433	25652.0725 433 413	28345.5553 126 330	31334.1705 262 368	588
50	25924.0649 300 597	28704.1209 051 387	31795.3714 528 258	35233.4981 887 879	600

MONTHLY Compounding

TABLE 2. FUTURE WORTH OF ONE DOLLAR PER PERIOD WITH INTEREST
Payable at end of each period

MONTHS	12% Nominal Annual Rate	12¼% Nominal Annual Rate	12½% Nominal Annual Rate	12¾% Nominal Annual Rate	MONTHS
1	1.0000 000 000	1.0000 000 000	1.0000 000 000	1.0000 000 000	1
2	2.0100 000 000	2.0102 083 333	2.0104 166 667	2.0106 250 000	2
3	3.0301 000 000	3.0307 292 101	3.0313 585 069	3.0319 878 906	3
4	4.0604 010 000	4.0616 679 041	4.0629 351 581	4.0642 027 620	4
5	5.1010 050 100	5.1031 307 639	5.1052 573 993	5.1073 849 163	5
6	6.1520 150 601	6.1552 252 238	6.1584 371 639	6.1616 508 810	6
7	7.2135 352 107	7.2180 598 147	7.2225 875 510	7.2271 184 217	7
8	8.2856 705 628	8.2917 441 753	8.2978 228 380	8.3039 065 549	8
9	9.3685 272 684	9.3763 890 637	9.3842 584 925	9.3921 355 620	9
10	10.4622 125 411	10.4721 063 687	10.4820 111 852	10.4919 270 024	10
11	11.5668 346 665	11.5790 091 213	11.5911 988 017	11.6034 037 268	11
YEARS					
1	12.6825 030 132	12.6972 115 060	12.7119 404 559	12.7266 898 914	12
2	26.9734 648 532	27.0402 021 415	27.1071 458 092	27.1742 965 359	24
3	43.0768 783 592	43.2422 934 647	43.4085 073 427	43.5755 241 557	36
4	61.2226 077 682	61.5444 572 124	61.8684 307 217	62.1945 434 892	48
5	81.6696 698 564	82.2188 992 439	82.7727 441 716	83.3312 467 272	60
6	104.7099 312 100	105.5731 080 252	106.4451 241 616	107.3260 778 068	72
7	130.6722 744 040	131.9544 278 678	133.2521 071 191	134.5655 158 616	84
8	159.9272 925 559	161.7552 249 384	163.6087 647 762	165.4883 001 515	96
9	192.8925 792 665	195.4187 228 734	197.9851 310 227	200.5924 967 326	108
10	230.0386 894 574	233.4455 947 902	236.9134 797 776	240.4435 206 913	120
11	271.8958 561 925	276.4014 097 374	280.9965 665 680	285.6832 431 525	132
12	319.0615 593 601	324.9250 443 352	330.9169 614 251	337.0403 297 483	144
13	372.2090 542 531	379.7381 847 089	387.4476 176 047	395.3419 770 641	156
14	432.0969 817 873	441.6560 600 400	451.4638 397 768	461.5272 361 013	168
15	499.5801 975 356	511.5995 673 700	523.9568 369 953	536.6621 373 520	180
16	575.6219 741 546	590.6089 679 909	606.0490 702 984	621.9568 611 026	192
17	661.3077 513 846	679.8593 591 247	699.0116 325 768	718.7852 295 253	204
18	757.8606 298 936	780.6781 510 018	804.2839 298 168	828.7068 345 101	216
19	866.6588 301 289	894.5648 092 722	923.4959 684 543	953.4921 576 467	228
20	989.2553 653 874	1023.2131 563 762	1058.4935 939 333	1095.1510 869 580	240
21	1127.4002 099 240	1168.5365 635 595	1211.3670 712 537	1255.9652 896 960	252
22	1283.0652 785 316	1332.6964 082 118	1384.4834 500 427	1438.5249 626 230	264
23	1458.4725 741 559	1518.1342 197 703	1580.5232 152 806	1645.7705 517 052	276
24	1656.1259 053 330	1727.6079 922 900	1802.5217 911 715	1881.0401 131 881	288
25	1878.8466 261 924	1964.2332 037 551	2053.9165 407 916	2148.1230 788 884	300
26	2129.8139 091 858	2231.5291 522 043	2338.5999 892 461	2451.3212 916 859	312
27	2412.6101 254 070	2533.4712 978 236	2660.9800 944 247	2795.5182 943 010	324
28	2731.2719 802 717	2874.5503 894 825	3026.0484 985 740	3186.2579 873 755	336
29	3090.3481 344 814	3259.8392 550 970	3439.4578 174 720	3629.8339 237 839	348
30	3494.9641 327 685	3695.0682 491 831	3907.6091 639 296	4133.3906 774 179	360
31	3950.8955 672 302	4186.7104 797 238	4437.7512 608 091	4705.0389 191 679	372
32	4464.6505 196 056	4742.0780 819 181	5038.0926 781 957	5353.9860 536 022	384
33	5043.5624 592 965	5369.4309 706 800	5717.9289 325 720	6090.6845 204 799	396
34	5695.8949 231 825	6078.0996 893 500	6487.7864 159 625	6927.0001 497 537	408
35	6430.9594 714 568	6878.6241 817 334	7359.5853 836 069	7876.4032 817 189	420
36	7259.2486 032 150	7782.9105 514 047	8346.8245 238 156	8954.1857 306 349	432
37	8192.5855 290 664	8804.4081 397 406	9464.7899 678 372	10177.7070 864 017	444
38	9244.2929 386 622	9958.3095 563 406	10730.7919 759 851	11566.6743 214 156	456
39	10429.3831 721 700	11261.7766 368 657	12164.4329 648 057	13143.4592 061 659	468
40	11764.7725 102 515	12734.1956 889 359	13787.9110 253 447	14933.4586 461 109	480
41	13269.5226 413 731	14397.4658 223 296	15626.3636 321 023	16965.5037 436 963	492
42	14965.1127 532 153	16276.3246 517 844	17708.2568 645 686	19272.3241 741 807	504
43	16875.7461 320 834	18398.7162 165 373	20065.8261 679 368	21891.0753 548 624	516
44	19028.6956 467 975	20796.2065 886 273	22735.5754 776 071	24863.9368 986 982	528
45	21454.6930 485 879	23504.4533 512 522	25758.8424 357 838	28238.7919 914 669	540
46	24188.3676 439 604	26563.7359 296 736	29182.4384 518 201	32069.9986 350 468	552
47	27268.7406 022 620	30019.5546 622 184	33059.3735 168 231	36419.2651 790 420	564
48	30739.7819 538 180	33923.3075 212 857	37449.6769 953 426	41356.6442 427 410	576
49	34651.0382 293 743	38333.0545 491 498	42421.3271 030 508	46961.6610 362 762	588
50	39058.3396 999 319	43314.3813 779 189	48051.3034 621 818	53324.5942 545 885	600

TABLE 2. FUTURE WORTH OF ONE DOLLAR PER PERIOD WITH INTEREST
Payable at end of each period

MONTHLY Compounding

MONTHS	13% Nominal Annual Rate	13¼% Nominal Annual Rate	13½% Nominal Annual Rate	13¾% Nominal Annual Rate	MONTHS
1	1.0000 000 000	1.0000 000 000	1.0000 000 000	1.0000 000 000	1
2	2.0108 333 333	2.0110 416 667	2.0112 500 000	2.0114 583 333	2
3	3.0326 173 611	3.0332 469 184	3.0338 765 625	3.0345 062 934	3
4	4.0654 707 159	4.0667 390 198	4.0680 076 738	4.0692 766 780	4
5	5.1095 133 153	5.1116 425 965	5.1137 727 602	5.1159 038 066	5
6	6.1648 663 762	6.1680 836 501	6.1713 027 037	6.1745 235 377	6
7	7.2316 524 286	7.2361 895 738	7.2407 298 591	7.2452 732 866	7
8	8.3099 953 299	8.3160 891 670	8.3221 880 700	8.3282 920 430	8
9	9.4000 202 793	9.4079 126 515	9.4158 126 858	9.4237 203 893	9
10	10.5018 538 323	10.5117 916 871	10.5217 405 785	10.5317 005 188	10
11	11.6156 239 155	11.6278 593 869	11.6401 101 601	11.6523 762 539	11
YEARS					
1	12.7414 598 413	12.7562 503 343	12.7710 613 994	12.7858 930 652	12
2	27.2416 550 038	27.3092 218 973	27.3769 979 030	27.4449 837 097	24
3	43.7433 480 886	43.9119 833 485	44.0814 341 652	44.2517 047 913	36
4	62.5228 108 206	62.8532 481 350	63.1858 709 654	63.5206 949 601	48
5	83.8944 493 969	84.4623 950 692	85.0351 270 386	85.6126 890 097	60
6	108.2160 682 821	109.1151 960 563	110.0235 627 587	110.9412 711 932	72
7	135.8948 605 789	137.2403 505 734	138.6021 980 059	139.9806 179 353	84
8	167.3942 252 644	169.3269 405 323	171.2868 526 895	173.2743 748 893	96
9	203.2415 254 268	205.9329 351 613	208.6674 568 556	211.4458 345 283	108
10	244.0369 173 897	247.6948 938 017	251.4186 984 199	255.2096 048 048	120
11	290.4633 985 437	295.3390 353 463	300.3122 007 070	305.3849 873 268	132
12	343.2982 421 040	349.6938 668 107	356.2304 495 911	362.9113 155 048	144
13	403.4260 102 365	411.7045 906 424	420.1827 216 110	428.8655 398 137	156
14	471.8533 634 184	482.4495 413 033	493.3233 005 476	504.4823 893 843	168
15	549.7259 139 701	563.1589 369 492	576.9723 112 585	591.1774 873 694	180
16	638.3474 059 242	655.2362 722 878	672.6395 468 020	690.5738 528 266	192
17	739.2015 423 369	760.2827 246 273	782.0517 189 096	804.5322 852 607	204
18	853.9768 254 798	880.1249 975 224	907.1836 236 552	935.1862 006 538	216
19	984.5948 257 828	1016.8470 862 061	1050.2937 848 341	1084.9815 711 494	228
20	1133.2423 528 111	1172.8265 171 904	1213.9652 183 851	1256.7227 161 002	240
21	1302.4080 668 808	1350.7756 922 243	1401.1520 536 171	1453.6248 017 348	252
22	1494.9241 442 676	1553.7890 555 596	1615.2328 527 155	1679.3740 322 898	264
23	1714.0136 935 666	1785.3969 047 382	1860.0715 908 980	1938.1966 594 443	276
24	1963.3447 170 510	2049.6267 806 432	2140.0873 978 611	2234.9381 019 843	288
25	2247.0915 204 504	2351.0735 043 547	2460.3343 192 888	2575.1536 568 946	300
26	2570.0045 992 729	2694.9790 787 155	2826.5925 380 521	2965.2125 000 820	312
27	2937.4901 717 109	3087.3238 440 535	3245.4727 015 637	3412.4169 237 270	324
28	3355.7006 896 699	3534.9304 732 108	3724.5352 383 061	3925.1390 425 061	336
29	3831.6378 432 597	4045.5826 143 016	4272.4268 170 957	4512.9775 279 638	348
30	4373.2697 832 517	4628.1602 443 325	4899.0364 120 556	5186.9373 052 560	360
31	4989.6645 240 422	5292.7940 874 169	5615.6737 901 354	5959.6355 763 704	372
32	5691.1417 605 578	6051.0417 828 351	6435.2736 427 262	6845.5380 267 839	384
33	6489.4456 408 252	6916.0888 664 125	7372.6290 457 708	7861.2296 375 813	396
34	7397.9413 867 680	7902.9780 601 779	8444.6584 621 250	9025.7251 729 112	408
35	8431.8390 550 589	9028.8708 575 309	9670.7111 053 337	10360.8251 554 133	420
36	9608.4481 842 387	10313.3459 527 488	11072.9161 763 765	11891.5239 938 354	432
37	10947.4675 914 089	11778.7397 043 687	12676.5822 768 080	13646.4779 033 963	444
38	12471.3151 702 798	13450.5345 529 270	14510.6542 073 572	15658.5413 788 334	456
39	14205.5032 120 636	15357.8021 474 398	16608.2353 968 100	17965.3822 634 471	468
40	16179.0655 328 400	17533.7088 863 650	19007.1853 905 699	20610.1869 288 516	480
41	18425.0435 583 727	20016.0926 641 430	21750.8031 830 531	23642.4687 671 007	492
42	20981.0395 044 200	22848.1208 526 393	24888.6087 274 831	27118.9951 309 747	504
43	23889.8459 138 952	26079.0409 594 477	28477.2367 286 687	31104.8500 756 752	516
44	27200.1620 906 046	29765.0370 166 130	32581.4588 509 583	35674.6527 975 193	528
45	30967.4094 241 117	33970.2065 919 325	37275.3527 913 519	40913.9545 800 237	540
46	35254.6592 559 161	38767.6754 125 562	42643.6393 185 373	46920.8403 996 103	552
47	40133.6888 213 032	44240.8689 836 163	48783.2114 102 628	53807.7651 745 949	564
48	45686.1829 454 681	50484.9633 146 764	55804.8830 886 669	61703.6590 338 793	576
49	52005.1016 127 380	57608.5399 813 839	63835.3895 185 448	70756.3410 180 856	588
50	59196.2363 047 674	65735.4743 029 933	73019.6744 686 164	81135.2864 000 335	600

TABLE 2. FUTURE WORTH OF ONE DOLLAR PER PERIOD WITH INTEREST
Payable at end of each period

MONTHS	14% Nominal Annual Rate	14¼% Nominal Annual Rate	14½% Nominal Annual Rate	14¾% Nominal Annual Rate	MONTHS
1	1.0000 000 000	1.0000 000 000	1.0000 000 000	1.0000 000 000	1
2	2.0116 666 667	2.0118 750 000	2.0120 833 333	2.0122 916 667	2
3	3.0351 361 111	3.0357 660 156	3.0363 960 069	3.0370 260 851	3
4	4.0705 460 324	4.0718 157 371	4.0730 857 920	4.0743 561 974	4
5	5.1180 357 361	5.1201 685 489	5.1223 022 453	5.1244 368 256	5
6	6.1777 461 530	6.1809 705 505	6.1841 967 308	6.1874 246 949	6
7	7.2498 198 582	7.2543 695 757	7.2589 224 413	7.2634 784 568	7
8	8.3344 010 898	8.3405 152 145	8.3466 344 208	8.3527 587 128	8
9	9.4316 357 692	9.4395 588 326	9.4474 895 867	9.4554 280 387	9
10	10.5416 715 199	10.5516 535 938	10.5616 467 526	10.5716 510 083	10
11	11.6646 576 876	11.6769 544 802	11.6892 666 508	11.7015 942 186	11
YEARS					
1	12.8007 453 606	12.8156 183 146	12.8305 119 562	12.8454 263 142	12
2	27.5131 800 087	27.5815 874 936	27.6502 068 602	27.7190 388 065	24
3	44.4227 995 018	44.5947 225 950	44.7674 783 920	44.9410 712 372	36
4	63.8577 358 831	64.1970 096 152	64.5385 321 549	64.8823 196 191	48
5	86.1951 251 010	86.7824 798 494	87.3747 982 131	87.9721 255 771	60
6	111.8684 253 520	112.8051 304 295	113.7514 928 365	114.7076 202 146	72
7	141.3758 283 589	142.7880 502 534	144.2175 076 166	145.6644 275 093	84
8	175.2899 268 075	177.3339 347 473	179.4068 317 466	181.5090 576 861	96
9	214.2688 255 371	217.1372 008 227	220.0517 451 581	223.0132 574 018	108
10	259.0689 120 993	262.9979 455 532	266.9980 570 600	271.0706 257 031	120
11	310.5595 344 973	315.8380 291 599	321.2227 069 905	326.7158 535 085	132
12	369.7398 709 293	376.7196 055 922	383.8540 946 536	391.1470 008 424	144
13	437.7583 188 933	446.8664 731 951	456.1955 615 996	465.7512 914 617	156
14	515.9347 798 998	527.6886 746 370	539.7525 133 960	552.1349 802 382	168
15	605.7862 722 292	620.8108 405 885	636.2637 466 934	652.1579 363 537	180
16	709.0563 687 503	728.1048 468 987	747.7376 330 946	767.9736 868 939	192
17	827.7490 310 424	851.7274 417 178	876.4939 128 024	902.0757 829 937	204
18	964.1674 963 731	994.1635 989 212	1025.2119 677 605	1057.3514 868 118	216
19	1120.9589 721 377	1158.2764 692 956	1196.9865 788 373	1237.1439 352 331	228
20	1301.1660 050 553	1347.3649 335 685	1395.3923 273 452	1445.3241 187 034	240
21	1508.2855 219 463	1565.2299 141 730	1624.5579 810 713	1686.3742 249 247	252
22	1746.3366 877 781	1816.2507 786 997	1889.2524 127 734	1965.4841 418 278	264
23	2019.9388 977 704	2105.4733 708 433	2194.9838 390 797	2288.6631 975 639	276
24	2334.4014 169 985	2438.7114 383 799	2548.1144 449 267	2662.8695 433 123	288
25	2695.8264 069 578	2822.6634 970 088	2955.9927 788 370	3096.1599 645 602	300
26	3111.2273 383 237	3265.0474 791 724	3427.1066 741 462	3597.8633 463 393	312
27	3588.6650 877 144	3774.7558 744 702	3971.2598 784 256	4178.7815 271 836	324
28	4137.4043 594 191	4362.0344 801 880	4599.7760 667 098	4851.4218 662 595	336
29	4768.0934 674 659	5038.6883 550 618	5325.7344 839 877	5630.2665 309 155	348
30	5492.9709 667 073	5818.3191 162 097	6164.2421 206 092	6532.0843 024 995	360
31	6326.1031 426 120	6716.5983 492 097	7132.7480 845 033	7576.2916 137 277	372
32	7283.6569 682 640	7751.5826 272 170	8251.4067 122 024	8785.3705 908 554	384
33	8384.2138 253 140	8944.0764 714 140	9543.4969 749 141	10185.3531 012 371	396
34	9649.1300 766 537	10318.0505 487 648	11035.9069 073 598	11806.3812 279 777	408
35	11102.9514 877 456	11901.1235 133 913	12759.6931 402 105	13683.3562 388 780	420
36	12773.8895 384 748	13725.1171 772 046	14750.7271 798 298	15856.6900 221 901	432
37	14694.3688 683 793	15826.6961 694 375	17050.4418 842 263	18373.1751 678 393	444
38	16901.6564 784 622	18248.1049 430 629	19706.6936 691 673	21286.9924 272 491	456
39	19438.5848 992 786	21038.0169 428 781	22774.7583 867 230	24660.8772 427 083	468
40	22354.3833 584 131	24252.5130 046 311	26318.4816 001 903	28567.4704 620 415	480
41	25705.6330 761 938	27956.2086 522 751	30411.6071 922 972	33090.8823 199 128	492
42	29557.3652 272 078	32223.5529 534 831	35139.3119 546 474	38328.5033 587 940	504
43	33984.3228 736 167	37140.3250 420 957	40599.9780 927 817	44393.1012 793 205	516
44	39072.4113 581 545	42805.3583 895 379	46907.2405 321 864	51415.2488 659 109	528
45	44920.3653 017 587	49332.5274 852 865	54192.3516 291 115	59546.1352 616 864	540
46	51641.6645 540 107	56853.0368 612 343	62606.9124 951 647	68960.8211 203 621	552
47	59366.7362 755 026	65518.0584 722 964	72326.0277 737 770	79862.0077 195 995	564
48	68245.4858 836 529	75501.7704 480 176	83551.9495 185 516	92484.4011 860 670	576
49	78450.2059 751 066	87004.8582 980 134	96518.2860 015 772	107099.7657 954 084	588
50	90178.9196 725 090	100258.5489 499 976	111494.8630 358 240	124022.7751 463 259	600

TABLE 2. FUTURE WORTH OF ONE DOLLAR PER PERIOD WITH INTEREST
Payable at end of each period

MONTHLY Compounding

MONTHS	15% Nominal Annual Rate	15¼% Nominal Annual Rate	15½% Nominal Annual Rate	15¾% Nominal Annual Rate	MONTHS
1	1.0000 000 000	1.0000 000 000	1.0000 000 000	1.0000 000 000	1
2	2.0125 000 000	2.0127 083 333	2.0129 166 667	2.0131 250 000	2
3	3.0376 562 500	3.0382 865 017	3.0389 168 403	3.0395 472 656	3
4	4.0756 269 531	4.0768 980 594	4.0781 695 161	4.0794 413 235	4
5	5.1265 722 900	5.1287 086 389	5.1308 458 724	5.1329 839 909	5
6	6.1906 544 437	6.1938 859 778	6.1971 192 982	6.2003 544 057	6
7	7.2680 376 242	7.2725 999 455	7.2771 654 225	7.2817 340 573	7
8	8.3588 880 945	8.3650 225 698	8.3711 621 425	8.3773 068 168	8
9	9.4633 741 957	9.4713 280 649	9.4792 896 536	9.4872 589 688	9
10	10.5816 663 731	10.5916 928 591	10.6017 304 782	10.6117 792 428	10
11	11.7139 372 028	11.7262 956 225	11.7386 694 969	11.7510 588 453	11
YEARS					
1	12.8603 614 178	12.8753 172 960	12.8902 939 779	12.9052 914 927	12
2	27.7880 840 331	27.8573 432 429	27.9268 171 408	27.9965 064 345	24
3	45.1155 054 982	45.2907 855 660	45.4669 158 551	45.6439 008 038	36
4	65.2283 882 442	65.5767 543 869	65.9274 345 250	66.2804 452 586	48
5	88.5745 077 561	89.1819 909 993	89.7946 219 944	90.4124 478 718	60
6	115.6736 214 508	116.6496 066 919	117.6356 873 596	118.6319 761 652	72
7	147.1290 400 983	148.6115 786 995	150.1122 798 221	151.6313 832 129	84
8	183.6410 594 001	185.8032 907 886	187.9962 129 312	190.2202 942 029	96
9	226.0225 507 560	229.0804 530 298	232.1878 069 066	235.3454 702 172	108
10	275.2170 583 151	279.4387 900 474	283.7372 849 522	288.1140 365 769	120
11	332.3198 052 116	338.0369 507 366	343.8697 320 474	349.8206 456 497	132
12	398.6020 766 460	406.2231 665 555	414.0142 093 679	421.9792 405 469	144
13	475.5395 226 585	485.5662 717 487	495.8377 162 473	506.3601 990 179	156
14	564.8450 106 995	577.8917 992 193	591.2848 067 922	605.0337 688 485	168
15	668.5067 594 006	685.3239 825 447	702.6238 026 498	720.4208 604 335	180
16	788.8326 025 204	810.3346 305 233	832.5007 001 832	855.3524 426 930	192
17	928.5013 685 206	955.7999 987 611	984.0020 531 727	1013.1389 995 857	204
18	1090.6225 196 401	1125.0669 668 053	1160.7283 254 625	1197.6517 513 014	216
19	1278.8053 782 205	1322.0300 434 328	1366.8794 567 967	1413.4176 328 577	228
20	1497.2394 814 758	1551.2209 718 390	1607.3546 753 352	1665.7303 603 571	240
21	1750.7878 536 541	1817.9129 963 704	1887.8689 289 162	1960.7803 098 623	252
22	2045.0952 721 214	2128.2421 897 780	2215.0887 020 820	2305.8063 954 103	264
23	2386.7139 377 067	2489.3486 325 006	2596.7904 465 880	2709.2736 724 194	276
24	2783.2493 471 233	2909.5406 922 418	3042.0453 905 338	3181.0810 239 090	288
25	3243.5296 150 408	3398.4861 835 998	3561.4351 181 463	3732.8040 250 150	300
26	3777.8020 154 448	3967.4348 059 670	4167.3030 435 168	4377.9789 443 723	312
27	4397.9611 179 084	4629.4769 775 685	4874.0477 546 224	5132.4348 502 040	324
28	5117.8135 978 001	5399.8450 209 171	5698.4651 990 190	6014.6819 691 892	336
29	5953.3856 159 285	6296.2636 293 829	6660.1478 433 250	7046.3658 263 120	348
30	6923.2796 108 540	7339.3576 784 442	7781.9502 926 126	8252.7983 078 055	360
31	8049.0884 471 761	8553.1267 645 736	9090.5324 352 546	9663.5786 765 725	372
32	9355.8761 400 295	9965.4973 899 926	10616.9930 211 884	11313.3197 764 096	384
33	10872.7358 582 139	11608.9654 980 060	12397.6087 307 265	13242.4972 421 199	396
34	12633.4376 288 485	13521.3441 424 259	14474.6962 980 508	15498.4425 504 909	408
35	14677.1801 634 754	15746.6334 935 251	16897.6181 779 509	18136.5042 761 847	420
36	17049.4635 436 063	18336.0331 976 917	19723.9556 557 013	21221.4060 434 158	432
37	19803.1021 944 124	21349.1203 832 418	23020.8772 793 015	24828.8344 901 336	444
38	22999.4006 985 123	24855.2204 160 478	26866.7351 351 774	29047.2962 046 763	456
39	26709.5186 271 375	28935.0019 434 441	31352.9269 031 974	33980.2891 939 767	468
40	31016.0547 740 743	33682.3329 253 167	36586.0679 431 607	39748.8421 592 904	480
41	36014.8860 623 685	39206.4403 560 963	42690.5250 328 844	46494.4838 793 993	492
42	41817.3020 635 912	45634.4233 687 233	49811.3719 727 440	54382.7155 537 354	504
43	48552.4826 507 186	53114.1775 422 929	58117.8372 972 802	63607.0712 977 572	516
44	56370.3739 449 069	61817.7976 961 004	67807.3260 295 127	74393.8664 129 539	528
45	65445.0265 837 034	71945.5374 618 595	79110.1110 558 624	87007.7499 280 861	540
46	75978.4706 309 533	83730.4167 362 689	92294.8056 132 644	101758.1976 406 939	552
47	88205.2133 959 811	97443.5830 225 864	107674.7469 433 640	119007.1049 626 431	564
48	102397.4602 975 240	113400.5500 154 128	125615.4428 227 774	139177.6658 566 616	576
49	118871.1750 051 302	131968.4569 665 746	146543.2579 378 899	162764.7557 044 686	588
50	137993.1137 756 640	153574.5158 562 116	170955.5465 378 485	190347.0728 453 617	600

TABLE 2. FUTURE WORTH OF ONE DOLLAR PER PERIOD WITH INTEREST
Payable at end of each period

MONTHS	16% Nominal Annual Rate	16¼% Nominal Annual Rate	16½% Nominal Annual Rate	16¾% Nominal Annual Rate	MONTHS
1	1.0000 000 000	1.0000 000 000	1.0000 000 000	1.0000 000 000	1
2	2.0133 333 333	2.0135 416 667	2.0137 500 000	2.0139 583 333	2
3	3.0401 777 778	3.0408 083 767	3.0414 390 625	3.0420 698 351	3
4	4.0807 134 815	4.0819 859 902	4.0832 588 496	4.0845 320 599	4
5	5.1351 229 946	5.1372 628 838	5.1394 036 588	5.1415 453 199	5
6	6.2035 913 012	6.2068 299 853	6.2100 704 591	6.2133 127 233	6
7	7.2863 058 518	7.2908 808 081	7.2954 589 279	7.3000 402 134	7
8	8.3834 565 965	8.3896 114 857	8.3957 714 882	8.4019 366 080	8
9	9.4952 360 178	9.5032 208 079	9.5112 133 461	9.5192 136 398	9
10	10.6218 391 647	10.6319 102 563	10.6419 925 296	10.6520 859 969	10
11	11.7634 636 869	11.7758 840 410	11.7883 199 269	11.8007 713 639	11
YEARS					
1	12.9203 098 694	12.9353 491 374	12.9504 093 259	12.9654 904 642	12
2	28.0664 118 338	28.1365 340 509	28.2068 738 003	28.2774 317 992	24
3	45.8217 448 741	46.0004 525 519	46.1800 283 471	46.3604 767 940	36
4	66.6358 033 106	66.9935 255 279	67.3536 288 825	67.7161 304 720	48
5	91.0355 162 089	91.6638 750 346	92.2975 728 331	92.9366 585 491	60
6	119.6385 871 255	120.6556 355 774	121.6832 381 938	122.7215 129 994	72
7	153.1691 319 016	154.7257 722 468	156.3015 539 820	157.8967 302 633	84
8	192.4760 103 924	194.7638 448 210	197.0842 884 651	199.4378 400 791	96
9	238.5543 162 178	241.8152 338 724	245.1291 281 419	248.4969 202 770	108
10	292.5705 685 701	297.1084 353 010	301.7292 224 910	306.4345 478 591	120
11	355.8922 438 341	362.0871 359 486	368.4079 896 986	374.8575 324 791	132
12	430.1223 946 430	438.4479 077 752	446.9601 201 757	455.6634 787 991	144
13	517.1402 327 866	528.1845 047 807	539.4998 814 954	551.0934 135 926	156
14	619.1487 033 699	633.6399 192 494	648.5180 249 002	663.7939 371 238	168
15	738.7302 546 098	757.5675 564 885	776.9488 250 445	796.8906 224 741	180
16	878.9122 151 389	903.2031 253 121	928.2490 573 776	954.0746 984 320	192
17	1043.2434 339 097	1074.3491 213 067	1106.4910 388 834	1139.7054 199 615	204
18	1235.8841 229 171	1275.4741 087 093	1316.4722 364 081	1358.9309 653 327	216
19	1461.7111 771 969	1511.8293 931 119	1563.8443 927 398	1617.8312 128 097	228
20	1726.4416 383 860	1789.5861 312 800	1855.2656 459 261	1923.5863 565 825	240
21	2036.7774 274 475	2115.9964 579 743	2198.5797 361 941	2284.6760 382 438	252
22	2400.5750 106 190	2499.5828 367 437	2603.0271 239 116	2711.1145 164 111	264
23	2827.0442 938 481	2950.3605 785 742	3079.4937 009 281	3214.7283 965 557	276
24	3326.9817 809 319	3480.0993 382 811	3640.8037 894 787	3809.4846 234 430	288
25	3913.0438 979 952	4102.6304 162 272	4302.0653 148 549	4511.8778 325 411	300
26	4600.0674 037 942	4834.2078 889 104	5081.0764 423 263	5341.3878 029 860	312
27	5405.4449 973 599	5693.9329 974 196	5998.8046 231 380	6321.0196 988 453	324
28	6349.5656 318 690	6704.2528 743 975	7079.9509 433 320	7477.9420 814 300	336
29	7456.3306 817 376	7891.5466 311 040	8353.6149 651 073	8844.2403 869 292	348
30	8753.7590 302 321	9286.8141 071 144	9854.0779 552 357	10457.8067 658 936	360
31	10274.6963 960 054	10926.4852 656 765	11621.7255 814 969	12363.3909 628 766	372
32	12057.6468 558 822	12853.3713 677 649	13704.1349 119 391	14613.8413 807 406	384
33	14147.7476 147 381	15117.7827 596 670	16157.3549 740 647	17271.5707 486 071	396
34	16597.9116 997 636	17778.8424 591 576	19047.4153 407 929	20410.2870 414 658	408
35	19470.1675 075 816	20906.0298 375 540	22452.1033 475 000	24117.0376 557 935	420
36	22837.2291 162 161	24580.9947 026 690	26463.0577 747 735	28494.6235 332 050	432
37	26784.3371 159 569	28899.6891 477 570	31188.2353 493 330	33664.4501 840 836	444
38	31411.4165 616 271	33974.8728 283 091	36754.8164 501 554	39769.8946 798 839	456
39	36835.6066 770 100	39939.0570 786 300	43312.6282 282 496	46980.2819 923 797	468
40	43194.2263 534 779	46947.9647 380 877	51038.1772 749 629	55495.5809 574 203	480
41	50648.2505 174 356	55184.5960 219 319	60139.4003 799 844	65551.9500 984 175	492
42	59386.3853 743 591	64864.0065 951 982	70861.2612 479 335	77428.2871 143 217	504
43	69629.8456 983 786	76238.9226 035 946	83492.3438 117 960	91453.9636 719 094	516
44	81637.9551 093 500	89606.3392 679 352	98372.6196 053 419	108017.9600 147 744	528
45	95714.7111 141 294	105315.2753 291 940	115902.5982 570 117	127579.6527 231 390	540
46	112216.4811 127 476	123775.8858 101 267	136554.1073 951 209	150681.5548 061 658	552
47	131561.0242 017 121	145470.1710 245 903	160882.9921 106 071	177964.3614 533 408	564
48	154238.0671 705 657	170964.5614 431 846	189544.0757 893 378	210184.7187 153 524	576
49	180821.7024 338 145	200924.7070 018 123	223308.7849 918 238	248236.2079 010 941	588
50	211984.9217 644 860	236132.8569 970 163	263085.9127 622 745	293174.1276 602 813	600

TABLE 2. FUTURE WORTH OF ONE DOLLAR PER PERIOD WITH INTEREST
Payable at end of each period

MONTHLY Compounding

MONTHS	17% Nominal Annual Rate	17¼% Nominal Annual Rate	17½% Nominal Annual Rate	17¾% Nominal Annual Rate	MONTHS
1	1.0000 000 000	1.0000 000 000	1.0000 000 000	1.0000 000 000	1
2	2.0141 666 667	2.0143 750 000	2.0145 833 333	2.0147 916 667	2
3	3.0427 006 944	3.0433 316 406	3.0439 626 736	3.0445 937 934	3
4	4.0858 056 209	4.0870 795 330	4.0883 537 959	4.0896 284 099	4
5	5.1436 878 672	5.1458 313 012	5.1479 756 221	5.1501 208 302	5
6	6.2165 567 787	6.2198 026 262	6.2230 502 666	6.2262 997 008	6
7	7.3046 246 664	7.3092 122 890	7.3138 030 830	7.3183 970 505	7
8	8.4081 068 492	8.4142 822 156	8.4204 627 113	8.4266 483 402	8
9	9.5272 216 962	9.5352 375 225	9.5432 611 258	9.5512 925 136	9
10	10.6621 906 702	10.6723 065 618	10.6824 336 839	10.6925 720 487	10
11	11.8132 383 714	11.8257 209 687	11.8382 191 751	11.8507 330 102	11
YEARS					
1	12.9805 925 817	12.9957 157 076	13.0108 598 714	13.0260 251 027	12
2	28.3482 087 667	28.4192 054 248	28.4904 224 974	28.5618 607 112	24
3	46.5418 024 510	46.7240 099 009	46.9071 037 512	47.0910 886 341	36
4	68.0810 475 208	68.4483 973 810	68.8181 975 335	69.1904 655 886	48
5	93.5811 815 914	94.2311 918 380	94.8867 396 403	95.5478 758 278	60
6	123.7705 793 867	124.8305 581 319	125.9015 714 114	126.9837 428 184	72
7	159.5115 577 170	161.1462 964 878	162.8012 102 883	164.4765 664 487	84
8	201.8250 063 215	204.2463 018 824	206.7022 496 134	209.1933 806 594	96
9	251.9195 481 177	255.3979 663 979	258.9331 470 553	262.5260 795 481	108
10	311.2260 617 802	316.1054 479 573	321.0744 241 078	326.1347 426 640	120
11	381.4385 527 360	388.1539 013 594	395.0064 931 097	401.9993 080 751	132
12	464.5625 399 976	473.6619 722 644	482.9665 590 460	492.4812 016 268	144
13	562.9723 409 350	575.1440 977 595	587.6163 179 933	600.3968 407 179	156
14	679.4788 902 426	695.5844 455 069	712.1225 007 837	729.1053 005 355	168
15	817.4100 302 536	838.5246 657 157	860.2526 991 615	882.6128 715 250	180
16	980.7055 659 794	1008.1680 363 591	1036.4893 741 574	1065.6977 626 382	192
17	1174.0297 999 837	1209.5030 641 155	1246.1654 966 078	1284.0588 319 841	204
18	1402.9047 614 897	1448.4501 756 232	1495.6259 243 355	1544.4929 743 973	216
19	1673.8679 352 179	1732.0358 126 291	1792.4193 993 141	1855.1066 874 446	228
20	1994.6589 952 525	2068.5990 504 459	2145.5269 747 010	2225.5684 012 545	240
21	2374.4408 777 207	2468.0368 155 095	2565.6337 840 052	2667.4094 264 062	252
22	2824.0615 069 104	2942.0949 128 642	3065.4523 762 018	3194.3828 874 405	264
23	3356.3636 506 541	3504.7134 214 866	3660.1074 010 014	3822.8918 144 671	276
24	3986.5517 555 567	4172.4366 140 886	4367.5932 849 608	4572.4997 180 167	288
25	4732.6262 401 862	4964.8994 554 379	5209.3187 478 380	5466.5395 397 298	300
26	5615.8976 511 901	5905.4049 850 904	6210.7546 364 112	6532.8399 336 076	312
27	6661.5953 684 685	7021.6095 629 617	7402.2046 793 912	7804.5914 846 797	324
28	7899.5882 461 940	8346.3361 279 624	8819.7224 866 864	9321.3798 277 588	336
29	9365.2377 737 533	9918.5393 842 556	10506.2025 416 734	11130.4178 240 255	348
30	11100.4081 259 298	11784.4512 972 531	12512.6782 002 020	13288.0151 492 350	360
31	13154.6619 529 589	13998.9405 836 284	14899.8659 741 476	15861.3310 372 143	372
32	15586.6760 664 843	16627.1261 723 004	17740.0028 299 588	18930.4647 360 540	384
33	18465.9174 584 501	19746.2920 815 691	21119.0320 993 677	22590.9487 463 362	396
34	21874.6275 260 050	23448.1600 209 869	25139.2041 485 279	26956.7224 480 805	408
35	25910.1711 789 518	27841.5865 457 406	29922.1705 025 531	32163.6786 760 829	420
36	30687.8179 286 274	33055.7640 756 515	35612.6650 545 253	38373.8936 374 082	432
37	36344.0343 960 214	39244.0199 074 597	42382.8837 533 823	45780.6718 350 933	444
38	43040.3822 849 045	46588.3249 335 608	50437.6953 012 586	54614.5630 307 043	456
39	50968.1331 599 712	55304.6446 498 793	60020.8405 374 317	65150.5385 349 097	468
40	60353.7318 445 108	65649.2898 037 881	71422.3081 039 573	77716.5502 014 750	480
41	71465.2644 917 182	77926.4534 282 410	84987.1095 826 882	92703.7385 393 019	492
42	84620.1160 808 167	92497.1558 949 792	101125.7196 417 662	110578.6076 890 047	504
43	100194.0360 633 764	109789.8610 236 584	120326.4971 133 242	131897.5462 328 385	516
44	118631.8711 070 018	130313.0754 225 583	143170.4628 676 682	157324.1458 252 234	528
45	140460.2715 018 050	154670.3015 551 352	170348.8816 665 241	187649.8567 184 827	540
46	166302.7341 699 252	183577.7842 399 768	202684.1800 271 225	223818.6231 254 928	552
47	196897.4119 600 659	217885.5724 349 867	241154.8330 775 100	266956.2652 407 724	564
48	233118.1979 239 842	258602.5156 453 644	286924.9734 862 562	318405.5224 901 235	576
49	275999.6868 170 216	306925.9299 958 777	341379.6184 410 095	379767.8487 952 117	588
50	326766.7268 121 076	364276.8063 233 579	406166.5806 540 768	452953.2608 085 137	600

MONTHLY
Compounding

TABLE 2. FUTURE WORTH OF ONE DOLLAR PER PERIOD WITH INTEREST
Payable at end of each period

MONTHS	18% Nominal Annual Rate	18¼% Nominal Annual Rate	18½% Nominal Annual Rate	18¾% Nominal Annual Rate	MONTHS
1	1.0000 000 000	1.0000 000 000	1.0000 000 000	1.0000 000 000	1
2	2.0150 000 000	2.0152 083 333	2.0154 166 667	2.0156 250 000	2
3	3.0452 250 000	3.0458 562 934	3.0464 876 736	3.0471 191 406	3
4	4.0909 033 750	4.0921 786 912	4.0934 543 586	4.0947 303 772	4
5	5.1522 669 256	5.1544 139 088	5.1565 617 799	5.1587 105 393	5
6	6.2295 509 295	6.2328 039 537	6.2360 587 740	6.2393 153 915	6
7	7.3229 941 935	7.3275 945 138	7.3321 980 135	7.3368 046 945	7
8	8.4328 391 064	8.4390 350 137	8.4452 360 662	8.4514 422 679	8
9	9.5593 316 929	9.5673 786 712	9.5754 334 555	9.5834 960 533	9
10	10.7027 216 683	10.7128 825 551	10.7230 547 213	10.7332 381 791	10
11	11.8632 624 934	11.8758 076 440	11.8883 684 816	11.9009 450 257	11
YEARS					
1	13.0412 114 308	13.0564 188 853	13.0716 474 957	13.0868 972 917	12
2	28.6335 207 953	28.7054 034 809	28.7775 095 019	28.8498 395 947	24
3	47.2759 692 065	47.4617 501 504	47.6484 361 728	47.8360 320 061	36
4	69.5652 192 875	69.9424 765 028	70.3222 552 397	70.7045 736 370	48
5	96.2146 517 126	96.8871 190 943	97.5653 302 641	98.2493 380 105	60
6	128.0771 973 793	129.1820 615 708	130.2984 633 371	131.4265 321 073	72
7	166.1726 359 673	167.8896 935 618	169.6280 177 216	171.3878 907 598	84
8	211.7202 345 929	214.2833 595 498	216.8833 123 685	219.5206 587 299	96
9	266.1777 711 761	269.8892 474 094	273.6615 522 218	277.4957 484 311	108
10	331.2881 914 881	336.5365 946 023	341.8818 129 339	347.3257 450 759	120
11	409.1353 931 646	416.4178 636 338	423.8499 046 474	431.4347 728 766	132
12	502.2109 220 864	512.1608 663 316	522.3363 072 062	532.7426 476 793	144
13	613.4937 157 837	626.9152 095 803	640.6698 109 661	654.7662 373 631	156
14	746.5454 460 992	764.4559 062 723	782.8500 282 172	801.7415 486 930	168
15	905.6245 126 089	929.3075 599 089	953.6825 780 469	978.7707 788 322	180
16	1095.8223 352 269	1126.8932 080 867	1158.9415 138 224	1191.9994 363 536	192
17	1323.2263 081 215	1363.7127 212 952	1405.5644 832 606	1448.8296 804 474	204
18	1595.1146 303 768	1647.5566 257 162	1701.8872 173 951	1758.1772 843 202	216
19	1920.1892 490 734	1987.7623 840 398	2057.9252 740 487	2130.7811 431 823	228
20	2308.8543 702 680	2395.5215 650 328	2485.7125 585 982	2579.5760 712 854	240
21	2773.5494 517 816	2884.2480 066 526	2999.7080 638 605	3120.1418 295 311	252
22	3329.1473 354 280	3470.0190 839 749	3617.2845 767 015	3771.2439 714 888	264
23	3993.4302 611 412	4172.1045 980 922	4359.3158 694 036	4555.4852 831 062	276
24	4787.6589 981 156	5013.6006 845 611	5250.8822 225 607	5500.0904 306 148	288
25	5737.2533 083 391	6022.1895 947 493	6322.1181 258 167	6637.8510 554 151	300
26	6872.6055 211 588	7231.0503 442 070	7609.2308 083 008	8008.2641 245 796	312
27	8230.0532 578 151	8679.9501 851 807	9155.7240 245 719	9658.9030 544 217	324
28	9853.0424 385 707	10416.5528 088 619	11013.8684 594 139	11647.0692 052 097	336
29	11793.5177 951 676	12497.9863 126 092	13246.4684 504 179	14041.7810 780 946	348
30	14113.5853 927 881	14992.7225 127 295	15928.9847 426 752	16926.1702 685 369	360
31	16887.5003 715 223	17982.8294 255 787	19152.0850 236 126	20400.3673 509 265	372
32	20204.0435 261 863	21566.6710 156 585	23024.7084 447 502	24584.9778 768 845	384
33	24169.3627 883 389	25862.1430 228 941	27677.7477 096 599	29625.2691 553 268	396
34	28910.3705 538 150	31010.5513 163 907	33268.4731 808 269	35696.2131 569 138	408
35	34578.8055 892 585	37181.2603 588 186	39985.8485 379 767	43008.5606 055 706	420
36	41356.0895 213 839	44577.2646 995 001	48056.9176 544 191	51816.1571 170 685	432
37	49459.1333 437 873	53441.8667 786 571	57754.4785 645 824	62424.7553 618 908	444
38	59147.2797 820 020	64066.6807 190 115	69406.3038 989 417	75202.6291 635 719	456
39	70730.6037 113 118	76801.2254 012 343	83406.2194 323 548	90593.3579 972 682	468
40	84579.8362 871 199	92064.4224 015 687	100227.4151 951 112	109131.2256 980 125	480
41	101138.2304 155 531	110358.3770 331 962	120438.4390 554 811	131459.7679 394 892	492
42	120935.7473 257 298	132284.8958 389 688	144722.4133 487 274	158354.1123 526 490	504
43	144606.0182 933 541	158565.2839 027 240	173900.1240 648 759	190747.8868 136 647	516
44	172906.6243 856 641	190064.0732 408 535	208957.7629 980 555	229765.6300 131 489	528
45	206743.3432 930 049	227817.4628 544 651	251080.2605 279 587	276761.8294 283 488	540
46	247199.1392 812 578	273067.4060 194 806	301691.3356 644 945	333367.9418 880 368	552
47	295568.8241 057 536	327302.4661 662 101	362501.6170 267 916	401549.0290 327 665	564
48	353400.4982 297 880	392306.7853 626 486	435566.4612 211 852	483671.9737 509 324	576
49	422545.0986 985 254	470218.7762 917 719	523355.4228 499 815	582587.6457 006 461	588
50	505215.6394 773 956	563601.4684 817 456	628835.7242 019 912	701729.8682 651 403	600

TABLE 2. FUTURE WORTH OF ONE DOLLAR PER PERIOD WITH INTEREST
Payable at end of each period

MONTHLY Compounding

MONTHS	19% Nominal Annual Rate	19¼% Nominal Annual Rate	19½% Nominal Annual Rate	19¾% Nominal Annual Rate	MONTHS
1	1.0000 000 000	1.0000 000 000	1.0000 000 000	1.0000 000 000	1
2	2.0158 333 333	2.0160 416 667	2.0162 500 000	2.0164 583 333	2
3	3.0477 506 944	3.0483 823 351	3.0490 140 625	3.0496 458 767	3
4	4.0960 067 471	4.0972 834 684	4.0985 605 410	4.0998 379 651	4
5	5.1608 601 873	5.1630 107 240	5.1651 621 498	5.1673 144 650	5
6	6.2425 738 069	6.2458 340 210	6.2490 960 347	6.2523 598 489	6
7	7.3414 145 588	7.3460 276 085	7.3506 438 453	7.3552 632 714	7
8	8.4576 536 227	8.4638 701 347	8.4700 918 078	8.4763 186 461	8
9	9.5915 664 717	9.5996 447 181	9.6077 307 997	9.6158 247 238	9
10	10.7434 329 409	10.7536 390 188	10.7638 564 252	10.7740 851 724	10
11	11.9135 372 958	11.9261 453 114	11.9387 690 921	11.9514 086 575	11
YEARS					
1	13.1021 683 029	13.1174 605 591	13.1327 740 898	13.1481 089 250	12
2	28.9223 944 980	28.9951 749 529	29.0681 817 032	29.1414 154 949	24
3	48.0245 424 078	48.2139 721 612	48.4043 260 750	48.5956 089 839	36
4	71.0894 499 680	71.4769 026 417	71.8669 502 037	72.2596 113 371	48
5	98.9391 956 233	99.6349 568 985	100.3366 761 437	101.0444 081 825	60
6	132.5663 988 124	133.7181 959 036	134.8820 573 702	136.0581 187 571	72
7	173.1695 988 674	174.9734 321 671	176.7996 847 684	178.6486 548 233	84
8	222.1959 733 011	224.9098 398 805	227.6628 515 455	230.4556 108 026	96
9	281.3929 180 458	285.3541 626 180	289.3806 036 026	293.4733 827 240	108
10	352.8703 280 640	358.5175 381 687	364.2693 917 052	370.1279 458 589	120
11	439.1757 981 342	447.0763 850 471	455.1400 147 678	463.3702 467 251	132
12	543.3854 241 145	554.2703 096 220	565.4031 174 969	576.7898 047 430	144
13	669.2134 410 191	684.0206 154 448	699.1972 020 279	714.7528 968 318	156
14	821.1446 056 233	841.0737 500 123	861.5439 582 178	882.5706 445 935	168
15	1004.5940 419 717	1031.1749 364 494	1058.5367 425 981	1086.7034 748 848	180
16	1226.1002 469 969	1261.2783 417 989	1297.5692 801 655	1335.0098 248 301	192
17	1493.5581 353 465	1539.8014 701 697	1587.6131 728 677	1637.0486 655 943	204
18	1816.5004 295 919	1876.9330 867 991	1939.5546 305 035	2004.4474 910 789	216
19	2206.4374 251 168	2285.0059 373 233	2366.6030 625 489	2451.3499 378 829	228
20	2677.2672 395 711	2778.9478 968 458	2884.7868 665 755	2994.9602 684 169	240
21	3245.7711 689 831	3376.8280 524 689	3513.5550 216 755	3656.2056 779 612	252
22	3932.2118 059 925	4100.5176 957 489	4276.5070 664 823	4460.5419 222 961	264
23	4761.0552 383 062	4976.4904 051 039	5202.2788 600 335	5438.9332 798 961	276
24	5761.8430 679 467	6036.7904 863 058	6325.6173 707 155	6629.0445 739 829	288
25	6970.2453 317 622	7320.2051 979 633	7688.6848 333 142	8076.6911 433 346	300
26	8429.3318 513 486	8873.6836 436 424	9342.6412 230 646	9837.6025 809 189	312
27	10191.1073 257 809	10754.0542 356 803	11349.5644 416 563	11979.5681 384 404	324
28	12318.3648 808 646	13030.1035 579 194	13784.7802 854 855	14585.0463 877 622	336
29	14886.9241 390 296	15785.0926 750 650	16739.6896 467 901	17754.3396 025 160	348
30	17988.3335 790 564	19119.8029 387 793	20325.1990 609 357	21609.4550 630 650	360
31	21733.1335 030 258	23156.2227 103 547	24675.8833 584 907	26298.8019 322 590	372
32	26254.7959 090 190	28042.0098 654 335	29955.0366 588 044	32002.9045 161 253	384
33	31714.4816 943 412	33955.8933 254 325	36360.8012 838 943	38941.3518 510 869	396
34	38306.7847 453 035	41114.2112 112 402	44133.6046 290 093	47381.2511 537 751	408
35	46266.6676 441 619	49778.8247 939 846	53565.1831 177 341	57647.5105 632 243	420
36	55877.8361 953 844	60266.6977 462 496	65009.5319 375 047	70135.3470 269 289	432
37	67482.8512 557 516	72961.4911 161 363	78896.1915 316 710	85325.5008 429 035	444
38	81495.3382 737 029	88327.5981 845 208	95746.3695 296 639	103802.7425 671 691	456
39	98414.7297 098 086	106927.1326 202 013	116192.5032 192 459	126278.3847 412 397	468
40	118844.0657 870 827	129440.4913 833 870	141001.9967 986 050	153617.6650 664 770	480
41	143511.4880 247 157	156691.2445 972 735	171106.0243 379 476	186873.0551 867 287	492
42	173296.1916 268 343	189676.2628 939 865	207634.4795 113 930	227324.7773 569 442	504
43	209259.7617 202 116	229602.1843 353 087	251958.3838 665 360	276530.0887 551 652	516
44	252684.0103 257 699	277929.5549 191 074	305741.3453 401 447	336383.2307 204 926	528
45	305116.6626 475 865	336426.2573 928 692	371001.9984 111 112	409188.3507 639 186	540
46	368426.5210 281 551	407232.1828 750 010	450189.7694 552 718	497748.2046 076 530	552
47	444870.0727 212 269	492937.5110 621 743	546276.8110 011 701	605472.0529 873 490	564
48	537171.9155 136 109	596677.4626 220 864	662869.5554 527 645	736506.9068 863 625	576
49	648621.8677 224 921	722246.9899 465 677	804344.0752 220 234	895897.1737 083 942	588
50	783192.2237 586 206	874239.6018 130 525	976010.3297 397 051	1089778.8502 368 228	600

MONTHLY Compounding

TABLE 2. FUTURE WORTH OF ONE DOLLAR PER PERIOD WITH INTEREST
Payable at end of each period

MONTHS	20% Nominal Annual Rate	20¼% Nominal Annual Rate	20½% Nominal Annual Rate	20¾% Nominal Annual Rate	MONTHS
1	1.0000 000 000	1.0000 000 000	1.0000 000 000	1.0000 000 000	1
2	2.0166 666 667	2.0168 750 000	2.0170 833 333	2.0172 916 667	2
3	3.0502 777 778	3.0509 097 656	3.0515 418 403	3.0521 740 017	3
4	4.1011 157 407	4.1023 938 679	4.1036 723 467	4.1049 511 772	4
5	5.1694 676 698	5.1716 217 644	5.1737 767 493	5.1759 326 246	5
6	6.2556 254 642	6.2588 928 817	6.2621 621 021	6.2654 331 263	6
7	7.3598 858 887	7.3645 116 991	7.3691 407 047	7.3737 729 074	7
8	8.4825 506 535	8.4887 878 340	8.4950 301 917	8.5012 777 306	8
9	9.6239 264 977	9.6320 361 287	9.6401 536 242	9.6482 789 913	9
10	10.7843 252 726	10.7945 767 384	10.8048 395 819	10.8151 138 156	10
11	11.9640 640 272	11.9767 352 208	11.9894 222 581	12.0021 251 586	11
YEARS					
1	13.1634 650 943	13.1788 426 277	13.1942 415 550	13.2096 619 062	12
2	29.2148 770 768	29.2885 671 999	29.3624 866 178	29.4366 360 867	24
3	48.7878 257 483	48.9809 812 549	49.1750 804 165	49.3701 281 720	36
4	72.6549 048 638	73.0528 497 452	73.4534 650 838	73.8567 701 235	48
5	101.7582 083 598	102.4781 325 467	103.2042 371 455	103.9365 790 950	60
6	137.2465 171 842	138.4473 913 641	139.6608 816 215	140.8871 299 118	72
7	180.5206 445 830	182.4159 604 550	184.3349 130 615	186.2778 172 980	84
8	233.2887 297 402	236.1628 301 838	239.0785 438 532	242.0365 125 232	96
9	297.6336 623 484	301.8626 258 643	306.1614 780 694	310.5314 455 645	108
10	376.0952 995 296	382.1735 941 915	388.3650 147 728	394.6717 905 525	120
11	471.7707 204 155	480.3451 572 357	489.0973 623 584	498.0312 266 501	132
12	588.4364 756 883	600.3493 856 904	612.5349 449 376	624.9997 223 457	144
13	730.6976 575 817	747.0417 108 447	763.7955 594 093	780.9699 898 689	156
14	904.1696 745 105	926.3573 777 698	949.1505 624 181	972.5665 289 788	168
15	1115.6999 054 341	1145.5515 883 120	1176.2848 845 969	1207.9269 882 625	180
16	1373.6379 832 103	1413.4930 501 993	1454.6156 524 437	1497.0477 941 581	192
17	1688.1653 757 081	1741.0228 094 058	1795.6826 280 860	1852.2087 275 456	204
18	2071.6972 740 785	2141.3928 843 101	2213.6266 548 057	2288.4944 808 797	216
19	2539.3726 517 281	2630.8024 490 084	2725.7759 449 610	2824.4353 478 741	228
20	3109.6518 378 637	3229.0532 600 244	3353.3645 181 614	3482.7942 576 476	240
21	3805.0451 933 445	3960.3508 453 138	4122.4125 765 745	4291.5335 809 033	252
22	4653.0016 515 201	4854.2838 720 687	5064.8053 182 605	5285.0027 711 436	264
23	5686.9921 970 073	5947.0213 190 369	6219.6149 167 852	6505.3972 834 115	276
24	6947.8310 500 506	7282.7758 915 481	7634.7204 771 901	8004.5507 349 782	288
25	8485.2867 069 538	8915.5928 897 528	9368.7931 326 711	9846.1364 261 229	300
26	10360.0464 284 186	10911.5369 085 810	11493.7285 852 789	12108.3717 258 414	312
27	12646.1117 191 123	13351.3648 443 977	14097.6279 452 497	14887.3401 854 146	324
28	15433.7193 540 954	16333.7933 595 453	17288.4504 563 688	18301.0724 794 265	336
29	18832.9032 524 076	19979.4930 080 282	21198.4895 515 737	22494.5595 033 740	348
30	22977.8377 939 629	24435.9706 266 679	25989.8578 187 695	27645.9105 483 470	360
31	28032.1340 214 512	29883.5375 357 250	31861.2082 868 621	33973.9181 079 278	372
32	34195.2977 817 206	36542.6050 253 790	39055.9707 005 945	41747.3506 161 219	384
33	41710.6047 258 041	44682.6023 071 089	47872.4442 651 292	51296.3678 052 624	396
34	50874.7030 137 459	54632.8777 547 622	58676.1653 116 753	63026.5435 265 262	408
35	62049.3227 672 574	66796.0245 049 942	71915.0626 550 648	77436.0916 220 314	420
36	75675.5544 718 952	81664.1695 775 583	88138.0289 935 782	95137.0264 801 758	432
37	92291.2599 333 837	99838.8855 814 242	108017.6783 324 979	116881.1570 230 351	444
38	112552.3030 425 338	122055.5306 443 455	132378.2329 679 472	143592.0181 642 114	456
39	137258.4383 807 121	149213.0013 716 369	162229.6962 422 465	176404.0959 567 403	468
40	167384.8795 545 488	182410.1026 538 013	198809.7278 939 112	216711.0124 343 705	480
41	204120.7933 418 473	222990.0058 636 681	243634.9581 796 516	266224.7166 931 290	492
42	248916.2391 099 262	272594.5942 440 062	298563.8682 829 379	327048.1962 263 354	504
43	303539.4063 238 775	333230.8943 272 574	365873.8440 689 345	401764.7967 697 493	516
44	370146.4094 538 574	407352.2812 359 624	448355.5978 811 296	493547.9443 240 792	528
45	451366.3952 628 099	497957.7434 710 746	549428.8731 645 077	606295.9295 604 403	540
46	550405.3218 743 760	608713.2234 912 981	673284.2290 989 872	744797.4792 848 482	552
47	671172.5060 431 034	744099.9435 841 670	825056.7837 198 560	914935.1472 515 859	564
48	818434.9337 675 577	909595.7183 680 234	1011039.1190 201 578	1123935.1629 103 176	576
49	998005.4252 762 586	1111896.5899 196 902	1238942.1752 094 606	1380674.3498 720 776	588
50	1216972.0817 340 191	1359187.7529 962 968	1518214.9509 629 128	1696057.1497 921 299	600

TABLE 2. FUTURE WORTH OF ONE DOLLAR PER PERIOD WITH INTEREST

Payable at end of each period

MONTHLY Compounding

	21% Nominal Annual Rate	21¼% Nominal Annual Rate	21½% Nominal Annual Rate	21¾% Nominal Annual Rate	
MONTHS					MONTHS
1	1.0000 000 000	1.0000 000 000	1.0000 000 000	1.0000 000 000	1
2	2.0175 000 000	2.0177 083 333	2.0179 166 667	2.0181 250 000	2
3	3.0528 062 500	3.0534 385 851	3.0540 710 069	3.0547 035 156	3
4	4.1062 303 594	4.1075 098 933	4.1087 897 792	4.1100 700 168	4
5	5.1780 893 907	5.1802 470 477	5.1824 055 960	5.1845 650 359	5
6	6.2687 059 550	6.2719 805 892	6.2752 570 296	6.2785 352 772	6
7	7.3784 083 092	7.3830 469 121	7.3876 887 181	7.3923 337 291	7
8	8.5075 304 546	8.5137 883 678	8.5200 514 743	8.5263 197 779	8
9	9.6564 122 376	9.6645 533 702	9.6727 023 965	9.6808 593 239	9
10	10.8253 994 517	10.8356 965 028	10.8460 049 811	10.8563 248 991	10
11	12.0148 439 421	12.0275 786 284	12.0403 292 370	12.0530 957 879	11
YEARS					
1	13.2251 037 111	13.2405 669 999	13.2560 518 025	13.2715 581 491	12
2	29.5110 163 652	29.5856 282 145	29.6604 723 983	29.7355 496 828	24
3	49.5661 294 873	49.7630 893 544	49.9610 127 924	50.1599 048 473	36
4	74.2627 842 514	74.6715 269 983	75.0830 180 401	75.4972 771 989	48
5	104.6752 158 756	105.4202 055 143	106.1716 065 906	106.9294 782 411	60
6	142.1262 798 406	143.3784 766 834	144.6438 674 047	145.9226 006 786	72
7	188.2449 923 937	190.2367 619 716	192.2534 541 102	194.2954 014 058	84
8	245.0373 881 863	248.0818 332 178	251.1705 205 447	254.3041 338 160	96
9	314.9737 771 551	319.4897 442 604	324.0806 413 302	328.7477 862 684	108
10	401.0961 960 765	407.6405 520 929	414.3072 265 060	421.0986 353 510	120
11	507.1507 286 346	516.4599 365 008	525.9630 101 582	535.6642 033 384	132
12	637.7504 495 547	650.7940 250 259	664.1375 182 446	677.7881 740 292	144
13	798.5760 804 165	816.6252 088 543	835.1290 608 271	854.0996 382 829	156
14	996.6230 851 105	1021.3385 607 063	1046.7318 234 468	1072.8222 948 214	168
15	1240.5059 528 977	1274.0507 192 942	1308.5911 439 258	1344.1580 283 526	180
16	1540.8329 045 325	1586.0158 867 853	1632.6431 689 222	1680.7627 562 583	192
17	1910.6673 201 130	1971.1270 198 292	2033.6589 307 906	2098.3367 387 702	204
18	2366.0959 594 784	2446.5345 340 305	2529.9176 450 162	2616.3568 864 842	216
19	2926.9286 911 449	3033.4100 750 533	3144.0399 186 579	3258.9852 222 424	228
20	3617.5601 660 269	3757.8893 698 947	3904.0188 493 484	4056.1958 707 891	240
21	4468.0309 163 348	4652.2361 469 628	4844.4960 146 992	5045.1731 423 975	252
22	5515.3340 344 746	5756.2789 586 034	6008.3405 146 285	6272.0459 213 058	264
23	6805.0242 688 163	7119.1848 930 680	7448.6030 429 701	7794.0392 560 753	276
24	8393.1995 274 849	8801.6491 658 423	9230.9340 594 169	9682.1435 085 338	288
25	10348.9409 800 321	10878.5981 008 942	11436.5762 876 058	12024.4255 584 694	300
26	12757.3178 945 659	13442.5258 755 387	14166.0679 442 500	14930.1365 086 496	312
27	15723.0879 123 283	16607.6136 264 464	17543.8255 009 723	18534.8074 859 254	324
28	19375.2537 112 855	20514.8143 557 396	21723.8148 716 015	23006.5712 219 600	336
29	23872.6742 608 180	25338.1300 867 524	26896.5695 306 212	28554.0042 711 830	348
30	29410.9747 413 531	31292.3608 142 953	33297.8754 646 554	35435.8556 506 792	360
31	36231.0556 910 615	38642.6703 386 879	41219.5188 369 448	43973.1156 751 345	372
32	44629.5715 036 385	47716.3949 853 430	51022.5862 679 352	54563.9879 137 179	384
33	54971.8340 624 313	58917.6210 956 297	63153.9239 891 853	67702.4626 061 475	396
34	67707.7027 828 103	72745.1804 783 162	78166.5061 164 670	84001.3578 581 123	408
35	83391.1522 350 605	89814.8652 252 502	96744.6404 745 266	104220.9033 269 322	420
36	102704.3684 845 109	110886.8511 987 506	119735.1609 126 390	129304.1996 268 081	432
37	126487.4222 721 146	136899.5514 594 950	148186.0279 280 324	160421.2073 873 241	444
38	155774.8097 356 165	169011.4072 525 980	183394.0971 018 707	199023.3177 476 277	456
39	191840.4500 901 939	208652.4776 582 405	226964.2327 423 448	246911.0496 188 091	468
40	236253.0975 414 800	257588.1253 837 951	280882.4612 699 091	306318.0313 190 742	480
41	290944.5776 937 762	317997.6348 600 762	347606.4988 432 523	380015.1837 385 955	492
42	358293.8165 458 365	392571.2637 947 800	430177.7796 822 156	471439.9644 512 289	504
43	441230.3170 998 708	484630.0502 458 508	532360.0915 948 089	584856.7011 084 659	516
44	543361.5845 260 491	598273.7106 645 269	658811.1380 326 832	725555.4925 489 307	528
45	669130.0425 197 853	738563.2153 520 522	815294.8468 658 828	900098.9549 713 635	540
46	824006.2662 732 547	911746.1720 868 460	1008944.1033 963 474	1116628.3221 571 673	552
47	1014726.9371 534 632	1125535.0550 842 524	1248585.8835 817 467	1385243.1771 805 707	564
48	1249587.8694 479 982	1389450.6698 480 701	1545143.6077 855 200	1718472.5274 392 298	576
49	1538804.8550 200 754	1715246.1496 673 309	1912135.0552 571 643	2131859.1953 661 896	588
50	1894958.0216 033 518	2117430.3658 822 417	2366288.5354 234 345	2644684.7825 694 404	600

MONTHLY
Compounding

TABLE 2. FUTURE WORTH OF ONE DOLLAR PER PERIOD WITH INTEREST
Payable at end of each period

MONTHS	22% Nominal Annual Rate	22¼% Nominal Annual Rate	22½% Nominal Annual Rate	22¾% Nominal Annual Rate	MONTHS
1	1.0000 000 000	1.0000 000 000	1.0000 000 000	1.0000 000 000	1
2	2.0183 333 333	2.0185 416 667	2.0187 500 000	2.0189 583 333	2
3	3.0553 361 111	3.0559 687 934	3.0566 015 625	3.0572 344 184	3
4	4.1113 506 065	4.1126 315 481	4.1139 128 418	4.1151 944 876	4
5	5.1867 253 676	5.1888 865 914	5.1910 487 076	5.1932 117 164	5
6	6.2818 153 327	6.2850 971 970	6.2883 808 708	6.2916 663 552	6
7	7.3969 819 471	7.4016 333 741	7.4062 880 122	7.4109 458 632	7
8	8.5325 932 828	8.5388 719 930	8.5451 559 124	8.5514 450 452	8
9	9.6890 241 597	9.6971 969 112	9.7053 775 858	9.7135 661 908	9
10	10.8666 562 692	10.8769 991 039	10.8873 534 155	10.8977 192 165	10
11	12.0658 783 009	12.0786 767 956	12.0914 912 920	12.1043 218 100	11
YEARS					
1	13.2870 860 697	13.3026 355 945	13.3182 067 538	13.3337 995 777	12
2	29.8108 608 368	29.8864 066 317	29.9621 878 413	30.0382 052 422	24
3	50.3597 705 920	50.5606 151 266	50.7624 435 788	50.9652 611 036	36
4	75.9143 244 439	76.3341 798 927	76.7568 638 121	77.1823 966 198	48
5	107.6938 801 651	108.4648 726 306	109.2425 164 788	110.0268 731 303	60
6	147.2148 269 086	148.5206 982 483	149.8403 686 219	151.1739 937 449	72
7	196.3629 410 360	198.4564 148 234	200.5761 693 012	202.7225 557 787	84
8	257.4833 675 771	260.7089 274 457	263.9815 302 918	267.3019 044 198	96
9	333.4925 208 662	338.3162 112 416	343.2202 482 881	348.2060 481 315	108
10	428.0172 437 890	435.0655 671 224	442.2461 718 315	449.5616 766 329	120
11	545.5678 657 470	555.6784 452 638	566.0004 901 948	576.5386 515 763	132
12	691.7534 169 491	706.0408 558 565	720.6582 885 325	735.6137 064 516	144
13	873.5492 681 690	893.4906 113 692	913.9366 718 892	934.9008 062 968	156
14	1099.6299 666 306	1127.1754 179 857	1155.4798 328 191	1184.5650 179 223	168
15	1380.7831 495 767	1418.4992 913 833	1457.3402 766 970	1497.3410 009 888	180
16	1730.4242 857 667	1781.6790 823 170	1834.5802 168 689	1889.1825 666 913	192
17	2165.2368 062 412	2234.4382 709 285	2306.0231 480 218	2380.0764 361 850	204
18	2705.9681 687 507	2798.8718 875 270	2895.1930 997 315	2995.0617 062 507	216
19	3378.4198 407 548	3502.5247 687 053	3631.4884 370 031	3765.5070 222 368	228
20	4214.6784 388 921	4379.7357 685 998	4551.6487 780 300	4730.7106 032 291	240
21	5254.6467 698 123	5473.3135 239 378	5701.5882 253 396	5939.9047 321 700	252
22	6547.9478 273 153	6836.6255 516 184	7138.6863 847 787	7454.7669 542 536	264
23	8156.2925 966 780	8536.2026 285 537	8934.6514 894 588	9352.5660 726 683	276
24	10156.4246 480 123	10654.9855 497 004	11179.0984 926 391	11730.1034 099 594	288
25	12643.7820 224 888	13296.3727 088 156	13984.0206 689 984	14708.6503 675 188	300
26	15737.0511 415 128	16589.2660 272 885	17489.3778 479 757	18440.1341 340 345	312
27	19583.8300 325 923	20694.3614 766 339	21870.0801 204 918	23114.8870 582 521	324
28	24367.6710 976 479	25811.9911 774 504	27344.7154 916 087	28971.3549 594 608	336
29	30316.8394 755 813	32191.8997 758 861	34186.4569 709 879	36308.2595 689 441	348
30	37715.2049 119 948	40145.4321 930 323	42736.6933 424 575	45499.8354 738 592	360
31	46915.7868 511 013	50060.7275 196 938	53422.0637 599 663	57014.9187 566 122	372
32	58357.5990 656 721	62421.6605 314 169	66775.7461 611 172	71440.8609 868 051	384
33	72586.5975 811 957	77831.4551 856 881	83464.0617 461 916	89513.4883 503 051	396
34	90281.7314 426 779	97042.1224 598 814	104319.7230 312 792	112154.6340 451 995	408
35	112287.3393 590 867	120991.1591 212 797	130383.3844 847 646	140519.1583 651 520	420
36	139653.4380 595 208	150847.2983 601 019	162955.5690 382 040	176053.8548 305 613	432
37	173685.8247 550 715	188067.5449 550 184	203661.5614 973 505	220571.2470 013 348	444
38	216008.3843 889 418	234468.2783 353 415	254532.5069 006 461	276342.0401 363 092	456
39	268640.5747 194 742	292313.8934 293 019	318106.7604 659 491	346210.9433 948 907	468
40	334093.7865 042 469	364427.3050 465 757	397556.5462 787 286	433741.7703 412 209	480
41	415491.1766 952 657	454327.7085 021 409	496846.2447 289 451	543399.2189 139 143	492
42	516716.6925 904 285	566402.3193 161 082	620930.2069 131 351	680776.6029 393 837	504
43	642600.3977 583 178	706120.4730 317 428	775999.9665 322 300	852881.1511 240 007	516
44	799148.9427 240 772	880300.5334 033 903	969793.1846 487 592	1068491.4258 133 176	528
45	993832.1775 256 835	1097442.6342 990 151	1211979.7430 094 011	1338605.0924 302 802	540
46	1235939.5821 081 234	1368143.4934 028 668	1514644.2511 930 846	1676999.8790 349 222	552
47	1537023.5219 418 660	1705613.5409 768 601	1892889.0436 958 134	2100936.3389 534 227	564
48	1911450.4791 931 507	2126321.6000 004 261	2365587.7552 626 332	2632038.2623 947 132	576
49	2377086.5619 210 136	2650798.5786 234 506	2956327.0763 210 176	3297395.6443 412 075	588
50	2956150.0009 688 579	3304639.3958 019 208	3694583.6801 687 537	4130946.4679 612 813	600

TABLE 3. SINKING FUND FACTORS
Payable at end of each period

MONTHLY Compounding

MONTHS	5% Nominal Annual Rate	5¼% Nominal Annual Rate	5½% Nominal Annual Rate	5¾% Nominal Annual Rate	MONTHS
1	1.0000 000 000	1.0000 000 000	1.0000 000 000	1.0000 000 000	1
2	0.4989 604 990	0.4989 086 374	0.4988 567 865	0.4988 049 465	2
3	0.3319 482 944	0.3318 792 442	0.3318 102 131	0.3317 412 011	3
4	0.2484 429 140	0.2483 653 434	0.2482 877 996	0.2482 102 828	4
5	0.1983 402 633	0.1982 576 395	0.1981 750 502	0.1980 924 953	5
6	0.1649 389 774	0.1648 530 341	0.1647 671 327	0.1646 812 732	6
7	0.1410 813 285	0.1409 930 563	0.1409 048 335	0.1408 166 599	7
8	0.1231 884 527	0.1230 984 709	0.1230 085 457	0.1229 186 770	8
9	0.1092 720 923	0.1091 808 136	0.1090 895 988	0.1089 984 478	9
10	0.0981 392 927	0.0980 470 061	0.0979 547 905	0.0978 626 461	10
11	0.0890 309 010	0.0889 378 165	0.0888 448 104	0.0887 518 826	11
YEARS					
1	0.0814 408 151	0.0813 470 904	0.0812 534 512	0.0811 598 977	12
2	0.0397 047 231	0.0396 084 370	0.0395 123 228	0.0394 163 806	24
3	0.0258 042 304	0.0257 082 705	0.0256 125 685	0.0255 171 242	36
4	0.0188 626 269	0.0187 677 128	0.0186 731 419	0.0185 789 141	48
5	0.0147 045 670	0.0146 109 838	0.0145 178 288	0.0144 251 015	60
6	0.0119 382 660	0.0118 461 537	0.0117 545 538	0.0116 634 654	72
7	0.0099 672 424	0.0098 766 781	0.0097 867 093	0.0096 973 351	84
8	0.0084 932 533	0.0084 042 822	0.0083 159 888	0.0082 283 720	96
9	0.0073 506 065	0.0072 632 556	0.0071 766 637	0.0070 908 291	108
10	0.0064 398 849	0.0063 541 701	0.0062 692 945	0.0061 852 553	120
11	0.0056 978 216	0.0056 137 516	0.0055 305 993	0.0054 483 614	132
12	0.0050 822 375	0.0049 998 155	0.0049 183 884	0.0048 379 520	144
13	0.0045 639 303	0.0044 831 558	0.0044 034 518	0.0043 248 131	156
14	0.0041 220 404	0.0040 429 099	0.0039 649 237	0.0038 880 757	168
15	0.0037 412 696	0.0036 637 772	0.0035 875 012	0.0035 124 342	180
16	0.0034 101 433	0.0033 342 811	0.0032 597 057	0.0031 864 080	192
17	0.0031 198 861	0.0030 456 447	0.0029 727 584	0.0029 012 164	204
18	0.0028 636 719	0.0027 910 404	0.0027 198 302	0.0026 500 288	216
19	0.0026 361 109	0.0025 650 772	0.0024 955 289	0.0024 274 514	228
20	0.0024 328 907	0.0023 634 417	0.0022 955 397	0.0022 291 684	240
21	0.0022 505 198	0.0021 826 411	0.0021 163 691	0.0020 516 849	252
22	0.0020 861 409	0.0020 198 174	0.0019 551 578	0.0018 921 408	264
23	0.0019 373 930	0.0018 726 088	0.0018 095 433	0.0017 481 725	276
24	0.0018 023 085	0.0017 390 467	0.0016 775 561	0.0016 178 099	288
25	0.0016 792 337	0.0016 174 772	0.0015 575 416	0.0014 993 974	300
26	0.0015 667 695	0.0015 065 000	0.0014 480 989	0.0013 915 334	312
27	0.0014 637 233	0.0014 049 223	0.0013 480 345	0.0012 930 239	324
28	0.0013 690 728	0.0013 117 211	0.0012 563 249	0.0012 028 446	336
29	0.0012 819 364	0.0012 260 143	0.0011 720 873	0.0011 201 126	348
30	0.0012 015 496	0.0011 470 370	0.0010 945 567	0.0010 440 619	360
31	0.0011 272 465	0.0010 741 230	0.0010 230 661	0.0009 740 255	372
32	0.0010 584 442	0.0010 066 888	0.0009 570 319	0.0009 094 193	384
33	0.0009 946 304	0.0009 442 218	0.0008 959 411	0.0008 497 299	396
34	0.0009 353 526	0.0008 862 694	0.0008 393 407	0.0007 945 042	408
35	0.0008 802 101	0.0008 324 304	0.0007 868 295	0.0007 433 407	420
36	0.0008 288 466	0.0007 823 484	0.0007 380 506	0.0006 958 823	432
37	0.0007 809 441	0.0007 357 052	0.0006 926 858	0.0006 518 108	444
38	0.0007 362 181	0.0006 922 161	0.0006 504 502	0.0006 108 410	456
39	0.0006 944 132	0.0006 516 255	0.0006 110 881	0.0005 727 174	468
40	0.0006 552 993	0.0006 137 034	0.0005 743 695	0.0005 372 097	480
41	0.0006 186 690	0.0005 782 420	0.0005 400 866	0.0005 041 103	492
42	0.0005 843 345	0.0005 450 536	0.0005 080 515	0.0004 732 315	504
43	0.0005 521 252	0.0005 139 677	0.0004 780 939	0.0004 444 027	516
44	0.0005 218 864	0.0004 848 294	0.0004 500 589	0.0004 174 695	528
45	0.0004 934 769	0.0004 574 976	0.0004 238 055	0.0003 922 909	540
46	0.0004 667 679	0.0004 318 436	0.0003 992 050	0.0003 687 383	552
47	0.0004 416 414	0.0004 077 494	0.0003 761 397	0.0003 466 944	564
48	0.0004 179 896	0.0003 851 073	0.0003 545 020	0.0003 260 515	576
49	0.0003 957 132	0.0003 638 181	0.0003 341 928	0.0003 067 112	588
50	0.0003 747 210	0.0003 437 908	0.0003 151 214	0.0002 885 827	600

MONTHLY
Compounding

TABLE 3. SINKING FUND FACTORS
Payable at end of each period

MONTHS	6% Nominal Annual Rate	6¼% Nominal Annual Rate	6½% Nominal Annual Rate	6¾% Nominal Annual Rate	MONTHS
1	1.0000 000 000	1.0000 000 000	1.0000 000 000	1.0000 000 000	1
2	0.4987 531 172	0.4987 012 987	0.4986 494 910	0.4985 976 940	2
3	0.3316 722 084	0.3316 032 347	0.3315 342 802	0.3314 653 448	3
4	0.2481 327 930	0.2480 553 300	0.2479 778 940	0.2479 004 849	4
5	0.1980 099 750	0.1979 274 891	0.1978 450 376	0.1977 626 206	5
6	0.1645 954 556	0.1645 096 799	0.1644 239 461	0.1643 382 541	6
7	0.1407 285 355	0.1406 404 604	0.1405 524 345	0.1404 644 578	7
8	0.1228 288 649	0.1227 391 094	0.1226 494 103	0.1225 597 678	8
9	0.1089 073 606	0.1088 163 373	0.1087 253 777	0.1086 344 819	9
10	0.0977 705 727	0.0976 785 705	0.0975 866 392	0.0974 947 790	10
11	0.0886 590 331	0.0885 662 620	0.0884 735 691	0.0883 809 545	11
YEARS					
1	0.0810 664 297	0.0809 730 473	0.0808 797 503	0.0807 865 388	12
2	0.0393 206 103	0.0392 250 117	0.0391 295 848	0.0390 343 295	24
3	0.0254 219 375	0.0253 270 082	0.0252 323 362	0.0251 379 214	36
4	0.0184 850 290	0.0183 914 865	0.0182 982 863	0.0182 054 280	48
5	0.0143 328 015	0.0142 409 284	0.0141 494 816	0.0140 584 607	60
6	0.0115 728 879	0.0114 828 207	0.0113 932 630	0.0113 042 140	72
7	0.0096 085 545	0.0095 203 664	0.0094 327 698	0.0093 457 636	84
8	0.0081 414 302	0.0080 551 620	0.0079 695 659	0.0078 846 404	96
9	0.0070 057 496	0.0069 214 234	0.0068 378 484	0.0067 550 224	108
10	0.0061 020 502	0.0060 196 764	0.0059 381 311	0.0058 574 114	120
11	0.0053 670 346	0.0052 866 155	0.0052 071 005	0.0051 284 858	132
12	0.0047 585 021	0.0046 800 344	0.0046 025 442	0.0045 260 269	144
13	0.0042 472 344	0.0041 707 104	0.0040 952 352	0.0040 208 031	156
14	0.0038 123 592	0.0037 377 677	0.0036 642 941	0.0035 919 314	168
15	0.0034 385 683	0.0033 658 953	0.0032 944 070	0.0032 240 946	180
16	0.0031 143 786	0.0030 436 080	0.0029 740 860	0.0029 058 025	192
17	0.0028 310 077	0.0027 621 210	0.0026 945 444	0.0026 282 659	204
18	0.0025 816 232	0.0025 146 002	0.0024 489 462	0.0023 846 470	216
19	0.0023 608 299	0.0022 956 491	0.0022 318 930	0.0021 695 457	228
20	0.0021 643 106	0.0021 009 487	0.0020 390 647	0.0019 786 401	240
21	0.0019 885 692	0.0019 270 019	0.0018 669 626	0.0018 084 304	252
22	0.0018 307 445	0.0017 709 463	0.0017 127 233	0.0016 560 517	264
23	0.0016 884 720	0.0016 304 165	0.0015 739 800	0.0015 191 364	276
24	0.0015 597 807	0.0015 034 402	0.0014 487 600	0.0013 957 106	288
25	0.0014 430 140	0.0013 883 604	0.0013 354 049	0.0012 841 153	300
26	0.0013 367 699	0.0012 837 742	0.0012 325 114	0.0011 829 460	312
27	0.0012 398 535	0.0011 884 860	0.0011 388 831	0.0010 910 061	324
28	0.0011 512 402	0.0011 014 705	0.0010 534 942	0.0010 072 691	336
29	0.0010 700 461	0.0010 218 436	0.0009 754 600	0.0009 308 498	348
30	0.0009 955 053	0.0009 488 387	0.0009 040 136	0.0008 609 810	360
31	0.0009 269 500	0.0008 817 877	0.0008 384 866	0.0007 969 940	372
32	0.0008 637 959	0.0008 201 062	0.0007 782 942	0.0007 383 037	384
33	0.0008 055 294	0.0007 632 800	0.0007 229 221	0.0006 843 960	396
34	0.0007 516 970	0.0007 108 557	0.0006 719 169	0.0006 348 170	408
35	0.0007 018 971	0.0006 624 315	0.0006 248 765	0.0005 891 651	420
36	0.0006 557 726	0.0006 176 502	0.0005 814 439	0.0005 470 830	432
37	0.0006 130 050	0.0005 761 932	0.0005 413 006	0.0005 082 526	444
38	0.0005 733 093	0.0005 377 758	0.0005 041 618	0.0004 723 891	456
39	0.0005 364 298	0.0005 021 422	0.0004 697 720	0.0004 392 375	468
40	0.0005 021 364	0.0004 690 624	0.0004 379 014	0.0004 085 684	480
41	0.0004 702 216	0.0004 383 291	0.0004 083 431	0.0003 801 749	492
42	0.0004 404 975	0.0004 097 548	0.0003 809 097	0.0003 538 703	504
43	0.0004 127 943	0.0003 831 697	0.0003 554 319	0.0003 294 857	516
44	0.0003 869 572	0.0003 584 194	0.0003 317 556	0.0003 068 676	528
45	0.0003 628 457	0.0003 353 638	0.0003 097 412	0.0002 858 767	540
46	0.0003 403 315	0.0003 138 748	0.0002 892 611	0.0002 663 861	552
47	0.0003 192 974	0.0002 938 358	0.0002 701 990	0.0002 482 802	564
48	0.0002 996 364	0.0002 751 398	0.0002 524 487	0.0002 314 533	576
49	0.0002 812 499	0.0002 576 892	0.0002 359 128	0.0002 158 087	588
50	0.0002 640 479	0.0002 413 941	0.0002 205 022	0.0002 012 579	600

TABLE 3. SINKING FUND FACTORS
Payable at end of each period

MONTHLY Compounding

MONTHS	7% Nominal Annual Rate	7¼% Nominal Annual Rate	7½% Nominal Annual Rate	7¾% Nominal Annual Rate	MONTHS
1	1.0000 000 000	1.0000 000 000	1.0000 000 000	1.0000 000 000	1
2	0.4985 459 078	0.4984 941 323	0.4984 423 676	0.4983 906 136	2
3	0.3313 964 286	0.3313 275 315	0.3312 586 535	0.3311 897 946	3
4	0.2478 231 027	0.2477 457 474	0.2476 684 189	0.2475 911 173	4
5	0.1976 802 380	0.1975 978 899	0.1975 155 761	0.1974 332 968	5
6	0.1642 526 040	0.1641 669 957	0.1640 814 292	0.1639 959 045	6
7	0.1403 765 303	0.1402 886 519	0.1402 008 227	0.1401 130 426	7
8	0.1224 701 817	0.1223 806 521	0.1222 911 789	0.1222 017 622	8
9	0.1085 436 499	0.1084 528 816	0.1083 621 769	0.1082 715 360	9
10	0.0974 029 898	0.0973 112 715	0.0972 196 242	0.0971 280 478	10
11	0.0882 884 181	0.0881 959 599	0.0881 035 799	0.0880 112 780	11
YEARS					
1	0.0806 934 128	0.0806 003 721	0.0805 074 169	0.0804 145 470	12
2	0.0389 392 458	0.0388 443 335	0.0387 495 927	0.0386 550 231	24
3	0.0250 437 635	0.0249 498 625	0.0248 562 182	0.0247 628 303	36
4	0.0181 129 113	0.0180 207 361	0.0179 289 019	0.0178 374 086	48
5	0.0139 678 652	0.0138 776 947	0.0137 879 486	0.0136 986 264	60
6	0.0112 156 731	0.0111 276 395	0.0110 401 123	0.0109 530 907	72
7	0.0092 593 466	0.0091 735 178	0.0090 882 759	0.0090 036 196	84
8	0.0078 003 837	0.0077 167 944	0.0076 338 706	0.0075 516 106	96
9	0.0066 729 433	0.0065 916 086	0.0065 110 162	0.0064 311 635	108
10	0.0057 775 146	0.0056 984 374	0.0056 201 769	0.0055 427 298	120
11	0.0050 507 676	0.0049 739 421	0.0048 980 051	0.0048 229 526	132
12	0.0044 504 776	0.0043 758 914	0.0043 022 631	0.0042 295 875	144
13	0.0039 474 081	0.0038 750 439	0.0038 037 042	0.0037 333 825	156
14	0.0035 206 721	0.0034 505 087	0.0033 814 334	0.0033 134 383	168
15	0.0031 549 494	0.0030 869 621	0.0030 201 236	0.0029 544 242	180
16	0.0028 387 469	0.0027 729 084	0.0027 082 759	0.0026 448 382	192
17	0.0025 632 732	0.0024 995 535	0.0024 370 939	0.0023 758 812	204
18	0.0023 216 884	0.0022 600 555	0.0021 997 333	0.0021 407 066	216
19	0.0021 085 904	0.0020 490 104	0.0019 907 882	0.0019 339 064	228
20	0.0019 196 560	0.0018 620 932	0.0018 059 319	0.0017 511 523	240
21	0.0017 513 838	0.0016 958 011	0.0016 416 601	0.0015 889 383	252
22	0.0016 009 077	0.0015 472 667	0.0014 951 040	0.0014 443 944	264
23	0.0014 658 589	0.0014 141 201	0.0013 638 926	0.0013 151 484	276
24	0.0013 442 625	0.0012 943 854	0.0012 460 490	0.0011 992 224	288
25	0.0012 344 586	0.0011 864 020	0.0011 399 118	0.0010 949 543	300
26	0.0011 350 423	0.0010 887 640	0.0010 440 744	0.0010 009 369	312
27	0.0010 448 160	0.0010 002 733	0.0009 573 384	0.0009 159 712	324
28	0.0009 627 528	0.0009 199 027	0.0008 786 759	0.0008 390 292	336
29	0.0008 879 673	0.0008 467 663	0.0008 072 008	0.0007 692 246	348
30	0.0008 196 916	0.0007 800 961	0.0007 421 451	0.0007 057 891	360
31	0.0007 572 571	0.0007 192 233	0.0006 828 398	0.0006 480 541	372
32	0.0007 000 786	0.0006 635 626	0.0006 286 998	0.0005 954 344	384
33	0.0006 476 417	0.0006 125 998	0.0005 792 109	0.0005 474 164	396
34	0.0005 994 928	0.0005 658 813	0.0005 339 200	0.0005 035 471	408
35	0.0005 552 303	0.0005 230 058	0.0004 924 260	0.0004 634 261	420
36	0.0005 144 971	0.0004 836 166	0.0004 543 727	0.0004 266 977	432
37	0.0004 769 753	0.0004 473 961	0.0004 194 430	0.0003 930 454	444
38	0.0004 423 807	0.0004 140 604	0.0003 873 536	0.0003 621 868	456
39	0.0004 104 584	0.0003 833 554	0.0003 578 509	0.0003 338 691	468
40	0.0003 809 795	0.0003 550 525	0.0003 307 073	0.0003 078 653	480
41	0.0003 537 376	0.0003 289 463	0.0003 057 178	0.0002 839 715	492
42	0.0003 285 467	0.0003 048 510	0.0002 826 977	0.0002 620 039	504
43	0.0003 052 382	0.0002 825 990	0.0002 614 802	0.0002 417 967	516
44	0.0002 836 595	0.0002 620 383	0.0002 419 140	0.0002 231 997	528
45	0.0002 636 717	0.0002 430 310	0.0002 238 623	0.0002 060 771	540
46	0.0002 451 489	0.0002 254 517	0.0002 072 007	0.0001 903 054	552
47	0.0002 279 759	0.0002 091 863	0.0001 918 158	0.0001 757 726	564
48	0.0002 120 478	0.0001 941 308	0.0001 776 048	0.0001 623 767	576
49	0.0001 972 689	0.0001 801 901	0.0001 644 734	0.0001 500 248	588
50	0.0001 835 512	0.0001 672 773	0.0001 523 360	0.0001 386 322	600

TABLE 3. SINKING FUND FACTORS
Payable at end of each period

MONTHS	8% Nominal Annual Rate	8¼% Nominal Annual Rate	8½% Nominal Annual Rate	8¾% Nominal Annual Rate	MONTHS
1	1.0000 000 000	1.0000 000 000	1.0000 000 000	1.0000 000 000	1
2	0.4983 388 704	0.4982 871 380	0.4982 354 162	0.4981 837 052	2
3	0.3311 209 548	0.3310 521 341	0.3309 833 325	0.3309 145 500	3
4	0.2475 138 426	0.2474 365 948	0.2473 593 738	0.2472 821 796	4
5	0.1973 510 518	0.1972 688 412	0.1971 866 649	0.1971 045 230	5
6	0.1639 104 215	0.1638 249 804	0.1637 395 810	0.1636 542 234	6
7	0.1400 253 116	0.1399 376 297	0.1398 499 970	0.1397 624 132	7
8	0.1221 124 018	0.1220 230 979	0.1219 338 503	0.1218 446 590	8
9	0.1081 809 587	0.1080 904 451	0.1079 999 951	0.1079 096 086	9
10	0.0970 365 423	0.0969 451 076	0.0968 537 439	0.0967 624 509	10
11	0.0879 190 542	0.0878 269 085	0.0877 348 409	0.0876 428 513	11
YEARS					
1	0.0803 217 624	0.0802 290 631	0.0801 364 491	0.0800 439 203	12
2	0.0385 606 248	0.0384 663 976	0.0383 723 415	0.0382 784 565	24
3	0.0246 696 988	0.0245 768 234	0.0244 842 041	0.0243 918 406	36
4	0.0177 462 557	0.0176 554 429	0.0175 649 700	0.0174 748 366	48
5	0.0136 097 276	0.0135 212 517	0.0134 331 980	0.0133 455 660	60
6	0.0108 665 739	0.0107 805 611	0.0106 950 513	0.0106 100 436	72
7	0.0089 195 477	0.0088 360 590	0.0087 531 521	0.0086 708 256	84
8	0.0074 700 126	0.0073 890 748	0.0073 087 952	0.0072 291 721	96
9	0.0063 520 482	0.0062 736 677	0.0061 960 194	0.0061 191 006	108
10	0.0054 660 928	0.0053 902 625	0.0053 152 356	0.0052 410 084	120
11	0.0047 487 802	0.0046 754 837	0.0046 030 585	0.0045 315 002	132
12	0.0041 578 592	0.0040 870 727	0.0040 172 223	0.0039 483 024	144
13	0.0036 640 721	0.0035 957 663	0.0035 284 579	0.0034 621 400	156
14	0.0032 465 153	0.0031 806 560	0.0031 158 520	0.0030 520 946	168
15	0.0028 898 542	0.0028 264 036	0.0027 640 622	0.0027 028 198	180
16	0.0025 825 836	0.0025 215 004	0.0024 615 767	0.0024 028 001	192
17	0.0023 159 018	0.0022 571 419	0.0021 995 877	0.0021 432 249	204
18	0.0020 829 596	0.0020 264 765	0.0019 712 412	0.0019 172 374	216
19	0.0018 783 471	0.0018 240 921	0.0017 711 230	0.0017 194 211	228
20	0.0016 977 340	0.0016 456 565	0.0015 948 990	0.0015 454 404	240
21	0.0015 376 129	0.0014 876 608	0.0014 390 587	0.0013 917 831	252
22	0.0013 951 124	0.0013 472 323	0.0013 007 282	0.0012 555 739	264
23	0.0012 678 592	0.0012 219 967	0.0011 775 321	0.0011 344 367	276
24	0.0011 538 746	0.0011 099 742	0.0010 674 899	0.0010 263 901	288
25	0.0010 514 955	0.0010 095 013	0.0009 689 375	0.0009 297 697	300
26	0.0009 593 145	0.0009 191 700	0.0008 804 665	0.0008 431 667	312
27	0.0008 761 320	0.0008 377 805	0.0008 008 769	0.0007 653 813	324
28	0.0008 009 198	0.0007 643 045	0.0007 291 406	0.0006 953 853	336
29	0.0007 327 915	0.0006 978 556	0.0006 643 712	0.0006 322 930	348
30	0.0006 709 791	0.0006 376 660	0.0006 058 015	0.0005 753 374	360
31	0.0006 148 139	0.0005 830 675	0.0005 527 635	0.0005 238 514	372
32	0.0005 637 113	0.0005 334 757	0.0005 046 738	0.0004 772 523	384
33	0.0005 171 579	0.0004 883 782	0.0004 610 205	0.0004 350 292	396
34	0.0004 747 015	0.0004 473 231	0.0004 213 527	0.0003 967 323	408
35	0.0004 359 421	0.0004 099 114	0.0003 852 724	0.0003 619 648	420
36	0.0004 005 249	0.0003 757 892	0.0003 524 267	0.0003 303 750	432
37	0.0003 681 343	0.0003 446 418	0.0003 225 021	0.0003 016 508	444
38	0.0003 384 885	0.0003 161 887	0.0002 952 193	0.0002 755 143	456
39	0.0003 113 358	0.0002 901 790	0.0002 703 289	0.0002 517 175	468
40	0.0002 864 502	0.0002 663 882	0.0002 476 073	0.0002 300 385	480
41	0.0002 636 290	0.0002 446 144	0.0002 268 545	0.0002 102 787	492
42	0.0002 426 893	0.0002 246 764	0.0002 078 904	0.0001 922 596	504
43	0.0002 234 665	0.0002 064 106	0.0001 905 529	0.0001 758 207	516
44	0.0002 058 117	0.0001 896 694	0.0001 746 960	0.0001 608 177	528
45	0.0001 895 900	0.0001 743 195	0.0001 601 876	0.0001 471 201	540
46	0.0001 746 794	0.0001 602 400	0.0001 469 086	0.0001 346 102	552
47	0.0001 609 690	0.0001 473 215	0.0001 347 508	0.0001 231 817	564
48	0.0001 483 580	0.0001 354 645	0.0001 236 164	0.0001 127 383	576
49	0.0001 367 548	0.0001 245 787	0.0001 134 165	0.0001 031 925	588
50	0.0001 260 759	0.0001 145 820	0.0001 040 703	0.0000 944 653	600

TABLE 3. SINKING FUND FACTORS
Payable at end of each period

MONTHLY Compounding

MONTHS	9% Nominal Annual Rate	9¼% Nominal Annual Rate	9½% Nominal Annual Rate	9¾% Nominal Annual Rate	MONTHS
1	1.0000 000 000	1.0000 000 000	1.0000 000 000	1.0000 000 000	1
2	0.4981 320 050	0.4980 803 155	0.4980 286 366	0.4979 769 686	2
3	0.3308 457 866	0.3307 770 422	0.3307 083 169	0.3306 396 107	3
4	0.2472 050 123	0.2471 278 717	0.2470 507 580	0.2469 736 711	4
5	0.1970 224 155	0.1969 403 423	0.1968 583 034	0.1967 762 988	5
6	0.1635 689 074	0.1634 836 333	0.1633 984 008	0.1633 132 100	6
7	0.1396 748 786	0.1395 873 929	0.1394 999 563	0.1394 125 687	7
8	0.1217 555 241	0.1216 664 455	0.1215 774 232	0.1214 884 571	8
9	0.1078 192 858	0.1077 290 265	0.1076 388 308	0.1075 486 985	9
10	0.0966 712 287	0.0965 800 774	0.0964 889 967	0.0963 979 868	10
11	0.0875 509 398	0.0874 591 062	0.0873 673 505	0.0872 756 728	11
YEARS					
1	0.0799 514 768	0.0798 591 184	0.0797 668 451	0.0796 746 570	12
2	0.0381 847 423	0.0380 911 989	0.0379 978 263	0.0379 046 244	24
3	0.0242 997 327	0.0242 078 802	0.0241 162 831	0.0240 249 410	36
4	0.0173 850 424	0.0172 955 870	0.0172 064 700	0.0171 176 912	48
5	0.0132 583 552	0.0131 715 650	0.0130 851 946	0.0129 992 437	60
6	0.0105 255 372	0.0104 415 310	0.0103 580 241	0.0102 750 156	72
7	0.0085 890 783	0.0085 079 085	0.0084 273 150	0.0083 472 962	84
8	0.0071 502 033	0.0070 718 868	0.0069 942 207	0.0069 172 027	96
9	0.0060 429 087	0.0059 674 408	0.0058 926 941	0.0058 186 658	108
10	0.0051 675 774	0.0050 949 389	0.0050 230 891	0.0049 520 242	120
11	0.0044 608 039	0.0043 909 651	0.0043 219 789	0.0042 538 402	132
12	0.0038 803 070	0.0038 132 301	0.0037 470 657	0.0036 818 075	144
13	0.0033 968 051	0.0033 324 461	0.0032 690 553	0.0032 066 250	156
14	0.0029 893 750	0.0029 276 843	0.0028 670 134	0.0028 073 529	168
15	0.0026 426 658	0.0025 835 896	0.0025 255 802	0.0024 686 266	180
16	0.0023 451 584	0.0022 886 390	0.0022 332 290	0.0021 789 157	192
17	0.0020 880 390	0.0020 340 156	0.0019 811 398	0.0019 293 967	204
18	0.0018 644 484	0.0018 128 575	0.0017 624 478	0.0017 132 023	216
19	0.0016 689 678	0.0016 197 438	0.0015 717 301	0.0015 249 072	228
20	0.0014 972 596	0.0014 503 350	0.0014 046 452	0.0013 601 685	240
21	0.0013 458 102	0.0013 011 161	0.0012 576 769	0.0012 154 685	252
22	0.0012 117 432	0.0011 692 096	0.0011 279 467	0.0010 879 279	264
23	0.0010 926 815	0.0010 522 376	0.0010 130 759	0.0009 751 675	276
24	0.0009 866 433	0.0009 482 178	0.0009 110 820	0.0008 752 046	288
25	0.0008 919 636	0.0008 554 851	0.0008 202 999	0.0007 863 742	300
26	0.0008 072 338	0.0007 726 308	0.0007 393 211	0.0007 072 683	312
27	0.0007 312 540	0.0006 984 555	0.0006 669 467	0.0006 366 887	324
28	0.0006 629 964	0.0006 319 319	0.0006 021 500	0.0005 736 098	336
29	0.0006 015 759	0.0005 721 754	0.0005 440 477	0.0005 171 492	348
30	0.0005 462 262	0.0005 184 209	0.0004 918 754	0.0004 665 441	360
31	0.0004 962 810	0.0004 700 032	0.0004 449 694	0.0004 211 322	372
32	0.0004 511 587	0.0004 263 417	0.0004 027 507	0.0003 803 363	384
33	0.0004 103 496	0.0003 869 281	0.0003 647 124	0.0003 436 512	396
34	0.0003 734 051	0.0003 513 155	0.0003 304 093	0.0003 106 338	408
35	0.0003 399 297	0.0003 191 099	0.0002 994 493	0.0002 808 939	420
36	0.0003 095 734	0.0002 899 628	0.0002 714 859	0.0002 540 870	432
37	0.0002 820 255	0.0002 635 654	0.0002 462 119	0.0002 299 084	444
38	0.0002 570 096	0.0002 396 431	0.0002 233 551	0.0002 080 878	456
39	0.0002 342 795	0.0002 179 515	0.0002 026 728	0.0001 883 848	468
40	0.0002 136 150	0.0001 982 723	0.0001 839 489	0.0001 705 856	480
41	0.0001 948 191	0.0001 804 104	0.0001 669 904	0.0001 544 994	492
42	0.0001 777 151	0.0001 641 911	0.0001 516 246	0.0001 399 557	504
43	0.0001 621 444	0.0001 494 576	0.0001 376 968	0.0001 268 021	516
44	0.0001 479 643	0.0001 360 690	0.0001 250 682	0.0001 149 018	528
45	0.0001 350 461	0.0001 238 986	0.0001 136 141	0.0001 041 325	540
46	0.0001 232 739	0.0001 128 325	0.0001 032 225	0.0000 943 841	552
47	0.0001 125 431	0.0001 027 678	0.0000 937 925	0.0000 855 578	564
48	0.0001 027 589	0.0000 936 115	0.0000 852 331	0.0000 775 647	576
49	0.0000 938 359	0.0000 852 800	0.0000 774 624	0.0000 703 247	588
50	0.0000 856 964	0.0000 776 973	0.0000 704 063	0.0000 637 658	600

MONTHLY
Compounding

TABLE 3. SINKING FUND FACTORS
Payable at end of each period

MONTHS	10% Nominal Annual Rate	10¼% Nominal Annual Rate	10½% Nominal Annual Rate	10¾% Nominal Annual Rate	MONTHS
1	1.0000 000 000	1.0000 000 000	1.0000 000 000	1.0000 000 000	1
2	0.4979 253 112	0.4978 736 646	0.4978 220 286	0.4977 704 034	2
3	0.3305 709 235	0.3305 022 554	0.3304 336 063	0.3303 649 763	3
4	0.2468 966 110	0.2468 195 777	0.2467 425 712	0.2466 655 914	4
5	0.1966 943 285	0.1966 123 925	0.1965 304 908	0.1964 486 233	5
6	0.1632 280 609	0.1631 429 534	0.1630 578 876	0.1629 728 634	6
7	0.1393 252 301	0.1392 379 405	0.1391 506 998	0.1390 635 081	7
8	0.1213 995 474	0.1213 106 938	0.1212 218 965	0.1211 331 554	8
9	0.1074 586 298	0.1073 686 245	0.1072 786 826	0.1071 888 042	9
10	0.0963 070 477	0.0962 161 791	0.0961 253 813	0.0960 346 541	10
11	0.0871 840 730	0.0870 925 511	0.0870 011 070	0.0869 097 407	11
YEARS					
1	0.0795 825 539	0.0794 905 359	0.0793 986 029	0.0793 067 549	12
2	0.0378 115 930	0.0377 187 321	0.0376 260 416	0.0375 335 215	24
3	0.0239 338 539	0.0238 430 214	0.0237 524 435	0.0236 621 199	36
4	0.0170 292 501	0.0169 411 464	0.0168 533 798	0.0167 659 497	48
5	0.0129 137 114	0.0128 285 972	0.0127 439 004	0.0126 596 203	60
6	0.0101 925 044	0.0101 104 896	0.0100 289 700	0.0099 479 446	72
7	0.0082 678 507	0.0081 889 769	0.0081 106 731	0.0080 329 380	84
8	0.0068 408 308	0.0067 651 027	0.0066 900 162	0.0066 155 691	96
9	0.0057 453 529	0.0056 727 524	0.0056 008 612	0.0055 296 762	108
10	0.0048 817 404	0.0048 122 335	0.0047 434 997	0.0046 755 347	120
11	0.0041 865 441	0.0041 200 856	0.0040 544 593	0.0039 896 600	132
12	0.0036 174 493	0.0035 539 846	0.0034 914 068	0.0034 297 095	144
13	0.0031 451 476	0.0030 846 151	0.0030 250 196	0.0029 663 529	156
14	0.0027 486 935	0.0026 910 258	0.0026 343 401	0.0025 786 266	168
15	0.0024 127 178	0.0023 578 425	0.0023 039 892	0.0022 511 465	180
16	0.0021 256 860	0.0020 735 266	0.0020 224 244	0.0019 723 658	192
17	0.0018 787 712	0.0018 292 482	0.0017 808 122	0.0017 334 479	204
18	0.0016 651 036	0.0016 181 346	0.0015 722 776	0.0015 275 152	216
19	0.0014 792 558	0.0014 347 563	0.0013 913 890	0.0013 491 342	228
20	0.0013 168 831	0.0012 747 672	0.0012 337 989	0.0011 939 562	240
21	0.0011 744 667	0.0011 346 475	0.0010 959 865	0.0010 584 597	252
22	0.0010 491 266	0.0010 115 165	0.0009 750 708	0.0009 397 634	264
23	0.0009 384 833	0.0009 029 945	0.0008 686 723	0.0008 354 880	276
24	0.0008 405 540	0.0008 070 991	0.0007 748 088	0.0007 436 523	288
25	0.0007 536 741	0.0007 221 662	0.0006 918 171	0.0006 625 939	300
26	0.0006 764 363	0.0006 467 893	0.0006 182 918	0.0005 909 090	312
27	0.0006 076 433	0.0005 797 723	0.0005 530 385	0.0005 274 048	324
28	0.0005 462 706	0.0005 200 924	0.0004 950 357	0.0004 710 619	336
29	0.0004 914 374	0.0004 668 701	0.0004 434 063	0.0004 210 053	348
30	0.0004 423 824	0.0004 193 463	0.0003 973 929	0.0003 764 803	360
31	0.0003 984 451	0.0003 768 624	0.0003 563 396	0.0003 368 333	372
32	0.0003 590 502	0.0003 388 453	0.0003 196 756	0.0003 014 963	384
33	0.0003 236 947	0.0003 047 943	0.0002 869 027	0.0002 699 742	396
34	0.0002 919 376	0.0002 742 708	0.0002 575 852	0.0002 418 339	408
35	0.0002 633 909	0.0002 468 894	0.0002 313 402	0.0002 166 956	420
36	0.0002 377 126	0.0002 223 106	0.0002 078 310	0.0001 942 256	432
37	0.0002 146 001	0.0002 002 344	0.0001 867 605	0.0001 741 298	444
38	0.0001 937 857	0.0001 803 955	0.0001 678 662	0.0001 561 487	456
39	0.0001 750 314	0.0001 625 588	0.0001 509 157	0.0001 400 528	468
40	0.0001 581 258	0.0001 465 154	0.0001 357 028	0.0001 256 390	480
41	0.0001 428 804	0.0001 320 793	0.0001 220 445	0.0001 127 270	492
42	0.0001 291 273	0.0001 190 851	0.0001 097 779	0.0001 011 568	504
43	0.0001 167 162	0.0001 073 852	0.0000 987 579	0.0000 907 860	516
44	0.0001 055 129	0.0000 968 476	0.0000 888 552	0.0000 814 880	528
45	0.0000 953 971	0.0000 873 545	0.0000 799 545	0.0000 731 499	540
46	0.0000 862 610	0.0000 788 004	0.0000 719 526	0.0000 656 713	552
47	0.0000 780 080	0.0000 710 908	0.0000 647 574	0.0000 589 622	564
48	0.0000 705 512	0.0000 641 412	0.0000 582 865	0.0000 529 425	576
49	0.0000 638 126	0.0000 578 754	0.0000 524 660	0.0000 475 407	588
50	0.0000 577 221	0.0000 522 255	0.0000 472 299	0.0000 426 926	600

TABLE 3. SINKING FUND FACTORS
Payable at end of each period

MONTHLY Compounding

MONTHS	11% Nominal Annual Rate	11¼% Nominal Annual Rate	11½% Nominal Annual Rate	11¾% Nominal Annual Rate	MONTHS
1	1.0000 000 000	1.0000 000 000	1.0000 000 000	1.0000 000 000	1
2	0.4977 187 889	0.4976 671 851	0.4976 155 920	0.4975 640 095	2
3	0.3302 963 653	0.3302 277 733	0.3301 592 004	0.3300 906 464	3
4	0.2465 886 384	0.2465 117 122	0.2464 348 127	0.2463 579 399	4
5	0.1963 667 901	0.1962 849 912	0.1962 032 264	0.1961 214 959	5
6	0.1628 878 809	0.1628 029 400	0.1627 180 406	0.1626 331 829	6
7	0.1389 763 652	0.1388 892 713	0.1388 022 263	0.1387 152 302	7
8	0.1210 444 704	0.1209 558 416	0.1208 672 690	0.1207 787 525	8
9	0.1070 989 892	0.1070 092 376	0.1069 195 494	0.1068 299 244	9
10	0.0959 439 974	0.0958 534 114	0.0957 628 959	0.0956 724 510	10
11	0.0868 184 523	0.0867 272 416	0.0866 361 086	0.0865 450 533	11
YEARS					
1	0.0792 149 919	0.0791 233 137	0.0790 317 205	0.0789 402 122	12
2	0.0374 411 715	0.0373 489 917	0.0372 569 820	0.0371 651 422	24
3	0.0235 720 505	0.0234 822 349	0.0233 926 731	0.0233 033 648	36
4	0.0166 788 559	0.0165 920 980	0.0165 056 756	0.0164 195 882	48
5	0.0125 757 564	0.0124 923 079	0.0124 092 740	0.0123 266 542	60
6	0.0098 674 123	0.0097 873 721	0.0097 078 228	0.0096 287 634	72
7	0.0079 557 698	0.0078 791 668	0.0078 031 275	0.0077 276 501	84
8	0.0065 417 590	0.0064 685 836	0.0063 960 405	0.0063 241 272	96
9	0.0054 591 944	0.0053 894 123	0.0053 203 269	0.0052 519 348	108
10	0.0046 083 345	0.0045 418 947	0.0044 762 111	0.0044 112 793	120
11	0.0039 256 824	0.0038 625 210	0.0038 001 703	0.0037 386 248	132
12	0.0033 688 859	0.0033 089 292	0.0032 498 325	0.0031 915 889	144
13	0.0029 086 069	0.0028 517 733	0.0027 958 436	0.0027 408 094	156
14	0.0025 238 756	0.0024 700 770	0.0024 172 209	0.0023 652 970	168
15	0.0021 993 027	0.0021 484 460	0.0020 985 648	0.0020 496 470	180
16	0.0019 233 373	0.0018 753 254	0.0018 283 163	0.0017 822 962	192
17	0.0016 871 398	0.0016 418 721	0.0015 976 293	0.0015 543 956	204
18	0.0014 838 298	0.0014 412 036	0.0013 996 191	0.0013 590 584	216
19	0.0013 079 722	0.0012 678 832	0.0012 288 475	0.0011 908 452	228
20	0.0011 552 173	0.0011 175 601	0.0010 809 630	0.0010 454 040	240
21	0.0010 220 429	0.0009 867 120	0.0009 524 432	0.0009 192 126	252
22	0.0009 055 679	0.0008 724 580	0.0008 404 078	0.0008 093 916	264
23	0.0008 034 134	0.0007 724 200	0.0007 424 799	0.0007 135 653	276
24	0.0007 135 990	0.0006 846 188	0.0006 566 817	0.0006 297 581	288
25	0.0006 344 641	0.0006 073 955	0.0005 813 563	0.0005 563 152	300
26	0.0005 646 064	0.0005 393 498	0.0005 151 058	0.0004 918 415	312
27	0.0005 028 349	0.0004 792 931	0.0004 567 444	0.0004 351 542	324
28	0.0004 481 329	0.0004 262 113	0.0004 052 606	0.0003 852 451	336
29	0.0003 996 277	0.0003 792 345	0.0003 597 881	0.0003 412 513	348
30	0.0003 565 673	0.0003 376 139	0.0003 195 810	0.0003 024 307	360
31	0.0003 183 011	0.0003 007 019	0.0002 839 955	0.0002 681 432	372
32	0.0002 842 642	0.0002 679 368	0.0002 524 735	0.0002 378 345	384
33	0.0002 539 643	0.0002 388 301	0.0002 245 299	0.0002 110 236	396
34	0.0002 269 718	0.0002 129 551	0.0001 997 418	0.0001 872 915	408
35	0.0002 029 099	0.0001 899 388	0.0001 777 400	0.0001 662 727	420
36	0.0001 814 481	0.0001 694 541	0.0001 582 009	0.0001 476 476	432
37	0.0001 622 957	0.0001 512 136	0.0001 408 407	0.0001 311 363	444
38	0.0001 451 963	0.0001 349 643	0.0001 254 101	0.0001 164 931	456
39	0.0001 299 235	0.0001 204 832	0.0001 116 894	0.0001 035 021	468
40	0.0001 162 774	0.0001 075 734	0.0000 994 853	0.0000 919 732	480
41	0.0001 040 805	0.0000 960 610	0.0000 886 269	0.0000 817 391	492
42	0.0000 931 759	0.0000 857 917	0.0000 789 633	0.0000 726 522	504
43	0.0000 834 240	0.0000 766 291	0.0000 703 611	0.0000 645 821	516
44	0.0000 747 010	0.0000 684 522	0.0000 627 021	0.0000 574 136	528
45	0.0000 668 967	0.0000 611 535	0.0000 558 816	0.0000 510 449	540
46	0.0000 599 131	0.0000 546 375	0.0000 498 068	0.0000 453 859	552
47	0.0000 536 627	0.0000 488 194	0.0000 443 955	0.0000 403 569	564
48	0.0000 480 678	0.0000 436 237	0.0000 395 745	0.0000 358 871	576
49	0.0000 430 589	0.0000 389 832	0.0000 352 789	0.0000 319 140	588
50	0.0000 385 742	0.0000 348 382	0.0000 314 511	0.0000 283 821	600

MONTHLY
Compounding

TABLE 3. SINKING FUND FACTORS
Payable at end of each period

MONTHS	12% Nominal Annual Rate	12¼% Nominal Annual Rate	12½% Nominal Annual Rate	12¾% Nominal Annual Rate	MONTHS
1	1.0000 000 000	1.0000 000 000	1.0000 000 000	1.0000 000 000	1
2	0.4975 124 378	0.4974 608 768	0.4974 093 264	0.4973 577 868	2
3	0.3300 221 115	0.3299 535 955	0.3298 850 986	0.3298 166 207	3
4	0.2462 810 939	0.2462 042 746	0.2461 274 820	0.2460 507 161	4
5	0.1960 397 996	0.1959 581 375	0.1958 765 096	0.1957 949 159	5
6	0.1625 483 667	0.1624 635 921	0.1623 788 590	0.1622 941 675	6
7	0.1386 282 829	0.1385 413 845	0.1384 545 349	0.1383 677 341	7
8	0.1206 902 920	0.1206 018 877	0.1205 135 395	0.1204 252 472	8
9	0.1067 403 628	0.1066 508 645	0.1065 614 295	0.1064 720 578	9
10	0.0955 820 766	0.0954 917 726	0.0954 015 391	0.0953 113 760	10
11	0.0864 540 757	0.0863 631 758	0.0862 723 535	0.0861 816 087	11
YEARS					
1	0.0788 487 887	0.0787 574 500	0.0786 661 960	0.0785 750 269	12
2	0.0370 734 722	0.0369 819 721	0.0368 906 416	0.0367 994 807	24
3	0.0232 143 098	0.0231 255 079	0.0230 369 589	0.0229 486 626	36
4	0.0163 338 354	0.0162 484 169	0.0161 633 322	0.0160 785 809	48
5	0.0122 444 477	0.0121 626 537	0.0120 812 716	0.0120 003 005	60
6	0.0095 501 925	0.0094 721 091	0.0093 945 120	0.0093 174 000	72
7	0.0076 527 328	0.0075 783 740	0.0075 045 718	0.0074 313 244	84
8	0.0062 528 414	0.0061 821 805	0.0061 121 420	0.0060 427 233	96
9	0.0051 842 326	0.0051 172 169	0.0050 508 844	0.0049 852 313	108
10	0.0043 470 948	0.0042 836 533	0.0042 209 502	0.0041 589 809	120
11	0.0036 778 788	0.0036 179 266	0.0035 587 623	0.0035 003 803	132
12	0.0031 341 914	0.0030 776 329	0.0030 219 061	0.0029 670 040	144
13	0.0026 866 622	0.0026 333 933	0.0025 809 941	0.0025 294 557	156
14	0.0023 142 953	0.0022 642 053	0.0022 150 168	0.0021 667 194	168
15	0.0020 016 806	0.0019 546 537	0.0019 085 542	0.0018 633 698	180
16	0.0017 372 513	0.0016 931 677	0.0016 500 314	0.0016 078 286	192
17	0.0015 121 553	0.0014 708 925	0.0014 305 914	0.0013 912 362	204
18	0.0013 195 038	0.0012 809 376	0.0012 433 420	0.0012 066 994	216
19	0.0011 538 566	0.0011 178 620	0.0010 828 418	0.0010 487 763	228
20	0.0010 108 613	0.0009 773 135	0.0009 447 388	0.0009 131 160	240
21	0.0008 869 965	0.0008 557 713	0.0008 255 136	0.0007 962 003	252
22	0.0007 793 836	0.0007 503 584	0.0007 222 910	0.0006 951 565	264
23	0.0006 856 488	0.0006 587 033	0.0006 327 019	0.0006 076 181	276
24	0.0006 038 188	0.0005 788 350	0.0005 547 783	0.0005 316 208	288
25	0.0005 322 414	0.0005 091 045	0.0004 868 747	0.0004 655 227	300
26	0.0004 695 246	0.0004 481 232	0.0004 276 063	0.0004 079 433	312
27	0.0004 144 889	0.0003 947 153	0.0003 758 014	0.0003 577 154	324
28	0.0003 661 298	0.0003 478 805	0.0003 304 640	0.0003 138 478	336
29	0.0003 235 881	0.0003 067 636	0.0002 907 435	0.0002 754 947	348
30	0.0002 861 260	0.0002 706 310	0.0002 559 110	0.0002 419 321	360
31	0.0002 531 072	0.0002 388 510	0.0002 253 394	0.0002 125 381	372
32	0.0002 239 817	0.0002 108 780	0.0001 984 878	0.0001 867 767	384
33	0.0001 982 726	0.0001 862 395	0.0001 748 885	0.0001 641 852	396
34	0.0001 755 650	0.0001 645 251	0.0001 541 358	0.0001 443 626	408
35	0.0001 554 978	0.0001 453 779	0.0001 358 772	0.0001 269 615	420
36	0.0001 377 553	0.0001 284 866	0.0001 198 060	0.0001 116 796	432
37	0.0001 220 616	0.0001 135 795	0.0001 056 547	0.0000 982 540	444
38	0.0001 081 748	0.0001 004 186	0.0000 931 898	0.0000 864 553	456
39	0.0000 958 829	0.0000 887 959	0.0000 822 069	0.0000 760 835	468
40	0.0000 849 995	0.0000 785 287	0.0000 725 273	0.0000 669 637	480
41	0.0000 753 607	0.0000 694 567	0.0000 639 944	0.0000 589 431	492
42	0.0000 668 221	0.0000 614 389	0.0000 564 708	0.0000 518 879	504
43	0.0000 592 566	0.0000 543 516	0.0000 498 360	0.0000 456 807	516
44	0.0000 525 522	0.0000 480 857	0.0000 439 839	0.0000 402 189	528
45	0.0000 466 098	0.0000 425 451	0.0000 388 216	0.0000 354 123	540
46	0.0000 413 422	0.0000 376 453	0.0000 342 672	0.0000 311 818	552
47	0.0000 366 720	0.0000 333 116	0.0000 302 486	0.0000 274 580	564
48	0.0000 325 311	0.0000 294 783	0.0000 267 025	0.0000 241 799	576
49	0.0000 288 592	0.0000 260 871	0.0000 235 730	0.0000 212 940	588
50	0.0000 256 027	0.0000 230 870	0.0000 208 111	0.0000 187 531	600

TABLE 3. SINKING FUND FACTORS
Payable at end of each period

MONTHLY Compounding

MONTHS	13% Nominal Annual Rate	13¼% Nominal Annual Rate	13½% Nominal Annual Rate	13¾% Nominal Annual Rate	MONTHS
1	1.0000 000 000	1.0000 000 000	1.0000 000 000	1.0000 000 000	1
2	0.4973 062 578	0.4972 547 395	0.4972 032 318	0.4971 517 349	2
3	0.3297 481 617	0.3296 797 217	0.3296 113 007	0.3295 428 987	3
4	0.2459 739 769	0.2458 972 644	0.2458 205 786	0.2457 439 194	4
5	0.1957 133 563	0.1956 318 309	0.1955 503 396	0.1954 688 825	5
6	0.1622 095 174	0.1621 249 089	0.1620 403 419	0.1619 558 163	6
7	0.1382 809 821	0.1381 942 789	0.1381 076 244	0.1380 210 187	7
8	0.1203 370 111	0.1202 488 309	0.1201 607 067	0.1200 726 385	8
9	0.1063 827 492	0.1062 935 039	0.1062 043 217	0.1061 152 028	9
10	0.0952 212 834	0.0951 312 611	0.0950 413 092	0.0949 514 277	10
11	0.0860 909 416	0.0860 003 520	0.0859 098 399	0.0858 194 053	11
YEARS					
1	0.0784 839 424	0.0783 929 426	0.0783 020 274	0.0782 111 969	12
2	0.0367 084 893	0.0366 176 672	0.0365 270 145	0.0364 365 310	24
3	0.0228 606 187	0.0227 728 270	0.0226 852 873	0.0225 979 994	36
4	0.0159 941 626	0.0159 100 767	0.0158 263 230	0.0157 429 008	48
5	0.0119 197 397	0.0118 395 885	0.0117 598 460	0.0116 805 115	60
6	0.0092 407 719	0.0091 646 263	0.0090 889 622	0.0090 137 781	72
7	0.0073 586 300	0.0072 864 868	0.0072 148 928	0.0071 438 462	84
8	0.0059 739 217	0.0059 057 348	0.0058 381 597	0.0057 711 938	96
9	0.0049 202 544	0.0048 559 498	0.0047 923 141	0.0047 293 436	108
10	0.0040 977 407	0.0040 372 249	0.0039 774 289	0.0039 183 478	120
11	0.0034 427 746	0.0033 859 391	0.0033 298 680	0.0032 745 552	132
12	0.0029 129 191	0.0028 596 441	0.0028 071 716	0.0027 554 941	144
13	0.0024 787 693	0.0024 289 260	0.0023 799 170	0.0023 317 332	156
14	0.0021 193 025	0.0020 727 556	0.0020 270 683	0.0019 822 297	168
15	0.0018 190 883	0.0017 756 976	0.0017 331 854	0.0016 915 394	180
16	0.0015 665 451	0.0015 261 670	0.0014 866 804	0.0014 480 710	192
17	0.0013 528 110	0.0013 153 002	0.0012 786 878	0.0012 429 582	204
18	0.0011 709 920	0.0011 362 022	0.0011 023 127	0.0010 693 058	216
19	0.0010 156 462	0.0009 834 320	0.0009 521 146	0.0009 216 746	228
20	0.0008 824 238	0.0008 526 410	0.0008 237 468	0.0007 957 205	240
21	0.0007 678 085	0.0007 403 154	0.0007 136 984	0.0006 879 354	252
22	0.0006 689 303	0.0006 435 880	0.0006 191 058	0.0005 954 600	264
23	0.0005 834 259	0.0005 600 995	0.0005 376 137	0.0005 159 435	276
24	0.0005 093 349	0.0004 878 937	0.0004 672 706	0.0004 474 397	288
25	0.0004 450 197	0.0004 253 376	0.0004 064 488	0.0003 883 263	300
26	0.0003 891 044	0.0003 710 604	0.0003 537 829	0.0003 372 440	312
27	0.0003 404 267	0.0003 239 051	0.0003 081 215	0.0002 930 474	324
28	0.0002 980 004	0.0002 828 910	0.0002 684 899	0.0002 547 680	336
29	0.0002 609 850	0.0002 471 832	0.0002 340 590	0.0002 215 832	348
30	0.0002 286 619	0.0002 160 686	0.0002 041 218	0.0001 927 920	360
31	0.0002 004 143	0.0001 889 361	0.0001 780 730	0.0001 677 955	372
32	0.0001 757 117	0.0001 652 608	0.0001 553 935	0.0001 460 806	384
33	0.0001 540 964	0.0001 445 904	0.0001 356 368	0.0001 272 066	396
34	0.0001 351 727	0.0001 265 346	0.0001 184 181	0.0001 107 944	408
35	0.0001 185 981	0.0001 107 558	0.0001 034 050	0.0000 965 174	420
36	0.0001 040 751	0.0000 969 617	0.0000 903 104	0.0000 840 935	432
37	0.0000 913 453	0.0000 848 987	0.0000 788 856	0.0000 732 790	444
38	0.0000 801 840	0.0000 743 465	0.0000 689 149	0.0000 638 629	456
39	0.0000 703 953	0.0000 651 135	0.0000 602 111	0.0000 556 626	468
40	0.0000 618 083	0.0000 570 330	0.0000 526 117	0.0000 485 197	480
41	0.0000 542 740	0.0000 499 598	0.0000 459 753	0.0000 422 968	492
42	0.0000 476 621	0.0000 437 673	0.0000 401 790	0.0000 368 745	504
43	0.0000 418 588	0.0000 383 450	0.0000 351 158	0.0000 321 493	516
44	0.0000 367 645	0.0000 335 965	0.0000 306 923	0.0000 280 311	528
45	0.0000 322 920	0.0000 294 376	0.0000 268 274	0.0000 244 415	540
46	0.0000 283 650	0.0000 257 947	0.0000 234 502	0.0000 213 125	552
47	0.0000 249 167	0.0000 226 035	0.0000 204 989	0.0000 185 847	564
48	0.0000 218 885	0.0000 198 079	0.0000 179 196	0.0000 162 065	576
49	0.0000 192 289	0.0000 173 585	0.0000 156 653	0.0000 141 330	588
50	0.0000 168 930	0.0000 152 125	0.0000 136 949	0.0000 123 251	600

MONTHLY
Compounding

TABLE 3. SINKING FUND FACTORS
Payable at end of each period

MONTHS	14% Nominal Annual Rate	14¼% Nominal Annual Rate	14½% Nominal Annual Rate	14¾% Nominal Annual Rate	MONTHS
1	1.0000 000 000	1.0000 000 000	1.0000 000 000	1.0000 000 000	1
2	0.4971 002 486	0.4970 487 729	0.4969 973 079	0.4969 458 536	2
3	0.3294 745 156	0.3294 061 515	0.3293 378 063	0.3292 694 801	3
4	0.2456 672 869	0.2455 906 811	0.2455 141 019	0.2454 375 493	4
5	0.1953 874 595	0.1953 060 706	0.1952 247 158	0.1951 433 951	5
6	0.1618 713 322	0.1617 868 896	0.1617 024 884	0.1616 181 286	6
7	0.1379 344 618	0.1378 479 535	0.1377 614 940	0.1376 750 831	7
8	0.1199 846 263	0.1198 966 700	0.1198 087 696	0.1197 209 251	8
9	0.1060 261 469	0.1059 371 542	0.1058 482 246	0.1057 593 581	9
10	0.0948 616 164	0.0947 718 754	0.0946 822 047	0.0945 926 042	10
11	0.0857 290 481	0.0856 387 684	0.0855 485 660	0.0854 584 411	11
YEARS					
1	0.0781 204 509	0.0780 297 895	0.0779 392 127	0.0778 487 203	12
2	0.0363 462 166	0.0362 560 712	0.0361 660 947	0.0360 762 870	24
3	0.0225 109 631	0.0224 241 781	0.0223 376 441	0.0222 513 610	36
4	0.0156 598 098	0.0155 770 496	0.0154 946 195	0.0154 125 192	48
5	0.0116 015 842	0.0115 230 632	0.0114 449 477	0.0113 672 370	60
6	0.0089 390 728	0.0088 648 450	0.0087 910 934	0.0087 178 166	72
7	0.0070 733 449	0.0070 033 872	0.0069 339 709	0.0068 650 941	84
8	0.0057 048 344	0.0056 390 786	0.0055 739 237	0.0055 093 669	96
9	0.0046 670 345	0.0046 053 831	0.0045 443 857	0.0044 840 384	108
10	0.0038 599 768	0.0038 023 111	0.0037 453 456	0.0036 890 755	120
11	0.0032 199 945	0.0031 661 798	0.0031 131 050	0.0030 607 636	132
12	0.0027 046 042	0.0026 544 942	0.0026 051 565	0.0025 565 836	144
13	0.0022 843 655	0.0022 378 049	0.0021 920 424	0.0021 470 687	156
14	0.0019 382 295	0.0018 950 568	0.0018 527 010	0.0018 111 513	168
15	0.0016 507 472	0.0016 107 966	0.0015 716 753	0.0015 333 709	180
16	0.0014 103 251	0.0013 734 286	0.0013 373 675	0.0013 021 279	192
17	0.0012 080 956	0.0011 740 845	0.0011 409 092	0.0011 085 543	204
18	0.0010 371 642	0.0010 058 707	0.0009 754 080	0.0009 457 593	216
19	0.0008 920 933	0.0008 633 517	0.0008 354 313	0.0008 083 134	228
20	0.0007 685 414	0.0007 421 894	0.0007 166 443	0.0006 918 863	240
21	0.0006 630 044	0.0006 388 838	0.0006 155 521	0.0005 929 882	252
22	0.0005 726 273	0.0005 505 848	0.0005 293 099	0.0005 087 805	264
23	0.0004 950 645	0.0004 749 526	0.0004 555 842	0.0004 369 363	276
24	0.0004 283 753	0.0004 100 526	0.0003 924 471	0.0003 755 347	288
25	0.0003 709 438	0.0003 542 753	0.0003 382 958	0.0003 229 807	300
26	0.0003 214 166	0.0003 062 743	0.0002 917 913	0.0002 779 427	312
27	0.0002 786 551	0.0002 649 178	0.0002 518 093	0.0002 393 042	324
28	0.0002 416 974	0.0002 292 508	0.0002 174 019	0.0002 061 251	336
29	0.0002 097 274	0.0001 984 643	0.0001 877 675	0.0001 776 115	348
30	0.0001 820 508	0.0001 718 709	0.0001 622 259	0.0001 530 905	360
31	0.0001 580 752	0.0001 488 849	0.0001 401 984	0.0001 319 907	372
32	0.0001 372 937	0.0001 290 059	0.0001 211 915	0.0001 138 256	384
33	0.0001 192 718	0.0001 118 058	0.0001 047 834	0.0000 981 802	396
34	0.0001 036 363	0.0000 969 175	0.0000 906 133	0.0000 847 000	408
35	0.0000 900 661	0.0000 840 257	0.0000 783 718	0.0000 730 815	420
36	0.0000 782 847	0.0000 728 591	0.0000 677 933	0.0000 630 649	432
37	0.0000 680 533	0.0000 631 844	0.0000 586 495	0.0000 544 272	444
38	0.0000 591 658	0.0000 548 002	0.0000 507 442	0.0000 469 770	456
39	0.0000 514 441	0.0000 475 330	0.0000 439 083	0.0000 405 501	468
40	0.0000 447 340	0.0000 412 328	0.0000 379 961	0.0000 350 048	480
41	0.0000 389 020	0.0000 357 702	0.0000 328 822	0.0000 302 198	492
42	0.0000 338 325	0.0000 310 332	0.0000 284 582	0.0000 260 902	504
43	0.0000 294 253	0.0000 269 249	0.0000 246 306	0.0000 225 260	516
44	0.0000 255 935	0.0000 233 616	0.0000 213 187	0.0000 194 495	528
45	0.0000 222 616	0.0000 202 706	0.0000 184 528	0.0000 167 937	540
46	0.0000 193 642	0.0000 175 892	0.0000 159 727	0.0000 145 010	552
47	0.0000 168 444	0.0000 152 630	0.0000 138 263	0.0000 125 216	564
48	0.0000 146 530	0.0000 132 447	0.0000 119 686	0.0000 108 126	576
49	0.0000 127 469	0.0000 114 936	0.0000 103 607	0.0000 093 371	588
50	0.0000 110 891	0.0000 099 742	0.0000 089 690	0.0000 080 630	600

TABLE 3. SINKING FUND FACTORS
Payable at end of each period

MONTHLY Compounding

MONTHS	15% Nominal Annual Rate	15¼% Nominal Annual Rate	15½% Nominal Annual Rate	15¾% Nominal Annual Rate	MONTHS
1	1.0000 000 000	1.0000 000 000	1.0000 000 000	1.0000 000 000	1
2	0.4968 944 099	0.4968 429 769	0.4967 915 545	0.4967 401 428	2
3	0.3292 011 728	0.3291 328 844	0.3290 646 150	0.3289 963 645	3
4	0.2453 610 233	0.2452 845 240	0.2452 080 513	0.2451 316 052	4
5	0.1950 621 084	0.1949 808 559	0.1948 996 374	0.1948 184 529	5
6	0.1615 338 102	0.1614 495 332	0.1613 652 976	0.1612 811 034	6
7	0.1375 887 209	0.1375 024 073	0.1374 161 424	0.1373 299 261	7
8	0.1196 331 365	0.1195 454 037	0.1194 577 268	0.1193 701 057	8
9	0.1056 705 546	0.1055 818 142	0.1054 931 368	0.1054 045 223	9
10	0.0945 030 740	0.0944 136 139	0.0943 242 240	0.0942 349 042	10
11	0.0853 683 935	0.0852 784 231	0.0851 885 301	0.0850 987 144	11
YEARS					
1	0.0777 583 123	0.0776 679 888	0.0775 777 497	0.0774 875 950	12
2	0.0359 866 480	0.0358 971 777	0.0358 078 758	0.0357 187 423	24
3	0.0221 653 285	0.0220 795 464	0.0219 940 144	0.0219 087 322	36
4	0.0153 307 483	0.0152 493 061	0.0151 681 922	0.0150 874 062	48
5	0.0112 899 301	0.0112 130 262	0.0111 365 244	0.0110 604 239	60
6	0.0086 450 133	0.0085 726 821	0.0085 008 217	0.0084 294 305	72
7	0.0067 967 547	0.0067 289 508	0.0066 616 802	0.0065 949 408	84
8	0.0054 454 053	0.0053 820 360	0.0053 192 561	0.0052 570 626	96
9	0.0044 243 373	0.0043 652 786	0.0043 068 584	0.0042 490 726	108
10	0.0036 334 957	0.0035 786 012	0.0035 243 870	0.0034 708 479	120
11	0.0030 091 496	0.0029 582 565	0.0029 080 780	0.0028 586 077	132
12	0.0025 087 677	0.0024 617 011	0.0024 153 760	0.0023 697 848	144
13	0.0021 028 746	0.0020 594 511	0.0020 167 889	0.0019 748 788	156
14	0.0017 703 972	0.0017 304 277	0.0016 912 324	0.0016 528 003	168
15	0.0014 958 712	0.0014 591 639	0.0014 232 367	0.0013 880 775	180
16	0.0012 676 961	0.0012 340 581	0.0012 012 002	0.0011 691 087	192
17	0.0010 770 043	0.0010 462 440	0.0010 162 580	0.0009 870 314	204
18	0.0009 169 075	0.0008 888 360	0.0008 615 280	0.0008 349 673	216
19	0.0007 819 798	0.0007 564 125	0.0007 315 934	0.0007 075 050	228
20	0.0006 678 958	0.0006 446 535	0.0006 221 402	0.0006 003 373	240
21	0.0005 711 714	0.0005 500 813	0.0005 296 978	0.0005 100 010	252
22	0.0004 889 748	0.0004 698 713	0.0004 514 492	0.0004 336 878	264
23	0.0004 189 861	0.0004 017 115	0.0003 850 908	0.0003 691 026	276
24	0.0003 592 923	0.0003 436 969	0.0003 287 262	0.0003 143 585	288
25	0.0003 083 061	0.0002 942 487	0.0002 807 857	0.0002 678 951	300
26	0.0002 647 042	0.0002 520 520	0.0002 399 634	0.0002 284 159	312
27	0.0002 273 781	0.0002 160 071	0.0002 051 683	0.0001 948 393	324
28	0.0001 953 959	0.0001 851 905	0.0001 754 858	0.0001 662 598	336
29	0.0001 679 716	0.0001 588 244	0.0001 501 468	0.0001 419 171	348
30	0.0001 444 402	0.0001 362 517	0.0001 285 025	0.0001 211 710	360
31	0.0001 242 377	0.0001 169 163	0.0001 100 046	0.0001 034 813	372
32	0.0001 068 847	0.0001 003 462	0.0000 941 886	0.0000 883 914	384
33	0.0000 919 732	0.0000 861 403	0.0000 806 607	0.0000 755 145	396
34	0.0000 791 550	0.0000 739 571	0.0000 690 861	0.0000 645 226	408
35	0.0000 681 330	0.0000 635 056	0.0000 591 799	0.0000 551 374	420
36	0.0000 586 529	0.0000 545 374	0.0000 506 998	0.0000 471 222	432
37	0.0000 504 971	0.0000 468 403	0.0000 434 388	0.0000 402 758	444
38	0.0000 434 794	0.0000 402 330	0.0000 372 207	0.0000 344 266	456
39	0.0000 374 398	0.0000 345 602	0.0000 318 949	0.0000 294 288	468
40	0.0000 322 414	0.0000 296 892	0.0000 273 328	0.0000 251 580	480
41	0.0000 277 663	0.0000 255 060	0.0000 234 244	0.0000 215 079	492
42	0.0000 239 135	0.0000 219 133	0.0000 200 757	0.0000 183 882	504
43	0.0000 205 963	0.0000 188 274	0.0000 172 064	0.0000 157 215	516
44	0.0000 177 398	0.0000 161 766	0.0000 147 477	0.0000 134 420	528
45	0.0000 152 800	0.0000 138 994	0.0000 126 406	0.0000 114 932	540
46	0.0000 131 616	0.0000 119 431	0.0000 108 348	0.0000 098 272	552
47	0.0000 113 372	0.0000 102 623	0.0000 092 872	0.0000 084 029	564
48	0.0000 097 659	0.0000 088 183	0.0000 079 608	0.0000 071 851	576
49	0.0000 084 125	0.0000 075 776	0.0000 068 239	0.0000 061 438	588
50	0.0000 072 467	0.0000 065 115	0.0000 058 495	0.0000 052 536	600

TABLE 3. SINKING FUND FACTORS
Payable at end of each period

	16% Nominal Annual Rate	16¼% Nominal Annual Rate	16½% Nominal Annual Rate	16¾% Nominal Annual Rate	
MONTHS					MONTHS
1	1.0000 000 000	1.0000 000 000	1.0000 000 000	1.0000 000 000	1
2	0.4966 887 417	0.4966 373 513	0.4965 859 714	0.4965 346 023	2
3	0.3289 281 329	0.3288 599 202	0.3287 917 264	0.3287 235 515	3
4	0.2450 551 857	0.2449 787 928	0.2449 024 264	0.2448 260 866	4
5	0.1947 373 025	0.1946 561 861	0.1945 751 037	0.1944 940 553	5
6	0.1611 969 505	0.1611 128 390	0.1610 287 688	0.1609 447 399	6
7	0.1372 437 584	0.1371 576 393	0.1370 715 687	0.1369 855 468	7
8	0.1192 825 404	0.1191 950 309	0.1191 075 771	0.1190 201 791	8
9	0.1053 159 709	0.1052 274 824	0.1051 390 568	0.1050 506 941	9
10	0.0941 456 545	0.0940 564 749	0.0939 673 653	0.0938 783 258	10
11	0.0850 089 758	0.0849 193 145	0.0848 297 303	0.0847 402 233	11
YEARS					
1	0.0773 975 245	0.0773 075 384	0.0772 176 365	0.0771 278 189	12
2	0.0356 297 772	0.0355 409 802	0.0354 523 513	0.0353 638 904	24
3	0.0218 236 997	0.0217 389 166	0.0216 543 826	0.0215 700 974	36
4	0.0150 069 475	0.0149 268 156	0.0148 470 100	0.0147 675 302	48
5	0.0109 847 238	0.0109 094 231	0.0108 345 211	0.0107 600 167	60
6	0.0083 585 073	0.0082 880 505	0.0082 180 587	0.0081 485 306	72
7	0.0065 287 306	0.0064 630 474	0.0063 978 890	0.0063 332 534	84
8	0.0051 954 527	0.0051 344 232	0.0050 739 712	0.0050 140 936	96
9	0.0041 919 174	0.0041 353 888	0.0040 794 825	0.0040 241 947	108
10	0.0034 179 788	0.0033 657 745	0.0033 142 299	0.0032 633 396	120
11	0.0028 098 393	0.0027 617 662	0.0027 143 820	0.0026 676 802	132
12	0.0023 249 196	0.0022 807 727	0.0022 373 361	0.0021 946 020	144
13	0.0019 337 115	0.0018 932 778	0.0018 535 685	0.0018 145 744	156
14	0.0016 151 209	0.0015 781 834	0.0015 419 772	0.0015 064 916	168
15	0.0013 536 741	0.0013 200 143	0.0012 870 861	0.0012 548 774	180
16	0.0011 377 701	0.0011 071 707	0.0010 772 971	0.0010 481 360	192
17	0.0009 585 490	0.0009 307 961	0.0009 037 579	0.0008 774 197	204
18	0.0008 091 373	0.0007 840 222	0.0007 596 058	0.0007 358 726	216
19	0.0006 841 297	0.0006 614 503	0.0006 394 498	0.0006 181 115	228
20	0.0005 792 261	0.0005 587 884	0.0005 390 064	0.0005 198 623	240
21	0.0004 909 717	0.0004 725 906	0.0004 548 391	0.0004 376 988	252
22	0.0004 165 669	0.0004 000 668	0.0003 841 681	0.0003 688 520	264
23	0.0003 537 263	0.0003 389 416	0.0003 247 287	0.0003 110 683	276
24	0.0003 005 727	0.0002 873 481	0.0002 746 646	0.0002 625 027	288
25	0.0002 555 555	0.0002 437 461	0.0002 324 465	0.0002 216 372	300
26	0.0002 173 881	0.0002 068 591	0.0001 968 087	0.0001 872 173	312
27	0.0001 849 986	0.0001 756 255	0.0001 666 999	0.0001 582 023	324
28	0.0001 574 911	0.0001 491 591	0.0001 412 439	0.0001 337 266	336
29	0.0001 341 142	0.0001 267 179	0.0001 197 087	0.0001 130 679	348
30	0.0001 142 366	0.0001 076 796	0.0001 014 808	0.0000 956 223	360
31	0.0000 973 265	0.0000 915 207	0.0000 860 457	0.0000 808 840	372
32	0.0000 829 349	0.0000 778 006	0.0000 729 707	0.0000 684 283	384
33	0.0000 706 826	0.0000 661 473	0.0000 618 913	0.0000 578 986	396
34	0.0000 602 485	0.0000 562 466	0.0000 525 006	0.0000 489 949	408
35	0.0000 513 606	0.0000 478 331	0.0000 445 393	0.0000 414 645	420
36	0.0000 437 881	0.0000 406 818	0.0000 377 885	0.0000 350 943	432
37	0.0000 373 353	0.0000 346 024	0.0000 320 634	0.0000 297 049	444
38	0.0000 318 356	0.0000 294 335	0.0000 272 073	0.0000 251 446	456
39	0.0000 271 476	0.0000 250 381	0.0000 230 880	0.0000 212 855	468
40	0.0000 231 512	0.0000 213 002	0.0000 195 932	0.0000 180 195	480
41	0.0000 197 440	0.0000 181 210	0.0000 166 280	0.0000 152 551	492
42	0.0000 168 389	0.0000 154 169	0.0000 141 121	0.0000 129 152	504
43	0.0000 143 617	0.0000 131 167	0.0000 119 771	0.0000 109 345	516
44	0.0000 122 492	0.0000 111 599	0.0000 101 654	0.0000 092 577	528
45	0.0000 104 477	0.0000 094 953	0.0000 086 279	0.0000 078 382	540
46	0.0000 089 113	0.0000 080 791	0.0000 073 231	0.0000 066 365	552
47	0.0000 076 010	0.0000 068 743	0.0000 062 157	0.0000 056 191	564
48	0.0000 064 835	0.0000 058 492	0.0000 052 758	0.0000 047 577	576
49	0.0000 055 303	0.0000 049 770	0.0000 044 781	0.0000 040 284	588
50	0.0000 047 173	0.0000 042 349	0.0000 038 010	0.0000 034 109	600

TABLE 3. SINKING FUND FACTORS
Payable at end of each period

MONTHLY Compounding

MONTHS	17% Nominal Annual Rate	17¼% Nominal Annual Rate	17½% Nominal Annual Rate	17¾% Nominal Annual Rate	MONTHS
1	1.0000 000 000	1.0000 000 000	1.0000 000 000	1.0000 000 000	1
2	0.4964 832 437	0.4964 318 957	0.4963 805 584	0.4963 292 317	2
3	0.3286 553 955	0.3285 872 583	0.3285 191 401	0.3284 510 407	3
4	0.2447 497 734	0.2446 734 868	0.2445 972 266	0.2445 209 930	4
5	0.1944 130 410	0.1943 320 605	0.1942 511 141	0.1941 702 016	5
6	0.1608 607 523	0.1607 768 060	0.1606 929 009	0.1606 090 372	6
7	0.1368 995 733	0.1368 136 484	0.1367 277 719	0.1366 419 440	7
8	0.1189 328 368	0.1188 455 503	0.1187 583 194	0.1186 711 442	8
9	0.1049 623 943	0.1048 741 573	0.1047 859 832	0.1046 978 719	9
10	0.0937 893 563	0.0937 004 568	0.0936 116 272	0.0935 228 676	10
11	0.0846 507 933	0.0845 614 405	0.0844 721 647	0.0843 829 659	11
YEARS					
1	0.0770 380 854	0.0769 484 361	0.0768 588 710	0.0767 693 899	12
2	0.0352 755 974	0.0351 874 722	0.0350 995 146	0.0350 117 246	24
3	0.0214 860 609	0.0214 022 727	0.0213 187 326	0.0212 354 403	36
4	0.0146 883 756	0.0146 095 459	0.0145 310 403	0.0144 528 584	48
5	0.0106 859 091	0.0106 121 973	0.0105 388 804	0.0104 659 574	60
6	0.0080 794 645	0.0080 108 590	0.0079 427 126	0.0078 750 238	72
7	0.0062 691 382	0.0062 055 413	0.0061 424 605	0.0060 798 935	84
8	0.0049 547 874	0.0048 960 495	0.0048 378 767	0.0047 802 660	96
9	0.0039 695 213	0.0039 154 580	0.0038 620 007	0.0038 091 454	108
10	0.0032 130 985	0.0031 635 013	0.0031 145 427	0.0030 662 173	120
11	0.0026 216 542	0.0025 762 977	0.0025 316 040	0.0024 875 665	132
12	0.0021 525 627	0.0021 112 102	0.0020 705 367	0.0020 305 344	144
13	0.0017 762 862	0.0017 386 947	0.0017 017 907	0.0016 655 651	156
14	0.0014 717 161	0.0014 376 400	0.0014 042 528	0.0013 715 440	168
15	0.0012 233 762	0.0011 925 708	0.0011 624 491	0.0011 329 996	180
16	0.0010 196 740	0.0009 918 981	0.0009 647 952	0.0009 383 524	192
17	0.0008 517 671	0.0008 267 858	0.0008 024 616	0.0007 787 805	204
18	0.0007 128 068	0.0006 903 931	0.0006 686 164	0.0006 474 617	216
19	0.0005 974 187	0.0005 773 553	0.0005 579 051	0.0005 390 526	228
20	0.0005 013 388	0.0004 834 190	0.0004 660 860	0.0004 493 234	240
21	0.0004 211 518	0.0004 051 803	0.0003 897 672	0.0003 748 956	252
22	0.0003 540 999	0.0003 398 939	0.0003 262 161	0.0003 130 495	264
23	0.0002 979 415	0.0002 853 300	0.0002 732 160	0.0002 615 821	276
24	0.0002 508 434	0.0002 396 681	0.0002 289 590	0.0002 186 988	288
25	0.0002 112 992	0.0002 014 139	0.0001 919 637	0.0001 829 311	300
26	0.0001 780 659	0.0001 693 364	0.0001 610 110	0.0001 530 728	312
27	0.0001 501 142	0.0001 424 175	0.0001 350 949	0.0001 281 297	324
28	0.0001 265 889	0.0001 198 131	0.0001 133 823	0.0001 072 803	336
29	0.0001 067 779	0.0001 008 213	0.0000 951 819	0.0000 898 439	348
30	0.0000 900 868	0.0000 848 576	0.0000 799 189	0.0000 752 558	360
31	0.0000 760 187	0.0000 714 340	0.0000 671 147	0.0000 630 464	372
32	0.0000 641 574	0.0000 601 427	0.0000 563 698	0.0000 528 249	384
33	0.0000 541 538	0.0000 506 424	0.0000 473 507	0.0000 442 655	396
34	0.0000 457 151	0.0000 426 473	0.0000 397 785	0.0000 370 965	408
35	0.0000 385 949	0.0000 359 175	0.0000 334 200	0.0000 310 910	420
36	0.0000 325 862	0.0000 302 519	0.0000 280 799	0.0000 260 594	432
37	0.0000 275 148	0.0000 254 816	0.0000 235 944	0.0000 218 433	444
38	0.0000 232 340	0.0000 214 646	0.0000 198 264	0.0000 183 101	456
39	0.0000 196 201	0.0000 180 817	0.0000 166 609	0.0000 153 491	468
40	0.0000 165 690	0.0000 152 325	0.0000 140 012	0.0000 128 673	480
41	0.0000 139 928	0.0000 128 326	0.0000 117 665	0.0000 107 871	492
42	0.0000 118 175	0.0000 108 111	0.0000 098 887	0.0000 090 433	504
43	0.0000 099 806	0.0000 091 083	0.0000 083 107	0.0000 075 816	516
44	0.0000 084 294	0.0000 076 738	0.0000 069 847	0.0000 063 563	528
45	0.0000 071 195	0.0000 064 654	0.0000 058 703	0.0000 053 291	540
46	0.0000 060 131	0.0000 054 473	0.0000 049 338	0.0000 044 679	552
47	0.0000 050 788	0.0000 045 896	0.0000 041 467	0.0000 037 459	564
48	0.0000 042 897	0.0000 038 669	0.0000 034 852	0.0000 031 406	576
49	0.0000 036 232	0.0000 032 581	0.0000 029 293	0.0000 026 332	588
50	0.0000 030 603	0.0000 027 452	0.0000 024 620	0.0000 022 077	600

MONTHLY
Compounding

TABLE 3. SINKING FUND FACTORS
Payable at end of each period

MONTHS	18% Nominal Annual Rate	18¼% Nominal Annual Rate	18½% Nominal Annual Rate	18¾% Nominal Annual Rate	MONTHS
1	1.0000 000 000	1.0000 000 000	1.0000 000 000	1.0000 000 000	1
2	0.4962 779 156	0.4962 266 102	0.4961 753 153	0.4961 240 310	2
3	0.3283 829 602	0.3283 148 986	0.3282 468 558	0.3281 788 318	3
4	0.2444 447 860	0.2443 686 054	0.2442 924 514	0.2442 163 239	4
5	0.1940 893 231	0.1940 084 785	0.1939 276 678	0.1938 468 911	5
6	0.1605 252 146	0.1604 414 333	0.1603 576 933	0.1602 739 944	6
7	0.1365 561 645	0.1364 704 335	0.1363 847 510	0.1362 991 168	7
8	0.1185 840 246	0.1184 969 607	0.1184 099 523	0.1183 229 996	8
9	0.1046 098 234	0.1045 218 376	0.1044 339 146	0.1043 460 543	9
10	0.0934 341 779	0.0933 455 580	0.0932 570 080	0.0931 685 278	10
11	0.0842 938 442	0.0842 047 994	0.0841 158 315	0.0840 269 405	11
YEARS					
1	0.0766 799 929	0.0765 906 799	0.0765 014 510	0.0764 123 060	12
2	0.0349 241 020	0.0348 366 467	0.0347 493 587	0.0346 622 378	24
3	0.0211 523 955	0.0210 695 981	0.0209 870 476	0.0209 047 439	36
4	0.0143 749 996	0.0142 974 634	0.0142 202 493	0.0141 433 566	48
5	0.0103 934 274	0.0103 212 894	0.0102 495 425	0.0101 781 856	60
6	0.0078 077 911	0.0077 410 129	0.0076 746 876	0.0076 088 137	72
7	0.0060 178 380	0.0059 562 918	0.0058 952 525	0.0058 347 179	84
8	0.0047 232 141	0.0046 667 179	0.0046 107 743	0.0045 553 799	96
9	0.0037 568 877	0.0037 052 236	0.0036 541 487	0.0036 036 588	108
10	0.0030 185 199	0.0029 714 451	0.0029 249 874	0.0028 791 416	120
11	0.0024 441 787	0.0024 014 340	0.0023 593 258	0.0023 178 475	132
12	0.0019 911 952	0.0019 525 115	0.0019 144 754	0.0018 770 789	144
13	0.0016 300 085	0.0015 951 120	0.0015 608 664	0.0015 272 626	156
14	0.0013 395 032	0.0013 081 199	0.0012 773 839	0.0012 472 847	168
15	0.0011 042 104	0.0010 760 700	0.0010 485 669	0.0010 216 897	180
16	0.0009 125 567	0.0008 873 955	0.0008 628 563	0.0008 389 266	192
17	0.0007 557 286	0.0007 332 923	0.0007 114 579	0.0006 902 123	204
18	0.0006 269 142	0.0006 069 594	0.0005 875 830	0.0005 687 709	216
19	0.0005 207 820	0.0005 030 782	0.0004 859 263	0.0004 693 115	228
20	0.0004 331 152	0.0004 174 456	0.0004 022 991	0.0003 876 606	240
21	0.0003 605 488	0.0003 467 108	0.0003 333 658	0.0003 204 983	252
22	0.0003 003 772	0.0002 881 829	0.0002 764 505	0.0002 651 645	264
23	0.0002 504 113	0.0002 396 872	0.0002 293 938	0.0002 195 156	276
24	0.0002 088 703	0.0001 994 574	0.0001 904 442	0.0001 818 152	288
25	0.0001 742 994	0.0001 660 526	0.0001 581 748	0.0001 506 512	300
26	0.0001 455 052	0.0001 382 925	0.0001 314 193	0.0001 248 710	312
27	0.0001 215 059	0.0001 152 080	0.0001 092 213	0.0001 035 314	324
28	0.0001 014 915	0.0000 960 010	0.0000 907 946	0.0000 858 585	336
29	0.0000 847 923	0.0000 800 129	0.0000 754 918	0.0000 712 160	348
30	0.0000 708 537	0.0000 666 990	0.0000 627 786	0.0000 590 801	360
31	0.0000 592 154	0.0000 556 086	0.0000 522 136	0.0000 490 187	372
32	0.0000 494 950	0.0000 463 678	0.0000 434 316	0.0000 406 752	384
33	0.0000 413 747	0.0000 386 666	0.0000 361 301	0.0000 337 550	396
34	0.0000 345 897	0.0000 322 471	0.0000 300 585	0.0000 280 142	408
35	0.0000 289 194	0.0000 268 953	0.0000 250 088	0.0000 232 512	420
36	0.0000 241 802	0.0000 224 330	0.0000 208 087	0.0000 192 990	432
37	0.0000 202 187	0.0000 187 119	0.0000 173 147	0.0000 160 193	444
38	0.0000 169 069	0.0000 156 087	0.0000 144 079	0.0000 132 974	456
39	0.0000 141 382	0.0000 130 206	0.0000 119 895	0.0000 110 383	468
40	0.0000 118 231	0.0000 108 620	0.0000 099 773	0.0000 091 633	480
41	0.0000 098 875	0.0000 090 614	0.0000 083 030	0.0000 076 069	492
42	0.0000 082 689	0.0000 075 594	0.0000 069 098	0.0000 063 150	504
43	0.0000 069 153	0.0000 063 066	0.0000 057 504	0.0000 052 425	516
44	0.0000 057 835	0.0000 052 614	0.0000 047 857	0.0000 043 523	528
45	0.0000 048 369	0.0000 043 895	0.0000 039 828	0.0000 036 132	540
46	0.0000 040 453	0.0000 036 621	0.0000 033 146	0.0000 029 997	552
47	0.0000 033 833	0.0000 030 553	0.0000 027 586	0.0000 024 904	564
48	0.0000 028 297	0.0000 025 490	0.0000 022 959	0.0000 020 675	576
49	0.0000 023 666	0.0000 021 267	0.0000 019 107	0.0000 017 165	588
50	0.0000 019 794	0.0000 017 743	0.0000 015 902	0.0000 014 250	600

TABLE 3. SINKING FUND FACTORS
Payable at end of each period

MONTHS	19% Nominal Annual Rate	19¼% Nominal Annual Rate	19½% Nominal Annual Rate	19¾% Nominal Annual Rate	MONTHS
1	1.0000 000 000	1.0000 000 000	1.0000 000 000	1.0000 000 000	1
2	0.4960 727 573	0.4960 214 943	0.4959 702 418	0.4959 189 999	2
3	0.3281 108 267	0.3280 428 405	0.3279 748 730	0.3279 069 244	3
4	0.2441 402 228	0.2440 641 483	0.2439 881 002	0.2439 120 786	4
5	0.1937 661 482	0.1936 854 393	0.1936 047 642	0.1935 241 230	5
6	0.1601 903 367	0.1601 067 202	0.1600 231 449	0.1599 396 107	6
7	0.1362 135 311	0.1361 279 937	0.1360 425 047	0.1359 570 641	7
8	0.1182 361 024	0.1181 492 608	0.1180 624 747	0.1179 757 442	8
9	0.1042 582 568	0.1041 705 219	0.1040 828 496	0.1039 952 400	9
10	0.0930 801 175	0.0929 917 769	0.0929 035 060	0.0928 153 049	10
11	0.0839 381 265	0.0838 493 892	0.0837 607 288	0.0836 721 452	11
YEARS					
1	0.0763 232 449	0.0762 342 677	0.0761 453 744	0.0760 565 649	12
2	0.0345 752 839	0.0344 884 968	0.0344 018 766	0.0343 154 230	24
3	0.0208 226 867	0.0207 408 756	0.0206 593 105	0.0205 779 909	36
4	0.0140 667 849	0.0139 905 335	0.0139 146 019	0.0138 389 895	48
5	0.0101 072 178	0.0100 366 381	0.0099 664 454	0.0098 966 387	60
6	0.0075 433 896	0.0074 784 138	0.0074 138 845	0.0073 498 003	72
7	0.0057 746 857	0.0057 151 534	0.0056 561 187	0.0055 975 792	84
8	0.0045 005 316	0.0044 462 261	0.0043 924 601	0.0043 392 304	96
9	0.0035 537 497	0.0035 044 171	0.0034 556 566	0.0034 074 640	108
10	0.0028 339 022	0.0027 892 638	0.0027 452 210	0.0027 017 684	120
11	0.0022 769 925	0.0022 367 542	0.0021 971 261	0.0021 581 014	132
12	0.0018 403 144	0.0018 041 739	0.0017 686 496	0.0017 337 338	144
13	0.0014 942 916	0.0014 619 442	0.0014 302 117	0.0013 990 849	156
14	0.0012 178 123	0.0011 889 564	0.0011 607 069	0.0011 330 538	168
15	0.0009 954 270	0.0009 697 676	0.0009 447 003	0.0009 202 142	180
16	0.0008 155 940	0.0007 928 464	0.0007 706 718	0.0007 490 582	192
17	0.0006 695 421	0.0006 494 344	0.0006 298 764	0.0006 108 554	204
18	0.0005 505 091	0.0005 327 840	0.0005 155 823	0.0004 988 906	216
19	0.0004 532 193	0.0004 376 356	0.0004 225 466	0.0004 079 385	228
20	0.0003 735 152	0.0003 598 484	0.0003 466 461	0.0003 338 942	240
21	0.0003 080 932	0.0002 961 359	0.0002 846 120	0.0002 735 076	252
22	0.0002 543 098	0.0002 438 716	0.0002 338 357	0.0002 241 880	264
23	0.0002 100 375	0.0002 009 448	0.0001 922 235	0.0001 838 596	276
24	0.0001 735 556	0.0001 656 509	0.0001 580 873	0.0001 508 513	288
25	0.0001 434 670	0.0001 366 082	0.0001 300 613	0.0001 238 131	300
26	0.0001 186 334	0.0001 126 928	0.0001 070 361	0.0001 016 508	312
27	0.0000 981 248	0.0000 929 882	0.0000 881 091	0.0000 834 755	324
28	0.0000 811 796	0.0000 767 454	0.0000 725 438	0.0000 685 634	336
29	0.0000 671 730	0.0000 633 509	0.0000 597 383	0.0000 563 243	348
30	0.0000 555 916	0.0000 523 018	0.0000 492 000	0.0000 462 760	360
31	0.0000 460 127	0.0000 431 849	0.0000 405 254	0.0000 380 245	372
32	0.0000 380 883	0.0000 356 608	0.0000 333 834	0.0000 312 472	384
33	0.0000 315 313	0.0000 294 500	0.0000 275 021	0.0000 256 796	396
34	0.0000 261 050	0.0000 243 225	0.0000 226 585	0.0000 211 054	408
35	0.0000 216 138	0.0000 200 889	0.0000 186 688	0.0000 173 468	420
36	0.0000 178 962	0.0000 165 929	0.0000 153 824	0.0000 142 581	432
37	0.0000 148 186	0.0000 137 059	0.0000 126 749	0.0000 117 198	444
38	0.0000 122 706	0.0000 113 215	0.0000 104 443	0.0000 096 337	456
39	0.0000 101 611	0.0000 093 522	0.0000 086 064	0.0000 079 190	468
40	0.0000 084 144	0.0000 077 256	0.0000 070 921	0.0000 065 097	480
41	0.0000 069 681	0.0000 063 820	0.0000 058 443	0.0000 053 512	492
42	0.0000 057 705	0.0000 052 721	0.0000 048 162	0.0000 043 990	504
43	0.0000 047 787	0.0000 043 554	0.0000 039 689	0.0000 036 162	516
44	0.0000 039 575	0.0000 035 980	0.0000 032 707	0.0000 029 728	528
45	0.0000 032 774	0.0000 029 724	0.0000 026 954	0.0000 024 439	540
46	0.0000 027 142	0.0000 024 556	0.0000 022 213	0.0000 020 090	552
47	0.0000 022 478	0.0000 020 287	0.0000 018 306	0.0000 016 516	564
48	0.0000 018 616	0.0000 016 759	0.0000 015 086	0.0000 013 578	576
49	0.0000 015 417	0.0000 013 846	0.0000 012 432	0.0000 011 162	588
50	0.0000 012 768	0.0000 011 439	0.0000 010 246	0.0000 009 176	600

MONTHLY
Compounding

TABLE 3. SINKING FUND FACTORS
Payable at end of each period

MONTHS	20% Nominal Annual Rate	20¼% Nominal Annual Rate	20½% Nominal Annual Rate	20¾% Nominal Annual Rate	MONTHS
1	1.0000 000 000	1.0000 000 000	1.0000 000 000	1.0000 000 000	1
2	0.4958 677 686	0.4958 165 479	0.4957 653 377	0.4957 141 382	2
3	0.3278 389 946	0.3277 710 837	0.3277 031 915	0.3276 353 181	3
4	0.2438 360 835	0.2437 601 148	0.2436 841 725	0.2436 082 567	4
5	0.1934 435 156	0.1933 629 421	0.1932 824 025	0.1932 018 966	5
6	0.1598 561 176	0.1597 726 657	0.1596 892 549	0.1596 058 852	6
7	0.1358 716 718	0.1357 863 278	0.1357 010 322	0.1356 157 848	7
8	0.1178 890 691	0.1178 024 495	0.1177 158 853	0.1176 293 766	8
9	0.1039 076 930	0.1038 202 086	0.1037 327 867	0.1036 454 274	9
10	0.0927 271 734	0.0926 391 117	0.0925 511 196	0.0924 631 971	10
11	0.0835 836 383	0.0834 952 081	0.0834 068 547	0.0833 185 779	11
YEARS					
1	0.0759 678 392	0.0758 791 973	0.0757 906 391	0.0757 021 646	12
2	0.0342 291 360	0.0341 430 154	0.0340 570 611	0.0339 712 730	24
3	0.0204 969 167	0.0204 160 875	0.0203 355 031	0.0202 551 631	36
4	0.0137 636 957	0.0136 887 199	0.0136 140 616	0.0135 397 202	48
5	0.0098 272 170	0.0097 581 794	0.0096 895 247	0.0096 212 518	60
6	0.0072 861 594	0.0072 229 602	0.0071 602 011	0.0070 978 804	72
7	0.0055 395 326	0.0054 819 765	0.0054 249 083	0.0053 683 257	84
8	0.0042 865 337	0.0042 343 666	0.0041 827 258	0.0041 316 080	96
9	0.0033 598 350	0.0033 127 652	0.0032 662 502	0.0032 202 858	108
10	0.0026 589 006	0.0026 166 120	0.0025 748 972	0.0025 337 509	120
11	0.0021 196 737	0.0020 818 363	0.0020 445 827	0.0020 079 062	132
12	0.0016 994 188	0.0016 656 967	0.0016 325 599	0.0016 000 007	144
13	0.0013 685 551	0.0013 386 133	0.0013 092 509	0.0012 804 589	156
14	0.0011 059 871	0.0010 794 970	0.0010 535 736	0.0010 282 073	168
15	0.0008 962 984	0.0008 729 419	0.0008 501 342	0.0008 278 646	180
16	0.0007 279 938	0.0007 074 672	0.0006 874 668	0.0006 679 813	192
17	0.0005 923 590	0.0005 743 750	0.0005 568 913	0.0005 398 960	204
18	0.0004 826 960	0.0004 669 858	0.0004 517 474	0.0004 369 685	216
19	0.0003 937 981	0.0003 801 122	0.0003 668 680	0.0003 540 531	228
20	0.0003 215 794	0.0003 096 883	0.0002 982 080	0.0002 871 258	240
21	0.0002 628 090	0.0002 525 029	0.0002 425 764	0.0002 330 169	252
22	0.0002 149 150	0.0002 060 036	0.0001 974 410	0.0001 892 147	264
23	0.0001 758 399	0.0001 681 514	0.0001 607 817	0.0001 537 185	276
24	0.0001 439 298	0.0001 373 103	0.0001 309 806	0.0001 249 289	288
25	0.0001 178 511	0.0001 121 630	0.0001 067 373	0.0001 015 627	300
26	0.0000 965 247	0.0000 916 461	0.0000 870 040	0.0000 825 875	312
27	0.0000 790 757	0.0000 748 987	0.0000 709 339	0.0000 671 712	324
28	0.0000 647 932	0.0000 612 228	0.0000 578 421	0.0000 546 416	336
29	0.0000 530 986	0.0000 500 513	0.0000 471 732	0.0000 444 552	348
30	0.0000 435 202	0.0000 409 233	0.0000 384 765	0.0000 361 717	360
31	0.0000 356 733	0.0000 334 632	0.0000 313 861	0.0000 294 343	372
32	0.0000 292 438	0.0000 273 653	0.0000 256 043	0.0000 239 536	384
33	0.0000 239 747	0.0000 223 801	0.0000 208 888	0.0000 194 946	396
34	0.0000 196 561	0.0000 183 040	0.0000 170 427	0.0000 158 663	408
35	0.0000 161 162	0.0000 149 710	0.0000 139 053	0.0000 129 139	420
36	0.0000 132 143	0.0000 122 453	0.0000 113 458	0.0000 105 112	432
37	0.0000 108 353	0.0000 100 161	0.0000 092 577	0.0000 085 557	444
38	0.0000 088 848	0.0000 081 930	0.0000 075 541	0.0000 069 642	456
39	0.0000 072 855	0.0000 067 018	0.0000 061 641	0.0000 056 688	468
40	0.0000 059 743	0.0000 054 822	0.0000 050 299	0.0000 046 144	480
41	0.0000 048 991	0.0000 044 845	0.0000 041 045	0.0000 037 562	492
42	0.0000 040 174	0.0000 036 685	0.0000 033 494	0.0000 030 577	504
43	0.0000 032 945	0.0000 030 009	0.0000 027 332	0.0000 024 890	516
44	0.0000 027 016	0.0000 024 549	0.0000 022 304	0.0000 020 261	528
45	0.0000 022 155	0.0000 020 082	0.0000 018 201	0.0000 016 494	540
46	0.0000 018 168	0.0000 016 428	0.0000 014 853	0.0000 013 426	552
47	0.0000 014 899	0.0000 013 439	0.0000 012 120	0.0000 010 930	564
48	0.0000 012 218	0.0000 010 994	0.0000 009 891	0.0000 008 897	576
49	0.0000 010 020	0.0000 008 994	0.0000 008 071	0.0000 007 243	588
50	0.0000 008 217	0.0000 007 357	0.0000 006 587	0.0000 005 896	600

TABLE 3. SINKING FUND FACTORS
Payable at end of each period

MONTHLY Compounding

MONTHS	21% Nominal Annual Rate	21¼% Nominal Annual Rate	21½% Nominal Annual Rate	21¾% Nominal Annual Rate	MONTHS
1	1.0000 000 000	1.0000 000 000	1.0000 000 000	1.0000 000 000	1
2	0.4956 629 492	0.4956 117 708	0.4955 606 029	0.4955 094 456	2
3	0.3275 674 635	0.3274 996 278	0.3274 318 108	0.3273 640 125	3
4	0.2435 323 673	0.2434 565 043	0.2433 806 677	0.2433 048 576	4
5	0.1931 214 246	0.1930 409 864	0.1929 605 820	0.1928 802 114	5
6	0.1595 225 565	0.1594 392 689	0.1593 560 224	0.1592 728 170	6
7	0.1355 305 857	0.1354 454 349	0.1353 603 323	0.1352 752 780	7
8	0.1175 429 233	0.1174 565 254	0.1173 701 829	0.1172 838 958	8
9	0.1035 581 306	0.1034 708 963	0.1033 837 245	0.1032 966 152	9
10	0.0923 753 442	0.0922 875 608	0.0921 998 470	0.0921 122 027	10
11	0.0832 303 778	0.0831 422 542	0.0830 542 073	0.0829 662 369	11
YEARS					
1	0.0756 137 738	0.0755 254 665	0.0754 372 429	0.0753 491 029	12
2	0.0338 856 510	0.0338 001 949	0.0337 149 047	0.0336 297 802	24
3	0.0201 750 673	0.0200 952 154	0.0200 156 071	0.0199 362 420	36
4	0.0134 656 950	0.0133 919 854	0.0133 185 909	0.0132 455 108	48
5	0.0095 533 598	0.0094 858 476	0.0094 187 140	0.0093 519 581	60
6	0.0070 359 964	0.0069 745 475	0.0069 135 320	0.0068 529 480	72
7	0.0053 122 263	0.0052 566 076	0.0052 014 670	0.0051 468 022	84
8	0.0040 810 099	0.0040 309 280	0.0039 813 590	0.0039 322 994	96
9	0.0031 748 675	0.0031 299 909	0.0030 856 518	0.0030 418 456	108
10	0.0024 931 675	0.0024 531 416	0.0024 136 678	0.0023 747 405	120
11	0.0019 718 004	0.0019 362 586	0.0019 012 744	0.0018 668 412	132
12	0.0015 680 114	0.0015 365 845	0.0015 057 123	0.0014 753 872	144
13	0.0012 522 288	0.0012 245 520	0.0011 974 197	0.0011 708 236	156
14	0.0010 033 884	0.0009 791 073	0.0009 553 545	0.0009 321 208	168
15	0.0008 061 227	0.0007 848 981	0.0007 641 806	0.0007 439 601	180
16	0.0006 489 996	0.0006 305 107	0.0006 125 037	0.0005 949 680	192
17	0.0005 233 774	0.0005 073 240	0.0004 917 245	0.0004 765 679	204
18	0.0004 226 371	0.0004 087 414	0.0003 952 698	0.0003 822 109	216
19	0.0003 416 551	0.0003 296 620	0.0003 180 621	0.0003 068 440	228
20	0.0002 764 294	0.0002 661 068	0.0002 561 463	0.0002 465 364	240
21	0.0002 238 122	0.0002 149 504	0.0002 064 198	0.0001 982 093	252
22	0.0001 813 127	0.0001 737 233	0.0001 664 353	0.0001 594 376	264
23	0.0001 469 502	0.0001 404 655	0.0001 342 534	0.0001 283 032	276
24	0.0001 191 441	0.0001 136 151	0.0001 083 314	0.0001 032 829	288
25	0.0000 966 282	0.0000 919 236	0.0000 874 388	0.0000 831 641	300
26	0.0000 783 864	0.0000 743 908	0.0000 705 912	0.0000 669 786	312
27	0.0000 636 007	0.0000 602 133	0.0000 570 001	0.0000 539 525	324
28	0.0000 516 122	0.0000 487 453	0.0000 460 324	0.0000 434 658	336
29	0.0000 418 889	0.0000 394 662	0.0000 371 795	0.0000 350 214	348
30	0.0000 340 009	0.0000 319 567	0.0000 300 319	0.0000 282 200	360
31	0.0000 276 006	0.0000 258 781	0.0000 242 604	0.0000 227 412	372
32	0.0000 224 067	0.0000 209 572	0.0000 195 992	0.0000 183 271	384
33	0.0000 181 911	0.0000 169 729	0.0000 158 343	0.0000 147 705	396
34	0.0000 147 694	0.0000 137 466	0.0000 127 932	0.0000 119 046	408
35	0.0000 119 917	0.0000 111 340	0.0000 103 365	0.0000 095 950	420
36	0.0000 097 367	0.0000 090 182	0.0000 083 518	0.0000 077 337	432
37	0.0000 079 059	0.0000 073 046	0.0000 067 483	0.0000 062 336	444
38	0.0000 064 195	0.0000 059 168	0.0000 054 527	0.0000 050 245	456
39	0.0000 052 127	0.0000 047 927	0.0000 044 060	0.0000 040 500	468
40	0.0000 042 327	0.0000 038 822	0.0000 035 602	0.0000 032 646	480
41	0.0000 034 371	0.0000 031 447	0.0000 028 768	0.0000 026 315	492
42	0.0000 027 910	0.0000 025 473	0.0000 023 246	0.0000 021 212	504
43	0.0000 022 664	0.0000 020 634	0.0000 018 784	0.0000 017 098	516
44	0.0000 018 404	0.0000 016 715	0.0000 015 179	0.0000 013 783	528
45	0.0000 014 945	0.0000 013 540	0.0000 012 266	0.0000 011 110	540
46	0.0000 012 136	0.0000 010 968	0.0000 009 911	0.0000 008 956	552
47	0.0000 009 855	0.0000 008 885	0.0000 008 009	0.0000 007 219	564
48	0.0000 008 003	0.0000 007 197	0.0000 006 472	0.0000 005 819	576
49	0.0000 006 499	0.0000 005 830	0.0000 005 230	0.0000 004 691	588
50	0.0000 005 277	0.0000 004 723	0.0000 004 226	0.0000 003 781	600

MONTHLY
Compounding

TABLE 3. SINKING FUND FACTORS
Payable at end of each period

MONTHS	22% Nominal Annual Rate	22¼% Nominal Annual Rate	22½% Nominal Annual Rate	22¾% Nominal Annual Rate	MONTHS
1	1.0000 000 000	1.0000 000 000	1.0000 000 000	1.0000 000 000	1
2	0.4954 582 989	0.4954 071 628	0.4953 560 372	0.4953 049 221	2
3	0.3272 962 331	0.3272 284 724	0.3271 607 305	0.3270 930 073	3
4	0.2432 290 738	0.2431 533 164	0.2430 775 854	0.2430 018 807	4
5	0.1927 998 745	0.1927 195 714	0.1926 393 021	0.1925 590 665	5
6	0.1591 896 525	0.1591 065 291	0.1590 234 467	0.1589 404 052	6
7	0.1351 902 718	0.1351 053 138	0.1350 204 041	0.1349 355 424	7
8	0.1171 976 639	0.1171 114 874	0.1170 253 662	0.1169 393 003	8
9	0.1032 095 682	0.1031 225 837	0.1030 356 615	0.1029 488 017	9
10	0.0920 246 279	0.0919 371 226	0.0918 496 867	0.0917 623 202	10
11	0.0828 783 430	0.0827 905 256	0.0827 027 846	0.0826 151 201	11
YEARS					
1	0.0752 610 463	0.0751 730 733	0.0750 851 837	0.0749 973 775	12
2	0.0335 448 213	0.0334 600 279	0.0333 753 999	0.0332 909 371	24
3	0.0198 571 198	0.0197 782 404	0.0196 996 033	0.0196 212 082	36
4	0.0131 727 445	0.0131 002 914	0.0130 281 508	0.0129 563 222	48
5	0.0092 855 787	0.0092 195 747	0.0091 539 451	0.0090 886 887	60
6	0.0067 927 940	0.0067 330 683	0.0066 737 690	0.0066 148 944	72
7	0.0050 926 106	0.0050 388 898	0.0049 856 371	0.0049 328 502	84
8	0.0038 837 460	0.0038 356 953	0.0037 881 438	0.0037 410 882	96
9	0.0029 985 680	0.0029 558 146	0.0029 135 810	0.0028 718 628	108
10	0.0023 363 545	0.0022 985 041	0.0022 611 841	0.0022 243 889	120
11	0.0018 329 525	0.0017 996 019	0.0017 667 829	0.0017 344 891	132
12	0.0014 456 018	0.0014 163 486	0.0013 876 202	0.0013 594 091	144
13	0.0011 447 551	0.0011 192 059	0.0010 941 677	0.0010 696 322	156
14	0.0009 093 968	0.0008 871 734	0.0008 654 413	0.0008 441 917	168
15	0.0007 242 267	0.0007 049 704	0.0006 861 815	0.0006 678 505	180
16	0.0005 778 930	0.0005 612 683	0.0005 450 838	0.0005 293 295	192
17	0.0004 618 432	0.0004 475 398	0.0004 336 470	0.0004 201 546	204
18	0.0003 695 535	0.0003 572 868	0.0003 454 001	0.0003 338 829	216
19	0.0002 959 964	0.0002 855 083	0.0002 753 692	0.0002 655 685	228
20	0.0002 372 660	0.0002 283 243	0.0002 197 006	0.0002 113 847	240
21	0.0001 903 077	0.0001 827 047	0.0001 753 897	0.0001 683 529	252
22	0.0001 527 196	0.0001 462 710	0.0001 400 818	0.0001 341 424	264
23	0.0001 226 047	0.0001 171 481	0.0001 119 238	0.0001 069 225	276
24	0.0000 984 598	0.0000 938 528	0.0000 894 527	0.0000 852 507	288
25	0.0000 790 903	0.0000 752 085	0.0000 715 102	0.0000 679 872	300
26	0.0000 635 443	0.0000 602 799	0.0000 571 776	0.0000 542 295	312
27	0.0000 510 625	0.0000 483 223	0.0000 457 246	0.0000 432 622	324
28	0.0000 410 380	0.0000 387 417	0.0000 365 701	0.0000 345 169	336
29	0.0000 329 850	0.0000 310 637	0.0000 292 513	0.0000 275 419	348
30	0.0000 265 145	0.0000 249 094	0.0000 233 991	0.0000 219 781	360
31	0.0000 213 148	0.0000 199 757	0.0000 187 189	0.0000 175 393	372
32	0.0000 171 357	0.0000 160 201	0.0000 149 755	0.0000 139 976	384
33	0.0000 137 766	0.0000 128 483	0.0000 119 812	0.0000 111 715	396
34	0.0000 110 764	0.0000 103 048	0.0000 095 859	0.0000 089 163	408
35	0.0000 089 057	0.0000 082 651	0.0000 076 697	0.0000 071 165	420
36	0.0000 071 606	0.0000 066 292	0.0000 061 366	0.0000 056 801	432
37	0.0000 057 575	0.0000 053 172	0.0000 049 101	0.0000 045 337	444
38	0.0000 046 294	0.0000 042 650	0.0000 039 288	0.0000 036 187	456
39	0.0000 037 224	0.0000 034 210	0.0000 031 436	0.0000 028 884	468
40	0.0000 029 932	0.0000 027 440	0.0000 025 154	0.0000 023 055	480
41	0.0000 024 068	0.0000 022 011	0.0000 020 127	0.0000 018 403	492
42	0.0000 019 353	0.0000 017 655	0.0000 016 105	0.0000 014 689	504
43	0.0000 015 562	0.0000 014 162	0.0000 012 887	0.0000 011 725	516
44	0.0000 012 513	0.0000 011 360	0.0000 010 311	0.0000 009 359	528
45	0.0000 010 062	0.0000 009 112	0.0000 008 251	0.0000 007 470	540
46	0.0000 008 091	0.0000 007 309	0.0000 006 602	0.0000 005 963	552
47	0.0000 006 506	0.0000 005 863	0.0000 005 283	0.0000 004 760	564
48	0.0000 005 232	0.0000 004 703	0.0000 004 227	0.0000 003 799	576
49	0.0000 004 207	0.0000 003 772	0.0000 003 383	0.0000 003 033	588
50	0.0000 003 383	0.0000 003 026	0.0000 002 707	0.0000 002 421	600

TABLE 4. PRESENT WORTH OF ONE DOLLAR
Payable at end of each period

MONTHLY Compounding

MONTHS	5% Nominal Annual Rate	5¼% Nominal Annual Rate	5½% Nominal Annual Rate	5¾% Nominal Annual Rate	MONTHS
1	0.9958 506 224	0.9956 440 572	0.9954 375 778	0.9952 311 839	1
2	0.9917 184 621	0.9913 070 887	0.9908 959 712	0.9904 851 094	2
3	0.9876 034 478	0.9869 890 118	0.9863 750 854	0.9857 616 681	3
4	0.9835 055 082	0.9826 897 442	0.9818 748 258	0.9810 607 520	4
5	0.9794 245 724	0.9784 092 039	0.9773 950 983	0.9763 822 537	5
6	0.9753 605 701	0.9741 473 094	0.9729 358 091	0.9717 260 663	6
7	0.9713 134 308	0.9699 039 795	0.9684 968 652	0.9670 920 834	7
8	0.9672 830 846	0.9656 791 333	0.9640 781 736	0.9624 801 991	8
9	0.9632 694 618	0.9614 726 903	0.9596 796 419	0.9578 903 081	9
10	0.9592 724 931	0.9572 845 703	0.9553 011 781	0.9533 223 053	10
11	0.9552 921 093	0.9531 146 935	0.9509 426 908	0.9487 760 866	11
YEARS					
1	0.9513 282 416	0.9489 629 805	0.9466 040 887	0.9442 515 479	12
2	0.9050 254 234	0.9005 307 383	0.8960 593 008	0.8916 109 858	24
3	0.8609 762 447	0.8545 703 334	0.8482 133 979	0.8419 050 534	36
4	0.8190 710 169	0.8109 556 106	0.8029 222 705	0.7949 701 499	48
5	0.7792 053 903	0.7695 668 533	0.7600 495 042	0.7506 517 946	60
6	0.7412 800 939	0.7302 904 548	0.7194 659 683	0.7088 041 190	72
7	0.7052 006 883	0.6930 186 066	0.6810 494 273	0.6692 893 866	84
8	0.6708 773 308	0.6576 490 024	0.6446 841 725	0.6319 775 393	96
9	0.6382 245 514	0.6240 845 575	0.6102 606 736	0.5967 457 697	108
10	0.6071 610 403	0.5922 331 417	0.5776 752 488	0.5634 781 168	120
11	0.5776 094 449	0.5620 073 273	0.5468 297 525	0.5320 650 840	132
12	0.5494 961 775	0.5333 241 484	0.5176 312 796	0.5024 032 791	144
13	0.5227 512 324	0.5061 048 734	0.4899 918 857	0.4743 950 740	156
14	0.4973 080 107	0.4802 747 891	0.4638 283 224	0.4479 482 830	168
15	0.4731 031 554	0.4557 629 953	0.4390 617 865	0.4229 758 596	180
16	0.4500 763 929	0.4325 022 104	0.4156 176 823	0.3993 956 101	192
17	0.4281 703 835	0.4104 285 867	0.3934 253 974	0.3771 299 231	204
18	0.4073 305 781	0.3894 815 349	0.3724 180 898	0.3561 055 137	216
19	0.3875 050 826	0.3696 035 582	0.3525 324 865	0.3362 531 825	228
20	0.3686 445 289	0.3507 400 941	0.3337 086 931	0.3175 075 881	240
21	0.3507 019 514	0.3328 393 651	0.3158 900 134	0.2998 070 315	252
22	0.3336 326 708	0.3158 522 359	0.2990 227 782	0.2830 932 536	264
23	0.3173 941 821	0.2997 320 792	0.2830 561 845	0.2673 112 429	276
24	0.3019 460 491	0.2844 346 472	0.2679 421 416	0.2524 090 549	288
25	0.2872 498 040	0.2699 179 506	0.2536 351 268	0.2383 376 408	300
26	0.2732 688 509	0.2561 421 429	0.2400 920 480	0.2250 506 862	312
27	0.2599 683 755	0.2430 694 113	0.2272 721 143	0.2125 044 588	324
28	0.2473 152 575	0.2306 638 730	0.2151 367 127	0.2006 576 642	336
29	0.2352 779 891	0.2188 914 764	0.2036 492 919	0.1894 713 100	348
30	0.2238 265 956	0.2077 199 079	0.1927 752 523	0.1789 085 778	360
31	0.2129 325 617	0.1971 185 029	0.1824 818 421	0.1689 347 015	372
32	0.2025 687 595	0.1870 581 620	0.1727 380 578	0.1595 168 534	384
33	0.1927 093 818	0.1775 112 709	0.1635 145 518	0.1506 240 357	396
34	0.1833 298 773	0.1684 516 247	0.1547 835 433	0.1422 269 789	408
35	0.1744 068 898	0.1598 543 559	0.1465 187 350	0.1342 980 450	420
36	0.1659 181 998	0.1516 958 660	0.1386 952 336	0.1268 111 369	432
37	0.1578 426 693	0.1439 537 611	0.1312 894 752	0.1197 416 123	444
38	0.1501 601 890	0.1366 067 902	0.1242 791 540	0.1130 662 027	456
39	0.1428 516 286	0.1296 347 868	0.1176 431 554	0.1067 629 370	468
40	0.1358 987 887	0.1230 186 136	0.1113 614 919	0.1008 110 685	480
41	0.1292 843 557	0.1167 401 103	0.1054 152 435	0.0951 910 075	492
42	0.1229 918 587	0.1107 820 430	0.0997 865 005	0.0898 842 561	504
43	0.1170 056 287	0.1051 280 577	0.0944 583 094	0.0848 733 480	516
44	0.1113 107 590	0.0997 626 349	0.0894 146 219	0.0801 417 902	528
45	0.1058 930 687	0.0946 710 474	0.0846 402 467	0.0756 740 095	540
46	0.1007 390 668	0.0898 393 193	0.0801 208 036	0.0714 553 006	552
47	0.0958 359 193	0.0852 541 882	0.0758 426 803	0.0674 717 782	564
48	0.0911 714 166	0.0809 030 685	0.0717 929 912	0.0637 103 310	576
49	0.0867 339 434	0.0767 740 171	0.0679 595 390	0.0601 585 787	588
50	0.0825 124 499	0.0728 557 000	0.0643 307 775	0.0568 048 310	600

MONTHLY
Compounding

TABLE 4. PRESENT WORTH OF ONE DOLLAR
Payable at end of each period

MONTHS	6% Nominal Annual Rate	6¼% Nominal Annual Rate	6½% Nominal Annual Rate	6¾% Nominal Annual Rate	MONTHS
1	0.9950 248 756	0.9948 186 528	0.9946 125 155	0.9944 064 636	1
2	0.9900 745 031	0.9896 641 521	0.9892 540 561	0.9888 442 149	2
3	0.9851 487 593	0.9845 363 585	0.9839 244 652	0.9833 130 789	3
4	0.9802 475 217	0.9794 351 339	0.9786 235 875	0.9778 128 814	4
5	0.9753 706 684	0.9743 603 404	0.9733 512 681	0.9723 434 495	5
6	0.9705 180 780	0.9693 118 413	0.9681 073 533	0.9669 046 111	6
7	0.9656 896 298	0.9642 895 001	0.9628 916 899	0.9614 961 950	7
8	0.9608 852 038	0.9592 931 815	0.9577 041 259	0.9561 180 310	8
9	0.9561 046 804	0.9543 227 505	0.9525 445 098	0.9507 699 501	9
10	0.9513 479 407	0.9493 780 730	0.9474 126 911	0.9454 517 838	10
11	0.9466 148 664	0.9444 590 156	0.9423 085 199	0.9401 633 649	11
YEARS					
1	0.9419 053 397	0.9395 654 456	0.9372 318 474	0.9349 045 269	12
2	0.8871 856 689	0.8827 832 266	0.8784 035 358	0.8740 464 744	24
3	0.8356 449 188	0.8294 326 156	0.8232 677 687	0.8171 500 057	36
4	0.7870 984 111	0.7793 062 251	0.7715 927 717	0.7639 572 394	48
5	0.7413 721 962	0.7322 092 006	0.7231 613 189	0.7142 270 815	60
6	0.6983 024 303	0.6879 584 639	0.6777 698 189	0.6677 341 317	72
7	0.6577 347 878	0.6463 820 007	0.6352 274 595	0.6242 676 625	84
8	0.6195 239 087	0.6073 181 925	0.5953 554 054	0.5836 306 637	96
9	0.5835 328 777	0.5706 151 881	0.5579 860 465	0.5456 389 495	108
10	0.5496 327 334	0.5361 303 135	0.5229 622 932	0.5101 203 240	120
11	0.5177 020 064	0.5037 295 169	0.4901 369 162	0.4769 138 001	132
12	0.4876 262 842	0.4732 868 480	0.4593 719 274	0.4458 688 707	144
13	0.4592 978 008	0.4446 839 682	0.4305 380 002	0.4168 448 256	156
14	0.4326 150 511	0.4178 096 908	0.4035 139 253	0.3897 101 145	168
15	0.4074 824 267	0.3925 595 483	0.3781 861 017	0.3643 417 502	180
16	0.3838 098 735	0.3688 353 869	0.3544 480 588	0.3406 247 516	192
17	0.3615 125 693	0.3465 449 847	0.3322 000 089	0.3184 516 223	204
18	0.3405 106 193	0.3256 016 929	0.3113 484 281	0.2977 218 632	216
19	0.3207 287 706	0.3059 240 997	0.2918 056 624	0.2783 415 177	228
20	0.3020 961 416	0.2874 357 131	0.2734 895 601	0.2602 227 449	240
21	0.2845 459 689	0.2700 646 638	0.2563 231 257	0.2432 834 222	252
22	0.2680 153 674	0.2537 434 262	0.2402 341 966	0.2274 467 728	264
23	0.2524 451 057	0.2384 085 553	0.2251 551 399	0.2126 410 175	276
24	0.2377 793 930	0.2240 004 405	0.2110 225 677	0.1987 990 499	288
25	0.2239 656 800	0.2104 630 737	0.1977 770 710	0.1858 581 317	300
26	0.2109 544 699	0.1977 438 316	0.1853 629 696	0.1737 596 086	312
27	0.1986 991 416	0.1857 932 713	0.1737 280 785	0.1624 486 447	324
28	0.1871 557 824	0.1745 649 377	0.1628 234 879	0.1518 739 733	336
29	0.1762 830 308	0.1640 151 835	0.1526 033 584	0.1419 876 652	348
30	0.1660 419 280	0.1541 029 990	0.1430 247 275	0.1327 449 109	360
31	0.1563 957 786	0.1447 898 529	0.1340 473 296	0.1241 038 182	372
32	0.1473 100 190	0.1360 395 426	0.1256 334 264	0.1160 252 214	384
33	0.1387 520 935	0.1278 180 535	0.1177 476 483	0.1084 725 047	396
34	0.1306 913 377	0.1200 934 264	0.1103 568 459	0.1014 114 357	408
35	0.1230 988 689	0.1128 356 337	0.1034 299 506	0.0948 100 103	420
36	0.1159 474 819	0.1060 164 624	0.0969 378 437	0.0886 383 079	432
37	0.1092 115 523	0.0996 094 048	0.0908 532 343	0.0828 683 553	444
38	0.1028 669 443	0.0935 895 548	0.0851 505 446	0.0774 740 005	456
39	0.0968 909 241	0.0879 335 117	0.0798 058 023	0.0724 307 938	468
40	0.0912 620 788	0.0826 192 891	0.0747 965 395	0.0677 158 770	480
41	0.0859 602 393	0.0776 262 292	0.0701 016 989	0.0633 078 799	492
42	0.0809 664 084	0.0729 349 226	0.0657 015 447	0.0591 868 235	504
43	0.0762 626 924	0.0685 271 331	0.0615 775 802	0.0553 340 293	516
44	0.0718 322 372	0.0643 857 263	0.0577 124 692	0.0517 320 344	528
45	0.0676 591 678	0.0604 946 037	0.0540 899 641	0.0483 645 132	540
46	0.0637 285 314	0.0568 386 392	0.0506 948 370	0.0452 162 023	552
47	0.0600 262 440	0.0534 036 214	0.0475 128 158	0.0422 728 322	564
48	0.0565 390 398	0.0501 761 973	0.0445 305 241	0.0395 210 622	576
49	0.0532 544 234	0.0471 438 212	0.0417 354 254	0.0369 484 200	588
50	0.0501 606 258	0.0442 947 054	0.0391 157 698	0.0345 432 451	600

TABLE 4. PRESENT WORTH OF ONE DOLLAR
Payable at end of each period

MONTHLY Compounding

MONTHS	7% Nominal Annual Rate	7¼% Nominal Annual Rate	7½% Nominal Annual Rate	7¾% Nominal Annual Rate	MONTHS
1	0.9942 004 971	0.9939 946 159	0.9937 888 199	0.9935 831 091	1
2	0.9884 346 284	0.9880 252 964	0.9876 162 185	0.9872 073 947	2
3	0.9827 021 989	0.9820 918 249	0.9814 819 563	0.9808 725 925	3
4	0.9770 030 147	0.9761 939 863	0.9753 857 951	0.9745 784 401	4
5	0.9713 368 829	0.9703 315 664	0.9693 274 982	0.9683 246 765	5
6	0.9657 036 118	0.9645 043 526	0.9633 068 305	0.9621 110 427	6
7	0.9601 030 109	0.9587 121 334	0.9573 235 583	0.9559 372 811	7
8	0.9545 348 907	0.9529 546 988	0.9513 774 492	0.9498 031 359	8
9	0.9489 990 628	0.9472 318 398	0.9454 682 725	0.9437 083 528	9
10	0.9434 953 400	0.9415 433 487	0.9395 957 988	0.9376 526 792	10
11	0.9380 235 361	0.9358 890 192	0.9337 598 000	0.9316 358 642	11
YEARS					
1	0.9325 834 658	0.9302 686 461	0.9279 600 497	0.9256 576 585	12
2	0.8697 119 208	0.8653 997 540	0.8611 098 539	0.8568 421 008	24
3	0.8110 789 574	0.8050 542 575	0.7990 755 428	0.7931 424 528	36
4	0.7563 988 251	0.7489 167 342	0.7415 101 804	0.7341 783 857	48
5	0.7054 050 379	0.6966 937 564	0.6880 918 239	0.6795 978 455	60
6	0.6578 490 751	0.6481 123 575	0.6385 217 231	0.6290 749 504	72
7	0.6134 991 704	0.6029 186 054	0.5925 226 499	0.5823 080 456	84
8	0.5721 391 827	0.5608 762 748	0.5498 373 476	0.5390 179 020	96
9	0.5335 675 419	0.5217 656 128	0.5102 270 924	0.4989 460 491	108
10	0.4975 962 675	0.4853 821 902	0.4734 703 581	0.4618 532 315	120
11	0.4640 500 517	0.4515 358 330	0.4393 615 770	0.4275 179 809	132
12	0.4327 654 056	0.4200 496 280	0.4077 099 908	0.3957 352 932	144
13	0.4035 898 618	0.3907 589 988	0.3783 385 834	0.3663 154 049	156
14	0.3763 812 321	0.3635 108 447	0.3510 830 906	0.3390 826 600	168
15	0.3510 069 139	0.3381 627 414	0.3257 910 822	0.3138 744 611	180
16	0.3273 432 443	0.3145 821 956	0.3023 211 089	0.2905 402 987	192
17	0.3052 748 973	0.2926 459 532	0.2805 419 112	0.2689 408 526	204
18	0.2846 943 218	0.2722 393 547	0.2603 316 859	0.2489 471 599	216
19	0.2655 012 173	0.2532 557 359	0.2415 774 042	0.2304 398 451	228
20	0.2476 020 454	0.2355 958 706	0.2241 741 800	0.2133 084 075	240
21	0.2309 095 737	0.2191 674 516	0.2080 246 832	0.1974 505 610	252
22	0.2153 424 505	0.2038 846 084	0.1930 385 953	0.1827 716 240	264
23	0.2008 248 089	0.1896 674 587	0.1791 321 045	0.1691 839 535	276
24	0.1872 858 963	0.1764 416 900	0.1662 274 366	0.1566 064 223	288
25	0.1746 597 302	0.1641 381 721	0.1542 524 204	0.1449 639 341	300
26	0.1628 847 766	0.1526 925 951	0.1431 400 837	0.1341 869 759	312
27	0.1519 036 495	0.1420 451 337	0.1328 282 791	0.1242 112 019	324
28	0.1416 628 319	0.1321 401 342	0.1232 593 365	0.1149 770 503	336
29	0.1321 124 148	0.1229 258 238	0.1143 797 400	0.1064 293 872	348
30	0.1232 058 536	0.1143 540 397	0.1061 398 293	0.0985 171 773	360
31	0.1148 997 420	0.1063 799 777	0.0984 935 212	0.0911 931 797	372
32	0.1071 535 996	0.0989 619 578	0.0913 980 529	0.0844 136 652	384
33	0.0999 296 753	0.0920 612 065	0.0848 137 417	0.0781 381 557	396
34	0.0931 927 629	0.0856 416 539	0.0787 037 639	0.0723 291 822	408
35	0.0869 100 299	0.0796 697 455	0.0730 339 487	0.0669 520 614	420
36	0.0810 508 569	0.0741 142 662	0.0677 725 867	0.0619 746 884	432
37	0.0755 866 890	0.0689 461 781	0.0628 902 529	0.0573 673 450	444
38	0.0704 908 964	0.0641 384 678	0.0583 596 422	0.0531 025 222	456
39	0.0657 386 445	0.0596 660 056	0.0541 554 165	0.0491 547 564	468
40	0.0613 067 729	0.0555 054 142	0.0502 540 630	0.0455 004 767	480
41	0.0571 736 828	0.0516 349 466	0.0466 337 628	0.0421 178 647	492
42	0.0533 192 312	0.0480 343 718	0.0432 742 688	0.0389 867 240	504
43	0.0497 246 334	0.0446 848 700	0.0401 567 926	0.0360 883 597	516
44	0.0463 723 710	0.0415 689 336	0.0372 638 993	0.0334 054 665	528
45	0.0432 461 065	0.0386 702 755	0.0345 794 098	0.0309 220 259	540
46	0.0403 306 039	0.0359 737 449	0.0320 883 109	0.0286 232 101	552
47	0.0376 116 543	0.0334 652 469	0.0297 766 706	0.0264 952 937	564
48	0.0350 760 069	0.0311 316 700	0.0276 315 607	0.0245 255 715	576
49	0.0327 113 041	0.0289 608 165	0.0256 409 844	0.0227 022 831	588
50	0.0305 060 214	0.0269 413 395	0.0237 938 092	0.0210 145 422	600

MONTHLY
Compounding

TABLE 4. PRESENT WORTH OF ONE DOLLAR
Payable at end of each period

MONTHS	8% Nominal Annual Rate	8¼% Nominal Annual Rate	8½% Nominal Annual Rate	8¾% Nominal Annual Rate	MONTHS
1	0.9933 774 834	0.9931 719 429	0.9929 664 874	0.9927 611 169	1
2	0.9867 988 246	0.9863 905 081	0.9859 824 451	0.9855 746 351	2
3	0.9802 637 331	0.9796 553 774	0.9790 475 251	0.9784 401 755	3
4	0.9737 719 203	0.9729 662 346	0.9721 613 820	0.9713 573 614	4
5	0.9673 230 996	0.9663 227 656	0.9653 236 726	0.9643 258 190	5
6	0.9609 169 864	0.9597 246 585	0.9585 340 564	0.9573 451 771	6
7	0.9545 532 977	0.9531 716 038	0.9517 921 950	0.9504 150 672	7
8	0.9482 317 527	0.9466 632 936	0.9450 977 526	0.9435 351 236	8
9	0.9419 520 722	0.9401 994 226	0.9384 503 956	0.9367 049 831	9
10	0.9357 139 790	0.9337 796 872	0.9318 497 929	0.9299 242 852	10
11	0.9295 171 977	0.9274 037 862	0.9252 956 156	0.9231 926 720	11
YEARS					
1	0.9233 614 547	0.9210 714 202	0.9187 875 373	0.9165 097 881	12
2	0.8525 963 759	0.8483 725 611	0.8441 705 386	0.8399 901 917	24
3	0.7872 546 299	0.7814 117 197	0.7756 133 702	0.7698 592 326	36
4	0.7269 205 803	0.7197 360 024	0.7126 238 983	0.7055 835 221	48
5	0.6712 104 444	0.6629 282 619	0.6547 499 565	0.6466 742 043	60
6	0.6197 698 523	0.6106 042 756	0.6015 761 000	0.5926 832 380	72
7	0.5722 715 924	0.5624 101 473	0.5527 206 234	0.5431 999 888	84
8	0.5284 135 300	0.5180 199 131	0.5078 328 204	0.4978 481 067	96
9	0.4879 166 858	0.4771 333 371	0.4665 904 664	0.4562 826 627	108
10	0.4505 234 607	0.4394 738 804	0.4286 975 055	0.4181 875 265	120
11	0.4159 959 980	0.4047 868 312	0.3938 819 253	0.3832 729 613	132
12	0.3841 146 699	0.3728 375 814	0.3618 938 041	0.3512 734 206	144
13	0.3546 766 803	0.3434 100 406	0.3325 035 171	0.3219 455 283	156
14	0.3274 947 755	0.3163 051 738	0.3055 000 876	0.2950 662 279	168
15	0.3023 960 523	0.2913 396 557	0.2806 896 731	0.2704 310 860	180
16	0.2792 208 587	0.2683 446 304	0.2578 941 735	0.2478 527 373	192
17	0.2578 217 783	0.2471 645 698	0.2369 499 525	0.2271 594 598	204
18	0.2380 626 922	0.2276 562 213	0.2177 066 633	0.2081 938 683	216
19	0.2198 179 138	0.2096 876 391	0.2000 261 690	0.1908 117 181	228
20	0.2029 713 887	0.1931 372 916	0.1837 815 512	0.1748 808 074	240
21	0.1874 159 567	0.1778 932 394	0.1688 561 989	0.1602 799 717	252
22	0.1730 526 704	0.1638 523 787	0.1551 429 711	0.1468 981 629	264
23	0.1597 901 655	0.1509 197 431	0.1425 434 283	0.1346 336 041	276
24	0.1475 440 796	0.1390 078 621	0.1309 671 255	0.1233 930 160	288
25	0.1362 365 160	0.1280 361 690	0.1203 309 627	0.1130 909 069	300
26	0.1257 955 476	0.1179 304 560	0.1105 585 889	0.1036 489 232	312
27	0.1161 547 598	0.1086 223 726	0.1015 798 536	0.0949 952 526	324
28	0.1072 528 280	0.1000 489 630	0.0933 303 035	0.0870 640 788	336
29	0.0990 331 273	0.0921 522 404	0.0857 507 197	0.0797 950 804	348
30	0.0914 433 724	0.0848 787 950	0.0787 866 926	0.0731 329 723	360
31	0.0844 352 854	0.0781 794 322	0.0723 882 312	0.0670 270 849	372
32	0.0779 642 879	0.0720 088 407	0.0665 094 047	0.0614 309 794	384
33	0.0719 892 183	0.0663 252 851	0.0611 080 122	0.0563 020 939	396
34	0.0664 720 694	0.0610 903 246	0.0561 452 800	0.0516 014 202	408
35	0.0613 777 467	0.0562 685 520	0.0515 855 835	0.0472 932 067	420
36	0.0566 738 454	0.0518 273 551	0.0473 961 913	0.0433 446 868	432
37	0.0523 304 444	0.0477 366 956	0.0435 470 298	0.0397 258 297	444
38	0.0483 199 152	0.0439 689 060	0.0400 104 683	0.0364 091 118	456
39	0.0446 167 472	0.0404 985 027	0.0367 611 196	0.0333 693 073	468
40	0.0411 973 846	0.0373 020 134	0.0337 756 586	0.0305 832 968	480
41	0.0380 400 770	0.0343 578 184	0.0310 326 542	0.0280 298 909	492
42	0.0351 247 408	0.0316 460 046	0.0285 124 159	0.0256 896 693	504
43	0.0324 328 318	0.0291 482 304	0.0261 968 524	0.0235 448 334	516
44	0.0299 472 267	0.0268 476 020	0.0240 693 415	0.0215 790 703	528
45	0.0276 521 148	0.0247 285 589	0.0221 146 110	0.0197 774 291	540
46	0.0255 328 970	0.0227 767 689	0.0203 186 290	0.0181 262 074	552
47	0.0235 760 929	0.0209 790 308	0.0186 685 031	0.0166 128 465	564
48	0.0217 692 554	0.0193 231 857	0.0171 523 880	0.0152 258 364	576
49	0.0201 008 914	0.0177 980 341	0.0157 594 003	0.0139 546 281	588
50	0.0185 603 883	0.0163 932 606	0.0144 795 406	0.0127 895 532	600

TABLE 4. PRESENT WORTH OF ONE DOLLAR
Payable at end of each period

MONTHLY Compounding

MONTHS	9% Nominal Annual Rate	9¼% Nominal Annual Rate	9½% Nominal Annual Rate	9¾% Nominal Annual Rate	MONTHS
1	0.9925 558 313	0.9923 506 306	0.9921 455 147	0.9919 404 836	1
2	0.9851 670 782	0.9847 597 740	0.9843 527 223	0.9839 459 229	2
3	0.9778 333 282	0.9772 269 826	0.9766 211 383	0.9760 157 946	3
4	0.9705 541 719	0.9697 518 124	0.9689 502 819	0.9681 495 793	4
5	0.9633 292 029	0.9623 338 225	0.9613 396 761	0.9603 467 618	5
6	0.9561 580 178	0.9549 725 756	0.9537 888 477	0.9526 068 313	6
7	0.9490 402 162	0.9476 676 376	0.9462 973 272	0.9449 292 809	7
8	0.9419 754 006	0.9404 185 777	0.9388 646 488	0.9373 136 079	8
9	0.9349 631 768	0.9332 249 686	0.9314 903 502	0.9297 593 134	9
10	0.9280 031 532	0.9260 863 860	0.9241 739 729	0.9222 659 030	10
11	0.9210 949 411	0.9190 024 091	0.9169 150 620	0.9148 328 858	11
YEARS					
1	0.9142 381 550	0.9119 726 201	0.9097 131 661	0.9074 597 751	12
2	0.8358 314 040	0.8316 940 599	0.8275 780 445	0.8234 832 435	24
3	0.7641 489 606	0.7584 822 110	0.7528 586 430	0.7472 779 189	36
4	0.6986 141 359	0.6917 150 093	0.6848 854 197	0.6781 246 522	48
5	0.6386 996 986	0.6308 251 494	0.6230 492 836	0.6153 708 444	60
6	0.5839 236 340	0.5752 952 644	0.5667 961 364	0.5584 242 881	72
7	0.5338 452 658	0.5246 535 296	0.5156 219 077	0.5067 475 789	84
8	0.4880 617 108	0.4784 696 541	0.4690 680 382	0.4598 530 440	96
9	0.4462 046 380	0.4363 512 241	0.4267 173 701	0.4172 981 399	108
10	0.4079 373 050	0.3979 403 691	0.3881 904 098	0.3786 812 762	120
11	0.3729 518 490	0.3629 107 211	0.3531 419 267	0.3436 380 257	132
12	0.3409 668 104	0.3309 646 412	0.3212 578 602	0.3118 376 855	144
13	0.3117 248 676	0.3018 306 910	0.2922 525 051	0.2829 801 560	156
14	0.2849 907 678	0.2752 613 261	0.2658 659 517	0.2567 931 087	168
15	0.2605 494 337	0.2510 307 928	0.2418 617 567	0.2330 294 167	180
16	0.2382 042 336	0.2289 332 099	0.2200 248 244	0.2114 648 221	192
17	0.2177 753 990	0.2087 808 192	0.2001 594 797	0.1918 958 199	204
18	0.1990 985 790	0.1904 023 908	0.1820 877 140	0.1741 377 375	216
19	0.1820 235 175	0.1736 417 672	0.1656 475 908	0.1580 229 922	228
20	0.1664 128 448	0.1583 565 374	0.1506 917 942	0.1433 995 089	240
21	0.1521 409 722	0.1444 168 263	0.1370 863 092	0.1301 292 861	252
22	0.1390 930 817	0.1317 041 915	0.1247 092 204	0.1180 870 927	264
23	0.1271 642 024	0.1201 106 166	0.1134 496 197	0.1071 592 866	276
24	0.1162 583 658	0.1095 375 937	0.1032 066 128	0.0972 427 421	288
25	0.1062 878 338	0.0998 952 864	0.0938 884 144	0.0882 438 769	300
26	0.0971 723 931	0.0911 017 660	0.0854 115 268	0.0800 777 687	312
27	0.0888 387 094	0.0830 823 163	0.0776 999 904	0.0726 673 540	324
28	0.0812 197 377	0.0757 687 977	0.0706 847 043	0.0659 427 007	336
29	0.0742 541 832	0.0690 990 689	0.0643 028 061	0.0598 403 483	348
30	0.0678 860 074	0.0630 164 589	0.0584 971 094	0.0543 027 090	360
31	0.0620 639 782	0.0574 692 852	0.0532 155 906	0.0492 775 241	372
32	0.0567 412 569	0.0524 104 146	0.0484 109 234	0.0447 173 710	384
33	0.0518 750 220	0.0477 968 631	0.0440 400 544	0.0405 792 154	396
34	0.0474 261 244	0.0435 894 305	0.0400 638 173	0.0368 240 057	408
35	0.0433 587 725	0.0397 523 671	0.0364 465 821	0.0334 163 039	420
36	0.0396 402 442	0.0362 530 704	0.0331 559 356	0.0303 239 516	432
37	0.0362 406 237	0.0330 618 076	0.0301 623 911	0.0275 177 663	444
38	0.0331 325 609	0.0301 514 633	0.0274 391 243	0.0249 712 660	456
39	0.0302 910 514	0.0274 973 090	0.0249 617 327	0.0226 604 195	468
40	0.0276 932 349	0.0250 767 929	0.0227 080 169	0.0205 634 192	480
41	0.0253 182 120	0.0228 693 486	0.0206 577 819	0.0186 604 757	492
42	0.0231 468 754	0.0208 562 197	0.0187 926 562	0.0169 336 311	504
43	0.0211 617 567	0.0190 203 013	0.0170 959 268	0.0153 665 891	516
44	0.0193 468 854	0.0173 459 941	0.0155 523 897	0.0139 445 615	528
45	0.0176 876 608	0.0158 190 716	0.0141 482 136	0.0126 541 286	540
46	0.0161 707 344	0.0144 265 602	0.0128 708 162	0.0114 831 127	552
47	0.0147 839 024	0.0131 566 279	0.0117 087 510	0.0104 204 629	564
48	0.0135 160 076	0.0119 984 844	0.0106 516 049	0.0094 561 509	576
49	0.0123 568 499	0.0109 422 893	0.0096 899 052	0.0085 810 766	588
50	0.0112 971 036	0.0099 790 682	0.0088 150 344	0.0077 869 818	600

MONTHLY
Compounding

TABLE 4. PRESENT WORTH OF ONE DOLLAR
Payable at end of each period

MONTHS	10% Nominal Annual Rate	10¼% Nominal Annual Rate	10½% Nominal Annual Rate	10¾% Nominal Annual Rate	MONTHS
1	0.9917 355 372	0.9915 306 755	0.9913 258 984	0.9911 212 059	1
2	0.9835 393 757	0.9831 330 804	0.9827 270 368	0.9823 212 447	2
3	0.9754 109 511	0.9748 066 073	0.9742 027 626	0.9735 994 166	3
4	0.9673 497 036	0.9665 506 538	0.9657 524 289	0.9649 550 278	4
5	0.9593 550 780	0.9583 646 227	0.9573 753 942	0.9563 873 908	5
6	0.9514 265 236	0.9502 479 217	0.9490 710 227	0.9478 958 240	6
7	0.9435 634 945	0.9421 999 636	0.9408 386 843	0.9394 796 521	7
8	0.9357 654 491	0.9342 201 664	0.9326 777 539	0.9311 382 057	8
9	0.9280 318 503	0.9263 079 526	0.9245 876 123	0.9228 708 213	9
10	0.9203 621 656	0.9184 627 500	0.9165 676 454	0.9146 768 412	10
11	0.9127 558 667	0.9106 839 909	0.9086 172 445	0.9065 556 139	11
YEARS					
1	0.9052 124 298	0.9029 711 126	0.9007 358 062	0.8985 064 932	12
2	0.8194 095 430	0.8153 568 302	0.8113 249 926	0.8073 139 183	24
3	0.7417 397 035	0.7362 436 642	0.7307 894 713	0.7253 767 976	36
4	0.6714 319 992	0.6648 067 606	0.6582 482 436	0.6517 557 627	48
5	0.6077 885 915	0.6003 013 003	0.5929 077 624	0.5856 067 847	60
6	0.5501 777 877	0.5420 547 331	0.5340 532 514	0.5261 714 985	72
7	0.4980 277 720	0.4894 597 654	0.4810 408 859	0.4727 685 080	84
8	0.4508 209 296	0.4419 680 290	0.4332 907 502	0.4247 855 742	96
9	0.4080 887 091	0.3990 843 629	0.3902 804 932	0.3816 725 966	108
10	0.3694 069 719	0.3603 616 512	0.3515 396 147	0.3429 353 063	120
11	0.3343 917 826	0.3253 961 611	0.3166 443 183	0.3081 295 995	132
12	0.3026 955 981	0.2938 233 336	0.2852 128 753	0.2768 564 459	144
13	0.2740 038 178	0.2653 139 825	0.2569 014 492	0.2487 573 143	156
14	0.2480 316 617	0.2395 708 620	0.2314 003 339	0.2235 100 621	168
15	0.2245 213 431	0.2163 255 678	0.2084 305 663	0.2008 252 421	180
16	0.2032 395 106	0.1953 357 386	0.1877 408 742	0.1804 427 840	192
17	0.1839 749 312	0.1763 825 292	0.1691 049 277	0.1621 290 131	204
18	0.1665 363 945	0.1592 683 287	0.1523 188 634	0.1456 739 710	216
19	0.1507 508 143	0.1438 146 999	0.1371 990 542	0.1308 890 088	228
20	0.1364 615 109	0.1298 605 196	0.1235 801 007	0.1176 046 243	240
21	0.1235 266 559	0.1172 602 979	0.1113 130 216	0.1056 685 186	252
22	0.1118 178 643	0.1058 826 617	0.1002 636 243	0.0949 438 501	264
23	0.1012 189 206	0.0956 089 848	0.0903 110 365	0.0853 076 658	276
24	0.0916 246 251	0.0863 321 514	0.0813 463 842	0.0766 494 916	288
25	0.0829 397 495	0.0779 554 388	0.0732 716 010	0.0688 700 659	300
26	0.0750 780 922	0.0703 915 093	0.0659 983 546	0.0618 802 014	312
27	0.0679 616 222	0.0635 614 995	0.0594 470 811	0.0555 997 628	324
28	0.0615 197 052	0.0573 941 979	0.0535 461 145	0.0499 567 479	336
29	0.0556 884 018	0.0518 253 027	0.0482 309 027	0.0448 864 623	348
30	0.0504 098 335	0.0467 967 513	0.0434 433 010	0.0403 307 779	360
31	0.0456 316 079	0.0422 561 146	0.0391 309 367	0.0362 374 658	372
32	0.0413 062 987	0.0381 560 508	0.0352 466 358	0.0325 595 983	384
33	0.0373 909 750	0.0344 538 116	0.0317 479 070	0.0292 550 105	396
34	0.0338 467 753	0.0311 107 966	0.0285 964 766	0.0262 858 169	408
35	0.0306 385 217	0.0280 921 506	0.0257 578 704	0.0236 179 772	420
36	0.0277 343 707	0.0253 664 005	0.0232 010 361	0.0212 209 058	432
37	0.0251 054 971	0.0229 051 269	0.0208 980 040	0.0190 671 217	444
38	0.0227 258 080	0.0206 826 679	0.0188 235 805	0.0171 319 326	456
39	0.0205 716 839	0.0186 758 517	0.0169 550 729	0.0153 931 527	468
40	0.0186 217 440	0.0168 637 546	0.0152 720 413	0.0138 308 477	480
41	0.0168 566 341	0.0152 274 832	0.0137 560 744	0.0124 271 064	492
42	0.0152 588 347	0.0137 499 775	0.0123 905 888	0.0111 658 358	504
43	0.0138 124 868	0.0124 158 324	0.0111 606 470	0.0100 325 760	516
44	0.0125 032 348	0.0112 111 380	0.0100 527 944	0.0090 143 347	528
45	0.0113 180 835	0.0101 233 338	0.0090 549 118	0.0080 994 382	540
46	0.0102 452 699	0.0091 410 780	0.0081 560 833	0.0072 773 978	552
47	0.0092 741 457	0.0082 541 293	0.0073 464 763	0.0065 387 892	564
48	0.0083 950 719	0.0074 532 404	0.0066 172 342	0.0058 751 446	576
49	0.0075 993 235	0.0067 300 607	0.0059 603 798	0.0052 788 555	588
50	0.0068 790 020	0.0060 770 504	0.0053 687 275	0.0047 430 860	600

TABLE 4. PRESENT WORTH OF ONE DOLLAR
Payable at end of each period

MONTHLY Compounding

MONTHS	11% Nominal Annual Rate	11¼% Nominal Annual Rate	11½% Nominal Annual Rate	11¾% Nominal Annual Rate	MONTHS
1	0.9909 165 979	0.9907 120 743	0.9905 076 352	0.9903 032 804	1
2	0.9819 157 039	0.9815 104 142	0.9811 053 753	0.9807 005 871	2
3	0.9729 965 687	0.9723 942 184	0.9717 923 652	0.9711 910 085	3
4	0.9641 584 496	0.9633 626 931	0.9625 677 575	0.9617 736 416	4
5	0.9554 006 106	0.9544 150 520	0.9534 307 131	0.9524 475 923	5
6	0.9467 223 227	0.9455 505 159	0.9443 804 010	0.9432 119 750	6
7	0.9381 228 631	0.9367 683 130	0.9354 159 977	0.9340 659 129	7
8	0.9296 015 159	0.9280 676 785	0.9265 366 877	0.9250 085 377	8
9	0.9211 575 715	0.9194 478 549	0.9177 416 635	0.9160 389 892	9
10	0.9127 903 268	0.9109 080 915	0.9090 301 248	0.9071 564 160	10
11	0.9044 990 852	0.9024 476 448	0.9004 012 792	0.8983 599 746	11
YEARS					
1	0.8962 831 563	0.8940 657 782	0.8918 543 417	0.8896 488 298	12
2	0.8033 234 962	0.7993 536 157	0.7954 041 669	0.7914 750 403	24
3	0.7200 053 187	0.7146 747 124	0.7093 846 596	0.7041 348 434	36
4	0.6453 286 395	0.6389 662 029	0.6326 677 886	0.6264 327 395	48
5	0.5783 971 899	0.5712 778 154	0.5642 475 142	0.5573 051 536	60
6	0.5184 076 589	0.5107 599 446	0.5032 265 953	0.4958 058 778	72
7	0.4646 400 527	0.4566 529 873	0.4488 048 239	0.4410 931 189	84
8	0.4164 490 530	0.4082 778 085	0.4002 685 308	0.3924 179 771	96
9	0.3732 562 716	0.3650 272 165	0.3569 812 270	0.3491 141 941	108
10	0.3345 433 092	0.3263 583 424	0.3183 752 573	0.3105 890 343	120
11	0.2998 455 331	0.2917 858 254	0.2839 443 555	0.2763 151 709	132
12	0.2687 465 008	0.2608 757 210	0.2532 370 062	0.2458 234 684	144
13	0.2408 729 620	0.2332 400 545	0.2258 505 235	0.2186 965 610	156
14	0.2158 903 786	0.2085 319 508	0.2014 257 700	0.1945 631 396	168
15	0.1934 989 100	0.1864 412 809	0.1796 424 475	0.1730 928 694	180
16	0.1734 298 137	0.1666 907 689	0.1602 148 967	0.1539 918 688	192
17	0.1554 422 209	0.1490 325 120	0.1428 883 513	0.1369 986 858	204
18	0.1393 202 443	0.1332 448 688	0.1274 355 965	0.1218 807 205	216
19	0.1248 703 883	0.1191 296 773	0.1136 539 900	0.1084 310 404	228
20	0.1119 192 258	0.1065 097 677	0.1013 628 044	0.0964 655 482	240
21	0.1003 113 169	0.0952 267 383	0.0904 008 572	0.0858 204 621	252
22	0.0899 073 437	0.0851 389 679	0.0806 243 970	0.0763 500 737	264
23	0.0805 824 378	0.0761 198 376	0.0719 052 185	0.0679 247 537	276
24	0.0722 246 817	0.0680 561 418	0.0641 289 813	0.0604 291 776	288
25	0.0647 337 657	0.0608 466 674	0.0571 937 104	0.0537 607 472	300
26	0.0580 197 838	0.0544 009 230	0.0510 084 590	0.0478 281 858	312
27	0.0520 021 550	0.0486 380 036	0.0454 921 156	0.0425 502 895	324
28	0.0466 086 556	0.0434 855 745	0.0405 723 408	0.0378 548 153	336
29	0.0417 745 529	0.0388 789 640	0.0361 846 183	0.0336 774 921	348
30	0.0374 418 282	0.0347 603 512	0.0322 714 089	0.0299 611 415	360
31	0.0335 584 799	0.0310 780 405	0.0287 813 962	0.0266 548 944	372
32	0.0300 779 003	0.0277 858 124	0.0256 688 131	0.0237 134 956	384
33	0.0269 583 154	0.0248 423 440	0.0228 928 424	0.0210 966 836	396
34	0.0241 622 840	0.0222 106 896	0.0204 170 809	0.0187 686 399	408
35	0.0216 562 482	0.0198 578 175	0.0182 090 623	0.0166 974 985	420
36	0.0194 101 305	0.0177 541 951	0.0162 398 312	0.0148 549 100	432
37	0.0173 969 730	0.0158 734 182	0.0144 835 640	0.0132 156 533	444
38	0.0155 926 139	0.0141 918 800	0.0129 172 294	0.0117 572 905	456
39	0.0139 753 972	0.0126 884 743	0.0115 202 872	0.0104 598 598	468
40	0.0125 259 131	0.0113 443 306	0.0102 744 181	0.0093 056 020	480
41	0.0112 267 649	0.0101 425 778	0.0091 632 844	0.0082 787 179	492
42	0.0100 623 603	0.0090 681 317	0.0081 723 150	0.0073 651 517	504
43	0.0090 187 240	0.0081 075 062	0.0072 885 146	0.0065 523 986	516
44	0.0080 833 305	0.0072 486 439	0.0065 002 934	0.0058 293 337	528
45	0.0072 449 529	0.0064 807 644	0.0057 973 149	0.0051 860 599	540
46	0.0064 935 293	0.0057 942 297	0.0051 703 605	0.0046 137 722	552
47	0.0058 200 409	0.0051 804 225	0.0046 112 084	0.0041 046 370	564
48	0.0052 164 046	0.0046 316 384	0.0041 125 262	0.0036 516 855	576
49	0.0046 753 756	0.0041 409 894	0.0036 677 744	0.0032 487 177	588
50	0.0041 904 604	0.0037 023 169	0.0032 711 205	0.0028 902 179	600

MONTHLY
Compounding

TABLE 4. PRESENT WORTH OF ONE DOLLAR
Payable at end of each period

MONTHS	12% Nominal Annual Rate	12¼% Nominal Annual Rate	12½% Nominal Annual Rate	12¾% Nominal Annual Rate	MONTHS
1	0.9900 990 099	0.9898 948 237	0.9896 907 216	0.9894 867 038	1
2	0.9802 960 494	0.9798 917 619	0.9794 877 245	0.9790 839 369	2
3	0.9705 901 479	0.9699 897 829	0.9693 899 129	0.9687 905 375	3
4	0.9609 803 445	0.9601 878 651	0.9593 962 025	0.9586 053 556	4
5	0.9514 656 876	0.9504 849 974	0.9495 055 200	0.9485 272 535	5
6	0.9420 452 353	0.9408 801 789	0.9397 168 033	0.9385 551 055	6
7	0.9327 180 547	0.9313 724 188	0.9300 290 012	0.9286 877 977	7
8	0.9234 832 225	0.9219 607 363	0.9204 410 733	0.9189 242 277	8
9	0.9143 398 242	0.9126 441 605	0.9109 519 901	0.9092 633 051	9
10	0.9052 869 547	0.9034 217 303	0.9015 607 325	0.8997 039 507	10
11	0.8963 237 175	0.8942 924 945	0.8922 662 919	0.8902 450 965	11
YEARS					
1	0.8874 492 253	0.8852 555 111	0.8830 676 704	0.8808 856 861	12
2	0.7875 661 274	0.7836 773 200	0.7798 085 105	0.7759 595 920	24
3	0.6989 249 496	0.6937 546 664	0.6886 236 847	0.6835 316 975	36
4	0.6202 604 051	0.6141 501 418	0.6081 013 130	0.6021 132 883	48
5	0.5504 496 159	0.5436 797 977	0.5369 946 098	0.5303 929 771	60
6	0.4884 960 852	0.4812 955 372	0.4742 025 791	0.4672 155 815	72
7	0.4335 154 724	0.4260 695 268	0.4187 529 668	0.4115 635 181	84
8	0.3847 229 701	0.3771 803 967	0.3697 872 068	0.3625 404 120	96
9	0.3414 221 017	0.3339 010 249	0.3265 471 273	0.3193 566 596	108
10	0.3029 947 797	0.2955 877 224	0.2883 632 110	0.2813 167 102	120
11	0.2688 924 825	0.2616 706 603	0.2546 442 289	0.2478 078 632	132
12	0.2386 284 253	0.2316 453 941	0.2248 680 860	0.2182 903 996	144
13	0.2117 706 111	0.2050 653 618	0.1985 737 369	0.1922 888 884	156
14	0.1879 356 648	0.1815 352 417	0.1753 540 472	0.1693 845 294	168
15	0.1667 833 601	0.1607 050 731	0.1548 494 900	0.1492 084 074	180
16	0.1480 117 637	0.1422 650 517	0.1367 425 783	0.1314 355 503	192
17	0.1313 529 250	0.1259 409 210	0.1207 529 501	0.1157 796 949	204
18	0.1165 690 516	0.1114 898 944	0.1066 330 263	0.1019 886 760	216
19	0.1034 491 145	0.0986 970 435	0.0941 641 782	0.0898 403 648	228
20	0.0918 058 365	0.0873 721 017	0.0831 533 414	0.0791 390 914	240
21	0.0814 730 185	0.0773 466 345	0.0734 300 275	0.0697 124 928	252
22	0.0723 031 671	0.0684 715 345	0.0648 436 833	0.0614 087 371	264
23	0.0641 653 897	0.0606 148 032	0.0572 613 604	0.0540 940 775	276
24	0.0569 435 253	0.0536 595 886	0.0505 656 561	0.0476 506 986	288
25	0.0505 344 875	0.0475 024 466	0.0446 528 961	0.0419 748 183	300
26	0.0448 467 917	0.0420 518 026	0.0394 315 290	0.0369 750 166	312
27	0.0397 992 506	0.0372 265 900	0.0348 207 084	0.0325 707 629	324
28	0.0353 198 141	0.0329 550 440	0.0307 490 419	0.0286 911 188	336
29	0.0313 445 417	0.0291 736 343	0.0271 534 848	0.0252 735 959	348
30	0.0278 166 892	0.0258 261 205	0.0239 783 645	0.0222 631 488	360
31	0.0246 858 993	0.0228 627 155	0.0211 745 185	0.0196 112 891	372
32	0.0219 074 822	0.0202 393 449	0.0186 985 327	0.0172 753 039	384
33	0.0194 417 781	0.0179 169 916	0.0165 120 697	0.0152 175 679	396
34	0.0172 535 909	0.0158 611 156	0.0145 812 750	0.0134 049 378	408
35	0.0153 116 859	0.0140 411 400	0.0128 762 525	0.0118 082 178	420
36	0.0135 883 438	0.0124 299 966	0.0113 706 023	0.0104 016 900	432
37	0.0120 589 652	0.0110 037 230	0.0100 410 113	0.0091 626 999	444
38	0.0107 017 193	0.0097 411 064	0.0088 668 924	0.0080 712 912	456
39	0.0094 972 325	0.0086 233 681	0.0078 300 661	0.0071 098 848	468
40	0.0084 283 116	0.0076 338 841	0.0069 144 782	0.0062 629 958	480
41	0.0074 796 986	0.0067 579 380	0.0061 059 521	0.0055 169 833	492
42	0.0066 378 527	0.0059 825 019	0.0053 919 689	0.0048 598 317	504
43	0.0058 907 573	0.0052 960 428	0.0047 614 734	0.0042 809 561	516
44	0.0052 277 480	0.0046 883 510	0.0042 047 033	0.0037 710 330	528
45	0.0046 393 609	0.0041 503 886	0.0037 130 375	0.0033 218 490	540
46	0.0041 171 972	0.0036 741 544	0.0032 788 634	0.0029 261 692	552
47	0.0036 538 035	0.0032 525 654	0.0028 954 583	0.0025 776 206	564
48	0.0032 425 651	0.0028 793 515	0.0025 568 856	0.0022 705 891	576
49	0.0028 776 119	0.0025 489 617	0.0022 579 030	0.0020 001 294	588
50	0.0025 537 344	0.0022 564 824	0.0019 938 811	0.0017 618 854	600

TABLE 4. PRESENT WORTH OF ONE DOLLAR
Payable at end of each period

MONTHLY Compounding

MONTHS	13% Nominal Annual Rate	13¼% Nominal Annual Rate	13½% Nominal Annual Rate	13¾% Nominal Annual Rate	MONTHS
1	0.9892 827 700	0.9890 789 203	0.9888 751 545	0.9886 714 727	1
2	0.9786 803 990	0.9782 771 105	0.9778 740 712	0.9774 712 809	2
3	0.9681 916 561	0.9675 932 682	0.9669 953 733	0.9663 979 709	3
4	0.9578 153 234	0.9570 261 049	0.9562 376 991	0.9554 501 051	4
5	0.9475 501 963	0.9465 743 465	0.9455 997 025	0.9446 262 625	5
6	0.9373 950 829	0.9362 367 326	0.9350 800 519	0.9339 250 381	6
7	0.9273 488 042	0.9260 120 166	0.9246 774 308	0.9233 450 428	7
8	0.9174 101 937	0.9158 989 655	0.9143 905 373	0.9128 849 033	8
9	0.9075 780 977	0.9058 963 599	0.9042 180 838	0.9025 432 618	9
10	0.8978 513 744	0.8960 029 935	0.8941 587 974	0.8923 187 758	10
11	0.8882 288 947	0.8862 176 733	0.8842 114 189	0.8822 101 182	11
YEARS					
1	0.8787 095 414	0.8765 392 194	0.8743 747 035	0.8722 159 768	12
2	0.7721 304 581	0.7683 210 032	0.7645 311 221	0.7607 607 101	24
3	0.6784 784 007	0.6734 634 924	0.6684 866 732	0.6635 476 459	36
4	0.5961 854 444	0.5903 171 640	0.5845 078 366	0.5787 568 581	48
5	0.5238 738 384	0.5174 361 461	0.5110 788 663	0.5048 009 783	60
6	0.4603 329 403	0.4535 530 756	0.4468 744 322	0.4402 954 784	72
7	0.4044 989 468	0.3975 570 589	0.3907 356 992	0.3840 327 507	84
8	0.3554 370 841	0.3484 743 541	0.3416 494 111	0.3349 595 008	96
9	0.3123 259 571	0.3054 514 383	0.2987 296 025	0.2921 570 282	108
10	0.2744 437 986	0.2677 401 653	0.2612 016 076	0.2548 240 277	120
11	0.2411 563 844	0.2346 847 555	0.2283 880 782	0.2222 615 882	132
12	0.2119 064 159	0.2057 103 924	0.1996 967 582	0.1938 601 083	144
13	0.1862 041 895	0.1803 132 268	0.1746 097 937	0.1690 878 837	156
14	0.1636 193 980	0.1580 516 151	0.1526 743 866	0.1474 811 536	168
15	0.1437 739 262	0.1385 384 393	0.1334 946 215	0.1286 354 185	180
16	0.1263 355 207	0.1214 343 755	0.1167 243 201	0.1121 978 672	192
17	0.1110 122 275	0.1064 419 927	0.1020 607 928	0.0978 607 723	204
18	0.0975 475 035	0.0933 005 812	0.0892 393 754	0.0853 557 291	216
19	0.0857 159 221	0.0817 816 186	0.0780 286 524	0.0744 486 306	228
20	0.0753 193 986	0.0716 847 961	0.0682 262 798	0.0649 352 851	240
21	0.0661 838 742	0.0628 345 352	0.0596 553 332	0.0566 375 931	252
22	0.0581 564 017	0.0550 769 345	0.0521 611 143	0.0494 002 136	264
23	0.0511 025 851	0.0482 770 932	0.0456 083 588	0.0430 876 556	276
24	0.0449 043 291	0.0423 167 656	0.0398 787 952	0.0375 817 416	288
25	0.0394 578 624	0.0370 923 046	0.0348 690 097	0.0327 793 954	300
26	0.0346 720 002	0.0325 128 598	0.0304 885 801	0.0285 907 124	312
27	0.0304 666 174	0.0284 987 967	0.0266 584 431	0.0249 372 762	324
28	0.0267 713 074	0.0249 803 130	0.0233 094 683	0.0217 506 907	336
29	0.0235 242 032	0.0218 962 241	0.0203 812 095	0.0189 712 999	348
30	0.0206 709 418	0.0191 928 992	0.0178 208 140	0.0165 470 709	360
31	0.0181 637 538	0.0168 233 289	0.0155 820 689	0.0144 326 196	372
32	0.0159 606 638	0.0147 463 075	0.0136 245 669	0.0125 883 614	384
33	0.0140 247 876	0.0129 257 169	0.0119 129 766	0.0109 797 699	396
34	0.0123 237 146	0.0113 298 978	0.0104 164 054	0.0095 767 308	408
35	0.0108 289 656	0.0099 310 998	0.0091 078 414	0.0083 529 776	420
36	0.0095 155 154	0.0087 049 984	0.0079 636 661	0.0072 856 005	432
37	0.0083 613 742	0.0076 302 725	0.0069 632 282	0.0063 546 171	444
38	0.0073 472 193	0.0066 882 331	0.0060 884 706	0.0055 425 986	456
39	0.0064 560 717	0.0058 624 987	0.0053 236 047	0.0048 343 431	468
40	0.0056 730 118	0.0051 387 100	0.0046 548 253	0.0042 165 912	480
41	0.0049 849 296	0.0045 042 808	0.0040 700 615	0.0036 777 783	492
42	0.0043 803 052	0.0039 481 788	0.0035 587 588	0.0032 078 170	504
43	0.0038 490 160	0.0034 607 336	0.0031 116 887	0.0027 979 092	516
44	0.0033 821 671	0.0030 334 687	0.0027 207 818	0.0024 403 811	528
45	0.0029 719 425	0.0026 589 543	0.0023 789 828	0.0021 285 394	540
46	0.0026 114 742	0.0023 306 777	0.0020 801 224	0.0018 565 461	552
47	0.0022 947 273	0.0020 429 304	0.0018 188 064	0.0016 193 091	564
48	0.0020 163 988	0.0017 907 086	0.0015 903 183	0.0014 123 873	576
49	0.0017 718 288	0.0015 696 264	0.0013 905 341	0.0012 319 068	588
50	0.0015 569 229	0.0013 758 391	0.0012 158 478	0.0010 744 888	600

MONTHLY
Compounding

TABLE 4. PRESENT WORTH OF ONE DOLLAR
Payable at end of each period

MONTHS	14% Nominal Annual Rate	14¼% Nominal Annual Rate	14½% Nominal Annual Rate	14¾% Nominal Annual Rate	MONTHS
1	0.9884 678 748	0.9882 643 607	0.9880 609 304	0.9878 575 839	1
2	0.9770 687 395	0.9766 664 467	0.9762 644 022	0.9758 626 060	2
3	0.9658 010 605	0.9652 046 415	0.9646 087 136	0.9640 132 761	3
4	0.9546 633 217	0.9538 773 480	0.9530 921 831	0.9523 078 258	4
5	0.9436 540 248	0.9426 829 876	0.9417 131 492	0.9407 445 079	5
6	0.9327 716 884	0.9316 200 001	0.9304 699 704	0.9293 215 966	6
7	0.9220 148 485	0.9206 868 438	0.9193 610 247	0.9180 373 870	7
8	0.9113 820 578	0.9098 819 951	0.9083 847 094	0.9068 901 951	8
9	0.9008 718 858	0.8992 039 482	0.8975 394 412	0.8958 783 569	9
10	0.8904 829 184	0.8886 512 150	0.8868 236 553	0.8850 002 291	10
11	0.8802 137 579	0.8782 223 249	0.8762 358 060	0.8742 541 880	11
YEARS					
1	0.8700 630 227	0.8679 158 245	0.8657 743 658	0.8636 386 299	12
2	0.7570 096 634	0.7532 778 784	0.7495 652 524	0.7458 716 830	24
3	0.6586 461 159	0.6537 817 909	0.6489 543 810	0.6441 635 984	36
4	0.5730 636 305	0.5674 275 621	0.5618 480 676	0.5563 245 675	48
5	0.4986 014 745	0.4924 793 604	0.4864 336 544	0.4804 633 873	60
6	0.4338 147 060	0.4274 306 302	0.4211 417 886	0.4149 467 415	72
7	0.3774 461 344	0.3709 738 078	0.3646 137 649	0.3583 640 353	84
8	0.3284 019 246	0.3219 740 383	0.3156 732 511	0.3094 970 245	96
9	0.2857 303 711	0.2794 463 629	0.2733 018 087	0.2672 935 862	108
10	0.2486 034 304	0.2425 359 205	0.2366 177 001	0.2308 450 665	120
11	0.2163 006 521	0.2105 007 634	0.2048 575 392	0.1993 667 170	132
12	0.1881 951 992	0.1826 969 436	0.1773 604 061	0.1721 807 983	144
13	0.1637 416 838	0.1585 655 684	0.1535 540 931	0.1487 019 887	156
14	0.1424 655 844	0.1376 215 661	0.1329 431 976	0.1284 247 818	168
15	0.1239 540 370	0.1194 439 350	0.1150 988 126	0.1109 126 026	180
16	0.1078 478 241	0.1036 672 813	0.0996 496 014	0.0957 884 081	192
17	0.0938 344 038	0.0899 744 739	0.0862 740 705	0.0827 265 696	204
18	0.0816 418 450	0.0780 902 697	0.0746 938 787	0.0714 458 612	216
19	0.0710 335 504	0.0677 757 808	0.0646 680 454	0.0617 034 057	228
20	0.0618 036 656	0.0588 236 727	0.0559 879 360	0.0532 894 447	240
21	0.0537 730 841	0.0510 539 964	0.0484 729 198	0.0460 228 230	252
22	0.0467 859 721	0.0443 105 714	0.0419 666 114	0.0397 470 878	264
23	0.0407 067 443	0.0384 578 461	0.0363 336 164	0.0343 271 205	276
24	0.0354 174 330	0.0333 781 732	0.0314 567 137	0.0296 462 273	288
25	0.0308 153 988	0.0289 694 447	0.0272 344 163	0.0256 036 271	300
26	0.0268 113 390	0.0251 430 395	0.0235 788 595	0.0221 122 814	312
27	0.0233 275 547	0.0218 220 419	0.0204 139 721	0.0190 970 205	324
28	0.0202 964 427	0.0189 396 954	0.0176 738 938	0.0164 929 246	336
29	0.0176 591 843	0.0164 380 614	0.0153 016 042	0.0142 439 268	348
30	0.0153 646 033	0.0142 668 536	0.0132 477 367	0.0123 016 054	360
31	0.0133 681 732	0.0123 824 280	0.0114 695 508	0.0106 241 416	372
32	0.0116 311 532	0.0107 469 052	0.0099 300 431	0.0091 754 191	384
33	0.0101 198 363	0.0093 274 091	0.0085 971 767	0.0079 242 464	396
34	0.0088 048 953	0.0080 954 060	0.0074 432 152	0.0068 436 853	408
35	0.0076 608 138	0.0070 261 309	0.0064 441 450	0.0059 104 710	420
36	0.0066 653 909	0.0060 980 902	0.0055 791 755	0.0051 045 111	432
37	0.0057 993 101	0.0052 926 290	0.0048 303 071	0.0044 084 530	444
38	0.0050 457 653	0.0045 935 565	0.0041 819 561	0.0038 073 103	456
39	0.0043 901 338	0.0039 868 204	0.0036 206 304	0.0032 881 402	468
40	0.0038 196 931	0.0034 602 245	0.0031 346 490	0.0028 397 649	480
41	0.0033 233 737	0.0030 031 836	0.0027 138 987	0.0024 525 307	492
42	0.0028 915 446	0.0026 065 105	0.0023 496 240	0.0021 181 002	504
43	0.0025 158 260	0.0022 622 318	0.0020 342 442	0.0018 292 732	516
44	0.0021 889 272	0.0019 634 267	0.0017 611 965	0.0015 798 310	528
45	0.0019 045 046	0.0017 040 891	0.0015 247 988	0.0013 644 031	540
46	0.0016 570 390	0.0014 790 059	0.0013 201 317	0.0011 783 512	552
47	0.0014 417 284	0.0012 836 526	0.0011 429 362	0.0010 176 696	564
48	0.0012 543 946	0.0011 141 024	0.0009 895 248	0.0008 788 988	576
49	0.0010 914 023	0.0009 669 471	0.0008 567 052	0.0007 590 509	588
50	0.0009 495 888	0.0008 392 287	0.0007 417 134	0.0006 555 457	600

TABLE 4. PRESENT WORTH OF ONE DOLLAR
Payable at end of each period

MONTHLY Compounding

MONTHS	15% Nominal Annual Rate	15¼% Nominal Annual Rate	15½% Nominal Annual Rate	15¾% Nominal Annual Rate	MONTHS
1	0.9876 543 210	0.9874 511 417	0.9872 480 461	0.9870 450 339	1
2	0.9754 610 578	0.9750 597 573	0.9746 587 045	0.9742 578 990	2
3	0.9634 183 287	0.9628 238 706	0.9622 299 016	0.9616 364 210	3
4	0.9515 242 752	0.9507 415 304	0.9499 595 902	0.9491 784 538	4
5	0.9397 770 619	0.9388 108 096	0.9378 457 493	0.9368 818 791	5
6	0.9281 748 760	0.9270 298 059	0.9258 863 835	0.9247 446 062	6
7	0.9167 159 269	0.9153 966 402	0.9140 795 230	0.9127 645 712	7
8	0.9053 984 463	0.9039 094 575	0.9024 232 230	0.9009 397 371	8
9	0.8942 206 877	0.8925 664 259	0.8909 155 637	0.8892 680 934	9
10	0.8831 809 262	0.8813 657 363	0.8795 546 494	0.8777 476 554	10
11	0.8722 774 579	0.8703 056 026	0.8683 386 091	0.8663 764 643	11
YEARS					
1	0.8615 086 004	0.8593 842 610	0.8572 655 951	0.8551 525 866	12
2	0.7421 970 686	0.7385 413 080	0.7349 043 006	0.7312 859 464	24
3	0.6394 091 578	0.6346 907 762	0.6300 081 726	0.6253 610 686	36
4	0.5508 564 886	0.5454 432 636	0.5400 843 310	0.5347 791 354	48
5	0.4745 676 026	0.4687 453 560	0.4629 957 155	0.4573 177 609	60
6	0.4088 440 711	0.4028 323 813	0.3969 102 976	0.3910 764 661	72
7	0.3522 226 835	0.3461 878 083	0.3402 575 424	0.3344 300 516	84
8	0.3034 428 711	0.2975 083 538	0.2916 910 846	0.2859 887 236	96
9	0.2614 186 432	0.2556 739 968	0.2500 567 313	0.2445 639 968	108
10	0.2252 144 094	0.2197 222 088	0.2143 650 325	0.2091 395 344	120
11	0.1940 241 506	0.1888 258 080	0.1837 677 672	0.1788 462 138	132
12	0.1671 534 745	0.1622 739 275	0.1575 377 843	0.1529 408 024	144
13	0.1440 041 558	0.1394 556 592	0.1350 517 224	0.1307 877 227	156
14	0.1240 608 188	0.1198 459 986	0.1157 751 952	0.1118 434 594	168
15	0.1068 794 623	0.1029 937 650	0.0992 500 916	0.0956 432 236	180
16	0.0920 775 760	0.0885 112 206	0.0850 836 888	0.0817 895 501	192
17	0.0793 256 236	0.0760 651 499	0.0729 393 192	0.0699 425 453	204
18	0.0683 397 070	0.0653 691 926	0.0625 283 688	0.0598 115 485	216
19	0.0588 752 453	0.0561 772 553	0.0536 034 193	0.0511 480 004	228
20	0.0507 215 302	0.0482 778 490	0.0459 523 672	0.0437 393 449	240
21	0.0436 970 345	0.0414 892 236	0.0393 933 834	0.0374 038 139	252
22	0.0376 453 710	0.0356 551 858	0.0337 705 923	0.0319 859 682	264
23	0.0324 318 109	0.0306 415 055	0.0289 503 669	0.0273 528 834	276
24	0.0279 402 840	0.0263 328 275	0.0248 181 535	0.0233 908 890	288
25	0.0240 707 950	0.0226 300 175	0.0212 757 491	0.0200 027 793	300
26	0.0207 371 969	0.0194 478 809	0.0182 389 677	0.0171 054 284	312
27	0.0178 652 735	0.0167 132 027	0.0156 356 395	0.0146 277 514	324
28	0.0153 910 868	0.0143 630 634	0.0134 038 958	0.0125 089 594	336
29	0.0132 595 536	0.0123 433 906	0.0114 906 987	0.0106 970 690	348
30	0.0114 232 195	0.0106 077 156	0.0098 505 807	0.0091 476 262	360
31	0.0098 412 018	0.0091 161 039	0.0084 445 639	0.0078 226 162	372
32	0.0084 782 800	0.0078 342 362	0.0072 392 341	0.0066 895 305	384
33	0.0073 041 111	0.0067 326 193	0.0062 059 463	0.0057 205 693	396
34	0.0062 925 546	0.0057 859 070	0.0053 201 443	0.0048 919 596	408
35	0.0054 210 899	0.0049 723 174	0.0045 607 767	0.0041 833 719	420
36	0.0046 703 156	0.0042 731 313	0.0039 097 969	0.0035 774 213	432
37	0.0040 235 170	0.0036 722 618	0.0033 517 344	0.0030 592 411	444
38	0.0034 662 945	0.0031 558 840	0.0028 733 266	0.0026 161 179	456
39	0.0029 862 425	0.0027 121 170	0.0024 632 040	0.0022 371 800	468
40	0.0025 726 736	0.0023 307 507	0.0021 116 200	0.0019 131 303	480
41	0.0022 163 805	0.0020 030 105	0.0018 102 192	0.0016 360 183	492
42	0.0019 094 308	0.0017 213 557	0.0015 518 387	0.0013 990 453	504
43	0.0016 449 911	0.0014 793 060	0.0013 303 379	0.0011 963 972	516
44	0.0014 171 740	0.0012 712 923	0.0011 404 529	0.0010 231 022	528
45	0.0012 209 076	0.0010 925 286	0.0009 776 710	0.0008 749 085	540
46	0.0010 518 224	0.0009 389 019	0.0008 381 237	0.0007 481 802	552
47	0.0009 061 540	0.0008 068 775	0.0007 184 946	0.0006 398 083	564
48	0.0007 806 595	0.0006 934 178	0.0006 159 407	0.0005 471 337	576
49	0.0006 725 448	0.0005 959 123	0.0005 280 248	0.0004 678 828	588
50	0.0005 794 032	0.0005 121 177	0.0004 526 575	0.0004 001 112	600

MONTHLY
Compounding

TABLE 4. PRESENT WORTH OF ONE DOLLAR
Payable at end of each period

MONTHS	16% Nominal Annual Rate	16¼% Nominal Annual Rate	16½% Nominal Annual Rate	16¾% Nominal Annual Rate	MONTHS
1	0.9868 421 053	0.9866 392 600	0.9864 364 982	0.9862 338 196	1
2	0.9738 573 407	0.9734 570 294	0.9730 569 649	0.9726 571 469	2
3	0.9610 434 283	0.9604 509 232	0.9598 589 049	0.9592 673 732	3
4	0.9483 981 201	0.9476 185 881	0.9468 398 569	0.9460 619 255	4
5	0.9359 191 974	0.9349 577 026	0.9339 973 928	0.9330 382 663	5
6	0.9236 044 712	0.9224 659 758	0.9213 291 174	0.9201 938 932	6
7	0.9114 517 807	0.9101 411 478	0.9088 326 682	0.9075 263 381	7
8	0.8994 589 942	0.8979 809 885	0.8965 057 146	0.8950 331 668	8
9	0.8876 240 074	0.8859 832 980	0.8843 459 577	0.8827 119 788	9
10	0.8759 447 441	0.8741 459 056	0.8723 511 297	0.8705 604 064	10
11	0.8644 191 554	0.8624 666 694	0.8605 189 935	0.8585 761 148	11
YEARS					
1	0.8530 452 191	0.8509 434 765	0.8488 473 426	0.8467 568 012	12
2	0.7276 861 459	0.7241 048 002	0.7205 418 110	0.7169 970 803	24
3	0.6207 491 878	0.6161 722 561	0.6116 300 014	0.6071 221 541	36
4	0.5295 271 269	0.5243 277 617	0.5191 805 013	0.5140 848 132	48
5	0.4517 105 841	0.4461 732 884	0.4407 049 889	0.4353 048 119	60
6	0.3853 295 542	0.3796 682 491	0.3740 912 587	0.3685 973 101	72
7	0.3287 035 340	0.3230 762 199	0.3175 463 708	0.3121 122 792	84
8	0.2803 989 782	0.2749 196 017	0.2695 483 930	0.2642 831 951	96
9	0.2391 930 078	0.2339 410 416	0.2288 054 371	0.2237 835 929	108
10	0.2040 424 517	0.1990 706 033	0.1942 208 872	0.1894 902 793	120
11	0.1740 574 380	0.1693 978 312	0.1648 638 840	0.1604 521 827	132
12	0.1484 788 653	0.1441 479 794	0.1399 442 698	0.1358 639 770	144
13	0.1266 591 862	0.1226 617 827	0.1187 913 215	0.1150 437 465	156
14	0.1080 460 132	0.1043 782 438	0.1008 356 976	0.0974 140 748	168
15	0.0921 681 350	0.0888 199 857	0.0855 941 139	0.0824 860 304	180
16	0.0786 235 870	0.0755 807 874	0.0726 563 362	0.0698 456 072	192
17	0.0670 694 750	0.0643 149 780	0.0616 741 379	0.0591 422 429	204
18	0.0572 132 950	0.0547 284 110	0.0523 519 280	0.0500 790 964	216
19	0.0488 055 277	0.0465 707 843	0.0444 387 950	0.0424 048 155	228
20	0.0416 333 221	0.0396 291 051	0.0377 217 530	0.0359 065 659	240
21	0.0355 151 064	0.0337 221 285	0.0320 200 098	0.0304 041 289	252
22	0.0302 959 917	0.0286 956 252	0.0271 801 002	0.0257 449 029	264
23	0.0258 438 509	0.0244 183 551	0.0230 717 559	0.0217 996 717	276
24	0.0220 459 734	0.0207 786 400	0.0195 843 987	0.0184 590 202	288
25	0.0188 062 122	0.0176 814 481	0.0166 241 648	0.0156 303 009	300
26	0.0160 425 494	0.0150 459 129	0.0141 113 781	0.0132 350 636	312
27	0.0136 850 201	0.0128 032 215	0.0119 784 058	0.0112 068 801	324
28	0.0116 739 410	0.0108 948 178	0.0101 678 379	0.0094 895 020	336
29	0.0099 583 995	0.0092 708 741	0.0086 309 422	0.0080 353 003	348
30	0.0084 949 651	0.0078 889 899	0.0073 263 523	0.0068 039 452	360
31	0.0072 465 894	0.0067 130 845	0.0062 189 547	0.0057 612 869	372
32	0.0061 816 684	0.0057 124 554	0.0052 789 432	0.0048 784 088	384
33	0.0052 732 427	0.0048 609 767	0.0044 810 169	0.0041 308 259	396
34	0.0044 983 145	0.0041 364 164	0.0038 036 993	0.0034 978 049	408
35	0.0038 372 657	0.0035 198 565	0.0032 287 600	0.0029 617 901	420
36	0.0032 733 611	0.0029 951 990	0.0027 407 244	0.0025 079 159	432
37	0.0027 923 251	0.0025 487 450	0.0023 264 566	0.0021 235 948	444
38	0.0023 819 795	0.0021 688 379	0.0019 748 065	0.0017 981 684	456
39	0.0020 319 363	0.0018 455 585	0.0016 763 092	0.0015 226 113	468
40	0.0017 333 335	0.0015 704 660	0.0014 229 307	0.0012 892 815	480
41	0.0014 786 119	0.0013 363 778	0.0012 078 509	0.0010 917 079	492
42	0.0012 613 228	0.0011 371 819	0.0010 252 810	0.0009 244 111	504
43	0.0010 759 654	0.0009 676 776	0.0008 703 071	0.0007 827 513	516
44	0.0009 178 471	0.0008 234 389	0.0007 387 578	0.0006 628 000	528
45	0.0007 829 651	0.0007 007 000	0.0006 270 926	0.0005 612 304	540
46	0.0006 679 046	0.0005 962 561	0.0005 323 059	0.0004 752 257	552
47	0.0005 697 529	0.0005 073 802	0.0004 518 465	0.0004 024 006	564
48	0.0004 860 249	0.0004 317 519	0.0003 835 487	0.0003 407 354	576
49	0.0004 146 013	0.0003 673 964	0.0003 255 743	0.0002 885 200	588
50	0.0003 536 736	0.0003 126 336	0.0002 763 629	0.0002 443 063	600

TABLE 4. PRESENT WORTH OF ONE DOLLAR
Payable at end of each period

MONTHLY Compounding

MONTHS	17% Nominal Annual Rate	17¼% Nominal Annual Rate	17½% Nominal Annual Rate	17¾% Nominal Annual Rate	MONTHS
1	0.9860 312 243	0.9858 287 123	0.9856 262 834	0.9854 239 376	1
2	0.9722 575 753	0.9718 582 499	0.9714 591 705	0.9710 603 368	2
3	0.9586 763 274	0.9580 857 670	0.9574 956 916	0.9569 061 007	3
4	0.9452 847 928	0.9445 084 579	0.9437 329 199	0.9429 581 777	4
5	0.9320 803 216	0.9311 235 568	0.9301 679 703	0.9292 135 604	5
6	0.9190 603 007	0.9179 283 370	0.9167 979 995	0.9156 692 856	6
7	0.9062 221 535	0.9049 201 104	0.9036 202 048	0.9023 224 329	7
8	0.8935 633 395	0.8920 962 271	0.8906 318 241	0.8891 701 248	8
9	0.8810 813 537	0.8794 540 748	0.8778 301 346	0.8762 095 256	9
10	0.8687 737 259	0.8669 910 780	0.8652 124 530	0.8634 378 408	10
11	0.8566 380 206	0.8547 046 980	0.8527 761 344	0.8508 523 170	11
YEARS					
1	0.8446 718 362	0.8425 924 318	0.8405 185 719	0.8384 502 405	12
2	0.7134 705 109	0.7099 620 061	0.7064 714 696	0.7029 988 058	24
3	0.6026 484 466	0.5982 086 132	0.5938 023 907	0.5894 295 178	36
4	0.5090 401 700	0.5040 460 501	0.4991 019 374	0.4942 073 210	48
5	0.4299 718 951	0.4247 053 871	0.4195 044 477	0.4143 682 472	60
6	0.3631 851 502	0.3578 535 449	0.3526 012 792	0.3474 271 565	72
7	0.3067 722 677	0.3015 246 887	0.2963 679 237	0.2913 003 829	84
8	0.2591 218 946	0.2540 624 207	0.2491 027 439	0.2442 408 761	96
9	0.2188 729 666	0.2140 710 729	0.2093 754 826	0.2047 838 213	108
10	0.1848 758 306	0.1803 746 659	0.1759 839 816	0.1717 010 443	120
11	0.1561 594 073	0.1519 823 283	0.1479 178 049	0.1439 627 818	132
12	0.1319 034 533	0.1280 591 596	0.1243 276 621	0.1207 056 291	144
13	0.1114 151 321	0.1079 016 787	0.1044 997 090	0.1012 056 637	156
14	0.0941 092 242	0.0909 171 379	0.0878 339 462	0.0848 559 131	168
15	0.0794 914 112	0.0766 060 923	0.0738 260 630	0.0711 474 607	180
16	0.0671 441 563	0.0645 477 136	0.0620 521 770	0.0596 536 056	192
17	0.0567 147 778	0.0543 874 150	0.0521 560 072	0.0500 165 799	204
18	0.0479 053 755	0.0458 264 242	0.0438 380 927	0.0419 364 135	216
19	0.0404 643 215	0.0386 129 982	0.0368 467 311	0.0351 615 960	228
20	0.0341 790 727	0.0325 350 201	0.0309 703 618	0.0294 812 486	240
21	0.0288 701 001	0.0274 137 617	0.0260 311 643	0.0247 185 600	252
22	0.0243 857 605	0.0230 986 281	0.0218 796 770	0.0207 252 826	264
23	0.0205 979 651	0.0194 627 292	0.0183 902 749	0.0173 771 181	276
24	0.0173 985 210	0.0163 991 484	0.0154 573 676	0.0145 698 489	288
25	0.0146 960 407	0.0138 177 983	0.0129 922 045	0.0122 160 933	300
26	0.0124 133 317	0.0116 427 723	0.0109 201 892	0.0102 425 864	312
27	0.0104 851 916	0.0098 101 118	0.0091 786 218	0.0085 878 990	324
28	0.0088 565 461	0.0082 659 260	0.0077 148 021	0.0072 005 260	336
29	0.0074 808 750	0.0069 648 067	0.0064 844 344	0.0060 372 827	348
30	0.0063 188 845	0.0058 684 934	0.0054 502 876	0.0050 619 612	360
31	0.0053 373 837	0.0049 447 481	0.0045 810 679	0.0042 442 026	372
32	0.0045 083 377	0.0041 664 073	0.0038 504 727	0.0035 585 527	384
33	0.0038 080 659	0.0035 105 833	0.0032 363 938	0.0029 836 693	396
34	0.0032 165 660	0.0029 579 909	0.0027 202 491	0.0025 016 583	408
35	0.0027 169 427	0.0024 923 808	0.0022 864 199	0.0020 975 160	420
36	0.0022 949 250	0.0021 000 612	0.0019 217 784	0.0017 586 628	432
37	0.0019 384 585	0.0017 694 956	0.0016 152 904	0.0014 745 512	444
38	0.0016 373 613	0.0014 909 636	0.0013 576 816	0.0012 363 378	456
39	0.0013 830 330	0.0012 562 747	0.0011 411 566	0.0010 366 078	468
40	0.0011 682 090	0.0010 585 275	0.0009 591 633	0.0008 691 440	480
41	0.0009 867 533	0.0008 919 073	0.0008 061 946	0.0007 287 340	492
42	0.0008 334 827	0.0007 515 143	0.0006 776 215	0.0006 110 072	504
43	0.0007 040 193	0.0006 332 203	0.0005 695 535	0.0005 122 991	516
44	0.0005 946 653	0.0005 335 466	0.0004 787 203	0.0004 295 373	528
45	0.0005 022 970	0.0004 495 623	0.0004 023 733	0.0003 601 457	540
46	0.0004 242 762	0.0003 787 978	0.0003 382 022	0.0003 019 642	552
47	0.0003 583 741	0.0003 191 722	0.0002 842 652	0.0002 531 820	564
48	0.0003 027 085	0.0002 689 321	0.0002 389 302	0.0002 122 805	576
49	0.0002 556 894	0.0002 266 001	0.0002 008 253	0.0001 779 866	588
50	0.0002 159 736	0.0001 909 315	0.0001 687 974	0.0001 492 329	600

MONTHLY
Compounding

TABLE 4. PRESENT WORTH OF ONE DOLLAR
Payable at end of each period

MONTHS	18% Nominal Annual Rate	18¼% Nominal Annual Rate	18½% Nominal Annual Rate	18¾% Nominal Annual Rate	MONTHS
1	0.9852 216 749	0.9850 194 952	0.9848 173 984	0.9846 153 846	1
2	0.9706 617 486	0.9702 634 059	0.9698 653 083	0.9694 674 556	2
3	0.9563 169 937	0.9557 283 702	0.9551 402 297	0.9545 525 717	3
4	0.9421 842 303	0.9414 110 768	0.9406 387 162	0.9398 671 475	4
5	0.9282 603 254	0.9273 082 636	0.9263 573 733	0.9254 076 529	5
6	0.9145 421 925	0.9134 167 177	0.9122 928 584	0.9111 706 121	6
7	0.9010 267 907	0.8997 332 742	0.8984 418 795	0.8971 526 027	7
8	0.8877 111 238	0.8862 548 155	0.8848 011 944	0.8833 502 550	8
9	0.8745 922 402	0.8729 782 710	0.8713 676 104	0.8697 602 510	9
10	0.8616 672 317	0.8599 006 158	0.8581 379 832	0.8563 793 241	10
11	0.8489 332 332	0.8470 188 704	0.8451 092 161	0.8432 042 576	11
YEARS					
1	0.8363 874 219	0.8343 301 002	0.8322 782 596	0.8302 318 844	12
2	0.6995 439 195	0.6961 067 161	0.6926 871 014	0.6892 849 819	24
3	0.5850 897 353	0.5807 827 861	0.5765 084 152	0.5722 663 694	36
4	0.4893 616 953	0.4845 645 601	0.4798 154 204	0.4751 137 862	48
5	0.4092 959 667	0.4042 867 980	0.3993 399 430	0.3944 546 140	60
6	0.3423 299 984	0.3373 086 447	0.3323 619 527	0.3274 887 975	72
7	0.2863 205 048	0.2814 267 553	0.2766 176 276	0.2718 916 415	84
8	0.2394 748 688	0.2348 028 129	0.2302 228 376	0.2257 331 098	96
9	0.2002 937 682	0.1959 030 544	0.1916 094 626	0.1874 108 252	108
10	0.1675 231 884	0.1634 478 150	0.1594 723 901	0.1555 944 425	120
11	0.1401 142 876	0.1363 694 319	0.1327 254 033	0.1291 794 672	132
12	0.1171 898 278	0.1137 771 218	0.1104 644 676	0.1072 489 125	144
13	0.0980 160 979	0.0949 276 774	0.0919 371 749	0.0890 414 667	156
14	0.0819 794 315	0.0792 010 186	0.0765 173 119	0.0739 250 647	168
15	0.0685 665 653	0.0660 797 938	0.0636 836 952	0.0613 749 458	180
16	0.0573 482 128	0.0551 323 610	0.0530 025 550	0.0509 554 369	192
17	0.0479 653 239	0.0459 985 882	0.0441 128 742	0.0423 048 284	204
18	0.0401 175 936	0.0383 780 067	0.0367 141 862	0.0351 228 174	216
19	0.0335 538 507	0.0320 199 262	0.0305 564 190	0.0291 600 829	228
20	0.0280 640 186	0.0267 151 882	0.0254 314 432	0.0242 096 305	240
21	0.0234 723 922	0.0222 892 857	0.0211 660 373	0.0200 996 072	252
22	0.0196 320 136	0.0185 966 220	0.0176 160 327	0.0166 873 347	264
23	0.0164 199 692	0.0155 157 215	0.0146 614 410	0.0138 543 574	276
24	0.0137 334 557	0.0129 452 334	0.0122 023 986	0.0115 023 292	288
25	0.0114 864 896	0.0108 005 979	0.0101 557 911	0.0095 496 005	300
26	0.0096 071 555	0.0090 112 639	0.0084 524 441	0.0079 283 828	312
27	0.0080 353 040	0.0075 183 687	0.0070 347 855	0.0065 823 962	324
28	0.0067 206 272	0.0062 728 013	0.0058 548 990	0.0054 649 152	336
29	0.0056 210 480	0.0052 335 870	0.0048 729 052	0.0045 371 468	348
30	0.0047 013 739	0.0043 665 391	0.0040 556 130	0.0037 668 840	360
31	0.0039 321 700	0.0036 431 350	0.0033 753 986	0.0031 273 872	372
32	0.0032 888 175	0.0030 395 772	0.0028 092 708	0.0025 964 565	384
33	0.0027 507 256	0.0025 360 108	0.0023 380 950	0.0021 556 610	396
34	0.0023 006 723	0.0021 158 701	0.0019 459 457	0.0017 896 985	408
35	0.0019 242 534	0.0017 653 341	0.0016 195 683	0.0014 858 648	420
36	0.0016 094 213	0.0014 728 714	0.0013 479 315	0.0012 336 123	432
37	0.0013 460 997	0.0012 288 609	0.0011 218 541	0.0010 241 843	444
38	0.0011 258 609	0.0010 252 757	0.0009 336 947	0.0008 503 104	456
39	0.0009 416 559	0.0008 554 184	0.0007 770 938	0.0007 059 548	468
40	0.0007 875 891	0.0007 137 013	0.0006 467 583	0.0005 861 062	480
41	0.0006 587 297	0.0005 954 625	0.0005 382 829	0.0004 866 041	492
42	0.0005 509 532	0.0004 968 123	0.0004 480 011	0.0004 039 942	504
43	0.0004 608 103	0.0004 145 054	0.0003 728 616	0.0003 354 089	516
44	0.0003 854 160	0.0003 458 343	0.0003 103 246	0.0002 784 671	528
45	0.0003 223 571	0.0002 885 400	0.0002 582 764	0.0002 311 923	540
46	0.0002 696 154	0.0002 407 376	0.0002 149 579	0.0001 919 432	552
47	0.0002 255 029	0.0002 008 546	0.0001 789 047	0.0001 593 574	564
48	0.0001 886 078	0.0001 675 791	0.0001 488 985	0.0001 323 036	576
49	0.0001 577 492	0.0001 398 163	0.0001 239 250	0.0001 098 426	588
50	0.0001 319 394	0.0001 166 529	0.0001 031 401	0.0000 911 949	600

TABLE 4. PRESENT WORTH OF ONE DOLLAR
Payable at end of each period

MONTHLY Compounding

MONTHS	19% Nominal Annual Rate	19¼% Nominal Annual Rate	19½% Nominal Annual Rate	19¾% Nominal Annual Rate	MONTHS
1	0.9844 134 537	0.9842 116 055	0.9840 098 401	0.9838 081 574	1
2	0.9690 698 477	0.9686 724 844	0.9682 753 654	0.9678 784 906	2
3	0.9539 653 956	0.9533 787 011	0.9527 924 875	0.9522 067 544	3
4	0.9390 963 698	0.9383 263 820	0.9375 571 833	0.9367 887 725	4
5	0.9244 591 007	0.9235 117 149	0.9225 654 940	0.9216 204 362	5
6	0.9100 499 761	0.9089 309 476	0.9078 135 242	0.9066 977 032	6
7	0.8958 654 399	0.8945 803 873	0.8932 974 408	0.8920 165 967	7
8	0.8819 019 917	0.8804 563 992	0.8790 134 719	0.8775 732 044	8
9	0.8681 561 855	0.8665 554 062	0.8649 579 059	0.8633 636 772	9
10	0.8546 246 288	0.8528 738 876	0.8511 270 907	0.8493 842 284	10
11	0.8413 039 824	0.8394 083 782	0.8375 174 324	0.8356 311 327	11
YEARS					
1	0.8281 909 589	0.8261 554 676	0.8241 253 947	0.8221 007 249	12
2	0.6859 002 645	0.6825 328 566	0.6791 826 663	0.6758 496 019	24
3	0.5680 563 977	0.5638 782 513	0.5597 316 829	0.5556 164 477	36
4	0.4704 591 728	0.4658 511 003	0.4612 890 942	0.4567 726 844	48
5	0.3896 300 334	0.3848 654 336	0.3801 600 568	0.3755 131 550	60
6	0.3226 880 710	0.3179 586 823	0.3132 995 569	0.3087 096 369	72
7	0.2672 473 430	0.2626 833 038	0.2581 981 210	0.2537 904 163	84
8	0.2213 318 332	0.2170 172 477	0.2127 876 284	0.2086 412 852	96
9	0.1833 050 232	0.1792 899 857	0.1753 636 882	0.1715 241 518	108
10	0.1518 115 630	0.1481 214 020	0.1445 216 688	0.1410 101 296	120
11	0.1257 289 639	0.1223 713 061	0.1191 039 773	0.1159 245 297	132
12	0.1041 275 912	0.1010 977 236	0.0981 566 123	0.0953 016 399	144
13	0.0862 375 296	0.0835 224 371	0.0808 933 569	0.0783 475 473	156
14	0.0714 211 423	0.0690 025 181	0.0666 662 697	0.0644 095 754	168
15	0.0591 503 444	0.0570 068 076	0.0549 413 658	0.0529 511 586	180
16	0.0489 877 804	0.0470 964 858	0.0452 785 748	0.0435 311 859	192
17	0.0405 712 368	0.0389 090 192	0.0373 152 233	0.0357 870 195	204
18	0.0336 007 315	0.0321 448 990	0.0307 524 232	0.0294 205 347	216
19	0.0278 278 221	0.0265 566 841	0.0253 438 529	0.0241 866 429	228
20	0.0230 467 506	0.0219 399 497	0.0208 865 128	0.0198 838 566	240
21	0.0190 871 105	0.0181 258 094	0.0172 131 056	0.0163 465 330	252
22	0.0158 077 724	0.0149 747 366	0.0141 857 574	0.0134 384 966	264
23	0.0130 918 542	0.0123 714 605	0.0116 908 429	0.0110 477 978	276
24	0.0108 425 552	0.0102 207 497	0.0096 347 205	0.0090 824 026	288
25	0.0089 797 062	0.0084 439 283	0.0079 402 179	0.0074 666 497	300
26	0.0074 369 115	0.0069 759 975	0.0065 437 352	0.0061 383 382	312
27	0.0061 591 829	0.0057 632 585	0.0053 928 583	0.0050 463 323	324
28	0.0051 009 796	0.0047 613 475	0.0044 443 915	0.0041 485 934	336
29	0.0042 245 852	0.0039 336 133	0.0036 627 359	0.0034 105 616	348
30	0.0034 987 632	0.0032 497 761	0.0030 185 537	0.0028 038 252	360
31	0.0028 976 441	0.0026 848 203	0.0024 876 667	0.0023 050 267	372
32	0.0023 998 026	0.0022 180 790	0.0020 501 493	0.0018 949 641	384
33	0.0019 874 948	0.0018 324 781	0.0016 895 801	0.0015 578 514	396
34	0.0016 460 253	0.0015 139 118	0.0013 924 259	0.0012 807 108	408
35	0.0013 632 232	0.0012 507 265	0.0011 475 335	0.0010 528 732	420
36	0.0011 290 092	0.0010 332 945	0.0009 457 115	0.0008 655 679	432
37	0.0009 350 352	0.0008 536 619	0.0007 793 849	0.0007 115 840	444
38	0.0007 743 877	0.0007 052 575	0.0006 423 109	0.0005 849 937	456
39	0.0006 413 409	0.0005 826 523	0.0005 293 447	0.0004 809 237	468
40	0.0005 311 527	0.0004 813 614	0.0004 362 464	0.0003 953 678	480
41	0.0004 398 959	0.0003 976 793	0.0003 595 217	0.0003 250 321	492
42	0.0003 643 178	0.0003 285 450	0.0002 962 910	0.0002 672 091	504
43	0.0003 017 247	0.0002 714 292	0.0002 441 809	0.0002 196 728	516
44	0.0002 498 857	0.0002 242 427	0.0002 012 357	0.0001 805 932	528
45	0.0002 069 531	0.0001 852 594	0.0001 658 435	0.0001 484 658	540
46	0.0001 713 966	0.0001 530 530	0.0001 366 758	0.0001 220 538	552
47	0.0001 419 492	0.0001 264 456	0.0001 126 380	0.0001 003 405	564
48	0.0001 175 610	0.0001 044 637	0.0000 928 278	0.0000 824 900	576
49	0.0000 973 630	0.0000 863 033	0.0000 765 018	0.0000 678 151	588
50	0.0000 806 351	0.0000 712 999	0.0000 630 471	0.0000 557 509	600

MONTHLY
Compounding

TABLE 4. PRESENT WORTH OF ONE DOLLAR
Payable at end of each period

MONTHS	20% Nominal Annual Rate	20¼% Nominal Annual Rate	20½% Nominal Annual Rate	20¾% Nominal Annual Rate	MONTHS
1	0.9836 065 574	0.9834 050 400	0.9832 036 051	0.9830 022 527	1
2	0.9674 818 597	0.9670 854 726	0.9666 893 290	0.9662 934 288	2
3	0.9516 215 014	0.9510 367 278	0.9504 524 333	0.9498 686 173	3
4	0.9360 211 489	0.9352 543 113	0.9344 882 589	0.9337 229 906	4
5	0.9206 765 399	0.9197 338 034	0.9187 922 250	0.9178 518 032	5
6	0.9055 834 818	0.9044 708 577	0.9033 598 280	0.9022 503 902	6
7	0.8907 378 510	0.8894 611 999	0.8881 866 396	0.8869 141 661	7
8	0.8761 355 911	0.8747 006 268	0.8732 683 060	0.8718 386 232	8
9	0.8617 727 126	0.8601 850 049	0.8586 005 467	0.8570 193 306	9
10	0.8476 452 911	0.8459 102 691	0.8441 791 528	0.8424 519 326	10
11	0.8337 494 666	0.8318 724 220	0.8299 999 864	0.8281 321 476	11
YEARS					
1	0.8200 814 426	0.8180 675 324	0.8160 589 788	0.8140 557 666	12
2	0.6725 335 725	0.6692 344 875	0.6659 522 569	0.6626 867 911	24
3	0.5515 323 023	0.5474 790 058	0.5434 563 187	0.5394 640 038	36
4	0.4523 014 061	0.4478 747 993	0.4434 924 085	0.4391 537 831	48
5	0.3709 239 896	0.3663 918 318	0.3619 159 620	0.3574 956 696	60
6	0.3041 878 805	0.2997 332 617	0.2953 447 703	0.2910 214 114	72
7	0.2494 588 359	0.2452 020 498	0.2410 187 517	0.2369 076 581	84
8	0.2045 765 620	0.2005 918 358	0.1966 855 164	0.1928 560 453	96
9	0.1677 694 421	0.1640 976 681	0.1605 069 816	0.1569 955 758	108
10	0.1375 846 061	0.1342 429 744	0.1309 831 635	0.1278 031 538	120
11	0.1128 305 822	0.1098 198 188	0.1068 899 867	0.1040 388 943	132
12	0.0925 302 666	0.0898 400 282	0.0872 285 334	0.0846 934 619	144
13	0.0758 823 546	0.0734 952 102	0.0711 836 279	0.0689 452 010	156
14	0.0622 297 108	0.0601 240 452	0.0580 900 387	0.0561 252 385	168
15	0.0510 334 310	0.0491 855 293	0.0474 048 976	0.0456 890 740	180
16	0.0418 515 697	0.0402 370 846	0.0386 851 923	0.0371 934 542	192
17	0.0343 216 957	0.0329 166 525	0.0315 693 986	0.0302 775 459	204
18	0.0281 465 857	0.0269 280 447	0.0257 624 911	0.0246 476 108	216
19	0.0230 824 926	0.0220 289 591	0.0210 237 122	0.0200 645 297	228
20	0.0189 295 238	0.0180 211 762	0.0171 565 891	0.0163 336 461	240
21	0.0155 237 512	0.0147 425 391	0.0140 007 886	0.0132 964 988	252
22	0.0127 307 403	0.0120 603 926	0.0114 254 692	0.0108 240 915	264
23	0.0104 402 439	0.0098 662 156	0.0093 238 568	0.0088 114 141	276
24	0.0085 618 502	0.0080 712 307	0.0076 088 170	0.0071 729 825	288
25	0.0070 214 145	0.0066 028 118	0.0062 092 435	0.0058 392 078	300
26	0.0057 581 317	0.0054 015 459	0.0050 671 089	0.0047 534 407	312
27	0.0047 221 370	0.0044 188 293	0.0041 350 597	0.0038 695 659	324
28	0.0038 725 369	0.0036 149 008	0.0033 744 526	0.0031 500 424	336
29	0.0031 757 957	0.0029 572 330	0.0027 537 523	0.0025 643 102	348
30	0.0026 044 111	0.0024 192 163	0.0022 472 243	0.0020 874 915	360
31	0.0021 358 292	0.0019 790 823	0.0018 338 676	0.0016 993 345	372
32	0.0017 515 539	0.0016 190 230	0.0014 965 441	0.0013 833 530	384
33	0.0014 364 168	0.0013 244 701	0.0012 212 683	0.0011 261 265	396
34	0.0011 779 788	0.0010 835 060	0.0009 966 269	0.0009 167 298	408
35	0.0009 660 385	0.0008 863 811	0.0008 133 064	0.0007 462 692	420
36	0.0007 922 303	0.0007 251 196	0.0006 637 060	0.0006 075 047	432
37	0.0006 496 934	0.0005 931 968	0.0005 416 232	0.0004 945 427	444
38	0.0005 328 015	0.0004 852 750	0.0004 419 965	0.0004 025 854	456
39	0.0004 369 406	0.0003 969 878	0.0003 606 952	0.0003 277 269	468
40	0.0003 583 269	0.0003 247 628	0.0002 943 486	0.0002 667 880	480
41	0.0002 938 572	0.0002 656 779	0.0002 402 058	0.0002 171 803	492
42	0.0002 409 869	0.0002 173 425	0.0001 960 221	0.0001 767 969	504
43	0.0001 976 288	0.0001 778 008	0.0001 599 656	0.0001 439 225	516
44	0.0001 620 717	0.0001 454 531	0.0001 305 413	0.0001 171 610	528
45	0.0001 329 120	0.0001 189 904	0.0001 065 294	0.0000 953 756	540
46	0.0001 089 987	0.0000 973 422	0.0000 869 343	0.0000 776 410	552
47	0.0000 893 878	0.0000 796 325	0.0000 709 435	0.0000 632 041	564
48	0.0000 733 053	0.0000 651 448	0.0000 578 941	0.0000 514 517	576
49	0.0000 601 163	0.0000 532 928	0.0000 472 450	0.0000 418 845	588
50	0.0000 493 003	0.0000 435 971	0.0000 385 547	0.0000 340 963	600

TABLE 4. PRESENT WORTH OF ONE DOLLAR
Payable at end of each period

MONTHLY Compounding

MONTHS	21% Nominal Annual Rate	21¼% Nominal Annual Rate	21½% Nominal Annual Rate	21¾% Nominal Annual Rate	MONTHS
1	0.9828 009 828	0.9825 997 953	0.9823 986 901	0.9821 976 673	1
2	0.9658 977 718	0.9655 023 577	0.9651 071 864	0.9647 122 576	2
3	0.9492 852 794	0.9487 024 190	0.9481 200 357	0.9475 381 290	3
4	0.9329 585 056	0.9321 948 027	0.9314 318 812	0.9306 697 400	4
5	0.9169 125 362	0.9159 744 223	0.9150 374 600	0.9141 016 476	5
6	0.9011 425 417	0.9000 362 799	0.8989 316 022	0.8978 285 060	6
7	0.8856 437 756	0.8843 754 644	0.8831 092 285	0.8818 450 642	7
8	0.8704 115 731	0.8689 871 503	0.8675 653 493	0.8661 461 649	8
9	0.8554 413 495	0.8538 665 959	0.8522 950 628	0.8507 267 427	9
10	0.8407 285 990	0.8390 091 424	0.8372 935 533	0.8355 818 222	10
11	0.8262 688 934	0.8244 102 116	0.8225 560 900	0.8207 065 166	11
YEARS					
1	0.8120 578 805	0.8100 653 051	0.8080 780 254	0.8060 960 261	12
2	0.6594 380 012	0.6562 057 985	0.6529 900 951	0.6497 908 033	24
3	0.5355 018 255	0.5315 695 504	0.5276 669 466	0.5237 937 843	36
4	0.4348 584 774	0.4306 060 500	0.4263 960 643	0.4222 280 880	48
5	0.3531 302 535	0.3488 190 213	0.3445 612 897	0.3403 563 839	60
6	0.2867 622 052	0.2825 661 869	0.2784 324 066	0.2743 599 285	72
7	0.2328 675 085	0.2288 970 644	0.2249 951 093	0.2211 604 481	84
8	0.1891 018 954	0.1854 215 703	0.1818 136 036	0.1782 765 583	96
9	0.1535 616 844	0.1502 035 809	0.1469 195 778	0.1437 080 252	108
10	0.1247 009 759	0.1216 747 096	0.1187 224 823	0.1158 424 680	120
11	0.1012 644 102	0.0985 644 608	0.0959 370 291	0.0933 801 531	132
12	0.0822 325 623	0.0798 436 500	0.0775 246 050	0.0752 733 704	144
13	0.0667 776 003	0.0646 785 707	0.0626 459 298	0.0606 775 647	156
14	0.0542 272 765	0.0523 938 661	0.0506 227 992	0.0489 119 438	168
15	0.0440 356 872	0.0424 424 531	0.0409 071 716	0.0394 277 235	180
16	0.0357 595 268	0.0343 811 587	0.0330 561 865	0.0317 825 313	192
17	0.0290 388 056	0.0278 509 838	0.0267 119 779	0.0256 197 721	204
18	0.0235 811 909	0.0225 611 157	0.0215 853 623	0.0206 519 965	216
19	0.0191 492 919	0.0182 759 771	0.0174 426 570	0.0166 474 923	228
20	0.0155 503 334	0.0148 047 350	0.0140 950 278	0.0134 194 774	240
21	0.0126 277 708	0.0119 928 021	0.0113 898 822	0.0108 173 874	252
22	0.0102 544 808	0.0097 149 529	0.0092 039 136	0.0087 198 530	264
23	0.0083 272 319	0.0078 697 463	0.0074 374 803	0.0070 290 389	276
24	0.0067 621 943	0.0063 750 084	0.0060 100 644	0.0056 660 803	288
25	0.0054 912 932	0.0051 641 732	0.0048 566 010	0.0045 674 048	300
26	0.0044 592 479	0.0041 833 175	0.0039 245 125	0.0036 817 669	312
27	0.0036 211 674	0.0033 887 604	0.0031 713 123	0.0029 678 576	324
28	0.0029 405 975	0.0027 451 172	0.0025 626 678	0.0023 923 782	336
29	0.0023 879 354	0.0022 237 242	0.0020 708 355	0.0019 284 866	348
30	0.0019 391 418	0.0018 013 618	0.0016 733 967	0.0015 545 454	360
31	0.0015 746 953	0.0014 592 207	0.0013 522 351	0.0012 531 129	372
32	0.0012 787 438	0.0011 820 641	0.0010 927 115	0.0010 101 293	384
33	0.0010 384 139	0.0009 575 491	0.0008 829 961	0.0008 142 612	396
34	0.0008 432 522	0.0007 756 773	0.0007 135 298	0.0006 563 727	408
35	0.0006 847 696	0.0006 283 493	0.0005 765 877	0.0005 290 994	420
36	0.0005 560 726	0.0005 090 039	0.0004 659 279	0.0004 265 050	432
37	0.0004 515 631	0.0004 123 264	0.0003 765 061	0.0003 438 040	444
38	0.0003 666 954	0.0003 340 113	0.0003 042 463	0.0002 771 390	456
39	0.0002 977 779	0.0002 705 710	0.0002 458 547	0.0002 234 006	468
40	0.0002 418 129	0.0002 191 802	0.0001 986 698	0.0001 800 824	480
41	0.0001 963 660	0.0001 775 503	0.0001 605 407	0.0001 451 637	492
42	0.0001 594 606	0.0001 438 273	0.0001 297 294	0.0001 170 159	504
43	0.0001 294 912	0.0001 165 095	0.0001 048 315	0.0000 943 260	516
44	0.0001 051 544	0.0000 943 803	0.0000 847 120	0.0000 760 358	528
45	0.0000 853 914	0.0000 764 542	0.0000 684 539	0.0000 612 922	540
46	0.0000 693 428	0.0000 619 329	0.0000 553 161	0.0000 494 074	552
47	0.0000 563 104	0.0000 501 697	0.0000 446 997	0.0000 398 271	564
48	0.0000 457 273	0.0000 406 407	0.0000 361 209	0.0000 321 045	576
49	0.0000 371 332	0.0000 329 216	0.0000 291 885	0.0000 258 793	588
50	0.0000 301 543	0.0000 266 687	0.0000 235 866	0.0000 208 612	600

MONTHLY
Compounding

TABLE 4. PRESENT WORTH OF ONE DOLLAR
Payable at end of each period

	22% Nominal Annual Rate	22¼% Nominal Annual Rate	22½% Nominal Annual Rate	22¾% Nominal Annual Rate	
MONTHS					MONTHS
1	0.9819 967 267	0.9817 958 683	0.9815 950 920	0.9813 943 979	1
2	0.9643 175 712	0.9639 231 270	0.9635 289 247	0.9631 349 642	2
3	0.9469 566 984	0.9463 757 434	0.9457 952 635	0.9452 152 582	3
4	0.9299 083 781	0.9291 477 947	0.9283 879 887	0.9276 289 592	4
5	0.9131 669 834	0.9122 334 658	0.9113 010 932	0.9103 698 639	5
6	0.8967 269 886	0.8956 270 477	0.8945 286 805	0.8934 318 844	6
7	0.8805 829 676	0.8793 229 349	0.8780 649 624	0.8768 090 462	7
8	0.8647 295 917	0.8633 156 244	0.8619 042 576	0.8604 954 860	8
9	0.8491 616 285	0.8475 997 130	0.8460 409 890	0.8444 854 493	9
10	0.8338 739 396	0.8321 698 962	0.8304 696 825	0.8287 732 891	10
11	0.8188 614 792	0.8170 209 658	0.8151 849 644	0.8133 534 630	11
YEARS					
1	0.8041 192 922	0.8021 478 085	0.8001 815 602	0.7982 205 321	12
2	0.6466 078 360	0.6434 411 067	0.6402 905 292	0.6371 560 178	24
3	0.5199 498 354	0.5161 348 737	0.5123 486 746	0.5085 910 156	36
4	0.4181 016 936	0.4140 164 578	0.4099 719 618	0.4059 677 911	48
5	0.3362 036 379	0.3321 023 943	0.3280 520 040	0.3240 518 262	60
6	0.2703 478 314	0.2663 952 078	0.2625 011 644	0.2586 648 211	72
7	0.2173 919 068	0.2136 883 322	0.2100 485 912	0.2064 715 711	84
8	0.1748 090 262	0.1714 096 273	0.1680 770 095	0.1648 098 474	96
9	0.1405 673 104	0.1374 958 569	0.1344 921 237	0.1315 546 041	108
10	0.1130 328 862	0.1102 920 003	0.1076 181 173	0.1050 095 861	120
11	0.0908 919 244	0.0884 704 864	0.0861 140 330	0.0838 208 077	132
12	0.0730 879 499	0.0709 664 067	0.0689 068 613	0.0669 074 897	144
13	0.0587 714 306	0.0569 255 477	0.0551 379 998	0.0534 069 320	156
14	0.0472 592 411	0.0456 627 033	0.0441 204 107	0.0426 305 097	168
15	0.0380 020 675	0.0366 282 374	0.0353 043 391	0.0340 285 481	180
16	0.0305 581 956	0.0293 812 603	0.0282 498 811	0.0271 622 858	192
17	0.0245 724 347	0.0235 681 136	0.0226 050 339	0.0216 814 942	204
18	0.0197 591 688	0.0189 051 107	0.0180 881 313	0.0173 066 139	216
19	0.0158 887 288	0.0151 646 931	0.0144 737 891	0.0138 144 945	228
20	0.0127 764 334	0.0121 643 253	0.0115 816 592	0.0110 270 132	240
21	0.0102 737 765	0.0097 575 869	0.0092 674 301	0.0088 019 883	252
22	0.0082 613 419	0.0078 270 270	0.0074 156 267	0.0070 259 278	264
23	0.0066 431 044	0.0062 784 325	0.0059 338 477	0.0056 082 398	276
24	0.0053 418 484	0.0050 362 309	0.0047 481 555	0.0044 766 122	288
25	0.0042 954 834	0.0040 398 016	0.0037 993 865	0.0035 733 238	300
26	0.0034 540 810	0.0032 405 180	0.0030 401 990	0.0028 523 004	312
27	0.0027 774 932	0.0025 993 744	0.0024 327 112	0.0022 767 647	324
28	0.0022 334 359	0.0020 850 825	0.0019 466 106	0.0018 173 604	336
29	0.0017 959 489	0.0016 725 443	0.0015 576 419	0.0014 506 544	348
30	0.0014 441 571	0.0013 416 278	0.0012 463 964	0.0011 579 421	360
31	0.0011 612 746	0.0010 761 838	0.0009 973 434	0.0009 242 931	372
32	0.0009 338 033	0.0008 632 585	0.0007 980 558	0.0007 377 898	384
33	0.0007 508 893	0.0006 924 609	0.0006 385 895	0.0005 889 189	396
34	0.0006 038 045	0.0005 554 560	0.0005 109 876	0.0004 700 872	408
35	0.0004 855 309	0.0004 455 578	0.0004 088 828	0.0003 752 332	420
36	0.0003 904 248	0.0003 574 032	0.0003 271 805	0.0002 995 189	432
37	0.0003 139 481	0.0002 866 902	0.0002 618 038	0.0002 390 821	444
38	0.0002 524 517	0.0002 299 679	0.0002 094 906	0.0001 908 403	456
39	0.0002 030 013	0.0001 844 683	0.0001 676 305	0.0001 523 326	468
40	0.0001 632 372	0.0001 479 708	0.0001 341 348	0.0001 215 950	480
41	0.0001 312 622	0.0001 186 945	0.0001 073 322	0.0000 970 596	492
42	0.0001 055 505	0.0000 952 105	0.0000 858 853	0.0000 774 750	504
43	0.0000 848 752	0.0000 763 729	0.0000 687 238	0.0000 618 421	516
44	0.0000 682 498	0.0000 612 624	0.0000 549 915	0.0000 493 637	528
45	0.0000 548 810	0.0000 491 415	0.0000 440 032	0.0000 394 031	540
46	0.0000 441 308	0.0000 394 187	0.0000 352 105	0.0000 314 524	552
47	0.0000 354 865	0.0000 316 196	0.0000 281 748	0.0000 251 059	564
48	0.0000 285 353	0.0000 253 636	0.0000 225 450	0.0000 200 401	576
49	0.0000 229 458	0.0000 203 454	0.0000 180 401	0.0000 159 964	588
50	0.0000 184 512	0.0000 163 200	0.0000 144 353	0.0000 127 686	600

TABLE 5. PRESENT WORTH OF ONE DOLLAR PER PERIOD
Payable at end of each period

MONTHLY Compounding

MONTHS	5% Nominal Annual Rate	5¼% Nominal Annual Rate	5½% Nominal Annual Rate	5¾% Nominal Annual Rate	MONTHS
1	0.9958 506 224	0.9956 440 572	0.9954 375 778	0.9952 311 839	1
2	1.9875 690 846	1.9869 511 460	1.9863 335 490	1.9857 162 933	2
3	2.9751 725 323	2.9739 401 578	2.9727 086 344	2.9714 779 614	3
4	3.9586 780 405	3.9566 299 020	3.9545 834 602	3.9525 387 134	4
5	4.9381 026 129	4.9350 391 059	4.9319 785 585	4.9289 209 671	5
6	5.9134 631 830	5.9091 864 153	5.9049 143 677	5.9006 470 334	6
7	6.8847 766 138	6.8790 903 948	6.8734 112 328	6.8677 391 168	7
8	7.8520 596 984	7.8447 695 282	7.8374 894 064	7.8302 193 159	8
9	8.8153 291 602	8.8062 422 185	8.7971 690 483	8.7881 096 240	9
10	9.7746 016 533	9.7635 267 887	9.7524 702 264	9.7414 319 293	10
11	10.7298 937 626	10.7166 414 823	10.7034 129 172	10.6902 080 159	11
YEARS					
1	11.6812 220 043	11.6656 044 627	11.6500 170 059	11.6344 595 638	12
2	22.7938 983 940	22.7358 312 428	22.6779 707 374	22.6203 160 163	24
3	33.3657 012 837	33.2410 666 424	33.1170 768 299	32.9937 279 767	36
4	43.4229 559 379	43.2101 461 379	42.9987 773 396	42.7888 382 776	48
5	52.9907 063 239	52.6704 335 286	52.3528 354 457	52.0378 863 413	60
6	62.0927 774 752	61.6478 960 470	61.2074 250 950	60.7713 142 923	72
7	70.7518 348 188	70.1671 756 355	69.5892 158 610	69.0178 671 537	84
8	78.9894 406 159	78.2516 565 854	77.5234 532 710	76.8046 874 581	96
9	86.8261 076 543	85.9235 297 231	85.0340 348 441	84.1574 045 839	108
10	94.2813 503 282	93.2038 533 218	92.1435 820 700	91.1002 191 114	120
11	101.3737 332 323	100.1126 109 028	98.8735 085 429	97.6559 824 759	132
12	108.1209 173 896	106.6687 660 882	105.2440 844 590	103.8462 721 807	144
13	114.5397 042 300	112.8903 146 535	111.2744 976 687	109.6914 628 165	156
14	120.6460 774 284	118.7943 339 231	116.9829 114 697	115.2107 931 223	168
15	126.4552 427 061	124.3970 296 460	122.3865 193 138	120.4224 293 071	180
16	131.9816 656 951	129.7137 804 779	127.5015 965 929	125.3435 248 417	192
17	137.2391 079 599	134.7591 801 938	132.3435 496 595	129.9902 769 178	204
18	142.2406 612 652	139.5470 777 459	136.9269 622 297	134.3779 797 584	216
19	146.9987 801 767	144.0906 152 771	141.2656 393 089	138.5210 749 576	228
20	151.5253 130 743	148.4022 641 947	145.3726 487 718	142.4331 990 125	240
21	155.8315 316 566	152.4938 594 022	149.2603 607 218	146.1272 282 071	252
22	159.9281 590 086	156.3766 317 853	152.9404 847 494	149.6153 209 921	264
23	163.8253 963 041	160.0612 390 384	156.4241 052 010	152.9089 580 037	276
24	167.5329 482 076	163.5577 949 193	159.7217 145 640	156.0189 798 501	288
25	171.0600 470 409	166.8758 970 093	162.8432 450 700	158.9556 227 927	300
26	174.4154 757 721	170.0246 530 582	165.7980 986 101	161.7285 524 370	312
27	177.6075 898 869	173.0127 059 832	168.5951 750 527	164.3468 955 459	324
28	180.6443 381 949	175.8482 575 927	171.2428 990 497	166.8192 700 794	336
29	183.5332 826 230	178.5390 910 993	173.7492 454 111	169.1538 135 598	348
30	186.2816 170 461	181.0925 924 837	176.1217 631 246	171.3582 098 548	360
31	188.8961 852 002	183.5157 707 682	178.3675 980 928	173.4397 144 686	372
32	191.3834 977 250	185.8152 772 551	180.4935 146 562	175.4051 784 222	384
33	193.7497 483 756	187.9974 237 847	182.5059 159 674	177.2610 708 027	396
34	196.0008 294 463	190.0682 000 592	184.4108 632 768	179.0135 000 558	408
35	198.1423 464 432	192.0332 900 845	186.2140 941 887	180.6682 340 907	420
36	200.1796 320 423	193.8980 877 718	187.9210 399 427	182.2307 192 646	432
37	202.1177 593 690	195.6677 117 432	189.5368 417 728	183.7060 983 086	444
38	203.9615 546 308	197.3470 193 814	191.0663 663 916	185.0992 272 547	456
39	205.7156 091 351	198.9406 201 629	192.5142 206 497	186.4146 914 185	468
40	207.3842 907 225	200.4528 883 101	193.8847 654 102	187.6568 204 914	480
41	208.9717 546 429	201.8879 747 985	195.1821 286 843	188.8297 027 912	492
42	210.4819 539 030	203.2498 187 497	196.4102 180 641	189.9371 987 183	504
43	211.9186 491 096	204.5421 582 445	197.5727 324 923	190.9829 534 618	516
44	213.2854 178 344	205.7685 405 834	198.6731 734 033	191.9704 089 971	528
45	214.5856 635 220	206.9323 320 228	199.7148 552 690	192.9028 154 148	540
46	215.8226 239 657	208.0367 270 159	200.7009 155 823	193.7832 416 180	552
47	216.9993 793 696	209.0847 569 801	201.6343 243 065	194.6145 854 233	564
48	218.1188 600 188	210.0792 986 186	202.5178 928 213	195.3995 830 982	576
49	219.1838 535 765	211.0230 818 160	203.3542 823 901	196.1408 183 679	588
50	220.1970 120 250	211.9186 971 320	204.1460 121 757	196.8407 309 186	600

MONTHLY
Compounding

TABLE 5. PRESENT WORTH OF ONE DOLLAR PER PERIOD
Payable at end of each period

MONTHS	6% Nominal Annual Rate	6¼% Nominal Annual Rate	6½% Nominal Annual Rate	6¾% Nominal Annual Rate	MONTHS
1	0.9950 248 756	0.9948 186 528	0.9946 125 155	0.9944 064 636	1
2	1.9850 993 787	1.9844 828 049	1.9838 665 716	1.9832 506 786	2
3	2.9702 481 380	2.9690 191 634	2.9677 910 368	2.9665 637 574	3
4	3.9504 956 597	3.9484 542 973	3.9464 146 243	3.9443 766 388	4
5	4.9258 663 281	4.9228 146 377	4.9197 658 924	4.9167 200 883	5
6	5.8963 844 061	5.8921 264 790	5.8878 732 456	5.8836 246 994	6
7	6.8620 740 359	6.8564 159 791	6.8507 649 355	6.8451 208 944	7
8	7.8229 592 397	7.8157 091 605	7.8084 690 615	7.8012 389 254	8
9	8.7790 639 201	8.7700 319 110	8.7610 135 713	8.7520 088 755	9
10	9.7304 118 608	9.7194 099 840	9.7084 262 624	9.6974 606 593	10
11	10.6770 267 272	10.6638 689 996	10.6507 347 823	10.6376 240 242	11
YEARS					
1	11.6189 320 668	11.6034 344 452	11.5879 666 297	11.5725 285 511	12
2	22.5628 662 218	22.5056 205 002	22.4485 780 020	22.3917 378 811	24
3	32.8710 162 393	32.7489 377 990	32.6274 888 625	32.5066 656 613	36
4	42.5803 177 828	42.3732 047 812	42.1674 882 931	41.9631 574 322	48
5	51.7255 607 511	51.4158 334 769	51.1086 795 838	50.8040 743 975	60
6	60.3395 139 355	59.9119 749 367	59.4886 488 154	59.0694 876 902	72
7	68.4530 424 355	67.8946 558 733	67.3426 228 596	66.7968 599 944	84
8	76.0952 182 532	75.3949 070 445	74.7036 174 627	74.0212 153 425	96
9	83.2934 244 626	82.4418 838 783	81.6025 760 334	80.7752 978 614	108
10	90.0734 533 272	89.0629 798 073	88.0684 997 199	87.0897 201 834	120
11	96.4595 987 178	95.2839 327 541	94.1285 693 219	92.9931 021 970	132
12	102.4747 431 612	101.1289 251 817	99.8082 595 505	98.5122 007 656	144
13	108.1404 398 312	106.6206 780 964	105.1314 461 163	103.6720 310 017	156
14	113.4769 897 777	111.7805 393 708	110.1205 060 955	108.4959 796 475	168
15	118.5035 146 676	116.6285 667 283	114.7964 119 967	113.0059 110 740	180
16	123.2380 253 014	121.1836 057 128	119.1788 199 228	117.2222 663 806	192
17	127.6974 861 481	125.4633 629 459	123.2861 521 996	121.1641 560 438	204
18	131.8978 761 316	129.4844 749 577	127.1356 748 173	124.8494 465 345	216
19	135.8542 458 858	133.2625 728 568	130.7435 700 121	128.2948 412 971	228
20	139.5807 716 829	136.8123 430 930	134.1250 042 907	131.5159 564 577	240
21	143.0908 062 297	140.1475 845 466	137.2941 921 866	134.5273 916 030	252
22	146.3969 265 116	143.2812 621 692	140.2644 560 132	137.3427 959 528	264
23	149.5109 788 588	146.2255 573 811	143.0482 818 666	139.9749 302 245	276
24	152.4441 213 926	148.9919 154 238	145.6573 721 142	142.4357 244 705	288
25	155.2068 640 072	151.5910 898 508	148.1026 945 870	144.7363 321 508	300
26	157.8091 060 280	154.0331 843 296	150.3945 286 857	146.8871 806 858	312
27	160.2601 716 825	156.3276 919 167	152.5425 085 920	148.8980 187 178	324
28	162.5688 435 103	158.4835 319 602	154.5556 637 679	150.7779 602 968	336
29	164.7433 938 325	160.5090 847 713	156.4424 569 125	152.5355 261 894	348
30	166.7916 143 923	162.4122 242 009	158.2108 195 371	154.1786 824 986	360
31	168.7208 442 745	164.2003 482 471	159.8681 853 067	155.7148 767 705	372
32	170.5379 962 019	165.8804 078 133	161.4215 212 887	157.1510 717 496	384
33	172.2495 813 053	167.4589 337 283	162.8773 572 409	158.4937 769 370	396
34	173.8617 324 535	168.9420 621 330	164.2418 130 599	159.7490 780 949	408
35	175.3802 262 283	170.3355 583 334	165.5206 245 078	160.9226 648 302	420
36	176.8105 036 231	171.6448 392 119	166.7191 673 237	162.0198 563 816	432
37	178.1576 895 384	172.8749 942 839	167.8424 798 212	163.0456 257 300	444
38	179.4266 111 456	174.0308 054 823	168.8952 840 685	164.0046 221 373	456
39	180.6218 151 830	175.1167 657 459	169.8820 057 382	164.9011 922 198	468
40	181.7475 842 478	176.1370 964 850	170.8067 927 115	165.7393 996 486	480
41	182.8079 521 412	177.0957 639 904	171.6735 325 150	166.5230 435 683	492
42	183.8067 183 220	177.9964 948 524	172.4858 686 623	167.2556 758 163	504
43	184.7474 615 208	178.8427 904 460	173.2472 159 703	167.9406 170 215	516
44	185.6335 525 630	179.6379 405 426	173.9607 749 144	168.5809 716 548	528
45	186.4681 664 471	180.3850 360 974	174.6295 450 817	169.1796 421 004	540
46	187.2542 937 210	181.0869 812 653	175.2563 377 812	169.7393 418 101	552
47	187.9947 511 980	181.7465 046 897	175.8437 878 609	170.2626 076 024	564
48	188.6921 920 494	182.3661 701 098	176.3943 647 843	170.7518 111 604	576
49	189.3491 153 114	182.9483 863 264	176.9103 830 114	171.2091 697 813	588
50	189.9678 748 396	183.4954 165 654	177.3940 117 277	171.6367 564 265	600

TABLE 5. PRESENT WORTH OF ONE DOLLAR PER PERIOD
Payable at end of each period

MONTHLY Compounding

MONTHS	7% Nominal Annual Rate	7¼% Nominal Annual Rate	7½% Nominal Annual Rate	7¾% Nominal Annual Rate	MONTHS
1	0.9942 004 971	0.9939 946 159	0.9937 888 199	0.9935 831 091	1
2	1.9826 351 255	1.9820 199 122	1.9814 050 384	1.9807 905 038	2
3	2.9653 373 245	2.9641 117 371	2.9628 869 947	2.9616 630 963	3
4	3.9423 403 392	3.9403 057 234	3.9382 727 897	3.9362 415 363	4
5	4.9136 772 220	4.9106 372 898	4.9076 002 879	4.9045 662 129	5
6	5.8793 808 338	5.8751 416 424	5.8709 071 184	5.8666 772 556	6
7	6.8394 838 447	6.8338 537 758	6.8282 306 767	6.8226 145 367	7
8	7.7940 187 355	7.7868 084 746	7.7796 081 259	7.7724 176 726	8
9	8.7430 177 983	8.7340 403 144	8.7250 763 984	8.7161 260 253	9
10	9.6865 131 383	9.6755 836 631	9.6646 721 972	9.6537 787 045	10
11	10.6245 366 744	10.6114 726 823	10.5984 319 972	10.5854 145 688	11
YEARS					
1	11.5571 201 402	11.5417 413 284	11.5263 920 469	11.5110 722 273	12
2	22.3350 992 958	22.2786 614 081	22.2224 233 837	22.1663 843 924	24
3	32.3864 644 516	32.2668 815 144	32.1479 131 547	32.0295 557 021	36
4	41.7602 014 051	41.5586 095 100	41.3583 711 359	41.1594 757 624	48
5	50.5019 935 012	50.2024 127 327	49.9053 081 820	49.6106 561 879	60
6	58.6544 442 718	58.2434 718 543	57.8365 243 081	57.4335 560 724	72
7	66.2572 850 667	65.7238 170 369	65.1963 760 188	64.6748 832 625	84
8	73.3475 686 854	72.6825 476 225	72.0260 243 780	71.3778 732 339	96
9	79.9598 499 565	79.1560 365 033	78.3636 652 089	77.5825 472 360	108
10	86.1263 541 414	85.1781 202 402	84.2447 427 094	83.3259 512 447	120
11	91.8771 339 863	90.7802 759 251	89.7021 476 791	88.6423 771 514	132
12	97.2402 161 854	95.9917 857 095	94.7664 014 660	93.5635 675 080	144
13	102.2417 379 703	100.8398 898 610	99.4658 266 618	98.1189 050 507	156
14	106.9060 744 910	105.3499 291 464	103.8267 055 002	102.3355 881 342	168
15	111.2559 576 093	109.5454 772 865	107.8734 268 437	106.2387 931 241	180
16	115.3125 866 838	113.4484 641 746	111.6286 225 829	109.8518 247 159	192
17	119.0957 318 858	117.0792 905 029	115.1132 942 076	113.1962 550 792	204
18	122.6238 305 501	120.4569 343 956	118.3469 302 617	116.2920 526 586	216
19	125.9140 770 303	123.5990 506 069	121.3476 153 352	119.1577 013 971	228
20	128.9825 064 963	126.5220 628 008	124.1321 312 052	121.8103 110 986	240
21	131.8440 730 824	129.2412 493 971	126.7160 506 903	124.2657 195 839	252
22	134.5127 227 670	131.7708 234 306	129.1138 247 442	126.5385 872 531	264
23	137.0014 613 390	134.1240 068 420	131.3388 632 743	128.6424 846 180	276
24	139.3224 177 821	136.3130 995 883	133.4036 101 394	130.5899 733 265	288
25	141.4869 033 859	138.3495 439 337	135.3196 127 429	132.3926 811 645	300
26	143.5054 668 720	140.2439 842 578	137.0975 866 142	134.0613 714 808	312
27	145.3879 458 040	142.0063 226 933	138.7474 753 361	135.6060 074 518	324
28	147.1435 145 307	143.6457 708 838	140.2785 061 565	137.0358 115 680	336
29	148.7807 288 984	145.1708 981 323	141.6992 415 927	138.3593 206 984	348
30	150.3075 679 478	146.5896 761 930	143.0176 273 187	139.5844 370 610	360
31	151.7314 728 003	147.9095 209 387	144.2410 366 025	140.7184 754 047	372
32	153.0593 829 226	149.1373 311 234	145.3763 115 423	141.7682 066 826	384
33	154.2977 699 469	150.2795 244 417	146.4298 013 319	142.7398 984 794	396
34	155.4526 692 100	151.3420 710 734	147.4073 977 694	143.6393 524 329	408
35	156.5297 091 675	152.3305 248 901	148.3145 682 082	144.4719 388 734	420
36	157.5341 388 240	153.2500 524 838	149.1563 861 336	145.2426 288 884	432
37	158.4708 533 142	154.1054 601 735	149.9375 595 376	145.9560 240 032	444
38	159.3444 177 600	154.9012 191 270	150.6624 572 483	146.6163 836 547	456
39	160.1590 895 185	155.6414 887 312	151.3351 333 640	147.2276 506 236	468
40	160.9188 389 305	156.3301 383 337	151.9593 499 257	147.7934 745 747	480
41	161.6273 686 704	156.9707 674 672	152.5385 979 574	148.3172 338 484	492
42	162.2881 317 909	157.5667 246 638	153.0761 169 897	148.8020 556 314	504
43	162.9043 485 519	158.1211 249 582	153.5749 131 776	149.2508 346 278	516
44	163.4790 221 145	158.6368 661 696	154.0377 761 129	149.6662 503 428	528
45	164.0149 531 774	159.1166 440 480	154.4672 944 254	150.0507 830 809	540
46	164.5147 536 254	159.5629 663 654	154.8658 702 600	150.4067 287 549	552
47	164.9808 592 594	159.9781 660 234	155.2357 327 112	150.7362 125 940	564
48	165.4155 416 671	160.3644 132 471	155.5789 502 899	151.0412 018 330	576
49	165.8209 192 933	160.7237 269 289	155.8974 424 913	151.3235 174 579	588
50	166.1989 677 650	161.0579 851 813	156.1929 905 303	151.5848 450 782	600

MONTHLY
Compounding

TABLE 5. PRESENT WORTH OF ONE DOLLAR PER PERIOD
Payable at end of each period

MONTHS	8% Nominal Annual Rate	8¼% Nominal Annual Rate	8½% Nominal Annual Rate	8¾% Nominal Annual Rate	MONTHS
1	0.9933 774 834	0.9931 719 429	0.9929 664 874	0.9927 611 169	1
2	1.9801 763 081	1.9795 624 510	1.9789 489 324	1.9783 357 520	2
3	2.9604 400 411	2.9592 178 285	2.9579 964 575	2.9567 759 275	3
4	3.9342 119 614	3.9321 840 630	3.9301 578 395	3.9281 332 890	4
5	4.9015 350 610	4.8985 068 286	4.8954 815 121	4.8924 591 080	5
6	5.8624 520 473	5.8582 314 871	5.8540 155 685	5.8498 042 851	6
7	6.8170 053 450	6.8114 030 909	6.8058 077 635	6.8002 193 523	7
8	7.7652 370 977	7.7580 663 845	7.7509 055 161	7.7437 544 759	8
9	8.7071 891 699	8.6982 658 071	8.6893 559 117	8.6804 594 590	9
10	9.6429 031 489	9.6320 454 943	9.6212 057 047	9.6103 837 442	10
11	10.5724 203 466	10.5594 492 805	10.5465 013 203	10.5335 764 162	11
YEARS					
1	11.4957 818 013	11.4805 207 007	11.4652 888 576	11.4500 862 043	12
2	22.1105 436 077	22.0549 002 069	21.9994 533 710	21.9442 022 850	24
3	31.9118 055 101	31.7946 589 562	31.6781 124 414	31.5621 623 904	36
4	40.9619 129 579	40.7656 723 797	40.5707 437 726	40.3771 169 684	48
5	49.3184 333 356	49.0286 164 541	48.7411 826 131	48.4561 091 208	60
6	57.0345 221 475	56.6393 780 876	56.2480 799 938	55.8605 845 065	72
7	64.1592 611 371	63.6494 331 141	63.1453 237 506	62.6468 586 731	84
8	70.7379 704 946	70.1061 944 529	69.4824 253 558	68.8665 453 715	96
9	76.8124 971 368	76.0533 327 890	75.3048 753 330	74.5669 491 094	108
10	82.4214 808 934	81.5310 719 423	80.6544 698 084	79.7914 249 314	120
11	87.6006 002 941	86.5764 609 236	85.5696 105 417	84.5797 081 598	132
12	92.3827 995 177	91.2236 245 180	90.0855 805 914	88.9682 166 069	144
13	96.7984 979 493	95.5039 940 897	94.2347 975 917	92.9903 275 537	156
14	100.8757 836 765	99.4465 201 700	98.0470 464 609	96.6766 316 053	168
15	104.6405 921 566	103.0778 682 659	101.5496 932 109	100.0551 653 505	180
16	108.1168 711 913	106.4225 992 137	104.7678 813 922	103.1516 245 973	192
17	111.3267 332 575	109.5033 352 980	107.7247 125 858	105.9895 598 055	204
18	114.2905 961 643	112.3409 132 584	110.4414 122 362	108.5905 552 018	216
19	117.0273 129 293	114.9545 252 202	112.9374 820 174	110.9743 929 412	228
20	119.5542 917 024	117.3618 485 017	115.2308 398 246	113.1592 035 627	240
21	121.8876 064 982	119.5791 651 754	117.3379 483 963	115.1616 038 824	252
22	124.0420 994 423	121.6214 721 931	119.2739 334 916	116.9968 233 750	264
23	126.0314 751 811	123.5025 828 183	121.0526 924 695	118.6788 200 034	276
24	127.8683 880 572	125.2352 200 533	122.6869 940 502	120.2203 863 768	288
25	129.5645 226 026	126.8311 026 921	124.1885 699 746	121.6332 470 470	300
26	131.1306 678 637	128.3010 245 807	125.5681 992 203	122.9281 476 805	312
27	132.5767 860 302	129.6549 276 221	126.8357 853 772	124.1149 367 857	324
28	133.9120 758 040	130.9019 690 193	128.0004 277 406	125.2026 406 170	336
29	135.1450 309 120	132.0505 832 100	129.0704 866 294	126.1995 318 250	348
30	136.2834 941 340	133.1085 389 139	130.0536 434 006	127.1131 923 747	360
31	137.3347 071 907	134.0829 916 765	130.9569 555 892	127.9505 712 116	372
32	138.3053 568 079	134.9805 322 665	131.7869 075 703	128.7180 371 119	384
33	139.2016 172 505	135.8072 312 525	132.5494 571 070	129.4214 271 215	396
34	140.0291 895 964	136.5686 800 615	133.2500 781 179	130.0660 909 502	408
35	140.7933 380 016	137.2700 287 974	133.8937 999 711	130.6569 316 593	420
36	141.4989 231 846	137.9160 210 736	134.4852 435 872	131.1984 429 523	432
37	142.1504 333 456	138.5110 260 969	135.0286 546 108	131.6947 433 527	444
38	142.7520 127 156	139.0590 682 188	135.5279 338 868	132.1496 075 275	456
39	143.3074 879 177	139.5638 541 542	135.9866 654 632	132.5664 949 960	468
40	143.8203 923 084	140.0287 980 527	136.4081 423 185	132.9485 764 414	480
41	144.2939 884 526	140.4570 445 896	136.7953 900 005	133.2987 578 260	492
42	144.7312 888 773	140.8514 902 355	137.1511 883 445	133.6197 024 925	504
43	145.1350 752 336	141.2148 028 467	137.4780 914 287	133.9138 514 209	516
44	145.5079 159 909	141.5494 397 096	137.7784 459 084	134.1834 417 928	528
45	145.8521 827 749	141.8576 641 601	138.0544 078 611	134.4305 240 075	540
46	146.1700 654 534	142.1415 608 924	138.3079 582 640	134.6569 772 758	552
47	146.4635 860 658	142.4030 500 588	138.5409 172 143	134.8645 239 126	564
48	146.7346 116 854	142.6439 002 567	138.7549 569 945	135.0547 424 368	576
49	146.9848 662 958	142.8657 404 906	138.9516 140 770	135.2290 795 761	588
50	147.2159 417 569	143.0700 711 898	139.1323 001 535	135.3888 612 707	600

MONTHLY
Compounding

TABLE 5. PRESENT WORTH OF ONE DOLLAR PER PERIOD
Payable at end of each period

MONTHS	9% Nominal Annual Rate	9¼% Nominal Annual Rate	9½% Nominal Annual Rate	9¾% Nominal Annual Rate	MONTHS
1	0.9925 558 313	0.9923 506 306	0.9921 455 147	0.9919 404 836	1
2	1.9777 229 094	1.9771 104 045	1.9764 982 370	1.9758 864 065	2
3	2.9555 562 377	2.9543 373 872	2.9531 193 752	2.9519 022 011	3
4	3.9261 104 096	3.9240 891 996	3.9220 696 571	3.9200 517 804	4
5	4.8894 396 125	4.8864 230 221	4.8834 093 332	4.8803 985 423	5
6	5.8455 976 303	5.8413 955 977	5.8371 981 810	5.8330 053 736	6
7	6.7946 378 464	6.7890 632 353	6.7834 955 082	6.7779 346 545	7
8	7.7366 132 471	7.7294 818 130	7.7223 601 570	7.7152 482 624	8
9	8.6715 764 239	8.6627 067 815	8.6538 505 071	8.6450 075 758	9
10	9.5995 795 771	9.5887 931 675	9.5780 244 800	9.5672 734 788	10
11	10.5206 745 182	10.5077 955 766	10.4949 395 419	10.4821 063 646	11
YEARS					
1	11.4349 126 731	11.4197 681 968	11.4046 527 080	11.3895 661 397	12
2	21.8891 461 374	21.8342 841 207	21.7796 154 308	21.7251 392 676	24
3	31.4468 052 513	31.3320 374 954	31.2178 556 172	31.1042 561 338	36
4	40.1847 818 852	39.9937 285 261	39.8039 469 792	39.6154 274 160	48
5	48.1733 735 210	47.8929 535 903	47.6148 273 362	47.3389 729 937	60
6	55.4768 487 987	55.0968 305 692	54.7204 880 355	54.3477 799 268	72
7	62.1539 645 614	61.6665 691 330	61.1846 011 272	60.7079 902 901	84
8	68.2584 385 567	67.6579 908 246	67.0650 899 136	66.4796 253 560	96
9	73.8393 815 990	73.1220 033 632	72.4146 479 855	71.7171 520 150	108
10	78.9416 926 690	78.1050 331 945	77.2812 113 962	76.4699 967 792	120
11	83.6064 201 276	82.6494 199 661	81.7083 882 043	80.7830 122 200	132
12	87.8710 919 527	86.7937 762 771	85.7358 492 351	84.6969 002 420	144
13	91.7700 176 535	90.5733 157 609	89.3996 835 607	88.2485 961 862	156
14	95.3345 642 925	94.0201 522 869	92.7327 218 849	91.4716 173 891	168
15	98.5934 088 351	97.1635 728 247	95.7648 307 314	94.3963 794 850	180
16	101.5727 688 569	100.0302 862 889	98.5231 800 700	97.0504 834 388	192
17	104.2966 134 662	102.6446 504 780	101.0324 867 800	99.4589 760 159	204
18	106.7868 561 361	105.0288 790 376	103.3152 361 317	101.6445 861 482	216
19	109.0635 310 001	107.2032 302 041	105.3918 832 718	103.6279 394 274	228
20	111.1449 540 271	109.1861 789 345	107.2810 365 164	105.4277 527 482	240
21	113.0478 703 751	110.9945 738 838	108.9996 240 957	107.0610 109 394	252
22	114.7875 891 060	112.6437 805 640	110.5630 458 436	108.5431 270 504	264
23	116.3781 063 488	114.1478 119 013	111.9853 111 918	109.8880 878 031	276
24	117.8322 178 982	115.5194 473 008	113.2791 647 047	111.1085 855 853	288
25	119.1616 221 582	116.7703 412 300	114.4562 002 803	112.2161 382 283	300
26	120.3770 142 561	117.9111 222 441	115.5269 650 404	113.2211 977 006	312
27	121.4881 720 852	118.9514 832 945	116.5010 538 404	114.1332 487 434	324
28	122.5040 349 687	119.9002 640 876	117.3871 952 467	114.9608 983 775	336
29	123.4327 755 771	120.7655 261 934	118.1933 297 510	115.7119 571 283	348
30	124.2818 656 772	121.5546 215 431	118.9266 809 231	116.3935 127 335	360
31	125.0581 362 438	122.2742 548 968	119.5938 201 398	117.0119 970 297	372
32	125.7678 324 144	122.9305 408 119	120.2007 254 688	117.5732 466 500	384
33	126.4166 637 319	123.5290 555 974	120.7528 352 371	118.0825 581 042	396
34	127.0098 500 785	124.0748 846 946	121.2550 967 625	118.5447 377 620	408
35	127.5521 636 696	124.5726 658 865	121.7120 106 849	118.9641 472 102	420
36	128.0479 674 465	125.0266 287 043	122.1276 712 959	119.3447 444 139	432
37	128.5012 501 767	125.4406 303 648	122.5058 032 263	119.6901 210 666	444
38	128.9156 585 436	125.8181 885 438	122.8497 948 219	120.0035 364 863	456
39	129.2945 264 844	126.1625 112 656	123.1627 285 055	120.2879 483 726	468
40	129.6409 020 116	126.4765 241 603	123.4474 083 975	120.5460 407 189	480
41	129.9575 717 344	126.7628 953 227	123.7063 854 434	120.7802 491 415	492
42	130.2470 832 776	127.0240 579 820	123.9419 802 718	120.9927 838 640	504
43	130.5117 657 767	127.2622 311 767	124.1563 039 890	121.1856 505 754	516
44	130.7537 486 163	127.4794 386 091	124.3512 770 963	121.3606 693 580	528
45	130.9749 785 610	127.6775 258 403	124.5286 466 991	121.5194 918 631	540
46	131.1772 354 176	127.8581 759 716	124.6900 021 620	121.6636 168 979	552
47	131.3621 463 530	128.0229 239 452	124.8367 893 511	121.7944 045 695	564
48	131.5311 989 853	128.1731 695 863	124.9703 235 895	121.9130 891 206	576
49	131.6857 533 520	128.3101 894 973	125.0918 014 444	122.0207 905 767	588
50	131.8270 528 511	128.4351 479 046	125.2023 114 483	122.1185 253 158	600

MONTHLY
Compounding

TABLE 5. PRESENT WORTH OF ONE DOLLAR PER PERIOD
Payable at end of each period

MONTHS	10% Nominal Annual Rate	10¼% Nominal Annual Rate	10½% Nominal Annual Rate	10¾% Nominal Annual Rate	MONTHS
1	0.9917 355 372	0.9915 306 755	0.9913 258 984	0.9911 212 059	1
2	1.9752 749 129	1.9746 637 559	1.9740 529 352	1.9734 424 506	2
3	2.9506 858 640	2.9494 703 632	2.9482 556 978	2.9470 418 672	3
4	3.9180 355 677	3.9160 210 170	3.9140 081 267	3.9119 968 950	4
5	4.8773 906 456	4.8743 856 397	4.8713 835 209	4.8683 842 858	5
6	5.8288 171 692	5.8246 335 614	5.8204 545 437	5.8162 801 098	6
7	6.7723 806 637	6.7668 335 250	6.7612 932 279	6.7557 597 619	7
8	7.7081 461 127	7.7010 536 914	7.6939 709 818	7.6868 979 676	8
9	8.6361 779 630	8.6273 616 440	8.6185 585 941	8.6097 687 889	9
10	9.5565 401 286	9.5458 243 940	9.5351 262 395	9.5244 456 301	10
11	10.4692 959 953	10.4565 083 848	10.4437 434 841	10.4310 012 440	11
YEARS					
1	11.3745 084 251	11.3594 794 975	11.3444 792 903	11.3295 077 372	12
2	21.6708 548 343	21.6167 613 382	21.5628 579 898	21.5091 440 036	24
3	30.9912 355 853	30.8787 905 344	30.7669 175 659	30.6556 132 874	36
4	39.4281 600 915	39.2421 353 428	39.0573 435 886	38.8737 753 285	48
5	47.0653 690 238	46.7939 941 098	46.5248 271 560	46.2578 472 846	60
6	53.9786 654 781	53.6131 044 230	53.2510 569 874	52.8924 838 832	72
7	60.2366 673 594	59.7705 640 496	59.3096 130 374	58.8537 479 471	84
8	65.9014 884 480	65.3305 722 196	64.7667 714 055	64.2099 824 161	96
9	71.0293 549 100	70.3510 989 831	69.6822 293 478	69.0225 938 655	108
10	75.6711 633 697	74.8844 896 207	74.1097 583 204	73.3467 565 020	120
11	79.8729 860 841	78.9780 104 087	78.0977 921 990	77.2320 447 085	132
12	83.6765 282 329	82.6743 414 292	81.6899 571 099	80.7230 013 899	144
13	87.1195 418 633	86.0120 215 634	84.9255 486 669	83.8596 486 356	156
14	90.2362 005 974	89.0258 503 077	87.8399 618 366	86.6779 465 527	168
15	93.0574 388 230	91.7472 506 023	90.4650 781 326	89.2102 055 310	180
16	95.6112 587 322	94.2045 964 542	92.8296 143 759	91.4854 566 654	192
17	97.9230 082 574	96.4235 087 722	94.9594 368 354	93.5297 845 833	204
18	100.0156 326 622	98.4271 224 968	96.8778 441 854	95.3666 264 917	216
19	101.9099 022 844	100.2363 278 109	98.6058 223 765	97.0170 408 734	228
20	103.6246 186 917	101.8699 879 464	100.1622 742 056	98.4999 489 118	240
21	105.1768 012 971	103.3451 358 566	101.5642 260 987	99.8323 514 131	252
22	106.5818 562 849	104.6771 518 064	102.8270 143 674	101.0295 237 120	264
23	107.8537 295 244	105.8799 237 306	103.9644 529 767	102.1051 907 961	276
24	109.0050 449 899	106.9659 920 332	104.9889 846 594	103.0716 846 556	288
25	110.0472 300 598	107.9466 803 368	105.9118 170 306	103.9400 856 641	300
26	110.9906 289 393	108.8322 135 455	106.7430 451 905	104.7203 496 088	312
27	111.8446 053 313	109.6318 244 521	107.4917 621 573	105.4214 218 296	324
28	112.6176 353 760	110.3538 500 022	108.1661 583 380	106.0513 397 722	336
29	113.3173 917 811	111.0058 182 165	108.7736 111 255	106.6173 251 337	348
30	113.9508 199 769	111.5945 266 804	109.3207 656 018	107.1258 666 562	360
31	114.5242 070 530	112.1261 134 170	109.8136 072 301	107.5827 945 161	372
32	115.0432 441 614	112.6061 208 840	110.2575 273 315	107.9933 471 652	384
33	115.5130 830 035	113.0395 537 606	110.6573 820 619	108.3622 313 862	396
34	115.9383 869 633	113.4309 311 274	111.0175 455 349	108.6936 762 540	408
35	116.3233 773 942	113.7843 335 837	111.3419 576 712	108.9914 816 198	420
36	116.6718 755 176	114.1034 457 930	111.6341 672 982	109.2590 616 747	432
37	116.9873 403 506	114.3915 948 996	111.8973 709 722	109.4994 840 915	444
38	117.2729 030 387	114.6517 852 190	112.1344 479 457	109.7155 051 941	456
39	117.5313 979 333	114.8867 295 612	112.3479 916 646	109.9096 015 575	468
40	117.7653 907 251	115.0988 775 153	112.5403 381 384	110.0839 984 003	480
41	117.9772 039 086	115.2904 409 894	112.7135 914 945	110.2406 950 959	492
42	118.1689 398 351	115.4634 172 728	112.8696 469 959	110.3814 880 944	504
43	118.3425 015 791	115.6196 098 599	113.0102 117 738	110.5079 915 177	516
44	118.4996 118 270	115.7606 472 540	113.1368 235 023	110.6216 556 650	528
45	118.6418 299 763	115.8879 999 467	113.2508 672 197	110.7237 836 393	540
46	118.7705 676 128	116.0029 957 493	113.3535 904 794	110.8155 462 874	552
47	118.8871 025 215	116.1068 336 371	113.4461 169 975	110.8979 956 226	564
48	118.9925 913 694	116.2005 962 503	113.5294 589 454	110.9720 768 856	576
49	119.0880 811 857	116.2852 611 813	113.6045 280 221	111.0386 393 814	588
50	119.1745 197 543	116.3617 111 684	113.6721 454 274	111.0984 462 161	600

TABLE 5. PRESENT WORTH OF ONE DOLLAR PER PERIOD
Payable at end of each period

MONTHLY Compounding

MONTHS	11% Nominal Annual Rate	11¼% Nominal Annual Rate	11½% Nominal Annual Rate	11¾% Nominal Annual Rate	MONTHS
1	0.9909 165 979	0.9907 120 743	0.9905 076 352	0.9903 032 804	1
2	1.9728 323 018	1.9722 224 885	1.9716 130 105	1.9710 038 675	2
3	2.9458 288 704	2.9446 167 068	2.9434 053 756	2.9421 948 760	3
4	3.9099 873 200	3.9079 794 000	3.9059 731 331	3.9039 685 176	4
5	4.8653 879 306	4.8623 944 520	4.8594 038 462	4.8564 161 099	5
6	5.8121 102 533	5.8079 449 679	5.8037 842 472	5.7996 280 849	6
7	6.7502 331 164	6.7447 132 809	6.7392 002 449	6.7336 939 978	7
8	7.6798 346 323	7.6727 809 594	7.6657 369 326	7.6587 025 355	8
9	8.6009 922 038	8.5922 288 143	8.5834 785 960	8.5747 415 247	9
10	9.5137 825 306	9.5031 369 058	9.4925 087 208	9.4818 979 407	10
11	10.4182 816 157	10.4055 845 506	10.3929 100 000	10.3802 579 153	11
YEARS					
1	11.3145 647 720	11.2996 503 288	11.2847 643 417	11.2699 067 451	12
2	21.4556 185 975	21.4022 809 930	21.3491 304 152	21.2961 660 927	24
3	30.5448 743 280	30.4346 973 394	30.3250 789 945	30.2160 159 884	36
4	38.6914 211 422	38.5102 716 888	38.3303 177 061	38.1515 500 100	48
5	45.9930 338 334	45.7303 663 537	45.4698 246 076	45.2113 885 661	60
6	52.5373 463 020	52.1856 059 087	51.8372 248 355	51.4921 656 760	72
7	58.4029 033 369	57.9570 146 847	57.5160 183 742	57.0798 516 820	84
8	63.6601 033 094	63.1170 337 631	62.5806 750 475	62.0509 299 984	96
9	68.3720 430 938	67.7304 302 358	67.0976 110 909	66.4734 440 054	108
10	72.5952 753 558	71.8551 101 432	71.1260 601 126	70.4079 284 164	120
11	76.3804 872 972	75.5428 452 943	74.7188 498 629	73.9082 378 685	132
12	79.7731 090 032	78.8399 230 918	77.9230 950 007	77.0222 840 765	144
13	82.8138 586 938	81.7877 275 186	80.7808 149 387	79.7926 916 413	156
14	85.5392 314 238	84.4232 585 772	83.3294 848 729	82.2573 814 894	168
15	87.9819 370 963	86.7795 967 041	85.6025 272 193	84.4500 899 285	180
16	90.1712 930 463	88.8863 179 851	87.6297 499 049	86.4008 304 255	192
17	92.1335 759 073	90.7698 653 866	89.4377 372 587	88.1363 044 258	204
18	93.8923 369 834	92.4538 806 598	91.0501 986 300	89.6802 668 393	216
19	95.4686 849 118	93.9595 010 855	92.4882 793 048	91.0538 511 937	228
20	96.8815 390 084	95.3056 247 831	93.7708 377 984	92.2758 589 072	240
21	98.1478 563 375	96.5091 479 142	94.9146 931 594	93.3630 166 396	252
22	99.2828 352 300	97.5851 767 590	95.9348 455 295	94.3302 052 439	264
23	100.3000 976 940	98.5472 173 254	96.8446 728 499	95.1906 634 540	276
24	101.2118 529 060	99.4073 448 731	97.6561 062 959	95.9561 690 936	288
25	102.0290 437 452	100.1763 554 783	98.3797 867 377	96.6372 002 902	300
26	102.7614 781 298	100.8639 015 435	99.0252 042 817	97.2430 788 972	312
27	103.4179 467 318	101.4786 129 513	99.6008 227 206	97.7820 980 909	324
28	104.0063 284 824	102.0282 053 845	100.1141 905 245	98.2616 358 859	336
29	104.5336 851 348	102.5195 771 709	100.5720 398 293	98.6882 561 240	348
30	105.0063 460 198	102.9588 958 695	100.9803 747 196	99.0677 983 196	360
31	105.4299 840 096	103.3516 756 836	101.3445 499 644	99.4054 575 897	372
32	105.8096 836 042	103.7028 466 738	101.6693 412 377	99.7058 557 643	384
33	106.1500 019 553	104.0168 166 384	101.9590 077 449	99.9731 046 488	396
34	106.4550 235 611	104.2975 264 391	102.2173 480 770	100.2108 623 061	408
35	106.7284 092 888	104.5484 994 655	102.4477 500 238	100.4223 831 277	420
36	106.9734 403 116	104.7728 858 597	102.6532 350 004	100.6105 623 792	432
37	107.1930 574 901	104.9735 020 558	102.8364 976 690	100.7779 758 300	444
38	107.3898 966 680	105.1528 661 313	102.9999 412 756	100.9269 150 106	456
39	107.5663 203 077	105.3132 294 130	103.1457 091 658	101.0594 185 784	468
40	107.7244 458 443	105.4566 047 353	103.2757 128 916	101.1773 002 223	480
41	107.8661 710 993	105.5847 917 044	103.3916 572 788	101.2821 734 890	492
42	107.9931 970 582	105.6993 992 866	103.4950 627 840	101.3754 738 679	504
43	108.1070 482 856	105.8018 660 038	103.5872 854 328	101.4584 784 408	516
44	108.2090 912 230	105.8934 779 891	103.6695 346 025	101.5323 233 620	528
45	108.3005 505 890	105.9753 851 300	103.7428 888 816	101.5980 194 097	540
46	108.3825 240 783	106.0486 155 016	103.8083 102 138	101.6564 658 217	552
47	108.4559 955 359	106.1140 882 708	103.8666 565 131	101.7084 626 037	564
48	108.5218 467 659	106.1726 252 332	103.9186 929 134	101.7547 214 800	576
49	108.5808 681 141	106.2249 611 280	103.9651 018 029	101.7958 756 351	588
50	108.6337 679 544	106.2717 528 605	104.0064 917 726	101.8324 883 811	600

TABLE 5. PRESENT WORTH OF ONE DOLLAR PER PERIOD
Payable at end of each period

	12% Nominal Annual Rate	12¼% Nominal Annual Rate	12½% Nominal Annual Rate	12¾% Nominal Annual Rate	
MONTHS					MONTHS
1	0.9900 990 099	0.9898 948 237	0.9896 907 216	0.9894 867 038	1
2	1.9703 950 593	1.9697 865 856	1.9691 784 462	1.9685 706 407	2
3	2.9409 852 072	2.9397 763 685	2.9385 683 591	2.9373 611 782	3
4	3.9019 655 517	3.8999 642 336	3.8979 645 616	3.8959 665 338	4
5	4.8534 312 393	4.8504 492 311	4.8474 700 816	4.8444 937 873	5
6	5.7954 764 746	5.7913 294 100	5.7871 868 848	5.7830 488 928	6
7	6.7281 945 293	6.7227 018 288	6.7172 158 860	6.7117 366 905	7
8	7.6516 777 518	7.6446 625 652	7.6376 569 594	7.6306 609 182	8
9	8.5660 175 760	8.5573 067 257	8.5486 089 495	8.5399 242 233	9
10	9.4713 045 307	9.4607 284 560	9.4501 696 820	9.4396 281 740	10
11	10.3676 282 482	10.3550 209 505	10.3424 359 739	10.3298 732 705	11
YEARS					
1	11.2550 774 735	11.2402 764 616	11.2255 036 443	11.2107 589 566	12
2	21.2433 872 576	21.1907 931 457	21.1383 829 962	21.0861 560 516	24
3	30.1075 050 373	29.9995 428 789	29.8921 262 721	29.7852 519 970	36
4	37.9739 594 935	37.7975 371 262	37.6222 739 539	37.4481 610 972	48
5	44.9550 384 062	44.7007 545 094	44.4485 174 588	44.1983 080 374	60
6	51.1503 914 789	50.8118 657 423	50.4765 524 081	50.1444 158 559	72
7	56.6484 527 634	56.2217 606 403	55.7997 151 877	55.3822 571 212	84
8	61.5277 029 908	61.0108 999 134	60.5004 281 425	59.9961 965 178	96
9	65.8577 898 250	65.2505 118 484	64.6514 757 806	64.0605 496 887	108
10	69.7005 220 314	69.0036 516 789	68.3171 317 480	67.6407 802 202	120
11	73.1107 517 508	72.3261 393 978	71.5541 540 235	70.7945 540 483	132
12	76.1371 574 733	75.2673 899 616	74.4126 637 432	73.5726 682 706	144
13	78.8229 388 871	77.8711 482 328	76.9369 212 622	76.0198 693 233	156
14	81.2064 335 219	80.1761 395 920	79.1660 114 689	78.1755 737 016	168
15	83.3216 639 891	82.2166 458 959	81.1344 489 648	80.0745 028 319	180
16	85.1988 236 284	84.0230 153 468	82.8727 124 785	81.7472 423 217	192
17	86.8647 074 960	85.6221 138 584	84.4077 167 901	83.2207 345 948	204
18	88.3430 948 437	87.0377 246 286	85.7632 294 715	84.5187 128 467	216
19	89.6550 885 500	88.2909 018 645	86.9602 388 973	85.6620 833 097	228
20	90.8194 163 483	89.4002 839 190	88.0172 792 223	86.6692 619 844	240
21	91.8526 981 508	90.3823 704 967	88.9507 173 596	87.5564 712 623	252
22	92.7696 832 859	91.2517 680 520	89.7750 064 010	88.3380 012 158	264
23	93.5834 610 337	92.0214 070 292	90.5029 094 044	89.0264 397 651	276
24	94.3056 474 655	92.7027 341 753	91.1456 970 139	89.6328 754 288	288
25	94.9465 512 548	93.3058 827 863	91.7133 219 708	90.1670 759 246	300
26	95.5153 208 262	93.8398 234 182	92.2145 732 191	90.6376 454 948	312
27	96.0200 749 416	94.3124 973 052	92.6572 119 913	91.0521 634 935	324
28	96.4680 185 903	94.7309 344 686	93.0480 919 806	91.4173 064 652	336
29	96.8655 458 343	95.1013 582 736	93.3932 654 621	91.7389 556 824	348
30	97.2183 310 791	95.4292 779 884	93.6980 770 044	92.0222 918 737	360
31	97.5314 100 712	95.7195 707 232	93.9672 462 229	92.2718 786 690	372
32	97.8092 517 802	95.9765 539 664	94.2049 408 576	92.4917 361 044	384
33	98.0558 221 896	96.2040 497 988	94.4148 413 049	92.6854 053 722	396
34	98.2746 409 083	96.4054 417 382	94.6001 976 040	92.8560 058 581	408
35	98.4688 314 108	96.5837 250 624	94.7638 797 592	93.0062 853 841	420
36	98.6411 656 218	96.7415 513 577	94.9084 221 786	93.1386 644 675	432
37	98.7941 034 838	96.8812 679 554	95.0360 629 162	93.2552 753 072	444
38	98.9298 280 709	97.0049 528 435	95.1487 783 251	93.3579 961 267	456
39	99.0502 767 506	97.1144 455 724	95.2483 136 585	93.4484 814 263	468
40	99.1571 688 381	97.2113 746 140	95.3362 100 936	93.5281 886 315	480
41	99.2520 301 384	97.2971 815 823	95.4138 285 937	93.5984 015 677	492
42	99.3362 147 258	97.3731 426 739	95.4823 709 818	93.6602 511 381	504
43	99.4109 242 727	97.4403 876 489	95.5428 985 488	93.7147 335 394	516
44	99.4772 252 021	97.4999 166 335	95.5963 484 864	93.7627 263 068	528
45	99.5360 639 107	97.5526 149 953	95.6435 483 982	93.8050 024 487	540
46	99.5882 802 769	97.5992 665 105	95.6852 291 144	93.8422 428 969	552
47	99.6346 196 507	97.6405 650 214	95.7220 360 074	93.8750 474 747	564
48	99.6757 434 921	97.6771 247 558	95.7545 389 846	93.9039 445 577	576
49	99.7122 388 133	97.7094 894 621	95.7832 413 129	93.9293 995 845	588
50	99.7446 265 578	97.7381 404 968	95.8085 874 112	93.9518 225 533	600

TABLE 5. PRESENT WORTH OF ONE DOLLAR PER PERIOD
Payable at end of each period

MONTHS	13% Nominal Annual Rate	13¼% Nominal Annual Rate	13½% Nominal Annual Rate	13¾% Nominal Annual Rate	MONTHS
1	0.9892 827 700	0.9890 789 203	0.9888 751 545	0.9886 714 727	1
2	1.9679 631 690	1.9673 560 307	1.9667 492 257	1.9661 427 537	2
3	2.9361 548 251	2.9349 492 989	2.9337 445 990	2.9325 407 245	3
4	3.8939 701 484	3.8919 754 038	3.8899 822 981	3.8879 908 296	4
5	4.8415 203 447	4.8385 497 503	4.8355 820 006	4.8326 170 921	5
6	5.7789 154 276	5.7747 864 829	5.7706 620 525	5.7665 421 302	6
7	6.7062 642 317	6.7007 984 995	6.6953 394 833	6.6898 871 730	7
8	7.6236 744 255	7.6166 974 650	7.6097 300 206	7.6027 720 763	8
9	8.5312 525 231	8.5225 938 248	8.5139 481 044	8.5053 153 380	9
10	9.4291 038 976	9.4185 968 183	9.4081 069 018	9.3976 341 138	10
11	10.3173 327 923	10.3048 144 916	10.2923 183 207	10.2798 442 320	11
YEARS					
1	11.1960 423 337	11.1813 537 111	11.1666 930 242	11.1520 602 088	12
2	21.0341 115 581	20.9822 487 652	20.9305 669 260	20.8790 652 968	24
3	29.6789 168 543	29.5731 176 658	29.4678 512 737	29.3631 145 407	36
4	37.2751 897 516	37.1033 511 863	36.9326 367 438	36.7630 378 391	48
5	43.9501 072 254	43.7038 961 985	43.4596 563 256	43.2173 691 668	60
6	49.8154 208 975	49.4895 327 714	49.1667 171 372	48.8469 400 702	72
7	54.9693 279 845	54.5608 701 370	54.1568 267 420	53.7571 417 545	84
8	59.4981 153 172	59.0060 962 329	58.5200 523 480	58.0398 981 128	96
9	63.4776 039 573	62.9025 112 453	62.3351 464 435	61.7753 866 331	108
10	66.9744 185 952	66.3178 718 188	65.6709 682 119	65.0335 394 016	120
11	70.0471 029 820	69.3115 693 101	68.5877 263 816	67.8753 523 010	132
12	72.7471 000 704	71.9356 625 723	71.1380 659 413	70.3540 269 149	144
13	75.1196 132 736	74.2357 832 321	73.3680 183 376	72.5159 665 144	156
14	77.2043 632 624	76.2519 291 999	75.3178 323 029	74.4016 447 739	168
15	79.0362 529 689	78.0191 602 127	77.0227 003 106	76.0463 634 788	180
16	80.6459 519 328	79.5682 075 053	78.5133 937 693	77.4809 134 106	192
17	82.0604 097 711	80.9260 082 100	79.8168 184 203	78.7321 507 806	204
18	83.3033 073 695	82.1161 737 799	80.9564 999 630	79.8235 000 054	216
19	84.3954 533 482	83.1594 005 795	81.9530 086 739	80.7753 922 356	228
20	85.3551 324 403	84.0738 297 842	82.8243 306 826	81.6056 478 468	240
21	86.1984 116 152	84.8753 628 454	83.5861 926 055	82.3298 100 558	252
22	86.9394 090 722	85.5779 380 093	84.2523 453 985	82.9614 359 043	264
23	87.5905 306 078	86.1937 726 951	84.8348 125 493	83.5123 500 606	276
24	88.1626 773 137	86.7335 759 498	85.3441 070 916	83.9928 661 896	288
25	88.6654 280 833	87.2067 346 734	85.7894 213 560	84.4119 800 345	300
26	89.1071 999 815	87.6214 768 516	86.1787 928 839	84.7775 378 260	312
27	89.4953 891 635	87.9850 146 368	86.5192 494 981	85.0963 831 722	324
28	89.8364 947 016	88.3036 697 632	86.8169 361 492	85.3744 851 773	336
29	90.1362 273 926	88.5829 834 791	87.0772 258 265	85.6170 501 893	348
30	90.3996 053 680	88.8278 129 055	87.3048 165 359	85.8286 192 682	360
31	90.6310 381 080	89.0424 154 998	87.5038 160 950	86.0131 531 990	372
32	90.8344 002 648	89.2305 230 904	87.6778 162 754	86.1741 066 417	384
33	91.0130 965 324	89.3954 067 709	87.8299 576 316	86.3144 928 059	396
34	91.1701 186 477	89.5399 337 836	87.9629 861 848	86.4369 398 613	408
35	91.3080 954 786	89.6666 173 785	88.0793 029 865	86.5437 401 393	420
36	91.4293 370 365	89.7776 605 179	88.1810 074 556	86.6368 930 481	432
37	91.5358 731 501	89.8749 941 846	88.2699 352 705	86.7181 425 034	444
38	91.6294 874 497	89.9603 109 608	88.3476 915 024	86.7890 095 764	456
39	91.7117 472 280	90.0350 944 613	88.4156 795 845	86.8508 209 698	468
40	91.7840 296 800	90.1006 451 324	88.4751 266 437	86.9047 338 546	480
41	91.8475 449 603	90.1581 028 665	88.5271 056 485	86.9517 575 341	492
42	91.9033 564 431	90.2084 668 239	88.5725 547 753	86.9927 723 386	504
43	91.9523 985 255	90.2526 128 078	88.6122 943 421	87.0285 461 064	516
44	91.9954 922 713	90.2913 084 940	88.6470 416 141	87.0597 485 582	528
45	92.0333 591 569	90.3252 267 807	88.6774 237 497	87.0869 638 352	540
46	92.0666 331 506	90.3549 574 892	88.7039 891 205	87.1107 014 347	552
47	92.0958 713 263	90.3810 176 212	88.7272 172 087	87.1314 057 481	564
48	92.1215 631 903	90.4038 603 490	88.7475 272 615	87.1494 643 811	576
49	92.1441 388 763	90.4238 828 957	88.7652 858 579	87.1652 154 093	588
50	92.1639 763 470	90.4414 334 433	88.7808 135 253	87.1789 537 078	600

TABLE 5. PRESENT WORTH OF ONE DOLLAR PER PERIOD
Payable at end of each period

MONTHS	14% Nominal Annual Rate	14¼% Nominal Annual Rate	14½% Nominal Annual Rate	14¾% Nominal Annual Rate	MONTHS
1	0.9884 678 748	0.9882 643 607	0.9880 609 304	0.9878 575 839	1
2	1.9655 366 143	1.9649 308 074	1.9643 253 327	1.9637 201 899	2
3	2.9313 376 748	2.9301 354 489	2.9289 340 463	2.9277 334 660	3
4	3.8860 009 965	3.8840 127 970	3.8820 262 293	3.8800 412 918	4
5	4.8296 550 212	4.8266 957 845	4.8237 393 785	4.8207 857 997	5
6	5.7624 267 096	5.7583 157 846	5.7542 093 489	5.7501 073 963	6
7	6.6844 415 581	6.6790 026 284	6.6735 703 735	6.6681 447 833	7
8	7.5958 236 159	7.5888 846 235	7.5819 550 829	7.5750 349 784	8
9	8.4966 955 017	8.4880 885 717	8.4794 945 241	8.4709 133 353	9
10	9.3871 784 202	9.3767 397 867	9.3663 181 794	9.3559 135 644	10
11	10.2673 921 781	10.2549 621 116	10.2425 539 854	10.2301 677 524	11
YEARS					
1	11.1374 552 007	11.1228 779 361	11.1083 283 512	11.0938 063 823	12
2	20.8277 431 374	20.7765 997 110	20.7256 342 841	20.6748 461 265	24
3	29.2589 043 500	29.1552 176 048	29.0520 512 284	28.9494 021 641	36
4	36.5945 459 592	36.4271 526 623	36.2608 495 774	36.0956 284 033	48
5	42.9770 164 708	42.7385 801 735	42.5020 423 958	42.2673 854 413	60
6	48.5301 680 561	48.2163 679 858	47.9055 071 498	47.5975 532 336	72
7	53.3617 599 097	52.9706 267 113	52.5836 884 201	52.2008 920 429	84
8	57.5655 493 222	57.0969 230 930	56.6339 378 422	56.1765 132 649	96
9	61.2231 110 449	60.6782 010 193	60.1405 399 668	59.6100 133 301	108
10	64.4054 202 530	63.7864 488 035	63.1764 661 972	62.5753 166 221	120
11	67.1742 298 217	66.4841 462 419	65.8048 933 038	65.1362 670 944	132
12	69.5832 686 441	68.8255 205 384	68.0805 181 150	67.3480 028 515	144
13	71.6792 842 436	70.8576 363 414	70.0506 957 426	69.2581 432 904	156
14	73.5029 499 117	72.6213 418 041	71.7564 250 285	70.9078 143 619	168
15	75.0896 539 752	74.1520 896 850	73.2332 017 192	72.3325 340 259	180
16	76.4701 865 088	75.4806 499 941	74.5117 571 219	73.5629 769 645	192
17	77.6713 368 178	76.6337 285 102	75.6186 976 148	74.6256 350 181	204
18	78.7164 132 863	77.6345 036 012	76.5770 583 180	75.5433 875 636	216
19	79.6256 956 774	78.5030 921 395	77.4067 824 480	76.3359 941 145	228
20	80.4168 286 631	79.2569 538 768	78.1251 363 303	77.0205 197 502	240
21	81.1051 642 199	79.9112 424 082	78.7470 687 072	77.6117 025 324	252
22	81.7040 595 351	80.4791 097 783	79.2855 218 164	78.1222 708 203	264
23	82.2251 362 033	80.9719 708 551	79.7517 007 154	78.5632 173 170	276
24	82.6785 057 442	81.3997 327 829	80.1553 064 561	78.9440 357 453	288
25	83.0729 658 174	81.7709 941 292	80.5047 379 602	79.2729 252 509	300
26	83.4161 709 410	82.0932 177 266	80.8072 667 991	79.5569 669 329	312
27	83.7147 810 282	82.3728 806 859	81.0691 885 127	79.8022 763 020	324
28	83.9745 906 233	82.6156 045 938	81.2959 536 181	80.0141 349 494	336
29	84.2006 413 449	82.8262 685 144	81.4922 810 335	80.1971 042 613	348
30	84.3973 197 191	83.0091 070 647	81.6622 562 770	80.3551 236 272	360
31	84.5684 422 997	83.1677 955 359	81.8094 164 857	80.4915 952 559	372
32	84.7173 297 295	83.3055 237 713	81.9368 240 220	80.6094 574 263	384
33	84.8468 711 767	83.4250 602 862	82.0471 302 009	80.7112 477 497	396
34	84.9595 803 998	83.5288 079 191	82.1426 304 630	80.7991 578 051	408
35	85.0576 445 272	83.6188 521 314	82.2253 121 419	80.8750 803 249	420
36	85.1429 664 982	83.6970 029 282	82.2968 958 200	80.9406 499 459	432
37	85.2172 019 903	83.7648 312 415	82.3588 711 334	80.9972 784 035	444
38	85.2817 915 469	83.8237 005 079	82.4125 277 712	81.0461 849 270	456
39	85.3379 885 317	83.8747 940 758	82.4589 823 127	81.0884 224 900	468
40	85.3868 834 502	83.9191 389 919	82.4992 014 638	81.1249 004 811	480
41	85.4294 251 108	83.9576 266 463	82.5340 221 740	81.1564 042 833	492
42	85.4664 390 365	83.9910 306 906	82.5641 690 522	81.1836 121 838	504
43	85.4986 434 847	84.0200 225 893	82.5902 694 466	81.2071 099 778	516
44	85.5266 633 842	84.0451 851 169	82.6128 664 989	81.2274 035 804	528
45	85.5510 424 626	84.0670 240 729	82.6324 304 476	81.2449 299 195	540
46	85.5722 537 973	84.0859 784 483	82.6493 684 129	81.2600 663 430	552
47	85.5907 089 953	84.1024 292 507	82.6640 328 690	81.2731 387 431	564
48	85.6067 661 806	84.1167 071 624	82.6767 289 793	81.2844 285 728	576
49	85.6207 369 438	84.1290 991 879	82.6877 209 460	81.2941 789 058	588
50	85.6328 923 883	84.1398 544 230	82.6972 375 091	81.3025 996 701	600

TABLE 5. PRESENT WORTH OF ONE DOLLAR PER PERIOD
Payable at end of each period

MONTHLY Compounding

MONTHS	15% Nominal Annual Rate	15¼% Nominal Annual Rate	15½% Nominal Annual Rate	15¾% Nominal Annual Rate	MONTHS
1	0.9876 543 210	0.9874 511 417	0.9872 480 461	0.9870 450 339	1
2	1.9631 153 788	1.9625 108 991	1.9619 067 505	1.9613 029 329	2
3	2.9265 337 074	2.9253 347 697	2.9241 366 521	2.9229 393 539	3
4	3.8780 579 826	3.8760 763 001	3.8740 962 423	3.8721 178 077	4
5	4.8178 350 446	4.8148 871 097	4.8119 419 916	4.8089 996 868	5
6	5.7460 099 206	5.7419 169 156	5.7378 283 751	5.7337 442 930	6
7	6.6627 258 475	6.6573 135 558	6.6519 078 981	6.6465 088 641	7
8	7.5681 242 938	7.5612 230 133	7.5543 311 211	7.5474 486 012	8
9	8.4623 449 815	8.4537 894 392	8.4452 466 847	8.4367 166 946	9
10	9.3455 259 077	9.3351 551 755	9.3248 013 342	9.3144 643 500	10
11	10.2178 033 656	10.2054 607 781	10.1931 399 432	10.1808 408 143	11
YEARS					
1	11.0793 119 660	11.0648 450 391	11.0504 055 384	11.0359 934 009	12
2	20.6242 345 116	20.5737 987 157	20.5235 380 186	20.4734 517 036	24
3	28.8472 673 749	28.7456 438 435	28.6445 285 721	28.5439 185 821	36
4	35.9314 809 083	35.7683 989 294	35.6063 743 719	35.4453 992 085	48
5	42.0345 917 945	41.8036 441 188	41.5745 252 547	41.3472 182 176	60
6	47.2924 743 123	46.9902 388 457	46.6908 156 731	46.3941 740 090	72
7	51.8221 853 215	51.4475 167 219	51.0768 354 234	50.7100 913 085	84
8	55.7245 703 133	55.2780 311 754	54.8368 192 550	54.4008 591 507	96
9	59.0865 085 459	58.5699 150 082	58.0601 240 320	57.5570 288 176	108
10	61.9828 472 474	61.3989 081 630	60.8233 523 199	60.2560 354 721	120
11	64.4780 679 485	63.8301 003 546	63.1921 728 627	62.5640 979 939	132
12	66.6277 220 424	65.9194 286 594	65.2228 812 150	64.5378 436 295	144
13	68.4796 675 323	67.7149 645 206	66.9637 376 192	66.2256 973 151	156
14	70.0751 344 993	69.2580 197 796	68.4561 139 206	67.6690 697 602	168
15	71.4496 430 131	70.5840 971 831	69.7354 767 788	68.9033 734 401	180
16	72.6337 939 191	71.7237 072 324	70.8322 305 407	69.9588 914 245	192
17	73.6539 501 088	72.7030 701 724	71.7724 398 072	70.8615 203 592	204
18	74.5328 234 400	73.5447 192 689	72.5784 488 636	71.6334 058 274	216
19	75.2899 803 735	74.2680 192 556	73.2694 126 970	72.2934 856 821	228
20	75.9422 775 836	74.8896 118 801	73.8617 522 188	72.8579 546 773	240
21	76.5042 372 401	75.4237 987 984	74.3695 445 115	73.3406 617 985	252
22	76.9883 703 173	75.8828 706 284	74.8048 573 736	73.7534 500 418	264
23	77.4054 551 271	76.2773 897 337	75.1780 361 133	74.1064 469 758	276
24	77.7647 772 778	76.6164 332 435	75.4979 494 077	74.4083 132 170	288
25	78.0743 364 010	76.9078 018 995	75.7722 000 684	74.6664 549 139	300
26	78.3410 242 479	77.1581 995 367	76.0073 057 243	74.8872 054 538	312
27	78.5707 781 217	77.3733 873 251	76.2088 537 143	75.0759 808 489	324
28	78.7687 130 599	77.5583 163 235	76.3816 338 719	75.2374 126 164	336
29	78.9392 357 115	77.7172 413 942	76.5297 523 565	75.3754 614 099	348
30	79.0861 424 425	77.8538 190 986	76.6567 292 374	75.4935 141 927	360
31	79.2127 038 546	77.9711 918 282	76.7655 821 487	75.5944 673 353	372
32	79.3217 375 997	78.0720 601 047	76.8588 980 045	75.6807 976 764	384
33	79.4156 711 088	78.1587 447 139	76.9388 944 772	75.7546 232 908	396
34	79.4965 956 347	78.2332 401 027	77.0074 727 010	75.8177 554 559	408
35	79.5663 128 098	78.2972 602 674	77.0662 624 528	75.8717 430 902	420
36	79.6263 747 558	78.3522 781 893	77.1166 608 844	75.9179 107 554	432
37	79.6781 186 388	78.3995 597 254	77.1598 657 258	75.9573 911 536	444
38	79.7226 964 390	78.4401 927 335	77.1969 037 499	75.9911 529 183	456
39	79.7611 005 972	78.4751 121 010	77.2286 551 737	76.0200 243 787	468
40	79.7941 861 099	78.5051 212 559	77.2558 745 769	76.0447 138 828	480
41	79.8226 895 636	78.5309 106 513	77.2792 088 347	76.0658 271 760	492
42	79.8472 455 341	78.5530 736 518	77.2992 124 912	76.0838 822 633	504
43	79.8684 007 139	78.5721 201 856	77.3163 609 377	76.0993 221 180	516
44	79.8866 260 832	78.5884 884 770	77.3310 617 109	76.1125 255 496	528
45	79.9023 273 956	78.6025 551 290	77.3436 641 779	76.1238 164 983	540
46	79.9158 542 113	78.6146 437 883	77.3544 678 393	76.1334 719 823	552
47	79.9275 076 793	78.6250 325 918	77.3637 294 466	76.1417 288 944	564
48	79.9375 472 423	78.6339 605 661	77.3716 691 038	76.1487 898 141	576
49	79.9461 964 121	78.6416 331 267	77.3784 754 988	76.1548 279 779	588
50	79.9536 477 463	78.6482 268 045	77.3843 103 871	76.1599 915 293	600

TABLE 5. PRESENT WORTH OF ONE DOLLAR PER PERIOD
Payable at end of each period

MONTHS	16% Nominal Annual Rate	16¼% Nominal Annual Rate	16½% Nominal Annual Rate	16¾% Nominal Annual Rate	MONTHS
1	0.9868 421 053	0.9866 392 600	0.9864 364 982	0.9862 338 196	1
2	1.9606 994 460	1.9600 962 894	1.9594 934 630	1.9588 909 665	2
3	2.9217 428 743	2.9205 472 126	2.9193 523 680	2.9181 583 397	3
4	3.8701 409 944	3.8681 658 007	3.8661 922 249	3.8642 202 652	4
5	4.8060 601 918	4.8031 235 033	4.8001 896 176	4.7972 585 315	5
6	5.7296 646 630	5.7255 894 791	5.7215 187 350	5.7174 524 247	6
7	6.6411 164 438	6.6357 306 268	6.6303 514 032	6.6249 787 628	7
8	7.5405 754 379	7.5337 116 154	7.5268 571 179	7.5200 119 297	8
9	8.4281 994 453	8.4196 949 134	8.4112 030 756	8.4027 239 084	9
10	9.3041 441 895	9.2938 408 190	9.2835 542 053	9.2732 843 149	10
11	10.1685 633 449	10.1563 074 884	10.1440 731 988	10.1318 604 297	11
YEARS					
1	11.0216 085 640	11.0072 509 649	10.9929 205 413	10.9786 172 309	12
2	20.4235 390 568	20.3737 993 679	20.3242 319 298	20.2748 360 383	24
3	28.4438 109 145	28.3442 026 290	28.2450 908 044	28.1464 725 386	36
4	35.2854 654 789	35.1265 652 891	34.9686 908 109	34.8118 342 814	48
5	41.1217 061 961	40.8979 725 501	40.6760 008 089	40.4557 746 692	60
6	46.1002 834 378	45.8091 139 092	45.5206 357 338	45.2348 195 779	72
7	50.3472 349 519	49.9882 176 110	49.6329 912 154	49.2815 083 573	84
8	53.9700 766 370	53.5443 986 437	53.1237 532 377	52.7080 696 035	96
9	57.0605 244 161	56.5705 076 948	56.0868 773 038	55.6095 336 432	108
10	59.6968 161 192	59.1455 554 511	58.6021 172 930	58.0663 680 522	120
11	61.9456 921 528	61.3367 755 410	60.7371 720 737	60.1467 092 973	132
12	63.8640 851 016	63.2013 799 821	62.5495 076 505	61.9082 523 953	144
13	65.5005 610 351	64.7880 529 675	64.0879 038 887	63.3998 509 940	156
14	66.8965 490 064	66.1382 219 939	65.3937 674 472	64.6628 722 521	168
15	68.0873 898 714	67.2871 395 190	66.5022 462 587	65.7323 440 924	180
16	69.1032 309 779	68.2648 033 921	67.4431 755 521	66.6379 266 468	192
17	69.9697 893 773	69.0967 400 871	68.2418 808 823	67.4047 348 337	204
18	70.7090 028 770	69.8046 711 906	68.9198 597 793	68.0540 348 812	216
19	71.3395 854 189	70.4070 805 450	69.4953 603 644	68.6038 341 124	228
20	71.8775 008 415	70.9196 968 553	69.9838 725 067	69.0693 803 507	240
21	72.3363 670 210	71.3559 043 604	70.3985 447 404	69.4635 847 942	252
22	72.7278 006 217	71.7270 922 914	70.7505 381 641	69.7973 800 878	264
23	73.0617 111 834	72.0429 522 398	71.0493 268 464	70.0800 235 228	276
24	73.3465 519 917	72.3117 312 024	71.3029 528 253	70.3193 537 737	288
25	73.5895 340 814	72.5404 469 072	71.5182 425 636	70.5220 082 914	300
26	73.7968 087 914	72.7350 710 442	71.7009 906 857	70.6936 073 826	312
27	73.9736 234 918	72.9006 851 840	71.8561 159 436	70.8389 100 801	324
28	74.1244 544 266	73.0416 134 558	71.9877 936 065	70.9619 461 274	336
29	74.2531 200 345	73.1615 354 494	72.0995 678 407	71.0661 277 372	348
30	74.3628 776 161	73.2635 822 875	72.1944 471 024	71.1543 442 240	360
31	74.4565 057 964	73.3504 183 787	72.2749 851 116	71.2290 421 340	372
32	74.5363 748 680	73.4243 109 841	72.3433 495 866	71.2922 930 974	384
33	74.6045 067 977	73.4871 894 146	72.4013 805 896	71.3458 512 809	396
34	74.6626 264 146	73.5406 954 048	72.4506 400 522	71.3912 020 370	408
35	74.7122 050 759	73.5862 259 781	72.4924 538 162	71.4296 030 981	420
36	74.7544 979 159	73.6249 699 225	72.5279 473 186	71.4621 194 578	432
37	74.7905 756 208	73.6579 388 292	72.5580 758 838	71.4896 529 066	444
38	74.8213 515 346	73.6859 935 053	72.5836 504 364	71.5129 670 415	456
39	74.8476 047 807	73.7098 664 489	72.6053 593 273	71.5327 084 439	468
40	74.8699 999 867	73.7301 809 745	72.6237 868 617	71.5494 246 106	480
41	74.8891 041 102	73.7474 674 876	72.6394 290 253	71.5635 791 384	492
42	74.9054 007 914	73.7621 773 331	72.6527 068 343	71.5755 645 811	504
43	74.9193 025 973	73.7746 945 802	72.6639 776 672	71.5857 133 363	516
44	74.9311 614 665	73.7853 460 500	72.6735 448 837	71.5943 068 637	528
45	74.9412 776 181	73.7944 098 487	72.6816 659 900	71.6015 834 915	540
46	74.9499 071 528	73.8021 226 290	72.6885 595 696	71.6077 450 256	552
47	74.9572 685 362	73.8086 857 692	72.6944 111 662	71.6129 623 465	564
48	74.9635 481 291	73.8142 706 305	72.6993 782 785	71.6173 801 484	576
49	74.9689 049 058	73.8190 230 318	72.7035 945 986	71.6211 209 523	588
50	74.9734 744 786	73.8230 670 566	72.7071 736 106	71.6242 885 034	600

TABLE 5. PRESENT WORTH OF ONE DOLLAR PER PERIOD
Payable at end of each period

MONTHLY Compounding

MONTHS	17% Nominal Annual Rate	17¼% Nominal Annual Rate	17½% Nominal Annual Rate	17¾% Nominal Annual Rate	MONTHS
1	0.9860 312 243	0.9858 287 123	0.9856 262 834	0.9854 239 376	1
2	1.9582 887 997	1.9576 869 622	1.9570 854 538	1.9564 842 744	2
3	2.9169 651 270	2.9157 727 292	2.9145 811 455	2.9133 903 751	3
4	3.8622 499 198	3.8602 811 871	3.8583 140 653	3.8563 485 527	4
5	4.7943 302 414	4.7914 047 439	4.7884 820 357	4.7855 621 131	5
6	5.7133 905 421	5.7093 330 809	5.7052 800 351	5.7012 313 987	6
7	6.6196 126 955	6.6142 531 913	6.6089 002 400	6.6035 538 316	7
8	7.5131 760 350	7.5063 494 184	7.4995 320 640	7.4927 239 564	8
9	8.3942 573 887	8.3858 034 932	8.3773 621 986	8.3689 334 820	9
10	9.2630 311 146	9.2527 945 712	9.2425 746 516	9.2323 713 228	10
11	10.1196 691 352	10.1074 992 692	10.0953 507 860	10.0832 236 398	11
YEARS					
1	10.9643 409 714	10.9500 917 010	10.9358 693 579	10.9216 738 804	12
2	20.2256 109 929	20.1765 560 958	20.1276 706 527	20.0789 539 722	24
3	28.0483 449 478	27.9507 051 671	27.8535 503 498	27.7568 776 677	36
4	34.6559 880 019	34.5011 443 382	34.3472 957 192	34.1944 346 370	48
5	40.2372 779 936	40.0204 948 087	39.8054 093 032	39.5920 058 261	60
6	44.9516 364 595	44.6710 577 437	44.3930 551 379	44.1176 006 879	72
7	48.9337 222 816	48.5895 868 762	48.2490 566 631	47.9120 867 883	84
8	52.2972 780 250	51.8913 098 671	51.4900 975 581	51.0935 745 718	96
9	55.1383 788 310	54.6733 166 711	54.2142 526 226	53.7610 937 691	108
10	57.5381 766 658	57.0174 145 494	56.5039 555 469	55.9976 758 817	120
11	59.5652 183 095	58.9925 336 810	58.4284 933 788	57.8729 386 919	132
12	61.2774 032 969	60.6567 541 132	60.0461 031 688	59.4452 532 462	144
13	62.7236 377 341	62.0590 136 542	61.4057 342 394	60.7635 607 624	156
14	63.9452 312 318	63.2405 469 309	62.5485 294 050	61.8688 960 164	168
15	64.9770 768 547	64.2360 979 278	63.5090 699 656	62.7956 646 260	180
16	65.8486 477 916	65.0749 416 632	64.3164 221 458	63.5727 139 896	192
17	66.5848 392 154	65.7817 450 461	64.9950 166 473	64.2242 312 154	204
18	67.2066 793 771	66.3772 922 273	65.5653 879 285	64.7704 959 901	216
19	67.7319 302 484	66.8790 957 750	66.0447 955 833	65.2285 118 219	228
20	68.1755 948 663	67.3019 116 465	66.4477 466 206	65.6125 353 061	240
21	68.5503 458 737	67.6581 730 999	66.7864 344 510	65.9345 198 889	252
22	68.8668 874 954	67.9583 563 043	67.0711 078 626	66.2044 879 398	264
23	69.1342 612 881	68.2112 884 004	67.3103 811 519	66.4308 427 169	276
24	69.3601 044 006	68.4244 070 704	67.5114 947 953	66.6206 299 343	288
25	69.5508 677 172	68.6039 792 488	67.6805 345 476	66.7797 570 723	300
26	69.7120 001 181	68.7552 854 073	67.8226 155 989	66.9131 772 595	312
27	69.8481 041 190	68.8827 748 313	67.9420 373 611	67.0250 434 475	324
28	69.9630 673 354	68.9901 964 551	68.0424 135 702	67.1188 376 798	336
29	70.0601 735 264	69.0807 091 023	68.1267 816 381	67.1974 794 764	348
30	70.1421 963 912	69.1569 743 739	68.1976 945 661	67.2634 167 096	360
31	70.2114 787 949	69.2212 349 145	68.2572 981 990	67.3187 017 987	372
32	70.2699 996 901	69.2753 803 597	68.3073 961 594	67.3650 555 950	384
33	70.3194 306 421	69.3210 029 020	68.3495 044 255	67.4039 209 466	396
34	70.3611 835 751	69.3594 441 109	68.3848 972 053	67.4365 076 100	408
35	70.3964 511 017	69.3918 343 825	68.4146 454 939	67.4638 299 058	420
36	70.4262 405 882	69.4191 261 803	68.4396 494 830	67.4867 382 912	432
37	70.4514 029 284	69.4421 220 426	68.4606 658 003	67.5059 458 325	444
38	70.4726 568 485	69.4614 981 821	68.4783 304 052	67.5220 504 002	456
39	70.4906 094 362	69.4778 243 706	68.4931 778 337	67.5355 532 788	468
40	70.5057 734 815	69.4915 806 934	68.5056 573 731	67.5468 747 706	480
41	70.5185 821 234	69.5031 716 670	68.5161 466 577	67.5563 672 781	492
42	70.5294 012 225	69.5129 381 336	68.5249 630 963	67.5643 262 733	504
43	70.5385 398 108	69.5211 672 844	68.5323 734 766	67.5709 994 948	516
44	70.5462 589 190	69.5281 011 046	68.5386 020 389	67.5765 946 589	528
45	70.5527 790 323	69.5339 434 890	68.5438 372 612	67.5812 859 256	540
46	70.5582 863 883	69.5388 662 379	68.5482 375 628	67.5852 193 193	552
47	70.5629 382 969	69.5430 141 089	68.5519 360 979	67.5885 172 742	564
48	70.5668 676 330	69.5465 090 736	68.5550 447 855	67.5912 824 453	576
49	70.5701 866 326	69.5494 539 044	68.5576 576 950	67.5936 009 037	588
50	70.5729 900 980	69.5519 351 965	68.5598 538 941	67.5955 448 156	600

MONTHLY
Compounding

TABLE 5. PRESENT WORTH OF ONE DOLLAR PER PERIOD
Payable at end of each period

MONTHS	18% Nominal Annual Rate	18¼% Nominal Annual Rate	18½% Nominal Annual Rate	18¾% Nominal Annual Rate	MONTHS
1	0.9852 216 749	0.9850 194 952	0.9848 173 984	0.9846 153 846	1
2	1.9558 834 235	1.9552 829 011	1.9546 827 067	1.9540 828 402	2
3	2.9122 004 173	2.9110 112 713	2.9098 229 364	2.9086 354 119	3
4	3.8543 846 476	3.8524 223 481	3.8504 616 526	3.8485 025 594	4
5	4.7826 449 730	4.7797 306 117	4.7768 190 260	4.7739 102 124	5
6	5.6971 871 655	5.6931 473 294	5.6891 118 844	5.6850 808 245	6
7	6.5982 139 561	6.5928 806 036	6.5875 537 639	6.5822 334 272	7
8	7.4859 250 799	7.4791 354 191	7.4723 549 583	7.4655 836 822	8
9	8.3605 173 201	8.3521 136 900	8.3437 225 687	8.3353 439 332	9
10	9.2221 845 519	9.2120 143 058	9.2018 605 519	9.1917 232 573	10
11	10.0711 177 851	10.0590 331 762	10.0469 697 679	10.0349 275 149	11
YEARS					
1	10.9075 052 070	10.8933 632 764	10.8792 480 275	10.8651 593 993	12
2	20.0304 053 663	19.9820 241 500	19.9338 096 413	19.8857 611 615	24
3	27.6606 843 109	27.5649 674 871	27.4697 244 225	27.3749 523 608	36
4	34.0425 536 456	33.8916 453 612	33.7417 024 609	33.5927 176 828	48
5	39.3802 688 853	39.1701 831 456	38.9617 334 268	38.7549 047 027	60
6	43.8446 667 735	43.5742 261 040	43.3062 517 140	43.0407 169 598	72
7	47.5786 330 136	47.2486 517 066	46.9220 998 328	46.5989 349 462	84
8	50.7016 754 105	50.3143 355 877	49.9314 916 120	49.5530 809 700	96
9	53.3137 487 893	52.8721 279 274	52.4361 429 644	52.0057 071 902	108
10	55.4984 541 085	55.0061 710 663	54.5207 098 328	54.0419 556 786	120
11	57.3257 141 579	56.7866 674 922	56.2556 495 180	55.7325 140 982	132
12	58.8540 114 798	58.2721 892 536	57.6996 020 996	57.1360 696 006	144
13	60.1322 601 368	59.5116 047 736	58.9013 724 412	58.3013 461 302	156
14	61.2013 712 355	60.5456 864 485	59.9015 797 695	59.2687 958 592	168
15	62.0955 623 111	61.4084 519 159	60.7340 305 839	60.0720 034 708	180
16	62.8434 524 795	62.1282 831 148	61.4268 612 989	60.7388 520 397	192
17	63.4689 784 093	62.7288 599 510	62.0034 892 406	61.2924 909 837	204
18	63.9921 604 291	63.2299 392 830	62.4834 041 403	61.7521 396 874	216
19	64.4297 432 898	63.6480 048 522	62.8828 268 778	62.1337 546 968	228
20	64.7957 320 905	63.9968 095 404	63.2152 577 386	62.4505 836 452	240
21	65.1018 405 200	64.2878 277 909	63.4919 327 168	62.7136 251 401	252
22	65.3578 657 601	64.5306 330 770	63.7222 032 862	62.9320 105 760	264
23	65.5720 020 507	64.7332 128 357	63.9138 524 749	63.1133 211 280	276
24	65.7511 029 506	64.9022 312 260	64.0733 579 281	63.2638 509 293	288
25	65.9009 006 906	65.0432 483 565	64.2061 108 491	63.3888 255 698	300
26	66.0261 896 362	65.1609 031 932	64.3165 982 191	63.4925 835 011	312
27	66.1309 797 344	65.2590 661 648	64.4085 544 552	63.5787 266 440	324
28	66.2186 248 544	65.3409 664 868	64.4850 876 312	63.6502 454 278	336
29	66.2919 301 304	65.4092 983 906	64.5487 845 298	63.7096 226 024	348
30	66.3532 417 412	65.4663 097 548	64.6017 980 737	63.7589 194 260	360
31	66.4045 220 013	65.5138 760 520	64.6459 200 938	63.7998 472 208	372
32	66.4474 121 659	65.5535 620 455	64.6826 418 919	63.8338 267 810	384
33	66.4832 849 600	65.5866 732 644	64.7132 046 460	63.8620 376 952	396
34	66.5132 885 138	65.6142 989 510	64.7386 413 619	63.8854 592 957	408
35	66.5383 831 088	65.6373 478 928	64.7598 117 875	63.9049 046 553	420
36	66.5593 719 124	65.6565 783 188	64.7774 314 725	63.9210 488 127	432
37	66.5769 266 838	65.6726 228 421	64.7920 959 532	63.9344 522 070	444
38	66.5916 092 738	65.6860 092 707	64.8043 008 817	63.9455 801 323	456
39	66.6038 896 073	65.6971 779 711	64.8144 587 784	63.9548 188 907	468
40	66.6141 607 238	65.7064 963 540	64.8229 129 749	63.9624 892 025	480
41	66.6227 513 565	65.7142 709 614	64.8299 492 189	63.9688 573 399	492
42	66.6299 364 536	65.7207 575 503	64.8358 053 318	63.9741 443 706	504
43	66.6359 459 785	65.7261 695 067	64.8406 792 473	63.9785 338 321	516
44	66.6409 722 695	65.7306 848 648	64.8447 357 012	63.9821 781 030	528
45	66.6451 761 960	65.7344 521 640	64.8481 117 995	63.9852 036 928	540
46	66.6486 923 073	65.7375 953 351	64.8509 216 528	63.9877 156 340	552
47	66.6516 331 386	65.7402 177 773	64.8532 602 326	63.9898 011 277	564
48	66.6540 928 129	65.7424 057 599	64.8552 065 817	63.9915 325 710	576
49	66.6561 500 535	65.7442 312 595	64.8568 264 858	63.9929 700 705	588
50	66.6578 707 037	65.7457 543 289	64.8581 746 967	63.9941 635 284	600

TABLE 5. PRESENT WORTH OF ONE DOLLAR PER PERIOD
Payable at end of each period

	19% Nominal Annual Rate	19¼% Nominal Annual Rate	19½% Nominal Annual Rate	19¾% Nominal Annual Rate	
MONTHS					MONTHS
1	0.9844 134 537	0.9842 116 055	0.9840 098 401	0.9838 081 574	1
2	1.9534 833 014	1.9528 840 899	1.9522 852 055	1.9516 866 480	2
3	2.9074 486 970	2.9062 627 909	2.9050 776 930	2.9038 934 024	3
4	3.8465 450 668	3.8445 891 730	3.8426 348 763	3.8406 821 750	4
5	4.7710 041 675	4.7681 008 879	4.7652 003 702	4.7623 026 111	5
6	5.6810 541 435	5.6770 318 355	5.6730 138 945	5.6690 003 143	6
7	6.5769 195 835	6.5716 122 228	6.5663 113 353	6.5610 169 110	7
8	7.4588 215 752	7.4520 686 220	7.4453 248 071	7.4385 901 153	8
9	8.3269 777 606	8.3186 240 282	8.3102 827 131	8.3019 537 925	9
10	9.1816 023 895	9.1714 979 158	9.1614 098 037	9.1513 380 209	10
11	10.0229 063 719	10.0109 062 940	9.9989 272 362	9.9869 691 536	11
YEARS					
1	10.8510 973 308	10.8370 617 616	10.8230 526 309	10.8090 698 785	12
2	19.8378 780 347	19.7901 595 883	19.7426 051 527	19.6952 140 613	24
3	27.2806 485 635	27.1868 103 096	27.0934 348 957	27.0005 196 357	36
4	33.4446 838 248	33.2975 937 448	33.1514 403 594	33.0062 166 441	48
5	38.5496 820 988	38.3460 508 909	38.1439 965 036	37.9435 045 084	60
6	42.7775 955 146	42.5168 613 650	42.2584 888 067	42.0024 524 407	72
7	46.2791 151 808	45.9625 992 424	45.6493 464 002	45.3393 164 782	84
8	49.1790 421 107	48.8093 144 296	48.4438 382 529	48.0825 548 225	96
9	51.5807 353 757	51.1611 437 462	50.7468 499 542	50.3377 730 539	108
10	53.5697 960 239	53.1041 203 949	52.6448 203 816	52.1917 895 968	120
11	55.2171 180 695	54.7093 211 765	54.2089 860 093	53.7159 779 407	132
12	56.5814 152 940	56.0354 665 789	55.4980 546 247	54.9690 142 831	144
13	57.7113 139 207	57.1310 688 538	56.5604 088 062	55.9991 363 686	156
14	58.6470 857 479	58.0362 066 635	57.4359 218 654	56.8460 004 818	168
15	59.4220 835 147	58.7839 912 140	58.1574 544 110	57.5422 080 832	180
16	60.0639 296 584	59.4017 775 088	58.7520 877 049	58.1145 608 570	192
17	60.5955 008 317	59.9121 650 342	59.2421 401 029	58.5850 924 872	204
18	61.0357 432 714	60.3338 244 788	59.6460 047 289	58.9719 168 815	216
19	61.4003 480 796	60.6821 807 344	59.9788 398 233	59.2899 254 965	228
20	61.7023 104 855	60.9699 771 597	60.2531 376 768	59.5513 606 094	240
21	61.9523 930 199	61.2077 417 499	60.4791 935 036	59.7662 866 053	252
22	62.1595 091 139	61.4041 722 662	60.6654 918 511	59.9429 774 222	264
23	62.3310 407 904	61.5664 544 112	60.8190 250 502	60.0882 350 710	276
24	62.4731 017 740	61.7005 246 926	60.9455 556 586	60.2076 514 893	288
25	62.5907 553 963	61.8112 875 886	61.0498 327 462	60.3058 238 134	300
26	62.6881 950 626	61.9027 949 607	61.1357 701 421	60.3865 313 521	312
27	62.7688 937 132	61.9783 942 765	61.2065 933 325	60.4528 810 783	324
28	62.8357 276 060	62.0408 510 646	61.2649 605 222	60.5074 272 362	336
29	62.8910 788 318	62.0924 500 816	61.3130 624 055	60.5522 696 722	348
30	62.9369 202 166	62.1350 788 916	61.3527 043 890	60.5891 346 714	360
31	62.9748 856 370	62.1702 969 161	61.3853 743 544	60.6194 414 139	372
32	63.0063 282 550	62.1993 924 795	61.4122 985 024	60.6443 566 089	384
33	63.0323 687 469	62.2234 299 384	61.4344 873 766	60.6648 394 087	396
34	63.0539 352 469	62.2432 886 164	61.4527 737 913	60.6816 783 334	408
35	63.0717 964 271	62.2596 949 719	61.4678 440 900	60.6955 216 255	420
36	63.0865 888 952	62.2732 491 721	61.4802 639 059	60.7069 022 060	432
37	63.0988 398 835	62.2844 470 488	61.4904 993 915	60.7162 581 895	444
38	63.1089 860 412	62.2936 982 358	61.4989 347 152	60.7239 497 503	456
39	63.1173 889 973	62.3013 411 545	61.5058 864 796	60.7302 729 880	468
40	63.1243 482 496	62.3076 553 936	61.5116 156 052	60.7354 713 263	480
41	63.1301 118 394	62.3128 719 368	61.5163 371 231	60.7397 448 840	492
42	63.1348 851 923	62.3171 816 124	61.5202 282 460	60.7432 581 789	504
43	63.1388 384 401	62.3207 420 745	61.5234 350 191	60.7461 464 611	516
44	63.1421 124 842	62.3236 835 698	61.5260 778 022	60.7485 209 201	528
45	63.1448 240 179	62.3261 137 021	61.5282 557 870	60.7504 729 645	540
46	63.1470 696 856	62.3281 213 693	61.5300 507 195	60.7520 777 416	552
47	63.1489 295 272	62.3297 800 145	61.5315 299 689	60.7533 970 301	564
48	63.1504 698 313	62.3311 503 133	61.5327 490 560	60.7544 816 180	576
49	63.1517 454 972	62.3322 823 931	61.5337 537 366	60.7553 732 586	588
50	63.1528 019 922	62.3332 176 670	61.5345 817 194	60.7561 062 770	600

MONTHLY
Compounding

TABLE 5. PRESENT WORTH OF ONE DOLLAR PER PERIOD
Payable at end of each period

MONTHS	20% Nominal Annual Rate	20¼% Nominal Annual Rate	20½% Nominal Annual Rate	20¾% Nominal Annual Rate	MONTHS
1	0.9836 065 574	0.9834 050 400	0.9832 036 051	0.9830 022 527	1
2	1.9510 884 171	1.9504 905 126	1.9498 929 341	1.9492 956 816	2
3	2.9027 099 185	2.9015 272 404	2.9003 453 674	2.8991 642 989	3
4	3.8387 310 673	3.8367 815 517	3.8348 336 263	3.8328 872 895	4
5	4.7594 076 072	4.7565 153 551	4.7536 258 514	4.7507 390 927	5
6	5.6649 910 891	5.6609 862 127	5.6569 856 793	5.6529 894 829	6
7	6.5557 289 401	6.5504 474 126	6.5451 723 189	6.5399 036 490	7
8	7.4318 645 312	7.4251 480 395	7.4184 406 249	7.4117 422 722	8
9	8.2936 372 438	8.2853 330 444	8.2770 411 715	8.2687 616 028	9
10	9.1412 825 349	9.1312 433 134	9.1212 203 243	9.1112 135 354	10
11	9.9750 320 015	9.9631 157 354	9.9512 203 107	9.9393 456 830	11
YEARS					
1	10.7951 134 441	10.7811 832 678	10.7672 792 895	10.7534 014 496	12
2	19.6479 856 504	19.6009 192 595	19.5540 142 310	19.5072 699 102	24
3	26.9080 618 605	26.8160 589 183	26.7245 081 743	26.6334 070 106	36
4	32.8619 156 322	32.7185 304 146	32.5760 541 393	32.4344 800 108	48
5	37.7445 606 223	37.5471 507 063	37.3512 607 639	37.1568 769 390	60
6	41.7487 271 695	41.4972 881 931	41.2481 110 055	41.0011 713 907	72
7	45.0324 698 479	44.7287 674 194	44.4281 706 343	44.1306 414 576	84
8	47.7254 062 807	47.3723 356 559	47.0232 868 474	46.6782 046 119	96
9	49.9338 334 754	49.5349 529 997	49.1410 547 342	48.7520 630 885	108
10	51.7449 236 351	51.3041 200 337	50.8692 782 333	50.4402 995 405	120
11	53.2301 650 659	52.7514 181 434	52.2796 105 371	51.8146 181 596	132
12	54.4481 840 011	53.9354 057 367	53.4305 248 767	52.9333 901 566	144
13	55.4470 587 266	54.9039 875 454	54.3697 388 573	53.8441 329 523	156
14	56.2662 173 524	55.6963 528 756	55.1361 928 593	54.5855 283 770	168
15	56.9379 941 400	56.3445 612 259	55.7616 645 294	55.1890 655 979	180
16	57.4889 058 171	56.8748 394 316	56.2720 863 018	55.6803 785 528	192
17	57.9406 982 600	57.3086 428 147	56.6886 205 721	56.0803 346 971	204
18	58.3112 048 583	57.6635 232 779	57.0285 371 034	56.4059 213 026	216
19	58.6150 504 440	57.9538 394 627	57.3059 290 408	56.6709 669 564	228
20	58.8642 285 702	58.1913 377 076	57.5322 972 220	56.8867 288 993	240
21	59.0685 749 274	58.3856 273 107	57.7170 270 087	57.0623 711 531	252
22	59.2361 555 828	58.5445 693 269	57.8677 774 099	57.2053 537 427	264
23	59.3735 853 684	58.6745 946 299	57.9907 986 283	57.3217 495 443	276
24	59.4862 889 852	58.7809 641 087	58.0911 911 982	57.4165 022 178	288
25	59.5787 151 299	58.8679 815 257	58.1731 174 562	57.4936 361 780	300
26	59.6545 120 960	58.9391 676 493	58.2399 741 147	57.5564 275 232	312
27	59.7166 717 813	58.9974 027 058	58.2945 330 911	57.6075 431 798	324
28	59.7676 477 857	59.0450 429 147	58.3390 564 337	57.6491 541 748	336
29	59.8094 522 609	59.0840 158 229	58.3753 901 072	57.6830 278 452	348
30	59.8437 353 352	59.1158 982 937	58.4050 405 277	57.7106 029 020	360
31	59.8718 502 483	59.1419 803 079	58.4292 370 196	57.7330 505 360	372
32	59.8949 067 667	59.1633 171 569	58.4489 827 840	57.7513 241 619	384
33	59.9138 149 897	59.1807 721 404	58.4650 964 924	57.7661 999 124	396
34	59.9293 212 724	59.1950 514 956	58.4782 462 288	57.7783 096 029	408
35	59.9420 376 871	59.2067 329 725	58.4889 771 892	57.7881 675 663	420
36	59.9524 661 828	59.2162 892 094	58.4977 342 858	57.7961 924 982	432
37	59.9610 183 986	59.2241 068 566	58.5048 805 932	57.8027 252 403	444
38	59.9680 319 121	59.2305 022 200	58.5107 124 014	57.8080 432 567	456
39	59.9737 835 644	59.2357 340 591	58.5154 715 009	57.8123 724 186	468
40	59.9785 003 877	59.2400 140 568	58.5193 552 068	57.8158 965 979	480
41	59.9823 685 669	59.2435 153 840	58.5225 245 399	57.8187 654 763	492
42	59.9855 407 889	59.2463 797 061	58.5251 109 026	57.8211 009 033	504
43	59.9881 422 693	59.2487 229 150	58.5272 215 270	57.8230 020 711	516
44	59.9902 756 951	59.2506 398 181	58.5289 439 211	57.8245 497 278	528
45	59.9920 252 780	59.2522 079 743	58.5303 494 963	57.8258 096 066	540
46	59.9934 600 785	59.2534 908 320	58.5314 965 285	57.8268 352 182	552
47	59.9946 367 317	59.2545 402 962	58.5324 325 744	57.8276 701 232	564
48	59.9956 016 832	59.2553 988 288	58.5331 964 431	57.8283 497 825	576
49	59.9963 930 220	59.2561 011 664	58.5338 198 050	57.8289 030 630	588
50	59.9970 419 843	59.2566 757 260	58.5343 285 051	57.8293 534 643	600

TABLE 5. PRESENT WORTH OF ONE DOLLAR PER PERIOD
Payable at end of each period

MONTHLY Compounding

MONTHS	21% Nominal Annual Rate	21¼% Nominal Annual Rate	21½% Nominal Annual Rate	21¾% Nominal Annual Rate	MONTHS
1	0.9828 009 828	0.9825 997 953	0.9823 986 901	0.9821 976 673	1
2	1.9486 987 546	1.9481 021 530	1.9475 058 765	1.9469 099 249	2
3	2.8979 840 340	2.8968 045 720	2.8956 259 123	2.8944 480 539	3
4	3.8309 425 396	3.8289 993 748	3.8270 577 935	3.8251 177 939	4
5	4.7478 550 757	4.7449 737 971	4.7420 952 535	4.7392 194 415	5
6	5.6489 976 174	5.6450 100 770	5.6410 268 557	5.6370 479 475	6
7	6.5346 413 930	6.5293 855 414	6.5241 360 842	6.5188 930 116	7
8	7.4050 529 661	7.3983 726 916	7.3917 014 335	7.3850 391 766	8
9	8.2604 943 156	8.2522 392 876	8.2439 964 962	8.2357 659 193	9
10	9.1012 229 146	9.0912 484 300	9.0812 900 495	9.0713 477 415	10
11	9.9274 918 080	9.9156 586 415	9.9038 461 395	9.8920 542 580	11
YEARS					
1	10.7395 496 884	10.7257 239 466	10.7119 241 649	10.6981 502 841	12
2	19.4606 856 454	19.4142 607 880	19.3679 946 921	19.3218 867 148	24
3	26.5427 528 258	26.4525 430 354	26.3627 750 712	26.2734 463 817	36
4	32.2938 012 895	32.1540 112 916	32.0151 033 880	31.8770 710 044	48
5	36.9639 855 154	36.7725 729 141	36.5826 256 930	36.3941 305 445	60
6	40.7564 454 191	40.5139 094 440	40.2735 400 980	40.0353 142 894	72
7	43.8361 423 702	43.5446 363 617	43.2560 869 223	42.9704 580 365	84
8	46.3370 345 488	45.9997 230 869	45.6662 174 707	45.3364 657 470	96
9	48.3679 037 506	47.9885 036 641	47.6137 910 052	47.2436 951 602	108
10	50.0170 870 901	49.5995 458 092	49.1875 823 812	48.7811 052 111	120
11	51.3563 194 172	50.9045 951 559	50.4593 286 086	50.0204 053 436	132
12	52.4438 535 822	51.9617 703 532	51.4869 987 889	51.0194 002 555	144
13	53.3269 942 712	52.8181 513 019	52.3174 364 789	51.8246 860 841	156
14	54.0441 556 272	53.5118 757 965	52.9884 949 277	52.4738 237 904	168
15	54.6265 321 579	54.0738 379 408	53.5307 625 139	52.9970 911 159	180
16	55.0994 556 090	54.5290 639 767	53.9689 570 341	53.4188 948 275	192
17	55.4834 968 244	54.8978 267 944	54.3230 523 968	53.7589 091 232	204
18	55.7953 605 197	55.1965 487 588	54.6091 890 783	54.0329 932 958	216
19	56.0486 118 912	55.4385 330 580	54.8404 098 428	54.2539 314 582	228
20	56.2542 666 631	55.6345 561 432	55.0272 542 616	54.4320 288 329	240
21	56.4212 702 412	55.7933 476 436	55.1782 391 307	54.5755 924 189	252
22	56.5568 868 130	55.9219 791 287	55.3002 466 855	54.6913 184 551	264
23	56.6670 153 188	56.0261 790 320	55.3988 383 095	54.7846 047 529	276
24	56.7564 460 398	56.1105 877 584	55.4785 080 343	54.8598 024 669	288
25	56.8290 689 615	56.1789 643 392	55.5428 873 882	54.9204 190 454	300
26	56.8880 429 774	56.2343 538 349	55.5949 109 294	54.9692 818 284	312
27	56.9359 332 917	56.2792 229 437	55.6369 500 099	55.0086 699 235	324
28	56.9748 229 989	56.3155 698 519	55.6709 208 670	55.0404 205 106	336
29	57.0064 036 921	56.3450 132 213	55.6983 719 701	55.0660 145 326	348
30	57.0320 490 428	56.3688 642 733	55.7205 546 033	55.0866 457 720	360
31	57.0528 745 520	56.3881 851 829	55.7384 799 018	55.1032 765 321	372
32	57.0697 860 709	56.4038 363 816	55.7529 649 415	55.1166 825 218	384
33	57.0835 192 030	56.4165 148 745	55.7646 699 839	55.1274 890 368	396
34	57.0946 713 012	56.4267 852 818	55.7741 285 714	55.1362 001 255	408
35	57.1037 274 504	56.4351 049 824	55.7817 718 481	55.1432 220 996	420
36	57.1110 815 677	56.4418 444 832	55.7879 482 120	55.1488 824 850	432
37	57.1170 535 367	56.4473 039 190	55.7929 391 960	55.1534 452 991	444
38	57.1219 031 211	56.4517 264 185	55.7969 723 005	55.1571 233 655	456
39	57.1258 412 644	56.4553 089 319	55.8002 313 636	55.1600 882 402	468
40	57.1290 392 646	56.4582 110 018	55.8028 649 409	55.1624 782 139	480
41	57.1316 362 260	56.4605 618 678	55.8049 930 768	55.1644 047 622	492
42	57.1337 451 089	56.4624 662 229	55.8067 127 767	55.1659 577 451	504
43	57.1354 576 438	56.4640 088 748	55.8081 024 284	55.1672 095 985	516
44	57.1368 483 214	56.4652 585 236	55.8092 253 754	55.1682 187 125	528
45	57.1379 776 320	56.4662 708 208	55.8101 328 042	55.1690 321 553	540
46	57.1388 946 976	56.4670 908 476	55.8108 660 774	55.1696 878 683	552
47	57.1396 394 080	56.4677 551 229	55.8114 586 194	55.1702 164 359	564
48	57.1402 441 559	56.4682 932 292	55.8119 374 396	55.1706 425 122	576
49	57.1407 352 462	56.4687 291 305	55.8123 243 637	55.1709 859 706	588
50	57.1411 340 400	56.4690 822 390	55.8126 370 285	55.1712 628 311	600

TABLE 5. PRESENT WORTH OF ONE DOLLAR PER PERIOD
Payable at end of each period

MONTHS	22% Nominal Annual Rate	22¼% Nominal Annual Rate	22½% Nominal Annual Rate	22¾% Nominal Annual Rate	MONTHS
1	0.9819 967 267	0.9817 958 683	0.9815 950 920	0.9813 943 979	1
2	1.9463 142 979	1.9457 189 952	1.9451 240 167	1.9445 293 621	2
3	2.8932 709 963	2.8920 947 386	2.8909 192 802	2.8897 446 203	3
4	3.8231 793 744	3.8212 425 333	3.8193 072 689	3.8173 735 795	4
5	4.7363 463 579	4.7334 759 992	4.7306 083 621	4.7277 434 434	5
6	5.6330 733 465	5.6291 030 468	5.6251 370 426	5.6211 753 278	6
7	6.5136 563 141	6.5084 259 818	6.5032 020 050	6.4979 843 741	7
8	7.3783 859 058	7.3717 416 062	7.3651 062 626	7.3584 798 600	8
9	8.2275 475 343	8.2193 413 192	8.2111 472 516	8.2029 653 094	9
10	9.0614 214 740	9.0515 112 154	9.0416 169 341	9.0317 385 985	10
11	9.8802 829 532	9.8685 321 812	9.8568 018 985	9.8450 920 615	11
YEARS					
1	10.6844 022 453	10.6706 799 897	10.6569 834 586	10.6433 125 935	12
2	19.2759 362 161	19.2301 425 590	19.1845 051 091	19.1390 232 350	24
3	26.1845 544 313	26.0960 967 010	26.0080 706 875	25.9204 739 037	36
4	31.7399 076 204	31.6036 067 695	31.4681 620 379	31.3335 670 648	48
5	36.2070 742 946	36.0214 439 013	35.8372 264 532	35.6544 091 680	60
6	39.7992 091 986	39.5652 022 750	39.3332 712 334	39.1033 940 506	72
7	42.6877 141 750	42.4078 202 884	42.1307 418 000	41.8564 445 988	84
8	45.0104 167 521	44.6880 200 984	44.3692 261 625	44.0539 860 722	96
9	46.8781 467 042	46.5170 773 789	46.1604 200 720	45.8081 087 964	108
10	48.3800 243 913	47.9842 516 682	47.5937 004 090	47.2082 855 706	120
11	49.5877 132 140	49.1611 423 090	48.7405 849 053	48.3259 354 203	132
12	50.5588 390 953	50.1051 825 574	49.6583 007 308	49.2180 664 780	144
13	51.3397 401 515	50.8624 423 738	50.3926 400 118	49.9301 838 056	156
14	51.9676 777 561	51.4698 766 761	50.9802 447 634	50.4986 104 778	168
15	52.4726 144 982	51.9571 287 704	51.4504 352 503	50.9523 403 184	180
16	52.8786 438 739	52.3479 769 701	51.8266 730 076	51.3145 167 933	192
17	53.2051 399 281	52.6614 949 970	52.1277 315 233	51.6036 134 917	204
18	53.4676 817 040	52.9129 827 951	52.3686 329 961	51.8343 764 122	216
19	53.6787 966 111	53.1147 131 813	52.5613 979 124	52.0185 761 134	228
20	53.8485 581 807	53.2765 307 685	52.7156 448 439	52.1656 080 968	240
21	53.9850 667 339	53.4063 323 914	52.8390 703 941	52.2829 720 449	252
22	54.0948 358 951	53.5104 524 788	52.9378 332 435	52.3766 543 580	264
23	54.1831 033 953	53.5939 721 787	53.0168 614 544	52.4514 335 038	276
24	54.2540 809 951	53.6609 673 230	53.0800 983 715	52.5111 237 533	288
25	54.3111 554 524	53.7147 073 311	53.1306 993 865	52.5587 697 361	300
26	54.3570 501 246	53.7578 147 609	53.1711 893 856	52.5968 017 378	312
27	54.3939 549 159	53.7923 932 912	53.2035 887 363	52.6271 596 624	324
28	54.4236 307 706	53.8201 303 835	53.2295 140 992	52.6513 919 812	336
29	54.4474 936 978	53.8423 796 313	53.2502 590 966	52.6707 347 156	348
30	54.4666 823 380	53.8602 268 167	53.2668 588 610	52.6861 744 833	360
31	54.4821 122 937	53.8745 428 973	53.2801 416 864	52.6984 988 229	372
32	54.4945 198 188	53.8860 265 100	53.2907 703 583	52.7083 363 638	384
33	54.5044 969 491	53.8952 380 648	53.2992 752 255	52.7161 888 909	396
34	54.5125 197 521	53.9026 270 933	53.3060 806 635	52.7224 569 393	408
35	54.5189 710 427	53.9085 541 863	53.3115 262 495	52.7274 602 243	420
36	54.5241 586 500	53.9133 085 909	53.3158 837 069	52.7314 539 490	432
37	54.5283 301 051	53.9171 223 262	53.3193 704 641	52.7346 418 221	444
38	54.5316 844 526	53.9201 815 056	53.3221 605 028	52.7371 864 479	456
39	54.5343 817 481	53.9226 354 197	53.3243 930 404	52.7392 176 204	468
40	54.5365 506 955	53.9246 038 214	53.3261 794 758	52.7408 389 440	480
41	54.5382 947 879	53.9261 827 706	53.3276 089 484	52.7421 331 178	492
42	54.5396 972 463	53.9274 493 212	53.3287 527 861	52.7431 661 539	504
43	54.5408 249 901	53.9284 652 820	53.3296 680 639	52.7439 907 446	516
44	54.5417 318 307	53.9292 802 328	53.3304 004 523	52.7446 489 497	528
45	54.5424 610 387	53.9299 339 437	53.3309 864 960	52.7451 743 426	540
46	54.5430 474 089	53.9304 583 165	53.3314 554 374	52.7455 937 220	552
47	54.5435 189 205	53.9308 789 410	53.3318 306 756	52.7459 284 792	564
48	54.5438 980 721	53.9312 163 440	53.3321 309 343	52.7461 956 893	576
49	54.5442 029 552	53.9314 869 911	53.3323 711 958	52.7464 089 819	588
50	54.5444 481 176	53.9317 040 901	53.3325 634 487	52.7465 792 364	600

TABLE 6. PARTIAL PAYMENT TO AMORTIZE ONE
Payable at end of each period

MONTHLY Compounding

MONTHS	5% Nominal Annual Rate	5¼% Nominal Annual Rate	5½% Nominal Annual Rate	5¾% Nominal Annual Rate	MONTHS
1	1.0041 666 667	1.0043 750 000	1.0045 833 333	1.0047 916 667	1
2	0.5031 271 656	0.5032 836 374	0.5034 401 199	0.5035 966 131	2
3	0.3361 149 611	0.3362 542 442	0.3363 935 464	0.3365 328 678	3
4	0.2526 095 807	0.2527 403 434	0.2528 711 330	0.2530 019 495	4
5	0.2025 069 300	0.2026 326 395	0.2027 583 835	0.2028 841 620	5
6	0.1691 056 440	0.1692 280 341	0.1693 504 660	0.1694 729 399	6
7	0.1452 479 951	0.1453 680 563	0.1454 881 668	0.1456 083 266	7
8	0.1273 551 193	0.1274 734 709	0.1275 918 790	0.1277 103 437	8
9	0.1134 387 590	0.1135 558 136	0.1136 729 321	0.1137 901 145	9
10	0.1023 059 594	0.1024 220 061	0.1025 381 239	0.1026 543 128	10
11	0.0931 975 677	0.0933 128 165	0.0934 281 437	0.0935 435 492	11
YEARS					
1	0.0856 074 818	0.0857 220 904	0.0858 367 846	0.0859 515 644	12
2	0.0438 713 897	0.0439 834 370	0.0440 956 562	0.0442 080 473	24
3	0.0299 708 971	0.0300 832 705	0.0301 959 018	0.0303 087 908	36
4	0.0230 292 936	0.0231 427 128	0.0232 564 752	0.0233 705 807	48
5	0.0188 712 336	0.0189 859 838	0.0191 011 622	0.0192 167 682	60
6	0.0161 049 327	0.0162 211 537	0.0163 378 871	0.0164 551 320	72
7	0.0141 339 091	0.0142 516 781	0.0143 700 427	0.0144 890 018	84
8	0.0126 599 200	0.0127 792 822	0.0128 993 222	0.0130 200 387	96
9	0.0115 172 732	0.0116 382 556	0.0117 599 971	0.0118 824 957	108
10	0.0106 065 515	0.0107 291 701	0.0108 526 278	0.0109 769 220	120
11	0.0098 644 882	0.0099 887 516	0.0101 139 326	0.0102 400 281	132
12	0.0092 489 041	0.0093 748 155	0.0095 017 217	0.0096 296 187	144
13	0.0087 305 970	0.0088 581 558	0.0089 867 851	0.0091 164 798	156
14	0.0082 887 071	0.0084 179 099	0.0085 482 571	0.0086 797 423	168
15	0.0079 079 363	0.0080 387 772	0.0081 708 345	0.0083 041 009	180
16	0.0075 768 100	0.0077 092 811	0.0078 430 390	0.0079 780 747	192
17	0.0072 865 528	0.0074 206 447	0.0075 560 917	0.0076 928 831	204
18	0.0070 303 385	0.0071 660 404	0.0073 031 636	0.0074 416 954	216
19	0.0068 027 775	0.0069 400 772	0.0070 788 622	0.0072 191 181	228
20	0.0065 995 574	0.0067 384 417	0.0068 788 731	0.0070 208 351	240
21	0.0064 171 865	0.0065 576 411	0.0066 997 024	0.0068 433 516	252
22	0.0062 528 075	0.0063 948 174	0.0065 384 911	0.0066 838 075	264
23	0.0061 040 597	0.0062 476 088	0.0063 928 766	0.0065 398 392	276
24	0.0059 689 751	0.0061 140 467	0.0062 608 895	0.0064 094 766	288
25	0.0058 459 004	0.0059 924 772	0.0061 408 749	0.0062 910 640	300
26	0.0057 334 362	0.0058 815 000	0.0060 314 323	0.0061 832 001	312
27	0.0056 303 900	0.0057 799 223	0.0059 313 678	0.0060 846 905	324
28	0.0055 357 395	0.0056 867 211	0.0058 396 582	0.0059 945 113	336
29	0.0054 486 030	0.0056 010 143	0.0057 554 207	0.0059 117 792	348
30	0.0053 682 162	0.0055 220 370	0.0056 778 900	0.0058 357 286	360
31	0.0052 939 132	0.0054 491 230	0.0056 063 994	0.0057 656 921	372
32	0.0052 251 109	0.0053 816 888	0.0055 403 653	0.0057 010 860	384
33	0.0051 612 970	0.0053 192 218	0.0054 792 744	0.0056 413 966	396
34	0.0051 020 192	0.0052 612 694	0.0054 226 740	0.0055 861 709	408
35	0.0050 468 767	0.0052 074 304	0.0053 701 628	0.0055 350 073	420
36	0.0049 955 132	0.0051 573 484	0.0053 213 839	0.0054 875 490	432
37	0.0049 476 108	0.0051 107 052	0.0052 760 191	0.0054 434 774	444
38	0.0049 028 848	0.0050 672 161	0.0052 337 835	0.0054 025 077	456
39	0.0048 610 798	0.0050 266 255	0.0051 944 215	0.0053 643 841	468
40	0.0048 219 660	0.0049 887 034	0.0051 577 028	0.0053 288 764	480
41	0.0047 853 357	0.0049 532 420	0.0051 234 199	0.0052 957 770	492
42	0.0047 510 011	0.0049 200 536	0.0050 913 848	0.0052 648 981	504
43	0.0047 187 919	0.0048 889 677	0.0050 614 272	0.0052 360 694	516
44	0.0046 885 531	0.0048 598 294	0.0050 333 922	0.0052 091 362	528
45	0.0046 601 436	0.0048 324 976	0.0050 071 388	0.0051 839 575	540
46	0.0046 334 345	0.0048 068 436	0.0049 825 383	0.0051 604 050	552
47	0.0046 083 081	0.0047 827 494	0.0049 594 731	0.0051 383 610	564
48	0.0045 846 563	0.0047 601 073	0.0049 378 353	0.0051 177 182	576
49	0.0045 623 799	0.0047 388 181	0.0049 175 261	0.0050 983 778	588
50	0.0045 413 877	0.0047 187 908	0.0048 984 547	0.0050 802 494	600

TABLE 6. PARTIAL PAYMENT TO AMORTIZE ONE
Payable at end of each period

	6% Nominal Annual Rate	6¼% Nominal Annual Rate	6½% Nominal Annual Rate	6¾% Nominal Annual Rate	
MONTHS					MONTHS
1	1.0050 000 000	1.0052 083 333	1.0054 166 667	1.0056 250 000	1
2	0.5037 531 172	0.5039 096 320	0.5040 661 576	0.5042 226 940	2
3	0.3366 722 084	0.3368 115 680	0.3369 509 469	0.3370 903 448	3
4	0.2531 327 930	0.2532 636 634	0.2533 945 607	0.2535 254 849	4
5	0.2030 099 750	0.2031 358 224	0.2032 617 043	0.2033 876 206	5
6	0.1695 954 556	0.1697 180 133	0.1698 406 128	0.1699 632 541	6
7	0.1457 285 355	0.1458 487 938	0.1459 691 012	0.1460 894 578	7
8	0.1278 288 649	0.1279 474 427	0.1280 660 770	0.1281 847 678	8
9	0.1139 073 606	0.1140 246 706	0.1141 420 444	0.1142 594 819	9
10	0.1027 705 727	0.1028 869 038	0.1030 033 059	0.1031 197 790	10
11	0.0936 590 331	0.0937 745 953	0.0938 902 358	0.0940 059 545	11
YEARS					
1	0.0860 664 297	0.0861 813 806	0.0862 964 170	0.0864 115 388	12
2	0.0443 206 103	0.0444 333 450	0.0445 462 514	0.0446 593 295	24
3	0.0304 219 375	0.0305 353 415	0.0306 490 029	0.0307 629 214	36
4	0.0234 850 290	0.0235 998 199	0.0237 149 529	0.0238 304 280	48
5	0.0193 328 015	0.0194 492 617	0.0195 661 482	0.0196 834 607	60
6	0.0165 728 879	0.0166 911 540	0.0168 099 296	0.0169 292 140	72
7	0.0146 085 545	0.0147 286 997	0.0148 494 365	0.0149 707 636	84
8	0.0131 414 302	0.0132 634 954	0.0133 862 326	0.0135 096 404	96
9	0.0120 057 496	0.0121 297 568	0.0122 545 151	0.0123 800 224	108
10	0.0111 020 502	0.0112 280 097	0.0113 547 977	0.0114 824 114	120
11	0.0103 670 346	0.0104 949 488	0.0106 237 671	0.0107 534 858	132
12	0.0097 585 021	0.0098 883 677	0.0100 192 109	0.0101 510 269	144
13	0.0092 472 344	0.0093 790 437	0.0095 119 019	0.0096 458 031	156
14	0.0088 123 592	0.0089 461 010	0.0090 809 608	0.0092 169 314	168
15	0.0084 385 683	0.0085 742 287	0.0087 110 737	0.0088 490 946	180
16	0.0081 143 786	0.0082 519 413	0.0083 907 527	0.0085 308 025	192
17	0.0078 310 077	0.0079 704 543	0.0081 112 110	0.0082 532 659	204
18	0.0075 816 232	0.0077 229 336	0.0078 656 129	0.0080 096 470	216
19	0.0073 608 299	0.0075 039 824	0.0076 485 597	0.0077 945 457	228
20	0.0071 643 106	0.0073 092 820	0.0074 557 314	0.0076 036 401	240
21	0.0069 885 692	0.0071 353 352	0.0072 836 293	0.0074 334 304	252
22	0.0068 307 445	0.0069 792 797	0.0071 293 899	0.0072 810 517	264
23	0.0066 884 720	0.0068 387 498	0.0069 906 467	0.0071 441 364	276
24	0.0065 597 807	0.0067 117 736	0.0068 654 266	0.0070 207 106	288
25	0.0064 430 140	0.0065 966 938	0.0067 520 716	0.0069 091 153	300
26	0.0063 367 699	0.0064 921 076	0.0066 491 781	0.0068 079 460	312
27	0.0062 398 535	0.0063 968 193	0.0065 555 497	0.0067 160 061	324
28	0.0061 512 402	0.0063 098 038	0.0064 701 608	0.0066 322 691	336
29	0.0060 700 461	0.0062 301 769	0.0063 921 267	0.0065 558 498	348
30	0.0059 955 053	0.0061 571 720	0.0063 206 802	0.0064 859 810	360
31	0.0059 269 500	0.0060 901 211	0.0062 551 533	0.0064 219 940	372
32	0.0058 637 959	0.0060 284 395	0.0061 949 608	0.0063 633 037	384
33	0.0058 055 294	0.0059 716 133	0.0061 395 888	0.0063 093 960	396
34	0.0057 516 970	0.0059 191 890	0.0060 885 835	0.0062 598 170	408
35	0.0057 018 971	0.0058 707 648	0.0060 415 432	0.0062 141 651	420
36	0.0056 557 726	0.0058 259 835	0.0059 981 106	0.0061 720 830	432
37	0.0056 130 050	0.0057 845 266	0.0059 579 673	0.0061 332 526	444
38	0.0055 733 093	0.0057 461 091	0.0059 208 284	0.0060 973 891	456
39	0.0055 364 298	0.0057 104 755	0.0058 864 386	0.0060 642 375	468
40	0.0055 021 364	0.0056 773 957	0.0058 545 681	0.0060 335 684	480
41	0.0054 702 216	0.0056 466 624	0.0058 250 097	0.0060 051 749	492
42	0.0054 404 975	0.0056 180 882	0.0057 975 764	0.0059 788 703	504
43	0.0054 127 943	0.0055 915 030	0.0057 720 985	0.0059 544 857	516
44	0.0053 869 572	0.0055 667 528	0.0057 484 223	0.0059 318 676	528
45	0.0053 628 457	0.0055 436 971	0.0057 264 079	0.0059 108 767	540
46	0.0053 403 315	0.0055 222 081	0.0057 059 277	0.0058 913 861	552
47	0.0053 192 974	0.0055 021 691	0.0056 868 657	0.0058 732 802	564
48	0.0052 996 364	0.0054 834 732	0.0056 691 153	0.0058 564 533	576
49	0.0052 812 499	0.0054 660 225	0.0056 525 795	0.0058 408 087	588
50	0.0052 640 479	0.0054 497 274	0.0056 371 689	0.0058 262 579	600

TABLE 6. PARTIAL PAYMENT TO AMORTIZE ONE
Payable at end of each period

MONTHLY Compounding

MONTHS	7% Nominal Annual Rate	7¼% Nominal Annual Rate	7½% Nominal Annual Rate	7¾% Nominal Annual Rate	MONTHS
1	1.0058 333 333	1.0060 416 667	1.0062 500 000	1.0064 583 333	1
2	0.5043 792 411	0.5045 357 990	0.5046 923 676	0.5048 489 470	2
3	0.3372 297 619	0.3373 691 982	0.3375 086 535	0.3376 481 279	3
4	0.2536 564 360	0.2537 874 140	0.2539 184 189	0.2540 494 507	4
5	0.2035 135 714	0.2036 395 565	0.2037 655 761	0.2038 916 301	5
6	0.1700 859 373	0.1702 086 623	0.1703 314 292	0.1704 542 378	6
7	0.1462 098 636	0.1463 303 186	0.1464 508 227	0.1465 713 759	7
8	0.1283 035 150	0.1284 223 188	0.1285 411 789	0.1286 600 955	8
9	0.1143 769 832	0.1144 945 482	0.1146 121 769	0.1147 298 693	9
10	0.1032 363 231	0.1033 529 382	0.1034 696 242	0.1035 863 811	10
11	0.0941 217 514	0.0942 376 266	0.0943 535 799	0.0944 696 113	11
YEARS					
1	0.0865 267 461	0.0866 420 388	0.0867 574 169	0.0868 728 803	12
2	0.0447 725 791	0.0448 860 002	0.0449 995 927	0.0451 133 564	24
3	0.0308 770 969	0.0309 915 292	0.0311 062 182	0.0312 211 636	36
4	0.0239 462 447	0.0240 624 028	0.0241 789 019	0.0242 957 419	48
5	0.0198 011 985	0.0199 193 614	0.0200 379 486	0.0201 569 598	60
6	0.0170 490 065	0.0171 693 062	0.0172 901 123	0.0174 114 241	72
7	0.0150 926 800	0.0152 151 845	0.0153 382 759	0.0154 619 529	84
8	0.0136 337 171	0.0137 584 610	0.0138 838 706	0.0140 099 439	96
9	0.0125 062 766	0.0126 332 753	0.0127 610 162	0.0128 894 969	108
10	0.0116 108 479	0.0117 401 041	0.0118 701 769	0.0120 010 631	120
11	0.0108 841 009	0.0110 156 087	0.0111 480 051	0.0112 812 859	132
12	0.0102 838 110	0.0104 175 581	0.0105 522 631	0.0106 879 208	144
13	0.0097 807 414	0.0099 167 106	0.0100 537 042	0.0101 917 159	156
14	0.0093 540 054	0.0094 921 753	0.0096 314 334	0.0097 717 717	168
15	0.0089 882 827	0.0091 286 288	0.0092 701 236	0.0094 127 575	180
16	0.0086 720 802	0.0088 145 750	0.0089 582 759	0.0091 031 715	192
17	0.0083 966 065	0.0085 412 202	0.0086 870 939	0.0088 342 145	204
18	0.0081 550 217	0.0083 017 221	0.0084 497 333	0.0085 990 399	216
19	0.0079 419 238	0.0080 906 770	0.0082 407 882	0.0083 922 398	228
20	0.0077 529 894	0.0079 037 598	0.0080 559 319	0.0082 094 856	240
21	0.0075 847 171	0.0077 374 678	0.0078 916 601	0.0080 472 716	252
22	0.0074 342 410	0.0075 889 334	0.0077 451 040	0.0079 027 277	264
23	0.0072 991 922	0.0074 557 868	0.0076 138 926	0.0077 734 817	276
24	0.0071 775 958	0.0073 360 521	0.0074 960 490	0.0076 575 557	288
25	0.0070 677 920	0.0072 280 686	0.0073 899 118	0.0075 532 876	300
26	0.0069 683 756	0.0071 304 306	0.0072 940 744	0.0074 592 703	312
27	0.0068 781 493	0.0070 419 400	0.0072 073 384	0.0073 743 046	324
28	0.0067 960 861	0.0069 615 694	0.0071 286 759	0.0072 973 626	336
29	0.0067 213 006	0.0068 884 330	0.0070 572 008	0.0072 275 579	348
30	0.0066 530 250	0.0068 217 628	0.0069 921 451	0.0071 641 225	360
31	0.0065 905 905	0.0067 608 900	0.0069 328 398	0.0071 063 874	372
32	0.0065 334 119	0.0067 052 293	0.0068 786 998	0.0070 537 677	384
33	0.0064 809 751	0.0066 542 665	0.0068 292 109	0.0070 057 497	396
34	0.0064 328 262	0.0066 075 480	0.0067 839 200	0.0069 618 805	408
35	0.0063 885 636	0.0065 646 724	0.0067 424 260	0.0069 217 594	420
36	0.0063 478 304	0.0065 252 832	0.0067 043 727	0.0068 850 310	432
37	0.0063 103 087	0.0064 890 627	0.0066 694 430	0.0068 513 787	444
38	0.0062 757 140	0.0064 557 271	0.0066 373 536	0.0068 205 202	456
39	0.0062 437 917	0.0064 250 221	0.0066 078 509	0.0067 922 024	468
40	0.0062 143 128	0.0063 967 192	0.0065 807 073	0.0067 661 986	480
41	0.0061 870 710	0.0063 706 129	0.0065 557 178	0.0067 423 048	492
42	0.0061 618 800	0.0063 465 177	0.0065 326 977	0.0067 203 373	504
43	0.0061 385 716	0.0063 242 657	0.0065 114 802	0.0067 001 300	516
44	0.0061 169 928	0.0063 037 050	0.0064 919 140	0.0066 815 331	528
45	0.0060 970 051	0.0062 846 977	0.0064 738 623	0.0066 644 104	540
46	0.0060 784 822	0.0062 671 184	0.0064 572 007	0.0066 486 387	552
47	0.0060 613 092	0.0062 508 530	0.0064 418 158	0.0066 341 059	564
48	0.0060 453 812	0.0062 357 975	0.0064 276 048	0.0066 207 100	576
49	0.0060 306 022	0.0062 218 567	0.0064 144 734	0.0066 083 582	588
50	0.0060 168 845	0.0062 089 439	0.0064 023 360	0.0065 969 655	600

MONTHLY
Compounding

TABLE 6. PARTIAL PAYMENT TO AMORTIZE ONE
Payable at end of each period

MONTHS	8% Nominal Annual Rate	8¼% Nominal Annual Rate	8½% Nominal Annual Rate	8¾% Nominal Annual Rate	MONTHS
1	1.0066 666 667	1.0068 750 000	1.0070 833 333	1.0072 916 667	1
2	0.5050 055 371	0.5051 621 380	0.5053 187 496	0.5054 753 719	2
3	0.3377 876 215	0.3379 271 341	0.3380 666 659	0.3382 062 167	3
4	0.2541 805 093	0.2543 115 948	0.2544 427 071	0.2545 738 463	4
5	0.2040 177 184	0.2041 438 412	0.2042 699 983	0.2043 961 897	5
6	0.1705 770 882	0.1706 999 804	0.1708 229 143	0.1709 458 900	6
7	0.1466 919 783	0.1468 126 297	0.1469 333 303	0.1470 540 799	7
8	0.1287 790 685	0.1288 980 979	0.1290 171 836	0.1291 363 257	8
9	0.1148 476 254	0.1149 654 451	0.1150 833 284	0.1152 012 753	9
10	0.1037 032 089	0.1038 201 076	0.1039 370 772	0.1040 541 176	10
11	0.0945 857 209	0.0947 019 085	0.0948 181 743	0.0949 345 180	11
YEARS					
1	0.0869 884 291	0.0871 040 631	0.0872 197 825	0.0873 355 870	12
2	0.0452 272 915	0.0453 413 976	0.0454 556 749	0.0455 701 231	24
3	0.0313 363 655	0.0314 518 234	0.0315 675 374	0.0316 835 072	36
4	0.0244 129 223	0.0245 304 429	0.0246 483 034	0.0247 665 033	48
5	0.0202 763 943	0.0203 962 517	0.0205 165 313	0.0206 372 327	60
6	0.0175 332 406	0.0176 555 611	0.0177 783 846	0.0179 017 103	72
7	0.0155 862 144	0.0157 110 590	0.0158 364 854	0.0159 624 923	84
8	0.0141 366 793	0.0142 640 748	0.0143 921 286	0.0145 208 387	96
9	0.0130 187 149	0.0131 486 677	0.0132 793 527	0.0134 107 673	108
10	0.0121 327 594	0.0122 652 625	0.0123 985 689	0.0125 326 750	120
11	0.0114 154 469	0.0115 504 837	0.0116 863 919	0.0118 231 668	132
12	0.0108 245 258	0.0109 620 727	0.0111 005 556	0.0112 399 690	144
13	0.0103 307 388	0.0104 707 663	0.0106 117 912	0.0107 538 066	156
14	0.0099 131 820	0.0100 556 560	0.0101 991 854	0.0103 437 613	168
15	0.0095 565 208	0.0097 014 036	0.0098 473 956	0.0099 944 865	180
16	0.0092 492 503	0.0093 965 004	0.0095 449 100	0.0096 944 668	192
17	0.0089 825 684	0.0091 321 419	0.0092 829 210	0.0094 348 915	204
18	0.0087 496 262	0.0089 014 765	0.0090 545 745	0.0092 089 040	216
19	0.0085 450 138	0.0086 990 921	0.0088 544 563	0.0090 110 878	228
20	0.0083 644 007	0.0085 206 565	0.0086 782 323	0.0088 371 071	240
21	0.0082 042 796	0.0083 626 608	0.0085 223 921	0.0086 834 497	252
22	0.0080 617 791	0.0082 222 323	0.0083 840 616	0.0085 472 406	264
23	0.0079 345 259	0.0080 969 967	0.0082 608 654	0.0084 261 033	276
24	0.0078 205 412	0.0079 849 742	0.0081 508 232	0.0083 180 568	288
25	0.0077 181 622	0.0078 845 013	0.0080 522 708	0.0082 214 364	300
26	0.0076 259 811	0.0077 941 700	0.0079 637 998	0.0081 348 334	312
27	0.0075 427 986	0.0077 127 805	0.0078 842 103	0.0080 570 480	324
28	0.0074 675 864	0.0076 393 045	0.0078 124 739	0.0079 870 520	336
29	0.0073 994 581	0.0075 728 556	0.0077 477 046	0.0079 239 597	348
30	0.0073 376 457	0.0075 126 660	0.0076 891 348	0.0078 670 041	360
31	0.0072 814 806	0.0074 580 675	0.0076 360 969	0.0078 155 181	372
32	0.0072 303 779	0.0074 084 757	0.0075 880 072	0.0077 689 190	384
33	0.0071 838 246	0.0073 633 782	0.0075 443 538	0.0077 266 958	396
34	0.0071 413 682	0.0073 223 231	0.0075 046 860	0.0076 883 990	408
35	0.0071 026 088	0.0072 849 114	0.0074 686 057	0.0076 536 314	420
36	0.0070 671 916	0.0072 507 892	0.0074 357 600	0.0076 220 417	432
37	0.0070 348 009	0.0072 196 418	0.0074 058 355	0.0075 933 175	444
38	0.0070 051 552	0.0071 911 887	0.0073 785 527	0.0075 671 810	456
39	0.0069 780 024	0.0071 651 790	0.0073 536 622	0.0075 433 842	468
40	0.0069 531 169	0.0071 413 882	0.0073 309 407	0.0075 217 052	480
41	0.0069 302 956	0.0071 196 144	0.0073 101 879	0.0075 019 454	492
42	0.0069 093 560	0.0070 996 764	0.0072 912 237	0.0074 839 263	504
43	0.0068 901 332	0.0070 814 106	0.0072 738 863	0.0074 674 874	516
44	0.0068 724 783	0.0070 646 694	0.0072 580 293	0.0074 524 844	528
45	0.0068 562 567	0.0070 493 195	0.0072 435 210	0.0074 387 867	540
46	0.0068 413 461	0.0070 352 400	0.0072 302 419	0.0074 262 769	552
47	0.0068 276 356	0.0070 223 215	0.0072 180 842	0.0074 148 484	564
48	0.0068 150 247	0.0070 104 645	0.0072 069 497	0.0074 044 049	576
49	0.0068 034 215	0.0069 995 787	0.0071 967 498	0.0073 948 592	588
50	0.0067 927 426	0.0069 895 820	0.0071 874 036	0.0073 861 320	600

TABLE 6. PARTIAL PAYMENT TO AMORTIZE ONE
Payable at end of each period

MONTHLY Compounding

MONTHS	9% Nominal Annual Rate	9¼% Nominal Annual Rate	9½% Nominal Annual Rate	9¾% Nominal Annual Rate	MONTHS
1	1.0075 000 000	1.0077 083 333	1.0079 166 667	1.0081 250 000	1
2	0.5056 320 050	0.5057 886 488	0.5059 453 033	0.5061 019 686	2
3	0.3383 457 866	0.3384 853 756	0.3386 249 836	0.3387 646 107	3
4	0.2547 050 123	0.2548 362 051	0.2549 674 247	0.2550 986 711	4
5	0.2045 224 155	0.2046 486 756	0.2047 749 701	0.2049 012 988	5
6	0.1710 689 074	0.1711 919 666	0.1713 150 674	0.1714 382 100	6
7	0.1471 748 786	0.1472 957 263	0.1474 166 230	0.1475 375 687	7
8	0.1292 555 241	0.1293 747 788	0.1294 940 898	0.1296 134 571	8
9	0.1153 192 858	0.1154 373 598	0.1155 554 974	0.1156 736 985	9
10	0.1041 712 287	0.1042 884 107	0.1044 056 634	0.1045 229 868	10
11	0.0950 509 398	0.0951 674 395	0.0952 840 172	0.0954 006 728	11
YEARS					
1	0.0874 514 768	0.0875 674 517	0.0876 835 118	0.0877 996 570	12
2	0.0456 847 423	0.0457 995 323	0.0459 144 930	0.0460 296 244	24
3	0.0317 997 327	0.0319 162 136	0.0320 329 497	0.0321 499 410	36
4	0.0248 850 424	0.0250 039 203	0.0251 231 367	0.0252 426 912	48
5	0.0207 583 552	0.0208 798 983	0.0210 018 613	0.0211 242 437	60
6	0.0180 255 372	0.0181 498 643	0.0182 746 908	0.0184 000 156	72
7	0.0160 890 783	0.0162 162 419	0.0163 439 817	0.0164 722 962	84
8	0.0146 502 033	0.0147 802 202	0.0149 108 873	0.0150 422 027	96
9	0.0135 429 087	0.0136 757 741	0.0138 093 608	0.0139 436 658	108
10	0.0126 675 774	0.0128 032 722	0.0129 397 558	0.0130 770 242	120
11	0.0119 608 039	0.0120 992 985	0.0122 386 455	0.0123 788 402	132
12	0.0113 803 070	0.0115 215 634	0.0116 637 324	0.0118 068 075	144
13	0.0108 968 051	0.0110 407 794	0.0111 857 219	0.0113 316 250	156
14	0.0104 893 750	0.0106 360 177	0.0107 836 800	0.0109 323 529	168
15	0.0101 426 658	0.0102 919 229	0.0104 422 468	0.0105 936 266	180
16	0.0098 451 584	0.0099 969 723	0.0101 498 957	0.0103 039 157	192
17	0.0095 880 390	0.0097 423 489	0.0098 978 065	0.0100 543 967	204
18	0.0093 644 484	0.0095 211 908	0.0096 791 145	0.0098 382 023	216
19	0.0091 689 678	0.0093 280 771	0.0094 883 967	0.0096 499 072	228
20	0.0089 972 596	0.0091 586 683	0.0093 213 119	0.0094 851 685	240
21	0.0088 458 102	0.0090 094 494	0.0091 743 436	0.0093 404 685	252
22	0.0087 117 432	0.0088 775 429	0.0090 446 133	0.0092 129 279	264
23	0.0085 926 815	0.0087 605 709	0.0089 297 426	0.0091 001 675	276
24	0.0084 866 433	0.0086 565 511	0.0088 277 487	0.0090 002 046	288
25	0.0083 919 636	0.0085 638 184	0.0087 369 666	0.0089 113 742	300
26	0.0083 072 338	0.0084 809 641	0.0086 559 878	0.0088 322 683	312
27	0.0082 312 540	0.0084 067 888	0.0085 836 133	0.0087 616 887	324
28	0.0081 629 964	0.0083 402 652	0.0085 188 167	0.0086 986 098	336
29	0.0081 015 759	0.0082 805 088	0.0084 607 143	0.0086 421 492	348
30	0.0080 462 262	0.0082 267 543	0.0084 085 421	0.0085 915 441	360
31	0.0079 962 810	0.0081 783 365	0.0083 616 361	0.0085 461 322	372
32	0.0079 511 587	0.0081 346 750	0.0083 194 173	0.0085 053 363	384
33	0.0079 103 496	0.0080 952 614	0.0082 813 791	0.0084 686 512	396
34	0.0078 734 051	0.0080 596 488	0.0082 470 760	0.0084 356 338	408
35	0.0078 399 297	0.0080 274 432	0.0082 161 160	0.0084 058 939	420
36	0.0078 095 734	0.0079 982 961	0.0081 881 525	0.0083 790 870	432
37	0.0077 820 255	0.0079 718 987	0.0081 628 786	0.0083 549 084	444
38	0.0077 570 096	0.0079 479 765	0.0081 400 217	0.0083 330 878	456
39	0.0077 342 795	0.0079 262 848	0.0081 193 394	0.0083 133 848	468
40	0.0077 136 150	0.0079 066 056	0.0081 006 156	0.0082 955 856	480
41	0.0076 948 191	0.0078 887 438	0.0080 836 571	0.0082 794 994	492
42	0.0076 777 151	0.0078 725 244	0.0080 682 913	0.0082 649 557	504
43	0.0076 621 444	0.0078 577 909	0.0080 543 635	0.0082 518 021	516
44	0.0076 479 643	0.0078 444 023	0.0080 417 349	0.0082 399 018	528
45	0.0076 350 461	0.0078 322 320	0.0080 302 808	0.0082 291 325	540
46	0.0076 232 739	0.0078 211 659	0.0080 198 892	0.0082 193 841	552
47	0.0076 125 431	0.0078 111 011	0.0080 104 591	0.0082 105 578	564
48	0.0076 027 589	0.0078 019 448	0.0080 018 997	0.0082 025 647	576
49	0.0075 938 359	0.0077 936 133	0.0079 941 290	0.0081 953 247	588
50	0.0075 856 964	0.0077 860 307	0.0079 870 730	0.0081 887 658	600

MONTHLY
Compounding

TABLE 6. PARTIAL PAYMENT TO AMORTIZE ONE
Payable at end of each period

MONTHS	10% Nominal Annual Rate	10¼% Nominal Annual Rate	10½% Nominal Annual Rate	10¾% Nominal Annual Rate	MONTHS
1	1.0083 333 333	1.0085 416 667	1.0087 500 000	1.0089 583 333	1
2	0.5062 586 445	0.5064 153 312	0.5065 720 286	0.5067 287 367	2
3	0.3389 042 569	0.3390 439 221	0.3391 836 063	0.3393 233 096	3
4	0.2552 299 444	0.2553 612 444	0.2554 925 712	0.2556 239 248	4
5	0.2050 276 619	0.2051 540 592	0.2052 804 908	0.2054 069 567	5
6	0.1715 613 942	0.1716 846 201	0.1718 078 876	0.1719 311 968	6
7	0.1476 585 635	0.1477 796 072	0.1479 006 998	0.1480 218 414	7
8	0.1297 328 807	0.1298 523 605	0.1299 718 965	0.1300 914 887	8
9	0.1157 919 631	0.1159 102 911	0.1160 286 826	0.1161 471 376	9
10	0.1046 403 810	0.1047 578 458	0.1048 753 813	0.1049 929 874	10
11	0.0955 174 064	0.0956 342 178	0.0957 511 070	0.0958 680 741	11
YEARS					
1	0.0879 158 872	0.0880 322 026	0.0881 486 029	0.0882 650 882	12
2	0.0461 449 263	0.0462 603 988	0.0463 760 416	0.0464 918 548	24
3	0.0322 671 872	0.0323 846 881	0.0325 024 435	0.0326 204 532	36
4	0.0253 625 834	0.0254 828 131	0.0256 033 798	0.0257 242 831	48
5	0.0212 470 447	0.0213 702 638	0.0214 939 004	0.0216 179 537	60
6	0.0185 258 378	0.0186 521 562	0.0187 789 700	0.0189 062 779	72
7	0.0166 011 840	0.0167 306 435	0.0168 606 731	0.0169 912 713	84
8	0.0151 741 641	0.0153 067 693	0.0154 400 162	0.0155 739 024	96
9	0.0140 786 862	0.0142 144 190	0.0143 508 612	0.0144 880 096	108
10	0.0132 150 737	0.0133 539 002	0.0134 934 997	0.0136 338 680	120
11	0.0125 198 775	0.0126 617 522	0.0128 044 593	0.0129 479 933	132
12	0.0119 507 826	0.0120 956 512	0.0122 414 068	0.0123 880 428	144
13	0.0114 784 809	0.0116 262 818	0.0117 750 196	0.0119 246 863	156
14	0.0110 820 269	0.0112 326 925	0.0113 843 401	0.0115 369 600	168
15	0.0107 460 512	0.0108 995 092	0.0110 539 892	0.0112 094 798	180
16	0.0104 590 193	0.0106 151 933	0.0107 724 244	0.0109 306 991	192
17	0.0102 121 046	0.0103 709 149	0.0105 308 122	0.0106 917 813	204
18	0.0099 984 370	0.0101 598 012	0.0103 222 776	0.0104 858 485	216
19	0.0098 125 891	0.0099 764 229	0.0101 413 890	0.0103 074 675	228
20	0.0096 502 165	0.0098 164 339	0.0099 837 989	0.0101 522 895	240
21	0.0095 078 001	0.0096 763 141	0.0098 459 865	0.0100 167 930	252
22	0.0093 824 600	0.0095 531 831	0.0097 250 708	0.0098 980 967	264
23	0.0092 718 166	0.0094 446 611	0.0096 186 723	0.0097 938 214	276
24	0.0091 738 873	0.0093 487 657	0.0095 248 088	0.0097 019 856	288
25	0.0090 870 075	0.0092 638 328	0.0094 418 171	0.0096 209 272	300
26	0.0090 097 696	0.0091 884 559	0.0093 682 918	0.0095 492 424	312
27	0.0089 409 766	0.0091 214 390	0.0093 030 385	0.0094 857 381	324
28	0.0088 796 040	0.0090 617 591	0.0092 450 357	0.0094 293 953	336
29	0.0088 247 707	0.0090 085 368	0.0091 934 063	0.0093 793 387	348
30	0.0087 757 157	0.0089 610 130	0.0091 473 929	0.0093 348 136	360
31	0.0087 317 784	0.0089 185 291	0.0091 063 396	0.0092 951 666	372
32	0.0086 923 835	0.0088 805 119	0.0090 696 756	0.0092 598 297	384
33	0.0086 570 281	0.0088 464 610	0.0090 369 027	0.0092 283 076	396
34	0.0086 252 709	0.0088 159 375	0.0090 075 852	0.0092 001 672	408
35	0.0085 967 243	0.0087 885 561	0.0089 813 402	0.0091 750 290	420
36	0.0085 710 459	0.0087 639 772	0.0089 578 310	0.0091 525 589	432
37	0.0085 479 335	0.0087 419 010	0.0089 367 605	0.0091 324 631	444
38	0.0085 271 190	0.0087 220 622	0.0089 178 662	0.0091 144 820	456
39	0.0085 083 647	0.0087 042 255	0.0089 009 157	0.0090 983 862	468
40	0.0084 914 591	0.0086 881 820	0.0088 857 028	0.0090 839 724	480
41	0.0084 762 138	0.0086 737 460	0.0088 720 445	0.0090 710 604	492
42	0.0084 624 606	0.0086 607 518	0.0088 597 779	0.0090 594 901	504
43	0.0084 500 495	0.0086 490 518	0.0088 487 579	0.0090 491 193	516
44	0.0084 388 462	0.0086 385 142	0.0088 388 552	0.0090 398 213	528
45	0.0084 287 304	0.0086 290 211	0.0088 299 545	0.0090 314 833	540
46	0.0084 195 943	0.0086 204 670	0.0088 219 526	0.0090 240 046	552
47	0.0084 113 413	0.0086 127 575	0.0088 147 574	0.0090 172 955	564
48	0.0084 038 845	0.0086 058 078	0.0088 082 865	0.0090 112 759	576
49	0.0083 971 460	0.0085 995 421	0.0088 024 660	0.0090 058 740	588
50	0.0083 910 554	0.0085 938 922	0.0087 972 299	0.0090 010 260	600

TABLE 6. PARTIAL PAYMENT TO AMORTIZE ONE
Payable at end of each period

MONTHLY Compounding

MONTHS	11% Nominal Annual Rate	11¼% Nominal Annual Rate	11½% Nominal Annual Rate	11¾% Nominal Annual Rate	MONTHS
1	1.0091 666 667	1.0093 750 000	1.0095 833 333	1.0097 916 667	1
2	0.5068 854 556	0.5070 421 851	0.5071 989 253	0.5073 556 762	2
3	0.3394 630 320	0.3396 027 733	0.3397 425 337	0.3398 823 131	3
4	0.2557 553 051	0.2558 867 122	0.2560 181 460	0.2561 496 066	4
5	0.2055 334 568	0.2056 599 912	0.2057 865 598	0.2059 131 626	5
6	0.1720 545 476	0.1721 779 400	0.1723 013 740	0.1724 248 496	6
7	0.1481 430 319	0.1482 642 713	0.1483 855 597	0.1485 068 969	7
8	0.1302 111 371	0.1303 308 416	0.1304 506 023	0.1305 704 191	8
9	0.1162 656 559	0.1163 842 376	0.1165 028 827	0.1166 215 911	9
10	0.1051 106 641	0.1052 284 114	0.1053 462 293	0.1054 641 177	10
11	0.0959 851 189	0.0961 022 416	0.0962 194 419	0.0963 367 200	11
YEARS					
1	0.0883 816 585	0.0884 983 137	0.0886 150 539	0.0887 318 789	12
2	0.0466 078 382	0.0467 239 917	0.0468 403 153	0.0469 568 088	24
3	0.0327 387 171	0.0328 572 349	0.0329 760 064	0.0330 950 315	36
4	0.0258 455 226	0.0259 670 980	0.0260 890 089	0.0262 112 548	48
5	0.0217 424 231	0.0218 673 079	0.0219 926 074	0.0221 183 209	60
6	0.0190 340 790	0.0191 623 721	0.0192 911 562	0.0194 204 300	72
7	0.0171 224 364	0.0172 541 668	0.0173 864 608	0.0175 193 167	84
8	0.0157 084 257	0.0158 435 836	0.0159 793 738	0.0161 157 939	96
9	0.0146 258 610	0.0147 644 123	0.0149 036 603	0.0150 436 015	108
10	0.0137 750 011	0.0139 168 947	0.0140 595 444	0.0142 029 459	120
11	0.0130 923 490	0.0132 375 210	0.0133 835 037	0.0135 302 915	132
12	0.0125 355 526	0.0126 839 292	0.0128 331 658	0.0129 832 556	144
13	0.0120 752 736	0.0122 267 733	0.0123 791 769	0.0125 324 761	156
14	0.0116 905 423	0.0118 450 770	0.0120 005 542	0.0121 569 637	168
15	0.0113 659 693	0.0115 234 460	0.0116 818 981	0.0118 413 136	180
16	0.0110 900 040	0.0112 503 254	0.0114 116 496	0.0115 739 628	192
17	0.0108 538 064	0.0110 168 721	0.0111 809 627	0.0113 460 623	204
18	0.0106 504 964	0.0108 162 036	0.0109 829 524	0.0111 507 251	216
19	0.0104 746 389	0.0106 428 832	0.0108 121 808	0.0109 825 119	228
20	0.0103 218 839	0.0104 925 601	0.0106 642 963	0.0108 370 706	240
21	0.0101 887 095	0.0103 617 120	0.0105 357 766	0.0107 108 793	252
22	0.0100 722 345	0.0102 474 580	0.0104 237 412	0.0106 010 582	264
23	0.0099 700 800	0.0101 474 200	0.0103 258 132	0.0105 052 320	276
24	0.0098 802 657	0.0100 596 188	0.0102 400 151	0.0104 214 248	288
25	0.0098 011 308	0.0099 823 955	0.0101 646 896	0.0103 479 819	300
26	0.0097 312 730	0.0099 143 498	0.0100 984 392	0.0102 835 082	312
27	0.0096 695 016	0.0098 542 931	0.0100 400 777	0.0102 268 209	324
28	0.0096 147 995	0.0098 012 113	0.0099 885 940	0.0101 769 118	336
29	0.0095 662 943	0.0097 542 345	0.0099 431 214	0.0101 329 179	348
30	0.0095 232 340	0.0097 126 139	0.0099 029 143	0.0100 940 973	360
31	0.0094 849 678	0.0096 757 019	0.0098 673 288	0.0100 598 098	372
32	0.0094 509 308	0.0096 429 368	0.0098 358 068	0.0100 295 012	384
33	0.0094 206 310	0.0096 138 301	0.0098 078 632	0.0100 026 903	396
34	0.0093 936 384	0.0095 879 551	0.0097 830 752	0.0099 789 581	408
35	0.0093 695 765	0.0095 649 388	0.0097 610 733	0.0099 579 393	420
36	0.0093 481 148	0.0095 444 541	0.0097 415 342	0.0099 393 143	432
37	0.0093 289 624	0.0095 262 136	0.0097 241 740	0.0099 228 030	444
38	0.0093 118 630	0.0095 099 643	0.0097 087 434	0.0099 081 598	456
39	0.0092 965 902	0.0094 954 832	0.0096 950 228	0.0098 951 687	468
40	0.0092 829 440	0.0094 825 734	0.0096 828 187	0.0098 836 399	480
41	0.0092 707 472	0.0094 710 610	0.0096 719 603	0.0098 734 058	492
42	0.0092 598 425	0.0094 607 917	0.0096 622 967	0.0098 643 189	504
43	0.0092 500 907	0.0094 516 291	0.0096 536 944	0.0098 562 487	516
44	0.0092 413 677	0.0094 434 522	0.0096 460 354	0.0098 490 802	528
45	0.0092 335 634	0.0094 361 535	0.0096 392 149	0.0098 427 116	540
46	0.0092 265 797	0.0094 296 375	0.0096 331 401	0.0098 370 526	552
47	0.0092 203 294	0.0094 238 194	0.0096 277 288	0.0098 320 236	564
48	0.0092 147 345	0.0094 186 237	0.0096 229 078	0.0098 275 538	576
49	0.0092 097 256	0.0094 139 832	0.0096 186 122	0.0098 235 807	588
50	0.0092 052 409	0.0094 098 382	0.0096 147 845	0.0098 200 487	600

MONTHLY
Compounding

TABLE 6. PARTIAL PAYMENT TO AMORTIZE ONE
Payable at end of each period

MONTHS	12% Nominal Annual Rate	12¼% Nominal Annual Rate	12½% Nominal Annual Rate	12¾% Nominal Annual Rate	MONTHS
1	1.0100 000 000	1.0102 083 333	1.0104 166 667	1.0106 250 000	1
2	0.5075 124 378	0.5076 692 101	0.5078 259 931	0.5079 827 868	2
3	0.3400 221 115	0.3401 619 289	0.3403 017 653	0.3404 416 207	3
4	0.2562 810 939	0.2564 126 079	0.2565 441 487	0.2566 757 161	4
5	0.2060 397 996	0.2061 664 708	0.2062 931 763	0.2064 199 159	5
6	0.1725 483 667	0.1726 719 254	0.1727 955 257	0.1729 191 675	6
7	0.1486 282 829	0.1487 497 178	0.1488 712 015	0.1489 927 341	7
8	0.1306 902 920	0.1308 102 211	0.1309 302 061	0.1310 502 472	8
9	0.1167 403 628	0.1168 591 979	0.1169 780 962	0.1170 970 578	9
10	0.1055 820 766	0.1057 001 059	0.1058 182 058	0.1059 363 760	10
11	0.0964 540 757	0.0965 715 091	0.0966 890 201	0.0968 066 087	11
YEARS					
1	0.0888 487 887	0.0889 657 833	0.0890 828 627	0.0892 000 269	12
2	0.0470 734 722	0.0471 903 054	0.0473 073 082	0.0474 244 807	24
3	0.0332 143 098	0.0333 338 413	0.0334 536 256	0.0335 736 626	36
4	0.0263 338 354	0.0264 567 503	0.0265 799 989	0.0267 035 809	48
5	0.0222 444 477	0.0223 709 870	0.0224 979 382	0.0226 253 005	60
6	0.0195 501 925	0.0196 804 425	0.0198 111 787	0.0199 424 000	72
7	0.0176 527 328	0.0177 867 073	0.0179 212 384	0.0180 563 244	84
8	0.0162 528 414	0.0163 905 138	0.0165 288 086	0.0166 677 233	96
9	0.0151 842 326	0.0153 255 503	0.0154 675 510	0.0156 102 313	108
10	0.0143 470 948	0.0144 919 867	0.0146 376 169	0.0147 839 809	120
11	0.0136 778 788	0.0138 262 599	0.0139 754 290	0.0141 253 803	132
12	0.0131 341 914	0.0132 859 662	0.0134 385 728	0.0135 920 040	144
13	0.0126 866 622	0.0128 417 267	0.0129 976 607	0.0131 544 557	156
14	0.0123 142 953	0.0124 725 387	0.0126 316 835	0.0127 917 194	168
15	0.0120 016 806	0.0121 629 871	0.0123 252 208	0.0124 883 698	180
16	0.0117 372 513	0.0119 015 010	0.0120 666 981	0.0122 328 286	192
17	0.0115 121 553	0.0116 792 258	0.0118 472 580	0.0120 162 362	204
18	0.0113 195 038	0.0114 892 709	0.0116 600 087	0.0118 316 994	216
19	0.0111 538 566	0.0113 261 953	0.0114 995 084	0.0116 737 763	228
20	0.0110 108 613	0.0111 856 468	0.0113 614 055	0.0115 381 160	240
21	0.0108 869 965	0.0110 641 046	0.0112 421 803	0.0114 212 003	252
22	0.0107 793 836	0.0109 586 918	0.0111 389 577	0.0113 201 565	264
23	0.0106 856 488	0.0108 670 366	0.0110 493 685	0.0112 326 181	276
24	0.0106 038 188	0.0107 871 683	0.0109 714 450	0.0111 566 208	288
25	0.0105 322 414	0.0107 174 379	0.0109 035 414	0.0110 905 227	300
26	0.0104 695 246	0.0106 564 565	0.0108 442 729	0.0110 329 433	312
27	0.0104 144 889	0.0106 030 487	0.0107 924 680	0.0109 827 154	324
28	0.0103 661 298	0.0105 562 138	0.0107 471 306	0.0109 388 478	336
29	0.0103 235 881	0.0105 150 969	0.0107 074 102	0.0109 004 947	348
30	0.0102 861 260	0.0104 789 643	0.0106 725 776	0.0108 669 321	360
31	0.0102 531 072	0.0104 471 843	0.0106 420 060	0.0108 375 381	372
32	0.0102 239 817	0.0104 192 113	0.0106 151 545	0.0108 117 767	384
33	0.0101 982 726	0.0103 945 728	0.0105 915 552	0.0107 891 852	396
34	0.0101 755 650	0.0103 728 584	0.0105 708 024	0.0107 693 626	408
35	0.0101 554 978	0.0103 537 112	0.0105 525 439	0.0107 519 615	420
36	0.0101 377 553	0.0103 368 200	0.0105 364 727	0.0107 366 796	432
37	0.0101 220 616	0.0103 219 128	0.0105 223 214	0.0107 232 540	444
38	0.0101 081 748	0.0103 087 520	0.0105 098 564	0.0107 114 553	456
39	0.0100 958 829	0.0102 971 293	0.0104 988 735	0.0107 010 835	468
40	0.0100 849 995	0.0102 868 620	0.0104 891 940	0.0106 919 637	480
41	0.0100 753 607	0.0102 777 900	0.0104 806 611	0.0106 839 431	492
42	0.0100 668 221	0.0102 697 723	0.0104 731 375	0.0106 768 879	504
43	0.0100 592 566	0.0102 626 850	0.0104 665 026	0.0106 706 807	516
44	0.0100 525 522	0.0102 564 190	0.0104 606 506	0.0106 652 189	528
45	0.0100 466 098	0.0102 508 785	0.0104 554 883	0.0106 604 123	540
46	0.0100 413 422	0.0102 459 786	0.0104 509 339	0.0106 561 818	552
47	0.0100 366 720	0.0102 416 450	0.0104 469 153	0.0106 524 580	564
48	0.0100 325 311	0.0102 378 116	0.0104 433 692	0.0106 491 799	576
49	0.0100 288 592	0.0102 344 205	0.0104 402 397	0.0106 462 940	588
50	0.0100 256 027	0.0102 314 204	0.0104 374 778	0.0106 437 531	600

TABLE 6. PARTIAL PAYMENT TO AMORTIZE ONE
Payable at end of each period

MONTHS	13% Nominal Annual Rate	13¼% Nominal Annual Rate	13½% Nominal Annual Rate	13¾% Nominal Annual Rate	MONTHS
1	1.0108 333 333	1.0110 416 667	1.0112 500 000	1.0114 583 333	1
2	0.5081 395 911	0.5082 964 061	0.5084 532 318	0.5086 100 682	2
3	0.3405 814 950	0.3407 213 884	0.3408 613 007	0.3410 012 320	3
4	0.2568 073 102	0.2569 389 311	0.2570 705 786	0.2572 022 527	4
5	0.2065 466 896	0.2066 734 976	0.2068 003 396	0.2069 272 158	5
6	0.1730 428 508	0.1731 665 756	0.1732 903 419	0.1734 141 497	6
7	0.1491 143 154	0.1492 359 455	0.1493 576 244	0.1494 793 521	7
8	0.1311 703 444	0.1312 904 976	0.1314 107 067	0.1315 309 719	8
9	0.1172 160 825	0.1173 351 706	0.1174 543 217	0.1175 735 361	9
10	0.1060 546 167	0.1061 729 278	0.1062 913 092	0.1064 097 610	10
11	0.0969 242 749	0.0970 420 186	0.0971 598 399	0.0972 777 386	11
YEARS					
1	0.0893 172 757	0.0894 346 092	0.0895 520 274	0.0896 695 302	12
2	0.0475 418 226	0.0476 593 339	0.0477 770 145	0.0478 948 643	24
3	0.0336 939 520	0.0338 144 937	0.0339 352 873	0.0340 563 328	36
4	0.0268 274 959	0.0269 517 434	0.0270 763 230	0.0272 012 341	48
5	0.0227 530 730	0.0228 812 552	0.0230 098 460	0.0231 388 449	60
6	0.0200 741 052	0.0202 062 930	0.0203 389 622	0.0204 721 114	72
7	0.0181 919 633	0.0183 281 534	0.0184 648 928	0.0186 021 795	84
8	0.0168 072 551	0.0169 474 014	0.0170 881 597	0.0172 295 271	96
9	0.0157 535 877	0.0158 976 165	0.0160 423 141	0.0161 876 769	108
10	0.0149 310 740	0.0150 788 916	0.0152 274 289	0.0153 766 812	120
11	0.0142 761 079	0.0144 276 058	0.0145 798 680	0.0147 328 885	132
12	0.0137 462 524	0.0139 013 108	0.0140 571 716	0.0142 138 275	144
13	0.0133 121 026	0.0134 705 927	0.0136 299 170	0.0137 900 665	156
14	0.0129 526 358	0.0131 144 223	0.0132 770 683	0.0134 405 631	168
15	0.0126 524 217	0.0128 173 643	0.0129 831 854	0.0131 498 727	180
16	0.0123 998 784	0.0125 678 337	0.0127 366 804	0.0129 064 044	192
17	0.0121 861 444	0.0123 569 668	0.0125 286 878	0.0127 012 915	204
18	0.0120 043 253	0.0121 778 689	0.0123 523 127	0.0125 276 391	216
19	0.0118 489 795	0.0120 250 987	0.0122 021 146	0.0123 800 080	228
20	0.0117 157 571	0.0118 943 077	0.0120 737 468	0.0122 540 538	240
21	0.0116 011 418	0.0117 819 820	0.0119 636 984	0.0121 462 688	252
22	0.0115 022 636	0.0116 852 547	0.0118 691 058	0.0120 537 933	264
23	0.0114 167 592	0.0116 017 662	0.0117 876 137	0.0119 742 768	276
24	0.0113 426 682	0.0115 295 604	0.0117 172 706	0.0119 057 730	288
25	0.0112 783 530	0.0114 670 043	0.0116 564 488	0.0118 466 597	300
26	0.0112 224 377	0.0114 127 271	0.0116 037 829	0.0117 955 773	312
27	0.0111 737 600	0.0113 655 718	0.0115 581 215	0.0117 513 808	324
28	0.0111 313 337	0.0113 245 577	0.0115 184 899	0.0117 131 014	336
29	0.0110 943 183	0.0112 888 499	0.0114 840 590	0.0116 799 165	348
30	0.0110 619 952	0.0112 577 352	0.0114 541 218	0.0116 511 253	360
31	0.0110 337 476	0.0112 306 028	0.0114 280 730	0.0116 261 288	372
32	0.0110 090 450	0.0112 069 275	0.0114 053 935	0.0116 044 139	384
33	0.0109 874 297	0.0111 862 571	0.0113 856 368	0.0115 855 399	396
34	0.0109 685 061	0.0111 682 012	0.0113 684 181	0.0115 691 278	408
35	0.0109 519 314	0.0111 524 225	0.0113 534 050	0.0115 548 507	420
36	0.0109 374 084	0.0111 386 284	0.0113 403 104	0.0115 424 268	432
37	0.0109 246 787	0.0111 265 654	0.0113 288 856	0.0115 316 123	444
38	0.0109 135 173	0.0111 160 132	0.0113 189 149	0.0115 221 962	456
39	0.0109 037 286	0.0111 067 802	0.0113 102 111	0.0115 139 959	468
40	0.0108 951 416	0.0110 986 997	0.0113 026 117	0.0115 068 530	480
41	0.0108 876 073	0.0110 916 265	0.0112 959 753	0.0115 006 301	492
42	0.0108 809 954	0.0110 854 339	0.0112 901 790	0.0114 952 079	504
43	0.0108 751 921	0.0110 800 116	0.0112 851 158	0.0114 904 827	516
44	0.0108 700 978	0.0110 752 631	0.0112 806 923	0.0114 863 644	528
45	0.0108 656 253	0.0110 711 042	0.0112 768 274	0.0114 827 749	540
46	0.0108 616 984	0.0110 674 614	0.0112 734 502	0.0114 796 458	552
47	0.0108 582 501	0.0110 642 702	0.0112 704 989	0.0114 769 180	564
48	0.0108 552 218	0.0110 614 745	0.0112 679 196	0.0114 745 398	576
49	0.0108 525 622	0.0110 590 252	0.0112 656 653	0.0114 724 663	588
50	0.0108 502 263	0.0110 568 792	0.0112 636 949	0.0114 706 584	600

TABLE 6. PARTIAL PAYMENT TO AMORTIZE ONE
Payable at end of each period

MONTHS	14% Nominal Annual Rate	14¼% Nominal Annual Rate	14½% Nominal Annual Rate	14¾% Nominal Annual Rate	MONTHS
1	1.0116 666 667	1.0118 750 000	1.0120 833 333	1.0122 916 667	1
2	0.5087 669 152	0.5089 237 729	0.5090 806 413	0.5092 375 203	2
3	0.3411 411 823	0.3412 811 515	0.3414 211 396	0.3415 611 467	3
4	0.2573 339 536	0.2574 656 811	0.2575 974 352	0.2577 292 160	4
5	0.2070 541 261	0.2071 810 706	0.2073 080 491	0.2074 350 617	5
6	0.1735 379 989	0.1736 618 896	0.1737 858 217	0.1739 097 953	6
7	0.1496 011 284	0.1497 229 535	0.1498 448 273	0.1499 667 497	7
8	0.1316 512 929	0.1317 716 700	0.1318 921 029	0.1320 125 917	8
9	0.1176 928 136	0.1178 121 542	0.1179 315 580	0.1180 510 248	9
10	0.1065 282 831	0.1066 468 754	0.1067 655 381	0.1068 842 709	10
11	0.0973 957 148	0.0975 137 684	0.0976 318 994	0.0977 501 077	11
YEARS					
1	0.0897 871 176	0.0899 047 895	0.0900 225 460	0.0901 403 869	12
2	0.0480 128 833	0.0481 310 712	0.0482 494 280	0.0483 679 537	24
3	0.0341 776 298	0.0342 991 781	0.0344 209 774	0.0345 430 277	36
4	0.0273 264 765	0.0274 520 496	0.0275 779 529	0.0277 041 859	48
5	0.0232 682 508	0.0233 980 632	0.0235 282 811	0.0236 589 037	60
6	0.0206 057 395	0.0207 398 450	0.0208 744 268	0.0210 094 833	72
7	0.0187 400 116	0.0188 783 872	0.0190 173 042	0.0191 567 608	84
8	0.0173 715 010	0.0175 140 786	0.0176 572 571	0.0178 010 336	96
9	0.0163 337 012	0.0164 803 831	0.0166 277 190	0.0167 757 050	108
10	0.0155 266 435	0.0156 773 111	0.0158 286 789	0.0159 807 422	120
11	0.0148 866 612	0.0150 411 798	0.0151 964 383	0.0153 524 303	132
12	0.0143 712 708	0.0145 294 942	0.0146 884 899	0.0148 482 502	144
13	0.0139 510 322	0.0141 128 049	0.0142 753 757	0.0144 387 353	156
14	0.0136 048 961	0.0137 700 568	0.0139 360 343	0.0141 028 180	168
15	0.0133 174 139	0.0134 857 966	0.0136 550 086	0.0138 250 376	180
16	0.0130 769 918	0.0132 484 286	0.0134 207 008	0.0135 937 946	192
17	0.0128 747 623	0.0130 490 845	0.0132 242 426	0.0134 002 210	204
18	0.0127 038 309	0.0128 808 707	0.0130 587 414	0.0132 374 260	216
19	0.0125 587 600	0.0127 383 517	0.0129 187 646	0.0130 999 801	228
20	0.0124 352 081	0.0126 171 894	0.0127 999 777	0.0129 835 530	240
21	0.0123 296 711	0.0125 138 838	0.0126 988 854	0.0128 846 549	252
22	0.0122 392 939	0.0124 255 848	0.0126 126 432	0.0128 004 472	264
23	0.0121 617 311	0.0123 499 526	0.0125 389 176	0.0127 286 030	276
24	0.0120 950 420	0.0122 850 526	0.0124 757 804	0.0126 672 014	288
25	0.0120 376 104	0.0122 292 753	0.0124 216 292	0.0126 146 474	300
26	0.0119 880 832	0.0121 812 743	0.0123 751 247	0.0125 696 094	312
27	0.0119 453 218	0.0121 399 178	0.0123 351 426	0.0125 309 709	324
28	0.0119 083 641	0.0121 042 508	0.0123 007 352	0.0124 977 918	336
29	0.0118 763 941	0.0120 734 643	0.0122 711 009	0.0124 692 782	348
30	0.0118 487 175	0.0120 468 709	0.0122 455 593	0.0124 447 572	360
31	0.0118 247 419	0.0120 238 849	0.0122 235 318	0.0124 236 574	372
32	0.0118 039 603	0.0120 040 059	0.0122 045 248	0.0124 054 923	384
33	0.0117 859 384	0.0119 868 058	0.0121 881 167	0.0123 898 469	396
34	0.0117 703 030	0.0119 719 175	0.0121 739 466	0.0123 763 666	408
35	0.0117 567 328	0.0119 590 257	0.0121 617 051	0.0123 647 482	420
36	0.0117 449 514	0.0119 478 591	0.0121 511 266	0.0123 547 315	432
37	0.0117 347 199	0.0119 381 844	0.0121 419 828	0.0123 460 938	444
38	0.0117 258 325	0.0119 298 002	0.0121 340 775	0.0123 386 437	456
39	0.0117 181 107	0.0119 225 330	0.0121 272 416	0.0123 322 167	468
40	0.0117 114 006	0.0119 162 328	0.0121 213 294	0.0123 266 715	480
41	0.0117 055 686	0.0119 107 702	0.0121 162 155	0.0123 218 865	492
42	0.0117 004 992	0.0119 060 332	0.0121 117 915	0.0123 177 569	504
43	0.0116 960 920	0.0119 019 249	0.0121 079 639	0.0123 141 927	516
44	0.0116 922 602	0.0118 983 616	0.0121 046 520	0.0123 111 161	528
45	0.0116 889 283	0.0118 952 706	0.0121 017 861	0.0123 084 604	540
46	0.0116 860 309	0.0118 925 892	0.0120 993 060	0.0123 061 677	552
47	0.0116 835 111	0.0118 902 630	0.0120 971 596	0.0123 041 883	564
48	0.0116 813 197	0.0118 882 447	0.0120 953 019	0.0123 024 793	576
49	0.0116 794 136	0.0118 864 936	0.0120 936 941	0.0123 010 038	588
50	0.0116 777 557	0.0118 849 742	0.0120 923 024	0.0122 997 297	600

TABLE 6. PARTIAL PAYMENT TO AMORTIZE ONE
Payable at end of each period

MONTHS	15% Nominal Annual Rate	15¼% Nominal Annual Rate	15½% Nominal Annual Rate	15¾% Nominal Annual Rate	MONTHS
1	1.0125 000 000	1.0127 083 333	1.0129 166 667	1.0131 250 000	1
2	0.5093 944 099	0.5095 513 103	0.5097 082 212	0.5098 651 428	2
3	0.3417 011 728	0.3418 412 177	0.3419 812 816	0.3421 213 645	3
4	0.2578 610 233	0.2579 928 574	0.2581 247 180	0.2582 566 052	4
5	0.2075 621 084	0.2076 891 892	0.2078 163 041	0.2079 434 529	5
6	0.1740 338 102	0.1741 578 666	0.1742 819 643	0.1744 061 034	6
7	0.1500 887 209	0.1502 107 407	0.1503 328 091	0.1504 549 261	7
8	0.1321 331 365	0.1322 537 370	0.1323 743 934	0.1324 951 057	8
9	0.1181 705 546	0.1182 901 475	0.1184 098 034	0.1185 295 223	9
10	0.1070 030 740	0.1071 219 472	0.1072 408 906	0.1073 599 042	10
11	0.0978 683 935	0.0979 867 565	0.0981 051 968	0.0982 237 144	11
YEARS					
1	0.0902 583 123	0.0903 763 222	0.0904 944 164	0.0906 125 950	12
2	0.0484 866 480	0.0486 055 110	0.0487 245 425	0.0488 437 423	24
3	0.0346 653 285	0.0347 878 797	0.0349 106 810	0.0350 337 322	36
4	0.0278 307 483	0.0279 576 394	0.0280 848 589	0.0282 124 062	48
5	0.0237 899 301	0.0239 213 595	0.0240 531 911	0.0241 854 239	60
6	0.0211 450 133	0.0212 810 155	0.0214 174 883	0.0215 544 305	72
7	0.0192 967 547	0.0194 372 841	0.0195 783 469	0.0197 199 408	84
8	0.0179 454 053	0.0180 903 693	0.0182 359 228	0.0183 820 626	96
9	0.0169 243 373	0.0170 736 119	0.0172 235 250	0.0173 740 726	108
10	0.0161 334 957	0.0162 869 346	0.0164 410 537	0.0165 958 479	120
11	0.0155 091 496	0.0156 665 898	0.0158 247 447	0.0159 836 077	132
12	0.0150 087 677	0.0151 700 344	0.0153 320 427	0.0154 947 848	144
13	0.0146 028 746	0.0147 677 844	0.0149 334 556	0.0150 998 788	156
14	0.0142 703 972	0.0144 387 611	0.0146 078 990	0.0147 778 003	168
15	0.0139 958 712	0.0141 674 972	0.0143 399 034	0.0145 130 775	180
16	0.0137 676 961	0.0139 423 914	0.0141 178 669	0.0142 941 087	192
17	0.0135 770 043	0.0137 545 773	0.0139 329 247	0.0141 120 314	204
18	0.0134 169 075	0.0135 971 693	0.0137 781 947	0.0139 599 673	216
19	0.0132 819 798	0.0134 647 458	0.0136 482 601	0.0138 325 050	228
20	0.0131 678 958	0.0133 529 868	0.0135 388 069	0.0137 253 373	240
21	0.0130 711 714	0.0132 584 147	0.0134 463 645	0.0136 350 010	252
22	0.0129 889 748	0.0131 782 047	0.0133 681 159	0.0135 586 878	264
23	0.0129 189 861	0.0131 100 448	0.0133 017 574	0.0134 941 026	276
24	0.0128 592 923	0.0130 520 302	0.0132 453 929	0.0134 393 585	288
25	0.0128 083 061	0.0130 025 820	0.0131 974 524	0.0133 928 951	300
26	0.0127 647 042	0.0129 603 854	0.0131 566 300	0.0133 534 159	312
27	0.0127 273 781	0.0129 243 405	0.0131 218 349	0.0133 198 393	324
28	0.0126 953 959	0.0128 935 238	0.0130 921 525	0.0132 912 598	336
29	0.0126 679 716	0.0128 671 577	0.0130 668 135	0.0132 669 171	348
30	0.0126 444 402	0.0128 445 850	0.0130 451 692	0.0132 461 710	360
31	0.0126 242 377	0.0128 252 496	0.0130 266 712	0.0132 284 813	372
32	0.0126 068 847	0.0128 086 796	0.0130 108 553	0.0132 133 914	384
33	0.0125 919 732	0.0127 944 737	0.0129 973 274	0.0132 005 145	396
34	0.0125 791 550	0.0127 822 905	0.0129 857 527	0.0131 895 226	408
35	0.0125 681 330	0.0127 718 390	0.0129 758 466	0.0131 801 374	420
36	0.0125 586 529	0.0127 628 708	0.0129 673 664	0.0131 721 222	432
37	0.0125 504 971	0.0127 551 737	0.0129 601 055	0.0131 652 758	444
38	0.0125 434 794	0.0127 485 663	0.0129 538 874	0.0131 594 266	456
39	0.0125 374 398	0.0127 428 936	0.0129 485 616	0.0131 544 288	468
40	0.0125 322 414	0.0127 380 225	0.0129 439 995	0.0131 501 580	480
41	0.0125 277 663	0.0127 338 393	0.0129 400 911	0.0131 465 079	492
42	0.0125 239 135	0.0127 302 466	0.0129 367 424	0.0131 433 882	504
43	0.0125 205 963	0.0127 271 607	0.0129 338 731	0.0131 407 215	516
44	0.0125 177 398	0.0127 245 099	0.0129 314 143	0.0131 384 420	528
45	0.0125 152 800	0.0127 222 327	0.0129 293 073	0.0131 364 932	540
46	0.0125 131 616	0.0127 202 764	0.0129 275 015	0.0131 348 272	552
47	0.0125 113 372	0.0127 185 957	0.0129 259 539	0.0131 334 029	564
48	0.0125 097 659	0.0127 171 516	0.0129 246 275	0.0131 321 851	576
49	0.0125 084 125	0.0127 159 109	0.0129 234 906	0.0131 311 438	588
50	0.0125 072 467	0.0127 148 448	0.0129 225 161	0.0131 302 536	600

MONTHLY
Compounding

TABLE 6. PARTIAL PAYMENT TO AMORTIZE ONE
Payable at end of each period

MONTHS	16% Nominal Annual Rate	16¼% Nominal Annual Rate	16½% Nominal Annual Rate	16¾% Nominal Annual Rate	MONTHS
1	1.0133 333 333	1.0135 416 667	1.0137 500 000	1.0139 583 333	1
2	0.5100 220 751	0.5101 790 179	0.5103 359 714	0.5104 929 356	2
3	0.3422 614 662	0.3424 015 868	0.3425 417 264	0.3426 818 848	3
4	0.2583 885 190	0.2585 204 594	0.2586 524 264	0.2587 844 200	4
5	0.2080 706 358	0.2081 978 528	0.2083 251 037	0.2084 523 887	5
6	0.1745 302 839	0.1746 545 056	0.1747 787 688	0.1749 030 732	6
7	0.1505 770 917	0.1506 993 060	0.1508 215 687	0.1509 438 801	7
8	0.1326 158 737	0.1327 366 975	0.1328 575 771	0.1329 785 124	8
9	0.1186 493 042	0.1187 691 490	0.1188 890 568	0.1190 090 274	9
10	0.1074 789 878	0.1075 981 416	0.1077 173 653	0.1078 366 592	10
11	0.0983 423 091	0.0984 609 811	0.0985 797 303	0.0986 985 566	11
YEARS					
1	0.0907 308 579	0.0908 492 051	0.0909 676 365	0.0910 861 522	12
2	0.0489 631 105	0.0490 826 469	0.0492 023 513	0.0493 222 238	24
3	0.0351 570 330	0.0352 805 832	0.0354 043 826	0.0355 284 307	36
4	0.0283 402 808	0.0284 684 822	0.0285 970 100	0.0287 258 635	48
5	0.0243 180 571	0.0244 510 898	0.0245 845 211	0.0247 183 501	60
6	0.0216 918 406	0.0218 297 172	0.0219 680 587	0.0221 068 639	72
7	0.0198 620 639	0.0200 047 141	0.0201 478 890	0.0202 915 867	84
8	0.0185 287 860	0.0186 760 898	0.0188 239 712	0.0189 724 269	96
9	0.0175 252 508	0.0176 770 554	0.0178 294 825	0.0179 825 281	108
10	0.0167 513 121	0.0169 074 412	0.0170 642 299	0.0172 216 730	120
11	0.0161 431 726	0.0163 034 328	0.0164 643 820	0.0166 260 135	132
12	0.0156 582 530	0.0158 224 393	0.0159 873 361	0.0161 529 354	144
13	0.0152 670 448	0.0154 349 445	0.0156 035 685	0.0157 729 077	156
14	0.0149 484 542	0.0151 198 501	0.0152 919 772	0.0154 648 249	168
15	0.0146 870 074	0.0148 616 810	0.0150 370 861	0.0152 132 107	180
16	0.0144 711 034	0.0146 488 373	0.0148 272 971	0.0150 064 693	192
17	0.0142 918 824	0.0144 724 628	0.0146 537 579	0.0148 357 530	204
18	0.0141 424 707	0.0143 256 889	0.0145 096 058	0.0146 942 059	216
19	0.0140 174 630	0.0142 031 170	0.0143 894 498	0.0145 764 448	228
20	0.0139 125 594	0.0141 004 551	0.0142 890 064	0.0144 781 956	240
21	0.0138 243 050	0.0140 142 572	0.0142 048 391	0.0143 960 322	252
22	0.0137 499 002	0.0139 417 334	0.0141 341 681	0.0143 271 853	264
23	0.0136 870 597	0.0138 806 083	0.0140 747 287	0.0142 694 016	276
24	0.0136 339 061	0.0138 290 148	0.0140 246 646	0.0142 208 360	288
25	0.0135 888 889	0.0137 854 127	0.0139 824 465	0.0141 799 705	300
26	0.0135 507 215	0.0137 485 258	0.0139 468 087	0.0141 455 506	312
27	0.0135 183 320	0.0137 172 922	0.0139 166 999	0.0141 165 357	324
28	0.0134 908 244	0.0136 908 257	0.0138 912 439	0.0140 920 600	336
29	0.0134 674 476	0.0136 683 845	0.0138 697 087	0.0140 714 013	348
30	0.0134 475 700	0.0136 493 462	0.0138 514 808	0.0140 539 557	360
31	0.0134 306 598	0.0136 331 874	0.0138 360 457	0.0140 392 173	372
32	0.0134 162 683	0.0136 194 673	0.0138 229 707	0.0140 267 616	384
33	0.0134 040 160	0.0136 078 139	0.0138 118 913	0.0140 162 319	396
34	0.0133 935 819	0.0135 979 133	0.0138 025 006	0.0140 073 282	408
35	0.0133 846 940	0.0135 894 998	0.0137 945 393	0.0139 997 978	420
36	0.0133 771 215	0.0135 823 485	0.0137 877 885	0.0139 934 277	432
37	0.0133 706 686	0.0135 762 691	0.0137 820 634	0.0139 880 383	444
38	0.0133 651 689	0.0135 711 002	0.0137 772 073	0.0139 834 780	456
39	0.0133 604 810	0.0135 667 048	0.0137 730 880	0.0139 796 189	468
40	0.0133 564 846	0.0135 629 668	0.0137 695 932	0.0139 763 528	480
41	0.0133 530 774	0.0135 597 877	0.0137 666 280	0.0139 735 884	492
42	0.0133 501 722	0.0135 570 835	0.0137 641 121	0.0139 712 485	504
43	0.0133 476 950	0.0135 547 833	0.0137 619 771	0.0139 692 678	516
44	0.0133 455 825	0.0135 528 266	0.0137 601 654	0.0139 675 911	528
45	0.0133 437 810	0.0135 511 620	0.0137 586 279	0.0139 661 716	540
46	0.0133 422 447	0.0135 497 458	0.0137 573 231	0.0139 649 698	552
47	0.0133 409 344	0.0135 485 409	0.0137 562 157	0.0139 639 524	564
48	0.0133 398 168	0.0135 475 158	0.0137 552 758	0.0139 630 911	576
49	0.0133 388 636	0.0135 466 437	0.0137 544 781	0.0139 623 618	588
50	0.0133 380 506	0.0135 459 016	0.0137 538 010	0.0139 617 443	600

TABLE 6. PARTIAL PAYMENT TO AMORTIZE ONE
Payable at end of each period

MONTHLY Compounding

MONTHS	17% Nominal Annual Rate	17¼% Nominal Annual Rate	17½% Nominal Annual Rate	17¾% Nominal Annual Rate	MONTHS
1	1.0141 666 667	1.0143 750 000	1.0145 833 333	1.0147 916 667	1
2	0.5106 499 104	0.5108 068 957	0.5109 638 918	0.5111 208 984	2
3	0.3428 220 621	0.3429 622 583	0.3431 024 734	0.3432 427 074	3
4	0.2589 164 401	0.2590 484 868	0.2591 805 600	0.2593 126 597	4
5	0.2085 797 076	0.2087 070 605	0.2088 344 474	0.2089 618 683	5
6	0.1750 274 189	0.1751 518 060	0.1752 762 343	0.1754 007 038	6
7	0.1510 662 400	0.1511 886 484	0.1513 111 053	0.1514 336 107	7
8	0.1330 995 035	0.1332 205 503	0.1333 416 527	0.1334 628 108	8
9	0.1191 290 609	0.1192 491 573	0.1193 693 165	0.1194 895 386	9
10	0.1079 560 230	0.1080 754 568	0.1081 949 606	0.1083 145 343	10
11	0.0988 174 600	0.0989 364 405	0.0990 554 980	0.0991 746 326	11
YEARS					
1	0.0912 047 521	0.0913 234 361	0.0914 422 043	0.0915 610 566	12
2	0.0494 422 641	0.0495 624 722	0.0496 828 479	0.0498 033 912	24
3	0.0356 527 275	0.0357 772 727	0.0359 020 659	0.0360 271 069	36
4	0.0288 550 423	0.0289 845 459	0.0291 143 736	0.0292 445 250	48
5	0.0248 525 758	0.0249 871 973	0.0251 222 137	0.0252 576 241	60
6	0.0222 461 311	0.0223 858 590	0.0225 260 460	0.0226 666 905	72
7	0.0204 358 049	0.0205 805 413	0.0207 257 938	0.0208 715 601	84
8	0.0191 214 541	0.0192 710 495	0.0194 212 100	0.0195 719 326	96
9	0.0181 361 879	0.0182 904 580	0.0184 453 341	0.0186 008 120	108
10	0.0173 797 652	0.0175 385 013	0.0176 978 760	0.0178 578 840	120
11	0.0167 883 209	0.0169 512 977	0.0171 149 373	0.0172 792 331	132
12	0.0163 192 294	0.0164 862 102	0.0166 538 701	0.0168 222 010	144
13	0.0159 429 529	0.0161 136 947	0.0162 851 241	0.0164 572 317	156
14	0.0156 383 827	0.0158 126 400	0.0159 875 861	0.0161 632 107	168
15	0.0153 900 429	0.0155 675 708	0.0157 457 825	0.0159 246 662	180
16	0.0151 863 407	0.0153 668 981	0.0155 481 286	0.0157 300 190	192
17	0.0150 184 338	0.0152 017 858	0.0153 857 950	0.0155 704 472	204
18	0.0148 794 734	0.0150 653 931	0.0152 519 497	0.0154 391 283	216
19	0.0147 640 854	0.0149 523 553	0.0151 412 385	0.0153 307 192	228
20	0.0146 680 055	0.0148 584 190	0.0150 494 193	0.0152 409 901	240
21	0.0145 878 184	0.0147 801 803	0.0149 731 006	0.0151 665 622	252
22	0.0145 207 666	0.0147 148 939	0.0149 095 495	0.0151 047 162	264
23	0.0144 646 082	0.0146 603 300	0.0148 565 494	0.0150 532 487	276
24	0.0144 175 100	0.0146 146 681	0.0148 122 924	0.0150 103 654	288
25	0.0143 779 658	0.0145 764 139	0.0147 752 970	0.0149 745 977	300
26	0.0143 447 326	0.0145 443 364	0.0147 443 444	0.0149 447 395	312
27	0.0143 167 809	0.0145 174 175	0.0147 184 282	0.0149 197 964	324
28	0.0142 932 555	0.0144 948 131	0.0146 967 156	0.0148 989 469	336
29	0.0142 734 445	0.0144 758 213	0.0146 785 152	0.0148 815 106	348
30	0.0142 567 534	0.0144 598 576	0.0146 632 523	0.0148 669 225	360
31	0.0142 426 853	0.0144 464 340	0.0146 504 480	0.0148 547 131	372
32	0.0142 308 240	0.0144 351 427	0.0146 397 031	0.0148 444 916	384
33	0.0142 208 205	0.0144 256 424	0.0146 306 840	0.0148 359 322	396
34	0.0142 123 817	0.0144 176 473	0.0146 231 118	0.0148 287 632	408
35	0.0142 052 615	0.0144 109 175	0.0146 167 534	0.0148 227 576	420
36	0.0141 992 529	0.0144 052 519	0.0146 114 132	0.0148 177 260	432
37	0.0141 941 815	0.0144 004 816	0.0146 069 278	0.0148 135 099	444
38	0.0141 899 007	0.0143 964 646	0.0146 031 598	0.0148 099 768	456
39	0.0141 862 868	0.0143 930 817	0.0145 999 942	0.0148 070 157	468
40	0.0141 832 357	0.0143 902 325	0.0145 973 346	0.0148 045 339	480
41	0.0141 806 595	0.0143 878 326	0.0145 950 998	0.0148 024 537	492
42	0.0141 784 842	0.0143 858 111	0.0145 932 220	0.0148 007 100	504
43	0.0141 766 473	0.0143 841 083	0.0145 916 441	0.0147 992 483	516
44	0.0141 750 961	0.0143 826 738	0.0145 903 180	0.0147 980 230	528
45	0.0141 737 861	0.0143 814 654	0.0145 892 036	0.0147 969 957	540
46	0.0141 726 798	0.0143 804 473	0.0145 882 671	0.0147 961 346	552
47	0.0141 717 455	0.0143 795 896	0.0145 874 800	0.0147 954 126	564
48	0.0141 709 563	0.0143 788 669	0.0145 868 186	0.0147 948 073	576
49	0.0141 702 899	0.0143 782 581	0.0145 862 626	0.0147 942 999	588
50	0.0141 697 270	0.0143 777 452	0.0145 857 954	0.0147 938 744	600

MONTHLY Compounding

TABLE 6. PARTIAL PAYMENT TO AMORTIZE ONE
Payable at end of each period

MONTHS	18% Nominal Annual Rate	18¼% Nominal Annual Rate	18½% Nominal Annual Rate	18¾% Nominal Annual Rate	MONTHS
1	1.0150 000 000	1.0152 083 333	1.0154 166 667	1.0156 250 000	1
2	0.5112 779 156	0.5114 349 435	0.5115 919 819	0.5117 490 310	2
3	0.3433 829 602	0.3435 232 319	0.3436 635 224	0.3438 038 318	3
4	0.2594 447 860	0.2595 769 388	0.2597 091 181	0.2598 413 239	4
5	0.2090 893 231	0.2092 168 118	0.2093 443 345	0.2094 718 911	5
6	0.1755 252 146	0.1756 497 667	0.1757 743 599	0.1758 989 944	6
7	0.1515 561 645	0.1516 787 669	0.1518 014 176	0.1519 241 168	7
8	0.1335 840 246	0.1337 052 940	0.1338 266 190	0.1339 479 996	8
9	0.1196 098 234	0.1197 301 710	0.1198 505 813	0.1199 710 543	9
10	0.1084 341 779	0.1085 538 913	0.1086 736 747	0.1087 935 278	10
11	0.0992 938 442	0.0994 131 327	0.0995 324 982	0.0996 519 405	11
YEARS					
1	0.0916 799 929	0.0917 990 133	0.0919 181 176	0.0920 373 060	12
2	0.0499 241 020	0.0500 449 801	0.0501 660 254	0.0502 872 378	24
3	0.0361 523 955	0.0362 779 314	0.0364 037 143	0.0365 297 439	36
4	0.0293 749 996	0.0295 057 968	0.0296 369 160	0.0297 683 566	48
5	0.0253 934 274	0.0255 296 228	0.0256 662 092	0.0258 031 856	60
6	0.0228 077 911	0.0229 493 462	0.0230 913 543	0.0232 338 137	72
7	0.0210 178 380	0.0211 646 251	0.0213 119 192	0.0214 597 179	84
8	0.0197 232 141	0.0198 750 513	0.0200 274 410	0.0201 803 799	96
9	0.0187 568 877	0.0189 135 569	0.0190 708 153	0.0192 286 588	108
10	0.0180 185 199	0.0181 797 784	0.0183 416 541	0.0185 041 416	120
11	0.0174 441 787	0.0176 097 673	0.0177 759 924	0.0179 428 475	132
12	0.0169 911 952	0.0171 608 449	0.0173 311 420	0.0175 020 789	144
13	0.0166 300 085	0.0168 034 454	0.0169 775 331	0.0171 522 626	156
14	0.0163 395 032	0.0165 164 533	0.0166 940 505	0.0168 722 847	168
15	0.0161 042 104	0.0162 844 033	0.0164 652 336	0.0166 466 897	180
16	0.0159 125 567	0.0160 957 289	0.0162 795 230	0.0164 639 266	192
17	0.0157 557 286	0.0159 416 256	0.0161 281 246	0.0163 152 123	204
18	0.0156 269 142	0.0158 152 927	0.0160 042 497	0.0161 937 709	216
19	0.0155 207 820	0.0157 114 116	0.0159 025 930	0.0160 943 115	228
20	0.0154 331 152	0.0156 257 790	0.0158 189 658	0.0160 126 606	240
21	0.0153 605 488	0.0155 550 442	0.0157 500 324	0.0159 454 983	252
22	0.0153 003 772	0.0154 965 162	0.0156 931 171	0.0158 901 645	264
23	0.0152 504 113	0.0154 480 205	0.0156 460 605	0.0158 445 156	276
24	0.0152 088 703	0.0154 077 908	0.0156 071 109	0.0158 068 152	288
25	0.0151 742 994	0.0153 743 859	0.0155 748 415	0.0157 756 512	300
26	0.0151 455 052	0.0153 466 258	0.0155 480 860	0.0157 498 710	312
27	0.0151 215 059	0.0153 235 414	0.0155 258 880	0.0157 285 314	324
28	0.0151 014 915	0.0153 043 344	0.0155 074 613	0.0157 108 585	336
29	0.0150 847 923	0.0152 883 462	0.0154 921 585	0.0156 962 160	348
30	0.0150 708 537	0.0152 750 324	0.0154 794 453	0.0156 840 801	360
31	0.0150 592 154	0.0152 639 419	0.0154 688 803	0.0156 740 187	372
32	0.0150 494 950	0.0152 547 012	0.0154 600 983	0.0156 656 752	384
33	0.0150 413 747	0.0152 469 999	0.0154 527 968	0.0156 587 550	396
34	0.0150 345 897	0.0152 405 804	0.0154 467 252	0.0156 530 142	408
35	0.0150 289 194	0.0152 352 286	0.0154 416 755	0.0156 482 512	420
36	0.0150 241 802	0.0152 307 663	0.0154 374 753	0.0156 442 990	432
37	0.0150 202 187	0.0152 270 453	0.0154 339 813	0.0156 410 193	444
38	0.0150 169 069	0.0152 239 421	0.0154 310 746	0.0156 382 974	456
39	0.0150 141 382	0.0152 213 540	0.0154 286 562	0.0156 360 383	468
40	0.0150 118 231	0.0152 191 953	0.0154 266 440	0.0156 341 633	480
41	0.0150 098 875	0.0152 173 947	0.0154 249 697	0.0156 326 069	492
42	0.0150 082 689	0.0152 158 928	0.0154 235 764	0.0156 313 150	504
43	0.0150 069 153	0.0152 146 399	0.0154 224 171	0.0156 302 425	516
44	0.0150 057 835	0.0152 135 947	0.0154 214 523	0.0156 293 523	528
45	0.0150 048 369	0.0152 127 228	0.0154 206 495	0.0156 286 132	540
46	0.0150 040 453	0.0152 119 954	0.0154 199 813	0.0156 279 997	552
47	0.0150 033 833	0.0152 113 886	0.0154 194 253	0.0156 274 904	564
48	0.0150 028 297	0.0152 108 824	0.0154 189 625	0.0156 270 675	576
49	0.0150 023 666	0.0152 104 600	0.0154 185 774	0.0156 267 165	588
50	0.0150 019 794	0.0152 101 076	0.0154 182 569	0.0156 264 250	600

TABLE 6. PARTIAL PAYMENT TO AMORTIZE ONE
Payable at end of each period

MONTHLY Compounding

MONTHS	19% Nominal Annual Rate	19¼% Nominal Annual Rate	19½% Nominal Annual Rate	19¾% Nominal Annual Rate	MONTHS
1	1.0158 333 333	1.0160 416 667	1.0162 500 000	1.0164 583 333	1
2	0.5119 060 907	0.5120 631 609	0.5122 202 418	0.5123 773 332	2
3	0.3439 441 601	0.3440 845 071	0.3442 248 730	0.3443 652 577	3
4	0.2599 735 562	0.2601 058 150	0.2602 381 002	0.2603 704 119	4
5	0.2095 994 816	0.2097 271 059	0.2098 547 642	0.2099 824 563	5
6	0.1760 236 700	0.1761 483 869	0.1762 731 449	0.1763 979 440	6
7	0.1520 468 644	0.1521 696 604	0.1522 925 047	0.1524 153 974	7
8	0.1340 694 358	0.1341 909 275	0.1343 124 747	0.1344 340 775	8
9	0.1200 915 901	0.1202 121 885	0.1203 328 496	0.1204 535 733	9
10	0.1089 134 508	0.1090 334 435	0.1091 535 060	0.1092 736 382	10
11	0.0997 714 598	0.0998 910 559	0.1000 107 288	0.1001 304 785	11
YEARS					
1	0.0921 565 782	0.0922 759 344	0.0923 953 744	0.0925 148 983	12
2	0.0504 086 172	0.0505 301 635	0.0506 518 766	0.0507 737 563	24
3	0.0366 560 200	0.0367 825 423	0.0369 093 105	0.0370 363 242	36
4	0.0299 001 182	0.0300 322 002	0.0301 646 019	0.0302 973 228	48
5	0.0259 405 511	0.0260 783 047	0.0262 164 454	0.0263 549 720	60
6	0.0233 767 230	0.0235 200 805	0.0236 638 845	0.0238 081 336	72
7	0.0216 080 190	0.0217 568 200	0.0219 061 187	0.0220 559 126	84
8	0.0203 338 649	0.0204 878 928	0.0206 424 601	0.0207 975 638	96
9	0.0193 870 830	0.0195 460 837	0.0197 056 566	0.0198 657 974	108
10	0.0186 672 355	0.0188 309 305	0.0189 952 210	0.0191 601 018	120
11	0.0181 103 258	0.0182 784 209	0.0184 471 261	0.0186 164 348	132
12	0.0176 736 477	0.0178 458 405	0.0180 186 496	0.0181 920 672	144
13	0.0173 276 249	0.0175 036 109	0.0176 802 117	0.0178 574 183	156
14	0.0170 511 456	0.0172 306 230	0.0174 107 069	0.0175 913 871	168
15	0.0168 287 603	0.0170 114 342	0.0171 947 003	0.0173 785 476	180
16	0.0166 489 273	0.0168 345 131	0.0170 206 718	0.0172 073 915	192
17	0.0165 028 754	0.0166 911 010	0.0168 798 764	0.0170 691 887	204
18	0.0163 838 424	0.0165 744 507	0.0167 655 823	0.0169 572 239	216
19	0.0162 865 526	0.0164 793 023	0.0166 725 466	0.0168 662 718	228
20	0.0162 068 485	0.0164 015 151	0.0165 966 461	0.0167 922 276	240
21	0.0161 414 265	0.0163 378 026	0.0165 346 120	0.0167 318 409	252
22	0.0160 876 431	0.0162 855 383	0.0164 838 357	0.0166 825 213	264
23	0.0160 433 708	0.0162 426 115	0.0164 422 235	0.0166 421 929	276
24	0.0160 068 889	0.0162 073 176	0.0164 080 873	0.0166 091 846	288
25	0.0159 768 003	0.0161 782 749	0.0163 800 613	0.0165 821 464	300
26	0.0159 519 667	0.0161 543 594	0.0163 570 361	0.0165 599 841	312
27	0.0159 314 581	0.0161 346 549	0.0163 381 091	0.0165 418 088	324
28	0.0159 145 129	0.0161 184 120	0.0163 225 438	0.0165 268 967	336
29	0.0159 005 064	0.0161 050 176	0.0163 097 383	0.0165 146 576	348
30	0.0158 889 249	0.0160 939 685	0.0162 992 000	0.0165 046 094	360
31	0.0158 793 460	0.0160 848 516	0.0162 905 254	0.0164 963 579	372
32	0.0158 714 216	0.0160 773 274	0.0162 833 834	0.0164 895 805	384
33	0.0158 648 647	0.0160 711 166	0.0162 775 021	0.0164 840 130	396
34	0.0158 594 384	0.0160 659 892	0.0162 726 585	0.0164 794 387	408
35	0.0158 549 472	0.0160 617 555	0.0162 686 688	0.0164 756 801	420
36	0.0158 512 295	0.0160 582 596	0.0162 653 824	0.0164 725 915	432
37	0.0158 481 519	0.0160 553 725	0.0162 626 749	0.0164 700 532	444
38	0.0158 456 040	0.0160 529 882	0.0162 604 443	0.0164 679 670	456
39	0.0158 434 944	0.0160 510 188	0.0162 586 064	0.0164 662 523	468
40	0.0158 417 477	0.0160 493 922	0.0162 570 921	0.0164 648 430	480
41	0.0158 403 014	0.0160 480 486	0.0162 558 443	0.0164 636 846	492
42	0.0158 391 038	0.0160 469 388	0.0162 548 162	0.0164 627 323	504
43	0.0158 381 121	0.0160 460 220	0.0162 539 689	0.0164 619 496	516
44	0.0158 372 908	0.0160 452 647	0.0162 532 707	0.0164 613 061	528
45	0.0158 366 108	0.0160 446 391	0.0162 526 954	0.0164 607 772	540
46	0.0158 360 476	0.0160 441 223	0.0162 522 213	0.0164 603 424	552
47	0.0158 355 812	0.0160 436 953	0.0162 518 306	0.0164 599 849	564
48	0.0158 351 949	0.0160 433 426	0.0162 515 086	0.0164 596 911	576
49	0.0158 348 751	0.0160 430 512	0.0162 512 432	0.0164 594 495	588
50	0.0158 346 102	0.0160 428 105	0.0162 510 246	0.0164 592 510	600

MONTHLY
Compounding

TABLE 6. PARTIAL PAYMENT TO AMORTIZE ONE
Payable at end of each period

MONTHS	20% Nominal Annual Rate	20¼% Nominal Annual Rate	20½% Nominal Annual Rate	20¾% Nominal Annual Rate	MONTHS
1	1.0166 666 667	1.0168 750 000	1.0170 833 333	1.0172 916 667	1
2	0.5125 344 353	0.5126 915 479	0.5128 486 711	0.5130 058 048	2
3	0.3445 056 613	0.3446 460 837	0.3447 865 248	0.3449 269 848	3
4	0.2605 027 501	0.2606 351 148	0.2607 675 058	0.2608 999 233	4
5	0.2101 101 823	0.2102 379 421	0.2103 657 358	0.2104 935 633	5
6	0.1765 227 843	0.1766 476 657	0.1767 725 882	0.1768 975 518	6
7	0.1525 383 385	0.1526 613 278	0.1527 843 655	0.1529 074 515	7
8	0.1345 557 358	0.1346 774 495	0.1347 992 187	0.1349 210 433	8
9	0.1205 743 597	0.1206 952 086	0.1208 161 201	0.1209 370 941	9
10	0.1093 938 401	0.1095 141 117	0.1096 344 529	0.1097 548 637	10
11	0.1002 503 049	0.1003 702 081	0.1004 901 880	0.1006 102 446	11
YEARS					
1	0.0926 345 059	0.0927 541 973	0.0928 739 724	0.0929 938 313	12
2	0.0508 958 026	0.0510 180 154	0.0511 403 944	0.0512 629 396	24
3	0.0371 635 834	0.0372 910 875	0.0374 188 364	0.0375 468 298	36
4	0.0304 303 623	0.0305 637 199	0.0306 973 950	0.0308 313 868	48
5	0.0264 938 837	0.0266 331 794	0.0267 728 580	0.0269 129 185	60
6	0.0239 528 261	0.0240 979 602	0.0242 435 344	0.0243 895 471	72
7	0.0222 061 993	0.0223 569 765	0.0225 082 416	0.0226 599 924	84
8	0.0209 532 004	0.0211 093 666	0.0212 660 592	0.0214 232 747	96
9	0.0200 265 017	0.0201 877 652	0.0203 495 836	0.0205 119 525	108
10	0.0193 255 672	0.0194 916 120	0.0196 582 306	0.0198 254 176	120
11	0.0187 863 404	0.0189 568 363	0.0191 279 160	0.0192 995 729	132
12	0.0183 660 855	0.0185 406 967	0.0187 158 933	0.0188 916 674	144
13	0.0180 352 218	0.0182 136 133	0.0183 925 842	0.0185 721 256	156
14	0.0177 726 538	0.0179 544 970	0.0181 369 070	0.0183 198 740	168
15	0.0175 629 650	0.0177 479 419	0.0179 334 675	0.0181 195 313	180
16	0.0173 946 605	0.0175 824 672	0.0177 708 002	0.0179 596 480	192
17	0.0172 590 257	0.0174 493 750	0.0176 402 246	0.0178 315 626	204
18	0.0171 493 627	0.0173 419 858	0.0175 350 807	0.0177 286 352	216
19	0.0170 604 647	0.0172 551 122	0.0174 502 013	0.0176 457 197	228
20	0.0169 882 461	0.0171 846 883	0.0173 815 413	0.0175 787 924	240
21	0.0169 294 756	0.0171 275 029	0.0173 259 097	0.0175 246 836	252
22	0.0168 815 817	0.0170 810 036	0.0172 807 743	0.0174 808 813	264
23	0.0168 425 065	0.0170 431 514	0.0172 441 150	0.0174 453 852	276
24	0.0168 105 965	0.0170 123 103	0.0172 143 139	0.0174 165 956	288
25	0.0167 845 177	0.0169 871 630	0.0171 900 707	0.0173 932 293	300
26	0.0167 631 913	0.0169 666 461	0.0171 703 373	0.0173 742 542	312
27	0.0167 457 424	0.0169 498 987	0.0171 542 673	0.0173 588 378	324
28	0.0167 314 599	0.0169 362 228	0.0171 411 754	0.0173 463 083	336
29	0.0167 197 652	0.0169 250 513	0.0171 305 065	0.0173 361 219	348
30	0.0167 101 869	0.0169 159 233	0.0171 218 099	0.0173 278 384	360
31	0.0167 023 400	0.0169 084 632	0.0171 147 195	0.0173 211 010	372
32	0.0166 959 105	0.0169 023 653	0.0171 089 376	0.0173 156 203	384
33	0.0166 906 414	0.0168 973 801	0.0171 042 222	0.0173 111 612	396
34	0.0166 863 228	0.0168 933 040	0.0171 003 760	0.0173 075 330	408
35	0.0166 827 829	0.0168 899 710	0.0170 972 386	0.0173 045 805	420
36	0.0166 798 810	0.0168 872 453	0.0170 946 792	0.0173 021 778	432
37	0.0166 775 019	0.0168 850 161	0.0170 925 911	0.0173 002 224	444
38	0.0166 755 514	0.0168 831 930	0.0170 908 874	0.0172 986 308	456
39	0.0166 739 522	0.0168 817 018	0.0170 894 974	0.0172 973 355	468
40	0.0166 726 409	0.0168 804 822	0.0170 883 633	0.0172 962 811	480
41	0.0166 715 657	0.0168 794 845	0.0170 874 378	0.0172 954 229	492
42	0.0166 706 841	0.0168 786 685	0.0170 866 827	0.0172 947 243	504
43	0.0166 699 611	0.0168 780 009	0.0170 860 665	0.0172 941 557	516
44	0.0166 693 683	0.0168 774 549	0.0170 855 637	0.0172 936 928	528
45	0.0166 688 822	0.0168 770 082	0.0170 851 534	0.0172 933 160	540
46	0.0166 684 835	0.0168 766 428	0.0170 848 186	0.0172 930 093	552
47	0.0166 681 566	0.0168 763 439	0.0170 845 454	0.0172 927 596	564
48	0.0166 678 885	0.0168 760 994	0.0170 843 224	0.0172 925 564	576
49	0.0166 676 687	0.0168 758 994	0.0170 841 405	0.0172 923 910	588
50	0.0166 674 884	0.0168 757 357	0.0170 839 920	0.0172 922 563	600

TABLE 6. PARTIAL PAYMENT TO AMORTIZE ONE
Payable at end of each period

MONTHLY Compounding

MONTHS	21% Nominal Annual Rate	21¼% Nominal Annual Rate	21½% Nominal Annual Rate	21¾% Nominal Annual Rate	MONTHS
1	1.0175 000 000	1.0177 083 333	1.0179 166 667	1.0181 250 000	1
2	0.5131 629 492	0.5133 201 041	0.5134 772 696	0.5136 344 456	2
3	0.3450 674 635	0.3452 079 611	0.3453 484 774	0.3454 890 125	3
4	0.2610 323 673	0.2611 648 376	0.2612 973 344	0.2614 298 576	4
5	0.2106 214 246	0.2107 493 198	0.2108 772 487	0.2110 052 114	5
6	0.1770 225 565	0.1771 476 023	0.1772 726 891	0.1773 978 170	6
7	0.1530 305 857	0.1531 537 682	0.1532 769 990	0.1534 002 780	7
8	0.1350 429 233	0.1351 648 588	0.1352 868 496	0.1354 088 958	8
9	0.1210 581 306	0.1211 792 297	0.1213 003 912	0.1214 216 152	9
10	0.1098 753 442	0.1099 958 942	0.1101 165 137	0.1102 372 027	10
11	0.1007 303 778	0.1008 505 876	0.1009 708 739	0.1010 912 369	11
YEARS					
1	0.0931 137 738	0.0932 337 999	0.0933 539 096	0.0934 741 029	12
2	0.0513 856 510	0.0515 085 282	0.0516 315 714	0.0517 547 802	24
3	0.0376 750 673	0.0378 035 487	0.0379 322 737	0.0380 612 420	36
4	0.0309 656 950	0.0311 003 187	0.0312 352 576	0.0313 705 108	48
5	0.0270 533 598	0.0271 941 809	0.0273 353 807	0.0274 769 581	60
6	0.0245 359 964	0.0246 828 809	0.0248 301 986	0.0249 779 480	72
7	0.0228 122 263	0.0229 649 409	0.0231 181 337	0.0232 718 022	84
8	0.0215 810 099	0.0217 392 613	0.0218 980 256	0.0220 572 994	96
9	0.0206 748 675	0.0208 383 243	0.0210 023 184	0.0211 668 456	108
10	0.0199 931 675	0.0201 614 749	0.0203 303 344	0.0204 997 405	120
11	0.0194 718 004	0.0196 445 919	0.0198 179 411	0.0199 918 412	132
12	0.0190 680 114	0.0192 449 178	0.0194 223 789	0.0196 003 872	144
13	0.0187 522 288	0.0189 328 853	0.0191 140 864	0.0192 958 236	156
14	0.0185 033 884	0.0186 874 406	0.0188 720 212	0.0190 571 208	168
15	0.0183 061 227	0.0184 932 314	0.0186 808 473	0.0188 689 601	180
16	0.0181 489 996	0.0183 388 440	0.0185 291 704	0.0187 199 680	192
17	0.0180 233 774	0.0182 156 573	0.0184 083 912	0.0186 015 679	204
18	0.0179 226 371	0.0181 170 748	0.0183 119 365	0.0185 072 109	216
19	0.0178 416 551	0.0180 379 953	0.0182 347 288	0.0184 318 440	228
20	0.0177 764 294	0.0179 744 402	0.0181 728 130	0.0183 715 364	240
21	0.0177 238 122	0.0179 232 837	0.0181 230 865	0.0183 232 093	252
22	0.0176 813 127	0.0178 820 567	0.0180 831 020	0.0182 844 376	264
23	0.0176 469 502	0.0178 487 989	0.0180 509 200	0.0182 533 032	276
24	0.0176 191 441	0.0178 219 484	0.0180 249 981	0.0182 282 829	288
25	0.0175 966 282	0.0178 002 569	0.0180 041 054	0.0182 081 641	300
26	0.0175 783 864	0.0177 827 241	0.0179 872 579	0.0181 919 786	312
27	0.0175 636 007	0.0177 685 467	0.0179 736 668	0.0181 789 525	324
28	0.0175 516 122	0.0177 570 786	0.0179 626 991	0.0181 684 658	336
29	0.0175 418 889	0.0177 477 995	0.0179 538 461	0.0181 600 214	348
30	0.0175 340 009	0.0177 402 900	0.0179 466 986	0.0181 532 200	360
31	0.0175 276 006	0.0177 342 115	0.0179 409 270	0.0181 477 412	372
32	0.0175 224 067	0.0177 292 905	0.0179 362 658	0.0181 433 271	384
33	0.0175 181 911	0.0177 253 062	0.0179 325 010	0.0181 397 705	396
34	0.0175 147 694	0.0177 220 799	0.0179 294 599	0.0181 369 046	408
35	0.0175 119 917	0.0177 194 673	0.0179 270 032	0.0181 345 950	420
36	0.0175 097 367	0.0177 173 515	0.0179 250 184	0.0181 327 337	432
37	0.0175 079 059	0.0177 156 380	0.0179 234 149	0.0181 312 336	444
38	0.0175 064 195	0.0177 142 501	0.0179 221 194	0.0181 300 245	456
39	0.0175 052 127	0.0177 131 260	0.0179 210 726	0.0181 290 500	468
40	0.0175 042 327	0.0177 122 155	0.0179 202 269	0.0181 282 646	480
41	0.0175 034 371	0.0177 114 780	0.0179 195 435	0.0181 276 315	492
42	0.0175 027 910	0.0177 108 806	0.0179 189 913	0.0181 271 212	504
43	0.0175 022 664	0.0177 103 968	0.0179 185 451	0.0181 267 098	516
44	0.0175 018 404	0.0177 100 048	0.0179 181 846	0.0181 263 783	528
45	0.0175 014 945	0.0177 096 873	0.0179 178 932	0.0181 261 110	540
46	0.0175 012 136	0.0177 094 301	0.0179 176 578	0.0181 258 956	552
47	0.0175 009 855	0.0177 092 218	0.0179 174 676	0.0181 257 219	564
48	0.0175 008 003	0.0177 090 530	0.0179 173 139	0.0181 255 819	576
49	0.0175 006 499	0.0177 089 163	0.0179 171 896	0.0181 254 691	588
50	0.0175 005 277	0.0177 088 056	0.0179 170 893	0.0181 253 781	600

MONTHLY
Compounding

TABLE 6. PARTIAL PAYMENT TO AMORTIZE ONE
Payable at end of each period

	22% Nominal Annual Rate	22¼% Nominal Annual Rate	22½% Nominal Annual Rate	22¾% Nominal Annual Rate	
MONTHS					MONTHS
1	1.0183 333 333	1.0185 416 667	1.0187 500 000	1.0189 583 333	1
2	0.5137 916 323	0.5139 488 294	0.5141 060 372	0.5142 632 554	2
3	0.3456 295 664	0.3457 701 391	0.3459 107 305	0.3460 513 407	3
4	0.2615 624 071	0.2616 949 831	0.2618 275 854	0.2619 602 141	4
5	0.2111 332 078	0.2112 612 381	0.2113 893 021	0.2115 173 998	5
6	0.1775 229 859	0.1776 481 958	0.1777 734 467	0.1778 987 386	6
7	0.1535 236 051	0.1536 469 805	0.1537 704 041	0.1538 938 758	7
8	0.1355 309 973	0.1356 531 541	0.1357 753 662	0.1358 976 336	8
9	0.1215 429 016	0.1216 642 504	0.1217 856 615	0.1219 071 351	9
10	0.1103 579 613	0.1104 787 893	0.1105 996 867	0.1107 206 535	10
11	0.1012 116 763	0.1013 321 922	0.1014 527 846	0.1015 734 534	11
YEARS					
1	0.0935 943 796	0.0937 147 399	0.0938 351 837	0.0939 557 108	12
2	0.0518 781 546	0.0520 016 946	0.0521 253 999	0.0522 492 704	24
3	0.0381 904 532	0.0383 199 071	0.0384 496 033	0.0385 795 416	36
4	0.0315 060 778	0.0316 419 581	0.0317 781 508	0.0319 146 555	48
5	0.0276 189 120	0.0277 612 414	0.0279 039 451	0.0280 470 220	60
6	0.0251 261 274	0.0252 747 349	0.0254 237 690	0.0255 732 277	72
7	0.0234 259 440	0.0235 805 564	0.0237 356 371	0.0238 911 835	84
8	0.0222 170 793	0.0223 773 619	0.0225 381 438	0.0226 994 215	96
9	0.0213 319 013	0.0214 974 813	0.0216 635 810	0.0218 301 961	108
10	0.0206 696 878	0.0208 401 708	0.0210 111 841	0.0211 827 222	120
11	0.0201 662 859	0.0203 412 686	0.0205 167 829	0.0206 928 224	132
12	0.0197 789 352	0.0199 580 153	0.0201 376 202	0.0203 177 425	144
13	0.0194 780 885	0.0196 608 726	0.0198 441 677	0.0200 279 655	156
14	0.0192 427 302	0.0194 288 400	0.0196 154 413	0.0198 025 251	168
15	0.0190 575 600	0.0192 466 371	0.0194 361 815	0.0196 261 839	180
16	0.0189 112 263	0.0191 029 350	0.0192 950 838	0.0194 876 628	192
17	0.0187 951 766	0.0189 892 064	0.0191 836 470	0.0193 784 879	204
18	0.0187 028 868	0.0188 989 535	0.0190 954 001	0.0192 922 163	216
19	0.0186 293 297	0.0188 271 750	0.0190 253 692	0.0192 239 018	228
20	0.0185 705 994	0.0187 699 909	0.0189 697 006	0.0191 697 181	240
21	0.0185 236 411	0.0187 243 713	0.0189 253 897	0.0191 266 862	252
22	0.0184 860 529	0.0186 879 377	0.0188 900 818	0.0190 924 757	264
23	0.0184 559 381	0.0186 588 148	0.0188 619 238	0.0190 652 559	276
24	0.0184 317 932	0.0186 355 194	0.0188 394 527	0.0190 435 841	288
25	0.0184 124 236	0.0186 168 751	0.0188 215 102	0.0190 263 205	300
26	0.0183 968 776	0.0186 019 466	0.0188 071 776	0.0190 125 629	312
27	0.0183 843 959	0.0185 899 890	0.0187 957 246	0.0190 015 955	324
28	0.0183 743 713	0.0185 804 084	0.0187 865 701	0.0189 928 502	336
29	0.0183 663 183	0.0185 727 304	0.0187 792 513	0.0189 858 753	348
30	0.0183 598 478	0.0185 665 761	0.0187 733 991	0.0189 803 114	360
31	0.0183 546 481	0.0185 616 424	0.0187 687 189	0.0189 758 726	372
32	0.0183 504 691	0.0185 576 867	0.0187 649 755	0.0189 723 309	384
33	0.0183 471 100	0.0185 545 149	0.0187 619 812	0.0189 695 048	396
34	0.0183 444 098	0.0185 519 715	0.0187 595 859	0.0189 672 496	408
35	0.0183 422 391	0.0185 499 317	0.0187 576 697	0.0189 654 498	420
36	0.0183 404 939	0.0185 482 959	0.0187 561 366	0.0189 640 134	432
37	0.0183 390 909	0.0185 469 839	0.0187 549 101	0.0189 628 670	444
38	0.0183 379 628	0.0185 459 316	0.0187 539 288	0.0189 619 520	456
39	0.0183 370 558	0.0185 450 876	0.0187 531 436	0.0189 612 217	468
40	0.0183 363 265	0.0185 444 107	0.0187 525 154	0.0189 606 389	480
41	0.0183 357 401	0.0185 438 677	0.0187 520 127	0.0189 601 736	492
42	0.0183 352 686	0.0185 434 322	0.0187 516 105	0.0189 598 022	504
43	0.0183 348 895	0.0185 430 829	0.0187 512 887	0.0189 595 058	516
44	0.0183 345 847	0.0185 428 026	0.0187 510 311	0.0189 592 692	528
45	0.0183 343 395	0.0185 425 779	0.0187 508 251	0.0189 590 804	540
46	0.0183 341 424	0.0185 423 976	0.0187 506 602	0.0189 589 296	552
47	0.0183 339 839	0.0185 422 530	0.0187 505 283	0.0189 588 093	564
48	0.0183 338 565	0.0185 421 370	0.0187 504 227	0.0189 587 133	576
49	0.0183 337 540	0.0185 420 439	0.0187 503 383	0.0189 586 366	588
50	0.0183 336 716	0.0185 419 693	0.0187 502 707	0.0189 585 754	600

TABLE 1. FUTURE WORTH OF ONE DOLLAR WITH INTEREST
Payable at beginning of each period

QUARTERLY Compounding

QUARTERS	5% Nominal Annual Rate	5¼% Nominal Annual Rate	5½% Nominal Annual Rate	5¾% Nominal Annual Rate	QUARTERS
1	1.0125 000 000	1.0131 250 000	1.0137 500 000	1.0143 750 000	1
2	1.0251 562 500	1.0264 222 656	1.0276 890 625	1.0289 566 406	2
3	1.0379 707 031	1.0398 940 579	1.0418 197 871	1.0437 478 923	3
YEARS					
1	1.0509 453 369	1.0535 426 674	1.0561 448 092	1.0587 517 683	4
2	1.1044 861 012	1.1099 521 520	1.1154 418 580	1.1209 553 068	8
3	1.1607 545 177	1.1693 819 508	1.1780 681 282	1.1868 134 133	12
4	1.2198 895 477	1.2319 937 797	1.2442 105 385	1.2565 408 000	16
5	1.2820 372 317	1.2979 580 128	1.3140 665 018	1.3303 647 939	20
6	1.3473 510 504	1.3674 541 470	1.3878 445 148	1.4085 260 780	24
7	1.4159 923 036	1.4406 712 895	1.4657 647 802	1.4912 794 757	28
8	1.4881 305 086	1.5178 086 731	1.5480 598 641	1.5788 947 819	32
9	1.5639 438 187	1.5990 761 980	1.6349 753 898	1.6716 576 423	36
10	1.6436 194 635	1.6846 950 030	1.7267 707 710	1.7698 704 848	40
11	1.7273 542 108	1.7748 980 672	1.8237 199 865	1.8738 535 054	44
12	1.8153 548 531	1.8699 308 440	1.9261 123 971	1.9839 457 124	48
13	1.9078 387 177	1.9700 519 292	2.0342 536 101	2.1005 060 311	52
14	2.0050 342 039	2.0755 337 644	2.1484 663 909	2.2239 144 748	56
15	2.1071 813 470	2.1866 633 783	2.2690 916 265	2.3545 733 827	60
16	2.2145 324 106	2.3037 431 682	2.3964 893 428	2.4929 087 325	64
17	2.3273 525 104	2.4270 917 224	2.5310 397 797	2.6393 715 287	68
18	2.4459 202 681	2.5570 446 872	2.6731 445 252	2.7944 392 731	72
19	2.5705 285 003	2.6939 556 803	2.8232 277 144	2.9586 175 218	76
20	2.7014 849 408	2.8381 972 532	2.9817 372 958	3.1324 415 329	80
21	2.8391 130 012	2.9901 619 047	3.1491 463 673	3.3164 780 120	84
22	2.9837 525 696	3.1502 631 489	3.3259 545 891	3.5113 269 597	88
23	3.1357 608 495	3.3189 366 408	3.5126 896 749	3.7176 236 276	92
24	3.2955 132 425	3.4966 413 614	3.7099 089 664	3.9360 405 896	96
25	3.4634 042 749	3.6838 608 667	3.9182 010 974	4.1672 899 342	100
26	3.6398 485 726	3.8811 046 038	4.1381 877 503	4.4121 255 868	104
27	3.8252 818 844	4.0889 092 966	4.3705 255 120	4.6713 457 670	108
28	4.0201 621 588	4.3078 404 070	4.6159 078 328	4.9457 955 911	112
29	4.2249 706 745	4.5384 936 730	4.8750 670 973	5.2363 698 276	116
30	4.4402 132 289	4.7814 967 301	5.1487 768 093	5.5440 158 144	120
31	4.6664 213 879	5.0375 108 190	5.4378 539 007	5.8697 365 469	124
32	4.9041 537 976	5.3072 325 852	5.7431 611 703	6.2145 939 484	128
33	5.1539 975 651	5.5913 959 742	6.0656 098 584	6.5797 123 320	132
34	5.4165 697 076	5.8907 742 289	6.4061 623 664	6.9662 820 664	136
35	5.6925 186 762	6.2061 819 940	6.7658 351 301	7.3755 634 561	140
36	5.9825 259 581	6.5384 775 322	7.1457 016 524	7.8088 908 513	144
37	6.2873 077 586	6.8885 650 598	7.5468 957 082	8.2676 769 972	148
38	6.6076 167 707	7.2573 972 075	7.9706 147 276	8.7534 176 404	152
39	6.9442 440 332	7.6459 776 121	8.4181 233 706	9.2676 964 053	156
40	7.2980 208 851	8.0553 636 481	8.8907 573 009	9.8121 899 570	160
41	7.6698 210 179	8.4866 693 045	9.3899 271 730	10.3886 734 678	164
42	8.0605 626 337	8.9410 682 161	9.9171 228 424	10.9990 264 042	168
43	8.4712 107 128	9.4197 968 576	10.4739 178 120	11.6452 386 548	172
44	8.9027 793 967	9.9241 579 074	11.0619 739 289	12.3294 170 179	176
45	9.3563 344 925	10.4555 237 932	11.6830 463 444	13.0537 920 697	180
46	9.8329 961 055	11.0153 404 258	12.3389 887 520	13.8207 254 366	184
47	10.3339 414 050	11.6051 311 342	13.0317 589 210	14.6327 174 950	188
48	10.8604 075 315	12.2265 008 103	13.7634 245 389	15.4924 155 227	192
49	11.4136 946 522	12.8811 402 763	14.5361 693 834	16.4026 223 296	196
50	11.9951 691 717	13.5708 308 855	15.3522 998 396	17.3663 053 960	200
51	12.6062 671 065	14.2974 493 696	16.2142 517 846	18.3866 065 467	204
52	13.2484 976 315	15.0629 729 454	17.1245 978 571	19.4668 521 941	208
53	13.9234 468 069	15.8694 846 954	18.0860 551 361	20.6105 641 834	212
54	14.6327 814 955	16.7191 792 358	19.1014 932 506	21.8214 712 746	216
55	15.3782 534 788	17.6143 686 884	20.1739 429 443	23.1035 212 986	220
56	16.1617 037 834	18.5574 889 720	21.3066 051 213	24.4608 940 285	224
57	16.9850 672 278	19.5511 064 313	22.5028 604 002	25.8980 148 065	228
58	17.8503 772 002	20.5979 248 196	23.7662 792 034	27.4195 689 715	232
59	18.7597 706 807	21.7007 926 568	25.1006 324 142	29.0305 171 343	236
60	19.7154 935 184	22.8627 109 797	26.5099 026 315	30.7361 113 502	240

QUARTERLY
Compounding

TABLE 1. FUTURE WORTH OF ONE DOLLAR WITH INTEREST
Payable at beginning of each period

	6% Nominal Annual Rate	6¼% Nominal Annual Rate	6½% Nominal Annual Rate	6¾% Nominal Annual Rate	
QUARTERS					QUARTERS
1	1.0150 000 000	1.0156 250 000	1.0162 500 000	1.0168 750 000	1
2	1.0302 250 000	1.0314 941 406	1.0327 640 625	1.0340 347 656	2
3	1.0456 783 750	1.0476 112 366	1.0495 464 785	1.0514 841 023	3
YEARS					
1	1.0613 635 506	1.0639 801 621	1.0666 016 088	1.0692 278 965	4
2	1.1264 925 866	1.1320 537 854	1.1376 389 919	1.1432 482 947	8
3	1.1956 181 715	1.2044 827 702	1.2134 075 790	1.2223 929 693	12
4	1.2689 855 477	1.2815 457 731	1.2942 224 758	1.3070 166 633	16
5	1.3468 550 066	1.3635 392 795	1.3804 197 749	1.3974 986 777	20
6	1.4295 028 119	1.4507 787 437	1.4723 579 527	1.4942 445 715	24
7	1.5172 221 801	1.5435 998 029	1.5704 193 610	1.5976 879 801	28
8	1.6103 243 202	1.6423 595 686	1.6750 118 170	1.7082 925 582	32
9	1.7091 395 381	1.7474 380 001	1.7865 702 987	1.8265 540 587	36
10	1.8140 184 087	1.8592 393 667	1.9055 587 548	1.9530 025 540	40
11	1.9253 330 191	1.9781 938 028	2.0324 720 336	2.0882 048 128	44
12	2.0434 782 893	2.1047 589 631	2.1678 379 408	2.2327 668 395	48
13	2.1688 733 728	2.2394 217 828	2.3122 194 353	2.3873 365 912	52
14	2.3019 631 438	2.3827 003 516	2.4662 169 695	2.5526 068 817	56
15	2.4432 197 757	2.5351 459 064	2.6304 709 873	2.7293 184 867	60
16	2.5931 444 161	2.6973 449 526	2.8056 645 870	2.9182 634 645	64
17	2.7522 689 647	2.8699 215 200	2.9925 263 622	3.1202 887 056	68
18	2.9211 579 607	3.0535 395 642	3.1918 334 323	3.3362 997 293	72
19	3.1004 105 851	3.2489 055 206	3.4044 146 738	3.5672 647 417	76
20	3.2906 627 870	3.4567 710 226	3.6311 541 681	3.8142 189 761	80
21	3.4925 895 395	3.6779 357 931	3.8729 948 775	4.0782 693 327	84
22	3.7069 072 345	3.9132 507 215	4.1309 425 672	4.3605 993 400	88
23	3.9343 762 243	4.1636 211 372	4.4060 699 880	4.6624 744 599	92
24	4.1758 035 189	4.4300 102 927	4.6995 213 376	4.9852 477 594	96
25	4.4320 456 495	4.7134 430 695	5.0125 170 192	5.3303 659 754	100
26	4.7040 117 071	5.0150 099 213	5.3463 587 168	5.6993 759 995	104
27	4.9926 665 676	5.3358 710 692	5.7024 348 085	6.0939 318 115	108
28	5.2990 343 153	5.6772 609 654	6.0822 261 408	6.5158 018 923	112
29	5.6242 018 758	6.0404 930 425	6.4873 121 868	6.9668 771 515	116
30	5.9693 228 723	6.4269 647 668	6.9193 776 152	7.4491 794 020	120
31	6.3356 217 186	6.8381 630 147	7.3802 192 962	7.9648 704 228	124
32	6.7243 979 627	7.2756 697 931	7.8717 537 746	8.5162 616 482	128
33	7.1370 308 975	7.7411 683 262	8.3960 252 400	9.1058 245 284	132
34	7.5749 844 543	8.2364 495 309	8.9552 140 284	9.7362 016 065	136
35	8.0398 123 963	8.7634 189 074	9.5516 456 898	10.4102 183 639	140
36	8.5331 638 313	9.3241 038 700	10.1878 006 593	11.1308 958 835	144
37	9.0567 890 620	9.9206 615 474	10.8663 245 733	11.9014 643 919	148
38	9.6125 457 962	10.5553 870 818	11.5900 392 715	12.7253 777 373	152
39	10.2024 057 368	11.2307 224 588	12.3619 545 330	13.6063 288 705	156
40	10.8284 615 777	11.9492 659 027	13.1852 805 927	14.5482 663 976	160
41	11.4929 344 279	12.7137 818 727	14.0634 414 925	15.5554 122 783	164
42	12.1981 816 915	13.5272 116 983	15.0000 893 210	16.6322 807 499	168
43	12.9467 054 312	14.3926 848 961	15.9991 194 018	17.7836 985 605	172
44	13.7411 612 454	15.3135 312 095	17.0646 864 932	19.0148 266 042	176
45	14.5843 676 891	16.2932 934 193	18.2012 220 672	20.3311 830 528	180
46	15.4793 162 742	17.3357 409 741	19.4134 527 389	21.7386 680 893	184
47	16.4291 820 820	18.4448 844 925	20.7064 199 235	23.2435 903 543	188
48	17.4373 350 284	19.6249 911 930	22.0855 008 027	24.8526 952 221	192
49	18.5073 518 192	20.8806 013 116	23.5564 306 871	26.5731 950 352	196
50	19.6430 286 395	22.2165 455 692	25.1253 268 683	28.4128 014 314	200
51	20.8483 946 218	23.6379 637 570	26.7987 140 591	30.3797 599 087	204
52	22.1277 261 406	25.1503 245 109	28.5835 515 290	32.4828 867 840	208
53	23.4855 619 839	26.7594 463 511	30.4872 620 458	34.7316 087 090	212
54	24.9267 194 557	28.4715 200 675	32.5177 627 457	37.1360 049 227	216
55	26.4563 114 669	30.2931 325 379	34.6834 980 588	39.7068 524 287	220
56	28.0797 646 749	32.2312 920 695	36.9934 748 281	42.4556 742 999	224
57	29.8028 387 361	34.2934 553 622	39.4572 997 664	45.3947 913 270	228
58	31.6316 467 397	36.4875 561 968	42.0852 194 094	48.5373 772 436	232
59	33.5726 768 957	38.8220 359 585	44.8881 627 284	51.8975 177 728	236
60	35.6328 155 540	41.3058 761 138	47.8777 865 819	55.4902 737 629	240

TABLE 1. FUTURE WORTH OF ONE DOLLAR WITH INTEREST
Payable at beginning of each period

QUARTERS	7% Nominal Annual Rate	7¼% Nominal Annual Rate	7½% Nominal Annual Rate	7¾% Nominal Annual Rate	QUARTERS
1	1.0175 000 000	1.0181 250 000	1.0187 500 000	1.0193 750 000	1
2	1.0353 062 500	1.0365 785 156	1.0378 515 625	1.0391 253 906	2
3	1.0534 241 094	1.0553 665 012	1.0573 112 793	1.0592 584 451	3
YEARS					
1	1.0718 590 313	1.0744 950 191	1.0771 358 658	1.0797 815 774	4
2	1.1488 817 830	1.1545 395 460	1.1602 216 734	1.1659 282 550	8
3	1.2314 393 149	1.2405 469 915	1.2497 163 766	1.2589 478 503	12
4	1.3199 293 512	1.3329 615 632	1.3461 143 313	1.3593 886 958	16
5	1.4147 781 958	1.4322 605 603	1.4499 480 257	1.4678 428 703	20
6	1.5164 427 864	1.5389 568 380	1.5617 910 220	1.5849 496 899	24
7	1.6254 128 960	1.6536 014 570	1.6822 611 247	1.7113 994 763	28
8	1.7422 134 922	1.7767 865 290	1.8120 237 930	1.8479 376 262	32
9	1.8674 072 660	1.9091 482 754	1.9517 958 171	1.9953 690 050	36
10	2.0015 973 432	2.0513 703 125	2.1023 492 773	2.1545 626 918	40
11	2.1454 301 893	2.2041 871 830	2.2645 158 090	2.3264 571 021	44
12	2.2995 987 244	2.3683 881 492	2.4391 911 965	2.5120 655 195	48
13	2.4648 456 611	2.5448 212 695	2.6273 403 212	2.7124 820 693	52
14	2.6419 670 826	2.7343 977 785	2.8300 024 916	2.9288 881 676	56
15	2.8318 162 778	2.9380 967 931	3.0482 971 840	3.1625 594 857	60
16	3.0353 078 523	3.1569 703 697	3.2834 302 264	3.4148 734 702	64
17	3.2534 221 343	3.3921 489 376	3.5367 004 597	3.6873 174 625	68
18	3.4872 098 972	3.6448 471 373	3.8095 069 117	3.9814 974 661	72
19	3.7377 974 223	3.9163 700 942	4.1033 565 255	4.2991 476 146	76
20	4.0063 919 242	4.2081 201 590	4.4198 724 837	4.6421 403 929	80
21	4.2942 873 669	4.5216 041 505	4.7608 031 744	5.0124 976 762	84
22	4.6028 706 972	4.8584 411 378	5.1280 318 491	5.4124 026 477	88
23	4.9336 285 266	5.2203 708 030	5.5235 870 255	5.8442 126 687	92
24	5.2881 542 933	5.6092 624 254	5.9496 536 930	6.3104 731 743	96
25	5.6681 559 381	6.0271 245 367	6.4085 853 817	6.8139 326 785	100
26	6.0754 641 330	6.4761 152 939	6.9029 171 636	7.3575 589 762	104
27	6.5120 411 002	6.9585 536 261	7.4353 796 554	7.9445 566 374	108
28	6.9799 900 654	7.4769 312 111	8.0089 141 026	8.5783 858 980	112
29	7.4815 653 899	8.0339 253 441	8.6266 886 258	9.2627 830 569	116
30	8.0191 834 313	8.6324 127 657	9.2921 157 218	10.0017 825 007	120
31	8.5954 341 844	9.2754 845 192	10.0088 711 130	10.7997 404 858	124
32	9.2130 937 584	9.9664 619 152	10.7809 140 518	11.6613 608 177	128
33	9.8751 377 511	10.7089 136 855	11.6125 091 912	12.5917 225 789	132
34	10.5847 555 837	11.5066 744 146	12.5082 501 415	13.5963 100 689	136
35	11.3453 658 664	12.3638 643 443	13.4730 848 456	14.6810 451 336	140
36	12.1606 328 672	13.2849 106 543	14.5123 429 100	15.8523 220 729	144
37	13.0344 841 649	14.2745 703 266	15.6317 650 449	17.1170 453 339	148
38	13.9711 295 703	15.3379 547 151	16.8375 347 754	18.4826 702 118	152
39	14.9750 814 073	16.4805 559 439	18.1363 125 979	19.9572 467 967	156
40	16.0511 762 507	17.7082 752 730	19.5352 727 723	21.5494 674 275	160
41	17.2045 982 271	19.0274 535 769	21.0421 429 509	23.2687 179 319	164
42	18.4409 039 894	20.4449 040 936	22.6652 468 654	25.1251 329 535	168
43	19.7660 494 862	21.9679 476 137	24.4135 503 055	27.1296 556 940	172
44	21.1864 186 547	23.6044 502 898	26.2967 106 452	29.2941 024 207	176
45	22.7088 541 757	25.3628 642 639	28.3251 301 881	31.6312 321 216	180
46	24.3406 904 385	27.2522 713 205	30.5100 136 286	34.1548 217 166	184
47	26.0897 888 743	29.2824 297 919	32.8634 299 449	36.8797 472 704	188
48	27.9645 758 293	31.4638 249 572	35.3983 790 663	39.8220 716 833	192
49	29.9740 831 588	33.8077 231 969	38.1288 636 829	42.9991 393 792	196
50	32.1279 917 384	36.3262 301 807	41.0699 665 944	46.4296 785 475	200
51	34.4366 781 020	39.0323 533 902	44.2379 340 254	50.1339 115 421	204
52	36.9112 644 312	41.9400 692 998	47.6502 653 669	54.1336 740 883	208
53	39.5636 721 369	45.0643 955 615	51.3258 098 408	58.4525 439 997	212
54	42.4066 792 909	48.4214 685 675	55.2848 706 200	63.1159 801 655	216
55	45.4539 821 849	52.0286 267 912	59.5493 169 800	68.1514 726 249	220
56	48.7202 613 129	55.9045 003 354	64.1427 051 021	73.5887 046 158	224
57	52.2212 520 950	60.0691 071 531	69.0904 081 938	79.4597 275 520	228
58	55.9738 206 833	64.5439 564 352	74.4197 566 472	85.7991 499 591	232
59	59.9960 452 151	69.3521 596 997	80.1601 890 076	92.6443 414 860	236
60	64.3073 029 055	74.5185 501 581	86.3434 145 881	100.0356 531 908	240

QUARTERLY
Compounding

TABLE 1. FUTURE WORTH OF ONE DOLLAR WITH INTEREST
Payable at beginning of each period

	8% Nominal Annual Rate	8¼% Nominal Annual Rate	8½% Nominal Annual Rate	8¾% Nominal Annual Rate	
QUARTERS					QUARTERS
1	1.0200 000 000	1.0206 250 000	1.0212 500 000	1.0218 750 000	1
2	1.0404 000 000	1.0416 753 906	1.0429 515 625	1.0442 285 156	2
3	1.0612 080 000	1.0631 599 456	1.0651 142 832	1.0670 710 144	3
YEARS					
1	1.0824 321 600	1.0850 876 194	1.0877 479 617	1.0904 131 928	4
2	1.1716 593 810	1.1774 151 418	1.1831 956 282	1.1890 009 311	8
3	1.2682 417 946	1.2775 985 934	1.2870 186 329	1.2965 023 016	12
4	1.3727 857 051	1.3863 064 163	1.3999 518 947	1.4137 232 142	16
5	1.4859 473 960	1.5042 639 290	1.5227 948 199	1.5415 424 438	20
6	1.6084 372 495	1.6322 581 657	1.6564 169 615	1.6809 182 181	24
7	1.7410 242 062	1.7711 431 274	1.8017 641 736	1.8328 954 011	28
8	1.8845 405 921	1.9218 454 797	1.9598 653 074	1.9986 133 264	32
9	2.0398 873 437	2.0853 707 365	2.1318 394 933	2.1793 143 385	36
10	2.2080 396 636	2.2628 099 681	2.3189 040 636	2.3763 531 061	40
11	2.3900 531 425	2.4553 470 816	2.5223 831 686	2.5912 067 778	44
12	2.5870 703 855	2.6642 667 196	2.7437 171 503	2.8254 860 559	48
13	2.8003 281 854	2.8909 628 323	2.9844 727 378	3.0809 472 715	52
14	3.0311 652 865	3.1369 479 776	3.2463 541 373	3.3595 055 513	56
15	3.2810 307 884	3.4038 634 133	3.5312 150 959	3.6632 491 746	60
16	3.5514 932 433	3.6934 900 480	3.8410 720 230	3.9944 552 286	64
17	3.8442 505 025	4.0077 603 236	4.1781 182 638	4.3556 066 795	68
18	4.1611 403 751	4.3487 711 088	4.5447 396 253	4.7494 109 862	72
19	4.5041 521 642	4.7187 976 899	4.9435 312 640	5.1788 203 976	76
20	4.8754 391 561	5.1203 089 519	5.3773 160 561	5.6470 540 849	80
21	5.2773 321 367	5.5559 838 514	5.8491 645 796	6.1576 222 749	84
22	5.7123 540 237	6.0287 292 910	6.3624 168 492	6.7143 525 651	88
23	6.1832 357 046	6.5416 995 145	6.9207 059 593	7.3214 186 184	92
24	6.6929 331 795	7.0983 171 533	7.5279 838 009	7.9833 714 518	96
25	7.2446 461 183	7.7022 960 618	8.1885 490 353	8.7051 735 544	100
26	7.8418 379 462	8.3576 660 979	8.9070 775 226	9.4922 360 897	104
27	8.4882 575 865	9.0688 000 102	9.6886 554 201	10.3504 594 619	108
28	9.1879 629 940	9.8404 426 142	10.5388 151 851	11.2862 775 492	112
29	9.9453 466 296	10.6777 424 504	11.4635 747 365	12.3067 059 378	116
30	10.7651 630 342	11.5862 861 364	12.4694 800 537	13.4193 945 150	120
31	11.6525 586 759	12.5721 356 419	13.5636 515 121	14.6326 848 191	124
32	12.6131 042 570	13.6418 687 348	14.7538 342 858	15.9556 725 735	128
33	13.6528 296 853	14.8026 228 701	16.0484 531 720	17.3982 758 749	132
34	14.7782 619 263	16.0621 428 115	17.4566 722 266	18.9713 095 467	136
35	15.9964 659 780	17.4288 323 063	18.9884 596 329	20.6865 662 153	140
36	17.3150 892 209	18.9118 101 568	20.6546 582 619	22.5569 047 158	144
37	18.7424 094 260	20.5209 710 622	22.4670 624 245	24.5963 464 918	148
38	20.2873 867 185	22.2670 516 384	24.4385 013 581	26.8201 807 104	152
39	21.9597 198 265	24.1617 020 541	26.5829 300 398	29.2450 788 811	156
40	23.7699 069 648	26.2175 637 634	28.9155 279 673	31.8892 198 378	160
41	25.7293 117 389	28.4483 538 513	31.4528 066 086	34.7724 260 206	164
42	27.8502 344 809	30.8689 565 573	34.2127 262 789	37.9163 120 801	168
43	30.1459 894 656	33.4955 225 852	37.2148 232 748	41.3444 469 161	172
44	32.6309 884 926	36.3455 768 637	40.4803 481 629	45.0825 303 682	176
45	35.3208 313 570	39.4381 354 760	44.0324 162 040	49.1585 858 803	180
46	38.2324 037 787	42.7938 325 385	47.8961 709 756	53.6031 705 854	184
47	41.3839 834 042	46.4350 578 757	52.0989 623 529	58.4496 043 846	188
48	44.7953 545 456	50.3861 064 086	56.6705 401 072	63.7342 197 375	192
49	48.4879 323 788	54.6733 402 554	61.6432 644 912	69.4966 340 375	196
50	52.4848 973 787	59.3253 646 242	67.0523 353 042	75.7800 466 127	200
51	56.8113 408 370	64.3732 186 722	72.9360 410 557	82.6315 625 809	204
52	61.4944 223 747	69.8505 826 043	79.3360 299 944	90.1025 459 835	208
53	66.5635 404 390	75.7940 023 941	86.2976 049 175	98.2490 048 493	212
54	72.0505 168 546	82.2431 336 252	93.8700 438 504	107.1320 110 715	216
55	77.9897 965 881	89.2410 060 801	102.1069 488 649	116.8181 582 484	220
56	84.4186 639 788	96.8343 108 434	111.0666 255 054	127.3800 609 178	224
57	91.3774 767 949	105.0737 118 325	120.8124 955 088	138.8968 989 301	228
58	98.9099 195 824	114.0141 838 374	131.4135 457 401	151.4550 110 385	232
59	107.0632 778 990	123.7153 793 218	142.9448 165 213	165.1485 421 588	236
60	115.8887 351 529	134.2420 264 357	155.4879 328 097	180.0801 491 490	240

TABLE 1. FUTURE WORTH OF ONE DOLLAR WITH INTEREST
Payable at beginning of each period

QUARTERLY Compounding

QUARTERS	9% Nominal Annual Rate	9¼% Nominal Annual Rate	9½% Nominal Annual Rate	9¾% Nominal Annual Rate	QUARTERS
1	1.0225 000 000	1.0231 250 000	1.0237 500 000	1.0243 750 000	1
2	1.0455 062 500	1.0467 847 656	1.0480 640 625	1.0493 441 406	2
3	1.0690 301 406	1.0709 916 633	1.0729 555 840	1.0749 219 041	3
YEARS					
1	1.0930 833 188	1.0957 583 455	1.0984 382 791	1.1011 231 255	4
2	1.1948 311 418	1.2006 863 518	1.2065 666 530	1.2124 721 374	8
3	1.3060 499 899	1.3156 620 904	1.3253 389 979	1.3350 811 095	12
4	1.4276 214 575	1.4416 477 155	1.4558 030 881	1.4700 886 840	16
5	1.5605 092 007	1.5796 975 156	1.5991 098 388	1.6187 486 465	20
6	1.7057 665 761	1.7309 667 361	1.7565 234 595	1.7824 415 690	24
7	1.8645 449 901	1.8967 212 470	1.9294 326 060	1.9626 876 314	28
8	2.0381 030 258	2.0783 481 355	2.1193 626 314	2.1611 607 390	32
9	2.2278 164 194	2.2773 673 145	2.3279 890 417	2.3797 040 675	36
10	2.4351 889 654	2.4954 442 407	2.5571 522 767	2.6203 471 805	40
11	2.6618 644 362	2.7344 038 526	2.8088 739 462	2.8853 248 772	44
12	2.9096 396 121	2.9962 458 415	3.0853 746 637	3.1770 979 468	48
13	3.1804 785 237	3.2831 613 862	3.3890 936 360	3.4983 760 210	52
14	3.4765 280 200	3.5975 514 887	3.7227 101 812	3.8521 427 383	56
15	3.8001 347 859	3.9420 470 672	4.0891 673 651	4.2416 834 518	60
16	4.1538 639 437	4.3195 309 724	4.4916 979 635	4.6706 157 396	64
17	4.5405 193 853	4.7331 621 119	4.9338 529 812	5.1429 230 011	68
18	4.9631 659 988	5.1864 018 849	5.4195 329 781	5.6629 914 490	72
19	5.4251 539 616	5.6830 431 488	5.9530 224 780	6.2356 508 438	76
20	5.9301 452 973	6.2272 419 583	6.5390 277 662	6.8662 193 464	80
21	6.4821 429 025	6.8235 523 456	7.1827 184 065	7.5605 529 068	84
22	7.0855 222 767	7.4769 644 289	7.8897 728 457	8.3250 996 470	88
23	7.7450 662 056	8.1929 461 723	8.6664 285 072	9.1669 597 431	92
24	8.4660 026 722	8.9774 891 429	9.5195 368 154	10.0939 513 633	96
25	9.2540 462 979	9.8371 586 504	10.4566 236 374	11.1146 832 735	100
26	10.1154 436 395	10.7791 486 876	11.4859 556 735	12.2386 347 846	104
27	11.0570 227 045	11.8113 421 323	12.6166 133 838	13.4762 437 855	108
28	12.0862 470 737	12.9423 767 136	13.8585 710 934	14.8390 036 766	112
29	13.2112 750 631	14.1817 172 951	15.2227 849 827	16.3395 701 071	116
30	14.4410 243 914	15.5397 350 803	16.7212 897 396	17.9918 785 051	120
31	15.7852 428 684	17.0277 944 017	18.3673 047 260	19.8112 734 925	124
32	17.2545 856 625	18.6583 478 219	20.1753 505 950	21.8146 513 875	128
33	18.8606 997 603	20.4450 403 399	22.1613 773 878	24.0206 171 167	132
34	20.6163 162 887	22.4028 235 775	24.3429 052 405	26.4496 569 951	136
35	22.5353 514 300	24.5480 808 988	26.7391 789 407	29.1243 289 779	140
36	24.6330 167 312	26.8987 645 120	29.3713 377 003	32.0694 721 512	144
37	26.9259 396 803	29.4745 456 988	32.2626 016 385	35.3124 374 071	148
38	29.4322 955 073	32.2969 794 306	35.4384 766 232	38.8833 414 454	152
39	32.1719 512 527	35.3896 847 470	38.9269 792 761	42.8153 464 609	156
40	35.1666 232 472	38.7785 424 077	42.7588 841 268	47.1449 681 128	160
41	38.4400 492 497	42.4919 114 713	46.9679 950 966	51.9124 146 383	164
42	42.0181 766 083	46.5608 666 128	51.5914 437 069	57.1619 602 569	168
43	45.9293 679 364	51.0194 581 668	56.6700 166 419	62.9423 563 357	172
44	50.2046 259 338	55.9049 970 714	62.2485 155 569	69.3072 841 324	176
45	54.8778 391 343	61.2583 670 986	68.3761 523 051	76.3158 533 213	180
46	59.9860 505 289	67.1243 669 828	75.1069 830 698	84.0331 509 316	184
47	65.5697 511 932	73.5520 853 108	82.5003 852 319	92.5308 457 964	188
48	71.6732 012 464	80.5953 113 115	90.6215 811 795	101.8878 541 252	192
49	78.3447 806 867	88.3129 849 813	99.5422 136 805	112.1910 723 812	196
50	85.6373 728 828	96.7696 903 132	109.3409 778 934	123.5361 842 695	200
51	93.6087 837 631	106.0361 957 565	120.1043 155 928	136.0285 493 308	204
52	102.3222 000 236	116.1900 464 300	131.9271 777 327	149.7841 813 914	208
53	111.8466 899 876	127.3162 130 449	144.9138 620 757	164.9308 259 588	212
54	122.2577 510 872	139.5078 029 670	159.1789 332 768	181.6091 465 651	216
55	133.6379 083 060	152.8668 393 697	174.8482 335 382	199.9740 310 786	220
56	146.0773 683 272	167.5051 149 964	192.0599 927 520	220.1960 301 129	224
57	159.6747 345 711	183.5451 276 787	210.9660 479 233	242.4629 408 927	228
58	174.5377 887 917	201.1211 054 380	231.7331 826 302	266.9815 512 850	232
59	190.7843 454 265	220.3801 297 488	254.5445 983 396	293.9795 601 921	236
60	208.5431 854 718	241.4833 663 645	279.6015 305 554	323.7076 921 413	240

TABLE 1. FUTURE WORTH OF ONE DOLLAR WITH INTEREST
Payable at beginning of each period

QUARTERS	10% Nominal Annual Rate	10¼% Nominal Annual Rate	10½% Nominal Annual Rate	10¾% Nominal Annual Rate	QUARTERS
1	1.0250 000 000	1.0256 250 000	1.0262 500 000	1.0268 750 000	1
2	1.0506 250 000	1.0519 066 406	1.0531 890 625	1.0544 722 656	2
3	1.0768 906 250	1.0788 617 483	1.0808 352 754	1.0828 112 078	3
YEARS					
1	1.1038 128 906	1.1065 075 806	1.1092 072 014	1.1119 117 590	4
2	1.2184 028 975	1.2243 590 259	1.2303 406 156	1.2363 477 597	8
3	1.3448 888 242	1.3547 625 435	1.3647 026 709	1.3747 096 122	12
4	1.4845 056 207	1.4990 550 243	1.5137 380 303	1.5285 557 830	16
5	1.6386 164 403	1.6587 157 481	1.6790 491 242	1.6996 191 494	20
6	1.8087 259 496	1.8353 815 493	1.8624 133 800	1.8898 265 180	24
7	1.9964 950 188	2.0308 635 976	2.0658 023 331	2.1013 203 278	28
8	2.2037 569 378	2.2471 659 659	2.2914 028 244	2.3364 827 818	32
9	2.4325 353 157	2.4865 061 761	2.5416 405 141	2.5979 626 797	36
10	2.6850 638 384	2.7513 379 331	2.8192 059 615	2.8887 052 529	40
11	2.9638 080 770	3.0443 762 797	3.1270 835 547	3.2119 853 390	44
12	3.2714 895 607	3.3686 254 317	3.4685 835 981	3.5714 442 680	48
13	3.6111 123 486	3.7274 095 763	3.8473 779 056	3.9711 308 781	52
14	3.9859 923 599	4.1244 069 522	4.2675 392 793	4.4155 471 198	56
15	4.3997 897 488	4.5636 875 580	4.7335 853 007	4.9096 987 648	60
16	4.8565 446 408	5.0497 548 784	5.2505 269 039	5.4591 517 896	64
17	5.3607 165 784	5.5875 920 531	5.8239 222 527	6.0700 950 689	68
18	5.9172 280 622	6.1827 129 640	6.4599 365 030	6.7494 100 852	72
19	6.5315 126 118	6.8412 187 633	7.1654 080 895	7.5047 484 398	76
20	7.2095 678 162	7.5698 604 221	7.9479 222 536	8.3446 180 384	80
21	7.9580 138 914	8.3761 079 410	8.8158 925 996	9.2784 789 210	84
22	8.7841 583 171	9.2682 269 326	9.7786 515 580	10.3168 498 176	88
23	9.6960 671 837	10.2553 633 595	10.8465 507 278	11.4714 266 278	92
24	10.7026 439 457	11.3476 372 990	12.0310 721 773	12.7552 141 596	96
25	11.8137 163 511	12.5562 466 932	13.3449 518 993	14.1826 726 123	100
26	13.0401 323 945	13.8935 821 498	14.8023 167 486	15.7698 804 513	104
27	14.3938 662 325	15.3733 539 703	16.4188 363 345	17.5347 155 114	108
28	15.8881 350 934	17.0107 327 073	18.2118 915 004	19.4970 563 673	112
29	17.5375 283 240	18.8225 046 920	20.2007 612 028	21.6790 062 402	116
30	19.3581 498 338	20.8272 441 274	22.4068 297 992	24.1051 419 613	120
31	21.3677 753 252	23.0455 035 098	24.8538 169 732	26.8027 907 984	124
32	23.5860 258 479	25.5000 243 321	27.5680 327 682	29.8023 382 621	128
33	26.0345 593 695	28.2159 702 287	30.5786 604 741	33.1375 703 584	132
34	28.7372 822 338	31.2211 849 518	33.9180 704 061	36.8460 541 453	136
35	31.7205 825 712	34.5464 778 242	37.6221 679 510	40.9695 608 759	140
36	35.0135 879 403	38.2259 395 952	41.7307 796 224	45.5545 364 979	144
37	38.6484 497 155	42.2972 919 373	46.2880 812 759	50.6526 248 065	148
38	42.6606 569 986	46.8022 741 671	51.3430 730 888	56.3212 491 452	152
39	47.0893 831 176	51.7870 711 548	56.9501 064 105	62.6242 592 045	156
40	51.9778 680 968	57.3027 868 094	63.1694 681 493	69.6326 502 064	160
41	57.3738 408 325	63.4059 679 936	70.0680 289 779	77.4253 625 730	164
42	63.3299 850 955	70.1591 842 396	77.7199 623 281	86.0901 710 876	168
43	69.9044 539 116	77.6316 692 092	86.2075 419 045	95.7246 735 642	172
44	77.1614 373 397	85.9000 304 739	95.6220 262 929	106.4373 901 598	176
45	85.1717 891 947	95.0490 348 924	106.0646 401 736	118.3489 857 130	180
46	94.0137 188 307	105.1724 776 363	117.6476 626 912	131.5936 288 768	184
47	103.7735 547 409	116.3741 437 741	130.4956 346 814	146.3205 033 539	188
48	114.5465 874 290	128.7688 722 708	144.7466 977 359	162.6954 882 580	192
49	126.4379 997 812	142.4837 333 118	160.5540 795 032	180.9030 265 258	196
50	139.5638 940 234	157.6593 310 204	178.0877 411 942	201.1482 024 277	200
51	154.0524 252 888	174.4512 449 250	197.5362 050 082	223.6590 515 755	204
52	170.0450 528 658	193.0316 249 530	219.1085 811 264	248.6891 294 474	208
53	187.6979 213 403	213.5909 563 043	243.0368 160 673	276.5203 673 611	212
54	207.1833 851 189	236.3400 122 964	269.5781 865 797	307.4662 480 642	216
55	228.6916 912 176	261.5120 152 029	299.0180 658 864	341.8753 367 097	220
56	252.4328 367 448	289.3650 272 376	331.6729 920 208	380.1352 069 901	224
57	278.6386 192 160	320.1845 961 963	367.8940 712 493	422.6768 066 517	228
58	307.5648 997 166	354.2866 828 797	408.0707 531 709	469.9793 115 609	232
59	339.4941 010 109	392.0209 003 088	452.6350 180 855	522.5755 229 983	236
60	374.7379 649 870	433.7740 979 418	502.0660 216 525	581.0578 689 729	240

TABLE 1. FUTURE WORTH OF ONE DOLLAR WITH INTEREST
Payable at beginning of each period

QUARTERLY Compounding

QUARTERS	11% Nominal Annual Rate	11¼% Nominal Annual Rate	11½% Nominal Annual Rate	11¾% Nominal Annual Rate	QUARTERS
1	1.0275 000 000	1.0281 250 000	1.0287 500 000	1.0293 750 000	1
2	1.0557 562 500	1.0570 410 156	1.0583 265 625	1.0596 128 906	2
3	1.0847 895 469	1.0867 702 942	1.0887 534 512	1.0907 390 193	3
YEARS					
1	1.1146 212 594	1.1173 357 087	1.1200 551 129	1.1227 794 780	4
2	1.2423 805 519	1.2484 390 860	1.2545 234 559	1.2606 337 562	8
3	1.3847 837 755	1.3949 255 709	1.4051 354 110	1.4154 137 107	12
4	1.5435 094 358	1.5586 001 514	1.5738 291 014	1.5891 974 672	16
5	1.7204 284 313	1.7414 796 047	1.7627 753 319	1.7843 183 026	20
6	1.9176 261 048	1.9458 173 484	1.9744 055 234	2.0033 959 724	24
7	2.1374 268 240	2.1741 312 060	2.2114 430 014	2.2493 718 840	28
8	2.3824 213 785	2.4292 344 318	2.4769 380 406	2.5255 485 897	32
9	2.6554 975 174	2.7142 703 755	2.7743 071 167	2.8356 341 272	36
10	2.9598 739 872	3.0327 512 137	3.1073 768 707	3.1837 918 051	40
11	3.2991 384 713	3.3886 012 267	3.4804 333 518	3.5746 961 009	44
12	3.6772 898 779	3.7862 051 532	3.8982 771 707	4.0135 954 221	48
13	4.0987 854 749	4.2304 622 182	4.3662 852 765	4.5063 825 728	52
14	4.5685 934 281	4.7268 465 007	4.8904 801 483	5.0596 738 727	56
15	5.0922 513 606	5.2814 743 849	5.4776 072 947	5.6808 979 895	60
16	5.6759 316 248	5.9011 799 249	6.1352 220 568	6.3783 956 791	64
17	6.3265 140 559	6.5935 990 536	6.8717 868 335	7.1615 317 710	68
18	7.0516 670 647	7.3672 636 715	7.6967 799 775	8.0408 209 033	72
19	7.8599 380 247	8.2317 067 757	8.6208 177 666	9.0280 686 964	76
20	8.7608 540 200	9.1975 799 241	9.6557 910 168	10.1365 302 581	80
21	9.7650 341 413	10.2767 844 830	10.8150 180 974	11.3810 881 517	84
22	10.8843 146 528	11.4826 182 736	12.1134 163 161	12.7784 522 137	88
23	12.1318 885 061	12.8299 394 266	13.5676 938 794	14.3473 839 059	92
24	13.5224 608 458	14.3353 494 620	15.1965 648 998	16.1089 482 123	96
25	15.0724 223 383	16.0173 978 508	17.0209 902 144	18.0867 964 645	100
26	16.8000 423 691	17.8968 105 794	19.0644 471 162	20.3074 838 928	104
27	18.7256 843 837	19.9967 455 324	21.3532 314 670	22.8008 261 642	108
28	20.8720 459 111	22.3430 778 414	23.9167 960 814	25.6002 996 981	112
29	23.2644 261 000	24.9647 187 148	26.7881 297 349	28.7434 911 311	116
30	25.9310 239 192	27.8939 716 780	30.0041 816 745	32.2726 019 675	120
31	28.9032 705 387	31.1669 306 137	33.6063 370 927	36.2350 151 901	124
32	32.2161 998 090	34.8239 245 056	37.6409 496 862	40.6839 314 397	128
33	35.9088 612 046	38.9100 143 677	42.1599 381 502	45.6790 833 039	132
34	40.0247 801 000	43.4755 484 796	47.2214 542 844	51.2875 373 065	136
35	44.6124 708 029	48.5767 827 722	52.8906 313 095	57.5845 943 639	140
36	49.7260 083 919	54.2765 740 057	59.2404 220 223	64.6548 007 995	144
37	55.4256 660 994	60.6451 542 833	66.3525 375 761	72.5930 834 904	148
38	61.7786 257 516	67.7609 964 411	74.3184 989 655	81.5060 243 863	152
39	68.8597 696 401	75.7117 809 817	83.2408 147 488	91.5132 915 125	156
40	76.7525 631 592	84.5954 764 611	93.2343 001 608	102.7492 456 725	160
41	85.5500 386 117	94.5215 466 456	104.4275 545 921	115.3647 444 189	164
42	95.3558 917 803	105.6122 993 100	116.9646 164 479	129.5291 675 158	168
43	106.2857 041 887	118.0043 932 984	131.0068 166 800	145.4326 910 864	172
44	118.4683 054 606	131.8505 224 174	146.7348 548 463	163.2888 409 790	176
45	132.0472 918 331	147.3212 969 095	164.3511 244 102	183.3373 596 342	180
46	147.1827 187 252	164.6073 456 910	184.0823 172 054	205.8474 249 440	184
47	164.0529 873 095	183.9216 652 571	206.1823 405 791	231.1212 643 219	188
48	182.8569 473 256	205.5022 441 978	230.9355 847 538	259.4982 125 051	192
49	203.8162 409 206	229.6149 956 630	258.6605 824 525	291.3592 675 729	196
50	227.1779 151 440	256.5570 339 103	289.7141 078 798	327.1322 063 498	200
51	253.2173 338 889	286.6603 353 096	324.4957 678 080	367.2973 278 754	204
52	282.2414 236 047	320.2958 289 132	363.4531 438 456	412.3939 020 549	208
53	314.5922 910 371	357.8779 669 968	407.0875 520 613	463.0274 100 708	212
54	350.6512 556 377	399.8698 318 873	455.9604 940 814	519.8776 737 691	216
55	390.8433 441 740	446.7888 420 049	510.7008 826 731	583.7079 831 672	220
56	435.6423 005 168	499.2131 274 269	572.0131 347 970	655.3753 446 325	224
57	485.5761 696 561	557.7886 535 326	640.6862 362 713	735.8419 873 266	228
58	541.2335 217 636	623.2371 805 072	717.6038 946 959	826.1882 824 053	232
59	603.2703 896 652	696.3651 567 787	803.7559 112 862	927.6272 484 311	236
60	672.4180 014 958	778.0736 559 727	900.2509 179 541	1041.5208 377 523	240

QUARTERLY
Compounding

TABLE 1. FUTURE WORTH OF ONE DOLLAR WITH INTEREST
Payable at beginning of each period

QUARTERS	12% Nominal Annual Rate	12¼% Nominal Annual Rate	12½% Nominal Annual Rate	12¾% Nominal Annual Rate	QUARTERS
1	1.0300 000 000	1.0306 250 000	1.0312 500 000	1.0318 750 000	1
2	1.0609 000 000	1.0621 878 906	1.0634 765 625	1.0647 660 156	2
3	1.0927 270 000	1.0947 173 948	1.0967 102 051	1.0987 054 324	3
YEARS					
1	1.1255 088 100	1.1282 431 150	1.1309 823 990	1.1337 266 680	4
2	1.2667 700 814	1.2729 325 265	1.2791 211 868	1.2853 361 578	8
3	1.4257 608 868	1.4361 773 589	1.4466 635 485	1.4572 198 795	12
4	1.6047 064 391	1.6203 572 171	1.6361 510 106	1.6520 890 386	16
5	1.8061 112 347	1.8281 568 740	1.8504 579 950	1.8730 174 010	20
6	2.0327 941 065	2.0626 054 062	2.0928 354 224	2.1234 897 772	24
7	2.2879 276 757	2.3271 203 485	2.3669 600 268	2.4074 569 897	28
8	2.5750 827 557	2.6255 575 109	2.6769 901 294	2.7293 981 913	32
9	2.8982 783 280	2.9622 671 847	3.0276 287 186	3.0943 915 172	36
10	3.2620 377 920	3.3421 575 559	3.4241 947 914	3.5081 941 843	40
11	3.6714 522 734	3.7707 662 517	3.8727 040 398	3.9773 333 034	44
12	4.1322 518 793	4.2543 410 617	4.3799 601 055	4.5092 088 337	48
13	4.6508 858 952	4.7999 310 117	4.9536 577 875	5.1122 103 065	52
14	5.2346 130 494	5.4154 891 164	5.6024 997 683	5.7958 491 571	56
15	5.8916 031 040	6.1099 883 099	6.3363 286 283	6.5709 087 532	60
16	6.6310 511 986	6.8935 522 433	7.1662 761 528	7.4496 144 867	64
17	7.4633 065 436	7.7776 028 563	8.1049 321 951	8.4458 266 101	68
18	8.4000 172 666	8.7750 268 738	9.1665 356 576	9.5752 588 615	72
19	9.4542 934 377	9.9003 636 542	10.3671 904 885	10.8557 263 245	76
20	10.6408 905 564	11.1700 171 287	11.7251 099 694	12.3074 264 350	80
21	11.9764 160 675	12.6024 949 198	13.2608 930 016	13.9532 575 641	84
22	13.4795 617 962	14.2186 781 250	14.9978 365 796	15.8191 802 064	88
23	15.1713 655 566	16.0421 256 988	16.9622 891 944	17.9346 264 663	92
24	17.0755 055 936	18.0994 178 694	19.1840 505 254	20.3329 643 060	96
25	19.2186 319 809	20.4205 435 965	21.6968 234 855	23.0520 238 738	100
26	21.6307 396 106	23.0393 377 172	24.5387 254 760	26.1346 942 178	104
27	24.3455 879 985	25.9939 741 533	27.7528 666 070	29.6295 997 956	108
28	27.4011 737 770	29.3275 223 697	31.3880 036 539	33.5918 674 513	112
29	30.8402 624 903	33.0885 751 934	35.4992 796 719	38.0839 959 585	116
30	34.7109 871 356	37.3319 571 468	40.1490 604 856	43.1768 418 432	120
31	39.0675 218 249	42.1195 236 199	45.4078 807 451	48.9507 370 390	124
32	43.9708 399 988	47.5210 625 309	51.3555 138 980	55.4967 560 008	128
33	49.4895 678 018	53.6153 116 175	58.0821 823 096	62.9181 522 673	132
34	55.7009 445 640	60.4911 061 905	65.6899 258 869	71.3319 871 286	136
35	62.6919 038 321	68.2486 740 776	74.2941 499 688	80.8709 760 913	140
36	70.5602 900 787	77.0010 966 353	84.0253 759 624	91.6855 822 643	144
37	79.4162 281 197	86.8759 571 254	95.0312 212 817	103.9463 896 869	148
38	89.3836 644 057	98.0172 004 850	107.4786 386 239	117.8467 940 334	152
39	100.6021 017 587	110.5872 315 978	121.5564 485 507	133.6060 531 375	156
40	113.2285 518 339	124.7692 826 561	137.4782 037 941	151.4727 454 522	160
41	127.4397 326 326	140.7700 841 190	155.4854 287 355	171.7286 909 989	164
42	143.4345 418 221	158.8228 782 039	175.8512 831 988	194.6933 966 514	168
43	161.4368 404 790	179.1908 188 365	198.8847 061 371	220.7290 958 730	172
44	181.6985 862 177	202.1708 076 218	224.9351 020 687	250.2464 624 013	176
45	204.5033 595 526	228.0978 217 513	254.3976 413 540	283.7110 880 045	180
46	230.1703 328 510	257.3497 969 352	287.7192 547 151	321.6508 264 865	184
47	259.0587 374 245	290.3531 365 363	325.4054 129 324	364.6641 197 816	188
48	291.5728 912 787	327.5889 272 130	368.0277 945 616	413.4294 374 701	192
49	328.1678 578 914	369.5999 516 751	416.2329 579 871	468.7159 786 085	196
50	369.3558 152 156	416.9986 007 782	470.7521 493 616	531.3958 046 802	200
51	415.7132 240 499	470.4758 002 887	532.4123 952 132	602.4575 950 451	204
52	467.8888 961 016	530.8110 824 453	602.1490 479 885	683.0222 418 599	208
53	526.6130 746 636	598.8839 491 295	681.0199 748 417	774.3605 304 541	212
54	592.7076 549 950	675.6866 922 836	770.2216 049 044	877.9131 840 456	216
55	667.0976 874 514	762.3388 584 596	871.1070 784 662	995.3135 889 676	220
56	750.8243 243 571	860.1035 683 466	985.2067 733 782	1128.4135 588 652	224
57	845.0593 918 262	970.4059 291 658	1114.2515 200 533	1279.3125 442 520	228
58	951.1217 904 737	1094.8538 083 271	1260.1988 572 246	1450.3907 481 638	232
59	1070.4959 545 611	1235.2612 711 661	1425.2627 267 443	1644.3466 702 571	236
60	1204.8526 279 279	1393.6750 244 074	1611.9470 578 797	1864.2396 715 568	240

TABLE 1. FUTURE WORTH OF ONE DOLLAR WITH INTEREST
Payable at beginning of each period

QUARTERLY Compounding

QUARTERS	13% Nominal Annual Rate	13¼% Nominal Annual Rate	13½% Nominal Annual Rate	13¾% Nominal Annual Rate	QUARTERS
1	1.0325 000 000	1.0331 250 000	1.0337 500 000	1.0343 750 000	1
2	1.0660 562 500	1.0673 472 656	1.0686 390 625	1.0699 316 406	2
3	1.1007 030 781	1.1027 031 438	1.1047 056 309	1.1067 105 408	3
YEARS					
1	1.1364 759 282	1.1392 301 854	1.1419 894 459	1.1447 537 156	4
2	1.2915 775 353	1.2978 454 154	1.3041 398 945	1.3104 610 694	8
3	1.4678 467 782	1.4785 446 733	1.4893 139 956	1.5001 551 784	12
4	1.6681 725 297	1.6844 027 223	1.7007 808 646	1.7173 082 144	16
5	1.8958 379 240	1.9189 224 257	1.9422 737 971	1.9658 949 593	20
6	2.1545 741 643	2.1860 943 508	2.2180 561 774	2.2504 655 592	24
7	2.4486 216 732	2.4904 646 727	2.5329 967 449	2.5762 288 107	28
8	2.7827 995 888	2.8372 125 309	2.8926 555 492	2.9491 475 033	32
9	3.1625 847 456	3.2322 381 577	3.3033 821 079	3.3760 475 623	36
10	3.5942 014 341	3.6822 632 758	3.7724 275 029	3.8647 429 910	40
11	4.0847 234 108	4.1949 454 745	4.3080 723 938	4.4241 788 989	44
12	4.6421 898 296	4.7790 085 108	4.9197 732 059	5.0645 952 330	48
13	5.2757 369 953	5.4443 907 520	5.6183 290 773	5.7977 142 111	52
14	5.9957 480 985	6.2024 142 860	6.4160 725 099	6.6369 548 851	56
15	6.8140 233 853	7.0659 775 772	7.3270 870 905	7.5976 787 651	60
16	7.7439 735 513	8.0497 749 455	8.3674 561 265	8.6974 709 964	64
17	8.8008 395 294	9.1705 466 039	9.5555 465 855	9.9564 622 395	68
18	10.0019 422 729	10.4473 635 081	10.9123 333 505	11.3976 971 430	72
19	11.3669 666 280	11.9019 518 667	12.4617 695 164	13.0475 561 539	76
20	12.9182 839 489	13.5590 628 322	14.2312 092 650	14.9362 383 868	80
21	14.6813 187 412	15.4468 936 646	16.2518 907 830	17.0983 143 905	84
22	16.6849 653 430	17.5975 675 340	18.5594 877 501	19.5733 589 292	88
23	18.9620 614 746	20.0476 801 250	21.1947 391 320	22.4066 753 612	92
24	21.5499 264 143	22.8389 223 464	24.2041 683 973	25.6501 248 742	96
25	24.4909 726 235	26.0187 897 399	27.6409 048 566	29.3630 757 556	100
26	27.8334 008 440	29.6413 906 602	31.5656 216 213	33.6134 900 730	104
27	31.6319 900 581	33.7683 669 784	36.0476 067 449	38.4791 676 557	108
28	35.9489 952 610	38.4699 429 748	41.1659 864 526	44.0491 701 475	112
29	40.8551 677 558	43.8261 202 689	47.0111 220 590	50.4254 511 959	116
30	46.4309 146 955	49.9280 391 209	53.6862 052 313	57.7247 226 179	120
31	52.7676 168 741	56.8795 292 662	61.3090 797 647	66.0805 906 994	124
32	59.9691 263 640	64.7988 766 736	70.0143 220 291	75.6460 017 329	128
33	68.1534 685 457	73.8208 362 889	79.9556 168 192	86.5960 415 548	132
34	77.4547 764 231	84.0989 250 146	91.3084 705 480	99.1311 403 270	136
35	88.0254 889 262	95.8080 339 394	104.2733 096 872	113.4807 412 220	140
36	100.0388 492 295	109.1474 042 712	119.0790 191 519	129.9075 001 641	144
37	113.6917 440 305	124.3440 176 078	135.9869 830 997	148.7120 934 986	148
38	129.2079 303 217	141.6564 582 374	155.2956 994 798	170.2387 215 887	152
39	146.8417 025 385	161.3793 131 861	177.3460 497 997	194.8814 090 794	156
40	166.8820 601 856	183.8481 848 868	202.5273 171 434	223.0912 171 471	160
41	189.6574 442 434	209.4454 017 608	231.2840 586 844	255.3844 997 492	164
42	215.5411 199 798	238.6065 238 870	264.1239 540 227	292.3523 549 972	168
43	244.9572 943 865	271.8277 544 543	301.6267 679 036	334.6714 446 506	172
44	278.3880 684 985	309.6743 831 139	344.4545 855 471	383.1163 797 725	176
45	316.3813 385 366	352.7904 049 000	393.3635 012 869	438.5738 992 558	180
46	359.5597 753 672	401.9094 783 947	449.2169 668 723	502.0591 007 429	184
47	408.6310 294 409	457.8674 096 005	513.0010 350 877	574.7340 210 314	188
48	464.3993 284 604	521.6163 739 448	585.8417 678 064	657.9289 060 635	192
49	527.7786 578 508	594.2411 184 162	669.0251 158 029	753.1665 598 238	196
50	599.8077 400 462	676.9774 195 277	764.0196 212 895	862.1902 178 318	200
51	681.6670 580 890	771.2331 111 853	872.5023 439 738	986.9954 554 260	204
52	774.6982 025 406	878.6120 402 709	996.3884 683 418	1129.8667 148 896	208
53	880.4258 587 793	1000.9413 575 652	1137.8651 148 637	1293.4191 200 145	212
54	1000.5827 950 359	1140.3026 083 907	1299.4299 520 331	1480.6463 434 783	216
55	1137.1382 606 934	1299.0671 520 114	1483.9352 909 093	1694.9754 032 019	220
56	1292.3302 602 724	1479.9365 124 813	1694.6384 406 183	1940.3293 906 838	224
57	1468.7022 320 376	1685.9883 475 493	1935.2592 138 040	2221.1992 794 935	228
58	1669.1447 323 516	1920.7288 178 235	2210.0455 972 466	2542.7261 283 116	232
59	1896.9428 089 394	2188.1522 473 035	2523.8487 470 154	2910.7951 831 646	236
60	2155.8298 394 636	2492.8090 904 603	2882.2086 321 417	3332.1436 013 088	240

QUARTERLY Compounding

TABLE 1. FUTURE WORTH OF ONE DOLLAR WITH INTEREST
Payable at beginning of each period

QUARTERS	14% Nominal Annual Rate	14¼% Nominal Annual Rate	14½% Nominal Annual Rate	14¾% Nominal Annual Rate	QUARTERS
1	1.0350 000 000	1.0356 250 000	1.0362 500 000	1.0368 750 000	1
2	1.0712 250 000	1.0725 191 406	1.0738 140 625	1.0751 097 656	2
3	1.1087 178 750	1.1107 276 350	1.1127 398 223	1.1147 544 382	3
YEARS					
1	1.1475 230 006	1.1502 973 070	1.1530 766 408	1.1558 610 081	4
2	1.3168 090 370	1.3231 838 945	1.3295 857 396	1.3360 146 701	8
3	1.5110 686 573	1.5220 548 705	1.5331 142 583	1.5442 472 635	12
4	1.7339 860 398	1.7508 156 187	1.7677 982 390	1.7849 351 988	16
5	1.9897 888 635	2.0139 584 912	2.0384 068 551	2.0631 369 984	20
6	2.2833 284 872	2.3166 510 289	2.3504 393 291	2.3846 996 109	24
7	2.6201 719 571	2.6648 374 398	2.7102 366 860	2.7563 812 964	28
8	3.0067 075 863	3.0653 553 306	3.1251 106 137	3.1859 936 641	32
9	3.4502 661 115	3.5260 699 818	3.6034 920 487	3.6825 658 485	36
10	3.9592 597 212	4.0560 288 044	4.1551 025 067	4.2565 342 742	40
11	4.5433 415 955	4.6656 390 109	4.7911 516 407	4.9199 619 973	44
12	5.2135 889 805	5.3668 719 897	5.5245 650 396	5.6867 922 342	48
13	5.9827 132 710	6.1734 983 968	6.3702 468 978	6.5731 414 050	52
14	6.8653 010 846	7.1013 585 806	7.3453 828 942	7.5976 378 510	56
15	7.8780 909 008	8.1686 736 514	8.4697 894 331	8.7818 133 460	60
16	9.0402 905 096	9.3964 033 030	9.7663 163 481	10.1505 556 274	64
17	10.3739 412 921	10.8086 574 150	11.2613 112 478	11.7326 314 607	68
18	11.9043 362 399	12.4331 695 168	12.9851 549 449	13.5612 912 283	72
19	13.6604 996 424	14.3018 414 128	14.9728 788 444	15.6749 677 509	76
20	15.6757 375 397	16.4513 696 624	17.2648 768 414	18.1180 840 271	80
21	17.9882 693 786	18.9239 662 192	19.9077 261 925	20.9419 868 692	84
22	20.6419 528 533	21.7681 873 798	22.9551 340 444	24.2060 260 551	88
23	23.6871 156 770	25.0398 873 214	26.4690 288 536	27.9788 016 792	92
24	27.1815 100 579	28.8033 149 536	30.5208 188 764	32.3396 059 155	96
25	31.1914 079 831	33.1323 756 240	35.1928 433 051	37.3800 894 964	100
26	35.7928 580 825	38.1120 824 551	40.5800 455 392	43.2061 879 298	104
27	41.0731 279 078	43.8402 258 125	46.7919 025 948	49.9403 479 385	108
28	47.1323 589 818	50.4292 936 907	53.9546 498 618	57.7241 009 152	112
29	54.0854 660 053	58.0086 807 266	62.2138 464 194	66.7210 374 779	116
30	62.0643 162 406	66.7272 292 229	71.7373 330 419	77.1202 456 435	120
31	71.2202 304 042	76.7561 520 791	82.7186 430 055	89.1402 848 777	124
32	81.7268 524 986	88.2923 950 328	95.3809 350 102	103.0337 795 448	128
33	93.7834 430 108	101.5625 042 355	109.9815 281 401	119.0927 282 974	132
34	107.6186 579 327	116.8270 751 149	126.8171 310 204	137.6546 409 922	136
35	123.4948 852 742	134.3858 698 902	146.2298 714 358	159.1096 321 127	140
36	141.7132 213 117	154.5837 042 345	168.6142 489 431	183.9086 197 789	144
37	162.6191 809 478	177.8172 186 881	194.4251 517 662	212.5728 026 637	148
38	186.6092 504 804	204.5426 677 964	224.1871 008 900	245.7046 139 905	152
39	214.1384 070 557	235.2848 799 343	258.5049 092 100	284.0003 828 323	156
40	245.7287 474 136	270.6475 637 678	298.0759 723 481	328.2649 688 133	160
41	281.9793 895 719	311.3251 637 501	343.7044 409 051	379.4286 777 903	164
42	323.5778 352 359	358.1164 974 653	396.3175 621 547	438.5668 140 288	168
43	371.3130 084 256	411.9404 426 291	456.9845 232 684	506.9222 798 010	172
44	426.0902 175 997	473.8539 818 035	526.9381 789 983	585.9316 973 806	176
45	488.9483 250 369	545.0729 591 831	607.6001 053 606	677.2556 024 368	180
46	561.0794 490 970	626.9959 570 707	700.6094 884 528	782.8133 434 026	184
47	643.8515 730 168	721.2317 609 227	807.8564 354 737	904.8234 202 925	188
48	738.8344 890 253	829.6309 523 173	931.5203 848 830	1045.8501 107 700	192
49	847.8295 698 116	954.3222 502 602	1074.1143 962 588	1208.8573 634 003	196
50	972.9039 319 688	1097.7543 144 912	1238.5362 198 975	1397.2710 907 601	200
51	1116.4296 393 327	1262.7438 317 145	1428.1271 839 767	1615.0511 716 139	204
52	1281.1286 897 137	1452.5308 290 609	1646.7400 959 675	1866.7746 754 230	208
53	1470.1246 382 071	1670.8423 010 133	1898.8175 381 664	2157.7320 583 088	212
54	1687.0018 361 281	1921.9653 992 890	2189.4821 484 442	2494.0383 522 177	216
55	1935.8734 090 536	2210.8316 229 628	2524.6407 208 695	2882.7616 841 398	220
56	2221.4592 631 874	2543.1136 621 400	2911.1042 417 045	3332.0718 264 636	224
57	2549.1755 994 590	2925.3367 969 723	3356.7263 001 095	3851.4119 005 386	228
58	2925.2376 330 112	3365.0070 396 457	3870.5626 862 917	4451.6968 421 276	232
59	3356.7774 661 742	3870.7585 357 640	4463.0554 204 031	5145.5427 998 852	236
60	3851.9793 504 146	4452.5231 197 636	5146.2449 519 642	5947.5322 881 144	240

TABLE 1. FUTURE WORTH OF ONE DOLLAR WITH INTEREST
Payable at beginning of each period

QUARTERLY Compounding

QUARTERS	15% Nominal Annual Rate	15¼% Nominal Annual Rate	15½% Nominal Annual Rate	15¾% Nominal Annual Rate	QUARTERS
1	1.0375 000 000	1.0381 250 000	1.0387 500 000	1.0393 750 000	1
2	1.0764 062 500	1.0777 035 156	1.0790 015 625	1.0803 003 906	2
3	1.1167 714 844	1.1187 909 622	1.1208 128 730	1.1228 372 185	3
YEARS					
1	1.1586 504 150	1.1614 448 676	1.1642 443 719	1.1670 489 340	4
2	1.3424 707 843	1.3489 541 805	1.3554 649 574	1.3620 032 143	8
3	1.5554 543 314	1.5667 359 095	1.5780 924 480	1.5895 243 993	12
4	1.8022 278 066	1.8196 773 810	1.8372 852 509	1.8550 527 558	16
5	2.0881 519 961	2.1134 549 548	2.1390 490 129	2.1649 373 411	20
6	2.4194 381 770	2.4546 614 101	2.4903 757 744	2.5265 878 161	24
7	2.8032 830 479	2.8509 538 965	2.8994 059 792	2.9486 516 174	28
8	3.2480 250 670	3.3112 257 708	3.3756 170 931	3.4412 207 268	32
9	3.7633 255 919	3.8458 061 769	3.9300 432 022	4.0160 729 808	36
10	4.3603 787 590	4.4666 918 459	4.5755 306 794	4.6869 536 911	40
11	5.0521 546 588	5.1878 163 195	5.3270 358 419	5.4699 043 088	44
12	5.8536 810 923	6.0253 626 383	6.2019 714 977	6.3836 459 926	48
13	6.7823 700 270	6.9981 265 117	7.2206 104 107	7.4500 272 506	52
14	7.8583 958 468	8.1279 381 197	8.4065 550 322	8.6945 463 610	56
15	9.1051 336 094	9.4401 520 132	9.7872 843 831	10.1469 610 620	60
16	10.5496 668 355	10.9642 161 051	11.3947 907 590	11.8420 000 906	64
17	12.2233 758 575	12.7343 325 224	13.2663 210 099	13.8201 935 820	68
18	14.1626 195 105	14.7902 251 503	15.4452 395 713	16.1288 421 874	72
19	16.4095 249 739	17.1780 310 913	17.9820 332 432	18.8231 480 812	76
20	19.0129 029 216	19.9513 360 463	20.9354 809 983	21.9675 349 024	80
21	22.0293 078 612	23.1723 768 526	24.3740 159 248	25.6371 881 901	84
22	25.5242 666 964	26.9134 381 653	28.3773 108 605	29.9198 531 476	88
23	29.5737 022 013	31.2584 746 263	33.0381 244 583	34.9179 327 208	92
24	34.2655 823 298	36.3049 949 234	38.4644 504 580	40.7509 361 588	96
25	39.7018 311 880	42.1662 500 217	44.7820 199 631	47.5583 366 030	100
26	46.0005 431 838	48.9737 746 732	52.1372 147 033	55.5029 060 346	104
27	53.2985 484 519	56.8803 392 408	60.7004 587 837	64.7746 073 207	108
28	61.7543 852 848	66.0633 780 780	70.6701 675 093	75.5951 364 229	112
29	71.5517 441 407	76.7289 714 044	82.2773 447 823	88.2232 233 768	116
30	82.9034 580 454	89.1164 700 331	95.7909 355 958	102.9608 187 946	120
31	96.0561 260 725	103.5038 667 377	111.5240 576 443	120.1603 138 164	124
32	111.2954 703 409	120.2140 347 983	129.8412 564 413	140.2329 661 467	128
33	128.9525 429 025	139.6219 737 288	151.1669 520 493	163.6587 336 510	132
34	149.4109 173 543	162.1632 247 902	175.9952 731 373	190.9977 506 446	136
35	173.1150 214 039	188.3436 451 445	204.9015 062 271	222.9037 212 832	140
36	200.5797 913 991	218.7507 599 964	238.5554 254 141	260.1395 503 048	144
37	232.4018 585 531	254.0669 474 793	277.7368 114 192	303.5955 848 704	148
38	269.2725 098 683	295.0847 521 742	323.3535 195 580	354.3109 036 854	152
39	311.9927 053 176	342.7246 709 170	376.4625 152 721	413.4981 624 452	156
40	361.4904 775 054	398.0558 100 331	438.2943 646 284	482.5725 896 862	160
41	418.8410 917 943	462.3198 775 776	510.2817 472 442	563.1858 263 634	164
42	485.2904 048 428	536.9590 489 975	594.0926 523 009	657.2654 182 926	168
43	562.2819 289 856	623.6483 315 644	691.6690 268 151	767.0609 057 633	172
44	651.4881 903 881	724.3331 538 769	805.2717 716 714	895.1976 123 723	176
45	754.8470 621 863	841.2730 239 959	937.5331 280 002	1044.7394 192 246	180
46	874.6038 618 931	977.0922 359 624	1091.5176 677 229	1219.2620 254 976	184
47	1013.3601 275 773	1134.8387 626 210	1270.7933 014 511	1422.9384 471 048	188
48	1174.1301 324 014	1318.0526 563 889	1479.5139 490 340	1660.6387 978 193	192
49	1360.4063 652 168	1530.8454 929 769	1722.5157 882 770	1938.0467 387 283	196
50	1576.2353 996 802	1777.9926 408 921	2005.4293 119 716	2261.7953 804 451	200
51	1826.3058 000 387	2065.0404 273 778	2334.8097 896 609	2639.6258 876 396	204
52	2116.0499 732 031	2398.4306 057 448	2718.2891 570 171	3080.5725 782 877	208
53	2451.7621 796 952	2785.6449 173 142	3164.7528 521 926	3595.1789 435 527	212
54	2840.7352 670 809	3235.3729 921 441	3684.5456 965 484	4195.7497 535 568	216
55	3291.4190 962 194	3757.7073 564 666	4289.7115 901 317	4896.6452 771 543	220
56	3813.6041 019 021	4364.3699 230 752	4994.2725 757 882	5714.6246 508 033	224
57	4418.6339 754 636	5068.9750 474 219	5814.5537 379 833	6669.2466 068 417	228
58	5119.6520 895 766	5887.3350 527 724	6769.5614 644 260	7783.3371 429 945	232
59	5931.8870 184 435	6837.8150 808 281	7881.4238 350 364	9083.5353 155 739	236
60	6872.9833 558 844	7941.7452 311 606	9175.9033 423 218	10600.9302 068 513	240

TABLE 1. FUTURE WORTH OF ONE DOLLAR WITH INTEREST
Payable at beginning of each period

QUARTERS	16% Nominal Annual Rate	16¼% Nominal Annual Rate	16½% Nominal Annual Rate	16¾% Nominal Annual Rate	QUARTERS
1	1.0400 000 000	1.0406 250 000	1.0412 500 000	1.0418 750 000	1
2	1.0816 000 000	1.0829 003 906	1.0842 015 625	1.0855 035 156	2
3	1.1248 640 000	1.1268 932 190	1.1289 248 770	1.1309 589 753	3
YEARS					
1	1.1698 585 600	1.1726 732 560	1.1754 930 281	1.1783 178 824	4
2	1.3685 690 504	1.3751 625 654	1.3817 838 592	1.3884 330 321	8
3	1.6010 322 186	1.6126 163 631	1.6242 772 928	1.6360 154 702	12
4	1.8729 812 457	1.8910 720 812	1.9093 266 335	1.9277 462 845	16
5	2.1911 231 430	2.2176 096 548	2.2444 001 461	2.2714 979 199	20
6	2.5633 041 649	2.6005 315 345	2.6382 767 240	2.6765 466 189	24
7	2.9987 033 192	3.0495 737 819	3.1012 758 954	3.1538 227 442	28
8	3.5080 587 468	3.5761 536 163	3.6455 281 933	3.7162 057 375	32
9	4.1039 325 540	4.1936 597 053	4.2852 929 751	4.3788 716 753	36
10	4.8010 206 279	4.9177 925 812	5.0373 320 157	5.1597 027 999	40
11	5.6165 150 783	5.7669 638 386	5.9213 486 648	6.0797 700 772	44
12	6.5705 282 418	6.7627 642 619	6.9605 040 726	7.1639 018 030	48
13	7.6865 887 073	7.9305 127 867	8.1820 240 096	8.4413 536 025	52
14	8.9922 215 965	9.2999 002 515	9.6179 121 792	9.9465 979 018	56
15	10.5196 274 081	10.9057 443 085	11.3057 887 118	11.7202 541 770	60
16	12.3064 761 713	12.7888 746 875	13.2898 758 083	13.8101 850 835	64
17	14.3968 364 925	14.9971 713 206	15.6221 563 573	16.2727 880 436	68
18	16.8422 624 076	17.5867 817 236	18.3637 358 823	19.1745 171 488	72
19	19.7030 648 473	20.6235 485 866	21.5864 435 000	22.5936 764 435	76
20	23.0497 990 699	24.1846 838 717	25.3747 138 364	26.6225 329 833	80
21	26.9650 047 482	28.3607 319 815	29.8277 992 054	31.3698 066 900	84
22	31.5452 416 251	33.2578 719 158	35.0623 700 103	36.9636 041 913	88
23	36.9034 709 424	39.0006 169 476	41.2155 714 967	43.5548 758 178	92
24	43.1718 413 757	45.7349 804 626	48.4486 169 447	51.3214 890 433	96
25	50.5049 481 843	53.6321 884 529	56.9510 114 409	60.4730 282 929	100
26	59.0836 459 557	62.8930 330 603	66.9455 168 936	71.2564 506 425	104
27	69.1195 089 773	73.7529 778 595	78.6939 883 728	83.9627 500 308	108
28	80.8600 492 401	86.4881 446 873	92.5042 346 877	98.9348 098 197	112
29	94.5948 207 656	101.4223 342 373	108.7380 829 477	116.5766 556 058	116
30	110.6625 608 043	118.9352 589 227	127.8208 583 970	137.3643 579 747	120
31	129.4595 440 284	139.4721 973 360	150.2525 278 949	161.8588 794 106	124
32	151.4493 557 553	163.5553 157 737	176.6207 989 990	190.7212 120 403	128
33	177.1743 252 368	191.7969 446 870	207.6165 178 456	224.7302 147 066	132
34	207.2689 009 905	224.9151 476 200	244.0517 692 516	264.8036 307 121	136
35	242.4752 980 455	263.7519 784 868	286.8811 532 574	312.0228 534 016	140
36	283.6618 030 071	309.2948 913 928	337.2267 955 553	367.6621 078 913	144
37	331.8441 883 929	362.7018 473 586	396.4077 470 730	433.2228 364 217	148
38	388.2107 643 777	425.3307 563 049	465.9745 429 800	510.4742 152 346	152
39	454.1516 857 914	498.7740 028 798	547.7498 265 579	601.5008 963 325	156
40	531.2932 371 615	584.8989 339 730	643.8761 022 768	708.7592 624 488	160
41	621.5379 413 635	685.8953 373 423	756.8718 692 042	835.1437 132 843	164
42	727.1114 810 689	804.3311 185 273	889.6976 054 353	984.0647 717 655	168
43	850.6175 902 027	943.2175 916 782	1045.8333 323 309	1159.5411 180 448	172
44	995.1022 691 852	1106.0860 443 646	1229.3697 907 383	1366.3080 348 100	176
45	1164.1289 076 818	1297.0775 230 786	1445.1156 180 033	1609.9451 903 302	180
46	1361.8661 675 950	1521.0481 222 935	1698.7233 338 010	1897.0272 075 051	184
47	1593.1907 937 354	1783.6924 541 266	1996.8374 356 005	2235.3010 820 675	188
48	1863.8078 877 645	2091.6884 379 114	2347.2684 838 523	2633.8952 376 247	192
49	2180.3916 116 968	2452.8670 910 562	2759.1977 379 116	3103.5658 589 516	196
50	2550.7497 910 957	2876.4116 382 428	3243.4177 041 401	3656.9871 509 150	200
51	2984.0164 775 316	3373.0910 014 598	3812.6148 985 218	4309.0933 557 554	204
52	3490.8772 194 213	3955.5336 075 194	4481.7022 321 472	5077.4817 581 651	208
53	4083.8325 970 491	4638.5484 748 097	5268.2097 280 322	5982.8875 533 795	212
54	4777.5065 212 649	5439.5017 431 421	6192.7438 060 150	7049.7433 927 403	216
55	5589.0068 993 575	6378.7582 202 339	7279.5271 689 501	8306.8387 062 385	220
56	6538.3475 631 125	7480.1991 714 591	8557.0334 351 651	9788.0965 940 577	224
57	7648.9418 649 623	8771.8295 180 414	10058.7331 444 900	11533.4892 517 718	228
58	8948.1801 156 685	10286.4898 821 370	11823.9706 831 424	13590.1166 322 258	232
59	10468.1051 047 365	12062.6915 830 589	13898.9951 028 171	16013.4774 521 185	236
60	12246.2023 637 557	14145.5958 150 198	16338.1718 413 390	18868.9668 417 887	240

TABLE 1. FUTURE WORTH OF ONE DOLLAR WITH INTEREST
Payable at beginning of each period

QUARTERLY Compounding

QUARTERS	17% Nominal Annual Rate	17¼% Nominal Annual Rate	17½% Nominal Annual Rate	17¾% Nominal Annual Rate	QUARTERS
1	1.0425 000 000	1.0431 250 000	1.0437 500 000	1.0443 750 000	1
2	1.0868 062 500	1.0881 097 656	1.0894 140 625	1.0907 191 406	2
3	1.1329 955 156	1.1350 344 993	1.1370 759 277	1.1391 198 025	3
YEARS					
1	1.1811 478 250	1.1839 828 620	1.1868 229 996	1.1896 682 437	4
2	1.3951 101 846	1.4018 154 176	1.4085 488 323	1.4153 105 301	8
3	1.6478 313 602	1.6597 254 302	1.6716 981 502	1.6837 499 927	12
4	1.9463 324 272	1.9650 864 651	1.9840 098 130	2.0031 038 967	16
5	2.2989 063 131	2.3266 286 971	2.3546 684 775	2.3830 290 948	20
6	2.7153 481 917	2.7546 885 037	2.7945 747 054	2.8350 140 379	24
7	3.2072 276 109	3.2615 039 787	3.3166 655 344	3.3727 261 714	28
8	3.7882 099 170	3.8615 648 153	3.9362 949 381	4.0124 252 210	32
9	4.4744 359 043	4.5720 265 620	4.6716 853 657	4.7734 548 657	36
10	5.2849 702 366	5.4132 010 942	5.5444 636 388	5.6788 276 666	40
11	6.2423 311 004	6.4091 373 244	6.5802 969 668	6.7559 209 365	44
12	7.3731 158 024	7.5883 087 526	7.8096 477 842	8.0373 045 953	48
13	8.7087 396 937	8.9844 275 150	9.2686 696 088	9.5617 260 422	52
14	10.2863 089 481	10.6374 082 031	11.0002 702 672	11.3752 818 276	56
15	12.1496 514 417	12.5945 090 090	13.0553 737 547	13.5328 115 537	60
16	14.3505 343 753	14.9116 828 226	15.4944 178 400	16.0995 561 538	64
17	16.9501 024 656	17.6551 769 063	18.3891 314 576	19.1531 306 942	68
18	20.0205 766 614	20.9034 268 835	21.8246 441 560	22.7858 713 548	72
19	23.6472 605 797	24.7492 991 881	25.9019 896 418	27.1076 275 565	76
20	27.9309 104 018	29.3027 460 864	30.7410 770 416	32.2490 836 667	80
21	32.9905 340 725	34.6939 491 773	36.4842 172 646	38.3657 107 275	84
22	38.9666 975 666	41.0770 412 427	43.3003 081 711	45.6424 677 005	88
23	46.0254 300 797	48.6345 128 550	51.3898 016 260	54.2993 943 885	92
24	54.3628 366 351	57.5824 297 244	60.9905 985 132	64.5982 651 576	96
25	64.2105 462 545	68.1766 099 488	72.3850 450 732	76.8505 046 577	100
26	75.8421 470 531	80.7199 377 719	85.9082 363 180	91.4266 049 056	104
27	89.5807 870 381	95.5710 229 476	101.9578 707 149	108.7673 284 879	108
28	105.8081 517 753	113.1544 532 784	121.0059 459 519	129.3970 366 569	112
29	124.9750 683 408	133.9729 334 460	143.6126 397 408	153.9395 453 429	116
30	147.6140 301 548	158.6216 571 785	170.4427 838 737	183.1369 885 481	120
31	174.3539 906 626	187.8053 236 490	202.2854 160 126	217.8722 595 272	124
32	205.9378 368 580	222.3582 846 019	240.0769 842 019	259.1957 083 483	128
33	243.2430 280 981	263.2683 982 032	284.9288 865 188	308.3569 031 319	132
34	287.3059 735 940	311.7052 715 915	338.1601 557 632	366.8424 153 897	136
35	339.3508 258 313	369.0536 995 745	401.3362 503 989	436.4207 720 407	140
36	400.8234 898 558	436.9532 554 719	476.3150 925 357	519.1959 333 991	144
37	473.4317 932 678	517.3451 659 950	565.3017 068 649	617.6709 142 365	148
38	559.1929 329 226	612.5278 103 017	670.9130 674 051	734.8234 717 402	152
39	660.4895 164 987	725.2224 299 253	796.2550 591 102	874.1961 490 736	156
40	780.1357 558 735	858.6509 282 047	945.0138 176 782	1040.0033 973 402	160
41	921.4556 512 852	1016.6279 834 764	1121.5641 337 345	1237.2590 151 825	164
42	1088.3753 383 855	1203.6701 095 150	1331.0981 094 120	1471.9277 596 261	168
43	1285.5321 637 602	1425.1247 812 257	1579.7778 509 380	1751.1057 126 855	172
44	1518.4035 192 431	1687.3233 172 519	1874.9166 877 088	2083.2348 577 887	176
45	1793.4590 142 857	1997.7618 903 610	2225.1942 472 556	2478.3583 545 337	180
46	2118.3402 140 202	2365.3158 406 411	2640.9117 111 599	2948.4242 309 611	184
47	2502.0729 364 828	2800.4934 186 509	3134.2947 586 456	3507.6466 766 059	188
48	2955.3180 070 157	3315.7362 129 622	3719.8531 070 010	4172.9358 613 681	192
49	3490.6674 362 854	3925.7748 512 208	4414.8072 224 209	4964.4092 773 740	196
50	4122.9942 503 032	4648.0501 441 064	5239.5947 502 490	5906.0000 661 493	200
51	4869.8656 913 942	5503.2117 125 640	6218.4715 580 362	7026.1807 261 399	204
52	5752.0312 696 226	6515.7083 539 004	7380.2250 672 664	8358.8240 845 665	208
53	6793.9992 236 714	7714.4870 251 242	8759.0208 518 551	9944.2275 682 986	212
54	8024.7174 063 565	9133.8204 272 425	10395.4074 007 190	11830.3317 463 869	216
55	9478.3775 110 711	10814.2868 508 836	12337.5085 931 021	14074.1699 914 170	220
56	11195.3649 821 008	12803.9302 967 225	14642.4389 557 201	16743.5930 955 865	224
57	13223.3809 991 269	15159.6340 381 830	17377.9833 224 887	19919.3209 916 848	228
58	15618.7677 067 816	17948.7468 961 356	20624.5902 933 213	23697.3836 203 869	232
59	18448.0735 066 554	21251.0087 202 706	24477.7381 168 787	28192.0247 525 608	236
60	21789.9018 985 468	25160.8301 260 435	29050.7425 746 303	33539.1565 744 515	240

TABLE 1. FUTURE WORTH OF ONE DOLLAR WITH INTEREST
Payable at beginning of each period

QUARTERS	18% Nominal Annual Rate	18¼% Nominal Annual Rate	18½% Nominal Annual Rate	18¾% Nominal Annual Rate	QUARTERS
1	1.0450 000 000	1.0456 250 000	1.0462 500 000	1.0468 750 000	1
2	1.0920 250 000	1.0933 316 406	1.0946 390 625	1.0959 472 656	2
3	1.1411 661 250	1.1432 148 967	1.1452 661 191	1.1473 197 937	3
YEARS					
1	1.1925 186 006	1.1953 740 764	1.1982 346 772	1.2011 004 090	4
2	1.4221 006 128	1.4289 191 825	1.4357 663 415	1.4426 421 926	8
3	1.6958 814 328	1.7080 929 480	1.7203 850 187	1.7327 581 276	12
4	2.0223 701 530	2.0418 100 301	2.0614 249 875	2.0812 164 958	16
5	2.4117 140 248	2.4407 267 790	2.4700 709 043	2.4997 499 844	20
6	2.8760 138 340	2.9175 815 191	2.9597 246 126	3.0024 507 287	24
7	3.4296 999 927	3.4876 013 137	3.5464 446 656	3.6062 447 984	28
8	4.0899 810 359	4.1689 881 992	4.2494 729 789	4.3314 621 024	32
9	4.8773 784 615	4.9835 004 181	5.0918 658 830	5.2025 209 029	36
10	5.8163 645 376	5.9571 472 095	6.1012 502 724	6.2487 499 844	40
11	6.9361 228 991	7.1210 193 435	7.3107 296 503	7.5053 761 622	44
12	8.2714 555 734	8.5122 819 207	8.7599 697 823	9.0147 103 784	48
13	9.8638 646 255	10.1753 611 389	10.4964 995 640	10.8275 723 228	52
14	11.7628 420 400	12.1633 629 234	12.5772 697 662	13.0050 015 457	56
15	14.0274 079 289	14.5397 687 203	15.0705 207 778	15.6203 126 760	60
16	16.7279 448 738	17.3804 626 050	18.0580 205 987	18.7615 639 443	64
17	19.9483 854 122	20.7761 544 337	21.6377 464 820	22.5345 221 275	68
18	23.7888 206 565	24.8352 764 172	25.9270 981 702	27.0662 237 447	72
19	28.3686 111 198	29.6874 456 091	31.0667 481 054	32.5092 524 107	76
20	33.8300 964 342	35.4876 028 755	37.2252 548 862	39.0468 763 677	80
21	40.3430 192 587	42.4209 605 106	44.6045 912 704	46.8992 191 767	84
22	48.1098 008 714	50.7089 164 900	53.4467 680 203	56.3306 713 363	88
23	57.3718 324 115	60.6161 242 141	64.0417 708 236	67.6587 923 831	92
24	68.4169 773 027	72.4589 434 969	76.7370 705 870	81.2650 032 058	96
25	81.5885 180 320	86.6155 426 589	91.9490 190 003	97.6074 285 904	100
26	97.2958 253 506	103.5379 743 071	110.1765 030 962	117.2363 224 044	104
27	116.0270 814 938	123.7666 104 088	132.0173 066 170	140.8125 947 932	108
28	138.3644 528 575	147.9473 976 055	158.1877 147 726	169.1300 652 028	112
29	165.0021 836 979	176.8524 837 673	189.5460 053 398	203.1421 904 946	116
30	196.7681 732 035	211.4048 744 409	227.1205 965 135	243.9941 680 944	120
31	234.6497 065 562	252.7079 065 295	272.1437 746 377	293.0614 950 994	124
32	279.8241 396 994	302.0804 803 646	326.0921 079 416	351.9962 816 351	128
33	333.6954 914 955	361.0991 752 118	390.7348 716 809	422.7828 778 493	132
34	397.9380 805 531	431.6485 930 546	468.1920 728 201	507.8046 875 160	136
35	474.5485 629 565	515.9815 382 484	561.0039 772 202	609.9244 178 833	140
36	565.9079 882 255	616.7909 547 189	672.2144 195 249	732.5804 677 976	144
37	674.8558 022 012	737.2959 178 239	805.4706 279 555	879.9026 995 198	148
38	804.7780 968 647	881.3444 267 962	965.1428 378 428	1056.8514 923 006	152
39	959.7128 498 867	1053.5362 801 645	1156.4676 167 071	1269.3847 596 872	156
40	1144.4754 247 487	1259.3699 578 468	1385.7196 013 404	1524.6585 540 779	160
41	1364.8082 319 710	1505.4182 001 967	1660.4172 791 338	1831.2680 129 354	164
42	1627.5592 029 116	1799.5378 906 435	1989.5695 623 986	2199.5367 593 820	168
43	1940.8946 230 905	2151.1209 439 599	2383.9712 422 700	2641.8645 013 722	172
44	2314.5529 398 884	2571.3942 115 930	2856.5570 118 183	3173.1445 332 024	176
45	2760.1474 329 482	3073.7779 807 221	3422.8256 688 192	3811.2651 967 436	180
46	3291.5271 542 581	3674.3145 147 390	4101.3484 102 213	4577.7121 867 341	184
47	3925.2073 559 150	4392.1803 194 289	4914.3778 882 048	5498.2919 799 121	188
48	4680.8827 832 388	5250.2984 926 834	5888.5780 022 705	6604.0007 460 438	192
49	5582.0397 863 575	6276.0707 114 724	7055.8983 614 284	7932.0679 973 137	196
50	6656.6862 746 602	7502.2522 300 957	8454.6220 951 156	9527.2101 160 345	200
51	7938.2222 010 574	8967.9978 304 086	10130.6213 765 735	11443.1359 672 925	204
52	9466.4776 306 553	10720.1121 236 080	12138.8618 344 963	13744.3552 909 114	208
53	11288.9506 569 569	12814.5441 285 739	14545.2051 912 368	16508.3507 617 799	212
54	13462.2836 399 589	15318.1738 520 754	17428.5692 464 149	19828.1868 523 996	216
55	16054.0236 475 406	18310.9479 204 330	20883.5160 441 797	23815.6433 387 585	220
56	19144.7218 145 658	21888.4324 582 451	25023.3531 049 729	28604.9789 555 173	224
57	22830.4368 676 609	26164.8647 334 380	29983.8494 289 697	34357.4519 237 925	228
58	27225.7206 250 804	31276.8010 146 487	35927.6881 402 620	41266.7495 589 271	232
59	32467.1782 608 281	37387.4771 253 743	43049.8017 995 243	49565.5097 746 036	236
60	38717.7139 858 451	44692.0209 373 622	51583.7653 606 624	59533.1540 641 022	240

TABLE 1. FUTURE WORTH OF ONE DOLLAR WITH INTEREST
Payable at beginning of each period

QUARTERLY Compounding

QUARTERS	19% Nominal Annual Rate	19¼% Nominal Annual Rate	19½% Nominal Annual Rate	19¾% Nominal Annual Rate	QUARTERS
1	1.0475 000 000	1.0481 250 000	1.0487 500 000	1.0493 750 000	1
2	1.0972 562 500	1.0985 660 156	1.0998 765 625	1.1011 878 906	2
3	1.1493 759 219	1.1514 345 051	1.1534 955 449	1.1555 590 427	3
YEARS					
1	1.2039 712 782	1.2068 472 907	1.2097 284 527	1.2126 147 705	4
2	1.4495 468 386	1.4564 803 830	1.4634 429 294	1.4704 345 815	8
3	1.7452 127 601	1.7577 494 042	1.7703 685 506	1.7830 706 926	12
4	2.1011 860 374	2.1213 351 062	2.1416 652 075	2.1621 778 586	16
5	2.5297 676 391	2.5601 275 255	2.5908 333 377	2.6218 888 077	20
6	3.0457 675 779	3.0896 829 680	3.1342 048 050	3.1793 410 947	24
7	3.6670 166 838	3.7287 755 190	3.7915 367 293	3.8553 159 717	28
8	4.4149 827 639	4.5000 626 327	4.5867 298 610	4.6750 130 921	32
9	5.3155 124 413	5.4308 883 962	5.5486 976 179	5.6689 899 276	36
10	6.3997 243 080	6.5542 529 469	6.7124 173 840	6.8743 009 198	40
11	7.7050 842 550	7.9099 824 115	8.1202 022 960	8.3358 788 319	44
12	9.2767 001 389	9.5461 408 427	9.8232 397 595	10.1082 097 963	48
13	11.1688 805 234	11.5207 342 125	11.8834 526 351	12.2573 645 019	52
14	13.4470 113 594	13.9037 668 710	14.3757 507 695	14.8634 612 419	56
15	16.1898 154 538	16.7797 233 786	17.3907 547 353	18.0236 526 421	60
16	19.4920 728 052	20.2505 636 980	21.0380 908 178	21.8557 474 115	64
17	23.4678 958 093	24.4393 379 338	25.4503 770 536	26.5026 021 306	68
18	28.2546 725 134	29.4945 487 715	30.7880 452 546	32.1374 467 991	72
19	34.0178 141 800	35.5954 162 749	37.2451 743 486	38.9703 426 735	76
20	40.9564 712 187	42.9582 316 922	45.0565 471 367	47.2560 131 357	80
21	49.3104 150 023	51.8440 255 304	54.5061 870 533	57.3033 395 213	84
22	59.3683 233 771	62.5678 217 497	65.9376 853 286	69.4868 759 002	88
23	71.4777 561 787	75.5098 061 627	79.7666 940 496	84.2608 120 697	92
24	86.0571 654 668	91.1288 049 877	96.4960 393 725	102.1759 052 865	96
25	103.6103 555 023	109.9785 514 029	116.7340 044 053	123.9000 119 355	100
26	124.7438 921 451	132.7273 167 942	141.2164 465 310	150.2429 845 331	104
27	150.1880 632 691	160.1816 026 731	170.8335 533 630	182.1868 622 026	108
28	180.8221 144 991	193.3147 332 038	206.6622 101 853	220.9224 800 905	112
29	217.7046 323 138	233.3013 620 168	250.0051 557 667	267.8938 624 842	116
30	262.1101 244 290	281.5591 166 633	302.4383 502 619	324.8520 545 637	120
31	315.5730 615 286	339.7988 571 131	365.8682 775 106	393.9203 995 780	124
32	379.9409 022 427	410.0853 300 852	442.6012 652 583	477.6736 949 134	128
33	457.4379 337 000	494.9103 695 635	535.4273 438 003	579.2341 779 118	132
34	550.7421 337 175	597.2812 386 402	647.7216 921 685	702.3879 196 906	136
35	663.0777 106 706	720.8272 446 306	783.5673 604 711	851.7259 660 089	140
36	798.3265 188 382	869.9284 072 353	947.9037 305 978	1032.8154 867 660	144
37	961.1621 992 779	1049.8707 413 629	1146.7061 133 595	1252.4073 144 114	148
38	1157.2116 815 876	1267.0336 597 845	1387.2030 122 583	1518.6876 080 863	152
39	1393.2496 273 874	1529.1161 395 191	1678.1389 536 511	1841.5830 252 787	156
40	1677.4325 346 872	1845.4096 701 231	2030.0924 398 777	2233.1307 774 798	160
41	2019.5805 928 213	2227.1276 605 942	2455.8605 862 059	2707.9273 651 389	164
42	2431.5170 276 944	2687.8029 832 003	2970.9244 270 882	3283.6727 202 979	168
43	2927.4766 637 109	3243.7677 481 736	3594.0118 103 795	3981.8300 419 870	172
44	3524.5978 206 035	3914.7323 184 985	4347.7783 464 882	4828.4259 223 713	176
45	4243.5145 430 863	4724.4840 923 416	5259.6311 719 398	5855.0205 915 352	180
46	5109.0696 283 474	5701.7308 267 325	6362.7254 795 971	7099.8844 506 380	184
47	6151.1730 906 706	6881.1184 004 640	7697.1700 496 221	8609.4247 533 968	188
48	7405.8357 281 831	8304.4590 984 909	9311.4856 145 815	10439.9156 211 255	192
49	8916.4135 075 337	10022.2139 636 280	11264.3690 852 088	12659.5958 845 239	196
50	10735.1057 673 046	12095.2817 686 817	13626.8277 845 061	15351.2129 576 173	200
51	12924.7590 118 882	14597.1580 326 195	16484.7612 914 616	18615.1075 768 705	204
52	15561.0386 275 055	17616.5406 233 850	19942.0847 708 556	22572.9544 013 989	208
53	18735.0435 659 181	21260.4743 225 953	24124.5073 541 936	27372.2979 200 369	212
54	22556.4543 485 178	25658.1458 349 275	29184.1029 546 265	33192.0527 592 447	216
55	27157.3231 728 343	30965.4637 849 133	35304.8397 118 123	40249.1734 377 191	220
56	32696.6370 919 118	37370.5860 736 639	42709.2691 186 920	48806.7422 093 497	224
57	39365.8119 512 156	45100.5905 543 562	51666.6180 484 756	59183.7765 010 489	228
58	47395.3069 308 712	54429.5255 188 719	62502.5779 099 264	71767.1215 567 243	232
59	57062.5882 645 390	65688.1254 057 852	75611.1468 670 376	87025.8716 330 202	236
60	68701.7173 282 067	79275.5361 762 265	91468.9557 091 176	105528.8573 542 811	240

QUARTERLY
Compounding

TABLE 1. FUTURE WORTH OF ONE DOLLAR WITH INTEREST
Payable at beginning of each period

	20% Nominal Annual Rate	20¼% Nominal Annual Rate	20½% Nominal Annual Rate	20¾% Nominal Annual Rate	
QUARTERS					QUARTERS
1	1.0500 000 000	1.0506 250 000	1.0512 500 000	1.0518 750 000	1
2	1.1025 000 000	1.1038 128 906	1.1051 265 625	1.1064 410 156	2
3	1.1576 250 000	1.1596 934 182	1.1617 642 988	1.1638 376 433	3
YEARS					
1	1.2155 062 500	1.2184 028 975	1.2213 047 191	1.2242 117 211	4
2	1.4774 554 438	1.4845 056 207	1.4915 852 170	1.4986 943 380	8
3	1.7958 563 260	1.8087 259 496	1.8216 800 645	1.8347 191 748	12
4	2.1828 745 884	2.2037 569 378	2.2248 264 596	2.2460 847 187	16
5	2.6532 977 051	2.6850 638 384	2.7171 910 544	2.7496 832 391	20
6	3.2250 999 437	3.2714 895 607	3.3185 182 575	3.3661 944 505	24
7	3.9201 291 385	3.9859 923 599	4.0529 220 084	4.1209 347 016	28
8	4.7649 414 686	4.8565 446 408	4.9498 527 752	5.0448 965 635	32
9	5.7918 161 360	5.9172 280 622	6.0452 785 535	6.1760 215 045	36
10	7.0399 887 121	7.2095 678 162	7.3831 272 259	7.5607 579 153	40
11	8.5571 502 795	8.7841 583 171	9.0170 481 230	9.2559 684 600	44
12	10.4012 696 469	10.7026 439 457	11.0125 634 253	11.3312 650 785	48
13	12.6428 082 638	13.0401 323 945	13.4496 956 812	13.8718 675 235	52
14	15.3674 124 622	15.8881 350 934	16.4261 768 065	16.9821 028 152	56
15	18.6791 858 941	19.3581 498 338	20.0613 672 513	20.7896 893 146	60
16	22.7046 671 992	23.5860 258 479	24.5010 424 965	25.4509 813 361	64
17	27.5976 648 848	28.7372 822 338	29.9232 388 249	31.1573 896 640	68
18	33.5451 341 529	35.0135 879 403	36.5453 927 888	38.1432 416 243	72
19	40.7743 202 199	42.6606 569 986	44.6330 606 759	46.6954 034 756	76
20	49.5614 410 668	51.9778 680 968	54.5105 676 333	57.1650 602 543	80
21	60.2422 413 758	63.3299 850 955	66.5740 134 937	69.9821 367 982	84
22	73.2248 209 062	77.1614 373 397	81.3071 568 522	85.6729 521 330	88
23	89.0052 274 667	94.0137 188 307	99.3008 143 637	104.8818 321 788	92
24	108.1864 102 684	114.5465 874 290	121.2765 531 971	128.3975 682 793	96
25	131.5012 578 463	139.5638 940 234	148.1156 267 411	157.1858 080 427	100
26	159.8406 007 950	170.0450 528 658	180.8943 139 177	192.4287 085 898	104
27	194.2872 492 701	207.1833 851 189	220.9270 792 539	235.5734 805 235	108
28	236.1573 657 832	252.4328 367 448	269.8192 844 792	288.3918 160 272	112
29	287.0507 540 930	307.5648 997 166	329.5315 654 503	353.0526 414 375	116
30	348.9119 856 672	374.7379 649 870	402.4584 559 910	432.2111 817 980	120
31	424.1046 992 784	456.5818 223 471	491.5244 115 609	529.1179 947 291	124
32	515.5019 126 273	556.3006 152 981	600.3010 834 133	647.7524 509 697	128
33	626.5957 966 854	677.7982 815 658	733.1505 460 794	792.9861 428 207	132
34	761.6311 070 948	825.8313 901 870	895.4002 217 691	970.7829 306 771	136
35	925.7673 708 682	1006.1953 586 584	1093.5565 163 683	1188.4438 423 372	140
36	1125.2760 253 363	1225.9513 404 505	1335.5657 340 903	1454.9068 816 075	144
37	1367.7800 417 715	1493.7026 654 110	1631.1327 337 702	1781.1140 575 108	148
38	1662.5451 893 985	1819.9316 555 551	1992.1101 053 023	2180.4607 057 447	152
39	2020.8340 686 213	2217.4100 023 983	2432.9734 726 583	2669.3455 532 774	156
40	2456.3364 406 221	2701.6987 718 896	2971.4019 837 075	3267.8441 138 744	160
41	2985.6922 956 789	3291.7576 118 693	3628.9872 651 730	4000.5330 667 931	164
42	3629.1276 459 746	4010.6870 122 019	4432.0992 726 659	4897.4994 708 453	168
43	4411.2273 357 299	4886.6326 766 721	5412.9437 574 175	5995.5762 560 807	172
44	5361.8743 967 505	5953.8874 123 240	6610.8537 553 899	7339.8547 271 867	176
45	6517.3918 409 652	7254.2336 746 234	8073.8668 890 224	8985.5361 878 796	180
46	7921.9305 163 922	8838.5793 283 751	9860.6517 332 960	11000.1987 211 866	184
47	9629.1560 547 405	10768.9506 635 635	12042.8604 957 007	13466.5722 084 360	188
48	11704.2993 667 624	13120.9206 916 271	14708.0023 553 808	16485.9355 400 315	192
49	14226.6490 321 707	15986.5677 886 763	17962.9526 857 939	20182.2755 207 014	196
50	17292.5808 151 600	19478.0805 149 620	21938.2388 849 037	24707.3782 500 501	200
51	21019.2400 594 570	23732.1497 373 612	26793.2746 798 209	30247.0620 503 071	204
52	25549.0176 625 204	28915.3200 041 401	32722.7528 077 617	37028.8078 895 328	208
53	31054.9906 501 539	35230.5096 754 708	39964.4524 274 713	45331.1006 351 444	212
54	37747.5352 289 537	42924.9550 693 448	48808.7743 476 393	55494.8647 259 710	216
55	45882.3649 928 884	52299.8896 319 728	59610.3864 463 609	67937.4638 560 220	220
56	55770.3014 136 370	63722.3370 670 445	72802.4462 768 825	83169.8395 514 475	224
57	67789.1499 326 597	77639.4801 185 907	88913.9712 031 162	101817.4924 173 355	228
58	82398.1354 253 349	94596.1675 376 546	108591.0526 281 165	124646.1676 259 630	232
59	100155.4485 978 410	115256.2446 212 121	132622.7650 314 317	152593.2993 925 746	236
60	121739.5737 422 294	140428.5424 025 967	161972.8087 986 896	186806.5056 711 927	240

TABLE 1. FUTURE WORTH OF ONE DOLLAR WITH INTEREST

Payable at beginning of each period

QUARTERLY Compounding

QUARTERS	21% Nominal Annual Rate	21¼% Nominal Annual Rate	21½% Nominal Annual Rate	21¾% Nominal Annual Rate	QUARTERS
1	1.0525 000 000	1.0531 250 000	1.0537 500 000	1.0543 750 000	1
2	1.1077 562 500	1.1090 722 656	1.1103 890 625	1.1117 066 406	2
3	1.1659 134 531	1.1679 917 297	1.1700 724 746	1.1721 556 892	3
YEARS					
1	1.2271 239 094	1.2300 412 904	1.2329 638 701	1.2358 916 548	4
2	1.5058 330 891	1.5130 015 760	1.5201 999 050	1.5274 281 824	8
3	1.8478 437 872	1.8610 544 109	1.8743 515 582	1.8877 357 440	12
4	2.2675 332 921	2.2891 737 691	2.3110 077 512	2.3330 368 525	16
5	2.7825 443 181	2.8157 782 568	2.8493 890 608	2.8833 807 763	20
6	3.4145 266 618	3.4635 235 205	3.5131 937 639	3.5635 462 391	24
7	4.1900 473 060	4.2602 769 404	4.3316 409 796	4.4041 570 585	28
8	5.1417 072 308	5.2403 165 451	5.3407 568 262	5.4430 609 550	32
9	6.3095 118 781	6.4458 057 251	6.5849 602 058	6.7270 336 109	36
10	7.7425 528 823	7.9286 071 916	8.1190 180 200	8.3138 847 014	40
11	9.5010 717 618	9.7525 142 209	10.0104 558 795	10.2750 607 215	44
12	11.6589 923 240	11.9959 951 767	12.3425 304 228	12.6988 617 983	48
13	14.3070 282 404	14.7555 693 865	15.2178 940 772	15.6944 173 221	52
14	17.5564 964 265	18.1499 596 085	18.7631 135 764	19.3965 993 955	56
15	21.5439 965 304	22.3251 997 371	23.1342 411 307	23.9720 953 246	60
16	26.4371 532 468	27.4609 174 926	28.5236 834 768	29.6269 125 600	64
17	32.4416 628 460	33.7780 623 876	35.1686 711 696	36.6156 539 907	68
18	39.8099 401 395	41.5484 114 458	43.3617 009 122	45.2529 812 025	72
19	48.8517 293 775	51.1062 616 279	53.4634 105 717	55.9277 818 234	76
20	59.9471 251 354	62.8628 119 992	65.9184 536 083	69.1206 788 275	80
21	73.5625 505 543	77.3238 543 884	81.2750 716 732	85.4256 701 377	84
22	90.2703 646 227	95.1115 336 289	100.2092 269 144	105.5768 728 297	88
23	110.7729 227 400	116.9911 135 548	123.5543 562 381	130.4815 760 712	92
24	135.9321 020 099	143.9039 002 798	152.3380 572 375	161.2610 909 728	96
25	166.8055 324 333	177.0077 391 907	187.8273 206 181	199.3012 365 788	100
26	204.6910 570 714	217.7268 279 211	231.5843 001 434	246.3147 350 810	104
27	251.1812 901 756	267.8129 883 661	285.5350 749 638	304.4183 255 433	108
28	308.2305 667 720	329.4210 337 899	352.0544 310 823	376.2280 681 101	112
29	378.2370 980 981	405.2014 734 808	434.0703 938 399	464.9771 296 824	116
30	464.1437 865 036	498.4145 433 036	535.1931 126 933	574.6613 542 519	120
31	569.5619 378 245	613.0704 679 887	659.8737 714 876	710.2191 720 615	124
32	698.9230 717 967	754.1019 895 378	813.6005 190 838	877.7539 478 367	128
33	857.6652 122 428	927.5765 842 881	1003.1400 447 410	1084.8087 791 077	132
34	1052.4614 882 159	1140.9574 986 626	1236.8354 318 358	1340.7061 171 635	136
35	1291.5006 559 272	1403.4248 339 221	1524.9734 007 373	1656.9675 017 547	140
36	1584.8313 339 122	1726.2704 936 669	1880.2371 060 026	2047.8323 077 096	144
37	1944.7844 222 323	2123.3839 855 725	2318.2644 189 595	2530.8988 595 480	148
38	2386.4914 631 772	2611.8499 775 827	2858.3362 699 609	3127.9167 796 828	152
39	2928.5207 340 774	3212.6833 167 011	3524.2253 495 143	3865.7662 449 493	156
40	3593.6578 120 011	3951.7331 324 527	4345.2425 261 109	4777.6682 415 779	160
41	4409.8634 233 592	4860.7949 214 739	5357.5270 416 021	5904.6803 092 156	164
42	5411.4488 440 547	5978.9784 574 754	6605.6372 754 843	7297.5451 184 789	168
43	6640.5182 611 106	7354.3903 769 787	8144.5120 997 875	9018.9751 125 255	172
44	8148.7387 291 095	9046.2038 292 466	10041.8891 587 902	11146.4760 765 068	176
45	9999.5121 260 586	11127.2042 311 541	12381.2865 205 343	13775.8367 634 910	180
46	12270.6404 123 623	13686.9206 507 946	15265.6789 454 180	17025.4416 940 195	184
47	15057.5962 338 322	16835.4775 386 126	18822.0305 925 463	21041.6013 090 882	188
48	18477.5363 568 387	20708.3325 157 344	23206.8836 828 959	26005.1394 617 355	192
49	22674.2266 505 444	25472.1040 492 425	28613.2491 190 794	32139.5348 429 219	196
50	27824.0856 503 565	31331.7397 333 874	35279.1023 705 572	39720.9829 018 335	200
51	34143.6007 591 372	38539.3335 714 614	43497.8585 931 488	49090.8312 892 157	204
52	41898.4288 450 254	47404.9715 965 706	53631.2880 729 251	60670.9487 180 137	208
53	51414.5638 026 145	58310.0724 330 051	66125.4405 018 944	74982.7192 099 818	212
54	63092.0405 342 831	71723.7967 375 615	81530.2790 345 810	92670.5169 265 572	216
55	77421.7514 333 399	88223.2314 899 205	100523.8883 704 102	114530.7185 164 353	220
56	95006.0822 925 639	108518.2175 032 292	123942.3224 446 545	141547.5592 338 238	224
57	116584.2351 209 651	133481.8882 872 544	152816.4055 529 762	174937.4472 157 677	228
58	143063.3023 776 870	164188.2341 110 226	188417.1068 083 682	216203.7311 276 837	232
59	175556.3989 073 934	201958.3073 509 010	232311.4852 071 892	267204.3870 394 294	236
60	215429.4545 498 952	248417.0569 765 743	286431.6678 742 949	330235.6720 705 781	240

QUARTERLY
Compounding

TABLE 1. FUTURE WORTH OF ONE DOLLAR WITH INTEREST
Payable at beginning of each period

QUARTERS	22% Nominal Annual Rate	22¼% Nominal Annual Rate	22½% Nominal Annual Rate	22¾% Nominal Annual Rate	QUARTERS
1	1.0550 000 000	1.0556 250 000	1.0562 500 000	1.0568 750 000	1
2	1.1130 250 000	1.1143 441 406	1.1156 640 625	1.1169 847 656	2
3	1.1742 413 750	1.1763 295 334	1.1784 201 660	1.1805 132 742	3
YEARS					
1	1.2388 246 506	1.2417 628 637	1.2447 063 004	1.2476 549 666	4
2	1.5346 865 150	1.5419 750 098	1.5492 937 741	1.5566 429 158	8
3	1.9012 074 858	1.9147 673 040	1.9284 157 218	1.9421 532 652	12
4	2.3552 626 993	2.3776 869 308	2.4003 111 986	2.4231 371 672	16
5	2.9177 574 906	2.9525 233 323	2.9876 824 717	3.0232 391 216	20
6	3.6145 899 039	3.6663 338 283	3.7187 871 960	3.7719 593 053	24
7	4.4778 430 749	4.5527 171 941	4.6287 978 525	4.7061 037 613	28
8	5.5472 623 828	5.6533 951 408	5.7614 938 501	5.8715 937 313	32
9	6.8720 853 833	7.0201 761 399	7.1713 676 947	7.3257 230 809	36
10	8.5133 087 740	8.7173 940 275	8.9262 465 517	9.1399 747 861	40
11	10.5464 967 676	10.8249 361 720	11.1105 553 214	11.4035 349 368	44
12	13.0652 601 734	13.4420 037 408	13.8293 782 090	14.2276 770 011	48
13	16.1855 663 697	16.6917 810 596	17.2135 141 867	17.7512 318 742	52
14	20.0510 786 021	20.7272 338 496	21.4257 695 594	22.1474 126 118	56
15	24.8397 704 451	25.7383 092 626	26.6687 903 605	27.6323 293 433	60
16	30.7721 199 432	31.9608 766 178	33.1948 113 846	34.4756 129 450	64
17	38.1212 607 377	39.6878 296 768	41.3177 908 694	43.0136 697 187	68
18	47.2255 575 147	49.2828 730 353	51.4285 146 119	53.6662 186 578	72
19	58.5041 847 888	61.1976 415 539	64.0133 961 553	66.9569 242 492	76
20	72.4764 262 811	75.9929 586 304	79.6778 775 015	83.5391 390 903	80
21	89.7855 834 662	94.3652 339 334	99.1755 561 250	104.2280 217 947	84
22	111.2285 940 687	117.1792 431 271	123.4444 395 499	130.0406 090 550	88
23	137.7927 241 866	145.5088 325 170	153.6520 716 514	162.2458 117 522	92
24	170.7010 233 992	180.6874 645 665	191.2517 016 470	202.4267 928 489	96
25	211.4686 356 738	224.3709 834 430	238.0521 979 934	252.5587 934 786	100
26	261.9725 587 067	278.6155 549 416	296.3050 706 555	315.1062 330 517	104
27	324.5380 635 132	345.9744 493 882	368.8127 882 718	393.1438 566 857	108
28	402.0457 531 462	429.6182 230 550	459.0636 012 130	490.5078 853 972	112
29	498.0641 896 767	533.4839 549 779	571.3993 566 931	611.9845 993 911	116
30	617.0141 957 650	662.4605 636 955	711.2243 792 941	763.5456 249 365	120
31	764.3723 954 992	822.6189 266 929	885.2654 658 727	952.6414 912 070	124
32	946.9233 658 018	1021.4976 341 812	1101.8955 028 576	1188.5678 879 302	128
33	1173.0720 078 080	1268.4578 275 299	1371.5362 747 386	1482.9226 285 629	132
34	1453.2305 202 307	1575.1238 244 536	1707.1598 423 312	1850.1757 826 669	136
35	1800.2977 915 024	1955.9302 710 069	2124.9126 114 609	2308.3810 043 983	140
36	2230.2532 825 789	2428.8015 746 116	2644.8921 151 871	2880.0630 250 311	144
37	2762.8927 435 961	3015.9955 987 587	3292.1138 795 300	3593.3249 374 115	148
38	3422.7396 377 998	3745.1513 317 577	4097.7148 873 339	4483.2297 049 069	152
39	4240.1742 359 777	4650.5898 428 829	5100.4515 373 189	5593.5238 079 076	156
40	5252.8323 664 742	5774.9297 614 029	6348.5641 631 511	6978.7877 599 456	160
41	6507.3382 211 890	7171.0933 184 475	7902.0978 120 758	8707.1192 098 110	164
42	8061.4509 983 632	8904.7973 752 999	9835.7909 327 043	10863.4805 272 328	168
43	9986.7242 165 779	11057.6466 898 237	12242.6709 429 018	13553.8754 347 808	172
44	12371.8001 384 903	13730.9750 198 389	15238.5296 557 908	16910.5600 034 016	176
45	15326.4909 841 676	17050.6148 626 500	18967.4938 706 941	21098.5441 768 796	180
46	18986.8348 387 686	21172.8203 404 619	23608.9591 227 789	26323.7034 311 222	184
47	23521.3590 356 121	26291.6220 195 360	29386.2201 649 231	32842.8993 261 542	188
48	29138.8393 895 173	32647.9598 514 873	36577.2133 828 696	40976.6064 630 792	192
49	36097.9125 263 368	40541.0241 206 234	45527.8879 470 506	51124.6665 696 453	196
50	44718.9838 737 310	50342.3382 111 914	56668.8489 695 050	63785.9441 633 469	200
51	55398.9795 736 798	62513.2460 647 619	70536.0733 461 524	79582.8500 371 153	204
52	68629.6215 153 454	77626.6274 553 915	87796.6948 961 880	99291.9381 080 408	208
53	85020.0668 962 738	96393.8632 118 941	109281.0992 875 434	123882.0797 276 434	212
54	105324.9546 688 905	119698.3196 294 714	136022.8727 928 167	154562.0920 496 807	216
55	130479.1501 697 822	148636.9281 685 891	169308.5267 574 702	192840.1617 997 958	220
56	161640.7876 229 274	184571.8175 809 271	210739.3899 586 776	240597.9856 368 555	224
57	200244.5922 537 228	229194.4287 659 616	262308.6464 143 253	300183.2717 430 019	228
58	248067.9370 382 637	284605.1302 188 817	326497.2248 292 413	374525.1498 919 016	232
59	307312.6754 326 915	353412.0815 371 940	406393.1527 930 544	467278.1633 935 983	236
60	380706.5177 755 381	438853.9984 518 028	505840.1177 022 422	583001.9213 596 629	240

TABLE 2. FUTURE WORTH OF ONE DOLLAR PER PERIOD WITH INTEREST
Payable at end of each period

QUARTERLY Compounding

QUARTERS	5% Nominal Annual Rate	5¼% Nominal Annual Rate	5½% Nominal Annual Rate	5¾% Nominal Annual Rate	QUARTERS
1	1.0000 000 000	1.0000 000 000	1.0000 000 000	1.0000 000 000	1
2	2.0125 000 000	2.0131 250 000	2.0137 500 000	2.0143 750 000	2
3	3.0376 562 500	3.0395 472 656	3.0414 390 625	3.0433 316 406	3
YEARS					
1	4.0756 269 531	4.0794 413 235	4.0832 588 496	4.0870 795 330	4
2	8.3588 880 945	8.3773 068 168	8.3957 714 882	8.4142 822 156	8
3	12.8603 614 178	12.9052 914 927	12.9504 093 259	12.9957 157 076	12
4	17.5911 638 162	17.6757 165 459	17.7607 664 360	17.8463 165 185	16
5	22.5629 785 367	22.7015 628 809	22.8412 001 280	22.9818 987 043	20
6	27.7880 840 331	27.9965 064 345	28.2068 738 003	28.4192 054 248	24
7	33.2793 842 895	33.5749 553 896	33.8738 021 971	34.1759 635 297	28
8	39.0504 406 876	39.4520 893 815	39.8588 992 073	40.2709 413 529	32
9	45.1155 054 982	45.6439 008 038	46.1800 283 471	46.7240 099 009	36
10	51.4895 570 790	52.1672 383 255	52.8560 560 763	53.5562 076 370	40
11	58.1883 368 650	59.0398 527 383	59.9069 081 085	60.7898 090 713	44
12	65.2283 882 442	66.2804 452 586	67.3536 288 825	68.4483 973 810	48
13	72.6270 974 128	73.9087 184 157	75.2184 443 735	76.5569 412 965	52
14	80.4027 363 127	81.9454 296 652	83.5248 284 294	85.1418 765 052	56
15	88.5745 077 561	90.4124 478 718	92.2975 728 331	94.2311 918 380	60
16	97.1625 928 489	99.3328 128 178	101.5628 612 974	103.8545 205 192	64
17	106.1882 008 301	108.7307 978 970	111.3483 476 146	114.0432 367 772	68
18	115.6736 214 508	118.6319 761 652	121.6832 381 938	124.8305 581 319	72
19	125.6422 800 208	129.0632 899 281	132.5983 792 324	136.2516 536 913	76
20	136.1187 952 603	140.0531 240 540	144.1263 487 819	148.3437 588 105	80
21	147.1290 400 983	151.6313 832 129	156.3015 539 820	161.1462 964 878	84
22	158.7002 055 690	163.8295 732 507	169.1603 337 548	174.7010 058 922	88
23	170.8608 679 632	176.6808 869 203	182.7410 672 642	189.0520 784 428	92
24	183.6410 594 001	190.2202 942 029	197.0842 884 651	204.2463 018 824	96
25	197.0723 419 957	204.4846 374 661	212.2328 070 834	220.3332 128 169	100
26	211.1878 858 082	219.5127 317 158	228.2318 363 889	237.3652 582 151	104
27	226.0225 507 560	235.3454 702 172	245.1291 281 419	255.3979 663 979	108
28	241.6129 727 076	252.0259 357 698	262.9751 151 160	274.4901 280 734	112
29	257.9976 539 581	269.5995 179 410	281.8230 616 234	294.7039 880 078	116
30	275.2170 583 151	288.1140 365 769	301.7292 224 910	316.1054 479 573	120
31	293.3137 110 286	307.6198 719 257	322.7530 109 620	338.7642 815 227	124
32	312.3323 038 116	328.1701 017 283	344.9571 760 251	362.7543 616 273	128
33	332.3198 052 116	349.8206 456 497	368.4079 896 986	388.1539 013 594	132
34	353.3255 766 044	372.6304 174 426	393.1754 448 310	415.0457 089 645	136
35	375.4014 940 980	396.6614 852 594	419.3334 640 058	443.5174 578 187	140
36	398.6020 766 460	421.9792 405 469	446.9601 201 757	473.6619 722 644	144
37	422.9846 206 885	448.6525 759 844	476.1378 696 846	505.5775 302 378	148
38	448.6093 416 521	476.7540 729 489	506.9537 983 720	539.3681 836 781	152
39	475.5395 226 585	506.3601 990 179	539.4998 814 954	575.1440 977 595	156
40	503.8416 708 094	537.5515 160 472	573.8732 582 453	613.0219 100 552	160
41	533.5856 814 332	570.4128 993 890	610.1765 216 738	653.1251 108 022	164
42	564.8450 106 995	605.0337 688 485	648.5180 249 002	695.5844 455 069	168
43	597.6968 570 269	641.5083 320 055	689.0122 045 090	740.5383 412 059	172
44	632.2223 517 338	679.9358 405 651	731.7799 221 049	788.1333 577 685	176
45	668.5067 594 006	720.4208 604 335	776.9488 250 445	838.5246 657 157	180
46	706.6396 884 407	763.0735 562 541	824.6537 274 205	891.8765 521 112	184
47	746.7153 123 983	808.0099 911 795	875.0370 124 374	948.3629 561 737	188
48	788.8326 025 204	855.3524 426 930	928.2490 573 776	1008.1680 363 591	192
49	833.0955 721 777	905.2297 353 403	984.4486 824 272	1071.4867 707 579	196
50	879.6135 337 370	957.7775 912 773	1043.8036 247 013	1138.5255 927 682	200
51	928.5013 685 206	1013.1389 995 857	1106.4910 388 834	1209.5030 641 155	204
52	979.8798 105 182	1071.4646 053 643	1172.6980 259 728	1284.6505 874 129	208
53	1033.8757 445 534	1132.9131 196 524	1242.6221 917 189	1364.2131 605 864	212
54	1090.6225 196 401	1197.6517 513 014	1316.4722 364 081	1448.4501 756 232	216
55	1150.2602 783 023	1265.8566 619 708	1394.4685 777 644	1537.6362 642 486	220
56	1212.9363 026 724	1337.7134 454 853	1476.8440 088 230	1632.0621 932 873	224
57	1278.8053 782 205	1413.4176 328 577	1563.8443 927 398	1732.0358 126 291	228
58	1348.0301 760 146	1493.1752 243 533	1655.7293 966 103	1837.8830 588 892	232
59	1420.7816 544 551	1577.2032 500 406	1752.7732 664 899	1949.9490 180 353	236
60	1497.2394 814 758	1665.7303 603 571	1855.2656 459 261	2068.5990 504 459	240

QUARTERLY
Compounding

TABLE 2. FUTURE WORTH OF ONE DOLLAR PER PERIOD WITH INTEREST

Payable at end of each period

QUARTERS	6% Nominal Annual Rate	6¼% Nominal Annual Rate	6½% Nominal Annual Rate	6¾% Nominal Annual Rate	QUARTERS
1	1.0000 000 000	1.0000 000 000	1.0000 000 000	1.0000 000 000	1
2	2.0150 000 000	2.0156 250 000	2.0162 500 000	2.0168 750 000	2
3	3.0452 250 000	3.0471 191 406	3.0490 140 625	3.0509 097 656	3
YEARS					
1	4.0909 033 750	4.0947 303 772	4.0985 605 410	4.1023 938 679	4
2	8.4328 391 064	8.4514 422 679	8.4700 918 078	8.4887 878 340	8
3	13.0412 114 308	13.0868 972 917	13.1327 740 898	13.1788 426 277	12
4	17.9323 698 436	18.0189 294 796	18.1059 985 131	18.1935 800 493	16
5	23.1236 671 033	23.2665 138 865	23.4104 476 839	23.5554 771 942	20
6	28.6335 207 953	28.8498 395 947	29.0681 817 032	29.2885 671 999	24
7	34.4814 786 732	34.7903 873 870	35.1027 299 103	35.4185 469 672	28
8	40.6882 880 103	41.1110 123 903	41.5391 887 363	41.9728 923 394	32
9	47.2759 692 065	47.8360 320 061	48.4043 260 750	48.9809 812 549	36
10	54.2678 939 113	54.9913 194 673	55.7266 926 051	56.4742 254 247	40
11	61.6888 679 416	62.6044 033 806	63.5367 405 262	64.4862 111 264	44
12	69.5652 192 875	70.7045 736 370	71.8669 502 037	73.0528 497 452	48
13	77.9248 915 180	79.3229 940 997	80.7519 652 472	82.2125 387 359	52
14	86.7975 429 186	88.4928 225 012	90.2287 365 867	92.0063 337 282	56
15	96.2146 517 126	98.2493 380 105	100.3366 761 437	102.4781 325 467	60
16	106.2096 277 389	108.6300 769 642	111.1178 207 366	113.6748 719 702	64
17	116.8179 309 825	119.6749 772 792	122.6170 069 041	125.6467 381 120	68
18	128.0771 973 793	131.4265 321 073	134.8820 573 702	138.4473 913 641	72
19	140.0273 723 395	143.9299 533 187	147.9639 799 291	152.1342 069 150	76
20	152.7108 524 660	157.2333 454 465	161.9171 795 766	166.7685 319 166	80
21	166.1726 359 673	171.3878 907 598	176.7996 847 684	182.4159 604 550	84
22	180.4604 823 019	186.4480 461 773	192.6733 887 488	199.1466 275 571	88
23	195.6250 816 185	202.4717 527 803	209.6043 069 518	217.0355 235 501	92
24	211.7202 345 929	219.5206 587 299	227.6628 515 455	236.1628 301 838	96
25	228.8030 433 017	237.6603 564 465	246.9241 242 615	256.6142 800 218	100
26	246.9341 138 075	256.9606 349 643	267.4682 287 277	278.4815 407 129	104
27	266.1777 711 761	277.4957 484 311	289.3806 036 026	301.8626 258 643	108
28	286.6022 876 880	299.3447 017 871	312.7523 778 966	326.8623 343 592	112
29	308.2801 250 527	322.5915 547 215	337.6807 499 589	353.5927 200 868	116
30	331.2881 914 881	347.3257 450 759	364.2693 917 052	382.1735 941 915	120
31	355.7081 145 729	373.6424 329 398	392.6288 797 672	412.7330 620 912	124
32	381.6265 308 443	401.6428 667 602	422.8771 553 588	445.4080 976 725	128
33	409.1353 931 646	431.4347 728 766	455.1400 147 678	480.3451 572 357	132
34	438.3322 969 505	463.1327 699 769	489.5516 325 178	517.7008 359 432	136
35	469.3208 264 200	496.8588 100 713	526.2551 193 710	557.6425 697 107	140
36	502.2109 220 864	532.7426 476 793	565.4031 174 969	600.3493 856 904	144
37	537.1192 708 033	570.9223 390 359	607.1584 352 789	646.0127 047 074	148
38	574.1697 197 439	611.5447 732 361	651.6947 244 008	694.8371 992 482	152
39	613.4937 157 837	654.7662 373 631	699.1972 020 279	747.0417 108 447	156
40	655.2307 718 453	700.7530 177 730	749.8634 210 865	802.8602 309 679	160
41	699.5289 618 595	749.6820 398 500	803.9040 918 457	862.5429 498 262	164
42	746.5454 460 992	801.7415 486 930	861.5439 582 178	926.3573 777 698	168
43	796.4470 287 498	857.1318 333 530	923.0227 324 207	994.5895 443 275	172
44	849.4107 496 936	916.0659 974 066	988.5960 918 920	1067.5452 802 512	176
45	905.6245 126 089	978.7707 788 322	1058.5367 425 981	1145.5515 883 120	180
46	965.2877 516 106	1045.4874 223 406	1133.1355 531 610	1228.9581 089 952	184
47	1028.6121 387 992	1116.4726 075 184	1212.7027 645 214	1318.1386 876 615	188
48	1095.8223 352 269	1191.9994 363 536	1297.5692 801 655	1413.4930 501 993	192
49	1167.1567 879 456	1272.3584 839 439	1388.0880 422 839	1515.4485 946 798	196
50	1242.8685 759 650	1357.8589 164 288	1484.6354 995 853	1624.4623 070 433	200
51	1323.2263 081 215	1448.8296 804 474	1587.6131 728 677	1741.0228 094 058	204
52	1408.5150 760 432	1545.6207 686 982	1697.4493 248 603	1865.6525 501 642	208
53	1499.0374 655 931	1648.6045 664 694	1814.6007 412 790	1998.9101 457 193	212
54	1595.1146 303 768	1758.1772 843 202	1939.5546 305 035	2141.3928 843 101	216
55	1697.0874 311 256	1874.7604 824 255	2072.8306 497 751	2293.7394 031 842	220
56	1805.3176 449 955	1998.8026 924 489	2214.9830 663 434	2456.6325 511 022	224
57	1920.1892 490 734	2130.7811 431 823	2366.6030 625 489	2630.8024 490 084	228
58	2042.1097 826 435	2271.2035 965 931	2528.3211 944 265	2817.0297 625 838	232
59	2171.5117 930 475	2420.6103 013 416	2700.8100 140 580	3016.1492 013 529	236
60	2308.8543 702 680	2579.5760 712 854	2884.7868 665 755	3229.0532 600 244	240

TABLE 2. FUTURE WORTH OF ONE DOLLAR PER PERIOD WITH INTEREST
Payable at end of each period

QUARTERLY Compounding

QUARTERS	7% Nominal Annual Rate	7¼% Nominal Annual Rate	7½% Nominal Annual Rate	7¾% Nominal Annual Rate	QUARTERS
1	1.0000 000 000	1.0000 000 000	1.0000 000 000	1.0000 000 000	1
2	2.0175 000 000	2.0181 250 000	2.0187 500 000	2.0193 750 000	2
3	3.0528 062 500	3.0547 035 156	3.0566 015 625	3.0585 003 906	3
YEARS					
1	4.1062 303 594	4.1100 700 168	4.1139 128 418	4.1177 588 357	4
2	8.5075 304 546	8.5263 197 779	8.5451 559 124	8.5640 389 668	8
3	13.2251 037 111	13.2715 581 491	13.3182 067 538	13.3650 503 406	12
4	18.2816 772 119	18.3702 931 431	18.4594 310 042	18.5490 939 750	16
5	23.7016 111 860	23.8488 584 977	23.9972 280 384	24.1467 287 881	20
6	29.5110 163 652	29.7355 496 828	29.9621 878 413	30.1909 517 366	24
7	35.7378 797 730	36.0607 700 399	36.3872 599 830	36.7173 923 263	28
8	42.4121 995 532	42.8571 878 080	43.3079 356 271	43.7645 226 413	32
9	49.5661 294 873	50.1599 048 473	50.7624 435 788	51.3738 841 293	36
10	57.2341 338 963	58.0066 379 316	58.7919 614 554	59.5903 324 802	40
11	65.4531 536 742	66.4379 135 464	67.4408 431 451	68.4623 020 414	44
12	74.2627 842 514	75.4972 771 989	76.7568 638 121	78.0420 913 292	48
13	83.7054 663 479	85.2315 183 193	86.7914 837 989	88.3861 713 180	52
14	93.8266 904 326	95.6909 119 175	97.6001 328 862	99.5555 183 255	56
15	104.6752 158 756	106.9294 782 411	109.2425 164 788	111.6159 734 562	60
16	116.3033 058 477	119.0052 617 770	121.7829 454 095	124.6386 307 219	64
17	128.7669 791 010	131.9806 310 377	135.2906 911 832	138.7002 561 267	68
18	142.1262 798 406	145.9226 006 786	149.8403 686 219	153.8837 401 877	72
19	156.4455 669 901	160.9031 776 136	165.5123 480 267	170.2785 865 582	76
20	171.7938 242 428	176.9997 329 128	182.3931 991 314	187.9814 396 341	80
21	188.2449 923 937	194.2954 014 058	200.5761 693 012	207.0966 542 535	84
22	205.8783 255 515	212.8795 110 527	220.1616 986 177	227.7369 108 484	88
23	224.7787 729 485	232.8480 443 019	241.2579 746 947	250.0238 796 732	92
24	245.0373 881 863	254.3041 338 160	263.9815 302 918	274.0889 380 273	96
25	266.7517 678 903	277.3585 951 274	288.4578 870 236	300.0739 446 981	100
26	290.0265 218 849	302.1304 989 734	314.8222 487 231	328.1320 761 909	104
27	314.9737 771 551	328.7477 862 684	343.2202 482 881	358.4287 296 743	108
28	341.7137 180 223	357.3479 288 878	373.8087 521 361	391.1424 979 638	112
29	370.3751 651 369	388.0786 396 765	406.7567 267 114	426.4662 222 915	116
30	401.0961 960 765	421.0986 353 510	442.2461 718 315	464.6081 290 671	120
31	434.0248 105 397	456.5784 562 325	480.4731 260 270	505.7930 573 320	124
32	469.3196 433 399	494.7013 470 466	521.6487 494 307	550.2637 841 406	128
33	507.1507 286 346	535.6642 033 384	566.0004 901 948	598.2824 556 840	132
34	547.7003 190 712	579.6785 883 902	613.7733 408 818	650.1321 325 898	136
35	591.1637 637 957	626.9718 258 951	665.2311 917 674	706.1184 585 089	140
36	637.7504 495 547	677.7881 740 292	720.6582 885 325	766.5714 618 250	144
37	687.6848 094 232	732.3900 869 858	780.3608 023 945	831.8475 011 068	148
38	741.2074 040 199	791.0595 704 886	844.6685 213 526	902.3313 657 716	152
39	798.5760 804 165	854.0996 382 829	913.9366 718 892	978.4385 443 436	156
40	860.0672 143 252	921.8358 771 288	988.5478 811 886	1060.6176 736 766	160
41	925.9770 415 494	994.6181 283 782	1068.9142 907 145	1149.3531 835 806	164
42	996.6230 851 105	1072.8222 948 214	1155.4798 328 191	1245.1681 524 399	168
43	1072.3456 849 262	1156.8522 821 339	1248.7226 829 610	1348.6273 906 572	172
44	1153.5096 374 114	1247.1420 849 525	1349.1579 010 768	1460.3407 701 004	176
45	1240.5059 528 977	1344.1580 283 526	1457.3402 766 970	1580.9668 191 770	180
46	1333.7537 393 407	1448.4011 763 050	1573.8673 935 233	1711.2166 047 294	184
47	1433.7022 213 872	1560.4099 195 504	1699.3829 303 932	1851.8579 236 345	188
48	1540.8329 045 325	1680.7627 562 583	1834.5802 168 689	2003.7198 288 155	192
49	1655.6618 947 898	1810.0812 798 301	1980.2060 630 886	2167.6975 163 450	196
50	1778.7423 850 510	1949.0333 892 795	2137.0648 850 368	2344.7576 024 508	200
51	1910.6673 201 130	2098.3367 387 702	2306.0231 480 218	2535.9438 215 281	204
52	2052.0722 532 113	2258.7624 441 263	2488.0141 529 035	2742.3831 787 485	208
53	2203.6384 078 216	2431.1390 654 598	2684.0431 915 116	2965.2925 935 340	212
54	2366.0959 594 784	2616.3568 864 842	2895.1930 997 315	3205.9860 730 576	216
55	2540.2275 534 229	2815.3725 126 152	3122.6302 389 320	3465.8824 580 575	220
56	2726.8720 750 250	3029.2138 116 072	3367.6109 387 762	3746.5137 866 240	224
57	2926.9286 911 449	3258.9852 222 424	3631.4884 370 031	4049.5343 252 631	228
58	3141.3611 819 021	3505.8734 584 912	3915.7203 545 166	4376.7303 204 720	232
59	3371.2025 837 220	3771.1536 386 039	4221.8767 470 709	4730.0305 283 113	236
60	3617.5601 660 269	4056.1958 707 891	4551.6487 780 300	5111.5175 840 424	240

QUARTERLY
Compounding

TABLE 2. FUTURE WORTH OF ONE DOLLAR PER PERIOD WITH INTEREST
Payable at end of each period

QUARTERS	8% Nominal Annual Rate	8¼% Nominal Annual Rate	8½% Nominal Annual Rate	8¾% Nominal Annual Rate	QUARTERS
1	1.0000 000 000	1.0000 000 000	1.0000 000 000	1.0000 000 000	1
2	2.0200 000 000	2.0206 250 000	2.0212 500 000	2.0218 750 000	2
3	3.0604 000 000	3.0623 003 906	3.0642 015 625	3.0661 035 156	3
YEARS					
1	4.1216 080 000	4.1254 603 362	4.1293 158 457	4.1331 745 300	4
2	8.5829 690 501	8.6019 462 714	8.6209 707 402	8.6400 425 659	8
3	13.4120 897 281	13.4593 257 384	13.5067 591 964	13.5543 909 306	12
4	18.6392 852 545	18.7300 080 608	18.8212 656 310	18.9130 612 218	16
5	24.2973 697 989	24.4491 601 948	24.6021 091 729	24.7562 260 033	20
6	30.4218 624 738	30.6549 413 692	30.8902 099 525	31.1276 899 691	24
7	37.0512 103 087	37.3887 576 903	37.7300 787 587	38.0752 183 351	28
8	44.2270 296 051	44.6955 384 120	45.1701 321 111	45.6508 949 230	32
9	51.9943 671 858	52.6240 357 109	53.2630 349 802	53.9115 126 192	36
10	60.4019 831 807	61.2271 499 707	62.0660 735 805	62.9189 991 363	40
11	69.5026 571 226	70.5622 827 427	71.6415 608 749	72.7408 812 688	44
12	79.3535 192 750	80.6917 197 392	82.0572 776 619	83.4507 911 246	48
13	90.0164 092 724	91.6830 464 160	93.3869 523 668	95.1290 181 256	52
14	101.5582 643 242	103.6095 989 142	105.7107 829 341	107.8631 109 165	56
15	114.0515 394 183	116.5509 533 725	119.1160 045 142	121.7485 336 947	60
16	127.5746 621 638	130.5934 568 738	133.6975 069 644	136.8893 818 801	64
17	142.2125 251 273	145.8308 035 690	149.5585 065 334	153.3991 624 924	68
18	158.0570 187 526	162.3646 598 210	166.8112 764 855	171.4016 450 831	72
19	175.2076 082 115	180.3053 425 415	185.5779 418 349	191.0317 896 038	76
20	193.7719 578 048	199.7725 552 458	205.9913 438 171	212.4367 581 667	80
21	213.8666 068 341	220.8961 867 360	228.1959 802 149	235.7770 182 801	84
22	235.6177 011 873	243.8171 777 435	252.3490 281 975	261.2275 458 322	88
23	259.1617 852 304	268.6884 613 110	278.6214 569 098	288.9791 368 398	92
24	284.6466 589 764	295.6759 831 894	307.1992 376 912	319.2398 377 969	96
25	312.2323 059 126	324.9598 090 589	338.2846 604 866	352.2365 053 453	100
26	342.0918 973 108	356.7353 259 596	372.0977 657 715	388.2165 069 600	104
27	374.4128 793 246	391.2145 459 496	408.8779 021 247	427.4495 753 992	108
28	409.3981 496 991	428.6275 206 885	448.8854 204 747	470.2298 308 210	112
29	447.2673 314 788	469.2238 763 838	492.4035 170 134	516.8779 857 262	116
30	488.2581 517 101	513.2744 793 430	539.7402 378 213	567.7437 492 567	120
31	532.6279 337 932	561.0732 432 425	591.2306 593 948	623.2084 488 745	124
32	580.6552 128 521	612.9390 901 742	647.2392 605 094	683.6878 890 749	128
33	632.6414 842 627	669.2180 785 512	708.1625 022 108	749.6354 685 652	132
34	688.9130 963 161	730.2857 120 733	774.4316 341 929	821.5455 792 776	136
35	749.8232 988 977	796.5494 451 563	846.5157 474 314	899.9573 126 974	140
36	815.7544 610 442	868.4514 015 421	924.9250 946 791	985.4585 012 920	144
37	887.1204 712 977	946.4713 242 294	1010.2147 023 277	1078.6901 253 395	148
38	964.3693 359 270	1031.1297 764 065	1102.9882 992 034	1180.3511 181 912	152
39	1047.9859 913 252	1122.9916 147 444	1203.9025 901 065	1291.2036 059 943	156
40	1138.4953 482 399	1222.6697 582 233	1313.6719 043 449	1412.0786 211 545	160
41	1236.4655 869 453	1330.8292 776 403	1433.0732 521 673	1543.8823 323 704	164
42	1342.5117 240 428	1448.1918 330 836	1562.9518 248 879	1687.6028 379 461	168
43	1457.2994 732 810	1575.5404 889 803	1704.2269 776 359	1844.3175 733 081	172
44	1581.5494 246 304	1713.7249 388 453	1857.8987 370 794	2015.2013 882 599	176
45	1716.0415 678 495	1863.6671 745 920	2025.0548 801 882	2201.5353 545 270	180
46	1861.6201 889 371	2026.3676 382 311	2206.8786 341 440	2404.7163 696 196	184
47	2019.1991 702 108	2202.9118 970 019	2404.6570 519 019	2626.2676 290 121	188
48	2189.7677 272 814	2394.4778 864 763	2619.7901 226 904	2867.8500 451 450	192
49	2374.3966 189 395	2602.3437 699 595	2853.8006 819 395	3131.2746 988 555	196
50	2574.2448 689 354	2827.8964 666 297	3108.3451 907 840	3418.5164 165 819	200
51	2790.5670 418 507	3072.6409 053 165	3385.2254 614 469	3731.7285 751 261	204
52	3024.7211 187 353	3338.2100 656 609	3686.4014 115 012	4073.2592 449 619	208
53	3278.1770 219 502	3626.3758 736 539	4014.0049 372 923	4445.6687 931 119	212
54	3552.5258 427 319	3939.0610 242 513	4370.3550 047 241	4851.7490 775 559	216
55	3849.4898 294 042	4278.3518 099 452	4757.9740 642 324	5294.5443 770 676	220
56	4170.9331 989 400	4646.5120 408 897	5179.6059 061 368	5777.3742 133 846	224
57	4518.8738 397 443	5045.9981 494 554	5638.2350 827 650	6303.8582 368 036	228
58	4895.4959 791 219	5479.4755 799 959	6137.1080 348 283	6877.9433 617 614	232
59	5303.1638 949 523	5949.8365 731 792	6679.7560 715 929	7503.9333 558 312	236
60	5744.4367 576 472	6460.2194 635 471	7270.0203 675 157	8186.5211 039 534	240

TABLE 2. FUTURE WORTH OF ONE DOLLAR PER PERIOD WITH INTEREST
Payable at end of each period

QUARTERLY Compounding

QUARTERS	9% Nominal Annual Rate	9¼% Nominal Annual Rate	9½% Nominal Annual Rate	9¾% Nominal Annual Rate	QUARTERS
1	1.0000 000 000	1.0000 000 000	1.0000 000 000	1.0000 000 000	1
2	2.0225 000 000	2.0231 250 000	2.0237 500 000	2.0243 750 000	2
3	3.0680 062 500	3.0699 097 656	3.0718 140 625	3.0737 191 406	3
YEARS					
1	4.1370 363 906	4.1409 014 290	4.1447 696 465	4.1486 410 447	4
2	8.6591 618 584	8.6783 287 278	8.6975 432 843	8.7168 056 382	8
3	13.6022 217 728	13.6502 525 578	13.6984 841 241	13.7469 173 131	12
4	19.0053 981 089	19.0982 795 880	19.1917 089 741	19.2856 896 020	16
5	24.9115 200 304	25.0680 006 730	25.2256 774 250	25.3845 598 559	20
6	31.3674 033 816	31.6093 723 726	31.8536 193 465	32.1001 669 318	24
7	38.4242 217 807	38.7771 350 036	39.1340 044 646	39.4948 771 845	28
8	46.1379 122 566	46.6312 707 255	47.1310 581 651	47.6373 636 499	32
9	54.5696 186 421	55.2375 054 897	55.9153 280 697	56.6032 437 957	36
10	63.7861 762 410	64.6678 590 564	65.5643 063 869	66.4757 817 644	40
11	73.8606 416 090	75.0012 476 785	76.1631 135 247	77.3466 616 288	44
12	84.8728 716 484	86.3241 444 989	87.8052 489 978	89.3168 388 416	48
13	96.9101 566 073	98.7313 031 857	100.5934 162 519	102.4974 777 865	52
14	110.0679 119 993	112.3265 508 611	114.6404 286 834	117.0109 841 371	56
15	124.4504 349 310	127.2236 569 613	130.0702 048 453	132.9921 416 113	60
16	140.1717 308 297	143.5472 852 950	147.0188 616 194	150.5893 636 779	64
17	157.3564 171 264	161.4340 372 712	165.6359 149 995	169.9660 718 393	68
18	176.1407 110 559	181.0335 950 238	186.0855 990 764	191.3022 132 912	72
19	196.6735 094 054	202.5099 740 003	208.5483 148 620	214.7959 320 521	76
20	219.1175 687 694	226.0428 954 958	233.2222 217 335	240.6654 090 829	80
21	243.6507 956 661	251.8292 906 195	260.3249 855 363	269.1508 884 851	84
22	270.4676 567 429	280.0849 482 778	290.0956 987 667	300.5169 085 948	88
23	299.7807 202 482	311.0463 209 658	322.7969 897 753	335.0547 586 914	92
24	331.8223 409 885	344.9725 034 782	358.7173 395 952	373.0851 841 365	96
25	366.8465 021 267	382.1474 010 986	398.1736 268 362	414.9613 650 654	100
26	405.1308 284 215	422.8821 054 109	441.5139 230 930	461.0721 962 923	104
27	446.9787 868 653	467.5174 976 144	489.1205 635 293	511.8458 988 906	108
28	492.7220 921 657	516.4271 011 281	541.4135 197 240	567.7539 969 870	112
29	542.7233 361 358	570.0202 073 554	598.8541 045 357	629.3156 967 017	116
30	597.3788 618 382	628.7453 007 677	661.9490 416 671	697.1027 079 004	120
31	657.1219 052 632	693.0938 119 671	731.2549 358 298	771.7445 535 374	124
32	722.4260 294 447	763.6042 301 373	807.3831 829 457	853.9344 158 957	128
33	793.8088 782 356	840.8666 092 950	891.0053 636 988	944.4355 740 170	132
34	871.8362 794 966	925.5275 060 537	982.8591 680 203	1044.0884 921 057	136
35	957.1267 302 235	1018.2953 902 184	1083.7549 027 683	1153.8186 247 331	140
36	1050.3562 991 651	1119.9465 734 904	1194.5826 400 138	1274.6450 113 294	144
37	1152.2639 857 930	1231.3317 058 951	1316.3200 689 907	1407.6897 397 768	148
38	1263.6575 781 023	1353.3828 942 971	1450.0411 209 787	1554.1883 669 914	152
39	1385.4200 556 757	1487.1215 025 723	1596.9254 432 044	1715.5013 932 660	156
40	1518.5165 887 655	1633.6666 987 114	1758.2688 053 373	1893.1268 969 356	160
41	1664.0021 888 747	1794.2448 203 802	1935.4945 303 835	2088.7144 466 984	164
42	1823.0300 714 780	1970.1996 373 107	2130.1660 508 161	2304.0804 207 951	168
43	1996.8607 971 741	2163.0035 964 011	2344.0007 007 107	2541.2248 753 111	172
44	2186.8722 637 255	2374.2701 436 284	2578.8848 655 538	2802.3501 182 541	176
45	2394.5706 281 914	2605.7672 258 871	2836.8906 233 727	3089.8811 619 011	180
46	2621.6022 457 289	2859.4320 857 414	3120.2940 239 903	3406.4882 433 496	184
47	2869.7667 196 968	3137.3874 728 980	3431.5951 676 569	3755.1116 224 182	188
48	3141.0311 665 072	3441.9594 080 640	3773.5402 601 891	4138.9888 871 881	192
49	3437.5458 082 962	3775.6966 478 408	4149.1458 391 783	4561.6850 207 661	196
50	3761.6610 170 125	4141.3920 135 452	4561.7253 849 851	5027.1255 084 930	200
51	4115.9459 450 261	4542.1057 624 428	5014.9185 512 745	5539.6327 930 564	204
52	4503.2088 899 361	4981.1911 969 718	5512.7232 729 552	6103.9664 160 580	208
53	4926.5195 550 024	5462.3227 262 641	6059.5310 347 680	6725.3672 188 218	212
54	5389.2333 816 519	5989.5266 147 906	6660.1656 116 544	7409.6060 129 270	216
55	5895.0181 469 354	6567.2146 754 472	7319.9256 226 598	8163.0371 724 559	220
56	6447.8830 367 646	7200.2211 890 331	8044.6312 737 702	8992.6576 456 583	224
57	7052.2104 253 809	7893.8433 590 790	8840.6757 020 328	9906.1719 340 598	228
58	7712.7906 129 649	8653.8856 405 614	9715.0813 739 040	10912.0636 424 606	232
59	8434.8597 967 354	9486.7083 134 626	10675.5620 353 530	12019.6742 642 932	236
60	9224.1415 765 266	10399.2807 076 528	11730.5907 602 277	13239.2899 340 026	240

TABLE 2. FUTURE WORTH OF ONE DOLLAR PER PERIOD WITH INTEREST
Payable at end of each period

QUARTERS	10% Nominal Annual Rate	10¼% Nominal Annual Rate	10½% Nominal Annual Rate	10¾% Nominal Annual Rate	QUARTERS
1	1.0000 000 000	1.0000 000 000	1.0000 000 000	1.0000 000 000	1
2	2.0250 000 000	2.0256 250 000	2.0262 500 000	2.0268 750 000	2
3	3.0756 250 000	3.0775 316 406	3.0794 390 625	3.0813 472 656	3
YEARS					
1	4.1525 156 250	4.1563 933 889	4.1602 743 379	4.1641 584 734	4
2	8.7361 159 004	8.7554 741 817	8.7748 805 932	8.7943 352 462	8
3	13.7955 529 699	13.8443 919 426	13.8934 350 830	13.9426 832 460	12
4	19.3802 248 264	19.4753 180 221	19.5709 725 837	19.6671 919 262	16
5	25.5446 576 116	25.7059 804 148	25.8685 380 655	26.0323 404 421	20
6	32.3490 379 833	32.6002 555 844	32.8538 430 491	33.1098 239 245	24
7	39.8598 007 503	40.2288 233 222	40.6019 936 406	40.9793 610 326	28
8	48.1502 775 109	48.6698 913 532	49.1962 980 740	49.7295 918 807	32
9	57.3014 126 287	58.0099 971 178	58.7291 624 423	59.4590 764 544	36
10	67.4025 535 356	68.3448 949 498	69.3030 842 493	70.2774 047 607	40
11	78.5523 230 786	79.7805 377 456	81.0317 544 643	82.3064 312 168	44
12	90.8595 824 277	92.4341 631 880	94.0412 799 293	95.6816 471 824	48
13	104.4444 939 455	106.4354 956 620	108.4715 392 615	110.5537 070 934	52
14	119.4396 943 969	121.9280 761 829	124.4776 868 304	127.0901 253 885	56
15	135.9915 899 526	139.0707 339 722	142.2318 209 800	145.4771 633 421	60
16	154.2617 856 313	158.0392 147 675	161.9248 344 329	165.9219 270 554	64
17	174.4286 631 356	179.0279 825 598	183.7684 667 714	188.6547 002 377	68
18	196.6891 224 886	202.2522 132 293	207.9975 810 654	213.9315 380 530	72
19	221.2605 044 736	227.9500 005 184	234.8726 891 231	242.0371 512 496	76
20	248.3827 126 492	256.3847 969 582	264.6827 525 183	273.2881 130 560	80
21	278.3205 556 556	287.8481 147 715	297.7482 895 095	308.0364 249 677	84
22	311.3663 326 835	322.6625 144 424	334.4248 212 573	346.6734 815 868	88
23	347.8426 873 477	361.1849 115 919	375.1066 943 932	389.6344 791 736	92
24	388.1057 578 290	403.8102 360 605	420.2313 210 408	437.4033 175 675	96
25	432.5486 540 425	450.9754 807 101	470.2838 818 775	490.5180 506 902	100
26	481.6052 957 796	503.1641 814 553	525.8025 428 044	549.5769 470 241	104
27	535.7546 492 998	560.9113 744 510	587.3842 413 150	615.2452 283 295	108
28	595.5254 037 344	624.8090 812 587	655.6911 047 756	688.2625 625 046	112
29	661.5011 329 617	695.5123 782 237	731.4575 696 289	769.4513 949 827	116
30	734.3259 933 511	773.7461 122 883	815.4982 780 666	859.7262 125 123	120
31	814.7110 130 070	860.3123 320 887	908.7168 370 739	960.1038 436 626	124
32	903.4410 339 162	956.0985 105 210	1012.1155 340 261	1071.7149 120 763	128
33	1001.3823 747 813	1062.0866 430 721	1126.8061 132 978	1195.8165 714 770	132
34	1109.4912 893 533	1179.3633 151 926	1254.0217 297 551	1333.8066 658 727	136
35	1228.8233 028 493	1309.1308 419 205	1395.1302 076 562	1487.2394 744 529	140
36	1360.5435 176 105	1452.7195 939 594	1551.6487 475 185	1657.8432 185 253	144
37	1505.9379 886 197	1611.6016 365 780	1725.2602 390 816	1847.5395 276 842	148
38	1666.4262 799 453	1787.4058 211 553	1917.8313 557 638	2058.4650 844 717	152
39	1843.5753 247 049	1981.9344 840 897	2131.4326 251 636	2292.9956 913 314	156
40	2039.1147 238 725	2197.1819 242 688	2368.3606 914 036	2553.7730 309 376	160
41	2254.9536 332 987	2435.3548 485 298	2631.1630 086 835	2843.7344 213 193	164
42	2493.1994 038 218	2698.8949 947 161	2922.6652 315 470	3166.1459 009 327	168
43	2756.1781 564 620	2990.5041 642 613	3246.0015 963 624	3524.6390 163 424	172
44	3046.4574 935 868	3313.1719 209 330	3604.6486 206 804	3923.2517 268 772	176
45	3366.8715 677 873	3670.2062 397 024	4002.4624 828 037	4366.4738 869 966	180
46	3720.5487 532 274	4065.2674 199 519	4443.7204 834 755	4859.2978 186 705	184
47	4110.9421 896 362	4502.4056 106 952	4933.1670 354 827	5407.2745 434 016	188
48	4541.8634 971 596	4986.1023 325 185	5476.0646 756 545	6016.5763 072 733	192
49	5017.5199 912 489	5521.3164 219 230	6078.2506 477 397	6694.0661 032 849	196
50	5542.5557 609 342	6113.5348 690 881	6746.1996 645 404	7447.3749 740 539	200
51	6122.0970 115 520	6768.8290 702 421	7487.0935 241 235	8284.9879 656 000	204
52	6761.8021 146 329	7493.9170 713 364	8308.8983 286 236	9216.3397 003 682	208
53	7467.9168 536 121	8296.2324 411 427	9220.4501 358 953	10251.9206 459 963	212
54	8247.3354 047 578	9184.0004 798 581	10231.5499 649 425	11403.3952 768 078	216
55	9107.6676 487 046	10166.3225 445 031	11353.0691 766 253	12683.7334 589 654	220
56	10057.3134 697 934	11253.2693 556 145	12597.0663 626 982	14107.3565 391 676	224
57	11105.5447 686 394	12455.9842 418 084	13976.9169 999 738	15690.2997 823 889	228
58	12262.5959 886 622	13786.7973 806 716	15507.4572 636 545	17450.3929 883 125	232
59	13539.7640 404 368	15259.3522 071 738	17205.1435 461 152	19407.4613 208 662	236
60	14949.5185 994 799	16888.7452 855 343	19088.2293 962 871	21583.5486 129 450	240

TABLE 2. FUTURE WORTH OF ONE DOLLAR PER PERIOD WITH INTEREST
Payable at end of each period

QUARTERLY Compounding

QUARTERS	11% Nominal Annual Rate	11¼% Nominal Annual Rate	11½% Nominal Annual Rate	11¾% Nominal Annual Rate	QUARTERS
1	1.0000 000 000	1.0000 000 000	1.0000 000 000	1.0000 000 000	1
2	2.0275 000 000	2.0281 250 000	2.0287 500 000	2.0293 750 000	2
3	3.0832 562 500	3.0851 660 156	3.0870 765 625	3.0889 878 906	3
YEARS					
1	4.1680 457 969	4.1719 363 098	4.1758 300 137	4.1797 269 099	4
2	8.8138 382 523	8.8333 897 232	8.8529 897 711	8.8726 385 079	8
3	13.9921 372 899	14.0417 980 766	14.0916 664 711	14.1417 433 421	12
4	19.7639 794 848	19.8613 387 153	19.9592 730 939	20.0577 861 173	16
5	26.1973 975 013	26.3637 192 793	26.5313 158 921	26.7001 975 361	20
6	33.3682 219 932	33.6290 612 751	33.8923 660 304	34.1581 607 614	24
7	41.3609 754 193	41.7468 873 230	42.1371 478 740	42.5318 088 183	28
8	50.2698 683 093	50.8172 242 434	51.3717 579 327	51.9335 690 124	32
9	60.1999 097 224	60.9518 355 747	61.7150 301 445	62.4896 724 153	36
10	71.2681 449 883	72.2755 987 090	73.3000 650 694	74.3418 486 834	40
11	83.6050 353 198	84.9280 436 161	86.2759 426 700	87.6492 289 666	44
12	97.3559 955 584	99.0650 721 132	100.8096 407 209	102.5904 824 543	48
13	112.6831 081 777	114.8608 788 682	117.0881 835 320	119.3662 152 455	52
14	129.7670 337 485	132.5100 978 035	135.3210 486 381	138.2016 637 515	56
15	148.8091 403 841	152.2302 003 508	155.7428 624 228	159.3497 187 927	60
16	170.0338 772 641	174.2641 751 064	178.6164 193 669	183.0943 209 920	64
17	193.6914 202 161	198.8835 219 057	204.2360 637 722	209.7542 730 541	68
18	220.0606 205 358	226.3915 972 097	232.9314 774 789	239.6875 201 134	72
19	249.4522 918 060	257.1273 520 249	265.0719 223 177	273.2959 556 209	76
20	282.2128 734 534	291.4695 084 142	301.0709 918 900	311.0308 172 956	80
21	318.7285 142 283	329.8412 260 622	341.3919 338 238	353.3987 455 883	84
22	359.4296 237 372	372.7153 163 950	386.5536 109 935	400.9685 859 999	88
23	404.7959 456 776	420.6200 685 024	437.1371 784 142	454.3790 265 847	92
24	455.3622 125 737	474.1457 586 490	493.7935 617 322	514.3471 731 832	96
25	511.7244 486 654	533.9519 235 835	557.2518 335 455	581.6781 775 163	100
26	574.5469 952 412	600.7754 872 659	628.3285 953 453	657.2760 474 133	104
27	644.5703 412 252	675.4398 411 518	707.9384 858 071	742.1557 843 125	108
28	722.6198 513 143	758.8649 899 165	797.1059 506 557	837.4570 109 991	112
29	809.6154 945 464	852.0788 876 360	896.9784 255 631	944.4592 725 491	116
30	906.5826 879 693	956.2301 041 064	1008.8411 017 204	1064.5992 159 147	120
31	1014.6643 832 242	1072.6019 773 748	1134.1334 640 923	1199.4898 788 111	124
32	1135.1345 385 088	1202.6284 268 674	1274.4678 151 733	1350.9423 468 821	128
33	1269.4131 347 140	1347.9116 219 628	1431.6500 226 162	1520.9900 699 215	132
34	1419.0829 127 286	1510.2417 237 188	1607.7027 577 185	1711.9161 636 271	136
35	1585.9080 291 953	1691.6189 430 099	1804.8915 238 085	1926.2840 634 504	140
36	1771.8548 506 135	1894.2781 868 710	2025.7538 094 728	2166.9719 421 094	144
37	1979.1151 308 866	2120.7165 967 379	2273.1317 417 762	2437.2113 528 659	148
38	2210.1318 455 111	2373.7243 179 065	2550.2086 596 697	2740.6306 174 044	152
39	2467.6279 869 116	2656.4188 793 484	2860.5500 782 209	3081.3035 408 516	156
40	2754.6386 603 336	2972.2836 075 066	3208.1495 708 116	3463.8041 080 010	160
41	3074.5468 586 086	3325.2105 474 008	3597.4801 597 269	3893.2678 951 117	164
42	3431.1233 374 668	3719.5484 199 116	4033.5518 764 472	4375.4610 218 145	168
43	3828.5710 614 091	4160.1562 061 661	4521.9762 323 477	4916.8575 688 988	172
44	4271.5747 440 209	4652.4630 192 854	5069.0384 294 357	5524.7265 014 136	176
45	4765.3560 666 587	5202.5350 012 265	5681.7782 403 545	6207.2292 641 420	180
46	5315.7352 263 725	5817.1500 690 122	6368.0805 984 474	6973.5293 597 972	184
47	5929.1995 385 279	6503.8814 313 625	7136.7770 636 198	7833.9153 811 719	188
48	6612.9799 027 481	7271.1909 048 101	7997.7594 696 990	8799.9391 491 112	192
49	7375.1360 334 778	8128.5331 791 271	8962.1072 157 389	9884.5708 109 930	196
50	8224.6514 597 820	9086.4723 168 113	10042.2298 392 979	11102.3729 821 198	200
51	9171.5394 141 408	10156.8119 221 200	11252.0267 063 666	12469.6962 680 989	204
52	10226.9608 583 522	11352.7405 835 819	12607.0658 728 889	14004.8987 933 585	208
53	11403.3560 377 117	12688.9943 821 071	14124.7844 195 226	15728.5926 832 611	212
54	12714.5911 140 980	14182.0384 671 035	15824.7128 376 123	17663.9208 091 609	216
55	14176.1216 063 277	15850.2699 379 535	17728.7263 538 459	19836.8675 120 761	220
56	15805.1745 642 487	17714.2445 307 338	19861.3264 277 208	22276.6074 768 507	224
57	17620.9516 238 589	19796.9299 033 821	22249.9560 442 205	25015.8974 409 040	228
58	19644.8553 368 568	22123.9886 402 573	24925.3528 589 888	28091.5159 967 760	232
59	21900.7414 423 712	24724.0944 632 419	27921.9447 403 879	31544.7573 933 995	236
60	24415.2000 543 944	27629.2855 456 965	31278.2927 984 028	35421.9859 660 348	240

TABLE 2. FUTURE WORTH OF ONE DOLLAR PER PERIOD WITH INTEREST

Payable at end of each period

QUARTERS	12% Nominal Annual Rate	12¼% Nominal Annual Rate	12½% Nominal Annual Rate	12¾% Nominal Annual Rate	QUARTERS
1	1.0000 000 000	1.0000 000 000	1.0000 000 000	1.0000 000 000	1
2	2.0300 000 000	2.0306 250 000	2.0312 500 000	2.0318 750 000	2
3	3.0909 000 000	3.0928 128 906	3.0947 265 625	3.0966 410 156	3
YEARS					
1	4.1836 270 000	4.1875 302 854	4.1914 367 676	4.1953 464 480	4
2	8.8923 360 463	8.9120 824 987	8.9318 779 782	8.9517 225 977	8
3	14.1920 295 615	14.2425 260 048	14.2932 335 508	14.3441 530 818	12
4	20.1568 813 033	20.2565 621 904	20.3568 323 381	20.4576 953 272	16
5	26.8703 744 890	27.0418 571 101	27.2146 558 411	27.3887 812 069	20
6	34.4264 702 153	34.6973 193 864	34.9707 335 184	35.2467 381 070	24
7	42.9309 225 246	43.3345 419 917	43.7427 208 565	44.1555 134 010	28
8	52.5027 585 228	53.0794 289 288	53.6636 841 401	54.2556 295 313	32
9	63.2759 442 668	64.0740 305 220	64.8841 189 948	65.7064 005 384	36
10	75.4012 597 333	76.4786 140 715	77.5742 333 245	78.6884 449 986	40
11	89.0484 091 149	90.4740 000 556	91.9265 292 725	93.4065 350 087	44
12	104.4083 959 753	106.2641 979 338	108.1587 233 747	110.0928 261 557	48
13	121.6961 965 082	124.0793 799 741	126.5170 492 012	129.0105 194 195	52
14	141.1537 683 135	144.1792 364 535	147.2799 925 859	150.4580 127 702	56
15	163.0534 368 015	166.8567 611 386	170.7625 161 052	174.7736 079 444	60
16	187.7017 066 209	192.4425 222 297	197.3208 368 892	202.3408 466 424	64
17	215.4435 514 539	221.3094 810 224	227.3578 302 426	233.5945 603 182	68
18	246.6672 422 190	253.8784 285 310	261.3291 410 438	269.0277 289 875	72
19	281.8097 812 559	290.6241 193 201	299.7500 956 305	309.1992 572 406	76
20	321.3630 185 477	332.0821 919 585	343.2035 190 203	354.7427 901 168	80
21	365.8805 355 836	378.8569 769 734	392.3485 760 499	406.3767 078 947	84
22	415.9853 932 069	431.6303 061 218	447.9307 705 475	464.9154 574 545	88
23	472.3788 518 856	491.1714 513 885	510.7932 542 214	531.2823 989 435	92
24	535.8501 864 550	558.3483 385 943	581.8896 168 132	606.5243 703 851	96
25	607.2877 326 952	634.1401 990 707	662.2983 515 365	691.8281 999 637	100
26	687.6913 203 534	719.6518 438 256	753.2392 152 333	788.5394 264 420	104
27	778.1862 666 183	816.1297 682 717	856.0917 314 231	898.1835 229 983	108
28	880.0391 258 999	924.9803 222 767	972.4161 169 253	1022.4899 592 562	112
29	994.6754 163 450	1047.7902 103 957	1103.9769 495 012	1163.4194 810 496	116
30	1123.6995 711 867	1186.3496 211 186	1252.7699 355 405	1323.1950 382 195	120
31	1268.9173 941 639	1342.6783 222 840	1421.0521 838 438	1504.3368 482 824	124
32	1432.3613 332 937	1519.0551 030 491	1611.3764 447 367	1709.7021 490 458	128
33	1616.3189 267 254	1718.0509 915 916	1826.6298 339 067	1942.5302 672 093	132
34	1823.3648 187 992	1942.5667 327 510	2070.0776 283 803	2206.4937 138 385	136
35	2056.3967 944 025	2195.8750 719 211	2345.4127 990 020	2505.7561 126 672	140
36	2318.6763 359 558	2481.6684 615 594	2656.8120 307 973	2845.0378 749 578	144
37	2613.8742 706 567	2804.1128 857 286	3008.9990 810 157	3229.6906 568 429	148
38	2946.1221 468 565	3167.9085 872 645	3407.3164 359 639	3665.7817 735 979	152
39	3320.0700 586 231	3578.3585 827 855	3857.8063 536 212	4160.1899 023 540	156
40	3740.9517 277 975	4041.4459 642 799	4367.3025 214 127	4720.7135 828 156	160
41	4214.6577 544 208	4563.9211 140 899	4943.5337 195 361	5356.1942 274 172	164
42	4747.8180 607 354	5153.4001 046 166	5595.2410 623 607	6076.6555 812 189	168
43	5347.8946 826 349	5818.4757 171 098	6332.3105 963 858	6893.4618 313 088	172
44	6023.2862 072 577	6568.8426 978 532	7165.9232 661 977	7819.4968 596 493	176
45	6783.4453 184 200	7415.4390 775 932	8108.7245 233 273	8869.3674 668 087	180
46	7639.0110 950 350	8370.6056 142 106	9175.0161 508 835	10059.6337 721 262	184
47	8601.9579 141 496	9448.2656 828 184	10380.9732 138 366	11409.0704 245 220	188
48	9685.7630 426 246	10664.1282 355 252	11744.8894 259 703	12938.9627 441 603	192
49	10905.5952 630 464	12035.9167 893 913	13287.4546 555 864	14673.4424 661 483	196
50	12278.5271 738 530	13583.6277 805 133	15032.0687 795 712	16639.8683 821 233	200
51	13823.7741 349 960	15329.8220 502 417	17005.1966 468 219	18869.2578 837 694	204
52	15562.9632 033 881	17299.9537 124 984	19236.7695 356 327	21396.7762 152 115	208
53	17520.4358 221 191	19522.7411 960 641	21760.6391 949 340	24262.2911 515 019	212
54	19723.5884 998 347	22030.5858 704 839	24615.0913 569 406	27511.0018 524 125	216
55	22203.2562 483 786	24860.0443 578 634	27843.4265 109 199	31194.1518 107 491	220
56	24994.1441 452 377	28052.3614 154 004	31494.6167 481 008	35369.8371 408 686	224
57	28135.3130 608 749	31654.0711 564 329	35624.0486 417 050	40103.9229 569 265	228
58	31670.7263 491 228	35717.6753 739 466	40294.3634 311 862	45471.0822 953 337	232
59	35649.8651 520 368	40302.4088 544 024	45576.4072 558 172	51555.9739 688 517	236
60	40128.4209 309 294	45475.1028 377 925	51550.3058 521 518	58454.5779 311 925	240

TABLE 2. FUTURE WORTH OF ONE DOLLAR PER PERIOD WITH INTEREST
Payable at end of each period

QUARTERLY Compounding

QUARTERS	13% Nominal Annual Rate	13¼% Nominal Annual Rate	13½% Nominal Annual Rate	13¾% Nominal Annual Rate	QUARTERS
1	1.0000 000 000	1.0000 000 000	1.0000 000 000	1.0000 000 000	1
2	2.0325 000 000	2.0331 250 000	2.0337 500 000	2.0343 750 000	2
3	3.0985 562 500	3.1004 722 656	3.1023 890 625	3.1043 066 406	3
YEARS					
1	4.1992 593 281	4.2031 754 094	4.2070 946 934	4.2110 171 814	4
2	8.9716 164 707	8.9915 597 105	9.0115 524 311	9.0315 947 463	8
3	14.3952 854 837	14.4466 316 458	14.4981 924 608	14.5499 688 251	12
4	20.5591 547 595	20.6612 142 582	20.7638 774 683	20.8671 480 560	16
5	27.5642 438 156	27.7410 543 602	27.9192 236 181	28.0987 624 527	20
6	35.5253 589 026	35.8066 219 124	36.0905 534 030	36.3771 799 031	24
7	44.5729 745 604	44.9951 599 306	45.4221 257 763	45.8539 290 389	28
8	54.8553 719 627	55.4630 198 009	56.0786 829 403	56.7024 728 241	32
9	66.5410 690 942	67.3883 217 421	68.2483 587 512	69.1213 836 310	36
10	79.8215 825 880	80.9739 856 840	82.1460 000 872	83.3379 779 212	40
11	94.9145 664 873	96.4511 841 358	98.0169 598 160	99.6124 770 581	44
12	112.0673 793 731	114.0832 757 981	116.1414 283 225	118.2427 704 148	48
13	131.5611 383 180	134.1702 868 521	136.8393 800 695	139.5698 679 579	52
14	153.7153 261 084	157.0540 161 801	160.4762 225 163	163.9841 421 134	56
15	178.8930 272 403	183.1238 513 860	187.4692 471 251	191.9324 731 669	60
16	207.5068 785 031	212.8233 945 818	218.2949 963 412	223.9264 289 856	64
17	240.0258 316 753	246.6580 106 842	253.4976 766 079	260.5516 287 860	68
18	276.9828 391 647	285.2034 266 608	293.6987 659 400	302.4784 623 426	72
19	318.9835 885 533	329.1155 280 515	339.6079 856 710	350.4743 608 402	76
20	366.7164 291 984	379.1415 194 618	392.0358 300 733	405.4178 439 794	80
21	420.9636 535 744	436.1326 389 328	451.9078 750 520	468.3146 004 516	84
22	482.6143 182 474	501.0586 425 360	520.2811 185 222	540.3158 961 231	88
23	552.6788 146 036	575.0243 056 606	598.3626 409 473	622.7396 468 717	92
24	632.3054 281 314	659.2882 217 781	687.5309 154 765	717.0945 417 957	96
25	722.7991 576 469	755.2842 185 622	789.3601 438 981	825.1076 583 461	100
26	825.6431 028 911	864.6457 557 798	905.6480 480 398	948.7560 748 518	104
27	942.5227 710 185	989.2337 201 039	1038.4476 072 555	1090.3030 590 760	108
28	1075.3537 003 372	1131.1680 898 041	1190.1033 023 002	1252.3394 952 001	112
29	1226.3128 540 235	1292.8640 081 175	1363.2925 054 520	1437.8313 075 175	116
30	1397.8742 983 240	1477.0728 791 222	1561.0727 475 953	1650.1737 488 832	120
31	1592.8497 499 726	1686.9291 853 960	1786.9356 967 307	1893.2535 476 183	124
32	1814.4346 573 541	1926.0038 241 075	2044.8688 008 633	2171.5200 504 103	128
33	2066.2605 706 377	2198.3648 691 001	2339.4256 835 313	2490.0666 634 113	132
34	2352.4546 591 724	2508.6467 928 928	2675.8065 347 555	2854.7240 822 393	136
35	2677.7073 515 749	2862.1293 264 731	3059.9499 166 568	3272.1670 173 676	140
36	3047.3492 070 610	3264.8272 987 525	3498.6376 045 006	3750.0363 684 111	144
37	3467.4382 778 627	3723.5929 843 875	3999.6143 140 650	4297.0790 835 945	148
38	3944.8593 945 138	4246.2327 015 058	4571.7244 290 297	4923.3082 643 984	152
39	4487.4370 011 849	4841.6396 433 552	5225.0681 422 125	5640.1864 459 474	156
40	5104.0633 903 275	5519.9452 041 289	5971.1797 672 130	6460.8354 079 157	160
41	5804.8444 382 588	6292.6913 739 122	6823.2313 684 274	7400.2763 563 407	164
42	6601.2652 301 463	7173.0271 362 102	7796.2653 043 773	8475.7048 726 470	168
43	7506.3782 888 158	8175.9322 099 400	8907.4597 897 354	9706.8056 625 621	172
44	8535.0174 922 606	9318.4719 430 610	10176.4321 643 577	11116.1128 661 085	176
45	9704.0411 857 415	10620.0876 950 939	11625.5852 233 161	12729.4225 238 048	180
46	11032.6084 728 360	12102.9276 496 502	13280.5027 221 415	14576.2647 488 830	184
47	12542.4932 135 651	13792.2236 860 530	15170.4010 396 369	16690.4442 481 876	188
48	14258.4408 757 060	15716.7207 228 624	17328.6449 720 424	19110.6590 854 841	192
49	16208.5740 877 185	17909.1658 389 801	19793.3367 645 291	21881.2090 130 550	196
50	18424.8535 398 839	20406.8654 951 756	22607.9887 789 474	25052.8063 369 262	200
51	20943.6017 873 546	23252.3203 376 696	25822.2916 732 968	28683.5041 578 480	204
52	23806.0985 397 105	26493.9483 855 371	29492.9916 545 725	32839.7589 786 073	208
53	27059.2571 932 107	30186.9089 076 275	33684.8922 922 578	37597.6471 276 955	212
54	30756.3936 934 124	34394.0410 080 207	38471.9985 787 597	43044.2572 648 234	216
55	34958.1003 290 283	39186.9328 909 103	43938.8234 343 505	49279.2844 567 824	220
56	39733.2387 776 130	44647.1399 994 349	50181.8797 220 238	56416.8550 017 100	224
57	45160.0686 780 801	50867.5727 562 047	57311.3841 127 119	64587.6154 034 480	228
58	51327.5302 262 021	57954.0775 191 989	65453.2028 813 817	73941.1237 327 007	232
59	58336.7018 135 201	66027.2376 544 462	74751.0739 856 402	84648.5871 466 066	236
60	66302.4565 988 785	75224.4253 723 879	85369.1446 560 503	96905.9956 744 388	240

TABLE 2. FUTURE WORTH OF ONE DOLLAR PER PERIOD WITH INTEREST
Payable at end of each period

QUARTERS	14% Nominal Annual Rate	14¼% Nominal Annual Rate	14½% Nominal Annual Rate	14¾% Nominal Annual Rate	QUARTERS
1	1.0000 000 000	1.0000 000 000	1.0000 000 000	1.0000 000 000	1
2	2.0350 000 000	2.0356 250 000	2.0362 500 000	2.0368 750 000	2
3	3.1062 250 000	3.1081 441 406	3.1100 640 625	3.1119 847 656	3
YEARS					
1	4.2149 428 750	4.2188 717 756	4.2228 038 848	4.2267 392 039	4
2	9.0516 867 704	9.0718 286 178	9.0920 204 031	9.1122 622 412	8
3	14.6019 616 385	14.6541 718 043	14.7066 002 294	14.7592 478 244	12
4	20.9710 297 094	21.0755 261 385	21.1806 410 752	21.2863 782 736	16
5	28.2796 818 133	28.4619 927 365	28.6457 063 463	28.8308 338 549	20
6	36.6665 282 061	36.9586 253 725	37.2534 987 325	37.5511 758 889	24
7	46.2906 273 446	46.7322 790 123	47.1789 430 621	47.6306 792 238	28
8	57.3345 024 663	57.9748 864 738	58.6237 410 684	59.2811 841 099	32
9	70.0076 031 845	70.9072 275 605	71.8204 703 084	72.7475 484 330	36
10	84.5502 777 478	85.7832 646 858	87.0373 105 303	88.3127 938 755	40
11	101.2383 312 998	102.8951 301 299	104.5834 935 373	106.3040 541 647	44
12	120.3882 565 864	122.5788 628 682	124.8155 872 983	127.0994 504 203	48
13	142.3632 363 131	145.2210 076 289	148.1447 420 090	151.1360 381 010	52
14	167.5800 309 877	171.2662 057 720	175.0450 453 560	178.9189 925 699	56
15	196.5168 828 788	201.2259 270 565	206.0631 567 765	211.0322 263 315	60
16	229.7225 859 896	235.6885 137 687	241.8294 164 980	248.1506 610 818	64
17	267.8268 940 611	275.3307 344 563	283.0706 551 124	291.0544 124 931	68
18	311.5524 639 960	320.9310 741 570	330.6249 639 973	340.6451 858 524	72
19	361.7285 612 119	373.3850 221 132	385.4587 267 429	397.9652 271 420	76
20	419.3067 868 486	433.7226 571 892	448.6862 576 933	464.2192 278 537	80
21	485.3791 251 019	503.1288 763 283	521.5924 466 891	540.7996 439 099	84
22	561.1986 529 527	582.9666 632 936	605.6588 701 915	629.3159 608 165	88
23	648.2033 050 580	674.8038 546 371	702.5938 994 097	731.6285 201 132	92
24	748.0431 445 102	780.4439 285 226	814.3674 172 787	849.8876 180 475	96
25	862.6116 566 603	901.9614 210 251	943.2508 497 959	986.5786 982 079	100
26	994.0816 594 999	1041.7426 654 050	1091.8633 252 207	1144.5745 879 261	104
27	1144.9465 116 506	1202.5326 543 853	1263.2248 991 678	1327.1958 762 981	108
28	1318.0673 994 794	1387.4889 457 030	1460.8179 272 208	1538.2807 027 840	112
29	1516.7276 001 516	1600.2436 695 198	1688.6578 322 582	1782.2654 231 295	116
30	1744.6947 497 318	1844.9748 553 793	1951.3747 046 041	2064.2778 479 594	120
31	2006.2922 972 619	2126.4884 794 140	2254.3073 932 561	2390.2450 136 319	124
32	2306.4814 999 598	2450.3128 430 270	2603.6120 002 824	2767.0177 503 674	128
33	2650.9555 145 949	2822.8071 364 342	3006.3869 831 763	3202.5146 656 910	132
34	3046.2473 695 063	3251.2863 190 160	3470.8174 074 589	3705.8885 692 798	136
35	3499.8538 649 769	3744.1647 688 484	4006.3412 809 866	4287.7188 369 544	140
36	4020.3777 517 623	4311.1215 223 724	4623.8413 501 543	4960.2337 567 165	144
37	4617.6908 842 232	4963.2903 491 404	5335.8662 556 181	5737.5675 298 634	148
38	5303.1214 422 976	5713.4783 942 857	6156.8855 417 923	6636.0573 285 559	152
39	6089.6687 730 191	6576.4176 823 650	7103.5837 023 449	7674.5866 530 782	156
40	6992.2499 261 022	7569.0544 215 533	8195.1992 371 878	8874.9822 051 059	160
41	8027.9825 591 957	8710.8817 894 777	9453.9156 111 745	10262.4726 180 420	164
42	9216.5095 781 684	10024.3227 358 681	10905.3120 594 397	11866.2186 855 260	168
43	10580.3716 693 039	11535.1703 194 136	12578.8834 005 073	13719.9262 318 923	172
44	12145.4347 885 624	13273.0942 260 640	14508.6394 206 428	15862.5545 052 361	176
45	13941.3807 153 413	15272.2234 156 671	16733.7960 099 482	18339.1349 813 373	180
46	16002.2699 741 990	17571.8163 388 266	19299.5720 952 490	21201.7177 871 891	184
47	18367.1878 004 792	20217.0318 855 492	22258.1085 647 911	24510.4656 350 515	188
48	21080.9854 007 238	23259.8162 053 973	25669.5278 588 422	28334.9182 581 703	192
49	24195.1305 660 454	26759.9228 143 217	29603.1557 588 647	32755.4539 227 206	196
50	27768.6837 705 370	30786.0860 208 048	34138.9302 040 692	37864.9787 324 765	200
51	31869.4182 666 484	35417.3707 147 928	39369.0257 648 753	43770.8792 302 087	204
52	36575.1054 203 926	40744.7250 262 700	45399.7267 853 117	50597.2793 335 052	208
53	41974.9896 630 596	46872.7663 442 343	52353.5872 597 627	58487.6490 388 838	212
54	48171.4810 322 325	53921.8357 695 161	60371.9213 363 929	67607.8197 211 578	216
55	55282.0974 015 327	62030.3613 463 232	69617.6750 584 683	78149.4694 004 002	220
56	63441.6932 339 253	71357.5764 811 216	80278.7377 021 934	90334.1512 261 318	224
57	72805.0171 273 997	82086.6469 325 550	92571.7600 030 209	104417.9498 451 143	228
58	83549.6466 574 632	94428.2677 795 271	106746.5568 632 182	120696.8635 153 238	232
59	95879.3561 764 057	108624.8010 039 005	123091.1840 111 195	139513.0250 816 327	236
60	110027.9814 404 172	124955.0349 407 324	141937.7917 783 219	161261.8925 590 338	240

TABLE 2. FUTURE WORTH OF ONE DOLLAR PER PERIOD WITH INTEREST
Payable at end of each period

QUARTERLY Compounding

QUARTERS	15% Nominal Annual Rate	15¼% Nominal Annual Rate	15½% Nominal Annual Rate	15¾% Nominal Annual Rate	QUARTERS
1	1.0000 000 000	1.0000 000 000	1.0000 000 000	1.0000 000 000	1
2	2.0375 000 000	2.0381 250 000	2.0387 500 000	2.0393 750 000	2
3	3.1139 062 500	3.1158 285 156	3.1177 515 625	3.1196 753 906	3
YEARS					
1	4.2306 777 344	4.2346 194 778	4.2385 644 355	4.2425 126 091	4
2	9.1325 542 472	9.1528 965 365	9.1732 892 245	9.1937 324 270	8
3	14.8121 155 033	14.8652 041 836	14.9185 147 867	14.9720 482 374	12
4	21.3927 415 098	21.4997 345 825	21.6073 613 128	21.7156 255 442	16
5	29.0173 865 636	29.2053 758 632	29.3948 132 351	29.5857 102 513	20
6	37.8516 847 196	38.1550 533 802	38.4613 103 069	38.7704 842 191	24
7	48.0875 479 447	48.5496 103 989	49.0169 284 954	49.4895 648 871	28
8	59.9473 351 187	60.6223 152 990	61.3062 475 630	61.9992 565 539	32
9	73.6886 824 501	74.6440 964 433	75.6140 181 217	76.5986 788 782	36
10	89.6101 002 389	90.9296 221 878	92.2717 594 687	93.6369 191 386	40
11	108.0574 575 679	109.8443 624 797	111.6654 410 803	113.5213 792 714	44
12	129.4314 957 935	131.8127 905 136	134.2444 257 465	136.7275 172 723	48
13	154.1965 340 546	157.3279 085 026	160.5318 815 668	163.8102 158 881	52
14	182.8905 559 143	186.9623 113 369	191.1369 040 566	195.4170 504 372	56
15	216.1368 962 512	221.3810 364 129	226.7686 292 415	232.3037 730 042	60
16	254.6577 822 811	261.3564 880 014	268.2526 647 483	275.3523 832 543	64
17	299.2900 228 673	307.7857 710 785	316.5502 196 099	325.5922 179 562	68
18	351.0031 869 466	361.7108 236 143	372.7803 760 329	384.2245 634 885	72
19	410.9206 659 701	424.3417 991 165	438.2460 191 782	452.6513 798 391	76
20	480.3440 779 088	497.0842 241 657	514.4640 257 615	532.5088 229 170	80
21	560.7815 429 649	581.5705 403 953	603.2004 109 618	625.7063 667 317	84
22	653.9804 452 369	679.6967 387 617	706.5112 480 120	734.4724 608 907	88
23	761.9653 920 356	793.6649 082 305	826.7903 086 016	861.4078 151 326	92
24	887.0821 954 618	926.0326 537 288	966.8245 279 477	1009.5475 849 856	96
25	1032.0488 316 799	1079.7704 923 723	1129.8585 796 918	1182.4339 454 732	100
26	1200.0144 849 009	1258.3285 160 193	1319.6700 568 591	1384.2007 881 808	104
27	1394.6279 587 177	1465.7138 161 511	1540.6570 008 690	1619.6725 668 761	108
28	1620.1169 409 277	1706.5804 086 030	1797.9398 066 908	1894.4796 551 858	112
29	1881.3798 437 521	1986.3336 761 802	2097.4798 653 498	2215.1929 746 491	116
30	2184.0922 145 438	2311.2516 729 994	2446.2176 927 953	2589.4811 122 434	120
31	2534.8300 285 992	2688.6260 127 928	2852.2337 456 594	3026.2936 842 259	124
32	2941.2125 424 243	3126.9255 029 063	3324.9356 500 985	3536.0753 307 091	128
33	3412.0678 107 324	3635.9861 961 661	3875.2761 819 174	4131.0154 578 021	132
34	3957.6244 627 809	4227.2321 256 447	4516.0070 487 035	4825.3396 989 107	136
35	4589.7339 041 042	4913.9316 759 215	5261.9743 542 475	5635.6500 643 361	140
36	5322.1277 706 435	5711.4953 441 671	6130.4625 913 316	6581.3219 125 024	144
37	6170.7162 280 814	6637.8215 732 276	7141.5951 333 986	7684.9672 348 041	148
38	7153.9335 964 892	7713.6984 176 843	8318.8005 047 222	8972.9753 316 933	152
39	8293.1388 084 685	8963.2700 568 381	9689.3552 328 295	10476.1438 081 312	156
40	9613.0794 001 429	10414.5786 238 199	11285.0158 613 786	12230.4149 761 573	160
41	11142.4291 145 134	12100.1935 102 309	13142.7547 675 932	14277.7352 727 219	164
42	12914.4107 958 087	14057.9422 687 872	15305.6168 335 713	16667.0582 423 525	168
43	14967.5181 062 831	16331.7595 164 440	17823.7168 210 336	19455.5150 670 046	172
44	17346.3517 436 839	18972.6728 885 737	20755.4005 592 612	22709.7806 316 768	176
45	20102.5883 249 673	22039.9481 703 849	24168.5968 516 173	26507.6677 898 300	180
46	23296.1029 838 172	25602.4193 039 316	28142.3914 251 058	30939.9879 491 462	184
47	26996.2700 687 269	29740.0331 179 287	32768.8593 922 870	36112.7224 661 544	188
48	31283.4701 973 714	34545.6434 462 671	38155.1986 847 489	42149.5567 700 137	192
49	36250.8364 057 809	40127.0948 977 556	44426.2138 910 200	49194.8378 089 739	196
50	42006.2773 248 056	46609.6430 397 923	51727.2080 508 790	57417.0255 351 139	200
51	48674.8213 343 663	54138.7653 082 691	60227.3494 106 049	67012.7209 559 262	204
52	56401.3326 187 501	62883.4257 244 527	70123.5911 488 285	78211.3670 676 254	208
53	65353.6581 252 054	73039.8666 836 509	81645.2348 952 939	91280.7350 743 539	212
54	75726.2737 888 246	84836.0129 086 973	95059.2437 818 931	106533.3270 744 580	216
55	87744.5092 325 177	98536.5863 991 244	110676.4281 324 303	124333.8483 086 803	220
56	101669.4427 173 898	114449.0471 626 272	128858.6471 171 156	145107.9276 394 484	224
57	117803.5726 790 283	132930.4930 471 324	150027.1932 382 787	169352.2947 769 314	228
58	136497.3890 553 749	154395.6735 153 423	174672.5539 206 708	197646.6575 998 604	232
59	158156.9871 584 929	179326.2972 020 482	203365.7763 880 354	230667.5635 701 311	236
60	183252.8894 902 498	208281.8421 288 026	236771.6991 566 921	269204.5766 819 389	240

TABLE 2. FUTURE WORTH OF ONE DOLLAR PER PERIOD WITH INTEREST
Payable at end of each period

QUARTERS	16% Nominal Annual Rate	16¼% Nominal Annual Rate	16½% Nominal Annual Rate	16¾% Nominal Annual Rate	QUARTERS
1	1.0000 000 000	1.0000 000 000	1.0000 000 000	1.0000 000 000	1
2	2.0400 000 000	2.0406 250 000	2.0412 500 000	2.0418 750 000	2
3	3.1216 000 000	3.1235 253 906	3.1254 515 625	3.1273 785 156	3
YEARS					
1	4.2464 640 000	4.2504 186 096	4.2543 764 395	4.2583 374 910	4
2	9.2142 262 601	9.2347 708 400	9.2553 662 831	9.2760 127 060	8
3	15.0258 054 642	15.0797 873 991	15.1339 949 780	15.1884 291 401	12
4	21.8245 311 432	21.9340 819 990	22.0442 820 238	22.1551 351 529	16
5	29.7780 785 758	29.9719 299 651	30.1672 762 685	30.3641 294 294	20
6	39.0826 041 223	39.3976 993 108	39.7157 993 706	40.0369 341 821	24
7	49.9675 829 796	50.4510 469 400	50.9400 217 061	51.4345 729 956	28
8	62.7014 686 711	63.4130 120 941	64.1340 168 077	64.8646 146 271	32
9	77.5983 138 495	78.6131 619 758	79.6434 660 627	80.6894 728 433	36
10	95.0255 156 984	96.4379 712 295	97.8747 155 320	99.3361 862 664	40
11	115.4128 769 582	117.3406 483 348	119.3054 221 773	121.3079 421 414	44
12	139.2632 060 438	141.8526 587 554	144.4970 684 267	147.1976 549 975	48
13	167.1647 176 834	170.5972 378 269	174.1096 729 598	177.7039 666 269	52
14	199.8055 399 119	204.3052 369 593	208.9190 831 333	213.6500 991 470	56
15	237.9906 852 013	243.8337 060 558	249.8373 021 054	256.0060 698 997	60
16	282.6619 042 830	290.1876 846 165	297.9363 832 306	305.9148 676 655	64
17	334.9209 123 114	344.5457 555 845	354.4765 177 525	364.7232 965 637	68
18	396.0565 601 905	408.2900 116 573	420.9390 516 924	434.0183 199 724	72
19	467.5766 211 830	483.0411 959 785	499.0652 969 704	515.6698 852 185	76
20	551.2449 767 468	570.6999 106 875	590.9021 536 085	611.8813 846 767	80
21	649.1251 187 043	673.4949 410 834	698.8557 383 118	725.2491 149 841	84
22	763.6310 406 272	794.0399 240 801	825.7544 244 918	858.8323 388 964	88
23	897.5867 735 595	935.3998 017 871	974.9229 453 750	1016.2358 404 254	92
24	1054.2960 343 913	1101.1687 498 478	1150.2695 016 892	1201.7072 010 348	96
25	1237.6237 046 067	1295.5615 619 165	1356.3881 561 427	1420.2514 219 202	100
26	1452.0911 488 931	1523.5208 137 911	1598.6791 974 199	1677.7659 854 922	104
27	1702.9877 244 328	1790.8425 319 258	1883.4906 272 189	1981.2000 007 363	108
28	1996.5012 310 027	2104.3235 615 346	2218.2844 772 786	2338.7417 270 373	112
29	2339.8705 191 390	2471.9343 812 252	2611.8323 138 838	2760.0395 368 542	116
30	2741.5640 201 064	2903.0217 580 983	3074.4450 520 478	3256.4622 799 917	120
31	3211.4886 007 095	3408.5463 959 634	3618.2431 004 826	3841.4060 754 778	124
32	3761.2338 938 824	4001.3616 190 448	4257.4739 151 269	4530.6558 099 179	128
33	4404.3581 309 205	4696.5401 769 115	5008.8852 811 056	5342.8110 974 718	132
34	5156.7225 247 629	5511.7574 798 773	5892.1641 030 693	6299.7881 961 101	136
35	6036.8824 511 387	6467.7410 089 067	6930.4522 001 802	7427.4114 245 156	140
36	7066.5450 751 784	7588.7973 265 910	8150.9526 195 217	8756.1100 391 940	144
37	8271.1047 098 233	8903.4300 888 269	9585.6423 532 843	10321.7393 772 352	148
38	9680.2691 094 431	10445.0647 705 831	11272.1101 328 483	12166.5484 235 128	152
39	11328.7921 447 856	12252.8985 324 250	13254.5412 498 873	14340.3199 124 182	156
40	13257.3309 290 382	14372.8968 362 594	15584.8752 067 096	16901.7137 301 211	160
41	15513.4485 340 881	16858.9621 499 648	18324.1665 261 628	19919.8498 694 768	164
42	18152.7870 267 224	19774.3044 560 556	21544.1843 741 900	23476.1736 541 008	168
43	21240.4397 550 682	23193.0484 105 396	25329.2929 049 920	27666.6535 652 494	172
44	24852.5567 296 308	27202.1180 151 286	29778.6615 936 554	32604.3709 805 372	176
45	29078.2226 920 442	31903.4467 219 360	35008.8634 667 478	38422.5717 093 777	180
46	34021.6541 898 742	37416.5691 641 482	41156.9293 042 670	45278.2616 717 625	184
47	39804.7698 433 842	43881.6604 092 708	48383.9378 327 393	53356.4437 508 653	188
48	46570.1971 941 128	51463.1000 101 278	56879.2359 721 761	62875.1101 522 319	192
49	54484.7902 924 209	60353.6514 721 518	66865.3997 069 480	74091.1249 898 881	196
50	63743.7447 773 934	70779.3634 028 993	78604.0655 549 115	87307.1558 427 461	200
51	74575.4119 382 890	83005.3169 590 115	92402.7854 187 102	102879.8413 314 713	204
52	87246.9304 855 336	97342.3657 235 553	108623.0844 156 893	121229.4151 203 602	208
53	102070.8149 262 264	114155.0393 799 299	127689.9328 007 808	142851.0460 508 546	212
54	119412.6630 316 217	133870.8121 388 813	150102.8801 458 188	168328.2004 236 493	216
55	139700.1724 839 383	156990.9715 749 880	176449.1434 896 984	198348.3870 146 508	220
56	163433.6890 778 116	184103.3642 205 312	207418.9923 676 384	233721.7097 088 404	224
57	191198.5466 240 564	215897.3419 825 585	243823.8338 058 174	275402.7284 005 207	228
58	223679.5028 917 115	253181.2894 064 484	286617.4711 064 817	324516.2180 830 031	232
59	261677.6276 184 135	296903.1774 291 423	336921.0934 016 271	382387.5212 446 215	236
60	306130.0590 938 934	348174.6662 158 721	396052.6506 991 266	450578.3126 397 292	240

TABLE 2. FUTURE WORTH OF ONE DOLLAR PER PERIOD WITH INTEREST
Payable at end of each period

QUARTERLY Compounding

QUARTERS	17% Nominal Annual Rate	17¼% Nominal Annual Rate	17½% Nominal Annual Rate	17¾% Nominal Annual Rate	QUARTERS
1	1.0000 000 000	1.0000 000 000	1.0000 000 000	1.0000 000 000	1
2	2.0425 000 000	2.0431 250 000	2.0437 500 000	2.0443 750 000	2
3	3.1293 062 500	3.1312 347 656	3.1331 640 625	3.1350 941 406	3
YEARS					
1	4.2623 017 656	4.2662 692 649	4.2702 399 902	4.2742 139 431	4
2	9.2967 102 258	9.3174 589 594	9.3382 590 243	9.3591 105 381	8
3	15.2430 908 288	15.2979 809 907	15.3531 005 763	15.4084 505 398	12
4	22.2666 453 449	22.3788 165 818	22.4916 528 689	22.6051 582 354	16
5	30.5625 014 857	30.7624 045 707	30.9638 509 135	31.1668 528 402	20
6	40.3611 339 232	40.6884 290 720	41.0188 504 097	41.3524 290 239	24
7	51.9347 673 151	52.4406 719 698	52.9523 550 725	53.4698 855 538	28
8	65.6049 392 238	66.3551 261 514	67.1153 128 718	67.8856 387 821	32
9	81.7514 330 416	82.8296 014 372	83.9242 369 300	85.0356 026 072	36
10	100.8228 290 966	102.3350 978 369	103.8734 546 004	105.4383 699 510	40
11	123.3489 670 674	125.4292 712 898	127.5496 449 551	129.7108 943 441	44
12	149.9556 659 380	152.7723 768 713	155.6490 922 102	158.5871 458 095	48
13	181.3821 104 406	185.1461 452 749	188.9981 624 880	192.9403 051 758	52
14	218.5013 870 136	223.4761 322 447	228.5776 061 079	233.8091 679 455	56
15	262.3447 398 047	268.8581 799 195	275.5514 001 064	282.4295 561 398	60
16	314.1302 205 964	322.5897 466 111	331.3009 792 010	340.2716 879 722	64
17	375.2965 286 021	386.2070 007 250	397.4658 618 869	409.0846 353 626	68
18	447.5429 802 687	461.5287 393 264	475.9918 664 227	490.9492 136 301	72
19	532.8767 195 215	550.7083 869 702	569.1883 346 702	588.3409 026 810	76
20	633.6684 800 424	656.2955 614 240	679.7960 466 654	704.2047 023 476	80
21	752.7184 487 635	781.3089 664 294	811.0678 231 913	842.0441 854 084	84
22	893.3340 603 895	929.3226 954 822	966.8641 867 671	1006.0274 411 374	88
23	1059.4218 842 279	1104.5684 140 285	1151.7668 943 086	1201.1131 129 810	92
24	1255.5961 561 203	1312.0563 414 347	1371.2136 803 022	1433.2003 415 791	96
25	1487.3069 706 945	1557.7184 915 656	1631.6581 731 017	1709.3071 472 167	100
26	1760.9916 953 668	1848.5782 671 746	1940.7596 872 682	2037.7826 457 602	104
27	2084.2538 126 600	2192.9512 567 550	2307.6084 734 837	2428.5595 152 195	108
28	2466.0741 594 184	2600.6829 745 705	2742.9930 503 297	2893.4543 471 977	112
29	2917.0604 315 477	3083.4303 407 776	3259.7174 797 898	3446.5249 654 744	116
30	3449.7418 859 957	3654.9949 490 659	3872.9779 171 140	4104.4955 165 760	120
31	4078.9174 273 555	4331.7176 498 328	4600.8095 088 586	4887.2621 865 282	124
32	4822.0667 496 006	5132.9457 298 998	5464.6167 817 566	5818.4948 360 173	128
33	5699.8359 552 495	6081.5860 452 913	6489.8031 204 302	6926.3527 466 351	132
34	6736.6111 433 880	7204.7599 209 631	7706.5178 460 158	8244.3361 214 575	136
35	7961.1959 019 123	8534.5785 408 590	9150.5428 662 597	9812.2990 882 421	140
36	9407.6115 260 192	10109.0609 964 488	10864.3449 722 437	11677.6548 371 638	144
37	11116.0421 945 357	11973.2212 404 631	12898.3247 283 416	13896.8093 349 071	148
38	13133.9513 628 839	14180.3550 214 882	15312.2986 835 441	16536.8669 687 935	152
39	15517.4003 882 047	16793.5635 924 702	18177.2584 939 479	19677.6596 974 338	156
40	18332.6060 205 540	19887.5577 554 711	21577.4586 897 868	23414.1610 668 220	160
41	21657.7800 302 410	23550.7938 197 423	25612.8944 853 602	27859.3580 886 208	164
42	25585.3020 796 592	27888.0025 394 773	30402.2425 008 459	33147.6678 225 591	168
43	30224.2862 061 225	33023.1833 327 709	36086.3508 785 824	39439.0019 760 111	172
44	35703.6122 174 853	39103.1493 855 510	42832.3814 333 443	46923.6024 290 402	176
45	42175.5062 184 865	46301.7249 938 794	50838.7256 515 563	55827.7939 049 842	180
46	49819.7697 416 524	54824.7151 453 004	60340.8391 122 265	66420.8277 399 681	184
47	58848.7749 760 653	64915.7894 179 910	71618.1659 118 999	79023.0236 981 608	188
48	69513.3648 709 583	76863.4484 165 151	85002.3567 314 504	94015.4560 308 315	192
49	82109.8220 302 448	91009.2719 123 671	100887.0222 267 635	111851.4766 732 168	196
50	96988.1000 071 338	107757.6845 010 187	119739.3085 771 207	133070.4240 258 994	200
51	114561.5456 798 628	127587.5179 724 995	142113.6356 122 563	158313.9318 566 742	204
52	135318.3828 146 488	151065.7009 600 084	168668.0015 375 175	188345.3314 831 889	208
53	159835.2758 510 913	178863.4672 492 573	200183.3337 566 887	224072.7339 334 905	212
54	188793.3507 378 007	211775.5461 389 573	237586.4548 735 772	266576.4900 594 235	216
55	222997.1179 075 558	250742.8834 987 501	281977.3392 709 059	317141.8589 615 092	220
56	263396.8231 082 545	296879.5431 124 068	334661.4618 450 308	377297.8725 765 976	224
57	311114.8470 382 791	351504.5574 071 411	397188.1902 283 124	448863.5716 436 015	228
58	367476.8872 183 896	416179.6381 712 604	471396.3495 616 296	534003.0111 636 487	232
59	434048.7883 918 913	492753.8253 975 798	559468.2998 143 699	635290.6986 492 570	236
60	512680.0446 716 883	583416.3507 488 345	663994.1159 915 495	755789.4439 313 021	240

QUARTERLY
Compounding

TABLE 2. FUTURE WORTH OF ONE DOLLAR PER PERIOD WITH INTEREST
Payable at end of each period

QUARTERS	18% Nominal Annual Rate	18¼% Nominal Annual Rate	18½% Nominal Annual Rate	18¾% Nominal Annual Rate	QUARTERS
1	1.0000 000 000	1.0000 000 000	1.0000 000 000	1.0000 000 000	1
2	2.0450 000 000	2.0456 250 000	2.0462 500 000	2.0468 750 000	2
3	3.1370 250 000	3.1389 566 406	3.1408 890 625	3.1428 222 656	3
YEARS					
1	4.2781 911 250	4.2821 715 374	4.2861 551 816	4.2901 420 593	4
2	9.3800 136 186	9.4009 683 838	9.4219 749 519	9.4430 334 416	8
3	15.4640 318 393	15.5198 454 363	15.5758 922 963	15.6321 733 885	12
4	22.7193 367 340	22.8341 924 415	22.9497 294 586	23.0659 519 103	16
5	31.3714 227 742	31.5775 732 373	31.7853 168 502	31.9946 663 335	20
6	41.6891 963 113	42.0291 839 805	42.3724 240 558	42.7189 488 793	24
7	53.9933 331 713	54.5227 685 196	55.0582 630 402	55.5998 890 316	28
8	68.6662 452 415	69.4572 755 988	70.2588 752 201	71.0711 915 172	32
9	86.1639 658 106	87.3095 982 049	88.4727 758 480	89.6537 792 610	36
10	107.0303 230 577	108.6498 018 517	110.2973 031 865	111.9733 330 009	40
11	131.9138 422 022	134.1593 280 760	136.4482 086 559	138.7813 581 272	44
12	161.5879 016 311	164.6527 544 255	167.7831 304 283	170.9804 880 718	48
13	196.9747 694 560	201.1038 057 841	205.3297 203 018	209.6548 762 187	52
14	239.1742 675 551	244.6764 476 354	250.3193 462 969	256.1066 996 409	56
15	289.4979 539 753	296.7620 541 444	304.2274 762 763	311.9000 037 536	60
16	349.5098 860 835	359.0238 379 183	368.8220 669 981	378.9133 641 445	64
17	421.0752 313 819	433.4499 601 916	446.2215 455 572	459.4031 387 206	68
18	506.4182 368 104	522.4170 173 634	538.9642 847 601	556.0794 398 867	72
19	608.1913 582 171	628.7659 311 594	650.0918 509 270	672.1973 847 609	76
20	729.5576 985 382	755.8926 657 637	783.2487 542 956	811.6666 958 452	80
21	874.2893 168 610	907.8566 687 259	942.8019 734 139	979.1833 424 358	84
22	1046.8844 638 095	1089.5104 984 117	1133.9841 734 124	1180.3876 551 752	88
23	1252.7073 869 232	1306.6547 772 953	1363.0653 151 047	1422.0542 375 053	92
24	1498.1550 511 712	1566.2234 191 096	1637.5582 829 616	1712.3200 683 911	96
25	1790.8559 562 670	1876.5050 445 786	1966.4652 756 819	2060.9584 765 957	100
26	2139.9072 300 134	2247.4076 560 450	2360.5730 399 168	2479.7082 112 941	104
27	2556.1573 665 279	2690.7750 226 579	2832.8066 295 574	2982.6686 889 220	108
28	3052.5433 968 342	3220.7648 790 250	3398.6532 923 802	3586.7747 243 273	112
29	3644.4929 710 648	3854.3010 140 769	4076.6703 857 246	4312.3667 305 506	116
30	4350.4038 489 668	4611.6136 863 753	4889.0939 786 710	5183.8755 860 149	120
31	5192.2157 012 485	5516.8856 225 639	5862.5681 002 747	6230.6452 287 872	124
32	6196.0919 933 210	6599.0242 271 686	7029.0185 500 894	7487.9206 748 822	128
33	7393.2331 443 440	7892.5846 621 758	8426.6999 282 355	8998.0347 274 513	132
34	8820.8462 345 124	9438.8732 724 295	10101.4502 231 383	10811.8333 336 755	136
35	10523.3013 990 341	11287.2665 917 465	12108.1941 020 594	12990.3875 815 110	140
36	12553.5108 494 562	13496.7880 486 339	14512.7442 059 430	15607.0499 796 823	144
37	14974.5733 822 493	16137.9927 194 283	17393.9595 233 630	18749.9242 564 217	148
38	17861.7354 858 813	19295.2203 133 408	20846.3316 290 339	22524.8318 357 461	152
39	21304.7299 974 820	23069.2883 323 726	24983.0836 044 773	27058.8748 733 265	156
40	25410.5649 944 157	27580.7114 048 623	29939.8832 722 259	32504.7158 203 281	160
41	30306.8495 993 563	32973.5495 933 521	35879.2925 218 122	39045.7176 092 890	164
42	36145.7600 647 017	39420.0085 620 484	42996.0986 464 573	46902.1175 334 820	168
43	43108.7694 020 101	47125.9384 977 510	51523.7025 355 667	56338.4426 959 405	172
44	51412.2875 530 759	56337.4073 773 810	61741.7732 285 043	67672.4167 083 182	176
45	61314.3873 988 491	67348.5584 815 802	73985.4198 663 613	81285.6575 305 308	180
46	73122.8256 501 797	80511.0030 627 723	88656.1818 426 233	97636.5266 503 267	184
47	87204.6079 092 232	96245.0480 970 725	106235.1975 828 070	117275.5622 381 245	188
48	103997.3951 830 836	115053.1176 478 553	127298.9838 328 762	140864.0159 156 012	192
49	124023.1063 635 010	137535.7964 158 343	152538.3429 498 030	169196.1172 760 251	196
50	147904.1394 368 927	164411.0077 829 196	182781.0182 727 689	203225.8158 087 356	200
51	176382.7155 790 532	196536.9387 486 823	219018.8405 745 618	244098.9006 355 729	204
52	210343.9473 478 949	234939.4438 051 063	262440.2558 810 015	293191.5795 394 425	208
53	250843.3479 323 753	280844.8028 180 587	314469.3014 321 475	352156.8162 513 035	212
54	299139.6364 435 312	335718.8789 495 985	376812.3080 305 934	422979.9861 845 245	216
55	356733.8588 342 360	401313.9270 231 888	451513.8604 146 972	508045.7245 601 822	220
56	425416.0403 236 844	479724.5470 300 295	541023.8509 183 334	610218.2177 177 014	224
57	507320.8192 813 537	573454.5695 000 115	648277.8254 912 360	732937.6410 409 060	228
58	604993.7916 684 534	685497.0085 402 446	776793.2570 867 467	880335.9905 904 449	232
59	721470.6280 184 019	819429.6356 246 426	930784.9037 734 992	1057376.2085 248 778	236
60	860371.4219 076 695	979529.2260 243 762	1115303.0348 251 323	1270019.2867 008 474	240

TABLE 2. FUTURE WORTH OF ONE DOLLAR PER PERIOD WITH INTEREST
Payable at end of each period

QUARTERLY Compounding

QUARTERS	19% Nominal Annual Rate	19¼% Nominal Annual Rate	19½% Nominal Annual Rate	19¾% Nominal Annual Rate	QUARTERS
1	1.0000 000 000	1.0000 000 000	1.0000 000 000	1.0000 000 000	1
2	2.0475 000 000	2.0481 250 000	2.0487 500 000	2.0493 750 000	2
3	3.1447 562 500	3.1466 910 156	3.1486 265 625	3.1505 628 906	3
YEARS					
1	4.2941 321 719	4.2981 255 208	4.3021 221 074	4.3061 219 333	4
2	9.4641 439 715	9.4853 066 605	9.5065 216 279	9.5277 889 931	8
3	15.6886 896 859	15.7454 421 653	15.8024 318 073	15.8596 595 962	12
4	23.1828 639 457	23.3004 697 386	23.4187 734 871	23.5377 794 142	16
5	32.2056 345 081	32.4182 342 965	32.6324 787 230	32.8483 809 148	20
6	43.0687 911 147	43.4219 837 503	43.7785 601 019	44.1385 538 163	24
7	56.1477 196 592	56.7018 289 660	57.2622 918 826	57.8291 842 377	28
8	71.8943 739 760	72.7285 741 854	73.5739 458 667	74.4306 449 036	32
9	90.8528 935 006	92.0704 082 318	93.3066 178 025	94.5618 213 183	36
10	113.6784 064 847	115.4130 482 477	117.1777 924 917	118.9731 831 854	40
11	141.1596 685 269	143.5840 501 083	146.0554 317 136	148.5747 611 525	44
12	174.2463 187 134	177.5821 473 798	180.9895 335 281	184.4700 718 243	48
13	214.0816 952 286	218.6126 589 602	223.2503 104 639	227.9972 557 352	52
14	262.0423 444 078	268.1302 206 966	274.3743 747 580	280.7789 618 620	56
15	319.7855 885 017	327.8903 559 196	336.2206 099 540	344.7828 383 214	60
16	389.3067 958 987	400.0117 132 044	411.0377 603 653	422.3948 842 827	64
17	473.0083 328 280	487.0511 778 442	501.5461 959 705	516.5083 975 809	68
18	573.7825 792 290	592.0945 199 276	611.0368 257 349	630.6318 339 061	72
19	695.1118 774 745	718.8657 927 255	743.4907 558 689	769.0195 984 497	76
20	841.1888 677 618	871.8593 598 385	903.7240 438 288	936.8306 457 860	80
21	1017.0613 684 685	1056.4992 318 012	1097.5628 113 495	1140.3208 004 322	84
22	1228.8068 079 382	1279.3313 610 321	1332.0550 836 628	1387.0759 675 992	88
23	1483.7422 353 419	1548.2557 124 722	1615.7270 574 270	1686.2949 279 931	92
24	1790.6771 677 225	1872.8063 374 073	1958.8931 153 336	2049.1322 589 680	96
25	2160.2180 105 739	2264.4893 798 006	2374.0308 595 967	2489.1141 657 823	100
26	2605.1345 714 755	2737.1909 983 208	2876.2348 006 368	3022.6427 247 200	104
27	3140.8013 319 807	3307.6696 659 348	3483.7651 971 896	3669.6073 357 497	108
28	3785.7287 262 960	3996.1503 003 391	4218.7120 038 020	4454.1261 790 487	112
29	4562.2027 855 529	4827.0412 886 598	5107.7980 670 090	5405.4453 161 365	116
30	5497.0552 511 377	5829.7998 267 702	6183.3507 746 023	6559.0289 531 896	120
31	6622.5907 690 226	7039.9762 517 012	7484.4774 873 961	7957.8815 104 402	124
32	7977.7032 051 095	8500.4743 913 814	9058.4874 924 786	9654.1507 830 568	128
33	9609.2196 568 411	10263.0726 143 067	10962.6121 805 194	11711.0719 577 077	132
34	11573.5186 045 781	12390.2595 042 124	13266.0859 932 009	14205.3249 557 595	136
35	13938.4781 193 813	14957.4492 390 783	16052.6638 045 359	17229.8929 824 591	140
36	16785.8214 492 252	18055.6552 152 786	19423.6662 686 730	20897.5288 458 934	144
37	20213.9410 374 293	21794.7167 036 436	23501.6638 637 855	25344.9582 665 596	148
38	24341.2985 597 386	26307.1929 305 861	28434.9335 847 854	30737.9768 726 340	152
39	29310.5184 713 134	31753.0626 393 574	34402.8503 313 040	37277.6308 917 206	156
40	35293.3165 197 305	38325.3957 428 180	41622.4090 231 320	45207.7119 489 576	160
41	42496.4335 330 806	46257.1981 422 167	50356.1145 888 398	54823.8453 699 014	164
42	51168.7795 304 091	55829.6723 781 891	60921.5267 095 025	66484.5107 908 435	168
43	61610.0350 254 936	67382.1869 750 357	73702.8063 667 585	80624.4059 136 601	172
44	74181.0067 495 481	81324.3079 168 528	89164.6840 305 273	97770.6515 923 305	176
45	89316.0956 439 222	98150.3188 019 038	107869.3573 731 244	118562.4423 602 075	180
46	107538.3079 652 085	118456.7444 515 840	130496.9329 148 119	143774.8749 496 310	184
47	129477.3282 246 446	142963.4992 304 209	157870.1548 640 429	174347.8431 067 713	188
48	155891.2784 880 650	172539.4098 387 711	190984.3202 991 077	211421.0758 708 964	192
49	187692.9159 480 774	208233.0174 260 355	231043.4684 145 395	256376.6255 093 442	196
50	225981.1740 485 185	251309.7510 375 414	279504.1596 821 758	310890.3890 150 348	200
51	272079.1370 923 822	303296.7902 881 979	338128.4367 479 300	376994.5838 353 516	204
52	327579.7605 790 625	366037.2077 586 493	409047.8927 354 993	457153.5068 637 761	208
53	394400.9171 772 233	441755.3105 993 838	494841.1764 962 783	554355.4009 121 407	212
54	474851.6704 951 119	533135.4978 686 225	598627.7529 154 160	672223.8533 517 916	216
55	571712.0667 965 120	643417.4292 968 996	724181.3274 217 908	815152.8797 512 727	220
56	688329.2019 349 863	776510.8794 527 558	876067.0588 449 643	988470.7282 906 274	224
57	828732.8831 834 864	937134.3491 814 280	1059807.5497 123 195	1198638.5114 136 484	228
58	997774.8827 551 827	1130982.3484 440 909	1282083.6494 343 884	1453491.0695 032 762	232
59	1201296.5950 429 268	1364927.2811 591 738	1550977.3716 315 410	1762529.0457 320 541	236
60	1446330.8911 201 406	1647263.0893 761 341	1876265.7581 357 457	2137273.0603 398 698	240

QUARTERLY
Compounding

TABLE 2. FUTURE WORTH OF ONE DOLLAR PER PERIOD WITH INTEREST
Payable at end of each period

QUARTERS	20% Nominal Annual Rate	20¼% Nominal Annual Rate	20½% Nominal Annual Rate	20¾% Nominal Annual Rate	QUARTERS
1	1.0000 000 000	1.0000 000 000	1.0000 000 000	1.0000 000 000	1
2	2.0500 000 000	2.0506 250 000	2.0512 500 000	2.0518 750 000	2
3	3.1525 000 000	3.1544 378 906	3.1563 765 625	3.1583 160 156	3
YEARS					
1	4.3101 250 000	4.3141 313 088	4.3181 408 613	4.3221 536 589	4
2	9.5491 088 758	9.5704 813 958	9.5919 066 732	9.6133 848 284	8
3	15.9171 265 204	15.9748 335 720	16.0327 817 469	16.0909 720 449	12
4	23.6574 917 676	23.7779 148 202	23.8990 528 698	24.0209 102 395	16
5	33.0659 541 029	33.2852 116 225	33.5061 669 142	33.7288 335 246	20
6	44.5019 988 743	44.8689 295 939	45.2393 806 341	45.6133 869 974	24
7	58.4025 827 692	58.9825 651 343	59.5692 099 208	60.1625 966 582	28
8	75.2988 293 721	76.1786 595 710	77.0702 980 533	77.9739 096 572	32
9	95.8363 227 194	97.1304 308 586	98.4444 595 796	99.7787 277 979	36
10	120.7997 742 425	122.6581 297 033	124.5488 239 193	126.4724 417 414	40
11	151.1430 055 903	153.7611 519 425	156.4302 072 777	159.1511 992 294	44
12	188.0253 929 388	191.6571 643 600	195.3670 912 262	199.1569 171 759	48
13	232.8561 652 759	237.8297 756 936	242.9208 913 411	248.1323 859 954	52
14	287.3482 492 439	294.0866 191 281	300.9985 718 346	308.0887 289 684	56
15	353.5837 178 825	362.6301 201 734	371.9291 170 983	381.4879 867 876	60
16	434.0933 439 844	446.1437 204 525	458.5569 267 602	471.3442 185 269	64
17	531.9532 976 964	547.8969 330 140	564.3558 795 093	581.3472 706 322	68
18	650.9026 830 581	671.8733 420 299	693.5686 397 822	716.0142 963 715	72
19	795.4864 043 989	822.9265 579 977	851.3767 936 769	880.8752 477 215	76
20	971.2288 213 368	1006.9702 340 111	1044.1086 367 478	1082.6999 567 088	80
21	1184.8448 275 151	1231.2095 821 342	1279.4929 462 195	1329.7761 310 501	84
22	1444.4964 181 247	1504.4234 536 231	1566.9689 141 895	1632.2496 796 727	88
23	1760.1045 493 332	1837.3080 262 851	1918.0646 705 114	2002.5413 432 062	92
24	2143.7282 053 680	2242.8955 541 529	2346.8595 745 785	2455.8567 379 138	96
25	2610.0251 569 261	2737.0645 733 008	2870.5488 144 602	3010.8107 574 505	100
26	3176.8120 159 009	3339.1615 380 903	3510.1329 544 920	3690.1919 728 152	104
27	3865.7449 854 026	4072.7582 245 717	4291.2600 830 021	4521.8984 197 307	108
28	4703.1473 156 630	4966.5745 529 844	5245.2543 313 020	5540.0832 005 237	112
29	5721.0150 818 591	6055.6029 573 641	6410.3720 087 861	6786.5569 433 726	116
30	6958.2397 133 440	7382.4783 207 308	7833.3357 266 544	8312.5047 093 583	120
31	8462.0939 855 679	8999.1471 080 914	9571.2080 304 563	10180.5878 501 993	124
32	10290.0382 525 452	10968.9010 429 254	11693.6796 763 576	12467.5171 271 262	128
33	12511.9159 337 077	13368.8549 445 088	14285.8643 137 443	15267.2027 531 693	132
34	15212.6221 418 963	16292.9657 320 881	17451.7116 442 747	18694.6107 118 468	136
35	18495.3474 173 634	19855.7107 883 148	21318.1759 291 381	22890.4837 077 047	140
36	22485.5205 067 265	24196.5696 879 105	26040.3070 066 398	28027.1206 093 018	144
37	27335.6008 354 293	29485.4847 488 597	31807.4679 760 047	34315.4517 110 523	148
38	33230.9037 879 695	35929.5141 838 040	38850.9288 839 479	42013.7003 517 043	152
39	40396.6813 724 256	43780.9383 189 793	47453.1409 299 185	51437.9865 692 038	156
40	49106.7288 124 419	53347.1362 348 562	57959.0630 967 318	62975.3082 192 653	160
41	59693.8459 135 782	65002.6194 937 140	70789.9954 180 106	77099.4326 128 784	164
42	72562.5529 194 913	79203.6940 681 847	86460.4736 129 937	94390.3512 452 107	168
43	88204.5467 145 974	96506.3244 774 742	105598.9025 837 552	115558.0965 027 597	172
44	107217.4879 350 101	117587.8995 026 958	128972.7562 027 305	141471.8983 554 058	176
45	130327.8368 193 043	143273.7515 974 984	157519.3539 321 442	173195.8783 205 711	180
46	158418.6103 278 445	174569.4682 148 172	192383.4484 545 560	212032.7464 325 127	184
47	192563.1210 948 096	212700.2600 210 077	234963.1316 234 274	259577.2955 843 075	188
48	234065.9873 352 479	259158.9272 420 176	286965.8996 171 867	317781.8899 283 187	192
49	284512.9806 434 147	315764.3019 985 451	350477.1255 764 669	389036.6365 436 416	196
50	345831.6163 031 995	384732.4546 165 331	428043.6855 590 975	476267.5325 310 865	200
51	420364.8011 891 409	468763.4516 021 958	522776.0913 135 779	583056.6178 372 451	204
52	510960.3532 504 082	571147.0618 101 746	638473.2255 173 006	713789.0677 500 304	208
53	621079.8130 030 790	695891.5491 451 019	779774.6815 116 358	873833.2652 557 962	212
54	754930.7045 790 738	847880.5939 623 666	952346.8165 393 037	1069761.2477 295 611	216
55	917627.2998 577 678	1033064.4865 574 867	1163109.9794 411 890	1309618.5803 570 498	220
56	1115386.0282 727 408	1258693.0778 675 466	1420516.0249 147 804	1603254.7383 411 566	224
57	1355762.9986 531 932	1533599.6072 808 048	1734887.2429 876 324	1962727.5646 715 278	228
58	1647942.7085 066 979	1868546.5192 623 140	2118830.2951 827 604	2402798.4120 667 567	232
59	2003088.9719 568 194	2276646.8073 325 844	2587741.7567 108 630	2941538.3015 436 062	236
60	2434771.4748 445 887	2773877.3807 920 341	3160425.5375 354 071	3601069.9888 422 697	240

TABLE 2. FUTURE WORTH OF ONE DOLLAR PER PERIOD WITH INTEREST
Payable at end of each period

QUARTERLY Compounding

QUARTERS	21% Nominal Annual Rate	21¼% Nominal Annual Rate	21½% Nominal Annual Rate	21¾% Nominal Annual Rate	QUARTERS
1	1.0000 000 000	1.0000 000 000	1.0000 000 000	1.0000 000 000	1
2	2.0525 000 000	2.0531 250 000	2.0537 500 000	2.0543 750 000	2
3	3.1602 562 500	3.1621 972 656	3.1641 390 625	3.1660 816 406	3
YEARS					
1	4.3261 697 031	4.3301 889 954	4.3342 115 371	4.3382 373 298	4
2	9.6349 159 820	9.6565 002 548	9.6781 377 678	9.6998 286 424	8
3	16.1494 054 698	16.2080 830 293	16.2670 057 349	16.3261 746 020	12
4	24.1434 912 780	24.2668 003 593	24.3908 418 832	24.5156 202 754	16
5	33.9532 251 071	34.1793 554 227	34.4072 383 409	34.6368 878 407	20
6	45.9909 840 337	46.3722 074 438	46.7570 932 821	47.1456 779 608	24
7	60.7628 058 284	61.3699 188 772	61.9840 182 257	62.6051 872 819	28
8	78.8896 615 383	79.8177 232 015	80.7582 665 343	81.7114 658 393	32
9	101.1335 595 823	102.5092 842 372	103.9062 363 874	105.3247 560 629	36
10	128.4295 787 107	130.4208 412 543	132.4468 468 828	134.5082 243 928	40
11	161.9251 764 150	164.7532 088 641	167.6363 884 549	170.5758 293 602	44
12	203.0284 252 181	206.9834 386 205	211.0238 218 194	215.1514 813 484	48
13	253.4672 045 789	258.9283 649 232	264.5189 595 749	270.2421 576 483	52
14	315.3618 366 943	322.8227 691 010	330.4765 316 546	338.3282 647 451	56
15	391.3142 196 274	401.4155 244 640	411.7998 349 897	422.4753 163 145	60
16	484.5172 047 016	498.0878 586 850	512.0685 298 007	526.4719 551 261	64
17	598.8888 161 150	616.9988 214 142	635.6962 078 066	655.0005 331 615	68
18	739.2369 550 385	763.2642 154 498	788.1246 681 347	813.8479 301 601	72
19	911.4615 119 533	943.1766 894 670	976.0634 524 972	1010.1661 024 988	76
20	1122.8023 835 317	1164.4764 611 623	1207.7851 834 104	1252.7940 933 798	80
21	1382.1438 200 820	1436.6843 178 989	1493.4897 055 480	1552.6560 025 328	84
22	1700.3878 975 746	1771.5112 212 504	1845.7530 588 733	1923.2528 336 504	88
23	2090.9128 140 953	2183.3621 375 023	2280.0810 462 907	2381.2703 645 275	92
24	2570.1352 763 797	2689.9557 699 724	2815.5917 625 581	2947.3304 086 950	96
25	3158.2006 177 771	3313.0868 553 535	3475.8571 277 777	3646.9192 934 030	100
26	3879.8296 585 037	4079.5638 196 907	4289.9404 677 849	4511.5353 578 111	104
27	4765.3579 081 068	5022.3621 339 494	5293.6758 132 799	5580.1071 364 276	108
28	5852.0107 956 564	6182.0429 889 870	6531.2452 294 374	6900.7460 801 849	112
29	7185.4685 352 023	7608.4983 243 447	8057.1236 063 246	8532.9127 297 913	116
30	8821.7864 095 923	9363.0972 857 155	9938.4765 152 233	10550.0938 712 985	120
31	10829.7511 966 579	11521.3264 562 570	12258.1166 788 399	13043.1112 103 269	124
32	13293.7727 961 275	14176.0374 501 225	15118.1491 922 576	16124.2105 349 280	128
33	16317.4326 141 495	17441.4415 865 990	18644.4659 486 689	19932.1154 778 423	132
34	20027.8378 707 788	21458.0235 042 380	22992.2871 039 216	24638.2734 190 989	136
35	24580.9648 748 042	26398.5851 091 220	28352.9935 020 899	30454.5747 449 143	140
36	30168.2158 840 426	32475.6798 807 883	34962.5508 093 506	37642.8930 153 484	144
37	37024.4651 853 768	39950.7573 754 816	43111.8961 666 882	46526.8755 778 941	148
38	45437.9326 319 476	49145.4113 427 339	53159.7445 574 125	57506.5154 884 195	152
39	55762.2996 967 115	60455.2153 731 974	65548.3785 956 153	71076.1608 266 536	156
40	68431.5773 714 503	74366.7413 167 575	80823.1167 648 536	87846.7722 589 047	160
41	83978.3509 211 281	91478.4926 395 091	99656.3170 530 617	108573.4309 740 805	164
42	103056.1684 581 839	112526.6533 171 837	122876.9725 671 489	134189.3355 122 554	168
43	126467.0144 973 440	138416.7600 372 461	151507.2018 565 124	165847.8181 613 882	172
44	155195.0234 116 088	170262.6603 152 305	186807.2401 635 385	204974.2726 713 900	176
45	190447.8500 201 634	209434.4325 864 297	230330.9120 099 405	253330.3312 825 933	180
46	233707.4364 259 491	257617.3298 973 110	283994.0268 914 971	313093.1805 796 694	184
47	286792.3092 158 523	316884.2830 797 657	350158.7086 985 353	386953.5872 935 768	188
48	351934.0258 445 464	389785.0826 491 186	431737.3708 445 750	478237.0475 721 471	192
49	431870.9838 198 926	479456.0762 210 350	532320.9138 433 377	591053.5143 525 868	196
50	529963.5361 972 671	589755.1008 637 635	656336.7882 894 363	730482.4441 716 507	200
51	650335.2525 549 945	725427.4554 628 031	809243.8808 027 680	902801.4949 740 822	204
52	798046.2637 147 697	892310.0535 825 047	997772.8013 567 456	1115769.1718 255 400	208
53	979305.9771 926 572	1097582.5399 153 908	1230222.1488 724 539	1378974.1463 904 705	212
54	1201734.1054 149 154	1350076.1738 835 116	1516823.7959 922 041	1704266.9779 596 735	216
55	1474680.9796 826 651	1660653.7692 220 333	1870193.2720 076 315	2106293.6738 654 762	220
56	1809620.6150 964 548	2042677.0353 549 020	2305885.0687 377 583	2603155.1123 461 841	224
57	2220633.0499 231 451	2512581.4265 836 120	2843077.3126 135 101	3217222.0177 612 453	228
58	2724996.2357 654 659	3090583.2303 251 311	3505415.9406 208 045	3976142.1816 585 510	232
59	3343912.3601 408 260	3801549.3148 404 905	4322055.5387 384 034	4914085.2788 860 582	236
60	4103399.1342 837 180	4676066.9548 531 630	5328942.6581 264 166	6073281.3254 359 189	240

QUARTERLY
Compounding

TABLE 2. FUTURE WORTH OF ONE DOLLAR PER PERIOD WITH INTEREST
Payable at end of each period

QUARTERS	22% Nominal Annual Rate	22¼% Nominal Annual Rate	22½% Nominal Annual Rate	22¾% Nominal Annual Rate	QUARTERS
1	1.0000 000 000	1.0000 000 000	1.0000 000 000	1.0000 000 000	1
2	2.0550 000 000	2.0556 250 000	2.0562 500 000	2.0568 750 000	2
3	3.1680 250 000	3.1699 691 406	3.1719 140 625	3.1738 597 656	3
YEARS					
1	4.3422 663 750	4.3462 986 741	4.3503 342 285	4.3543 730 398	4
2	9.7215 729 999	9.7433 709 623	9.7652 226 514	9.7871 281 895	8
3	16.3855 906 502	16.4452 549 027	16.5051 683 871	16.5653 321 345	12
4	24.6411 399 875	24.7674 054 971	24.8944 213 083	25.0221 919 515	16
5	34.8683 180 110	35.1015 430 517	35.3365 772 746	35.5734 351 042	20
6	47.5379 982 528	47.9340 912 958	48.3339 945 952	48.7377 460 280	24
7	63.2335 104 520	63.8690 731 526	64.5119 618 224	65.1622 639 343	28
8	82.6774 978 685	83.6565 418 568	84.6487 795 571	85.6543 952 749	32
9	106.7651 887 865	108.2278 856 612	109.7132 034 605	111.2215 047 189	36
10	136.6056 140 723	138.7396 679 098	140.9110 498 078	143.1204 357 993	40
11	173.5726 685 015	176.6280 660 128	179.7432 057 138	182.9192 955 922	44
12	219.3683 667 895	223.6764 717 440	228.0778 348 263	232.5745 406 794	48
13	276.1012 067 211	282.0994 347 793	288.2402 522 079	294.5271 538 321	52
14	346.3832 473 284	354.6469 006 665	363.1247 921 673	371.8226 393 283	56
15	433.4503 717 290	444.7336 496 641	456.3340 508 539	468.2607 357 063	60
16	541.3112 716 955	556.6000 290 849	572.3522 023 925	588.5822 056 255	64
17	674.9320 134 125	695.5115 447 512	716.7607 265 679	738.7018 851 634	68
18	840.4646 820 864	868.0067 062 522	896.5069 264 339	925.9994 489 291	72
19	1045.5306 325 233	1082.2047 919 799	1120.2381 538 718	1159.6821 846 005	76
20	1299.5713 869 284	1348.1880 203 219	1398.7178 222 497	1451.2376 103 786	80
21	1614.2833 357 488	1678.4761 156 561	1745.3432 200 001	1814.9981 854 010	84
22	2004.1562 557 938	2088.6156 067 792	2176.7900 364 428	2268.8458 734 949	88
23	2487.1404 397 566	2597.9115 958 113	2713.8146 071 367	2835.0911 956 426	92
24	3085.4731 527 118	3230.3364 416 458	3382.2524 737 243	3541.5699 841 560	96
25	3826.7024 667 960	4015.6581 293 129	4214.2612 976 610	4423.0117 534 692	100
26	4744.9556 128 494	4990.8414 371 516	5249.8679 227 653	5522.7469 547 554	104
27	5882.5102 456 943	6201.7878 541 700	6538.8940 137 208	6894.8370 406 271	108
28	7291.7409 662 953	7705.4961 448 088	8143.3529 104 539	8606.7320 509 402	112
29	9037.5307 213 937	9572.7452 580 300	10140.4330 078 766	10742.5863 629 207	116
30	11200.2581 048 183	11891.4258 641 894	12626.2111 874 502	13407.3956 032 790	120
31	13879.4980 999 864	14770.6773 338 044	15720.2749 488 480	16732.1580 871 559	124
32	17198.6066 509 410	18346.0248 841 564	19571.4756 063 569	20880.3145 130 576	128
33	21310.4001 419 637	22785.7586 971 661	24365.0893 286 856	26055.7824 802 267	132
34	26404.1912 769 222	28298.8552 710 757	30331.7305 303 316	32512.9807 941 427	136
35	32714.5053 000 438	35144.8138 607 980	37758.4464 259 721	40569.3363 410 688	140
36	40531.8778 650 714	43645.8710 042 530	47002.5264 922 151	50620.8883 521 955	144
37	50216.2317 017 473	54202.1680 675 719	58508.6911 916 447	63161.7571 413 012	148
38	62213.4479 599 961	67310.5857 394 646	72830.4868 859 355	78808.4343 719 886	152
39	77075.8951 995 938	83588.1320 068 831	90656.9162 190 020	98330.0889 302 427	156
40	95487.8612 086 210	103800.9844 746 589	112845.5851 226 854	122686.3781 968 464	160
41	118297.0585 670 733	128900.5540 395 048	140463.9611 035 691	153074.6234 692 045	164
42	146553.6545 156 948	160068.2674 211 215	174840.7276 925 207	190988.6686 106 860	168
43	181558.6221 195 976	198771.1764 462 696	217629.7056 515 879	238292.3153 368 055	172
44	224923.6388 816 418	246831.0115 926 101	270889.4161 029 473	297310.9451 147 537	176
45	278645.2906 212 286	306509.9301 150 554	337182.1132 567 844	370945.8316 814 000	180
46	345196.9970 685 201	380616.9948 847 078	419697.0510 716 253	462816.7636 241 268	184
47	427642.8915 565 836	472640.3958 568 276	522403.9140 430 767	577439.9881 521 625	188
48	529778.8979 912 244	586911.6377 795 462	650243.7934 732 376	720450.2235 266 673	192
49	656307.5004 788 511	728809.4223 932 298	809366.8968 364 550	898877.6539 717 857	196
50	813054.2522 496 547	905012.8217 742 270	1007428.4261 245 332	1121493.5237 511 540	200
51	1007235.9922 487 241	1123815.6595 912 256	1253956.8594 871 531	1399241.3193 338 959	204
52	1247793.1184 608 258	1395516.8980 744 537	1560812.3537 100 084	1745774.7359 655 531	208
53	1545801.2162 958 867	1732905.4060 565 234	1942757.3206 674 380	2178128.8743 321 921	212
54	1914980.9939 798 269	2151861.9259 230 821	2418166.6274 278 524	2717557.6624 119 677	216
55	2372330.0030 869 493	2672106.5738 173 320	3009911.5867 994 696	3390578.6690 073 981	220
56	2938905.2295 077 701	3318127.0576 346 453	3746460.2659 320 456	4230276.6705 381 193	224
57	3640792.5864 313 237	4120331.3036 577 370	4663247.0473 657 826	5277930.0526 242 088	228
58	4510307.9461 502 497	5116478.7455 079 862	5804377.3302 976 241	6585039.9980 993 689	232
59	5587485.0078 671 193	6353457.6456 124 763	7224749.3829 876 343	8215862.2135 138 171	236
60	6921918.5050 097 843	7889492.1069 987 020	8992695.4258 176 391	10250565.6502 797 879	240

TABLE 3. SINKING FUND FACTORS
Payable at end of each period

QUARTERLY Compounding

QUARTERS	5% Nominal Annual Rate	5¼% Nominal Annual Rate	5½% Nominal Annual Rate	5¾% Nominal Annual Rate	QUARTERS
1	1.0000 000 000	1.0000 000 000	1.0000 000 000	1.0000 000 000	1
2	0.4968 944 099	0.4967 401 428	0.4965 859 714	0.4964 318 957	2
3	0.3292 011 728	0.3289 963 645	0.3287 917 264	0.3285 872 583	3
YEARS					
1	0.2453 610 233	0.2451 316 052	0.2449 024 264	0.2446 734 868	4
2	0.1196 331 365	0.1193 701 057	0.1191 075 771	0.1188 455 503	8
3	0.0777 583 123	0.0774 875 950	0.0772 176 365	0.0769 484 361	12
4	0.0568 467 221	0.0565 747 927	0.0563 038 765	0.0560 339 720	16
5	0.0443 203 896	0.0440 498 306	0.0437 805 367	0.0435 125 058	20
6	0.0359 866 480	0.0357 187 423	0.0354 523 513	0.0351 874 722	24
7	0.0300 486 329	0.0297 841 051	0.0295 213 391	0.0292 603 309	28
8	0.0256 079 056	0.0253 472 000	0.0250 885 002	0.0248 318 010	32
9	0.0221 653 285	0.0219 087 322	0.0216 543 826	0.0214 022 727	36
10	0.0194 214 139	0.0191 691 190	0.0189 193 079	0.0186 719 718	40
11	0.0171 855 745	0.0169 377 116	0.0166 925 657	0.0164 501 257	44
12	0.0153 307 483	0.0150 874 062	0.0148 470 100	0.0146 095 459	48
13	0.0137 689 655	0.0135 302 035	0.0132 946 116	0.0130 621 728	52
14	0.0124 373 877	0.0122 032 431	0.0119 724 879	0.0117 451 017	56
15	0.0112 899 301	0.0110 604 239	0.0108 345 211	0.0106 121 973	60
16	0.0102 920 267	0.0100 671 668	0.0098 461 188	0.0096 288 539	64
17	0.0094 172 421	0.0091 970 262	0.0089 808 248	0.0087 686 042	68
18	0.0086 450 133	0.0084 294 305	0.0082 180 587	0.0080 108 590	72
19	0.0079 591 042	0.0077 481 366	0.0075 415 703	0.0073 393 605	76
20	0.0073 465 240	0.0071 401 478	0.0069 383 566	0.0067 410 992	80
21	0.0067 967 547	0.0065 949 408	0.0063 978 890	0.0062 055 413	84
22	0.0063 011 891	0.0061 039 041	0.0059 115 514	0.0057 240 655	88
23	0.0058 527 152	0.0056 599 218	0.0054 722 237	0.0052 895 478	92
24	0.0054 454 053	0.0052 570 626	0.0050 739 712	0.0048 960 495	96
25	0.0050 742 788	0.0048 903 429	0.0047 118 069	0.0045 385 804	100
26	0.0047 351 201	0.0045 555 444	0.0043 815 097	0.0042 129 164	104
27	0.0044 243 373	0.0042 490 726	0.0040 794 825	0.0039 154 580	108
28	0.0041 388 506	0.0039 678 456	0.0038 026 412	0.0036 431 183	112
29	0.0038 760 042	0.0037 092 054	0.0035 483 257	0.0033 932 354	116
30	0.0036 334 957	0.0034 708 479	0.0033 142 299	0.0031 635 013	120
31	0.0034 093 190	0.0032 507 653	0.0030 983 444	0.0029 519 051	124
32	0.0032 017 181	0.0030 472 002	0.0028 989 106	0.0027 566 864	128
33	0.0030 091 496	0.0028 586 077	0.0027 143 820	0.0025 762 977	132
34	0.0028 302 508	0.0026 836 242	0.0025 433 938	0.0024 093 732	136
35	0.0026 638 147	0.0025 210 413	0.0023 847 369	0.0022 547 027	140
36	0.0025 087 677	0.0023 697 848	0.0022 373 361	0.0021 112 102	144
37	0.0023 641 521	0.0022 288 962	0.0021 002 320	0.0019 779 360	148
38	0.0022 291 110	0.0020 975 175	0.0019 725 663	0.0018 540 211	152
39	0.0021 028 746	0.0019 748 788	0.0018 535 685	0.0017 386 947	156
40	0.0019 847 505	0.0018 602 868	0.0017 425 450	0.0016 312 631	160
41	0.0018 741 133	0.0017 531 160	0.0016 388 700	0.0015 311 002	164
42	0.0017 703 972	0.0016 528 003	0.0015 419 772	0.0014 376 400	168
43	0.0016 730 889	0.0015 588 262	0.0014 513 531	0.0013 503 690	172
44	0.0015 817 220	0.0014 707 270	0.0013 665 311	0.0012 688 208	176
45	0.0014 958 712	0.0013 880 775	0.0012 870 861	0.0011 925 708	180
46	0.0014 151 484	0.0013 104 897	0.0012 126 302	0.0011 212 314	184
47	0.0013 391 985	0.0012 376 085	0.0011 428 088	0.0010 544 486	188
48	0.0012 676 961	0.0011 691 087	0.0010 772 971	0.0009 918 981	192
49	0.0012 003 425	0.0011 046 919	0.0010 157 970	0.0009 332 826	196
50	0.0011 368 629	0.0010 440 837	0.0009 580 346	0.0008 783 290	200
51	0.0010 770 043	0.0009 870 314	0.0009 037 579	0.0008 267 858	204
52	0.0010 205 333	0.0009 333 019	0.0008 527 344	0.0007 784 218	208
53	0.0009 672 342	0.0008 826 802	0.0008 047 498	0.0007 330 233	212
54	0.0009 169 075	0.0008 349 673	0.0007 596 058	0.0006 903 931	216
55	0.0008 693 685	0.0007 899 789	0.0007 171 191	0.0006 503 489	220
56	0.0008 244 456	0.0007 475 443	0.0006 771 196	0.0006 127 217	224
57	0.0007 819 798	0.0007 075 050	0.0006 394 498	0.0005 773 553	228
58	0.0007 418 232	0.0006 697 138	0.0006 039 634	0.0005 441 043	232
59	0.0007 038 379	0.0006 340 337	0.0005 705 244	0.0005 128 339	236
60	0.0006 678 958	0.0006 003 373	0.0005 390 064	0.0004 834 190	240

QUARTERLY
Compounding

TABLE 3. SINKING FUND FACTORS
Payable at end of each period

QUARTERS	6% Nominal Annual Rate	6¼% Nominal Annual Rate	6½% Nominal Annual Rate	6¾% Nominal Annual Rate	QUARTERS
1	1.0000 000 000	1.0000 000 000	1.0000 000 000	1.0000 000 000	1
2	0.4962 779 156	0.4961 240 310	0.4959 702 418	0.4958 165 479	2
3	0.3283 829 602	0.3281 788 318	0.3279 748 730	0.3277 710 837	3
YEARS					
1	0.2444 447 860	0.2442 163 239	0.2439 881 002	0.2437 601 148	4
2	0.1185 840 246	0.1183 229 996	0.1180 624 747	0.1178 024 495	8
3	0.0766 799 929	0.0764 123 060	0.0761 453 744	0.0758 791 973	12
4	0.0557 650 778	0.0554 971 926	0.0552 303 149	0.0549 644 434	16
5	0.0432 457 359	0.0429 802 249	0.0427 159 708	0.0424 529 714	20
6	0.0349 241 020	0.0346 622 378	0.0344 018 766	0.0341 430 154	24
7	0.0290 010 765	0.0287 435 719	0.0284 878 128	0.0282 337 952	28
8	0.0245 770 970	0.0243 243 827	0.0240 736 526	0.0238 249 009	32
9	0.0211 523 955	0.0209 047 439	0.0206 593 105	0.0204 160 875	36
10	0.0184 271 017	0.0181 846 882	0.0179 447 219	0.0177 071 928	40
11	0.0162 103 801	0.0159 733 173	0.0157 389 251	0.0155 071 911	44
12	0.0143 749 996	0.0141 433 566	0.0139 146 019	0.0136 887 199	48
13	0.0128 328 700	0.0126 066 850	0.0123 835 995	0.0121 635 947	52
14	0.0115 210 635	0.0113 003 515	0.0110 829 436	0.0108 688 170	56
15	0.0103 934 274	0.0101 781 856	0.0099 664 454	0.0097 581 794	60
16	0.0094 153 423	0.0092 055 536	0.0089 994 566	0.0087 970 189	64
17	0.0085 603 297	0.0083 559 657	0.0081 554 755	0.0079 588 218	68
18	0.0078 077 911	0.0076 088 137	0.0074 138 845	0.0072 229 602	72
19	0.0071 414 609	0.0069 478 241	0.0067 584 016	0.0065 731 437	76
20	0.0065 483 231	0.0063 599 741	0.0061 759 969	0.0059 963 351	80
21	0.0060 178 380	0.0058 347 179	0.0056 561 187	0.0054 819 765	84
22	0.0055 413 794	0.0053 634 244	0.0051 901 303	0.0050 214 257	88
23	0.0051 118 190	0.0049 389 606	0.0047 708 943	0.0046 075 407	92
24	0.0047 232 141	0.0045 553 799	0.0043 924 601	0.0042 343 666	96
25	0.0043 705 712	0.0042 076 853	0.0040 498 271	0.0038 968 993	100
26	0.0040 496 632	0.0038 916 467	0.0037 387 618	0.0035 909 023	104
27	0.0037 568 877	0.0036 036 588	0.0034 556 566	0.0033 127 652	108
28	0.0034 891 557	0.0033 406 304	0.0031 974 177	0.0030 593 920	112
29	0.0032 438 030	0.0030 998 952	0.0029 613 770	0.0028 281 125	116
30	0.0030 185 199	0.0028 791 416	0.0027 452 210	0.0026 166 120	120
31	0.0028 112 938	0.0026 763 556	0.0025 469 344	0.0024 228 735	124
32	0.0026 203 629	0.0024 897 741	0.0023 647 529	0.0022 451 321	128
33	0.0024 441 787	0.0023 178 475	0.0021 971 261	0.0020 818 363	132
34	0.0022 813 742	0.0021 592 080	0.0020 426 855	0.0019 316 175	136
35	0.0021 307 386	0.0020 126 442	0.0019 002 190	0.0017 932 634	140
36	0.0019 911 952	0.0018 770 789	0.0017 686 496	0.0016 656 967	144
37	0.0018 617 839	0.0017 515 517	0.0016 470 166	0.0015 479 572	148
38	0.0017 416 453	0.0016 352 032	0.0015 344 608	0.0014 391 860	152
39	0.0016 300 085	0.0015 272 626	0.0014 302 117	0.0013 386 133	156
40	0.0015 261 798	0.0014 270 363	0.0013 335 762	0.0012 455 468	160
41	0.0014 295 334	0.0013 338 988	0.0012 439 295	0.0011 593 626	164
42	0.0013 395 032	0.0012 472 847	0.0011 607 069	0.0010 794 970	168
43	0.0012 555 763	0.0011 666 817	0.0010 833 969	0.0010 054 399	172
44	0.0011 772 867	0.0010 916 244	0.0010 115 355	0.0009 367 284	176
45	0.0011 042 104	0.0010 216 897	0.0009 447 003	0.0008 729 419	180
46	0.0010 359 605	0.0009 564 917	0.0008 825 069	0.0008 136 974	184
47	0.0009 721 837	0.0008 956 780	0.0008 246 044	0.0007 586 455	188
48	0.0009 125 567	0.0008 389 266	0.0007 706 718	0.0007 074 672	192
49	0.0008 567 829	0.0007 859 420	0.0007 204 154	0.0006 598 706	196
50	0.0008 045 903	0.0007 364 535	0.0006 735 660	0.0006 155 883	200
51	0.0007 557 286	0.0006 902 123	0.0006 298 764	0.0005 743 750	204
52	0.0007 099 676	0.0006 469 892	0.0005 891 192	0.0005 360 055	208
53	0.0006 670 947	0.0006 065 736	0.0005 510 854	0.0005 002 726	212
54	0.0006 269 142	0.0005 687 709	0.0005 155 823	0.0004 669 858	216
55	0.0005 892 448	0.0005 334 015	0.0004 824 321	0.0004 359 693	220
56	0.0005 539 191	0.0005 002 995	0.0004 514 707	0.0004 070 613	224
57	0.0005 207 820	0.0004 693 115	0.0004 225 466	0.0003 801 122	228
58	0.0004 896 896	0.0004 402 952	0.0003 955 194	0.0003 549 838	232
59	0.0004 605 087	0.0004 131 190	0.0003 702 593	0.0003 315 486	236
60	0.0004 331 152	0.0003 876 606	0.0003 466 461	0.0003 096 883	240

TABLE 3. SINKING FUND FACTORS
Payable at end of each period

QUARTERLY Compounding

QUARTERS	7% Nominal Annual Rate	7¼% Nominal Annual Rate	7½% Nominal Annual Rate	7¾% Nominal Annual Rate	QUARTERS
1	1.0000 000 000	1.0000 000 000	1.0000 000 000	1.0000 000 000	1
2	0.4956 629 492	0.4955 094 456	0.4953 560 372	0.4952 027 236	2
3	0.3275 674 635	0.3273 640 125	0.3271 607 305	0.3269 576 172	3
YEARS					
1	0.2435 323 673	0.2433 048 576	0.2430 775 854	0.2428 505 505	4
2	0.1175 429 233	0.1172 838 958	0.1170 253 662	0.1167 673 342	8
3	0.0756 137 738	0.0753 491 029	0.0750 851 837	0.0748 220 152	12
4	0.0546 995 764	0.0544 357 127	0.0541 728 507	0.0539 109 889	16
5	0.0421 912 246	0.0419 307 281	0.0416 714 797	0.0414 134 771	20
6	0.0338 856 510	0.0336 297 802	0.0333 753 999	0.0331 225 067	24
7	0.0279 815 145	0.0277 309 663	0.0274 821 462	0.0272 350 496	28
8	0.0235 781 216	0.0233 333 089	0.0230 904 564	0.0228 495 580	32
9	0.0201 750 673	0.0199 362 420	0.0196 996 033	0.0194 651 430	36
10	0.0174 720 911	0.0172 394 063	0.0170 091 280	0.0167 812 455	40
11	0.0152 781 026	0.0150 516 467	0.0148 278 099	0.0146 065 787	44
12	0.0134 656 950	0.0132 455 108	0.0130 281 508	0.0128 135 982	48
13	0.0119 466 511	0.0117 327 489	0.0115 218 678	0.0113 139 871	52
14	0.0106 579 481	0.0104 503 132	0.0102 458 877	0.0100 446 466	56
15	0.0095 533 598	0.0093 519 581	0.0091 539 451	0.0089 592 911	60
16	0.0085 982 079	0.0084 029 898	0.0082 113 304	0.0080 231 947	64
17	0.0077 659 661	0.0075 768 694	0.0073 914 915	0.0072 097 920	68
18	0.0070 359 964	0.0068 529 480	0.0066 737 690	0.0064 984 124	72
19	0.0063 919 996	0.0062 149 177	0.0060 418 453	0.0058 727 290	76
20	0.0058 209 310	0.0056 497 260	0.0054 826 606	0.0053 196 741	80
21	0.0053 122 263	0.0051 468 022	0.0049 856 371	0.0048 286 632	84
22	0.0048 572 379	0.0046 974 929	0.0045 421 161	0.0043 910 317	88
23	0.0044 488 187	0.0042 946 463	0.0041 449 407	0.0039 996 180	92
24	0.0040 810 099	0.0039 322 994	0.0037 881 438	0.0036 484 508	96
25	0.0037 488 036	0.0036 054 408	0.0034 667 105	0.0033 325 119	100
26	0.0034 479 605	0.0033 098 280	0.0031 763 956	0.0030 475 533	104
27	0.0031 748 675	0.0030 418 456	0.0029 135 810	0.0027 899 549	108
28	0.0029 264 263	0.0027 983 932	0.0026 751 648	0.0025 566 130	112
29	0.0026 999 650	0.0025 767 973	0.0024 584 719	0.0023 448 516	116
30	0.0024 931 675	0.0023 747 405	0.0022 611 841	0.0021 523 515	120
31	0.0023 040 158	0.0021 902 041	0.0020 812 819	0.0019 770 932	124
32	0.0021 307 440	0.0020 214 216	0.0019 169 987	0.0018 173 102	128
33	0.0019 718 004	0.0018 668 412	0.0017 667 829	0.0016 714 513	132
34	0.0018 258 160	0.0017 250 939	0.0016 292 659	0.0015 381 489	136
35	0.0016 915 786	0.0015 949 680	0.0015 032 368	0.0014 161 930	140
36	0.0015 680 114	0.0014 753 872	0.0013 876 202	0.0013 045 098	144
37	0.0014 541 546	0.0013 653 926	0.0012 814 585	0.0012 021 434	148
38	0.0013 491 500	0.0012 641 273	0.0011 838 964	0.0011 082 403	152
39	0.0012 522 288	0.0011 708 236	0.0010 941 677	0.0010 220 366	156
40	0.0011 626 998	0.0010 847 918	0.0010 115 848	0.0009 428 468	160
41	0.0010 799 404	0.0010 054 110	0.0009 355 287	0.0008 700 546	164
42	0.0010 033 884	0.0009 321 208	0.0008 654 413	0.0008 031 044	168
43	0.0009 325 351	0.0008 644 146	0.0008 008 183	0.0007 414 947	172
44	0.0008 669 195	0.0008 018 333	0.0007 412 031	0.0006 847 717	176
45	0.0008 061 227	0.0007 439 601	0.0006 861 815	0.0006 325 243	180
46	0.0007 497 636	0.0006 904 165	0.0006 353 775	0.0005 843 796	184
47	0.0006 974 949	0.0006 408 572	0.0005 884 489	0.0005 399 982	188
48	0.0006 489 996	0.0005 949 680	0.0005 450 838	0.0004 990 718	192
49	0.0006 039 881	0.0005 524 614	0.0005 049 979	0.0004 613 190	196
50	0.0005 621 950	0.0005 130 748	0.0004 679 315	0.0004 264 833	200
51	0.0005 233 774	0.0004 765 679	0.0004 336 470	0.0003 943 305	204
52	0.0004 873 123	0.0004 427 203	0.0004 019 270	0.0003 646 463	208
53	0.0004 537 950	0.0004 113 298	0.0003 725 722	0.0003 372 348	212
54	0.0004 226 371	0.0003 822 109	0.0003 454 001	0.0003 119 165	216
55	0.0003 936 655	0.0003 551 928	0.0003 202 428	0.0002 885 268	220
56	0.0003 667 205	0.0003 301 187	0.0002 969 464	0.0002 669 148	224
57	0.0003 416 551	0.0003 068 440	0.0002 753 692	0.0002 469 420	228
58	0.0003 183 333	0.0002 852 356	0.0002 553 809	0.0002 284 811	232
59	0.0002 966 301	0.0002 651 708	0.0002 368 615	0.0002 114 151	236
60	0.0002 764 294	0.0002 465 364	0.0002 197 006	0.0001 956 366	240

TABLE 3. SINKING FUND FACTORS
Payable at end of each period

QUARTERS	8% Nominal Annual Rate	8¼% Nominal Annual Rate	8½% Nominal Annual Rate	8¾% Nominal Annual Rate	QUARTERS
1	1.0000 000 000	1.0000 000 000	1.0000 000 000	1.0000 000 000	1
2	0.4950 495 050	0.4948 963 811	0.4947 433 519	0.4945 904 173	2
3	0.3267 546 726	0.3265 518 964	0.3263 492 886	0.3261 468 489	3
YEARS					
1	0.2426 237 527	0.2423 971 917	0.2421 708 674	0.2419 447 794	4
2	0.1165 097 991	0.1162 527 605	0.1159 962 178	0.1157 401 705	8
3	0.0745 595 966	0.0742 979 269	0.0740 370 051	0.0737 768 303	12
4	0.0536 501 259	0.0533 902 600	0.0531 313 898	0.0528 735 136	16
5	0.0411 567 181	0.0409 012 004	0.0406 469 215	0.0403 938 791	20
6	0.0328 710 973	0.0326 211 682	0.0323 727 162	0.0321 257 376	24
7	0.0269 896 716	0.0267 460 077	0.0265 040 528	0.0262 638 021	28
8	0.0226 106 073	0.0223 735 978	0.0221 385 228	0.0219 053 756	32
9	0.0192 328 526	0.0190 027 235	0.0187 747 469	0.0185 489 138	36
10	0.0165 557 478	0.0163 326 237	0.0161 118 618	0.0158 934 505	40
11	0.0143 879 391	0.0141 718 771	0.0139 583 782	0.0137 474 276	44
12	0.0126 018 355	0.0123 928 453	0.0121 866 095	0.0119 831 099	48
13	0.0111 090 856	0.0109 071 419	0.0107 081 340	0.0105 120 395	52
14	0.0098 465 645	0.0096 516 154	0.0094 597 729	0.0092 710 102	56
15	0.0087 679 658	0.0085 799 384	0.0083 951 775	0.0082 136 513	60
16	0.0078 385 471	0.0076 573 515	0.0074 795 710	0.0073 051 685	64
17	0.0070 317 294	0.0068 572 618	0.0066 863 465	0.0065 189 404	68
18	0.0063 268 307	0.0061 589 757	0.0059 947 986	0.0058 342 497	72
19	0.0057 075 147	0.0055 461 474	0.0053 885 715	0.0052 347 308	76
20	0.0051 607 055	0.0050 056 926	0.0048 545 729	0.0047 072 833	80
21	0.0046 758 118	0.0045 270 134	0.0043 821 981	0.0042 412 955	84
22	0.0042 441 633	0.0041 014 337	0.0039 627 654	0.0038 280 802	88
23	0.0038 585 936	0.0037 217 825	0.0035 890 990	0.0034 604 574	92
24	0.0035 131 275	0.0033 820 806	0.0032 552 164	0.0031 324 411	96
25	0.0032 027 435	0.0030 773 036	0.0029 560 903	0.0028 390 016	100
26	0.0029 231 911	0.0028 031 987	0.0026 874 657	0.0025 758 822	104
27	0.0026 708 483	0.0025 561 422	0.0024 457 179	0.0023 394 572	108
28	0.0024 426 100	0.0023 330 280	0.0022 277 400	0.0021 266 197	112
29	0.0022 357 993	0.0021 311 788	0.0020 308 547	0.0019 346 926	116
30	0.0020 480 969	0.0019 482 753	0.0018 527 431	0.0017 613 580	120
31	0.0018 774 832	0.0017 822 985	0.0016 913 873	0.0016 045 996	124
32	0.0017 221 924	0.0016 314 835	0.0015 450 237	0.0014 626 557	128
33	0.0015 806 741	0.0014 942 812	0.0014 121 053	0.0013 339 817	132
34	0.0014 515 619	0.0013 693 271	0.0012 912 696	0.0012 172 179	136
35	0.0013 336 475	0.0012 554 148	0.0011 813 129	0.0011 111 638	140
36	0.0012 258 591	0.0011 514 749	0.0010 811 686	0.0010 147 561	144
37	0.0011 272 426	0.0010 565 560	0.0009 898 886	0.0009 270 503	148
38	0.0010 369 471	0.0009 698 100	0.0009 066 279	0.0008 472 055	152
39	0.0009 542 112	0.0008 904 786	0.0008 306 320	0.0007 744 712	156
40	0.0008 783 523	0.0008 178 823	0.0007 612 251	0.0007 081 759	160
41	0.0008 087 568	0.0007 514 112	0.0006 978 010	0.0006 477 178	164
42	0.0007 448 725	0.0006 905 163	0.0006 398 150	0.0005 925 565	168
43	0.0006 862 008	0.0006 347 028	0.0005 867 763	0.0005 422 060	172
44	0.0006 322 913	0.0005 835 242	0.0005 382 425	0.0004 962 283	176
45	0.0005 827 365	0.0005 365 765	0.0004 938 138	0.0004 542 285	180
46	0.0005 371 665	0.0004 934 939	0.0004 531 287	0.0004 158 495	184
47	0.0004 952 458	0.0004 539 446	0.0004 158 597	0.0003 807 685	188
48	0.0004 566 694	0.0004 176 276	0.0003 817 100	0.0003 486 933	192
49	0.0004 211 596	0.0003 842 690	0.0003 504 099	0.0003 193 588	196
50	0.0003 884 634	0.0003 536 197	0.0003 217 146	0.0002 925 246	200
51	0.0003 583 501	0.0003 254 529	0.0002 954 013	0.0002 679 723	204
52	0.0003 306 090	0.0002 995 617	0.0002 712 673	0.0002 455 036	208
53	0.0003 050 476	0.0002 757 574	0.0002 491 277	0.0002 249 380	212
54	0.0002 814 899	0.0002 538 676	0.0002 288 144	0.0002 061 112	216
55	0.0002 597 747	0.0002 337 349	0.0002 101 735	0.0001 888 737	220
56	0.0002 397 545	0.0002 152 152	0.0001 930 649	0.0001 730 890	224
57	0.0002 212 941	0.0001 981 768	0.0001 773 605	0.0001 586 330	228
58	0.0002 042 694	0.0001 824 992	0.0001 629 432	0.0001 453 923	232
59	0.0001 885 667	0.0001 680 718	0.0001 497 061	0.0001 332 634	236
60	0.0001 740 815	0.0001 547 935	0.0001 375 512	0.0001 221 520	240

TABLE 3. SINKING FUND FACTORS
Payable at end of each period

QUARTERLY Compounding

QUARTERS	9% Nominal Annual Rate	9¼% Nominal Annual Rate	9½% Nominal Annual Rate	9¾% Nominal Annual Rate	QUARTERS
1	1.0000 000 000	1.0000 000 000	1.0000 000 000	1.0000 000 000	1
2	0.4944 375 773	0.4942 848 316	0.4941 321 804	0.4939 796 233	2
3	0.3259 445 772	0.3257 424 733	0.3255 405 372	0.3253 387 685	3
YEARS					
1	0.2417 189 277	0.2414 933 118	0.2412 679 317	0.2410 427 871	4
2	0.1154 846 181	0.1152 295 599	0.1149 749 955	0.1147 209 243	8
3	0.0735 174 015	0.0732 587 178	0.0730 007 781	0.0727 435 815	12
4	0.0526 166 300	0.0523 607 373	0.0521 058 339	0.0518 519 182	16
5	0.0401 420 708	0.0398 914 941	0.0396 421 465	0.0393 940 256	20
6	0.0318 802 289	0.0316 361 865	0.0313 936 068	0.0311 524 860	24
7	0.0260 252 506	0.0257 883 931	0.0255 532 245	0.0253 197 395	28
8	0.0216 741 493	0.0214 448 370	0.0212 174 315	0.0209 919 257	32
9	0.0183 252 151	0.0181 036 416	0.0178 841 837	0.0176 668 320	36
10	0.0156 773 781	0.0154 636 324	0.0152 522 013	0.0150 430 724	40
11	0.0135 390 105	0.0133 331 115	0.0131 297 153	0.0129 288 062	44
12	0.0117 823 279	0.0115 842 445	0.0113 888 408	0.0111 960 971	48
13	0.0103 188 359	0.0101 285 000	0.0099 410 084	0.0097 563 376	52
14	0.0090 853 000	0.0089 026 147	0.0087 229 262	0.0085 462 062	56
15	0.0080 353 275	0.0078 601 734	0.0076 881 558	0.0075 192 413	60
16	0.0071 341 061	0.0069 663 456	0.0068 018 483	0.0066 405 752	64
17	0.0063 549 998	0.0061 944 805	0.0060 373 380	0.0058 835 272	68
18	0.0056 772 792	0.0055 238 366	0.0053 738 710	0.0052 273 311	72
19	0.0050 845 689	0.0049 380 284	0.0047 950 519	0.0046 555 817	76
20	0.0045 637 600	0.0044 239 391	0.0042 877 561	0.0041 551 464	80
21	0.0041 042 345	0.0039 709 440	0.0038 413 524	0.0037 153 881	84
22	0.0036 972 998	0.0035 703 454	0.0034 471 383	0.0033 275 998	88
23	0.0033 357 716	0.0032 149 552	0.0030 979 223	0.0029 845 868	92
24	0.0030 136 609	0.0028 987 818	0.0027 877 102	0.0026 803 530	96
25	0.0027 259 358	0.0026 167 913	0.0025 114 672	0.0024 098 629	100
26	0.0024 683 384	0.0023 647 253	0.0022 649 342	0.0021 688 577	104
27	0.0022 372 426	0.0021 389 574	0.0020 444 857	0.0019 537 130	108
28	0.0020 295 416	0.0019 363 817	0.0018 470 170	0.0017 613 262	112
29	0.0018 425 594	0.0017 543 238	0.0016 698 558	0.0015 890 276	116
30	0.0016 739 796	0.0015 904 691	0.0015 106 903	0.0014 345 088	120
31	0.0015 217 877	0.0014 428 061	0.0013 675 121	0.0012 957 655	124
32	0.0013 842 248	0.0013 095 789	0.0012 385 693	0.0011 710 501	128
33	0.0012 597 491	0.0011 892 493	0.0011 223 277	0.0010 588 335	132
34	0.0011 470 043	0.0010 804 649	0.0010 174 398	0.0009 577 732	136
35	0.0010 447 937	0.0009 820 333	0.0009 227 179	0.0008 666 873	140
36	0.0009 520 579	0.0008 928 997	0.0008 371 124	0.0007 845 322	144
37	0.0008 678 567	0.0008 121 288	0.0007 596 937	0.0007 103 838	148
38	0.0007 913 536	0.0007 388 892	0.0006 896 356	0.0006 434 227	152
39	0.0007 218 027	0.0006 724 400	0.0006 262 033	0.0005 829 200	156
40	0.0006 585 374	0.0006 121 200	0.0005 687 413	0.0005 282 266	160
41	0.0006 009 607	0.0005 573 375	0.0005 166 638	0.0004 787 634	164
42	0.0005 485 373	0.0005 075 628	0.0004 694 470	0.0004 340 126	168
43	0.0005 007 860	0.0004 623 201	0.0004 266 210	0.0003 935 110	172
44	0.0004 572 741	0.0004 211 821	0.0003 877 645	0.0003 568 433	176
45	0.0004 176 114	0.0003 837 641	0.0003 524 986	0.0003 236 370	180
46	0.0003 814 461	0.0003 497 198	0.0003 204 826	0.0002 935 574	184
47	0.0003 484 604	0.0003 187 365	0.0002 914 097	0.0002 663 037	188
48	0.0003 183 668	0.0002 905 322	0.0002 650 031	0.0002 416 049	192
49	0.0002 909 052	0.0002 648 518	0.0002 410 135	0.0002 192 172	196
50	0.0002 658 400	0.0002 414 647	0.0002 192 153	0.0001 989 208	200
51	0.0002 429 575	0.0002 201 622	0.0001 994 050	0.0001 805 174	204
52	0.0002 220 639	0.0002 007 552	0.0001 813 985	0.0001 638 279	208
53	0.0002 029 831	0.0001 830 723	0.0001 650 293	0.0001 486 908	212
54	0.0001 855 551	0.0001 669 581	0.0001 501 464	0.0001 349 599	216
55	0.0001 696 348	0.0001 522 716	0.0001 366 134	0.0001 225 034	220
56	0.0001 550 897	0.0001 388 846	0.0001 243 065	0.0001 112 018	224
57	0.0001 417 995	0.0001 266 810	0.0001 131 135	0.0001 009 472	228
58	0.0001 296 548	0.0001 155 550	0.0001 029 327	0.0000 916 417	232
59	0.0001 185 556	0.0001 054 106	0.0000 936 719	0.0000 831 969	236
60	0.0001 084 112	0.0000 961 605	0.0000 852 472	0.0000 755 328	240

QUARTERLY
Compounding

TABLE 3. SINKING FUND FACTORS
Payable at end of each period

QUARTERS	10% Nominal Annual Rate	10¼% Nominal Annual Rate	10½% Nominal Annual Rate	10¾% Nominal Annual Rate	QUARTERS
1	1.0000 000 000	1.0000 000 000	1.0000 000 000	1.0000 000 000	1
2	0.4938 271 605	0.4936 747 917	0.4935 225 170	0.4933 703 361	2
3	0.3251 371 672	0.3249 357 332	0.3247 344 661	0.3245 333 660	3
YEARS					
1	0.2408 178 777	0.2405 932 034	0.2403 687 639	0.2401 445 590	4
2	0.1144 673 458	0.1142 142 595	0.1139 616 647	0.1137 095 610	8
3	0.0724 871 270	0.0722 314 136	0.0719 764 402	0.0717 222 060	12
4	0.0515 989 886	0.0513 470 434	0.0510 960 810	0.0508 460 996	16
5	0.0391 471 287	0.0389 014 534	0.0386 569 971	0.0384 137 570	20
6	0.0309 128 204	0.0306 746 061	0.0304 378 394	0.0302 025 164	24
7	0.0250 879 327	0.0248 577 989	0.0246 293 325	0.0244 025 279	28
8	0.0207 683 123	0.0205 465 838	0.0203 267 327	0.0201 087 514	32
9	0.0174 515 767	0.0172 384 080	0.0170 273 159	0.0168 182 902	36
10	0.0148 362 332	0.0146 316 707	0.0144 293 722	0.0142 293 245	40
11	0.0127 303 683	0.0125 343 853	0.0123 408 410	0.0121 497 189	44
12	0.0110 059 938	0.0108 185 109	0.0106 336 281	0.0104 513 251	48
13	0.0095 744 635	0.0093 953 619	0.0092 190 081	0.0090 453 774	52
14	0.0083 724 260	0.0082 015 565	0.0080 335 683	0.0078 684 319	56
15	0.0073 533 959	0.0071 905 855	0.0070 307 755	0.0068 739 311	60
16	0.0064 824 869	0.0063 275 435	0.0061 757 049	0.0060 269 310	64
17	0.0057 330 027	0.0055 857 190	0.0054 416 300	0.0053 006 896	68
18	0.0050 841 652	0.0049 443 217	0.0048 077 482	0.0046 743 926	72
19	0.0045 195 594	0.0043 869 269	0.0042 576 257	0.0041 315 971	76
20	0.0040 260 451	0.0039 003 873	0.0037 781 079	0.0036 591 420	80
21	0.0035 929 793	0.0034 740 544	0.0033 585 415	0.0032 463 693	84
22	0.0032 116 510	0.0030 992 134	0.0029 902 087	0.0028 845 587	88
23	0.0028 748 628	0.0027 686 649	0.0026 659 082	0.0025 665 080	92
24	0.0025 766 173	0.0024 764 107	0.0023 796 418	0.0022 862 195	96
25	0.0023 118 787	0.0022 174 155	0.0021 263 752	0.0020 386 610	100
26	0.0020 763 891	0.0019 874 229	0.0019 018 546	0.0018 195 814	104
27	0.0018 665 260	0.0017 828 128	0.0017 024 631	0.0016 253 682	108
28	0.0016 791 895	0.0016 004 889	0.0015 251 084	0.0014 529 339	112
29	0.0015 117 132	0.0014 377 889	0.0013 671 333	0.0012 996 272	116
30	0.0013 617 930	0.0012 924 136	0.0012 262 442	0.0011 631 610	120
31	0.0012 274 291	0.0011 623 686	0.0011 004 528	0.0010 415 540	124
32	0.0011 068 791	0.0010 459 173	0.0009 880 295	0.0009 330 840	128
33	0.0009 986 195	0.0009 415 428	0.0008 874 641	0.0008 362 487	132
34	0.0009 013 140	0.0008 479 151	0.0007 974 343	0.0007 497 338	136
35	0.0008 137 867	0.0007 638 656	0.0007 167 790	0.0006 723 867	140
36	0.0007 350 004	0.0006 883 641	0.0006 444 758	0.0006 031 933	144
37	0.0006 640 380	0.0006 205 007	0.0005 796 227	0.0005 412 604	148
38	0.0006 000 866	0.0005 594 700	0.0005 214 223	0.0004 857 989	152
39	0.0005 424 243	0.0005 045 575	0.0004 691 680	0.0004 361 107	156
40	0.0004 904 089	0.0004 551 284	0.0004 222 330	0.0003 915 775	160
41	0.0004 434 681	0.0004 106 178	0.0003 800 601	0.0003 516 503	164
42	0.0004 010 911	0.0003 705 220	0.0003 421 535	0.0003 158 414	168
43	0.0003 628 212	0.0003 343 918	0.0003 080 713	0.0002 837 170	172
44	0.0003 282 501	0.0003 018 256	0.0002 774 196	0.0002 548 906	176
45	0.0002 970 116	0.0002 724 643	0.0002 498 462	0.0002 290 177	180
46	0.0002 687 776	0.0002 459 863	0.0002 250 367	0.0002 057 910	184
47	0.0002 432 532	0.0002 221 035	0.0002 027 095	0.0001 849 361	188
48	0.0002 201 739	0.0002 005 575	0.0001 826 129	0.0001 662 075	192
49	0.0001 993 016	0.0001 811 162	0.0001 645 210	0.0001 493 860	196
50	0.0001 804 222	0.0001 635 715	0.0001 482 316	0.0001 342 755	200
51	0.0001 633 427	0.0001 477 360	0.0001 335 632	0.0001 207 002	204
52	0.0001 478 896	0.0001 334 416	0.0001 203 529	0.0001 085 029	208
53	0.0001 339 062	0.0001 205 366	0.0001 084 546	0.0000 975 427	212
54	0.0001 212 513	0.0001 088 850	0.0000 977 369	0.0000 876 932	216
55	0.0001 097 976	0.0000 983 640	0.0000 880 819	0.0000 788 411	220
56	0.0000 994 301	0.0000 888 631	0.0000 793 836	0.0000 708 850	224
57	0.0000 900 451	0.0000 802 827	0.0000 715 465	0.0000 637 336	228
58	0.0000 815 488	0.0000 725 332	0.0000 644 851	0.0000 573 053	232
59	0.0000 738 565	0.0000 655 336	0.0000 581 222	0.0000 515 266	236
60	0.0000 668 918	0.0000 592 110	0.0000 523 883	0.0000 463 316	240

TABLE 3. SINKING FUND FACTORS
Payable at end of each period

QUARTERLY Compounding

QUARTERS	11% Nominal Annual Rate	11¼% Nominal Annual Rate	11½% Nominal Annual Rate	11¾% Nominal Annual Rate	QUARTERS
1	1.0000 000 000	1.0000 000 000	1.0000 000 000	1.0000 000 000	1
2	0.4932 182 491	0.4930 662 558	0.4929 143 561	0.4927 625 500	2
3	0.3243 324 326	0.3241 316 658	0.3239 310 654	0.3237 306 313	3
YEARS					
1	0.2399 205 884	0.2396 968 520	0.2394 733 494	0.2392 500 806	4
2	0.1134 579 478	0.1132 068 245	0.1129 561 906	0.1127 060 456	8
3	0.0714 687 098	0.0712 159 507	0.0709 639 277	0.0707 126 396	12
4	0.0505 970 977	0.0503 490 734	0.0501 020 250	0.0498 559 509	16
5	0.0381 717 306	0.0379 309 152	0.0376 913 080	0.0374 529 064	20
6	0.0299 686 330	0.0297 361 854	0.0295 051 694	0.0292 755 809	24
7	0.0241 773 795	0.0239 538 817	0.0237 320 286	0.0235 118 145	28
8	0.0198 926 322	0.0196 783 672	0.0194 659 486	0.0192 553 683	32
9	0.0166 113 206	0.0164 063 968	0.0162 035 082	0.0160 026 443	36
10	0.0140 315 144	0.0138 359 283	0.0136 425 527	0.0134 513 739	40
11	0.0119 610 021	0.0117 746 737	0.0115 907 166	0.0114 091 135	44
12	0.0102 715 811	0.0100 943 751	0.0099 196 862	0.0097 474 929	48
13	0.0088 744 446	0.0087 061 845	0.0085 405 715	0.0083 775 799	52
14	0.0077 061 174	0.0075 465 947	0.0073 898 334	0.0072 358 029	56
15	0.0067 200 173	0.0065 689 988	0.0064 208 400	0.0062 755 053	60
16	0.0058 811 810	0.0057 384 141	0.0055 985 894	0.0054 616 658	64
17	0.0051 628 513	0.0050 280 686	0.0048 962 949	0.0047 674 833	68
18	0.0045 442 024	0.0044 171 251	0.0042 931 080	0.0041 720 987	72
19	0.0040 087 826	0.0038 891 234	0.0037 725 610	0.0036 590 370	76
20	0.0035 434 245	0.0034 308 906	0.0033 214 758	0.0032 151 155	80
21	0.0031 374 664	0.0030 317 617	0.0029 291 846	0.0028 296 648	84
22	0.0027 821 858	0.0026 830 129	0.0025 869 633	0.0024 939 610	88
23	0.0024 703 805	0.0023 774 424	0.0022 876 114	0.0022 008 058	92
24	0.0021 960 540	0.0021 090 561	0.0020 251 378	0.0019 442 121	96
25	0.0019 541 767	0.0018 728 278	0.0017 945 208	0.0017 191 637	100
26	0.0017 405 017	0.0016 645 153	0.0015 915 239	0.0015 214 308	104
27	0.0015 514 211	0.0014 805 168	0.0014 125 521	0.0013 474 260	108
28	0.0013 838 535	0.0013 177 575	0.0012 545 384	0.0011 940 911	112
29	0.0012 351 542	0.0011 736 003	0.0011 148 540	0.0010 588 069	116
30	0.0011 030 433	0.0010 457 734	0.0009 912 364	0.0009 393 206	120
31	0.0009 855 476	0.0009 323 123	0.0008 817 304	0.0008 336 877	124
32	0.0008 809 528	0.0008 315 120	0.0007 846 412	0.0007 402 240	128
33	0.0007 877 656	0.0007 418 884	0.0006 984 947	0.0006 574 665	132
34	0.0007 046 805	0.0006 621 457	0.0006 220 055	0.0005 841 408	136
35	0.0006 305 536	0.0005 911 497	0.0005 540 499	0.0005 191 342	140
36	0.0005 643 803	0.0005 279 056	0.0004 936 434	0.0004 614 734	144
37	0.0005 052 763	0.0004 715 387	0.0004 399 217	0.0004 103 050	148
38	0.0004 524 617	0.0004 212 789	0.0003 921 248	0.0003 648 795	152
39	0.0004 052 475	0.0003 764 467	0.0003 495 831	0.0003 245 380	156
40	0.0003 630 240	0.0003 364 416	0.0003 117 062	0.0002 886 999	160
41	0.0003 252 512	0.0003 007 328	0.0002 779 723	0.0002 568 536	164
42	0.0002 914 497	0.0002 688 498	0.0002 479 205	0.0002 285 473	168
43	0.0002 611 941	0.0002 403 756	0.0002 211 423	0.0002 033 819	172
44	0.0002 341 057	0.0002 149 399	0.0001 972 761	0.0001 810 044	176
45	0.0002 098 479	0.0001 922 140	0.0001 760 012	0.0001 611 025	180
46	0.0001 881 207	0.0001 719 055	0.0001 570 332	0.0001 433 994	184
47	0.0001 686 568	0.0001 537 543	0.0001 401 193	0.0001 276 501	188
48	0.0001 512 178	0.0001 375 291	0.0001 250 350	0.0001 136 371	192
49	0.0001 355 907	0.0001 230 234	0.0001 115 809	0.0001 011 678	196
50	0.0001 215 857	0.0001 100 537	0.0000 995 795	0.0000 900 708	200
51	0.0001 090 330	0.0000 984 561	0.0000 888 729	0.0000 801 944	204
52	0.0000 977 808	0.0000 880 845	0.0000 793 206	0.0000 714 036	208
53	0.0000 876 935	0.0000 788 085	0.0000 707 975	0.0000 635 785	212
54	0.0000 786 498	0.0000 705 117	0.0000 631 923	0.0000 566 126	216
55	0.0000 705 412	0.0000 630 904	0.0000 564 056	0.0000 504 112	220
56	0.0000 632 704	0.0000 564 517	0.0000 503 491	0.0000 448 901	224
57	0.0000 567 506	0.0000 505 129	0.0000 449 439	0.0000 399 746	228
58	0.0000 509 039	0.0000 451 998	0.0000 401 198	0.0000 355 979	232
59	0.0000 456 606	0.0000 404 464	0.0000 358 141	0.0000 317 010	236
60	0.0000 409 581	0.0000 361 935	0.0000 319 711	0.0000 282 311	240

TABLE 3. SINKING FUND FACTORS
Payable at end of each period

QUARTERS	12% Nominal Annual Rate	12¼% Nominal Annual Rate	12½% Nominal Annual Rate	12¾% Nominal Annual Rate	QUARTERS
1	1.0000 000 000	1.0000 000 000	1.0000 000 000	1.0000 000 000	1
2	0.4926 108 374	0.4924 592 182	0.4923 076 923	0.4921 562 596	2
3	0.3235 303 633	0.3233 302 613	0.3231 303 250	0.3229 305 544	3
YEARS					
1	0.2390 270 452	0.2388 042 430	0.2385 816 739	0.2383 593 375	4
2	0.1124 563 888	0.1122 072 198	0.1119 585 380	0.1117 103 428	8
3	0.0704 620 855	0.0702 122 643	0.0699 631 750	0.0697 148 165	12
4	0.0496 108 493	0.0493 667 183	0.0491 235 563	0.0488 813 615	16
5	0.0372 157 076	0.0369 797 088	0.0367 449 071	0.0365 112 997	20
6	0.0290 474 159	0.0288 206 702	0.0285 953 396	0.0283 714 197	24
7	0.0232 932 334	0.0230 762 794	0.0228 609 465	0.0226 472 285	28
8	0.0190 466 183	0.0188 396 903	0.0186 345 760	0.0184 312 671	32
9	0.0158 037 942	0.0156 069 470	0.0154 120 918	0.0152 192 175	36
10	0.0132 623 779	0.0130 755 508	0.0128 908 783	0.0127 083 462	40
11	0.0112 298 469	0.0110 528 992	0.0108 782 525	0.0107 058 890	44
12	0.0095 777 738	0.0094 105 072	0.0092 456 713	0.0090 832 440	48
13	0.0082 171 837	0.0080 593 568	0.0079 040 731	0.0077 513 059	52
14	0.0070 844 726	0.0069 358 115	0.0067 897 885	0.0066 463 725	56
15	0.0061 329 587	0.0059 931 644	0.0058 560 861	0.0057 216 877	60
16	0.0053 276 021	0.0051 963 568	0.0050 678 885	0.0049 421 559	64
17	0.0046 415 871	0.0045 185 592	0.0043 983 530	0.0042 809 216	68
18	0.0040 540 446	0.0039 388 931	0.0038 265 920	0.0037 170 890	72
19	0.0035 484 929	0.0034 408 706	0.0033 361 124	0.0032 341 604	76
20	0.0031 117 457	0.0030 113 027	0.0029 137 230	0.0028 189 438	80
21	0.0027 331 325	0.0026 395 185	0.0025 487 540	0.0024 607 710	84
22	0.0024 039 306	0.0023 167 975	0.0022 324 878	0.0021 509 287	88
23	0.0021 169 449	0.0020 359 489	0.0019 577 392	0.0018 822 382	92
24	0.0018 661 932	0.0017 909 966	0.0017 185 390	0.0016 487 384	96
25	0.0016 466 659	0.0015 769 384	0.0015 098 935	0.0014 454 456	100
26	0.0014 541 408	0.0013 895 608	0.0013 275 995	0.0012 681 674	104
27	0.0012 850 394	0.0012 252 953	0.0011 680 991	0.0011 133 582	108
28	0.0011 363 131	0.0010 811 041	0.0010 283 663	0.0009 780 047	112
29	0.0010 053 531	0.0009 543 895	0.0009 058 160	0.0008 595 352	116
30	0.0008 899 176	0.0008 429 218	0.0007 982 312	0.0007 557 465	120
31	0.0007 880 734	0.0007 447 800	0.0007 037 039	0.0006 647 447	124
32	0.0006 981 479	0.0006 583 040	0.0006 205 875	0.0005 848 972	128
33	0.0006 186 898	0.0005 820 549	0.0005 474 563	0.0005 147 925	132
34	0.0005 484 366	0.0005 147 828	0.0004 830 737	0.0004 532 077	136
35	0.0004 862 875	0.0004 553 993	0.0004 263 642	0.0003 990 811	140
36	0.0004 312 805	0.0004 029 547	0.0003 763 909	0.0003 514 892	144
37	0.0003 825 739	0.0003 566 190	0.0003 323 364	0.0003 096 272	148
38	0.0003 394 292	0.0003 156 657	0.0002 934 861	0.0002 727 931	152
39	0.0003 011 985	0.0002 794 577	0.0002 592 147	0.0002 403 736	156
40	0.0002 673 117	0.0002 474 362	0.0002 289 743	0.0002 118 324	160
41	0.0002 372 672	0.0002 191 098	0.0002 022 845	0.0001 866 997	164
42	0.0002 106 231	0.0001 940 466	0.0001 787 233	0.0001 645 642	168
43	0.0001 869 895	0.0001 718 663	0.0001 579 202	0.0001 450 650	172
44	0.0001 660 223	0.0001 522 338	0.0001 395 494	0.0001 278 855	176
45	0.0001 474 177	0.0001 348 538	0.0001 233 240	0.0001 127 476	180
46	0.0001 309 070	0.0001 194 657	0.0001 089 916	0.0000 994 072	184
47	0.0001 162 526	0.0001 058 395	0.0000 963 301	0.0000 876 496	188
48	0.0001 032 443	0.0000 937 723	0.0000 851 434	0.0000 772 859	192
49	0.0000 916 960	0.0000 830 847	0.0000 752 590	0.0000 681 503	196
50	0.0000 814 430	0.0000 736 180	0.0000 665 244	0.0000 600 966	200
51	0.0000 723 391	0.0000 652 323	0.0000 588 056	0.0000 529 963	204
52	0.0000 642 551	0.0000 578 036	0.0000 519 838	0.0000 467 360	208
53	0.0000 570 762	0.0000 512 223	0.0000 459 545	0.0000 412 162	212
54	0.0000 507 007	0.0000 453 914	0.0000 406 255	0.0000 363 491	216
55	0.0000 450 384	0.0000 402 252	0.0000 359 151	0.0000 320 573	220
56	0.0000 400 094	0.0000 356 476	0.0000 317 515	0.0000 282 727	224
57	0.0000 355 425	0.0000 315 915	0.0000 280 709	0.0000 249 352	228
58	0.0000 315 749	0.0000 279 973	0.0000 248 174	0.0000 219 920	232
59	0.0000 280 506	0.0000 248 124	0.0000 219 412	0.0000 193 964	236
60	0.0000 249 200	0.0000 219 901	0.0000 193 985	0.0000 171 073	240

TABLE 3. SINKING FUND FACTORS
Payable at end of each period

QUARTERLY Compounding

QUARTERS	13% Nominal Annual Rate	13¼% Nominal Annual Rate	13½% Nominal Annual Rate	13¾% Nominal Annual Rate	QUARTERS
1	1.0000 000 000	1.0000 000 000	1.0000 000 000	1.0000 000 000	1
2	0.4920 049 200	0.4918 536 735	0.4917 025 200	0.4915 514 593	2
3	0.3227 309 493	0.3225 315 095	0.3223 322 349	0.3221 331 253	3
YEARS					
1	0.2381 372 337	0.2379 153 622	0.2376 937 228	0.2374 723 153	4
2	0.1114 626 337	0.1112 154 100	0.1109 686 713	0.1107 224 170	8
3	0.0694 671 878	0.0692 202 878	0.0689 741 154	0.0687 286 696	12
4	0.0486 401 319	0.0483 998 659	0.0481 605 616	0.0479 222 171	16
5	0.0362 788 839	0.0360 476 566	0.0358 176 149	0.0355 887 560	20
6	0.0281 489 063	0.0279 277 951	0.0277 080 816	0.0274 897 615	24
7	0.0224 351 193	0.0222 246 126	0.0220 157 023	0.0218 083 820	28
8	0.0182 297 552	0.0180 300 316	0.0178 320 878	0.0176 359 152	32
9	0.0150 283 128	0.0148 393 664	0.0146 523 670	0.0144 673 030	36
10	0.0125 279 400	0.0123 496 453	0.0121 734 473	0.0119 993 312	40
11	0.0105 357 906	0.0103 679 391	0.0102 023 160	0.0100 389 031	44
12	0.0089 232 032	0.0087 655 267	0.0086 101 920	0.0084 571 767	48
13	0.0076 010 288	0.0074 532 150	0.0073 078 378	0.0071 648 703	52
14	0.0065 055 322	0.0063 672 361	0.0062 314 528	0.0060 981 506	56
15	0.0055 899 328	0.0054 607 851	0.0053 342 082	0.0052 101 658	60
16	0.0048 191 174	0.0046 987 316	0.0045 809 570	0.0044 657 525	64
17	0.0041 662 182	0.0040 541 963	0.0039 448 093	0.0038 380 109	68
18	0.0036 103 320	0.0035 062 692	0.0034 048 492	0.0033 060 205	72
19	0.0031 349 575	0.0030 384 467	0.0029 445 715	0.0028 532 758	76
20	0.0027 269 026	0.0026 375 376	0.0025 507 873	0.0024 665 910	80
21	0.0023 755 020	0.0022 928 804	0.0022 128 404	0.0021 353 167	84
22	0.0020 720 479	0.0019 957 744	0.0019 220 378	0.0018 507 692	88
23	0.0018 093 692	0.0017 390 569	0.0016 712 273	0.0016 058 075	92
24	0.0015 815 142	0.0015 167 873	0.0014 544 800	0.0013 945 163	96
25	0.0013 835 102	0.0013 240 049	0.0012 668 489	0.0012 119 631	100
26	0.0012 111 771	0.0011 565 430	0.0011 041 817	0.0010 540 117	104
27	0.0010 609 823	0.0010 108 835	0.0009 629 759	0.0009 171 762	108
28	0.0009 299 266	0.0008 840 419	0.0008 402 632	0.0007 985 055	112
29	0.0008 154 526	0.0007 734 766	0.0007 335 183	0.0006 954 919	116
30	0.0007 153 719	0.0006 770 147	0.0006 405 851	0.0006 059 968	120
31	0.0006 278 056	0.0005 927 931	0.0005 596 172	0.0005 281 913	124
32	0.0005 511 359	0.0005 192 098	0.0004 890 289	0.0004 605 069	128
33	0.0004 839 661	0.0004 548 835	0.0004 274 553	0.0004 015 957	132
34	0.0004 250 879	0.0003 986 213	0.0003 737 191	0.0003 502 966	136
35	0.0003 734 538	0.0003 493 902	0.0003 268 027	0.0003 056 079	140
36	0.0003 281 541	0.0003 062 949	0.0002 858 255	0.0002 666 641	144
37	0.0002 883 973	0.0002 685 578	0.0002 500 241	0.0002 327 162	148
38	0.0002 534 945	0.0002 355 029	0.0002 187 358	0.0002 031 155	152
39	0.0002 228 444	0.0002 065 416	0.0001 913 851	0.0001 772 991	156
40	0.0001 959 223	0.0001 811 612	0.0001 674 711	0.0001 547 787	160
41	0.0001 722 699	0.0001 589 145	0.0001 465 581	0.0001 351 301	164
42	0.0001 514 861	0.0001 394 112	0.0001 282 665	0.0001 179 843	168
43	0.0001 332 200	0.0001 223 102	0.0001 122 655	0.0001 030 205	172
44	0.0001 171 644	0.0001 073 137	0.0000 982 663	0.0000 899 595	176
45	0.0001 030 499	0.0000 941 612	0.0000 860 172	0.0000 785 582	180
46	0.0000 906 404	0.0000 826 246	0.0000 752 984	0.0000 686 047	184
47	0.0000 797 290	0.0000 725 046	0.0000 659 178	0.0000 599 145	188
48	0.0000 701 339	0.0000 636 265	0.0000 577 079	0.0000 523 268	192
49	0.0000 616 957	0.0000 558 373	0.0000 505 221	0.0000 457 013	196
50	0.0000 542 745	0.0000 490 031	0.0000 442 322	0.0000 399 157	200
51	0.0000 477 473	0.0000 430 065	0.0000 387 262	0.0000 348 632	204
52	0.0000 420 060	0.0000 377 445	0.0000 339 064	0.0000 304 509	208
53	0.0000 369 559	0.0000 331 269	0.0000 296 869	0.0000 265 974	212
54	0.0000 325 136	0.0000 290 748	0.0000 259 929	0.0000 232 319	216
55	0.0000 286 057	0.0000 255 187	0.0000 227 589	0.0000 202 925	220
56	0.0000 251 678	0.0000 223 979	0.0000 199 275	0.0000 177 252	224
57	0.0000 221 435	0.0000 196 589	0.0000 174 485	0.0000 154 828	228
58	0.0000 194 827	0.0000 172 550	0.0000 152 781	0.0000 135 243	232
59	0.0000 171 419	0.0000 151 453	0.0000 133 777	0.0000 118 135	236
60	0.0000 150 824	0.0000 132 936	0.0000 117 138	0.0000 103 193	240

TABLE 3. SINKING FUND FACTORS
Payable at end of each period

QUARTERS	14% Nominal Annual Rate	14¼% Nominal Annual Rate	14½% Nominal Annual Rate	14¾% Nominal Annual Rate	QUARTERS
1	1.0000 000 000	1.0000 000 000	1.0000 000 000	1.0000 000 000	1
2	0.4914 004 914	0.4912 496 162	0.4910 988 336	0.4909 481 436	2
3	0.3219 341 806	0.3217 354 005	0.3215 367 851	0.3213 383 340	3
YEARS					
1	0.2372 511 395	0.2370 301 951	0.2368 094 819	0.2365 889 996	4
2	0.1104 766 465	0.1102 313 593	0.1099 865 548	0.1097 422 323	8
3	0.0684 839 493	0.0682 399 533	0.0679 966 807	0.0677 541 303	12
4	0.0476 848 306	0.0474 484 003	0.0472 129 241	0.0469 784 003	16
5	0.0353 610 768	0.0351 345 744	0.0349 092 457	0.0346 850 877	20
6	0.0272 728 303	0.0270 572 834	0.0268 431 163	0.0266 303 245	24
7	0.0216 026 452	0.0213 984 856	0.0211 958 966	0.0209 948 717	28
8	0.0174 415 048	0.0172 488 479	0.0170 579 356	0.0168 687 589	32
9	0.0142 841 628	0.0141 029 347	0.0139 236 070	0.0137 461 677	36
10	0.0118 272 823	0.0116 572 854	0.0114 893 256	0.0113 233 877	40
11	0.0098 776 816	0.0097 186 329	0.0095 617 383	0.0094 069 790	44
12	0.0083 064 580	0.0081 580 134	0.0080 118 199	0.0078 678 546	48
13	0.0070 242 854	0.0068 860 561	0.0067 501 552	0.0066 165 556	52
14	0.0059 672 981	0.0058 388 635	0.0057 128 152	0.0055 891 216	56
15	0.0050 886 213	0.0049 695 385	0.0048 528 811	0.0047 386 128	60
16	0.0043 530 765	0.0042 428 881	0.0041 351 462	0.0040 298 099	64
17	0.0037 337 550	0.0036 319 955	0.0035 326 869	0.0034 357 837	68
18	0.0032 097 323	0.0031 159 339	0.0030 245 750	0.0029 356 058	72
19	0.0027 645 038	0.0026 782 006	0.0025 943 115	0.0025 127 824	76
20	0.0023 848 887	0.0023 056 208	0.0022 287 288	0.0021 541 546	80
21	0.0020 602 452	0.0019 875 623	0.0019 172 057	0.0018 491 136	84
22	0.0017 819 002	0.0017 153 640	0.0016 510 945	0.0015 890 269	88
23	0.0015 427 259	0.0014 819 121	0.0014 232 973	0.0013 668 139	92
24	0.0013 368 213	0.0012 813 220	0.0012 279 470	0.0011 766 262	96
25	0.0011 592 702	0.0011 086 949	0.0010 601 634	0.0010 136 039	100
26	0.0010 059 536	0.0009 599 300	0.0009 158 655	0.0008 736 871	104
27	0.0008 734 032	0.0008 315 782	0.0007 916 247	0.0007 534 683	108
28	0.0007 586 865	0.0007 207 265	0.0006 845 480	0.0006 500 764	112
29	0.0006 593 142	0.0006 249 048	0.0005 921 863	0.0005 610 837	116
30	0.0005 731 662	0.0005 420 128	0.0005 124 592	0.0004 844 309	120
31	0.0004 984 319	0.0004 702 588	0.0004 435 952	0.0004 183 672	124
32	0.0004 335 608	0.0004 081 112	0.0003 840 818	0.0003 613 999	128
33	0.0003 772 225	0.0003 542 573	0.0003 326 252	0.0003 122 546	132
34	0.0003 282 727	0.0003 075 706	0.0002 881 166	0.0002 698 408	136
35	0.0002 857 262	0.0002 670 823	0.0002 496 043	0.0002 332 242	140
36	0.0002 487 328	0.0002 319 582	0.0002 162 704	0.0002 016 034	144
37	0.0002 165 585	0.0002 014 792	0.0001 874 110	0.0001 742 899	148
38	0.0001 885 682	0.0001 750 247	0.0001 624 198	0.0001 506 919	152
39	0.0001 642 125	0.0001 520 585	0.0001 407 740	0.0001 303 002	156
40	0.0001 430 155	0.0001 321 169	0.0001 220 227	0.0001 126 763	160
41	0.0001 245 643	0.0001 147 989	0.0001 057 763	0.0000 974 424	164
42	0.0001 085 009	0.0000 997 574	0.0000 916 984	0.0000 842 728	168
43	0.0000 945 146	0.0000 866 914	0.0000 794 983	0.0000 728 867	172
44	0.0000 823 355	0.0000 753 404	0.0000 689 245	0.0000 630 415	176
45	0.0000 717 289	0.0000 654 784	0.0000 597 593	0.0000 545 282	180
46	0.0000 624 911	0.0000 569 093	0.0000 518 146	0.0000 471 660	184
47	0.0000 544 449	0.0000 494 632	0.0000 449 274	0.0000 407 989	188
48	0.0000 474 361	0.0000 429 926	0.0000 389 567	0.0000 352 921	192
49	0.0000 413 306	0.0000 373 693	0.0000 337 802	0.0000 305 293	196
50	0.0000 360 118	0.0000 324 822	0.0000 292 921	0.0000 264 096	200
51	0.0000 313 780	0.0000 282 347	0.0000 254 007	0.0000 228 462	204
52	0.0000 273 410	0.0000 245 431	0.0000 220 266	0.0000 197 639	208
53	0.0000 238 237	0.0000 213 343	0.0000 191 009	0.0000 170 976	212
54	0.0000 207 592	0.0000 185 454	0.0000 165 640	0.0000 147 912	216
55	0.0000 180 890	0.0000 161 211	0.0000 143 642	0.0000 127 960	220
56	0.0000 157 625	0.0000 140 139	0.0000 124 566	0.0000 110 700	224
57	0.0000 137 353	0.0000 121 822	0.0000 108 024	0.0000 095 769	228
58	0.0000 119 689	0.0000 105 900	0.0000 093 680	0.0000 082 852	232
59	0.0000 104 298	0.0000 092 060	0.0000 081 241	0.0000 071 678	236
60	0.0000 090 886	0.0000 080 029	0.0000 070 453	0.0000 062 011	240

TABLE 3. SINKING FUND FACTORS
Payable at end of each period

QUARTERS	15% Nominal Annual Rate	15¼% Nominal Annual Rate	15½% Nominal Annual Rate	15¾% Nominal Annual Rate	QUARTERS
1	1.0000 000 000	1.0000 000 000	1.0000 000 000	1.0000 000 000	1
2	0.4907 975 460	0.4906 470 408	0.4904 966 278	0.4903 463 071	2
3	0.3211 400 472	0.3209 419 244	0.3207 439 656	0.3205 461 706	3
YEARS					
1	0.2363 687 482	0.2361 487 272	0.2359 289 366	0.2357 093 761	4
2	0.1094 983 915	0.1092 550 316	0.1090 121 521	0.1087 697 524	8
3	0.0675 123 010	0.0672 711 917	0.0670 308 013	0.0667 911 287	12
4	0.0467 448 270	0.0465 122 021	0.0462 805 238	0.0460 497 902	16
5	0.0344 620 973	0.0342 402 715	0.0340 196 072	0.0338 001 012	20
6	0.0264 189 033	0.0262 088 481	0.0260 001 542	0.0257 928 169	24
7	0.0207 954 043	0.0205 974 876	0.0204 011 151	0.0202 062 799	28
8	0.0166 813 087	0.0164 955 758	0.0163 115 513	0.0161 292 257	32
9	0.0135 706 050	0.0133 969 068	0.0132 250 610	0.0130 550 554	36
10	0.0111 594 563	0.0109 975 163	0.0108 375 521	0.0106 795 483	40
11	0.0092 543 358	0.0091 037 899	0.0089 553 222	0.0088 089 134	44
12	0.0077 260 947	0.0075 865 172	0.0074 490 989	0.0073 138 167	48
13	0.0064 852 301	0.0063 561 514	0.0062 292 922	0.0061 046 254	52
14	0.0054 677 509	0.0053 486 716	0.0052 318 520	0.0051 172 607	56
15	0.0046 266 973	0.0045 170 987	0.0044 097 810	0.0043 047 084	60
16	0.0039 268 386	0.0038 261 916	0.0037 278 288	0.0036 317 100	64
17	0.0033 412 407	0.0032 490 131	0.0031 590 564	0.0030 713 265	68
18	0.0028 489 770	0.0027 646 394	0.0026 825 446	0.0026 026 446	72
19	0.0024 335 598	0.0023 565 908	0.0022 818 234	0.0022 092 057	76
20	0.0020 818 410	0.0020 117 315	0.0019 437 705	0.0018 779 032	80
21	0.0017 832 256	0.0017 194 819	0.0016 578 238	0.0015 981 937	84
22	0.0015 290 977	0.0014 712 444	0.0014 154 056	0.0013 615 214	88
23	0.0013 123 956	0.0012 599 776	0.0012 094 965	0.0011 608 903	92
24	0.0011 272 913	0.0010 798 755	0.0010 343 139	0.0009 905 427	96
25	0.0009 689 464	0.0009 261 227	0.0008 850 665	0.0008 457 132	100
26	0.0008 333 233	0.0007 947 050	0.0007 577 652	0.0007 224 385	104
27	0.0007 170 371	0.0006 822 614	0.0006 490 737	0.0006 174 087	108
28	0.0006 172 394	0.0005 859 671	0.0005 561 921	0.0005 278 494	112
29	0.0005 315 248	0.0005 034 401	0.0004 767 626	0.0004 514 279	116
30	0.0004 578 561	0.0004 326 660	0.0004 087 944	0.0003 861 778	120
31	0.0003 945 038	0.0003 719 372	0.0003 506 024	0.0003 304 372	124
32	0.0003 399 958	0.0003 198 029	0.0003 007 577	0.0002 827 994	128
33	0.0002 930 774	0.0002 750 285	0.0002 580 461	0.0002 420 712	132
34	0.0002 526 768	0.0002 365 614	0.0002 214 346	0.0002 072 393	136
35	0.0002 178 776	0.0002 035 030	0.0001 900 427	0.0001 774 418	140
36	0.0001 878 948	0.0001 750 855	0.0001 631 198	0.0001 519 452	144
37	0.0001 620 557	0.0001 506 518	0.0001 400 247	0.0001 301 242	148
38	0.0001 397 832	0.0001 296 395	0.0001 202 096	0.0001 114 458	152
39	0.0001 205 816	0.0001 115 664	0.0001 032 060	0.0000 954 550	156
40	0.0001 040 249	0.0000 960 192	0.0000 886 131	0.0000 817 634	160
41	0.0000 897 470	0.0000 826 433	0.0000 760 875	0.0000 700 391	164
42	0.0000 774 329	0.0000 711 342	0.0000 653 355	0.0000 599 986	168
43	0.0000 668 113	0.0000 612 304	0.0000 561 050	0.0000 513 993	172
44	0.0000 576 490	0.0000 527 074	0.0000 481 802	0.0000 440 339	176
45	0.0000 497 448	0.0000 453 722	0.0000 413 760	0.0000 377 249	180
46	0.0000 429 256	0.0000 390 588	0.0000 355 336	0.0000 323 206	184
47	0.0000 370 422	0.0000 336 247	0.0000 305 168	0.0000 276 911	188
48	0.0000 319 658	0.0000 289 472	0.0000 262 087	0.0000 237 250	192
49	0.0000 275 856	0.0000 249 208	0.0000 225 092	0.0000 203 273	196
50	0.0000 238 060	0.0000 214 548	0.0000 193 322	0.0000 174 164	200
51	0.0000 205 445	0.0000 184 711	0.0000 166 038	0.0000 149 225	204
52	0.0000 177 301	0.0000 159 024	0.0000 142 605	0.0000 127 859	208
53	0.0000 153 014	0.0000 136 912	0.0000 122 481	0.0000 109 552	212
54	0.0000 132 055	0.0000 117 874	0.0000 105 198	0.0000 093 867	216
55	0.0000 113 967	0.0000 101 485	0.0000 090 353	0.0000 080 429	220
56	0.0000 098 358	0.0000 087 375	0.0000 077 604	0.0000 068 914	224
57	0.0000 084 887	0.0000 075 227	0.0000 066 655	0.0000 059 049	228
58	0.0000 073 261	0.0000 064 769	0.0000 057 250	0.0000 050 595	232
59	0.0000 063 228	0.0000 055 764	0.0000 049 172	0.0000 043 352	236
60	0.0000 054 569	0.0000 048 012	0.0000 042 235	0.0000 037 146	240

TABLE 3. SINKING FUND FACTORS
Payable at end of each period

QUARTERS	16% Nominal Annual Rate	16¼% Nominal Annual Rate	16½% Nominal Annual Rate	16¾% Nominal Annual Rate	QUARTERS
1	1.0000 000 000	1.0000 000 000	1.0000 000 000	1.0000 000 000	1
2	0.4901 960 784	0.4900 459 418	0.4898 958 971	0.4897 459 443	2
3	0.3203 485 392	0.3201 510 713	0.3199 537 667	0.3197 566 252	3
YEARS					
1	0.2354 900 454	0.2352 709 443	0.2350 520 727	0.2348 334 302	4
2	0.1085 278 320	0.1082 863 904	0.1080 454 268	0.1078 049 407	8
3	0.0665 521 727	0.0663 139 323	0.0660 764 062	0.0658 395 935	12
4	0.0458 199 992	0.0455 911 490	0.0453 632 375	0.0451 362 627	16
5	0.0335 817 503	0.0333 645 515	0.0331 485 014	0.0329 335 969	20
6	0.0255 868 313	0.0253 821 928	0.0251 788 965	0.0249 769 374	24
7	0.0200 129 752	0.0198 211 942	0.0196 309 300	0.0194 421 756	28
8	0.0159 485 897	0.0157 696 341	0.0155 923 494	0.0154 167 261	32
9	0.0128 868 780	0.0127 205 162	0.0125 559 578	0.0123 931 904	36
10	0.0105 234 893	0.0103 693 596	0.0102 171 434	0.0100 668 250	40
11	0.0086 645 444	0.0085 221 960	0.0083 818 487	0.0082 434 833	44
12	0.0071 806 476	0.0070 495 683	0.0069 205 556	0.0067 935 865	48
13	0.0059 821 236	0.0058 617 596	0.0057 435 063	0.0056 273 364	52
14	0.0050 048 662	0.0048 946 371	0.0047 865 422	0.0046 805 501	56
15	0.0042 018 451	0.0041 011 557	0.0040 026 049	0.0039 061 574	60
16	0.0035 377 955	0.0034 460 456	0.0033 564 212	0.0032 688 833	64
17	0.0029 857 795	0.0029 023 721	0.0028 210 613	0.0027 418 046	68
18	0.0025 248 919	0.0024 492 394	0.0023 756 408	0.0023 040 502	72
19	0.0021 386 869	0.0020 702 168	0.0020 037 458	0.0019 392 251	76
20	0.0018 140 755	0.0017 522 344	0.0016 923 276	0.0016 343 037	80
21	0.0015 405 351	0.0014 847 921	0.0014 309 105	0.0013 788 366	84
22	0.0013 095 329	0.0012 593 825	0.0012 110 138	0.0011 643 716	88
23	0.0011 140 984	0.0010 690 616	0.0010 257 221	0.0009 840 236	92
24	0.0009 485 002	0.0009 081 260	0.0008 693 615	0.0008 321 495	96
25	0.0008 080 000	0.0007 718 661	0.0007 372 521	0.0007 041 007	100
26	0.0006 886 620	0.0006 563 744	0.0006 255 164	0.0005 960 307	104
27	0.0005 872 033	0.0005 583 964	0.0005 309 291	0.0005 047 446	108
28	0.0005 008 762	0.0004 752 121	0.0004 507 988	0.0004 275 803	112
29	0.0004 273 741	0.0004 045 415	0.0003 828 730	0.0003 623 137	116
30	0.0003 647 553	0.0003 444 687	0.0003 252 620	0.0003 070 817	120
31	0.0003 113 821	0.0002 933 802	0.0002 763 772	0.0002 603 213	124
32	0.0002 658 702	0.0002 499 149	0.0002 348 811	0.0002 207 186	128
33	0.0002 270 478	0.0002 129 227	0.0001 996 452	0.0001 871 674	132
34	0.0001 939 216	0.0001 814 303	0.0001 697 169	0.0001 587 355	136
35	0.0001 656 484	0.0001 546 135	0.0001 442 907	0.0001 346 364	140
36	0.0001 415 119	0.0001 317 732	0.0001 226 850	0.0001 142 060	144
37	0.0001 209 028	0.0001 123 163	0.0001 043 227	0.0000 968 829	148
38	0.0001 033 029	0.0000 957 390	0.0000 887 145	0.0000 821 926	152
39	0.0000 882 707	0.0000 816 133	0.0000 754 458	0.0000 697 335	156
40	0.0000 754 300	0.0000 695 754	0.0000 641 648	0.0000 591 656	160
41	0.0000 644 602	0.0000 593 156	0.0000 545 727	0.0000 502 012	164
42	0.0000 550 880	0.0000 505 707	0.0000 464 162	0.0000 425 964	168
43	0.0000 470 800	0.0000 431 164	0.0000 394 800	0.0000 361 446	172
44	0.0000 402 373	0.0000 367 618	0.0000 335 811	0.0000 306 707	176
45	0.0000 343 900	0.0000 313 446	0.0000 285 642	0.0000 260 264	180
46	0.0000 293 930	0.0000 267 261	0.0000 242 972	0.0000 220 857	184
47	0.0000 251 226	0.0000 227 886	0.0000 206 680	0.0000 187 419	188
48	0.0000 214 730	0.0000 194 314	0.0000 175 811	0.0000 159 045	192
49	0.0000 183 537	0.0000 165 690	0.0000 149 554	0.0000 134 969	196
50	0.0000 156 878	0.0000 141 284	0.0000 127 220	0.0000 114 538	200
51	0.0000 134 092	0.0000 120 474	0.0000 108 222	0.0000 097 201	204
52	0.0000 114 617	0.0000 102 730	0.0000 092 061	0.0000 082 488	208
53	0.0000 097 971	0.0000 087 600	0.0000 078 315	0.0000 070 003	212
54	0.0000 083 743	0.0000 074 699	0.0000 066 621	0.0000 059 408	216
55	0.0000 071 582	0.0000 063 698	0.0000 056 674	0.0000 050 416	220
56	0.0000 061 187	0.0000 054 317	0.0000 048 212	0.0000 042 786	224
57	0.0000 052 302	0.0000 046 318	0.0000 041 013	0.0000 036 310	228
58	0.0000 044 707	0.0000 039 497	0.0000 034 890	0.0000 030 815	232
59	0.0000 038 215	0.0000 033 681	0.0000 029 681	0.0000 026 151	236
60	0.0000 032 666	0.0000 028 721	0.0000 025 249	0.0000 022 194	240

TABLE 3. SINKING FUND FACTORS
Payable at end of each period

QUARTERLY Compounding

QUARTERS	17% Nominal Annual Rate	17¼% Nominal Annual Rate	17½% Nominal Annual Rate	17¾% Nominal Annual Rate	QUARTERS
1	1.0000 000 000	1.0000 000 000	1.0000 000 000	1.0000 000 000	1
2	0.4895 960 832	0.4894 463 139	0.4892 966 361	0.4891 470 498	2
3	0.3195 596 468	0.3193 628 312	0.3191 661 784	0.3189 696 880	3
YEARS					
1	0.2346 150 167	0.2343 968 320	0.2341 788 757	0.2339 611 478	4
2	0.1075 649 316	0.1073 253 989	0.1070 863 420	0.1068 477 604	8
3	0.0656 034 928	0.0653 681 032	0.0651 334 234	0.0648 994 522	12
4	0.0449 102 226	0.0446 851 153	0.0444 609 387	0.0442 376 908	16
5	0.0327 198 348	0.0325 072 118	0.0322 957 245	0.0320 853 698	20
6	0.0247 763 108	0.0245 770 118	0.0243 790 352	0.0241 823 763	24
7	0.0192 549 240	0.0190 691 683	0.0188 849 013	0.0187 021 160	28
8	0.0152 427 548	0.0150 704 257	0.0148 997 294	0.0147 306 561	32
9	0.0122 322 015	0.0120 729 785	0.0119 155 090	0.0117 597 802	36
10	0.0099 183 886	0.0097 718 185	0.0096 270 987	0.0094 842 134	40
11	0.0081 070 805	0.0079 726 207	0.0078 400 845	0.0077 094 527	44
12	0.0066 686 377	0.0065 456 859	0.0064 247 082	0.0063 056 813	48
13	0.0055 132 229	0.0054 011 386	0.0052 910 567	0.0051 829 502	52
14	0.0045 766 300	0.0044 747 508	0.0043 748 818	0.0042 769 923	56
15	0.0038 117 784	0.0037 194 330	0.0036 290 870	0.0035 407 059	60
16	0.0031 833 932	0.0030 999 125	0.0030 184 034	0.0029 388 281	64
17	0.0026 645 597	0.0025 892 850	0.0025 159 393	0.0024 444 819	68
18	0.0022 344 223	0.0021 667 123	0.0021 008 762	0.0020 368 706	72
19	0.0018 766 067	0.0018 158 431	0.0017 568 877	0.0016 996 948	76
20	0.0015 781 123	0.0015 237 037	0.0014 710 294	0.0014 200 416	80
21	0.0013 285 180	0.0012 799 034	0.0012 329 425	0.0011 875 861	84
22	0.0011 194 021	0.0010 760 525	0.0010 342 714	0.0009 940 087	88
23	0.0009 439 110	0.0009 053 310	0.0008 682 312	0.0008 325 611	92
24	0.0007 964 344	0.0007 621 624	0.0007 292 809	0.0006 977 392	96
25	0.0006 723 562	0.0006 419 645	0.0006 128 735	0.0005 850 324	100
26	0.0005 678 618	0.0005 409 563	0.0005 152 621	0.0004 907 295	104
27	0.0004 797 880	0.0004 560 065	0.0004 333 491	0.0004 117 667	108
28	0.0004 055 028	0.0003 845 144	0.0003 645 653	0.0003 456 077	112
29	0.0003 428 109	0.0003 243 141	0.0003 067 751	0.0002 901 473	116
30	0.0002 898 768	0.0002 735 982	0.0002 581 993	0.0002 436 353	120
31	0.0002 451 631	0.0002 308 553	0.0002 173 531	0.0002 046 135	124
32	0.0002 073 800	0.0001 948 199	0.0001 829 954	0.0001 718 658	128
33	0.0001 754 436	0.0001 644 308	0.0001 540 879	0.0001 443 761	132
34	0.0001 484 426	0.0001 387 971	0.0001 297 603	0.0001 212 954	136
35	0.0001 256 093	0.0001 171 704	0.0001 092 831	0.0001 019 129	140
36	0.0001 062 969	0.0000 989 212	0.0000 920 442	0.0000 856 336	144
37	0.0000 899 601	0.0000 835 197	0.0000 775 294	0.0000 719 590	148
38	0.0000 761 385	0.0000 705 201	0.0000 653 070	0.0000 604 709	152
39	0.0000 644 438	0.0000 595 466	0.0000 550 138	0.0000 508 191	156
40	0.0000 545 476	0.0000 502 827	0.0000 463 447	0.0000 427 092	160
41	0.0000 461 728	0.0000 424 614	0.0000 390 428	0.0000 358 946	164
42	0.0000 390 849	0.0000 358 577	0.0000 328 923	0.0000 301 680	168
43	0.0000 330 860	0.0000 302 818	0.0000 277 113	0.0000 253 556	172
44	0.0000 280 084	0.0000 255 734	0.0000 233 468	0.0000 213 112	176
45	0.0000 237 104	0.0000 215 975	0.0000 196 700	0.0000 179 122	180
46	0.0000 200 724	0.0000 182 399	0.0000 165 725	0.0000 150 555	184
47	0.0000 169 927	0.0000 154 046	0.0000 139 629	0.0000 126 545	188
48	0.0000 143 857	0.0000 130 101	0.0000 117 644	0.0000 106 365	192
49	0.0000 121 788	0.0000 109 879	0.0000 099 121	0.0000 089 404	196
50	0.0000 103 105	0.0000 092 801	0.0000 083 515	0.0000 075 148	200
51	0.0000 087 289	0.0000 078 378	0.0000 070 366	0.0000 063 166	204
52	0.0000 073 900	0.0000 066 196	0.0000 059 288	0.0000 053 094	208
53	0.0000 062 564	0.0000 055 909	0.0000 049 954	0.0000 044 628	212
54	0.0000 052 968	0.0000 047 220	0.0000 042 090	0.0000 037 513	216
55	0.0000 044 844	0.0000 039 881	0.0000 035 464	0.0000 031 532	220
56	0.0000 037 966	0.0000 033 684	0.0000 029 881	0.0000 026 504	224
57	0.0000 032 142	0.0000 028 449	0.0000 025 177	0.0000 022 278	228
58	0.0000 027 213	0.0000 024 028	0.0000 021 214	0.0000 018 726	232
59	0.0000 023 039	0.0000 020 294	0.0000 017 874	0.0000 015 741	236
60	0.0000 019 505	0.0000 017 140	0.0000 015 060	0.0000 013 231	240

TABLE 3. SINKING FUND FACTORS
Payable at end of each period

QUARTERS	18% Nominal Annual Rate	18¼% Nominal Annual Rate	18½% Nominal Annual Rate	18¾% Nominal Annual Rate	QUARTERS
1	1.0000 000 000	1.0000 000 000	1.0000 000 000	1.0000 000 000	1
2	0.4889 975 550	0.4888 481 515	0.4886 988 393	0.4885 496 183	2
3	0.3187 733 601	0.3185 771 944	0.3183 811 908	0.3181 853 492	3
YEARS					
1	0.2337 436 479	0.2335 263 759	0.2333 093 315	0.2330 925 145	4
2	0.1066 096 533	0.1063 720 203	0.1061 348 608	0.1058 981 742	8
3	0.0646 661 886	0.0644 336 314	0.0642 017 793	0.0639 706 313	12
4	0.0440 153 694	0.0437 939 727	0.0435 734 984	0.0433 539 445	16
5	0.0318 761 443	0.0316 680 447	0.0314 610 675	0.0312 552 095	20
6	0.0239 870 299	0.0237 929 911	0.0236 002 547	0.0234 088 157	24
7	0.0185 208 051	0.0183 409 615	0.0181 625 781	0.0179 856 474	28
8	0.0145 631 962	0.0143 973 398	0.0142 330 773	0.0140 703 987	32
9	0.0116 057 796	0.0114 534 945	0.0113 029 120	0.0111 540 195	36
10	0.0093 431 466	0.0092 038 824	0.0090 664 048	0.0089 306 978	40
11	0.0075 807 056	0.0074 538 239	0.0073 287 880	0.0072 055 787	44
12	0.0061 885 821	0.0060 733 876	0.0059 600 748	0.0058 486 206	48
13	0.0050 767 923	0.0049 725 563	0.0048 702 156	0.0047 697 436	52
14	0.0041 810 518	0.0040 870 301	0.0039 948 970	0.0039 046 226	56
15	0.0034 542 558	0.0033 697 031	0.0032 870 141	0.0032 061 558	60
16	0.0028 611 494	0.0027 853 304	0.0027 113 345	0.0026 391 257	64
17	0.0023 748 725	0.0023 070 714	0.0022 410 393	0.0021 767 374	68
18	0.0019 746 524	0.0019 141 796	0.0018 554 105	0.0017 983 042	72
19	0.0016 442 194	0.0015 904 170	0.0015 382 442	0.0014 876 583	76
20	0.0013 706 935	0.0013 229 391	0.0012 767 336	0.0012 320 328	80
21	0.0011 437 861	0.0011 014 955	0.0010 606 681	0.0010 212 592	84
22	0.0009 552 152	0.0009 178 434	0.0008 818 465	0.0008 471 793	88
23	0.0007 982 710	0.0007 653 131	0.0007 336 406	0.0007 032 081	92
24	0.0006 674 877	0.0006 384 785	0.0006 106 653	0.0005 840 030	96
25	0.0005 583 922	0.0005 329 056	0.0005 085 267	0.0004 852 111	100
26	0.0004 673 100	0.0004 449 571	0.0004 236 260	0.0004 032 733	104
27	0.0003 912 122	0.0003 716 401	0.0003 530 068	0.0003 352 702	108
28	0.0003 275 957	0.0003 104 853	0.0002 942 342	0.0002 788 020	112
29	0.0002 743 866	0.0002 594 504	0.0002 452 982	0.0002 318 912	116
30	0.0002 298 637	0.0002 168 438	0.0002 045 369	0.0001 929 059	120
31	0.0001 925 960	0.0001 812 617	0.0001 705 737	0.0001 604 970	124
32	0.0001 613 921	0.0001 515 376	0.0001 422 674	0.0001 335 484	128
33	0.0001 352 588	0.0001 267 012	0.0001 186 704	0.0001 111 354	132
34	0.0001 133 678	0.0001 059 448	0.0000 989 957	0.0000 924 913	136
35	0.0000 950 272	0.0000 885 954	0.0000 825 887	0.0000 769 800	140
36	0.0000 796 590	0.0000 740 917	0.0000 689 050	0.0000 640 736	144
37	0.0000 667 799	0.0000 619 656	0.0000 574 912	0.0000 533 335	148
38	0.0000 559 856	0.0000 518 263	0.0000 479 701	0.0000 443 954	152
39	0.0000 469 379	0.0000 433 477	0.0000 400 271	0.0000 369 565	156
40	0.0000 393 537	0.0000 362 572	0.0000 334 003	0.0000 307 648	160
41	0.0000 329 958	0.0000 303 273	0.0000 278 712	0.0000 256 110	164
42	0.0000 276 658	0.0000 253 678	0.0000 232 579	0.0000 213 210	168
43	0.0000 231 971	0.0000 212 197	0.0000 194 085	0.0000 177 499	172
44	0.0000 194 506	0.0000 177 502	0.0000 161 965	0.0000 147 771	176
45	0.0000 163 094	0.0000 148 481	0.0000 135 162	0.0000 123 023	180
46	0.0000 136 756	0.0000 124 207	0.0000 112 795	0.0000 102 421	184
47	0.0000 114 673	0.0000 103 901	0.0000 094 131	0.0000 085 269	188
48	0.0000 096 156	0.0000 086 916	0.0000 078 555	0.0000 070 990	192
49	0.0000 080 630	0.0000 072 708	0.0000 065 557	0.0000 059 103	196
50	0.0000 067 611	0.0000 060 823	0.0000 054 710	0.0000 049 206	200
51	0.0000 056 695	0.0000 050 881	0.0000 045 658	0.0000 040 967	204
52	0.0000 047 541	0.0000 042 564	0.0000 038 104	0.0000 034 107	208
53	0.0000 039 866	0.0000 035 607	0.0000 031 800	0.0000 028 396	212
54	0.0000 033 429	0.0000 029 787	0.0000 026 538	0.0000 023 642	216
55	0.0000 028 032	0.0000 024 918	0.0000 022 148	0.0000 019 683	220
56	0.0000 023 506	0.0000 020 845	0.0000 018 483	0.0000 016 388	224
57	0.0000 019 711	0.0000 017 438	0.0000 015 425	0.0000 013 644	228
58	0.0000 016 529	0.0000 014 588	0.0000 012 873	0.0000 011 359	232
59	0.0000 013 861	0.0000 012 204	0.0000 010 744	0.0000 009 457	236
60	0.0000 011 623	0.0000 010 209	0.0000 008 966	0.0000 007 874	240

TABLE 3. SINKING FUND FACTORS
Payable at end of each period

QUARTERLY Compounding

QUARTERS	19% Nominal Annual Rate	19¼% Nominal Annual Rate	19½% Nominal Annual Rate	19¾% Nominal Annual Rate	QUARTERS
1	1.0000 000 000	1.0000 000 000	1.0000 000 000	1.0000 000 000	1
2	0.4884 004 884	0.4882 514 495	0.4881 025 015	0.4879 536 444	2
3	0.3179 896 693	0.3177 941 511	0.3175 987 943	0.3174 035 989	3
YEARS					
1	0.2328 759 246	0.2326 595 617	0.2324 434 256	0.2322 275 160	4
2	0.1056 619 598	0.1054 262 172	0.1051 909 457	0.1049 561 447	8
3	0.0637 401 861	0.0635 104 425	0.0632 813 995	0.0630 530 557	12
4	0.0431 353 090	0.0429 175 897	0.0427 007 845	0.0424 848 913	16
5	0.0310 504 673	0.0308 468 373	0.0306 443 163	0.0304 429 008	20
6	0.0232 186 689	0.0230 298 092	0.0228 422 314	0.0226 559 303	24
7	0.0178 101 623	0.0176 361 154	0.0174 634 994	0.0172 923 069	28
8	0.0139 092 942	0.0137 497 539	0.0135 917 680	0.0134 353 263	32
9	0.0110 068 041	0.0108 612 530	0.0107 173 534	0.0105 750 924	36
10	0.0087 967 454	0.0086 645 316	0.0085 340 403	0.0084 052 555	40
11	0.0070 841 765	0.0069 645 619	0.0068 467 156	0.0067 306 183	44
12	0.0057 390 022	0.0056 311 967	0.0055 251 814	0.0054 209 335	48
13	0.0046 711 140	0.0045 743 005	0.0044 792 771	0.0043 860 177	52
14	0.0038 161 771	0.0037 295 311	0.0036 446 552	0.0035 615 204	56
15	0.0031 270 953	0.0030 498 000	0.0029 742 377	0.0029 003 764	60
16	0.0025 686 682	0.0024 999 268	0.0024 328 665	0.0023 674 529	64
17	0.0021 141 277	0.0020 531 723	0.0019 938 343	0.0019 360 769	68
18	0.0017 428 204	0.0016 889 195	0.0016 365 626	0.0015 857 113	72
19	0.0014 386 173	0.0013 910 802	0.0013 450 066	0.0013 003 570	76
20	0.0011 887 937	0.0011 469 740	0.0011 065 325	0.0010 674 288	80
21	0.0009 832 248	0.0009 465 222	0.0009 111 096	0.0008 769 462	84
22	0.0008 137 976	0.0007 816 583	0.0007 507 197	0.0007 209 410	88
23	0.0006 739 715	0.0006 458 881	0.0006 189 164	0.0005 930 161	92
24	0.0005 584 480	0.0005 339 580	0.0005 104 924	0.0004 880 114	96
25	0.0004 629 162	0.0004 416 007	0.0004 212 245	0.0004 017 494	100
26	0.0003 838 573	0.0003 653 380	0.0003 476 768	0.0003 308 363	104
27	0.0003 183 901	0.0003 023 277	0.0002 870 458	0.0002 725 087	108
28	0.0002 641 499	0.0002 502 408	0.0002 370 392	0.0002 245 109	112
29	0.0002 191 924	0.0002 071 662	0.0001 957 791	0.0001 849 986	116
30	0.0001 819 156	0.0001 715 325	0.0001 617 246	0.0001 524 616	120
31	0.0001 509 983	0.0001 420 459	0.0001 336 099	0.0001 256 616	124
32	0.0001 253 494	0.0001 176 405	0.0001 103 937	0.0001 035 824	128
33	0.0001 040 667	0.0000 974 367	0.0000 912 191	0.0000 853 893	132
34	0.0000 864 041	0.0000 807 086	0.0000 753 802	0.0000 703 961	136
35	0.0000 717 438	0.0000 668 563	0.0000 622 950	0.0000 580 387	140
36	0.0000 595 741	0.0000 553 843	0.0000 514 836	0.0000 478 525	144
37	0.0000 494 708	0.0000 458 827	0.0000 425 502	0.0000 394 556	148
38	0.0000 410 824	0.0000 380 124	0.0000 351 680	0.0000 325 330	152
39	0.0000 341 174	0.0000 314 930	0.0000 290 674	0.0000 268 257	156
40	0.0000 283 340	0.0000 260 924	0.0000 240 255	0.0000 221 201	160
41	0.0000 235 314	0.0000 216 183	0.0000 198 586	0.0000 182 402	164
42	0.0000 195 432	0.0000 179 116	0.0000 164 146	0.0000 150 411	168
43	0.0000 162 311	0.0000 148 407	0.0000 135 680	0.0000 124 032	172
44	0.0000 134 805	0.0000 122 964	0.0000 112 152	0.0000 102 280	176
45	0.0000 111 962	0.0000 101 885	0.0000 092 705	0.0000 084 344	180
46	0.0000 092 990	0.0000 084 419	0.0000 076 630	0.0000 069 553	184
47	0.0000 077 234	0.0000 069 948	0.0000 063 343	0.0000 057 357	188
48	0.0000 064 147	0.0000 057 958	0.0000 052 360	0.0000 047 299	192
49	0.0000 053 279	0.0000 048 023	0.0000 043 282	0.0000 039 005	196
50	0.0000 044 251	0.0000 039 792	0.0000 035 778	0.0000 032 166	200
51	0.0000 036 754	0.0000 032 971	0.0000 029 575	0.0000 026 526	204
52	0.0000 030 527	0.0000 027 320	0.0000 024 447	0.0000 021 874	208
53	0.0000 025 355	0.0000 022 637	0.0000 020 209	0.0000 018 039	212
54	0.0000 021 059	0.0000 018 757	0.0000 016 705	0.0000 014 876	216
55	0.0000 017 491	0.0000 015 542	0.0000 013 809	0.0000 012 268	220
56	0.0000 014 528	0.0000 012 878	0.0000 011 415	0.0000 010 117	224
57	0.0000 012 067	0.0000 010 671	0.0000 009 436	0.0000 008 343	228
58	0.0000 010 022	0.0000 008 842	0.0000 007 800	0.0000 006 880	232
59	0.0000 008 324	0.0000 007 326	0.0000 006 448	0.0000 005 674	236
60	0.0000 006 914	0.0000 006 071	0.0000 005 330	0.0000 004 679	240

TABLE 3. SINKING FUND FACTORS
Payable at end of each period

QUARTERS	20% Nominal Annual Rate	20¼% Nominal Annual Rate	20½% Nominal Annual Rate	20¾% Nominal Annual Rate	QUARTERS
1	1.0000 000 000	1.0000 000 000	1.0000 000 000	1.0000 000 000	1
2	0.4878 048 780	0.4876 562 024	0.4875 076 173	0.4873 591 228	2
3	0.3172 085 646	0.3170 136 914	0.3168 189 790	0.3166 244 274	3
YEARS					
1	0.2320 118 326	0.2317 963 753	0.2315 811 439	0.2313 661 380	4
2	0.1047 218 136	0.1044 879 519	0.1042 545 590	0.1040 216 342	8
3	0.0628 254 100	0.0625 984 612	0.0623 722 081	0.0621 466 495	12
4	0.0422 699 080	0.0420 558 324	0.0418 426 624	0.0416 303 958	16
5	0.0302 425 872	0.0300 433 722	0.0298 452 521	0.0296 482 237	20
6	0.0224 709 008	0.0222 871 374	0.0221 046 351	0.0219 233 884	24
7	0.0171 225 304	0.0169 541 626	0.0167 871 960	0.0166 216 230	28
8	0.0132 804 189	0.0131 270 359	0.0129 751 672	0.0128 248 026	32
9	0.0104 344 571	0.0102 954 346	0.0101 580 120	0.0100 221 763	36
10	0.0082 781 612	0.0081 527 413	0.0080 289 799	0.0079 068 609	40
11	0.0066 162 506	0.0065 035 933	0.0063 926 272	0.0062 833 331	44
12	0.0053 184 306	0.0052 176 500	0.0051 185 693	0.0050 211 663	48
13	0.0042 944 966	0.0042 046 880	0.0041 165 665	0.0040 301 067	52
14	0.0034 800 978	0.0034 003 587	0.0033 222 749	0.0032 458 182	56
15	0.0028 281 845	0.0027 576 308	0.0026 886 844	0.0026 213 145	60
16	0.0023 036 520	0.0022 414 302	0.0021 807 543	0.0021 215 917	64
17	0.0018 798 643	0.0018 251 608	0.0017 719 316	0.0017 201 422	68
18	0.0015 363 280	0.0014 883 758	0.0014 418 184	0.0013 966 202	72
19	0.0012 570 925	0.0012 151 753	0.0011 745 681	0.0011 352 345	76
20	0.0010 296 235	0.0009 930 780	0.0009 577 547	0.0009 236 169	80
21	0.0008 439 924	0.0008 122 094	0.0007 815 596	0.0007 520 063	84
22	0.0006 922 828	0.0006 647 065	0.0006 381 748	0.0006 126 514	88
23	0.0005 681 481	0.0005 442 746	0.0005 213 589	0.0004 993 655	92
24	0.0004 664 770	0.0004 458 522	0.0004 261 013	0.0004 071 899	96
25	0.0003 831 381	0.0003 653 549	0.0003 483 654	0.0003 321 365	100
26	0.0003 147 810	0.0002 994 764	0.0002 848 895	0.0002 709 886	104
27	0.0002 586 824	0.0002 455 338	0.0002 330 318	0.0002 211 461	108
28	0.0002 126 236	0.0002 013 460	0.0001 906 485	0.0001 805 027	112
29	0.0001 747 942	0.0001 651 363	0.0001 559 972	0.0001 473 501	116
30	0.0001 437 145	0.0001 354 559	0.0001 276 595	0.0001 203 007	120
31	0.0001 181 741	0.0001 111 216	0.0001 044 800	0.0000 982 262	124
32	0.0000 971 814	0.0000 911 668	0.0000 855 163	0.0000 802 084	128
33	0.0000 799 238	0.0000 748 007	0.0000 699 993	0.0000 654 999	132
34	0.0000 657 349	0.0000 613 762	0.0000 573 010	0.0000 534 914	136
35	0.0000 540 677	0.0000 503 633	0.0000 469 083	0.0000 436 863	140
36	0.0000 444 731	0.0000 413 282	0.0000 384 020	0.0000 356 797	144
37	0.0000 365 823	0.0000 339 150	0.0000 314 392	0.0000 291 414	148
38	0.0000 300 925	0.0000 278 323	0.0000 257 394	0.0000 238 018	152
39	0.0000 247 545	0.0000 228 410	0.0000 210 734	0.0000 194 409	156
40	0.0000 203 638	0.0000 187 451	0.0000 172 536	0.0000 158 792	160
41	0.0000 167 521	0.0000 153 840	0.0000 141 263	0.0000 129 703	164
42	0.0000 137 812	0.0000 126 257	0.0000 115 660	0.0000 105 943	168
43	0.0000 113 373	0.0000 103 620	0.0000 094 698	0.0000 086 537	172
44	0.0000 093 268	0.0000 085 043	0.0000 077 536	0.0000 070 685	176
45	0.0000 076 730	0.0000 069 796	0.0000 063 484	0.0000 057 738	180
46	0.0000 063 124	0.0000 057 284	0.0000 051 980	0.0000 047 163	184
47	0.0000 051 931	0.0000 047 015	0.0000 042 560	0.0000 038 524	188
48	0.0000 042 723	0.0000 038 586	0.0000 034 847	0.0000 031 468	192
49	0.0000 035 148	0.0000 031 669	0.0000 028 533	0.0000 025 705	196
50	0.0000 028 916	0.0000 025 992	0.0000 023 362	0.0000 020 997	200
51	0.0000 023 789	0.0000 021 333	0.0000 019 129	0.0000 017 151	204
52	0.0000 019 571	0.0000 017 509	0.0000 015 662	0.0000 014 010	208
53	0.0000 016 101	0.0000 014 370	0.0000 012 824	0.0000 011 444	212
54	0.0000 013 246	0.0000 011 794	0.0000 010 500	0.0000 009 348	216
55	0.0000 010 898	0.0000 009 680	0.0000 008 598	0.0000 007 636	220
56	0.0000 008 966	0.0000 007 945	0.0000 007 040	0.0000 006 237	224
57	0.0000 007 376	0.0000 006 521	0.0000 005 764	0.0000 005 095	228
58	0.0000 006 068	0.0000 005 352	0.0000 004 720	0.0000 004 162	232
59	0.0000 004 992	0.0000 004 392	0.0000 003 864	0.0000 003 400	236
60	0.0000 004 107	0.0000 003 605	0.0000 003 164	0.0000 002 777	240

TABLE 3. SINKING FUND FACTORS
Payable at end of each period

QUARTERLY Compounding

QUARTERS	21% Nominal Annual Rate	21¼% Nominal Annual Rate	21½% Nominal Annual Rate	21¾% Nominal Annual Rate	QUARTERS
1	1.0000 000 000	1.0000 000 000	1.0000 000 000	1.0000 000 000	1
2	0.4872 107 186	0.4870 624 049	0.4869 141 814	0.4867 660 481	2
3	0.3164 300 363	0.3162 358 057	0.3160 417 353	0.3158 478 250	3
YEARS					
1	0.2311 513 576	0.2309 368 023	0.2307 224 720	0.2305 083 664	4
2	0.1037 891 770	0.1035 571 867	0.1033 256 628	0.1030 946 047	8
3	0.0619 217 842	0.0616 976 109	0.0614 741 284	0.0612 513 356	12
4	0.0414 190 304	0.0412 085 642	0.0409 989 948	0.0407 903 202	16
5	0.0294 522 832	0.0292 574 271	0.0290 636 520	0.0288 709 541	20
6	0.0217 433 921	0.0215 646 409	0.0213 871 293	0.0212 108 520	24
7	0.0164 574 362	0.0162 946 280	0.0161 331 909	0.0159 731 173	28
8	0.0126 759 322	0.0125 285 458	0.0123 826 333	0.0122 381 846	32
9	0.0098 879 146	0.0097 552 140	0.0096 240 614	0.0094 944 440	36
10	0.0077 863 683	0.0076 674 862	0.0075 501 986	0.0074 344 896	40
11	0.0061 756 919	0.0060 696 845	0.0059 652 920	0.0058 624 953	44
12	0.0049 254 187	0.0048 313 044	0.0047 388 015	0.0046 478 881	48
13	0.0039 452 836	0.0038 620 720	0.0037 804 474	0.0037 003 849	52
14	0.0031 709 607	0.0030 976 749	0.0030 259 335	0.0029 557 093	56
15	0.0025 554 911	0.0024 911 842	0.0024 283 643	0.0023 670 022	60
16	0.0020 639 102	0.0020 076 779	0.0019 528 636	0.0018 994 364	64
17	0.0016 697 590	0.0016 207 486	0.0015 730 784	0.0015 267 163	68
18	0.0013 527 462	0.0013 101 623	0.0012 688 348	0.0012 287 308	72
19	0.0010 971 390	0.0010 602 467	0.0010 245 236	0.0009 899 362	76
20	0.0008 906 287	0.0008 587 550	0.0008 279 618	0.0007 982 158	80
21	0.0007 235 137	0.0006 960 471	0.0006 695 727	0.0006 440 577	84
22	0.0005 881 011	0.0005 644 898	0.0005 417 843	0.0005 199 524	88
23	0.0004 782 600	0.0004 580 092	0.0004 385 809	0.0004 199 439	92
24	0.0003 890 846	0.0003 717 533	0.0003 551 651	0.0003 392 901	96
25	0.0003 166 360	0.0003 018 333	0.0002 876 988	0.0002 742 040	100
26	0.0002 577 433	0.0002 451 242	0.0002 331 035	0.0002 216 540	104
27	0.0002 098 478	0.0001 991 095	0.0001 889 047	0.0001 792 080	108
28	0.0001 708 814	0.0001 617 588	0.0001 531 102	0.0001 449 119	112
29	0.0001 391 698	0.0001 314 320	0.0001 241 138	0.0001 171 933	116
30	0.0001 133 557	0.0001 068 023	0.0001 006 190	0.0000 947 859	120
31	0.0000 923 382	0.0000 867 956	0.0000 815 786	0.0000 766 688	124
32	0.0000 752 232	0.0000 705 416	0.0000 661 457	0.0000 620 185	128
33	0.0000 612 842	0.0000 573 347	0.0000 536 352	0.0000 501 703	132
34	0.0000 499 305	0.0000 466 026	0.0000 434 928	0.0000 405 873	136
35	0.0000 406 819	0.0000 378 808	0.0000 352 696	0.0000 328 358	140
36	0.0000 331 475	0.0000 307 923	0.0000 286 020	0.0000 265 654	144
37	0.0000 270 092	0.0000 250 308	0.0000 231 955	0.0000 214 930	148
38	0.0000 220 080	0.0000 203 478	0.0000 188 112	0.0000 173 893	152
39	0.0000 179 333	0.0000 165 412	0.0000 152 559	0.0000 140 694	156
40	0.0000 146 131	0.0000 134 469	0.0000 123 727	0.0000 113 835	160
41	0.0000 119 078	0.0000 109 315	0.0000 100 345	0.0000 092 104	164
42	0.0000 097 034	0.0000 088 868	0.0000 081 382	0.0000 074 522	168
43	0.0000 079 072	0.0000 072 246	0.0000 066 003	0.0000 060 296	172
44	0.0000 064 435	0.0000 058 733	0.0000 053 531	0.0000 048 787	176
45	0.0000 052 508	0.0000 047 748	0.0000 043 416	0.0000 039 474	180
46	0.0000 042 789	0.0000 038 817	0.0000 035 212	0.0000 031 939	184
47	0.0000 034 868	0.0000 031 557	0.0000 028 558	0.0000 025 843	188
48	0.0000 028 414	0.0000 025 655	0.0000 023 162	0.0000 020 910	192
49	0.0000 023 155	0.0000 020 857	0.0000 018 786	0.0000 016 919	196
50	0.0000 018 869	0.0000 016 956	0.0000 015 236	0.0000 013 690	200
51	0.0000 015 377	0.0000 013 785	0.0000 012 357	0.0000 011 077	204
52	0.0000 012 531	0.0000 011 207	0.0000 010 022	0.0000 008 962	208
53	0.0000 010 211	0.0000 009 111	0.0000 008 129	0.0000 007 252	212
54	0.0000 008 321	0.0000 007 407	0.0000 006 593	0.0000 005 868	216
55	0.0000 006 781	0.0000 006 022	0.0000 005 347	0.0000 004 748	220
56	0.0000 005 526	0.0000 004 896	0.0000 004 337	0.0000 003 841	224
57	0.0000 004 503	0.0000 003 980	0.0000 003 517	0.0000 003 108	228
58	0.0000 003 670	0.0000 003 236	0.0000 002 853	0.0000 002 515	232
59	0.0000 002 991	0.0000 002 631	0.0000 002 314	0.0000 002 035	236
60	0.0000 002 437	0.0000 002 139	0.0000 001 877	0.0000 001 647	240

QUARTERLY
Compounding

TABLE 3. SINKING FUND FACTORS
Payable at end of each period

QUARTERS	22% Nominal Annual Rate	22¼% Nominal Annual Rate	22½% Nominal Annual Rate	22¾% Nominal Annual Rate	QUARTERS
1	1.0000 000 000	1.0000 000 000	1.0000 000 000	1.0000 000 000	1
2	0.4866 180 049	0.4864 700 517	0.4863 221 884	0.4861 744 151	2
3	0.3156 540 747	0.3154 604 842	0.3152 670 534	0.3150 737 820	3
YEARS					
1	0.2302 944 853	0.2300 808 285	0.2298 673 958	0.2296 541 869	4
2	0.1028 640 118	0.1026 338 835	0.1024 042 191	0.1021 750 181	8
3	0.0610 292 312	0.0608 078 139	0.0605 870 826	0.0603 670 359	12
4	0.0405 825 380	0.0403 756 461	0.0401 696 423	0.0399 645 244	16
5	0.0286 793 300	0.0284 887 761	0.0282 992 886	0.0281 108 641	20
6	0.0210 358 037	0.0208 619 789	0.0206 893 721	0.0205 179 780	24
7	0.0158 143 996	0.0156 570 301	0.0155 010 012	0.0153 463 054	28
8	0.0120 951 895	0.0119 536 378	0.0118 135 194	0.0116 748 241	32
9	0.0093 663 488	0.0092 397 629	0.0091 146 732	0.0089 910 670	36
10	0.0073 203 434	0.0072 077 439	0.0070 966 755	0.0069 871 224	40
11	0.0057 612 757	0.0056 616 144	0.0055 634 926	0.0054 668 918	44
12	0.0045 585 424	0.0044 707 429	0.0043 844 681	0.0042 996 968	48
13	0.0036 218 603	0.0035 448 494	0.0034 693 281	0.0033 952 727	52
14	0.0028 869 756	0.0028 197 060	0.0027 538 742	0.0026 894 543	56
15	0.0023 070 692	0.0022 485 369	0.0021 913 771	0.0021 355 624	60
16	0.0018 473 659	0.0017 966 223	0.0017 471 759	0.0016 989 980	64
17	0.0014 816 307	0.0014 377 907	0.0013 951 657	0.0013 537 261	68
18	0.0011 898 180	0.0011 520 648	0.0011 154 404	0.0010 799 142	72
19	0.0009 564 521	0.0009 240 395	0.0008 926 673	0.0008 623 052	76
20	0.0007 694 845	0.0007 417 363	0.0007 149 405	0.0006 890 670	80
21	0.0006 194 699	0.0005 957 785	0.0005 729 532	0.0005 509 647	84
22	0.0004 989 631	0.0004 787 860	0.0004 593 920	0.0004 407 527	88
23	0.0004 020 682	0.0003 849 246	0.0003 684 850	0.0003 527 223	92
24	0.0003 240 994	0.0003 095 653	0.0002 956 610	0.0002 823 606	96
25	0.0002 613 216	0.0002 490 252	0.0002 372 895	0.0002 260 903	100
26	0.0002 107 501	0.0002 003 670	0.0001 904 810	0.0001 810 693	104
27	0.0001 699 955	0.0001 612 438	0.0001 529 311	0.0001 450 361	108
28	0.0001 371 415	0.0001 297 775	0.0001 227 995	0.0001 161 881	112
29	0.0001 106 497	0.0001 044 632	0.0000 986 151	0.0000 930 875	116
30	0.0000 892 837	0.0000 840 942	0.0000 792 003	0.0000 745 857	120
31	0.0000 720 487	0.0000 677 017	0.0000 636 121	0.0000 597 652	124
32	0.0000 581 442	0.0000 545 077	0.0000 510 948	0.0000 478 920	128
33	0.0000 469 254	0.0000 438 871	0.0000 410 423	0.0000 383 792	132
34	0.0000 378 728	0.0000 353 371	0.0000 329 688	0.0000 307 569	136
35	0.0000 305 675	0.0000 284 537	0.0000 264 841	0.0000 246 492	140
36	0.0000 246 719	0.0000 229 117	0.0000 212 755	0.0000 197 547	144
37	0.0000 199 139	0.0000 184 494	0.0000 170 915	0.0000 158 324	148
38	0.0000 160 737	0.0000 148 565	0.0000 137 305	0.0000 126 890	152
39	0.0000 129 742	0.0000 119 634	0.0000 110 306	0.0000 101 698	156
40	0.0000 104 725	0.0000 096 338	0.0000 088 617	0.0000 081 509	160
41	0.0000 084 533	0.0000 077 579	0.0000 071 193	0.0000 065 328	164
42	0.0000 068 234	0.0000 062 473	0.0000 057 195	0.0000 052 359	168
43	0.0000 055 079	0.0000 050 309	0.0000 045 950	0.0000 041 965	172
44	0.0000 044 460	0.0000 040 514	0.0000 036 915	0.0000 033 635	176
45	0.0000 035 888	0.0000 032 625	0.0000 029 658	0.0000 026 958	180
46	0.0000 028 969	0.0000 026 273	0.0000 023 827	0.0000 021 607	184
47	0.0000 023 384	0.0000 021 158	0.0000 019 142	0.0000 017 318	188
48	0.0000 018 876	0.0000 017 038	0.0000 015 379	0.0000 013 880	192
49	0.0000 015 237	0.0000 013 721	0.0000 012 355	0.0000 011 125	196
50	0.0000 012 299	0.0000 011 050	0.0000 009 926	0.0000 008 917	200
51	0.0000 009 928	0.0000 008 898	0.0000 007 975	0.0000 007 147	204
52	0.0000 008 014	0.0000 007 166	0.0000 006 407	0.0000 005 728	208
53	0.0000 006 469	0.0000 005 771	0.0000 005 147	0.0000 004 591	212
54	0.0000 005 222	0.0000 004 647	0.0000 004 135	0.0000 003 680	216
55	0.0000 004 215	0.0000 003 742	0.0000 003 322	0.0000 002 949	220
56	0.0000 003 403	0.0000 003 014	0.0000 002 669	0.0000 002 364	224
57	0.0000 002 747	0.0000 002 427	0.0000 002 144	0.0000 001 895	228
58	0.0000 002 217	0.0000 001 954	0.0000 001 723	0.0000 001 519	232
59	0.0000 001 790	0.0000 001 574	0.0000 001 384	0.0000 001 217	236
60	0.0000 001 445	0.0000 001 268	0.0000 001 112	0.0000 000 976	240

TABLE 4. PRESENT WORTH OF ONE DOLLAR
Payable at end of each period

QUARTERLY Compounding

QUARTERS	5% Nominal Annual Rate	5¼% Nominal Annual Rate	5½% Nominal Annual Rate	5¾% Nominal Annual Rate	QUARTERS
1	0.9876 543 210	0.9870 450 339	0.9864 364 982	0.9858 287 123	1
2	0.9754 610 578	0.9742 578 990	0.9730 569 649	0.9718 582 499	2
3	0.9634 183 287	0.9616 364 210	0.9598 589 049	0.9580 857 670	3
YEARS					
1	0.9515 242 752	0.9491 784 538	0.9468 398 569	0.9445 084 579	4
2	0.9053 984 463	0.9009 397 371	0.8965 057 146	0.8920 962 271	8
3	0.8615 086 004	0.8551 525 866	0.8488 473 426	0.8425 924 318	12
4	0.8197 463 466	0.8116 924 099	0.8037 224 964	0.7958 356 784	16
5	0.7800 085 483	0.7704 409 466	0.7609 964 935	0.7516 735 294	20
6	0.7421 970 686	0.7312 859 464	0.7205 418 110	0.7099 620 061	24
7	0.7062 185 278	0.6941 208 639	0.6822 377 052	0.6705 651 196	28
8	0.6719 840 728	0.6588 445 683	0.6459 698 512	0.6333 544 271	32
9	0.6394 091 578	0.6253 610 686	0.6116 300 014	0.5982 086 132	36
10	0.6084 133 355	0.5935 792 522	0.5791 156 630	0.5650 130 948	40
11	0.5789 200 581	0.5634 126 368	0.5483 297 915	0.5336 596 469	44
12	0.5508 564 886	0.5347 791 354	0.5191 805 013	0.5040 460 501	48
13	0.5241 533 211	0.5076 008 328	0.4915 807 916	0.4760 757 575	52
14	0.4987 446 090	0.4818 037 736	0.4654 482 864	0.4496 575 796	56
15	0.4745 676 026	0.4573 177 609	0.4407 049 889	0.4247 053 871	60
16	0.4515 625 941	0.4340 761 652	0.4172 770 486	0.4011 378 303	64
17	0.4296 727 700	0.4120 157 433	0.3950 945 410	0.3788 780 735	68
18	0.4088 440 711	0.3910 764 661	0.3740 912 587	0.3578 535 449	72
19	0.3890 250 584	0.3712 013 554	0.3542 045 138	0.3379 956 999	76
20	0.3701 667 868	0.3523 363 286	0.3353 749 512	0.3192 397 973	80
21	0.3522 226 835	0.3344 300 516	0.3175 463 708	0.3015 246 887	84
22	0.3351 484 336	0.3174 337 993	0.3006 655 603	0.2847 926 187	88
23	0.3189 018 704	0.3013 013 227	0.2846 821 361	0.2689 890 371	92
24	0.3034 428 711	0.2859 887 236	0.2695 483 930	0.2540 624 207	96
25	0.2887 332 580	0.2714 543 345	0.2552 191 618	0.2399 641 052	100
26	0.2747 367 040	0.2576 586 055	0.2416 516 747	0.2266 481 269	104
27	0.2614 186 432	0.2445 639 968	0.2288 054 371	0.2140 710 729	108
28	0.2487 461 850	0.2321 348 763	0.2166 421 073	0.2021 919 389	112
29	0.2366 880 334	0.2203 374 230	0.2051 253 819	0.1909 719 964	116
30	0.2252 144 094	0.2091 395 344	0.1942 208 872	0.1803 746 659	120
31	0.2142 969 777	0.1985 107 399	0.1838 960 771	0.1703 653 975	124
32	0.2039 087 764	0.1884 221 172	0.1741 201 353	0.1609 115 589	128
33	0.1940 241 506	0.1788 462 138	0.1648 638 840	0.1519 823 283	132
34	0.1846 186 893	0.1697 569 727	0.1560 996 963	0.1435 485 946	136
35	0.1756 691 645	0.1611 296 609	0.1478 014 141	0.1355 828 617	140
36	0.1671 534 745	0.1529 408 024	0.1399 442 698	0.1280 591 596	144
37	0.1590 505 886	0.1451 681 143	0.1325 048 124	0.1209 529 594	148
38	0.1513 404 961	0.1377 904 463	0.1254 608 376	0.1142 410 931	152
39	0.1440 041 558	0.1307 877 227	0.1187 913 215	0.1079 016 787	156
40	0.1370 234 500	0.1241 408 884	0.1124 763 579	0.1019 140 482	160
41	0.1303 811 390	0.1178 318 565	0.1064 970 986	0.0962 586 805	164
42	0.1240 608 188	0.1118 434 594	0.1008 356 976	0.0909 171 379	168
43	0.1180 468 807	0.1061 594 019	0.0954 752 575	0.0858 720 057	172
44	0.1123 244 726	0.1007 642 169	0.0903 997 791	0.0811 068 357	176
45	0.1068 794 623	0.0956 432 236	0.0855 941 139	0.0766 060 923	180
46	0.1016 984 029	0.0907 824 871	0.0810 439 186	0.0723 551 021	184
47	0.0967 684 991	0.0861 687 807	0.0767 356 123	0.0683 400 059	188
48	0.0920 775 760	0.0817 895 501	0.0726 563 362	0.0645 477 136	192
49	0.0876 140 488	0.0776 328 787	0.0687 939 149	0.0609 658 614	196
50	0.0833 668 943	0.0736 874 557	0.0651 368 206	0.0575 827 718	200
51	0.0793 256 236	0.0699 425 453	0.0616 741 379	0.0543 874 150	204
52	0.0754 802 565	0.0663 879 570	0.0583 955 319	0.0513 693 734	208
53	0.0718 212 964	0.0630 140 184	0.0552 912 170	0.0485 188 077	212
54	0.0683 397 070	0.0598 115 485	0.0523 519 280	0.0458 264 242	216
55	0.0650 268 902	0.0567 718 331	0.0495 688 920	0.0432 834 453	220
56	0.0618 746 645	0.0538 866 008	0.0469 338 027	0.0408 815 802	224
57	0.0588 752 453	0.0511 480 004	0.0444 387 950	0.0386 129 982	228
58	0.0560 212 251	0.0485 485 800	0.0420 764 223	0.0364 703 034	232
59	0.0533 055 556	0.0460 812 661	0.0398 396 337	0.0344 465 100	236
60	0.0507 215 302	0.0437 393 449	0.0377 217 530	0.0325 350 201	240

TABLE 4. PRESENT WORTH OF ONE DOLLAR
Payable at end of each period

QUARTERS	6% Nominal Annual Rate	6¼% Nominal Annual Rate	6½% Nominal Annual Rate	6¾% Nominal Annual Rate	QUARTERS
1	0.9852 216 749	0.9846 153 846	0.9840 098 401	0.9834 050 400	1
2	0.9706 617 486	0.9694 674 556	0.9682 753 654	0.9670 854 726	2
3	0.9563 169 937	0.9545 525 717	0.9527 924 875	0.9510 367 278	3
YEARS					
1	0.9421 842 303	0.9398 671 475	0.9375 571 833	0.9352 543 113	4
2	0.8877 111 238	0.8833 502 550	0.8790 134 719	0.8747 006 268	8
3	0.8363 874 219	0.8302 318 844	0.8241 253 947	0.8180 675 324	12
4	0.7880 310 393	0.7803 076 729	0.7726 646 838	0.7651 011 866	16
5	0.7424 704 182	0.7333 855 468	0.7244 173 245	0.7155 641 833	20
6	0.6995 439 195	0.6892 849 819	0.6791 826 663	0.6692 344 875	24
7	0.6590 992 494	0.6478 363 097	0.6367 725 875	0.6259 044 397	28
8	0.6209 929 189	0.6088 800 645	0.5970 107 135	0.5853 798 257	32
9	0.5850 897 353	0.5722 663 694	0.5597 316 829	0.5474 790 058	36
10	0.5512 623 219	0.5378 543 602	0.5247 804 600	0.5120 321 005	40
11	0.5193 906 665	0.5055 116 433	0.4920 116 899	0.4788 802 295	44
12	0.4893 616 953	0.4751 137 862	0.4612 890 942	0.4478 747 993	48
13	0.4610 688 722	0.4465 438 390	0.4324 849 038	0.4188 768 369	52
14	0.4344 118 205	0.4196 918 842	0.4054 793 282	0.3917 563 677	56
15	0.4092 959 667	0.3944 546 140	0.3801 600 568	0.3663 918 318	60
16	0.3856 322 054	0.3707 349 329	0.3564 217 921	0.3426 695 404	64
17	0.3633 365 826	0.3484 415 839	0.3341 658 114	0.3204 831 650	68
18	0.3423 299 984	0.3274 887 975	0.3132 995 569	0.2997 332 617	72
19	0.3225 379 260	0.3077 959 620	0.2937 362 501	0.2803 268 253	76
20	0.3038 901 476	0.2892 873 128	0.2753 945 312	0.2621 768 719	80
21	0.2863 205 048	0.2718 916 415	0.2581 981 210	0.2452 020 498	84
22	0.2697 666 644	0.2555 420 215	0.2420 755 030	0.2293 262 742	88
23	0.2541 698 971	0.2401 755 508	0.2269 596 268	0.2144 783 867	92
24	0.2394 748 688	0.2257 331 098	0.2127 876 284	0.2005 918 358	96
25	0.2256 294 450	0.2121 591 340	0.1995 005 695	0.1876 043 793	100
26	0.2125 845 049	0.1994 014 001	0.1870 431 920	0.1754 578 045	104
27	0.2002 937 682	0.1874 108 252	0.1753 636 882	0.1640 976 681	108
28	0.1887 136 298	0.1761 412 776	0.1644 134 856	0.1534 730 516	112
29	0.1778 030 060	0.1655 494 002	0.1541 470 444	0.1435 363 332	116
30	0.1675 231 884	0.1555 944 425	0.1445 216 688	0.1342 429 744	120
31	0.1578 377 063	0.1462 381 049	0.1354 973 287	0.1255 513 206	124
32	0.1487 121 978	0.1374 443 905	0.1270 364 939	0.1174 224 139	128
33	0.1401 142 876	0.1291 794 672	0.1191 039 773	0.1098 198 188	132
34	0.1320 134 722	0.1214 115 374	0.1116 667 895	0.1027 094 590	136
35	0.1243 810 117	0.1141 107 153	0.1046 940 006	0.0960 594 644	140
36	0.1171 898 278	0.1072 489 125	0.0981 566 123	0.0898 400 282	144
37	0.1104 144 077	0.1007 997 295	0.0920 274 370	0.0840 232 737	148
38	0.1040 307 137	0.0947 383 542	0.0862 809 846	0.0785 831 290	152
39	0.0980 160 979	0.0890 414 667	0.0808 933 569	0.0734 952 102	156
40	0.0923 492 218	0.0836 871 493	0.0758 421 478	0.0687 367 122	160
41	0.0870 099 805	0.0786 548 023	0.0711 063 505	0.0642 863 064	164
42	0.0819 794 315	0.0739 250 647	0.0666 662 697	0.0601 240 452	168
43	0.0772 397 275	0.0694 797 397	0.0625 034 400	0.0562 312 725	172
44	0.0727 740 532	0.0653 017 248	0.0586 005 492	0.0525 905 400	176
45	0.0685 665 653	0.0613 749 458	0.0549 413 658	0.0491 855 293	180
46	0.0646 023 366	0.0576 842 952	0.0515 106 722	0.0460 009 783	184
47	0.0608 673 028	0.0542 155 740	0.0482 942 007	0.0430 226 133	188
48	0.0573 482 128	0.0509 554 369	0.0452 785 748	0.0402 370 846	192
49	0.0540 325 817	0.0478 913 411	0.0424 512 530	0.0376 319 068	196
50	0.0509 086 464	0.0450 114 982	0.0398 004 772	0.0351 954 031	200
51	0.0479 653 239	0.0423 048 284	0.0373 152 233	0.0329 166 525	204
52	0.0451 921 717	0.0397 609 184	0.0349 851 557	0.0307 854 412	208
53	0.0425 793 515	0.0373 699 809	0.0328 005 840	0.0287 922 166	212
54	0.0401 175 936	0.0351 228 174	0.0307 524 232	0.0269 280 447	216
55	0.0377 981 640	0.0330 107 822	0.0288 321 552	0.0251 845 699	220
56	0.0356 128 341	0.0310 257 497	0.0270 317 942	0.0235 539 776	224
57	0.0335 538 507	0.0291 600 829	0.0253 438 529	0.0220 289 591	228
58	0.0316 139 090	0.0274 066 039	0.0237 613 113	0.0206 026 789	232
59	0.0297 861 265	0.0257 585 666	0.0222 775 881	0.0192 687 443	236
60	0.0280 640 186	0.0242 096 305	0.0208 865 128	0.0180 211 762	240

TABLE 4. PRESENT WORTH OF ONE DOLLAR
Payable at end of each period

QUARTERLY Compounding

QUARTERS	7% Nominal Annual Rate	7¼% Nominal Annual Rate	7½% Nominal Annual Rate	7¾% Nominal Annual Rate	QUARTERS
1	0.9828 009 828	0.9821 976 673	0.9815 950 920	0.9809 932 557	1
2	0.9658 977 718	0.9647 122 576	0.9635 289 247	0.9623 477 677	2
3	0.9492 852 794	0.9475 381 290	0.9457 952 635	0.9440 566 697	3
YEARS					
1	0.9329 585 056	0.9306 697 400	0.9283 879 887	0.9261 132 259	4
2	0.8704 115 731	0.8661 461 649	0.8619 042 576	0.8576 857 073	8
3	0.8120 578 805	0.8060 960 261	0.8001 815 602	0.7943 140 772	12
4	0.7576 163 066	0.7502 091 790	0.7428 789 492	0.7356 247 725	16
5	0.7068 245 772	0.6981 969 816	0.6896 798 935	0.6812 718 311	20
6	0.6594 380 012	0.6497 908 033	0.6402 905 292	0.6309 348 532	24
7	0.6152 282 921	0.6047 406 379	0.5944 380 366	0.5843 171 123	28
8	0.5739 824 680	0.5628 138 123	0.5518 691 332	0.5411 438 058	32
9	0.5355 018 255	0.5237 937 843	0.5123 486 746	0.5011 604 357	36
10	0.4996 009 829	0.4874 790 251	0.4756 583 555	0.4641 313 079	40
11	0.4661 069 864	0.4536 819 775	0.4415 955 040	0.4298 381 428	44
12	0.4348 584 774	0.4222 280 880	0.4099 719 618	0.3980 787 890	48
13	0.4057 049 152	0.3929 549 049	0.3806 130 450	0.3686 660 315	52
14	0.3785 058 514	0.3657 112 392	0.3533 565 794	0.3414 264 877	56
15	0.3531 302 535	0.3403 563 839	0.3280 520 040	0.3161 995 860	60
16	0.3294 558 736	0.3167 593 873	0.3045 595 402	0.2928 366 186	64
17	0.3073 686 594	0.2947 983 766	0.2827 494 190	0.2711 998 655	68
18	0.2867 622 052	0.2743 599 285	0.2625 011 644	0.2511 617 823	72
19	0.2675 372 384	0.2553 384 833	0.2437 029 280	0.2326 042 485	76
20	0.2496 011 421	0.2376 357 999	0.2262 508 712	0.2154 178 709	80
21	0.2328 675 085	0.2211 604 481	0.2100 485 912	0.1995 013 394	84
22	0.2172 557 227	0.2058 273 367	0.1950 065 892	0.1847 608 290	88
23	0.2026 905 744	0.1915 572 739	0.1810 417 751	0.1711 094 474	92
24	0.1891 018 954	0.1782 765 583	0.1680 770 095	0.1584 667 223	96
25	0.1764 242 217	0.1659 165 982	0.1560 406 768	0.1467 581 274	100
26	0.1645 964 782	0.1544 135 573	0.1448 662 900	0.1359 146 428	104
27	0.1535 616 844	0.1437 080 252	0.1344 921 237	0.1258 723 483	108
28	0.1432 666 796	0.1337 447 105	0.1248 608 722	0.1165 720 465	112
29	0.1336 618 673	0.1244 721 549	0.1159 193 340	0.1079 589 141	116
30	0.1247 009 759	0.1158 424 680	0.1076 181 173	0.0999 821 782	120
31	0.1163 408 361	0.1078 110 796	0.0999 113 675	0.0925 948 176	124
32	0.1085 411 726	0.1003 365 094	0.0927 565 135	0.0857 532 852	128
33	0.1012 644 102	0.0933 801 531	0.0861 140 330	0.0794 172 516	132
34	0.0944 754 928	0.0869 060 828	0.0799 472 339	0.0735 493 671	136
35	0.0881 417 146	0.0808 808 615	0.0742 220 517	0.0681 150 416	140
36	0.0822 325 623	0.0752 733 704	0.0689 068 613	0.0630 822 409	144
37	0.0767 195 684	0.0700 546 480	0.0639 723 024	0.0584 212 976	148
38	0.0715 761 739	0.0651 977 411	0.0593 911 171	0.0541 047 364	152
39	0.0667 776 003	0.0606 775 647	0.0551 379 998	0.0501 071 120	156
40	0.0623 007 301	0.0564 707 734	0.0511 894 567	0.0464 048 591	160
41	0.0581 239 961	0.0525 556 400	0.0475 236 768	0.0429 761 538	164
42	0.0542 272 765	0.0489 119 438	0.0441 204 107	0.0398 007 844	168
43	0.0505 917 989	0.0455 208 660	0.0409 608 593	0.0368 600 328	172
44	0.0472 000 491	0.0423 648 925	0.0380 275 698	0.0341 365 639	176
45	0.0440 356 872	0.0394 277 235	0.0353 043 391	0.0316 143 233	180
46	0.0410 834 690	0.0366 941 892	0.0327 761 243	0.0292 784 430	184
47	0.0383 291 718	0.0341 501 715	0.0304 289 601	0.0271 151 533	188
48	0.0357 595 268	0.0317 825 313	0.0282 498 811	0.0251 117 021	192
49	0.0333 621 547	0.0295 790 401	0.0262 268 503	0.0232 562 794	196
50	0.0311 255 060	0.0275 283 176	0.0243 486 928	0.0215 379 480	200
51	0.0290 388 056	0.0256 197 721	0.0226 050 339	0.0199 465 785	204
52	0.0270 920 007	0.0238 435 467	0.0209 862 420	0.0184 727 901	208
53	0.0252 757 124	0.0221 904 674	0.0194 833 750	0.0171 078 953	212
54	0.0235 811 909	0.0206 519 965	0.0180 881 313	0.0158 438 481	216
55	0.0220 002 726	0.0192 201 882	0.0167 928 039	0.0146 731 972	220
56	0.0205 253 415	0.0178 876 476	0.0155 902 374	0.0135 890 420	224
57	0.0191 492 919	0.0166 474 923	0.0144 737 891	0.0125 849 916	228
58	0.0178 654 948	0.0154 933 173	0.0134 372 920	0.0116 551 271	232
59	0.0166 677 653	0.0144 191 616	0.0124 750 205	0.0107 939 674	236
60	0.0155 503 334	0.0134 194 774	0.0115 816 592	0.0099 964 360	240

TABLE 4. PRESENT WORTH OF ONE DOLLAR
Payable at end of each period

QUARTERS	8% Nominal Annual Rate	8¼% Nominal Annual Rate	8½% Nominal Annual Rate	8¾% Nominal Annual Rate	QUARTERS
1	0.9803 921 569	0.9797 917 942	0.9791 921 665	0.9785 932 722	1
2	0.9611 687 812	0.9599 919 601	0.9588 172 989	0.9576 447 923	2
3	0.9423 223 345	0.9405 922 450	0.9388 663 881	0.9371 447 509	3
YEARS					
1	0.9238 454 260	0.9215 845 634	0.9193 306 126	0.9170 835 483	4
2	0.8534 903 712	0.8493 181 075	0.8451 687 753	0.8410 422 346	8
3	0.7884 931 756	0.7827 184 573	0.7769 895 279	0.7713 059 967	12
4	0.7284 458 137	0.7213 412 477	0.7143 102 587	0.7073 520 403	16
5	0.6729 713 331	0.6647 769 588	0.6566 872 877	0.6487 009 190	20
6	0.6217 214 879	0.6126 481 834	0.6037 127 265	0.5949 129 406	24
7	0.5743 745 529	0.5646 071 086	0.5550 115 907	0.5455 848 705	28
8	0.5306 333 035	0.5203 331 956	0.5102 391 456	0.5003 469 089	32
9	0.4902 231 504	0.4795 310 409	0.4690 784 663	0.4588 599 186	36
10	0.4528 904 152	0.4419 284 050	0.4312 381 938	0.4208 128 823	40
11	0.4184 007 386	0.4072 743 962	0.3964 504 729	0.3859 205 713	44
12	0.3865 376 086	0.3753 377 966	0.3644 690 561	0.3539 214 069	48
13	0.3571 010 017	0.3459 055 194	0.3350 675 606	0.3245 754 996	52
14	0.3299 061 270	0.3187 811 870	0.3080 378 658	0.2976 628 509	56
15	0.3047 822 665	0.2937 838 211	0.2831 886 398	0.2729 817 035	60
16	0.2815 717 028	0.2707 466 345	0.2603 439 857	0.2503 470 293	64
17	0.2601 287 297	0.2495 159 189	0.2393 421 959	0.2295 891 419	68
18	0.2403 187 371	0.2299 500 192	0.2200 346 076	0.2105 524 249	72
19	0.2220 173 661	0.2119 183 881	0.2022 845 506	0.1930 941 649	76
20	0.2051 097 282	0.1953 007 151	0.1859 663 798	0.1770 834 819	80
21	0.1894 896 842	0.1799 861 243	0.1709 645 859	0.1624 003 480	84
22	0.1750 591 780	0.1658 724 338	0.1571 729 775	0.1489 346 873	88
23	0.1617 276 209	0.1528 654 745	0.1444 939 296	0.1365 855 515	92
24	0.1494 113 228	0.1408 784 615	0.1328 376 929	0.1252 603 622	96
25	0.1380 329 672	0.1298 314 155	0.1221 217 576	0.1148 742 175	100
26	0.1275 211 254	0.1196 506 283	0.1122 702 702	0.1053 492 550	104
27	0.1178 098 084	0.1102 681 721	0.1032 134 963	0.0966 140 686	108
28	0.1088 380 526	0.1016 214 452	0.0948 873 267	0.0886 031 728	112
29	0.1005 495 371	0.0936 527 552	0.0872 328 242	0.0812 565 121	116
30	0.0928 922 299	0.0863 089 335	0.0801 958 057	0.0745 190 104	120
31	0.0858 180 618	0.0795 409 808	0.0737 264 592	0.0683 401 585	124
32	0.0792 826 238	0.0733 037 401	0.0677 789 909	0.0626 736 351	128
33	0.0732 448 894	0.0675 555 953	0.0623 113 012	0.0574 769 596	132
34	0.0676 669 560	0.0622 581 938	0.0572 846 867	0.0527 111 741	136
35	0.0625 138 078	0.0573 761 904	0.0526 635 662	0.0483 405 506	140
36	0.0577 530 954	0.0528 770 113	0.0484 152 285	0.0443 323 236	144
37	0.0533 549 330	0.0487 306 374	0.0445 096 017	0.0406 564 447	148
38	0.0492 917 108	0.0449 094 032	0.0409 190 394	0.0372 853 565	152
39	0.0455 379 216	0.0413 878 127	0.0376 181 256	0.0341 937 871	156
40	0.0420 700 006	0.0381 423 693	0.0345 834 944	0.0313 585 596	160
41	0.0388 661 776	0.0351 514 188	0.0317 936 651	0.0287 584 191	164
42	0.0359 063 404	0.0323 950 049	0.0292 288 896	0.0263 738 730	168
43	0.0331 719 084	0.0298 547 365	0.0268 710 130	0.0241 870 450	172
44	0.0306 457 158	0.0275 136 643	0.0247 033 448	0.0221 815 411	176
45	0.0283 119 044	0.0253 561 683	0.0227 105 411	0.0203 423 264	180
46	0.0261 558 234	0.0233 678 533	0.0208 784 957	0.0186 556 129	184
47	0.0241 639 378	0.0215 354 529	0.0191 942 402	0.0171 087 557	188
48	0.0223 237 434	0.0198 467 409	0.0176 458 526	0.0156 901 584	192
49	0.0206 236 882	0.0182 904 501	0.0162 223 725	0.0143 891 861	196
50	0.0190 531 000	0.0168 561 964	0.0149 137 237	0.0131 960 858	200
51	0.0176 021 193	0.0155 344 104	0.0137 106 427	0.0121 019 132	204
52	0.0162 616 374	0.0143 162 729	0.0126 046 136	0.0110 984 655	208
53	0.0150 232 394	0.0131 936 561	0.0115 878 071	0.0101 782 201	212
54	0.0138 791 510	0.0121 590 698	0.0106 530 258	0.0093 342 782	216
55	0.0128 221 901	0.0112 056 110	0.0097 936 527	0.0085 603 130	220
56	0.0118 457 217	0.0103 269 181	0.0090 036 048	0.0078 505 222	224
57	0.0109 436 158	0.0095 171 283	0.0082 772 895	0.0071 995 848	228
58	0.0101 102 094	0.0087 708 386	0.0076 095 656	0.0066 026 208	232
59	0.0093 402 707	0.0080 830 694	0.0069 957 066	0.0060 551 549	236
60	0.0086 289 664	0.0074 492 320	0.0064 313 673	0.0055 530 829	240

TABLE 4. PRESENT WORTH OF ONE DOLLAR
Payable at end of each period

QUARTERLY Compounding

QUARTERS	9% Nominal Annual Rate	9¼% Nominal Annual Rate	9½% Nominal Annual Rate	9¾% Nominal Annual Rate	QUARTERS
1	0.9779 951 100	0.9773 976 787	0.9768 009 768	0.9762 050 031	1
2	0.9564 744 352	0.9553 062 223	0.9541 401 483	0.9529 762 080	2
3	0.9354 273 205	0.9337 140 841	0.9320 050 288	0.9303 001 420	3
YEARS					
1	0.9148 433 453	0.9126 099 783	0.9103 834 226	0.9081 636 530	4
2	0.8369 383 464	0.8328 569 726	0.8287 979 761	0.8247 612 206	8
3	0.7656 674 765	0.7600 735 837	0.7545 239 381	0.7490 181 629	12
4	0.7004 657 956	0.6936 507 368	0.6869 060 851	0.6802 310 710	16
5	0.6408 164 717	0.6330 325 839	0.6253 479 128	0.6177 611 343	20
6	0.5862 466 846	0.5777 118 527	0.5693 063 731	0.5610 282 084	24
7	0.5363 238 781	0.5272 256 013	0.5182 870 844	0.5095 054 272	28
8	0.4906 523 308	0.4811 513 446	0.4718 399 698	0.4627 143 099	32
9	0.4488 700 197	0.4391 035 182	0.4295 552 866	0.4202 203 180	36
10	0.4106 457 504	0.4007 302 522	0.3910 600 120	0.3816 288 191	40
11	0.3756 765 320	0.3657 104 268	0.3560 145 521	0.3465 814 224	44
12	0.3436 851 753	0.3337 509 847	0.3241 097 465	0.3147 526 506	48
13	0.3144 180 954	0.3045 844 789	0.2950 641 403	0.2858 469 170	52
14	0.2876 433 022	0.2779 668 347	0.2686 215 019	0.2595 957 803	56
15	0.2631 485 609	0.2536 753 070	0.2445 485 623	0.2357 554 521	60
16	0.2407 397 097	0.2315 066 164	0.2226 329 571	0.2141 045 326	64
17	0.2202 391 214	0.2112 752 482	0.2026 813 535	0.1944 419 545	68
18	0.2014 842 946	0.1928 118 997	0.1845 177 442	0.1765 851 157	72
19	0.1843 265 660	0.1759 620 636	0.1679 818 955	0.1603 681 837	76
20	0.1686 299 323	0.1605 847 351	0.1529 279 330	0.1456 405 555	80
21	0.1542 699 714	0.1465 512 316	0.1392 230 550	0.1322 654 589	84
22	0.1411 328 567	0.1337 441 163	0.1267 463 613	0.1201 186 823	88
23	0.1291 144 547	0.1220 562 151	0.1153 877 862	0.1090 874 214	92
24	0.1181 194 997	0.1113 897 198	0.1050 471 278	0.0990 692 311	96
25	0.1080 608 382	0.1016 553 698	0.0956 331 637	0.0899 710 748	100
26	0.0988 587 387	0.0927 717 048	0.0870 628 469	0.0817 084 599	104
27	0.0904 402 593	0.0846 643 835	0.0792 605 725	0.0742 046 535	108
28	0.0827 386 693	0.0772 655 612	0.0721 575 113	0.0673 899 692	112
29	0.0756 929 210	0.0705 133 221	0.0656 910 021	0.0612 011 206	116
30	0.0692 471 651	0.0643 511 614	0.0598 039 993	0.0555 806 332	120
31	0.0633 503 082	0.0587 275 120	0.0544 445 696	0.0504 763 109	124
32	0.0579 556 078	0.0535 953 135	0.0495 654 336	0.0458 407 509	128
33	0.0530 203 021	0.0489 116 178	0.0451 235 491	0.0416 309 038	132
34	0.0485 052 706	0.0446 372 305	0.0410 797 310	0.0378 076 737	136
35	0.0443 747 240	0.0407 363 820	0.0373 983 061	0.0343 355 550	140
36	0.0405 959 210	0.0371 764 287	0.0340 467 979	0.0311 823 031	144
37	0.0371 389 081	0.0339 275 798	0.0309 956 404	0.0283 186 343	148
38	0.0339 762 829	0.0309 626 478	0.0282 179 172	0.0257 179 543	152
39	0.0310 829 764	0.0282 568 214	0.0256 891 241	0.0233 561 114	156
40	0.0284 360 541	0.0257 874 571	0.0233 869 527	0.0212 111 714	160
41	0.0260 145 348	0.0235 338 907	0.0212 910 940	0.0192 632 149	164
42	0.0237 992 241	0.0214 772 635	0.0193 830 591	0.0174 941 516	168
43	0.0217 725 618	0.0196 003 650	0.0176 460 156	0.0158 875 526	172
44	0.0199 184 832	0.0178 874 886	0.0160 646 401	0.0144 284 978	176
45	0.0182 222 918	0.0163 243 006	0.0146 249 820	0.0131 034 373	180
46	0.0166 705 424	0.0148 977 196	0.0133 143 412	0.0119 000 655	184
47	0.0152 509 348	0.0135 958 076	0.0121 211 555	0.0108 072 070	188
48	0.0139 522 162	0.0124 076 697	0.0110 348 990	0.0098 147 125	192
49	0.0127 640 921	0.0113 233 632	0.0100 459 892	0.0089 133 652	196
50	0.0116 771 448	0.0103 338 142	0.0091 457 020	0.0080 947 943	200
51	0.0106 827 582	0.0094 307 420	0.0083 260 955	0.0073 513 980	204
52	0.0097 730 502	0.0086 065 892	0.0075 799 393	0.0066 762 724	208
53	0.0089 408 100	0.0078 544 592	0.0069 006 511	0.0060 631 480	212
54	0.0081 794 405	0.0071 680 578	0.0062 822 384	0.0055 063 306	216
55	0.0074 829 067	0.0065 416 411	0.0057 192 457	0.0050 006 493	220
56	0.0068 456 874	0.0059 699 669	0.0052 067 064	0.0045 414 079	224
57	0.0062 627 316	0.0054 482 514	0.0047 400 992	0.0041 243 416	228
58	0.0057 294 183	0.0049 721 286	0.0043 153 078	0.0037 455 772	232
59	0.0052 415 202	0.0045 376 142	0.0039 285 846	0.0034 015 970	236
60	0.0047 951 699	0.0041 410 720	0.0035 765 183	0.0030 892 068	240

QUARTERLY
Compounding

TABLE 4. PRESENT WORTH OF ONE DOLLAR
Payable at end of each period

QUARTERS	10% Nominal Annual Rate	10¼% Nominal Annual Rate	10½% Nominal Annual Rate	10¾% Nominal Annual Rate	QUARTERS
1	0.9756 097 561	0.9750 152 346	0.9744 214 373	0.9738 283 628	1
2	0.9518 143 962	0.9506 547 077	0.9494 971 374	0.9483 416 801	2
3	0.9285 994 109	0.9269 028 229	0.9252 103 653	0.9235 220 257	3
YEARS					
1	0.9059 506 448	0.9037 443 733	0.9015 448 140	0.8993 519 422	4
2	0.8207 465 708	0.8167 538 923	0.8127 830 516	0.8088 339 160	8
3	0.7435 558 850	0.7381 367 346	0.7327 603 450	0.7274 263 532	12
4	0.6736 249 335	0.6670 869 206	0.6606 162 889	0.6542 123 036	16
5	0.6102 709 429	0.6028 760 510	0.5955 751 893	0.5883 671 059	20
6	0.5528 753 542	0.5448 458 389	0.5369 377 232	0.5291 490 994	24
7	0.5008 777 836	0.4924 013 613	0.4840 734 198	0.4758 912 703	28
8	0.4537 705 510	0.4450 049 597	0.4364 138 812	0.4279 937 382	32
9	0.4110 937 233	0.4021 707 284	0.3934 466 713	0.3849 169 997	36
10	0.3724 306 237	0.3634 595 329	0.3547 098 061	0.3461 758 513	40
11	0.3374 037 637	0.3284 745 078	0.3197 867 862	0.3113 339 242	44
12	0.3056 711 573	0.2968 569 882	0.2883 021 186	0.2799 987 694	48
13	0.2769 229 820	0.2682 828 328	0.2599 172 799	0.2518 174 371	52
14	0.2508 785 541	0.2424 591 006	0.2343 270 758	0.2264 725 011	56
15	0.2272 835 879	0.2191 210 479	0.2112 563 599	0.2036 784 837	60
16	0.2059 077 130	0.1980 294 141	0.1904 570 757	0.1831 786 399	64
17	0.1865 422 253	0.1789 679 688	0.1717 055 889	0.1647 420 656	68
18	0.1689 980 493	0.1617 412 948	0.1548 002 832	0.1481 610 967	72
19	0.1531 038 918	0.1461 727 851	0.1395 593 925	0.1332 489 700	76
20	0.1387 045 695	0.1321 028 321	0.1258 190 465	0.1198 377 200	80
21	0.1256 594 941	0.1193 871 912	0.1134 315 089	0.1077 762 862	84
22	0.1138 412 997	0.1078 955 023	0.1022 635 886	0.0969 288 123	88
23	0.1031 345 989	0.0975 099 531	0.0921 952 080	0.0871 731 156	92
24	0.0934 348 564	0.0881 240 714	0.0831 181 116	0.0783 993 109	96
25	0.0846 473 684	0.0796 416 337	0.0749 347 025	0.0705 085 725	100
26	0.0766 863 380	0.0719 756 784	0.0675 569 924	0.0634 120 216	104
27	0.0694 740 373	0.0650 476 143	0.0609 056 561	0.0570 297 248	108
28	0.0629 400 489	0.0587 864 154	0.0549 091 784	0.0512 897 938	112
29	0.0570 205 779	0.0531 278 922	0.0495 030 851	0.0461 275 756	116
30	0.0516 578 293	0.0480 140 336	0.0446 292 496	0.0414 849 247	120
31	0.0467 994 438	0.0433 924 127	0.0402 352 685	0.0373 095 476	124
32	0.0423 979 863	0.0392 156 489	0.0362 738 977	0.0335 544 141	128
33	0.0384 104 830	0.0354 409 220	0.0327 025 443	0.0301 772 275	132
34	0.0347 980 018	0.0320 295 338	0.0294 828 093	0.0271 399 482	136
35	0.0315 252 722	0.0289 465 110	0.0265 800 738	0.0244 083 651	140
36	0.0285 603 407	0.0261 602 464	0.0239 631 277	0.0219 517 106	144
37	0.0258 742 591	0.0236 421 755	0.0216 038 335	0.0197 423 135	148
38	0.0234 408 017	0.0213 664 831	0.0194 768 240	0.0177 552 880	152
39	0.0212 362 094	0.0193 098 389	0.0175 592 297	0.0159 682 528	156
40	0.0192 389 576	0.0174 511 582	0.0158 304 325	0.0143 610 791	160
41	0.0174 295 460	0.0157 713 861	0.0142 718 443	0.0129 156 644	164
42	0.0157 903 085	0.0142 533 014	0.0128 667 072	0.0116 157 279	168
43	0.0143 052 401	0.0128 813 410	0.0115 999 132	0.0104 466 274	172
44	0.0129 598 415	0.0116 414 394	0.0104 578 416	0.0093 951 947	176
45	0.0117 409 768	0.0105 208 854	0.0094 282 128	0.0084 495 866	180
46	0.0106 367 455	0.0095 081 909	0.0084 999 564	0.0075 991 521	184
47	0.0096 363 664	0.0085 929 741	0.0076 630 916	0.0068 343 122	188
48	0.0087 300 724	0.0077 658 520	0.0069 086 205	0.0061 464 519	192
49	0.0079 090 147	0.0070 183 450	0.0062 284 310	0.0055 278 235	196
50	0.0071 651 770	0.0063 427 898	0.0056 152 096	0.0049 714 588	200
51	0.0064 912 967	0.0057 322 606	0.0050 623 631	0.0044 710 911	204
52	0.0058 807 944	0.0051 804 983	0.0045 639 472	0.0040 210 845	208
53	0.0053 277 095	0.0046 818 462	0.0041 146 029	0.0036 163 701	212
54	0.0048 266 419	0.0042 311 921	0.0037 094 989	0.0032 523 895	216
55	0.0043 726 993	0.0038 239 161	0.0033 442 795	0.0029 250 428	220
56	0.0039 614 498	0.0034 558 426	0.0030 150 179	0.0026 306 429	224
57	0.0035 888 780	0.0031 231 983	0.0027 181 737	0.0023 658 738	228
58	0.0032 513 463	0.0028 225 729	0.0024 505 554	0.0021 277 532	232
59	0.0029 455 593	0.0025 508 844	0.0022 092 855	0.0019 135 990	236
60	0.0026 685 313	0.0023 053 474	0.0019 917 699	0.0017 209 990	240

TABLE 4. PRESENT WORTH OF ONE DOLLAR
Payable at end of each period

QUARTERLY Compounding

	11% Nominal Annual Rate	11¼% Nominal Annual Rate	11½% Nominal Annual Rate	11¾% Nominal Annual Rate	
QUARTERS					QUARTERS
1	0.9732 360 097	0.9726 443 769	0.9720 534 629	0.9714 632 665	1
2	0.9471 883 306	0.9460 370 839	0.9448 870 348	0.9437 408 782	2
3	0.9218 377 914	0.9201 576 500	0.9184 815 891	0.9168 095 964	3
YEARS					
1	0.8971 657 337	0.8949 861 641	0.8928 132 094	0.8906 468 453	4
2	0.8049 063 537	0.8010 002 340	0.7971 154 268	0.7932 518 030	8
3	0.7221 343 994	0.7168 841 269	0.7116 751 824	0.7065 072 158	12
4	0.6478 742 383	0.6416 013 749	0.6353 930 036	0.6292 484 230	16
5	0.5812 505 663	0.5742 243 534	0.5672 872 668	0.5604 381 228	20
6	0.5214 780 908	0.5139 228 514	0.5064 815 653	0.4991 524 460	24
7	0.4678 522 739	0.4599 538 415	0.4521 934 318	0.4445 685 514	28
8	0.4197 410 286	0.4116 523 242	0.4037 242 691	0.3959 535 778	32
9	0.3765 772 679	0.3684 231 346	0.3604 503 604	0.3526 548 049	36
10	0.3378 522 208	0.3297 336 080	0.3218 148 431	0.3140 908 895	40
11	0.3031 094 356	0.2951 070 171	0.2873 205 429	0.2797 440 599	44
12	0.2719 393 992	0.2641 166 972	0.2565 235 760	0.2491 531 644	48
13	0.2439 747 106	0.2363 807 897	0.2290 276 371	0.2219 074 799	52
14	0.2188 857 502	0.2115 575 363	0.2044 788 998	0.1976 411 969	56
15	0.1963 767 947	0.1893 410 679	0.1825 614 627	0.1760 285 085	60
16	0.1761 825 311	0.1694 576 361	0.1629 932 854	0.1567 792 358	64
17	0.1580 649 298	0.1516 622 397	0.1455 225 583	0.1396 349 317	68
18	0.1418 104 387	0.1357 356 061	0.1299 244 623	0.1243 654 114	72
19	0.1272 274 663	0.1214 814 895	0.1159 982 762	0.1107 656 614	76
20	0.1141 441 231	0.1087 242 523	0.1035 647 932	0.0986 530 869	80
21	0.1024 061 960	0.0973 067 015	0.0924 640 154	0.0878 650 606	84
22	0.0918 753 299	0.0870 881 515	0.0825 530 943	0.0782 567 390	88
23	0.0824 273 978	0.0779 426 907	0.0737 044 931	0.0696 991 177	92
24	0.0739 510 368	0.0697 576 297	0.0658 043 450	0.0620 772 993	96
25	0.0663 463 362	0.0624 321 135	0.0587 509 885	0.0552 889 508	100
26	0.0595 236 594	0.0558 758 777	0.0524 536 586	0.0492 429 296	104
27	0.0534 025 876	0.0500 081 375	0.0468 313 193	0.0438 580 599	108
28	0.0479 109 717	0.0447 565 912	0.0418 116 204	0.0390 620 427	112
29	0.0429 840 820	0.0400 565 298	0.0373 299 670	0.0347 904 851	116
30	0.0385 638 455	0.0358 500 400	0.0333 286 877	0.0309 860 358	120
31	0.0345 981 607	0.0320 852 898	0.0297 562 926	0.0275 976 150	124
32	0.0310 402 843	0.0287 158 904	0.0265 668 111	0.0245 797 288	128
33	0.0278 482 794	0.0257 003 246	0.0237 191 999	0.0218 918 579	132
34	0.0249 845 220	0.0230 014 349	0.0211 768 150	0.0194 979 142	136
35	0.0224 152 570	0.0205 859 660	0.0189 069 401	0.0173 657 557	140
36	0.0201 102 005	0.0184 241 548	0.0168 803 659	0.0154 667 556	144
37	0.0180 421 828	0.0164 893 636	0.0150 710 137	0.0137 754 170	148
38	0.0161 868 282	0.0147 577 523	0.0134 556 001	0.0122 690 317	152
39	0.0145 222 676	0.0132 079 841	0.0120 133 375	0.0109 273 744	156
40	0.0130 288 808	0.0118 209 630	0.0107 256 664	0.0097 324 315	160
41	0.0116 890 654	0.0105 795 984	0.0095 760 166	0.0086 681 595	164
42	0.0104 870 290	0.0094 685 942	0.0085 495 941	0.0077 202 689	168
43	0.0094 086 030	0.0084 742 608	0.0076 331 906	0.0068 760 331	172
44	0.0084 410 763	0.0075 843 461	0.0068 150 134	0.0061 241 172	176
45	0.0075 730 444	0.0067 878 849	0.0060 845 340	0.0054 544 257	180
46	0.0067 942 759	0.0060 750 630	0.0054 323 523	0.0048 579 670	184
47	0.0060 955 915	0.0054 370 974	0.0048 500 759	0.0043 267 330	188
48	0.0054 687 558	0.0048 661 269	0.0043 302 118	0.0038 535 911	192
49	0.0049 063 804	0.0043 551 163	0.0038 660 703	0.0034 321 887	196
50	0.0044 018 363	0.0038 977 688	0.0034 516 786	0.0030 568 681	200
51	0.0039 491 767	0.0034 884 491	0.0030 817 043	0.0027 225 899	204
52	0.0035 430 660	0.0031 221 137	0.0027 513 863	0.0024 248 661	208
53	0.0031 787 174	0.0027 942 486	0.0024 564 740	0.0021 596 994	212
54	0.0028 518 364	0.0025 008 138	0.0021 931 725	0.0019 235 294	216
55	0.0025 585 699	0.0022 381 938	0.0019 580 933	0.0017 131 854	220
56	0.0022 954 612	0.0020 031 525	0.0017 482 116	0.0015 258 432	224
57	0.0020 594 091	0.0017 927 937	0.0015 608 264	0.0013 589 874	228
58	0.0018 476 313	0.0016 045 256	0.0013 935 264	0.0012 103 779	232
59	0.0016 576 315	0.0014 360 282	0.0012 441 588	0.0010 780 192	236
60	0.0014 871 702	0.0012 852 254	0.0011 108 014	0.0009 601 344	240

QUARTERLY
Compounding

TABLE 4. PRESENT WORTH OF ONE DOLLAR
Payable at end of each period

QUARTERS	12% Nominal Annual Rate	12¼% Nominal Annual Rate	12½% Nominal Annual Rate	12¾% Nominal Annual Rate	QUARTERS
1	0.9708 737 864	0.9702 850 212	0.9696 969 697	0.9691 096 305	1
2	0.9425 959 091	0.9414 530 224	0.9403 122 130	0.9391 734 760	2
3	0.9151 416 594	0.9134 777 658	0.9118 179 036	0.9101 620 603	3
YEARS					
1	0.8884 870 479	0.8863 337 934	0.8841 870 580	0.8820 468 180	4
2	0.7894 092 343	0.7855 875 933	0.7817 867 535	0.7780 065 891	8
3	0.7013 798 802	0.6962 928 317	0.6912 457 296	0.6862 382 363	12
4	0.6231 669 392	0.6171 478 668	0.6111 905 280	0.6052 942 527	16
5	0.5536 757 542	0.5469 990 099	0.5404 067 548	0.5338 978 695	20
6	0.4919 337 363	0.4848 237 074	0.4778 206 586	0.4709 229 170	24
7	0.4370 767 532	0.4297 156 357	0.4224 828 424	0.4153 760 604	28
8	0.3883 370 341	0.3808 714 895	0.3735 538 615	0.3663 811 324	32
9	0.3450 324 251	0.3375 792 721	0.3302 914 898	0.3231 653 120	36
10	0.3065 568 408	0.2992 079 168	0.2920 394 606	0.2850 469 351	40
11	0.2723 717 825	0.2651 980 879	0.2582 175 115	0.2514 247 421	44
12	0.2419 988 009	0.2350 540 273	0.2283 125 818	0.2217 683 937	48
13	0.2150 128 003	0.2083 363 277	0.2018 710 300	0.1956 101 060	52
14	0.1910 360 882	0.1846 555 276	0.1784 917 521	0.1725 372 716	56
15	0.1697 330 900	0.1636 664 343	0.1578 200 972	0.1521 859 514	60
16	0.1508 056 521	0.1450 630 915	0.1395 424 874	0.1342 351 342	64
17	0.1339 888 686	0.1285 743 202	0.1233 816 614	0.1184 016 729	68
18	0.1190 473 743	0.1139 597 650	0.1090 924 682	0.1044 358 189	72
19	0.1057 720 502	0.1010 063 908	0.0964 581 485	0.0921 172 817	76
20	0.0939 770 966	0.0895 253 775	0.0852 870 466	0.0812 517 552	80
21	0.0834 974 332	0.0793 493 674	0.0754 097 028	0.0716 678 521	84
22	0.0741 863 879	0.0703 300 258	0.0666 762 833	0.0632 144 009	88
23	0.0659 136 448	0.0623 358 786	0.0589 543 067	0.0557 580 612	92
24	0.0585 634 197	0.0552 503 957	0.0521 266 350	0.0491 812 205	96
25	0.0520 328 399	0.0489 702 928	0.0460 896 961	0.0433 801 390	100
26	0.0462 305 043	0.0434 040 254	0.0407 519 128	0.0382 633 136	104
27	0.0410 752 043	0.0384 704 545	0.0360 323 139	0.0337 500 340	108
28	0.0364 947 870	0.0340 976 639	0.0318 593 056	0.0297 691 101	112
29	0.0324 251 455	0.0302 219 118	0.0281 695 857	0.0262 577 488	116
30	0.0288 093 218	0.0267 867 017	0.0249 071 831	0.0231 605 638	120
31	0.0255 967 093	0.0237 419 589	0.0220 226 089	0.0204 287 016	124
32	0.0227 423 447	0.0210 433 005	0.0194 721 058	0.0180 190 712	128
33	0.0202 062 787	0.0186 513 884	0.0172 169 839	0.0158 936 645	132
34	0.0179 530 169	0.0165 313 558	0.0152 230 344	0.0140 189 562	136
35	0.0159 510 230	0.0146 522 993	0.0134 600 100	0.0123 653 757	140
36	0.0141 722 773	0.0129 868 280	0.0119 011 666	0.0109 068 403	144
37	0.0125 918 849	0.0115 106 646	0.0105 228 575	0.0096 203 437	148
38	0.0111 877 266	0.0102 022 910	0.0093 041 744	0.0084 855 936	152
39	0.0099 401 502	0.0090 426 353	0.0082 266 306	0.0074 846 908	156
40	0.0088 316 947	0.0080 147 932	0.0072 738 803	0.0066 018 477	160
41	0.0078 468 463	0.0071 037 821	0.0064 314 708	0.0058 231 388	164
42	0.0069 718 213	0.0062 963 221	0.0056 866 233	0.0051 362 810	168
43	0.0061 943 730	0.0055 806 431	0.0050 280 387	0.0045 304 403	172
44	0.0055 036 201	0.0049 463 125	0.0044 457 267	0.0039 960 605	176
45	0.0048 898 952	0.0043 840 840	0.0039 308 541	0.0035 247 124	180
46	0.0043 446 086	0.0038 857 618	0.0034 756 103	0.0031 089 614	184
47	0.0038 601 284	0.0034 440 820	0.0030 730 896	0.0027 422 495	188
48	0.0034 296 741	0.0030 526 062	0.0027 171 861	0.0024 187 924	192
49	0.0030 472 210	0.0027 056 281	0.0024 025 008	0.0021 334 882	196
50	0.0027 074 164	0.0023 980 896	0.0021 242 601	0.0018 818 365	200
51	0.0024 055 044	0.0021 255 078	0.0018 782 433	0.0016 598 679	204
52	0.0021 372 595	0.0018 839 094	0.0016 607 184	0.0014 640 812	208
53	0.0018 989 274	0.0016 697 726	0.0014 683 857	0.0012 913 881	212
54	0.0016 871 724	0.0014 799 759	0.0012 983 276	0.0011 390 648	216
55	0.0014 990 308	0.0013 117 526	0.0011 479 645	0.0010 047 085	220
56	0.0013 318 695	0.0011 626 507	0.0010 150 154	0.0008 861 999	224
57	0.0011 833 488	0.0010 304 966	0.0008 974 634	0.0007 816 698	228
58	0.0010 513 901	0.0009 133 640	0.0007 935 256	0.0006 894 694	232
59	0.0009 341 465	0.0008 095 453	0.0007 016 250	0.0006 081 443	236
60	0.0008 299 770	0.0007 175 274	0.0006 203 678	0.0005 364 117	240

TABLE 4. PRESENT WORTH OF ONE DOLLAR
Payable at end of each period

QUARTERLY Compounding

QUARTERS	13% Nominal Annual Rate	13¼% Nominal Annual Rate	13½% Nominal Annual Rate	13¾% Nominal Annual Rate	QUARTERS
1	0.9685 230 024	0.9679 370 841	0.9673 518 742	0.9667 673 716	1
2	0.9380 368 062	0.9369 021 988	0.9357 696 486	0.9346 391 508	2
3	0.9085 102 239	0.9068 623 823	0.9052 185 234	0.9035 786 352	3
YEARS					
1	0.8799 130 498	0.8777 857 300	0.8756 648 352	0.8735 503 422	4
2	0.7742 469 752	0.7705 077 879	0.7667 889 037	0.7630 902 003	8
3	0.6812 700 173	0.6763 407 411	0.6714 500 790	0.6665 977 056	12
4	0.5994 583 787	0.5936 822 511	0.5879 652 228	0.5823 066 539	16
5	0.5274 712 502	0.5211 258 082	0.5148 604 700	0.5086 741 767	20
6	0.4641 288 365	0.4574 367 980	0.4508 452 086	0.4443 525 012	24
7	0.4083 930 200	0.4015 314 937	0.3947 892 953	0.3881 642 794	28
8	0.3593 503 478	0.3524 586 153	0.3457 031 032	0.3390 810 391	32
9	0.3161 970 605	0.3093 831 430	0.3027 200 510	0.2962 043 578	36
10	0.2782 259 198	0.2715 721 080	0.2650 813 035	0.2587 494 181	40
11	0.2448 146 176	0.2383 821 211	0.2321 223 760	0.2260 306 427	44
12	0.2154 155 769	0.2092 484 242	0.2032 614 021	0.1974 491 453	48
13	0.1895 469 772	0.1836 752 808	0.1779 888 622	0.1724 817 684	52
14	0.1667 848 588	0.1612 275 404	0.1558 585 877	0.1506 715 078	56
15	0.1467 561 738	0.1415 232 343	0.1364 798 845	0.1316 191 472	60
16	0.1291 326 724	0.1242 270 755	0.1195 106 356	0.1149 759 511	64
17	0.1136 255 236	0.1090 447 542	0.1046 512 610	0.1004 372 814	68
18	0.0999 805 810	0.0957 179 291	0.0916 394 292	0.0877 370 216	72
19	0.0879 742 180	0.0840 198 323	0.0802 454 257	0.0766 427 052	76
20	0.0774 096 625	0.0737 514 098	0.0702 680 975	0.0669 512 614	80
21	0.0681 137 722	0.0647 379 351	0.0615 313 020	0.0584 852 973	84
22	0.0599 341 970	0.0568 260 356	0.0538 807 974	0.0510 898 514	88
23	0.0527 368 821	0.0498 810 832	0.0471 815 196	0.0446 295 572	92
24	0.0464 038 708	0.0437 849 030	0.0413 151 976	0.0389 861 650	96
25	0.0408 313 714	0.0384 337 631	0.0361 782 657	0.0340 563 778	100
26	0.0359 280 566	0.0337 366 088	0.0316 800 351	0.0297 499 604	104
27	0.0316 135 658	0.0296 135 138	0.0277 410 927	0.0259 880 881	108
28	0.0278 171 891	0.0259 943 198	0.0242 918 994	0.0227 019 033	112
29	0.0244 767 077	0.0228 174 430	0.0212 715 621	0.0198 312 554	116
30	0.0215 373 745	0.0200 288 258	0.0186 267 589	0.0173 235 999	120
31	0.0189 510 169	0.0175 810 175	0.0163 107 977	0.0151 330 366	124
32	0.0166 752 471	0.0154 323 663	0.0142 827 920	0.0132 194 693	128
33	0.0146 727 675	0.0135 463 109	0.0125 069 387	0.0115 478 720	132
34	0.0129 107 596	0.0118 907 584	0.0109 518 864	0.0100 876 475	136
35	0.0113 603 459	0.0104 375 381	0.0095 901 818	0.0088 120 679	140
36	0.0099 961 166	0.0091 619 220	0.0083 977 850	0.0076 977 850	144
37	0.0087 957 134	0.0080 422 044	0.0073 536 450	0.0067 244 027	148
38	0.0077 394 630	0.0070 593 322	0.0064 393 283	0.0058 741 043	152
39	0.0068 100 545	0.0061 965 811	0.0056 386 934	0.0051 313 258	156
40	0.0059 922 558	0.0054 392 705	0.0049 376 055	0.0044 824 714	160
41	0.0052 726 641	0.0047 745 140	0.0043 236 875	0.0039 156 644	164
42	0.0046 394 860	0.0041 910 002	0.0037 861 011	0.0034 205 300	168
43	0.0040 823 442	0.0036 788 002	0.0033 153 556	0.0029 880 051	172
44	0.0035 921 080	0.0032 291 983	0.0029 031 403	0.0026 101 729	176
45	0.0031 607 427	0.0028 345 442	0.0025 421 779	0.0022 801 174	180
46	0.0027 811 787	0.0024 881 225	0.0022 260 958	0.0019 917 974	184
47	0.0024 471 955	0.0021 840 384	0.0019 493 138	0.0017 399 353	188
48	0.0021 533 192	0.0019 171 177	0.0017 069 456	0.0015 199 211	192
49	0.0018 947 337	0.0016 828 186	0.0014 947 122	0.0013 277 276	196
50	0.0016 672 009	0.0014 771 541	0.0013 088 669	0.0011 598 369	200
51	0.0014 669 918	0.0012 966 248	0.0011 461 287	0.0010 131 759	204
52	0.0012 908 252	0.0011 381 588	0.0010 036 246	0.0008 850 601	208
53	0.0011 358 140	0.0009 990 595	0.0008 788 388	0.0007 731 446	212
54	0.0009 994 175	0.0008 769 602	0.0007 695 682	0.0006 753 807	216
55	0.0008 794 005	0.0007 697 831	0.0006 738 838	0.0005 899 791	220
56	0.0007 737 960	0.0006 757 047	0.0005 900 964	0.0005 153 764	224
57	0.0006 808 732	0.0005 931 239	0.0005 167 266	0.0004 502 072	228
58	0.0005 991 092	0.0005 206 357	0.0004 524 794	0.0003 932 787	232
59	0.0005 271 640	0.0004 570 066	0.0003 962 203	0.0003 435 487	236
60	0.0004 638 585	0.0004 011 539	0.0003 469 561	0.0003 001 071	240

QUARTERLY
Compounding

TABLE 4. PRESENT WORTH OF ONE DOLLAR
Payable at end of each period

QUARTERS	14% Nominal Annual Rate	14¼% Nominal Annual Rate	14½% Nominal Annual Rate	14¾% Nominal Annual Rate	QUARTERS
1	0.9661 835 749	0.9656 004 828	0.9650 180 941	0.9644 364 075	1
2	0.9335 107 004	0.9323 842 924	0.9312 599 219	0.9301 375 841	2
3	0.9019 427 057	0.9003 107 229	0.8986 826 750	0.8970 585 500	3
YEARS					
1	0.8714 422 277	0.8693 404 687	0.8672 450 422	0.8651 559 253	4
2	0.7594 115 562	0.7557 528 505	0.7521 139 632	0.7484 947 751	8
3	0.6617 832 983	0.6570 065 373	0.6522 671 057	0.6475 646 897	12
4	0.5767 059 117	0.5711 623 710	0.5656 754 136	0.5602 444 283	16
5	0.5025 658 844	0.4965 345 633	0.4905 791 979	0.4846 987 867	20
6	0.4379 571 339	0.4316 575 900	0.4254 523 772	0.4193 400 273	24
7	0.3816 543 404	0.3752 574 116	0.3689 714 648	0.3627 945 093	28
8	0.3325 897 086	0.3262 264 541	0.3199 886 736	0.3138 738 194	32
9	0.2898 327 166	0.2836 018 585	0.2775 085 907	0.2715 497 947	36
10	0.2525 724 682	0.2465 465 726	0.2406 679 494	0.2349 329 139	40
11	0.2201 023 143	0.2143 329 130	0.2087 180 860	0.2032 536 025	44
12	0.1918 064 511	0.1863 282 750	0.1810 097 253	0.1758 460 585	48
13	0.1671 482 411	0.1619 827 099	0.1569 797 868	0.1521 342 595	52
14	0.1456 600 355	0.1408 181 250	0.1361 399 418	0.1316 198 560	56
15	0.1269 343 059	0.1224 188 948	0.1180 666 896	0.1138 716 983	60
16	0.1106 159 143	0.1064 236 993	0.1023 927 512	0.0985 167 745	64
17	0.0963 953 788	0.0925 184 287	0.0887 996 058	0.0852 323 712	68
18	0.0840 030 036	0.0804 300 141	0.0770 110 179	0.0737 392 910	72
19	0.0732 037 646	0.0699 210 662	0.0667 874 235	0.0637 959 845	76
20	0.0637 928 517	0.0607 852 124	0.0579 210 619	0.0551 934 740	80
21	0.0555 917 848	0.0528 430 451	0.0502 317 538	0.0477 509 611	84
22	0.0484 450 288	0.0459 385 976	0.0435 632 394	0.0413 120 269	88
23	0.0422 170 438	0.0399 362 819	0.0377 800 034	0.0357 413 449	92
24	0.0367 897 147	0.0347 182 261	0.0327 645 206	0.0309 218 363	96
25	0.0320 601 109	0.0301 819 589	0.0284 148 681	0.0267 522 099	100
26	0.0279 385 345	0.0262 383 983	0.0246 426 535	0.0231 448 329	104
27	0.0243 468 187	0.0228 101 015	0.0213 712 190	0.0200 238 893	108
28	0.0212 168 460	0.0198 297 443	0.0185 340 838	0.0173 237 865	112
29	0.0184 892 555	0.0172 387 992	0.0160 735 923	0.0149 877 765	116
30	0.0161 123 180	0.0149 863 858	0.0139 397 432	0.0129 667 637	120
31	0.0140 409 543	0.0130 282 716	0.0120 891 732	0.0112 182 724	124
32	0.0122 358 805	0.0113 260 038	0.0104 842 755	0.0097 055 549	128
33	0.0106 628 630	0.0098 461 534	0.0090 924 359	0.0083 968 183	132
34	0.0092 920 690	0.0085 596 596	0.0078 853 700	0.0072 645 571	136
35	0.0080 975 013	0.0074 412 585	0.0068 385 480	0.0062 849 746	140
36	0.0070 565 046	0.0064 689 872	0.0059 306 969	0.0054 374 830	144
37	0.0061 493 361	0.0056 237 523	0.0051 433 675	0.0047 042 707	148
38	0.0053 587 912	0.0048 889 555	0.0044 605 599	0.0040 699 276	152
39	0.0046 698 769	0.0042 501 669	0.0038 683 985	0.0035 211 220	156
40	0.0040 695 279	0.0036 948 421	0.0033 548 494	0.0030 463 196	160
41	0.0035 463 585	0.0032 120 757	0.0029 094 765	0.0026 355 414	164
42	0.0030 904 465	0.0027 923 874	0.0025 232 291	0.0022 801 543	168
43	0.0026 931 456	0.0024 275 354	0.0021 882 579	0.0019 726 890	172
44	0.0023 469 208	0.0021 103 547	0.0018 977 558	0.0017 066 836	176
45	0.0020 452 059	0.0018 346 168	0.0016 458 193	0.0014 765 474	180
46	0.0017 822 788	0.0015 949 066	0.0014 273 287	0.0012 774 437	184
47	0.0015 531 530	0.0013 865 169	0.0012 378 437	0.0011 051 880	188
48	0.0013 534 831	0.0012 053 552	0.0010 735 138	0.0009 561 600	192
49	0.0011 794 823	0.0010 478 641	0.0009 309 995	0.0008 272 275	196
50	0.0010 278 507	0.0009 109 506	0.0008 074 047	0.0007 156 807	200
51	0.0008 957 125	0.0007 919 263	0.0007 002 177	0.0006 191 754	204
52	0.0007 805 617	0.0006 884 535	0.0006 072 604	0.0005 356 833	208
53	0.0006 802 144	0.0005 985 005	0.0005 266 435	0.0004 634 496	212
54	0.0005 927 676	0.0005 203 007	0.0004 567 290	0.0004 009 561	216
55	0.0005 165 627	0.0004 523 185	0.0003 960 960	0.0003 468 896	220
56	0.0004 501 546	0.0003 932 188	0.0003 435 123	0.0003 001 136	224
57	0.0003 922 837	0.0003 418 410	0.0002 979 093	0.0002 596 450	228
58	0.0003 418 526	0.0002 971 762	0.0002 583 604	0.0002 246 334	232
59	0.0002 979 048	0.0002 583 473	0.0002 240 617	0.0001 943 430	236
60	0.0002 596 068	0.0002 245 918	0.0001 943 164	0.0001 681 370	240

TABLE 4. PRESENT WORTH OF ONE DOLLAR
Payable at end of each period

QUARTERLY Compounding

QUARTERS	15% Nominal Annual Rate	15¼% Nominal Annual Rate	15½% Nominal Annual Rate	15¾% Nominal Annual Rate	QUARTERS
1	0.9638 554 217	0.9632 751 355	0.9626 955 475	0.9621 166 566	1
2	0.9290 172 739	0.9278 989 866	0.9267 827 172	0.9256 684 610	2
3	0.8954 383 363	0.8938 220 220	0.8922 095 954	0.8906 010 449	3
YEARS					
1	0.8630 730 952	0.8609 965 293	0.8589 262 050	0.8568 620 997	4
2	0.7448 951 677	0.7413 150 235	0.7377 542 256	0.7342 126 579	8
3	0.6428 989 780	0.6382 696 624	0.6336 764 372	0.6291 189 996	12
4	0.5548 688 109	0.5495 479 641	0.5442 812 974	0.5390 682 270	16
5	0.4788 923 421	0.4731 588 898	0.4674 974 692	0.4619 071 328	20
6	0.4133 190 959	0.4073 881 619	0.4015 458 271	0.3957 907 157	24
7	0.3567 245 915	0.3507 597 935	0.3448 982 334	0.3391 380 637	28
8	0.3078 793 973	0.3020 029 648	0.2962 421 307	0.2905 945 533	32
9	0.2657 224 244	0.2600 235 046	0.2544 501 291	0.2489 994 591	36
10	0.2293 378 753	0.2238 793 350	0.2185 538 837	0.2133 581 994	40
11	0.1979 353 499	0.1927 593 304	0.1877 216 579	0.1828 185 547	44
12	0.1708 326 751	0.1659 651 145	0.1612 390 512	0.1566 502 906	48
13	0.1474 410 856	0.1428 953 875	0.1384 924 464	0.1342 276 969	52
14	0.1272 524 341	0.1230 324 327	0.1189 547 914	0.1150 146 262	56
15	0.1098 281 522	0.1059 304 976	0.1021 733 875	0.0985 516 741	60
16	0.0947 897 233	0.0912 057 908	0.0877 594 000	0.0844 451 944	64
17	0.0818 104 599	0.0785 278 693	0.0753 788 484	0.0723 578 866	68
18	0.0706 084 068	0.0676 122 229	0.0647 448 682	0.0620 007 306	72
19	0.0609 402 162	0.0582 138 893	0.0556 110 639	0.0531 260 762	76
20	0.0525 958 610	0.0501 219 566	0.0477 658 001	0.0455 217 212	80
21	0.0453 940 726	0.0431 548 307	0.0410 272 974	0.0390 058 376	84
22	0.0391 784 027	0.0371 561 595	0.0352 394 208	0.0334 226 239	88
23	0.0338 138 253	0.0319 913 243	0.0302 680 620	0.0286 385 797	92
24	0.0291 838 029	0.0275 444 192	0.0259 980 316	0.0245 393 136	96
25	0.0251 877 551	0.0237 156 494	0.0223 303 907	0.0210 268 077	100
26	0.0217 388 737	0.0204 190 918	0.0191 801 577	0.0180 170 746	104
27	0.0187 622 370	0.0175 807 672	0.0164 743 401	0.0154 381 484	108
28	0.0161 931 820	0.0151 369 795	0.0141 502 424	0.0132 283 642	112
29	0.0139 758 997	0.0130 328 868	0.0121 540 140	0.0113 348 840	116
30	0.0120 622 230	0.0112 212 703	0.0104 394 011	0.0097 124 325	120
31	0.0104 105 802	0.0096 614 748	0.0089 666 752	0.0083 222 153	124
32	0.0089 850 916	0.0083 184 963	0.0077 017 123	0.0071 309 909	128
33	0.0077 547 909	0.0071 621 964	0.0066 152 025	0.0061 102 758	132
34	0.0066 929 513	0.0061 666 263	0.0056 819 708	0.0052 356 638	136
35	0.0057 765 062	0.0053 094 438	0.0048 803 936	0.0044 862 418	140
36	0.0049 855 471	0.0045 714 127	0.0041 918 980	0.0038 440 906	144
37	0.0043 028 916	0.0039 359 705	0.0036 005 310	0.0032 938 555	148
38	0.0037 137 100	0.0033 888 569	0.0030 925 904	0.0028 223 800	152
39	0.0032 052 031	0.0029 177 940	0.0026 563 070	0.0024 183 904	156
40	0.0027 663 246	0.0025 122 105	0.0022 815 717	0.0020 722 271	160
41	0.0023 875 403	0.0021 630 046	0.0019 597 017	0.0017 756 129	164
42	0.0020 606 218	0.0018 623 394	0.0016 832 391	0.0015 214 554	168
43	0.0017 784 673	0.0016 034 678	0.0014 457 782	0.0013 036 774	172
44	0.0015 349 472	0.0013 805 802	0.0012 418 168	0.0011 170 718	176
45	0.0013 247 717	0.0011 886 747	0.0010 666 290	0.0009 571 765	180
46	0.0011 433 748	0.0010 234 448	0.0009 161 556	0.0008 201 682	184
47	0.0009 868 160	0.0008 811 824	0.0007 869 100	0.0007 027 711	188
48	0.0008 516 944	0.0007 586 950	0.0006 758 976	0.0006 021 779	192
49	0.0007 350 745	0.0006 532 338	0.0005 805 462	0.0005 159 834	196
50	0.0006 344 230	0.0005 624 320	0.0004 986 463	0.0004 421 266	200
51	0.0005 475 534	0.0004 842 520	0.0004 283 004	0.0003 788 416	204
52	0.0004 725 786	0.0004 169 393	0.0003 678 784	0.0003 246 150	208
53	0.0004 078 699	0.0003 589 833	0.0003 159 804	0.0002 781 503	212
54	0.0003 520 215	0.0003 090 834	0.0002 714 039	0.0002 383 364	216
55	0.0003 038 203	0.0002 661 197	0.0002 331 159	0.0002 042 215	220
56	0.0002 622 191	0.0002 291 281	0.0002 002 294	0.0001 749 896	224
57	0.0002 263 143	0.0001 972 785	0.0001 719 822	0.0001 499 420	228
58	0.0001 953 258	0.0001 698 561	0.0001 477 201	0.0001 284 796	232
59	0.0001 685 804	0.0001 462 455	0.0001 268 806	0.0001 100 893	236
60	0.0001 454 972	0.0001 259 169	0.0001 089 811	0.0000 943 313	240

TABLE 4. PRESENT WORTH OF ONE DOLLAR
Payable at end of each period

QUARTERS	16% Nominal Annual Rate	16¼% Nominal Annual Rate	16½% Nominal Annual Rate	16¾% Nominal Annual Rate	QUARTERS
1	0.9615 384 615	0.9609 609 610	0.9603 841 537	0.9598 080 384	1
2	0.9245 562 130	0.9234 459 685	0.9223 377 226	0.9212 314 706	2
3	0.8889 963 587	0.8873 955 253	0.8857 985 331	0.8842 053 707	3
YEARS					
1	0.8548 041 910	0.8527 524 567	0.8507 068 745	0.8486 674 224	4
2	0.7306 902 050	0.7271 867 524	0.7237 021 864	0.7202 363 938	8
3	0.6245 970 496	0.6201 102 896	0.6156 584 251	0.6112 411 638	12
4	0.5339 081 757	0.5288 005 729	0.5237 448 546	0.5187 404 629	16
5	0.4563 869 462	0.4509 359 877	0.4455 533 483	0.4402 381 315	20
6	0.3901 214 743	0.3845 367 713	0.3790 352 964	0.3736 157 603	24
7	0.3334 774 713	0.3279 146 764	0.3224 479 323	0.3170 755 242	28
8	0.2850 579 401	0.2796 300 459	0.2743 086 727	0.2690 916 679	32
9	0.2436 687 219	0.2384 552 086	0.2333 562 736	0.2283 693 321	36
10	0.2082 890 447	0.2033 432 650	0.1985 177 862	0.1938 096 124	40
11	0.1780 463 483	0.1734 014 688	0.1688 804 454	0.1644 799 042	44
12	0.1521 947 647	0.1478 685 285	0.1436 677 559	0.1395 887 363	48
13	0.1300 967 228	0.1260 952 509	0.1222 191 476	0.1184 644 131	52
14	0.1112 072 239	0.1075 280 350	0.1039 726 691	0.1005 368 881	56
15	0.0950 604 010	0.0916 947 960	0.0884 502 643	0.0853 223 817	60
16	0.0812 580 292	0.0781 929 626	0.0752 452 479	0.0724 103 257	64
17	0.0694 597 039	0.0666 792 409	0.0640 116 497	0.0614 522 845	68
18	0.0593 744 460	0.0568 608 865	0.0544 551 504	0.0521 525 519	72
19	0.0507 535 253	0.0484 882 607	0.0463 253 708	0.0442 601 718	76
20	0.0433 843 261	0.0413 484 834	0.0394 093 114	0.0375 621 659	80
21	0.0370 851 038	0.0352 600 208	0.0335 257 722	0.0318 777 865	84
22	0.0317 005 022	0.0300 680 694	0.0285 206 048	0.0270 536 389	88
23	0.0270 977 221	0.0256 406 200	0.0242 626 746	0.0229 595 420	92
24	0.0231 632 464	0.0218 651 017	0.0206 404 241	0.0194 850 153	96
25	0.0198 000 401	0.0186 455 192	0.0175 589 507	0.0165 362 977	100
26	0.0169 251 573	0.0159 000 123	0.0149 375 200	0.0140 338 172	104
27	0.0144 676 954	0.0135 587 746	0.0127 074 510	0.0119 100 434	108
28	0.0123 670 466	0.0115 622 783	0.0108 103 159	0.0101 076 659	112
29	0.0105 714 033	0.0098 597 612	0.0091 964 101	0.0085 780 467	116
30	0.0090 364 798	0.0084 079 356	0.0078 234 493	0.0072 799 088	120
31	0.0077 244 208	0.0071 698 878	0.0066 554 621	0.0061 782 214	124
32	0.0066 028 673	0.0061 141 394	0.0056 618 473	0.0052 432 553	128
33	0.0056 441 586	0.0052 138 474	0.0048 165 724	0.0044 497 799	132
34	0.0048 246 505	0.0044 461 212	0.0040 974 913	0.0037 763 833	136
35	0.0041 241 314	0.0037 914 408	0.0034 857 640	0.0032 048 935	140
36	0.0035 253 248	0.0032 331 604	0.0029 653 634	0.0027 198 887	144
37	0.0030 134 624	0.0027 570 855	0.0025 226 550	0.0023 082 809	148
38	0.0025 759 203	0.0023 511 114	0.0021 460 400	0.0019 589 628	152
39	0.0022 019 075	0.0020 049 160	0.0018 256 510	0.0016 625 079	156
40	0.0018 821 998	0.0017 096 971	0.0015 530 938	0.0014 109 163	160
41	0.0016 089 122	0.0014 579 484	0.0013 212 276	0.0011 973 987	164
42	0.0013 753 049	0.0012 432 691	0.0011 239 774	0.0010 161 933	168
43	0.0011 756 164	0.0010 602 008	0.0009 561 753	0.0008 624 101	172
44	0.0010 049 218	0.0009 040 888	0.0008 134 249	0.0007 318 994	176
45	0.0008 590 114	0.0007 709 639	0.0006 919 862	0.0006 211 392	180
46	0.0007 342 865	0.0006 574 414	0.0005 886 774	0.0005 271 406	184
47	0.0006 276 712	0.0005 606 348	0.0005 007 919	0.0004 473 670	188
48	0.0005 365 360	0.0004 780 827	0.0004 260 271	0.0003 796 658	192
49	0.0004 586 332	0.0004 076 862	0.0003 624 242	0.0003 222 100	196
50	0.0003 920 416	0.0003 476 554	0.0003 083 167	0.0002 734 491	200
51	0.0003 351 188	0.0002 964 640	0.0002 622 872	0.0002 320 674	204
52	0.0002 864 609	0.0002 528 104	0.0002 231 295	0.0001 969 480	208
53	0.0002 448 680	0.0002 155 847	0.0001 898 178	0.0001 671 434	212
54	0.0002 093 142	0.0001 838 404	0.0001 614 793	0.0001 418 491	216
55	0.0001 789 227	0.0001 567 703	0.0001 373 716	0.0001 203 827	220
56	0.0001 529 438	0.0001 336 863	0.0001 168 629	0.0001 021 649	224
57	0.0001 307 370	0.0001 140 013	0.0000 994 161	0.0000 867 040	228
58	0.0001 117 546	0.0000 972 149	0.0000 845 740	0.0000 735 829	232
59	0.0000 955 283	0.0000 829 002	0.0000 719 476	0.0000 624 474	236
60	0.0000 816 580	0.0000 706 934	0.0000 612 064	0.0000 529 971	240

TABLE 4. PRESENT WORTH OF ONE DOLLAR
Payable at end of each period

QUARTERLY Compounding

QUARTERS	17% Nominal Annual Rate	17¼% Nominal Annual Rate	17½% Nominal Annual Rate	17¾% Nominal Annual Rate	QUARTERS
1	0.9592 326 139	0.9586 578 790	0.9580 838 323	0.9575 104 728	1
2	0.9201 272 076	0.9190 249 289	0.9179 246 298	0.9168 263 055	2
3	0.8826 160 265	0.8810 304 891	0.8794 487 471	0.8778 707 892	3
YEARS					
1	0.8466 340 781	0.8446 068 200	0.8425 856 260	0.8405 704 744	4
2	0.7167 892 623	0.7133 606 803	0.7099 505 371	0.7065 587 224	8
3	0.6068 582 163	0.6025 092 957	0.5981 941 177	0.5939 124 005	12
4	0.5137 868 465	0.5088 834 602	0.5040 297 651	0.4992 252 282	16
5	0.4349 894 532	0.4298 064 411	0.4246 882 351	0.4196 339 869	20
6	0.3682 768 947	0.3630 174 514	0.3578 362 024	0.3527 319 395	24
7	0.3117 957 692	0.3066 070 152	0.3015 076 406	0.2964 960 537	28
8	0.2639 769 236	0.2589 623 761	0.2540 460 041	0.2492 258 285	32
9	0.2234 918 594	0.2187 213 890	0.2140 555 114	0.2094 918 729	36
10	0.1892 158 244	0.1847 335 768	0.1803 600 971	0.1760 926 830	40
11	0.1601 965 650	0.1560 272 388	0.1519 688 253	0.1480 183 101	44
12	0.1356 278 711	0.1317 816 700	0.1280 467 478	0.1244 198 211	48
13	0.1148 271 777	0.1113 036 972	0.1078 903 491	0.1045 836 281	52
14	0.0972 166 017	0.0940 078 618	0.0909 068 574	0.0879 099 099	56
15	0.0823 068 880	0.0793 996 812	0.0765 968 113	0.0738 944 746	60
16	0.0696 838 162	0.0670 615 122	0.0645 393 722	0.0621 135 136	64
17	0.0589 966 935	0.0566 406 106	0.0543 799 473	0.0522 107 856	68
18	0.0499 486 112	0.0478 390 460	0.0458 197 620	0.0438 868 448	72
19	0.0422 881 964	0.0404 051 845	0.0386 070 728	0.0368 899 860	76
20	0.0358 026 282	0.0341 264 944	0.0325 297 646	0.0310 086 330	80
21	0.0303 117 251	0.0288 234 699	0.0274 091 121	0.0260 649 414	84
22	0.0256 629 394	0.0243 444 993	0.0230 945 239	0.0219 094 201	88
23	0.0217 271 191	0.0205 615 301	0.0194 591 138	0.0184 164 117	92
24	0.0183 949 194	0.0173 664 086	0.0163 959 696	0.0154 802 919	96
25	0.0155 737 657	0.0146 677 871	0.0138 150 083	0.0130 122 763	100
26	0.0131 852 807	0.0123 885 130	0.0116 403 274	0.0109 377 353	104
27	0.0111 631 080	0.0104 634 226	0.0098 079 726	0.0091 939 373	108
28	0.0094 510 676	0.0088 374 781	0.0082 640 567	0.0077 281 523	112
29	0.0080 015 959	0.0074 641 943	0.0069 631 754	0.0064 960 566	116
30	0.0067 744 238	0.0063 043 094	0.0058 670 715	0.0054 603 934	120
31	0.0057 354 581	0.0053 246 627	0.0049 435 101	0.0045 898 455	124
32	0.0048 558 342	0.0044 972 464	0.0041 653 306	0.0038 580 886	128
33	0.0041 111 147	0.0037 984 050	0.0035 096 477	0.0032 429 953	132
34	0.0034 806 098	0.0032 081 588	0.0029 571 787	0.0027 259 661	136
35	0.0029 468 029	0.0027 096 328	0.0024 916 762	0.0022 913 666	140
36	0.0024 948 638	0.0022 885 743	0.0020 994 506	0.0019 260 551	144
37	0.0021 122 367	0.0019 329 455	0.0017 689 669	0.0016 189 851	148
38	0.0017 882 916	0.0016 325 789	0.0014 905 061	0.0013 608 711	152
39	0.0015 140 286	0.0013 788 873	0.0012 558 790	0.0011 439 080	156
40	0.0012 818 282	0.0011 646 176	0.0010 581 856	0.0009 615 353	160
41	0.0010 852 394	0.0009 836 440	0.0008 916 120	0.0008 082 382	164
42	0.0009 188 007	0.0008 307 924	0.0007 512 594	0.0006 793 812	168
43	0.0007 778 880	0.0007 016 929	0.0006 330 004	0.0005 710 678	172
44	0.0006 585 865	0.0005 926 546	0.0005 333 570	0.0004 800 227	176
45	0.0005 575 817	0.0005 005 602	0.0004 493 990	0.0004 034 929	180
46	0.0004 720 677	0.0004 227 765	0.0003 786 571	0.0003 391 642	184
47	0.0003 996 686	0.0003 570 799	0.0003 190 510	0.0002 850 914	188
48	0.0003 383 731	0.0003 015 921	0.0002 688 278	0.0002 396 394	192
49	0.0002 864 782	0.0002 547 268	0.0002 265 105	0.0002 014 338	196
50	0.0002 425 422	0.0002 151 440	0.0001 908 545	0.0001 693 193	200
51	0.0002 053 445	0.0001 817 121	0.0001 608 112	0.0001 423 248	204
52	0.0001 738 516	0.0001 534 753	0.0001 354 972	0.0001 196 341	208
53	0.0001 471 887	0.0001 296 262	0.0001 141 680	0.0001 005 609	212
54	0.0001 246 150	0.0001 094 832	0.0000 961 963	0.0000 845 285	216
55	0.0001 055 033	0.0000 924 703	0.0000 810 536	0.0000 710 521	220
56	0.0000 893 227	0.0000 781 010	0.0000 682 946	0.0000 597 243	224
57	0.0000 756 236	0.0000 659 647	0.0000 575 441	0.0000 502 025	228
58	0.0000 640 255	0.0000 557 142	0.0000 484 858	0.0000 421 988	232
59	0.0000 542 062	0.0000 470 566	0.0000 408 534	0.0000 354 710	236
60	0.0000 458 928	0.0000 397 443	0.0000 344 225	0.0000 298 159	240

QUARTERLY Compounding

TABLE 4. PRESENT WORTH OF ONE DOLLAR
Payable at end of each period

QUARTERS	18% Nominal Annual Rate	18¼% Nominal Annual Rate	18½% Nominal Annual Rate	18¾% Nominal Annual Rate	QUARTERS
1	0.9569 377 990	0.9563 658 099	0.9557 945 042	0.9552 238 806	1
2	0.9157 299 512	0.9146 355 624	0.9135 431 342	0.9124 526 621	2
3	0.8762 966 041	0.8747 261 804	0.8731 595 070	0.8715 965 727	3
YEARS					
1	0.8385 613 436	0.8365 582 120	0.8345 610 581	0.8325 698 605	4
2	0.7031 851 270	0.6998 296 420	0.6964 921 597	0.6931 725 726	8
3	0.5896 638 649	0.5854 482 340	0.5812 652 337	0.5771 145 921	12
4	0.4944 693 228	0.4897 615 279	0.4851 013 285	0.4804 882 154	16
5	0.4146 428 597	0.4097 140 281	0.4048 466 780	0.4000 400 065	20
6	0.3477 034 735	0.3427 496 347	0.3378 692 719	0.3330 612 524	24
7	0.2915 706 919	0.2867 300 216	0.2819 725 371	0.2772 967 605	28
8	0.2444 999 112	0.2398 663 542	0.2353 232 989	0.2308 689 252	32
9	0.2050 281 740	0.2006 621 684	0.1963 916 613	0.1922 145 088	36
10	0.1719 287 011	0.1678 655 848	0.1639 008 327	0.1600 320 068	40
11	0.1441 727 626	0.1404 293 335	0.1367 852 523	0.1332 378 256	44
12	0.1208 977 055	0.1174 773 121	0.1141 556 449	0.1109 297 979	48
13	0.1013 801 424	0.0982 766 102	0.0952 698 558	0.0923 568 063	52
14	0.0850 134 684	0.0822 141 053	0.0795 085 117	0.0768 934 934	56
15	0.0712 890 083	0.0687 768 849	0.0663 547 076	0.0640 192 050	60
16	0.0597 802 066	0.0575 358 679	0.0553 770 550	0.0533 004 606	64
17	0.0501 293 703	0.0481 321 028	0.0462 155 336	0.0443 763 571	68
18	0.0420 365 521	0.0402 653 058	0.0385 696 846	0.0369 464 174	72
19	0.0352 502 276	0.0336 842 722	0.0321 887 568	0.0307 604 736	76
20	0.0295 594 783	0.0281 788 546	0.0268 634 830	0.0256 102 432	80
21	0.0247 874 358	0.0235 732 522	0.0224 192 168	0.0213 223 166	84
22	0.0207 857 855	0.0197 203 977	0.0187 102 053	0.0177 523 182	88
23	0.0174 301 562	0.0164 972 606	0.0156 148 087	0.0147 800 451	92
24	0.0146 162 552	0.0138 009 189	0.0130 315 113	0.0123 054 201	96
25	0.0122 566 266	0.0115 452 720	0.0108 755 918	0.0102 451 219	100
26	0.0102 779 333	0.0096 582 921	0.0090 763 454	0.0085 297 797	104
27	0.0086 186 775	0.0080 797 236	0.0075 747 644	0.0071 016 375	108
28	0.0072 272 898	0.0067 591 591	0.0063 216 034	0.0059 126 093	112
29	0.0060 605 259	0.0056 544 301	0.0052 757 640	0.0049 226 603	116
30	0.0050 821 227	0.0047 302 599	0.0044 029 472	0.0040 984 586	120
31	0.0042 616 716	0.0039 571 378	0.0036 745 283	0.0034 122 531	124
32	0.0035 736 731	0.0033 103 761	0.0030 666 182	0.0028 409 391	128
33	0.0029 967 441	0.0027 693 223	0.0025 592 801	0.0023 652 803	132
34	0.0025 129 538	0.0023 166 993	0.0021 358 755	0.0019 692 611	136
35	0.0021 072 659	0.0019 380 538	0.0017 825 186	0.0016 395 474	140
36	0.0017 670 717	0.0016 212 949	0.0014 876 206	0.0013 650 378	144
37	0.0014 817 980	0.0013 563 075	0.0012 415 102	0.0011 364 893	148
38	0.0012 425 785	0.0011 346 302	0.0010 361 161	0.0009 462 067	152
39	0.0010 419 783	0.0009 491 842	0.0008 647 021	0.0007 877 832	156
40	0.0008 737 628	0.0007 940 478	0.0007 216 467	0.0006 558 846	160
41	0.0007 327 037	0.0006 642 672	0.0006 022 582	0.0005 460 697	164
42	0.0006 144 170	0.0005 556 982	0.0005 026 213	0.0004 546 412	168
43	0.0005 152 263	0.0004 648 739	0.0004 194 681	0.0003 785 205	172
44	0.0004 320 489	0.0003 888 941	0.0003 500 718	0.0003 151 448	176
45	0.0003 622 995	0.0003 253 325	0.0002 921 563	0.0002 623 801	180
46	0.0003 038 103	0.0002 721 596	0.0002 438 223	0.0002 184 497	184
47	0.0002 547 636	0.0002 276 774	0.0002 034 846	0.0001 818 747	188
48	0.0002 136 349	0.0001 904 654	0.0001 698 203	0.0001 514 234	192
49	0.0001 791 460	0.0001 593 354	0.0001 417 254	0.0001 260 705	196
50	0.0001 502 249	0.0001 332 933	0.0001 182 785	0.0001 049 625	200
51	0.0001 259 728	0.0001 115 076	0.0000 987 106	0.0000 873 886	204
52	0.0001 056 359	0.0000 932 826	0.0000 823 800	0.0000 727 571	208
53	0.0000 885 822	0.0000 780 363	0.0000 687 512	0.0000 605 754	212
54	0.0000 742 816	0.0000 652 819	0.0000 573 771	0.0000 504 333	216
55	0.0000 622 897	0.0000 546 121	0.0000 478 847	0.0000 419 892	220
56	0.0000 522 337	0.0000 456 862	0.0000 399 627	0.0000 349 589	224
57	0.0000 438 012	0.0000 382 192	0.0000 333 513	0.0000 291 058	228
58	0.0000 367 300	0.0000 319 726	0.0000 278 337	0.0000 242 326	232
59	0.0000 308 003	0.0000 267 469	0.0000 232 289	0.0000 201 753	236
60	0.0000 258 280	0.0000 223 754	0.0000 193 859	0.0000 167 974	240

TABLE 4. PRESENT WORTH OF ONE DOLLAR
Payable at end of each period

QUARTERLY Compounding

QUARTERS	19% Nominal Annual Rate	19¼% Nominal Annual Rate	19½% Nominal Annual Rate	19¾% Nominal Annual Rate	QUARTERS
1	0.9546 539 379	0.9540 846 750	0.9535 160 906	0.9529 481 834	1
2	0.9113 641 412	0.9102 775 671	0.9091 929 350	0.9081 102 403	2
3	0.8700 373 663	0.8684 818 768	0.8669 300 930	0.8653 820 039	3
YEARS					
1	0.8305 845 979	0.8286 052 492	0.8266 317 931	0.8246 642 086	4
2	0.6898 707 743	0.6865 866 589	0.6833 201 213	0.6800 710 569	8
3	0.5729 960 397	0.5689 093 096	0.5648 541 371	0.5608 302 599	12
4	0.4759 216 853	0.4714 012 402	0.4669 263 882	0.4624 966 425	16
5	0.3952 932 216	0.3906 055 421	0.3859 761 975	0.3814 044 276	20
6	0.3283 244 615	0.3236 578 026	0.3190 601 962	0.3145 305 805	24
7	0.2727 012 409	0.2681 845 541	0.2637 453 021	0.2593 821 122	28
8	0.2265 014 505	0.2222 191 293	0.2180 202 520	0.2139 031 443	32
9	0.1881 286 162	0.1841 319 370	0.1802 224 718	0.1763 982 672	36
10	0.1562 567 311	0.1525 726 895	0.1489 776 250	0.1454 693 374	40
11	0.1297 844 341	0.1264 225 314	0.1231 496 413	0.1199 633 560	44
12	0.1077 969 520	0.1047 543 732	0.1017 994 088	0.0989 294 860	48
13	0.0895 344 881	0.0868 000 235	0.0841 506 278	0.0815 836 063	52
14	0.0743 659 668	0.0719 229 551	0.0695 615 844	0.0672 790 801	56
15	0.0617 672 266	0.0595 957 381	0.0575 018 172	0.0554 826 494	60
16	0.0513 029 071	0.0493 813 414	0.0475 328 303	0.0457 545 551	64
17	0.0426 114 045	0.0409 176 387	0.0392 921 487	0.0377 321 440	68
18	0.0353 923 762	0.0339 045 702	0.0324 801 393	0.0311 163 487	72
19	0.0293 963 626	0.0280 935 049	0.0268 491 158	0.0256 605 391	76
20	0.0244 161 660	0.0232 784 256	0.0221 943 328	0.0211 613 281	80
21	0.0202 796 914	0.0192 886 256	0.0183 465 411	0.0174 509 899	84
22	0.0168 439 993	0.0159 826 565	0.0151 658 342	0.0143 912 068	88
23	0.0139 903 664	0.0132 433 130	0.0125 365 607	0.0118 679 132	92
24	0.0116 201 829	0.0109 734 787	0.0103 631 196	0.0097 870 432	96
25	0.0096 515 449	0.0090 926 820	0.0085 664 842	0.0080 710 242	100
26	0.0080 164 246	0.0075 342 441	0.0070 813 282	0.0066 558 848	104
27	0.0066 583 188	0.0062 429 142	0.0058 536 510	0.0054 888 700	108
28	0.0055 302 970	0.0051 729 115	0.0048 388 140	0.0045 264 746	112
29	0.0045 933 795	0.0042 863 016	0.0039 999 175	0.0037 328 216	116
30	0.0038 151 903	0.0035 516 520	0.0033 064 590	0.0030 783 244	120
31	0.0031 688 383	0.0029 429 175	0.0027 332 241	0.0025 385 839	124
32	0.0026 319 883	0.0024 385 169	0.0022 593 700	0.0020 934 793	128
33	0.0021 860 889	0.0020 205 679	0.0018 676 670	0.0017 264 175	132
34	0.0018 157 318	0.0016 742 532	0.0015 438 730	0.0014 237 147	136
35	0.0015 081 189	0.0013 872 950	0.0012 762 145	0.0011 740 865	140
36	0.0012 526 203	0.0011 495 199	0.0010 549 595	0.0009 682 272	144
37	0.0010 404 071	0.0009 524 982	0.0008 720 630	0.0007 984 623	148
38	0.0008 641 461	0.0007 892 450	0.0007 208 750	0.0006 584 633	152
39	0.0007 177 465	0.0006 539 726	0.0005 958 982	0.0005 430 111	156
40	0.0005 961 492	0.0005 418 851	0.0004 925 884	0.0004 478 018	160
41	0.0004 951 523	0.0004 490 088	0.0004 071 892	0.0003 692 861	164
42	0.0004 112 659	0.0003 720 511	0.0003 365 956	0.0003 045 370	168
43	0.0003 415 911	0.0003 082 835	0.0002 782 406	0.0002 511 408	172
44	0.0002 837 203	0.0002 554 453	0.0002 300 025	0.0002 071 068	176
45	0.0002 356 537	0.0002 116 633	0.0001 901 274	0.0001 707 936	180
46	0.0001 957 304	0.0001 753 853	0.0001 571 654	0.0001 408 474	184
47	0.0001 625 706	0.0001 453 252	0.0001 299 179	0.0001 161 518	188
48	0.0001 350 286	0.0001 204 172	0.0001 073 942	0.0000 957 862	192
49	0.0001 121 527	0.0000 997 784	0.0000 887 755	0.0000 789 915	196
50	0.0000 931 523	0.0000 826 769	0.0000 733 847	0.0000 651 414	200
51	0.0000 773 709	0.0000 685 065	0.0000 606 621	0.0000 537 198	204
52	0.0000 642 631	0.0000 567 648	0.0000 501 452	0.0000 443 008	208
53	0.0000 533 759	0.0000 470 356	0.0000 414 516	0.0000 365 333	212
54	0.0000 443 332	0.0000 389 740	0.0000 342 652	0.0000 301 277	216
55	0.0000 368 225	0.0000 322 940	0.0000 283 247	0.0000 248 452	220
56	0.0000 305 842	0.0000 267 590	0.0000 234 141	0.0000 204 890	224
57	0.0000 254 028	0.0000 221 727	0.0000 193 549	0.0000 168 965	228
58	0.0000 210 991	0.0000 183 724	0.0000 159 993	0.0000 139 340	232
59	0.0000 175 246	0.0000 152 235	0.0000 132 256	0.0000 114 908	236
60	0.0000 145 557	0.0000 126 142	0.0000 109 327	0.0000 094 761	240

QUARTERLY
Compounding

TABLE 4. PRESENT WORTH OF ONE DOLLAR
Payable at end of each period

QUARTERS	20% Nominal Annual Rate	20¼% Nominal Annual Rate	20½% Nominal Annual Rate	20¾% Nominal Annual Rate	QUARTERS
1	0.9523 809 524	0.9518 143 962	0.9512 485 137	0.9506 833 036	1
2	0.9070 294 785	0.9059 506 448	0.9048 737 348	0.9037 987 438	2
3	0.8638 375 985	0.8622 968 660	0.8607 597 953	0.8592 263 756	3
YEARS					
1	0.8227 024 748	0.8207 465 708	0.8187 964 759	0.8168 521 693	4
2	0.6768 393 620	0.6736 249 335	0.6704 276 689	0.6672 474 665	8
3	0.5568 374 182	0.5528 753 542	0.5489 438 126	0.5450 425 404	12
4	0.4581 115 220	0.4537 705 510	0.4494 732 592	0.4452 191 815	16
5	0.3768 894 829	0.3724 306 237	0.3680 271 207	0.3636 782 542	20
6	0.3100 679 103	0.3056 711 573	0.3013 393 094	0.2970 713 709	24
7	0.2550 936 371	0.2508 785 541	0.2467 355 646	0.2426 633 937	28
8	0.2098 661 666	0.2059 077 130	0.2020 262 108	0.1982 201 196	32
9	0.1726 574 146	0.1689 980 493	0.1654 183 494	0.1619 165 347	36
10	0.1420 456 823	0.1387 045 695	0.1354 439 615	0.1322 618 726	40
11	0.1168 613 344	0.1138 412 997	0.1109 010 384	0.1080 383 975	44
12	0.0961 421 090	0.0934 348 564	0.0908 053 794	0.0882 513 994	48
13	0.0790 963 510	0.0766 863 380	0.0743 511 246	0.0720 883 470	52
14	0.0650 727 637	0.0629 400 489	0.0608 784 388	0.0588 855 227	56
15	0.0535 355 237	0.0516 578 293	0.0498 470 512	0.0481 007 669	60
16	0.0440 438 079	0.0423 979 863	0.0408 145 898	0.0392 912 158	64
17	0.0362 349 497	0.0347 980 018	0.0334 188 423	0.0320 951 149	68
18	0.0298 105 828	0.0285 603 407	0.0273 632 303	0.0262 169 642	72
19	0.0245 252 403	0.0234 408 017	0.0224 049 166	0.0214 153 841	76
20	0.0201 769 759	0.0192 389 576	0.0183 450 667	0.0174 932 029	80
21	0.0165 996 480	0.0157 903 085	0.0150 208 760	0.0142 893 608	84
22	0.0136 565 715	0.0129 598 415	0.0122 990 403	0.0116 722 953	88
23	0.0112 352 951	0.0106 367 455	0.0100 704 109	0.0095 345 398	92
24	0.0092 433 051	0.0087 300 724	0.0082 456 169	0.0077 883 095	96
25	0.0076 044 900	0.0071 651 770	0.0067 514 821	0.0063 618 975	100
26	0.0062 562 327	0.0058 807 944	0.0055 280 897	0.0051 967 298	104
27	0.0051 470 182	0.0048 266 419	0.0045 263 804	0.0042 449 600	108
28	0.0042 344 646	0.0039 614 498	0.0037 061 843	0.0034 675 048	112
29	0.0034 837 045	0.0032 513 463	0.0030 346 107	0.0028 324 388	116
30	0.0028 660 523	0.0026 685 313	0.0024 847 285	0.0023 136 838	120
31	0.0023 579 083	0.0021 901 879	0.0020 344 869	0.0018 899 376	124
32	0.0019 398 570	0.0017 975 892	0.0016 658 307	0.0015 437 996	128
33	0.0015 959 252	0.0014 753 652	0.0013 639 763	0.0012 610 561	132
34	0.0013 129 716	0.0012 109 009	0.0011 168 190	0.0010 300 964	136
35	0.0010 801 850	0.0009 938 428	0.0009 144 475	0.0008 414 365	140
36	0.0008 886 708	0.0008 156 931	0.0007 487 464	0.0006 873 292	144
37	0.0007 311 117	0.0006 694 773	0.0006 130 709	0.0005 614 464	148
38	0.0006 014 874	0.0005 494 712	0.0005 019 803	0.0004 586 187	152
39	0.0004 948 452	0.0004 509 766	0.0004 110 197	0.0003 746 237	156
40	0.0004 071 104	0.0003 701 375	0.0003 365 415	0.0003 060 121	160
41	0.0003 349 307	0.0003 037 891	0.0002 755 590	0.0002 499 667	164
42	0.0002 755 483	0.0002 493 338	0.0002 256 267	0.0002 041 858	168
43	0.0002 266 943	0.0002 046 399	0.0001 847 424	0.0001 667 896	172
44	0.0001 865 019	0.0001 679 575	0.0001 512 664	0.0001 362 425	176
45	0.0001 534 356	0.0001 378 505	0.0001 238 564	0.0001 112 900	180
46	0.0001 262 319	0.0001 131 404	0.0001 014 132	0.0000 909 074	184
47	0.0001 038 513	0.0000 928 596	0.0000 830 368	0.0000 742 579	188
48	0.0000 854 387	0.0000 762 142	0.0000 679 902	0.0000 606 578	192
49	0.0000 702 906	0.0000 625 525	0.0000 556 701	0.0000 495 484	196
50	0.0000 578 283	0.0000 513 398	0.0000 455 825	0.0000 404 737	200
51	0.0000 475 755	0.0000 421 369	0.0000 373 228	0.0000 330 611	204
52	0.0000 391 404	0.0000 345 837	0.0000 305 598	0.0000 270 060	208
53	0.0000 322 009	0.0000 283 845	0.0000 250 222	0.0000 220 599	212
54	0.0000 264 918	0.0000 232 965	0.0000 204 881	0.0000 180 197	216
55	0.0000 217 949	0.0000 191 205	0.0000 167 756	0.0000 147 194	220
56	0.0000 179 307	0.0000 156 931	0.0000 137 358	0.0000 120 236	224
57	0.0000 147 516	0.0000 128 800	0.0000 112 468	0.0000 098 215	228
58	0.0000 121 362	0.0000 105 713	0.0000 092 089	0.0000 080 227	232
59	0.0000 099 845	0.0000 086 763	0.0000 075 402	0.0000 065 534	236
60	0.0000 082 143	0.0000 071 211	0.0000 061 739	0.0000 053 531	240

TABLE 4. PRESENT WORTH OF ONE DOLLAR
Payable at end of each period

QUARTERLY Compounding

QUARTERS	21% Nominal Annual Rate	21¼% Nominal Annual Rate	21½% Nominal Annual Rate	21¾% Nominal Annual Rate	QUARTERS
1	0.9501 187 648	0.9495 548 961	0.9489 916 963	0.9484 291 642	1
2	0.9027 256 673	0.9016 545 008	0.9005 852 397	0.8995 178 795	2
3	0.8576 965 960	0.8561 704 459	0.8546 479 143	0.8531 289 906	3
YEARS					
1	0.8149 136 304	0.8129 808 388	0.8110 537 739	0.8091 324 155	4
2	0.6640 842 250	0.6609 378 442	0.6578 082 242	0.6546 952 659	8
3	0.5411 712 867	0.5373 298 030	0.5335 178 428	0.5297 351 619	12
4	0.4410 078 580	0.4368 388 340	0.4327 116 599	0.4286 258 912	16
5	0.3593 833 146	0.3551 416 016	0.3509 524 248	0.3468 151 027	20
6	0.2928 663 616	0.2887 233 172	0.2846 412 886	0.2806 193 418	24
7	0.2386 607 900	0.2347 265 246	0.2308 593 913	0.2270 582 059	28
8	0.1944 879 308	0.1908 281 668	0.1872 393 806	0.1837 201 546	32
9	0.1584 908 657	0.1551 396 431	0.1518 612 063	0.1486 539 325	36
10	0.1291 563 668	0.1261 255 572	0.1231 676 044	0.1202 807 154	40
11	0.1052 512 838	0.1025 376 613	0.0998 955 504	0.0973 230 258	44
12	0.0857 707 058	0.0833 611 539	0.0810 206 632	0.0787 472 150	48
13	0.0698 957 172	0.0677 710 208	0.0657 121 146	0.0637 169 243	52
14	0.0569 589 727	0.0550 965 413	0.0532 960 586	0.0515 554 288	56
15	0.0464 166 432	0.0447 924 324	0.0432 259 694	0.0417 151 687	60
16	0.0378 255 552	0.0364 153 893	0.0350 585 856	0.0337 530 952	64
17	0.0308 245 605	0.0296 050 137	0.0284 343 982	0.0273 107 234	68
18	0.0251 193 545	0.0240 683 089	0.0230 618 260	0.0220 979 916	72
19	0.0204 701 044	0.0195 670 739	0.0187 043 810	0.0178 802 013	76
20	0.0166 813 671	0.0159 076 562	0.0151 702 588	0.0144 674 505	80
21	0.0135 938 734	0.0129 326 197	0.0123 038 956	0.0117 060 832	84
22	0.0110 778 327	0.0105 139 720	0.0099 791 210	0.0094 717 714	88
23	0.0090 274 769	0.0085 476 578	0.0080 936 037	0.0076 639 172	92
24	0.0073 566 140	0.0069 490 820	0.0065 643 479	0.0062 011 239	96
25	0.0059 950 050	0.0056 494 705	0.0053 240 391	0.0050 175 303	100
26	0.0048 854 113	0.0045 929 113	0.0043 180 820	0.0040 598 464	104
27	0.0039 811 882	0.0037 339 489	0.0035 021 967	0.0032 849 534	108
28	0.0032 443 246	0.0030 356 289	0.0028 404 699	0.0026 579 622	112
29	0.0026 438 443	0.0024 679 081	0.0023 037 738	0.0021 506 434	116
30	0.0021 545 048	0.0020 063 620	0.0018 684 844	0.0017 401 553	120
31	0.0017 557 353	0.0016 311 339	0.0015 154 414	0.0014 080 161	124
32	0.0014 307 726	0.0013 260 806	0.0012 291 044	0.0011 392 714	128
33	0.0011 659 561	0.0010 780 781	0.0009 968 698	0.0009 218 214	132
34	0.0009 501 535	0.0008 764 568	0.0008 085 150	0.0007 458 756	136
35	0.0007 742 931	0.0007 125 426	0.0006 557 491	0.0006 035 121	140
36	0.0006 309 820	0.0005 792 835	0.0005 318 478	0.0004 883 212	144
37	0.0005 141 958	0.0004 709 464	0.0004 313 572	0.0003 951 165	148
38	0.0004 190 252	0.0003 828 704	0.0003 498 539	0.0003 197 016	152
39	0.0003 414 693	0.0003 112 663	0.0002 837 503	0.0002 586 809	156
40	0.0002 782 680	0.0002 530 535	0.0002 301 368	0.0002 093 071	160
41	0.0002 267 644	0.0002 057 277	0.0001 866 533	0.0001 693 572	164
42	0.0001 847 934	0.0001 672 527	0.0001 513 858	0.0001 370 324	168
43	0.0001 505 907	0.0001 359 732	0.0001 227 821	0.0001 108 773	172
44	0.0001 227 184	0.0001 105 436	0.0000 995 829	0.0000 897 145	176
45	0.0001 000 049	0.0000 898 698	0.0000 807 671	0.0000 725 909	180
46	0.0000 814 953	0.0000 730 625	0.0000 655 064	0.0000 587 356	184
47	0.0000 664 117	0.0000 593 984	0.0000 531 292	0.0000 475 249	188
48	0.0000 541 198	0.0000 482 897	0.0000 430 907	0.0000 384 539	192
49	0.0000 441 029	0.0000 392 586	0.0000 349 488	0.0000 311 143	196
50	0.0000 359 401	0.0000 319 165	0.0000 283 454	0.0000 251 756	200
51	0.0000 292 881	0.0000 259 475	0.0000 229 896	0.0000 203 704	204
52	0.0000 238 672	0.0000 210 948	0.0000 186 458	0.0000 164 824	208
53	0.0000 194 497	0.0000 171 497	0.0000 151 228	0.0000 133 364	212
54	0.0000 158 499	0.0000 139 424	0.0000 122 654	0.0000 107 909	216
55	0.0000 129 163	0.0000 113 349	0.0000 099 479	0.0000 087 313	220
56	0.0000 105 256	0.0000 092 150	0.0000 080 683	0.0000 070 648	224
57	0.0000 085 775	0.0000 074 917	0.0000 065 438	0.0000 057 163	228
58	0.0000 069 899	0.0000 060 906	0.0000 053 074	0.0000 046 253	232
59	0.0000 056 962	0.0000 049 515	0.0000 043 046	0.0000 037 425	236
60	0.0000 046 419	0.0000 040 255	0.0000 034 912	0.0000 030 281	240

QUARTERLY
Compounding

TABLE 4. PRESENT WORTH OF ONE DOLLAR
Payable at end of each period

QUARTERS	22% Nominal Annual Rate	22¼% Nominal Annual Rate	22½% Nominal Annual Rate	22¾% Nominal Annual Rate	QUARTERS
1	0.9478 672 986	0.9473 060 983	0.9467 455 621	0.9461 856 889	1
2	0.8984 524 157	0.8973 888 438	0.8963 271 594	0.8952 673 580	2
3	0.8516 136 642	0.8501 019 243	0.8485 937 604	0.8470 891 619	3
YEARS					
1	0.8072 167 433	0.8053 067 371	0.8034 023 767	0.8015 036 422	4
2	0.6515 988 707	0.6485 189 407	0.6454 553 789	0.6424 080 885	8
3	0.5259 815 183	0.5222 566 721	0.5185 603 855	0.5148 924 227	12
4	0.4245 810 883	0.4205 768 165	0.4166 126 461	0.4126 881 522	16
5	0.3427 289 633	0.3386 933 438	0.3347 075 901	0.3307 710 571	20
6	0.2766 565 576	0.2727 520 315	0.2689 048 734	0.2651 142 070	24
7	0.2233 218 055	0.2196 490 485	0.2160 388 144	0.2124 900 025	28
8	0.1802 691 005	0.1768 848 586	0.1735 660 969	0.1703 115 109	32
9	0.1455 162 362	0.1424 465 683	0.1394 434 148	0.1365 052 963	36
10	0.1174 631 423	0.1147 131 811	0.1120 291 709	0.1094 094 922	40
11	0.0948 182 152	0.0923 792 976	0.0900 045 021	0.0876 921 065	44
12	0.0765 388 509	0.0743 936 707	0.0723 098 309	0.0702 855 427	48
13	0.0617 834 419	0.0599 097 242	0.0580 938 900	0.0563 341 185	52
14	0.0498 726 288	0.0482 457 045	0.0466 727 693	0.0451 520 012	56
15	0.0402 580 210	0.0388 525 909	0.0374 970 138	0.0361 894 934	60
16	0.0324 969 486	0.0312 882 532	0.0301 251 900	0.0290 060 108	64
17	0.0262 320 810	0.0251 966 411	0.0242 026 492	0.0232 484 233	68
18	0.0211 749 750	0.0202 910 248	0.0194 444 659	0.0186 336 959	72
19	0.0170 927 944	0.0163 404 990	0.0156 217 301	0.0149 349 752	76
20	0.0137 975 898	0.0131 591 139	0.0125 505 351	0.0119 704 370	80
21	0.0111 376 455	0.0105 971 231	0.0100 831 297	0.0095 943 488	84
22	0.0089 904 939	0.0085 339 346	0.0081 008 104	0.0076 899 055	88
23	0.0072 572 772	0.0068 724 350	0.0065 082 103	0.0061 634 873	92
24	0.0058 581 957	0.0055 344 182	0.0052 287 116	0.0049 400 575	96
25	0.0047 288 336	0.0044 569 043	0.0042 007 594	0.0039 594 741	100
26	0.0038 171 937	0.0035 891 751	0.0033 749 001	0.0031 735 329	104
27	0.0030 813 027	0.0028 903 869	0.0027 114 027	0.0025 435 982	108
28	0.0024 872 791	0.0023 276 480	0.0021 783 474	0.0020 387 032	112
29	0.0020 077 733	0.0018 744 706	0.0017 500 895	0.0016 340 280	116
30	0.0016 207 083	0.0015 095 238	0.0014 060 260	0.0013 096 794	120
31	0.0013 082 628	0.0012 156 297	0.0011 296 047	0.0010 497 128	124
32	0.0010 560 517	0.0009 789 548	0.0009 075 271	0.0008 413 487	128
33	0.0008 524 626	0.0007 883 589	0.0007 291 094	0.0006 743 440	132
34	0.0006 881 221	0.0006 348 707	0.0005 857 682	0.0005 404 892	136
35	0.0005 554 637	0.0005 112 657	0.0004 706 076	0.0004 332 040	140
36	0.0004 483 796	0.0004 117 257	0.0003 780 873	0.0003 472 146	144
37	0.0003 619 395	0.0003 315 655	0.0003 037 562	0.0002 782 938	148
38	0.0002 921 636	0.0002 670 119	0.0002 440 385	0.0002 230 535	152
39	0.0002 358 394	0.0002 150 265	0.0001 960 611	0.0001 787 782	156
40	0.0001 903 735	0.0001 731 623	0.0001 575 159	0.0001 432 914	160
41	0.0001 536 727	0.0001 394 488	0.0001 265 487	0.0001 148 485	164
42	0.0001 240 471	0.0001 122 990	0.0001 016 695	0.0000 920 515	168
43	0.0001 001 329	0.0000 904 352	0.0000 816 815	0.0000 737 796	172
44	0.0000 808 290	0.0000 728 280	0.0000 656 231	0.0000 591 346	176
45	0.0000 652 465	0.0000 586 489	0.0000 527 218	0.0000 473 966	180
46	0.0000 526 681	0.0000 472 304	0.0000 423 568	0.0000 379 886	184
47	0.0000 425 146	0.0000 380 349	0.0000 340 296	0.0000 304 480	188
48	0.0000 343 185	0.0000 306 298	0.0000 273 394	0.0000 244 042	192
49	0.0000 277 024	0.0000 246 664	0.0000 219 646	0.0000 195 600	196
50	0.0000 223 619	0.0000 198 640	0.0000 176 464	0.0000 156 774	200
51	0.0000 180 509	0.0000 159 966	0.0000 141 771	0.0000 125 655	204
52	0.0000 145 710	0.0000 128 822	0.0000 113 900	0.0000 100 713	208
53	0.0000 117 619	0.0000 103 741	0.0000 091 507	0.0000 080 722	212
54	0.0000 094 944	0.0000 083 543	0.0000 073 517	0.0000 064 699	216
55	0.0000 076 641	0.0000 067 278	0.0000 059 064	0.0000 051 856	220
56	0.0000 061 866	0.0000 054 179	0.0000 047 452	0.0000 041 563	224
57	0.0000 049 939	0.0000 043 631	0.0000 038 123	0.0000 033 313	228
58	0.0000 040 312	0.0000 035 136	0.0000 030 628	0.0000 026 700	232
59	0.0000 032 540	0.0000 028 296	0.0000 024 607	0.0000 021 401	236
60	0.0000 026 267	0.0000 022 787	0.0000 019 769	0.0000 017 153	240

TABLE 5. PRESENT WORTH OF ONE DOLLAR PER PERIOD
Payable at end of each period

QUARTERLY Compounding

QUARTERS	5% Nominal Annual Rate	5¼% Nominal Annual Rate	5½% Nominal Annual Rate	5¾% Nominal Annual Rate	QUARTERS
1	0.9876 543 210	0.9870 450 339	0.9864 364 982	0.9858 287 123	1
2	1.9631 153 788	1.9613 029 329	1.9594 934 630	1.9576 869 622	2
3	2.9265 337 074	2.9229 393 539	2.9193 523 680	2.9157 727 292	3
YEARS					
1	3.8780 579 826	3.8721 178 077	3.8661 922 249	3.8602 811 871	4
2	7.5681 242 938	7.5474 486 012	7.5268 571 179	7.5063 494 184	8
3	11.0793 119 660	11.0359 934 009	10.9929 205 413	10.9500 917 010	12
4	14.4202 922 710	14.3472 449 599	14.2747 275 372	14.2027 354 139	16
5	17.5993 161 342	17.4902 135 946	17.3820 732 036	17.2748 849 114	20
6	20.6242 345 116	20.4734 517 036	20.3242 319 298	20.1765 560 958	24
7	23.5025 177 782	23.3050 770 391	23.1099 850 770	22.9172 090 716	28
8	26.2412 741 773	25.9927 947 968	25.7476 471 884	25.5057 789 875	32
9	28.8472 673 749	28.5439 185 821	28.2450 908 044	27.9507 051 671	36
10	31.3269 331 635	30.9653 903 121	30.6097 699 605	30.2599 586 227	40
11	33.6863 953 558	33.2637 991 047	32.8487 424 343	32.4410 680 430	44
12	35.9314 809 083	35.4453 992 085	34.9686 908 109	34.5011 443 382	48
13	38.0677 343 114	37.5161 270 218	36.9759 424 286	36.4469 038 230	52
14	40.1004 312 824	39.4816 172 459	38.8764 882 630	38.2846 901 135	56
15	42.0345 917 945	41.3472 182 176	40.6760 008 089	40.0204 948 087	60
16	43.8749 924 739	43.1180 064 634	42.3798 510 103	41.6599 770 247	64
17	45.6261 783 966	44.7988 005 124	43.9931 242 913	43.2084 818 444	68
18	47.2924 743 123	46.3941 740 090	45.5206 357 338	44.6710 577 437	72
19	48.8779 953 259	47.9084 681 577	46.9669 444 494	46.0524 730 509	76
20	50.3866 570 592	49.3458 035 363	48.3363 671 868	47.3572 314 926	80
21	51.8221 853 215	50.7100 913 085	49.6329 912 154	48.5895 868 762	84
22	53.1881 253 108	52.0050 438 666	50.8606 865 252	49.7535 569 593	88
23	54.4878 503 692	53.2341 849 335	52.0231 173 767	50.8529 365 475	92
24	55.7245 703 133	54.4008 591 507	53.1237 532 377	51.8913 098 671	96
25	56.9013 393 618	55.5082 411 804	54.1658 791 389	52.8720 622 500	100
26	58.0210 636 777	56.5593 443 430	55.1526 054 780	53.7983 911 707	104
27	59.0865 085 459	57.5570 288 176	56.0868 773 038	54.6733 166 711	108
28	60.1003 052 019	58.5040 094 247	56.9714 831 056	55.4996 912 064	112
29	61.0649 573 302	59.4028 630 130	57.8090 631 364	56.2802 089 443	116
30	61.9828 472 474	60.2560 354 721	58.6021 172 930	57.0174 145 494	120
31	62.8562 417 856	61.0658 483 876	59.3530 125 770	57.7137 114 786	124
32	63.6872 978 905	61.8345 053 587	60.0639 901 604	58.3713 698 175	128
33	64.4780 679 485	62.5640 979 939	60.7371 720 737	58.9925 336 810	132
34	65.2305 048 547	63.2566 116 033	61.3745 675 401	59.5792 282 039	136
35	65.9464 668 365	63.9139 306 003	61.9780 789 723	60.1333 661 429	140
36	66.6277 220 424	64.5378 436 295	62.5495 076 505	60.6567 541 132	144
37	67.2759 529 084	65.1300 484 339	63.0905 590 983	61.1510 984 780	148
38	67.8927 603 133	65.6921 564 744	63.6028 481 738	61.6180 109 116	152
39	68.4796 675 323	66.2256 973 151	64.0879 038 887	62.0590 136 542	156
40	69.0381 239 984	66.7321 227 854	64.5471 739 723	62.4755 444 747	160
41	69.5695 088 825	67.2128 109 302	64.9820 291 927	62.8689 613 576	164
42	70.0751 344 993	67.6690 697 602	65.3937 674 472	63.2405 469 309	168
43	70.5562 495 478	68.1021 408 110	65.7836 176 373	63.5915 126 478	172
44	71.0140 421 956	68.5132 025 214	66.1527 433 355	63.9230 027 359	176
45	71.4496 430 131	68.9033 734 401	66.5022 462 587	64.2360 979 278	180
46	71.8641 277 652	69.2737 152 693	66.8331 695 565	64.5318 189 847	184
47	72.2585 200 685	69.6252 357 542	67.1465 009 245	64.8111 300 241	188
48	72.6337 939 191	69.9588 914 245	67.4431 755 521	65.0749 416 632	192
49	72.9908 760 977	70.2755 901 978	67.7240 789 140	65.3241 139 876	196
50	73.3306 484 590	70.5761 938 497	67.9900 494 131	65.5594 593 556	200
51	73.6539 501 088	70.8615 203 592	68.2418 808 823	65.7817 450 461	204
52	73.9615 794 768	71.1323 461 343	68.4803 249 546	65.9916 957 609	208
53	74.2542 962 882	71.3894 081 248	68.7060 933 059	66.1899 959 868	212
54	74.5328 234 400	71.6334 058 274	68.9198 597 793	66.3772 922 273	216
55	74.7978 487 862	71.8650 031 895	69.1222 623 965	66.5541 951 107	220
56	75.0500 268 368	72.0848 304 156	69.3139 052 615	66.7212 813 802	224
57	75.2899 803 735	72.2934 856 821	69.4953 603 644	66.8790 957 750	228
58	75.5183 019 886	72.4915 367 654	69.6671 692 881	67.0281 528 057	232
59	75.7355 555 480	72.6795 225 864	69.8298 448 248	67.1689 384 318	236
60	75.9422 775 836	72.8579 546 773	69.9838 725 067	67.3019 116 465	240

QUARTERLY Compounding

TABLE 5. PRESENT WORTH OF ONE DOLLAR PER PERIOD
Payable at end of each period

QUARTERS	6% Nominal Annual Rate	6¼% Nominal Annual Rate	6½% Nominal Annual Rate	6¾% Nominal Annual Rate	QUARTERS
1	0.9852 216 749	0.9846 153 846	0.9840 098 401	0.9834 050 400	1
2	1.9558 834 235	1.9540 828 402	1.9522 852 055	1.9504 905 126	2
3	2.9122 004 173	2.9086 354 119	2.9050 776 930	2.9015 272 404	3
YEARS					
1	3.8543 846 476	3.8485 025 594	3.8426 348 763	3.8367 815 517	4
2	7.4859 250 799	7.4655 836 822	7.4453 248 071	7.4251 480 395	8
3	10.9075 052 070	10.8651 593 993	10.8230 526 309	10.7811 832 678	12
4	14.1312 640 453	14.0603 089 313	13.9898 656 152	13.9199 296 839	16
5	17.1686 387 851	17.0633 250 077	16.9589 338 766	16.8554 558 018	20
6	20.0304 053 663	19.8857 611 615	19.7426 051 527	19.6009 192 595	24
7	22.7267 167 100	22.5384 761 783	22.3524 561 535	22.1686 257 949	28
8	25.2671 387 379	25.0316 758 743	24.7993 407 065	24.5700 844 023	32
9	27.6606 843 109	27.3749 523 608	27.0934 348 957	26.8160 589 183	36
10	29.9158 452 042	29.5773 209 480	29.2442 793 820	28.9166 162 675	40
11	32.0406 222 346	31.6472 548 298	31.2608 190 801	30.8811 715 845	44
12	34.0425 536 456	33.5927 176 828	33.1514 403 594	32.7185 304 146	48
13	35.9287 418 511	35.4211 943 050	34.9240 059 207	34.4369 281 818	52
14	37.7058 786 337	37.1397 194 122	36.5858 874 954	36.0440 671 022	56
15	39.3802 688 853	38.7549 047 027	38.1439 965 036	37.5471 507 063	60
16	40.9578 529 758	40.2729 642 943	39.6048 127 965	38.9529 161 274	64
17	42.4442 278 277	41.6997 386 325	40.9744 116 053	40.2676 642 981	68
18	43.8446 667 735	43.0407 169 598	42.2584 888 067	41.4972 881 931	72
19	45.1641 382 638	44.3010 584 352	43.4623 846 107	42.6472 992 422	76
20	46.4073 234 941	45.4856 119 825	44.5911 057 697	43.7228 520 339	80
21	47.5786 330 136	46.5989 349 462	45.6493 464 002	44.7287 674 194	84
22	48.6822 223 715	47.6453 106 242	46.6415 075 049	45.6695 541 205	88
23	49.7220 068 613	48.6287 647 480	47.5717 152 756	46.5494 289 387	92
24	50.7016 754 105	49.5530 809 700	48.4438 382 529	47.3723 356 559	96
25	51.6247 036 684	50.4218 154 210	49.2615 034 150	48.1419 627 109	100
26	52.4943 663 372	51.2383 103 914	50.0281 112 612	48.8617 597 323	104
27	53.3137 487 893	52.0057 071 902	50.7468 499 542	49.5349 529 997	108
28	54.0857 580 143	52.7269 582 304	51.4207 085 787	50.1645 599 055	112
29	54.8131 329 318	53.4048 383 883	52.0524 895 725	50.7534 024 785	116
30	55.4984 541 085	54.0419 556 786	52.6448 203 816	51.3041 200 337	120
31	56.1441 529 138	54.6407 612 889	53.2001 643 865	51.8191 810 014	124
32	56.7525 201 458	55.2035 590 097	53.7208 311 475	52.3008 939 921	128
33	57.3257 141 579	55.7325 140 982	54.2089 860 093	52.7514 181 434	132
34	57.8657 685 171	56.2296 616 084	54.6666 591 066	53.1727 727 983	136
35	58.3745 992 178	56.6969 142 207	55.0957 538 065	53.5668 465 559	140
36	58.8540 114 798	57.1360 696 006	55.4980 546 247	53.9354 057 367	144
37	59.3057 061 530	57.5488 173 149	55.8752 346 467	54.2801 022 994	148
38	59.7312 857 509	57.9367 453 317	56.2288 624 856	54.6024 812 459	152
39	60.1322 601 368	58.3013 461 302	56.5604 088 062	54.9039 875 454	156
40	60.5100 518 799	58.6440 224 428	56.8712 524 407	55.1859 726 119	160
41	60.8660 013 027	58.9660 926 512	57.1626 861 231	55.4497 003 611	164
42	61.2013 712 355	59.2687 958 592	57.4359 218 654	55.6963 528 756	168
43	61.5173 514 976	59.5532 966 599	57.6920 959 984	55.9270 357 031	172
44	61.8150 631 176	59.8206 896 160	57.9322 738 969	56.1427 828 121	176
45	62.0955 623 111	60.0720 034 708	58.1574 544 110	56.3445 612 259	180
46	62.3598 442 279	60.3082 051 067	58.3685 740 194	56.5332 753 574	184
47	62.6088 464 822	60.5302 032 644	58.5665 107 249	56.7097 710 625	188
48	62.8434 524 795	60.7388 520 397	58.7520 877 049	56.8748 394 316	192
49	63.0644 945 505	60.9349 541 690	58.9260 767 355	57.0292 203 354	196
50	63.2727 569 041	61.1192 641 178	59.0892 014 010	57.1736 057 413	200
51	63.4689 784 093	61.2924 909 837	59.2421 401 029	57.3086 428 147	204
52	63.6538 552 172	61.4553 012 240	59.3855 288 815	57.4349 368 198	208
53	63.8280 432 302	61.6083 212 201	59.5199 640 609	57.5530 538 325	212
54	63.9921 604 291	61.7521 396 874	59.6460 047 289	57.6635 232 779	216
55	64.1467 890 658	61.8873 099 400	59.7641 750 627	57.7668 403 030	220
56	64.2924 777 289	62.0143 520 197	59.8749 665 079	57.8634 679 961	224
57	64.4297 432 898	62.1337 546 968	59.9788 398 233	57.9538 394 627	228
58	64.5590 727 366	62.2459 773 503	60.0762 269 962	58.0383 597 664	232
59	64.6809 249 019	62.3514 517 356	60.1675 330 398	58.1174 077 449	236
60	64.7957 320 905	62.4505 836 452	60.2531 376 768	58.1913 377 076	240

TABLE 5. PRESENT WORTH OF ONE DOLLAR PER PERIOD
Payable at end of each period

QUARTERLY Compounding

QUARTERS	7% Nominal Annual Rate	7¼% Nominal Annual Rate	7½% Nominal Annual Rate	7¾% Nominal Annual Rate	QUARTERS
1	0.9828 009 828	0.9821 976 673	0.9815 950 920	0.9809 932 557	1
2	1.9486 987 546	1.9469 099 249	1.9451 240 167	1.9433 410 233	2
3	2.8979 840 340	2.8944 480 539	2.8909 192 802	2.8873 976 930	3
YEARS					
1	3.8309 425 396	3.8251 177 939	3.8193 072 689	3.8135 109 190	4
2	7.4050 529 661	7.3850 391 766	7.3651 062 626	7.3452 538 183	8
3	10.7395 496 884	10.6981 502 841	10.6569 834 586	10.6160 476 281	12
4	13.8504 967 672	13.7815 625 372	13.7131 227 078	13.6451 730 346	16
5	16.7528 813 048	16.6512 010 170	16.5504 056 785	16.4504 861 366	20
6	19.4606 856 454	19.3218 867 148	19.1845 051 091	19.0485 237 033	24
7	21.9869 547 364	21.8074 130 788	21.6299 713 815	21.4546 006 554	28
8	24.3438 589 722	24.1206 172 537	23.9003 128 956	23.6829 003 433	32
9	26.5427 528 258	26.2734 463 817	26.0080 706 875	25.7465 581 556	36
10	28.5942 295 493	28.2770 193 065	27.9648 877 047	27.6577 389 495	40
11	30.5081 722 075	30.1416 839 994	29.7815 731 195	29.4277 087 598	44
12	32.2938 012 895	31.8770 710 044	31.4681 620 379	31.0669 012 107	48
13	33.9597 191 294	33.4921 431 770	33.0339 709 316	32.5849 790 193	52
14	35.5139 513 477	34.9952 419 760	34.4876 491 011	33.9908 909 559	56
15	36.9639 855 154	36.3941 305 445	35.8372 264 532	35.2929 245 949	60
16	38.3168 072 254	37.6960 338 047	37.0901 578 566	36.4987 551 686	64
17	39.5789 337 463	38.9076 757 734	38.2533 643 223	37.6154 908 111	68
18	40.7564 454 191	40.0353 142 894	39.3332 712 334	38.6497 144 596	72
19	41.8550 149 496	41.0847 733 339	40.3358 438 386	39.6075 226 590	76
20	42.8799 347 370	42.0614 731 099	41.2666 202 031	40.4945 615 004	80
21	43.8361 423 702	42.9704 580 365	42.1307 418 000	41.3160 599 033	84
22	44.7282 444 147	43.8164 228 018	42.9329 819 114	42.0768 604 394	88
23	45.5605 386 049	44.6037 366 099	43.6777 719 949	42.7814 478 781	92
24	46.3370 345 488	45.3364 657 470	44.3692 261 625	43.4339 756 240	96
25	47.0614 730 442	46.0183 945 826	45.0111 639 064	44.0382 901 997	100
26	47.7373 441 002	46.6530 451 146	45.6071 311 974	44.5979 539 209	104
27	48.3679 037 506	47.2436 951 602	46.1604 200 720	45.1162 658 952	108
28	48.9561 897 397	47.7933 952 846	46.6740 868 175	45.5962 814 698	112
29	49.5050 361 569	48.3049 845 565	47.1509 688 542	46.0408 302 420	116
30	50.0170 870 901	48.7811 052 111	47.5937 004 090	46.4525 327 396	120
31	50.4948 093 635	49.2242 162 969	48.0047 270 668	46.8338 158 678	124
32	50.9405 044 217	49.6366 063 759	48.3863 192 790	47.1869 272 156	128
33	51.3563 194 172	50.0204 053 436	48.7405 849 053	47.5139 483 050	132
34	51.7442 575 540	50.3775 954 290	49.0694 808 576	47.8168 068 611	136
35	52.1061 877 383	50.7100 214 329	49.3748 239 092	48.0972 881 755	140
36	52.4438 535 822	51.0194 002 555	49.6583 007 308	48.3570 456 304	144
37	52.7588 818 033	51.3073 297 639	49.9214 772 070	48.5976 104 449	148
38	53.0527 900 617	51.5752 970 446	50.1658 070 865	48.8204 007 013	152
39	53.3269 942 712	51.8246 860 841	50.3926 400 118	49.0267 297 044	156
40	53.5828 154 207	52.0567 849 166	50.6032 289 752	49.2178 137 230	160
41	53.8214 859 380	52.2727 922 767	50.7987 372 393	49.3947 791 600	164
42	54.0441 556 272	52.4738 237 904	50.9802 447 634	49.5586 691 917	168
43	54.2518 972 076	52.6609 177 370	51.1487 541 687	49.7104 499 176	172
44	54.4457 114 820	52.8350 404 116	51.3051 962 765	49.8510 160 553	176
45	54.6265 321 579	52.9970 911 159	51.4504 352 503	49.9811 962 146	180
46	54.7952 303 454	53.1479 068 027	51.5852 733 691	50.1017 577 819	184
47	54.9526 187 543	53.2882 663 987	51.7104 554 590	50.2134 114 438	188
48	55.0994 556 090	53.4188 948 275	51.8266 730 076	50.3168 153 769	192
49	55.2364 483 016	53.5404 667 533	51.9345 679 839	50.4125 791 270	196
50	55.3642 567 993	53.6536 100 659	52.0347 363 839	50.5012 672 025	200
51	55.4834 968 244	53.7589 091 232	52.1277 315 233	50.5834 024 021	204
52	55.5947 428 199	53.8569 077 695	52.2140 670 937	50.6594 688 969	208
53	55.6985 307 177	53.9481 121 442	52.2942 200 003	50.7299 150 837	212
54	55.7953 605 197	54.0329 932 958	52.3686 329 961	50.7951 562 291	216
55	55.8856 987 071	54.1119 896 152	52.4377 171 275	50.8555 769 167	220
56	55.9699 804 874	54.1855 090 992	52.5018 540 053	50.9115 333 146	224
57	56.0486 118 912	54.2539 314 582	52.5613 979 124	50.9633 552 747	228
58	56.1219 717 281	54.3176 100 773	52.6166 777 605	51.0113 482 774	232
59	56.1904 134 120	54.3768 738 412	52.6679 989 074	51.0557 952 320	236
60	56.2542 666 631	54.4320 288 329	52.7156 448 439	51.0969 581 444	240

TABLE 5. PRESENT WORTH OF ONE DOLLAR PER PERIOD
Payable at end of each period

QUARTERS	8% Nominal Annual Rate	8¼% Nominal Annual Rate	8½% Nominal Annual Rate	8¾% Nominal Annual Rate	QUARTERS
1	0.9803 921 569	0.9797 917 942	0.9791 921 665	0.9785 932 722	1
2	1.9415 609 381	1.9397 837 543	1.9380 094 653	1.9362 380 645	2
3	2.8838 832 726	2.8803 759 993	2.8768 758 534	2.8733 828 154	3
YEARS					
1	3.8077 286 987	3.8019 605 627	3.7962 064 660	3.7904 663 637	4
2	7.3254 814 405	7.3057 887 280	7.2861 752 820	7.2666 407 062	8
3	10.5753 412 209	10.5348 626 778	10.4946 104 515	10.4545 830 068	12
4	13.5777 093 143	13.5107 273 841	13.4442 231 214	13.3781 924 435	16
5	16.3514 333 446	16.2532 383 601	16.1558 923 441	16.0593 865 596	20
6	18.9139 256 031	18.7806 941 406	18.6488 128 718	18.5182 655 732	24
7	21.2812 723 553	21.1099 583 725	20.9406 310 277	20.7732 630 638	28
8	23.4683 348 241	23.2565 723 327	23.0475 696 169	22.8412 841 639	32
9	25.4888 424 824	25.2348 586 220	24.9845 427 608	24.7378 322 923	36
10	27.3554 792 407	27.0580 167 282	26.7652 614 677	26.4771 253 795	40
11	29.0799 630 720	28.7382 110 954	28.4023 306 875	28.0722 024 553	44
12	30.6731 195 718	30.2866 522 878	29.9073 385 361	29.5350 213 999	48
13	32.1449 499 170	31.7136 717 881	31.2909 383 236	30.8765 485 880	52
14	33.5046 936 494	33.0287 909 311	32.5629 239 638	32.1068 411 019	56
15	34.7608 866 770	34.2407 844 324	33.7322 993 016	33.2351 221 260	60
16	35.9214 148 599	35.3577 389 341	34.8073 418 473	34.2698 500 910	64
17	36.9935 635 134	36.3871 069 609	35.7956 613 694	35.2187 820 846	68
18	37.9840 631 429	37.3357 566 445	36.7042 537 610	36.0890 320 045	72
19	38.8991 316 952	38.2100 175 489	37.5395 505 611	36.8871 238 889	76
20	39.7445 135 917	39.0157 229 028	38.3074 644 800	37.6190 408 261	80
21	40.5255 157 900	39.7582 485 196	39.0134 312 534	38.2902 698 079	84
22	41.2470 410 986	40.4425 486 660	39.6624 481 198	38.9058 428 643	88
23	41.9136 189 548	41.0731 891 176	40.2591 091 931	39.4703 747 870	92
24	42.5294 338 582	41.6543 776 228	40.8076 379 831	39.9880 977 259	96
25	43.0983 516 401	42.1899 919 777	41.3119 172 916	40.4628 929 157	100
26	43.6239 437 307	42.6836 058 991	41.7755 166 973	40.8983 197 731	104
27	44.1095 095 795	43.1385 128 693	42.2017 178 229	41.2976 425 804	108
28	44.5580 973 680	43.5577 481 108	42.5935 375 648	41.6638 549 576	112
29	44.9725 231 445	43.9441 088 379	42.9537 494 482	41.9997 023 038	116
30	45.3553 885 026	44.3001 729 198	43.2849 032 595	42.3077 023 798	120
31	45.7090 969 125	44.6283 160 813	43.5893 430 958	42.5901 641 823	124
32	46.0358 688 091	44.9307 277 535	43.8692 239 570	42.8492 052 544	128
33	46.3377 555 311	45.2094 256 824	44.1265 270 006	43.0867 675 600	132
34	46.6166 521 984	45.4662 693 915	44.3630 735 652	43.3046 320 422	136
35	46.8743 096 088	45.7029 725 891	44.5805 380 634	43.5044 319 745	140
36	47.1123 452 289	45.9211 146 020	44.7804 598 338	43.6876 652 054	144
37	47.3322 533 478	46.1221 509 138	44.9642 540 374	43.8557 053 869	148
38	47.5354 144 576	46.3074 228 754	45.1332 216 752	44.0098 122 729	152
39	47.7231 039 196	46.4781 666 552	45.2885 587 972	44.1511 411 627	156
40	47.8964 999 706	46.6355 214 870	45.4313 649 686	44.2807 515 624	160
41	48.0566 911 192	46.7805 372 710	45.5626 510 538	44.3996 151 277	164
42	48.2046 829 791	46.9141 815 789	45.6833 463 708	44.5086 229 479	168
43	48.3414 045 820	47.0373 461 101	45.7943 052 706	44.6085 922 264	172
44	48.4677 142 094	47.1508 526 408	45.8963 131 839	44.7002 724 071	176
45	48.5844 047 810	47.2554 585 074	45.9900 921 813	44.7843 507 925	180
46	48.6922 088 318	47.3518 616 592	46.0763 060 845	44.8614 576 966	184
47	48.7918 031 111	47.4407 053 158	46.1555 651 649	44.9321 711 697	188
48	48.8838 128 304	47.5225 822 583	46.2284 304 638	44.9970 213 326	192
49	48.9688 155 888	47.5980 387 846	46.2954 177 637	45.0564 943 500	196
50	49.0473 449 983	47.6675 783 544	46.3570 012 392	45.1110 360 759	200
51	49.1198 940 341	47.7316 649 485	46.4136 168 134	45.1610 553 954	204
52	49.1869 181 290	47.7907 261 644	46.4656 652 439	45.2069 272 904	208
53	49.2488 380 325	47.8451 560 692	46.5135 149 594	45.2489 956 507	212
54	49.3060 424 521	47.8953 178 292	46.5575 046 677	45.2875 758 518	216
55	49.3588 904 935	47.9415 461 330	46.5979 457 532	45.3229 571 195	220
56	49.4077 139 149	47.9841 494 241	46.6351 244 811	45.3554 046 980	224
57	49.4528 192 094	48.0234 119 596	46.6693 040 237	45.3851 618 385	228
58	49.4944 895 294	48.0595 957 062	46.7007 263 236	45.4124 516 224	232
59	49.5329 864 639	48.0929 420 885	46.7296 138 059	45.4374 786 343	236
60	49.5685 516 808	48.1236 735 997	46.7561 709 526	45.4604 304 952	240

TABLE 5. PRESENT WORTH OF ONE DOLLAR PER PERIOD
Payable at end of each period

QUARTERLY Compounding

QUARTERS	9% Nominal Annual Rate	9¼% Nominal Annual Rate	9½% Nominal Annual Rate	9¾% Nominal Annual Rate	QUARTERS
1	0.9779 951 100	0.9773 976 787	0.9768 009 768	0.9762 050 031	1
2	1.9344 695 453	1.9327 039 010	1.9309 411 251	1.9291 812 110	2
3	2.8698 968 658	2.8664 179 851	2.8629 461 539	2.8594 813 531	3
YEARS					
1	3.7847 402 110	3.7790 279 634	3.7733 295 765	3.7676 450 060	4
2	7.2471 846 066	7.2278 065 913	7.2085 062 708	7.1892 832 578	8
3	10.4147 788 202	10.3751 963 802	10.3358 341 868	10.2966 907 518	12
4	13.3126 313 069	13.2475 357 072	13.1829 016 785	13.1187 252 927	16
5	15.9637 123 700	15.8688 612 383	15.7748 247 258	15.6815 944 903	20
6	18.3890 362 382	18.2611 090 745	18.1344 685 006	18.0090 991 428	24
7	20.6078 276 392	20.4442 983 205	20.2826 490 763	20.1228 542 704	28
8	22.6376 741 868	22.4366 986 110	22.2383 170 611	22.0424 898 486	32
9	24.4946 657 928	24.2549 829 969	24.0187 247 745	23.7858 331 077	36
10	26.1935 222 057	25.9143 674 710	25.6395 784 422	25.3690 740 902	40
11	27.7477 096 897	27.4287 383 000	27.1151 767 517	26.8069 160 045	44
12	29.1695 477 666	28.8107 682 294	28.4585 369 910	28.1127 117 697	48
13	30.4703 068 693	30.0720 225 334	29.6815 098 833	29.2985 880 219	52
14	31.6602 976 782	31.2230 557 964	30.7948 841 308	30.3755 577 311	56
15	32.7489 528 506	32.2735 002 377	31.8084 815 887	31.3536 224 764	60
16	33.7449 017 904	33.2321 463 165	32.7312 439 116	32.2418 653 283	64
17	34.6560 390 501	34.1070 162 937	33.5713 114 334	33.0485 352 014	68
18	35.4895 869 088	34.9054 313 647	34.3360 949 790	33.7811 234 601	72
19	36.2521 526 203	35.6340 729 253	35.0323 412 407	34.4464 334 892	76
20	36.9497 807 868	36.2990 384 841	35.6661 922 954	35.0506 438 757	80
21	37.5880 012 723	36.9058 926 884	36.2432 397 880	35.5993 657 874	84
22	38.1718 730 363	37.4597 138 906	36.7685 742 593	36.0976 950 832	88
23	38.7060 242 341	37.9651 366 460	37.2468 300 533	36.5502 596 369	92
24	39.1946 889 028	38.4263 904 958	37.6822 261 999	36.9612 623 152	96
25	39.6417 405 229	38.8473 353 617	38.0786 036 339	37.3345 200 089	100
26	40.0507 227 226	39.2314 938 467	38.4394 590 790	37.6734 990 795	104
27	40.4248 773 664	39.5820 807 133	38.7679 758 941	37.9813 475 505	108
28	40.7671 702 523	39.9020 297 861	39.0670 521 566	38.2609 243 425	112
29	41.0803 146 211	40.1940 185 024	39.3393 262 281	38.5148 258 232	116
30	41.3667 926 630	40.4604 903 186	39.5872 000 292	38.7454 099 195	120
31	41.6288 751 932	40.7036 751 569	39.8128 602 286	38.9548 180 146	124
32	41.8686 396 518	40.9256 080 670	40.0182 975 332	39.1449 948 353	128
33	42.0879 865 712	41.1281 462 552	40.2053 242 497	39.3177 065 115	132
34	42.2886 546 408	41.3129 846 268	40.3755 902 720	39.4745 569 782	136
35	42.4722 344 888	41.4816 699 691	40.5305 976 361	39.6170 028 710	140
36	42.6401 812 911	41.6356 138 957	40.6717 137 708	39.7463 670 534	144
37	42.7938 263 055	41.7761 046 592	40.8001 835 605	39.8638 509 019	148
38	42.9343 874 245	41.9043 179 318	40.9171 403 273	39.9705 454 628	152
39	43.0629 788 288	42.0213 266 437	41.0236 158 289	40.0674 415 851	156
40	43.1806 198 193	42.1281 099 618	41.1205 493 606	40.1554 391 214	160
41	43.2882 428 965	42.2255 614 834	41.2087 960 408	40.2353 552 855	164
42	43.3867 011 526	42.3144 967 145	41.2891 343 557	40.3079 322 410	168
43	43.4767 750 329	42.3956 598 937	41.3622 730 257	40.3738 439 940	172
44	43.5591 785 229	42.4697 302 210	41.4288 572 584	40.4337 026 524	176
45	43.6345 648 073	42.5373 275 408	41.4894 744 401	40.4880 641 102	180
46	43.7035 314 480	42.5990 175 293	41.5446 593 174	40.5374 332 104	184
47	43.7666 251 202	42.6553 164 284	41.5948 987 149	40.5822 684 327	188
48	43.8243 459 464	42.7066 953 655	41.6406 358 295	40.6229 861 520	192
49	43.8771 514 601	42.7535 842 961	41.6822 741 405	40.6599 645 047	196
50	43.9254 602 329	42.7963 756 021	41.7201 809 685	40.6935 469 006	200
51	43.9696 551 922	42.8354 273 749	41.7546 907 163	40.7240 452 119	204
52	44.0100 866 567	42.8710 664 125	41.7861 078 187	40.7517 426 697	208
53	44.0470 751 128	42.9035 909 538	41.8147 094 279	40.7768 964 942	212
54	44.0809 137 558	42.9332 731 747	41.8407 478 587	40.7997 402 833	216
55	44.1118 708 131	42.9603 614 657	41.8644 528 145	40.8204 861 823	220
56	44.1401 916 710	42.9850 825 104	41.8860 334 133	40.8393 268 537	224
57	44.1661 008 194	43.0076 431 824	41.9056 800 327	40.8564 372 666	228
58	44.1898 036 314	43.0282 322 768	41.9235 659 893	40.8719 763 217	232
59	44.2114 879 912	43.0470 220 899	41.9398 490 677	40.8860 883 268	236
60	44.2313 257 835	43.0641 698 607	41.9546 729 123	40.8989 043 369	240

QUARTERLY
Compounding

TABLE 5. PRESENT WORTH OF ONE DOLLAR PER PERIOD
Payable at end of each period

QUARTERS	10% Nominal Annual Rate	10¼% Nominal Annual Rate	10½% Nominal Annual Rate	10¾% Nominal Annual Rate	QUARTERS
1	0.9756 097 561	0.9750 152 346	0.9744 214 373	0.9738 283 628	1
2	1.9274 241 523	1.9256 699 423	1.9239 185 747	1.9221 700 428	2
3	2.8560 235 632	2.8525 727 652	2.8491 289 400	2.8456 920 685	3
YEARS					
1	3.7619 742 080	3.7563 171 386	3.7506 737 540	3.7450 440 107	4
2	7.1701 371 675	7.1510 676 169	7.1320 742 257	7.1131 566 154	8
3	10.2577 645 982	10.2190 542 606	10.1805 582 849	10.1422 752 281	12
4	13.0550 026 599	12.9917 299 273	12.9289 032 789	12.8665 189 355	16
5	15.5891 622 856	15.4975 199 601	15.4066 594 553	15.3165 728 049	20
6	17.8849 858 326	17.7621 136 030	17.6404 676 863	17.5200 335 108	24
7	19.9648 886 553	19.8087 273 656	19.6543 459 123	19.5017 201 763	28
8	21.8491 779 586	21.6583 430 379	21.4699 473 830	21.2839 539 278	32
9	23.5562 510 680	23.3299 227 946	23.1067 934 731	22.8868 093 136	36
10	25.1027 750 521	24.8406 035 943	24.5824 835 768	24.3283 404 179	40
11	26.5038 494 527	26.2058 728 669	25.9128 843 369	25.6247 842 164	44
12	27.7731 537 094	27.4397 272 901	27.1123 002 426	26.7907 434 645	48
13	28.9230 807 191	28.5548 162 825	28.1936 274 321	27.8393 511 788	52
14	29.9648 578 351	29.5625 716 852	29.1684 923 521	28.7824 185 633	56
15	30.9086 564 851	30.4733 249 600	30.0473 767 650	29.6305 680 472	60
16	31.7636 914 805	31.2964 131 077	30.8397 304 495	30.3933 529 328	64
17	32.5383 109 860	32.0402 743 899	31.5540 728 046	31.0793 650 012	68
18	33.2400 780 265	32.7125 348 382	32.1980 844 502	31.6963 312 872	72
19	33.8758 443 293	33.3200 864 357	32.7786 898 094	32.2512 011 149	76
20	34.4518 172 213	33.8691 577 735	33.3021 315 600	32.7502 243 720	80
21	34.9736 202 342	34.3653 779 056	33.7740 377 557	33.1990 219 076	84
22	35.4463 480 101	34.8138 340 579	34.1994 823 390	33.6026 488 429	88
23	35.8746 160 436	35.2191 237 823	34.5830 396 968	33.9656 515 110	92
24	36.2626 057 446	35.5854 020 902	34.9288 338 435	34.2921 186 656	96
25	36.6141 052 645	35.9164 240 501	35.2405 827 632	34.5857 275 352	100
26	36.9325 464 811	36.2155 832 837	35.5216 383 850	34.8497 852 423	104
27	37.2210 385 067	36.4859 467 579	35.7750 226 233	35.0872 660 541	108
28	37.4823 980 433	36.7302 862 264	36.0034 598 692	35.3008 448 834	112
29	37.7191 768 839	36.9511 066 463	36.2094 062 836	35.4929 274 183	116
30	37.9336 868 273	37.1506 718 583	36.3950 762 055	35.6656 772 191	120
31	38.1280 222 489	37.3310 277 957	36.5624 659 606	35.8210 400 881	124
32	38.3040 805 493	37.4940 234 593	36.7133 753 263	35.9607 659 860	128
33	38.4635 806 801	37.6413 298 732	36.8494 268 823	36.0864 287 436	132
34	38.6080 799 265	37.7744 572 159	36.9720 834 570	36.1994 437 888	136
35	38.7389 891 119	37.8947 703 028	37.0826 638 559	36.3010 840 892	140
36	38.8575 863 728	38.0035 025 782	37.1823 570 410	36.3924 944 907	144
37	38.9650 296 378	38.1017 687 602	37.2722 349 150	36.4747 046 129	148
38	39.0623 679 330	38.1905 762 693	37.3532 638 463	36.5486 404 459	152
39	39.1505 516 243	38.2708 355 560	37.4263 150 590	36.6151 347 810	156
40	39.2304 416 963	38.3433 694 347	37.4921 740 010	36.6749 365 903	160
41	39.3028 181 586	38.4089 215 194	37.5515 487 886	36.7287 194 637	164
42	39.3683 876 612	38.4681 638 472	37.6050 778 204	36.7770 891 954	168
43	39.4277 903 944	38.5217 037 676	37.6533 366 414	36.8205 906 075	172
44	39.4816 063 389	38.5700 901 694	37.6968 441 313	36.8597 136 869	176
45	39.5303 609 284	38.6138 191 078	37.7360 680 831	36.8948 991 045	180
46	39.5745 301 803	38.6533 388 898	37.7714 302 335	36.9265 431 780	184
47	39.6145 453 425	38.6890 546 704	37.8033 107 968	36.9550 023 370	188
48	39.6507 971 045	38.7213 326 062	37.8320 525 532	36.9805 971 370	192
49	39.6836 394 117	38.7505 036 090	37.8579 645 347	37.0036 158 700	196
50	39.7133 929 210	38.7768 667 387	37.8813 253 473	37.0243 178 123	200
51	39.7403 481 320	38.8006 922 688	37.9023 861 667	37.0429 361 443	204
52	39.7647 682 227	38.8222 244 576	37.9213 734 392	37.0596 805 773	208
53	39.7868 916 197	38.8416 840 520	37.9384 913 162	37.0747 397 157	212
54	39.8069 343 255	38.8592 705 510	37.9539 238 495	37.0882 831 810	216
55	39.8250 920 277	38.8751 642 505	37.9678 369 699	37.1004 635 229	220
56	39.8415 420 097	38.8895 280 921	37.9803 802 714	37.1114 179 370	224
57	39.8564 448 815	38.9025 093 330	37.9916 886 198	37.1212 698 106	228
58	39.8699 461 478	38.9142 410 565	38.0018 836 027	37.1301 301 122	232
59	39.8821 776 288	38.9248 435 355	38.0110 748 366	37.1380 986 417	236
60	39.8932 587 468	38.9344 254 663	38.0193 611 459	37.1452 651 542	240

TABLE 5. PRESENT WORTH OF ONE DOLLAR PER PERIOD
Payable at end of each period

QUARTERLY Compounding

QUARTERS	11% Nominal Annual Rate	11¼% Nominal Annual Rate	11½% Nominal Annual Rate	11¾% Nominal Annual Rate	QUARTERS
1	0.9732 360 097	0.9726 443 769	0.9720 534 629	0.9714 632 665	1
2	1.9204 243 404	1.9186 814 608	1.9169 413 978	1.9152 041 448	2
3	2.8422 621 317	2.8388 391 108	2.8354 229 869	2.8320 137 411	3
YEARS					
1	3.7394 278 654	3.7338 252 750	3.7282 361 962	3.7226 605 864	4
2	7.0943 144 100	7.0755 472 354	7.0568 547 199	7.0382 364 937	8
3	10.1042 036 582	10.0663 421 544	10.0286 893 066	9.9912 437 159	12
4	12.8045 731 539	12.7430 622 266	12.6819 824 818	12.6213 302 823	16
5	15.2272 521 338	15.1386 896 566	15.0508 776 768	14.9638 085 855	20
6	17.4007 966 983	17.2827 430 609	17.1658 585 985	17.0501 294 964	24
7	19.3508 264 022	19.2016 411 928	19.0541 415 030	18.9083 046 339	28
8	21.1003 262 323	20.9190 284 714	20.7400 254 231	20.5632 824 581	32
9	22.6699 175 310	22.4560 663 241	22.2452 048 564	22.0372 832 362	36
10	24.0781 010 600	23.8316 939 361	23.5890 489 369	23.3500 973 791	40
11	25.3414 750 691	25.0628 616 158	24.7888 506 833	24.5193 511 540	44
12	26.4749 309 389	26.1647 396 549	25.8600 495 311	25.5607 433 399	48
13	27.4918 287 059	27.1509 052 545	26.8164 300 123	26.4882 560 049	52
14	28.4041 545 371	28.0335 098 217	27.6702 991 390	27.3143 422 340	56
15	29.2226 620 109	28.8234 286 977	28.4326 447 744	28.0500 933 279	60
16	29.9569 988 691	29.5303 951 625	29.1132 770 278	28.7053 877 185	64
17	30.6158 207 353	30.1631 203 670	29.7209 544 944	29.2890 236 003	68
18	31.2068 931 383	30.7294 006 708	30.2634 969 636	29.8088 370 572	72
19	31.7371 830 443	31.2362 137 077	30.7478 860 467	30.2718 072 727	76
20	32.2129 409 770	31.6898 043 635	31.1803 550 186	30.6841 502 346	80
21	32.6397 746 917	32.0957 617 247	31.5664 690 293	31.0514 021 928	84
22	33.0227 152 746	32.4590 879 461	31.9111 967 184	31.3784 939 907	88
23	33.3662 764 435	32.7842 598 874	32.2189 741 528	31.6698 172 687	92
24	33.6745 077 517	33.0752 842 758	32.4937 619 119	31.9292 834 272	96
25	33.9510 423 195	33.3357 470 769	32.7390 960 529	32.1603 761 427	100
26	34.1991 396 579	33.5688 576 801	32.9581 336 147	32.3661 981 407	104
27	34.4217 240 886	33.7774 884 447	33.1536 932 432	32.5495 128 540	108
28	34.6214 192 126	33.9642 100 924	33.3282 914 628	32.7127 815 250	112
29	34.8005 788 351	34.1313 233 837	33.4841 750 596	32.8581 962 518	116
30	34.9613 147 092	34.2808 874 672	33.6233 499 939	32.9877 094 195	120
31	35.1055 214 276	34.4147 452 526	33.7476 072 136	33.1030 599 137	124
32	35.2348 987 540	34.5345 461 185	33.8585 457 008	33.2057 964 675	128
33	35.3509 716 579	34.6417 662 359	33.9575 930 476	33.2972 984 550	132
34	35.4551 082 900	34.7377 267 576	34.0460 238 271	33.3787 944 115	136
35	35.5485 361 078	34.8236 100 967	34.1249 759 952	33.4513 785 281	140
36	35.6323 563 446	34.9004 744 970	34.1954 655 338	33.5160 253 425	144
37	35.7075 569 888	34.9692 670 717	34.2583 995 250	33.5736 028 238	148
38	35.7750 244 300	35.0308 354 743	34.3145 878 236	33.6248 840 260	152
39	35.8355 539 063	35.0859 383 428	34.3647 534 788	33.6705 574 668	156
40	35.8898 588 783	35.1352 546 477	34.4095 420 385	33.7112 363 729	160
41	35.9385 794 384	35.1793 920 583	34.4495 298 561	33.7474 669 122	164
42	35.9822 898 555	35.2188 944 300	34.4852 315 080	33.7797 355 278	168
43	36.0215 053 438	35.2542 485 062	34.5171 064 143	33.8084 754 684	172
44	36.0566 881 362	35.2858 899 152	34.5455 647 518	33.8340 726 059	176
45	36.0882 529 320	35.3142 085 385	34.5709 727 314	33.8568 706 156	180
46	36.1165 717 851	35.3395 533 145	34.5936 573 112	33.8771 755 911	184
47	36.1419 784 898	35.3622 365 384	34.6139 104 037	33.8952 601 534	188
48	36.1647 725 146	35.3825 377 100	34.6319 926 322	33.9113 671 118	192
49	36.1852 225 326	35.4007 069 776	34.6481 366 846	33.9257 127 234	196
50	36.2035 695 880	35.4169 682 207	34.6625 503 079	33.9384 895 972	200
51	36.2200 299 375	35.4315 218 084	34.6754 189 812	33.9498 692 796	204
52	36.2347 975 989	35.4445 470 679	34.6869 083 027	33.9600 045 577	208
53	36.2480 466 388	35.4562 044 950	34.6971 661 207	33.9690 315 112	212
54	36.2599 332 233	35.4666 377 310	34.7063 244 361	33.9770 713 389	216
55	36.2705 974 597	35.4759 753 328	34.7145 011 010	33.9842 319 861	220
56	36.2801 650 471	35.4843 323 573	34.7218 013 355	33.9906 095 939	224
57	36.2887 487 587	35.4918 117 785	34.7283 190 813	33.9962 897 901	228
58	36.2964 497 706	35.4985 057 571	34.7341 382 108	34.0013 488 390	232
59	36.3033 588 546	35.5044 967 752	34.7393 336 065	34.0058 546 650	236
60	36.3095 574 480	35.5098 586 536	34.7439 721 244	34.0098 677 646	240

TABLE 5. PRESENT WORTH OF ONE DOLLAR PER PERIOD
Payable at end of each period

QUARTERS	12% Nominal Annual Rate	12¼% Nominal Annual Rate	12½% Nominal Annual Rate	12¾% Nominal Annual Rate	QUARTERS
1	0.9708 737 864	0.9702 850 212	0.9696 969 697	0.9691 096 305	1
2	1.9134 696 955	1.9117 380 436	1.9100 091 827	1.9082 831 065	2
3	2.8286 113 549	2.8252 158 095	2.8218 270 863	2.8184 451 668	3
YEARS					
1	3.7170 984 028	3.7115 496 029	3.7060 141 443	3.7004 919 848	4
2	7.0196 921 895	7.0012 214 418	6.9828 238 874	6.9644 991 650	8
3	9.9540 039 936	9.9169 687 620	9.8801 366 537	9.8435 063 121	12
4	12.5611 020 260	12.5012 941 448	12.4419 031 047	12.3829 254 052	16
5	14.8774 748 605	14.7918 690 648	14.7069 838 462	14.6228 119 358	20
6	16.9355 421 220	16.8220 830 227	16.7097 389 232	16.5984 967 228	24
7	18.7641 082 277	18.6215 302 615	18.4805 490 426	18.3411 432 024	28
8	20.3887 655 288	20.2164 411 587	20.0462 764 323	19.8782 389 847	32
9	21.8322 524 981	21.6300 645 844	21.4306 723 267	21.2340 294 284	36
10	23.1147 719 742	22.8830 067 977	22.6547 372 596	22.4299 000 751	40
11	24.2542 739 174	23.9935 318 225	23.7370 396 314	23.4847 139 738	44
12	25.2667 066 350	24.9778 276 805	24.6939 973 814	24.4151 092 166	48
13	26.1662 399 915	25.8502 423 621	25.5401 270 390	25.2357 613 801	52
14	26.9654 637 279	26.6234 929 763	26.2882 639 316	25.9596 150 095	56
15	27.6755 636 661	27.3088 511 265	26.9497 568 896	26.5980 878 000	60
16	28.3064 782 639	27.9163 072 155	27.5346 404 021	27.1612 506 933	64
17	28.8670 377 124	28.4547 160 753	28.0517 868 343	27.6579 867 313	68
18	29.3650 875 220	28.9319 260 423	28.5090 410 167	28.0961 311 730	72
19	29.8075 983 270	29.3548 933 627	28.9133 392 470	28.4825 950 836	76
20	30.2007 634 458	29.7297 835 922	29.2708 145 098	28.8234 743 462	80
21	30.5500 855 616	30.0620 614 715	29.5868 895 107	29.1241 458 152	84
22	30.8604 537 370	30.3565 705 847	29.8663 589 358	29.3893 521 276	88
23	31.1362 118 409	30.6176 039 642	30.1134 621 847	29.6232 765 116	92
24	31.3812 193 446	30.8489 666 696	30.3319 476 793	29.8296 087 701	96
25	31.5989 053 383	31.0540 312 540	30.5251 297 260	30.0116 034 822	100
26	31.7923 165 242	31.2357 869 250	30.6959 387 915	30.1721 313 389	104
27	31.9641 598 578	31.3968 831 183	30.8469 659 566	30.3137 244 241	108
28	32.1168 404 340	31.5396 681 184	30.9805 022 214	30.4386 161 543	112
29	32.2524 951 484	31.6662 232 892	31.0985 732 585	30.5487 765 076	116
30	32.3730 226 051	31.7783 934 138	31.2029 701 414	30.6459 430 966	120
31	32.4801 096 893	31.8778 135 859	31.2952 765 142	30.7316 485 773	124
32	32.5752 551 767	31.9659 330 442	31.3768 926 144	30.8072 448 238	128
33	32.6597 907 098	32.0440 362 979	31.4490 565 139	30.8739 242 525	132
34	32.7348 994 361	32.1132 618 510	31.5128 628 999	30.9327 386 304	136
35	32.8016 325 666	32.1746 187 981	31.5692 796 807	30.9846 156 653	140
36	32.8609 240 888	32.2290 015 338	31.6191 626 680	31.0303 736 389	144
37	32.9136 038 382	32.2772 027 902	31.6632 685 599	31.0707 343 138	148
38	32.9604 091 133	32.3199 251 926	31.7022 664 186	31.1063 343 188	152
39	33.0019 949 940	32.3577 915 016	31.7367 478 206	31.1377 351 898	156
40	33.0389 435 103	32.3913 536 910	31.7672 358 300	31.1654 322 282	160
41	33.0717 717 886	32.4211 009 935	31.7941 929 333	31.1898 623 128	164
42	33.1009 392 886	32.4474 670 331	31.8180 280 552	31.2114 107 912	168
43	33.1268 542 345	32.4708 361 449	31.8391 027 615	31.2304 175 580	172
44	33.1498 793 284	32.4915 489 784	31.8577 367 440	31.2471 824 161	176
45	33.1703 368 261	32.5099 074 628	31.8742 126 703	31.2619 698 059	180
46	33.1885 130 478	32.5261 792 078	31.8887 804 710	31.2750 129 761	184
47	33.2046 623 853	32.5406 014 053	31.9016 611 318	31.2865 176 628	188
48	33.2190 108 626	32.5533 842 864	31.9130 500 455	31.2966 653 351	192
49	33.2317 592 988	32.5647 141 858	31.9231 199 755	31.3056 160 571	196
50	33.2430 861 192	32.5747 562 586	31.9320 236 773	31.3135 110 130	200
51	33.2531 498 525	32.5836 568 870	31.9398 962 153	31.3204 747 338	204
52	33.2620 913 492	32.5915 458 148	31.9468 570 114	31.3266 170 615	208
53	33.2700 357 531	32.5985 380 380	31.9530 116 572	31.3320 348 821	212
54	33.2770 942 532	32.6047 354 818	31.9584 535 155	31.3368 136 535	216
55	33.2833 656 390	32.6102 284 857	31.9632 651 361	31.3410 287 537	220
56	33.2889 376 841	32.6150 971 206	31.9675 195 087	31.3447 466 693	224
57	33.2938 883 740	32.6194 123 563	31.9712 811 700	31.3480 260 450	228
58	33.2982 869 979	32.6232 370 955	31.9746 071 822	31.3509 186 079	232
59	33.3021 951 182	32.6266 270 911	31.9775 479 991	31.3534 699 838	236
60	33.3056 674 325	32.6296 317 588	31.9801 482 314	31.3557 204 168	240

TABLE 5. PRESENT WORTH OF ONE DOLLAR PER PERIOD
Payable at end of each period

QUARTERLY Compounding

QUARTERS	13% Nominal Annual Rate	13¼% Nominal Annual Rate	13½% Nominal Annual Rate	13¾% Nominal Annual Rate	QUARTERS
1	0.9685 230 024	0.9679 370 841	0.9673 518 742	0.9667 673 716	1
2	1.9065 598 086	1.9048 392 828	1.9031 215 228	1.9014 065 224	2
3	2.8150 700 326	2.8117 016 652	2.8083 400 463	2.8049 851 576	3
YEARS					
1	3.6949 830 824	3.6894 873 952	3.6840 048 815	3.6785 354 998	4
2	6.9462 469 155	6.9280 667 819	6.9099 584 092	6.8919 214 444	8
3	9.8070 763 906	9.7708 455 531	9.7348 124 735	9.6989 758 359	12
4	12.3243 575 791	12.2661 961 921	12.2084 378 423	12.1510 791 602	16
5	14.5393 461 469	14.4565 793 744	14.3745 045 933	14.2931 148 582	20
6	16.4883 434 930	16.3792 664 752	16.2712 530 780	16.1642 908 752	24
7	18.2032 916 918	18.0669 737 755	17.9321 690 274	17.7988 573 252	28
8	19.7122 969 917	19.5484 191 603	19.3865 747 186	19.2267 334 069	32
9	21.0400 904 474	20.8488 107 788	20.6601 466 385	20.4740 550 467	36
10	22.2084 332 365	21.9902 759 850	21.7753 687 839	21.5636 532 919	40
11	23.2364 733 033	22.9922 378 544	22.7519 296 002	22.5154 722 119	44
12	24.1410 591 738	23.8717 456 853	23.6070 695 665	23.3469 339 552	48
13	24.9370 160 860	24.6437 651 088	24.3558 855 641	24.0732 576 455	52
14	25.6373 889 601	25.3214 327 420	25.0115 974 014	24.7077 379 538	56
15	26.2536 561 917	25.9162 797 201	25.5857 811 993	25.2619 884 442	60
16	26.7959 177 710	26.4384 279 091	26.0885 737 601	25.7461 541 497	64
17	27.2730 608 111	26.8967 621 384	26.5288 515 251	26.1690 972 675	68
18	27.6929 051 987	27.2990 813 844	26.9143 872 815	26.5385 593 727	72
19	28.0623 317 542	27.6522 314 774	27.2519 873 862	26.8613 031 212	76
20	28.3873 950 014	27.9622 215 897	27.5476 119 263	27.1432 360 331	80
21	28.6734 223 945	28.2343 264 867	27.8064 799 404	27.3895 186 248	84
22	28.9251 016 304	28.4731 762 823	28.0331 615 574	27.6046 588 670	88
23	29.1465 574 744	28.6828 352 246	28.2316 586 782	27.7925 946 992	92
24	29.3414 193 615	28.8668 708 523	28.4054 756 268	27.9567 661 098	96
25	29.5128 808 789	29.0284 147 000	28.5576 810 164	28.1001 781 017	100
26	29.6637 521 056	29.1702 155 844	28.6909 619 238	28.2254 556 962	104
27	29.7965 056 668	29.2946 863 772	28.8076 713 277	28.3348 919 818	108
28	29.9133 172 577	29.4039 450 629	28.9098 696 486	28.4304 900 866	112
29	30.0161 013 009	29.4998 507 781	28.9993 611 244	28.5139 998 437	116
30	30.1065 423 219	29.5840 354 464	29.0777 256 628	28.5869 498 206	120
31	30.1861 225 564	29.6579 315 469	29.1463 467 335	28.6506 752 979	124
32	30.2561 462 433	29.7227 964 894	29.2064 357 920	28.7063 427 103	128
33	30.3177 609 992	29.7797 340 103	29.2590 536 675	28.7549 709 976	132
34	30.3719 766 270	29.8297 129 536	29.3051 292 908	28.7974 502 545	136
35	30.4196 816 654	29.8735 837 569	29.3454 760 939	28.8345 580 240	140
36	30.4616 579 512	29.9120 929 220	29.3808 063 706	28.8669 735 287	144
37	30.4985 934 329	29.9458 957 176	29.4117 438 515	28.8952 901 039	148
38	30.5310 934 452	29.9755 673 292	29.4388 347 156	28.9200 260 578	152
39	30.5596 906 302	30.0016 126 464	29.4625 572 327	28.9416 341 589	156
40	30.5848 536 664	30.0244 748 542	29.4833 302 067	28.9605 099 230	160
41	30.6069 949 504	30.0445 429 740	29.5015 203 695	28.9769 988 531	164
42	30.6264 773 551	30.0621 584 832	29.5174 488 555	28.9914 027 637	168
43	30.6436 201 772	30.0776 211 258	29.5313 968 705	29.0039 853 047	172
44	30.6587 043 701	30.0911 940 128	29.5436 106 568	29.0149 767 878	176
45	30.6719 771 483	30.1031 080 993	29.5543 058 400	29.0245 784 015	180
46	30.6836 560 390	30.1135 661 144	29.5636 712 358	29.0329 658 945	184
47	30.6939 324 474	30.1227 460 109	29.5718 721 835	29.0402 927 918	188
48	30.7029 747 932	30.1308 039 930	29.5790 534 651	29.0466 932 055	192
49	30.7109 312 713	30.1378 771 747	29.5853 418 609	29.0522 842 891	196
50	30.7179 322 802	30.1440 859 127	29.5908 483 879	29.0571 683 821	200
51	30.7240 925 593	30.1495 358 543	29.5956 702 600	29.0614 348 832	204
52	30.7295 130 693	30.1543 197 352	29.5998 926 038	29.0651 618 867	208
53	30.7342 826 467	30.1585 189 577	29.6035 899 618	29.0684 176 118	212
54	30.7384 794 602	30.1622 049 752	29.6068 276 082	29.0712 616 517	216
55	30.7421 722 911	30.1654 405 088	29.6096 627 013	29.0737 460 636	220
56	30.7454 216 612	30.1682 806 140	29.6121 452 926	29.0759 163 226	224
57	30.7482 808 244	30.1707 736 178	29.6143 192 105	29.0778 121 530	228
58	30.7507 966 394	30.1729 619 410	29.6162 228 340	29.0794 682 563	232
59	30.7530 103 378	30.1748 828 199	29.6178 897 702	29.0809 149 459	236
60	30.7549 581 999	30.1765 689 399	29.6193 494 475	29.0821 787 021	240

QUARTERLY
Compounding

TABLE 5. PRESENT WORTH OF ONE DOLLAR PER PERIOD
Payable at end of each period

QUARTERS	14% Nominal Annual Rate	14¼% Nominal Annual Rate	14½% Nominal Annual Rate	14¾% Nominal Annual Rate	QUARTERS
1	0.9661 835 749	0.9656 004 828	0.9650 180 941	0.9644 364 075	1
2	1.8996 942 752	1.8979 847 752	1.8962 780 160	1.8945 739 915	2
3	2.8016 369 809	2.7982 954 981	2.7949 606 910	2.7916 325 416	3
YEARS					
1	3.6730 792 086	3.6676 359 668	3.6622 057 331	3.6567 884 669	4
2	6.8739 555 367	6.8560 603 370	6.8382 354 986	6.8204 806 765	8
3	9.6633 343 346	9.6278 866 735	9.5926 315 665	9.5575 677 374	12
4	12.0941 168 081	12.0375 474 799	11.9813 679 006	11.9255 748 262	16
5	14.2124 033 020	14.1323 631 348	14.0529 876 434	13.9742 701 901	20
6	16.0583 676 030	15.9534 711 579	15.8495 895 946	15.7467 111 234	24
7	17.6670 188 458	17.5366 340 603	17.4076 837 295	17.2801 488 990	28
8	19.0688 654 684	18.9129 416 399	18.7589 331 433	18.6068 116 766	32
9	20.2904 938 121	20.1094 215 162	19.9307 974 981	19.7545 818 395	36
10	21.3550 723 373	21.1495 698 926	20.9470 910 500	20.7475 819 968	40
11	22.2827 910 189	22.0538 129 697	21.8284 665 942	21.6066 819 668	44
12	23.0912 442 535	22.8399 080 701	22.5928 351 652	22.3499 373 961	48
13	23.7957 645 412	23.5232 923 531	23.2557 300 188	22.9929 692 349	52
14	24.4097 132 702	24.1173 859 660	23.8306 222 941	23.5492 920 403	56
15	24.9447 341 182	24.6338 555 859	24.3291 947 696	24.0305 980 118	60
16	25.4109 738 780	25.0828 435 273	24.7615 792 771	24.4470 027 249	64
17	25.8172 748 928	25.4731 669 147	25.1365 625 976	24.8072 577 297	68
18	26.1713 427 543	25.8124 908 313	25.4617 650 232	25.1189 344 818	72
19	26.4798 924 403	26.1074 788 439	25.7437 952 145	25.3885 834 706	76
20	26.7487 756 660	26.3639 238 611	25.9883 844 997	25.6218 718 910	80
21	26.9830 918 632	26.5868 618 925	26.2005 033 446	25.8237 027 503	84
22	27.1872 848 921	26.7806 709 452	26.3844 623 612	25.9983 179 141	88
23	27.3652 273 200	26.9491 569 980	26.5439 999 063	26.1493 872 576	92
24	27.5202 938 659	27.0956 287 420	26.6823 580 513	26.2800 857 954	96
25	27.6554 254 020	27.2229 625 566	26.8023 484 667	26.3931 604 097	100
26	27.7731 847 289	27.3336 589 947	26.9064 095 595	26.4909 875 823	104
27	27.8758 051 790	27.4298 918 881	26.9966 560 263	26.5756 233 403	108
28	27.9652 329 727	27.5135 510 367	27.0749 218 272	26.6488 464 679	112
29	28.0431 641 285	27.5862 793 202	27.1427 974 550	26.7121 958 905	116
30	28.1110 766 284	27.6495 049 602	27.2016 622 567	26.7670 030 189	120
31	28.1702 584 487	27.7044 695 678	27.2527 124 642	26.8144 197 308	124
32	28.2218 319 860	27.7522 525 254	27.2969 855 035	26.8554 425 800	128
33	28.2667 753 442	27.7937 921 843	27.3353 810 773	26.8909 337 411	132
34	28.3059 408 844	27.8299 042 907	27.3686 794 484	26.9216 391 294	136
35	28.3400 713 901	27.8612 980 063	27.3975 572 956	26.9482 040 780	140
36	28.3698 141 539	27.8885 898 337	27.4226 014 654	26.9711 869 008	144
37	28.3957 332 543	27.9123 157 237	27.4443 208 975	26.9910 706 260	148
38	28.4183 202 529	27.9329 416 001	27.4631 569 673	27.0082 731 487	152
39	28.4380 035 172	27.9508 725 091	27.4794 924 555	27.0231 560 132	156
40	28.4551 563 450	27.9664 605 740	27.4936 593 266	27.0360 320 115	160
41	28.4701 040 434	27.9800 119 096	27.5059 454 754	27.0471 717 578	164
42	28.4831 300 990	27.9917 926 340	27.5166 005 769	27.0568 093 753	168
43	28.4944 815 539	28.0020 340 945	27.5258 411 610	27.0651 474 172	172
44	28.5043 736 911	28.0109 374 106	27.5338 550 117	27.0723 611 236	176
45	28.5129 941 171	28.0186 774 236	27.5408 049 839	27.0786 021 044	180
46	28.5205 063 204	28.0254 061 301	27.5468 323 129	27.0840 015 259	184
47	28.5270 527 715	28.0312 556 670	27.5520 594 841	27.0886 728 674	188
48	28.5327 576 255	28.0363 409 061	27.5565 927 224	27.0927 143 062	192
49	28.5377 290 762	28.0407 617 102	27.5605 241 508	27.0962 107 809	196
50	28.5420 614 082	28.0446 048 942	27.5639 336 627	27.0992 357 767	200
51	28.5458 367 853	28.0479 459 295	27.5668 905 449	27.1018 528 698	204
52	28.5491 268 083	28.0508 504 268	27.5694 548 863	27.1041 170 633	208
53	28.5519 938 733	28.0533 754 238	27.5716 787 988	27.1060 759 438	212
54	28.5544 923 548	28.0555 705 058	27.5736 074 758	27.1077 706 808	216
55	28.5566 696 371	28.0574 787 795	27.5752 801 113	27.1092 368 927	220
56	28.5585 670 128	28.0591 377 190	27.5767 306 962	27.1105 053 945	224
57	28.5602 204 661	28.0605 799 023	27.5779 887 088	27.1116 028 464	228
58	28.5616 613 552	28.0618 336 506	27.5790 797 140	27.1125 523 133	232
59	28.5629 170 067	28.0629 235 847	27.5800 258 828	27.1133 737 503	236
60	28.5640 112 345	28.0638 711 085	27.5808 464 430	27.1140 844 214	240

TABLE 5. PRESENT WORTH OF ONE DOLLAR PER PERIOD
Payable at end of each period

QUARTERLY Compounding

QUARTERS	15% Nominal Annual Rate	15¼% Nominal Annual Rate	15½% Nominal Annual Rate	15¾% Nominal Annual Rate	QUARTERS
1	0.9638 554 217	0.9632 751 355	0.9626 955 475	0.9621 166 566	1
2	1.8928 726 956	1.8911 741 221	1.8894 782 648	1.8877 851 176	2
3	2.7883 110 319	2.7849 961 441	2.7816 878 602	2.7783 861 625	3
YEARS					
1	3.6513 841 271	3.6459 926 734	3.6406 140 652	3.6352 482 622	4
2	6.8027 955 276	6.7851 797 111	6.7676 328 879	6.7501 547 209	8
3	9.5226 939 194	9.4880 088 555	9.4535 112 983	9.4192 000 095	12
4	11.8701 650 431	11.8151 353 682	11.7604 826 483	11.7062 037 596	16
5	13.8962 042 118	13.8187 832 190	13.7420 007 949	13.6658 505 948	20
6	15.6448 241 082	15.5439 170 644	15.4439 786 567	15.3449 976 967	24
7	17.1540 108 946	17.0292 513 180	16.9058 520 425	16.7837 952 081	28
8	18.4565 494 056	18.3081 189 552	18.1614 934 019	18.0166 462 648	32
9	19.5807 353 499	19.4092 195 524	19.2399 966 695	19.0730 296 097	36
10	20.5509 899 925	20.3572 633 449	20.1663 513 882	19.9782 044 608	40
11	21.3883 906 701	21.1735 257 600	20.9620 217 313	20.7538 144 842	44
12	22.1111 286 648	21.8763 248 663	21.6454 438 394	21.4184 053 174	48
13	22.7349 043 829	22.4814 324 577	22.2324 529 971	21.9878 680 142	52
14	23.2732 684 227	23.0024 279 938	22.7366 505 453	22.4758 190 162	56
15	23.7379 159 409	23.4510 033 421	23.1697 190 319	22.8939 257 364	60
16	24.1389 407 126	23.8372 251 602	23.5416 929 035	23.2521 855 385	64
17	24.4850 544 036	24.1697 608 051	23.8611 910 095	23.5591 647 848	68
18	24.7837 758 182	24.4560 728 413	24.1356 163 051	23.8222 036 663	72
19	25.0415 942 341	24.7025 865 107	24.3713 273 828	24.0475 917 146	76
20	25.2641 103 723	24.9148 339 245	24.5737 858 043	24.2407 181 909	80
21	25.4561 580 645	25.0975 782 111	24.7476 826 479	24.4062 009 489	84
22	25.6219 092 606	25.2549 204 077	24.8970 472 039	24.5479 968 524	88
23	25.7649 646 584	25.3903 914 928	25.0253 403 351	24.6694 963 880	92
24	25.8884 319 234	25.5070 316 270	25.1355 346 674	24.7736 047 351	96
25	25.9949 931 980	25.6074 583 777	25.2301 834 670	24.8628 112 321	100
26	26.0869 633 671	25.6939 254 614	25.3114 798 013	24.9392 488 984	104
27	26.1663 403 456	25.7683 733 205	25.3813 073 532	25.0047 454 376	108
28	26.2348 484 801	25.8324 726 687	25.4412 840 674	25.0608 669 397	112
29	26.2939 760 078	25.8876 619 851	25.4927 996 388	25.1089 553 279	116
30	26.3450 073 862	25.9351 797 949	25.5370 477 131	25.1501 604 451	120
31	26.3890 511 958	25.9760 924 643	25.5750 535 437	25.1854 675 484	124
32	26.4270 642 230	26.0113 181 306	25.6076 977 475	25.2157 208 670	128
33	26.4598 722 440	26.0416 473 071	25.6357 367 095	25.2416 437 892	132
34	26.4881 879 642	26.0677 606 228	25.6598 201 088	25.2638 561 586	136
35	26.5126 265 005	26.0902 440 969	25.6805 059 716	25.2828 890 962	140
36	26.5337 187 436	26.1096 022 901	25.6982 736 012	25.2991 976 990	144
37	26.5519 228 912	26.1262 696 273	25.7135 346 838	25.3131 719 227	148
38	26.5676 344 013	26.1406 201 468	25.7266 428 276	25.3251 459 054	152
39	26.5811 945 828	26.1529 758 942	25.7379 017 558	25.3354 059 573	156
40	26.5928 980 107	26.1636 141 499	25.7475 723 443	25.3441 974 069	160
41	26.6029 989 244	26.1727 736 511	25.7558 786 662	25.3517 304 669	164
42	26.6117 167 513	26.1806 599 498	25.7630 131 837	25.3581 852 605	168
43	26.6192 408 731	26.1874 500 257	25.7691 412 078	25.3637 161 284	172
44	26.6257 347 403	26.1932 962 574	25.7744 047 282	25.3684 553 196	176
45	26.6313 394 222	26.1983 298 427	25.7789 257 039	25.3725 161 529	180
46	26.6361 766 725	26.2026 637 421	25.7828 088 883	25.3759 957 270	184
47	26.6403 515 730	26.2063 952 145	25.7861 442 572	25.3789 772 422	188
48	26.6439 548 173	26.2096 079 992	25.7890 090 929	25.3815 319 896	192
49	26.6470 646 806	26.2123 741 957	25.7914 697 754	25.3837 210 558	196
50	26.6497 487 198	26.2147 558 813	25.7935 833 201	25.3855 967 837	200
51	26.6520 652 419	26.2168 065 044	25.7953 986 990	25.3872 040 238	204
52	26.6540 645 698	26.2185 720 837	25.7969 579 755	25.3885 812 069	208
53	26.6557 901 359	26.2200 922 414	25.7982 972 790	25.3897 612 629	212
54	26.6572 794 256	26.2214 010 918	25.7994 476 418	25.3907 724 082	216
55	26.6585 647 915	26.2225 280 076	25.8004 357 186	25.3916 388 203	220
56	26.6596 741 562	26.2234 982 781	25.8012 844 036	25.3923 812 160	224
57	26.6606 316 190	26.2243 336 776	25.8020 133 614	25.3930 173 467	228
58	26.6614 579 794	26.2250 529 537	25.8026 394 824	25.3935 624 230	232
59	26.6621 711 888	26.2256 722 480	25.8031 772 741	25.3940 294 782	236
60	26.6627 867 407	26.2262 054 582	25.8036 391 975	25.3944 296 801	240

QUARTERLY
Compounding

TABLE 5. PRESENT WORTH OF ONE DOLLAR PER PERIOD
Payable at end of each period

QUARTERS	16% Nominal Annual Rate	16¼% Nominal Annual Rate	16½% Nominal Annual Rate	16¾% Nominal Annual Rate	QUARTERS
1	0.9615 384 615	0.9609 609 610	0.9603 841 537	0.9598 080 384	1
2	1.8860 946 746	1.8844 069 295	1.8827 218 763	1.8810 395 090	2
3	2.7750 910 332	2.7718 024 547	2.7685 204 094	2.7652 448 796	3
YEARS					
1	3.6298 952 243	3.6245 549 115	3.6192 272 839	3.6139 123 020	4
2	6.7327 448 750	6.7154 030 167	6.6981 288 149	6.6809 219 399	8
3	9.3850 737 605	9.3511 313 318	9.3173 715 133	9.2837 931 037	12
4	11.6522 956 079	11.5987 551 278	11.5455 792 829	11.4927 650 649	16
5	13.5903 263 450	13.5154 218 416	13.4411 309 504	13.3674 476 054	20
6	15.2469 631 414	15.1498 640 905	15.0536 897 850	14.9584 296 047	24
7	16.6630 632 180	16.5436 387 337	16.4255 046 712	16.3086 441 971	28
8	17.8735 514 984	17.7321 834 847	17.5925 170 254	17.4545 273 348	32
9	18.9082 819 537	18.7457 179 411	18.5853 024 579	18.4270 010 236	36
10	19.7927 738 834	19.6100 119 387	19.4298 718 502	19.2523 077 624	40
11	20.5488 412 919	20.3470 407 686	20.1483 528 383	19.9527 187 051	44
12	21.1951 308 814	20.9755 439 139	20.7595 695 541	20.5471 346 544	48
13	21.7475 819 311	21.5115 015 151	21.2795 358 160	21.0515 961 059	52
14	22.2198 194 037	21.9685 406 762	21.7218 746 896	21.4797 161 056	56
15	22.6234 899 745	22.3582 819 437	22.0981 754 102	21.8430 476 022	60
16	22.9685 492 702	22.6906 347 670	22.4182 970 202	22.1513 952 069	64
17	23.2635 074 023	22.9740 494 536	22.6906 266 744	22.4130 797 738	68
18	23.5156 388 498	23.2157 320 239	22.9222 993 834	22.6351 629 407	72
19	23.7311 618 678	23.4218 274 294	23.1193 849 496	22.8236 376 894	76
20	23.9153 918 468	23.5975 757 928	23.2870 469 957	22.9835 900 686	80
21	24.0728 724 050	23.7474 456 415	23.4296 782 508	23.1193 364 420	84
22	24.2074 874 462	23.8752 475 231	23.5510 156 401	23.2345 399 667	88
23	24.3225 569 476	23.9842 308 916	23.6542 381 913	23.3323 094 451	92
24	24.4209 188 396	24.0771 667 269	23.7420 503 252	23.4152 832 164	96
25	24.5049 989 972	24.1564 179 887	23.8167 527 112	23.4857 003 529	100
26	24.5768 710 682	24.2239 996 969	23.8803 025 446	23.5454 610 827	104
27	24.6383 076 158	24.2816 301 647	23.9343 648 246	23.5961 780 672	108
28	24.6908 238 341	24.3307 746 876	23.9803 559 779	23.6392 199 197	112
29	24.7357 149 176	24.3726 828 002	24.0194 809 682	23.6757 481 377	116
30	24.7740 880 039	24.4084 200 463	24.0527 648 664	23.7067 484 463	120
31	24.8068 894 790	24.4388 950 706	24.0810 797 074	23.7330 573 983	124
32	24.8349 283 173	24.4648 827 225	24.1051 673 373	23.7553 849 488	128
33	24.8588 960 338	24.4870 437 565	24.1256 588 497	23.7743 336 135	132
34	24.8793 837 383	24.5059 416 327	24.1430 911 201	23.7904 147 280	136
35	24.8968 967 140	24.5220 568 430	24.1579 208 724	23.8040 622 459	140
36	24.9118 668 790	24.5357 991 282	24.1705 366 446	23.8156 444 498	144
37	24.9246 634 388	24.5475 178 957	24.1812 689 688	23.8254 738 889	148
38	24.9356 019 918	24.5575 111 034	24.1903 990 307	23.8338 158 136	152
39	24.9449 523 127	24.5660 328 359	24.1981 660 372	23.8408 953 334	156
40	24.9529 450 062	24.5732 997 642	24.2047 734 830	23.8469 034 912	160
41	24.9597 771 941	24.5794 966 551	24.2103 944 825	23.8520 024 190	164
42	24.9656 173 769	24.5847 810 691	24.2151 763 055	23.8563 297 129	168
43	24.9706 095 897	24.5892 873 661	24.2192 442 352	23.8600 021 463	172
44	24.9748 769 541	24.5931 301 219	24.2227 048 509	23.8631 188 208	176
45	24.9785 247 151	24.5964 070 414	24.2256 488 205	23.8657 638 410	180
46	24.9816 428 364	24.5992 014 426	24.2281 532 757	23.8680 085 834	184
47	24.9843 082 196	24.6015 843 750	24.2302 838 329	23.8699 136 232	188
48	24.9865 866 004	24.6036 164 265	24.2320 963 126	23.8715 303 684	192
49	24.9885 341 698	24.6053 492 634	24.2336 382 015	23.8729 024 474	196
50	24.9901 989 603	24.6068 269 443	24.2349 498 970	23.8740 668 862	200
51	24.9916 220 302	24.6080 870 404	24.2360 657 654	23.8750 551 074	204
52	24.9928 384 763	24.6091 615 904	24.2370 150 423	23.8758 937 785	208
53	24.9938 782 995	24.6100 779 155	24.2378 225 987	23.8766 055 314	212
54	24.9947 671 448	24.6108 593 140	24.2385 095 925	23.8772 095 729	216
55	24.9955 269 334	24.6115 256 535	24.2390 940 228	23.8777 222 032	220
56	24.9961 764 039	24.6120 938 762	24.2395 912 017	23.8781 572 559	224
57	24.9967 315 741	24.6125 784 294	24.2400 141 552	23.8785 264 709	228
58	24.9972 061 358	24.6129 916 334	24.2403 739 647	23.8788 398 117	232
59	24.9976 117 932	24.6133 439 941	24.2406 800 570	23.8791 057 338	236
60	24.9979 585 508	24.6136 444 706	24.2409 404 519	23.8793 314 132	240

TABLE 5. PRESENT WORTH OF ONE DOLLAR PER PERIOD
Payable at end of each period

QUARTERS	17% Nominal Annual Rate	17¼% Nominal Annual Rate	17½% Nominal Annual Rate	17¾% Nominal Annual Rate	QUARTERS
1	0.9592 326 139	0.9586 578 790	0.9580 838 323	0.9575 104 728	1
2	1.8793 598 215	1.8776 828 079	1.8760 084 621	1.8743 367 782	2
3	2.7619 758 480	2.7587 132 969	2.7554 572 092	2.7522 075 674	3
YEARS					
1	3.6086 099 261	3.6033 201 169	3.5980 428 352	3.5927 780 418	4
2	6.6637 820 642	6.6467 088 621	6.6297 020 097	6.6127 611 848	8
3	9.2503 949 110	9.2171 757 521	9.1841 344 529	9.1512 698 480	12
4	11.4403 094 940	11.3882 096 179	11.3364 625 121	11.2850 652 793	16
5	13.2943 658 082	13.2218 796 273	13.1499 831 971	13.0786 707 172	20
6	14.8640 730 666	14.7706 098 228	14.6780 296 587	14.5863 224 910	24
7	16.1930 407 243	16.0786 779 082	15.9655 396 430	15.8536 100 578	28
8	17.3181 900 320	17.1834 811 341	17.0503 770 491	16.9188 545 689	32
9	18.2707 797 789	18.1166 054 734	17.9644 454 540	17.8142 676 530	36
10	19.0772 747 211	18.9047 286 542	18.7346 263 531	18.5669 254 539	40
11	19.7600 808 230	19.5703 828 677	19.3835 697 080	19.1995 873 787	44
12	20.3381 677 377	20.1325 989 562	19.9303 600 510	19.7313 843 129	48
13	20.8275 958 198	20.6074 504 988	20.3910 777 343	20.1783 971 142	52
14	21.2419 623 129	21.0085 133 501	20.7792 718 320	20.5541 428 766	56
15	21.5927 791 068	21.3472 537 696	21.1063 585 987	20.8699 836 704	60
16	21.8897 925 596	21.6333 562 381	21.3819 572 069	21.1354 701 162	64
17	22.1412 542 705	21.8750 003 342	21.6141 726 326	21.3586 301 839	68
18	22.3541 503 243	22.0790 945 858	21.8098 340 124	21.5462 119 480	72
19	22.5343 953 785	22.2514 739 826	21.9746 954 787	21.7038 876 403	76
20	22.6869 969 839	22.3970 667 967	22.1136 053 804	21.8364 251 718	80
21	22.8161 947 033	22.5200 354 805	22.2306 488 668	21.9478 323 076	84
22	22.9255 778 954	22.6238 956 694	22.3292 680 262	22.0414 778 565	88
23	23.0181 854 334	22.7116 166 933	22.4123 631 123	22.1201 935 400	92
24	23.0965 901 310	22.7857 064 684	22.4823 778 374	22.1863 596 195	96
25	23.1629 702 199	22.8482 831 977	22.5413 712 384	22.2419 768 722	100
26	23.2191 698 652	22.9011 359 300	22.5910 782 301	22.2887 270 928	104
27	23.2667 504 001	22.9457 757 082	22.6329 606 268	22.3280 239 478	108
28	23.3070 337 024	22.9834 787 693	22.6682 501 323	22.3610 557 239	112
29	23.3411 389 190	23.0153 230 318	22.6979 845 623	22.3888 212 596	116
30	23.3700 135 575	23.0422 189 131	22.7230 383 657	22.4121 601 492	120
31	23.3944 598 105	23.0649 353 579	22.7441 483 402	22.4317 781 306	124
32	23.4151 568 414	23.0841 218 221	22.7619 353 014	22.4482 684 266	128
33	23.4326 796 530	23.1003 268 406	22.7769 223 392	22.4621 296 825	132
34	23.4475 150 625	23.1140 137 097	22.7895 502 018	22.4737 810 449	136
35	23.4600 752 257	23.1255 737 328	22.8001 902 573	22.4835 748 362	140
36	23.4707 090 879	23.1353 374 070	22.8091 554 152	22.4918 072 079	144
37	23.4797 120 781	23.1435 838 729	22.8167 093 283	22.4987 270 966	148
38	23.4873 343 163	23.1505 488 943	22.8230 741 470	22.5045 437 507	152
39	23.4937 875 630	23.1564 315 988	22.8284 370 516	22.5094 330 583	156
40	23.4992 511 015	23.1614 001 711	22.8329 557 580	22.5135 428 660	160
41	23.5038 767 194	23.1655 966 612	22.8367 631 551	22.5169 974 490	164
42	23.5077 929 252	23.1691 410 454	22.8399 712 131	22.5199 012 695	168
43	23.5111 085 184	23.1721 346 564	22.8426 742 767	22.5223 421 352	172
44	23.5139 156 127	23.1746 630 807	22.8449 518 393	22.5243 938 549	176
45	23.5162 921 943	23.1767 986 051	22.8468 708 807	22.5261 184 699	180
46	23.5183 042 893	23.1786 022 836	22.8484 878 375	22.5275 681 303	184
47	23.5200 077 975	23.1801 256 827	22.8498 502 620	22.5287 866 720	188
48	23.5214 500 456	23.1814 123 560	22.8509 982 213	22.5298 109 423	192
49	23.5226 711 020	23.1824 990 891	22.8519 654 753	22.5306 719 136	196
50	23.5237 048 900	23.1834 169 512	22.8527 804 696	22.5313 956 206	200
51	23.5245 801 301	23.1841 921 839	22.8534 671 721	22.5320 039 474	204
52	23.5253 211 382	23.1848 469 506	22.8540 457 778	22.5325 152 890	208
53	23.5259 485 009	23.1853 999 711	22.8545 333 026	22.5329 451 076	212
54	23.5264 796 475	23.1858 670 559	22.8549 440 840	22.5333 064 004	216
55	23.5269 293 344	23.1862 615 590	22.8552 902 025	22.5336 100 925	220
56	23.5273 100 546	23.1865 947 590	22.8555 818 370	22.5338 653 670	224
57	23.5276 323 853	23.1868 761 820	22.8558 275 640	22.5340 799 433	228
58	23.5279 052 815	23.1871 138 737	22.8560 346 100	22.5342 603 098	232
59	23.5281 363 247	23.1873 146 298	22.8562 090 640	22.5344 119 206	236
60	23.5283 319 337	23.1874 841 898	22.8563 560 565	22.5345 393 601	240

QUARTERLY
Compounding

TABLE 5. PRESENT WORTH OF ONE DOLLAR PER PERIOD
Payable at end of each period

QUARTERS	18% Nominal Annual Rate	18¼% Nominal Annual Rate	18½% Nominal Annual Rate	18¾% Nominal Annual Rate	QUARTERS
1	0.9569 377 990	0.9563 658 099	0.9557 945 042	0.9552 238 806	1
2	1.8726 677 503	1.8710 013 723	1.8693 376 384	1.8676 765 427	2
3	2.7489 643 543	2.7457 275 527	2.7424 971 454	2.7392 731 154	3
YEARS					
1	3.5875 256 979	3.5822 857 647	3.5770 582 035	3.5718 429 759	4
2	6.5958 860 674	6.5790 763 388	6.5623 316 827	6.5456 517 841	8
3	9.1185 807 808	9.0860 661 032	9.0537 246 761	9.0215 553 687	12
4	11.2340 150 491	11.1833 089 780	11.1329 442 489	11.0829 180 707	16
5	13.0079 364 515	12.9377 747 274	12.8681 799 355	12.7991 465 280	20
6	14.4954 783 660	14.4054 874 578	14.3163 400 661	14.2280 266 153	24
7	15.7428 735 126	15.6333 145 951	15.5249 181 170	15.4176 691 102	28
8	16.7888 908 627	16.6604 634 698	16.5335 502 940	16.4081 295 963	32
9	17.6660 405 772	17.5197 332 959	17.3753 154 308	17.2327 571 450	36
10	18.4015 844 203	18.2385 625 252	18.0778 198 341	17.9193 171 883	40
11	19.0183 830 536	18.8399 050 199	18.6641 026 521	18.4909 263 877	44
12	19.5356 065 444	19.3429 630 221	19.1533 914 611	18.9668 309 791	48
13	19.9693 301 697	19.7638 003 250	19.5617 328 473	19.3630 547 984	52
14	20.3330 340 357	20.1158 552 266	19.9025 186 666	19.6929 388 083	56
15	20.6380 220 382	20.4103 696 457	20.1869 252 405	19.9675 902 925	60
16	20.8937 731 874	20.6567 481 014	20.4242 798 918	20.1962 568 403	64
17	21.1082 362 147	20.8628 580 219	20.6223 668 406	20.3866 377 162	68
18	21.2880 766 190	21.0352 809 684	20.7876 824 943	20.5451 430 954	72
19	21.4388 838 301	21.1795 228 002	20.9256 485 012	20.6771 098 969	76
20	21.5653 449 276	21.3001 894 892	21.0407 895 578	20.7869 814 784	80
21	21.6713 903 155	21.4011 341 987	21.1368 817 999	20.8784 572 457	84
22	21.7603 158 784	21.4855 803 244	21.2170 766 431	20.9546 172 125	88
23	21.8348 854 179	21.5562 244 244	21.2840 041 363	21.0180 257 054	92
24	21.8974 165 512	21.6153 223 263	21.3398 592 158	21.0708 177 056	96
25	21.9498 527 423	21.6647 611 615	21.3864 736 901	21.1147 707 337	100
26	21.9938 237 052	21.7061 196 251	21.4253 763 151	21.1513 647 003	104
27	22.0306 960 549	21.7407 183 874	21.4578 429 310	21.1818 317 339	108
28	22.0616 157 820	21.7696 622 661	21.4849 383 043	21.2071 976 678	112
29	22.0875 438 699	21.7938 755 056	21.5075 510 477	21.2283 165 799	116
30	22.1092 861 622	21.8141 312 899	21.5264 227 627	21.2458 995 496	120
31	22.1275 184 080	21.8310 764 326	21.5421 723 612	21.2605 386 002	124
32	22.1428 072 645	21.8452 520 309	21.5553 163 628	21.2727 266 325	128
33	22.1556 279 086	21.8571 107 440	21.5662 858 347	21.2828 740 209	132
34	22.1663 788 051	21.8670 312 479	21.5754 405 287	21.2913 224 306	136
35	22.1753 940 913	21.8753 303 269	21.5830 806 798	21.2983 563 219	140
36	22.1829 539 619	21.8822 729 895	21.5894 568 525	21.3042 125 278	144
37	22.1892 933 771	21.8880 809 310	21.5947 781 578	21.3090 882 283	148
38	22.1946 093 656	21.8929 396 121	21.5992 191 121	21.3131 475 897	152
39	22.1990 671 481	21.8970 041 817	21.6029 253 596	21.3165 272 915	156
40	22.2028 052 721	21.9004 044 308	21.6060 184 494	21.3193 411 295	160
41	22.2059 399 185	21.9032 489 371	21.6085 998 217	21.3216 838 461	164
42	22.2085 685 117	21.9056 285 322	21.6107 541 345	21.3236 343 214	168
43	22.2107 727 484	21.9076 192 020	21.6125 520 401	21.3252 582 283	172
44	22.2126 211 361	21.9092 845 132	21.6140 525 020	21.3266 102 443	176
45	22.2141 711 225	21.9106 776 429	21.6153 047 292	21.3277 358 920	180
46	22.2154 708 812	21.9118 430 771	21.6163 497 892	21.3286 730 724	184
47	22.2165 608 086	21.9128 180 306	21.6172 219 556	21.3294 533 405	188
48	22.2174 747 796	21.9136 336 359	21.6179 498 317	21.3301 029 683	192
49	22.2182 412 004	21.9143 159 373	21.6185 572 887	21.3306 438 287	196
50	22.2188 838 912	21.9148 867 221	21.6190 642 487	21.3310 941 329	200
51	22.2194 228 269	21.9153 642 168	21.6194 873 378	21.3314 690 425	204
52	22.2198 747 575	21.9157 636 689	21.6198 404 314	21.3317 811 810	208
53	22.2202 537 291	21.9160 978 339	21.6201 351 097	21.3320 410 581	212
54	22.2205 715 199	21.9163 773 823	21.6203 810 366	21.3322 574 239	216
55	22.2208 380 071	21.9166 112 408	21.6205 862 777	21.3324 375 636	220
56	22.2210 614 729	21.9168 068 771	21.6207 575 639	21.3325 875 424	224
57	22.2212 488 627	21.9169 705 382	21.6209 005 127	21.3327 124 103	228
58	22.2214 060 006	21.9171 074 503	21.6210 198 122	21.3328 163 715	232
59	22.2215 377 703	21.9172 219 852	21.6211 193 749	21.3329 029 265	236
60	22.2216 482 673	21.9173 178 004	21.6212 024 661	21.3329 749 896	240

TABLE 5. PRESENT WORTH OF ONE DOLLAR PER PERIOD
Payable at end of each period

QUARTERLY Compounding

QUARTERS	19% Nominal Annual Rate	19¼% Nominal Annual Rate	19½% Nominal Annual Rate	19¾% Nominal Annual Rate	QUARTERS
1	0.9546 539 379	0.9540 846 750	0.9535 160 906	0.9529 481 834	1
2	1.8660 180 792	1.8643 622 421	1.8627 090 256	1.8610 584 238	2
3	2.7360 554 455	2.7328 441 189	2.7296 391 186	2.7264 404 277	3
YEARS					
1	3.5666 400 435	3.5614 493 681	3.5562 709 116	3.5511 046 362	4
2	6.5290 363 299	6.5124 850 090	6.4959 975 119	6.4795 735 307	8
3	8.9895 570 585	8.9577 286 316	8.9260 689 826	8.8945 770 139	12
4	11.0332 276 785	10.9838 703 328	10.9348 433 196	10.8861 439 501	16
5	12.7306 690 187	12.6627 419 819	12.5953 600 518	12.5285 179 214	20
6	14.1405 376 518	14.0538 638 431	13.9679 959 754	13.8829 249 526	24
7	15.3115 528 236	15.2065 547 194	15.1026 604 702	14.9998 559 552	28
8	16.2841 799 892	16.1616 804 303	16.0406 102 161	15.9209 489 764	32
9	17.0920 291 325	16.9531 026 079	16.8159 492 963	16.6805 414 238	36
10	17.7630 161 884	17.6088 791 785	17.4568 692 304	17.3069 501 283	40
11	18.3203 277 024	18.1522 590 872	17.9866 740 247	17.8235 269 668	44
12	18.7832 220 622	18.6025 065 319	18.4246 275 118	18.2495 293 965	48
13	19.1676 949 880	18.9755 839 280	18.7866 537 882	18.6008 383 531	52
14	19.4870 322 784	19.2847 178 167	19.0859 162 181	18.8905 502 757	56
15	19.7522 689 134	19.5408 677 796	19.3332 960 571	19.1294 653 291	60
16	19.9725 703 772	19.7531 149 834	19.5377 880 971	19.3264 900 225	64
17	20.1555 493 799	19.9289 841 306	19.7068 277 187	19.4889 692 354	68
18	20.3075 289 214	20.0747 102 291	19.8465 612 442	19.6229 600 269	72
19	20.4337 607 877	20.1954 596 393	19.9620 694 190	19.7334 574 369	76
20	20.5386 070 316	20.2955 132 345	20.0575 521 486	19.8245 806 961	80
21	20.6256 907 070	20.3784 181 686	20.1364 812 086	19.8997 267 866	84
22	20.6980 210 664	20.4471 136 322	20.2017 264 790	19.9616 970 777	88
23	20.7580 975 490	20.5040 350 539	20.2556 602 938	20.0128 017 589	92
24	20.8079 961 501	20.5512 004 427	20.3002 436 999	20.0549 459 603	96
25	20.8494 411 596	20.5902 819 315	20.3370 977 608	20.0897 007 748	100
26	20.8838 647 462	20.6226 650 582	20.3675 624 992	20.1183 618 264	104
27	20.9124 564 470	20.6494 978 870	20.3927 456 206	20.1419 975 699	108
28	20.9362 042 734	20.6717 317 098	20.4135 627 893	20.1614 891 215	112
29	20.9559 288 522	20.6901 547 721	20.4307 709 229	20.1775 631 066	116
30	20.9723 117 835	20.7054 202 182	20.4449 957 132	20.1908 187 467	120
31	20.9859 191 939	20.7180 692 469	20.4567 543 771	20.2017 501 987	124
32	20.9972 212 995	20.7285 502 986	20.4664 744 625	20.2107 649 759	128
33	21.0066 086 542	20.7372 349 530	20.4745 093 941	20.2181 991 400	132
34	21.0144 056 465	20.7444 311 032	20.4811 513 241	20.2243 298 290	136
35	21.0208 817 082	20.7503 938 711	20.4866 417 546	20.2293 855 889	140
36	21.0262 606 254	20.7553 346 518	20.4911 803 189	20.2335 548 931	144
37	21.0307 282 711	20.7594 286 087	20.4949 320 405	20.2369 931 690	148
38	21.0344 390 288	20.7628 208 828	20.4980 333 329	20.2398 285 921	152
39	21.0375 211 270	20.7656 317 390	20.5005 969 598	20.2421 668 641	156
40	21.0400 810 703	20.7679 608 291	20.5027 161 353	20.2440 951 533	160
41	21.0422 073 197	20.7698 907 255	20.5044 679 131	20.2456 853 443	164
42	21.0439 733 498	20.7714 898 477	20.5059 159 883	20.2469 967 180	168
43	21.0454 401 872	20.7728 148 888	20.5071 130 133	20.2480 781 609	172
44	21.0466 585 197	20.7739 128 248	20.5081 025 123	20.2489 699 882	176
45	21.0476 704 479	20.7748 225 803	20.5089 204 636	20.2497 054 462	180
46	21.0485 109 399	20.7755 764 085	20.5095 966 081	20.2503 119 521	184
47	21.0492 090 397	20.7762 010 345	20.5101 555 307	20.2508 121 159	188
48	21.0497 888 705	20.7767 186 029	20.5106 175 539	20.2512 245 830	192
49	21.0502 704 691	20.7771 474 628	20.5109 994 769	20.2515 647 299	196
50	21.0506 704 775	20.7775 028 184	20.5113 151 866	20.2518 452 368	200
51	21.0510 027 183	20.7777 972 678	20.5115 761 623	20.2520 765 609	204
52	21.0512 786 724	20.7780 412 502	20.5117 918 932	20.2522 673 255	208
53	21.0515 078 756	20.7782 434 153	20.5119 702 231	20.2524 246 423	212
54	21.0516 982 482	20.7784 109 303	20.5121 176 363	20.2525 543 758	216
55	21.0518 563 688	20.7785 497 342	20.5122 394 927	20.2526 613 624	220
56	21.0519 877 014	20.7786 647 478	20.5123 402 232	20.2527 495 904	224
57	21.0520 967 841	20.7787 600 487	20.5124 234 901	20.2528 223 489	228
58	21.0521 873 866	20.7788 390 155	20.5124 923 212	20.2528 823 502	232
59	21.0522 626 396	20.7789 044 478	20.5125 492 192	20.2529 318 312	236
60	21.0523 251 436	20.7789 586 653	20.5125 962 529	20.2529 726 363	240

QUARTERLY
Compounding

TABLE 5. PRESENT WORTH OF ONE DOLLAR PER PERIOD
Payable at end of each period

	20% Nominal Annual Rate	20¼% Nominal Annual Rate	20½% Nominal Annual Rate	20¾% Nominal Annual Rate	
QUARTERS					QUARTERS
1	0.9523 809 524	0.9518 143 962	0.9512 485 137	0.9506 833 036	1
2	1.8594 104 308	1.8577 650 410	1.8561 222 484	1.8544 820 474	2
3	2.7232 480 294	2.7200 619 070	2.7168 820 437	2.7137 084 230	3
YEARS					
1	3.5459 505 042	3.5408 084 778	3.5356 785 196	3.5305 605 923	4
2	6.4632 127 594	6.4469 148 938	6.4306 796 312	6.4145 066 708	8
3	8.8632 516 364	8.8320 917 692	8.8010 963 391	8.7702 642 811	12
4	10.8377 695 602	10.7897 175 104	10.7419 851 858	10.6945 699 954	16
5	12.4622 103 425	12.3964 321 245	12.3311 781 336	12.2664 432 925	20
6	13.7986 417 943	13.7151 376 343	13.6324 037 187	13.5504 314 050	24
7	14.8981 272 571	14.7974 606 593	14.6978 426 421	14.5992 598 801	28
8	15.8026 766 684	15.6857 735 706	15.5702 202 779	15.4559 976 951	32
9	16.5468 517 076	16.4148 533 464	16.2845 200 116	16.1558 258 379	36
10	17.1590 863 540	17.0132 430 722	16.8693 861 164	16.7274 819 744	40
11	17.6627 733 128	17.5043 693 877	17.3482 724 218	17.1944 405 296	44
12	18.0771 578 203	17.9074 596 270	17.7403 828 410	17.5758 766 383	48
13	18.4180 729 801	18.2382 945 586	18.0614 414 704	17.8874 535 512	52
14	18.6985 447 258	18.5098 261 942	18.3243 231 447	18.1419 658 284	56
15	18.9292 895 251	18.7326 848 530	18.5395 697 332	18.3498 647 341	60
16	19.1191 238 425	18.9155 953 330	18.7158 128 813	18.5196 874 063	64
17	19.2753 010 052	19.0657 184 822	18.8601 201 498	18.6584 074 244	68
18	19.4037 883 435	19.1889 315 421	18.9782 784 328	18.7717 211 721	72
19	19.5094 951 947	19.2900 582 385	19.0750 260 185	18.8642 817 528	76
20	19.5964 604 828	19.3730 576 278	19.1542 426 006	18.9398 900 638	80
21	19.6680 070 405	19.4411 790 920	19.2191 048 590	19.0016 508 768	84
22	19.7268 685 706	19.4970 895 501	19.2722 138 475	19.0521 003 308	88
23	19.7752 940 971	19.5429 778 668	19.3156 993 002	19.0933 100 767	92
24	19.8151 338 976	19.5806 405 454	19.3513 050 356	19.1269 723 471	96
25	19.8479 102 000	19.6115 520 598	19.3804 588 862	19.1544 694 457	100
26	19.8748 753 452	19.6369 225 791	19.4043 299 564	19.1769 305 103	104
27	19.8970 596 368	19.6577 453 459	19.4238 755 045	19.1952 778 797	108
28	19.9153 107 085	19.6748 355 603	19.4398 793 304	19.2102 649 681	112
29	19.9303 259 103	19.6888 622 952	19.4529 832 067	19.2225 072 039	116
30	19.9426 789 539	19.7003 746 898	19.4637 126 144	19.2325 073 007	120
31	19.9528 418 336	19.7098 234 481	19.4724 978 156	19.2406 759 014	124
32	19.9612 028 598	19.7175 784 842	19.4796 911 074	19.2473 484 407	128
33	19.9680 814 967	19.7239 434 034	19.4855 809 494	19.2527 989 189	132
34	19.9737 405 683	19.7291 673 890	19.4904 035 313	19.2572 511 538	136
35	19.9783 963 006	19.7334 549 573	19.4943 522 443	19.2608 879 715	140
36	19.9822 265 830	19.7369 739 643	19.4975 854 366	19.2638 587 140	144
37	19.9853 777 659	19.7398 621 772	19.5002 327 631	19.2662 853 714	148
38	19.9879 702 518	19.7422 326 680	19.5024 003 847	19.2682 675 918	152
39	19.9901 030 964	19.7441 782 402	19.5041 752 256	19.2698 867 728	156
40	19.9918 577 929	19.7457 750 619	19.5056 284 591	19.2712 094 044	160
41	19.9933 013 861	19.7470 856 479	19.5068 183 615	19.2722 897 988	164
42	19.9944 890 337	19.7481 613 068	19.5077 926 495	19.2731 723 213	168
43	19.9954 661 144	19.7490 441 502	19.5085 903 930	19.2738 932 118	172
44	19.9962 699 611	19.7497 687 409	19.5092 435 826	19.2744 820 727	176
45	19.9969 312 878	19.7503 634 462	19.5097 784 119	19.2749 630 850	180
46	19.9974 753 629	19.7508 515 485	19.5102 163 283	19.2753 560 010	184
47	19.9979 229 748	19.7512 521 569	19.5105 748 927	19.2756 769 552	188
48	19.9982 912 262	19.7515 809 548	19.5108 684 839	19.2759 391 274	192
49	19.9985 941 876	19.7518 508 145	19.5111 088 754	19.2761 532 833	196
50	19.9988 434 346	19.7520 723 010	19.5113 057 071	19.2763 282 171	200
51	19.9990 484 908	19.7522 540 853	19.5114 668 722	19.2764 711 121	204
52	19.9992 171 910	19.7524 032 841	19.5115 988 336	19.2765 878 361	208
53	19.9993 559 811	19.7525 257 385	19.5117 068 832	19.2766 831 825	212
54	19.9994 701 641	19.7526 262 425	19.5117 953 538	19.2767 610 663	216
55	19.9995 641 027	19.7527 087 309	19.5118 677 932	19.2768 246 859	220
56	19.9996 413 862	19.7527 764 329	19.5119 271 063	19.2768 766 537	224
57	19.9997 049 675	19.7528 319 991	19.5119 756 717	19.2769 191 037	228
58	19.9997 572 761	19.7528 776 049	19.5120 154 368	19.2769 537 791	232
59	19.9998 003 104	19.7529 150 357	19.5120 479 964	19.2769 821 038	236
60	19.9998 357 149	19.7529 457 569	19.5120 746 561	19.2770 052 408	240

TABLE 5. PRESENT WORTH OF ONE DOLLAR PER PERIOD
Payable at end of each period

QUARTERLY Compounding

QUARTERS	21% Nominal Annual Rate	21¼% Nominal Annual Rate	21½% Nominal Annual Rate	21¾% Nominal Annual Rate	QUARTERS
1	0.9501 187 648	0.9495 548 961	0.9489 916 963	0.9484 291 642	1
2	1.8528 444 322	1.8512 093 969	1.8495 769 360	1.8479 470 437	2
3	2.7105 410 282	2.7073 798 428	2.7042 248 503	2.7010 760 343	3
YEARS					
1	3.5254 546 586	3.5203 606 816	3.5152 786 243	3.5102 084 499	4
2	6.3983 957 133	6.3823 464 613	6.3663 586 189	6.3504 318 920	8
3	8.7395 945 382	8.7090 860 612	8.6787 378 084	8.6485 487 463	12
4	10.6474 693 722	10.6006 807 727	10.5542 016 769	10.5080 295 879	16
5	12.2022 225 795	12.1385 110 279	12.0753 037 253	12.0125 958 129	20
6	13.4692 121 601	13.3887 375 587	13.3089 992 822	13.2299 891 168	24
7	14.5016 992 389	14.4051 477 724	14.3095 927 195	14.2150 215 015	28
8	15.3430 870 327	15.2314 698 005	15.1211 278 031	15.0120 431 343	32
9	16.0287 454 143	15.9032 537 760	15.7793 263 952	15.6569 391 733	36
10	16.5874 977 753	16.4494 012 759	16.3131 608 475	16.1787 454 631	40
11	17.0428 326 903	16.8934 087 285	16.7461 292 946	16.6009 558 468	44
12	17.4138 913 190	17.2543 782 797	17.0972 899 876	16.9425 799 544	48
13	17.7162 720 532	17.5478 396 082	17.3821 001 930	17.2189 990 939	52
14	17.9626 862 350	17.7864 180 452	17.6130 965 849	17.4426 587 798	56
15	18.1634 925 105	17.9803 777 431	17.8004 470 803	17.6236 290 818	60
16	18.3271 322 815	18.1380 632 609	17.9523 984 067	17.7700 580 194	64
17	18.4604 845 614	18.2662 585 655	18.0756 391 034	17.8885 384 194	68
18	18.5691 551 519	18.3704 788 917	18.1755 939 355	17.9844 047 516	72
19	18.6577 122 973	18.4552 080 200	18.2566 626 794	18.0619 733 085	76
20	18.7298 787 222	18.5240 911 777	18.3224 137 900	18.1247 365 424	80
21	18.7886 881 255	18.5800 918 651	18.3757 414 765	18.1755 203 094	84
22	18.8366 127 099	18.6256 193 509	18.4189 930 978	18.2166 111 015	88
23	18.8756 671 069	18.6626 323 245	18.4540 724 885	18.2498 589 933	92
24	18.9074 930 673	18.6927 231 628	18.4825 237 607	18.2767 609 404	96
25	18.9334 284 763	18.7171 864 377	18.5055 992 725	18.2985 281 778	100
26	18.9545 635 946	18.7370 746 115	18.5243 147 533	18.3161 407 552	104
27	18.9717 868 906	18.7532 433 158	18.5394 940 147	18.3303 916 624	108
28	18.9858 223 892	18.7663 881 625	18.5518 052 119	18.3419 225 335	112
29	18.9972 601 084	18.7770 746 710	18.5617 902 549	18.3512 525 350	116
30	19.0065 808 616	18.7857 625 976	18.5698 886 617	18.3588 017 417	120
31	19.0141 764 705	18.7928 257 155	18.5764 569 051	18.3649 100 495	124
32	19.0203 662 357	18.7985 678 951	18.5817 841 037	18.3698 524 794	128
33	19.0254 103 597	18.8032 361 770	18.5861 047 482	18.3738 515 596	132
34	19.0295 208 851	18.8070 314 007	18.5896 090 232	18.3770 873 450	136
35	19.0328 706 083	18.8101 168 449	18.5924 511 787	18.3797 055 239	140
36	19.0356 003 434	18.8126 252 519	18.5947 563 197	18.3818 239 773	144
37	19.0378 248 417	18.8146 645 387	18.5966 259 129	18.3835 380 866	148
38	19.0396 376 157	18.8163 224 399	18.5981 422 536	18.3849 250 280	152
39	19.0411 148 700	18.8176 702 817	18.5993 720 874	18.3860 472 473	156
40	19.0423 187 046	18.8187 660 513	18.6003 695 488	18.3869 552 713	160
41	19.0432 997 259	18.8196 568 910	18.6011 785 436	18.3876 899 829	164
42	19.0440 991 734	18.8203 811 266	18.6018 346 819	18.3882 844 619	168
43	19.0447 506 542	18.8209 699 162	18.6023 668 453	18.3887 654 741	172
44	19.0452 815 547	18.8214 485 909	18.6027 984 585	18.3891 546 767	176
45	19.0457 141 928	18.8218 377 443	18.6031 485 200	18.3894 695 932	180
46	19.0460 667 554	18.8221 541 185	18.6034 324 387	18.3897 244 023	184
47	19.0463 540 636	18.8224 113 247	18.6036 627 120	18.3899 305 766	188
48	19.0465 881 949	18.8226 204 284	18.6038 494 760	18.3900 973 989	192
49	19.0467 789 917	18.8227 904 257	18.6040 009 517	18.3902 323 802	196
50	19.0469 344 746	18.8229 286 303	18.6041 238 067	18.3903 415 980	200
51	19.0470 611 797	18.8230 409 879	18.6042 234 486	18.3904 299 696	204
52	19.0471 644 335	18.8231 323 325	18.6043 042 636	18.3905 014 740	208
53	19.0472 485 763	18.8232 065 940	18.6043 698 089	18.3905 593 305	212
54	19.0473 171 455	18.8232 669 671	18.6044 229 696	18.3906 061 440	216
55	19.0473 730 235	18.8233 160 493	18.6044 660 859	18.3906 440 224	220
56	19.0474 185 592	18.8233 559 521	18.6045 010 555	18.3906 746 710	224
57	19.0474 556 669	18.8233 883 924	18.6045 294 177	18.3906 994 698	228
58	19.0474 859 064	18.8234 147 657	18.6045 524 210	18.3907 195 353	232
59	19.0475 105 490	18.8234 362 067	18.6045 710 779	18.3907 357 710	236
60	19.0475 306 307	18.8234 536 379	18.6045 862 096	18.3907 489 078	240

QUARTERLY
Compounding

TABLE 5. PRESENT WORTH OF ONE DOLLAR PER PERIOD
Payable at end of each period

QUARTERS	22% Nominal Annual Rate	22¼% Nominal Annual Rate	22½% Nominal Annual Rate	22¾% Nominal Annual Rate	QUARTERS
1	0.9478 672 986	0.9473 060 983	0.9467 455 621	0.9461 856 889	1
2	1.8463 197 143	1.8446 949 421	1.8430 727 215	1.8414 530 469	2
3	2.6979 333 785	2.6947 968 664	2.6916 664 819	2.6885 422 088	3
YEARS					
1	3.5051 501 218	3.5001 036 035	3.4950 688 586	3.4900 458 510	4
2	6.3345 659 879	6.3187 606 158	6.3030 154 864	6.2873 303 121	8
3	8.6185 178 487	8.5886 440 972	8.5589 264 808	8.5293 639 960	12
4	10.4621 620 317	10.4165 965 571	10.3713 307 353	10.3263 621 597	16
5	11.9503 824 849	11.8886 589 882	11.8274 206 210	11.7666 627 329	20
6	13.1516 989 525	13.0741 207 812	12.9972 466 958	12.9210 688 882	24
7	14.1214 217 191	14.0287 811 497	13.9370 877 446	13.8463 296 264	28
8	14.9041 981 727	14.7975 755 760	14.6921 582 769	14.5879 294 780	32
9	15.5360 684 322	15.4166 909 069	15.2987 837 372	15.1823 244 601	36
10	16.0461 246 854	15.9152 686 540	15.7861 480 738	15.6587 342 032	40
11	16.4578 506 329	16.3167 766 726	16.1776 977 401	16.0405 783 475	44
12	16.7902 027 114	16.6401 137 850	16.4922 696 726	16.3466 278 199	48
13	17.0584 828 739	16.9004 993 399	16.7449 975 108	16.5919 275 867	52
14	17.2750 431 129	17.1101 895 815	16.9480 396 567	16.7885 362 433	56
15	17.4498 541 638	17.2790 545 458	17.1111 641 992	16.9461 187 976	60
16	17.5909 645 710	17.4150 426 392	17.2422 188 444	17.0724 217 889	64
17	17.7048 712 543	17.5245 547 669	17.3475 084 579	17.1736 540 964	68
18	17.7968 186 363	17.6127 456 212	17.4320 983 835	17.2547 921 595	72
19	17.8710 401 025	17.6837 663 103	17.5000 581 309	17.3198 246 127	76
20	17.9309 529 127	17.7409 597 497	17.5546 571 534	17.3719 483 608	80
21	17.9793 155 363	17.7870 180 118	17.5985 221 379	17.4137 257 347	84
22	18.0183 546 558	17.8241 090 405	17.6337 633 706	17.4472 104 520	88
23	18.0498 676 867	17.8539 786 958	17.6620 762 608	17.4740 485 750	92
24	18.0753 055 329	17.8780 329 305	17.6848 229 040	17.4955 594 282	96
25	18.0958 393 882	17.8974 039 677	17.7030 976 113	17.5128 004 555	100
26	18.1124 146 600	17.9130 035 945	17.7177 795 545	17.5266 192 016	104
27	18.1257 944 970	17.9255 660 790	17.7295 750 626	17.5376 949 770	108
28	18.1365 949 254	17.9356 827 325	17.7390 516 019	17.5465 722 513	112
29	18.1453 132 121	17.9438 297 417	17.7466 650 760	17.5536 874 189	116
30	18.1523 507 590	17.9503 905 830	17.7527 817 592	17.5593 902 518	120
31	18.1580 315 847	17.9556 740 728	17.7576 959 171	17.5639 610 930	124
32	18.1626 172 424	17.9599 289 027	17.7616 439 632	17.5676 246 389	128
33	18.1663 188 620	17.9633 553 459	17.7648 158 328	17.5705 609 843	132
34	18.1693 068 714	17.9661 146 836	17.7673 641 203	17.5729 144 759	136
35	18.1717 188 425	17.9683 367 969	17.7694 114 206	17.5748 008 079	140
36	18.1736 658 261	17.9701 262 798	17.7710 562 266	17.5763 127 099	144
37	18.1752 374 638	17.9715 673 623	17.7723 776 676	17.5775 245 049	148
38	18.1765 061 160	17.9727 278 758	17.7734 393 164	17.5784 957 629	152
39	18.1775 301 934	17.9736 624 452	17.7742 922 476	17.5792 742 298	156
40	18.1783 568 457	17.9744 150 601	17.7749 774 945	17.5798 981 739	160
41	18.1790 241 334	17.9750 211 461	17.7755 280 236	17.5803 982 673	164
42	18.1795 627 791	17.9755 092 311	17.7759 703 199	17.5807 990 940	168
43	18.1799 975 830	17.9759 022 893	17.7763 256 618	17.5811 203 580	172
44	18.1803 485 640	17.9762 188 218	17.7766 111 444	17.5813 778 524	176
45	18.1806 318 817	17.9764 737 274	17.7768 405 017	17.5815 842 350	180
46	18.1808 605 805	17.9766 790 047	17.7770 247 680	17.5817 496 514	184
47	18.1810 451 900	17.9768 443 159	17.7771 728 079	17.5818 822 333	188
48	18.1811 942 099	17.9769 774 421	17.7772 917 435	17.5819 884 981	192
49	18.1813 145 012	17.9770 846 495	17.7773 872 967	17.5820 736 698	196
50	18.1814 116 024	17.9771 709 843	17.7774 640 644	17.5821 419 352	200
51	18.1814 899 841	17.9772 405 104	17.7775 257 397	17.5821 966 502	204
52	18.1815 532 551	17.9772 965 002	17.7775 752 898	17.5822 405 044	208
53	18.1816 043 286	17.9773 415 891	17.7776 150 984	17.5822 756 538	212
54	18.1816 455 559	17.9773 778 996	17.7776 470 808	17.5823 038 261	216
55	18.1816 788 353	17.9774 071 406	17.7776 727 755	17.5823 264 063	220
56	18.1817 056 990	17.9774 306 886	17.7776 934 187	17.5823 445 044	224
57	18.1817 273 838	17.9774 496 520	17.7777 100 035	17.5823 590 101	228
58	18.1817 448 881	17.9774 649 233	17.7777 233 278	17.5823 706 365	232
59	18.1817 590 179	17.9774 772 214	17.7777 340 325	17.5823 799 551	236
60	18.1817 704 237	17.9774 871 252	17.7777 426 327	17.5823 874 240	240

TABLE 6. PARTIAL PAYMENT TO AMORTIZE ONE
Payable at end of each period

QUARTERLY Compounding

QUARTERS	5% Nominal Annual Rate	5¼% Nominal Annual Rate	5½% Nominal Annual Rate	5¾% Nominal Annual Rate	QUARTERS
1	1.0125 000 000	1.0131 250 000	1.0137 500 000	1.0143 750 000	1
2	0.5093 944 099	0.5098 651 428	0.5103 359 714	0.5108 068 957	2
3	0.3417 011 728	0.3421 213 645	0.3425 417 264	0.3429 622 583	3
YEARS					
1	0.2578 610 233	0.2582 566 052	0.2586 524 264	0.2590 484 868	4
2	0.1321 331 365	0.1324 951 057	0.1328 575 771	0.1332 205 503	8
3	0.0902 583 123	0.0906 125 950	0.0909 676 365	0.0913 234 361	12
4	0.0693 467 221	0.0696 997 927	0.0700 538 765	0.0704 089 720	16
5	0.0568 203 896	0.0571 748 306	0.0575 305 367	0.0578 875 058	20
6	0.0484 866 480	0.0488 437 423	0.0492 023 513	0.0495 624 722	24
7	0.0425 486 329	0.0429 091 051	0.0432 713 391	0.0436 353 309	28
8	0.0381 079 056	0.0384 722 000	0.0388 385 002	0.0392 068 010	32
9	0.0346 653 285	0.0350 337 322	0.0354 043 826	0.0357 772 727	36
10	0.0319 214 139	0.0322 941 190	0.0326 693 079	0.0330 469 718	40
11	0.0296 855 745	0.0300 627 116	0.0304 425 657	0.0308 251 257	44
12	0.0278 307 483	0.0282 124 062	0.0285 970 100	0.0289 845 459	48
13	0.0262 689 655	0.0266 552 035	0.0270 446 116	0.0274 371 728	52
14	0.0249 373 877	0.0253 282 431	0.0257 224 879	0.0261 201 017	56
15	0.0237 899 301	0.0241 854 239	0.0245 845 211	0.0249 871 973	60
16	0.0227 920 267	0.0231 921 668	0.0235 961 188	0.0240 038 539	64
17	0.0219 172 421	0.0223 220 262	0.0227 308 248	0.0231 436 042	68
18	0.0211 450 133	0.0215 544 305	0.0219 680 587	0.0223 858 590	72
19	0.0204 591 042	0.0208 731 366	0.0212 915 703	0.0217 143 605	76
20	0.0198 465 240	0.0202 651 478	0.0206 883 566	0.0211 160 992	80
21	0.0192 967 547	0.0197 199 408	0.0201 478 890	0.0205 805 413	84
22	0.0188 011 891	0.0192 289 041	0.0196 615 514	0.0200 990 655	88
23	0.0183 527 152	0.0187 849 218	0.0192 222 237	0.0196 645 478	92
24	0.0179 454 053	0.0183 820 626	0.0188 239 712	0.0192 710 495	96
25	0.0175 742 788	0.0180 153 429	0.0184 618 069	0.0189 135 804	100
26	0.0172 351 201	0.0176 805 444	0.0181 315 097	0.0185 879 164	104
27	0.0169 243 373	0.0173 740 726	0.0178 294 825	0.0182 904 580	108
28	0.0166 388 506	0.0170 928 456	0.0175 526 412	0.0180 181 183	112
29	0.0163 760 042	0.0168 342 054	0.0172 983 257	0.0177 682 354	116
30	0.0161 334 957	0.0165 958 479	0.0170 642 299	0.0175 385 013	120
31	0.0159 093 190	0.0163 757 653	0.0168 483 444	0.0173 269 051	124
32	0.0157 017 181	0.0161 722 002	0.0166 489 106	0.0171 316 864	128
33	0.0155 091 496	0.0159 836 077	0.0164 643 820	0.0169 512 977	132
34	0.0153 302 508	0.0158 086 242	0.0162 933 938	0.0167 843 732	136
35	0.0151 638 147	0.0156 460 413	0.0161 347 369	0.0166 297 027	140
36	0.0150 087 677	0.0154 947 848	0.0159 873 361	0.0164 862 102	144
37	0.0148 641 521	0.0153 538 962	0.0158 502 320	0.0163 529 360	148
38	0.0147 291 110	0.0152 225 175	0.0157 225 663	0.0162 290 211	152
39	0.0146 028 746	0.0150 998 788	0.0156 035 685	0.0161 136 947	156
40	0.0144 847 505	0.0149 852 868	0.0154 925 450	0.0160 062 631	160
41	0.0143 741 133	0.0148 781 160	0.0153 888 700	0.0159 061 002	164
42	0.0142 703 972	0.0147 778 003	0.0152 919 772	0.0158 126 400	168
43	0.0141 730 889	0.0146 838 262	0.0152 013 531	0.0157 253 690	172
44	0.0140 817 220	0.0145 957 270	0.0151 165 311	0.0156 438 208	176
45	0.0139 958 712	0.0145 130 775	0.0150 370 861	0.0155 675 708	180
46	0.0139 151 484	0.0144 354 897	0.0149 626 302	0.0154 962 314	184
47	0.0138 391 985	0.0143 626 085	0.0148 928 088	0.0154 294 486	188
48	0.0137 676 961	0.0142 941 087	0.0148 272 971	0.0153 668 981	192
49	0.0137 003 425	0.0142 296 919	0.0147 657 970	0.0153 082 826	196
50	0.0136 368 629	0.0141 690 837	0.0147 080 346	0.0152 533 290	200
51	0.0135 770 043	0.0141 120 314	0.0146 537 579	0.0152 017 858	204
52	0.0135 205 333	0.0140 583 019	0.0146 027 344	0.0151 534 218	208
53	0.0134 672 342	0.0140 076 802	0.0145 547 498	0.0151 080 233	212
54	0.0134 169 075	0.0139 599 673	0.0145 096 058	0.0150 653 931	216
55	0.0133 693 685	0.0139 149 789	0.0144 671 191	0.0150 253 489	220
56	0.0133 244 456	0.0138 725 443	0.0144 271 196	0.0149 877 217	224
57	0.0132 819 798	0.0138 325 050	0.0143 894 498	0.0149 523 553	228
58	0.0132 418 232	0.0137 947 138	0.0143 539 634	0.0149 191 043	232
59	0.0132 038 379	0.0137 590 337	0.0143 205 244	0.0148 878 339	236
60	0.0131 678 958	0.0137 253 373	0.0142 890 064	0.0148 584 190	240

QUARTERLY
Compounding

TABLE 6. PARTIAL PAYMENT TO AMORTIZE ONE
Payable at end of each period

QUARTERS	6% Nominal Annual Rate	6¼% Nominal Annual Rate	6½% Nominal Annual Rate	6¾% Nominal Annual Rate	QUARTERS
1	1.0150 000 000	1.0156 250 000	1.0162 500 000	1.0168 750 000	1
2	0.5112 779 156	0.5117 490 310	0.5122 202 418	0.5126 915 479	2
3	0.3433 829 602	0.3438 038 318	0.3442 248 730	0.3446 460 837	3
YEARS					
1	0.2594 447 860	0.2598 413 239	0.2602 381 002	0.2606 351 148	4
2	0.1335 840 246	0.1339 479 996	0.1343 124 747	0.1346 774 495	8
3	0.0916 799 929	0.0920 373 060	0.0923 953 744	0.0927 541 973	12
4	0.0707 650 778	0.0711 221 926	0.0714 803 149	0.0718 394 434	16
5	0.0582 457 359	0.0586 052 249	0.0589 659 708	0.0593 279 714	20
6	0.0499 241 020	0.0502 872 378	0.0506 518 766	0.0510 180 154	24
7	0.0440 010 765	0.0443 685 719	0.0447 378 128	0.0451 087 952	28
8	0.0395 770 970	0.0399 493 827	0.0403 236 526	0.0406 999 009	32
9	0.0361 523 955	0.0365 297 439	0.0369 093 105	0.0372 910 875	36
10	0.0334 271 017	0.0338 096 882	0.0341 947 219	0.0345 821 928	40
11	0.0312 103 801	0.0315 983 173	0.0319 889 251	0.0323 821 911	44
12	0.0293 749 996	0.0297 683 566	0.0301 646 019	0.0305 637 199	48
13	0.0278 328 700	0.0282 316 850	0.0286 335 995	0.0290 385 947	52
14	0.0265 210 635	0.0269 253 515	0.0273 329 436	0.0277 438 170	56
15	0.0253 934 274	0.0258 031 856	0.0262 164 454	0.0266 331 794	60
16	0.0244 153 423	0.0248 305 536	0.0252 494 566	0.0256 720 189	64
17	0.0235 603 297	0.0239 809 657	0.0244 054 755	0.0248 338 218	68
18	0.0228 077 911	0.0232 338 137	0.0236 638 845	0.0240 979 602	72
19	0.0221 414 609	0.0225 728 241	0.0230 084 016	0.0234 481 437	76
20	0.0215 483 231	0.0219 849 741	0.0224 259 969	0.0228 713 351	80
21	0.0210 178 380	0.0214 597 179	0.0219 061 187	0.0223 569 765	84
22	0.0205 413 794	0.0209 884 244	0.0214 401 303	0.0218 964 257	88
23	0.0201 118 190	0.0205 639 606	0.0210 208 943	0.0214 825 407	92
24	0.0197 232 141	0.0201 803 799	0.0206 424 601	0.0211 093 666	96
25	0.0193 705 712	0.0198 326 853	0.0202 998 271	0.0207 718 993	100
26	0.0190 496 632	0.0195 166 467	0.0199 887 618	0.0204 659 023	104
27	0.0187 568 877	0.0192 286 588	0.0197 056 566	0.0201 877 652	108
28	0.0184 891 557	0.0189 656 304	0.0194 474 177	0.0199 343 920	112
29	0.0182 438 030	0.0187 248 952	0.0192 113 770	0.0197 031 125	116
30	0.0180 185 199	0.0185 041 416	0.0189 952 210	0.0194 916 120	120
31	0.0178 112 938	0.0183 013 556	0.0187 969 344	0.0192 978 735	124
32	0.0176 203 629	0.0181 147 741	0.0186 147 529	0.0191 201 321	128
33	0.0174 441 787	0.0179 428 475	0.0184 471 261	0.0189 568 363	132
34	0.0172 813 742	0.0177 842 080	0.0182 926 855	0.0188 066 175	136
35	0.0171 307 386	0.0176 376 442	0.0181 502 190	0.0186 682 634	140
36	0.0169 911 952	0.0175 020 789	0.0180 186 496	0.0185 406 967	144
37	0.0168 617 839	0.0173 765 517	0.0178 970 166	0.0184 229 572	148
38	0.0167 416 453	0.0172 602 032	0.0177 844 608	0.0183 141 860	152
39	0.0166 300 085	0.0171 522 626	0.0176 802 117	0.0182 136 133	156
40	0.0165 261 798	0.0170 520 363	0.0175 835 762	0.0181 205 468	160
41	0.0164 295 334	0.0169 588 988	0.0174 939 295	0.0180 343 626	164
42	0.0163 395 032	0.0168 722 847	0.0174 107 069	0.0179 544 970	168
43	0.0162 555 763	0.0167 916 817	0.0173 333 969	0.0178 804 399	172
44	0.0161 772 867	0.0167 166 244	0.0172 615 355	0.0178 117 284	176
45	0.0161 042 104	0.0166 466 897	0.0171 947 003	0.0177 479 419	180
46	0.0160 359 605	0.0165 814 917	0.0171 325 069	0.0176 886 974	184
47	0.0159 721 837	0.0165 206 780	0.0170 746 044	0.0176 336 455	188
48	0.0159 125 567	0.0164 639 266	0.0170 206 718	0.0175 824 672	192
49	0.0158 567 829	0.0164 109 420	0.0169 704 154	0.0175 348 706	196
50	0.0158 045 903	0.0163 614 535	0.0169 235 660	0.0174 905 883	200
51	0.0157 557 286	0.0163 152 123	0.0168 798 764	0.0174 493 750	204
52	0.0157 099 676	0.0162 719 892	0.0168 391 192	0.0174 110 055	208
53	0.0156 670 947	0.0162 315 736	0.0168 010 854	0.0173 752 726	212
54	0.0156 269 142	0.0161 937 709	0.0167 655 823	0.0173 419 858	216
55	0.0155 892 448	0.0161 584 015	0.0167 324 321	0.0173 109 693	220
56	0.0155 539 191	0.0161 252 995	0.0167 014 707	0.0172 820 613	224
57	0.0155 207 820	0.0160 943 115	0.0166 725 466	0.0172 551 122	228
58	0.0154 896 896	0.0160 652 952	0.0166 455 194	0.0172 299 838	232
59	0.0154 605 087	0.0160 381 190	0.0166 202 593	0.0172 065 486	236
60	0.0154 331 152	0.0160 126 606	0.0165 966 461	0.0171 846 883	240

TABLE 6. PARTIAL PAYMENT TO AMORTIZE ONE
Payable at end of each period

QUARTERLY Compounding

QUARTERS	7% Nominal Annual Rate	7¼% Nominal Annual Rate	7½% Nominal Annual Rate	7¾% Nominal Annual Rate	QUARTERS
1	1.0175 000 000	1.0181 250 000	1.0187 500 000	1.0193 750 000	1
2	0.5131 629 492	0.5136 344 456	0.5141 060 372	0.5145 777 236	2
3	0.3450 674 635	0.3454 890 125	0.3459 107 305	0.3463 326 172	3
YEARS					
1	0.2610 323 673	0.2614 298 576	0.2618 275 854	0.2622 255 505	4
2	0.1350 429 233	0.1354 088 958	0.1357 753 662	0.1361 423 342	8
3	0.0931 137 738	0.0934 741 029	0.0938 351 837	0.0941 970 152	12
4	0.0721 995 764	0.0725 607 127	0.0729 228 507	0.0732 859 889	16
5	0.0596 912 246	0.0600 557 281	0.0604 214 797	0.0607 884 771	20
6	0.0513 856 510	0.0517 547 802	0.0521 253 999	0.0524 975 067	24
7	0.0454 815 145	0.0458 559 663	0.0462 321 462	0.0466 100 496	28
8	0.0410 781 216	0.0414 583 089	0.0418 404 564	0.0422 245 580	32
9	0.0376 750 673	0.0380 612 420	0.0384 496 033	0.0388 401 430	36
10	0.0349 720 911	0.0353 644 063	0.0357 591 280	0.0361 562 455	40
11	0.0327 781 026	0.0331 766 467	0.0335 778 099	0.0339 815 787	44
12	0.0309 656 950	0.0313 705 108	0.0317 781 508	0.0321 885 982	48
13	0.0294 466 511	0.0298 577 489	0.0302 718 678	0.0306 889 871	52
14	0.0281 579 481	0.0285 753 132	0.0289 958 877	0.0294 196 466	56
15	0.0270 533 598	0.0274 769 581	0.0279 039 451	0.0283 342 911	60
16	0.0260 982 079	0.0265 279 898	0.0269 613 304	0.0273 981 947	64
17	0.0252 659 661	0.0257 018 694	0.0261 414 915	0.0265 847 920	68
18	0.0245 359 964	0.0249 779 480	0.0254 237 690	0.0258 734 124	72
19	0.0238 919 996	0.0243 399 177	0.0247 918 453	0.0252 477 290	76
20	0.0233 209 310	0.0237 747 260	0.0242 326 606	0.0246 946 741	80
21	0.0228 122 263	0.0232 718 022	0.0237 356 371	0.0242 036 632	84
22	0.0223 572 379	0.0228 224 929	0.0232 921 161	0.0237 660 317	88
23	0.0219 488 187	0.0224 196 463	0.0228 949 407	0.0233 746 180	92
24	0.0215 810 099	0.0220 572 994	0.0225 381 438	0.0230 234 508	96
25	0.0212 488 036	0.0217 304 408	0.0222 167 105	0.0227 075 119	100
26	0.0209 479 605	0.0214 348 280	0.0219 263 956	0.0224 225 533	104
27	0.0206 748 675	0.0211 668 456	0.0216 635 810	0.0221 649 549	108
28	0.0204 264 263	0.0209 233 932	0.0214 251 648	0.0219 316 130	112
29	0.0201 999 650	0.0207 017 973	0.0212 084 719	0.0217 198 516	116
30	0.0199 931 675	0.0204 997 405	0.0210 111 841	0.0215 273 515	120
31	0.0198 040 158	0.0203 152 041	0.0208 312 819	0.0213 520 932	124
32	0.0196 307 440	0.0201 464 216	0.0206 669 987	0.0211 923 102	128
33	0.0194 718 004	0.0199 918 412	0.0205 167 829	0.0210 464 513	132
34	0.0193 258 160	0.0198 500 939	0.0203 792 659	0.0209 131 489	136
35	0.0191 915 786	0.0197 199 680	0.0202 532 368	0.0207 911 930	140
36	0.0190 680 114	0.0196 003 872	0.0201 376 202	0.0206 795 098	144
37	0.0189 541 546	0.0194 903 926	0.0200 314 585	0.0205 771 434	148
38	0.0188 491 500	0.0193 891 273	0.0199 338 964	0.0204 832 403	152
39	0.0187 522 288	0.0192 958 236	0.0198 441 677	0.0203 970 366	156
40	0.0186 626 998	0.0192 097 918	0.0197 615 848	0.0203 178 468	160
41	0.0185 799 404	0.0191 304 110	0.0196 855 287	0.0202 450 546	164
42	0.0185 033 884	0.0190 571 208	0.0196 154 413	0.0201 781 044	168
43	0.0184 325 351	0.0189 894 146	0.0195 508 183	0.0201 164 947	172
44	0.0183 669 195	0.0189 268 333	0.0194 912 031	0.0200 597 717	176
45	0.0183 061 227	0.0188 689 601	0.0194 361 815	0.0200 075 243	180
46	0.0182 497 636	0.0188 154 165	0.0193 853 775	0.0199 593 796	184
47	0.0181 974 949	0.0187 658 572	0.0193 384 489	0.0199 149 982	188
48	0.0181 489 996	0.0187 199 680	0.0192 950 838	0.0198 740 718	192
49	0.0181 039 881	0.0186 774 614	0.0192 549 979	0.0198 363 190	196
50	0.0180 621 950	0.0186 380 748	0.0192 179 315	0.0198 014 833	200
51	0.0180 233 774	0.0186 015 679	0.0191 836 470	0.0197 693 305	204
52	0.0179 873 123	0.0185 677 203	0.0191 519 270	0.0197 396 463	208
53	0.0179 537 950	0.0185 363 298	0.0191 225 722	0.0197 122 348	212
54	0.0179 226 371	0.0185 072 109	0.0190 954 001	0.0196 869 165	216
55	0.0178 936 655	0.0184 801 928	0.0190 702 428	0.0196 635 268	220
56	0.0178 667 205	0.0184 551 187	0.0190 469 464	0.0196 419 148	224
57	0.0178 416 551	0.0184 318 440	0.0190 253 692	0.0196 219 420	228
58	0.0178 183 333	0.0184 102 356	0.0190 053 809	0.0196 034 811	232
59	0.0177 966 301	0.0183 901 708	0.0189 868 615	0.0195 864 151	236
60	0.0177 764 294	0.0183 715 364	0.0189 697 006	0.0195 706 366	240

TABLE 6. PARTIAL PAYMENT TO AMORTIZE ONE
Payable at end of each period

	8% Nominal Annual Rate	8¼% Nominal Annual Rate	8½% Nominal Annual Rate	8¾% Nominal Annual Rate	
QUARTERS					QUARTERS
1	1.0200 000 000	1.0206 250 000	1.0212 500 000	1.0218 750 000	1
2	0.5150 495 050	0.5155 213 811	0.5159 933 519	0.5164 654 173	2
3	0.3467 546 726	0.3471 768 964	0.3475 992 886	0.3480 218 489	3
YEARS					
1	0.2626 237 527	0.2630 221 917	0.2634 208 674	0.2638 197 794	4
2	0.1365 097 991	0.1368 777 605	0.1372 462 178	0.1376 151 705	8
3	0.0945 595 966	0.0949 229 269	0.0952 870 051	0.0956 518 303	12
4	0.0736 501 259	0.0740 152 600	0.0743 813 898	0.0747 485 136	16
5	0.0611 567 181	0.0615 262 004	0.0618 969 215	0.0622 688 791	20
6	0.0528 710 973	0.0532 461 682	0.0536 227 162	0.0540 007 376	24
7	0.0469 896 716	0.0473 710 077	0.0477 540 528	0.0481 388 021	28
8	0.0426 106 073	0.0429 985 978	0.0433 885 228	0.0437 803 756	32
9	0.0392 328 526	0.0396 277 235	0.0400 247 469	0.0404 239 138	36
10	0.0365 557 478	0.0369 576 237	0.0373 618 618	0.0377 684 505	40
11	0.0343 879 391	0.0347 968 771	0.0352 083 782	0.0356 224 276	44
12	0.0326 018 355	0.0330 178 453	0.0334 366 095	0.0338 581 099	48
13	0.0311 090 856	0.0315 321 419	0.0319 581 340	0.0323 870 395	52
14	0.0298 465 645	0.0302 766 154	0.0307 097 729	0.0311 460 102	56
15	0.0287 679 658	0.0292 049 384	0.0296 451 775	0.0300 886 513	60
16	0.0278 385 471	0.0282 823 515	0.0287 295 710	0.0291 801 685	64
17	0.0270 317 294	0.0274 822 618	0.0279 363 465	0.0283 939 404	68
18	0.0263 268 307	0.0267 839 757	0.0272 447 986	0.0277 092 497	72
19	0.0257 075 147	0.0261 711 474	0.0266 385 715	0.0271 097 308	76
20	0.0251 607 055	0.0256 306 926	0.0261 045 729	0.0265 822 833	80
21	0.0246 758 118	0.0251 520 134	0.0256 321 981	0.0261 162 955	84
22	0.0242 441 633	0.0247 264 337	0.0252 127 654	0.0257 030 802	88
23	0.0238 585 936	0.0243 467 825	0.0248 390 990	0.0253 354 574	92
24	0.0235 131 275	0.0240 070 806	0.0245 052 164	0.0250 074 411	96
25	0.0232 027 435	0.0237 023 036	0.0242 060 903	0.0247 140 016	100
26	0.0229 231 911	0.0234 281 987	0.0239 374 657	0.0244 508 822	104
27	0.0226 708 483	0.0231 811 422	0.0236 957 179	0.0242 144 572	108
28	0.0224 426 100	0.0229 580 280	0.0234 777 400	0.0240 016 197	112
29	0.0222 357 993	0.0227 561 788	0.0232 808 547	0.0238 096 926	116
30	0.0220 480 969	0.0225 732 753	0.0231 027 431	0.0236 363 580	120
31	0.0218 774 832	0.0224 072 985	0.0229 413 873	0.0234 795 996	124
32	0.0217 221 924	0.0222 564 835	0.0227 950 237	0.0233 376 557	128
33	0.0215 806 741	0.0221 192 812	0.0226 621 053	0.0232 089 817	132
34	0.0214 515 619	0.0219 943 271	0.0225 412 696	0.0230 922 179	136
35	0.0213 336 475	0.0218 804 148	0.0224 313 129	0.0229 861 638	140
36	0.0212 258 591	0.0217 764 749	0.0223 311 686	0.0228 897 561	144
37	0.0211 272 426	0.0216 815 560	0.0222 398 886	0.0228 020 503	148
38	0.0210 369 471	0.0215 948 100	0.0221 566 279	0.0227 222 055	152
39	0.0209 542 112	0.0215 154 786	0.0220 806 320	0.0226 494 712	156
40	0.0208 783 523	0.0214 428 823	0.0220 112 251	0.0225 831 759	160
41	0.0208 087 568	0.0213 764 112	0.0219 478 010	0.0225 227 178	164
42	0.0207 448 725	0.0213 155 163	0.0218 898 150	0.0224 675 565	168
43	0.0206 862 008	0.0212 597 028	0.0218 367 763	0.0224 172 060	172
44	0.0206 322 913	0.0212 085 242	0.0217 882 425	0.0223 712 283	176
45	0.0205 827 365	0.0211 615 765	0.0217 438 138	0.0223 292 285	180
46	0.0205 371 665	0.0211 184 939	0.0217 031 287	0.0222 908 495	184
47	0.0204 952 458	0.0210 789 446	0.0216 658 597	0.0222 557 685	188
48	0.0204 566 694	0.0210 426 276	0.0216 317 100	0.0222 236 933	192
49	0.0204 211 596	0.0210 092 690	0.0216 004 099	0.0221 943 588	196
50	0.0203 884 634	0.0209 786 197	0.0215 717 146	0.0221 675 246	200
51	0.0203 583 501	0.0209 504 529	0.0215 454 013	0.0221 429 723	204
52	0.0203 306 090	0.0209 245 617	0.0215 212 673	0.0221 205 036	208
53	0.0203 050 476	0.0209 007 574	0.0214 991 277	0.0220 999 380	212
54	0.0202 814 899	0.0208 788 676	0.0214 788 144	0.0220 811 112	216
55	0.0202 597 747	0.0208 587 349	0.0214 601 735	0.0220 638 737	220
56	0.0202 397 545	0.0208 402 152	0.0214 430 649	0.0220 480 890	224
57	0.0202 212 941	0.0208 231 768	0.0214 273 605	0.0220 336 330	228
58	0.0202 042 694	0.0208 074 992	0.0214 129 432	0.0220 203 923	232
59	0.0201 885 667	0.0207 930 718	0.0213 997 061	0.0220 082 634	236
60	0.0201 740 815	0.0207 797 935	0.0213 875 512	0.0219 971 520	240

TABLE 6. PARTIAL PAYMENT TO AMORTIZE ONE
Payable at end of each period

QUARTERLY
Compounding

QUARTERS	9% Nominal Annual Rate	9¼% Nominal Annual Rate	9½% Nominal Annual Rate	9¾% Nominal Annual Rate	QUARTERS
1	1.0225 000 000	1.0231 250 000	1.0237 500 000	1.0243 750 000	1
2	0.5169 375 773	0.5174 098 316	0.5178 821 804	0.5183 546 233	2
3	0.3484 445 772	0.3488 674 733	0.3492 905 372	0.3497 137 685	3
YEARS					
1	0.2642 189 277	0.2646 183 118	0.2650 179 317	0.2654 177 871	4
2	0.1379 846 181	0.1383 545 599	0.1387 249 955	0.1390 959 243	8
3	0.0960 174 015	0.0963 837 178	0.0967 507 781	0.0971 185 815	12
4	0.0751 166 300	0.0754 857 373	0.0758 558 339	0.0762 269 182	16
5	0.0626 420 708	0.0630 164 941	0.0633 921 465	0.0637 690 256	20
6	0.0543 802 289	0.0547 611 865	0.0551 436 068	0.0555 274 860	24
7	0.0485 252 506	0.0489 133 931	0.0493 032 245	0.0496 947 395	28
8	0.0441 741 493	0.0445 698 370	0.0449 674 315	0.0453 669 257	32
9	0.0408 252 151	0.0412 286 416	0.0416 341 837	0.0420 418 320	36
10	0.0381 773 781	0.0385 886 324	0.0390 022 013	0.0394 180 724	40
11	0.0360 390 105	0.0364 581 115	0.0368 797 153	0.0373 038 062	44
12	0.0342 823 279	0.0347 092 445	0.0351 388 408	0.0355 710 971	48
13	0.0328 188 359	0.0332 535 000	0.0336 910 084	0.0341 313 376	52
14	0.0315 853 000	0.0320 276 147	0.0324 729 262	0.0329 212 062	56
15	0.0305 353 275	0.0309 851 734	0.0314 381 558	0.0318 942 413	60
16	0.0296 341 061	0.0300 913 456	0.0305 518 483	0.0310 155 752	64
17	0.0288 549 998	0.0293 194 805	0.0297 873 380	0.0302 585 272	68
18	0.0281 772 792	0.0286 488 366	0.0291 238 710	0.0296 023 311	72
19	0.0275 845 689	0.0280 630 284	0.0285 450 519	0.0290 305 817	76
20	0.0270 637 600	0.0275 489 391	0.0280 377 561	0.0285 301 464	80
21	0.0266 042 345	0.0270 959 440	0.0275 913 524	0.0280 903 881	84
22	0.0261 972 998	0.0266 953 454	0.0271 971 383	0.0277 025 998	88
23	0.0258 357 716	0.0263 399 552	0.0268 479 223	0.0273 595 868	92
24	0.0255 136 609	0.0260 237 818	0.0265 377 102	0.0270 553 530	96
25	0.0252 259 358	0.0257 417 913	0.0262 614 672	0.0267 848 629	100
26	0.0249 683 384	0.0254 897 253	0.0260 149 342	0.0265 438 577	104
27	0.0247 372 426	0.0252 639 574	0.0257 944 857	0.0263 287 130	108
28	0.0245 295 416	0.0250 613 817	0.0255 970 170	0.0261 363 262	112
29	0.0243 425 594	0.0248 793 238	0.0254 198 558	0.0259 640 276	116
30	0.0241 739 796	0.0247 154 691	0.0252 606 903	0.0258 095 088	120
31	0.0240 217 877	0.0245 678 061	0.0251 175 121	0.0256 707 655	124
32	0.0238 842 248	0.0244 345 789	0.0249 885 693	0.0255 460 501	128
33	0.0237 597 491	0.0243 142 493	0.0248 723 277	0.0254 338 335	132
34	0.0236 470 043	0.0242 054 649	0.0247 674 398	0.0253 327 732	136
35	0.0235 447 937	0.0241 070 333	0.0246 727 179	0.0252 416 873	140
36	0.0234 520 579	0.0240 178 997	0.0245 871 124	0.0251 595 322	144
37	0.0233 678 567	0.0239 371 288	0.0245 096 937	0.0250 853 838	148
38	0.0232 913 536	0.0238 638 892	0.0244 396 356	0.0250 184 227	152
39	0.0232 218 027	0.0237 974 400	0.0243 762 033	0.0249 579 200	156
40	0.0231 585 374	0.0237 371 200	0.0243 187 413	0.0249 032 266	160
41	0.0231 009 607	0.0236 823 375	0.0242 666 638	0.0248 537 634	164
42	0.0230 485 373	0.0236 325 628	0.0242 194 470	0.0248 090 126	168
43	0.0230 007 860	0.0235 873 201	0.0241 766 210	0.0247 685 110	172
44	0.0229 572 741	0.0235 461 821	0.0241 377 645	0.0247 318 433	176
45	0.0229 176 114	0.0235 087 641	0.0241 024 986	0.0246 986 370	180
46	0.0228 814 461	0.0234 747 198	0.0240 704 826	0.0246 685 574	184
47	0.0228 484 604	0.0234 437 365	0.0240 414 097	0.0246 413 037	188
48	0.0228 183 668	0.0234 155 322	0.0240 150 031	0.0246 166 049	192
49	0.0227 909 052	0.0233 898 518	0.0239 910 135	0.0245 942 172	196
50	0.0227 658 400	0.0233 664 647	0.0239 692 153	0.0245 739 208	200
51	0.0227 429 575	0.0233 451 622	0.0239 494 050	0.0245 555 174	204
52	0.0227 220 639	0.0233 257 552	0.0239 313 985	0.0245 388 279	208
53	0.0227 029 831	0.0233 080 723	0.0239 150 293	0.0245 236 908	212
54	0.0226 855 551	0.0232 919 581	0.0239 001 464	0.0245 099 599	216
55	0.0226 696 348	0.0232 772 716	0.0238 866 134	0.0244 975 034	220
56	0.0226 550 897	0.0232 638 846	0.0238 743 065	0.0244 862 018	224
57	0.0226 417 995	0.0232 516 810	0.0238 631 135	0.0244 759 472	228
58	0.0226 296 548	0.0232 405 550	0.0238 529 327	0.0244 666 417	232
59	0.0226 185 556	0.0232 304 106	0.0238 436 719	0.0244 581 969	236
60	0.0226 084 112	0.0232 211 605	0.0238 352 472	0.0244 505 328	240

QUARTERLY
Compounding

TABLE 6. PARTIAL PAYMENT TO AMORTIZE ONE
Payable at end of each period

	10% Nominal Annual Rate	10¼% Nominal Annual Rate	10½% Nominal Annual Rate	10¾% Nominal Annual Rate	
QUARTERS					QUARTERS
1	1.0250 000 000	1.0256 250 000	1.0262 500 000	1.0268 750 000	1
2	0.5188 271 605	0.5192 997 917	0.5197 725 170	0.5202 453 361	2
3	0.3501 371 672	0.3505 607 332	0.3509 844 661	0.3514 083 660	3
YEARS					
1	0.2658 178 777	0.2662 182 034	0.2666 187 639	0.2670 195 590	4
2	0.1394 673 458	0.1398 392 595	0.1402 116 647	0.1405 845 610	8
3	0.0974 871 270	0.0978 564 136	0.0982 264 402	0.0985 972 060	12
4	0.0765 989 886	0.0769 720 434	0.0773 460 810	0.0777 210 996	16
5	0.0641 471 287	0.0645 264 534	0.0649 069 971	0.0652 887 570	20
6	0.0559 128 204	0.0562 996 061	0.0566 878 394	0.0570 775 164	24
7	0.0500 879 327	0.0504 827 989	0.0508 793 325	0.0512 775 279	28
8	0.0457 683 123	0.0461 715 838	0.0465 767 327	0.0469 837 514	32
9	0.0424 515 767	0.0428 634 080	0.0432 773 159	0.0436 932 902	36
10	0.0398 362 332	0.0402 566 707	0.0406 793 722	0.0411 043 245	40
11	0.0377 303 683	0.0381 593 853	0.0385 908 410	0.0390 247 189	44
12	0.0360 059 938	0.0364 435 109	0.0368 836 281	0.0373 263 251	48
13	0.0345 744 635	0.0350 203 619	0.0354 690 081	0.0359 203 774	52
14	0.0333 724 260	0.0338 265 565	0.0342 835 683	0.0347 434 319	56
15	0.0323 533 959	0.0328 155 855	0.0332 807 755	0.0337 489 311	60
16	0.0314 824 869	0.0319 525 435	0.0324 257 049	0.0329 019 310	64
17	0.0307 330 027	0.0312 107 190	0.0316 916 300	0.0321 756 896	68
18	0.0300 841 652	0.0305 693 217	0.0310 577 482	0.0315 493 926	72
19	0.0295 195 594	0.0300 119 269	0.0305 076 257	0.0310 065 971	76
20	0.0290 260 451	0.0295 253 873	0.0300 281 079	0.0305 341 420	80
21	0.0285 929 793	0.0290 990 544	0.0296 085 415	0.0301 213 693	84
22	0.0282 116 510	0.0287 242 134	0.0292 402 087	0.0297 595 587	88
23	0.0278 748 628	0.0283 936 649	0.0289 159 082	0.0294 415 080	92
24	0.0275 766 173	0.0281 014 107	0.0286 296 418	0.0291 612 195	96
25	0.0273 118 787	0.0278 424 155	0.0283 763 752	0.0289 136 610	100
26	0.0270 763 891	0.0276 124 229	0.0281 518 546	0.0286 945 814	104
27	0.0268 665 260	0.0274 078 128	0.0279 524 631	0.0285 003 682	108
28	0.0266 791 895	0.0272 254 889	0.0277 751 084	0.0283 279 339	112
29	0.0265 117 132	0.0270 627 889	0.0276 171 333	0.0281 746 272	116
30	0.0263 617 930	0.0269 174 136	0.0274 762 442	0.0280 381 610	120
31	0.0262 274 291	0.0267 873 686	0.0273 504 528	0.0279 165 540	124
32	0.0261 068 791	0.0266 709 173	0.0272 380 295	0.0278 080 840	128
33	0.0259 986 195	0.0265 665 428	0.0271 374 641	0.0277 112 487	132
34	0.0259 013 140	0.0264 729 151	0.0270 474 343	0.0276 247 338	136
35	0.0258 137 867	0.0263 888 656	0.0269 667 790	0.0275 473 867	140
36	0.0257 350 004	0.0263 133 641	0.0268 944 758	0.0274 781 933	144
37	0.0256 640 380	0.0262 455 007	0.0268 296 227	0.0274 162 604	148
38	0.0256 000 866	0.0261 844 700	0.0267 714 223	0.0273 607 989	152
39	0.0255 424 243	0.0261 295 575	0.0267 191 680	0.0273 111 107	156
40	0.0254 904 089	0.0260 801 284	0.0266 722 330	0.0272 665 775	160
41	0.0254 434 681	0.0260 356 178	0.0266 300 601	0.0272 266 503	164
42	0.0254 010 911	0.0259 955 220	0.0265 921 535	0.0271 908 414	168
43	0.0253 628 212	0.0259 593 918	0.0265 580 713	0.0271 587 170	172
44	0.0253 282 501	0.0259 268 256	0.0265 274 196	0.0271 298 906	176
45	0.0252 970 116	0.0258 974 643	0.0264 998 462	0.0271 040 177	180
46	0.0252 687 776	0.0258 709 863	0.0264 750 367	0.0270 807 910	184
47	0.0252 432 532	0.0258 471 035	0.0264 527 095	0.0270 599 361	188
48	0.0252 201 739	0.0258 255 575	0.0264 326 129	0.0270 412 075	192
49	0.0251 993 016	0.0258 061 162	0.0264 145 210	0.0270 243 860	196
50	0.0251 804 222	0.0257 885 715	0.0263 982 316	0.0270 092 755	200
51	0.0251 633 427	0.0257 727 360	0.0263 835 632	0.0269 957 002	204
52	0.0251 478 896	0.0257 584 416	0.0263 703 529	0.0269 835 029	208
53	0.0251 339 062	0.0257 455 366	0.0263 584 546	0.0269 725 427	212
54	0.0251 212 513	0.0257 338 850	0.0263 477 369	0.0269 626 932	216
55	0.0251 097 976	0.0257 233 640	0.0263 380 819	0.0269 538 411	220
56	0.0250 994 301	0.0257 138 631	0.0263 293 836	0.0269 458 850	224
57	0.0250 900 451	0.0257 052 827	0.0263 215 465	0.0269 387 336	228
58	0.0250 815 488	0.0256 975 332	0.0263 144 851	0.0269 323 053	232
59	0.0250 738 565	0.0256 905 336	0.0263 081 222	0.0269 265 266	236
60	0.0250 668 918	0.0256 842 110	0.0263 023 883	0.0269 213 316	240

TABLE 6. PARTIAL PAYMENT TO AMORTIZE ONE
Payable at end of each period

QUARTERS	11% Nominal Annual Rate	11¼% Nominal Annual Rate	11½% Nominal Annual Rate	11¾% Nominal Annual Rate	QUARTERS
1	1.0275 000 000	1.0281 250 000	1.0287 500 000	1.0293 750 000	1
2	0.5207 182 491	0.5211 912 558	0.5216 643 561	0.5221 375 500	2
3	0.3518 324 326	0.3522 566 658	0.3526 810 654	0.3531 056 313	3
YEARS					
1	0.2674 205 884	0.2678 218 520	0.2682 233 494	0.2686 250 806	4
2	0.1409 579 478	0.1413 318 245	0.1417 061 906	0.1420 810 456	8
3	0.0989 687 098	0.0993 409 507	0.0997 139 277	0.1000 876 396	12
4	0.0780 970 977	0.0784 740 734	0.0788 520 250	0.0792 309 509	16
5	0.0656 717 306	0.0660 559 152	0.0664 413 080	0.0668 279 064	20
6	0.0574 686 330	0.0578 611 854	0.0582 551 694	0.0586 505 809	24
7	0.0516 773 795	0.0520 788 817	0.0524 820 286	0.0528 868 145	28
8	0.0473 926 322	0.0478 033 672	0.0482 159 486	0.0486 303 683	32
9	0.0441 113 206	0.0445 313 968	0.0449 535 082	0.0453 776 443	36
10	0.0415 315 144	0.0419 609 283	0.0423 925 527	0.0428 263 739	40
11	0.0394 610 021	0.0398 996 737	0.0403 407 166	0.0407 841 135	44
12	0.0377 715 811	0.0382 193 751	0.0386 696 862	0.0391 224 929	48
13	0.0363 744 446	0.0368 311 845	0.0372 905 715	0.0377 525 799	52
14	0.0352 061 174	0.0356 715 947	0.0361 398 334	0.0366 108 029	56
15	0.0342 200 173	0.0346 939 988	0.0351 708 400	0.0356 505 053	60
16	0.0333 811 810	0.0338 634 141	0.0343 485 894	0.0348 366 658	64
17	0.0326 628 513	0.0331 530 686	0.0336 462 949	0.0341 424 833	68
18	0.0320 442 024	0.0325 421 251	0.0330 431 080	0.0335 470 987	72
19	0.0315 087 826	0.0320 141 234	0.0325 225 610	0.0330 340 370	76
20	0.0310 434 245	0.0315 558 906	0.0320 714 758	0.0325 901 155	80
21	0.0306 374 664	0.0311 567 617	0.0316 791 846	0.0322 046 648	84
22	0.0302 821 858	0.0308 080 129	0.0313 369 633	0.0318 689 610	88
23	0.0299 703 805	0.0305 024 424	0.0310 376 114	0.0315 758 058	92
24	0.0296 960 540	0.0302 340 561	0.0307 751 378	0.0313 192 121	96
25	0.0294 541 767	0.0299 978 278	0.0305 445 208	0.0310 941 637	100
26	0.0292 405 017	0.0297 895 153	0.0303 415 239	0.0308 964 308	104
27	0.0290 514 211	0.0296 055 168	0.0301 625 521	0.0307 224 260	108
28	0.0288 838 535	0.0294 427 575	0.0300 045 384	0.0305 690 911	112
29	0.0287 351 542	0.0292 986 003	0.0298 648 540	0.0304 338 069	116
30	0.0286 030 433	0.0291 707 734	0.0297 412 364	0.0303 143 206	120
31	0.0284 855 476	0.0290 573 123	0.0296 317 304	0.0302 086 877	124
32	0.0283 809 528	0.0289 565 120	0.0295 346 412	0.0301 152 240	128
33	0.0282 877 656	0.0288 668 884	0.0294 484 947	0.0300 324 665	132
34	0.0282 046 805	0.0287 871 457	0.0293 720 055	0.0299 591 408	136
35	0.0281 305 536	0.0287 161 497	0.0293 040 499	0.0298 941 342	140
36	0.0280 643 803	0.0286 529 056	0.0292 436 434	0.0298 364 734	144
37	0.0280 052 763	0.0285 965 387	0.0291 899 217	0.0297 853 050	148
38	0.0279 524 617	0.0285 462 789	0.0291 421 248	0.0297 398 795	152
39	0.0279 052 475	0.0285 014 467	0.0290 995 831	0.0296 995 380	156
40	0.0278 630 240	0.0284 614 416	0.0290 617 062	0.0296 636 999	160
41	0.0278 252 512	0.0284 257 328	0.0290 279 723	0.0296 318 536	164
42	0.0277 914 497	0.0283 938 498	0.0289 979 205	0.0296 035 473	168
43	0.0277 611 941	0.0283 653 756	0.0289 711 423	0.0295 783 819	172
44	0.0277 341 057	0.0283 399 399	0.0289 472 761	0.0295 560 044	176
45	0.0277 098 479	0.0283 172 140	0.0289 260 012	0.0295 361 025	180
46	0.0276 881 207	0.0282 969 055	0.0289 070 332	0.0295 183 994	184
47	0.0276 686 568	0.0282 787 543	0.0288 901 193	0.0295 026 501	188
48	0.0276 512 178	0.0282 625 291	0.0288 750 350	0.0294 886 371	192
49	0.0276 355 907	0.0282 480 234	0.0288 615 809	0.0294 761 678	196
50	0.0276 215 857	0.0282 350 537	0.0288 495 795	0.0294 650 708	200
51	0.0276 090 330	0.0282 234 561	0.0288 388 729	0.0294 551 944	204
52	0.0275 977 808	0.0282 130 845	0.0288 293 206	0.0294 464 036	208
53	0.0275 876 935	0.0282 038 085	0.0288 207 975	0.0294 385 785	212
54	0.0275 786 498	0.0281 955 117	0.0288 131 923	0.0294 316 126	216
55	0.0275 705 412	0.0281 880 904	0.0288 064 056	0.0294 254 112	220
56	0.0275 632 704	0.0281 814 517	0.0288 003 491	0.0294 198 901	224
57	0.0275 567 506	0.0281 755 129	0.0287 949 439	0.0294 149 746	228
58	0.0275 509 039	0.0281 701 998	0.0287 901 198	0.0294 105 979	232
59	0.0275 456 606	0.0281 654 464	0.0287 858 141	0.0294 067 010	236
60	0.0275 409 581	0.0281 611 935	0.0287 819 711	0.0294 032 311	240

TABLE 6. PARTIAL PAYMENT TO AMORTIZE ONE
Payable at end of each period

	12% Nominal Annual Rate	12¼% Nominal Annual Rate	12½% Nominal Annual Rate	12¾% Nominal Annual Rate	
QUARTERS					QUARTERS
1	1.0300 000 000	1.0306 250 000	1.0312 500 000	1.0318 750 000	1
2	0.5226 108 374	0.5230 842 182	0.5235 576 923	0.5240 312 596	2
3	0.3535 303 633	0.3539 552 613	0.3543 803 250	0.3548 055 544	3
YEARS					
1	0.2690 270 452	0.2694 292 430	0.2698 316 739	0.2702 343 375	4
2	0.1424 563 888	0.1428 322 198	0.1432 085 380	0.1435 853 428	8
3	0.1004 620 855	0.1008 372 643	0.1012 131 750	0.1015 898 165	12
4	0.0796 108 493	0.0799 917 183	0.0803 735 563	0.0807 563 615	16
5	0.0672 157 076	0.0676 047 088	0.0679 949 071	0.0683 862 997	20
6	0.0590 474 159	0.0594 456 702	0.0598 453 396	0.0602 464 197	24
7	0.0532 932 334	0.0537 012 794	0.0541 109 465	0.0545 222 285	28
8	0.0490 466 183	0.0494 646 903	0.0498 845 760	0.0503 062 671	32
9	0.0458 037 942	0.0462 319 470	0.0466 620 918	0.0470 942 175	36
10	0.0432 623 779	0.0437 005 508	0.0441 408 783	0.0445 833 462	40
11	0.0412 298 469	0.0416 778 992	0.0421 282 525	0.0425 808 890	44
12	0.0395 777 738	0.0400 355 072	0.0404 956 713	0.0409 582 440	48
13	0.0382 171 837	0.0386 843 568	0.0391 540 731	0.0396 263 059	52
14	0.0370 844 726	0.0375 608 115	0.0380 397 885	0.0385 213 725	56
15	0.0361 329 587	0.0366 181 644	0.0371 060 861	0.0375 966 877	60
16	0.0353 276 021	0.0358 213 568	0.0363 178 885	0.0368 171 559	64
17	0.0346 415 871	0.0351 435 592	0.0356 483 530	0.0361 559 216	68
18	0.0340 540 446	0.0345 638 931	0.0350 765 920	0.0355 920 890	72
19	0.0335 484 929	0.0340 658 706	0.0345 861 124	0.0351 091 604	76
20	0.0331 117 457	0.0336 363 027	0.0341 637 230	0.0346 939 438	80
21	0.0327 331 325	0.0332 645 185	0.0337 987 540	0.0343 357 710	84
22	0.0324 039 306	0.0329 417 975	0.0334 824 878	0.0340 259 287	88
23	0.0321 169 449	0.0326 609 489	0.0332 077 392	0.0337 572 382	92
24	0.0318 661 932	0.0324 159 966	0.0329 685 390	0.0335 237 384	96
25	0.0316 466 659	0.0322 019 384	0.0327 598 935	0.0333 204 456	100
26	0.0314 541 408	0.0320 145 608	0.0325 775 995	0.0331 431 674	104
27	0.0312 850 394	0.0318 502 953	0.0324 180 991	0.0329 883 582	108
28	0.0311 363 131	0.0317 061 041	0.0322 783 663	0.0328 530 047	112
29	0.0310 053 531	0.0315 793 895	0.0321 558 160	0.0327 345 352	116
30	0.0308 899 176	0.0314 679 218	0.0320 482 312	0.0326 307 465	120
31	0.0307 880 734	0.0313 697 800	0.0319 537 039	0.0325 397 447	124
32	0.0306 981 479	0.0312 833 040	0.0318 705 875	0.0324 598 972	128
33	0.0306 186 898	0.0312 070 549	0.0317 974 563	0.0323 897 925	132
34	0.0305 484 366	0.0311 397 828	0.0317 330 737	0.0323 282 077	136
35	0.0304 862 875	0.0310 803 993	0.0316 763 642	0.0322 740 811	140
36	0.0304 312 805	0.0310 279 547	0.0316 263 909	0.0322 264 892	144
37	0.0303 825 739	0.0309 816 190	0.0315 823 364	0.0321 846 272	148
38	0.0303 394 292	0.0309 406 657	0.0315 434 861	0.0321 477 931	152
39	0.0303 011 985	0.0309 044 577	0.0315 092 147	0.0321 153 736	156
40	0.0302 673 117	0.0308 724 362	0.0314 789 743	0.0320 868 324	160
41	0.0302 372 672	0.0308 441 098	0.0314 522 845	0.0320 616 997	164
42	0.0302 106 231	0.0308 190 466	0.0314 287 233	0.0320 395 642	168
43	0.0301 869 895	0.0307 968 663	0.0314 079 202	0.0320 200 650	172
44	0.0301 660 223	0.0307 772 338	0.0313 895 494	0.0320 028 855	176
45	0.0301 474 177	0.0307 598 538	0.0313 733 240	0.0319 877 476	180
46	0.0301 309 070	0.0307 444 657	0.0313 589 916	0.0319 744 072	184
47	0.0301 162 526	0.0307 308 395	0.0313 463 301	0.0319 626 496	188
48	0.0301 032 443	0.0307 187 723	0.0313 351 434	0.0319 522 859	192
49	0.0300 916 960	0.0307 080 847	0.0313 252 590	0.0319 431 503	196
50	0.0300 814 430	0.0306 986 180	0.0313 165 244	0.0319 350 966	200
51	0.0300 723 391	0.0306 902 323	0.0313 088 056	0.0319 279 963	204
52	0.0300 642 551	0.0306 828 036	0.0313 019 838	0.0319 217 360	208
53	0.0300 570 762	0.0306 762 223	0.0312 959 545	0.0319 162 162	212
54	0.0300 507 007	0.0306 703 914	0.0312 906 255	0.0319 113 491	216
55	0.0300 450 384	0.0306 652 252	0.0312 859 151	0.0319 070 573	220
56	0.0300 400 094	0.0306 606 476	0.0312 817 515	0.0319 032 727	224
57	0.0300 355 425	0.0306 565 915	0.0312 780 709	0.0318 999 352	228
58	0.0300 315 749	0.0306 529 973	0.0312 748 174	0.0318 969 920	232
59	0.0300 280 506	0.0306 498 124	0.0312 719 412	0.0318 943 964	236
60	0.0300 249 200	0.0306 469 901	0.0312 693 985	0.0318 921 073	240

TABLE 6. PARTIAL PAYMENT TO AMORTIZE ONE
Payable at end of each period

QUARTERS	13% Nominal Annual Rate	13¼% Nominal Annual Rate	13½% Nominal Annual Rate	13¾% Nominal Annual Rate	QUARTERS
1	1.0325 000 000	1.0331 250 000	1.0337 500 000	1.0343 750 000	1
2	0.5245 049 200	0.5249 786 735	0.5254 525 200	0.5259 264 593	2
3	0.3552 309 493	0.3556 565 095	0.3560 822 349	0.3565 081 253	3
YEARS					
1	0.2706 372 337	0.2710 403 622	0.2714 437 228	0.2718 473 153	4
2	0.1439 626 337	0.1443 404 100	0.1447 186 713	0.1450 974 170	8
3	0.1019 671 878	0.1023 452 878	0.1027 241 154	0.1031 036 696	12
4	0.0811 401 319	0.0815 248 659	0.0819 105 616	0.0822 972 171	16
5	0.0687 788 839	0.0691 726 566	0.0695 676 149	0.0699 637 560	20
6	0.0606 489 063	0.0610 527 951	0.0614 580 816	0.0618 647 615	24
7	0.0549 351 193	0.0553 496 126	0.0557 657 023	0.0561 833 820	28
8	0.0507 297 552	0.0511 550 316	0.0515 820 878	0.0520 109 152	32
9	0.0475 283 128	0.0479 643 664	0.0484 023 670	0.0488 423 030	36
10	0.0450 279 400	0.0454 746 453	0.0459 234 473	0.0463 743 312	40
11	0.0430 357 906	0.0434 929 391	0.0439 523 160	0.0444 139 031	44
12	0.0414 232 032	0.0418 905 267	0.0423 601 920	0.0428 321 767	48
13	0.0401 010 288	0.0405 782 150	0.0410 578 378	0.0415 398 703	52
14	0.0390 055 322	0.0394 922 361	0.0399 814 528	0.0404 731 506	56
15	0.0380 899 328	0.0385 857 851	0.0390 842 082	0.0395 851 658	60
16	0.0373 191 174	0.0378 237 316	0.0383 309 570	0.0388 407 525	64
17	0.0366 662 182	0.0371 791 963	0.0376 948 093	0.0382 130 109	68
18	0.0361 103 320	0.0366 312 692	0.0371 548 492	0.0376 810 205	72
19	0.0356 349 575	0.0361 634 467	0.0366 945 715	0.0372 282 758	76
20	0.0352 269 026	0.0357 625 376	0.0363 007 873	0.0368 415 910	80
21	0.0348 755 020	0.0354 178 804	0.0359 628 404	0.0365 103 167	84
22	0.0345 720 479	0.0351 207 744	0.0356 720 378	0.0362 257 692	88
23	0.0343 093 692	0.0348 640 569	0.0354 212 273	0.0359 808 075	92
24	0.0340 815 142	0.0346 417 873	0.0352 044 800	0.0357 695 163	96
25	0.0338 835 102	0.0344 490 049	0.0350 168 489	0.0355 869 631	100
26	0.0337 111 771	0.0342 815 430	0.0348 541 817	0.0354 290 117	104
27	0.0335 609 823	0.0341 358 835	0.0347 129 759	0.0352 921 762	108
28	0.0334 299 266	0.0340 090 419	0.0345 902 632	0.0351 735 055	112
29	0.0333 154 526	0.0338 984 766	0.0344 835 183	0.0350 704 919	116
30	0.0332 153 719	0.0338 020 147	0.0343 905 851	0.0349 809 968	120
31	0.0331 278 056	0.0337 177 931	0.0343 096 172	0.0349 031 913	124
32	0.0330 511 359	0.0336 442 098	0.0342 390 289	0.0348 355 069	128
33	0.0329 839 661	0.0335 798 835	0.0341 774 553	0.0347 765 957	132
34	0.0329 250 879	0.0335 236 213	0.0341 237 191	0.0347 252 966	136
35	0.0328 734 538	0.0334 743 902	0.0340 768 027	0.0346 806 079	140
36	0.0328 281 541	0.0334 312 949	0.0340 358 255	0.0346 416 641	144
37	0.0327 883 973	0.0333 935 578	0.0340 000 241	0.0346 077 162	148
38	0.0327 534 945	0.0333 605 029	0.0339 687 358	0.0345 781 155	152
39	0.0327 228 444	0.0333 315 416	0.0339 413 851	0.0345 522 991	156
40	0.0326 959 223	0.0333 061 612	0.0339 174 711	0.0345 297 787	160
41	0.0326 722 699	0.0332 839 145	0.0338 965 581	0.0345 101 301	164
42	0.0326 514 861	0.0332 644 112	0.0338 782 665	0.0344 929 843	168
43	0.0326 332 200	0.0332 473 102	0.0338 622 655	0.0344 780 205	172
44	0.0326 171 644	0.0332 323 137	0.0338 482 663	0.0344 649 595	176
45	0.0326 030 499	0.0332 191 612	0.0338 360 172	0.0344 535 582	180
46	0.0325 906 404	0.0332 076 246	0.0338 252 984	0.0344 436 047	184
47	0.0325 797 290	0.0331 975 046	0.0338 159 178	0.0344 349 145	188
48	0.0325 701 339	0.0331 886 265	0.0338 077 079	0.0344 273 268	192
49	0.0325 616 957	0.0331 808 373	0.0338 005 221	0.0344 207 013	196
50	0.0325 542 745	0.0331 740 031	0.0337 942 322	0.0344 149 157	200
51	0.0325 477 473	0.0331 680 065	0.0337 887 262	0.0344 098 632	204
52	0.0325 420 060	0.0331 627 445	0.0337 839 064	0.0344 054 509	208
53	0.0325 369 559	0.0331 581 269	0.0337 796 869	0.0344 015 974	212
54	0.0325 325 136	0.0331 540 748	0.0337 759 929	0.0343 982 319	216
55	0.0325 286 057	0.0331 505 187	0.0337 727 589	0.0343 952 925	220
56	0.0325 251 678	0.0331 473 979	0.0337 699 275	0.0343 927 252	224
57	0.0325 221 435	0.0331 446 589	0.0337 674 485	0.0343 904 828	228
58	0.0325 194 827	0.0331 422 550	0.0337 652 781	0.0343 885 243	232
59	0.0325 171 419	0.0331 401 453	0.0337 633 777	0.0343 868 135	236
60	0.0325 150 824	0.0331 382 936	0.0337 617 138	0.0343 853 193	240

TABLE 6. PARTIAL PAYMENT TO AMORTIZE ONE
Payable at end of each period

QUARTERS	14% Nominal Annual Rate	14¼% Nominal Annual Rate	14½% Nominal Annual Rate	14¾% Nominal Annual Rate	QUARTERS
1	1.0350 000 000	1.0356 250 000	1.0362 500 000	1.0368 750 000	1
2	0.5264 004 914	0.5268 746 162	0.5273 488 336	0.5278 231 436	2
3	0.3569 341 806	0.3573 604 005	0.3577 867 851	0.3582 133 340	3
YEARS					
1	0.2722 511 395	0.2726 551 951	0.2730 594 819	0.2734 639 996	4
2	0.1454 766 465	0.1458 563 593	0.1462 365 548	0.1466 172 323	8
3	0.1034 839 493	0.1038 649 533	0.1042 466 807	0.1046 291 303	12
4	0.0826 848 306	0.0830 734 003	0.0834 629 241	0.0838 534 003	16
5	0.0703 610 768	0.0707 595 744	0.0711 592 457	0.0715 600 877	20
6	0.0622 728 303	0.0626 822 834	0.0630 931 163	0.0635 053 245	24
7	0.0566 026 452	0.0570 234 856	0.0574 458 966	0.0578 698 717	28
8	0.0524 415 048	0.0528 738 479	0.0533 079 356	0.0537 437 589	32
9	0.0492 841 628	0.0497 279 347	0.0501 736 070	0.0506 211 677	36
10	0.0468 272 823	0.0472 822 854	0.0477 393 256	0.0481 983 877	40
11	0.0448 776 816	0.0453 436 329	0.0458 117 383	0.0462 819 790	44
12	0.0433 064 580	0.0437 830 134	0.0442 618 199	0.0447 428 546	48
13	0.0420 242 854	0.0425 110 561	0.0430 001 552	0.0434 915 556	52
14	0.0409 672 981	0.0414 638 635	0.0419 628 152	0.0424 641 216	56
15	0.0400 886 213	0.0405 945 385	0.0411 028 811	0.0416 136 128	60
16	0.0393 530 765	0.0398 678 881	0.0403 851 462	0.0409 048 099	64
17	0.0387 337 550	0.0392 569 955	0.0397 826 869	0.0403 107 837	68
18	0.0382 097 323	0.0387 409 339	0.0392 745 750	0.0398 106 058	72
19	0.0377 645 038	0.0383 032 006	0.0388 443 115	0.0393 877 824	76
20	0.0373 848 887	0.0379 306 208	0.0384 787 288	0.0390 291 546	80
21	0.0370 602 452	0.0376 125 623	0.0381 672 057	0.0387 241 136	84
22	0.0367 819 002	0.0373 403 640	0.0379 010 945	0.0384 640 269	88
23	0.0365 427 259	0.0371 069 121	0.0376 732 973	0.0382 418 139	92
24	0.0363 368 213	0.0369 063 220	0.0374 779 470	0.0380 516 262	96
25	0.0361 592 702	0.0367 336 949	0.0373 101 634	0.0378 886 039	100
26	0.0360 059 536	0.0365 849 300	0.0371 658 655	0.0377 486 871	104
27	0.0358 734 032	0.0364 565 782	0.0370 416 247	0.0376 284 683	108
28	0.0357 586 865	0.0363 457 265	0.0369 345 480	0.0375 250 764	112
29	0.0356 593 142	0.0362 499 048	0.0368 421 863	0.0374 360 837	116
30	0.0355 731 662	0.0361 670 128	0.0367 624 592	0.0373 594 309	120
31	0.0354 984 319	0.0360 952 588	0.0366 935 952	0.0372 933 672	124
32	0.0354 335 608	0.0360 331 112	0.0366 340 818	0.0372 363 999	128
33	0.0353 772 225	0.0359 792 573	0.0365 826 252	0.0371 872 546	132
34	0.0353 282 727	0.0359 325 706	0.0365 381 166	0.0371 448 408	136
35	0.0352 857 262	0.0358 920 823	0.0364 996 043	0.0371 082 242	140
36	0.0352 487 328	0.0358 569 582	0.0364 662 704	0.0370 766 034	144
37	0.0352 165 585	0.0358 264 792	0.0364 374 110	0.0370 492 899	148
38	0.0351 885 682	0.0358 000 247	0.0364 124 198	0.0370 256 919	152
39	0.0351 642 125	0.0357 770 585	0.0363 907 740	0.0370 053 002	156
40	0.0351 430 155	0.0357 571 169	0.0363 720 227	0.0369 876 763	160
41	0.0351 245 643	0.0357 397 989	0.0363 557 763	0.0369 724 424	164
42	0.0351 085 009	0.0357 247 574	0.0363 416 984	0.0369 592 728	168
43	0.0350 945 146	0.0357 116 914	0.0363 294 983	0.0369 478 867	172
44	0.0350 823 355	0.0357 003 404	0.0363 189 245	0.0369 380 415	176
45	0.0350 717 289	0.0356 904 784	0.0363 097 593	0.0369 295 282	180
46	0.0350 624 911	0.0356 819 093	0.0363 018 146	0.0369 221 660	184
47	0.0350 544 449	0.0356 744 632	0.0362 949 274	0.0369 157 989	188
48	0.0350 474 361	0.0356 679 926	0.0362 889 567	0.0369 102 921	192
49	0.0350 413 306	0.0356 623 693	0.0362 837 802	0.0369 055 293	196
50	0.0350 360 118	0.0356 574 822	0.0362 792 921	0.0369 014 096	200
51	0.0350 313 780	0.0356 532 347	0.0362 754 007	0.0368 978 462	204
52	0.0350 273 410	0.0356 495 431	0.0362 720 266	0.0368 947 639	208
53	0.0350 238 237	0.0356 463 343	0.0362 691 009	0.0368 920 976	212
54	0.0350 207 592	0.0356 435 454	0.0362 665 640	0.0368 897 912	216
55	0.0350 180 890	0.0356 411 211	0.0362 643 642	0.0368 877 960	220
56	0.0350 157 625	0.0356 390 139	0.0362 624 566	0.0368 860 700	224
57	0.0350 137 353	0.0356 371 822	0.0362 608 024	0.0368 845 769	228
58	0.0350 119 689	0.0356 355 900	0.0362 593 680	0.0368 832 852	232
59	0.0350 104 298	0.0356 342 060	0.0362 581 241	0.0368 821 678	236
60	0.0350 090 886	0.0356 330 029	0.0362 570 453	0.0368 812 011	240

TABLE 6. PARTIAL PAYMENT TO AMORTIZE ONE
Payable at end of each period

QUARTERLY Compounding

QUARTERS	15% Nominal Annual Rate	15¼% Nominal Annual Rate	15½% Nominal Annual Rate	15¾% Nominal Annual Rate	QUARTERS
1	1.0375 000 000	1.0381 250 000	1.0387 500 000	1.0393 750 000	1
2	0.5282 975 460	0.5287 720 408	0.5292 466 278	0.5297 213 071	2
3	0.3586 400 472	0.3590 669 244	0.3594 939 656	0.3599 211 706	3
YEARS					
1	0.2738 687 482	0.2742 737 272	0.2746 789 366	0.2750 843 761	4
2	0.1469 983 915	0.1473 800 316	0.1477 621 521	0.1481 447 524	8
3	0.1050 123 010	0.1053 961 917	0.1057 808 013	0.1061 661 287	12
4	0.0842 448 270	0.0846 372 021	0.0850 305 238	0.0854 247 902	16
5	0.0719 620 973	0.0723 652 715	0.0727 696 072	0.0731 751 012	20
6	0.0639 189 033	0.0643 338 481	0.0647 501 542	0.0651 678 169	24
7	0.0582 954 043	0.0587 224 876	0.0591 511 151	0.0595 812 799	28
8	0.0541 813 087	0.0546 205 758	0.0550 615 513	0.0555 042 257	32
9	0.0510 706 050	0.0515 219 068	0.0519 750 610	0.0524 300 554	36
10	0.0486 594 563	0.0491 225 163	0.0495 875 521	0.0500 545 483	40
11	0.0467 543 358	0.0472 287 899	0.0477 053 222	0.0481 839 134	44
12	0.0452 260 947	0.0457 115 172	0.0461 990 989	0.0466 888 167	48
13	0.0439 852 301	0.0444 811 514	0.0449 792 922	0.0454 796 254	52
14	0.0429 677 509	0.0434 736 716	0.0439 818 520	0.0444 922 607	56
15	0.0421 266 973	0.0426 420 987	0.0431 597 810	0.0436 797 084	60
16	0.0414 268 386	0.0419 511 916	0.0424 778 288	0.0430 067 100	64
17	0.0408 412 407	0.0413 740 131	0.0419 090 564	0.0424 463 265	68
18	0.0403 489 770	0.0408 896 394	0.0414 325 446	0.0419 776 446	72
19	0.0399 335 598	0.0404 815 908	0.0410 318 234	0.0415 842 057	76
20	0.0395 818 410	0.0401 367 315	0.0406 937 705	0.0412 529 032	80
21	0.0392 832 256	0.0398 444 819	0.0404 078 238	0.0409 731 937	84
22	0.0390 290 977	0.0395 962 444	0.0401 654 056	0.0407 365 214	88
23	0.0388 123 956	0.0393 849 776	0.0399 594 965	0.0405 358 903	92
24	0.0386 272 913	0.0392 048 755	0.0397 843 139	0.0403 655 427	96
25	0.0384 689 464	0.0390 511 227	0.0396 350 665	0.0402 207 132	100
26	0.0383 333 233	0.0389 197 050	0.0395 077 652	0.0400 974 385	104
27	0.0382 170 371	0.0388 072 614	0.0393 990 737	0.0399 924 087	108
28	0.0381 172 394	0.0387 109 671	0.0393 061 921	0.0399 028 494	112
29	0.0380 315 248	0.0386 284 401	0.0392 267 626	0.0398 264 279	116
30	0.0379 578 561	0.0385 576 660	0.0391 587 944	0.0397 611 778	120
31	0.0378 945 038	0.0384 969 372	0.0391 006 024	0.0397 054 372	124
32	0.0378 399 958	0.0384 448 029	0.0390 507 577	0.0396 577 994	128
33	0.0377 930 774	0.0384 000 285	0.0390 080 461	0.0396 170 712	132
34	0.0377 526 768	0.0383 615 614	0.0389 714 346	0.0395 822 393	136
35	0.0377 178 776	0.0383 285 030	0.0389 400 427	0.0395 524 418	140
36	0.0376 878 948	0.0383 000 855	0.0389 131 198	0.0395 269 452	144
37	0.0376 620 557	0.0382 756 518	0.0388 900 247	0.0395 051 242	148
38	0.0376 397 832	0.0382 546 395	0.0388 702 096	0.0394 864 458	152
39	0.0376 205 816	0.0382 365 664	0.0388 532 060	0.0394 704 550	156
40	0.0376 040 249	0.0382 210 192	0.0388 386 131	0.0394 567 634	160
41	0.0375 897 470	0.0382 076 433	0.0388 260 875	0.0394 450 391	164
42	0.0375 774 329	0.0381 961 342	0.0388 153 355	0.0394 349 986	168
43	0.0375 668 113	0.0381 862 304	0.0388 061 050	0.0394 263 993	172
44	0.0375 576 490	0.0381 777 074	0.0387 981 802	0.0394 190 339	176
45	0.0375 497 448	0.0381 703 722	0.0387 913 760	0.0394 127 249	180
46	0.0375 429 256	0.0381 640 588	0.0387 855 336	0.0394 073 206	184
47	0.0375 370 422	0.0381 586 247	0.0387 805 168	0.0394 026 911	188
48	0.0375 319 658	0.0381 539 472	0.0387 762 087	0.0393 987 250	192
49	0.0375 275 856	0.0381 499 208	0.0387 725 092	0.0393 953 273	196
50	0.0375 238 060	0.0381 464 548	0.0387 693 322	0.0393 924 164	200
51	0.0375 205 445	0.0381 434 711	0.0387 666 038	0.0393 899 225	204
52	0.0375 177 301	0.0381 409 024	0.0387 642 605	0.0393 877 859	208
53	0.0375 153 014	0.0381 386 912	0.0387 622 481	0.0393 859 552	212
54	0.0375 132 055	0.0381 367 874	0.0387 605 198	0.0393 843 867	216
55	0.0375 113 967	0.0381 351 485	0.0387 590 353	0.0393 830 429	220
56	0.0375 098 358	0.0381 337 375	0.0387 577 604	0.0393 818 914	224
57	0.0375 084 887	0.0381 325 227	0.0387 566 655	0.0393 809 049	228
58	0.0375 073 261	0.0381 314 769	0.0387 557 250	0.0393 800 595	232
59	0.0375 063 228	0.0381 305 764	0.0387 549 172	0.0393 793 352	236
60	0.0375 054 569	0.0381 298 012	0.0387 542 235	0.0393 787 146	240

TABLE 6. PARTIAL PAYMENT TO AMORTIZE ONE
Payable at end of each period

QUARTERS	16% Nominal Annual Rate	16¼% Nominal Annual Rate	16½% Nominal Annual Rate	16¾% Nominal Annual Rate	QUARTERS
1	1.0400 000 000	1.0406 250 000	1.0412 500 000	1.0418 750 000	1
2	0.5301 960 784	0.5306 709 418	0.5311 458 971	0.5316 209 443	2
3	0.3603 485 392	0.3607 760 713	0.3612 037 667	0.3616 316 252	3
YEARS					
1	0.2754 900 454	0.2758 959 443	0.2763 020 727	0.2767 084 302	4
2	0.1485 278 320	0.1489 113 904	0.1492 954 268	0.1496 799 407	8
3	0.1065 521 727	0.1069 389 323	0.1073 264 062	0.1077 145 935	12
4	0.0858 199 992	0.0862 161 490	0.0866 132 375	0.0870 112 627	16
5	0.0735 817 503	0.0739 895 515	0.0743 985 014	0.0748 085 969	20
6	0.0655 868 313	0.0660 071 928	0.0664 288 965	0.0668 519 374	24
7	0.0600 129 752	0.0604 461 942	0.0608 809 300	0.0613 171 756	28
8	0.0559 485 897	0.0563 946 341	0.0568 423 494	0.0572 917 261	32
9	0.0528 868 780	0.0533 455 162	0.0538 059 578	0.0542 681 904	36
10	0.0505 234 893	0.0509 943 596	0.0514 671 434	0.0519 418 250	40
11	0.0486 645 444	0.0491 471 960	0.0496 318 487	0.0501 184 833	44
12	0.0471 806 476	0.0476 745 683	0.0481 705 556	0.0486 685 865	48
13	0.0459 821 236	0.0464 867 596	0.0469 935 063	0.0475 023 364	52
14	0.0450 048 662	0.0455 196 371	0.0460 365 422	0.0465 555 501	56
15	0.0442 018 451	0.0447 261 557	0.0452 526 049	0.0457 811 574	60
16	0.0435 377 955	0.0440 710 456	0.0446 064 212	0.0451 438 833	64
17	0.0429 857 795	0.0435 273 721	0.0440 710 613	0.0446 168 046	68
18	0.0425 248 919	0.0430 742 394	0.0436 256 408	0.0441 790 502	72
19	0.0421 386 869	0.0426 952 168	0.0432 537 458	0.0438 142 251	76
20	0.0418 140 755	0.0423 772 344	0.0429 423 276	0.0435 093 037	80
21	0.0415 405 351	0.0421 097 921	0.0426 809 105	0.0432 538 366	84
22	0.0413 095 329	0.0418 843 825	0.0424 610 138	0.0430 393 716	88
23	0.0411 140 984	0.0416 940 616	0.0422 757 221	0.0428 590 236	92
24	0.0409 485 002	0.0415 331 260	0.0421 193 615	0.0427 071 495	96
25	0.0408 080 000	0.0413 968 661	0.0419 872 521	0.0425 791 007	100
26	0.0406 886 620	0.0412 813 744	0.0418 755 164	0.0424 710 307	104
27	0.0405 872 033	0.0411 833 964	0.0417 809 291	0.0423 797 446	108
28	0.0405 008 762	0.0411 002 121	0.0417 007 988	0.0423 025 803	112
29	0.0404 273 741	0.0410 295 415	0.0416 328 730	0.0422 373 137	116
30	0.0403 647 553	0.0409 694 687	0.0415 752 620	0.0421 820 817	120
31	0.0403 113 821	0.0409 183 802	0.0415 263 772	0.0421 353 213	124
32	0.0402 658 702	0.0408 749 149	0.0414 848 811	0.0420 957 186	128
33	0.0402 270 478	0.0408 379 227	0.0414 496 452	0.0420 621 674	132
34	0.0401 939 216	0.0408 064 303	0.0414 197 169	0.0420 337 355	136
35	0.0401 656 484	0.0407 796 135	0.0413 942 907	0.0420 096 364	140
36	0.0401 415 119	0.0407 567 732	0.0413 726 850	0.0419 892 060	144
37	0.0401 209 028	0.0407 373 163	0.0413 543 227	0.0419 718 829	148
38	0.0401 033 029	0.0407 207 390	0.0413 387 145	0.0419 571 926	152
39	0.0400 882 707	0.0407 066 133	0.0413 254 458	0.0419 447 335	156
40	0.0400 754 300	0.0406 945 754	0.0413 141 648	0.0419 341 656	160
41	0.0400 644 602	0.0406 843 156	0.0413 045 727	0.0419 252 012	164
42	0.0400 550 880	0.0406 755 707	0.0412 964 162	0.0419 175 964	168
43	0.0400 470 800	0.0406 681 164	0.0412 894 800	0.0419 111 446	172
44	0.0400 402 373	0.0406 617 618	0.0412 835 811	0.0419 056 707	176
45	0.0400 343 900	0.0406 563 446	0.0412 785 642	0.0419 010 264	180
46	0.0400 293 930	0.0406 517 261	0.0412 742 972	0.0418 970 857	184
47	0.0400 251 226	0.0406 477 886	0.0412 706 680	0.0418 937 419	188
48	0.0400 214 730	0.0406 444 314	0.0412 675 811	0.0418 909 045	192
49	0.0400 183 537	0.0406 415 690	0.0412 649 554	0.0418 884 969	196
50	0.0400 156 878	0.0406 391 284	0.0412 627 220	0.0418 864 538	200
51	0.0400 134 092	0.0406 370 474	0.0412 608 222	0.0418 847 201	204
52	0.0400 114 617	0.0406 352 730	0.0412 592 061	0.0418 832 488	208
53	0.0400 097 971	0.0406 337 600	0.0412 578 315	0.0418 820 003	212
54	0.0400 083 743	0.0406 324 699	0.0412 566 621	0.0418 809 408	216
55	0.0400 071 582	0.0406 313 698	0.0412 556 674	0.0418 800 416	220
56	0.0400 061 187	0.0406 304 317	0.0412 548 212	0.0418 792 786	224
57	0.0400 052 302	0.0406 296 318	0.0412 541 013	0.0418 786 310	228
58	0.0400 044 707	0.0406 289 497	0.0412 534 890	0.0418 780 815	232
59	0.0400 038 215	0.0406 283 681	0.0412 529 681	0.0418 776 151	236
60	0.0400 032 666	0.0406 278 721	0.0412 525 249	0.0418 772 194	240

TABLE 6. PARTIAL PAYMENT TO AMORTIZE ONE
Payable at end of each period

QUARTERS	17% Nominal Annual Rate	17¼% Nominal Annual Rate	17½% Nominal Annual Rate	17¾% Nominal Annual Rate	QUARTERS
1	1.0425 000 000	1.0431 250 000	1.0437 500 000	1.0443 750 000	1
2	0.5320 960 832	0.5325 713 139	0.5330 466 361	0.5335 220 498	2
3	0.3620 596 468	0.3624 878 312	0.3629 161 784	0.3633 446 880	3
YEARS					
1	0.2771 150 167	0.2775 218 320	0.2779 288 757	0.2783 361 478	4
2	0.1500 649 316	0.1504 503 989	0.1508 363 420	0.1512 227 604	8
3	0.1081 034 928	0.1084 931 032	0.1088 834 234	0.1092 744 522	12
4	0.0874 102 226	0.0878 101 153	0.0882 109 387	0.0886 126 908	16
5	0.0752 198 348	0.0756 322 118	0.0760 457 245	0.0764 603 698	20
6	0.0672 763 108	0.0677 020 118	0.0681 290 352	0.0685 573 763	24
7	0.0617 549 240	0.0621 941 683	0.0626 349 013	0.0630 771 160	28
8	0.0577 427 548	0.0581 954 257	0.0586 497 294	0.0591 056 561	32
9	0.0547 322 015	0.0551 979 785	0.0556 655 090	0.0561 347 802	36
10	0.0524 183 886	0.0528 968 185	0.0533 770 987	0.0538 592 134	40
11	0.0506 070 805	0.0510 976 207	0.0515 900 845	0.0520 844 527	44
12	0.0491 686 377	0.0496 706 859	0.0501 747 082	0.0506 806 813	48
13	0.0480 132 229	0.0485 261 386	0.0490 410 567	0.0495 579 502	52
14	0.0470 766 300	0.0475 997 508	0.0481 248 818	0.0486 519 923	56
15	0.0463 117 784	0.0468 444 330	0.0473 790 870	0.0479 157 059	60
16	0.0456 833 932	0.0462 249 125	0.0467 684 034	0.0473 138 281	64
17	0.0451 645 597	0.0457 142 850	0.0462 659 393	0.0468 194 819	68
18	0.0447 344 223	0.0452 917 123	0.0458 508 762	0.0464 118 706	72
19	0.0443 766 067	0.0449 408 431	0.0455 068 877	0.0460 746 948	76
20	0.0440 781 123	0.0446 487 037	0.0452 210 294	0.0457 950 416	80
21	0.0438 285 180	0.0444 049 034	0.0449 829 425	0.0455 625 861	84
22	0.0436 194 021	0.0442 010 525	0.0447 842 714	0.0453 690 087	88
23	0.0434 439 110	0.0440 303 310	0.0446 182 312	0.0452 075 611	92
24	0.0432 964 344	0.0438 871 624	0.0444 792 809	0.0450 727 392	96
25	0.0431 723 562	0.0437 669 645	0.0443 628 735	0.0449 600 324	100
26	0.0430 678 618	0.0436 659 563	0.0442 652 621	0.0448 657 295	104
27	0.0429 797 880	0.0435 810 065	0.0441 833 491	0.0447 867 667	108
28	0.0429 055 028	0.0435 095 144	0.0441 145 653	0.0447 206 077	112
29	0.0428 428 109	0.0434 493 141	0.0440 567 751	0.0446 651 473	116
30	0.0427 898 768	0.0433 985 982	0.0440 081 993	0.0446 186 353	120
31	0.0427 451 631	0.0433 558 553	0.0439 673 531	0.0445 796 135	124
32	0.0427 073 800	0.0433 198 199	0.0439 329 954	0.0445 468 658	128
33	0.0426 754 436	0.0432 894 308	0.0439 040 879	0.0445 193 761	132
34	0.0426 484 426	0.0432 637 971	0.0438 797 603	0.0444 962 954	136
35	0.0426 256 093	0.0432 421 704	0.0438 592 831	0.0444 769 129	140
36	0.0426 062 969	0.0432 239 212	0.0438 420 442	0.0444 606 336	144
37	0.0425 899 601	0.0432 085 197	0.0438 275 294	0.0444 469 590	148
38	0.0425 761 385	0.0431 955 201	0.0438 153 070	0.0444 354 709	152
39	0.0425 644 438	0.0431 845 466	0.0438 050 138	0.0444 258 191	156
40	0.0425 545 476	0.0431 752 827	0.0437 963 447	0.0444 177 092	160
41	0.0425 461 728	0.0431 674 614	0.0437 890 428	0.0444 108 946	164
42	0.0425 390 849	0.0431 608 577	0.0437 828 923	0.0444 051 680	168
43	0.0425 330 860	0.0431 552 818	0.0437 777 113	0.0444 003 556	172
44	0.0425 280 084	0.0431 505 734	0.0437 733 468	0.0443 963 112	176
45	0.0425 237 104	0.0431 465 975	0.0437 696 700	0.0443 929 122	180
46	0.0425 200 724	0.0431 432 399	0.0437 665 725	0.0443 900 555	184
47	0.0425 169 927	0.0431 404 046	0.0437 639 629	0.0443 876 545	188
48	0.0425 143 857	0.0431 380 101	0.0437 617 644	0.0443 856 365	192
49	0.0425 121 788	0.0431 359 879	0.0437 599 121	0.0443 839 404	196
50	0.0425 103 105	0.0431 342 801	0.0437 583 515	0.0443 825 148	200
51	0.0425 087 289	0.0431 328 378	0.0437 570 366	0.0443 813 166	204
52	0.0425 073 900	0.0431 316 196	0.0437 559 288	0.0443 803 094	208
53	0.0425 062 564	0.0431 305 909	0.0437 549 954	0.0443 794 628	212
54	0.0425 052 968	0.0431 297 220	0.0437 542 090	0.0443 787 513	216
55	0.0425 044 844	0.0431 289 881	0.0437 535 464	0.0443 781 532	220
56	0.0425 037 966	0.0431 283 684	0.0437 529 881	0.0443 776 504	224
57	0.0425 032 142	0.0431 278 449	0.0437 525 177	0.0443 772 278	228
58	0.0425 027 213	0.0431 274 028	0.0437 521 214	0.0443 768 726	232
59	0.0425 023 039	0.0431 270 294	0.0437 517 874	0.0443 765 741	236
60	0.0425 019 505	0.0431 267 140	0.0437 515 060	0.0443 763 231	240

TABLE 6. PARTIAL PAYMENT TO AMORTIZE ONE
Payable at end of each period

QUARTERS	18% Nominal Annual Rate	18¼% Nominal Annual Rate	18½% Nominal Annual Rate	18¾% Nominal Annual Rate	QUARTERS
1	1.0450 000 000	1.0456 250 000	1.0462 500 000	1.0468 750 000	1
2	0.5339 975 550	0.5344 731 515	0.5349 488 393	0.5354 246 183	2
3	0.3637 733 601	0.3642 021 944	0.3646 311 908	0.3650 603 492	3
YEARS					
1	0.2787 436 479	0.2791 513 759	0.2795 593 315	0.2799 675 145	4
2	0.1516 096 533	0.1519 970 203	0.1523 848 608	0.1527 731 742	8
3	0.1096 661 886	0.1100 586 314	0.1104 517 793	0.1108 456 313	12
4	0.0890 153 694	0.0894 189 727	0.0898 234 984	0.0902 289 445	16
5	0.0768 761 443	0.0772 930 447	0.0777 110 675	0.0781 302 095	20
6	0.0689 870 299	0.0694 179 911	0.0698 502 547	0.0702 838 157	24
7	0.0635 208 051	0.0639 659 615	0.0644 125 781	0.0648 606 474	28
8	0.0595 631 962	0.0600 223 398	0.0604 830 773	0.0609 453 987	32
9	0.0566 057 796	0.0570 784 945	0.0575 529 120	0.0580 290 195	36
10	0.0543 431 466	0.0548 288 824	0.0553 164 048	0.0558 056 978	40
11	0.0525 807 056	0.0530 788 239	0.0535 787 880	0.0540 805 787	44
12	0.0511 885 821	0.0516 983 876	0.0522 100 748	0.0527 236 206	48
13	0.0500 767 923	0.0505 975 563	0.0511 202 156	0.0516 447 436	52
14	0.0491 810 518	0.0497 120 301	0.0502 448 970	0.0507 796 226	56
15	0.0484 542 558	0.0489 947 031	0.0495 370 141	0.0500 811 558	60
16	0.0478 611 494	0.0484 103 304	0.0489 613 345	0.0495 141 257	64
17	0.0473 748 725	0.0479 320 714	0.0484 910 393	0.0490 517 374	68
18	0.0469 746 524	0.0475 391 796	0.0481 054 105	0.0486 733 042	72
19	0.0466 442 194	0.0472 154 170	0.0477 882 442	0.0483 626 583	76
20	0.0463 706 935	0.0469 479 391	0.0475 267 336	0.0481 070 328	80
21	0.0461 437 861	0.0467 264 955	0.0473 106 681	0.0478 962 592	84
22	0.0459 552 152	0.0465 428 434	0.0471 318 465	0.0477 221 793	88
23	0.0457 982 710	0.0463 903 131	0.0469 836 406	0.0475 782 081	92
24	0.0456 674 877	0.0462 634 785	0.0468 606 653	0.0474 590 030	96
25	0.0455 583 922	0.0461 579 056	0.0467 585 267	0.0473 602 111	100
26	0.0454 673 100	0.0460 699 571	0.0466 736 260	0.0472 782 733	104
27	0.0453 912 122	0.0459 966 401	0.0466 030 068	0.0472 102 702	108
28	0.0453 275 957	0.0459 354 853	0.0465 442 342	0.0471 538 020	112
29	0.0452 743 866	0.0458 844 504	0.0464 952 982	0.0471 068 912	116
30	0.0452 298 637	0.0458 418 438	0.0464 545 369	0.0470 679 059	120
31	0.0451 925 960	0.0458 062 617	0.0464 205 737	0.0470 354 970	124
32	0.0451 613 921	0.0457 765 376	0.0463 922 674	0.0470 085 484	128
33	0.0451 352 588	0.0457 517 012	0.0463 686 704	0.0469 861 354	132
34	0.0451 133 678	0.0457 309 448	0.0463 489 957	0.0469 674 913	136
35	0.0450 950 272	0.0457 135 954	0.0463 325 887	0.0469 519 800	140
36	0.0450 796 590	0.0456 990 917	0.0463 189 050	0.0469 390 736	144
37	0.0450 667 799	0.0456 869 656	0.0463 074 912	0.0469 283 335	148
38	0.0450 559 856	0.0456 768 263	0.0462 979 701	0.0469 193 954	152
39	0.0450 469 379	0.0456 683 477	0.0462 900 271	0.0469 119 565	156
40	0.0450 393 537	0.0456 612 572	0.0462 834 003	0.0469 057 648	160
41	0.0450 329 958	0.0456 553 273	0.0462 778 712	0.0469 006 110	164
42	0.0450 276 658	0.0456 503 678	0.0462 732 579	0.0468 963 210	168
43	0.0450 231 971	0.0456 462 197	0.0462 694 085	0.0468 927 499	172
44	0.0450 194 506	0.0456 427 502	0.0462 661 965	0.0468 897 771	176
45	0.0450 163 094	0.0456 398 481	0.0462 635 162	0.0468 873 023	180
46	0.0450 136 756	0.0456 374 207	0.0462 612 795	0.0468 852 421	184
47	0.0450 114 673	0.0456 353 901	0.0462 594 131	0.0468 835 269	188
48	0.0450 096 156	0.0456 336 916	0.0462 578 555	0.0468 820 990	192
49	0.0450 080 630	0.0456 322 708	0.0462 565 557	0.0468 809 103	196
50	0.0450 067 611	0.0456 310 823	0.0462 554 710	0.0468 799 206	200
51	0.0450 056 695	0.0456 300 881	0.0462 545 658	0.0468 790 967	204
52	0.0450 047 541	0.0456 292 564	0.0462 538 104	0.0468 784 107	208
53	0.0450 039 866	0.0456 285 607	0.0462 531 800	0.0468 778 396	212
54	0.0450 033 429	0.0456 279 787	0.0462 526 538	0.0468 773 642	216
55	0.0450 028 032	0.0456 274 918	0.0462 522 148	0.0468 769 683	220
56	0.0450 023 506	0.0456 270 845	0.0462 518 483	0.0468 766 388	224
57	0.0450 019 711	0.0456 267 438	0.0462 515 425	0.0468 763 644	228
58	0.0450 016 529	0.0456 264 588	0.0462 512 873	0.0468 761 359	232
59	0.0450 013 861	0.0456 262 204	0.0462 510 744	0.0468 759 457	236
60	0.0450 011 623	0.0456 260 209	0.0462 508 966	0.0468 757 874	240

TABLE 6. PARTIAL PAYMENT TO AMORTIZE ONE
Payable at end of each period

QUARTERS	19% Nominal Annual Rate	19¼% Nominal Annual Rate	19½% Nominal Annual Rate	19¾% Nominal Annual Rate	QUARTERS
1	1.0475 000 000	1.0481 250 000	1.0487 500 000	1.0493 750 000	1
2	0.5359 004 884	0.5363 764 495	0.5368 525 015	0.5373 286 444	2
3	0.3654 896 693	0.3659 191 511	0.3663 487 943	0.3667 785 989	3
YEARS					
1	0.2803 759 246	0.2807 845 617	0.2811 934 256	0.2816 025 160	4
2	0.1531 619 598	0.1535 512 172	0.1539 409 457	0.1543 311 447	8
3	0.1112 401 861	0.1116 354 425	0.1120 313 995	0.1124 280 557	12
4	0.0906 353 090	0.0910 425 897	0.0914 507 845	0.0918 598 913	16
5	0.0785 504 673	0.0789 718 373	0.0793 943 163	0.0798 179 008	20
6	0.0707 186 689	0.0711 548 092	0.0715 922 314	0.0720 309 303	24
7	0.0653 101 623	0.0657 611 154	0.0662 134 994	0.0666 673 069	28
8	0.0614 092 942	0.0618 747 539	0.0623 417 680	0.0628 103 263	32
9	0.0585 068 041	0.0589 862 530	0.0594 673 534	0.0599 500 924	36
10	0.0562 967 454	0.0567 895 316	0.0572 840 403	0.0577 802 555	40
11	0.0545 841 765	0.0550 895 619	0.0555 967 156	0.0561 056 183	44
12	0.0532 390 022	0.0537 561 967	0.0542 751 814	0.0547 959 335	48
13	0.0521 711 140	0.0526 993 005	0.0532 292 771	0.0537 610 177	52
14	0.0513 161 771	0.0518 545 311	0.0523 946 552	0.0529 365 204	56
15	0.0506 270 953	0.0511 748 000	0.0517 242 377	0.0522 753 764	60
16	0.0500 686 682	0.0506 249 268	0.0511 828 665	0.0517 424 529	64
17	0.0496 141 277	0.0501 781 723	0.0507 438 343	0.0513 110 769	68
18	0.0492 428 204	0.0498 139 195	0.0503 865 626	0.0509 607 113	72
19	0.0489 386 173	0.0495 160 802	0.0500 950 066	0.0506 753 570	76
20	0.0486 887 937	0.0492 719 740	0.0498 565 325	0.0504 424 288	80
21	0.0484 832 248	0.0490 715 222	0.0496 611 096	0.0502 519 462	84
22	0.0483 137 976	0.0489 066 583	0.0495 007 197	0.0500 959 410	88
23	0.0481 739 715	0.0487 708 881	0.0493 689 164	0.0499 680 161	92
24	0.0480 584 480	0.0486 589 580	0.0492 604 924	0.0498 630 114	96
25	0.0479 629 162	0.0485 666 007	0.0491 712 245	0.0497 767 494	100
26	0.0478 838 573	0.0484 903 380	0.0490 976 768	0.0497 058 363	104
27	0.0478 183 901	0.0484 273 277	0.0490 370 458	0.0496 475 087	108
28	0.0477 641 499	0.0483 752 408	0.0489 870 392	0.0495 995 109	112
29	0.0477 191 924	0.0483 321 662	0.0489 457 791	0.0495 599 986	116
30	0.0476 819 156	0.0482 965 325	0.0489 117 246	0.0495 274 616	120
31	0.0476 509 983	0.0482 670 459	0.0488 836 099	0.0495 006 616	124
32	0.0476 253 494	0.0482 426 405	0.0488 603 937	0.0494 785 824	128
33	0.0476 040 667	0.0482 224 367	0.0488 412 191	0.0494 603 893	132
34	0.0475 864 041	0.0482 057 086	0.0488 253 802	0.0494 453 961	136
35	0.0475 717 438	0.0481 918 563	0.0488 122 950	0.0494 330 387	140
36	0.0475 595 741	0.0481 803 843	0.0488 014 836	0.0494 228 525	144
37	0.0475 494 708	0.0481 708 827	0.0487 925 502	0.0494 144 556	148
38	0.0475 410 824	0.0481 630 124	0.0487 851 680	0.0494 075 330	152
39	0.0475 341 174	0.0481 564 930	0.0487 790 674	0.0494 018 257	156
40	0.0475 283 340	0.0481 510 924	0.0487 740 255	0.0493 971 201	160
41	0.0475 235 314	0.0481 466 183	0.0487 698 586	0.0493 932 402	164
42	0.0475 195 432	0.0481 429 116	0.0487 664 146	0.0493 900 411	168
43	0.0475 162 311	0.0481 398 407	0.0487 635 680	0.0493 874 032	172
44	0.0475 134 805	0.0481 372 964	0.0487 612 152	0.0493 852 280	176
45	0.0475 111 962	0.0481 351 885	0.0487 592 705	0.0493 834 344	180
46	0.0475 092 990	0.0481 334 419	0.0487 576 630	0.0493 819 553	184
47	0.0475 077 234	0.0481 319 948	0.0487 563 343	0.0493 807 357	188
48	0.0475 064 147	0.0481 307 958	0.0487 552 360	0.0493 797 299	192
49	0.0475 053 279	0.0481 298 023	0.0487 543 282	0.0493 789 005	196
50	0.0475 044 251	0.0481 289 792	0.0487 535 778	0.0493 782 166	200
51	0.0475 036 754	0.0481 282 971	0.0487 529 575	0.0493 776 526	204
52	0.0475 030 527	0.0481 277 320	0.0487 524 447	0.0493 771 874	208
53	0.0475 025 355	0.0481 272 637	0.0487 520 209	0.0493 768 039	212
54	0.0475 021 059	0.0481 268 757	0.0487 516 705	0.0493 764 876	216
55	0.0475 017 491	0.0481 265 542	0.0487 513 809	0.0493 762 268	220
56	0.0475 014 528	0.0481 262 878	0.0487 511 415	0.0493 760 117	224
57	0.0475 012 067	0.0481 260 671	0.0487 509 436	0.0493 758 343	228
58	0.0475 010 022	0.0481 258 842	0.0487 507 800	0.0493 756 880	232
59	0.0475 008 324	0.0481 257 326	0.0487 506 448	0.0493 755 674	236
60	0.0475 006 914	0.0481 256 071	0.0487 505 330	0.0493 754 679	240

QUARTERLY
Compounding

TABLE 6. PARTIAL PAYMENT TO AMORTIZE ONE
Payable at end of each period

QUARTERS	20% Nominal Annual Rate	20¼% Nominal Annual Rate	20½% Nominal Annual Rate	20¾% Nominal Annual Rate	QUARTERS
1	1.0500 000 000	1.0506 250 000	1.0512 500 000	1.0518 750 000	1
2	0.5378 048 780	0.5382 812 024	0.5387 576 173	0.5392 341 228	2
3	0.3672 085 646	0.3676 386 914	0.3680 689 790	0.3684 994 274	3
YEARS					
1	0.2820 118 326	0.2824 213 753	0.2828 311 439	0.2832 411 380	4
2	0.1547 218 136	0.1551 129 519	0.1555 045 590	0.1558 966 342	8
3	0.1128 254 100	0.1132 234 612	0.1136 222 081	0.1140 216 495	12
4	0.0922 699 080	0.0926 808 324	0.0930 926 624	0.0935 053 958	16
5	0.0802 425 872	0.0806 683 722	0.0810 952 521	0.0815 232 237	20
6	0.0724 709 008	0.0729 121 374	0.0733 546 351	0.0737 983 884	24
7	0.0671 225 304	0.0675 791 626	0.0680 371 960	0.0684 966 230	28
8	0.0632 804 189	0.0637 520 359	0.0642 251 672	0.0646 998 026	32
9	0.0604 344 571	0.0609 204 346	0.0614 080 120	0.0618 971 763	36
10	0.0582 781 612	0.0587 777 413	0.0592 789 799	0.0597 818 609	40
11	0.0566 162 506	0.0571 285 933	0.0576 426 272	0.0581 583 331	44
12	0.0553 184 306	0.0558 426 500	0.0563 685 693	0.0568 961 663	48
13	0.0542 944 966	0.0548 296 880	0.0553 665 665	0.0559 051 067	52
14	0.0534 800 978	0.0540 253 587	0.0545 722 749	0.0551 208 182	56
15	0.0528 281 845	0.0533 826 308	0.0539 386 844	0.0544 963 145	60
16	0.0523 036 520	0.0528 664 302	0.0534 307 543	0.0539 965 917	64
17	0.0518 798 643	0.0524 501 608	0.0530 219 316	0.0535 951 422	68
18	0.0515 363 280	0.0521 133 758	0.0526 918 184	0.0532 716 202	72
19	0.0512 570 925	0.0518 401 753	0.0524 245 681	0.0530 102 345	76
20	0.0510 296 235	0.0516 180 780	0.0522 077 547	0.0527 986 169	80
21	0.0508 439 924	0.0514 372 094	0.0520 315 596	0.0526 270 063	84
22	0.0506 922 828	0.0512 897 065	0.0518 881 748	0.0524 876 514	88
23	0.0505 681 481	0.0511 692 746	0.0517 713 589	0.0523 743 655	92
24	0.0504 664 770	0.0510 708 522	0.0516 761 013	0.0522 821 899	96
25	0.0503 831 381	0.0509 903 549	0.0515 983 654	0.0522 071 365	100
26	0.0503 147 810	0.0509 244 764	0.0515 348 895	0.0521 459 886	104
27	0.0502 586 824	0.0508 705 338	0.0514 830 318	0.0520 961 461	108
28	0.0502 126 236	0.0508 263 460	0.0514 406 485	0.0520 555 027	112
29	0.0501 747 942	0.0507 901 363	0.0514 059 972	0.0520 223 501	116
30	0.0501 437 145	0.0507 604 559	0.0513 776 595	0.0519 953 007	120
31	0.0501 181 741	0.0507 361 216	0.0513 544 800	0.0519 732 262	124
32	0.0500 971 814	0.0507 161 668	0.0513 355 163	0.0519 552 084	128
33	0.0500 799 238	0.0506 998 007	0.0513 199 993	0.0519 404 999	132
34	0.0500 657 349	0.0506 863 762	0.0513 073 010	0.0519 284 914	136
35	0.0500 540 677	0.0506 753 633	0.0512 969 083	0.0519 186 863	140
36	0.0500 444 731	0.0506 663 282	0.0512 884 020	0.0519 106 797	144
37	0.0500 365 823	0.0506 589 150	0.0512 814 392	0.0519 041 414	148
38	0.0500 300 925	0.0506 528 323	0.0512 757 394	0.0518 988 018	152
39	0.0500 247 545	0.0506 478 410	0.0512 710 734	0.0518 944 409	156
40	0.0500 203 638	0.0506 437 451	0.0512 672 536	0.0518 908 792	160
41	0.0500 167 521	0.0506 403 840	0.0512 641 263	0.0518 879 703	164
42	0.0500 137 812	0.0506 376 257	0.0512 615 660	0.0518 855 943	168
43	0.0500 113 373	0.0506 353 620	0.0512 594 698	0.0518 836 537	172
44	0.0500 093 268	0.0506 335 043	0.0512 577 536	0.0518 820 685	176
45	0.0500 076 730	0.0506 319 796	0.0512 563 484	0.0518 807 738	180
46	0.0500 063 124	0.0506 307 284	0.0512 551 980	0.0518 797 163	184
47	0.0500 051 931	0.0506 297 015	0.0512 542 560	0.0518 788 524	188
48	0.0500 042 723	0.0506 288 586	0.0512 534 847	0.0518 781 468	192
49	0.0500 035 148	0.0506 281 669	0.0512 528 533	0.0518 775 705	196
50	0.0500 028 916	0.0506 275 992	0.0512 523 362	0.0518 770 997	200
51	0.0500 023 789	0.0506 271 333	0.0512 519 129	0.0518 767 151	204
52	0.0500 019 571	0.0506 267 509	0.0512 515 662	0.0518 764 010	208
53	0.0500 016 101	0.0506 264 370	0.0512 512 824	0.0518 761 444	212
54	0.0500 013 246	0.0506 261 794	0.0512 510 500	0.0518 759 348	216
55	0.0500 010 898	0.0506 259 680	0.0512 508 598	0.0518 757 636	220
56	0.0500 008 966	0.0506 257 945	0.0512 507 040	0.0518 756 237	224
57	0.0500 007 376	0.0506 256 521	0.0512 505 764	0.0518 755 095	228
58	0.0500 006 068	0.0506 255 352	0.0512 504 720	0.0518 754 162	232
59	0.0500 004 992	0.0506 254 392	0.0512 503 864	0.0518 753 400	236
60	0.0500 004 107	0.0506 253 605	0.0512 503 164	0.0518 752 777	240

TABLE 6. PARTIAL PAYMENT TO AMORTIZE ONE
Payable at end of each period

QUARTERLY Compounding

QUARTERS	21% Nominal Annual Rate	21¼% Nominal Annual Rate	21½% Nominal Annual Rate	21¾% Nominal Annual Rate	QUARTERS
1	1.0525 000 000	1.0531 250 000	1.0537 500 000	1.0543 750 000	1
2	0.5397 107 186	0.5401 874 049	0.5406 641 814	0.5411 410 481	2
3	0.3689 300 363	0.3693 608 057	0.3697 917 353	0.3702 228 250	3
YEARS					
1	0.2836 513 576	0.2840 618 023	0.2844 724 720	0.2848 833 664	4
2	0.1562 891 770	0.1566 821 867	0.1570 756 628	0.1574 696 047	8
3	0.1144 217 842	0.1148 226 109	0.1152 241 284	0.1156 263 356	12
4	0.0939 190 304	0.0943 335 642	0.0947 489 948	0.0951 653 202	16
5	0.0819 522 832	0.0823 824 271	0.0828 136 520	0.0832 459 541	20
6	0.0742 433 921	0.0746 896 409	0.0751 371 293	0.0755 858 520	24
7	0.0689 574 362	0.0694 196 280	0.0698 831 909	0.0703 481 173	28
8	0.0651 759 322	0.0656 535 458	0.0661 326 333	0.0666 131 846	32
9	0.0623 879 146	0.0628 802 140	0.0633 740 614	0.0638 694 440	36
10	0.0602 863 683	0.0607 924 862	0.0613 001 986	0.0618 094 896	40
11	0.0586 756 919	0.0591 946 845	0.0597 152 920	0.0602 374 953	44
12	0.0574 254 187	0.0579 563 044	0.0584 888 015	0.0590 228 881	48
13	0.0564 452 836	0.0569 870 720	0.0575 304 474	0.0580 753 849	52
14	0.0556 709 607	0.0562 226 749	0.0567 759 335	0.0573 307 093	56
15	0.0550 554 911	0.0556 161 842	0.0561 783 643	0.0567 420 022	60
16	0.0545 639 102	0.0551 326 779	0.0557 028 636	0.0562 744 364	64
17	0.0541 697 590	0.0547 457 486	0.0553 230 784	0.0559 017 163	68
18	0.0538 527 462	0.0544 351 623	0.0550 188 348	0.0556 037 308	72
19	0.0535 971 390	0.0541 852 467	0.0547 745 236	0.0553 649 362	76
20	0.0533 906 287	0.0539 837 550	0.0545 779 618	0.0551 732 158	80
21	0.0532 235 137	0.0538 210 471	0.0544 195 727	0.0550 190 577	84
22	0.0530 881 011	0.0536 894 898	0.0542 917 843	0.0548 949 524	88
23	0.0529 782 600	0.0535 830 092	0.0541 885 809	0.0547 949 439	92
24	0.0528 890 846	0.0534 967 533	0.0541 051 651	0.0547 142 901	96
25	0.0528 166 360	0.0534 268 333	0.0540 376 988	0.0546 492 040	100
26	0.0527 577 433	0.0533 701 242	0.0539 831 035	0.0545 966 540	104
27	0.0527 098 478	0.0533 241 095	0.0539 389 047	0.0545 542 080	108
28	0.0526 708 814	0.0532 867 588	0.0539 031 102	0.0545 199 119	112
29	0.0526 391 698	0.0532 564 320	0.0538 741 138	0.0544 921 933	116
30	0.0526 133 557	0.0532 318 023	0.0538 506 190	0.0544 697 859	120
31	0.0525 923 382	0.0532 117 956	0.0538 315 786	0.0544 516 688	124
32	0.0525 752 232	0.0531 955 416	0.0538 161 457	0.0544 370 185	128
33	0.0525 612 842	0.0531 823 347	0.0538 036 352	0.0544 251 703	132
34	0.0525 499 305	0.0531 716 026	0.0537 934 928	0.0544 155 873	136
35	0.0525 406 819	0.0531 628 808	0.0537 852 696	0.0544 078 358	140
36	0.0525 331 475	0.0531 557 923	0.0537 786 020	0.0544 015 654	144
37	0.0525 270 092	0.0531 500 308	0.0537 731 955	0.0543 964 930	148
38	0.0525 220 080	0.0531 453 478	0.0537 688 112	0.0543 923 893	152
39	0.0525 179 333	0.0531 415 412	0.0537 652 559	0.0543 890 694	156
40	0.0525 146 131	0.0531 384 469	0.0537 623 727	0.0543 863 835	160
41	0.0525 119 078	0.0531 359 315	0.0537 600 345	0.0543 842 104	164
42	0.0525 097 034	0.0531 338 868	0.0537 581 382	0.0543 824 522	168
43	0.0525 079 072	0.0531 322 246	0.0537 566 003	0.0543 810 296	172
44	0.0525 064 435	0.0531 308 733	0.0537 553 531	0.0543 798 787	176
45	0.0525 052 508	0.0531 297 748	0.0537 543 416	0.0543 789 474	180
46	0.0525 042 789	0.0531 288 817	0.0537 535 212	0.0543 781 939	184
47	0.0525 034 868	0.0531 281 557	0.0537 528 558	0.0543 775 843	188
48	0.0525 028 414	0.0531 275 655	0.0537 523 162	0.0543 770 910	192
49	0.0525 023 155	0.0531 270 857	0.0537 518 786	0.0543 766 919	196
50	0.0525 018 869	0.0531 266 956	0.0537 515 236	0.0543 763 690	200
51	0.0525 015 377	0.0531 263 785	0.0537 512 357	0.0543 761 077	204
52	0.0525 012 531	0.0531 261 207	0.0537 510 022	0.0543 758 962	208
53	0.0525 010 211	0.0531 259 111	0.0537 508 129	0.0543 757 252	212
54	0.0525 008 321	0.0531 257 407	0.0537 506 593	0.0543 755 868	216
55	0.0525 006 781	0.0531 256 022	0.0537 505 347	0.0543 754 748	220
56	0.0525 005 526	0.0531 254 896	0.0537 504 337	0.0543 753 841	224
57	0.0525 004 503	0.0531 253 980	0.0537 503 517	0.0543 753 108	228
58	0.0525 003 670	0.0531 253 236	0.0537 502 853	0.0543 752 515	232
59	0.0525 002 991	0.0531 252 631	0.0537 502 314	0.0543 752 035	236
60	0.0525 002 437	0.0531 252 139	0.0537 501 877	0.0543 751 647	240

TABLE 6. PARTIAL PAYMENT TO AMORTIZE ONE
Payable at end of each period

QUARTERS	22% Nominal Annual Rate	22¼% Nominal Annual Rate	22½% Nominal Annual Rate	22¾% Nominal Annual Rate	QUARTERS
1	1.0550 000 000	1.0556 250 000	1.0562 500 000	1.0568 750 000	1
2	0.5416 180 049	0.5420 950 517	0.5425 721 884	0.5430 494 151	2
3	0.3706 540 747	0.3710 854 842	0.3715 170 534	0.3719 487 820	3
YEARS					
1	0.2852 944 853	0.2857 058 285	0.2861 173 958	0.2865 291 869	4
2	0.1578 640 118	0.1582 588 835	0.1586 542 191	0.1590 500 181	8
3	0.1160 292 312	0.1164 328 139	0.1168 370 826	0.1172 420 359	12
4	0.0955 825 380	0.0960 006 461	0.0964 196 423	0.0968 395 244	16
5	0.0836 793 300	0.0841 137 761	0.0845 492 886	0.0849 858 641	20
6	0.0760 358 037	0.0764 869 789	0.0769 393 721	0.0773 929 780	24
7	0.0708 143 996	0.0712 820 301	0.0717 510 012	0.0722 213 054	28
8	0.0670 951 895	0.0675 786 378	0.0680 635 194	0.0685 498 241	32
9	0.0643 663 488	0.0648 647 629	0.0653 646 732	0.0658 660 670	36
10	0.0623 203 434	0.0628 327 439	0.0633 466 755	0.0638 621 224	40
11	0.0607 612 757	0.0612 866 144	0.0618 134 926	0.0623 418 918	44
12	0.0595 585 424	0.0600 957 429	0.0606 344 681	0.0611 746 968	48
13	0.0586 218 603	0.0591 698 494	0.0597 193 281	0.0602 702 727	52
14	0.0578 869 756	0.0584 447 060	0.0590 038 742	0.0595 644 543	56
15	0.0573 070 692	0.0578 735 369	0.0584 413 771	0.0590 105 624	60
16	0.0568 473 659	0.0574 216 223	0.0579 971 759	0.0585 739 980	64
17	0.0564 816 307	0.0570 627 907	0.0576 451 657	0.0582 287 261	68
18	0.0561 898 180	0.0567 770 648	0.0573 654 404	0.0579 549 142	72
19	0.0559 564 521	0.0565 490 395	0.0571 426 673	0.0577 373 052	76
20	0.0557 694 845	0.0563 667 363	0.0569 649 405	0.0575 640 670	80
21	0.0556 194 699	0.0562 207 785	0.0568 229 532	0.0574 259 647	84
22	0.0554 989 631	0.0561 037 860	0.0567 093 920	0.0573 157 527	88
23	0.0554 020 682	0.0560 099 246	0.0566 184 850	0.0572 277 223	92
24	0.0553 240 994	0.0559 345 653	0.0565 456 610	0.0571 573 606	96
25	0.0552 613 216	0.0558 740 252	0.0564 872 895	0.0571 010 903	100
26	0.0552 107 501	0.0558 253 670	0.0564 404 810	0.0570 560 693	104
27	0.0551 699 955	0.0557 862 438	0.0564 029 311	0.0570 200 361	108
28	0.0551 371 415	0.0557 547 775	0.0563 727 995	0.0569 911 881	112
29	0.0551 106 497	0.0557 294 632	0.0563 486 151	0.0569 680 875	116
30	0.0550 892 837	0.0557 090 942	0.0563 292 003	0.0569 495 857	120
31	0.0550 720 487	0.0556 927 017	0.0563 136 121	0.0569 347 652	124
32	0.0550 581 442	0.0556 795 077	0.0563 010 948	0.0569 228 920	128
33	0.0550 469 254	0.0556 688 871	0.0562 910 423	0.0569 133 792	132
34	0.0550 378 728	0.0556 603 371	0.0562 829 688	0.0569 057 569	136
35	0.0550 305 675	0.0556 534 537	0.0562 764 841	0.0568 996 492	140
36	0.0550 246 719	0.0556 479 117	0.0562 712 755	0.0568 947 547	144
37	0.0550 199 139	0.0556 434 494	0.0562 670 915	0.0568 908 324	148
38	0.0550 160 737	0.0556 398 565	0.0562 637 305	0.0568 876 890	152
39	0.0550 129 742	0.0556 369 634	0.0562 610 306	0.0568 851 698	156
40	0.0550 104 725	0.0556 346 338	0.0562 588 617	0.0568 831 509	160
41	0.0550 084 533	0.0556 327 579	0.0562 571 193	0.0568 815 328	164
42	0.0550 068 234	0.0556 312 473	0.0562 557 195	0.0568 802 359	168
43	0.0550 055 079	0.0556 300 309	0.0562 545 950	0.0568 791 965	172
44	0.0550 044 460	0.0556 290 514	0.0562 536 915	0.0568 783 635	176
45	0.0550 035 888	0.0556 282 625	0.0562 529 658	0.0568 776 958	180
46	0.0550 028 969	0.0556 276 273	0.0562 523 827	0.0568 771 607	184
47	0.0550 023 384	0.0556 271 158	0.0562 519 142	0.0568 767 318	188
48	0.0550 018 876	0.0556 267 038	0.0562 515 379	0.0568 763 880	192
49	0.0550 015 237	0.0556 263 721	0.0562 512 355	0.0568 761 125	196
50	0.0550 012 299	0.0556 261 050	0.0562 509 926	0.0568 758 917	200
51	0.0550 009 928	0.0556 258 898	0.0562 507 975	0.0568 757 147	204
52	0.0550 008 014	0.0556 257 166	0.0562 506 407	0.0568 755 728	208
53	0.0550 006 469	0.0556 255 771	0.0562 505 147	0.0568 754 591	212
54	0.0550 005 222	0.0556 254 647	0.0562 504 135	0.0568 753 680	216
55	0.0550 004 215	0.0556 253 742	0.0562 503 322	0.0568 752 949	220
56	0.0550 003 403	0.0556 253 014	0.0562 502 669	0.0568 752 364	224
57	0.0550 002 747	0.0556 252 427	0.0562 502 144	0.0568 751 895	228
58	0.0550 002 217	0.0556 251 954	0.0562 501 723	0.0568 751 519	232
59	0.0550 001 790	0.0556 251 574	0.0562 501 384	0.0568 751 217	236
60	0.0550 001 445	0.0556 251 268	0.0562 501 112	0.0568 750 976	240

TABLE 1. FUTURE WORTH OF ONE DOLLAR WITH INTEREST
Payable at beginning of each period

SEMI ANNUAL Compounding

HALF YEARS	5% Nominal Annual Rate	5¼% Nominal Annual Rate	5½% Nominal Annual Rate	5¾% Nominal Annual Rate	HALF YEARS
1	1.0250 000 000	1.0262 500 000	1.0275 000 000	1.0287 500 000	1
YEARS					
1	1.0506 250 000	1.0531 890 625	1.0557 562 500	1.0583 265 625	2
2	1.1038 128 906	1.1092 072 014	1.1146 212 594	1.1200 551 129	4
3	1.1596 934 182	1.1682 048 925	1.1767 683 610	1.1853 840 774	6
4	1.2184 028 975	1.2303 406 156	1.2423 805 519	1.2545 234 559	8
5	1.2800 845 442	1.2957 812 795	1.3116 510 326	1.3276 954 967	10
6	1.3448 888 242	1.3647 026 709	1.3847 837 755	1.4051 354 110	12
7	1.4129 738 210	1.4372 899 266	1.4619 941 259	1.4870 921 294	14
8	1.4845 056 207	1.5137 380 303	1.5435 094 358	1.5738 291 014	16
9	1.5596 587 177	1.5942 523 370	1.6295 697 338	1.6656 251 429	18
10	1.6386 164 403	1.6790 491 242	1.7204 284 313	1.7627 753 319	20
11	1.7215 713 976	1.7683 561 730	1.8163 530 690	1.8655 919 575	22
12	1.8087 259 496	1.8624 133 800	1.9176 261 048	1.9744 055 234	24
13	1.9002 927 008	1.9614 734 017	2.0245 457 453	2.0895 658 105	26
14	1.9964 950 188	2.0658 023 331	2.1374 268 240	2.2114 430 014	28
15	2.0975 675 791	2.1756 804 225	2.2566 017 284	2.3404 288 698	30
16	2.2037 569 378	2.2914 028 244	2.3824 213 785	2.4769 380 406	32
17	2.3153 221 327	2.4132 803 925	2.5152 562 605	2.6214 093 220	34
18	2.4325 353 157	2.5416 405 141	2.6554 975 174	2.7743 071 167	36
19	2.5556 824 161	2.6768 279 903	2.8035 581 008	2.9361 229 141	38
20	2.6850 638 384	2.8192 059 615	2.9598 739 872	3.1073 768 707	40
21	2.8209 951 952	2.9691 568 836	3.1249 054 612	3.2886 194 820	42
22	2.9638 080 770	3.1270 835 547	3.2991 384 713	3.4804 333 518	44
23	3.1138 508 609	3.2934 101 973	3.4830 860 607	3.6834 350 652	46
24	3.2714 895 607	3.4685 835 981	3.6772 898 779	3.8982 771 707	48
25	3.4371 087 197	3.6530 743 079	3.8823 217 716	4.1256 502 778	50
26	3.6111 123 486	3.8473 779 056	4.0987 854 749	4.3662 852 765	52
27	3.7939 249 113	4.0520 163 295	4.3273 183 825	4.6209 556 876	54
28	3.9859 923 599	4.2675 392 793	4.5685 934 281	4.8904 801 483	56
29	4.1877 832 231	4.4945 256 927	4.8233 210 654	5.1757 250 444	58
30	4.3997 897 488	4.7335 853 007	5.0922 513 606	5.4776 072 947	60
31	4.6225 291 048	4.9853 602 651	5.3761 762 005	5.7970 972 989	62
32	4.8565 446 408	5.2505 269 039	5.6759 316 248	6.1352 220 568	64
33	5.1024 072 132	5.5297 975 075	5.9924 002 874	6.4930 684 695	66
34	5.3607 165 784	5.8239 222 527	6.3265 140 559	6.8717 868 335	68
35	5.6321 028 552	6.1336 912 174	6.6792 567 553	7.2725 945 377	70
36	5.9172 280 622	6.4599 365 030	7.0516 670 647	7.6967 799 775	72
37	6.2167 877 329	6.8035 344 694	7.4448 415 765	8.1457 066 959	74
38	6.5315 126 118	7.1654 080 895	7.8599 380 247	8.6208 177 666	76
39	6.8621 704 378	7.5465 294 282	8.2981 786 942	9.1236 404 329	78
40	7.2095 678 162	7.9479 222 536	8.7608 540 200	9.6557 910 168	80
41	7.5745 521 869	8.3706 647 871	9.2493 263 869	10.2189 801 151	82
42	7.9580 138 914	8.8158 925 996	9.7650 341 413	10.8150 180 974	84
43	8.3608 883 446	9.2848 016 621	10.3094 958 261	11.4458 209 264	86
44	8.7841 583 171	9.7786 515 580	10.8843 146 528	12.1134 163 161	88
45	9.2288 563 319	10.2987 688 669	11.4911 832 216	12.8199 502 499	90
46	9.6960 671 837	10.8465 507 278	12.1318 885 061	13.5676 938 794	92
47	10.1869 305 849	11.4234 685 924	12.8083 171 147	14.3590 508 244	94
48	10.7026 439 457	12.0310 721 773	13.5224 608 458	15.1965 648 998	96
49	11.2444 652 955	12.6709 936 273	14.2764 225 533	16.0829 282 922	98
50	11.8137 163 511	13.3449 518 993	15.0724 223 383	17.0209 902 144	100
51	12.4117 857 413	14.0547 573 799	15.9128 040 863	18.0137 660 640	102
52	13.0401 323 945	14.8023 167 486	16.8000 423 691	19.0644 471 162	104
53	13.7002 890 970	15.5896 380 993	17.7367 497 315	20.1764 107 824	106
54	14.3938 662 325	16.4188 363 345	18.7256 843 837	21.3532 314 670	108
55	15.1225 557 105	17.2921 388 465	19.7697 583 236	22.5986 920 567	110
56	15.8881 350 934	18.2118 915 004	20.8720 459 111	23.9167 960 814	112
57	16.6924 719 325	19.1805 649 356	22.0357 929 210	25.3117 805 828	114
58	17.5375 283 240	20.2007 612 028	23.2644 261 000	26.7881 297 349	116
59	18.4253 656 954	21.2752 207 529	24.5615 632 578	28.3505 892 582	118
60	19.3581 498 338	22.4068 297 992	25.9310 239 192	30.0041 816 745	120

SEMI ANNUAL
Compounding

TABLE 1. FUTURE WORTH OF ONE DOLLAR WITH INTEREST
Payable at beginning of each period

HALF YEARS	6% Nominal Annual Rate	6¼% Nominal Annual Rate	6½% Nominal Annual Rate	6¾% Nominal Annual Rate	HALF YEARS
1	1.0300 000 000	1.0312 500 000	1.0325 000 000	1.0337 500 000	1
YEARS					
1	1.0609 000 000	1.0634 765 625	1.0660 562 500	1.0686 390 625	2
2	1.1255 088 100	1.1309 823 990	1.1364 759 282	1.1419 894 459	4
3	1.1940 522 965	1.2027 732 739	1.2115 472 662	1.2203 745 309	6
4	1.2667 700 814	1.2791 211 868	1.2915 775 353	1.3041 398 945	8
5	1.3439 163 793	1.3603 154 028	1.3768 943 039	1.3936 548 343	10
6	1.4257 608 868	1.4466 635 485	1.4678 467 782	1.4893 139 956	12
7	1.5125 897 249	1.5384 927 776	1.5648 072 320	1.5915 391 120	14
8	1.6047 064 391	1.6361 510 106	1.6681 725 297	1.7007 808 646	16
9	1.7024 330 612	1.7400 082 524	1.7783 657 513	1.8175 208 686	18
10	1.8061 112 347	1.8504 579 950	1.8958 379 240	1.9422 737 971	20
11	1.9161 034 089	1.9679 187 076	2.0210 698 679	2.0755 896 497	22
12	2.0327 941 065	2.0928 354 224	2.1545 741 643	2.2180 561 774	24
13	2.1565 912 675	2.2256 814 209	2.2968 972 540	2.3703 014 739	26
14	2.2879 276 757	2.3669 600 268	2.4486 216 732	2.5329 967 449	28
15	2.4272 624 712	2.5172 065 128	2.6103 684 386	2.7068 592 668	30
16	2.5750 827 557	2.6769 901 294	2.7827 995 888	2.8926 555 492	32
17	2.7319 052 955	2.8469 162 606	2.9666 208 941	3.0912 047 143	34
18	2.8982 783 280	3.0276 287 186	3.1625 847 456	3.3033 821 079	36
19	3.0747 834 782	3.2198 121 822	3.3714 932 342	3.5301 231 588	38
20	3.2620 377 920	3.4241 947 914	3.5942 014 341	3.7724 275 029	40
21	3.4606 958 935	3.6415 509 061	3.8316 209 026	4.0313 633 901	42
22	3.6714 522 734	3.8727 040 398	4.0847 234 108	4.3080 723 938	44
23	3.8950 437 169	4.1185 299 798	4.3545 449 216	4.6037 744 441	46
24	4.1322 518 793	4.3799 601 055	4.6421 898 296	4.9197 732 059	48
25	4.3839 060 187	4.6579 849 168	4.9488 354 816	5.2574 618 264	50
26	4.6508 858 952	4.9536 577 875	5.2757 369 953	5.6183 290 773	52
27	4.9341 248 463	5.2680 989 557	5.6242 323 972	6.0039 659 180	54
28	5.2346 130 494	5.6024 997 683	5.9957 480 985	6.4160 725 099	56
29	5.5534 009 841	5.9581 271 950	6.3918 047 339	6.8564 657 119	58
30	5.8916 031 040	6.3363 286 283	6.8140 233 853	7.3270 870 905	60
31	6.2504 017 331	6.7385 369 885	7.2641 322 176	7.8300 114 792	62
32	6.6310 511 986	7.1662 761 528	7.7439 735 513	8.3674 561 265	64
33	7.0348 822 166	7.6211 667 289	8.2555 114 043	8.9417 904 705	66
34	7.4633 065 436	8.1049 321 951	8.8008 395 294	9.5555 465 855	68
35	7.9178 219 121	8.6194 054 301	9.3821 899 856	10.2114 303 448	70
36	8.4000 172 666	9.1665 356 576	10.0019 422 729	10.9123 333 505	72
37	8.9115 783 181	9.7483 958 312	10.6626 330 721	11.6613 456 813	74
38	9.4542 934 377	10.3671 904 885	11.3669 666 280	12.4617 695 164	76
39	10.0300 599 080	11.0252 641 034	12.1178 258 173	13.3171 336 931	78
40	10.6408 905 564	11.7251 099 694	12.9182 839 489	14.2312 092 650	80
41	11.2889 207 913	12.4693 796 452	13.7716 173 431	15.2080 261 272	82
42	11.9764 160 675	13.2608 930 016	14.6813 187 412	16.2518 907 830	84
43	12.7057 798 060	14.1026 489 050	15.6511 116 023	17.3674 053 302	86
44	13.4795 617 962	14.9978 365 796	16.6849 653 430	18.5594 877 501	88
45	14.3004 671 096	15.9498 476 906	17.7871 115 850	19.8333 935 898	90
46	15.1713 655 566	16.9622 891 944	18.9620 614 746	21.1947 391 320	92
47	16.0953 017 190	18.0389 970 046	20.2146 241 479	22.6495 261 559	94
48	17.0755 055 936	19.1840 505 254	21.5499 264 143	24.2041 683 973	96
49	18.1154 038 843	20.4017 881 076	22.9734 337 410	25.8655 198 247	98
50	19.2186 319 809	21.6968 234 855	24.4909 726 235	27.6409 048 566	100
51	20.3890 466 685	23.0740 632 575	26.1087 544 339	29.5381 506 526	102
52	21.6307 396 106	24.5387 254 760	27.8334 008 440	31.5656 216 213	104
53	22.9480 516 529	26.0963 594 174	29.6719 709 285	33.7322 562 967	106
54	24.3455 879 985	27.7528 666 070	31.6319 900 581	36.0476 067 449	108
55	25.8282 343 077	29.5145 231 787	33.7214 807 014	38.5218 806 772	110
56	27.4011 737 770	31.3880 036 539	35.9489 952 610	41.1659 864 526	112
57	29.0699 052 600	33.3804 062 296	38.3236 510 792	43.9915 811 696	114
58	30.8402 624 903	35.4992 796 719	40.8551 677 558	47.0111 220 590	116
59	32.7184 344 760	37.7526 519 167	43.5539 069 308	50.2379 214 042	118
60	34.7109 871 356	40.1490 604 856	46.4309 146 955	53.6862 052 313	120

TABLE 1. FUTURE WORTH OF ONE DOLLAR WITH INTEREST
Payable at beginning of each period

SEMI ANNUAL Compounding

HALF YEARS	7% Nominal Annual Rate	7¼% Nominal Annual Rate	7½% Nominal Annual Rate	7¾% Nominal Annual Rate	HALF YEARS
1	1.0350 000 000	1.0362 500 000	1.0375 000 000	1.0387 500 000	1
YEARS					
1	1.0712 250 000	1.0738 140 625	1.0764 062 500	1.0790 015 625	2
2	1.1475 230 006	1.1530 766 408	1.1586 504 150	1.1642 443 719	4
3	1.2292 553 263	1.2381 899 121	1.2471 785 483	1.2562 214 964	6
4	1.3168 090 370	1.3295 857 396	1.3424 707 843	1.3554 649 574	8
5	1.4105 987 606	1.4277 278 645	1.4450 439 426	1.4625 488 070	10
6	1.5110 686 573	1.5331 142 583	1.5554 543 314	1.5780 924 480	12
7	1.6186 945 225	1.6462 796 500	1.6743 007 639	1.7027 642 171	14
8	1.7339 860 398	1.7677 982 390	1.8022 278 066	1.8372 852 509	16
9	1.8574 891 955	1.8982 866 087	1.9399 292 750	1.9824 336 564	18
10	1.9897 888 635	2.0384 068 551	2.0881 519 961	2.1390 490 129	20
11	2.1315 115 753	2.1888 699 461	2.2476 998 596	2.3080 372 271	22
12	2.2833 284 872	2.3504 393 291	2.4194 381 770	2.4903 757 744	24
13	2.4459 585 587	2.5239 348 046	2.6042 983 752	2.6871 193 518	26
14	2.6201 719 571	2.7102 366 860	2.8032 830 479	2.8994 059 792	28
15	2.8067 937 047	2.9102 902 661	3.0174 713 933	3.1284 635 819	30
16	3.0067 075 863	3.1251 106 137	3.2480 250 670	3.3756 170 931	32
17	3.2208 603 342	3.3557 877 239	3.4961 944 822	3.6422 961 178	34
18	3.4502 661 115	3.6034 920 487	3.7633 255 919	3.9300 432 022	36
19	3.6960 113 152	3.8694 804 360	4.0508 671 879	4.2405 227 559	38
20	3.9592 597 212	4.1551 025 067	4.3603 787 590	4.5755 306 794	40
21	4.2412 579 948	4.4618 075 028	4.6935 389 485	4.9370 047 524	42
22	4.5433 415 955	4.7911 516 407	5.0521 546 588	5.3270 358 419	44
23	4.8669 411 006	5.1448 060 074	5.4381 708 507	5.7478 799 969	46
24	5.2135 889 805	5.5245 650 396	5.8536 810 923	6.2019 714 977	48
25	5.5849 268 557	5.9323 556 287	6.3009 389 132	6.6919 369 366	50
26	5.9827 132 710	6.3702 468 978	6.7823 700 270	7.2206 104 107	52
27	6.4088 320 237	6.8404 607 005	7.3005 854 869	7.7910 499 154	54
28	6.8653 010 846	7.3453 828 942	7.8583 958 468	8.4065 550 322	56
29	7.3542 821 543	7.8875 754 462	8.4588 264 045	9.0706 860 150	58
30	7.8780 909 008	8.4697 894 331	9.1051 336 094	9.7872 843 831	60
31	8.4392 079 252	9.0949 789 997	9.8008 227 243	10.5604 951 420	62
32	9.0402 905 096	9.7663 163 481	10.5496 668 355	11.3947 907 590	64
33	9.6841 852 012	10.4872 078 334	11.3557 273 172	12.2949 970 333	66
34	10.3739 412 921	11.2613 112 478	12.2233 758 575	13.2663 210 099	68
35	11.1128 252 607	12.0925 543 801	13.1573 181 691	14.3143 810 983	70
36	11.9043 362 399	12.9851 549 449	14.1626 195 105	15.4452 395 713	72
37	12.7522 225 885	13.9436 419 836	15.2447 321 575	16.6654 376 306	74
38	13.6604 996 424	14.9728 788 444	16.4095 249 739	17.9820 332 432	76
39	14.6334 687 294	16.0780 878 593	17.6633 152 414	19.4026 419 663	78
40	15.6757 375 397	17.2648 768 414	19.0129 029 216	20.9354 809 983	80
41	16.7922 419 460	18.5392 675 396	20.4656 075 354	22.5894 167 088	82
42	17.9882 693 786	19.9077 261 925	22.0293 078 612	24.3740 159 248	84
43	19.2694 838 651	21.3771 963 379	23.7124 846 650	26.2996 012 672	86
44	20.6419 528 533	22.9551 340 444	25.5242 666 964	28.3773 108 605	88
45	22.1121 759 453	24.6495 457 435	27.4744 801 987	30.6191 627 580	90
46	23.6871 156 770	26.4690 288 536	29.5737 022 013	33.0381 244 583	92
47	25.3742 304 911	28.4228 154 037	31.8333 178 852	35.6481 879 126	94
48	27.1815 100 579	30.5208 188 764	34.2655 823 298	38.4644 504 580	96
49	29.1175 131 117	32.7736 845 084	36.8836 869 797	41.5032 021 449	98
50	31.1914 079 831	35.1928 433 051	39.7018 311 880	44.7820 199 631	100
51	33.4130 160 167	37.7905 700 404	42.7352 992 272	48.3198 695 120	102
52	35.7928 580 825	40.5800 455 392	46.0005 431 838	52.1372 147 033	104
53	38.3422 043 994	43.5754 235 569	49.5152 721 864	56.2561 361 292	106
54	41.0731 279 078	46.7919 025 948	53.2985 484 519	60.7004 587 837	108
55	43.9985 614 430	50.2458 030 175	57.3708 906 696	65.4958 898 720	110
56	47.1323 589 818	53.9546 498 618	61.7543 852 848	70.6701 675 093	112
57	50.4893 612 503	57.9372 617 588	66.4728 062 855	76.2532 211 646	114
58	54.0854 660 053	62.2138 464 194	71.5517 441 407	82.2773 447 823	116
59	57.9377 033 215	66.8061 031 673	77.0187 445 915	88.7773 835 785	118
60	62.0643 162 406	71.7373 330 419	82.9034 580 454	95.7909 355 958	120

TABLE 1. FUTURE WORTH OF ONE DOLLAR WITH INTEREST
Payable at beginning of each period

HALF YEARS	8% Nominal Annual Rate	8¼% Nominal Annual Rate	8½% Nominal Annual Rate	8¾% Nominal Annual Rate	HALF YEARS
1	1.0400 000 000	1.0412 500 000	1.0425 000 000	1.0437 500 000	1
YEARS					
1	1.0816 000 000	1.0842 015 625	1.0868 062 500	1.0894 140 625	2
2	1.1698 585 600	1.1754 930 281	1.1811 478 250	1.1868 229 996	4
3	1.2653 190 185	1.2744 713 778	1.2836 788 384	1.2929 416 654	6
4	1.3685 690 504	1.3817 838 592	1.3951 101 846	1.4085 488 323	8
5	1.4802 442 849	1.4981 322 192	1.5162 144 681	1.5344 929 056	10
6	1.6010 322 186	1.6242 772 928	1.6478 313 602	1.6716 981 502	12
7	1.7316 764 476	1.7610 439 788	1.7908 734 212	1.8211 714 731	14
8	1.8729 812 457	1.9093 266 335	1.9463 324 272	1.9840 098 130	16
9	2.0258 165 154	2.0700 949 193	2.1152 862 464	2.1614 081 904	18
10	2.1911 231 430	2.2444 001 461	2.2989 063 131	2.3546 684 775	20
11	2.3699 187 915	2.4333 821 452	2.4984 657 493	2.5652 089 519	22
12	2.5633 041 649	2.6382 767 240	2.7153 481 917	2.7945 747 054	24
13	2.7724 697 847	2.8604 237 465	2.9510 573 857	3.0444 489 828	26
14	2.9987 033 192	3.1012 758 954	3.2072 276 109	3.3166 655 344	28
15	3.2433 975 100	3.3624 081 715	3.4856 350 127	3.6132 220 738	30
16	3.5080 587 468	3.6455 281 933	3.7882 099 170	3.9362 949 381	32
17	3.7943 163 406	3.9524 873 633	4.1170 502 141	4.2882 550 598	34
18	4.1039 325 540	4.2852 929 751	4.4744 359 043	4.6716 853 657	36
19	4.4388 134 504	4.6461 213 394	4.8628 449 060	5.0893 997 330	38
20	4.8010 206 279	5.0373 320 157	5.2849 702 366	5.5444 636 388	40
21	5.1927 839 112	5.4614 832 422	5.7437 386 842	6.0402 166 571	42
22	5.6165 150 783	5.9213 486 648	6.2423 311 004	6.5802 969 668	44
23	6.0748 227 087	6.4199 354 745	6.7842 044 544	7.1686 680 510	46
24	6.5705 282 418	6.9605 040 726	7.3731 158 024	7.8096 477 842	48
25	7.1066 833 463	7.5465 893 913	8.0131 483 360	8.5079 401 193	50
26	7.6865 887 073	8.1820 240 096	8.7087 396 937	9.2686 696 088	52
27	8.3138 143 459	8.8709 632 156	9.4647 127 288	10.0974 190 125	54
28	8.9922 215 965	9.6179 121 792	10.2863 089 481	11.0002 702 672	56
29	9.7259 868 787	10.4277 554 127	11.1792 248 542	11.9838 491 204	58
30	10.5196 274 081	11.3057 887 118	12.1496 514 417	13.0553 737 547	60
31	11.3780 290 045	12.2577 537 867	13.2043 171 222	14.2227 077 595	62
32	12.3064 761 713	13.2898 758 083	14.3505 343 753	15.4944 178 400	64
33	13.3106 846 269	14.4089 041 167	15.5962 504 500	16.8798 366 852	66
34	14.3968 364 925	15.6221 563 573	16.9501 024 656	18.3891 314 576	68
35	15.5716 183 502	16.9375 663 322	18.4214 772 977	20.0333 784 070	70
36	16.8422 624 076	18.3637 358 823	20.0205 766 614	21.8246 441 560	72
37	18.2165 910 201	19.9099 911 369	21.7584 878 442	23.7760 742 526	74
38	19.7030 648 473	21.5864 435 000	23.6472 605 797	25.9019 896 418	76
39	21.3108 349 389	23.4040 557 716	25.6999 905 934	28.2179 917 625	78
40	23.0497 990 699	25.3747 138 364	27.9309 104 018	30.7410 770 416	80
41	24.9306 626 740	27.5113 043 894	30.3554 879 929	33.4897 616 255	82
42	26.9650 047 482	29.8277 992 054	32.9905 340 725	36.4842 172 646	84
43	29.1653 491 356	32.3393 465 044	35.8543 186 208	39.7464 193 474	86
44	31.5452 416 251	35.0623 700 103	38.9666 975 666	43.3003 081 711	88
45	34.1193 333 417	38.0146 763 501	42.3492 504 572	47.1719 646 321	90
46	36.9034 709 424	41.2155 714 967	46.0254 300 797	51.3898 016 260	92
47	39.9147 941 713	44.6859 870 161	50.0207 250 695	55.9847 725 605	94
48	43.1718 413 757	48.4486 169 447	54.3628 366 351	60.9905 985 132	96
49	46.6946 636 319	52.5280 661 924	59.0818 706 228	66.4440 157 006	98
50	50.5049 481 843	56.9510 114 409	64.2105 462 545	72.3850 450 732	100
51	54.6261 519 561	61.7463 755 902	69.7844 229 853	78.8572 860 174	102
52	59.0836 459 557	66.9455 168 936	75.8421 470 531	85.9082 363 180	104
53	63.9048 714 657	72.5824 340 184	82.4257 194 307	93.5896 407 294	106
54	69.1195 089 773	78.6939 883 728	89.5807 870 381	101.9578 707 149	108
55	74.7596 609 099	85.3201 451 531	97.3569 592 329	111.0743 381 394	110
56	80.8600 492 401	92.5042 346 877	105.8081 517 753	121.0059 459 519	112
57	87.4582 292 581	100.2932 357 863	114.9929 606 503	131.8255 791 661	114
58	94.5948 207 656	108.7380 829 477	124.9750 683 408	143.6126 397 408	116
59	102.3137 581 400	117.8939 994 352	135.8236 853 669	156.4536 292 864	118
60	110.6625 608 043	127.8208 583 970	147.6140 301 548	170.4427 838 737	120

TABLE 1. FUTURE WORTH OF ONE DOLLAR WITH INTEREST
Payable at beginning of each period

SEMI ANNUAL Compounding

HALF YEARS	9% Nominal Annual Rate	9¼% Nominal Annual Rate	9½% Nominal Annual Rate	9¾% Nominal Annual Rate	HALF YEARS
1	1.0450 000 000	1.0462 500 000	1.0475 000 000	1.0487 500 000	1
YEARS					
1	1.0920 250 000	1.0946 390 625	1.0972 562 500	1.0998 765 625	2
2	1.1925 186 006	1.1982 346 772	1.2039 712 782	1.2097 284 527	4
3	1.3022 601 248	1.3116 344 837	1.3210 650 098	1.3305 519 722	6
4	1.4221 006 128	1.4357 663 415	1.4495 468 386	1.4634 429 294	8
5	1.5529 694 217	1.5716 459 221	1.5905 243 284	1.6096 065 786	10
6	1.6958 814 328	1.7203 850 187	1.7452 127 601	1.7703 685 506	12
7	1.8519 449 216	1.8832 006 440	1.9149 456 086	1.9471 868 758	14
8	2.0223 701 530	2.0614 249 875	2.1011 860 374	2.1416 652 075	16
9	2.2084 787 664	2.2565 163 157	2.3055 395 120	2.3555 673 664	18
10	2.4117 140 248	2.4700 709 043	2.5297 676 391	2.5908 333 377	20
11	2.6336 520 080	2.7038 360 990	2.7758 033 531	2.8495 968 655	22
12	2.8760 138 340	2.9597 246 126	3.0457 675 779	3.1342 048 050	24
13	3.1406 790 071	3.2398 301 752	3.3419 875 110	3.4472 384 071	26
14	3.4296 999 927	3.5464 446 656	3.6670 166 838	3.7915 367 293	28
15	3.7453 181 345	3.8820 768 640	4.0236 569 752	4.1702 223 844	30
16	4.0899 810 359	4.2494 729 789	4.4149 827 639	4.5867 298 610	32
17	4.4663 615 407	4.6516 391 178	4.8443 674 313	5.0448 366 726	34
18	4.8773 784 615	5.0918 658 830	5.3155 124 413	5.5486 976 179	36
19	5.3262 192 144	5.5737 552 965	5.8324 792 481	6.1028 824 623	38
20	5.8163 645 376	6.1012 502 724	6.3997 243 080	6.7124 173 840	40
21	6.3516 154 842	6.6786 668 782	7.0221 374 953	7.3828 305 583	42
22	6.9361 228 991	7.3107 296 503	7.7050 842 550	8.1202 022 960	44
23	7.5744 196 089	8.0026 102 506	8.4544 518 556	8.9312 201 882	46
24	8.2714 555 734	8.7599 697 823	9.2767 001 389	9.8232 397 595	48
25	9.0326 362 725	9.5890 051 100	10.1789 172 068	10.8043 511 793	50
26	9.8638 646 255	10.4964 995 640	11.1688 805 234	11.8834 526 351	52
27	10.7715 867 677	11.4898 784 422	12.2551 239 598	13.0703 310 349	54
28	11.7628 420 400	12.5772 697 662	13.4470 113 594	14.3757 507 695	56
29	12.8453 175 787	13.7675 707 857	14.7548 172 579	15.8115 513 397	58
30	14.0274 079 289	15.0705 207 778	16.1898 154 538	17.3907 547 353	60
31	15.3182 801 435	16.4967 807 356	17.7643 761 931	19.1276 835 375	62
32	16.7279 448 738	18.0580 205 987	19.4920 728 052	21.0380 908 178	64
33	18.2673 340 008	19.7670 147 387	21.3877 987 109	23.1393 030 103	66
34	19.9483 854 122	21.6377 464 820	23.4678 958 093	25.4503 770 536	68
35	21.7841 355 797	23.6855 225 237	25.7502 953 511	27.9922 732 280	70
36	23.7888 206 565	25.9270 981 702	28.2546 725 134	30.7880 452 546	72
37	25.9779 868 774	28.3808 144 343	31.0026 160 070	33.8630 493 807	74
38	28.3686 111 198	31.0667 481 054	34.0178 141 800	37.2451 743 486	76
39	30.9792 325 581	34.0068 760 210	37.3262 592 204	40.9650 943 323	78
40	33.8300 964 342	37.2252 548 862	40.9564 712 187	45.0565 471 367	80
41	36.9433 110 586	40.7482 181 099	44.9397 440 227	49.5566 401 828	82
42	40.3430 192 587	44.6045 912 704	49.3104 150 023	54.5061 870 533	84
43	44.0555 856 060	48.8259 279 714	54.1061 610 513	59.9500 776 512	86
44	48.1098 008 714	53.4467 680 203	59.3683 233 771	65.9376 853 286	88
45	52.5371 052 966	58.5049 200 394	65.1422 638 775	72.5233 146 784	90
46	57.3718 324 115	64.0417 708 236	71.4777 561 787	79.7666 940 496	92
47	62.6514 752 892	70.1026 239 752	78.4294 147 031	87.7335 172 532	94
48	68.4169 773 027	76.7370 705 870	86.0571 654 668	96.4960 393 725	96
49	74.7130 496 390	83.9993 950 063	94.4267 626 657	106.1337 320 799	98
50	81.5885 180 320	91.9490 190 003	103.6103 555 023	116.7340 044 053	100
51	89.0967 014 039	100.6509 879 563	113.6871 101 396	128.3929 954 922	102
52	97.2958 253 506	110.1765 030 962	124.7438 921 451	141.2164 465 310	104
53	106.2494 736 785	120.6035 040 587	136.8760 153 055	155.3206 597 790	106
54	116.0270 814 938	132.0173 066 170	150.1880 632 691	170.8335 533 630	108
55	126.7044 736 682	144.5113 007 490	164.7947 910 974	187.8958 214 325	110
56	138.3644 528 575	158.1877 147 726	180.8221 144 991	206.6622 101 853	112
57	151.0974 416 318	173.1584 517 977	198.4081 952 723	227.3029 213 373	114
58	165.0021 836 979	189.5460 053 398	217.7046 323 138	250.0051 557 667	116
59	180.1865 096 527	207.4844 615 857	238.8777 684 602	274.9748 113 319	118
60	196.7681 732 035	227.1205 965 135	262.1101 244 290	302.4383 502 619	120

SEMI ANNUAL
Compounding

TABLE 1. FUTURE WORTH OF ONE DOLLAR WITH INTEREST
Payable at beginning of each period

HALF YEARS	10% Nominal Annual Rate	10¼% Nominal Annual Rate	10½% Nominal Annual Rate	10¾% Nominal Annual Rate	HALF YEARS
1	1.0500 000 000	1.0512 500 000	1.0525 000 000	1.0537 500 000	1
YEARS					
1	1.1025 000 000	1.1051 265 625	1.1077 562 500	1.1103 890 625	2
2	1.2155 062 500	1.2213 047 191	1.2271 239 094	1.2329 638 701	4
3	1.3400 956 406	1.3496 962 860	1.3593 541 802	1.3690 695 958	6
4	1.4774 554 438	1.4915 852 170	1.5058 330 891	1.5201 999 050	8
5	1.6288 946 268	1.6483 904 435	1.6680 960 159	1.6880 133 473	10
6	1.7958 563 260	1.8216 800 645	1.8478 437 872	1.8743 515 582	12
7	1.9799 315 994	2.0131 870 277	2.0469 605 043	2.0812 594 696	14
8	2.1828 745 884	2.2248 264 596	2.2675 332 921	2.3110 077 512	16
9	2.4066 192 337	2.4587 148 174	2.5118 741 764	2.5661 177 303	18
10	2.6532 977 051	2.7171 910 544	2.7825 443 181	2.8493 890 608	20
11	2.9252 607 199	3.0028 400 096	3.0823 808 593	3.1639 304 479	22
12	3.2250 999 437	3.3185 182 575	3.4145 266 618	3.5131 937 639	24
13	3.5556 726 879	3.6673 826 745	3.7824 632 504	3.9010 119 299	26
14	3.9201 291 385	4.0529 220 084	4.1900 473 060	4.3316 409 796	28
15	4.3219 423 752	4.4789 917 673	4.6415 510 910	4.8098 067 665	30
16	4.7649 414 686	4.9498 527 752	5.1417 072 308	5.3407 568 262	32
17	5.2533 479 691	5.4702 137 824	5.6957 583 205	5.9303 179 653	34
18	5.7918 161 360	6.0452 785 535	6.3095 118 781	6.5849 602 058	36
19	6.3854 772 899	6.6807 979 071	6.9894 012 174	7.3118 677 895	38
20	7.0399 887 121	7.3831 272 259	7.7425 528 823	8.1190 180 200	40
21	7.7615 875 551	8.1592 900 116	8.5768 613 463	9.0152 688 076	42
22	8.5571 502 795	9.0170 481 230	9.5010 717 618	10.0104 558 795	44
23	9.4342 581 832	9.9649 793 961	10.5248 716 258	11.1155 007 192	46
24	10.4012 696 469	11.0125 634 253	11.6589 923 240	12.3425 304 228	48
25	11.4673 997 858	12.1702 763 626	12.9153 216 156	13.7050 107 850	50
26	12.6428 082 638	13.4496 956 812	14.3070 282 404	15.2178 940 772	52
27	13.9386 961 108	14.8636 159 549	15.8486 999 522	16.8977 831 376	54
28	15.3674 124 622	16.4261 768 065	17.5564 964 265	18.7631 135 764	56
29	16.9425 722 396	18.1530 043 092	19.4483 186 445	20.8343 560 937	58
30	18.6791 858 941	20.0613 672 513	21.5439 965 304	23.1342 411 307	60
31	20.5938 024 483	22.1703 498 295	23.8654 968 066	25.6880 083 208	62
32	22.7046 671 992	24.5010 424 965	26.4371 532 468	28.5236 834 768	64
33	25.0318 955 871	27.0767 528 718	29.2859 217 414	31.6723 861 548	66
34	27.5976 648 848	29.9232 388 249	32.4416 628 460	35.1686 711 696	68
35	30.4264 255 355	33.0689 660 614	35.9374 547 781	39.0509 078 094	70
36	33.5451 341 529	36.5453 927 888	39.8099 401 395	43.3617 009 122	72
37	36.9835 104 036	40.3872 843 079	44.0997 100 017	48.1483 584 243	74
38	40.7743 202 199	44.6330 606 759	48.8517 293 775	53.4634 105 717	76
39	44.9536 880 425	49.3251 809 187	54.1158 085 413	59.3651 863 428	78
40	49.5614 410 668	54.5105 676 333	59.9471 251 354	65.9184 536 083	80
41	54.6414 887 762	60.2410 762 285	66.4068 025 383	73.1951 299 036	82
42	60.2422 413 758	66.5740 134 937	73.5625 505 543	81.2750 716 732	84
43	66.4170 711 168	73.5727 106 842	81.4893 751 425	90.2469 506 398	86
44	73.2248 209 062	81.3071 568 522	90.2703 646 227	100.2092 269 144	88
45	80.7303 650 491	89.8546 987 587	99.9975 606 005	111.2712 295 274	90
46	89.0052 274 667	99.3008 143 637	110.7729 227 400	123.5543 562 381	92
47	98.1282 632 820	109.7399 676 312	122.7093 974 960	137.1934 057 910	94
48	108.1864 102 684	121.2765 531 971	135.9321 020 099	152.3380 572 375	96
49	119.2755 173 209	134.0259 403 466	150.5796 355 771	169.1545 125 590	98
50	131.5012 578 463	148.1156 267 411	166.8055 324 333	187.8273 206 181	100
51	144.9801 367 755	163.6865 134 329	184.7798 710 876	208.5614 024 530	102
52	159.8406 007 950	180.8943 139 177	204.6910 570 714	231.5843 001 434	104
53	176.2242 623 765	199.9111 113 157	226.7477 977 900	257.1486 739 260	106
54	194.2872 492 701	220.9270 792 539	251.1812 901 756	285.5350 749 638	108
55	214.2016 923 203	244.1523 836 590	278.2476 440 751	317.0550 241 999	110
56	236.1573 657 832	269.8192 844 792	308.2305 667 720	352.0544 310 823	112
57	260.3634 957 759	298.1844 583 527	341.4443 367 827	390.9173 896 784	114
58	287.0507 540 930	329.5315 654 503	378.2370 980 981	434.0703 938 399	116
59	316.4734 563 875	364.1740 861 613	418.9945 094 001	481.9870 176 749	118
60	348.9119 856 672	402.4584 559 910	464.1437 865 036	535.1931 126 933	120

TABLE 1. FUTURE WORTH OF ONE DOLLAR WITH INTEREST
Payable at beginning of each period

SEMI ANNUAL Compounding

HALF YEARS	11% Nominal Annual Rate	11¼% Nominal Annual Rate	11½% Nominal Annual Rate	11¾% Nominal Annual Rate	HALF YEARS
1	1.0550 000 000	1.0562 500 000	1.0575 000 000	1.0587 500 000	1
YEARS					
1	1.1130 250 000	1.1156 640 625	1.1183 062 500	1.1209 515 625	2
2	1.2388 246 506	1.2447 063 004	1.2506 088 688	1.2565 324 055	4
3	1.3788 428 068	1.3886 740 877	1.3985 637 143	1.4085 119 632	6
4	1.5346 865 150	1.5492 937 741	1.5640 225 427	1.5788 736 860	8
5	1.7081 444 584	1.7284 913 861	1.7490 561 846	1.7698 409 253	10
6	1.9012 074 858	1.9284 157 218	1.9559 804 629	1.9839 059 506	12
7	2.1160 914 618	2.1514 641 183	2.1873 851 765	2.2238 624 752	14
8	2.3552 626 993	2.4003 111 986	2.4461 665 141	2.4928 421 163	16
9	2.6214 662 659	2.6779 409 431	2.7355 633 012	2.7943 552 654	18
10	2.9177 574 906	2.9876 824 717	3.0591 975 370	3.1323 369 009	20
11	3.2475 370 310	3.3332 499 638	3.4211 197 256	3.5111 979 433	22
12	3.6145 899 039	3.7187 871 960	3.8258 595 712	3.9358 828 208	24
13	4.0231 289 278	4.1489 172 306	4.2784 826 701	4.4119 339 978	26
14	4.4778 430 749	4.6287 978 525	4.7846 539 104	4.9455 643 085	28
15	4.9839 512 884	5.1641 834 166	5.3507 083 721	5.5437 380 391	30
16	5.5472 623 828	5.7614 938 501	5.9837 306 145	6.2142 618 170	32
17	6.1742 417 136	6.4278 916 349	6.6916 433 445	6.9658 864 936	34
18	6.8720 853 833	7.1713 676 947	7.4833 065 749	7.8084 213 491	36
19	7.6488 028 337	8.0008 372 159	8.3686 285 134	8.7528 621 120	38
20	8.5133 087 740	8.9262 465 517	9.3586 895 705	9.8115 344 608	40
21	9.4755 254 982	9.9586 924 907	10.4658 810 385	10.9982 548 843	42
22	10.5464 967 676	11.1105 553 214	11.7040 601 771	12.3285 109 974	44
23	11.7385 145 647	12.3956 472 865	13.0887 236 464	13.8196 636 658	46
24	13.0652 601 734	13.8293 782 090	14.6372 014 583	15.4911 735 794	48
25	14.5419 612 045	15.4289 402 745	16.3688 738 733	17.3648 552 288	50
26	16.1855 663 697	17.2135 141 867	18.3054 139 580	19.4651 616 013	52
27	18.0149 400 086	19.2044 991 674	20.4710 588 380	21.8195 033 113	54
28	20.0510 786 031	21.4257 695 594	22.8929 130 427	24.4586 063 297	56
29	22.3173 517 622	23.9039 611 088	25.6012 877 363	27.4169 129 819	58
30	24.8397 704 451	26.6687 903 605	28.6300 800 836	30.7330 314 460	60
31	27.6472 854 997	29.7534 109 956	32.0171 974 955	34.4502 396 197	62
32	30.7721 199 432	33.1948 113 846	35.8050 320 667	38.6170 499 303	64
33	34.2501 387 998	37.0342 581 232	40.0409 911 416	43.2878 424 585	66
34	38.1212 607 377	41.3177 908 694	44.7780 906 499	48.5235 746 411	68
35	42.4299 162 326	46.0967 744 149	50.0756 186 368	54.3925 768 120	70
36	47.2255 575 147	51.4285 146 119	55.9998 772 942	60.9714 439 658	72
37	52.5632 261 529	57.3769 455 403	62.6250 127 773	68.3460 353 813	74
38	58.5041 847 888	64.0133 961 553	70.0339 431 952	76.6125 951 514	76
39	65.1166 202 745	71.4174 456 090	78.3193 963 873	85.8790 082 421	78
40	72.4764 262 811	79.6778 775 015	87.5850 704 762	96.2662 084 750	80
41	80.6680 743 615	88.8937 445 047	97.9469 317 202	107.9097 568 060	82
42	89.7855 834 662	99.1755 561 250	109.5346 659 110	120.9616 105 006	84
43	99.9335 990 375	110.6466 038 471	122.4933 014 800	135.5921 062 932	86
44	111.2285 940 687	123.4444 395 499	136.9850 246 282	151.9921 834 120	88
45	123.8002 059 133	137.7225 249 213	153.1912 091 981	170.3758 754 835	90
46	137.7927 241 866	153.6520 716 514	171.3146 866 913	190.9831 038 355	92
47	153.3667 468 378	171.4240 944 702	191.5822 848 437	214.0828 086 556	94
48	170.7010 233 992	191.2517 016 470	214.2476 665 299	239.9764 588 668	96
49	189.9945 065 688	213.3726 504 195	239.5945 045 283	269.0019 865 300	98
50	211.4686 356 738	238.0521 979 934	267.9400 318 797	301.5381 971 164	100
51	235.3698 782 208	265.5862 823 004	299.6390 122 763	338.0097 132 111	102
52	261.9725 587 067	296.3050 706 555	335.0881 801 724	378.8925 161 641	104
53	291.5820 071 545	330.5769 188 669	374.7312 061 879	424.7201 580 137	106
54	324.5380 635 132	368.8127 882 718	419.0642 499 500	476.0907 247 507	108
55	361.2189 781 418	411.4711 736 653	468.6421 698 706	533.6746 418 011	110
56	402.0457 531 462	459.0636 012 130	524.0854 675 799	598.2234 235 936	112
57	447.4869 743 956	512.1607 622 752	586.0880 539 287	670.5794 814 013	114
58	498.0641 896 767	571.3993 566 931	655.4259 337 588	751.6871 174 572	116
59	554.3578 947 149	637.4897 275 981	732.9669 181 346	842.6048 488 248	118
60	617.0141 957 650	711.2243 792 941	819.6814 855 932	944.5192 218 603	120

SEMI ANNUAL Compounding

TABLE 1. FUTURE WORTH OF ONE DOLLAR WITH INTEREST
Payable at beginning of each period

HALF YEARS	12% Nominal Annual Rate	12¼% Nominal Annual Rate	12½% Nominal Annual Rate	12¾% Nominal Annual Rate	HALF YEARS
1	1.0600 000 000	1.0612 500 000	1.0625 000 000	1.0637 500 000	1
YEARS					
1	1.1236 000 000	1.1262 515 625	1.1289 062 500	1.1315 640 625	2
2	1.2624 769 600	1.2684 425 820	1.2744 293 213	1.2804 372 275	4
3	1.4185 191 123	1.4285 854 400	1.4387 112 260	1.4488 967 510	6
4	1.5938 480 745	1.6089 465 839	1.6241 700 950	1.6395 194 937	8
5	1.7908 476 965	1.8120 786 041	1.8335 357 713	1.8552 213 388	10
6	2.0121 964 718	2.0408 563 593	2.0698 899 918	2.0993 017 950	12
7	2.2609 039 558	2.2985 176 635	2.3367 117 485	2.3754 944 675	14
8	2.5403 516 847	2.5887 091 099	2.6379 284 974	2.6880 241 701	16
9	2.8543 391 529	2.9155 376 799	2.9779 739 677	3.0416 715 501	18
10	3.2071 354 722	3.2836 288 675	3.3618 534 245	3.4418 462 160	20
11	3.6035 374 166	3.6981 921 427	3.7952 173 425	3.8946 694 866	22
12	4.0489 346 413	4.1650 946 791	4.2844 445 781	4.4070 680 264	24
13	4.5493 829 629	4.6909 443 903	4.8367 362 620	4.9868 797 997	26
14	5.1116 866 971	5.2831 834 492	5.4602 217 957	5.6429 739 653	28
15	5.7434 911 729	5.9501 936 146	6.1640 785 116	6.3853 865 448	30
16	6.4533 866 819	6.7014 148 557	6.9586 667 572	7.2254 739 392	32
17	7.2510 252 758	7.5474 789 521	7.8556 823 939	8.1760 866 442	34
18	8.1472 519 999	8.5003 599 628	8.8683 289 525	9.2517 658 184	36
19	9.1542 523 470	9.5735 436 899	10.0115 119 815	10.4689 657 148	38
20	10.2857 179 371	10.7822 185 394	11.3020 584 479	11.8463 053 744	40
21	11.5570 326 742	12.1434 904 772	12.7589 644 197	13.4048 534 351	42
22	12.9854 819 127	13.6766 251 242	14.4036 746 769	15.1684 504 102	44
23	14.5904 874 771	15.4033 204 158	16.2603 983 657	17.1640 733 680	46
24	16.3938 717 293	17.3480 136 860	18.3564 653 425	19.4222 485 894	48
25	18.4201 542 750	19.5382 275 202	20.7227 284 531	21.9775 185 167	50
26	20.6968 853 434	22.0049 592 731	23.3940 176 678	24.8689 701 364	52
27	23.2550 203 718	24.7831 197 640	26.4096 527 578	28.1408 328 778	54
28	26.1293 408 898	27.9120 273 579	29.8140 220 586	31.8431 551 733	56
29	29.3589 274 238	31.4359 644 244	33.6572 358 395	36.0325 700 307	58
30	32.9876 908 533	35.4048 040 516	37.9958 638 970	40.7731 613 263	60
31	37.0649 694 428	39.8747 158 831	42.8937 682 275	46.1374 440 713	62
32	41.6461 996 659	44.9089 610 676	48.4230 430 380	52.2074 736 467	64
33	46.7936 699 446	50.5787 875 727	54.6650 759 296	59.0761 009 725	66
34	52.5773 675 498	56.9644 385 331	61.7117 458 737	66.8483 928 131	68
35	59.0759 301 790	64.1562 879 048	69.6667 756 152	75.6432 389 432	70
36	66.3777 151 491	72.2561 194 970	78.6472 584 094	85.5951 707 592	72
37	74.5820 007 415	81.3785 674 837	88.7853 815 637	96.8564 191 547	74
38	83.8003 360 332	91.6527 387 825	100.2303 721 559	109.5992 431 379	76
39	94.1580 575 669	103.2240 402 612	113.1506 935 666	124.0185 648 120	78
40	105.7959 934 821	116.2562 366 318	127.7365 251 592	140.3349 510 241	80
41	118.8723 782 765	130.9337 681 569	144.2025 616 055	158.7979 872 916	82
42	133.5650 042 315	147.4643 609 707	162.7911 730 625	179.6900 956 165	84
43	150.0736 387 545	166.0819 669 563	183.7759 727 151	203.3308 545 868	86
44	168.6227 405 045	187.0500 747 876	207.4658 441 979	230.0818 878 479	88
45	189.4645 112 309	210.6654 389 953	234.2094 881 765	260.3523 957 208	90
46	212.8823 248 190	237.2622 798 332	264.4005 550 117	294.6054 145 835	92
47	239.1945 801 667	267.2170 133 845	298.4834 390 562	333.3648 997 606	94
48	268.7590 302 753	300.9535 788 508	336.9598 198 721	377.2237 402 680	96
49	301.9776 464 173	338.9494 384 207	380.3960 466 524	426.8528 280 091	98
50	339.3020 835 145	381.7423 346 298	429.4314 745 412	483.0113 201 515	100
51	381.2398 210 369	429.9379 008 492	484.7878 755 563	546.5582 516 642	102
52	428.3610 629 170	484.2182 326 094	547.2800 626 397	618.4656 756 460	104
53	481.3064 902 936	545.3515 410 674	617.8278 832 144	699.8335 324 508	106
54	540.7959 724 939	614.2030 252 389	697.4697 587 850	791.9064 750 538	108
55	607.6383 546 941	691.7471 168 675	787.3779 698 784	896.0929 080 319	110
56	682.7424 553 343	779.0812 712 269	888.8759 113 080	1013.9865 313 900	112
57	767.1294 228 136	877.4414 990 338	1003.4575 717 501	1147.3907 187 799	114
58	861.9466 194 734	988.2198 592 892	1132.8095 243 585	1298.3461 030 174	116
59	968.4832 216 403	1112.9841 606 180	1278.8357 521 078	1469.1617 908 614	118
60	1088.1877 478 350	1253.5001 499 337	1443.6856 732 780	1662.4506 845 370	120

TABLE 1. FUTURE WORTH OF ONE DOLLAR WITH INTEREST
Payable at beginning of each period

HALF YEARS	13% Nominal Annual Rate	13¼% Nominal Annual Rate	13½% Nominal Annual Rate	13¾% Nominal Annual Rate	HALF YEARS
1	1.0650 000 000	1.0662 500 000	1.0675 000 000	1.0687 500 000	1
YEARS					
1	1.1342 250 000	1.1368 890 625	1.1395 562 500	1.1422 265 625	2
2	1.2864 663 506	1.2925 167 404	1.2985 884 469	1.3046 815 201	4
3	1.4591 422 965	1.4694 481 453	1.4798 145 809	1.4902 418 878	6
4	1.6549 956 713	1.6705 995 243	1.6863 319 545	1.7021 938 688	8
5	1.8771 374 653	1.8992 863 270	1.9216 701 183	1.9442 910 515	10
6	2.1290 962 415	2.1592 778 517	2.1898 511 937	2.2208 208 843	12
7	2.4148 741 846	2.4548 593 725	2.4954 586 144	2.5366 806 046	14
8	2.7390 106 720	2.7909 027 706	2.8437 154 606	2.8974 639 671	16
9	3.1066 543 794	3.1729 468 344	3.2405 737 264	3.3095 603 071	18
10	3.5236 450 635	3.6072 885 519	3.6928 160 435	3.7802 676 930	20
11	3.9966 063 222	4.1010 868 999	4.2081 716 025	4.3179 221 723	22
12	4.5330 508 058	4.6624 808 409	4.7954 482 506	4.9320 454 000	24
13	5.1414 995 502	5.3007 234 721	5.4646 830 256	5.6335 132 633	26
14	5.8316 173 273	6.0263 345 388	6.2273 136 961	6.4347 484 896	28
15	6.6143 661 630	6.8512 738 241	7.0963 742 431	7.3499 406 478	30
16	7.5021 794 613	7.7891 382 748	8.0867 176 210	8.3952 974 407	32
17	8.5091 594 995	8.8553 861 110	9.2152 696 070	9.5893 317 369	34
18	9.6513 014 333	10.0675 916 138	10.5013 180 761	10.9531 894 265	36
19	10.9467 473 682	11.4457 347 914	11.9668 426 469	12.5110 239 070	38
20	12.4160 745 337	13.0125 306 966	13.6368 903 310	14.2904 238 307	40
21	14.0826 221 379	14.7938 038 245	15.5400 036 073	16.3229 016 888	42
22	15.9728 620 944	16.8189 137 608	17.7087 082 357	18.6444 518 860	44
23	18.1168 195 090	19.1212 390 978	20.1800 691 494	21.2961 881 875	46
24	20.5485 496 076	21.7387 275 917	22.9963 239 246	24.3250 718 277	48
25	23.3066 786 787	24.7145 216 317	26.2056 046 553	27.7847 431 764	50
26	26.4350 176 243	28.0976 693 280	29.8627 605 700	31.7364 716 883	52
27	29.9832 578 650	31.9439 329 407	34.0302 954 498	36.2502 409 624	54
28	34.0077 606 519	36.3167 079 735	38.7794 358 692	41.4059 881 243	56
29	38.5724 523 254	41.2880 680 811	44.1913 485 162	47.2950 194 821	58
30	43.7498 397 388	46.9399 530 132	50.3585 273 976	54.0216 275 264	60
31	49.6221 619 777	53.3655 191 750	57.3863 746 367	61.7049 379 101	62
32	56.2826 966 692	60.6706 750 646	65.3950 018 821	70.4810 191 184	64
33	63.8372 416 296	68.9758 268 955	74.5212 831 135	80.5052 921 891	66
34	72.4057 953 873	78.4178 631 744	84.9211 939 300	91.9552 831 602	68
35	82.1244 632 732	89.1524 109 476	96.7724 773 004	105.0337 669 878	70
36	93.1476 193 560	101.3564 009 018	110.2776 813 356	119.9723 586 129	72
37	105.6503 585 641	115.2309 835 996	125.6676 210 015	137.0356 147 734	74
38	119.8312 779 424	131.0048 449 155	143.2053 229 349	156.5257 192 027	76
39	135.9156 312 242	148.9379 753 190	163.1905 207 837	178.7878 341 878	78
40	154.1589 068 252	169.3259 551 310	185.9647 778 999	204.2162 132 611	80
41	174.8508 860 939	192.5048 263 858	211.9173 249 357	233.2611 832 800	82
42	198.3202 462 798	218.8566 315 965	241.4917 121 137	266.4371 195 426	84
43	224.9397 813 367	248.8157 107 176	275.1933 898 624	304.3315 551 775	86
44	255.1323 234 866	282.8758 600 931	313.5983 473 764	347.6155 861 307	88
45	289.3774 596 066	321.5984 713 851	357.3629 567 424	397.0557 560 175	90
46	328.2191 491 223	365.6217 846 344	407.2351 908 743	453.5276 313 167	92
47	372.2743 644 133	415.6714 079 626	464.0674 069 807	518.0313 073 177	94
48	422.2428 909 767	472.5722 773 067	528.8309 140 462	591.7091 194 248	96
49	478.9184 430 180	537.2622 533 106	602.6325 732 945	675.8658 734 805	98
50	543.2012 710 321	610.8075 794 830	686.7337 153 514	771.9919 533 767	100
51	616.1124 616 364	694.4204 564 063	782.5716 974 144	881.7897 151 831	102
52	698.8101 567 995	789.4790 216 646	891.7844 688 616	1007.2036 352 215	104
53	792.6079 500 959	897.5500 648 037	1016.2385 651 442	1150.4547 459 965	106
54	898.9957 521 976	1020.4148 517 215	1158.0610 084 011	1314.0799 698 314	108
55	1019.6634 570 363	1160.0984 841 347	1319.6756 600 048	1500.9770 467 907	110
56	1156.5277 845 570	1318.9032 780 355	1503.8446 463 314	1714.4558 525 471	112
57	1311.7627 264 392	1499.4467 112 940	1713.7155 657 559	1958.2970 150 129	114
58	1487.8340 783 954	1704.7045 658 718	1952.8752 836 795	2236.8188 678 122	116
59	1687.5386 075 681	1938.0599 757 334	2225.4112 349 875	2554.9539 263 163	118
60	1914.0484 771 689	2203.3591 888 803	2535.9812 816 502	2918.3362 406 021	120

SEMI ANNUAL
Compounding

TABLE 1. FUTURE WORTH OF ONE DOLLAR WITH INTEREST
Payable at beginning of each period

HALF YEARS	14% Nominal Annual Rate	14¼% Nominal Annual Rate	14½% Nominal Annual Rate	14¾% Nominal Annual Rate	HALF YEARS
1	1.0700 000 000	1.0712 500 000	1.0725 000 000	1.0737 500 000	1
YEARS					
1	1.1449 000 000	1.1475 765 625	1.1502 562 500	1.1529 390 625	2
2	1.3107 960 100	1.3169 319 668	1.3230 894 407	1.3292 684 818	4
3	1.5007 303 518	1.5112 802 595	1.5218 918 984	1.5325 655 573	6
4	1.7181 861 798	1.7343 098 052	1.7505 656 680	1.7669 546 968	8
5	1.9671 513 573	1.9902 532 845	2.0135 991 006	2.0371 910 916	10
6	2.2521 915 890	2.2839 680 228	2.3161 549 505	2.3487 571 873	12
7	2.5785 341 502	2.6210 281 724	2.6641 717 078	2.7079 739 096	14
8	2.9521 637 486	3.0078 305 003	3.0644 801 580	3.1221 289 006	16
9	3.3799 322 757	3.4517 157 862	3.5249 374 547	3.5996 243 676	18
10	3.8696 844 625	3.9611 081 366	4.0545 813 381	4.1501 475 438	20
11	4.4304 017 411	4.5456 748 591	4.6638 075 253	4.7848 672 184	22
12	5.0723 669 534	5.2165 099 290	5.3645 737 548	5.5166 603 249	24
13	5.8073 529 249	5.9863 445 326	6.1706 344 900	6.3603 731 831	26
14	6.6488 383 638	6.8697 886 807	7.0978 108 886	7.3331 226 949	28
15	7.6122 550 427	7.8836 084 793	8.1643 013 360	8.4546 436 051	30
16	8.7152 707 983	9.0470 443 188	9.3910 386 386	9.7476 888 718	32
17	9.9781 135 370	10.3821 760 201	10.8021 008 880	11.2384 912 694	34
18	11.4239 421 885	11.9143 418 684	12.4251 840 596	12.9572 955 881	36
19	13.0792 714 117	13.6726 194 858	14.2921 456 219	14.9389 722 278	38
20	14.9744 578 392	15.6903 776 699	16.4396 298 275	17.2237 246 351	40
21	17.1442 567 801	18.0059 096 707	18.9097 869 568	19.8579 049 335	42
22	19.6284 595 875	20.6631 599 246	21.7511 006 332	22.8949 542 973	44
23	22.4726 233 818	23.7125 580 367	25.0193 394 478	26.3964 871 435	46
24	25.7289 065 098	27.2119 758 398	28.7786 515 707	30.4335 411 405	48
25	29.4570 250 631	31.2278 256 931	33.1028 238 357	35.0880 183 911	50
26	33.7253 479 947	35.8363 208 633	38.0767 300 097	40.4543 470 288	52
27	38.6121 509 191	41.1249 219 089	43.7979 966 732	46.6413 969 374	54
28	44.2070 515 873	47.1939 965 173	50.3789 194 108	53.7746 884 587	56
29	50.6126 533 623	54.1587 242 940	57.9486 669 206	61.9989 388 978	58
30	57.9464 268 345	62.1512 826 546	66.6558 163 046	71.4809 984 888	60
31	66.3428 640 829	71.3233 553 038	76.6712 693 032	82.4132 353 843	62
32	75.9559 450 885	81.8490 109 055	88.1916 067 114	95.0174 383 415	64
33	86.9619 615 318	93.9280 065 789	101.4429 468 173	109.5493 162 826	66
34	99.5627 497 577	107.7895 789 123	116.6853 835 950	126.3036 860 124	68
35	113.9893 921 976	123.6967 944 415	134.2180 917 638	145.6204 533 415	70
36	130.5064 551 271	141.9515 421 575	154.3851 989 144	167.8915 089 563	72
37	149.4168 404 750	162.9002 627 907	177.5825 399 588	193.5686 789 378	74
38	171.0673 406 598	186.9405 236 037	204.2654 264 785	223.1728 912 239	76
39	195.8549 983 214	214.5285 634 690	234.9575 834 658	257.3047 439 831	78
40	224.2343 875 782	246.1879 514 239	270.2614 288 665	296.6566 903 047	80
41	256.7259 503 383	282.5195 230 239	310.8698 976 876	342.0270 864 043	82
42	293.9255 405 423	324.2127 830 709	357.5800 427 520	394.3363 883 485	84
43	336.5153 513 669	372.0589 911 151	411.3086 790 508	454.6458 258 922	86
44	385.2764 257 799	426.9661 780 711	473.1103 787 574	524.1789 322 737	88
45	441.1029 798 754	489.9763 789 346	544.1981 701 055	604.3463 667 579	90
46	505.0188 016 594	562.2854 086 439	625.9673 464 025	696.7745 335 151	92
47	578.1960 260 198	645.2655 563 955	720.0228 524 954	803.3385 774 448	94
48	661.9766 301 901	740.4916 291 080	828.2107 862 256	926.2004 263 493	96
49	757.8970 439 046	849.7708 382 918	952.6546 331 734	1067.8526 512 422	98
50	867.7163 255 664	975.1770 975 196	1095.7969 458 992	1231.1690 346 113	100
51	993.4484 211 410	1119.0903 814 003	1260.4472 857 514	1419.4628 725 438	102
52	1137.3990 973 643	1284.2418 930 142	1449.8373 682 311	1636.5541 935 242	104
53	1302.2082 265 724	1473.7658 970 037	1667.6844 942 914	1886.8472 576 123	106
54	1490.8981 986 027	1691.2592 020 132	1918.2645 125 868	2175.4199 082 722	108
55	1706.9293 475 803	1940.8494 213 428	2206.4957 447 562	2508.1265 895 872	110
56	1954.2634 100 447	2227.2733 072 747	2538.0355 210 042	2891.7171 188 300	112
57	2237.4361 781 601	2555.9666 457 103	2919.3912 207 571	3333.9736 239 990	114
58	2561.6406 803 755	2933.1674 171 489	3358.0479 978 709	3843.8684 244 532	116
59	2932.8224 149 620	3366.0341 818 088	3862.6156 973 510	4431.7460 576 624	118
60	3357.7883 828 899	3862.7819 356 176	4442.9978 472 261	5109.5331 449 594	120

TABLE 1. FUTURE WORTH OF ONE DOLLAR WITH INTEREST
Payable at beginning of each period

SEMI ANNUAL Compounding

HALF YEARS	15% Nominal Annual Rate	15¼% Nominal Annual Rate	15½% Nominal Annual Rate	15¾% Nominal Annual Rate	HALF YEARS
1	1.0750 000 000	1.0762 500 000	1.0775 000 000	1.0787 500 000	1
YEARS					
1	1.1556 250 000	1.1583 140 625	1.1610 062 500	1.1637 015 625	2
2	1.3354 691 406	1.3416 914 674	1.3479 355 125	1.3542 013 266	4
3	1.5433 015 256	1.5541 000 942	1.5649 615 547	1.5758 861 997	6
4	1.7834 778 256	1.8001 359 937	1.8169 301 460	1.8338 612 329	8
5	2.0610 315 622	2.0851 228 359	2.1094 672 553	2.1340 671 821	10
6	2.3817 795 990	2.4152 271 028	2.4491 046 675	2.4834 173 143	12
7	2.7524 440 491	2.7975 915 173	2.8434 258 259	2.8899 566 090	14
8	3.1807 931 543	3.2404 895 957	3.3012 351 553	3.3630 470 214	16
9	3.6758 040 889	3.7535 046 680	3.8327 546 480	3.9135 830 736	18
10	4.2478 511 002	4.3477 372 406	4.4498 521 011	4.5542 427 377	20
11	4.9089 229 277	5.0360 451 859	5.1663 061 009	5.2997 793 899	22
12	5.6728 740 583	5.8333 219 582	5.9981 136 726	6.1673 615 569	24
13	6.5557 150 837	6.7568 188 553	6.9638 474 621	7.1769 682 803	26
14	7.5759 482 436	7.8265 182 978	8.0850 704 275	8.3518 492 018	28
15	8.7549 551 890	9.0655 662 048	9.3868 172 981	9.7190 599 659	30
16	10.1174 450 903	10.5007 728 195	10.8981 535 507	11.3100 852 683	32
17	11.6919 724 824	12.1631 928 240	12.6528 243 858	13.1615 638 987	34
18	13.5115 357 000	14.0887 972 929	14.6900 081 921	15.3161 324 739	36
19	15.6142 684 433	16.3192 520 281	17.0551 913 235	17.8234 072 913	38
20	18.0442 389 698	18.9028 191 136	19.8011 837 216	20.7411 269 140	40
21	20.8523 736 595	21.8954 012 002	22.9892 980 581	24.1364 817 978	42
22	24.0975 243 102	25.3617 511 142	26.6907 187 286	28.0876 615 814	44
23	27.8477 015 310	29.3768 729 653	30.9880 912 609	32.6856 556 693	46
24	32.1815 000 818	34.0276 450 679	35.9773 676 295	38.0363 485 737	48
25	37.1897 460 320	39.4146 997 959	41.7699 486 764	44.2629 582 670	50
26	42.9774 002 582	45.6546 010 429	48.4951 714 754	51.5088 736 961	52
27	49.6657 581 734	52.8823 664 058	56.3031 971 778	59.9409 568 028	54
28	57.3949 917 892	61.2543 886 661	65.3683 638 184	69.7533 850 892	56
29	66.3270 873 864	70.9518 197 818	75.8930 789 455	81.1721 232 179	58
30	76.6492 403 609	82.1844 906 132	88.1123 389 874	94.4601 266 201	60
31	88.5777 783 920	95.1954 511 966	102.2989 762 665	109.9233 969 418	62
32	102.3626 951 543	110.2662 298 071	118.7697 508 140	127.9180 287 765	64
33	118.2928 895 877	127.7229 246 044	137.8924 230 060	148.8584 099 591	66
34	136.7022 205 297	147.9432 596 729	160.0939 649 376	173.2267 642 607	68
35	157.9765 035 997	171.3647 581 312	185.8700 938 799	201.5842 562 370	70
36	182.5615 969 724	198.4942 091 603	215.7963 406 826	234.5839 139 584	72
37	210.9727 455 012	229.9186 337 952	250.5409 002 596	272.9856 672 107	74
38	243.8053 790 198	266.3179 867 558	290.8795 510 821	317.6738 474 732	76
39	281.7475 911 298	308.4798 691 559	337.7129 768 035	369.6775 526 700	78
40	325.5945 599 993	357.3165 704 415	392.0868 767 749	430.1943 456 632	80
41	376.2652 133 992	413.8848 083 066	455.2153 144 787	500.6178 322 269	82
42	434.8214 872 345	479.4085 937 167	528.5078 252 055	582.5697 535 778	84
43	502.4905 811 854	555.3057 157 854	613.6008 882 375	677.9373 325 038	86
44	580.6906 778 823	643.2184 195 808	712.3944 662 492	788.9167 331 117	88
45	671.0606 646 278	745.0489 406 595	827.0944 277 808	918.0636 350 045	90
46	775.4944 805 605	863.0006 652 166	960.2617 999 937	1068.3520 865 292	92
47	896.1808 090 977	999.6258 064 673	1114.8699 514 289	1243.2429 923 941	94
48	1035.6489 475 135	1157.8806 288 689	1294.3709 815 461	1446.7638 128 162	96
49	1196.8218 149 703	1341.1894 151 152	1502.7727 993 937	1683.6013 095 427	98
50	1383.0772 099 251	1553.5185 600 041	1744.7286 124 261	1959.2094 745 419	100
51	1598.3186 007 197	1799.4623 944 075	2025.6408 235 805	2279.9351 267 892	102
52	1847.0569 329 567	2084.3425 963 822	2351.7816 564 321	2653.1640 694 433	104
53	2134.5051 681 481	2414.3233 404 572	2730.4332 017 530	3087.4911 731 800	106
54	2466.6875 349 411	2796.5446 766 736	3170.0500 124 428	3592.9183 024 345	108
55	2850.5657 825 663	3239.2770 254 005	3680.4478 772 587	4181.0846 424 779	110
56	3294.1850 824 782	3752.1001 308 546	4273.0229 882 965	4865.5347 313 962	112
57	3806.8426 359 389	4346.1103 454 769	4961.0063 958 059	5662.0303 693 238	114
58	4399.2825 211 568	5034.1607 303 427	5759.7594 318 207	6588.9135 877 046	116
59	5083.9208 635 119	5831.1391 668 412	6687.1166 988 403	7667.5290 371 893	118
60	5875.1060 478 959	6754.2904 973 467	7763.7842 818 329	8922.7155 210 913	120

TABLE 1. FUTURE WORTH OF ONE DOLLAR WITH INTEREST
Payable at beginning of each period

HALF YEARS	16% Nominal Annual Rate	16¼% Nominal Annual Rate	16½% Nominal Annual Rate	16¾% Nominal Annual Rate	HALF YEARS
1	1.0800 000 000	1.0812 500 000	1.0825 000 000	1.0837 500 000	1
YEARS					
1	1.1664 000 000	1.1691 015 625	1.1718 062 500	1.1745 140 625	2
2	1.3604 889 600	1.3667 984 634	1.3731 298 875	1.3794 832 830	4
3	1.5868 743 229	1.5979 262 192	1.6090 421 843	1.6202 225 149	6
4	1.8509 302 103	1.8681 380 397	1.8854 856 881	1.9029 741 281	8
5	2.1589 249 973	2.1840 431 011	2.2094 239 135	2.2350 698 740	10
6	2.5181 701 168	2.5533 682 021	2.5890 167 508	2.6251 209 977	12
7	2.9371 936 243	2.9851 467 547	3.0338 260 099	3.0832 415 276	14
8	3.4259 426 433	3.4899 397 352	3.5550 562 799	3.6213 105 322	16
9	3.9960 194 992	4.0800 939 975	4.1658 371 678	4.2532 801 448	18
10	4.6609 571 438	4.7700 442 676	4.8815 540 297	4.9955 373 418	20
11	5.4365 404 126	5.5766 662 065	5.7202 355 218	5.8673 288 577	22
12	6.3411 807 372	6.5196 891 755	6.7030 077 359	6.8912 602 527	24
13	7.3963 532 119	7.6221 788 021	7.8546 263 587	8.0938 820 751	26
14	8.6271 063 864	8.9111 011 472	9.2041 002 586	9.5063 783 174	28
15	10.0626 568 891	10.4179 822 748	10.7854 222 086	11.1653 750 173	30
16	11.7370 829 954	12.1796 793 555	12.6384 251 529	13.1138 899 709	32
17	13.6901 336 059	14.2392 821 653	14.8097 855 844	15.4024 481 849	34
18	15.9681 718 379	16.6471 670 284	17.3541 993 089	18.0903 919 901	36
19	18.6252 756 317	19.4622 289 840	20.3357 592 139	21.2474 197 885	38
20	21.7245 214 968	22.7533 223 150	23.8295 697 454	24.9553 933 334	40
21	25.3394 818 739	26.6009 446 705	27.9236 387 624	29.3104 604 053	42
22	29.5559 716 577	31.0992 059 783	32.7210 944 246	34.4255 479 244	44
23	34.4740 853 415	36.3581 303 017	38.3427 829 535	40.4332 901 464	46
24	40.2105 731 423	42.5063 469 453	44.9303 127 073	47.4894 678 701	48
25	46.9016 125 132	49.6942 366 299	52.6496 212 449	55.7770 478 341	50
26	54.7060 408 354	58.0976 096 913	61.6951 552 349	65.5109 270 459	52
27	63.8091 260 304	67.9220 062 676	72.2947 684 990	76.9435 050 628	54
28	74.4269 646 019	79.4077 236 556	84.7154 615 694	90.3712 287 143	56
29	86.8116 115 117	92.8356 938 003	99.2701 073 387	106.1422 789 704	58
30	101.2570 636 672	108.5343 546 777	116.3253 322 177	124.6655 992 765	60
31	118.1062 390 614	126.8876 836 386	136.3107 513 260	146.4214 994 603	62
32	137.7591 172 413	148.3445 892 039	159.7297 903 460	171.9741 101 684	64
33	160.6822 343 502	173.4298 910 267	187.1723 666 386	201.9860 107 788	66
34	187.4197 581 461	202.7571 565 836	219.3297 490 544	237.2354 100 879	68
35	218.6064 059 016	237.0437 085 699	257.0119 707 529	278.6363 252 712	70
36	254.9825 118 436	277.1281 700 699	301.1682 336 531	327.2622 823 544	72
37	297.4116 018 144	323.9909 766 415	352.9108 184 961	384.3741 527 511	74
38	346.9008 923 563	378.7783 570 274	413.5431 028 064	451.4528 476 676	76
39	404.6252 008 444	442.8303 690 419	484.5923 925 129	530.2377 181 413	78
40	471.9548 342 649	517.7136 763 694	567.8483 942 491	622.7716 564 249	80
41	550.4881 186 866	605.2598 679 711	665.4082 974 335	731.4540 681 975	82
42	642.0893 416 361	707.6102 573 635	779.7296 017 345	859.1030 891 707	84
43	748.9330 080 843	827.2682 575 247	913.6920 206 225	1009.0286 593 682	86
44	873.5554 606 295	967.1606 124 788	1070.6700 203 406	1185.1183 498 935	88
45	1018.9150 892 783	1130.7089 832 374	1254.6178 215 227	1391.9381 676 767	90
46	1188.4625 601 342	1321.9136 390 357	1470.1690 046 217	1634.8509 520 668	92
47	1386.2227 301 405	1545.4513 008 866	1722.7532 281 719	1920.1554 332 940	94
48	1616.8901 924 359	1806.7895 306 342	2018.7329 999 796	2255.2495 585 895	96
49	1885.9407 204 572	2112.3204 633 731	2365.5639 464 573	2648.8223 210 103	98
50	2199.7612 563 413	2469.5171 542 302	2771.9826 172 333	3111.0790 650 905	100
51	2565.8015 293 965	2887.1163 636 311	3248.2265 557 654	3654.0061 114 982	102
52	2992.7509 038 880	3375.3322 518 405	3806.2921 794 618	4291.6815 624 156	104
53	3490.7446 542 950	3946.1062 095 833	4460.2369 652 195	5040.6403 468 290	106
54	4071.6045 647 697	4613.3989 354 148	5226.5335 523 253	5920.3029 713 556	108
55	4749.1195 643 474	5393.5319 038 293	6124.4846 824 494	6953.4790 941 177	110
56	5539.3730 598 548	6305.5865 761 605	7176.7094 289 235	8166.9589 793 410	112
57	6461.1247 370 146	7371.8711 186 682	8409.7129 632 465	9592.2081 690 966	114
58	7536.2558 932 539	8618.4660 433 836	9854.5542 110 383	11266.1833 850 313	116
59	8790.2888 738 913	10075.8621 176 730	11547.6282 154 585	13232.2908 164 232	118
60	10252.9929 425 068	11779.7061 453 061	13531.5829 155 506	15541.5116 429 786	120

TABLE 1. FUTURE WORTH OF ONE DOLLAR WITH INTEREST
Payable at beginning of each period

SEMI ANNUAL Compounding

HALF YEARS	17% Nominal Annual Rate	17¼% Nominal Annual Rate	17½% Nominal Annual Rate	17¾% Nominal Annual Rate	HALF YEARS
1	1.0850 000 000	1.0862 500 000	1.0875 000 000	1.0887 500 000	1
YEARS					
1	1.1772 250 000	1.1799 390 625	1.1826 562 500	1.1853 765 625	2
2	1.3858 587 006	1.3922 561 912	1.3986 758 057	1.4051 175 949	4
3	1.6314 675 088	1.6427 774 650	1.6541 526 833	1.6655 934 646	6
4	1.9206 043 381	1.9383 773 020	1.9562 940 094	1.9743 554 556	8
5	2.2609 834 419	2.2871 670 965	2.3136 233 370	2.3403 546 831	10
6	2.6616 862 324	2.6987 177 996	2.7362 210 996	2.7742 015 893	12
7	3.1334 035 750	3.1843 225 504	3.2360 089 849	3.2884 735 435	14
8	3.6887 210 235	3.7573 065 648	3.8270 862 510	3.8980 794 649	16
9	4.3424 546 069	4.4333 927 856	4.5261 274 741	4.6206 920 365	18
10	5.1120 461 246	5.2311 333 271	5.3528 529 455	5.4772 600 426	20
11	6.0180 284 991	6.1724 185 538	6.3305 849 913	6.4926 156 812	22
12	7.0845 735 998	7.2830 777 618	7.4869 059 061	7.6961 944 578	24
13	8.3401 371 560	8.5935 879 463	8.8544 360 631	9.1228 885 307	26
14	9.8182 179 635	10.1399 101 049	10.4717 541 502	10.8140 582 466	28
15	11.5582 516 421	11.9644 760 230	12.3844 854 942	12.8187 311 910	30
16	13.6066 627 894	14.1173 526 219	14.6465 891 727	15.1950 235 149	32
17	16.0181 036 022	16.6576 158 177	17.3218 802 263	18.0118 247 411	34
18	18.8569 120 131	19.6549 715 914	20.4858 299 114	21.3507 948 960	36
19	22.1988 282 446	23.1916 687 530	24.2276 947 812	25.3087 318 605	38
20	26.1330 155 803	27.3647 558 862	28.6530 346 560	30.0003 775 740	40
21	30.7644 392 665	32.2887 444 059	33.8866 905 174	35.5617 444 424	42
22	36.2166 670 155	38.0987 508 036	40.0763 063 323	42.1540 583 836	44
23	42.6351 658 273	44.9542 043 056	47.3964 941 608	49.9684 328 222	46
24	50.1911 830 911	53.0432 216 838	56.0537 600 473	59.2314 091 323	48
25	59.0863 155 144	62.5877 692 656	66.2923 296 559	70.2115 241 492	50
26	69.5578 877 815	73.8497 537 912	78.4010 379 947	83.2270 951 439	52
27	81.8852 844 435	87.1382 092 543	92.7214 775 909	98.6554 479 485	54
28	96.3974 039 790	102.8177 769 354	109.6576 349 821	116.9438 557 611	56
29	113.4814 338 992	121.3187 113 255	129.6872 873 718	138.6225 057 476	58
30	133.5931 810 220	143.1486 865 051	153.3754 809 558	164.3198 693 483	60
31	157.2692 325 286	168.9067 269 529	181.3904 711 491	194.7809 218 785	62
32	185.1412 722 635	199.2996 450 508	214.5225 743 949	230.8887 396 169	64
33	217.9529 342 404	235.1614 363 378	253.7064 633 743	273.6901 004 871	66
34	256.5796 430 111	277.4761 647 286	300.0475 345 750	324.4258 305 057	68
35	302.0519 702 438	327.4049 656 760	354.8530 920 622	384.5667 757 510	70
36	355.5831 306 703	386.3179 082 575	419.6692 271 591	455.8564 426 914	72
37	418.6013 510 033	455.8315 904 964	496.3244 344 324	540.3615 430 310	74
38	492.7879 754 348	537.8534 995 482	586.9811 944 092	640.5319 083 853	76
39	580.1223 243 813	634.6343 540 192	694.1969 782 005	759.2715 117 334	78
40	682.9345 033 198	748.8298 647 117	820.9963 950 000	900.0226 545 827	80
41	803.9675 706 706	883.5736 085 400	970.9565 177 742	1066.8657 604 613	82
42	946.4507 233 827	1042.5630 153 104	1148.3077 942 239	1264.6376 677 846	84
43	1114.1854 528 342	1230.1608 268 825	1358.0533 897 626	1499.0718 514 465	86
44	1311.6469 697 127	1451.5148 127 960	1606.1103 292 364	1776.9646 382 082	88
45	1544.1036 039 201	1712.6990 274 153	1899.4764 190 610	2106.3722 345 233	90
46	1817.7573 651 248	2020.8804 847 531	2246.4276 587 301	2496.8442 787 047	92
47	2139.9094 141 591	2384.5158 246 041	2656.7517 107 701	2959.7006 881 887	94
48	2519.1548 600 834	2813.5833 665 998	3142.0240 154 404	3508.3598 277 941	96
49	2965.6120 801 617	3319.8569 198 514	3715.9343 395 107	4158.7275 126 836	98
50	3491.1926 810 683	3917.2288 616 436	4394.6729 712 119	4929.6581 233 591	100
51	4109.9193 039 707	4622.0913 506 056	5197.3874 561 099	5843.5012 005 676	102
52	4838.2997 526 169	5453.7861 350 230	6146.7227 586 399	6926.7493 660 934	104
53	5695.7674 262 744	6435.1352 992 345	7269.4600 875 228	8210.8063 528 789	106
54	6705.1998 083 959	7593.0675 120 394	8597.2724 066 343	9732.8974 099 287	108
55	7893.5288 444 388	8959.3569 616 550	10167.6179 446 587	11537.1484 749 465	110
56	9292.4594 938 945	10571.4952 539 381	12024.7969 098 627	13675.8654 002 842	112
57	10939.3156 277 000	12473.7201 991 549	14221.2012 204 298	16211.0503 174 015	114
58	12878.0358 398 191	14718.2297 176 781	16818.7925 058 490	19216.1990 997 560	116
59	15160.3457 415 310	17366.6141 747 367	19890.8500 744 954	22778.4320 331 843	118
60	17847.1380 155 739	20491.5464 481 381	23524.0381 584 150	27001.0194 626 359	120

TABLE 1. FUTURE WORTH OF ONE DOLLAR WITH INTEREST
Payable at beginning of each period

HALF YEARS	18% Nominal Annual Rate	18¼% Nominal Annual Rate	18½% Nominal Annual Rate	18¾% Nominal Annual Rate	HALF YEARS
1	1.0900 000 000	1.0912 500 000	1.0925 000 000	1.0937 500 000	1
YEARS					
1	1.1881 000 000	1.1908 265 625	1.1935 562 500	1.1962 890 625	2
2	1.4115 816 100	1.4180 679 020	1.4245 765 219	1.4311 075 211	4
3	1.6771 001 108	1.6886 729 251	1.7003 122 113	1.7120 182 747	6
4	1.9925 626 417	2.0109 165 746	2.0294 182 668	2.0480 687 368	8
5	2.3673 636 746	2.3946 528 720	2.4222 248 562	2.4500 822 291	10
6	2.8126 647 818	2.8516 162 479	2.8910 616 160	2.9310 065 729	12
7	3.3417 270 272	3.3957 803 740	3.4506 446 609	3.5063 311 053	14
8	3.9703 058 811	4.0437 854 698	4.1185 385 016	4.1945 855 508	16
9	4.7171 204 173	4.8154 471 505	4.9157 073 694	5.0179 368 161	18
10	5.6044 107 678	5.7343 623 772	5.8671 732 539	6.0029 029 294	20
11	6.6586 004 332	6.8286 310 377	7.0028 013 071	7.1812 071 177	22
12	7.9110 831 747	8.1317 152 252	8.3582 372 676	8.5907 995 305	24
13	9.3991 579 198	9.6834 624 889	9.9760 263 297	10.2770 795 164	26
14	11.1671 395 246	11.5313 243 487	11.9069 485 760	12.2943 578 199	28
15	13.2676 784 691	13.7318 073 353	14.2116 128 913	14.7076 057 905	30
16	15.7633 287 892	16.3522 009 260	16.9623 593 890	17.5945 479 427	32
17	18.7284 109 344	19.4726 352 180	20.2455 300 634	21.0481 652 635	34
18	22.2512 250 312	23.1885 312 595	24.1641 789 418	25.1796 898 904	36
19	26.4366 804 595	27.6135 189 691	28.8413 068 021	30.1221 876 130	38
20	31.4094 200 540	32.8829 118 725	34.4237 219 918	36.0348 435 800	40
21	37.3175 319 661	39.1578 449 102	41.0866 485 316	43.1080 892 437	42
22	44.3369 597 290	46.6302 018 493	49.0392 261 464	51.5697 356 675	44
23	52.6767 418 540	55.5284 829 769	58.5310 748 622	61.6923 107 350	46
24	62.5852 369 967	66.1247 925 042	69.8601 302 210	73.8018 365 726	48
25	74.3575 200 758	78.7431 593 538	83.3819 950 511	88.2883 298 843	50
26	88.3441 696 021	93.7694 457 736	99.5211 013 307	105.6183 633 869	52
27	104.9617 079 042	111.6631 467 781	118.7840 325 002	126.3500 929 189	54
28	124.7050 051 610	132.9714 412 358	141.7754 243 908	151.1512 342 048	56
29	148.1620 166 318	158.3459 242 774	169.2169 438 780	180.8205 682 626	58
30	176.0312 919 602	188.5625 326 932	201.9699 409 715	216.3136 680 876	60
31	209.1427 779 780	224.5452 726 233	241.0624 853 586	258.7736 752 024	62
32	248.4825 345 156	267.3944 751 237	287.7216 360 404	309.5681 173 076	64
33	295.2220 992 580	318.4204 436 430	343.4119 569 562	370.3329 528 337	66
34	350.7533 761 285	379.1835 223 331	409.8814 875 498	443.0252 609 583	68
35	416.7300 861 782	451.5418 104 566	489.2166 112 243	529.9862 740 957	70
36	495.1170 153 883	537.7079 819 711	583.9075 439 306	634.0167 829 758	72
37	588.2485 259 829	640.3169 477 994	696.9264 984 806	758.4673 429 153	74
38	698.8980 737 203	762.5064 298 585	831.8209 780 521	907.3461 865 931	76
39	830.3608 013 870	908.0129 107 525	992.8251 272 352	1085.4483 189 224	78
40	986.5516 681 279	1081.2858 932 170	1184.9926 357 686	1298.5099 518 358	80
41	1172.1220 369 028	1287.6239 632 994	1414.3553 666 256	1553.3932 529 286	82
42	1392.5981 920 442	1533.3368 180 084	1688.1126 875 570	1858.3073 582 398	84
43	1654.5459 119 677	1825.9382 121 437	2014.8574 489 380	2223.0727 674 256	86
44	1965.7659 980 089	2174.3757 245 044	2404.8457 010 390	2659.4376 368 128	88
45	2335.5265 822 343	2589.3043 695 951	2870.3186 167 607	3181.4561 573 200	90
46	2774.8391 323 526	3083.4124 217 111	3425.8867 245 261	3805.9412 038 252	92
47	3296.7863 731 482	3671.8094 149 161	4088.9885 118 501	4553.0058 346 542	94
48	3916.9118 899 373	4372.4881 837 196	4880.4377 944 969	5446.7110 814 954	96
49	4653.6830 164 345	5206.8750 733 907	5825.0770 323 580	6515.8408 933 905	98
50	5529.0407 918 259	6200.4851 450 128	6952.5570 987 023	7794.8291 937 533	100
51	6569.0533 647 683	7383.7024 110 679	8298.2679 786 380	9324.8689 085 428	102
52	7804.6923 026 812	8792.7089 606 950	9904.4496 100 783	11155.2386 845 361	104
53	9272.7549 248 156	10470.5913 867 274	11821.5177 349 190	13344.8900 278 874	106
54	11016.9601 261 734	12468.6583 483 986	14109.6463 769 984	15964.3459 806 270	108
55	13089.2503 259 066	14848.0095 600 105	16840.6566 185 563	19097.9724 865 899	110
56	15551.3383 122 097	17681.4041 843 144	20100.2709 611 818	22846.6956 016 335	112
57	18476.5450 487 363	21055.4857 649 803	23990.8040 324 120	27331.2520 625 010	114
58	21951.9831 724 036	25073.4317 352 791	28634.3740 954 106	32696.0779 068 005	116
59	26081.1512 071 327	29858.1085 234 009	34176.7361 664 154	39113.9603 865 533	118
60	30987.0157 491 944	35555.8287 356 734	40791.8570 560 261	46791.6030 014 920	120

TABLE 1. FUTURE WORTH OF ONE DOLLAR WITH INTEREST
Payable at beginning of each period

SEMI ANNUAL Compounding

HALF YEARS	19% Nominal Annual Rate	19¼% Nominal Annual Rate	19½% Nominal Annual Rate	19¾% Nominal Annual Rate	HALF YEARS
1	1.0950 000 000	1.0962 500 000	1.0975 000 000	1.0987 500 000	1
YEARS					
1	1.1990 250 000	1.2017 640 625	1.2045 062 500	1.2072 515 625	2
2	1.4376 609 506	1.4442 368 619	1.4508 353 063	1.4574 563 352	4
3	1.7237 914 213	1.7356 319 584	1.7475 401 941	1.7595 164 379	6
4	2.0668 690 090	2.0858 201 133	2.1049 230 860	2.1241 789 689	8
5	2.4782 276 135	2.5066 636 530	2.5353 930 128	2.5644 183 792	10
6	2.9714 568 642	3.0124 182 950	3.0538 967 302	3.0958 980 952	12
7	3.5628 510 666	3.6202 160 481	3.6784 376 983	3.7375 278 128	14
8	4.2719 475 002	4.3506 455 451	4.4307 011 979	4.5121 362 919	16
9	5.1221 718 514	5.2284 494 648	5.3368 072 847	5.4472 835 886	18
10	6.1416 121 041	6.2833 626 694	6.4282 177 295	6.5762 416 237	20
11	7.3639 464 531	7.5511 194 477	7.7428 284 315	7.9391 779 756	22
12	8.8295 558 960	9.0746 639 839	9.3262 852 385	9.5845 850 160	24
13	10.5868 582 582	10.9056 050 552	11.2335 688 590	11.5710 052 365	26
14	12.6939 077 230	13.1059 642 351	13.5309 039 005	13.9691 141 515	28
15	15.2203 127 076	15.7502 768 222	16.2980 583 163	16.8642 348 861	30
16	18.2495 354 442	18.9281 166 593	19.6311 131 048	20.3593 739 166	32
17	21.8816 492 360	22.7471 303 720	23.6457 984 292	24.5788 859 724	34
18	26.2366 444 751	27.3366 838 060	28.4815 119 942	29.6728 984 946	36
19	31.4583 926 418	32.8522 441 860	34.3061 592 065	35.8226 530 715	38
20	37.7193 992 373	39.4806 464 352	41.3219 831 777	43.2469 538 935	40
21	45.2265 026 705	47.4464 220 501	49.7725 869 999	52.2099 526 613	42
22	54.2277 073 646	57.0194 049 140	59.9513 921 201	63.0305 469 284	44
23	65.0203 768 228	68.5238 716 908	72.2118 265 048	76.0937 262 646	46
24	77.9610 573 199	82.3495 264 214	86.9795 963 490	91.8642 699 294	48
25	93.4772 567 530	98.9647 014 171	104.7674 674 248	110.9032 834 101	50
26	112.0815 677 783	118.9322 216 191	126.1930 693 099	133.8881 621 833	52
27	134.3886 018 054	142.9284 698 152	152.0003 406 904	161.6366 929 960	54
28	161.1352 932 797	171.7662 985 320	183.0853 603 638	195.1361 501 768	56
29	193.2052 450 247	206.4225 647 244	220.5274 608 417	235.5784 222 011	58
30	231.6579 189 157	248.0712 199 748	265.6267 048 804	284.4024 182 936	60
31	277.7636 362 280	298.1230 771 063	319.9490 261 953	343.3452 638 637	62
32	333.0455 439 282	358.2736 002 683	385.3806 017 337	414.5041 062 765	64
33	399.3299 333 085	430.5603 373 449	464.1933 434 170	500.4107 299 649	66
34	478.8065 732 853	517.4319 401 589	559.1237 833 542	604.1216 356 419	68
35	574.1010 515 334	621.8311 104 727	673.4680 915 738	729.3267 885 688	70
36	688.3615 133 148	747.2942 815 105	811.1965 254 762	880.4809 050 727	72
37	825.3626 635 023	898.0714 116 311	977.0912 849 143	1062.9619 484 005	74
38	989.6304 676 058	1079.2699 480 569	1176.9125 594 999	1283.2624 730 845	76
39	1186.5916 714 211	1297.0278 373 110	1417.5985 336 211	1549.2206 257 289	78
40	1422.7530 788 256	1558.7214 429 425	1707.5062 937 374	1870.2990 210 684	80
41	1705.9165 103 389	1873.2154 135 764	2056.7020 027 211	2257.9214 155 271	82
42	2045.4365 438 091	2251.1629 653 572	2477.3104 166 650	2725.8791 568 973	84
43	2452.5295 519 407	2705.3667 505 973	2983.9358 800 631	3290.8218 713 504	86
44	2940.6442 460 157	3251.2125 367 502	3594.1694 171 353	3972.8498 460 970	88
45	3525.9059 670 790	3907.1903 862 158	4329.1995 264 983	4796.2291 842 785	90
46	4227.6494 021 769	4695.5209 914 997	5214.5478 871 643	5790.2551 768 283	92
47	5069.0573 244 452	5642.9083 822 987	6280.9555 210 137	6990.2946 094 997	94
48	6077.9264 584 429	6781.4445 018 266	7565.4501 810 330	8439.0440 896 538	96
49	7287.5857 718 345	8149.6962 941 334	9112.6320 271 178	10188.0491 632 410	98
50	8737.9975 300 739	9794.0121 265 790	10976.2222 306 136	12299.5382 711 495	100
51	10477.0774 884 968	11770.0918 014 118	13220.9282 781 630	14848.6367 958 738	102
52	12562.2778 356 449	14144.8733 392 626	15924.6907 418 491	17926.0399 728 136	104
53	15062.4851 818 841	16998.8004 477 402	19181.3895 278 744	21641.2397 666 167	106
54	18060.2962 952 086	20428.5474 837 031	23104.1035 700 092	26126.4205 226 851	108
55	21654.7467 653 625	24550.2942 149 891	27829.0371 507 234	31541.1619 985 437	110
56	25964.5827 403 388	29503.6613 113 756	33520.2491 795 286	38078.1171 058 075	112
57	31132.1838 202 347	35456.4398 761 828	40375.3496 382 995	45969.8663 730 440	114
58	37328.2667 050 569	42610.2752 273 884	48632.3609 852 670	55497.1930 067 736	116
59	44757.5249 860 309	51207.4974 615 094	58577.9827 590 103	66999.0729 717 915	118
60	53665.3913 963 756	61539.3301 798 020	70557.5463 456 202	80884.7355 312 469	120

SEMI ANNUAL
Compounding

TABLE 1. FUTURE WORTH OF ONE DOLLAR WITH INTEREST

Payable at beginning of each period

HALF YEARS	20% Nominal Annual Rate	20¼% Nominal Annual Rate	20½% Nominal Annual Rate	20¾% Nominal Annual Rate	HALF YEARS
1	1.1000 000 000	1.1012 500 000	1.1025 000 000	1.1037 500 000	1
YEARS					
1	1.2100 000 000	1.2127 515 625	1.2155 062 500	1.2182 640 625	2
2	1.4641 000 000	1.4707 663 523	1.4774 554 438	1.4841 673 260	4
3	1.7715 610 000	1.7836 741 919	1.7958 563 260	1.8081 077 160	6
4	2.1435 888 100	2.1631 536 632	2.1828 745 884	2.2027 526 515	8
5	2.5937 424 601	2.6233 679 850	2.6532 977 051	2.6835 343 939	10
6	3.1384 283 767	3.1814 936 228	3.2250 999 437	3.2692 535 126	12
7	3.7974 983 358	3.8583 613 621	3.9201 291 385	3.9828 140 656	14
8	4.5949 729 864	4.6792 337 706	4.7649 414 686	4.8521 192 437	16
9	5.5599 173 135	5.6747 480 666	5.7918 161 360	5.9111 625 016	18
10	6.7274 999 493	6.8820 595 845	7.0399 887 121	7.2013 568 433	20
11	8.1402 749 387	8.3462 285 144	8.5571 502 795	8.7731 542 434	22
12	9.8497 326 758	10.1219 016 718	10.4012 696 469	10.6880 185 295	24
13	11.9181 765 377	12.2753 520 679	12.6428 082 638	13.0208 288 738	26
14	14.4209 936 106	14.8869 524 006	15.3674 124 622	15.8628 078 809	28
15	17.4494 022 689	18.0541 747 847	18.6791 858 941	19.3250 887 717	30
16	21.1137 767 454	21.8952 286 798	22.7046 671 992	23.5430 611 551	32
17	25.5476 698 619	26.5534 727 927	27.5976 648 848	28.6816 653 266	34
18	30.9126 805 329	32.2027 656 192	33.5451 341 529	34.9418 421 200	36
19	37.4043 434 448	39.0539 543 215	40.7743 202 199	42.5683 905 323	38
20	45.2592 555 682	47.3627 441 252	49.5614 410 668	51.8595 403 840	40
21	54.7636 992 375	57.4392 419 421	60.2422 413 758	63.1786 143 476	42
22	66.2640 760 774	69.6595 304 141	73.2248 209 062	76.9682 353 782	44
23	80.1795 320 536	84.4797 043 528	89.0052 274 667	93.7676 351 153	46
24	97.0172 337 849	102.4528 934 533	108.1864 102 684	114.2337 400 866	48
25	117.3908 528 797	124.2499 066 182	131.5012 578 463	139.1668 602 725	50
26	142.0429 319 844	150.6842 683 917	159.8406 007 950	169.5419 845 610	52
27	171.8719 477 012	182.7425 819 362	194.2872 492 701	206.5469 068 756	54
28	207.9650 567 184	221.6213 517 784	236.1573 657 832	251.6286 738 670	56
29	251.6377 186 293	268.7716 406 526	287.0507 540 930	306.5501 704 667	58
30	304.4816 395 414	325.9532 271 572	348.9119 856 672	373.4590 560 329	60
31	368.4227 838 451	395.3002 855 368	424.1046 992 784	454.9717 467 800	62
32	445.7915 684 526	479.4010 389 414	515.5019 126 273	554.2757 285 550	64
33	539.4077 978 276	581.3943 590 403	626.5957 966 854	675.2542 008 145	66
34	652.6834 353 714	705.0869 173 548	761.6311 070 948	822.6379 259 045	68
35	789.7469 567 994	855.0952 607 204	925.7673 708 682	1002.1902 215 790	70
36	955.5938 177 273	1037.0181 135 250	1125.2760 253 363	1220.9323 307 386	72
37	1156.2685 194 501	1257.6453 375 182	1367.7800 417 715	1487.4179 812 832	74
38	1399.0849 085 346	1525.2113 481 460	1662.5451 893 985	1812.0678 725 136	76
39	1692.8927 393 268	1849.7024 456 068	2020.8340 686 213	2207.5771 678 941	78
40	2048.4002 145 855	2243.2295 310 698	2456.3364 406 221	2689.4119 288 409	80
41	2478.5642 596 484	2720.4801 188 510	2985.6922 956 789	3276.4139 021 657	82
42	2999.0627 541 746	3299.2665 148 867	3629.1276 459 746	3991.5373 108 839	84
43	3628.8659 325 512	4001.1906 210 328	4411.2273 357 299	4862.7464 599 777	86
44	4390.9277 783 870	4852.4501 775 179	5361.8743 967 505	5924.1092 572 399	88
45	5313.0226 118 483	5884.8165 347 382	6517.3918 409 652	7217.1294 104 190	90
46	6428.7573 603 364	7136.8204 475 296	7921.9305 163 922	8792.3693 951 252	92
47	7778.7964 060 071	8655.1901 490 235	9629.1560 547 405	10711.4276 583 059	94
48	9412.3436 512 685	10496.5953 769 628	11704.2993 667 624	13049.3473 741 827	96
49	11388.9358 180 349	12729.7624 443 419	14226.6490 321 707	15897.5509 450 455	98
50	13780.6123 398 223	15438.0392 946 295	17292.5808 151 600	19367.4149 981 118	100
51	16674.5409 311 849	18722.5062 764 983	21019.2400 594 570	23594.6256 757 231	102
52	20176.1945 267 338	22705.7487 407 394	25549.0176 625 204	28744.4845 288 733	104
53	24413.1953 773 479	27536.4322 630 641	31054.9906 501 540	35018.3724 966 135	106
54	29539.9664 065 909	33394.8512 527 064	37747.5352 289 537	42661.6247 398 627	108
55	35743.3593 519 750	40499.6580 361 748	45882.3649 928 884	51973.1242 684 356	110
56	43249.4648 158 898	49116.0235 640 866	55770.3014 136 370	63316.9895 120 817	112
57	52331.8524 272 266	59565.5343 211 329	67789.1499 326 597	77136.8128 682 586	114
58	63321.5414 369 442	72238.1948 191 013	82398.1354 253 349	93973.0070 131 870	116
59	76619.0651 387 025	87606.9836 390 444	100155.4485 978 410	114483.9372 892 261	118
60	92709.0688 178 300	106245.5062 941 631	121739.5737 422 294	139471.6665 329 679	120

TABLE 2. FUTURE WORTH OF ONE DOLLAR PER PERIOD WITH INTEREST
Payable at end of each period

HALF YEARS	7% Nominal Annual Rate	7¼% Nominal Annual Rate	7½% Nominal Annual Rate	7¾% Nominal Annual Rate	HALF YEARS
1	1.0000 000 000	1.0000 000 000	1.0000 000 000	1.0000 000 000	1
YEARS					
1	2.0350 000 000	2.0362 500 000	2.0375 000 000	2.0387 500 000	2
2	4.2149 428 750	4.2228 038 848	4.2306 777 344	4.2385 644 355	4
3	6.5501 521 813	6.5707 561 946	6.5914 279 550	6.6121 676 487	6
4	9.0516 867 704	9.0920 204 031	9.1325 542 472	9.1732 892 245	8
5	11.7313 931 606	11.7993 893 653	11.8678 384 702	11.9367 434 065	10
6	14.6019 616 385	14.7066 002 294	14.8121 155 033	14.9185 147 867	12
7	17.6769 863 562	17.8284 041 379	17.9813 537 034	18.1358 507 651	14
8	20.9710 297 094	21.1806 410 752	21.3927 415 098	21.6073 613 128	16
9	24.4996 913 004	24.7803 202 393	25.0647 806 658	25.3531 266 180	18
10	28.2796 818 133	28.6457 063 463	29.0173 865 636	29.3948 132 351	20
11	32.3289 021 505	32.7964 123 049	33.2719 962 557	33.7557 994 100	22
12	36.6665 282 061	37.2534 987 325	37.8516 847 196	38.4613 103 069	24
13	41.3131 016 776	42.0395 808 163	42.7812 900 052	43.5385 639 169	26
14	46.2906 273 446	47.1789 430 621	48.0875 479 447	49.0169 284 954	28
15	51.6226 772 772	52.6976 625 140	53.7992 371 548	54.9280 924 354	30
16	57.3345 024 663	58.6237 410 684	59.9473 351 187	61.3062 475 630	32
17	63.4531 524 044	64.9872 475 556	66.5651 861 926	68.1882 869 115	34
18	70.0076 031 845	71.8204 703 084	73.6886 824 501	75.6140 181 217	36
19	77.0288 947 213	79.1580 809 925	81.3564 583 436	83.6263 937 002	38
20	84.5502 777 478	87.0373 105 303	89.6101 002 389	92.2717 594 687	40
21	92.6073 712 804	95.4981 380 096	98.4943 719 603	101.6001 226 414	42
22	101.2383 312 998	104.5834 935 373	108.0574 575 679	111.6654 410 803	44
23	110.4840 314 467	114.3394 760 657	118.3512 226 852	122.5259 354 029	46
24	120.3882 565 864	124.8155 872 983	129.4314 957 935	134.2444 257 465	48
25	130.9979 101 618	136.0649 828 601	141.3583 710 189	146.8886 951 373	50
26	142.3632 363 131	148.1447 420 090	154.1965 340 546	160.5318 815 668	52
27	154.5380 578 195	161.1161 572 547	168.0156 129 847	175.2529 010 416	54
28	167.5800 309 877	175.0450 453 560	182.8905 559 143	191.1369 040 566	56
29	181.5509 186 948	190.0020 812 742	198.9020 374 521	208.2757 681 284	58
30	196.5168 828 788	206.0631 567 765	216.1368 962 512	226.7686 292 415	60
31	212.5487 978 619	223.3097 655 098	234.6886 059 804	246.7224 552 775	62
32	229.7225 859 896	241.8294 164 980	254.6577 822 811	268.2526 647 483	64
33	248.1195 771 767	261.7160 781 617	276.1527 284 585	291.4837 944 082	66
34	267.8268 940 611	283.0706 551 124	299.2900 228 673	316.5502 196 099	68
35	288.9378 645 906	306.0015 001 408	324.1951 511 770	343.5969 315 688	70
36	311.5524 639 960	330.6249 639 973	351.0031 869 466	372.7803 760 329	72
37	335.7777 882 442	357.0659 857 538	379.8595 241 992	404.2693 582 089	74
38	361.7285 612 119	385.4587 267 429	410.9206 659 701	438.2460 191 782	76
39	389.5276 779 842	415.9472 512 899	444.3550 731 044	474.9068 894 527	78
40	419.3067 868 486	448.6862 576 933	480.3440 779 088	514.4640 257 615	80
41	451.2069 127 419	483.8418 631 615	519.0828 676 115	557.1462 376 467	82
42	485.3791 251 019	521.5924 466 891	560.7815 429 649	603.2004 109 618	84
43	521.9852 532 873	562.1295 541 485	605.6662 577 321	652.8929 359 284	86
44	561.1986 529 527	605.6588 701 915	653.9804 452 369	706.5112 480 120	88
45	603.2050 270 092	652.4012 618 895	705.9861 386 308	764.3654 905 287	90
46	648.2033 050 580	702.5938 994 097	761.9653 920 356	826.7903 086 016	92
47	696.4065 854 607	756.4914 594 128	822.2218 102 708	894.1467 848 410	94
48	748.0431 445 102	814.3674 172 787	887.0821 954 618	966.8245 279 477	96
49	803.3575 174 779	876.5154 347 156	956.8983 194 588	1045.2439 263 189	98
50	862.6116 566 603	943.2508 497 959	1032.0488 316 799	1129.8585 796 918	100
51	926.0861 719 059	1014.9122 769 760	1112.9413 127 255	1221.1579 228 915	102
52	994.0816 594 999	1091.8633 252 207	1200.0144 849 009	1319.6700 568 591	104
53	1066.9201 256 978	1174.4944 429 500	1293.7405 916 379	1425.9648 033 355	106
54	1144.9465 116 506	1263.2248 991 678	1394.6279 587 177	1540.6570 008 690	108
55	1228.5303 269 429	1358.5049 108 265	1503.2237 511 885	1664.4100 612 142	110
56	1318.0673 994 794	1460.8179 272 208	1620.1169 409 277	1797.9398 066 908	112
57	1413.9817 500 074	1570.6830 830 018	1745.9415 009 455	1942.0186 107 004	114
58	1516.7276 001 516	1688.6578 322 582	1881.3798 437 521	2097.4798 653 498	116
59	1626.7915 234 724	1815.3407 770 296	2027.1665 224 387	2265.2228 020 247	118
60	1744.6947 497 318	1951.3747 046 041	2184.0922 145 438	2446.2176 927 953	120

TABLE 2. FUTURE WORTH OF ONE DOLLAR PER PERIOD WITH INTEREST
Payable at end of each period

HALF YEARS	8% Nominal Annual Rate	8¼% Nominal Annual Rate	8½% Nominal Annual Rate	8¾% Nominal Annual Rate	HALF YEARS
1	1.0000 000 000	1.0000 000 000	1.0000 000 000	1.0000 000 000	1
YEARS					
1	2.0400 000 000	2.0412 500 000	2.0425 000 000	2.0437 500 000	2
2	4.2464 640 000	4.2543 764 395	4.2623 017 656	4.2702 399 902	4
3	6.6329 754 624	6.6538 515 831	6.6747 961 983	6.6958 094 956	6
4	9.2142 262 601	9.2553 662 831	9.2967 102 258	9.3382 590 243	8
5	12.0061 071 230	12.0759 325 856	12.1462 227 778	12.2169 807 004	10
6	15.0258 054 642	15.1339 949 780	15.2430 908 288	15.3531 005 763	12
7	18.2919 111 901	18.4495 510 020	18.6087 863 820	18.7696 336 708	14
8	21.8245 311 432	22.0442 820 238	22.2666 453 449	22.4916 528 689	16
9	25.6454 128 845	25.9416 950 143	26.2420 293 274	26.5464 729 243	18
10	29.7780 785 758	30.1672 762 685	30.5625 014 857	30.9638 509 135	20
11	34.2479 697 876	34.7486 580 666	35.2580 176 303	35.7762 046 143	22
12	39.0826 041 223	39.7157 993 706	40.3611 339 232	41.0188 504 097	24
13	44.3117 446 187	45.1011 817 336	45.9072 326 048	46.7302 624 639	26
14	49.9675 829 796	50.9400 217 061	51.9347 673 151	52.9523 550 725	28
15	56.0849 377 507	57.2705 011 276	58.4855 297 104	59.7307 902 585	30
16	62.7014 686 711	64.1340 168 077	65.6049 392 238	67.1153 128 718	32
17	69.8579 085 147	71.5754 512 323	73.3423 579 793	75.1601 156 516	34
18	77.5983 138 495	79.6434 660 627	81.7514 330 416	83.9242 369 300	36
19	85.9703 362 596	88.3908 203 481	90.8904 683 761	93.4719 938 962	38
20	95.0255 156 984	97.8747 155 320	100.8228 290 966	103.8734 546 004	40
21	104.8195 977 794	108.1571 695 091	111.6173 808 049	115.2049 521 621	42
22	115.4128 769 582	119.3054 221 773	123.3489 670 674	127.5496 449 551	44
23	126.8705 677 180	131.3923 751 393	136.0989 283 398	140.9981 268 809	46
24	139.2632 060 438	144.4970 684 267	149.9556 659 380	155.6490 922 102	48
25	152.6670 836 570	158.7051 973 649	165.0152 549 644	171.6100 598 692	50
26	167.1647 176 834	174.1096 729 598	181.3821 104 406	188.9981 624 880	52
27	182.8453 586 463	190.8112 294 694	199.1697 112 651	207.9410 060 010	54
28	199.8055 399 119	208.9190 831 333	218.5013 870 136	228.5776 061 079	56
29	218.1496 719 687	228.5516 463 692	239.5111 730 400	251.0594 084 666	58
30	237.9906 852 013	249.8373 021 054	262.3447 398 047	275.5514 001 064	60
31	259.4507 251 137	272.9152 433 135	287.1604 028 744	302.2333 202 175	62
32	282.6619 042 830	297.9363 832 306	314.1302 205 964	331.3009 792 010	64
33	307.7671 156 725	325.0643 422 242	343.4411 870 581	362.9676 956 616	66
34	334.9209 123 114	354.4765 177 525	375.2965 286 021	397.4658 618 869	68
35	364.2904 587 560	386.3652 444 168	409.9171 128 881	435.0486 493 033	70
36	396.0565 601 905	420.9390 516 924	447.5429 802 687	475.9918 664 227	72
37	430.4147 755 021	458.4240 275 622	488.4350 080 997	520.5959 829 165	74
38	467.5766 211 830	499.0652 969 704	532.8767 195 215	569.1883 346 702	76
39	507.7708 734 716	543.1286 247 649	581.1762 492 555	622.1255 260 007	78
40	551.2449 767 468	590.9021 536 085	633.6684 800 424	679.7960 466 654	80
41	598.2665 668 494	642.6982 882 270	690.7173 645 381	742.6231 228 692	82
42	649.1251 187 043	698.8557 383 118	752.7184 487 635	811.0678 231 913	84
43	704.1337 283 906	759.7417 334 397	820.1016 146 065	885.6324 422 259	86
44	763.6310 406 272	825.7544 244 918	893.3340 603 895	966.8641 867 671	88
45	827.9833 335 424	897.3254 872 753	972.9235 401 691	1055.3591 915 917	90
46	897.5867 735 595	974.9229 453 750	1059.4218 842 279	1151.7668 943 086	92
47	972.8698 542 819	1059.0542 306 926	1153.4288 251 657	1256.7948 013 818	94
48	1054.2960 343 913	1150.2695 016 892	1255.5961 561 203	1371.2136 803 022	96
49	1142.3665 907 976	1249.1652 410 275	1366.6322 499 475	1495.8632 160 136	98
50	1237.6237 046 067	1356.3881 561 427	1487.3069 706 945	1631.6581 731 017	100
51	1340.6537 989 026	1472.6394 082 464	1618.4570 114 193	1779.5951 089 700	102
52	1452.0911 488 931	1598.6791 974 199	1760.9916 953 668	1940.7596 872 682	104
53	1572.6217 866 428	1735.3317 337 789	1915.8992 807 228	2116.3346 452 431	106
54	1702.9877 244 328	1883.4906 272 189	2084.2538 126 600	2307.6084 734 837	108
55	1843.9915 227 465	2044.1247 309 848	2267.2225 701 852	2515.9848 717 573	110
56	1996.5012 310 027	2218.2844 772 786	2466.0741 594 184	2742.9930 503 297	112
57	2161.4557 314 525	2407.1087 463 350	2682.1873 094 194	2990.2989 523 690	114
58	2339.8705 191 390	2611.8323 138 838	2917.0604 315 477	3259.7174 797 898	116
59	2532.8439 535 007	2833.7939 257 008	3172.3220 086 337	3553.2258 122 600	118
60	2741.5640 201 064	3074.4450 520 478	3449.7418 859 957	3872.9779 171 140	120

TABLE 2. FUTURE WORTH OF ONE DOLLAR PER PERIOD WITH INTEREST
Payable at end of each period

SEMI ANNUAL Compounding

HALF YEARS	9% Nominal Annual Rate	9¼% Nominal Annual Rate	9½% Nominal Annual Rate	9¾% Nominal Annual Rate	HALF YEARS
1	1.0000 000 000	1.0000 000 000	1.0000 000 000	1.0000 000 000	1
YEARS					
1	2.0450 000 000	2.0462 500 000	2.0475 000 000	2.0487 500 000	2
2	4.2781 911 250	4.2861 551 816	4.2941 321 719	4.3021 221 074	4
3	6.7168 916 633	6.7380 428 898	6.7592 633 639	6.7805 532 750	6
4	9.3800 136 186	9.4219 749 519	9.4641 439 715	9.5065 216 279	8
5	12.2882 093 718	12.3599 118 283	12.4320 911 236	12.5047 503 294	10
6	15.4640 318 393	15.5758 922 963	15.6886 896 859	15.8024 318 073	12
7	18.9321 093 693	19.0962 301 408	19.2620 128 122	19.4294 743 753	14
8	22.7193 367 340	22.9497 294 586	23.1828 639 457	23.4187 734 871	16
9	26.8550 836 970	27.1679 203 392	27.4850 423 574	27.8065 100 810	18
10	31.3714 227 742	31.7853 168 502	32.2056 345 081	32.6324 787 230	20
11	36.3033 779 550	36.8396 994 382	37.3853 337 493	37.9404 485 237	22
12	41.6891 963 113	42.3724 240 558	43.0687 911 147	43.7785 601 019	24
13	47.5706 446 018	48.4287 605 443	49.3050 002 306	50.1997 621 961	26
14	53.9933 331 713	55.0582 630 402	56.1477 196 592	57.2622 918 826	28
15	61.0070 696 564	62.3151 754 372	63.6559 363 194	65.0302 027 567	30
16	68.6662 452 415	70.2588 752 201	71.8943 739 760	73.5739 458 667	32
17	77.0302 564 599	78.9543 593 033	80.9340 511 850	82.9710 086 694	34
18	86.1639 658 106	88.4727 758 480	90.8528 935 006	93.3066 178 025	36
19	96.1382 047 643	98.8920 064 110	101.7364 052 241	104.6745 120 471	38
20	107.0303 230 577	110.2973 031 865	113.6784 064 847	117.1777 924 917	40
21	118.9247 885 371	122.7819 865 564	126.7818 420 053	130.9298 576 072	42
22	131.9138 422 022	136.4482 086 559	141.1596 685 269	146.0554 317 136	44
23	146.0982 135 309	151.4077 892 029	156.9358 285 390	162.6916 961 676	46
24	161.5879 016 311	167.7831 304 283	174.2463 187 134	180.9895 335 281	48
25	178.5030 282 787	185.7082 185 954	193.2403 622 478	201.1148 959 854	50
26	196.9747 694 560	205.3297 203 018	214.0816 952 286	223.2503 104 639	52
27	217.1463 726 152	226.8081 825 345	236.9499 781 002	247.5965 340 501	54
28	239.1742 675 551	250.3193 462 969	262.0423 444 078	274.3743 747 580	56
29	263.2292 795 269	276.0555 845 561	289.5751 001 661	303.8266 941 469	58
30	289.4979 539 753	304.2274 762 763	319.7855 885 017	336.2206 099 540	60
31	318.1840 031 899	335.0655 294 179	352.9342 356 434	371.8499 187 178	62
32	349.5098 860 835	368.8220 669 981	389.3067 958 987	411.0377 603 653	64
33	383.7185 333 503	405.7732 916 481	429.2168 149 673	454.1395 489 283	66
34	421.0752 313 819	446.2215 455 572	473.0083 328 280	501.5461 959 705	68
35	461.8696 795 498	490.4977 842 960	521.0588 494 975	553.6876 559 590	70
36	506.4182 368 104	538.9642 847 601	573.7825 792 290	611.0368 257 349	72
37	555.0663 750 528	592.0176 093 908	631.6340 212 001	674.1138 334 502	74
38	608.1913 582 171	650.0918 509 270	695.1118 774 745	743.4907 558 689	76
39	666.2051 679 570	713.6621 842 377	764.7633 520 081	819.7968 068 156	78
40	729.5576 985 382	783.2487 542 956	841.1888 677 618	903.7240 438 288	80
41	798.7402 457 462	859.4209 321 064	925.0472 425 821	996.0336 447 751	82
42	874.2893 168 610	942.8019 734 139	1017.0613 684 685	1097.5628 113 495	84
43	956.7907 912 452	1034.0741 183 009	1118.0244 431 856	1209.2323 620 750	86
44	1046.8844 638 095	1133.9841 734 124	1228.8068 079 382	1332.0550 836 628	88
45	1145.2690 065 916	1243.3496 224 740	1350.3634 500 527	1467.1449 164 797	90
46	1252.7073 869 232	1363.0653 151 047	1483.7422 353 419	1615.7270 574 270	92
47	1370.0327 842 048	1494.1107 886 524	1630.0929 411 179	1779.1490 718 610	94
48	1498.1550 511 712	1637.5582 829 616	1790.6771 677 225	1958.8931 153 336	96
49	1638.0677 697 552	1794.5815 136 502	1966.8792 140 158	2156.5893 759 980	98
50	1790.8559 562 670	1966.4652 756 819	2160.2180 105 739	2374.0308 595 967	100
51	1957.7044 756 424	2154.6159 558 113	2372.3602 134 648	2613.1896 511 222	102
52	2139.9072 300 134	2360.5730 399 168	2605.1345 714 755	2876.2348 006 368	104
53	2338.8771 928 554	2586.0217 093 773	2860.5476 906 426	3165.5519 954 673	106
54	2556.1573 665 279	2832.8066 295 574	3140.8013 319 807	3483.7651 971 896	108
55	2793.4327 481 827	3102.9470 432 225	3448.3113 915 241	3833.7604 396 420	110
56	3052.5433 968 342	3398.6532 923 802	3785.7287 262 960	4218.7120 038 020	112
57	3335.4987 029 278	3722.3449 037 336	4155.9620 057 329	4642.1112 069 192	114
58	3644.4929 710 648	4076.6703 857 246	4562.2027 855 529	5107.7980 670 090	116
59	3981.9224 367 270	4464.5288 991 511	5007.9530 202 154	5619.9961 298 860	118
60	4350.4038 489 668	4889.0939 786 710	5497.0552 511 377	6183.3507 746 023	120

TABLE 2. FUTURE WORTH OF ONE DOLLAR PER PERIOD WITH INTEREST
Payable at end of each period

HALF YEARS	10% Nominal Annual Rate	10¼% Nominal Annual Rate	10½% Nominal Annual Rate	10¾% Nominal Annual Rate	HALF YEARS
1	1.0000 000 000	1.0000 000 000	1.0000 000 000	1.0000 000 000	1
YEARS					
1	2.0500 000 000	2.0512 500 000	2.0525 000 000	2.0537 500 000	2
2	4.3101 250 000	4.3181 408 613	4.3261 697 031	4.3342 115 371	4
3	6.8019 128 125	6.8233 421 665	6.8448 415 272	6.8664 110 854	6
4	9.5491 088 758	9.5919 066 732	9.6349 159 820	9.6781 377 678	8
5	12.5778 925 355	12.6515 208 496	12.7256 383 973	12.8002 483 228	10
6	15.9171 265 204	16.0327 817 469	16.1494 054 698	16.2670 057 349	12
7	19.5986 319 888	19.7695 029 792	19.9421 048 430	20.1164 552 476	14
8	23.6574 917 676	23.8990 528 698	24.1434 912 780	24.3908 418 832	16
9	28.1323 846 738	28.4627 281 450	28.7976 033 600	29.1370 740 523	18
10	33.0659 541 029	33.5061 669 142	33.9532 251 071	34.4072 383 409	20
11	38.5052 143 984	39.0798 050 645	39.6643 973 200	40.2591 711 246	22
12	44.5019 988 743	45.2393 806 341	45.9909 840 337	46.7570 932 821	24
13	51.1134 537 589	52.0464 912 098	52.9993 000 070	53.9723 149 747	26
14	58.4025 827 692	59.5692 099 208	60.7628 058 284	61.9840 182 257	28
15	66.4388 475 030	67.8827 661 907	69.3628 779 240	70.8801 258 877	30
16	75.2988 293 721	77.0702 980 533	78.8896 615 383	80.7582 665 343	32
17	85.0669 593 827	87.2236 835 585	89.4430 156 294	91.7268 458 661	34
18	95.8363 227 194	98.4444 595 796	101.1335 595 823	103.9062 363 874	36
19	107.7095 457 982	110.8448 372 123	114.0838 327 120	117.4300 984 101	38
20	120.7997 742 425	124.5488 239 193	128.4295 787 107	132.4468 468 828	40
21	135.2317 511 023	139.6934 636 414	144.3211 685 017	149.1212 801 413	42
22	151.1430 055 903	156.4302 072 777	161.9251 764 150	167.6363 884 549	44
23	168.6851 636 633	174.9264 272 400	181.4261 262 061	188.1953 622 173	46
24	188.0253 929 388	195.3670 912 262	203.0284 252 181	211.0238 218 194	48
25	209.3479 957 151	217.9566 119 524	226.9585 069 630	236.3722 936 752	50
26	232.8561 652 759	242.9208 913 411	253.4672 045 789	264.5189 595 749	52
27	258.7739 222 166	270.5095 796 072	282.8323 800 424	295.7727 095 359	54
28	287.3482 492 439	300.9985 718 346	315.3618 366 943	330.4765 316 546	56
29	318.8514 447 913	334.6927 670 090	351.3965 456 096	369.0112 761 622	58
30	353.5837 178 825	371.9291 170 983	391.3142 196 274	411.7998 349 897	60
31	391.8760 489 654	413.0799 966 725	435.5332 725 061	459.3117 827 119	62
32	434.0933 439 844	458.5569 267 602	484.5172 047 016	512.0685 298 007	64
33	480.6379 117 428	508.8146 901 811	538.7794 617 408	570.6490 447 411	66
34	531.9532 976 964	564.3558 795 093	598.8888 161 150	635.6962 078 066	68
35	588.5285 107 103	625.7359 231 488	665.4753 291 065	707.9238 662 212	70
36	650.9026 830 581	693.5686 397 822	739.2369 550 385	788.1246 681 347	72
37	719.6702 080 715	768.5323 767 403	820.9468 571 749	877.1787 613 832	74
38	795.4864 043 989	851.3767 936 769	911.4615 119 533	976.0634 524 972	76
39	879.0737 608 497	942.9303 593 884	1011.7296 865 007	1085.8639 319 589	78
40	971.2288 213 368	1044.1086 367 478	1122.8023 835 317	1207.7851 834 104	80
41	1072.8297 755 239	1155.9234 386 057	1245.8438 578 722	1343.1652 075 085	82
42	1184.8448 275 151	1279.4929 462 195	1382.1438 200 820	1493.4897 055 480	84
43	1308.3414 223 354	1416.0528 913 986	1533.1309 550 947	1660.4083 839 968	86
44	1444.4964 181 247	1566.9689 141 895	1700.3878 975 746	1845.7530 588 733	88
45	1594.6073 009 825	1733.7502 196 826	1885.6678 209 627	2051.5577 586 489	90
46	1760.1045 493 332	1918.0646 705 114	2090.9128 140 953	2280.0810 462 907	92
47	1942.5652 656 399	2121.7554 659 750	2318.2742 380 191	2533.8308 054 148	94
48	2143.7282 053 680	2346.8595 745 785	2570.1352 763 797	2815.5917 625 581	96
49	2365.5103 464 182	2595.6281 043 242	2849.1359 157 551	3128.4560 476 097	98
50	2610.0251 569 261	2870.5488 144 602	3158.2006 177 771	3475.8571 277 777	100
51	2879.6027 355 110	3174.3709 938 128	3500.5689 730 965	3861.6074 874 971	102
52	3176.8120 159 009	3510.1329 544 920	3879.8296 585 037	4289.9404 677 849	104
53	3504.4852 475 307	3881.1924 159 158	4299.9580 531 428	4765.5567 242 044	106
54	3865.7449 854 026	4291.2600 830 021	4765.3579 081 068	5293.6758 132 799	108
55	4264.0338 464 064	4744.4367 543 215	5280.9075 061 923	5880.0934 734 868	110
56	4703.1473 156 630	5245.2543 313 020	5852.0107 956 564	6531.2452 294 374	112
57	5187.2699 155 185	5798.7211 385 900	6484.6540 339 558	7254.2770 172 726	114
58	5721.0150 818 591	6410.3720 087 861	7185.4685 352 023	8057.1236 063 246	116
59	6309.4691 277 497	7086.3236 324 160	7961.8001 790 487	8948.5956 776 734	118
60	6958.2397 133 440	7833.3357 266 544	8821.7864 095 923	9938.4765 152 233	120

TABLE 2. FUTURE WORTH OF ONE DOLLAR PER PERIOD WITH INTEREST
Payable at end of each period

SEMI ANNUAL Compounding

YEARS	11% Nominal Annual Rate	11¼% Nominal Annual Rate	11½% Nominal Annual Rate	11¾% Nominal Annual Rate	HALF YEARS
HALF YEARS 1	1.0000 000 000	1.0000 000 000	1.0000 000 000	1.0000 000 000	1
1	2.0550 000 000	2.0562 500 000	2.0575 000 000	2.0587 500 000	2
2	4.3422 663 750	4.3503 342 285	4.3584 151 094	4.3665 090 293	4
3	6.8880 510 320	6.9097 615 586	6.9315 428 569	6.9533 951 191	6
4	9.7215 729 999	9.7652 226 514	9.8090 876 990	9.8531 691 234	8
5	12.8753 537 882	12.9509 579 745	13.0270 640 806	13.1036 753 244	10
6	16.3855 906 502	16.5051 683 871	16.6257 471 805	16.7473 353 294	12
7	20.2925 720 334	20.4704 732 150	20.6501 769 829	20.8317 017 052	14
8	24.6411 399 875	24.8944 213 083	25.1507 219 836	25.4100 785 760	16
9	29.4812 048 346	29.8300 612 104	30.1837 095 862	30.5422 172 830	18
10	34.8683 180 110	35.3365 772 746	35.8121 310 785	36.2950 961 856	20
11	40.8643 096 542	41.4799 993 571	42.1064 300 109	42.7437 947 804	22
12	47.5379 982 528	48.3339 945 952	49.1453 838 463	49.9724 735 462	24
13	54.9659 805 054	55.9807 507 669	57.0170 899 140	58.0754 723 036	26
14	63.2335 104 520	64.5119 618 224	65.8200 680 076	67.1585 414 217	28
15	72.4354 779 708	74.0299 274 066	75.6644 934 284	77.3402 219 419	30
16	82.6774 978 685	84.6487 795 571	86.6735 759 040	88.7533 926 298	32
17	94.0771 220 651	96.4958 512 863	98.9851 016 433	101.5470 041 456	34
18	106.7651 887 865	109.7132 034 605	112.7531 578 246	115.8880 229 642	36
19	120.8873 242 490	124.4593 282 826	128.1500 611 025	131.9636 104 167	38
20	136.6056 140 723	140.9110 498 078	145.3685 142 688	149.9835 652 898	40
21	154.1004 636 028	159.2656 442 797	164.6240 180 600	170.1830 618 609	42
22	173.5726 685 015	179.7432 057 138	186.1575 682 966	192.8257 191 040	44
23	195.2457 193 589	202.5892 850 934	210.2386 721 109	218.2070 411 198	46
24	219.3683 667 895	228.0778 348 263	237.1687 210 134	246.6582 736 918	48
25	246.2174 764 458	256.5144 937 685	267.2847 630 138	278.5507 272 983	50
26	276.1012 067 211	288.2402 522 079	300.9637 210 081	314.3006 230 006	52
27	309.3625 456 108	323.6355 407 543	338.6271 102 266	354.3745 244 472	54
28	346.3832 473 284	363.1247 921 673	380.7463 137 858	399.2954 268 893	56
29	387.5882 138 577	407.1815 308 239	427.8484 823 711	449.6495 826 707	58
30	433.4503 717 290	456.3340 508 539	480.5231 318 886	506.0941 522 722	60
31	484.4960 999 937	511.1717 510 328	539.4295 216 606	569.3657 807 616	62
32	541.3112 716 955	572.3522 023 925	605.3049 055 076	640.2902 115 788	64
33	604.5479 781 788	640.6090 333 020	678.9737 589 848	719.7930 631 227	66
34	674.9320 134 125	716.7607 265 679	761.3580 982 587	808.9119 087 840	68
35	753.2712 042 284	801.7204 340 432	853.4890 197 708	908.8098 180 763	70
36	840.4646 820 864	896.5069 264 339	956.5196 051 161	1020.7905 355 880	72
37	937.5132 027 792	1002.2568 096 046	1071.7393 526 489	1146.3154 958 526	74
38	1045.5306 325 233	1120.2381 538 718	1200.5903 164 382	1287.0228 961 939	76
39	1165.7567 322 642	1251.8656 997 161	1344.6851 545 623	1444.7490 764 618	78
40	1299.5713 869 284	1398.7178 222 497	1505.8273 126 292	1621.5524 846 803	80
41	1448.5104 429 360	1562.5554 578 622	1686.0335 951 340	1819.7405 413 781	82
42	1614.2833 357 488	1745.3432 200 001	1887.5594 071 483	2041.8997 532 024	84
43	1798.7927 097 718	1949.2729 572 822	2112.9269 822 602	2290.9294 688 206	86
44	2004.1562 557 938	2176.7900 364 428	2364.9569 500 552	2570.0797 176 518	88
45	2232.7310 166 049	2430.6226 652 673	2646.8036 382 277	2882.9936 252 513	90
46	2487.1404 397 566	2713.8146 071 367	2961.9945 511 528	3233.7549 589 030	92
47	2770.3044 879 601	3029.7616 794 700	3314.4745 190 201	3626.9414 239 244	94
48	3085.4731 527 118	3382.2524 737 243	3708.6550 700 859	4067.6844 062 440	96
49	3436.2637 557 971	3775.5137 852 359	4149.4696 439 713	4561.7359 409 362	98
50	3826.7024 667 960	4214.2612 976 610	4642.4353 370 384	5115.5437 807 048	100
51	4261.2705 131 057	4703.7561 297 850	5193.7219 526 309	5736.3355 440 182	102
52	4744.9556 128 494	5249.8679 227 653	5810.2292 203 893	6432.2130 410 915	104
53	5283.3092 209 917	5859.1452 243 007	6499.6731 510 940	7212.2580 087 444	106
54	5882.5102 456 943	6538.8940 137 208	7270.6826 078 256	8086.6506 340 551	108
55	6549.4359 662 139	7297.2653 096 047	8132.9073 020 977	9066.8024 136 357	110
56	7291.7409 662 953	8143.3529 104 539	9097.1385 666 065	10165.5050 824 437	112
57	8117.9449 890 108	9087.3024 404 482	10175.4444 161 520	11397.0975 557 670	114
58	9037.5307 213 937	10140.4330 078 766	11381.3205 871 104	12777.6530 631 019	116
59	10061.0526 311 793	11315.3729 350 767	12729.8594 458 193	14325.1889 161 670	118
60	11200.2581 048 183	12626.2111 874 502	14237.9388 798 812	16059.9016 486 851	120

SEMI ANNUAL
Compounding

TABLE 2. FUTURE WORTH OF ONE DOLLAR PER PERIOD WITH INTEREST
Payable at end of each period

HALF YEARS / YEARS	12% Nominal Annual Rate	12¼% Nominal Annual Rate	12½% Nominal Annual Rate	12¾% Nominal Annual Rate	HALF YEARS
1	1.0000 000 000	1.0000 000 000	1.0000 000 000	1.0000 000 000	1
YEARS					
1	2.0600 000 000	2.0612 500 000	2.0625 000 000	2.0637 500 000	2
2	4.3746 160 000	4.3827 360 332	4.3908 691 406	4.3990 153 340	4
3	6.9753 185 376	6.9973 133 054	7.0193 796 158	7.0415 176 623	6
4	9.8974 679 088	9.9419 850 435	9.9867 215 194	10.0316 783 321	8
5	13.1807 949 424	13.2584 261 896	13.3365 723 402	13.4152 366 872	10
6	16.8699 411 973	16.9935 732 124	17.1182 398 685	17.2439 497 252	12
7	21.0150 659 292	21.2002 883 829	21.3873 879 765	21.5763 838 046	14
8	25.6725 280 781	25.9381 079 167	26.2068 559 579	26.4788 105 120	16
9	30.9056 525 485	31.2740 845 694	31.6475 834 837	32.0262 203 931	18
10	36.7855 912 035	37.2837 366 121	37.7896 547 921	38.3034 700 545	20
11	43.3922 902 763	44.0521 166 152	44.7234 774 802	45.4065 801 827	22
12	50.8155 773 545	51.6750 151 693	52.5511 132 491	53.4442 043 358	24
13	59.1563 827 155	60.2603 165 766	61.3877 801 914	62.5392 909 753	26
14	68.5281 116 191	69.9295 257 012	71.3635 487 317	72.8309 641 619	28
15	79.0581 862 152	80.8194 875 858	82.6252 561 854	84.4766 516 828	30
16	90.8897 780 314	93.0843 241 740	95.3386 681 155	97.6544 931 646	32
17	104.1837 545 961	106.8976 155 452	109.6909 183 023	112.5660 650 067	34
18	119.1208 666 642	122.4548 565 353	125.8932 632 397	129.4394 638 187	36
19	135.9042 057 839	139.9762 235 086	144.1841 917 042	148.5327 955 265	38
20	154.7619 656 188	159.7096 904 395	164.8329 351 660	170.1381 235 204	40
21	175.9505 445 692	181.9345 384 038	188.1434 307 148	194.5859 362 369	42
22	199.7580 318 780	206.9653 081 500	214.4587 948 303	222.2502 025 136	44
23	226.5081 246 181	235.1562 516 873	244.1663 738 514	253.5540 920 477	46
24	256.5645 288 209	266.9063 458 944	277.7034 454 807	288.9764 484 610	48
25	290.3359 045 832	302.6649 391 048	315.5636 552 497	329.0591 139 873	50
26	328.2814 223 897	342.9381 105 807	358.3042 826 843	374.4152 178 262	52
27	370.9170 061 970	388.2958 328 823	406.5544 441 240	425.7385 549 452	54
28	418.8223 481 630	439.3800 384 960	461.0243 529 369	483.8141 987 966	56
29	472.6487 903 959	496.9137 048 874	522.5157 734 327	549.5305 102 855	58
30	533.1281 808 889	561.7110 865 571	591.9338 223 517	623.8927 266 864	60
31	601.0828 240 467	634.6892 389 085	670.3002 916 392	708.0383 383 734	62
32	677.4366 610 989	716.8809 970 226	758.7686 886 084	803.2544 885 756	64
33	763.2278 324 107	809.4495 930 233	858.6412 148 743	910.9976 623 140	66
34	859.6227 924 967	913.7051 189 075	971.3879 339 792	1032.9159 656 960	68
35	967.9321 696 493	1031.1230 678 338	1098.6684 098 437	1170.8743 363 641	70
36	1089.6285 858 180	1163.3652 162 776	1242.3561 345 501	1326.9830 707 331	72
37	1226.3666 790 251	1312.3031 425 908	1404.5661 050 194	1503.6301 043 875	74
38	1380.0056 005 526	1480.0447 148 165	1587.6859 544 946	1703.5175 394 180	76
39	1552.6342 927 808	1668.9639 226 320	1794.4110 970 661	1929.7029 774 438	78
40	1746.5998 913 686	1881.7344 756 204	2027.7844 025 473	2185.6462 905 747	80
41	1964.5396 379 417	2121.3676 433 776	2291.2409 856 882	2475.2625 457 508	82
42	2209.4167 371 913	2391.2548 729 910	2588.6587 689 996	2802.9818 920 238	84
43	2484.5606 459 082	2695.2157 870 418	2924.4155 634 409	3173.8173 268 524	86
44	2793.7123 417 424	3037.5522 414 305	3303.4535 071 657	3593.4413 780 060	88
45	3141.0751 871 818	3423.1092 080 865	3731.3518 108 238	4068.2728 740 521	90
46	3531.3720 803 174	3857.3433 442 156	4214.4088 801 878	4605.5751 307 209	92
47	3969.9096 694 447	4346.4002 185 217	4759.7350 248 995	5213.5670 550 676	94
48	4462.6505 045 880	4897.2012 873 605	5375.3571 179 530	5901.5488 669 484	96
49	5016.2941 069 551	5517.5418 517 667	6070.3367 464 391	6680.0443 609 264	98
50	5638.3680 585 748	6216.2013 817 114	6854.9035 926 597	7560.9618 847 301	100
51	6337.3303 506 146	7003.0677 689 671	7740.6060 089 010	8557.7764 966 928	102
52	7122.6843 819 506	7889.2772 670 926	8740.4810 022 359	9685.7360 885 648	104
53	8005.1081 715 597	8887.3720 990 588	9869.2461 314 304	10962.0946 266 792	106
54	8996.5995 415 644	10011.4779 630 839	11143.5161 405 601	12406.3760 792 746	108
55	10110.6392 449 018	11277.5039 488 575	12582.0475 180 542	14040.6730 671 667	110
56	11362.3742 555 716	12703.3676 935 007	14206.0145 809 284	15889.9848 061 175	112
57	12768.8237 135 603	14309.2489 638 172	16039.3211 480 012	17982.5995 102 736	114
58	14349.1103 245 564	16117.8752 537 006	18108.9523 897 357	20350.5271 061 557	116
59	16124.7203 606 715	18154.8434 386 604	20445.3720 337 251	23029.9888 762 579	118
60	18119.7957 972 505	20448.9820 397 342	23082.9707 724 474	26061.9715 221 483	120

TABLE 2. FUTURE WORTH OF ONE DOLLAR PER PERIOD WITH INTEREST
Payable at end of each period

SEMI ANNUAL Compounding

HALF YEARS	13% Nominal Annual Rate	13¼% Nominal Annual Rate	13½% Nominal Annual Rate	13¾% Nominal Annual Rate	HALF YEARS
1	1.0000 000 000	1.0000 000 000	1.0000 000 000	1.0000 000 000	1
YEARS					
1	2.0650 000 000	2.0662 500 000	2.0675 000 000	2.0687 500 000	2
2	4.4071 746 250	4.4153 470 254	4.4235 325 469	4.4317 312 012	4
3	7.0637 276 390	7.0860 097 403	7.1083 641 609	7.1307 910 958	6
4	10.0768 564 814	10.1222 569 705	10.1678 808 068	10.2137 290 013	8
5	13.4944 225 426	13.5741 332 376	13.6543 721 226	13.7351 425 675	10
6	17.3707 114 084	17.4985 336 108	17.6274 250 922	17.7573 946 803	12
7	21.7672 951 472	21.9601 414 719	22.1549 424 352	22.3517 178 846	14
8	26.7540 103 383	27.0324 946 503	27.3143 031 204	27.5994 758 853	16
9	32.4100 673 760	32.7991 975 000	33.1936 848 353	33.5936 044 673	18
10	38.8253 086 695	39.3552 988 965	39.8935 710 146	40.4402 573 527	20
11	46.1016 357 257	46.8088 588 669	47.5284 681 845	48.2606 861 425	22
12	54.3546 277 809	55.2827 296 739	56.2288 629 725	57.1933 876 365	24
13	63.7153 776 948	64.9165 807 114	66.1434 522 307	67.3965 565 578	26
14	74.3325 742 659	75.8692 005 857	77.4416 843 861	79.0508 871 213	28
15	86.3748 640 468	88.3211 143 265	90.3166 554 527	92.3627 730 591	30
16	100.0335 301 735	102.4775 588 656	104.9884 092 003	107.5679 627 743	32
17	115.5255 307 610	118.5718 658 260	121.7076 978 817	124.9357 343 548	34
18	133.0969 451 274	136.8693 073 778	140.7602 677 942	144.7736 643 855	36
19	153.0268 825 871	157.6714 685 497	162.4717 429 166	167.4330 750 116	38
20	175.6319 159 024	181.3212 180 625	187.2131 900 890	193.3152 557 193	40
21	201.2711 098 144	208.2083 596 144	215.4074 608 483	222.8785 700 191	42
22	230.3517 245 292	238.7760 567 667	247.5364 183 063	256.6465 728 878	44
23	263.3356 847 541	273.5281 373 250	284.1491 725 836	295.2172 827 270	46
24	300.7469 170 403	313.0373 976 107	325.8714 655 500	339.2737 720 399	48
25	343.1796 719 800	357.9550 434 971	373.4163 652 641	389.5962 643 835	50
26	391.3079 634 515	409.0214 238 186	427.5964 528 890	447.0759 518 296	52
27	445.8962 748 458	467.0782 330 675	489.3377 103 675	512.7307 776 348	54
28	507.8117 023 369	533.0823 845 063	559.6953 462 100	587.7234 636 257	56
29	578.0377 280 831	608.1217 823 566	639.8718 298 695	673.3821 015 578	58
30	657.6898 421 351	693.4332 530 293	731.2374 429 267	771.2236 731 114	60
31	748.0332 611 957	790.4229 309 428	835.3536 983 212	882.9809 150 567	62
32	850.5030 256 796	900.6894 349 380	954.0000 278 825	1010.6330 053 583	64
33	966.7267 943 015	1026.0502 172 903	1089.2041 942 737	1156.4406 136 594	66
34	1098.5506 982 666	1168.5715 196 131	1243.2769 471 108	1322.9859 368 756	68
35	1248.0686 657 414	1330.6024 293 972	1418.8515 155 610	1513.2184 289 133	70
36	1417.6556 824 006	1514.8135 985 176	1618.9286 123 795	1730.5070 343 693	72
37	1610.0055 163 708	1724.2412 618 809	1846.9277 185 409	1978.6998 512 497	74
38	1828.1735 068 057	1962.3372 817 436	2106.7455 249 615	2262.1922 793 122	76
39	2075.6250 957 567	2233.0260 425 503	2402.8225 301 295	2586.0048 609 128	78
40	2356.2908 742 346	2540.7691 340 531	2740.2189 318 498	2955.8721 928 887	80
41	2674.6290 168 287	2890.6388 888 425	3124.7011 101 578	3378.3444 840 726	82
42	3035.6960 966 126	3288.4019 863 622	3562.8401 794 623	3860.9035 569 831	84
43	3445.2274 051 804	3740.6145 013 985	4062.1242 942 573	4412.0953 480 368	86
44	3909.7280 536 407	4254.7299 636 688	4631.0866 277 978	5041.6812 528 103	88
45	4436.5763 016 407	4839.2222 095 861	5279.4512 109 984	5760.8109 966 182	90
46	5034.1407 557 284	5503.7250 510 855	6018.2991 240 633	6582.2200 918 794	92
47	5711.9132 986 660	6259.1910 635 864	6860.2578 811 958	7520.4553 791 658	94
48	6480.6598 611 795	7118.0721 102 891	7819.7172 451 285	8592.1326 461 792	96
49	7352.5914 310 463	8094.5245 782 739	8913.0751 599 189	9816.2308 869 893	98
50	8341.5580 158 785	9204.6427 091 771	10159.0180 052 054	11214.4284 127 521	100
51	9463.2686 405 598	10466.7238 702 838	11578.8399 616 943	12811.4867 663 002	102
52	10735.5408 738 389	11901.5701 383 333	13196.8069 460 985	14635.6892 395 853	104
53	12178.5838 476 299	13532.8311 668 477	15040.5713 354 700	16719.3417 599 498	106
54	13815.3192 645 781	15387.3939 882 483	17141.6445 689 057	19099.3450 157 301	108
55	15671.7454 928 661	17495.8261 756 178	19535.9357 037 750	21817.8479 533 190	110
56	17777.3505 316 460	19892.8796 684 610	22264.3651 308 350	24922.9942 188 672	112
57	20165.5804 067 562	22618.0635 667 020	25373.5639 371 250	28469.7747 638 240	114
58	22874.3704 368 530	25716.2953 339 132	28916.6708 693 254	32521.0017 136 320	116
59	25946.7478 087 396	29238.6411 431 457	32954.2405 183 327	37148.4207 464 184	118
60	29431.5150 333 677	33243.1575 680 049	37555.2782 466 693	42433.9816 814 852	120

SEMI ANNUAL
Compounding

TABLE 2. FUTURE WORTH OF ONE DOLLAR PER PERIOD WITH INTEREST
Payable at end of each period

HALF YEARS	14% Nominal Annual Rate	14¼% Nominal Annual Rate	14½% Nominal Annual Rate	14¾% Nominal Annual Rate	HALF YEARS
1	1.0000 000 000	1.0000 000 000	1.0000 000 000	1.0000 000 000	1
YEARS					
1	2.0700 000 000	2.0712 500 000	2.0725 000 000	2.0737 500 000	2
2	4.4399 430 000	4.4481 679 551	4.4564 060 781	4.4646 573 809	4
3	7.1532 907 407	7.1758 632 913	7.1985 089 439	7.2212 278 951	6
4	10.2598 025 690	10.3061 025 288	10.3526 299 034	10.3993 857 194	8
5	13.8164 479 613	13.8982 917 128	13.9806 772 503	14.0636 080 220	10
6	17.8884 512 709	18.0206 038 284	18.1538 613 864	18.2882 330 482	12
7	22.5504 878 600	22.7512 725 956	22.9540 925 214	23.1589 682 654	14
8	27.8880 535 509	28.1800 771 977	28.4755 883 858	28.7746 291 603	16
9	33.9990 325 105	34.4100 461 215	34.8267 235 132	35.2491 439 679	18
10	40.9954 923 212	41.5594 124 436	42.1321 563 880	42.7138 650 003	20
11	49.0057 391 586	49.7638 576 716	50.5352 762 113	51.3202 334 692	22
12	58.1766 707 627	59.1790 867 235	60.2010 173 076	61.2428 518 632	24
13	68.6764 703 562	69.9837 829 140	71.3190 964 144	72.6830 262 120	26
14	80.6976 909 108	82.3829 990 272	84.1077 363 950	85.8728 501 006	28
15	94.4607 863 237	96.6120 488 321	98.8179 494 617	101.0799 132 891	30
16	110.2181 542 621	112.9409 728 948	115.7384 639 805	118.6127 304 652	32
17	128.2587 648 146	131.6796 634 400	135.2013 915 589	138.8270 002 631	34
18	148.9134 598 363	153.1837 455 216	157.5887 456 494	162.1328 215 330	36
19	172.5610 201 665	177.8613 261 166	183.3399 396 129	189.0030 132 587	38
20	199.6351 119 887	206.1807 392 266	212.9604 114 143	219.9827 069 162	40
21	230.6322 397 158	238.6794 339 753	247.0315 442 319	255.7004 058 782	42
22	266.1208 512 507	275.9741 743 809	286.2220 776 999	296.8807 362 341	44
23	306.7517 625 969	318.7727 443 748	331.3012 337 623	344.3591 477 080	46
24	353.2700 929 972	367.8873 802 083	383.1538 147 678	399.0988 629 218	48
25	406.5289 294 724	424.2501 851 665	442.7975 701 480	462.2104 188 618	50
26	467.5049 713 530	488.9308 191 334	511.4031 725 475	534.9741 970 003	52
27	537.3164 417 021	563.1567 987 214	590.3171 954 926	618.8663 991 512	54
28	617.2435 941 047	648.3367 932 252	681.0885 435 978	715.5889 960 501	56
29	708.7521 908 905	746.0873 585 117	785.4988 540 768	827.1042 562 414	58
30	813.5203 833 505	858.2636 162 055	905.5974 662 697	955.6745 557 807	60
31	933.4694 868 980	986.9944 604 040	1043.7416 455 609	1103.9082 763 969	62
32	1070.7992 155 495	1134.7229 600 769	1202.6428 511 917	1274.8127 232 750	64
33	1228.0280 218 826	1304.2527 239 149	1385.4199 561 010	1471.8551 360 358	66
34	1408.0392 822 534	1498.8011 075 416	1595.6604 633 799	1699.0330 306 769	68
35	1614.1341 742 519	1722.0602 728 637	1837.4909 208 807	1960.9552 995 451	70
36	1850.0922 161 010	1978.2672 583 508	2115.6579 160 612	2262.9357 146 620	72
37	2120.2405 782 140	2272.2843 900 445	2435.6212 408 114	2611.1007 313 601	74
38	2429.5334 379 972	2609.6915 593 496	2803.6610 548 761	3012.5137 793 074	76
39	2783.6428 331 631	2996.8921 188 637	3227.0011 512 528	3475.3185 624 830	78
40	3189.0626 796 884	3441.2344 059 490	3713.9507 429 858	4008.9042 753 180	80
41	3653.2278 619 752	3951.1512 003 357	4274.0675 543 115	4624.0960 868 374	82
42	4184.6505 791 754	4536.3197 623 989	4918.3454 172 690	5333.3747 572 682	84
43	4793.0764 480 980	5207.8454 893 346	5659.4300 558 726	6151.1298 426 060	86
44	5489.6632 254 273	5978.4726 746 817	6511.8672 932 053	7093.9516 240 499	88
45	6287.1854 267 918	6862.8263 710 114	7492.3885 531 799	8180.9676 848 525	90
46	7200.2685 951 339	7877.6899 458 797	8620.2392 607 237	9434.2309 629 166	92
47	8245.6575 145 688	9042.3235 985 334	9917.5565 861 428	10879.1671 517 936	94
48	9442.5232 884 298	10378.8298 822 176	11409.8039 479 394	12545.0905 267 697	96
49	10812.8149 129 233	11912.5731 690 075	13126.2708 023 920	14465.7986 609 115	98
50	12381.6617 938 059	13672.6610 178 194	15100.6475 296 439	16680.2580 964 250	100
51	14177.8345 877 284	15692.4965 810 569	17371.6867 000 199	19233.3948 819 503	102
52	16234.2728 194 902	18010.4125 335 323	19983.9636 997 398	22177.0060 138 881	104
53	18588.6889 510 343	20670.3985 544 379	22988.7516 453 988	25570.8102 727 090	106
54	21284.2599 800 392	23722.9361 686 068	26445.0277 598 178	29483.6597 731 824	108
55	24370.4192 511 469	27225.9567 907 768	30420.6309 621 539	33994.9368 079 619	110
56	27903.7630 006 381	31245.9411 547 331	34993.5933 931 610	39196.1643 231 184	112
57	31949.0882 594 305	35859.1809 924 259	40253.6720 104 422	45192.8626 982 920	114
58	36580.5811 482 220	41153.2269 073 535	46304.1103 154 612	52106.6905 010 600	116
59	41883.1773 565 994	47228.5499 201 232	53263.6647 910 487	60077.9126 462 698	118
60	47954.1197 555 706	54200.4482 191 947	61268.9358 238 087	69268.2460 333 472	120

TABLE 2. FUTURE WORTH OF ONE DOLLAR PER PERIOD WITH INTEREST
Payable at end of each period

SEMI ANNUAL Compounding

HALF YEARS	15% Nominal Annual Rate	15¼% Nominal Annual Rate	15½% Nominal Annual Rate	15¾% Nominal Annual Rate	HALF YEARS
1	1.0000 000 000	1.0000 000 000	1.0000 000 000	1.0000 000 000	1
YEARS					
1	2.0750 000 000	2.0762 500 000	2.0775 000 000	2.0787 500 000	2
2	4.4729 218 750	4.4811 995 723	4.4894 904 844	4.4977 946 230	4
3	7.2440 203 418	7.2668 864 814	7.2898 265 117	7.3128 406 306	6
4	10.4463 710 075	10.4935 868 020	10.5410 341 415	10.5887 140 682	8
5	14.1470 874 955	14.2311 191 588	14.3157 065 197	14.4008 531 060	10
6	18.4237 279 870	18.5603 554 468	18.6981 247 425	18.8370 452 608	12
7	23.3659 206 550	23.5749 707 190	23.7861 396 894	23.9994 490 029	14
8	29.0772 420 569	29.3834 701 069	29.6933 568 427	30.0069 463 038	16
9	35.6773 878 520	36.1115 366 299	36.5516 728 779	36.9978 802 996	18
10	43.3046 813 365	43.9047 506 968	44.5142 206 592	45.1332 411 138	20
11	52.1189 723 695	52.9317 401 427	53.7587 883 992	54.6003 732 048	22
12	62.3049 874 445	63.3878 289 599	64.4917 893 239	65.6172 896 116	24
13	74.0762 011 156	75.4992 636 756	76.9528 704 787	78.4376 924 480	26
14	87.6793 099 142	89.5281 088 238	91.4202 635 813	93.3568 152 606	28
15	103.3994 025 196	105.7779 174 397	108.2169 973 945	110.7182 217 888	30
16	121.5659 345 367	124.6002 992 723	127.7181 103 312	130.9217 176 928	32
17	142.5596 330 990	146.4025 288 389	150.3590 243 328	154.4325 574 443	34
18	166.8204 760 000	171.6563 579 396	176.6452 669 942	181.7921 583 989	36
19	194.8569 125 775	200.9082 233 190	207.1637 590 132	213.6305 687 790	38
20	227.2565 195 974	234.7910 703 423	242.5959 189 879	250.6809 766 859	40
21	264.6983 154 597	274.0380 485 269	283.7328 781 694	293.7965 942 584	42
22	307.9669 908 031	319.4983 752 688	331.4931 448 852	343.9703 057 957	44
23	357.9693 537 469	372.1557 110 197	386.9431 130 438	402.3575 323 080	46
24	415.7533 344 237	433.1494 435 138	451.3208 726 383	470.3028 390 305	48
25	482.5299 470 934	503.7993 415 861	526.0638 538 886	549.3708 986 280	50
26	559.6986 701 098	585.6341 120 374	612.8409 222 637	641.3825 231 254	52
27	648.8767 756 457	680.4244 774 527	713.5896 410 039	748.4565 943 212	54
28	751.9332 238 555	790.2214 907 026	830.5595 331 408	873.0588 582 750	56
29	871.0278 318 180	917.4009 151 706	966.3623 089 736	1018.0587 075 291	58
30	1008.6565 381 447	1064.7146 309 924	1124.0301 804 828	1186.7952 586 683	60
31	1167.7037 118 935	1235.3501 796 280	1307.0835 647 291	1383.1542 468 799	62
32	1351.5026 020 569	1432.9997 351 750	1519.6096 879 228	1611.6575 082 727	64
33	1563.9051 945 020	1661.9399 948 120	1766.3538 452 389	1877.5671 105 918	66
34	1809.3629 403 964	1927.1247 170 220	2052.8253 540 339	2187.0065 302 943	68
35	2093.0200 479 956	2234.2919 099 179	2385.4205 661 918	2547.1016 665 012	70
36	2420.8212 929 649	2590.0879 889 878	2771.5656 862 272	2966.1449 391 537	72
37	2799.6366 066 826	3002.2115 907 570	3219.8825 839 953	3453.7862 502 947	74
38	3237.4050 535 975	3479.5801 541 743	3740.3813 042 847	4021.2552 060 089	76
39	3743.3012 150 636	4032.5228 741 760	4344.6835 716 577	4681.6197 164 439	78
40	4327.9274 666 579	4673.0042 025 110	5046.2822 809 670	5450.0869 290 565	80
41	5003.5361 786 566	5414.8827 318 901	5860.8427 674 669	6344.3534 251 039	82
42	5784.2864 964 600	6274.2110 651 367	6806.5525 832 964	7385.0127 438 457	84
43	6686.5410 824 716	7269.5831 578 409	7904.5275 901 607	8596.0296 190 956	86
44	7729.2090 384 312	8422.5366 502 403	9179.2834 354 740	10005.2918 490 378	88
45	8934.1421 950 371	9758.0188 938 950	10659.2829 391 068	11645.2525 079 938	90
46	10326.5930 741 397	11304.9267 569 392	12377.5716 128 214	13553.6772 892 595	92
47	11935.7441 213 027	13096.7318 880 952	14372.5155 023 082	15774.5141 891 320	94
48	13795.3193 001 804	15172.2049 687 729	16688.6578 264 017	18358.9055 595 713	96
49	15944.2908 662 710	17576.2546 244 620	19377.7135 405 638	21366.3658 354 631	98
50	18427.6961 323 344	20360.8991 475 950	22499.7240 313 043	24866.1520 576 750	100
51	21297.5813 429 290	23586.3920 578 036	26124.3977 236 194	28938.8587 528 790	102
52	24614.0924 394 223	27322.5258 541 922	30332.6665 346 079	33678.2738 976 921	104
53	28446.7355 753 074	31650.1421 699 306	35218.4929 258 457	39193.5387 070 473	106
54	32875.8337 992 146	36662.8810 055 549	40890.9679 024 876	45611.6609 832 951	108
55	37994.2104 342 174	42469.2068 904 984	47476.7468 033 375	53080.4399 044 808	110
56	43909.1344 330 425	49194.7558 144 862	55122.8772 683 423	61771.8696 050 317	112
57	50744.5684 791 847	56985.0537 111 730	64000.0825 265 284	71886.0999 279 217	114
58	58643.7669 487 579	66008.6653 159 695	74306.5733 138 152	83656.0455 581 536	116
59	67772.2781 801 583	76460.8415 323 434	86272.4735 334 227	97352.7496 785 945	118
60	78321.4139 719 454	88567.7442 274 975	100164.9584 752 633	113291.6256 646 518	120

TABLE 2. FUTURE WORTH OF ONE DOLLAR PER PERIOD WITH INTEREST
Payable at end of each period

HALF YEARS	16% Nominal Annual Rate	16¼% Nominal Annual Rate	16½% Nominal Annual Rate	16¾% Nominal Annual Rate	HALF YEARS
1	1.0000 000 000	1.0000 000 000	1.0000 000 000	1.0000 000 000	1
YEARS					
1	2.0800 000 000	2.0812 500 000	2.0825 000 000	2.0837 500 000	2
2	4.5061 120 000	4.5144 426 270	4.5227 865 156	4.5311 436 777	4
3	7.3359 290 368	7.3590 919 290	7.3823 295 064	7.4056 419 687	6
4	10.6366 276 285	10.6847 758 728	10.7331 598 552	10.7817 806 341	8
5	14.4865 624 659	14.5728 381 678	14.6596 838 006	14.7471 029 735	10
6	18.9771 264 602	19.1183 778 720	19.2608 091 005	19.4044 298 235	12
7	24.2149 203 032	24.4325 754 427	24.6524 364 840	24.8745 257 025	14
8	30.3242 830 417	30.6454 121 259	30.9703 791 497	31.2992 302 357	16
9	37.4502 437 398	37.9088 491 999	38.3737 838 525	38.8451 360 572	18
10	45.7619 642 981	46.4005 448 322	47.0491 397 545	47.7079 085 589	20
11	55.4567 551 573	56.3281 994 641	57.2149 760 215	58.1173 594 949	22
12	66.7647 592 155	67.9346 360 063	69.1273 664 956	70.3434 060 021	24
13	79.9544 151 490	81.5037 391 028	83.0863 801 056	84.7030 695 536	26
14	95.3388 298 297	97.3673 987 347	99.4436 394 976	101.5686 963 277	28
15	113.2832 111 134	115.9136 279 973	118.6111 782 860	121.3776 121 466	30
16	134.2135 374 427	137.5960 536 067	141.0718 200 354	144.6434 623 389	32
17	158.6266 700 732	162.9450 112 655	167.3913 404 164	171.9695 305 657	34
18	187.1021 479 733	192.5805 172 720	198.2327 188 958	204.0643 819 710	36
19	220.3159 453 961	227.2274 336 498	234.3728 389 566	241.7602 362 803	38
20	259.0565 187 100	267.7331 977 228	276.7220 575 195	286.0345 472 645	40
21	304.2435 234 233	315.0885 497 909	326.3471 365 143	338.0353 481 230	42
22	356.9496 457 210	370.4517 658 864	384.4981 142 370	399.1110 199 925	44
23	418.4260 667 690	435.1769 883 287	452.6397 933 761	470.8452 554 800	46
24	490.1321 642 793	510.8473 470 191	532.4886 388 769	555.0981 238 226	48
25	573.7701 564 154	599.3136 815 990	626.0560 150 899	654.0543 024 970	50
26	671.3255 104 429	702.7398 115 850	735.6988 513 325	770.2797 259 214	52
27	785.1140 753 806	823.6554 617 550	864.1790 121 092	906.7881 201 533	54
28	917.8370 575 239	965.0181 372 994	1014.7328 675 084	1067.1191 488 280	56
29	1072.6451 438 959	1130.2854 621 576	1191.1528 162 267	1255.4301 966 616	58
30	1253.2132 958 402	1323.4997 498 795	1397.8828 147 596	1476.6041 704 661	60
31	1463.8279 882 680	1549.3868 755 524	1640.1303 191 029	1736.3761 129 586	62
32	1709.4889 655 158	1813.4718 671 253	1923.9974 587 393	2041.4819 124 590	64
33	1996.0279 293 777	2122.2140 434 060	2256.6347 471 348	2399.8329 645 225	66
34	2330.2469 768 261	2483.1650 041 054	2646.4212 006 597	2820.7213 144 827	68
35	2720.0800 737 700	2905.1533 362 450	3103.1754 030 656	3315.0606 002 534	70
36	3174.7813 980 453	3398.5005 547 061	3638.4028 321 585	3895.6690 430 374	72
37	3705.1450 226 800	3975.2735 586 640	4265.5856 787 410	4577.6018 238 933	74
38	4323.7611 544 540	4649.5797 787 990	5000.5224 582 592	5378.5414 646 883	76
39	5045.3150 105 551	5437.9122 343 624	5861.7259 698 535	6319.2563 360 158	78
40	5886.9354 283 115	6359.5529 399 309	6870.8896 272 616	7424.1391 811 928	80
41	6868.6014 835 825	7437.0445 288 747	8053.4339 082 854	8721.8396 202 681	82
42	8013.6167 704 506	8696.7416 290 895	9439.1466 876 907	10246.0070 348 746	84
43	9349.1626 010 536	10169.4554 772 273	11062.9335 833 028	12036.1630 969 341	86
44	10906.9432 578 690	11891.2075 382 006	12965.6972 162 491	14138.7265 658 927	88
45	12723.9386 159 783	13904.1105 629 221	15195.3675 336 083	16608.2169 274 833	90
46	14843.2820 016 771	16257.3986 342 850	17808.1091 469 293	19508.6680 843 797	92
47	17315.2841 267 562	19008.6313 955 279	20869.7360 990 539	22915.2887 557 488	94
48	20198.6274 054 485	22225.1019 154 983	24457.3696 967 220	26916.4126 398 751	96
49	23561.7590 057 151	25985.4826 261 308	28661.3811 691 794	31615.7889 075 861	98
50	27484.5157 042 661	30381.7495 905 261	33587.6680 876 767	37135.2724 189 914	100
51	32060.0191 174 559	35521.4321 677 678	39360.3218 880 652	43617.9834 208 738	102
52	37396.8862 986 006	41530.2430 995 751	46124.7536 904 466	51232.0186 557 081	104
53	43621.8081 786 877	48555.1533 487 181	54051.3571 541 758	60174.8101 113 915	106
54	50882.5570 596 214	56767.9868 974 134	63339.8006 342 455	70678.2444 340 965	108
55	59351.4945 543 424	66369.6234 317 455	74224.0567 569 628	83014.6757 506 587	110
56	69229.6632 481 849	77594.9117 065 903	86978.2961 081 637	97503.9878 130 264	112
57	80751.5592 126 829	90718.4137 682 243	101923.7934 938 969	114521.8885 862 281	114
58	94190.6986 656 734	106061.1205 339 525	119437.0207 398 578	134509.6523 585 832	116
59	109866.1109 236 414	123998.3029 867 447	139959.1298 843 450	157985.5619 871 422	118
60	128149.9117 813 353	144968.6910 191 516	164007.0656 430 372	185558.3479 758 640	120

TABLE 2. FUTURE WORTH OF ONE DOLLAR PER PERIOD WITH INTEREST
Payable at end of each period

HALF YEARS	17% Nominal Annual Rate	17¼% Nominal Annual Rate	17½% Nominal Annual Rate	17¾% Nominal Annual Rate	HALF YEARS
1	1.0000 000 000	1.0000 000 000	1.0000 000 000	1.0000 000 000	1
YEARS					
1	2.0850 000 000	2.0862 500 000	2.0875 000 000	2.0887 500 000	2
2	4.5395 141 250	4.5478 978 691	4.5562 949 219	4.5647 052 949	4
3	7.4290 295 158	7.4524 923 481	7.4760 306 662	7.4996 446 713	6
4	10.8306 392 717	10.8797 368 345	10.9290 743 926	10.9786 530 205	8
5	14.8350 993 167	14.9236 764 807	15.0128 381 371	15.1025 879 783	10
6	19.5492 497 931	19.6952 788 357	19.8425 268 531	19.9910 038 225	12
7	25.0988 655 877	25.3254 788 451	25.5543 883 986	25.7856 173 921	14
8	31.6320 120 414	31.9687 717 658	32.3095 571 545	32.6544 165 062	16
9	39.3229 953 755	39.8074 525 866	40.2985 997 035	40.7965 299 885	18
10	48.3770 132 309	49.0566 182 856	49.7468 908 056	50.4480 004 797	20
11	59.0356 294 007	59.9700 701 893	60.9209 713 293	61.8886 273 937	22
12	71.5832 188 213	72.8472 783 972	74.1360 674 987	75.4500 783 977	24
13	86.3545 547 769	88.0415 993 777	89.7649 835 777	91.5255 045 715	26
14	103.7437 407 472	105.9699 722 307	108.2486 188 593	110.5809 379 900	28
15	124.2147 252 011	127.1243 596 870	130.1084 056 479	133.1688 021 526	30
16	148.3136 798 749	152.0852 477 900	155.9610 191 170	159.9439 269 279	32
17	176.6835 717 907	181.5375 746 975	186.5357 740 151	191.6825 322 946	34
18	210.0813 178 013	216.2895 256 970	222.6951 989 875	229.3047 312 226	36
19	249.3979 793 487	257.2947 101 795	265.4593 689 276	273.9012 040 617	38
20	295.6825 362 387	305.6783 291 154	316.0346 817 833	326.7648 177 352	40
21	350.1698 737 236	362.7680 510 830	375.8478 916 277	389.4281 063 929	42
22	414.3137 295 943	430.1304 440 999	446.5863 580 829	463.7077 000 969	44
23	489.8254 803 217	509.6139 629 639	530.2456 475 514	551.7569 895 457	46
24	578.7198 010 717	603.3996 716 966	629.1858 291 120	656.1285 536 030	48
25	683.3684 178 166	714.0610 929 345	746.1980 532 108	779.8481 594 280	50
26	806.5633 856 641	844.6348 265 648	884.5832 913 675	926.5024 804 948	52
27	951.5915 816 884	998.7038 754 117	1048.2454 581 814	1100.3430 754 766	54
28	1122.3223 997 532	1180.4959 644 684	1241.8015 426 523	1306.4096 423 791	56
29	1323.3109 870 494	1394.9995 515 999	1470.7118 556 774	1550.6761 211 002	58
30	1559.9197 767 293	1648.1007 131 027	1741.4340 680 660	1840.2238 799 806	60
31	1838.4615 591 601	1946.7446 603 240	2061.6053 845 612	2183.4470 070 818	62
32	2166.3679 089 823	2299.1263 194 296	2440.2579 930 849	2590.2956 576 556	64
33	2552.3874 616 517	2714.9152 039 168	2888.0738 671 343	3072.5645 125 305	66
34	3006.8193 295 429	3205.5207 504 766	3417.6861 094 281	3644.2347 099 228	68
35	3541.7878 852 211	3784.4053 991 417	4044.0353 378 533	4321.8791 633 915	70
36	4171.5662 431 794	4467.4540 087 832	4784.7911 675 331	5125.1430 162 414	72
37	4912.9570 706 269	5273.4097 448 855	5660.8506 792 278	6077.3131 609 131	74
38	5785.7408 874 688	6224.3884 005 585	6696.9279 361 055	7205.9933 339 192	76
39	6813.2038 162 504	7346.4852 639 909	7922.2511 794 348	8543.9043 575 591	78
40	8022.7588 625 854	8670.4911 850 635	9371.3873 714 284	10129.8327 276 922	80
41	9446.6773 020 071	10232.7374 903 183	11085.2173 459 909	12009.7550 474 517	82
42	11122.9496 868 553	12076.0929 311 348	13112.0890 768 445	14238.1709 046 154	84
43	13096.2994 451 082	14251.1400 218 261	15509.1815 972 869	16879.6828 332 005	86
44	15419.3761 142 675	16817.5630 469 097	18344.1180 484 163	20010.8691 629 094	88
45	18154.1600 461 186	19845.7858 251 052	21696.8733 606 974	23722.5040 509 668	90
46	21373.6160 602 919	23418.9041 710 505	25662.0303 854 873	28122.1890 558 274	92
47	25163.6401 665 772	27634.9660 823 666	30351.4481 230 864	33337.4725 429 718	94
48	29625.3512 950 988	32609.6622 214 470	35897.4173 193 189	39519.5473 554 260	96
49	34877.7891 783 727	38479.5005 200 158	42456.3924 515 508	46847.6339 457 309	98
50	41061.0903 655 098	45405.5520 190 557	50213.4053 852 793	55534.1760 378 488	100
51	48340.2271 055 373	53577.8707 316 596	59387.2852 126 843	65830.9994 430 151	102
52	56909.4088 543 161	63220.7088 118 606	70236.8315 273 136	78036.6125 757 006	104
53	66997.2638 385 223	74598.6701 360 523	83068.1152 859 745	92504.8603 141 282	106
54	78872.9389 223 044	88023.9711 540 803	98243.1132 186 783	109655.1820 837 040	108
55	92853.2805 228 098	103865.0082 510 725	116189.9193 675 275	129984.7715 486 926	110
56	109311.2881 634 648	122556.4667 123 253	137414.8218 270 024	154082.9904 257 371	112
57	128686.0662 082 349	144611.2486 858 536	162516.5853 763 408	182648.4542 805 806	114
58	151494.5392 919 893	170634.5474 513 404	192203.3429 239 881	216509.2856 310 531	116
59	178345.2440 180 121	201340.4541 998 464	227312.5722 799 478	256647.1215 006 683	118
60	209954.5648 891 043	237571.5530 218 909	268834.7218 104 570	304225.5714 099 821	120

SEMI ANNUAL
Compounding

TABLE 2. FUTURE WORTH OF ONE DOLLAR PER PERIOD WITH INTEREST
Payable at end of each period

HALF YEARS	18% Nominal Annual Rate	18¼% Nominal Annual Rate	18½% Nominal Annual Rate	18¾% Nominal Annual Rate	HALF YEARS
1	1.0000 000 000	1.0000 000 000	1.0000 000 000	1.0000 000 000	1
YEARS					
1	2.0900 000 000	2.0912 500 000	2.0925 000 000	2.0937 500 000	2
2	4.5731 290 000	4.5815 660 488	4.5900 164 531	4.5984 802 246	4
3	7.5233 345 649	7.5471 005 488	7.5709 428 252	7.5948 615 968	6
4	11.0284 737 966	11.0785 378 034	11.1288 461 274	11.1793 998 595	8
5	15.1929 297 177	15.2838 670 899	15.3754 038 507	15.4675 437 772	10
6	20.1407 197 976	20.2916 849 084	20.4439 093 623	20.5974 034 444	12
7	26.0191 891 915	26.2551 273 868	26.4934 557 938	26.7341 984 565	14
8	33.0033 986 784	33.3565 530 940	33.7139 297 468	34.0755 792 082	16
9	41.3013 379 699	41.8131 194 578	42.3319 715 613	42.8579 927 051	18
10	51.1601 196 420	51.8834 233 113	52.6180 892 318	53.3642 979 138	20
11	62.8733 381 466	63.8754 086 325	64.8951 492 657	65.9328 759 223	22
12	76.7898 130 520	78.1557 832 901	79.5485 110 008	80.9685 283 250	24
13	93.3239 768 871	95.1612 327 549	97.0381 224 832	98.9555 148 419	26
14	112.9682 169 396	115.4117 736 848	117.9129 575 780	120.4731 500 794	28
15	136.3075 385 459	139.5266 557 291	142.8282 474 733	146.2144 617 649	30
16	164.0369 865 464	168.2432 978 190	172.5660 474 483	177.0085 113 887	32
17	196.9823 437 158	202.4398 380 054	208.0597 844 697	213.8470 961 437	34
18	236.1247 225 687	243.1619 864 051	250.4235 561 274	257.9166 921 641	36
19	282.6297 828 839	291.6550 024 014	300.9871 005 631	310.6366 678 721	38
20	337.8824 450 443	349.4017 739 456	361.3375 350 465	373.7049 981 868	40
21	403.5281 329 572	418.1681 633 991	433.3691 733 143	449.1529 519 324	42
22	481.5217 747 664	500.0570 065 674	519.3429 853 666	539.4105 137 864	44
23	574.1860 206 000	597.5724 161 847	621.9575 660 780	647.3846 478 401	46
24	684.2804 110 748	713.6963 562 101	744.4338 402 272	776.5529 234 415	48
25	815.0835 563 980	851.9798 285 344	890.6161 627 146	931.0755 187 655	50
26	970.4907 733 565	1016.6514 605 330	1065.0929 873 591	1115.9292 094 607	52
27	1155.1300 878 248	1212.7468 140 071	1273.3408 918 936	1337.0676 578 021	54
28	1374.5000 573 447	1446.2623 697 069	1521.8964 799 002	1601.6131 648 512	56
29	1635.1335 181 312	1724.3388 961 912	1818.5615 554 378	1918.0860 614 675	58
30	1944.7921 328 917	2055.4798 103 364	2172.6480 105 026	2296.6791 262 672	60
31	2312.6975 330 886	2449.8112 068 311	2595.2701 119 854	2749.5858 688 255	62
32	2749.8059 390 625	2919.3915 082 046	3099.6933 625 984	3291.3932 512 806	64
33	3269.1344 362 002	3478.5802 043 070	3701.7508 860 128	3939.5514 968 932	66
34	3886.1486 236 495	4144.4769 570 754	4420.3404 059 436	4714.9361 168 889	68
35	4619.2231 797 579	4937.4444 981 546	5278.0174 186 416	5642.5202 570 204	70
36	5490.1890 598 704	5881.7313 092 720	6301.7031 776 285	6752.1790 184 082	72
37	6524.9836 220 320	7006.2131 265 690	7523.5297 133 034	8079.6516 577 637	74
38	7754.4230 413 362	8345.2759 436 545	8981.8484 113 739	9667.6926 569 927	76
39	9215.1200 154 116	9939.8675 150 961	10722.4338 079 479	11567.4487 351 720	78
40	10950.5740 903 105	11838.7495 147 073	12799.9203 866 875	13840.1061 529 157	80
41	13012.4670 766 979	14099.9886 388 974	15279.5174 770 333	16558.8613 645 720	82
42	15462.2021 338 247	16792.7322 521 472	18239.0560 816 974	19811.2784 878 913	84
43	18372.7323 551 972	19999.3228 728 074	21771.4318 804 104	23702.1095 192 059	86
44	21830.7333 112 098	23817.8161 589 529	25987.5210 923 131	28356.6681 260 031	88
45	25939.1842 470 483	28364.9793 928 228	31019.6607 217 371	33924.8656 780 799	90
46	30820.4348 039 181	33779.8621 557 385	37025.8024 273 088	40586.0395 074 686	92
47	36619.8485 905 351	40228.0483 826 419	44194.4703 983 796	48554.7289 029 776	94
48	43510.1321 104 148	47906.7198 215 851	52750.6788 594 260	58087.5848 692 848	96
49	51696.4779 603 838	57050.6857 357 888	62962.9949 444 107	69491.6361 961 659	98
50	61422.6754 647 320	67939.5632 330 172	75151.9686 346 198	83134.1780 667 023	100
51	72978.3707 196 481	80906.3277 925 253	89700.1943 636 545	99454.6016 911 234	102
52	86707.6922 520 139	96347.4954 596 711	107064.3201 089 546	118978.5459 683 849	104
53	103019.4991 646 177	114735.2480 737 245	127789.3809 180 434	142334.8269 641 323	106
54	122399.5569 574 822	136631.8723 112 180	152525.9067 783 615	170275.6904 600 216	108
55	145425.0036 211 846	162706.9540 823 067	182050.3418 222 307	203701.0398 569 594	110
56	172781.5368 023 295	193757.8540 746 787	217289.4157 965 598	243687.4197 507 571	112
57	205283.8338 748 476	230734.0905 751 262	259349.2327 828 327	291522.6886 666 772	114
58	243899.8130 267 065	274766.3751 811 412	309549.9902 206 549	348747.4976 725 386	116
59	289779.4578 570 300	327201.1892 975 437	369467.4180 153 015	417204.9107 899 021	118
60	344289.0638 799 373	389641.9587 471 057	440982.2384 435 257	499099.7653 492 482	120

TABLE 2. FUTURE WORTH OF ONE DOLLAR PER PERIOD WITH INTEREST
Payable at end of each period

HALF YEARS	19% Nominal Annual Rate	19¼% Nominal Annual Rate	19½% Nominal Annual Rate	19¾% Nominal Annual Rate	HALF YEARS
1	1.0000 000 000	1.0000 000 000	1.0000 000 000	1.0000 000 000	1
YEARS					
1	2.0950 000 000	2.0962 500 000	2.0975 000 000	2.0987 500 000	2
2	4.6069 573 750	4.6154 479 160	4.6239 518 594	4.6324 692 168	4
3	7.6188 570 666	7.6429 294 378	7.6670 789 143	7.6913 057 002	6
4	11.2302 000 942	11.2812 479 306	11.3325 444 715	11.3840 908 242	8
5	15.5602 906 680	15.6536 483 431	15.7476 206 444	15.8422 114 352	10
6	20.7521 775 182	20.9082 420 258	21.0656 074 888	21.2242 845 086	12
7	26.9773 796 487	27.2230 238 766	27.4711 558 803	27.7218 006 360	14
8	34.4415 526 333	34.8119 017 675	35.1866 789 525	35.5659 371 331	16
9	43.3912 826 462	43.9319 424 915	44.4800 747 150	45.0357 831 757	18
10	54.1222 326 748	54.8920 796 821	55.6740 279 947	56.4682 696 073	20
11	66.9889 100 329	68.0635 786 778	69.1572 146 823	70.2701 567 151	22
12	82.4163 778 522	83.8926 128 201	85.3977 973 175	86.9325 064 914	24
13	100.9142 974 543	102.9153 771 965	104.9596 806 051	107.0481 542 937	26
14	123.0937 655 051	125.7762 517 933	128.5220 912 869	131.3328 015 339	28
15	149.6875 021 848	153.2496 293 212	156.9031 622 181	160.6504 798 593	30
16	181.5740 573 071	186.2661 471 097	191.0883 395 365	196.0442 928 265	32
17	219.8068 340 627	225.9442 116 567	232.2645 992 738	238.7735 288 340	34
18	265.6488 892 120	273.6278 836 989	281.8616 614 791	290.3584 657 684	36
19	320.6146 593 874	330.9324 071 273	341.6016 328 869	352.6344 614 840	38
20	386.5199 919 720	399.7989 240 022	413.5588 018 225	427.8172 546 179	40
21	465.5421 333 742	482.5602 290 921	500.2316 615 377	518.5817 991 020	42
22	560.2916 564 690	582.0197 913 146	604.6296 627 700	628.1574 372 499	44
23	673.8987 033 977	701.5467 188 656	730.3777 077 419	760.4427 976 160	46
24	810.1163 928 415	845.1898 848 975	881.8420 138 358	920.1445 056 137	48
25	973.4448 079 267	1017.8150 796 584	1064.2817 171 778	1112.9446 421 280	50
26	1169.2796 608 244	1225.2698 350 040	1284.0314 801 014	1345.7029 081 850	52
27	1404.0905 453 199	1474.5815 045 731	1548.7214 429 789	1626.7006 885 672	54
28	1685.6346 661 022	1774.1953 094 231	1867.5421 575 770	1965.9356 979 925	56
29	2023.2131 055 232	2134.2604 127 208	2251.5637 009 400	2375.4776 931 760	58
30	2427.9780 938 500	2566.9737 140 242	2714.1200 500 554	2869.8979 067 706	60
31	2913.3014 339 785	3086.9930 088 965	3271.2720 635 420	3466.7874 821 643	62
32	3495.2162 518 760	3711.9335 092 805	3942.3651 459 868	4187.3833 546 983	64
33	4192.9466 664 057	4462.9645 438 429	4750.7009 581 233	5057.3238 477 460	66
34	5029.5428 766 871	5365.5266 510 021	5724.3464 959 404	6107.5608 672 599	68
35	6032.6426 477 197	6450.1933 555 602	6897.1086 315 259	7375.4611 500 634	70
36	7235.3843 506 821	7753.7068 208 886	8309.7079 536 019	8906.1357 475 720	72
37	8677.5017 210 766	9320.2224 585 050	10011.1926 657 881	10754.0450 470 934	74
38	10406.6365 011 139	11202.8046 551 367	12060.6416 358 960	12984.9364 362 989	76
39	12479.9123 307 481	13465.2242 837 510	14529.2157 294 469	15678.1835 516 851	78
40	14965.8218 823 753	16184.1188 877 143	17502.6286 537 171	18929.6103 399 336	80
41	17946.4895 825 150	19451.5887 124 825	21084.1231 048 314	22854.9004 104 010	82
42	21520.3846 716 750	23378.3165 231 922	25398.0555 555 388	27593.7129 812 385	84
43	25805.5742 309 552	28097.3168 893 223	30594.2141 544 937	33314.6518 617 767	86
44	30943.6236 422 710	33768.4419 402 618	36853.0196 629 262	40221.2642 642 735	88
45	37104.2733 376 740	40583.7962 204 244	44391.7900 153 674	48559.2828 787 696	90
46	44491.0463 387 046	48774.2440 675 294	53472.2860 221 977	58625.3688 792 740	92
47	53347.9718 362 652	58617.2299 459 606	64409.8002 155 247	70777.6669 316 425	94
48	63967.6469 309 779	70446.1766 423 543	77584.1044 208 509	85448.5477 433 299	96
49	76700.9028 614 158	84661.7796 793 083	93452.6361 755 675	103159.9915 264 909	98
50	91968.3950 534 091	101745.5805 358 855	112566.3818 524 472	124542.1597 078 429	100
51	110274.4998 789 138	122276.2784 562 267	135589.0079 811 592	150355.8156 544 179	102
52	132223.9772 173 147	146949.3333 949 362	163319.9050 446 062	181519.3921 297 580	104
53	158541.9492 829 907	176600.5241 323 655	196721.9438 756 347	219141.6685 227 005	106
54	190097.8557 390 380	212234.2595 709 408	236954.9084 103 512	264561.2204 828 873	108
55	227934.1764 775 000	255057.6022 336 533	285415.7656 484 456	319394.0455 548 727	110
56	273300.8709 509 344	306521.1564 818 243	343787.1710 720 880	385591.0592 993 162	112
57	327696.6717 919 441	368368.2065 057 953	414095.8937 261 492	465507.5075 751 296	114
58	392918.5968 953 358	442693.7685 962 435	498783.1895 924 825	561986.7646 255 558	116
59	471121.3156 424 300	532015.5580 416 566	600789.5667 590 801	678461.4984 485 220	118
60	564888.3304 881 646	639359.2745 953 457	723656.8855 961 042	819075.8028 480 695	120

TABLE 2. FUTURE WORTH OF ONE DOLLAR PER PERIOD WITH INTEREST
Payable at end of each period

HALF YEARS	20% Nominal Annual Rate	20¼% Nominal Annual Rate	20½% Nominal Annual Rate	20¾% Nominal Annual Rate	HALF YEARS
1	1.0000 000 000	1.0000 000 000	1.0000 000 000	1.0000 000 000	1
YEARS					
1	2.1000 000 000	2.1012 500 000	2.1025 000 000	2.1037 500 000	2
2	4.6410 000 000	4.6495 442 207	4.6581 018 906	4.6666 730 215	4
3	7.7156 100 000	7.7399 920 186	7.7644 519 612	7.7889 900 335	6
4	11.4358 881 000	11.4879 374 143	11.5402 398 867	11.5927 966 410	8
5	15.9374 246 010	16.0332 640 490	16.1297 337 087	16.2268 375 316	10
6	21.3842 837 672	21.5456 160 275	21.7082 921 338	21.8723 230 128	12
7	27.9749 833 583	28.2307 295 023	28.4890 647 655	28.7500 150 899	14
8	35.9497 298 636	36.3381 113 145	36.7311 362 791	37.1288 601 803	16
9	45.5991 731 349	46.1703 512 749	46.7494 257 168	47.3365 060 393	18
10	57.2749 994 933	58.0944 156 498	58.9267 191 427	59.7721 141 519	20
11	71.4027 493 868	72.5553 433 518	73.7282 954 099	74.9219 686 109	22
12	88.4973 267 581	90.0928 560 177	91.7197 038 726	93.3784 918 505	24
13	109.1817 653 773	111.3615 019 055	113.5883 733 053	115.8634 108 319	26
14	134.2099 361 065	137.1550 854 382	140.1698 776 799	143.2559 795 751	28
15	164.4940 226 889	168.4362 941 701	172.4798 623 817	176.6273 616 546	30
16	201.1377 674 535	206.3726 289 364	211.7528 507 241	217.2825 171 580	32
17	245.4766 986 188	252.3799 781 999	259.4894 135 104	266.8112 320 632	34
18	299.1268 053 287	308.1754 629 057	317.5135 039 308	327.1502 854 939	36
19	364.0434 344 477	375.8415 241 630	388.0421 484 873	400.6591 858 539	38
20	442.5925 556 818	457.9036 456 810	473.7701 567 497	490.2124 374 363	40
21	537.6369 923 749	557.4246 117 741	577.9730 865 927	599.3119 455 191	42
22	652.6407 607 737	678.1188 189 050	704.6323 990 852	732.2239 554 529	44
23	791.7953 205 361	824.4909 071 877	858.5875 850 406	894.1458 806 299	46
24	960.1723 378 487	1002.0038 859 590	1045.7210 757 893	1091.4095 430 038	48
25	1163.9085 287 970	1217.2830 283 278	1273.1830 033 786	1331.7287 737 111	50
26	1410.4293 198 443	1478.3631 446 093	1549.6643 980 004	1624.5010 560 094	52
27	1708.7194 770 116	1794.9884 635 673	1885.7292 611 720	1981.1750 060 295	54
28	2069.6505 671 841	2178.9763 138 608	2294.2182 027 625	2415.6980 613 690	56
29	2506.3771 862 927	2644.6581 792 851	2790.7390 643 215	2945.0618 840 168	58
30	3034.8163 954 142	3209.4145 892 065	3394.2632 748 020	3589.9668 051 362	60
31	3674.2278 384 512	3894.3238 077 704	4127.8507 246 673	4375.6312 942 653	62
32	4447.9156 845 259	4724.9485 327 545	5019.5308 549 001	5332.7781 065 538	64
33	5384.0779 782 763	5732.2899 658 301	6103.3736 261 989	6498.8356 705 013	66
34	6516.8343 537 144	6953.9448 627 636	7420.7912 887 299	7919.4016 954 648	68
35	7887.4695 679 944	8435.5087 478 554	9022.1206 913 968	9650.0262 320 864	70
36	9545.9381 772 732	10232.2776 644 440	10968.5465 886 471	11758.3839 107 331	72
37	11552.6851 945 006	12411.3119 754 883	13334.4394 319 167	14326.9203 015 244	74
38	13980.8490 853 457	15053.9392 409 485	16210.1969 697 412	17456.0758 796 488	76
39	16918.9273 932 683	18258.7895 862 403	19705.6982 304 515	21268.2136 664 492	78
40	20474.0021 458 547	22145.4768 500 717	23954.5018 597 278	25912.4041 334 064	80
41	24775.6425 964 841	26859.0629 022 320	29118.9492 261 357	31570.2544 787 055	82
42	29980.6275 417 458	32575.4717 519 676	35396.3672 778 006	38463.0102 253 866	84
43	36278.6593 255 124	39508.0555 163 733	43026.6081 534 621	46860.2068 431 585	86
44	43899.2777 838 700	47915.5573 088 185	52301.2136 268 342	57090.2097 083 366	88
45	53120.2261 184 827	58111.7682 443 279	63574.5545 460 021	69553.0545 582 551	90
46	64277.5736 033 641	70477.2389 879 466	77277.3708 916 315	84736.0905 554 240	92
47	77777.9640 600 706	85473.4829 533 181	93933.2298 023 461	103233.0376 704 187	94
48	94113.4365 126 854	103660.2012 539 537	114178.5304 074 380	125767.2036 065 799	96
49	113879.3581 803 493	125716.1722 897 968	138786.8198 260 559	153219.7681 450 167	98
50	137796.1233 982 227	152464.5856 259 703	168698.3494 161 949	186664.2409 456 561	100
51	166735.4093 118 494	184903.7656 938 105	205056.0005 800 688	227408.4402 479 338	102
52	201751.9452 673 378	224244.4320 073 025	249248.9528 050 772	277045.6340 132 363	104
53	244121.9537 734 787	271954.8865 487 812	302965.7624 405 264	337516.8433 408 535	106
54	295389.6640 659 093	329815.8148 415 446	368258.8802 824 751	411186.7444 806 042	108
55	357423.5935 197 502	399986.7460 362 939	447623.0731 013 502	500936.1375 270 904	110
56	432484.6481 588 977	485086.6524 848 061	544090.7454 988 980	610274.5977 068 118	112
57	523308.5242 722 663	588291.6969 988 431	661347.8042 210 699	743477.7143 928 537	114
58	633205.4143 694 422	713453.7759 911 235	803874.4919 544 869	905754.2844 644 527	116
59	766180.6513 870 250	865244.2828 547 600	977116.5716 862 535	1103449.9979 684 448	118
60	927080.6881 783 003	1049328.4572 263 021	1187693.4023 632 142	1344295.5810 406 542	120

TABLE 2. FUTURE WORTH OF ONE DOLLAR PER PERIOD WITH INTEREST
Payable at end of each period

SEMI ANNUAL Compounding

HALF YEARS	21% Nominal Annual Rate	21¼% Nominal Annual Rate	21½% Nominal Annual Rate	21¾% Nominal Annual Rate	HALF YEARS
1	1.0000 000 000	1.0000 000 000	1.0000 000 000	1.0000 000 000	1
YEARS					
1	2.1050 000 000	2.1062 500 000	2.1075 000 000	2.1087 500 000	2
2	4.6752 576 250	4.6838 557 129	4.6924 672 969	4.7010 923 887	4
3	7.8136 064 416	7.8383 013 918	7.8630 750 909	7.8879 277 462	6
4	11.6456 088 053	11.6986 775 118	11.7520 038 970	11.8055 891 014	8
5	16.3245 794 915	16.4229 635 847	16.5219 938 298	16.6216 742 684	10
6	22.0377 196 736	22.2044 932 088	22.3726 547 945	22.5422 156 913	12
7	29.0136 066 645	29.2798 659 272	29.5488 195 672	29.8204 945 269	14
8	37.5313 390 775	37.9386 296 732	38.3507 893 203	38.7678 760 288	16
9	47.9317 032 971	48.5351 300 403	49.1469 003 333	49.7671 297 740	18
10	60.6308 080 183	61.5030 112 904	62.3889 377 719	63.2888 045 705	20
11	76.1367 323 606	77.3729 625 280	78.6310 415 550	79.9113 585 674	22
12	95.0698 536 306	96.7944 352 750	98.5528 954 633	100.3459 057 324	24
13	118.1876 680 293	120.5622 212 004	122.9881 698 861	125.4666 373 549	26
14	146.4150 973 555	149.6489 776 557	152.9594 084 498	156.3482 200 080	28
15	180.8814 942 485	185.2450 320 694	189.7208 184 304	194.3117 698 554	30
16	222.9658 265 147	228.8070 941 289	234.8107 556 010	240.9813 700 897	32
17	274.3518 483 201	282.1178 692 174	290.1160 998 496	298.3535 493 189	34
18	337.0954 655 951	347.3590 126 841	357.9512 154 962	368.8826 931 938	36
19	413.7069 908 783	427.2004 104 836	441.1548 005 619	455.5860 431 897	38
20	507.2515 785 371	524.9094 398 453	543.2086 778 467	562.1727 743 974	40
21	621.4718 586 833	644.4846 812 857	668.3834 988 671	693.2026 742 810	42
22	760.9376 762 488	790.8195 539 062	821.9174 579 323	854.2812 106 897	44
23	931.2289 261 417	969.9025 704 815	1010.2354 950 110	1052.2993 341 455	46
24	1139.1587 995 421	1189.0624 074 459	1241.2181 603 776	1295.7282 731 661	48
25	1393.0463 732 109	1457.2678 188 622	1524.5313 922 246	1594.9819 339 853	50
26	1703.0494 478 499	1785.4946 678 568	1872.0310 074 543	1962.8624 081 558	52
27	2081.5709 520 609	2187.1750 956 753	2298.2588 323 869	2415.1076 468 786	54
28	2543.7551 717 401	2678.7472 098 598	2821.0512 349 819	2971.0647 316 048	56
29	3108.0936 585 740	3280.3277 866 288	3462.2855 238 372	3654.5175 434 687	58
30	3797.1650 594 603	4016.5355 166 911	4248.7954 485 471	4494.7042 393 083	60
31	4638.5384 667 276	4917.4984 844 694	5213.4941 123 870	5527.5680 619 631	62
32	5665.8764 313 360	6020.0871 101 540	6396.7512 878 865	6797.2949 945 978	64
33	6920.2817 695 720	7369.4230 107 037	7848.0827 718 527	8358.2040 400 074	66
34	8451.9420 476 917	9020.7255 274 350	9628.2224 743 332	10277.0709 911 759	68
35	10322.1375 387 828	11041.5714 862 895	11811.6639 522 839	12635.9851 041 508	70
36	12605.6929 882 922	13514.6606 677 329	14489.7777 435 735	15535.8608 818 868	72
37	15393.9712 810 295	16541.2001 585 705	17774.6349 524 910	19100.7552 034 082	74
38	18798.5287 834 191	20245.0460 846 818	21803.6970 924 462	23483.1744 853 598	76
39	22955.5786 077 743	24777.7722 182 421	26745.5684 418 468	28870.5989 166 750	78
40	28031.4403 695 576	30324.8728 838 010	32807.0516 321 499	35493.5028 735 523	80
41	34229.1944 772 391	37113.3540 068 985	40241.8017 234 862	43635.2146 286 280	82
42	41796.8071 865 708	45421.0229 563 330	49360.9409 152 028	53644.0371 533 609	84
43	51037.0514 949 826	55587.8453 515 217	60546.0780 854 227	65948.1485 423 635	86
44	62319.6208 016 612	68029.9180 846 025	74265.2779 886 632	81073.9195 008 231	88
45	76095.9199 893 483	83256.3759 247 075	91092.6483 749 823	99668.4315 183 485	90
46	92917.1257 049 940	101890.3484 900 453	111732.3646 933 868	122527.1590 582 181	92
47	113456.2384 139 403	124694.4003 064 308	137048.1377 419 530	150628.0000 079 299	94
48	138535.0085 093 815	152601.7495 000 067	168099.3573 982 533	185173.1102 159 985	96
49	169156.8137 651 676	186754.4582 064 730	206185.4249 378 113	227640.3317 992 671	98
50	206546.8035 276 137	228550.1695 761 951	252900.1291 163 783	279846.4153 271 524	100
51	252200.9157 773 045	279699.3040 098 678	310198.3414 935 008	344024.7405 320 756	102
52	307945.7281 869 833	342295.0552 861 386	380477.8219 984 878	422920.8604 432 509	104
53	376011.5377 595 112	418899.0510 570 092	466679.5580 586 327	519909.9563 282 438	106
54	459121.5928 928 072	512646.1832 251 969	572410.8361 840 538	639141.2281 725 251	108
55	560601.0479 619 399	627372.8982 133 669	702096.1961 892 773	785715.3977 313 585	110
56	684509.9995 877 276	767774.1971 924 442	861162.5850 371 842	965902.9177 464 112	112
57	835805.9272 466 051	939595.7712 438 315	1056266.4584 435 148	1187412.2223 319 159	114
58	1020542.0373 162 860	1149869.1342 694 529	1295572.3337 692 583	1459719.4942 997 799	116
59	1246109.4461 141 181	1407199.3760 753 004	1589094.4508 117 698	1794474.0568 917 867	118
60	1521532.8914 414 911	1722117.3114 477 768	1949115.8379 834 938	2205996.7326 042 096	120

SEMI ANNUAL
Compounding

TABLE 2. FUTURE WORTH OF ONE DOLLAR PER PERIOD WITH INTEREST
Payable at end of each period

HALF YEARS	22% Nominal Annual Rate	22¼% Nominal Annual Rate	22½% Nominal Annual Rate	22¾% Nominal Annual Rate	HALF YEARS
1	1.0000 000 000	1.0000 000 000	1.0000 000 000	1.0000 000 000	1
YEARS					
1	2.1100 000 000	2.1112 500 000	2.1125 000 000	2.1137 500 000	2
2	4.7097 310 000	4.7183 831 426	4.7270 488 281	4.7357 280 684	4
3	7.9128 595 651	7.9378 707 557	7.9629 615 262	7.9881 320 854	6
4	11.8594 342 702	11.9135 405 523	11.9679 091 014	12.0225 410 751	8
5	16.7220 089 643	16.8230 020 045	16.9246 574 988	17.0269 795 801	10
6	22.7131 872 449	22.8855 808 862	23.0594 081 325	23.2346 805 875	12
7	30.0949 180 044	30.3721 174 556	30.6521 205 964	30.9349 554 055	14
8	39.1899 484 732	39.6170 659 994	40.0492 886 319	40.4866 770 816	16
9	50.3959 355 139	51.0334 362 776	51.6797 523 834	52.3350 057 629	18
10	64.2028 321 466	65.1312 443 631	66.0742 685 357	67.0321 354 844	20
11	81.2143 094 879	82.5402 971 504	83.8897 314 174	85.2630 292 977	22
12	102.1741 507 200	104.0383 284 129	105.9391 503 996	107.8773 421 279	24
13	127.9987 711 021	130.5857 433 587	133.2287 516 118	135.9290 191 341	26
14	159.8172 858 749	163.3685 238 703	167.0038 971 120	170.7254 150 613	28
15	199.0208 779 265	203.8512 111 777	208.8059 170 350	213.8882 238 036	30
16	247.3236 236 932	253.8423 329 206	260.5424 482 554	267.4290 578 147	32
17	306.8374 367 524	315.5751 974 939	324.5744 894 736	333.8431 997 609	34
18	380.1644 058 226	391.8076 650 916	403.8241 454 875	416.2258 957 334	36
19	470.5105 644 141	485.9453 526 294	501.9079 775 635	518.4166 098 918	38
20	581.8260 664 146	602.1937 766 179	623.3020 453 563	645.1779 635 586	40
21	718.9778 964 294	745.7462 308 288	773.5461 720 731	802.4176 982 622	42
22	887.9626 661 906	923.0157 920 232	959.4967 545 298	997.4640 073 658	44
23	1096.1688 010 135	1141.9218 183 868	1189.6396 550 985	1239.4070 681 744	46
24	1352.6995 797 287	1412.2437 397 333	1474.4774 543 805	1539.5226 917 021	48
25	1668.7711 521 837	1746.0579 447 340	1827.0087 368 982	1911.7978 343 924	50
26	2058.2029 366 056	2158.2772 827 189	2263.3212 820 266	2373.5824 633 832	52
27	2538.0218 381 917	2667.3172 818 058	2803.3262 304 582	2946.3981 556 456	54
28	3129.2067 068 360	3295.9188 460 532	3471.6667 299 156	3656.9411 159 407	56
29	3857.6055 834 927	4072.1641 848 931	4298.8425 261 971	4538.3263 594 752	58
30	4755.0658 394 213	5030.7313 605 764	5322.6018 203 136	5631.6310 446 664	60
31	5860.8266 207 510	6214.4434 994 095	6589.6639 091 725	6987.8088 833 919	62
32	7223.2344 794 273	7676.1818 764 013	8157.8512 225 868	8670.0648 502 439	64
33	8901.8572 021 024	9481.2483 386 553	10098.7280 522 047	10756.8008 646 507	66
34	10970.0882 587 104	11710.2826 066 475	12500.8663 908 614	13345.2697 300 465	68
35	13518.3557 435 571	14462.8647 812 004	15473.8879 190 646	16556.1076 227 485	70
36	16658.0761 116 367	17861.9639 949 110	19153.4665 948 298	20538.9563 682 113	72
37	20526.5255 771 475	22059.4319 475 345	23707.5201 402 573	25479.4375 321 124	74
38	25292.8421 636 035	27242.7867 440 740	29343.8729 735 903	31607.8033 553 608	76
39	31165.4208 297 759	33643.5900 974 427	36319.7402 849 702	39209.6677 118 081	78
40	38401.0250 043 668	41547.7921 396 891	44953.4660 620 701	48639.3172 073 718	80
41	47316.0129 078 804	51308.5059 869 238	55639.0507 308 840	60336.2227 873 523	82
42	58300.1695 037 994	63361.7827 501 431	68864.1313 811 456	74845.5213 791 345	84
43	71833.7488 456 313	78246.0917 263 686	85232.2351 046 960	92843.4221 218 573	86
44	88508.4719 527 023	96626.3760 301 177	105490.3209 787 964	115168.7212 461 284	88
45	109053.3982 929 245	119323.7583 289 041	130562.8675 739 135	142861.8943 618 714	90
46	134366.8020 367 122	147352.2237 597 779	161594.0615 707 763	177213.5880 592 137	92
47	165555.4467 894 331	181963.9188 032 053	200000.0127 659 562	219824.7707 844 323	94
48	203982.9759 892 606	224705.0898 007 313	247533.3782 998 654	272681.3463 361 186	96
49	251329.5347 163 679	277485.1601 193 809	306363.3452 364 428	338246.7073 604 127	98
50	309665.2297 240 369	342662.0319 229 832	379174.6215 027 912	419576.5423 218 622	100
51	381540.6395 429 859	423147.4233 303 187	469289.9526 443 139	520461.2465 547 223	102
52	470098.3319 809 129	522536.9468 028 763	580821.7554 524 391	645602.5744 939 211	104
53	579210.2648 336 828	645270.7398 971 812	718859.7882 716 828	800832.7660 028 259	106
54	713647.0773 015 806	796831.8244 160 628	889703.4223 281 249	993386.3592 298 272	108
55	879286.6739 432 774	983991.0554 755 111	1101149.1137 907 933	1232237.3578 933 351	110
56	1083371.2209 655 121	1215109.6033 663 460	1362846.1953 651 365	1528517.4667 526 855	112
57	1334823.7913 516 074	1500512.4813 157 717	1686737.2239 823 822	1896034.8872 235 762	114
58	1644638.5033 243 154	1852949.8061 655 657	2087602.9798 694 453	2351917.8517 249 060	116
59	2026361.2099 458 890	2288166.3983 727 750	2583736.9880 540 431	2917412.8888 206 564	118
60	2496681.7567 743 299	2825605.1677 005 780	3197780.3441 212 617	3618875.0224 841 117	120

TABLE 3. SINKING FUND FACTORS
Payable at end of each period

SEMI ANNUAL Compounding

HALF YEARS	5% Nominal Annual Rate	5¼% Nominal Annual Rate	5½% Nominal Annual Rate	5¾% Nominal Annual Rate	HALF YEARS
1	1.0000 000 000	1.0000 000 000	1.0000 000 000	1.0000 000 000	1
YEARS					
1	0.4938 271 605	0.4935 225 170	0.4932 182 491	0.4929 143 561	2
2	0.2408 178 777	0.2403 687 639	0.2399 205 884	0.2394 733 494	4
3	0.1565 499 711	0.1560 596 699	0.1555 708 264	0.1550 834 376	6
4	0.1144 673 458	0.1139 616 647	0.1134 579 478	0.1129 561 906	8
5	0.0892 587 632	0.0887 480 102	0.0882 397 205	0.0877 338 880	10
6	0.0724 871 270	0.0719 764 402	0.0714 687 098	0.0709 639 277	12
7	0.0605 365 249	0.0600 288 239	0.0595 245 664	0.0590 237 416	14
8	0.0515 989 886	0.0510 960 810	0.0505 970 977	0.0501 020 250	16
9	0.0446 700 805	0.0441 731 540	0.0436 806 259	0.0431 924 790	18
10	0.0391 471 287	0.0386 569 971	0.0381 717 306	0.0376 913 080	20
11	0.0346 466 061	0.0341 638 434	0.0336 864 049	0.0332 142 642	22
12	0.0309 128 204	0.0304 378 394	0.0299 686 330	0.0295 051 694	24
13	0.0277 687 467	0.0273 018 473	0.0268 411 636	0.0263 866 576	26
14	0.0250 879 327	0.0246 293 325	0.0241 773 795	0.0237 320 286	28
15	0.0227 776 407	0.0223 274 961	0.0218 844 200	0.0214 483 593	30
16	0.0207 683 123	0.0203 267 327	0.0198 926 322	0.0194 659 486	32
17	0.0190 067 508	0.0185 738 089	0.0181 487 453	0.0177 314 880	34
18	0.0174 515 767	0.0170 273 159	0.0166 113 206	0.0162 035 082	36
19	0.0160 701 180	0.0156 545 574	0.0152 476 374	0.0148 492 639	38
20	0.0148 362 332	0.0144 293 722	0.0140 315 144	0.0136 425 527	40
21	0.0137 287 567	0.0133 305 783	0.0129 417 522	0.0125 621 582	42
22	0.0127 303 683	0.0123 408 410	0.0119 610 021	0.0115 907 166	44
23	0.0118 267 568	0.0114 458 373	0.0110 749 283	0.0107 138 795	46
24	0.0110 059 938	0.0106 336 281	0.0102 715 811	0.0099 196 862	48
25	0.0102 580 569	0.0098 941 820	0.0095 409 195	0.0091 980 860	50
26	0.0095 744 635	0.0092 190 081	0.0088 744 446	0.0085 405 715	52
27	0.0089 479 856	0.0086 008 714	0.0082 649 139	0.0079 398 928	54
28	0.0083 724 260	0.0080 335 683	0.0077 061 174	0.0073 898 334	56
29	0.0078 424 404	0.0075 117 490	0.0071 926 996	0.0068 850 319	58
30	0.0073 533 959	0.0070 307 755	0.0067 200 173	0.0064 208 400	60
31	0.0069 012 558	0.0065 866 065	0.0062 840 249	0.0059 932 076	62
32	0.0064 824 869	0.0061 757 049	0.0058 811 810	0.0055 985 894	64
33	0.0060 939 830	0.0057 949 610	0.0055 083 724	0.0052 338 689	66
34	0.0057 330 027	0.0054 416 300	0.0051 628 513	0.0048 962 949	68
35	0.0053 971 168	0.0051 132 799	0.0048 421 829	0.0045 834 303	70
36	0.0050 841 652	0.0048 077 482	0.0045 442 024	0.0042 931 080	72
37	0.0047 922 211	0.0045 231 057	0.0042 669 784	0.0040 233 949	74
38	0.0045 195 594	0.0042 576 257	0.0040 087 826	0.0037 725 610	76
39	0.0042 646 321	0.0040 097 582	0.0037 680 634	0.0035 390 537	78
40	0.0040 260 451	0.0037 781 079	0.0035 434 245	0.0033 214 758	80
41	0.0038 025 404	0.0035 614 155	0.0033 336 055	0.0031 185 662	82
42	0.0035 929 793	0.0033 585 415	0.0031 374 664	0.0029 291 846	84
43	0.0033 963 292	0.0031 684 524	0.0029 539 731	0.0027 522 968	86
44	0.0032 116 510	0.0029 902 087	0.0027 821 858	0.0025 869 633	88
45	0.0030 380 893	0.0028 229 543	0.0026 212 487	0.0024 323 283	90
46	0.0028 748 628	0.0026 659 082	0.0024 703 805	0.0022 876 114	92
47	0.0027 212 571	0.0025 183 556	0.0023 288 670	0.0021 520 990	94
48	0.0025 766 173	0.0023 796 418	0.0021 960 540	0.0020 251 378	96
49	0.0024 403 421	0.0022 491 658	0.0020 713 411	0.0019 061 285	98
50	0.0023 118 787	0.0021 263 752	0.0019 541 767	0.0017 945 208	100
51	0.0021 907 176	0.0020 107 612	0.0018 440 529	0.0016 898 081	102
52	0.0020 763 891	0.0019 018 546	0.0017 405 017	0.0015 915 239	104
53	0.0019 684 591	0.0017 992 221	0.0016 430 908	0.0014 992 378	106
54	0.0018 665 260	0.0017 024 631	0.0015 514 211	0.0014 125 521	108
55	0.0017 702 178	0.0016 112 065	0.0014 651 228	0.0013 310 991	110
56	0.0016 791 895	0.0015 251 084	0.0013 838 535	0.0012 545 384	112
57	0.0015 931 206	0.0014 438 495	0.0013 072 956	0.0011 825 543	114
58	0.0015 117 132	0.0013 671 333	0.0012 351 542	0.0011 148 540	116
59	0.0014 346 901	0.0012 946 838	0.0011 671 552	0.0010 511 657	118
60	0.0013 617 930	0.0012 262 442	0.0011 030 433	0.0009 912 364	120

SEMI ANNUAL
Compounding

TABLE 3. SINKING FUND FACTORS
Payable at end of each period

HALF YEARS	6% Nominal Annual Rate	6¼% Nominal Annual Rate	6½% Nominal Annual Rate	6¾% Nominal Annual Rate	HALF YEARS
1	1.0000 000 000	1.0000 000 000	1.0000 000 000	1.0000 000 000	1
YEARS					
1	0.4926 108 374	0.4923 076 923	0.4920 049 200	0.4917 025 200	2
2	0.2390 270 452	0.2385 816 739	0.2381 372 337	0.2376 937 228	4
3	0.1545 975 005	0.1541 130 120	0.1536 299 692	0.1531 483 691	6
4	0.1124 563 888	0.1119 585 380	0.1114 626 337	0.1109 686 713	8
5	0.0872 305 066	0.0867 295 701	0.0862 310 724	0.0857 350 071	10
6	0.0704 620 855	0.0699 631 750	0.0694 671 878	0.0689 741 154	12
7	0.0585 263 390	0.0580 323 475	0.0575 417 561	0.0570 545 536	14
8	0.0496 108 493	0.0491 235 563	0.0486 401 319	0.0481 605 616	16
9	0.0427 086 959	0.0422 292 588	0.0417 541 496	0.0412 833 498	18
10	0.0372 157 076	0.0367 449 071	0.0362 788 839	0.0358 176 149	20
11	0.0327 473 948	0.0322 857 692	0.0318 293 596	0.0313 781 376	22
12	0.0290 474 159	0.0285 953 396	0.0281 489 063	0.0277 080 816	24
13	0.0259 382 903	0.0254 960 216	0.0250 598 109	0.0246 296 167	26
14	0.0232 932 334	0.0228 609 465	0.0224 351 193	0.0220 157 023	28
15	0.0210 192 593	0.0205 970 642	0.0201 817 169	0.0197 731 592	30
16	0.0190 466 183	0.0186 345 760	0.0182 297 552	0.0178 320 878	32
17	0.0173 219 633	0.0169 200 958	0.0165 258 084	0.0161 390 225	34
18	0.0158 037 942	0.0154 120 918	0.0150 283 128	0.0146 523 670	36
19	0.0144 593 401	0.0140 777 676	0.0137 044 456	0.0133 392 716	38
20	0.0132 623 779	0.0128 908 783	0.0125 279 400	0.0121 734 473	40
21	0.0121 916 731	0.0118 301 714	0.0114 775 251	0.0111 336 041	42
22	0.0112 298 469	0.0108 782 525	0.0105 357 906	0.0102 023 160	44
23	0.0103 625 378	0.0100 207 470	0.0096 883 484	0.0093 651 810	46
24	0.0095 777 738	0.0092 456 713	0.0089 232 032	0.0086 101 920	48
25	0.0088 654 944	0.0085 429 549	0.0082 302 745	0.0079 272 584	50
26	0.0082 171 837	0.0079 040 731	0.0076 010 288	0.0073 078 378	52
27	0.0076 255 841	0.0073 217 609	0.0070 281 935	0.0067 446 503	54
28	0.0070 844 726	0.0067 897 885	0.0065 055 322	0.0062 314 528	56
29	0.0065 884 819	0.0063 027 830	0.0060 276 664	0.0057 628 614	58
30	0.0061 329 587	0.0058 560 861	0.0055 899 328	0.0053 342 082	60
31	0.0057 138 485	0.0054 456 389	0.0051 882 685	0.0049 414 265	62
32	0.0053 276 021	0.0050 678 885	0.0048 191 174	0.0045 809 570	64
33	0.0049 710 995	0.0047 197 120	0.0044 793 534	0.0042 496 714	66
34	0.0046 415 871	0.0043 983 530	0.0041 662 182	0.0039 448 093	68
35	0.0043 366 251	0.0041 013 699	0.0038 772 684	0.0036 639 261	70
36	0.0040 540 446	0.0038 265 920	0.0036 103 320	0.0034 048 492	72
37	0.0037 919 109	0.0035 720 835	0.0033 634 724	0.0031 656 417	74
38	0.0035 484 929	0.0033 361 124	0.0031 349 575	0.0029 445 715	76
39	0.0033 222 371	0.0031 171 249	0.0029 232 334	0.0027 400 855	78
40	0.0031 117 457	0.0029 137 230	0.0027 269 026	0.0025 507 873	80
41	0.0029 157 577	0.0027 246 461	0.0025 447 051	0.0023 754 179	82
42	0.0027 331 325	0.0025 487 540	0.0023 755 020	0.0022 128 404	84
43	0.0025 628 365	0.0023 850 139	0.0022 182 617	0.0020 620 251	86
44	0.0024 039 306	0.0022 324 878	0.0020 720 479	0.0019 220 378	88
45	0.0022 555 599	0.0020 903 223	0.0019 360 091	0.0017 920 297	90
46	0.0021 169 449	0.0019 577 392	0.0018 093 692	0.0016 712 273	92
47	0.0019 873 733	0.0018 340 281	0.0016 914 200	0.0015 589 256	94
48	0.0018 661 932	0.0017 185 390	0.0015 815 142	0.0014 544 800	96
49	0.0017 528 070	0.0016 106 763	0.0014 790 588	0.0013 573 012	98
50	0.0016 466 659	0.0015 098 935	0.0013 835 102	0.0012 668 489	100
51	0.0015 472 653	0.0014 156 886	0.0012 943 693	0.0011 826 274	102
52	0.0014 541 408	0.0013 275 995	0.0012 111 771	0.0011 041 817	104
53	0.0013 668 639	0.0012 452 005	0.0011 335 112	0.0010 310 930	106
54	0.0012 850 394	0.0011 680 991	0.0010 609 823	0.0009 629 759	108
55	0.0012 083 018	0.0010 959 328	0.0009 932 313	0.0008 994 752	110
56	0.0011 363 131	0.0010 283 663	0.0009 299 266	0.0008 402 632	112
57	0.0010 687 603	0.0009 650 898	0.0008 707 615	0.0007 850 374	114
58	0.0010 053 531	0.0009 058 160	0.0008 154 526	0.0007 335 183	116
59	0.0009 458 222	0.0008 502 788	0.0007 637 372	0.0006 854 473	118
60	0.0008 899 176	0.0007 982 312	0.0007 153 719	0.0006 405 851	120

TABLE 3. SINKING FUND FACTORS
Payable at end of each period

SEMI ANNUAL Compounding

HALF YEARS	7% Nominal Annual Rate	7¼% Nominal Annual Rate	7½% Nominal Annual Rate	7¾% Nominal Annual Rate	HALF YEARS
1	1.0000 000 000	1.0000 000 000	1.0000 000 000	1.0000 000 000	1
YEARS					
1	0.4914 004 914	0.4910 988 336	0.4907 975 460	0.4904 966 278	2
2	0.2372 511 395	0.2368 094 819	0.2363 687 482	0.2359 289 366	4
3	0.1526 682 087	0.1521 894 848	0.1517 121 945	0.1512 363 348	6
4	0.1104 766 465	0.1099 865 548	0.1094 983 915	0.1090 121 521	8
5	0.0852 413 679	0.0847 501 484	0.0842 613 423	0.0837 749 431	10
6	0.0684 839 493	0.0679 966 807	0.0675 123 010	0.0670 308 013	12
7	0.0565 707 287	0.0560 902 699	0.0556 131 655	0.0551 394 039	14
8	0.0476 848 306	0.0472 129 241	0.0467 448 270	0.0462 805 238	16
9	0.0408 168 408	0.0403 546 036	0.0398 966 188	0.0394 428 670	18
10	0.0353 610 768	0.0349 092 457	0.0344 620 973	0.0340 196 072	20
11	0.0309 320 742	0.0304 911 400	0.0300 553 051	0.0296 245 391	22
12	0.0272 728 303	0.0268 431 163	0.0264 189 033	0.0260 001 542	24
13	0.0242 053 963	0.0237 871 068	0.0233 747 042	0.0229 681 439	26
14	0.0216 026 452	0.0211 958 966	0.0207 954 043	0.0204 011 151	28
15	0.0193 713 316	0.0189 761 737	0.0185 876 242	0.0182 056 204	30
16	0.0174 415 048	0.0170 579 356	0.0166 813 087	0.0163 115 513	32
17	0.0157 596 583	0.0153 876 343	0.0150 228 679	0.0146 652 753	34
18	0.0142 841 628	0.0139 236 070	0.0135 706 050	0.0132 250 610	36
19	0.0129 821 414	0.0126 329 490	0.0122 915 872	0.0119 579 472	38
20	0.0118 272 823	0.0114 893 256	0.0111 594 563	0.0108 375 521	40
21	0.0107 982 765	0.0104 714 084	0.0101 528 644	0.0098 425 078	42
22	0.0098 776 816	0.0095 617 383	0.0092 543 358	0.0089 553 222	44
23	0.0090 510 817	0.0087 458 858	0.0084 494 269	0.0081 615 374	46
24	0.0083 064 580	0.0080 118 199	0.0077 260 947	0.0074 490 989	48
25	0.0076 337 096	0.0073 494 295	0.0070 742 185	0.0068 078 758	50
26	0.0070 242 854	0.0067 501 552	0.0064 852 301	0.0062 292 922	52
27	0.0064 708 979	0.0062 067 022	0.0059 518 278	0.0057 060 396	54
28	0.0059 672 981	0.0057 128 152	0.0054 677 509	0.0052 318 520	56
29	0.0055 080 966	0.0052 631 002	0.0050 276 006	0.0048 013 267	58
30	0.0050 886 213	0.0048 528 811	0.0046 266 973	0.0044 097 810	60
31	0.0047 048 020	0.0044 780 845	0.0042 609 653	0.0040 531 374	62
32	0.0043 530 765	0.0041 351 462	0.0039 268 386	0.0037 278 288	64
33	0.0040 303 148	0.0038 209 345	0.0036 211 846	0.0034 307 225	66
34	0.0037 337 550	0.0035 326 869	0.0033 412 407	0.0031 590 564	68
35	0.0034 609 517	0.0032 679 578	0.0030 845 619	0.0029 103 869	70
36	0.0032 097 323	0.0030 245 750	0.0028 489 770	0.0026 825 446	72
37	0.0029 781 601	0.0028 006 028	0.0026 325 521	0.0024 735 983	74
38	0.0027 645 038	0.0025 943 115	0.0024 335 598	0.0022 818 234	76
39	0.0025 672 117	0.0024 041 510	0.0022 504 525	0.0021 056 759	78
40	0.0023 848 887	0.0022 287 288	0.0020 818 410	0.0019 437 705	80
41	0.0022 162 781	0.0020 667 910	0.0019 264 747	0.0017 948 609	82
42	0.0020 602 452	0.0019 172 057	0.0017 832 256	0.0016 578 238	84
43	0.0019 157 629	0.0017 789 493	0.0016 510 743	0.0015 316 447	86
44	0.0017 819 002	0.0016 510 945	0.0015 290 977	0.0014 154 056	88
45	0.0016 578 111	0.0015 327 990	0.0014 164 584	0.0013 082 747	90
46	0.0015 427 259	0.0014 232 973	0.0013 123 956	0.0012 094 965	92
47	0.0014 359 428	0.0013 218 920	0.0012 162 168	0.0011 183 846	94
48	0.0013 368 213	0.0012 279 470	0.0011 272 913	0.0010 343 139	96
49	0.0012 447 758	0.0011 408 812	0.0010 450 431	0.0009 567 145	98
50	0.0011 592 702	0.0010 601 634	0.0009 689 464	0.0008 850 665	100
51	0.0010 798 131	0.0009 853 068	0.0008 985 200	0.0008 188 949	102
52	0.0010 059 536	0.0009 158 655	0.0008 333 233	0.0007 577 652	104
53	0.0009 372 773	0.0008 514 302	0.0007 729 525	0.0007 012 796	106
54	0.0008 734 032	0.0007 916 247	0.0007 170 371	0.0006 490 737	108
55	0.0008 139 807	0.0007 361 033	0.0006 652 370	0.0006 008 135	110
56	0.0007 586 865	0.0006 845 480	0.0006 172 394	0.0005 561 921	112
57	0.0007 072 227	0.0006 366 657	0.0005 727 569	0.0005 149 281	114
58	0.0006 593 142	0.0005 921 863	0.0005 315 248	0.0004 767 626	116
59	0.0006 147 069	0.0005 508 608	0.0004 932 994	0.0004 414 577	118
60	0.0005 731 662	0.0005 124 592	0.0004 578 561	0.0004 087 944	120

TABLE 3. SINKING FUND FACTORS
Payable at end of each period

HALF YEARS	8% Nominal Annual Rate	8¼% Nominal Annual Rate	8½% Nominal Annual Rate	8¾% Nominal Annual Rate	HALF YEARS
1	1.0000 000 000	1.0000 000 000	1.0000 000 000	1.0000 000 000	1
YEARS					
1	0.4901 960 784	0.4898 958 971	0.4895 960 832	0.4892 966 361	2
2	0.2354 900 454	0.2350 520 727	0.2346 150 167	0.2341 788 757	4
3	0.1507 619 025	0.1502 888 947	0.1498 173 083	0.1493 471 403	6
4	0.1085 278 320	0.1080 454 268	0.1075 649 316	0.1070 863 420	8
5	0.0832 909 443	0.0828 093 394	0.0823 301 217	0.0818 532 847	10
6	0.0665 521 727	0.0660 764 062	0.0656 034 928	0.0651 334 234	12
7	0.0546 689 731	0.0542 018 611	0.0537 380 557	0.0532 775 449	14
8	0.0458 199 992	0.0453 632 375	0.0449 102 226	0.0444 609 387	16
9	0.0389 933 281	0.0385 479 823	0.0381 068 090	0.0376 697 877	18
10	0.0335 817 503	0.0331 485 014	0.0327 198 348	0.0322 957 245	20
11	0.0291 988 111	0.0287 780 897	0.0283 623 433	0.0279 515 396	22
12	0.0255 868 313	0.0251 788 965	0.0247 763 108	0.0243 790 352	24
13	0.0225 673 805	0.0221 723 680	0.0217 830 600	0.0213 994 090	26
14	0.0200 129 752	0.0196 309 300	0.0192 549 240	0.0188 849 013	28
15	0.0178 300 991	0.0174 609 962	0.0170 982 464	0.0167 417 842	30
16	0.0159 485 897	0.0155 923 494	0.0152 427 548	0.0148 997 294	32
17	0.0143 147 715	0.0139 712 706	0.0136 346 857	0.0133 049 290	34
18	0.0128 868 780	0.0125 559 578	0.0122 322 015	0.0119 155 090	36
19	0.0116 319 191	0.0113 133 920	0.0110 022 538	0.0106 983 917	38
20	0.0105 234 893	0.0102 171 434	0.0099 183 886	0.0096 270 987	40
21	0.0095 402 007	0.0092 458 041	0.0089 591 782	0.0086 801 824	42
22	0.0086 645 444	0.0083 818 487	0.0081 070 805	0.0078 400 845	44
23	0.0078 820 488	0.0076 107 917	0.0073 475 964	0.0070 922 928	46
24	0.0071 806 476	0.0069 205 556	0.0066 686 377	0.0064 247 082	48
25	0.0065 502 004	0.0063 009 909	0.0060 600 458	0.0058 271 642	50
26	0.0059 821 236	0.0057 435 063	0.0055 132 229	0.0052 910 567	52
27	0.0054 691 025	0.0052 407 817	0.0050 208 438	0.0048 090 563	54
28	0.0050 048 662	0.0047 865 422	0.0045 766 300	0.0043 748 818	56
29	0.0045 840 087	0.0043 753 787	0.0041 751 706	0.0039 831 210	58
30	0.0042 018 451	0.0040 026 049	0.0038 117 784	0.0036 290 870	60
31	0.0038 542 964	0.0036 641 412	0.0034 823 743	0.0033 087 020	62
32	0.0035 377 955	0.0033 564 212	0.0031 833 932	0.0030 184 034	64
33	0.0032 492 100	0.0030 763 140	0.0029 117 067	0.0027 550 661	66
34	0.0029 857 795	0.0028 210 613	0.0026 645 597	0.0025 159 393	68
35	0.0027 450 623	0.0025 882 245	0.0024 395 176	0.0022 985 935	70
36	0.0025 248 919	0.0023 756 408	0.0022 344 223	0.0021 008 762	72
37	0.0023 233 403	0.0021 813 865	0.0020 473 553	0.0019 208 754	74
38	0.0021 386 869	0.0020 037 458	0.0018 766 067	0.0017 568 877	76
39	0.0019 693 922	0.0018 411 845	0.0017 206 484	0.0016 073 927	78
40	0.0018 140 755	0.0016 923 276	0.0015 781 123	0.0014 710 294	80
41	0.0016 714 957	0.0015 559 400	0.0014 477 702	0.0013 465 781	82
42	0.0015 405 351	0.0014 309 105	0.0013 285 180	0.0012 329 425	84
43	0.0014 201 848	0.0013 162 368	0.0012 193 611	0.0011 291 366	86
44	0.0013 095 329	0.0012 110 138	0.0011 194 021	0.0010 342 714	88
45	0.0012 077 538	0.0011 144 228	0.0010 278 300	0.0009 475 447	90
46	0.0011 140 984	0.0010 257 221	0.0009 439 110	0.0008 682 312	92
47	0.0010 278 867	0.0009 442 387	0.0008 669 802	0.0007 956 748	94
48	0.0009 485 002	0.0008 693 615	0.0007 964 344	0.0007 292 809	96
49	0.0008 753 757	0.0008 005 346	0.0007 317 257	0.0006 685 103	98
50	0.0008 080 000	0.0007 372 521	0.0006 723 562	0.0006 128 735	100
51	0.0007 459 047	0.0006 790 529	0.0006 178 725	0.0005 619 256	102
52	0.0006 886 620	0.0006 255 164	0.0005 678 618	0.0005 152 621	104
53	0.0006 358 808	0.0005 762 587	0.0005 219 481	0.0004 725 151	106
54	0.0005 872 033	0.0005 309 291	0.0004 797 880	0.0004 333 491	108
55	0.0005 423 018	0.0004 892 069	0.0004 410 683	0.0003 974 587	110
56	0.0005 008 762	0.0004 507 988	0.0004 055 028	0.0003 645 653	112
57	0.0004 626 512	0.0004 154 362	0.0003 728 300	0.0003 344 147	114
58	0.0004 273 741	0.0003 828 730	0.0003 428 109	0.0003 067 751	116
59	0.0003 948 131	0.0003 528 838	0.0003 152 265	0.0002 814 344	118
60	0.0003 647 553	0.0003 252 620	0.0002 898 768	0.0002 581 993	120

TABLE 3. SINKING FUND FACTORS
Payable at end of each period

SEMI ANNUAL Compounding

HALF YEARS	9% Nominal Annual Rate	9¼% Nominal Annual Rate	9½% Nominal Annual Rate	9¾% Nominal Annual Rate	HALF YEARS
1	1.0000 000 000	1.0000 000 000	1.0000 000 000	1.0000 000 000	1
YEARS					
1	0.4889 975 550	0.4886 988 393	0.4884 004 884	0.4881 025 015	2
2	0.2337 436 479	0.2333 093 315	0.2328 759 246	0.2324 434 256	4
3	0.1488 783 875	0.1484 110 470	0.1479 451 156	0.1474 805 904	6
4	0.1066 096 533	0.1061 348 608	0.1056 619 598	0.1051 909 457	8
5	0.0813 788 217	0.0809 067 260	0.0804 369 909	0.0799 696 094	10
6	0.0646 661 886	0.0642 017 793	0.0637 401 861	0.0632 813 995	12
7	0.0528 203 160	0.0523 663 567	0.0519 156 544	0.0514 681 962	14
8	0.0440 153 694	0.0435 734 984	0.0431 353 090	0.0427 007 845	16
9	0.0372 368 975	0.0368 081 173	0.0363 834 258	0.0359 628 014	18
10	0.0318 761 443	0.0314 610 675	0.0310 504 673	0.0306 443 163	20
11	0.0275 456 461	0.0271 446 297	0.0267 484 572	0.0263 570 948	22
12	0.0239 870 299	0.0236 002 547	0.0232 186 689	0.0228 422 314	24
13	0.0210 213 674	0.0206 488 869	0.0202 819 186	0.0199 204 131	26
14	0.0185 208 051	0.0181 625 781	0.0178 101 623	0.0174 634 994	28
15	0.0163 915 429	0.0160 474 554	0.0157 094 539	0.0153 774 701	30
16	0.0145 631 962	0.0142 330 773	0.0139 092 942	0.0135 917 680	32
17	0.0129 819 119	0.0126 655 451	0.0123 557 388	0.0120 524 026	34
18	0.0116 057 796	0.0113 029 120	0.0110 068 041	0.0107 173 534	36
19	0.0104 016 920	0.0101 120 408	0.0098 293 231	0.0095 534 240	38
20	0.0093 431 466	0.0090 664 048	0.0087 967 454	0.0085 340 403	40
21	0.0084 086 759	0.0081 445 172	0.0078 875 648	0.0076 376 773	42
22	0.0075 807 056	0.0073 287 880	0.0070 841 765	0.0068 467 156	44
23	0.0068 447 107	0.0066 046 800	0.0063 720 312	0.0061 465 952	46
24	0.0061 885 821	0.0059 600 748	0.0057 390 022	0.0055 251 814	48
25	0.0056 021 459	0.0053 847 913	0.0051 749 023	0.0049 722 821	50
26	0.0050 767 923	0.0048 702 156	0.0046 711 140	0.0044 792 771	52
27	0.0046 051 886	0.0044 090 120	0.0042 203 000	0.0040 388 287	54
28	0.0041 810 518	0.0039 948 970	0.0038 161 771	0.0036 446 552	56
29	0.0037 989 695	0.0036 224 589	0.0034 533 356	0.0032 913 500	58
30	0.0034 542 558	0.0032 870 141	0.0031 270 953	0.0029 742 377	60
31	0.0031 428 356	0.0029 844 908	0.0028 333 891	0.0026 892 570	62
32	0.0028 611 494	0.0027 113 345	0.0025 686 682	0.0024 328 665	64
33	0.0026 060 769	0.0024 644 303	0.0023 298 248	0.0022 019 663	66
34	0.0023 748 725	0.0022 410 393	0.0021 141 277	0.0019 938 343	68
35	0.0021 651 129	0.0020 387 452	0.0019 191 690	0.0018 060 724	70
36	0.0019 746 524	0.0018 554 105	0.0017 428 204	0.0016 365 626	72
37	0.0018 015 863	0.0016 891 389	0.0015 831 953	0.0014 834 290	74
38	0.0016 442 194	0.0015 382 442	0.0014 386 173	0.0013 450 066	76
39	0.0015 010 391	0.0014 012 232	0.0013 075 940	0.0012 198 145	78
40	0.0013 706 935	0.0012 767 336	0.0011 887 937	0.0011 065 325	80
41	0.0012 519 715	0.0011 635 742	0.0010 810 259	0.0010 039 821	82
42	0.0011 437 861	0.0010 606 681	0.0009 832 248	0.0009 111 096	84
43	0.0010 451 606	0.0009 670 487	0.0008 944 348	0.0008 269 709	86
44	0.0009 552 152	0.0008 818 465	0.0008 137 976	0.0007 507 197	88
45	0.0008 731 573	0.0008 042 790	0.0007 405 414	0.0006 815 959	90
46	0.0007 982 710	0.0007 336 406	0.0006 739 715	0.0006 189 164	92
47	0.0007 299 095	0.0006 692 944	0.0006 134 620	0.0005 620 664	94
48	0.0006 674 877	0.0006 106 653	0.0005 584 480	0.0005 104 924	96
49	0.0006 104 754	0.0005 572 330	0.0005 084 196	0.0004 636 951	98
50	0.0005 583 922	0.0005 085 267	0.0004 629 162	0.0004 212 245	100
51	0.0005 108 023	0.0004 641 198	0.0004 215 211	0.0003 826 741	102
52	0.0004 673 100	0.0004 236 260	0.0003 838 573	0.0003 476 768	104
53	0.0004 275 556	0.0003 866 944	0.0003 495 834	0.0003 159 007	106
54	0.0003 912 122	0.0003 530 068	0.0003 183 901	0.0002 870 458	108
55	0.0003 579 825	0.0003 222 743	0.0002 899 970	0.0002 608 405	110
56	0.0003 275 957	0.0002 942 342	0.0002 641 499	0.0002 370 392	112
57	0.0002 998 052	0.0002 686 479	0.0002 406 182	0.0002 154 192	114
58	0.0002 743 866	0.0002 452 982	0.0002 191 924	0.0001 957 791	116
59	0.0002 511 350	0.0002 239 878	0.0001 996 824	0.0001 779 361	118
60	0.0002 298 637	0.0002 045 369	0.0001 819 156	0.0001 617 246	120

SEMI ANNUAL
Compounding

TABLE 3. SINKING FUND FACTORS
Payable at end of each period

HALF YEARS	10% Nominal Annual Rate	10¼% Nominal Annual Rate	10½% Nominal Annual Rate	10¾% Nominal Annual Rate	HALF YEARS
1	1.0000 000 000	1.0000 000 000	1.0000 000 000	1.0000 000 000	1
YEARS					
1	0.4878 048 780	0.4875 076 173	0.4872 107 186	0.4869 141 814	2
2	0.2320 118 326	0.2315 811 439	0.2311 513 576	0.2307 224 720	4
3	0.1470 174 681	0.1465 557 458	0.1460 954 203	0.1456 364 886	6
4	0.1047 218 136	0.1042 545 590	0.1037 891 770	0.1033 256 628	8
5	0.0795 045 750	0.0790 418 806	0.0785 815 194	0.0781 234 844	10
6	0.0628 254 100	0.0623 722 081	0.0619 217 842	0.0614 741 284	12
7	0.0510 239 695	0.0505 829 611	0.0501 451 581	0.0497 105 473	14
8	0.0422 699 080	0.0418 426 624	0.0414 190 304	0.0409 989 948	16
9	0.0355 462 223	0.0351 336 666	0.0347 251 119	0.0343 205 360	18
10	0.0302 425 872	0.0298 452 521	0.0294 522 832	0.0290 636 520	20
11	0.0259 705 086	0.0255 886 640	0.0252 115 264	0.0248 390 608	22
12	0.0224 709 008	0.0221 046 351	0.0217 433 921	0.0213 871 293	24
13	0.0195 643 207	0.0192 135 911	0.0188 681 737	0.0185 280 176	26
14	0.0171 225 304	0.0167 871 960	0.0164 574 362	0.0161 331 909	28
15	0.0150 514 351	0.0147 312 795	0.0144 169 335	0.0141 083 271	30
16	0.0132 804 189	0.0129 751 672	0.0126 759 322	0.0123 826 333	32
17	0.0117 554 454	0.0114 647 761	0.0111 803 028	0.0109 019 338	34
18	0.0104 344 571	0.0101 580 120	0.0098 879 146	0.0096 240 614	36
19	0.0092 842 282	0.0090 216 200	0.0087 654 839	0.0085 157 044	38
20	0.0082 781 612	0.0080 289 799	0.0077 863 683	0.0075 501 986	40
21	0.0073 947 131	0.0071 585 311	0.0069 289 905	0.0067 059 510	42
22	0.0066 162 506	0.0063 926 272	0.0061 756 919	0.0059 652 920	44
23	0.0059 282 036	0.0057 166 891	0.0055 118 853	0.0053 136 272	46
24	0.0053 184 306	0.0051 185 693	0.0049 254 187	0.0047 388 015	48
25	0.0047 767 355	0.0045 880 691	0.0044 060 917	0.0042 306 143	50
26	0.0042 944 966	0.0041 165 665	0.0039 452 836	0.0037 804 474	52
27	0.0038 643 770	0.0036 967 268	0.0035 356 631	0.0033 809 745	54
28	0.0034 800 978	0.0033 222 749	0.0031 709 607	0.0030 259 335	56
29	0.0031 362 568	0.0029 878 148	0.0028 457 878	0.0027 099 443	58
30	0.0028 281 845	0.0026 886 844	0.0025 554 911	0.0024 283 643	60
31	0.0025 518 273	0.0024 208 386	0.0022 960 358	0.0021 771 704	62
32	0.0023 036 520	0.0021 807 543	0.0020 639 102	0.0019 528 636	64
33	0.0020 805 683	0.0019 653 521	0.0018 560 470	0.0017 523 906	66
34	0.0018 798 643	0.0017 719 316	0.0016 697 590	0.0015 730 784	68
35	0.0016 991 530	0.0015 981 183	0.0015 026 853	0.0014 125 813	70
36	0.0015 363 280	0.0014 418 184	0.0013 527 462	0.0012 688 348	72
37	0.0013 895 254	0.0013 011 814	0.0012 181 056	0.0011 400 185	74
38	0.0012 570 925	0.0011 745 681	0.0010 971 390	0.0010 245 236	76
39	0.0011 375 610	0.0010 605 237	0.0009 884 063	0.0009 209 257	78
40	0.0010 296 235	0.0009 577 547	0.0008 906 287	0.0008 279 618	80
41	0.0009 321 143	0.0008 651 092	0.0008 026 688	0.0007 445 101	82
42	0.0008 439 924	0.0007 815 596	0.0007 235 137	0.0006 695 727	84
43	0.0007 643 265	0.0007 061 883	0.0006 522 600	0.0006 022 615	86
44	0.0006 922 828	0.0006 381 748	0.0005 881 011	0.0005 417 843	88
45	0.0006 271 136	0.0005 767 844	0.0005 303 161	0.0004 874 345	90
46	0.0005 681 481	0.0005 213 589	0.0004 782 600	0.0004 385 809	92
47	0.0005 147 832	0.0004 713 078	0.0004 313 554	0.0003 946 593	94
48	0.0004 664 770	0.0004 261 013	0.0003 890 846	0.0003 551 651	96
49	0.0004 227 418	0.0003 852 632	0.0003 509 836	0.0003 196 465	98
50	0.0003 831 381	0.0003 483 654	0.0003 166 360	0.0002 876 988	100
51	0.0003 472 701	0.0003 150 230	0.0002 856 678	0.0002 589 595	102
52	0.0003 147 810	0.0002 848 895	0.0002 577 433	0.0002 331 035	104
53	0.0002 853 486	0.0002 576 528	0.0002 325 604	0.0002 098 391	106
54	0.0002 586 824	0.0002 330 318	0.0002 098 478	0.0001 889 047	108
55	0.0002 345 197	0.0002 107 732	0.0001 893 614	0.0001 700 653	110
56	0.0002 126 236	0.0001 906 485	0.0001 708 814	0.0001 531 102	112
57	0.0001 927 796	0.0001 724 518	0.0001 542 102	0.0001 378 497	114
58	0.0001 747 942	0.0001 559 972	0.0001 391 698	0.0001 241 138	116
59	0.0001 584 919	0.0001 411 169	0.0001 255 997	0.0001 117 494	118
60	0.0001 437 145	0.0001 276 595	0.0001 133 557	0.0001 006 190	120

TABLE 3. SINKING FUND FACTORS
Payable at end of each period

SEMI ANNUAL Compounding

HALF YEARS	11% Nominal Annual Rate	11¼% Nominal Annual Rate	11½% Nominal Annual Rate	11¾% Nominal Annual Rate	HALF YEARS
1	1.0000 000 000	1.0000 000 000	1.0000 000 000	1.0000 000 000	1
YEARS					
1	0.4866 180 049	0.4863 221 884	0.4860 267 315	0.4857 316 333	2
2	0.2302 944 853	0.2298 673 958	0.2294 412 017	0.2290 159 011	4
3	0.1451 789 476	0.1447 227 942	0.1442 680 253	0.1438 146 377	6
4	0.1028 640 118	0.1024 042 191	0.1019 462 799	0.1014 901 893	8
5	0.0776 677 687	0.0772 143 653	0.0767 632 671	0.0763 144 671	10
6	0.0610 292 312	0.0605 870 826	0.0601 476 727	0.0597 109 916	12
7	0.0492 791 154	0.0488 508 492	0.0484 257 351	0.0480 037 596	14
8	0.0405 825 380	0.0401 696 423	0.0397 602 900	0.0393 544 631	16
9	0.0339 199 163	0.0335 232 299	0.0331 304 539	0.0327 415 652	18
10	0.0286 793 300	0.0282 992 886	0.0279 234 988	0.0275 519 314	20
11	0.0244 712 319	0.0241 080 042	0.0237 493 418	0.0233 952 087	22
12	0.0210 358 037	0.0206 893 721	0.0203 477 910	0.0200 110 166	24
13	0.0181 930 713	0.0178 632 831	0.0175 386 012	0.0172 189 732	26
14	0.0158 143 996	0.0155 010 012	0.0151 929 348	0.0148 901 387	28
15	0.0138 053 897	0.0135 080 505	0.0132 162 386	0.0129 298 827	30
16	0.0120 951 895	0.0118 135 194	0.0115 375 417	0.0112 671 749	32
17	0.0106 295 769	0.0103 631 398	0.0101 025 304	0.0098 476 563	34
18	0.0093 663 488	0.0091 146 732	0.0088 689 312	0.0086 290 194	36
19	0.0082 721 659	0.0080 347 533	0.0078 033 517	0.0075 778 466	38
20	0.0073 203 434	0.0070 966 755	0.0068 790 687	0.0066 673 972	40
21	0.0064 892 731	0.0062 788 180	0.0060 744 478	0.0058 760 254	42
22	0.0057 612 757	0.0055 634 926	0.0053 717 934	0.0051 860 302	44
23	0.0051 217 512	0.0049 360 952	0.0047 564 988	0.0045 828 035	46
24	0.0045 585 424	0.0043 844 681	0.0042 164 076	0.0040 541 920	48
25	0.0040 614 501	0.0038 984 152	0.0037 413 281	0.0035 900 104	50
26	0.0036 218 603	0.0034 693 281	0.0033 226 596	0.0031 816 673	52
27	0.0032 324 534	0.0030 898 955	0.0029 531 008	0.0028 218 733	54
28	0.0028 869 756	0.0027 538 742	0.0026 264 207	0.0025 044 114	56
29	0.0025 800 578	0.0024 559 071	0.0023 372 760	0.0022 239 540	58
30	0.0023 070 692	0.0021 913 771	0.0020 810 653	0.0019 759 169	60
31	0.0020 640 001	0.0019 562 896	0.0018 538 103	0.0017 563 402	62
32	0.0018 473 659	0.0017 471 759	0.0016 520 600	0.0015 617 918	64
33	0.0016 541 284	0.0015 610 145	0.0014 728 110	0.0013 892 882	66
34	0.0014 816 307	0.0013 951 657	0.0013 134 424	0.0012 362 286	68
35	0.0013 275 431	0.0012 473 176	0.0011 716 612	0.0011 003 402	70
36	0.0011 898 180	0.0011 154 404	0.0010 454 569	0.0009 796 329	72
37	0.0010 666 516	0.0009 977 483	0.0009 330 627	0.0008 723 602	74
38	0.0009 564 521	0.0008 926 673	0.0008 329 236	0.0007 769 870	76
39	0.0008 578 119	0.0007 988 077	0.0007 436 685	0.0006 921 617	78
40	0.0007 694 845	0.0007 149 405	0.0006 640 868	0.0006 166 930	80
41	0.0006 903 644	0.0006 399 773	0.0005 931 080	0.0005 495 289	82
42	0.0006 194 699	0.0005 729 532	0.0005 297 847	0.0004 897 400	84
43	0.0005 559 284	0.0005 130 118	0.0004 732 771	0.0004 365 041	86
44	0.0004 989 631	0.0004 593 920	0.0004 228 407	0.0003 890 930	88
45	0.0004 478 820	0.0004 114 172	0.0003 778 142	0.0003 468 617	90
46	0.0004 020 682	0.0003 684 850	0.0003 376 103	0.0003 092 380	92
47	0.0003 609 712	0.0003 300 590	0.0003 017 070	0.0002 757 144	94
48	0.0003 240 994	0.0002 956 610	0.0002 696 395	0.0002 458 401	96
49	0.0002 910 137	0.0002 648 646	0.0002 409 947	0.0002 192 148	98
50	0.0002 613 216	0.0002 372 895	0.0002 154 042	0.0001 954 826	100
51	0.0002 346 718	0.0002 125 961	0.0001 925 401	0.0001 743 273	102
52	0.0002 107 501	0.0001 904 810	0.0001 721 102	0.0001 554 675	104
53	0.0001 892 753	0.0001 706 734	0.0001 538 539	0.0001 386 528	106
54	0.0001 699 955	0.0001 529 311	0.0001 375 387	0.0001 236 606	108
55	0.0001 526 849	0.0001 370 376	0.0001 229 573	0.0001 102 925	110
56	0.0001 371 415	0.0001 227 995	0.0001 099 247	0.0000 983 719	112
57	0.0001 231 839	0.0001 100 437	0.0000 982 758	0.0000 877 416	114
58	0.0001 106 497	0.0000 986 151	0.0000 878 633	0.0000 782 616	116
59	0.0000 993 932	0.0000 883 753	0.0000 785 555	0.0000 698 071	118
60	0.0000 892 837	0.0000 792 003	0.0000 702 349	0.0000 622 669	120

SEMI ANNUAL
Compounding

TABLE 3. SINKING FUND FACTORS
Payable at end of each period

HALF YEARS	12% Nominal Annual Rate	12¼% Nominal Annual Rate	12½% Nominal Annual Rate	12¾% Nominal Annual Rate	HALF YEARS
1	1.0000 000 000	1.0000 000 000	1.0000 000 000	1.0000 000 000	1
YEARS					
1	0.4854 368 932	0.4851 425 106	0.4848 484 848	0.4845 548 153	2
2	0.2285 914 924	0.2281 679 737	0.2277 453 433	0.2273 235 995	4
3	0.1433 626 285	0.1429 119 944	0.1424 627 324	0.1420 148 394	6
4	0.1010 359 426	0.1005 835 349	0.1001 329 614	0.0996 842 170	8
5	0.0758 679 582	0.0754 237 332	0.0749 817 850	0.0745 421 064	10
6	0.0592 770 294	0.0588 457 758	0.0584 172 209	0.0579 913 544	12
7	0.0475 849 090	0.0471 691 697	0.0467 565 278	0.0463 469 694	14
8	0.0389 521 436	0.0385 533 133	0.0381 579 538	0.0377 660 469	16
9	0.0323 565 406	0.0319 753 564	0.0315 979 892	0.0312 244 151	18
10	0.0271 845 570	0.0268 213 460	0.0264 622 687	0.0261 072 952	20
11	0.0230 455 685	0.0227 003 848	0.0223 596 209	0.0220 232 397	22
12	0.0196 790 050	0.0193 517 118	0.0190 290 926	0.0187 111 028	24
13	0.0169 043 467	0.0165 946 689	0.0162 898 870	0.0159 899 478	26
14	0.0145 925 515	0.0143 001 113	0.0140 127 561	0.0137 304 237	28
15	0.0126 489 115	0.0123 732 534	0.0121 028 369	0.0118 375 904	30
16	0.0110 023 374	0.0107 429 474	0.0104 889 235	0.0102 401 842	32
17	0.0095 984 254	0.0093 547 456	0.0091 165 250	0.0088 836 720	34
18	0.0083 948 348	0.0081 662 747	0.0079 432 368	0.0077 256 191	36
19	0.0073 581 240	0.0071 440 704	0.0069 355 731	0.0067 325 199	38
20	0.0064 615 359	0.0062 613 608	0.0060 667 487	0.0058 775 775	40
21	0.0056 834 152	0.0054 964 825	0.0053 150 939	0.0051 391 176	42
22	0.0050 060 565	0.0048 317 276	0.0046 629 004	0.0044 994 335	44
23	0.0044 148 527	0.0042 524 917	0.0040 955 681	0.0039 439 316	46
24	0.0038 976 549	0.0037 466 325	0.0036 009 636	0.0034 604 896	48
25	0.0034 442 864	0.0033 039 836	0.0031 689 327	0.0030 389 676	50
26	0.0030 461 669	0.0029 159 780	0.0027 909 239	0.0026 708 316	52
27	0.0026 960 209	0.0025 753 560	0.0024 596 952	0.0023 488 594	54
28	0.0023 876 472	0.0022 759 341	0.0021 690 828	0.0020 669 092	56
29	0.0021 157 359	0.0020 124 219	0.0019 138 178	0.0018 197 352	58
30	0.0018 757 215	0.0017 802 746	0.0016 893 780	0.0016 028 397	60
31	0.0016 636 642	0.0015 755 742	0.0014 918 687	0.0014 123 529	62
32	0.0014 761 528	0.0013 949 317	0.0013 179 247	0.0012 449 355	64
33	0.0013 102 248	0.0012 354 074	0.0011 646 308	0.0010 976 977	66
34	0.0011 633 009	0.0010 944 450	0.0010 294 548	0.0009 681 330	68
35	0.0010 331 302	0.0009 698 163	0.0009 101 927	0.0008 540 626	70
36	0.0009 177 439	0.0008 595 753	0.0008 049 222	0.0007 535 891	72
37	0.0008 154 168	0.0007 620 191	0.0007 119 636	0.0006 650 572	74
38	0.0007 246 347	0.0006 756 553	0.0006 298 475	0.0005 870 207	76
39	0.0006 440 667	0.0005 991 741	0.0005 572 859	0.0005 182 145	78
40	0.0005 725 410	0.0005 314 246	0.0004 931 491	0.0004 575 306	80
41	0.0005 090 251	0.0004 713 940	0.0004 364 447	0.0004 039 975	82
42	0.0004 526 081	0.0004 181 905	0.0003 863 004	0.0003 567 629	84
43	0.0004 024 856	0.0003 710 278	0.0003 419 487	0.0003 150 780	86
44	0.0003 579 467	0.0003 292 124	0.0003 027 135	0.0002 782 848	88
45	0.0003 183 623	0.0002 921 321	0.0002 679 994	0.0002 458 046	90
46	0.0002 831 761	0.0002 592 458	0.0002 372 812	0.0002 171 281	92
47	0.0002 518 949	0.0002 300 755	0.0002 100 957	0.0001 918 073	94
48	0.0002 240 821	0.0002 041 983	0.0001 860 342	0.0001 694 470	96
49	0.0001 993 504	0.0001 812 401	0.0001 647 355	0.0001 496 996	98
50	0.0001 773 563	0.0001 608 699	0.0001 458 810	0.0001 322 583	100
51	0.0001 577 952	0.0001 427 946	0.0001 291 889	0.0001 168 528	102
52	0.0001 403 965	0.0001 267 543	0.0001 144 102	0.0001 032 446	104
53	0.0001 249 202	0.0001 125 192	0.0001 013 249	0.0000 912 234	106
54	0.0001 111 531	0.0000 998 854	0.0000 897 383	0.0000 806 037	108
55	0.0000 989 057	0.0000 886 721	0.0000 794 783	0.0000 712 217	110
56	0.0000 880 098	0.0000 787 193	0.0000 703 927	0.0000 629 327	112
57	0.0000 783 157	0.0000 698 849	0.0000 623 468	0.0000 556 093	114
58	0.0000 696 907	0.0000 620 429	0.0000 552 213	0.0000 491 388	116
59	0.0000 620 166	0.0000 550 817	0.0000 489 108	0.0000 434 216	118
60	0.0000 551 883	0.0000 489 022	0.0000 433 220	0.0000 383 701	120

TABLE 3. SINKING FUND FACTORS
Payable at end of each period

HALF YEARS	13% Nominal Annual Rate	13¼% Nominal Annual Rate	13½% Nominal Annual Rate	13¾% Nominal Annual Rate	HALF YEARS
1	1.0000 000 000	1.0000 000 000	1.0000 000 000	1.0000 000 000	1
YEARS					
1	0.4842 615 012	0.4839 685 420	0.4836 759 371	0.4833 836 858	2
2	0.2269 027 404	0.2264 827 644	0.2260 636 696	0.2256 454 542	4
3	0.1415 683 122	0.1411 231 478	0.1406 793 430	0.1402 368 947	6
4	0.0992 372 971	0.0987 921 965	0.0983 489 106	0.0979 074 342	8
5	0.0741 046 901	0.0736 695 288	0.0732 366 154	0.0728 059 425	10
6	0.0575 681 661	0.0571 476 458	0.0567 297 830	0.0563 145 674	12
7	0.0459 404 806	0.0455 370 473	0.0451 366 553	0.0447 392 905	14
8	0.0373 775 740	0.0369 925 163	0.0366 108 553	0.0362 325 721	16
9	0.0308 546 103	0.0304 885 508	0.0301 262 124	0.0297 675 708	18
10	0.0257 563 954	0.0254 095 389	0.0250 666 956	0.0247 278 347	20
11	0.0216 912 043	0.0213 634 774	0.0210 400 217	0.0207 207 995	22
12	0.0183 976 975	0.0180 888 318	0.0177 844 606	0.0174 845 387	24
13	0.0156 947 983	0.0154 043 850	0.0151 186 545	0.0148 375 533	26
14	0.0134 530 522	0.0131 805 791	0.0129 129 423	0.0126 500 794	28
15	0.0115 774 422	0.0113 223 209	0.0110 721 549	0.0108 268 729	30
16	0.0099 966 481	0.0097 582 340	0.0095 248 610	0.0092 964 483	32
17	0.0086 560 953	0.0084 337 038	0.0082 164 072	0.0080 041 151	34
18	0.0075 133 205	0.0073 062 399	0.0071 042 775	0.0069 073 336	36
19	0.0065 347 995	0.0063 423 016	0.0061 549 164	0.0059 725 356	38
20	0.0056 937 260	0.0055 150 744	0.0053 415 040	0.0051 728 975	40
21	0.0049 684 229	0.0048 028 811	0.0046 423 647	0.0044 867 481	42
22	0.0043 411 874	0.0041 880 246	0.0040 398 096	0.0038 964 089	44
23	0.0037 974 344	0.0036 559 310	0.0035 192 782	0.0033 873 356	46
24	0.0033 250 549	0.0031 945 065	0.0030 686 946	0.0029 474 722	48
25	0.0029 139 255	0.0027 936 469	0.0026 779 758	0.0025 667 597	50
26	0.0025 555 319	0.0024 448 597	0.0023 386 536	0.0022 367 564	52
27	0.0022 426 740	0.0021 409 690	0.0020 435 785	0.0019 503 413	54
28	0.0019 692 339	0.0018 758 827	0.0017 866 863	0.0017 014 805	56
29	0.0017 299 909	0.0016 444 075	0.0015 628 130	0.0014 850 410	58
30	0.0015 204 735	0.0014 420 999	0.0013 675 449	0.0012 966 407	60
31	0.0013 368 390	0.0012 651 455	0.0011 970 977	0.0011 325 273	62
32	0.0011 757 748	0.0011 102 606	0.0010 482 180	0.0009 894 789	64
33	0.0010 344 184	0.0009 746 112	0.0009 181 015	0.0008 647 223	66
34	0.0009 102 903	0.0008 557 457	0.0008 043 260	0.0007 558 659	68
35	0.0008 012 380	0.0007 515 393	0.0007 047 954	0.0006 608 431	70
36	0.0007 053 899	0.0006 601 472	0.0006 176 925	0.0005 778 653	72
37	0.0006 211 159	0.0005 799 652	0.0005 414 397	0.0005 053 824	74
38	0.0005 469 940	0.0005 095 964	0.0004 746 658	0.0004 420 491	76
39	0.0004 817 826	0.0004 478 228	0.0004 161 772	0.0003 866 969	78
40	0.0004 243 958	0.0003 935 816	0.0003 649 343	0.0003 383 096	80
41	0.0003 738 836	0.0003 459 443	0.0003 200 306	0.0002 960 030	82
42	0.0003 294 137	0.0003 040 991	0.0002 806 750	0.0002 590 067	84
43	0.0002 902 566	0.0002 673 358	0.0002 461 766	0.0002 266 497	86
44	0.0002 557 723	0.0002 350 325	0.0002 159 320	0.0001 983 465	88
45	0.0002 253 990	0.0002 066 448	0.0001 894 136	0.0001 735 867	90
46	0.0001 986 436	0.0001 816 951	0.0001 661 599	0.0001 519 244	92
47	0.0001 750 727	0.0001 597 651	0.0001 457 671	0.0001 329 707	94
48	0.0001 543 053	0.0001 404 875	0.0001 278 819	0.0001 163 855	96
49	0.0001 360 065	0.0001 235 403	0.0001 121 947	0.0001 018 721	98
50	0.0001 198 817	0.0001 086 408	0.0000 984 347	0.0000 891 708	100
51	0.0001 056 717	0.0000 955 409	0.0000 863 644	0.0000 780 550	102
52	0.0000 931 485	0.0000 840 225	0.0000 757 759	0.0000 683 261	104
53	0.0000 821 114	0.0000 738 944	0.0000 664 868	0.0000 598 110	106
54	0.0000 723 834	0.0000 649 883	0.0000 583 375	0.0000 523 578	108
55	0.0000 638 091	0.0000 571 565	0.0000 511 877	0.0000 458 340	110
56	0.0000 562 514	0.0000 502 692	0.0000 449 148	0.0000 401 236	112
57	0.0000 495 894	0.0000 442 124	0.0000 394 111	0.0000 351 250	114
58	0.0000 437 171	0.0000 388 858	0.0000 345 821	0.0000 307 494	116
59	0.0000 385 405	0.0000 342 013	0.0000 303 451	0.0000 269 190	118
60	0.0000 339 772	0.0000 300 814	0.0000 266 274	0.0000 235 660	120

SEMI ANNUAL
Compounding

TABLE 3. SINKING FUND FACTORS
Payable at end of each period

HALF YEARS	14% Nominal Annual Rate	14¼% Nominal Annual Rate	14½% Nominal Annual Rate	14¾% Nominal Annual Rate	HALF YEARS
1	1.0000 000 000	1.0000 000 000	1.0000 000 000	1.0000 000 000	1
YEARS					
1	0.4830 917 874	0.4828 002 414	0.4825 090 470	0.4822 182 037	2
2	0.2252 281 167	0.2248 116 551	0.2243 960 677	0.2239 813 528	4
3	0.1397 957 998	0.1393 560 551	0.1389 176 575	0.1384 806 039	6
4	0.0974 677 625	0.0970 298 905	0.0965 938 133	0.0961 595 259	8
5	0.0723 775 027	0.0719 512 887	0.0715 272 931	0.0711 055 085	10
6	0.0559 019 887	0.0554 920 362	0.0550 846 995	0.0546 799 681	12
7	0.0443 449 386	0.0439 535 853	0.0435 652 161	0.0431 798 165	14
8	0.0358 576 477	0.0354 860 632	0.0351 177 994	0.0347 528 371	16
9	0.0294 126 017	0.0290 612 804	0.0287 135 825	0.0283 694 833	18
10	0.0243 929 257	0.0240 619 379	0.0237 348 402	0.0234 116 018	20
11	0.0204 057 732	0.0200 949 052	0.0197 881 574	0.0194 854 920	22
12	0.0171 890 207	0.0168 978 613	0.0166 110 150	0.0163 284 362	24
13	0.0145 610 279	0.0142 890 247	0.0140 214 900	0.0137 583 704	26
14	0.0123 919 283	0.0121 384 268	0.0118 895 127	0.0116 451 241	28
15	0.0105 864 035	0.0103 506 758	0.0101 196 190	0.0098 931 624	30
16	0.0090 729 155	0.0088 541 826	0.0086 401 700	0.0084 307 982	32
17	0.0077 967 381	0.0075 941 871	0.0073 963 736	0.0072 032 097	34
18	0.0067 153 097	0.0065 281 078	0.0063 456 308	0.0061 677 826	36
19	0.0057 950 515	0.0056 223 577	0.0054 543 489	0.0052 909 209	38
20	0.0050 091 389	0.0048 501 136	0.0046 957 084	0.0045 458 119	40
21	0.0043 359 072	0.0041 897 200	0.0040 480 660	0.0039 108 268	42
22	0.0037 576 913	0.0036 235 275	0.0034 937 906	0.0033 683 560	44
23	0.0032 599 650	0.0031 370 311	0.0030 184 011	0.0029 039 449	46
24	0.0028 306 953	0.0027 182 232	0.0026 099 179	0.0025 056 448	48
25	0.0024 598 495	0.0023 570 997	0.0022 583 683	0.0021 635 168	50
26	0.0021 390 147	0.0020 452 791	0.0019 554 044	0.0018 692 490	52
27	0.0018 611 007	0.0017 757 044	0.0016 940 045	0.0016 158 576	54
28	0.0016 201 059	0.0015 424 082	0.0014 682 379	0.0013 974 502	56
29	0.0014 109 304	0.0013 403 256	0.0012 730 763	0.0012 090 374	58
30	0.0012 292 255	0.0011 651 432	0.0011 042 434	0.0010 463 813	60
31	0.0010 712 723	0.0010 131 769	0.0009 580 915	0.0009 058 724	62
32	0.0009 338 819	0.0008 812 724	0.0008 315 021	0.0007 844 289	64
33	0.0008 143 137	0.0007 667 226	0.0007 218 028	0.0006 794 147	66
34	0.0007 102 075	0.0006 671 999	0.0006 266 997	0.0005 885 701	68
35	0.0006 195 272	0.0005 806 998	0.0005 442 204	0.0005 099 555	70
36	0.0005 405 136	0.0005 054 929	0.0004 726 662	0.0004 419 038	72
37	0.0004 716 446	0.0004 400 858	0.0004 105 729	0.0003 829 802	74
38	0.0004 116 017	0.0003 831 870	0.0003 566 765	0.0003 319 487	76
39	0.0003 592 415	0.0003 336 790	0.0003 098 852	0.0002 877 434	78
40	0.0003 135 718	0.0002 905 934	0.0002 692 551	0.0002 494 447	80
41	0.0002 737 305	0.0002 530 908	0.0002 339 692	0.0002 162 585	82
42	0.0002 389 686	0.0002 204 430	0.0002 033 204	0.0001 874 985	84
43	0.0002 086 343	0.0001 920 180	0.0001 766 962	0.0001 625 718	86
44	0.0001 821 605	0.0001 672 668	0.0001 535 658	0.0001 409 652	88
45	0.0001 590 537	0.0001 457 126	0.0001 334 688	0.0001 222 349	90
46	0.0001 388 837	0.0001 269 408	0.0001 160 061	0.0001 059 970	92
47	0.0001 212 760	0.0001 105 910	0.0001 008 313	0.0000 919 188	94
48	0.0001 059 039	0.0000 963 500	0.0000 876 439	0.0000 797 125	96
49	0.0000 924 829	0.0000 839 449	0.0000 761 831	0.0000 691 286	98
50	0.0000 807 646	0.0000 731 387	0.0000 662 223	0.0000 599 511	100
51	0.0000 705 326	0.0000 637 247	0.0000 575 649	0.0000 519 929	102
52	0.0000 615 981	0.0000 555 234	0.0000 500 401	0.0000 450 917	104
53	0.0000 537 962	0.0000 483 784	0.0000 434 995	0.0000 391 071	106
54	0.0000 469 831	0.0000 421 533	0.0000 378 143	0.0000 339 171	108
55	0.0000 410 334	0.0000 367 297	0.0000 328 724	0.0000 294 161	110
56	0.0000 358 375	0.0000 320 042	0.0000 285 767	0.0000 255 127	112
57	0.0000 312 998	0.0000 278 869	0.0000 248 425	0.0000 221 274	114
58	0.0000 273 369	0.0000 242 994	0.0000 215 964	0.0000 191 914	116
59	0.0000 238 759	0.0000 211 736	0.0000 187 745	0.0000 166 451	118
60	0.0000 208 533	0.0000 184 500	0.0000 163 215	0.0000 144 366	120

TABLE 3. SINKING FUND FACTORS
Payable at end of each period

SEMI ANNUAL Compounding

HALF YEARS	15% Nominal Annual Rate	15¼% Nominal Annual Rate	15½% Nominal Annual Rate	15¾% Nominal Annual Rate	HALF YEARS
1	1.0000 000 000	1.0000 000 000	1.0000 000 000	1.0000 000 000	1
YEARS					
1	0.4819 277 108	0.4816 375 677	0.4813 477 738	0.4810 583 283	2
2	0.2235 675 087	0.2231 545 335	0.2227 424 256	0.2223 311 831	4
3	0.1380 448 912	0.1376 105 162	0.1371 774 758	0.1367 457 669	6
4	0.0957 270 232	0.0952 963 004	0.0948 673 523	0.0944 401 741	8
5	0.0706 859 274	0.0702 685 424	0.0698 533 459	0.0694 403 306	10
6	0.0542 778 313	0.0538 782 785	0.0534 812 990	0.0530 868 821	12
7	0.0427 973 721	0.0424 178 682	0.0420 412 901	0.0416 676 233	14
8	0.0343 911 571	0.0340 327 401	0.0336 775 665	0.0333 256 170	16
9	0.0280 289 578	0.0276 919 814	0.0273 585 289	0.0270 285 755	18
10	0.0230 921 916	0.0227 765 785	0.0224 647 312	0.0221 566 184	20
11	0.0191 868 710	0.0188 922 563	0.0186 016 097	0.0183 148 931	22
12	0.0160 500 795	0.0157 758 992	0.0155 058 498	0.0152 398 858	24
13	0.0134 996 124	0.0132 451 623	0.0129 949 668	0.0127 489 727	26
14	0.0114 051 993	0.0111 696 764	0.0109 384 939	0.0107 115 908	28
15	0.0096 712 358	0.0094 537 690	0.0092 406 925	0.0090 319 370	30
16	0.0082 259 887	0.0080 256 629	0.0078 297 432	0.0076 381 522	32
17	0.0070 146 084	0.0068 304 831	0.0066 507 481	0.0064 753 185	34
18	0.0059 944 680	0.0058 255 926	0.0056 610 631	0.0055 007 873	36
19	0.0051 319 709	0.0049 773 971	0.0048 270 991	0.0046 809 780	38
20	0.0044 003 138	0.0042 591 058	0.0041 220 809	0.0039 891 340	40
21	0.0037 778 858	0.0036 491 283	0.0035 244 417	0.0034 037 154	42
22	0.0032 471 012	0.0031 299 064	0.0030 166 536	0.0029 072 277	44
23	0.0027 935 352	0.0026 870 473	0.0025 843 592	0.0024 853 518	46
24	0.0024 052 724	0.0023 086 720	0.0022 157 185	0.0021 262 895	48
25	0.0020 724 102	0.0019 849 172	0.0019 009 099	0.0018 202 639	50
26	0.0017 866 757	0.0017 075 508	0.0016 317 448	0.0015 591 320	52
27	0.0015 411 247	0.0014 696 708	0.0014 013 656	0.0013 360 828	54
28	0.0013 299 053	0.0012 654 680	0.0012 040 076	0.0011 453 981	56
29	0.0011 480 689	0.0010 900 360	0.0010 348 086	0.0009 822 616	58
30	0.0009 914 178	0.0009 392 188	0.0008 896 558	0.0008 426 053	60
31	0.0008 563 816	0.0008 094 871	0.0007 650 620	0.0007 229 852	62
32	0.0007 399 172	0.0006 978 368	0.0006 580 637	0.0006 204 792	64
33	0.0006 394 249	0.0006 017 064	0.0005 661 380	0.0005 326 041	66
34	0.0005 526 807	0.0005 189 078	0.0004 871 335	0.0004 572 460	68
35	0.0004 777 785	0.0004 475 691	0.0004 192 133	0.0003 926 031	70
36	0.0004 130 829	0.0003 860 873	0.0003 608 069	0.0003 371 379	72
37	0.0003 571 892	0.0003 330 878	0.0003 105 703	0.0002 895 373	74
38	0.0003 088 894	0.0002 873 910	0.0002 673 524	0.0002 486 786	76
39	0.0002 671 439	0.0002 479 837	0.0002 301 664	0.0002 136 013	78
40	0.0002 310 575	0.0002 139 951	0.0001 981 657	0.0001 834 833	80
41	0.0001 998 587	0.0001 846 762	0.0001 706 239	0.0001 576 205	82
42	0.0001 728 822	0.0001 593 826	0.0001 469 173	0.0001 354 094	84
43	0.0001 495 542	0.0001 375 595	0.0001 265 098	0.0001 163 328	86
44	0.0001 293 793	0.0001 187 291	0.0001 089 410	0.0000 999 471	88
45	0.0001 119 302	0.0001 024 798	0.0000 938 149	0.0000 858 719	90
46	0.0000 968 374	0.0000 884 570	0.0000 807 913	0.0000 737 807	92
47	0.0000 837 820	0.0000 763 549	0.0000 695 772	0.0000 633 934	94
48	0.0000 724 884	0.0000 659 100	0.0000 599 209	0.0000 544 695	96
49	0.0000 627 184	0.0000 568 949	0.0000 516 057	0.0000 468 025	98
50	0.0000 542 661	0.0000 491 137	0.0000 444 450	0.0000 402 153	100
51	0.0000 469 537	0.0000 423 973	0.0000 382 784	0.0000 345 556	102
52	0.0000 406 271	0.0000 365 998	0.0000 329 678	0.0000 296 927	104
53	0.0000 351 534	0.0000 315 954	0.0000 283 942	0.0000 255 144	106
54	0.0000 304 175	0.0000 272 755	0.0000 244 553	0.0000 219 242	108
55	0.0000 263 198	0.0000 235 465	0.0000 210 629	0.0000 188 393	110
56	0.0000 227 743	0.0000 203 274	0.0000 181 413	0.0000 161 886	112
57	0.0000 197 065	0.0000 175 485	0.0000 156 250	0.0000 139 109	114
58	0.0000 170 521	0.0000 151 495	0.0000 134 578	0.0000 119 537	116
59	0.0000 147 553	0.0000 130 786	0.0000 115 912	0.0000 102 719	118
60	0.0000 127 679	0.0000 112 908	0.0000 099 835	0.0000 088 268	120

TABLE 3. SINKING FUND FACTORS
Payable at end of each period

	16% Nominal Annual Rate	16¼% Nominal Annual Rate	16½% Nominal Annual Rate	16¾% Nominal Annual Rate	
HALF YEARS					HALF YEARS
1	1.0000 000 000	1.0000 000 000	1.0000 000 000	1.0000 000 000	1
YEARS					
1	0.4807 692 308	0.4804 804 805	0.4801 920 768	0.4799 040 192	2
2	0.2219 208 045	0.2215 112 878	0.2211 026 314	0.2206 948 336	4
3	0.1363 153 862	0.1358 863 308	0.1354 585 973	0.1350 321 828	6
4	0.0940 147 606	0.0935 911 068	0.0931 692 077	0.0927 490 582	8
5	0.0690 294 887	0.0686 208 128	0.0682 142 953	0.0678 099 286	10
6	0.0526 950 169	0.0523 056 928	0.0519 188 989	0.0515 346 243	12
7	0.0412 968 528	0.0409 289 640	0.0405 639 419	0.0402 017 716	14
8	0.0329 768 720	0.0326 313 119	0.0322 889 169	0.0319 496 675	16
9	0.0267 020 959	0.0263 790 651	0.0260 594 578	0.0257 432 487	18
10	0.0218 522 088	0.0215 514 711	0.0212 543 737	0.0209 608 853	20
11	0.0180 320 684	0.0177 530 972	0.0174 779 414	0.0172 065 629	22
12	0.0149 779 616	0.0147 200 318	0.0144 660 509	0.0142 159 736	24
13	0.0125 071 267	0.0122 693 757	0.0120 356 670	0.0118 059 476	26
14	0.0104 889 057	0.0102 703 781	0.0100 559 473	0.0098 455 532	28
15	0.0088 274 334	0.0086 271 133	0.0084 309 086	0.0082 387 516	30
16	0.0074 508 132	0.0072 676 503	0.0070 885 879	0.0069 135 513	32
17	0.0063 041 101	0.0061 370 397	0.0059 740 247	0.0058 149 836	34
18	0.0053 446 741	0.0051 926 333	0.0050 445 759	0.0049 004 142	36
19	0.0045 389 361	0.0044 008 771	0.0042 667 060	0.0041 363 295	38
20	0.0038 601 615	0.0037 350 617	0.0036 137 343	0.0034 960 812	40
21	0.0032 868 407	0.0031 737 110	0.0030 642 218	0.0029 582 705	42
22	0.0028 015 156	0.0026 994 068	0.0026 007 930	0.0025 055 685	44
23	0.0023 899 085	0.0022 979 156	0.0022 092 622	0.0021 238 400	46
24	0.0020 402 660	0.0019 575 319	0.0018 779 743	0.0018 014 833	48
25	0.0017 428 582	0.0016 685 753	0.0015 973 012	0.0015 289 250	50
26	0.0014 895 903	0.0014 230 018	0.0013 592 518	0.0012 982 297	52
27	0.0012 737 003	0.0012 140 999	0.0011 571 677	0.0011 027 935	54
28	0.0010 895 180	0.0010 362 500	0.0009 854 810	0.0009 371 025	56
29	0.0009 322 748	0.0008 847 322	0.0008 395 228	0.0007 965 397	58
30	0.0007 979 488	0.0007 555 725	0.0007 153 675	0.0006 772 296	60
31	0.0006 831 404	0.0006 454 166	0.0006 097 076	0.0005 759 121	62
32	0.0005 849 701	0.0005 514 285	0.0005 197 512	0.0004 898 402	64
33	0.0005 009 950	0.0004 712 060	0.0004 431 377	0.0004 166 957	66
34	0.0004 291 391	0.0004 027 119	0.0003 778 688	0.0003 545 192	68
35	0.0003 676 362	0.0003 442 159	0.0003 222 506	0.0003 016 536	70
36	0.0003 149 823	0.0002 942 474	0.0002 748 459	0.0002 566 953	72
37	0.0002 698 950	0.0002 515 550	0.0002 344 344	0.0002 184 550	74
38	0.0002 312 801	0.0002 150 732	0.0001 999 791	0.0001 859 240	76
39	0.0001 982 037	0.0001 838 941	0.0001 705 982	0.0001 582 465	78
40	0.0001 698 677	0.0001 572 438	0.0001 455 416	0.0001 346 958	80
41	0.0001 455 900	0.0001 344 620	0.0001 241 706	0.0001 146 547	82
42	0.0001 247 876	0.0001 149 856	0.0001 059 418	0.0000 975 990	84
43	0.0001 069 615	0.0000 983 337	0.0000 903 919	0.0000 830 830	86
44	0.0000 916 847	0.0000 840 957	0.0000 771 266	0.0000 707 277	88
45	0.0000 785 920	0.0000 719 212	0.0000 658 095	0.0000 602 112	90
46	0.0000 673 705	0.0000 615 105	0.0000 561 542	0.0000 512 593	92
47	0.0000 577 524	0.0000 526 077	0.0000 479 163	0.0000 436 390	94
48	0.0000 495 083	0.0000 449 942	0.0000 408 875	0.0000 371 521	96
49	0.0000 424 417	0.0000 384 830	0.0000 348 902	0.0000 316 298	98
50	0.0000 363 841	0.0000 329 145	0.0000 297 728	0.0000 269 286	100
51	0.0000 311 915	0.0000 281 520	0.0000 254 063	0.0000 229 263	102
52	0.0000 267 402	0.0000 240 788	0.0000 216 803	0.0000 195 190	104
53	0.0000 229 243	0.0000 205 951	0.0000 185 009	0.0000 166 182	106
54	0.0000 196 531	0.0000 176 156	0.0000 157 879	0.0000 141 486	108
55	0.0000 168 488	0.0000 150 671	0.0000 134 727	0.0000 120 461	110
56	0.0000 144 447	0.0000 128 874	0.0000 114 971	0.0000 102 560	112
57	0.0000 123 837	0.0000 110 231	0.0000 098 113	0.0000 087 320	114
58	0.0000 106 168	0.0000 094 285	0.0000 083 726	0.0000 074 344	116
59	0.0000 091 020	0.0000 080 646	0.0000 071 449	0.0000 063 297	118
60	0.0000 078 034	0.0000 068 980	0.0000 060 973	0.0000 053 891	120

TABLE 3. SINKING FUND FACTORS
Payable at end of each period

SEMI ANNUAL Compounding

HALF YEARS	17% Nominal Annual Rate	17¼% Nominal Annual Rate	17½% Nominal Annual Rate	17¾% Nominal Annual Rate	HALF YEARS
1	1.0000 000 000	1.0000 000 000	1.0000 000 000	1.0000 000 000	1
YEARS					
1	0.4796 163 070	0.4793 289 395	0.4790 419 162	0.4787 552 364	2
2	0.2202 878 926	0.2198 818 067	0.2194 765 741	0.2190 721 931	4
3	0.1346 070 840	0.1341 832 978	0.1337 608 210	0.1333 396 506	6
4	0.0923 306 533	0.0919 139 879	0.0914 990 569	0.0910 858 553	8
5	0.0674 077 051	0.0670 076 171	0.0666 096 571	0.0662 138 172	10
6	0.0511 528 581	0.0507 735 894	0.0503 968 072	0.0500 225 006	12
7	0.0398 424 382	0.0394 859 266	0.0391 322 220	0.0387 813 092	14
8	0.0316 135 439	0.0312 805 261	0.0309 505 944	0.0306 237 289	16
9	0.0254 304 127	0.0251 209 242	0.0248 147 580	0.0245 118 886	18
10	0.0206 709 744	0.0203 846 094	0.0201 017 588	0.0198 223 912	20
11	0.0169 389 233	0.0166 749 847	0.0164 147 087	0.0161 580 575	22
12	0.0139 697 546	0.0137 273 488	0.0134 887 111	0.0132 537 967	24
13	0.0115 801 651	0.0113 582 671	0.0111 402 014	0.0109 259 163	26
14	0.0096 391 357	0.0094 366 355	0.0092 379 932	0.0090 431 499	28
15	0.0080 505 753	0.0078 663 130	0.0076 858 985	0.0075 092 663	30
16	0.0067 424 664	0.0065 752 597	0.0064 118 586	0.0062 521 911	32
17	0.0056 598 358	0.0055 085 015	0.0053 609 020	0.0052 169 595	34
18	0.0047 600 615	0.0046 234 324	0.0044 904 426	0.0043 610 090	36
19	0.0040 096 556	0.0038 865 937	0.0037 670 548	0.0036 509 515	38
20	0.0033 820 056	0.0032 714 128	0.0031 642 097	0.0030 603 050	40
21	0.0028 557 568	0.0027 565 823	0.0026 606 508	0.0025 678 681	42
22	0.0024 136 299	0.0023 248 761	0.0022 392 086	0.0021 565 309	44
23	0.0020 415 434	0.0019 622 696	0.0018 859 184	0.0018 123 921	46
24	0.0017 279 519	0.0016 572 763	0.0015 893 556	0.0015 240 916	48
25	0.0014 633 395	0.0014 004 404	0.0013 401 268	0.0012 823 009	50
26	0.0012 398 282	0.0011 839 436	0.0011 304 758	0.0010 793 279	52
27	0.0010 508 710	0.0010 012 978	0.0009 539 750	0.0009 088 075	54
28	0.0008 910 096	0.0008 471 016	0.0008 052 817	0.0007 654 567	56
29	0.0007 556 803	0.0007 168 461	0.0006 799 428	0.0006 448 800	58
30	0.0006 410 586	0.0006 067 590	0.0005 742 394	0.0005 434 121	60
31	0.0005 439 330	0.0005 136 780	0.0004 850 589	0.0004 579 914	62
32	0.0004 616 021	0.0004 349 478	0.0004 097 927	0.0003 860 563	64
33	0.0003 917 900	0.0003 683 356	0.0003 462 515	0.0003 254 610	66
34	0.0003 325 773	0.0003 119 618	0.0002 925 956	0.0002 744 060	68
35	0.0002 823 433	0.0002 642 423	0.0002 472 778	0.0002 313 808	70
36	0.0002 397 181	0.0002 238 411	0.0002 089 955	0.0001 951 165	72
37	0.0002 035 434	0.0001 896 306	0.0001 766 519	0.0001 645 464	74
38	0.0001 728 387	0.0001 606 584	0.0001 493 222	0.0001 387 734	76
39	0.0001 467 738	0.0001 361 195	0.0001 262 267	0.0001 170 425	78
40	0.0001 246 454	0.0001 153 337	0.0001 067 078	0.0000 987 183	80
41	0.0001 058 573	0.0000 977 256	0.0000 902 102	0.0000 832 656	82
42	0.0000 899 042	0.0000 828 082	0.0000 762 655	0.0000 702 337	84
43	0.0000 763 574	0.0000 701 698	0.0000 644 779	0.0000 592 428	86
44	0.0000 648 535	0.0000 594 616	0.0000 545 134	0.0000 499 728	88
45	0.0000 550 838	0.0000 503 885	0.0000 460 896	0.0000 421 541	90
46	0.0000 467 867	0.0000 427 005	0.0000 389 681	0.0000 355 591	92
47	0.0000 397 399	0.0000 361 860	0.0000 329 474	0.0000 299 963	94
48	0.0000 337 549	0.0000 306 658	0.0000 278 572	0.0000 253 039	96
49	0.0000 286 715	0.0000 259 879	0.0000 235 536	0.0000 213 458	98
50	0.0000 243 540	0.0000 220 237	0.0000 199 150	0.0000 180 069	100
51	0.0000 206 867	0.0000 186 644	0.0000 168 386	0.0000 151 904	102
52	0.0000 175 718	0.0000 158 176	0.0000 142 375	0.0000 128 145	104
53	0.0000 149 260	0.0000 134 051	0.0000 120 383	0.0000 108 102	106
54	0.0000 126 786	0.0000 113 605	0.0000 101 788	0.0000 091 195	108
55	0.0000 107 697	0.0000 096 279	0.0000 086 066	0.0000 076 932	110
56	0.0000 091 482	0.0000 081 595	0.0000 072 772	0.0000 064 900	112
57	0.0000 077 708	0.0000 069 151	0.0000 061 532	0.0000 054 750	114
58	0.0000 066 009	0.0000 058 605	0.0000 052 028	0.0000 046 187	116
59	0.0000 056 071	0.0000 049 667	0.0000 043 992	0.0000 038 964	118
60	0.0000 047 629	0.0000 042 093	0.0000 037 198	0.0000 032 870	120

TABLE 3. SINKING FUND FACTORS
Payable at end of each period

HALF YEARS	18% Nominal Annual Rate	18¼% Nominal Annual Rate	18½% Nominal Annual Rate	18¾% Nominal Annual Rate	HALF YEARS
1	1.0000 000 000	1.0000 000 000	1.0000 000 000	1.0000 000 000	1
YEARS					
1	0.4784 688 995	0.4781 829 050	0.4778 972 521	0.4776 119 403	2
2	0.2186 686 621	0.2182 659 792	0.2178 641 428	0.2174 631 511	4
3	0.1329 197 833	0.1325 012 160	0.1320 839 456	0.1316 679 688	6
4	0.0906 743 778	0.0902 646 196	0.0898 565 753	0.0894 502 400	8
5	0.0658 200 899	0.0654 284 674	0.0650 389 420	0.0646 515 060	10
6	0.0496 506 585	0.0492 812 699	0.0489 143 237	0.0485 498 088	12
7	0.0384 331 730	0.0380 877 984	0.0377 451 703	0.0374 052 733	14
8	0.0302 999 097	0.0299 791 168	0.0296 613 301	0.0293 465 298	16
9	0.0242 122 907	0.0239 159 387	0.0236 228 071	0.0233 328 706	18
10	0.0195 464 750	0.0192 739 788	0.0190 048 710	0.0187 391 203	20
11	0.0159 049 930	0.0156 554 771	0.0154 094 722	0.0151 669 404	22
12	0.0130 225 607	0.0127 949 585	0.0125 709 455	0.0123 504 777	24
13	0.0107 153 599	0.0105 084 809	0.0103 052 282	0.0101 055 510	26
14	0.0088 520 473	0.0086 646 273	0.0084 808 321	0.0083 006 047	28
15	0.0073 363 514	0.0071 670 893	0.0070 014 162	0.0068 392 688	30
16	0.0060 961 861	0.0059 437 732	0.0057 948 827	0.0056 494 458	32
17	0.0050 765 971	0.0049 397 392	0.0048 063 109	0.0046 762 384	34
18	0.0042 350 500	0.0041 124 849	0.0039 932 346	0.0038 772 209	36
19	0.0035 381 975	0.0034 287 085	0.0033 224 015	0.0032 191 950	38
20	0.0029 596 092	0.0028 620 347	0.0027 674 955	0.0026 759 075	40
21	0.0024 781 420	0.0023 913 824	0.0023 075 015	0.0022 264 131	42
22	0.0020 767 493	0.0019 997 720	0.0019 255 098	0.0018 538 756	44
23	0.0017 415 959	0.0016 734 373	0.0016 078 267	0.0015 446 767	46
24	0.0014 613 892	0.0014 011 561	0.0013 433 027	0.0012 877 422	48
25	0.0012 268 681	0.0011 737 367	0.0011 228 182	0.0010 740 267	50
26	0.0010 304 065	0.0009 836 213	0.0009 388 852	0.0008 961 142	52
27	0.0008 657 034	0.0008 245 744	0.0007 853 357	0.0007 479 053	54
28	0.0007 275 373	0.0006 914 375	0.0006 570 749	0.0006 243 705	56
29	0.0006 115 709	0.0005 799 324	0.0005 498 852	0.0005 213 530	58
30	0.0005 141 938	0.0004 865 044	0.0004 602 678	0.0004 354 113	60
31	0.0004 323 955	0.0004 081 947	0.0003 853 163	0.0003 636 911	62
32	0.0003 636 620	0.0003 425 371	0.0003 226 126	0.0003 038 227	64
33	0.0003 058 914	0.0002 874 736	0.0002 701 424	0.0002 538 360	66
34	0.0002 573 242	0.0002 412 850	0.0002 262 269	0.0002 120 920	68
35	0.0002 164 866	0.0002 025 339	0.0001 894 651	0.0001 772 258	70
36	0.0001 821 431	0.0001 700 180	0.0001 586 873	0.0001 481 003	72
37	0.0001 532 571	0.0001 427 305	0.0001 329 163	0.0001 237 677	74
38	0.0001 289 587	0.0001 198 283	0.0001 113 357	0.0001 034 373	76
39	0.0001 085 173	0.0001 006 050	0.0000 932 624	0.0000 864 495	78
40	0.0000 913 194	0.0000 844 684	0.0000 781 255	0.0000 722 538	80
41	0.0000 768 494	0.0000 709 220	0.0000 654 471	0.0000 603 906	82
42	0.0000 646 738	0.0000 595 496	0.0000 548 274	0.0000 504 763	84
43	0.0000 544 285	0.0000 500 017	0.0000 459 318	0.0000 421 903	86
44	0.0000 458 070	0.0000 419 854	0.0000 384 800	0.0000 352 651	88
45	0.0000 385 517	0.0000 352 547	0.0000 322 376	0.0000 294 769	90
46	0.0000 324 460	0.0000 296 034	0.0000 270 082	0.0000 246 390	92
47	0.0000 273 076	0.0000 248 583	0.0000 226 273	0.0000 205 953	94
48	0.0000 229 832	0.0000 208 739	0.0000 189 571	0.0000 172 154	96
49	0.0000 193 437	0.0000 175 283	0.0000 158 823	0.0000 143 902	98
50	0.0000 162 806	0.0000 147 190	0.0000 133 064	0.0000 120 287	100
51	0.0000 137 027	0.0000 123 600	0.0000 111 482	0.0000 100 548	102
52	0.0000 115 330	0.0000 103 791	0.0000 093 402	0.0000 084 049	104
53	0.0000 097 069	0.0000 087 157	0.0000 078 254	0.0000 070 257	106
54	0.0000 081 700	0.0000 073 189	0.0000 065 563	0.0000 058 728	108
55	0.0000 068 764	0.0000 061 460	0.0000 054 930	0.0000 049 092	110
56	0.0000 057 877	0.0000 051 611	0.0000 046 022	0.0000 041 036	112
57	0.0000 048 713	0.0000 043 340	0.0000 038 558	0.0000 034 303	114
58	0.0000 041 000	0.0000 036 395	0.0000 032 305	0.0000 028 674	116
59	0.0000 034 509	0.0000 030 562	0.0000 027 066	0.0000 023 969	118
60	0.0000 029 045	0.0000 025 665	0.0000 022 677	0.0000 020 036	120

TABLE 3. SINKING FUND FACTORS
Payable at end of each period

SEMI ANNUAL Compounding

HALF YEARS	19% Nominal Annual Rate	19¼% Nominal Annual Rate	19½% Nominal Annual Rate	19¾% Nominal Annual Rate	HALF YEARS
1	1.0000 000 000	1.0000 000 000	1.0000 000 000	1.0000 000 000	1
YEARS					
1	0.4773 269 690	0.4770 423 375	0.4767 580 453	0.4764 740 917	2
2	0.2170 630 025	0.2166 636 951	0.2162 652 273	0.2158 675 974	4
3	0.1312 532 826	0.1308 398 839	0.1304 277 693	0.1300 169 359	6
4	0.0890 456 084	0.0886 426 755	0.0882 414 362	0.0878 418 853	8
5	0.0642 661 517	0.0638 828 711	0.0635 016 567	0.0631 225 005	10
6	0.0481 877 142	0.0478 280 287	0.0474 707 411	0.0471 158 403	12
7	0.0370 680 923	0.0367 336 121	0.0364 018 174	0.0360 726 929	14
8	0.0290 346 957	0.0287 258 078	0.0284 198 461	0.0281 167 904	16
9	0.0230 461 037	0.0227 624 809	0.0224 819 766	0.0222 045 656	18
10	0.0184 766 953	0.0182 175 645	0.0179 616 966	0.0177 090 605	20
11	0.0149 278 440	0.0146 921 455	0.0144 598 073	0.0142 307 922	22
12	0.0121 335 107	0.0119 200 007	0.0117 099 039	0.0115 031 769	24
13	0.0099 093 986	0.0097 167 209	0.0095 274 680	0.0093 415 903	26
14	0.0081 238 883	0.0079 506 265	0.0077 807 635	0.0076 142 440	28
15	0.0066 805 845	0.0065 253 013	0.0063 733 578	0.0062 246 935	30
16	0.0055 073 947	0.0053 686 621	0.0052 331 817	0.0051 008 881	32
17	0.0045 494 491	0.0044 258 713	0.0043 054 344	0.0041 880 689	34
18	0.0037 643 673	0.0036 545 983	0.0035 478 397	0.0034 440 187	36
19	0.0031 190 090	0.0030 217 651	0.0029 273 865	0.0028 357 977	38
20	0.0025 871 883	0.0025 012 574	0.0024 180 358	0.0023 374 466	40
21	0.0021 480 333	0.0020 722 802	0.0019 990 738	0.0019 283 361	42
22	0.0017 847 847	0.0017 181 546	0.0016 539 050	0.0015 919 576	44
23	0.0014 839 025	0.0014 254 218	0.0013 691 546	0.0013 150 233	46
24	0.0012 343 905	0.0011 831 661	0.0011 339 900	0.0010 867 858	48
25	0.0010 272 796	0.0009 824 967	0.0009 396 008	0.0008 985 173	50
26	0.0008 552 274	0.0008 161 468	0.0007 787 971	0.0007 431 061	52
27	0.0007 122 048	0.0006 781 585	0.0006 456 939	0.0006 147 412	54
28	0.0005 932 484	0.0005 636 358	0.0005 354 631	0.0005 086 636	56
29	0.0004 942 633	0.0004 685 464	0.0004 441 358	0.0004 209 680	58
30	0.0004 118 653	0.0003 895 638	0.0003 684 435	0.0003 484 445	60
31	0.0003 432 532	0.0003 239 398	0.0003 056 915	0.0002 884 515	62
32	0.0002 861 053	0.0002 694 014	0.0002 536 548	0.0002 388 126	64
33	0.0002 384 958	0.0002 240 663	0.0002 104 953	0.0001 977 330	66
34	0.0001 988 252	0.0001 863 750	0.0001 746 924	0.0001 637 315	68
35	0.0001 657 648	0.0001 550 341	0.0001 449 883	0.0001 355 847	70
36	0.0001 382 097	0.0001 289 706	0.0001 203 412	0.0001 122 821	72
37	0.0001 152 405	0.0001 072 936	0.0000 998 882	0.0000 929 883	74
38	0.0000 960 925	0.0000 892 634	0.0000 829 143	0.0000 770 123	76
39	0.0000 801 288	0.0000 742 654	0.0000 688 268	0.0000 637 829	78
40	0.0000 668 189	0.0000 617 890	0.0000 571 343	0.0000 528 273	80
41	0.0000 557 212	0.0000 514 097	0.0000 474 291	0.0000 437 543	82
42	0.0000 464 676	0.0000 427 747	0.0000 393 731	0.0000 362 401	84
43	0.0000 387 513	0.0000 355 906	0.0000 326 859	0.0000 300 168	86
44	0.0000 323 168	0.0000 296 134	0.0000 271 348	0.0000 248 625	88
45	0.0000 269 511	0.0000 246 404	0.0000 225 267	0.0000 205 934	90
46	0.0000 224 764	0.0000 205 026	0.0000 187 013	0.0000 170 575	92
47	0.0000 187 449	0.0000 170 598	0.0000 155 256	0.0000 141 288	94
48	0.0000 156 329	0.0000 141 952	0.0000 128 892	0.0000 117 029	96
49	0.0000 130 377	0.0000 118 117	0.0000 107 006	0.0000 096 937	98
50	0.0000 108 733	0.0000 098 284	0.0000 088 836	0.0000 080 294	100
51	0.0000 090 683	0.0000 081 782	0.0000 073 752	0.0000 066 509	102
52	0.0000 075 629	0.0000 068 051	0.0000 061 230	0.0000 055 091	104
53	0.0000 063 075	0.0000 056 625	0.0000 050 833	0.0000 045 633	106
54	0.0000 052 604	0.0000 047 118	0.0000 042 202	0.0000 037 798	108
55	0.0000 043 872	0.0000 039 207	0.0000 035 037	0.0000 031 309	110
56	0.0000 036 590	0.0000 032 624	0.0000 029 088	0.0000 025 934	112
57	0.0000 030 516	0.0000 027 147	0.0000 024 149	0.0000 021 482	114
58	0.0000 025 451	0.0000 022 589	0.0000 020 049	0.0000 017 794	116
59	0.0000 021 226	0.0000 018 796	0.0000 016 645	0.0000 014 739	118
60	0.0000 017 703	0.0000 015 641	0.0000 013 819	0.0000 012 209	120

SEMI ANNUAL
Compounding

TABLE 3. SINKING FUND FACTORS
Payable at end of each period

HALF YEARS	20% Nominal Annual Rate	20¼% Nominal Annual Rate	20½% Nominal Annual Rate	20¾% Nominal Annual Rate	HALF YEARS
1	1.0000 000 000	1.0000 000 000	1.0000 000 000	1.0000 000 000	1
YEARS					
1	0.4761 904 762	0.4759 071 981	0.4756 242 568	0.4753 416 518	2
2	0.2154 708 037	0.2150 748 444	0.2146 797 179	0.2142 854 225	4
3	0.1296 073 804	0.1291 990 996	0.1287 920 905	0.1283 863 499	6
4	0.0874 440 176	0.0870 478 280	0.0866 533 114	0.0862 604 625	8
5	0.0627 453 949	0.0623 703 319	0.0619 973 037	0.0616 263 026	10
6	0.0467 633 151	0.0464 131 542	0.0460 653 465	0.0457 198 808	12
7	0.0357 462 232	0.0354 223 932	0.0351 011 874	0.0347 825 904	14
8	0.0278 166 207	0.0275 193 169	0.0272 248 588	0.0269 332 265	16
9	0.0219 302 222	0.0216 589 212	0.0213 906 371	0.0211 253 446	18
10	0.0174 596 248	0.0172 133 584	0.0169 702 304	0.0167 302 096	20
11	0.0140 050 630	0.0137 825 824	0.0135 633 137	0.0133 472 200	22
12	0.0112 997 764	0.0110 996 592	0.0109 027 827	0.0107 091 042	24
13	0.0091 590 386	0.0089 797 639	0.0088 037 179	0.0086 308 524	26
14	0.0074 510 132	0.0072 910 166	0.0071 342 004	0.0069 805 114	28
15	0.0060 792 483	0.0059 369 627	0.0057 977 783	0.0056 616 370	30
16	0.0049 717 167	0.0048 456 038	0.0047 224 866	0.0046 023 031	32
17	0.0040 737 064	0.0039 622 794	0.0038 537 218	0.0037 479 682	34
18	0.0033 430 638	0.0032 449 047	0.0031 494 723	0.0030 566 992	36
19	0.0027 469 250	0.0026 606 959	0.0025 770 396	0.0024 958 869	38
20	0.0022 594 144	0.0021 838 656	0.0021 107 281	0.0020 399 319	40
21	0.0018 599 911	0.0017 939 646	0.0017 301 844	0.0016 685 801	42
22	0.0015 322 365	0.0014 746 678	0.0014 191 797	0.0013 657 024	44
23	0.0012 629 527	0.0012 128 697	0.0011 647 035	0.0011 183 857	46
24	0.0010 414 797	0.0009 980 001	0.0009 562 779	0.0009 162 463	48
25	0.0008 591 740	0.0008 215 016	0.0007 854 330	0.0007 509 037	50
26	0.0007 090 040	0.0006 764 238	0.0006 453 010	0.0006 155 736	52
27	0.0005 852 336	0.0005 571 066	0.0005 302 988	0.0005 047 510	54
28	0.0004 831 734	0.0004 589 311	0.0004 358 783	0.0004 139 590	56
29	0.0003 989 822	0.0003 781 207	0.0003 583 280	0.0003 395 514	58
30	0.0003 295 092	0.0003 115 833	0.0002 946 147	0.0002 785 541	60
31	0.0002 721 660	0.0002 567 840	0.0002 422 568	0.0002 285 385	62
32	0.0002 248 244	0.0002 116 425	0.0001 992 218	0.0001 875 195	64
33	0.0001 857 328	0.0001 744 504	0.0001 638 438	0.0001 538 737	66
34	0.0001 534 487	0.0001 438 033	0.0001 347 565	0.0001 262 722	68
35	0.0001 267 834	0.0001 185 465	0.0001 108 387	0.0001 036 267	70
36	0.0001 047 566	0.0000 977 300	0.0000 911 698	0.0000 850 457	72
37	0.0000 865 600	0.0000 805 717	0.0000 749 938	0.0000 697 987	74
38	0.0000 715 264	0.0000 664 278	0.0000 616 896	0.0000 572 866	76
39	0.0000 591 054	0.0000 547 681	0.0000 507 467	0.0000 470 185	78
40	0.0000 488 424	0.0000 451 559	0.0000 417 458	0.0000 385 916	80
41	0.0000 403 622	0.0000 372 314	0.0000 343 419	0.0000 316 754	82
42	0.0000 333 549	0.0000 306 979	0.0000 282 515	0.0000 259 990	84
43	0.0000 275 644	0.0000 253 113	0.0000 232 414	0.0000 213 401	86
44	0.0000 227 794	0.0000 208 700	0.0000 191 200	0.0000 175 161	88
45	0.0000 188 252	0.0000 172 082	0.0000 157 296	0.0000 143 775	90
46	0.0000 155 575	0.0000 141 890	0.0000 129 404	0.0000 118 013	92
47	0.0000 128 571	0.0000 116 995	0.0000 106 459	0.0000 096 868	94
48	0.0000 106 255	0.0000 096 469	0.0000 087 582	0.0000 079 512	96
49	0.0000 087 812	0.0000 079 544	0.0000 072 053	0.0000 065 266	98
50	0.0000 072 571	0.0000 065 589	0.0000 059 277	0.0000 053 572	100
51	0.0000 059 975	0.0000 054 082	0.0000 048 767	0.0000 043 974	102
52	0.0000 049 566	0.0000 044 594	0.0000 040 121	0.0000 036 095	104
53	0.0000 040 963	0.0000 036 771	0.0000 033 007	0.0000 029 628	106
54	0.0000 033 854	0.0000 030 320	0.0000 027 155	0.0000 024 320	108
55	0.0000 027 978	0.0000 025 001	0.0000 022 340	0.0000 019 963	110
56	0.0000 023 122	0.0000 020 615	0.0000 018 379	0.0000 016 386	112
57	0.0000 019 109	0.0000 016 998	0.0000 015 121	0.0000 013 450	114
58	0.0000 015 793	0.0000 014 016	0.0000 012 440	0.0000 011 041	116
59	0.0000 013 052	0.0000 011 557	0.0000 010 234	0.0000 009 062	118
60	0.0000 010 787	0.0000 009 530	0.0000 008 420	0.0000 007 439	120

TABLE 3. SINKING FUND FACTORS
Payable at end of each period

SEMI ANNUAL Compounding

HALF YEARS	21% Nominal Annual Rate	21¼% Nominal Annual Rate	21½% Nominal Annual Rate	21¾% Nominal Annual Rate	HALF YEARS
1	1.0000 000 000	1.0000 000 000	1.0000 000 000	1.0000 000 000	1
YEARS					
1	0.4750 593 824	0.4747 774 481	0.4744 958 482	0.4742 145 821	2
2	0.2138 919 564	0.2134 993 179	0.2131 075 054	0.2127 165 172	4
3	0.1279 818 746	0.1275 786 615	0.1271 767 074	0.1267 760 091	6
4	0.0858 692 763	0.0854 797 475	0.0850 918 710	0.0847 056 417	8
5	0.0612 573 206	0.0608 903 500	0.0605 253 827	0.0601 624 111	10
6	0.0453 767 456	0.0450 359 299	0.0446 974 223	0.0443 612 116	12
7	0.0344 665 871	0.0341 531 619	0.0338 422 994	0.0335 339 845	14
8	0.0266 443 997	0.0263 583 584	0.0260 750 826	0.0257 945 522	16
9	0.0208 630 182	0.0206 036 329	0.0203 471 632	0.0200 935 839	18
10	0.0164 932 653	0.0162 593 665	0.0160 284 825	0.0158 005 828	20
11	0.0131 342 647	0.0129 244 114	0.0127 176 237	0.0125 138 656	22
12	0.0105 185 815	0.0103 311 724	0.0101 468 353	0.0099 655 287	24
13	0.0084 611 196	0.0082 944 723	0.0081 308 633	0.0079 702 463	26
14	0.0068 298 968	0.0066 823 043	0.0065 376 822	0.0063 959 794	28
15	0.0055 284 815	0.0053 982 554	0.0052 709 028	0.0051 463 686	30
16	0.0044 849 922	0.0043 704 939	0.0042 587 487	0.0041 496 984	32
17	0.0036 449 545	0.0035 446 177	0.0034 468 959	0.0033 517 282	34
18	0.0029 665 187	0.0028 788 659	0.0027 936 768	0.0027 108 889	36
19	0.0024 171 697	0.0023 408 217	0.0022 667 780	0.0021 949 751	38
20	0.0019 714 084	0.0019 050 905	0.0018 409 132	0.0017 788 126	40
21	0.0016 090 833	0.0015 516 273	0.0014 961 470	0.0014 425 795	42
22	0.0013 141 681	0.0012 645 110	0.0012 166 672	0.0011 705 747	44
23	0.0010 738 498	0.0010 310 314	0.0009 898 682	0.0009 502 999	46
24	0.0008 778 407	0.0008 409 988	0.0008 056 601	0.0007 717 668	48
25	0.0007 178 512	0.0006 862 157	0.0006 559 393	0.0006 269 663	50
26	0.0005 871 820	0.0005 600 689	0.0005 341 792	0.0005 094 601	52
27	0.0004 804 064	0.0004 572 108	0.0004 351 120	0.0004 140 602	54
28	0.0003 931 196	0.0003 733 088	0.0003 544 778	0.0003 365 797	56
29	0.0003 217 406	0.0003 048 476	0.0002 888 266	0.0002 736 339	58
30	0.0002 633 544	0.0002 489 708	0.0002 353 608	0.0002 224 840	60
31	0.0002 155 851	0.0002 033 554	0.0001 918 099	0.0001 809 114	62
32	0.0001 764 952	0.0001 661 106	0.0001 563 294	0.0001 471 173	64
33	0.0001 445 028	0.0001 356 958	0.0001 274 197	0.0001 196 429	66
34	0.0001 183 160	0.0001 108 558	0.0001 038 613	0.0000 973 040	68
35	0.0000 968 792	0.0000 905 668	0.0000 846 621	0.0000 791 391	70
36	0.0000 793 292	0.0000 739 937	0.0000 690 142	0.0000 643 672	72
37	0.0000 649 605	0.0000 604 551	0.0000 562 599	0.0000 523 540	74
38	0.0000 531 957	0.0000 493 948	0.0000 458 638	0.0000 425 837	76
39	0.0000 435 624	0.0000 403 588	0.0000 373 894	0.0000 346 373	78
40	0.0000 356 742	0.0000 329 762	0.0000 304 813	0.0000 281 742	80
41	0.0000 292 148	0.0000 269 445	0.0000 248 498	0.0000 229 173	82
42	0.0000 239 253	0.0000 220 162	0.0000 202 589	0.0000 186 414	84
43	0.0000 195 936	0.0000 179 895	0.0000 165 163	0.0000 151 634	86
44	0.0000 160 463	0.0000 146 994	0.0000 134 652	0.0000 123 344	88
45	0.0000 131 413	0.0000 120 111	0.0000 109 778	0.0000 100 333	90
46	0.0000 107 623	0.0000 098 145	0.0000 089 500	0.0000 081 615	92
47	0.0000 088 140	0.0000 080 196	0.0000 072 967	0.0000 066 389	94
48	0.0000 072 184	0.0000 065 530	0.0000 059 489	0.0000 054 004	96
49	0.0000 059 117	0.0000 053 546	0.0000 048 500	0.0000 043 929	98
50	0.0000 048 415	0.0000 043 754	0.0000 039 541	0.0000 035 734	100
51	0.0000 039 651	0.0000 035 753	0.0000 032 237	0.0000 029 068	102
52	0.0000 032 473	0.0000 029 215	0.0000 026 283	0.0000 023 645	104
53	0.0000 026 595	0.0000 023 872	0.0000 021 428	0.0000 019 234	106
54	0.0000 021 781	0.0000 019 507	0.0000 017 470	0.0000 015 646	108
55	0.0000 017 838	0.0000 015 939	0.0000 014 243	0.0000 012 727	110
56	0.0000 014 609	0.0000 013 025	0.0000 011 612	0.0000 010 353	112
57	0.0000 011 964	0.0000 010 643	0.0000 009 467	0.0000 008 422	114
58	0.0000 009 799	0.0000 008 697	0.0000 007 719	0.0000 006 851	116
59	0.0000 008 025	0.0000 007 106	0.0000 006 293	0.0000 005 573	118
60	0.0000 006 572	0.0000 005 807	0.0000 005 131	0.0000 004 533	120

SEMI ANNUAL
Compounding

TABLE 3. SINKING FUND FACTORS
Payable at end of each period

HALF YEARS	22% Nominal Annual Rate	22¼% Nominal Annual Rate	22½% Nominal Annual Rate	22¾% Nominal Annual Rate	HALF YEARS
1	1.0000 000 000	1.0000 000 000	1.0000 000 000	1.0000 000 000	1
YEARS					
1	0.4739 336 493	0.4736 530 491	0.4733 727 811	0.4730 928 445	2
2	0.2123 263 515	0.2119 370 068	0.2115 484 812	0.2111 607 731	4
3	0.1263 765 636	0.1259 783 676	0.1255 814 180	0.1251 857 117	6
4	0.0843 210 542	0.0839 381 035	0.0835 567 844	0.0831 770 916	8
5	0.0598 014 271	0.0594 424 229	0.0590 853 907	0.0587 303 224	10
6	0.0440 272 864	0.0436 956 355	0.0433 662 475	0.0430 391 111	12
7	0.0332 282 015	0.0329 249 352	0.0326 241 702	0.0323 258 911	14
8	0.0255 167 470	0.0252 416 471	0.0249 692 325	0.0246 994 832	16
9	0.0198 428 701	0.0195 949 964	0.0193 499 379	0.0191 076 696	18
10	0.0155 756 369	0.0153 536 142	0.0151 344 846	0.0149 182 178	20
11	0.0123 131 011	0.0121 152 944	0.0119 204 101	0.0117 284 128	22
12	0.0097 872 113	0.0096 118 422	0.0094 393 810	0.0092 697 872	24
13	0.0078 125 750	0.0076 578 038	0.0075 058 873	0.0073 567 808	26
14	0.0062 571 454	0.0061 211 302	0.0059 878 842	0.0058 573 587	28
15	0.0050 245 985	0.0049 055 387	0.0047 891 363	0.0046 753 392	30
16	0.0040 432 854	0.0039 394 532	0.0038 381 462	0.0037 393 094	32
17	0.0032 590 547	0.0031 688 168	0.0030 809 569	0.0029 954 182	34
18	0.0026 304 409	0.0025 522 727	0.0024 763 254	0.0024 025 415	36
19	0.0021 253 508	0.0020 578 446	0.0019 923 971	0.0019 289 505	38
20	0.0017 187 267	0.0016 605 950	0.0016 043 586	0.0015 499 599	40
21	0.0013 908 633	0.0013 409 387	0.0012 927 477	0.0012 462 337	42
22	0.0011 261 735	0.0010 834 051	0.0010 422 130	0.0010 025 424	44
23	0.0009 122 683	0.0008 757 167	0.0008 405 907	0.0008 068 374	46
24	0.0007 392 624	0.0007 080 931	0.0006 782 064	0.0006 495 520	48
25	0.0005 992 433	0.0005 727 187	0.0005 473 428	0.0005 230 679	50
26	0.0004 858 607	0.0004 633 325	0.0004 418 286	0.0004 213 041	52
27	0.0003 940 076	0.0003 749 085	0.0003 567 191	0.0003 393 974	54
28	0.0003 195 698	0.0003 034 055	0.0002 880 461	0.0002 734 526	56
29	0.0002 592 282	0.0002 455 697	0.0002 326 208	0.0002 203 455	58
30	0.0002 103 020	0.0001 987 783	0.0001 878 780	0.0001 775 685	60
31	0.0001 706 244	0.0001 609 155	0.0001 517 528	0.0001 431 064	62
32	0.0001 384 421	0.0001 302 731	0.0001 225 813	0.0001 153 394	64
33	0.0001 123 361	0.0001 054 713	0.0000 990 224	0.0000 929 644	66
34	0.0000 911 570	0.0000 853 950	0.0000 799 945	0.0000 749 329	68
35	0.0000 739 735	0.0000 691 426	0.0000 646 250	0.0000 604 007	70
36	0.0000 600 309	0.0000 559 849	0.0000 522 099	0.0000 486 880	72
37	0.0000 487 175	0.0000 453 321	0.0000 421 807	0.0000 392 473	74
38	0.0000 395 369	0.0000 367 070	0.0000 340 787	0.0000 316 378	76
39	0.0000 320 868	0.0000 297 233	0.0000 275 332	0.0000 255 039	78
40	0.0000 260 410	0.0000 240 687	0.0000 222 452	0.0000 205 595	80
41	0.0000 211 345	0.0000 194 899	0.0000 179 730	0.0000 165 738	82
42	0.0000 171 526	0.0000 157 824	0.0000 145 213	0.0000 133 609	84
43	0.0000 139 210	0.0000 127 802	0.0000 117 327	0.0000 107 708	86
44	0.0000 112 984	0.0000 103 491	0.0000 094 795	0.0000 086 829	88
45	0.0000 091 698	0.0000 083 806	0.0000 076 591	0.0000 069 998	90
46	0.0000 074 423	0.0000 067 865	0.0000 061 883	0.0000 056 429	92
47	0.0000 060 403	0.0000 054 956	0.0000 050 000	0.0000 045 491	94
48	0.0000 049 024	0.0000 044 503	0.0000 040 399	0.0000 036 673	96
49	0.0000 039 788	0.0000 036 038	0.0000 032 641	0.0000 029 564	98
50	0.0000 032 293	0.0000 029 183	0.0000 026 373	0.0000 023 834	100
51	0.0000 026 210	0.0000 023 632	0.0000 021 309	0.0000 019 214	102
52	0.0000 021 272	0.0000 019 137	0.0000 017 217	0.0000 015 489	104
53	0.0000 017 265	0.0000 015 497	0.0000 013 911	0.0000 012 487	106
54	0.0000 014 013	0.0000 012 550	0.0000 011 240	0.0000 010 067	108
55	0.0000 011 373	0.0000 010 163	0.0000 009 081	0.0000 008 115	110
56	0.0000 009 230	0.0000 008 230	0.0000 007 338	0.0000 006 542	112
57	0.0000 007 492	0.0000 006 664	0.0000 005 929	0.0000 005 274	114
58	0.0000 006 080	0.0000 005 397	0.0000 004 790	0.0000 004 252	116
59	0.0000 004 935	0.0000 004 370	0.0000 003 870	0.0000 003 428	118
60	0.0000 004 005	0.0000 003 539	0.0000 003 127	0.0000 002 763	120

TABLE 4. PRESENT WORTH OF ONE DOLLAR
Payable at end of each period

HALF YEARS	5% Nominal Annual Rate	5¼% Nominal Annual Rate	5½% Nominal Annual Rate	5¾% Nominal Annual Rate	HALF YEARS
1	0.9756 097 561	0.9744 214 373	0.9732 360 097	0.9720 534 629	1
YEARS					
1	0.9518 143 962	0.9494 971 374	0.9471 883 306	0.9448 879 348	2
2	0.9059 506 448	0.9015 448 140	0.8971 657 337	0.8928 132 094	4
3	0.8622 968 660	0.8560 142 201	0.8497 849 136	0.8436 084 296	6
4	0.8207 465 708	0.8127 830 516	0.8049 063 537	0.7971 154 268	8
5	0.7811 984 017	0.7717 351 808	0.7623 979 055	0.7531 847 494	10
6	0.7435 558 850	0.7327 603 450	0.7221 343 994	0.7116 751 824	12
7	0.7077 271 958	0.6957 538 500	0.6839 972 763	0.6724 532 934	14
8	0.6736 249 335	0.6606 162 889	0.6478 742 383	0.6353 930 036	16
9	0.6411 659 093	0.6272 532 753	0.6136 589 182	0.6003 751 830	18
10	0.6102 709 429	0.5955 751 893	0.5812 505 663	0.5672 872 668	20
11	0.5808 646 690	0.5654 969 374	0.5505 537 536	0.5360 228 940	22
12	0.5528 753 542	0.5369 377 232	0.5214 780 908	0.5064 815 653	24
13	0.5262 347 214	0.5098 208 312	0.4939 379 623	0.4785 683 203	26
14	0.5008 777 836	0.4840 734 198	0.4678 522 739	0.4521 934 318	28
15	0.4767 426 852	0.4596 263 264	0.4431 442 143	0.4272 721 179	30
16	0.4537 705 510	0.4364 138 812	0.4197 410 286	0.4037 242 691	32
17	0.4319 053 430	0.4143 737 309	0.3975 738 042	0.3814 741 909	34
18	0.4110 937 233	0.3934 466 713	0.3765 772 679	0.3604 503 604	36
19	0.3912 849 240	0.3735 764 882	0.3566 895 937	0.3405 851 966	38
20	0.3724 306 237	0.3547 098 061	0.3378 522 208	0.3218 148 431	40
21	0.3544 848 292	0.3367 959 455	0.3200 096 811	0.3040 789 625	42
22	0.3374 037 637	0.3197 867 862	0.3031 094 356	0.2873 205 429	44
23	0.3211 457 596	0.3036 366 380	0.2871 017 203	0.2714 857 144	46
24	0.3056 711 573	0.2883 021 186	0.2719 393 992	0.2565 235 760	48
25	0.2909 422 080	0.2737 420 364	0.2575 778 255	0.2423 860 319	50
26	0.2769 229 820	0.2599 172 799	0.2439 747 106	0.2290 276 371	52
27	0.2635 792 809	0.2467 907 132	0.2310 899 988	0.2164 054 511	54
28	0.2508 785 541	0.2343 270 758	0.2188 857 502	0.2044 788 998	56
29	0.2387 898 195	0.2224 928 877	0.2073 260 284	0.1932 096 453	58
30	0.2272 835 879	0.2112 563 599	0.1963 767 947	0.1825 614 627	60
31	0.2163 317 910	0.2005 873 090	0.1860 058 083	0.1725 001 235	62
32	0.2059 077 130	0.1904 570 757	0.1761 825 311	0.1629 932 854	64
33	0.1959 859 255	0.1808 384 482	0.1668 780 375	0.1540 103 889	66
34	0.1865 422 253	0.1717 055 889	0.1580 649 298	0.1455 225 583	68
35	0.1775 535 756	0.1630 339 651	0.1497 172 570	0.1375 025 096	70
36	0.1689 980 493	0.1548 002 832	0.1418 104 387	0.1299 244 623	72
37	0.1608 547 763	0.1469 824 258	0.1343 211 927	0.1227 640 569	74
38	0.1531 038 918	0.1395 593 925	0.1272 274 663	0.1159 982 762	76
39	0.1457 264 883	0.1325 112 437	0.1205 083 714	0.1096 053 716	78
40	0.1387 045 695	0.1258 190 465	0.1141 441 231	0.1035 647 932	80
41	0.1320 210 060	0.1194 648 245	0.1081 159 814	0.0978 571 236	82
42	0.1256 594 941	0.1134 315 089	0.1024 061 960	0.0924 640 154	84
43	0.1196 045 155	0.1077 028 930	0.0969 979 538	0.0873 681 326	86
44	0.1138 412 997	0.1022 635 886	0.0918 753 299	0.0825 530 943	88
45	0.1083 557 880	0.0970 989 846	0.0870 232 404	0.0780 034 228	90
46	0.1031 345 989	0.0921 952 080	0.0824 273 978	0.0737 044 931	92
47	0.0981 649 960	0.0875 390 860	0.0780 742 693	0.0696 424 863	94
48	0.0934 348 564	0.0831 181 116	0.0739 510 368	0.0658 043 450	96
49	0.0889 326 414	0.0789 204 090	0.0700 455 591	0.0621 777 317	98
50	0.0846 473 684	0.0749 347 025	0.0663 463 362	0.0587 509 885	100
51	0.0805 685 838	0.0711 502 855	0.0628 424 754	0.0555 131 002	102
52	0.0766 863 380	0.0675 569 924	0.0595 236 594	0.0524 536 586	104
53	0.0729 911 605	0.0641 451 709	0.0563 801 156	0.0495 628 291	106
54	0.0694 740 373	0.0609 056 561	0.0534 025 876	0.0468 313 193	108
55	0.0661 263 889	0.0578 297 462	0.0505 823 078	0.0442 503 485	110
56	0.0629 400 489	0.0549 091 784	0.0479 109 717	0.0418 116 204	112
57	0.0599 072 447	0.0521 361 077	0.0453 807 133	0.0395 072 957	114
58	0.0570 205 779	0.0495 030 851	0.0429 840 820	0.0373 299 670	116
59	0.0542 730 069	0.0470 030 376	0.0407 140 209	0.0352 726 355	118
60	0.0516 578 293	0.0446 292 496	0.0385 638 455	0.0333 286 877	120

SEMI ANNUAL
Compounding

TABLE 4. PRESENT WORTH OF ONE DOLLAR
Payable at end of each period

HALF YEARS	6% Nominal Annual Rate	6¼% Nominal Annual Rate	6½% Nominal Annual Rate	6¾% Nominal Annual Rate	HALF YEARS
1	0.9708 737 864	0.9696 969 697	0.9685 230 024	0.9673 518 742	1
YEARS					
1	0.9425 959 091	0.9403 122 130	0.9380 368 062	0.9357 696 486	2
2	0.8884 870 479	0.8841 870 580	0.8799 130 498	0.8756 648 352	4
3	0.8374 842 567	0.8314 118 892	0.8253 908 270	0.8194 205 752	6
4	0.7894 092 343	0.7817 867 535	0.7742 469 752	0.7667 889 037	8
5	0.7440 939 149	0.7351 236 323	0.7262 721 599	0.7175 377 830	10
6	0.7013 798 802	0.6912 457 296	0.6812 700 173	0.6714 500 790	12
7	0.6611 178 058	0.6499 868 017	0.6390 563 512	0.6283 226 045	14
8	0.6231 669 392	0.6111 905 280	0.5994 583 787	0.5879 652 228	16
9	0.5873 946 076	0.5747 099 180	0.5623 140 230	0.5502 000 100	18
10	0.5536 757 542	0.5404 067 548	0.5274 712 502	0.5148 604 700	20
11	0.5218 925 009	0.5081 510 716	0.4947 874 469	0.4817 908 011	22
12	0.4919 337 363	0.4778 206 586	0.4641 288 365	0.4508 452 086	24
13	0.4636 947 274	0.4493 006 010	0.4353 699 314	0.4218 872 624	26
14	0.4370 767 532	0.4224 828 424	0.4083 930 200	0.3947 892 953	28
15	0.4119 867 595	0.3972 657 765	0.3830 876 842	0.3694 318 402	30
16	0.3883 370 341	0.3735 538 615	0.3593 503 478	0.3457 031 032	32
17	0.3660 448 997	0.3512 572 582	0.3370 838 525	0.3234 984 714	34
18	0.3450 324 251	0.3302 914 898	0.3161 970 605	0.3027 200 510	36
19	0.3252 261 524	0.3105 771 217	0.2966 044 807	0.2832 762 357	38
20	0.3065 568 408	0.2920 394 606	0.2782 259 198	0.2650 813 035	40
21	0.2889 592 240	0.2746 082 715	0.2609 861 532	0.2480 550 383	42
22	0.2723 717 825	0.2582 175 115	0.2448 146 176	0.2321 223 760	44
23	0.2567 365 279	0.2428 050 797	0.2296 451 220	0.2172 130 742	46
24	0.2419 988 009	0.2283 125 818	0.2154 155 769	0.2032 614 021	48
25	0.2281 070 798	0.2146 851 091	0.2020 677 397	0.1902 058 508	50
26	0.2150 128 003	0.2018 710 300	0.1895 469 772	0.1779 888 622	52
27	0.2026 701 859	0.1898 217 950	0.1778 020 411	0.1665 565 750	54
28	0.1910 360 882	0.1784 917 521	0.1667 848 588	0.1558 585 877	56
29	0.1800 698 352	0.1678 379 745	0.1564 503 363	0.1458 477 358	58
30	0.1697 330 900	0.1578 200 972	0.1467 561 738	0.1364 798 845	60
31	0.1599 897 163	0.1484 001 649	0.1376 626 925	0.1277 137 336	62
32	0.1508 056 521	0.1395 424 874	0.1291 326 724	0.1195 106 356	64
33	0.1421 487 907	0.1312 135 052	0.1211 311 996	0.1118 344 255	66
34	0.1339 888 686	0.1233 816 614	0.1136 255 236	0.1046 512 610	68
35	0.1262 973 594	0.1160 172 831	0.1065 849 233	0.0979 294 738	70
36	0.1190 473 743	0.1090 924 682	0.0999 805 810	0.0916 394 292	72
37	0.1122 135 680	0.1025 809 802	0.0937 854 649	0.0857 533 965	74
38	0.1057 720 502	0.0964 581 485	0.0879 742 180	0.0802 454 257	76
39	0.0997 003 018	0.0907 007 751	0.0825 230 545	0.0750 912 338	78
40	0.0939 770 966	0.0852 870 466	0.0774 096 625	0.0702 680 975	80
41	0.0885 824 268	0.0801 964 515	0.0726 131 125	0.0657 547 529	82
42	0.0834 974 332	0.0754 097 028	0.0681 137 722	0.0615 313 020	84
43	0.0787 043 389	0.0709 086 645	0.0638 932 253	0.0575 791 249	86
44	0.0741 863 879	0.0666 762 833	0.0599 341 970	0.0538 807 974	88
45	0.0699 277 857	0.0626 965 235	0.0562 204 827	0.0504 200 149	90
46	0.0659 136 448	0.0589 543 067	0.0527 368 821	0.0471 815 196	92
47	0.0621 299 319	0.0554 354 546	0.0494 691 364	0.0441 510 340	94
48	0.0585 634 197	0.0521 266 350	0.0464 038 708	0.0413 151 976	96
49	0.0552 016 398	0.0490 153 115	0.0435 285 387	0.0386 615 079	98
50	0.0520 328 399	0.0460 896 961	0.0408 313 714	0.0361 782 657	100
51	0.0490 459 420	0.0433 387 041	0.0383 013 293	0.0338 545 230	102
52	0.0462 305 043	0.0407 519 128	0.0359 280 566	0.0316 800 351	104
53	0.0435 766 842	0.0383 195 213	0.0337 018 394	0.0296 452 153	106
54	0.0410 752 043	0.0360 323 139	0.0316 135 658	0.0277 410 927	108
55	0.0387 173 195	0.0338 816 248	0.0296 546 883	0.0259 592 726	110
56	0.0364 947 870	0.0318 593 056	0.0278 171 891	0.0242 918 994	112
57	0.0343 998 369	0.0299 576 941	0.0260 935 472	0.0227 316 221	114
58	0.0324 251 455	0.0281 695 857	0.0244 767 077	0.0212 715 621	116
59	0.0305 638 095	0.0264 882 054	0.0229 600 527	0.0199 052 821	118
60	0.0288 093 218	0.0249 071 831	0.0215 373 745	0.0186 267 589	120

TABLE 4. PRESENT WORTH OF ONE DOLLAR
Payable at end of each period

SEMI ANNUAL Compounding

HALF YEARS	7% Nominal Annual Rate	7¼% Nominal Annual Rate	7½% Nominal Annual Rate	7¾% Nominal Annual Rate	HALF YEARS
1	0.9661 835 749	0.9650 180 941	0.9638 554 217	0.9626 955 475	1
YEARS					
1	0.9335 107 004	0.9312 599 219	0.9290 172 739	0.9267 827 172	2
2	0.8714 422 277	0.8672 450 422	0.8630 730 952	0.8589 262 050	4
3	0.8135 006 443	0.8076 305 503	0.8018 098 141	0.7960 379 622	6
4	0.7594 115 562	0.7521 139 632	0.7448 951 677	0.7377 542 256	8
5	0.7089 188 137	0.7004 135 906	0.6920 204 781	0.6837 378 658	10
6	0.6617 832 983	0.6522 671 057	0.6428 989 780	0.6336 764 372	12
7	0.6177 817 903	0.6074 302 139	0.5972 642 560	0.5872 803 703	14
8	0.5767 059 117	0.5656 754 136	0.5548 688 109	0.5442 812 974	16
9	0.5383 611 396	0.5267 908 415	0.5154 827 101	0.5044 304 997	18
10	0.5025 658 844	0.4905 791 979	0.4788 923 421	0.4674 974 692	20
11	0.4691 506 308	0.4568 567 456	0.4448 992 581	0.4332 685 748	22
12	0.4379 571 339	0.4254 523 772	0.4133 190 959	0.4015 458 271	24
13	0.4088 376 708	0.3962 067 476	0.3839 805 798	0.3721 457 327	26
14	0.3816 543 404	0.3689 714 648	0.3567 245 915	0.3448 982 334	28
15	0.3562 784 106	0.3436 083 375	0.3314 033 075	0.3196 457 219	30
16	0.3325 897 086	0.3199 886 736	0.3078 793 973	0.2962 421 307	32
17	0.3104 760 518	0.2979 926 271	0.2860 252 784	0.2745 520 868	34
18	0.2898 327 166	0.2775 085 907	0.2657 224 244	0.2544 501 291	36
19	0.2705 619 422	0.2584 326 285	0.2468 607 223	0.2358 199 820	38
20	0.2525 724 682	0.2406 679 494	0.2293 378 753	0.2185 538 837	40
21	0.2357 791 017	0.2241 244 158	0.2130 588 477	0.2025 519 622	42
22	0.2201 023 143	0.2087 180 860	0.1979 353 499	0.1877 216 579	44
23	0.2054 678 656	0.1943 707 884	0.1838 853 592	0.1739 771 882	46
24	0.1918 064 511	0.1810 097 253	0.1708 326 751	0.1612 390 512	48
25	0.1790 533 745	0.1685 671 026	0.1587 065 061	0.1494 335 660	50
26	0.1671 482 411	0.1569 797 868	0.1474 410 856	0.1384 924 464	52
27	0.1560 346 716	0.1461 889 840	0.1369 753 154	0.1283 524 058	54
28	0.1456 600 355	0.1361 399 418	0.1272 524 341	0.1189 547 914	56
29	0.1359 752 018	0.1267 816 716	0.1182 197 095	0.1102 452 448	58
30	0.1269 343 059	0.1180 666 896	0.1098 281 522	0.1021 733 875	60
31	0.1184 945 328	0.1099 507 761	0.1020 322 506	0.0946 925 297	62
32	0.1106 159 143	0.1023 927 512	0.0947 897 233	0.0877 594 000	64
33	0.1032 611 396	0.0953 542 655	0.0880 612 903	0.0813 338 952	66
34	0.0963 953 788	0.0887 996 058	0.0818 104 599	0.0753 788 484	68
35	0.0899 861 175	0.0826 955 140	0.0760 033 304	0.0698 598 139	70
36	0.0840 030 036	0.0770 110 179	0.0706 084 068	0.0647 448 682	72
37	0.0784 177 027	0.0717 172 745	0.0655 964 296	0.0600 044 249	74
38	0.0732 037 646	0.0667 874 235	0.0609 402 162	0.0556 110 639	76
39	0.0683 364 976	0.0621 964 508	0.0566 145 135	0.0515 393 729	78
40	0.0637 928 517	0.0579 210 619	0.0525 958 610	0.0477 658 001	80
41	0.0595 513 097	0.0539 395 636	0.0488 624 634	0.0442 685 180	82
42	0.0555 917 848	0.0502 317 538	0.0453 940 726	0.0410 272 974	84
43	0.0518 955 260	0.0467 788 191	0.0421 718 776	0.0380 233 902	86
44	0.0484 450 288	0.0435 632 394	0.0391 784 027	0.0352 394 208	88
45	0.0452 239 527	0.0405 686 989	0.0363 974 129	0.0326 592 862	90
46	0.0422 170 438	0.0377 800 034	0.0338 138 253	0.0302 680 620	92
47	0.0394 100 621	0.0351 830 030	0.0314 136 278	0.0280 519 168	94
48	0.0367 897 147	0.0327 645 206	0.0291 838 029	0.0259 980 316	96
49	0.0343 435 923	0.0305 122 849	0.0271 122 570	0.0240 945 264	98
50	0.0320 601 109	0.0284 148 681	0.0251 877 551	0.0223 303 907	100
51	0.0299 284 566	0.0264 616 278	0.0233 998 596	0.0206 954 201	102
52	0.0279 385 345	0.0246 426 535	0.0217 388 737	0.0191 801 577	104
53	0.0260 809 209	0.0229 487 155	0.0201 957 892	0.0177 758 387	106
54	0.0243 468 187	0.0213 712 190	0.0187 622 370	0.0164 743 401	108
55	0.0227 280 158	0.0199 021 598	0.0174 304 423	0.0152 681 336	110
56	0.0212 168 460	0.0185 340 838	0.0161 931 820	0.0141 502 424	112
57	0.0198 061 527	0.0172 600 494	0.0150 437 458	0.0131 142 001	114
58	0.0184 892 555	0.0160 735 923	0.0139 758 997	0.0121 540 140	116
59	0.0172 599 179	0.0149 686 923	0.0129 838 522	0.0112 641 301	118
60	0.0161 123 180	0.0139 397 432	0.0120 622 230	0.0104 394 011	120

SEMI ANNUAL
Compounding

TABLE 4. PRESENT WORTH OF ONE DOLLAR
Payable at end of each period

HALF YEARS	8% Nominal Annual Rate	8¼% Nominal Annual Rate	8½% Nominal Annual Rate	8¾% Nominal Annual Rate	HALF YEARS
1	0.9615 384 615	0.9603 841 537	0.9592 326 139	0.9580 838 323	1
YEARS					
1	0.9245 562 130	0.9223 377 226	0.9201 272 076	0.9179 246 298	2
2	0.8548 041 910	0.8507 068 745	0.8466 340 781	0.8425 856 260	4
3	0.7903 145 257	0.7846 390 413	0.7790 110 502	0.7734 300 988	6
4	0.7306 902 050	0.7237 021 864	0.7167 892 623	0.7099 505 371	8
5	0.6755 641 688	0.6674 978 264	0.6595 373 023	0.6516 810 839	10
6	0.6245 970 496	0.6156 584 251	0.6068 582 163	0.5981 941 177	12
7	0.5774 750 828	0.5678 449 897	0.5583 867 559	0.5490 971 140	14
8	0.5339 081 757	0.5237 448 546	0.5137 868 465	0.5040 297 651	16
9	0.4936 281 210	0.4830 696 364	0.4727 492 564	0.4626 613 355	18
10	0.4563 869 462	0.4455 533 483	0.4349 894 532	0.4246 882 351	20
11	0.4219 553 867	0.4109 506 606	0.4002 456 309	0.3898 317 910	22
12	0.3901 214 743	0.3790 352 964	0.3682 768 947	0.3578 362 024	24
13	0.3606 892 329	0.3495 985 520	0.3388 615 907	0.3284 666 636	26
14	0.3334 774 713	0.3224 479 323	0.3117 957 692	0.3015 076 406	28
15	0.3083 186 680	0.2974 058 915	0.2868 917 705	0.2767 612 894	30
16	0.2850 579 401	0.2743 086 727	0.2639 769 236	0.2540 460 041	32
17	0.2635 520 896	0.2530 052 365	0.2428 923 496	0.2331 950 843	34
18	0.2436 687 219	0.2333 562 736	0.2234 918 594	0.2140 555 114	36
19	0.2252 854 307	0.2152 332 940	0.2056 409 405	0.1964 868 260	38
20	0.2082 890 447	0.1985 177 862	0.1892 158 244	0.1803 600 971	40
21	0.1925 749 303	0.1831 004 428	0.1741 026 281	0.1655 569 753	42
22	0.1780 463 483	0.1688 804 454	0.1601 965 650	0.1519 688 253	44
23	0.1646 138 575	0.1557 648 054	0.1474 012 180	0.1394 959 277	46
24	0.1521 947 647	0.1436 677 559	0.1356 278 711	0.1280 467 478	48
25	0.1407 126 153	0.1325 101 908	0.1247 948 943	0.1175 372 635	50
26	0.1300 967 228	0.1222 191 476	0.1148 271 777	0.1078 903 491	52
27	0.1202 817 333	0.1127 273 302	0.1056 556 103	0.0990 352 088	54
28	0.1112 072 239	0.1039 726 691	0.0972 166 017	0.0909 068 574	56
29	0.1028 173 297	0.0958 979 148	0.0894 516 403	0.0834 456 434	58
30	0.0950 604 010	0.0884 502 643	0.0823 068 880	0.0765 968 113	60
31	0.0878 886 844	0.0815 810 154	0.0757 328 070	0.0703 100 997	62
32	0.0812 580 292	0.0752 452 479	0.0696 838 162	0.0645 393 722	64
33	0.0751 276 157	0.0694 015 306	0.0641 179 752	0.0592 422 793	66
34	0.0694 597 039	0.0640 116 497	0.0589 966 935	0.0543 799 473	68
35	0.0642 194 008	0.0590 403 592	0.0542 844 628	0.0499 166 930	70
36	0.0593 744 460	0.0544 551 504	0.0499 486 112	0.0458 197 620	72
37	0.0548 950 130	0.0502 260 394	0.0459 590 762	0.0420 590 880	74
38	0.0507 535 253	0.0463 253 708	0.0422 881 964	0.0386 070 728	76
39	0.0469 244 871	0.0427 276 370	0.0389 105 201	0.0354 383 830	78
40	0.0433 843 261	0.0394 093 114	0.0358 026 282	0.0325 297 646	80
41	0.0401 112 483	0.0363 486 946	0.0329 429 723	0.0298 598 721	82
42	0.0370 851 038	0.0335 257 722	0.0303 117 251	0.0274 091 121	84
43	0.0342 872 631	0.0309 220 843	0.0278 906 430	0.0251 594 991	86
44	0.0317 005 022	0.0285 206 048	0.0256 629 394	0.0230 945 239	88
45	0.0293 088 962	0.0263 056 297	0.0236 131 688	0.0211 990 323	90
46	0.0270 977 221	0.0242 626 746	0.0217 271 191	0.0194 591 138	92
47	0.0250 533 673	0.0223 783 800	0.0199 917 134	0.0178 619 999	94
48	0.0231 632 464	0.0206 404 241	0.0183 949 194	0.0163 959 696	96
49	0.0214 157 234	0.0190 374 417	0.0169 256 659	0.0150 502 643	98
50	0.0198 000 401	0.0175 589 507	0.0155 737 657	0.0138 150 083	100
51	0.0183 062 501	0.0161 952 826	0.0143 298 455	0.0126 811 364	102
52	0.0169 251 573	0.0149 375 200	0.0131 852 807	0.0116 403 274	104
53	0.0156 482 593	0.0137 774 382	0.0121 321 355	0.0106 849 433	106
54	0.0144 676 954	0.0127 074 510	0.0111 631 080	0.0098 079 726	108
55	0.0133 761 976	0.0117 205 614	0.0102 714 794	0.0090 029 796	110
56	0.0123 670 466	0.0108 103 159	0.0094 510 676	0.0082 640 567	112
57	0.0114 340 298	0.0099 707 622	0.0086 961 845	0.0075 857 812	114
58	0.0105 714 033	0.0091 964 101	0.0080 015 959	0.0069 631 754	116
59	0.0097 738 566	0.0084 821 959	0.0073 624 861	0.0063 916 702	118
60	0.0090 364 798	0.0078 234 493	0.0067 744 238	0.0058 670 715	120

TABLE 4. PRESENT WORTH OF ONE DOLLAR
Payable at end of each period

SEMI ANNUAL Compounding

HALF YEARS	9% Nominal Annual Rate	9¼% Nominal Annual Rate	9½% Nominal Annual Rate	9¾% Nominal Annual Rate	HALF YEARS
1	0.9569 377 990	0.9557 945 042	0.9546 539 379	0.9535 160 906	1
YEARS					
1	0.9157 299 512	0.9135 431 342	0.9113 641 412	0.9091 929 350	2
2	0.8385 613 436	0.8345 610 581	0.8305 845 979	0.8266 317 931	4
3	0.7678 957 383	0.7624 075 247	0.7569 650 188	0.7515 677 861	6
4	0.7031 851 270	0.6964 921 597	0.6898 707 743	0.6833 201 213	8
5	0.6439 276 820	0.6362 756 305	0.6287 234 858	0.6212 698 266	10
6	0.5896 638 649	0.5812 652 337	0.5729 960 397	0.5648 541 371	12
7	0.5399 728 622	0.5310 108 634	0.5222 080 437	0.5135 613 908	14
8	0.4944 693 228	0.4851 013 285	0.4759 216 853	0.4669 263 882	16
9	0.4528 003 688	0.4431 609 880	0.4337 379 580	0.4245 261 733	18
10	0.4146 428 597	0.4048 466 780	0.3952 932 216	0.3859 761 975	20
11	0.3797 008 857	0.3698 449 031	0.3602 560 675	0.3509 268 318	22
12	0.3477 034 735	0.3378 692 719	0.3283 244 615	0.3190 601 962	24
13	0.3184 024 849	0.3086 581 536	0.2992 231 409	0.2900 872 762	26
14	0.2915 706 919	0.2819 725 371	0.2727 012 409	0.2637 453 021	28
15	0.2670 000 155	0.2575 940 753	0.2485 301 322	0.2397 953 653	30
16	0.2444 999 112	0.2353 232 989	0.2265 014 505	0.2180 202 520	32
17	0.2238 958 917	0.2149 779 840	0.2064 252 999	0.1982 224 728	34
18	0.2050 281 740	0.1963 916 613	0.1881 286 162	0.1802 224 718	36
19	0.1877 504 398	0.1794 122 538	0.1714 536 748	0.1638 569 981	38
20	0.1719 287 011	0.1639 008 327	0.1562 567 311	0.1489 776 250	40
21	0.1574 402 611	0.1497 304 804	0.1424 067 815	0.1354 494 041	42
22	0.1441 727 626	0.1367 852 523	0.1297 844 341	0.1231 496 413	44
23	0.1320 233 169	0.1249 592 281	0.1182 808 794	0.1119 667 838	46
24	0.1208 977 055	0.1141 556 449	0.1077 969 520	0.1017 994 088	48
25	0.1107 096 500	0.1042 861 057	0.0982 422 766	0.0925 553 033	50
26	0.1013 801 424	0.0952 698 558	0.0895 344 881	0.0841 506 278	52
27	0.0928 368 328	0.0870 331 227	0.0815 985 218	0.0765 091 563	54
28	0.0850 134 684	0.0795 085 117	0.0743 659 668	0.0695 615 844	56
29	0.0778 493 793	0.0726 344 549	0.0677 744 754	0.0632 449 011	58
30	0.0712 890 083	0.0663 547 076	0.0617 672 266	0.0575 018 172	60
31	0.0652 814 801	0.0606 178 876	0.0562 924 354	0.0522 802 460	62
32	0.0597 802 066	0.0553 770 550	0.0513 029 071	0.0475 328 303	64
33	0.0547 425 256	0.0505 893 284	0.0467 556 299	0.0432 165 135	66
34	0.0501 293 703	0.0462 155 336	0.0426 114 045	0.0392 921 487	68
35	0.0459 049 659	0.0422 198 834	0.0388 345 060	0.0357 241 440	70
36	0.0420 365 521	0.0385 696 846	0.0353 923 762	0.0324 801 393	72
37	0.0384 941 298	0.0352 350 706	0.0322 553 426	0.0295 307 132	74
38	0.0352 502 276	0.0321 887 568	0.0293 963 626	0.0268 491 158	76
39	0.0322 796 892	0.0294 058 178	0.0267 907 907	0.0244 110 264	78
40	0.0295 594 783	0.0268 634 830	0.0244 161 660	0.0221 943 328	80
41	0.0270 684 996	0.0245 409 504	0.0222 520 182	0.0201 789 305	82
42	0.0247 874 358	0.0224 192 168	0.0202 796 914	0.0183 465 411	84
43	0.0226 985 974	0.0204 809 215	0.0184 821 836	0.0166 805 455	86
44	0.0207 857 855	0.0187 102 053	0.0168 439 993	0.0151 658 342	88
45	0.0190 341 663	0.0170 925 796	0.0153 510 170	0.0137 886 693	90
46	0.0174 301 562	0.0156 148 087	0.0139 903 664	0.0125 365 607	92
47	0.0159 613 161	0.0142 648 013	0.0127 503 183	0.0113 981 524	94
48	0.0146 162 552	0.0130 315 113	0.0116 201 829	0.0103 631 196	96
49	0.0133 845 427	0.0119 048 476	0.0105 902 180	0.0094 220 752	98
50	0.0122 566 266	0.0108 755 918	0.0096 515 449	0.0085 664 842	100
51	0.0112 237 601	0.0099 353 222	0.0087 960 719	0.0077 885 869	102
52	0.0102 779 333	0.0090 763 454	0.0080 164 246	0.0070 813 282	104
53	0.0094 118 113	0.0082 916 330	0.0073 058 819	0.0064 382 935	106
54	0.0086 186 775	0.0075 747 644	0.0066 583 188	0.0058 536 510	108
55	0.0078 923 812	0.0069 198 741	0.0060 681 530	0.0053 220 981	110
56	0.0072 272 898	0.0063 216 034	0.0055 302 970	0.0048 388 140	112
57	0.0066 182 457	0.0057 750 574	0.0050 401 144	0.0043 994 155	114
58	0.0060 605 259	0.0052 757 640	0.0045 933 795	0.0039 999 175	116
59	0.0055 498 050	0.0048 196 380	0.0041 862 414	0.0036 366 967	118
60	0.0050 821 227	0.0044 029 472	0.0038 151 903	0.0033 064 590	120

SEMI ANNUAL
Compounding

TABLE 4. PRESENT WORTH OF ONE DOLLAR
Payable at end of each period

HALF YEARS	10% Nominal Annual Rate	10¼% Nominal Annual Rate	10½% Nominal Annual Rate	10¾% Nominal Annual Rate	HALF YEARS
1	0.9523 809 524	0.9512 485 137	0.9501 187 648	0.9489 916 963	1
YEARS					
1	0.9070 294 785	0.9048 737 348	0.9027 256 673	0.9005 852 397	2
2	0.8227 024 748	0.8187 964 759	0.8149 136 304	0.8110 537 739	4
3	0.7462 153 966	0.7409 074 251	0.7356 434 508	0.7304 230 574	6
4	0.6768 393 620	0.6704 276 689	0.6640 842 250	0.6578 082 242	8
5	0.6139 132 535	0.6066 523 886	0.5994 858 752	0.5924 123 773	10
6	0.5568 374 182	0.5489 438 126	0.5411 712 867	0.5335 178 428	12
7	0.5050 679 530	0.4967 248 379	0.4885 292 110	0.4804 782 943	14
8	0.4581 115 220	0.4494 732 592	0.4410 078 580	0.4327 116 599	16
9	0.4155 206 549	0.4067 165 468	0.3981 091 129	0.3896 937 339	18
10	0.3768 894 829	0.3680 271 207	0.3593 833 146	0.3509 524 248	20
11	0.3418 498 711	0.3330 180 752	0.3244 245 425	0.3160 625 736	22
12	0.3100 679 103	0.3013 393 094	0.2928 663 616	0.2846 412 886	24
13	0.2812 407 350	0.2726 740 263	0.2643 779 817	0.2563 437 431	26
14	0.2550 936 371	0.2467 355 646	0.2386 607 900	0.2308 593 913	28
15	0.2313 774 487	0.2232 645 318	0.2154 452 209	0.2079 085 603	30
16	0.2098 661 666	0.2020 262 108	0.1944 879 308	0.1872 393 806	32
17	0.1903 547 996	0.1828 082 119	0.1755 692 471	0.1686 250 224	34
18	0.1726 574 146	0.1654 183 494	0.1584 908 657	0.1518 612 063	36
19	0.1566 053 647	0.1496 827 196	0.1430 737 725	0.1367 639 608	38
20	0.1420 456 823	0.1354 439 615	0.1291 563 668	0.1231 676 044	40
21	0.1288 396 211	0.1225 596 833	0.1165 927 674	0.1109 229 266	42
22	0.1168 613 344	0.1109 010 384	0.1052 512 838	0.0998 955 504	44
23	0.1059 966 752	0.1003 514 368	0.0950 130 354	0.0899 644 582	46
24	0.0961 421 090	0.0908 053 794	0.0857 707 058	0.0810 206 632	48
25	0.0872 037 270	0.0821 674 028	0.0774 274 176	0.0729 660 134	50
26	0.0790 963 510	0.0743 511 246	0.0698 957 172	0.0657 121 146	52
27	0.0717 427 220	0.0672 783 798	0.0630 966 580	0.0591 793 605	54
28	0.0650 727 637	0.0608 784 388	0.0569 589 727	0.0532 960 586	56
29	0.0590 229 149	0.0550 873 003	0.0514 183 266	0.0479 976 437	58
30	0.0535 355 237	0.0498 470 512	0.0464 166 432	0.0432 259 694	60
31	0.0485 582 982	0.0451 052 874	0.0419 014 952	0.0389 286 700	62
32	0.0440 438 079	0.0408 145 898	0.0378 255 552	0.0350 585 856	64
33	0.0399 490 321	0.0369 320 503	0.0341 460 996	0.0315 732 448	66
34	0.0362 349 497	0.0334 188 423	0.0308 245 605	0.0284 343 982	68
35	0.0328 661 676	0.0302 398 327	0.0278 261 220	0.0256 075 993	70
36	0.0298 105 828	0.0273 632 303	0.0251 193 545	0.0230 618 260	72
37	0.0270 390 774	0.0247 602 684	0.0226 758 861	0.0207 691 401	74
38	0.0245 252 403	0.0224 049 166	0.0204 701 044	0.0187 043 810	76
39	0.0222 451 159	0.0202 736 205	0.0184 788 886	0.0168 448 894	78
40	0.0201 769 759	0.0183 450 667	0.0166 813 671	0.0151 702 588	80
41	0.0183 011 119	0.0165 999 690	0.0150 586 982	0.0136 621 111	82
42	0.0165 996 480	0.0150 208 760	0.0135 938 734	0.0123 038 956	84
43	0.0150 563 700	0.0135 919 961	0.0122 715 384	0.0110 807 068	86
44	0.0136 565 715	0.0122 990 403	0.0110 778 327	0.0099 791 210	88
45	0.0123 869 129	0.0111 290 785	0.0100 002 439	0.0089 870 491	90
46	0.0112 352 951	0.0100 704 109	0.0090 274 769	0.0080 936 037	92
47	0.0101 907 439	0.0091 124 503	0.0081 493 351	0.0072 889 801	94
48	0.0092 433 051	0.0082 456 169	0.0073 566 140	0.0065 643 479	96
49	0.0083 839 502	0.0074 612 422	0.0066 410 043	0.0059 117 548	98
50	0.0076 044 900	0.0067 514 821	0.0059 950 050	0.0053 240 391	100
51	0.0068 974 966	0.0061 092 388	0.0054 118 449	0.0047 947 510	102
52	0.0062 562 327	0.0055 280 897	0.0048 854 113	0.0043 180 820	104
53	0.0056 745 875	0.0050 022 232	0.0044 101 862	0.0038 888 009	106
54	0.0051 470 182	0.0045 263 804	0.0039 811 882	0.0035 021 967	108
55	0.0046 684 972	0.0040 958 027	0.0035 939 208	0.0031 540 267	110
56	0.0042 344 646	0.0037 061 843	0.0032 443 246	0.0028 404 699	112
57	0.0038 407 842	0.0033 536 288	0.0029 287 351	0.0025 580 852	114
58	0.0034 837 045	0.0030 346 107	0.0026 438 443	0.0023 037 738	116
59	0.0031 598 227	0.0027 459 395	0.0023 866 661	0.0020 747 447	118
60	0.0028 660 523	0.0024 847 285	0.0021 545 048	0.0018 684 844	120

TABLE 4. PRESENT WORTH OF ONE DOLLAR
Payable at end of each period

SEMI ANNUAL Compounding

HALF YEARS	11% Nominal Annual Rate	11¼% Nominal Annual Rate	11½% Nominal Annual Rate	11¾% Nominal Annual Rate	HALF YEARS
1	0.9478 672 986	0.9467 455 621	0.9456 264 775	0.9445 100 354	1
YEARS					
1	0.8984 524 157	0.8963 271 594	0.8942 094 350	0.8920 992 070	2
2	0.8072 167 433	0.8034 023 767	0.7996 105 137	0.7958 409 951	4
3	0.7252 458 330	0.7201 113 702	0.7150 192 657	0.7099 691 207	6
4	0.6515 988 707	0.6454 553 789	0.6393 769 736	0.6333 628 896	8
5	0.5854 305 794	0.5785 391 863	0.5717 369 223	0.5650 225 315	10
6	0.5259 815 183	0.5185 603 855	0.5112 525 503	0.5040 561 523	12
7	0.4725 693 658	0.4647 997 573	0.4571 668 542	0.4496 680 938	14
8	0.4245 810 883	0.4166 126 461	0.4088 029 144	0.4011 485 499	16
9	0.3814 659 044	0.3734 212 297	0.3655 554 231	0.3578 643 032	18
10	0.3427 289 633	0.3347 075 901	0.3268 831 084	0.3192 504 611	20
11	0.3079 256 650	0.3000 075 034	0.2923 019 597	0.2848 030 832	22
12	0.2766 565 576	0.2689 048 734	0.2613 791 702	0.2540 726 047	24
13	0.2485 627 525	0.2410 267 413	0.2337 277 201	0.2266 579 692	26
14	0.2233 218 055	0.2160 388 144	0.2090 015 325	0.2022 013 945	28
15	0.2006 440 156	0.1936 414 568	0.1868 911 423	0.1803 837 037	30
16	0.1802 691 005	0.1735 660 969	0.1671 198 228	0.1609 201 591	32
17	0.1619 632 088	0.1555 720 066	0.1494 401 223	0.1435 567 463	34
18	0.1455 162 362	0.1394 434 148	0.1336 307 674	0.1280 668 595	36
19	0.1307 394 140	0.1249 869 199	0.1194 938 930	0.1142 483 438	38
20	0.1174 631 423	0.1120 291 709	0.1068 525 665	0.1019 208 569	40
21	0.1055 350 440	0.1004 147 885	0.0955 485 732	0.0909 235 156	42
22	0.0948 182 152	0.0900 045 021	0.0854 404 356	0.0811 127 962	44
23	0.0851 896 545	0.0806 734 797	0.0764 016 437	0.0723 606 612	46
24	0.0765 388 509	0.0723 098 309	0.0683 190 706	0.0645 528 884	48
25	0.0687 665 155	0.0648 132 653	0.0610 915 575	0.0575 875 806	50
26	0.0617 834 419	0.0580 938 900	0.0546 286 471	0.0513 738 350	52
27	0.0555 094 827	0.0520 711 314	0.0488 494 517	0.0458 305 574	54
28	0.0498 726 288	0.0466 727 693	0.0436 816 406	0.0408 854 040	56
29	0.0448 081 838	0.0418 340 707	0.0390 605 352	0.0364 738 364	58
30	0.0402 580 210	0.0374 970 138	0.0349 282 991	0.0325 382 806	60
31	0.0361 699 162	0.0336 095 919	0.0312 332 146	0.0290 273 743	62
32	0.0324 969 486	0.0301 251 900	0.0279 290 352	0.0258 952 976	64
33	0.0291 969 620	0.0270 020 260	0.0249 744 068	0.0231 011 744	66
34	0.0262 320 810	0.0242 026 492	0.0223 323 502	0.0206 085 394	68
35	0.0235 682 766	0.0216 934 918	0.0199 697 982	0.0183 848 617	70
36	0.0211 749 750	0.0194 444 659	0.0178 571 820	0.0164 011 205	72
37	0.0190 247 074	0.0174 286 029	0.0159 680 606	0.0146 314 266	74
38	0.0170 927 944	0.0156 217 301	0.0142 787 905	0.0130 526 841	76
39	0.0153 570 624	0.0140 021 810	0.0127 682 292	0.0116 442 891	78
40	0.0137 975 898	0.0125 505 351	0.0114 174 710	0.0103 878 611	80
41	0.0123 964 779	0.0112 493 855	0.0102 096 103	0.0092 670 026	82
42	0.0111 376 455	0.0100 831 297	0.0091 295 298	0.0082 670 857	84
43	0.0100 066 445	0.0090 377 830	0.0081 637 117	0.0073 750 606	86
44	0.0089 904 939	0.0081 008 104	0.0073 000 680	0.0065 792 857	88
45	0.0080 775 310	0.0072 609 764	0.0065 277 897	0.0058 693 756	90
46	0.0072 572 772	0.0065 082 103	0.0058 372 112	0.0052 360 653	92
47	0.0065 203 183	0.0058 334 857	0.0052 196 893	0.0046 710 897	94
48	0.0058 581 957	0.0052 287 116	0.0046 674 954	0.0041 670 754	96
49	0.0052 633 101	0.0046 866 363	0.0041 737 184	0.0037 174 447	98
50	0.0047 288 336	0.0042 007 594	0.0037 321 784	0.0033 163 294	100
51	0.0042 486 320	0.0037 652 547	0.0033 373 491	0.0029 584 949	102
52	0.0038 171 937	0.0033 749 001	0.0029 842 891	0.0026 392 709	104
53	0.0034 295 669	0.0030 250 146	0.0026 685 795	0.0023 544 915	106
54	0.0030 813 027	0.0027 114 027	0.0023 862 689	0.0021 004 400	108
55	0.0027 684 038	0.0024 303 039	0.0021 338 242	0.0018 738 009	110
56	0.0024 872 791	0.0021 783 474	0.0019 080 857	0.0016 716 163	112
57	0.0022 347 019	0.0019 525 119	0.0017 062 283	0.0014 912 475	114
58	0.0020 077 733	0.0017 500 895	0.0015 257 254	0.0013 303 407	116
59	0.0018 038 888	0.0015 686 527	0.0013 643 181	0.0011 867 959	118
60	0.0016 207 083	0.0014 060 260	0.0012 199 861	0.0010 587 397	120

SEMI ANNUAL
Compounding

TABLE 4. PRESENT WORTH OF ONE DOLLAR
Payable at end of each period

HALF YEARS	12% Nominal Annual Rate	12¼% Nominal Annual Rate	12½% Nominal Annual Rate	12¾% Nominal Annual Rate	HALF YEARS
1	0.9433 962 264	0.9422 850 412	0.9411 764 706	0.9400 705 053	1
YEARS					
1	0.8899 964 400	0.8879 010 989	0.8858 131 488	0.8837 325 549	2
2	0.7920 936 632	0.7883 683 615	0.7846 649 346	0.7809 832 286	4
3	0.7049 605 404	0.6999 931 345	0.6950 665 164	0.6901 803 040	6
4	0.6274 123 713	0.6215 246 733	0.6156 990 595	0.6099 348 034	8
5	0.5583 947 769	0.5518 524 405	0.5453 943 226	0.5390 192 421	10
6	0.4969 693 636	0.4899 903 883	0.4831 174 623	0.4763 488 520	12
7	0.4423 009 644	0.4350 630 043	0.4279 518 005	0.4209 649 880	14
8	0.3936 462 837	0.3862 929 196	0.3790 853 319	0.3720 204 644	16
9	0.3503 437 911	0.3429 899 078	0.3357 987 715	0.3287 665 955	18
10	0.3118 047 269	0.3045 411 161	0.2974 549 672	0.2905 417 434	20
11	0.2775 050 969	0.2704 023 916	0.2634 895 211	0.2567 611 972	22
12	0.2469 785 483	0.2400 905 807	0.2334 024 823	0.2269 082 288	24
13	0.2198 100 288	0.2131 766 904	0.2067 509 878	0.2005 261 888	26
14	0.1956 301 431	0.1892 798 177	0.1831 427 435	0.1772 115 211	28
15	0.1741 101 309	0.1680 617 581	0.1622 302 503	0.1566 075 903	30
16	0.1549 573 967	0.1492 222 197	0.1437 056 889	0.1383 992 259	32
17	0.1379 115 314	0.1324 945 729	0.1272 963 888	0.1223 079 015	34
18	0.1227 407 720	0.1176 420 769	0.1127 608 150	0.1080 874 743	36
19	0.1092 388 501	0.1044 545 293	0.0998 850 126	0.0955 204 198	38
20	0.0972 221 877	0.0927 452 914	0.0884 794 575	0.0844 145 046	40
21	0.0865 274 010	0.0823 486 461	0.0783 762 668	0.0745 998 459	42
22	0.0770 090 788	0.0731 174 534	0.0694 267 277	0.0659 263 124	44
23	0.0685 378 060	0.0649 210 672	0.0614 991 083	0.0582 612 285	46
24	0.0609 984 033	0.0576 434 869	0.0544 767 188	0.0514 873 443	48
25	0.0542 883 618	0.0511 817 154	0.0482 561 938	0.0455 010 423	50
26	0.0483 164 488	0.0454 443 013	0.0427 459 710	0.0402 107 524	52
27	0.0430 014 674	0.0403 500 451	0.0378 649 431	0.0355 355 509	54
28	0.0382 711 529	0.0358 268 494	0.0335 412 645	0.0314 039 232	56
29	0.0340 611 898	0.0318 106 989	0.0297 112 931	0.0277 526 693	58
30	0.0303 143 377	0.0282 447 545	0.0263 186 541	0.0245 259 373	60
31	0.0269 796 526	0.0250 785 486	0.0233 134 099	0.0216 743 693	62
32	0.0240 117 948	0.0222 672 709	0.0206 513 250	0.0191 543 457	64
33	0.0213 704 119	0.0197 711 343	0.0182 932 152	0.0169 273 189	66
34	0.0190 195 905	0.0175 548 118	0.0162 043 706	0.0149 592 228	68
35	0.0169 273 678	0.0155 869 367	0.0143 540 445	0.0132 199 522	70
36	0.0150 652 971	0.0138 396 582	0.0127 150 014	0.0116 829 021	72
37	0.0134 080 608	0.0122 882 478	0.0112 631 154	0.0103 245 609	74
38	0.0119 331 264	0.0109 107 487	0.0099 770 157	0.0091 241 506	76
39	0.0106 204 400	0.0096 876 658	0.0088 377 717	0.0080 633 089	78
40	0.0094 521 538	0.0086 016 891	0.0078 286 144	0.0071 258 086	80
41	0.0084 123 832	0.0076 374 492	0.0069 346 896	0.0062 973 090	82
42	0.0074 869 911	0.0067 812 995	0.0061 428 392	0.0055 651 370	84
43	0.0066 633 954	0.0060 211 233	0.0054 414 077	0.0049 180 927	86
44	0.0059 303 982	0.0053 461 620	0.0048 200 705	0.0043 462 787	88
45	0.0052 780 333	0.0047 468 631	0.0042 696 818	0.0038 409 479	90
46	0.0046 974 308	0.0042 147 450	0.0037 821 403	0.0033 943 707	92
47	0.0041 806 967	0.0037 422 767	0.0033 502 696	0.0029 997 159	94
48	0.0037 208 052	0.0033 227 716	0.0029 677 129	0.0026 509 466	96
49	0.0033 115 034	0.0029 502 925	0.0026 288 391	0.0023 427 278	98
50	0.0029 472 262	0.0026 195 680	0.0023 286 602	0.0020 703 449	100
51	0.0026 230 209	0.0023 259 173	0.0020 627 579	0.0018 296 311	102
52	0.0023 344 792	0.0020 651 845	0.0018 272 180	0.0016 169 046	104
53	0.0020 776 782	0.0018 336 796	0.0016 185 738	0.0014 289 112	106
54	0.0018 491 262	0.0016 281 261	0.0014 337 539	0.0012 627 754	108
55	0.0016 457 157	0.0014 456 150	0.0012 700 381	0.0011 159 557	110
56	0.0014 646 811	0.0012 835 631	0.0011 250 164	0.0009 862 064	112
57	0.0013 035 610	0.0011 396 771	0.0009 965 543	0.0008 715 427	114
58	0.0011 601 647	0.0010 119 206	0.0008 827 609	0.0007 702 107	116
59	0.0010 325 424	0.0008 984 854	0.0007 819 612	0.0006 806 602	118
60	0.0009 189 591	0.0007 977 662	0.0006 926 716	0.0006 015 216	120

TABLE 4. PRESENT WORTH OF ONE DOLLAR
Payable at end of each period

HALF YEARS	13% Nominal Annual Rate	13¼% Nominal Annual Rate	13½% Nominal Annual Rate	13¾% Nominal Annual Rate	HALF YEARS
1	0.9389 671 362	0.9378 663 540	0.9367 681 499	0.9356 725 146	1
YEARS					
1	0.8816 592 828	0.8795 932 980	0.8775 345 666	0.8754 830 546	2
2	0.7773 230 909	0.7736 843 700	0.7700 669 156	0.7664 705 789	4
3	0.6853 341 188	0.6805 275 866	0.6757 603 371	0.6710 320 037	6
4	0.6042 311 876	0.5985 875 043	0.5930 030 546	0.5874 771 483	8
5	0.5327 260 355	0.5265 135 571	0.5203 806 785	0.5143 262 884	10
6	0.4696 828 544	0.4631 177 962	0.4566 520 332	0.4502 839 500	12
7	0.4141 002 485	0.4073 553 097	0.4007 279 440	0.3942 159 680	14
8	0.3650 953 281	0.3583 070 004	0.3516 526 227	0.3451 293 998	16
9	0.3218 896 851	0.3151 644 362	0.3085 873 319	0.3021 549 412	18
10	0.2837 970 289	0.2772 165 258	0.2707 960 506	0.2645 315 309	20
11	0.2502 122 850	0.2438 377 982	0.2376 328 949	0.2315 928 727	22
12	0.2206 019 837	0.2144 780 931	0.2085 310 794	0.2027 556 356	24
13	0.1944 957 867	0.1886 534 933	0.1829 932 304	0.1775 091 232	26
14	0.1714 790 158	0.1659 383 484	0.1605 828 851	0.1554 062 294	28
15	0.1511 860 661	0.1459 582 591	0.1409 170 325	0.1360 555 204	30
16	0.1332 945 986	0.1283 839 065	0.1236 595 671	0.1191 143 026	32
17	0.1175 204 202	0.1129 256 237	0.1085 155 446	0.1042 825 535	34
18	0.1036 129 694	0.0993 286 218	0.0952 261 414	0.0912 976 085	36
19	0.0913 513 363	0.0873 687 901	0.0835 642 307	0.0799 295 092	38
20	0.0805 407 536	0.0768 490 022	0.0733 305 010	0.0699 769 308	40
21	0.0710 095 031	0.0675 958 673	0.0643 500 494	0.0612 636 172	42
22	0.0626 061 876	0.0594 568 718	0.0564 693 927	0.0536 352 587	44
23	0.0551 973 264	0.0522 978 660	0.0495 538 441	0.0469 567 601	46
24	0.0486 652 352	0.0460 008 524	0.0434 852 111	0.0411 098 478	48
25	0.0429 061 564	0.0404 620 415	0.0381 597 759	0.0359 909 751	50
26	0.0378 286 111	0.0355 901 405	0.0334 865 224	0.0315 094 888	52
27	0.0333 519 461	0.0313 048 491	0.0293 855 809	0.0275 860 235	54
28	0.0294 050 529	0.0275 355 355	0.0257 868 630	0.0241 510 961	56
29	0.0259 252 378	0.0242 200 724	0.0226 288 636	0.0211 438 754	58
30	0.0228 572 266	0.0213 038 134	0.0198 576 101	0.0185 111 046	60
31	0.0201 522 860	0.0187 386 915	0.0174 257 392	0.0162 061 584	62
32	0.0177 674 500	0.0164 824 274	0.0152 916 885	0.0141 882 171	64
33	0.0156 648 372	0.0144 978 327	0.0134 189 853	0.0124 215 436	66
34	0.0138 110 492	0.0127 521 965	0.0117 756 234	0.0108 748 510	68
35	0.0121 766 397	0.0112 167 466	0.0103 335 166	0.0095 207 477	70
36	0.0107 356 474	0.0098 661 751	0.0090 680 180	0.0083 352 533	72
37	0.0094 651 832	0.0086 782 215	0.0079 574 993	0.0072 973 730	74
38	0.0083 450 666	0.0076 333 055	0.0069 829 807	0.0063 887 264	76
39	0.0073 575 055	0.0067 142 043	0.0061 278 069	0.0055 932 217	78
40	0.0064 868 130	0.0059 057 691	0.0053 773 624	0.0048 967 708	80
41	0.0057 191 589	0.0051 946 750	0.0047 188 214	0.0042 870 399	82
42	0.0050 423 495	0.0045 692 013	0.0041 409 289	0.0037 532 308	84
43	0.0044 456 343	0.0040 190 388	0.0036 338 082	0.0032 858 900	86
44	0.0039 195 347	0.0035 351 196	0.0031 887 923	0.0028 767 410	88
45	0.0034 556 942	0.0031 094 675	0.0027 982 755	0.0025 185 380	90
46	0.0030 467 448	0.0027 350 668	0.0024 555 835	0.0022 049 373	92
47	0.0026 861 909	0.0024 057 464	0.0021 548 594	0.0019 303 853	94
48	0.0023 683 051	0.0021 160 784	0.0018 909 636	0.0016 900 196	96
49	0.0020 880 382	0.0018 612 884	0.0016 593 859	0.0014 795 835	98
50	0.0018 409 383	0.0016 371 768	0.0014 561 685	0.0012 953 503	100
51	0.0016 230 803	0.0014 400 497	0.0012 778 382	0.0011 340 572	102
52	0.0014 310 038	0.0012 666 581	0.0011 213 472	0.0009 928 479	104
53	0.0012 616 578	0.0011 141 440	0.0009 840 209	0.0008 692 215	106
54	0.0011 123 523	0.0009 799 936	0.0008 635 124	0.0007 609 887	108
55	0.0009 807 157	0.0008 619 958	0.0007 577 619	0.0006 662 327	110
56	0.0008 646 571	0.0007 582 057	0.0006 649 623	0.0005 832 754	112
57	0.0007 623 330	0.0006 669 127	0.0005 835 274	0.0005 106 478	114
58	0.0006 721 180	0.0005 866 119	0.0005 120 655	0.0004 470 635	116
59	0.0005 925 790	0.0005 159 799	0.0004 493 552	0.0003 913 965	118
60	0.0005 224 528	0.0004 538 525	0.0003 943 247	0.0003 426 610	120

SEMI ANNUAL
Compounding

TABLE 4. PRESENT WORTH OF ONE DOLLAR
Payable at end of each period

HALF YEARS	14% Nominal Annual Rate	14¼% Nominal Annual Rate	14½% Nominal Annual Rate	14¾% Nominal Annual Rate	HALF YEARS
1	0.9345 794 393	0.9334 889 148	0.9324 009 324	0.9313 154 831	1
YEARS					
1	0.8734 387 283	0.8714 015 541	0.8693 714 987	0.8673 485 291	2
2	0.7628 952 120	0.7593 406 685	0.7558 068 028	0.7522 934 709	4
3	0.6663 422 238	0.6616 906 386	0.6570 768 929	0.6525 006 355	6
4	0.5820 091 046	0.5765 982 508	0.5712 439 232	0.5659 454 664	8
5	0.5083 492 921	0.5024 486 118	0.4966 231 857	0.4908 719 678	10
6	0.4440 119 592	0.4378 345 012	0.4317 500 432	0.4257 570 793	12
7	0.3878 172 410	0.3815 296 648	0.3753 511 822	0.3692 797 765	14
8	0.3387 345 978	0.3324 655 428	0.3263 196 198	0.3202 942 709	16
9	0.2958 639 163	0.2897 109 907	0.2836 929 769	0.2778 067 648	18
10	0.2584 190 028	0.2524 546 075	0.2466 345 885	0.2409 552 888	20
11	0.2257 131 652	0.2199 893 373	0.2144 170 819	0.2089 922 153	22
12	0.1971 466 199	0.1916 990 504	0.1864 080 998	0.1812 690 906	24
13	0.1721 954 930	0.1670 468 505	0.1620 578 891	0.1572 234 791	26
14	0.1504 022 124	0.1455 648 851	0.1408 885 099	0.1363 675 533	28
15	0.1313 671 172	0.1268 454 671	0.1224 844 550	0.1182 781 968	30
16	0.1147 411 277	0.1105 333 372	0.1064 844 943	0.1025 884 200	32
17	0.1002 193 447	0.0963 189 218	0.0925 745 844	0.0889 799 152	34
18	0.0875 354 570	0.0839 324 581	0.0804 817 052	0.0771 765 986	36
19	0.0764 568 582	0.0731 388 745	0.0699 685 006	0.0669 390 092	38
20	0.0667 803 810	0.0637 333 289	0.0608 286 203	0.0580 594 512	40
21	0.0583 285 711	0.0555 373 218	0.0528 826 688	0.0503 577 796	42
22	0.0509 464 329	0.0483 953 085	0.0459 746 850	0.0436 777 461	44
23	0.0444 985 876	0.0421 717 471	0.0399 690 808	0.0378 838 288	46
24	0.0388 667 898	0.0367 485 259	0.0347 479 797	0.0328 584 832	48
25	0.0339 477 594	0.0320 227 226	0.0302 089 032	0.0284 997 571	50
26	0.0296 512 878	0.0279 046 503	0.0262 627 594	0.0247 192 224	52
27	0.0258 985 831	0.0243 161 556	0.0228 320 945	0.0214 401 812	54
28	0.0226 208 255	0.0211 891 358	0.0198 495 722	0.0185 961 096	56
29	0.0197 579 051	0.0184 642 458	0.0172 566 524	0.0161 293 083	58
30	0.0172 573 195	0.0160 897 725	0.0150 024 417	0.0139 897 318	60
31	0.0150 732 112	0.0140 206 528	0.0130 426 953	0.0121 339 733	62
32	0.0131 655 264	0.0122 176 186	0.0113 389 475	0.0105 243 839	64
33	0.0114 992 806	0.0106 464 519	0.0098 577 578	0.0091 283 089	66
34	0.0100 439 171	0.0092 773 347	0.0085 700 537	0.0079 174 253	68
35	0.0087 727 461	0.0080 842 839	0.0074 505 604	0.0068 671 672	70
36	0.0076 624 562	0.0070 446 575	0.0064 773 049	0.0059 562 274	72
37	0.0066 926 860	0.0061 387 255	0.0056 311 842	0.0051 661 250	74
38	0.0058 456 512	0.0053 492 950	0.0048 955 911	0.0044 808 310	76
39	0.0051 058 181	0.0046 613 839	0.0042 560 874	0.0038 864 421	78
40	0.0044 596 193	0.0040 619 372	0.0037 001 210	0.0033 708 999	80
41	0.0038 952 042	0.0035 395 784	0.0032 167 798	0.0029 237 450	82
42	0.0034 022 222	0.0030 843 941	0.0027 965 767	0.0025 359 060	84
43	0.0029 716 326	0.0026 877 458	0.0024 312 640	0.0021 995 143	86
44	0.0025 955 390	0.0023 421 059	0.0021 136 717	0.0019 077 455	88
45	0.0022 670 443	0.0020 409 147	0.0018 375 659	0.0016 546 803	90
46	0.0019 801 243	0.0017 784 563	0.0015 975 274	0.0014 351 845	92
47	0.0017 295 172	0.0015 497 495	0.0013 888 448	0.0012 448 052	94
48	0.0015 106 273	0.0013 504 542	0.0012 074 221	0.0010 796 799	96
49	0.0013 194 404	0.0011 767 879	0.0010 496 984	0.0009 364 588	98
50	0.0011 524 504	0.0010 254 548	0.0009 125 778	0.0008 122 362	100
51	0.0010 065 948	0.0008 935 829	0.0007 933 692	0.0007 044 918	102
52	0.0008 791 989	0.0007 786 695	0.0006 897 325	0.0006 110 400	104
53	0.0007 679 263	0.0006 785 338	0.0005 996 338	0.0005 299 846	106
54	0.0006 707 366	0.0005 912 754	0.0005 213 045	0.0004 596 814	108
55	0.0005 858 473	0.0005 152 383	0.0004 532 073	0.0003 987 040	110
56	0.0005 117 017	0.0004 489 795	0.0003 940 055	0.0003 458 153	112
57	0.0004 469 401	0.0003 912 414	0.0003 425 372	0.0002 999 424	114
58	0.0003 903 748	0.0003 409 284	0.0002 977 921	0.0002 601 546	116
59	0.0003 409 685	0.0002 970 855	0.0002 588 919	0.0002 256 447	118
60	0.0002 978 151	0.0002 588 808	0.0002 250 733	0.0001 957 126	120

TABLE 4. PRESENT WORTH OF ONE DOLLAR
Payable at end of each period

SEMI ANNUAL Compounding

HALF YEARS	15% Nominal Annual Rate	15¼% Nominal Annual Rate	15½% Nominal Annual Rate	15¾% Nominal Annual Rate	HALF YEARS
1	0.9302 325 581	0.9291 521 487	0.9280 742 459	0.9269 988 413	1
YEARS					
1	0.8653 326 122	0.8633 237 154	0.8613 218 060	0.8593 268 517	2
2	0.7488 005 298	0.7453 278 375	0.7418 752 535	0.7384 426 380	4
3	0.6479 615 185	0.6434 591 979	0.6389 933 331	0.6345 635 873	6
4	0.5607 022 334	0.5555 135 854	0.5503 788 917	0.5452 975 296	8
5	0.4851 939 283	0.4795 880 525	0.4740 533 410	0.4685 888 094	10
6	0.4198 541 294	0.4140 397 393	0.4083 124 798	0.4026 709 463	12
7	0.3633 134 706	0.3574 503 260	0.3516 884 425	0.3460 259 565	14
8	0.3143 869 945	0.3085 953 435	0.3029 169 244	0.2973 493 958	16
9	0.2720 493 192	0.2664 176 785	0.2609 089 524	0.2555 203 202	18
10	0.2354 131 481	0.2300 047 001	0.2247 265 701	0.2195 754 723	20
11	0.2037 106 744	0.1985 685 122	0.1935 618 952	0.1886 870 993	22
12	0.1762 774 900	0.1714 289 057	0.1667 190 811	0.1621 438 910	24
13	0.1525 386 609	0.1479 986 398	0.1435 987 800	0.1393 345 994	26
14	0.1319 966 779	0.1277 707 356	0.1236 847 606	0.1197 339 626	28
15	0.1142 210 301	0.1103 075 062	0.1065 323 813	0.1028 906 091	30
16	0.0988 391 823	0.0952 310 861	0.0917 586 631	0.0884 166 632	32
17	0.0855 287 678	0.0822 152 550	0.0790 337 374	0.0759 788 128	34
18	0.0740 108 321	0.0709 783 794	0.0680 734 814	0.0652 906 340	36
19	0.0640 439 867	0.0612 773 182	0.0586 331 740	0.0561 059 950	38
20	0.0554 193 503	0.0529 021 621	0.0505 020 313	0.0482 133 880	40
21	0.0479 561 711	0.0456 716 911	0.0434 985 008	0.0414 310 589	42
22	0.0414 980 388	0.0394 294 540	0.0374 662 073	0.0356 028 214	44
23	0.0359 096 064	0.0340 403 828	0.0322 704 613	0.0305 944 605	46
24	0.0310 737 535	0.0293 878 697	0.0277 952 520	0.0262 906 414	48
25	0.0268 891 323	0.0253 712 449	0.0239 406 567	0.0225 922 541	50
26	0.0232 680 431	0.0219 035 974	0.0206 206 096	0.0194 141 306	52
27	0.0201 345 965	0.0189 098 951	0.0177 609 807	0.0166 830 837	54
28	0.0174 231 230	0.0163 253 609	0.0152 979 200	0.0143 362 218	56
29	0.0150 767 965	0.0140 940 712	0.0131 764 321	0.0123 195 003	58
30	0.0130 464 437	0.0121 677 459	0.0113 491 483	0.0105 864 774	60
31	0.0112 895 132	0.0105 047 036	0.0097 752 689	0.0090 972 443	62
32	0.0097 691 840	0.0090 689 598	0.0084 196 523	0.0078 175 063	64
33	0.0084 535 935	0.0078 294 480	0.0072 520 301	0.0067 177 931	66
34	0.0073 151 701	0.0067 593 482	0.0062 463 316	0.0057 727 800	68
35	0.0063 300 553	0.0058 355 056	0.0053 801 017	0.0049 607 049	70
36	0.0054 776 033	0.0050 379 303	0.0046 339 989	0.0042 628 669	72
37	0.0047 399 487	0.0043 493 647	0.0039 913 643	0.0036 631 960	74
38	0.0041 016 322	0.0037 549 097	0.0034 378 491	0.0031 478 827	76
39	0.0035 492 761	0.0032 417 026	0.0029 610 944	0.0027 050 601	78
40	0.0030 713 044	0.0027 986 387	0.0025 504 552	0.0023 245 308	80
41	0.0026 576 998	0.0024 161 312	0.0021 967 626	0.0019 975 317	82
42	0.0022 997 944	0.0020 859 034	0.0018 921 196	0.0017 165 326	84
43	0.0019 900 871	0.0018 008 098	0.0016 297 238	0.0014 750 626	86
44	0.0017 220 872	0.0015 546 818	0.0014 037 167	0.0012 675 609	88
45	0.0014 901 782	0.0013 421 937	0.0012 090 518	0.0010 892 491	90
46	0.0012 894 998	0.0011 587 477	0.0010 413 827	0.0009 360 210	92
47	0.0011 158 463	0.0010 003 743	0.0008 969 656	0.0008 043 480	94
48	0.0009 655 782	0.0008 636 469	0.0007 725 760	0.0006 911 978	96
49	0.0008 355 463	0.0007 456 068	0.0006 654 366	0.0005 939 649	98
50	0.0007 230 254	0.0006 437 001	0.0005 731 550	0.0005 104 099	100
51	0.0006 256 575	0.0005 557 215	0.0004 936 709	0.0004 386 090	102
52	0.0005 414 018	0.0004 797 676	0.0004 252 095	0.0003 769 085	104
53	0.0004 684 927	0.0004 141 947	0.0003 662 423	0.0003 238 876	106
54	0.0004 054 020	0.0003 575 841	0.0003 154 524	0.0002 783 253	108
55	0.0003 508 076	0.0003 087 109	0.0002 717 061	0.0002 391 724	110
56	0.0003 035 652	0.0002 665 174	0.0002 340 264	0.0002 055 273	112
57	0.0002 626 849	0.0002 300 908	0.0002 015 720	0.0001 766 151	114
58	0.0002 273 098	0.0001 986 428	0.0001 736 184	0.0001 517 701	116
59	0.0001 966 986	0.0001 714 931	0.0001 495 413	0.0001 304 201	118
60	0.0001 702 097	0.0001 480 540	0.0001 288 032	0.0001 120 735	120

SEMI ANNUAL Compounding

TABLE 4. PRESENT WORTH OF ONE DOLLAR
Payable at end of each period

HALF YEARS	16% Nominal Annual Rate	16¼% Nominal Annual Rate	16½% Nominal Annual Rate	16¾% Nominal Annual Rate	HALF YEARS
1	0.9259 259 259	0.9248 554 913	0.9237 875 289	0.9227 220 300	1
YEARS					
1	0.8573 388 203	0.8553 576 798	0.8533 833 985	0.8514 159 446	2
2	0.7350 298 528	0.7316 367 605	0.7282 632 248	0.7249 091 108	4
3	0.6301 696 269	0.6258 111 219	0.6214 877 458	0.6171 991 753	6
4	0.5402 688 845	0.5352 923 493	0.5303 673 246	0.5254 932 189	8
5	0.4631 934 881	0.4578 664 219	0.4526 066 699	0.4474 133 053	10
6	0.3971 137 586	0.3916 395 603	0.3862 470 182	0.3809 348 220	12
7	0.3404 610 414	0.3349 919 056	0.3296 167 930	0.3243 339 813	14
8	0.2918 904 676	0.2865 378 992	0.2812 894 990	0.2761 431 231	16
9	0.2502 490 291	0.2450 923 926	0.2400 477 886	0.2351 126 580	18
10	0.2145 482 074	0.2096 416 603	0.2048 527 977	0.2001 786 658	20
11	0.1839 405 070	0.1793 186 042	0.1748 179 767	0.1704 353 078	22
12	0.1576 993 373	0.1533 815 452	0.1491 867 590	0.1451 113 386	24
13	0.1352 017 638	0.1311 960 826	0.1273 135 034	0.1235 501 074	26
14	0.1159 137 207	0.1122 195 768	0.1086 472 302	0.1051 925 314	28
15	0.0993 773 325	0.0959 878 769	0.0927 177 426	0.0895 625 985	30
16	0.0852 000 451	0.0821 039 677	0.0791 237 823	0.0762 550 244	32
17	0.0730 453 061	0.0702 282 593	0.0675 229 222	0.0649 247 437	34
18	0.0626 245 766	0.0600 702 809	0.0576 229 408	0.0552 779 619	36
19	0.0536 904 806	0.0513 815 761	0.0491 744 611	0.0470 645 382	38
20	0.0460 309 333	0.0439 496 257	0.0419 646 687	0.0400 714 982	40
21	0.0394 641 061	0.0375 926 499	0.0358 119 516	0.0341 175 125	42
22	0.0338 341 101	0.0321 551 618	0.0305 613 250	0.0290 481 942	44
23	0.0290 072 961	0.0275 041 646	0.0260 805 274	0.0247 320 957	46
24	0.0248 690 810	0.0235 258 984	0.0222 566 891	0.0210 573 006	48
25	0.0213 212 286	0.0201 230 579	0.0189 934 890	0.0179 285 215	50
26	0.0182 795 169	0.0172 124 121	0.0162 087 282	0.0152 646 290	52
27	0.0156 717 395	0.0147 227 689	0.0138 322 595	0.0129 965 486	54
28	0.0134 359 906	0.0125 932 334	0.0118 042 206	0.0110 654 687	56
29	0.0115 191 964	0.0107 717 189	0.0100 735 259	0.0094 213 165	58
30	0.0098 758 542	0.0092 136 725	0.0085 965 798	0.0080 214 591	60
31	0.0084 669 532	0.0078 809 855	0.0073 361 785	0.0068 295 981	62
32	0.0072 590 477	0.0067 410 615	0.0062 605 729	0.0058 148 287	64
33	0.0062 234 634	0.0057 660 187	0.0053 426 690	0.0049 508 379	66
34	0.0053 356 167	0.0049 320 084	0.0045 593 450	0.0042 152 223	68
35	0.0045 744 314	0.0042 186 313	0.0038 908 694	0.0035 889 075	70
36	0.0039 218 376	0.0036 084 387	0.0033 204 033	0.0030 556 531	72
37	0.0033 623 436	0.0030 865 057	0.0028 335 771	0.0026 016 318	74
38	0.0028 826 677	0.0026 400 664	0.0024 181 276	0.0022 150 708	76
39	0.0024 714 229	0.0022 582 010	0.0020 635 900	0.0018 859 466	78
40	0.0021 188 468	0.0019 315 696	0.0017 610 334	0.0016 057 250	80
41	0.0018 165 696	0.0016 521 829	0.0015 028 367	0.0013 671 398	82
42	0.0015 574 157	0.0014 132 073	0.0012 824 959	0.0011 640 047	84
43	0.0013 352 329	0.0012 087 977	0.0010 944 607	0.0009 910 521	86
44	0.0011 447 470	0.0010 339 544	0.0009 339 946	0.0008 437 976	88
45	0.0009 814 360	0.0008 844 009	0.0007 970 555	0.0007 184 227	90
46	0.0008 414 232	0.0007 564 791	0.0006 801 939	0.0006 116 766	92
47	0.0007 213 848	0.0006 470 602	0.0005 804 662	0.0005 207 912	94
48	0.0006 184 712	0.0005 534 679	0.0004 953 602	0.0004 434 099	96
49	0.0005 302 394	0.0004 734 130	0.0004 227 322	0.0003 775 263	98
50	0.0004 545 948	0.0004 049 375	0.0003 607 526	0.0003 214 319	100
51	0.0003 897 418	0.0003 463 664	0.0003 078 603	0.0002 736 722	102
52	0.0003 341 407	0.0002 962 671	0.0002 627 229	0.0002 330 089	104
53	0.0002 864 718	0.0002 534 144	0.0002 242 033	0.0001 983 875	106
54	0.0002 456 034	0.0002 167 599	0.0001 913 314	0.0001 689 103	108
55	0.0002 105 653	0.0001 854 073	0.0001 632 790	0.0001 438 129	110
56	0.0001 805 258	0.0001 585 895	0.0001 393 396	0.0001 224 446	112
57	0.0001 547 718	0.0001 356 508	0.0001 189 101	0.0001 042 513	114
58	0.0001 326 919	0.0001 160 299	0.0001 014 759	0.0000 887 612	116
59	0.0001 137 619	0.0000 992 471	0.0000 865 979	0.0000 755 727	118
60	0.0000 975 325	0.0000 848 918	0.0000 739 012	0.0000 643 438	120

TABLE 4. PRESENT WORTH OF ONE DOLLAR
Payable at end of each period

SEMI ANNUAL Compounding

HALF YEARS	17% Nominal Annual Rate	17¼% Nominal Annual Rate	17½% Nominal Annual Rate	17¾% Nominal Annual Rate	HALF YEARS
1	0.9216 589 862	0.9205 983 890	0.9195 402 299	0.9184 845 006	1
YEARS					
1	0.8494 552 868	0.8475 013 937	0.8455 542 344	0.8436 137 778	2
2	0.7215 742 843	0.7182 586 124	0.7149 619 633	0.7116 842 061	4
3	0.6129 450 906	0.6087 251 751	0.6045 391 155	0.6003 866 017	6
4	0.5206 694 477	0.5158 954 343	0.5111 706 089	0.5064 944 092	8
5	0.4422 854 150	0.4372 220 996	0.4322 224 729	0.4272 856 620	10
6	0.3757 016 841	0.3705 463 388	0.3654 675 421	0.3604 640 715	12
7	0.3191 417 818	0.3140 385 386	0.3090 226 278	0.3040 924 571	14
8	0.2710 966 738	0.2661 480 991	0.2612 953 914	0.2565 365 865	16
9	0.2302 845 028	0.2255 608 849	0.2209 394 246	0.2164 177 989	18
10	0.1956 163 884	0.1911 631 644	0.1868 162 661	0.1825 730 369	20
11	0.1661 673 753	0.1620 110 482	0.1579 632 848	0.1540 211 294	22
12	0.1411 517 554	0.1373 045 892	0.1335 665 243	0.1299 343 468	24
13	0.1199 021 049	0.1163 658 307	0.1129 377 402	0.1096 144 052	26
14	0.1018 514 769	0.0986 202 037	0.0954 949 845	0.0924 722 225	28
15	0.0865 182 755	0.0835 807 601	0.0807 461 885	0.0780 108 409	30
16	0.0734 934 065	0.0708 348 107	0.0682 752 816	0.0658 110 202	32
17	0.0624 293 627	0.0600 326 008	0.0577 304 534	0.0555 190 834	34
18	0.0530 309 522	0.0508 777 128	0.0488 142 294	0.0468 366 637	36
19	0.0450 474 227	0.0431 189 325	0.0412 750 783	0.0395 120 548	38
20	0.0382 657 714	0.0365 433 554	0.0349 003 173	0.0333 329 138	40
21	0.0325 050 618	0.0309 705 446	0.0295 101 110	0.0281 201 053	42
22	0.0276 115 966	0.0262 475 797	0.0249 523 993	0.0237 225 083	44
23	0.0234 548 167	0.0222 448 604	0.0210 986 069	0.0200 126 348	46
24	0.0199 238 181	0.0188 525 502	0.0178 400 164	0.0168 829 345	48
25	0.0169 243 926	0.0159 775 626	0.0150 847 014	0.0142 426 761	50
26	0.0143 765 148	0.0135 410 066	0.0127 549 332	0.0120 153 178	52
27	0.0122 122 065	0.0114 760 219	0.0107 849 878	0.0101 362 877	54
28	0.0103 737 233	0.0097 259 446	0.0091 192 921	0.0085 511 119	56
29	0.0088 120 141	0.0082 427 516	0.0077 108 560	0.0072 138 358	58
30	0.0074 854 120	0.0069 857 435	0.0065 199 470	0.0060 856 913	60
31	0.0063 585 228	0.0059 204 273	0.0055 129 688	0.0051 339 730	62
32	0.0054 012 808	0.0050 175 704	0.0046 615 141	0.0043 310 904	64
33	0.0045 881 465	0.0042 523 979	0.0039 415 630	0.0036 537 675	66
34	0.0038 974 253	0.0036 039 132	0.0033 328 053	0.0030 823 686	68
35	0.0033 106 886	0.0030 543 214	0.0028 180 676	0.0026 003 286	70
36	0.0028 122 819	0.0025 885 417	0.0023 828 290	0.0021 936 731	72
37	0.0023 889 077	0.0021 937 927	0.0020 148 111	0.0018 506 128	74
38	0.0020 292 703	0.0018 592 423	0.0017 036 321	0.0015 612 025	76
39	0.0017 237 744	0.0015 757 105	0.0014 405 133	0.0013 170 519	78
40	0.0014 642 693	0.0013 354 168	0.0012 180 321	0.0011 110 831	80
41	0.0012 438 313	0.0011 317 676	0.0010 299 122	0.0009 373 250	82
42	0.0010 565 790	0.0009 591 746	0.0008 708 467	0.0007 907 403	84
43	0.0008 975 167	0.0008 129 018	0.0007 363 481	0.0006 670 794	86
44	0.0007 624 003	0.0006 889 354	0.0006 226 222	0.0005 627 574	88
45	0.0006 476 249	0.0005 838 737	0.0005 264 609	0.0004 747 499	90
46	0.0005 501 284	0.0004 948 338	0.0004 451 512	0.0004 005 056	92
47	0.0004 673 095	0.0004 193 723	0.0003 763 995	0.0003 378 720	94
48	0.0003 969 585	0.0003 554 186	0.0003 182 662	0.0002 850 335	96
49	0.0003 371 985	0.0003 012 178	0.0002 691 113	0.0002 404 582	98
50	0.0002 864 351	0.0002 552 825	0.0002 275 482	0.0002 028 538	100
51	0.0002 433 138	0.0002 163 523	0.0001 924 044	0.0001 711 303	102
52	0.0002 066 842	0.0001 833 589	0.0001 626 883	0.0001 443 679	104
53	0.0001 755 690	0.0001 553 969	0.0001 375 618	0.0001 217 907	106
54	0.0001 491 380	0.0001 316 991	0.0001 163 160	0.0001 027 443	108
55	0.0001 266 861	0.0001 116 152	0.0000 983 515	0.0000 866 765	110
56	0.0001 076 141	0.0000 945 940	0.0000 831 615	0.0000 731 215	112
57	0.0000 914 134	0.0000 801 685	0.0000 703 175	0.0000 616 863	114
58	0.0000 776 516	0.0000 679 430	0.0000 594 573	0.0000 520 394	116
59	0.0000 659 616	0.0000 575 817	0.0000 502 744	0.0000 439 012	118
60	0.0000 560 314	0.0000 488 006	0.0000 425 097	0.0000 370 356	120

TABLE 4. PRESENT WORTH OF ONE DOLLAR
Payable at end of each period

HALF YEARS	18% Nominal Annual Rate	18¼% Nominal Annual Rate	18½% Nominal Annual Rate	18¾% Nominal Annual Rate	HALF YEARS
1	0.9174 311 927	0.9163 802 978	0.9153 318 078	0.9142 857 143	1
YEARS					
1	0.8416 799 933	0.8397 528 502	0.8378 323 183	0.8359 183 673	2
2	0.7084 252 111	0.7051 848 495	0.7019 629 936	0.6987 595 169	4
3	0.5962 673 269	0.5921 809 873	0.5881 272 824	0.5841 059 145	6
4	0.5018 662 797	0.4972 856 719	0.4927 520 444	0.4882 648 624	8
5	0.4224 108 069	0.4175 970 604	0.4128 435 878	0.4081 495 666	10
6	0.3555 347 251	0.3506 783 217	0.3458 937 002	0.3411 797 194	12
7	0.2992 464 650	0.2944 831 202	0.2898 009 208	0.2851 983 940	14
8	0.2518 697 627	0.2472 930 395	0.2428 045 773	0.2384 025 759	16
9	0.2119 937 402	0.2076 650 348	0.2034 295 219	0.1992 850 920	18
10	0.1784 308 898	0.1743 873 049	0.1704 398 280	0.1665 860 687	20
11	0.1501 817 101	0.1464 422 363	0.1427 999 962	0.1392 523 546	22
12	0.1264 049 408	0.1229 752 853	0.1196 424 519	0.1164 036 009	24
13	0.1063 925 097	0.1032 688 464	0.1002 403 128	0.0973 039 080	26
14	0.0895 484 468	0.0867 203 081	0.0839 845 737	0.0813 381 239	28
15	0.0753 711 361	0.0728 236 259	0.0703 649 901	0.0679 920 318	30
16	0.0634 383 773	0.0611 538 474	0.0589 540 628	0.0568 357 882	32
17	0.0533 948 130	0.0513 541 177	0.0493 936 191	0.0475 100 793	34
18	0.0449 413 459	0.0431 247 667	0.0413 835 704	0.0397 145 479	36
19	0.0378 262 317	0.0362 141 457	0.0346 724 927	0.0331 981 200	38
20	0.0318 375 824	0.0304 109 321	0.0290 497 350	0.0277 509 183	40
21	0.0267 970 562	0.0255 376 669	0.0243 388 068	0.0231 975 023	42
22	0.0225 545 461	0.0214 453 286	0.0203 918 389	0.0193 912 183	44
23	0.0189 837 102	0.0180 087 758	0.0170 849 417	0.0162 094 755	46
24	0.0159 782 090	0.0151 229 208	0.0143 143 163	0.0135 497 983	48
25	0.0134 485 389	0.0126 995 158	0.0119 929 968	0.0113 265 253	50
26	0.0113 193 661	0.0106 644 546	0.0100 481 203	0.0094 680 505	52
27	0.0095 272 840	0.0089 555 062	0.0084 186 399	0.0079 145 173	54
28	0.0080 189 243	0.0075 204 118	0.0070 534 086	0.0066 158 904	56
29	0.0067 493 682	0.0063 152 873	0.0059 095 737	0.0055 303 443	58
30	0.0056 808 082	0.0053 032 805	0.0049 512 318	0.0046 229 164	60
31	0.0047 814 226	0.0044 534 449	0.0041 483 020	0.0038 643 807	62
32	0.0040 244 277	0.0037 397 931	0.0034 755 815	0.0032 303 068	64
33	0.0033 872 803	0.0031 405 019	0.0029 119 545	0.0027 002 728	66
34	0.0028 510 061	0.0026 372 454	0.0024 397 296	0.0022 572 076	68
35	0.0023 996 348	0.0022 146 343	0.0020 440 843	0.0018 868 413	70
36	0.0020 197 246	0.0018 597 455	0.0017 125 999	0.0015 772 453	72
37	0.0016 999 618	0.0015 617 266	0.0014 348 715	0.0013 184 483	74
38	0.0014 308 238	0.0013 114 644	0.0012 021 818	0.0011 021 152	76
39	0.0012 042 958	0.0011 013 059	0.0010 072 267	0.0009 212 783	78
40	0.0010 136 317	0.0009 248 248	0.0008 438 871	0.0007 701 135	80
41	0.0008 531 535	0.0007 766 243	0.0007 070 359	0.0006 437 520	82
42	0.0007 180 822	0.0006 521 724	0.0005 923 775	0.0005 381 241	84
43	0.0006 043 954	0.0005 476 637	0.0004 963 130	0.0004 498 278	86
44	0.0005 087 075	0.0004 599 021	0.0004 158 271	0.0003 760 193	88
45	0.0004 281 690	0.0003 862 041	0.0003 483 934	0.0003 143 215	90
46	0.0003 603 813	0.0003 243 160	0.0002 918 952	0.0002 627 471	92
47	0.0003 033 257	0.0002 723 453	0.0002 445 593	0.0002 196 351	94
48	0.0002 553 032	0.0002 287 027	0.0002 048 997	0.0001 835 970	96
49	0.0002 148 836	0.0001 920 538	0.0001 716 715	0.0001 534 721	98
50	0.0001 808 632	0.0001 612 777	0.0001 438 320	0.0001 282 902	100
51	0.0001 522 289	0.0001 354 334	0.0001 205 071	0.0001 072 401	102
52	0.0001 281 280	0.0001 137 306	0.0001 009 647	0.0000 896 440	104
53	0.0001 078 428	0.0000 955 056	0.0000 845 915	0.0000 749 350	106
54	0.0000 907 691	0.0000 802 011	0.0000 708 735	0.0000 626 396	108
55	0.0000 763 986	0.0000 673 491	0.0000 593 801	0.0000 523 616	110
56	0.0000 643 031	0.0000 565 566	0.0000 497 506	0.0000 437 700	112
57	0.0000 541 227	0.0000 474 936	0.0000 416 826	0.0000 365 882	114
58	0.0000 455 540	0.0000 398 829	0.0000 349 231	0.0000 305 847	116
59	0.0000 383 419	0.0000 334 917	0.0000 292 597	0.0000 255 663	118
60	0.0000 322 716	0.0000 281 248	0.0000 245 147	0.0000 213 714	120

TABLE 4. PRESENT WORTH OF ONE DOLLAR
Payable at end of each period

SEMI ANNUAL Compounding

HALF YEARS	19% Nominal Annual Rate	19¼% Nominal Annual Rate	19½% Nominal Annual Rate	19¾% Nominal Annual Rate	HALF YEARS
1	0.9132 420 091	0.9122 006 842	0.9111 617 312	0.9101 251 422	1
YEARS					
1	0.8340 109 672	0.8321 100 882	0.8302 157 004	0.8283 277 745	2
2	0.6955 742 935	0.6924 071 988	0.6892 581 092	0.6861 269 020	4
3	0.5801 165 893	0.5761 590 153	0.5722 329 039	0.5683 379 697	6
4	0.4838 235 978	0.4794 277 290	0.4750 767 411	0.4707 701 256	8
5	0.4035 141 867	0.3989 366 498	0.3944 161 694	0.3899 519 704	10
6	0.3365 352 572	0.3319 592 109	0.3274 504 963	0.3230 080 478	12
7	0.2806 740 954	0.2762 266 082	0.2718 545 432	0.2675 565 374	14
8	0.2340 852 737	0.2298 509 473	0.2256 979 100	0.2216 245 112	16
9	0.1952 296 856	0.1912 612 920	0.1873 779 484	0.1835 777 381	18
10	0.1628 236 989	0.1591 504 506	0.1555 641 147	0.1520 625 392	20
11	0.1357 967 506	0.1324 306 955	0.1291 517 704	0.1259 576 247	22
12	0.1132 559 793	0.1101 969 177	0.1072 238 275	0.1043 341 990	24
13	0.0944 567 289	0.0916 959 669	0.0890 189 051	0.0864 229 148	26
14	0.0787 779 478	0.0763 011 391	0.0739 048 926	0.0715 865 007	28
15	0.0657 016 724	0.0634 909 476	0.0613 570 022	0.0592 970 868	30
16	0.0547 959 154	0.0528 314 580	0.0509 395 466	0.0491 174 239	32
17	0.0457 003 944	0.0439 615 892	0.0422 908 113	0.0406 853 265	34
18	0.0381 146 301	0.0365 808 818	0.0351 104 955	0.0337 007 859	36
19	0.0317 880 195	0.0304 393 208	0.0291 492 847	0.0279 152 970	38
20	0.0265 115 569	0.0253 288 659	0.0242 001 938	0.0231 230 158	40
21	0.0221 109 292	0.0210 764 049	0.0200 913 808	0.0191 534 363	42
22	0.0184 407 575	0.0175 378 891	0.0166 801 798	0.0158 653 232	44
23	0.0153 797 940	0.0145 934 544	0.0138 481 472	0.0131 416 879	46
24	0.0128 269 169	0.0121 433 607	0.0114 969 492	0.0108 856 251	48
25	0.0106 977 893	0.0101 046 129	0.0095 449 477	0.0090 168 656	50
26	0.0089 220 736	0.0084 081 503	0.0079 243 655	0.0074 689 202	52
27	0.0074 411 073	0.0069 965 067	0.0065 789 326	0.0061 867 141	54
28	0.0062 059 651	0.0058 218 638	0.0054 619 332	0.0051 246 271	56
29	0.0051 758 429	0.0048 444 316	0.0045 345 827	0.0042 448 709	58
30	0.0043 167 098	0.0040 311 004	0.0037 646 817	0.0035 161 445	60
31	0.0036 001 833	0.0033 543 193	0.0031 254 979	0.0029 125 202	62
32	0.0030 025 923	0.0027 911 630	0.0025 948 374	0.0024 125 213	64
33	0.0025 041 949	0.0023 225 549	0.0021 542 748	0.0019 983 584	66
34	0.0020 885 260	0.0019 326 213	0.0017 885 127	0.0016 552 958	68
35	0.0017 418 536	0.0016 081 537	0.0014 848 513	0.0013 711 275	70
36	0.0014 527 250	0.0013 381 609	0.0012 327 469	0.0011 357 430	72
37	0.0012 115 886	0.0011 134 972	0.0010 234 458	0.0009 407 674	74
38	0.0010 104 782	0.0009 265 523	0.0008 496 808	0.0007 792 638	76
39	0.0008 427 499	0.0007 709 935	0.0007 054 183	0.0006 454 859	78
40	0.0007 028 627	0.0006 415 514	0.0005 856 494	0.0005 346 739	80
41	0.0005 861 952	0.0005 338 414	0.0004 862 153	0.0004 428 852	82
42	0.0004 888 932	0.0004 442 148	0.0004 036 636	0.0003 668 541	84
43	0.0004 077 423	0.0003 696 357	0.0003 351 278	0.0003 038 755	86
44	0.0003 400 615	0.0003 075 776	0.0002 782 284	0.0002 517 085	88
45	0.0002 836 151	0.0002 559 384	0.0002 309 896	0.0002 084 971	90
46	0.0002 365 381	0.0002 129 689	0.0001 917 712	0.0001 727 040	92
47	0.0001 972 753	0.0001 772 136	0.0001 592 114	0.0001 430 555	94
48	0.0001 645 298	0.0001 474 612	0.0001 321 798	0.0001 184 968	96
49	0.0001 372 197	0.0001 227 040	0.0001 097 378	0.0000 981 542	98
50	0.0001 144 427	0.0001 021 032	0.0000 911 060	0.0000 813 039	100
51	0.0000 954 465	0.0000 849 611	0.0000 756 377	0.0000 673 462	102
52	0.0000 796 034	0.0000 706 970	0.0000 627 956	0.0000 557 848	104
53	0.0000 663 901	0.0000 588 277	0.0000 521 339	0.0000 462 081	106
54	0.0000 553 701	0.0000 489 511	0.0000 432 824	0.0000 382 754	108
55	0.0000 461 793	0.0000 407 327	0.0000 359 337	0.0000 317 046	110
56	0.0000 385 140	0.0000 338 941	0.0000 298 327	0.0000 262 618	112
57	0.0000 321 211	0.0000 282 036	0.0000 247 676	0.0000 217 534	114
58	0.0000 267 893	0.0000 234 685	0.0000 205 624	0.0000 180 189	116
59	0.0000 223 426	0.0000 195 284	0.0000 170 713	0.0000 149 256	118
60	0.0000 186 340	0.0000 162 498	0.0000 141 728	0.0000 123 633	120

SEMI ANNUAL
Compounding

TABLE 4. PRESENT WORTH OF ONE DOLLAR
Payable at end of each period

HALF YEARS	20% Nominal Annual Rate	20¼% Nominal Annual Rate	20½% Nominal Annual Rate	20¾% Nominal Annual Rate	HALF YEARS
1	0.9090 909 091	0.9080 590 238	0.9070 294 785	0.9060 022 650	1
YEARS					
1	0.8264 462 810	0.8245 711 908	0.8227 024 748	0.8208 401 042	2
2	0.6830 134 554	0.6799 176 486	0.6768 393 620	0.6737 784 767	4
3	0.5644 739 301	0.5606 405 052	0.5568 374 182	0.5530 643 950	6
4	0.4665 073 802	0.4622 880 089	0.4581 115 220	0.4539 774 356	8
5	0.3855 432 894	0.3811 893 740	0.3768 894 829	0.3726 428 855	10
6	0.3186 308 177	0.3143 177 760	0.3100 679 103	0.3058 802 250	12
7	0.2633 312 543	0.2591 773 829	0.2550 936 371	0.2510 787 558	14
8	0.2176 291 358	0.2137 102 032	0.2098 661 666	0.2060 955 120	16
9	0.1798 587 899	0.1762 192 767	0.1726 574 146	0.1691 714 616	18
10	0.1486 436 280	0.1453 053 389	0.1420 456 823	0.1388 627 201	20
11	0.1228 459 736	0.1198 145 963	0.1168 613 344	0.1139 840 897	22
12	0.1015 255 980	0.0987 956 643	0.0961 421 090	0.0935 627 120	24
13	0.0839 054 529	0.0814 640 586	0.0790 963 510	0.0768 000 263	26
14	0.0693 433 495	0.0671 729 158	0.0650 727 637	0.0630 405 416	28
15	0.0573 085 533	0.0553 888 512	0.0535 355 237	0.0517 462 047	30
16	0.0473 624 407	0.0456 720 510	0.0440 438 079	0.0424 753 601	32
17	0.0391 425 130	0.0376 598 574	0.0362 349 497	0.0348 654 790	34
18	0.0323 491 843	0.0310 532 335	0.0298 105 828	0.0286 189 834	36
19	0.0267 348 631	0.0256 056 017	0.0245 252 403	0.0234 916 093	38
20	0.0220 949 282	0.0211 136 415	0.0201 769 759	0.0192 828 550	40
21	0.0182 602 712	0.0174 097 005	0.0165 996 480	0.0158 281 407	42
22	0.0150 911 332	0.0143 555 375	0.0136 565 715	0.0129 923 727	44
23	0.0124 720 109	0.0118 371 626	0.0112 352 951	0.0106 646 606	46
24	0.0103 074 470	0.0097 605 833	0.0092 433 051	0.0087 539 811	48
25	0.0085 185 513	0.0080 482 958	0.0076 044 900	0.0071 856 187	50
26	0.0070 401 250	0.0066 363 928	0.0062 562 327	0.0058 982 440	52
27	0.0058 182 851	0.0054 721 783	0.0051 470 182	0.0048 415 153	54
28	0.0048 085 001	0.0045 122 006	0.0042 344 646	0.0039 741 099	56
29	0.0039 739 670	0.0037 206 306	0.0034 837 045	0.0032 621 088	58
30	0.0032 842 703	0.0030 679 248	0.0028 660 523	0.0026 776 697	60
31	0.0027 142 730	0.0025 297 224	0.0023 579 083	0.0021 979 387	62
32	0.0022 432 008	0.0020 859 362	0.0019 398 570	0.0018 041 562	64
33	0.0018 538 850	0.0017 200 029	0.0015 959 252	0.0014 809 238	66
34	0.0015 321 363	0.0014 182 649	0.0013 129 716	0.0012 156 016	68
35	0.0012 662 284	0.0011 694 603	0.0010 801 850	0.0009 978 146	70
36	0.0010 464 697	0.0009 643 033	0.0008 886 708	0.0008 190 462	72
37	0.0008 648 510	0.0007 951 367	0.0007 311 117	0.0006 723 060	74
38	0.0007 147 529	0.0006 556 468	0.0006 014 874	0.0005 518 557	76
39	0.0005 907 049	0.0005 406 275	0.0004 948 452	0.0004 529 853	78
40	0.0004 881 859	0.0004 457 859	0.0004 071 104	0.0003 718 285	80
41	0.0004 034 594	0.0003 675 822	0.0003 349 307	0.0003 052 117	82
42	0.0003 334 375	0.0003 030 977	0.0002 755 483	0.0002 505 300	84
43	0.0002 755 682	0.0002 499 256	0.0002 266 943	0.0002 056 451	86
44	0.0002 277 423	0.0002 060 815	0.0001 865 019	0.0001 688 017	88
45	0.0001 882 168	0.0001 699 288	0.0001 534 356	0.0001 385 592	90
46	0.0001 555 511	0.0001 401 184	0.0001 262 319	0.0001 137 350	92
47	0.0001 285 546	0.0001 155 376	0.0001 038 513	0.0000 933 582	94
48	0.0001 062 435	0.0000 952 690	0.0000 854 387	0.0000 766 322	96
49	0.0000 878 045	0.0000 785 561	0.0000 702 906	0.0000 629 028	98
50	0.0000 725 657	0.0000 647 751	0.0000 578 283	0.0000 516 331	100
51	0.0000 599 717	0.0000 534 117	0.0000 475 755	0.0000 423 825	102
52	0.0000 495 634	0.0000 440 417	0.0000 391 404	0.0000 347 893	104
53	0.0000 409 615	0.0000 363 155	0.0000 322 009	0.0000 285 564	106
54	0.0000 338 524	0.0000 299 447	0.0000 264 918	0.0000 234 403	108
55	0.0000 279 772	0.0000 246 916	0.0000 217 949	0.0000 192 407	110
56	0.0000 231 217	0.0000 203 600	0.0000 179 307	0.0000 157 935	112
57	0.0000 191 088	0.0000 167 882	0.0000 147 516	0.0000 129 640	114
58	0.0000 157 924	0.0000 138 431	0.0000 121 362	0.0000 106 414	116
59	0.0000 130 516	0.0000 114 146	0.0000 099 845	0.0000 087 348	118
60	0.0000 107 864	0.0000 094 122	0.0000 082 143	0.0000 071 699	120

TABLE 4. PRESENT WORTH OF ONE DOLLAR
Payable at end of each period

SEMI ANNUAL Compounding

HALF YEARS	21% Nominal Annual Rate	21¼% Nominal Annual Rate	21½% Nominal Annual Rate	21¾% Nominal Annual Rate	HALF YEARS
1	0.9049 773 756	0.9039 548 023	0.9029 345 372	0.9019 165 727	1
YEARS					
1	0.8189 840 503	0.8171 342 845	0.8152 907 786	0.8134 535 041	2
2	0.6707 348 746	0.6677 084 390	0.6646 990 536	0.6617 066 034	4
3	0.5493 211 643	0.5456 074 575	0.5419 230 089	0.5382 675 552	6
4	0.4498 852 720	0.4458 345 594	0.4418 248 318	0.4378 556 290	8
5	0.3684 488 623	0.3643 067 038	0.3602 157 111	0.3561 751 957	10
6	0.3017 537 415	0.2976 874 977	0.2936 805 476	0.2897 319 610	12
7	0.2471 315 014	0.2432 506 605	0.2394 350 423	0.2356 834 790	14
8	0.2023 967 580	0.1987 684 544	0.1952 091 820	0.1917 175 518	16
9	0.1657 597 166	0.1624 205 188	0.1591 522 460	0.1559 533 143	18
10	0.1357 545 641	0.1327 193 744	0.1297 553 586	0.1268 607 700	20
11	0.1111 808 227	0.1084 495 510	0.1057 883 473	0.1031 953 379	22
12	0.0910 553 205	0.0886 178 463	0.0862 482 640	0.0839 446 092	24
13	0.0745 728 552	0.0724 126 804	0.0703 174 143	0.0682 850 365	26
14	0.0610 739 790	0.0591 708 838	0.0573 291 395	0.0555 467 023	28
15	0.0500 186 147	0.0483 505 578	0.0467 399 188	0.0451 846 596	30
16	0.0409 644 476	0.0395 088 985	0.0381 066 248	0.0367 556 197	32
17	0.0335 492 293	0.0322 840 755	0.0310 679 798	0.0298 989 876	34
18	0.0274 762 837	0.0263 804 249	0.0253 294 374	0.0243 214 363	36
19	0.0225 026 381	0.0215 563 496	0.0206 508 567	0.0197 843 575	38
20	0.0184 293 017	0.0176 144 323	0.0168 364 531	0.0160 936 550	40
21	0.0150 933 041	0.0143 933 566	0.0137 266 049	0.0130 914 400	42
22	0.0123 611 753	0.0117 613 051	0.0111 911 744	0.0106 492 778	44
23	0.0101 236 055	0.0096 105 656	0.0091 240 613	0.0086 626 923	46
24	0.0082 910 714	0.0078 531 227	0.0074 387 630	0.0070 466 974	48
25	0.0067 902 552	0.0064 170 558	0.0060 647 549	0.0057 321 607	50
26	0.0055 611 107	0.0052 435 963	0.0049 445 388	0.0046 628 462	52
27	0.0045 544 610	0.0042 847 223	0.0040 312 369	0.0037 930 086	54
28	0.0037 300 309	0.0035 011 935	0.0032 866 302	0.0030 854 361	56
29	0.0030 548 358	0.0028 609 452	0.0026 795 593	0.0025 098 588	58
30	0.0025 018 618	0.0023 377 764	0.0021 846 200	0.0020 416 535	60
31	0.0020 489 849	0.0019 102 773	0.0017 811 005	0.0016 607 902	62
32	0.0016 780 860	0.0015 609 531	0.0014 521 148	0.0013 509 756	64
33	0.0013 743 256	0.0012 755 083	0.0011 838 958	0.0010 989 558	66
34	0.0011 255 508	0.0010 422 615	0.0009 652 194	0.0008 939 495	68
35	0.0009 218 081	0.0008 516 676	0.0007 869 344	0.0007 271 863	70
36	0.0007 549 462	0.0006 959 268	0.0006 415 804	0.0005 915 323	72
37	0.0006 182 889	0.0005 686 657	0.0005 230 746	0.0004 811 840	74
38	0.0005 063 687	0.0004 646 762	0.0004 264 579	0.0003 914 208	76
39	0.0004 147 079	0.0003 797 029	0.0003 476 872	0.0003 184 026	78
40	0.0003 396 392	0.0003 102 682	0.0002 834 662	0.0002 590 057	80
41	0.0002 781 591	0.0002 535 308	0.0002 311 073	0.0002 106 891	82
42	0.0002 278 078	0.0002 071 687	0.0001 884 197	0.0001 713 858	84
43	0.0001 865 710	0.0001 692 847	0.0001 536 168	0.0001 394 144	86
44	0.0001 527 987	0.0001 383 283	0.0001 252 424	0.0001 134 071	88
45	0.0001 251 397	0.0001 130 328	0.0001 021 090	0.0000 922 514	90
46	0.0001 024 874	0.0000 923 630	0.0000 832 485	0.0000 750 422	92
47	0.0000 839 355	0.0000 754 730	0.0000 678 717	0.0000 610 434	94
48	0.0000 687 419	0.0000 616 715	0.0000 553 352	0.0000 496 559	96
49	0.0000 562 985	0.0000 503 939	0.0000 451 143	0.0000 403 928	98
50	0.0000 461 076	0.0000 411 786	0.0000 367 813	0.0000 328 577	100
51	0.0000 377 614	0.0000 336 484	0.0000 299 874	0.0000 267 282	102
52	0.0000 309 260	0.0000 274 953	0.0000 244 485	0.0000 217 421	104
53	0.0000 253 279	0.0000 224 674	0.0000 199 326	0.0000 176 862	106
54	0.0000 207 431	0.0000 183 588	0.0000 162 509	0.0000 143 869	108
55	0.0000 169 883	0.0000 150 016	0.0000 132 492	0.0000 117 031	110
56	0.0000 139 131	0.0000 122 584	0.0000 108 019	0.0000 095 199	112
57	0.0000 113 946	0.0000 100 167	0.0000 088 067	0.0000 077 440	114
58	0.0000 093 320	0.0000 081 850	0.0000 071 800	0.0000 062 994	116
59	0.0000 076 428	0.0000 066 883	0.0000 058 538	0.0000 051 243	118
60	0.0000 062 593	0.0000 054 652	0.0000 047 726	0.0000 041 683	120

SEMI ANNUAL
Compounding

TABLE 4. PRESENT WORTH OF ONE DOLLAR
Payable at end of each period

HALF YEARS	22% Nominal Annual Rate	22¼% Nominal Annual Rate	22½% Nominal Annual Rate	22¾% Nominal Annual Rate	HALF YEARS
1	0.9009 009 009	0.8998 875 141	0.8988 764 045	0.8978 675 645	1
YEARS					
1	0.8116 224 332	0.8097 975 380	0.8079 787 906	0.8061 661 634	2
2	0.6587 309 741	0.6557 720 525	0.6528 297 260	0.6499 038 831	4
3	0.5346 408 361	0.5310 425 936	0.5274 725 724	0.5239 305 200	6
4	0.4339 264 963	0.4300 369 848	0.4261 866 511	0.4223 750 572	8
5	0.3521 844 788	0.3482 428 915	0.3443 497 749	0.3405 044 794	10
6	0.2858 408 236	0.2820 062 362	0.2782 273 147	0.2745 031 898	12
7	0.2319 948 248	0.2283 679 558	0.2248 017 692	0.2212 951 834	14
8	0.1882 922 042	0.1849 318 083	0.1816 350 616	0.1784 006 890	16
9	0.1528 221 769	0.1497 573 231	0.1467 572 774	0.1438 205 990	18
10	0.1240 339 071	0.1212 731 115	0.1185 767 675	0.1159 433 005	20
11	0.1006 687 015	0.0982 066 671	0.0958 075 132	0.0934 695 658	22
12	0.0817 049 764	0.0795 275 172	0.0774 104 386	0.0753 520 012	24
13	0.0663 135 918	0.0644 011 877	0.0625 459 926	0.0607 462 337	26
14	0.0538 215 987	0.0521 519 232	0.0505 358 354	0.0489 715 582	28
15	0.0436 828 169	0.0422 324 990	0.0408 318 832	0.0394 792 132	30
16	0.0354 539 542	0.0341 997 737	0.0329 912 956	0.0318 268 058	32
17	0.0287 752 245	0.0276 948 926	0.0266 562 671	0.0256 576 939	34
18	0.0233 546 178	0.0224 272 558	0.0215 376 985	0.0206 843 647	36
19	0.0189 551 317	0.0181 615 365	0.0174 020 036	0.0166 750 349	38
20	0.0153 844 101	0.0147 071 676	0.0140 604 498	0.0134 428 489	40
21	0.0124 863 324	0.0119 098 281	0.0113 605 452	0.0108 371 700	42
22	0.0101 341 875	0.0096 445 495	0.0091 790 796	0.0087 365 597	44
23	0.0082 251 339	0.0078 101 324	0.0074 165 016	0.0070 431 188	46
24	0.0066 757 032	0.0063 246 260	0.0059 923 760	0.0056 779 241	48
25	0.0054 181 505	0.0051 216 666	0.0048 417 127	0.0045 773 503	50
26	0.0043 974 925	0.0041 475 130	0.0039 120 012	0.0036 901 049	52
27	0.0035 691 035	0.0033 586 458	0.0031 608 140	0.0029 748 377	54
28	0.0028 967 645	0.0027 198 231	0.0025 538 707	0.0023 982 135	56
29	0.0023 510 790	0.0022 025 060	0.0020 634 733	0.0019 333 586	58
30	0.0019 081 885	0.0017 835 840	0.0016 672 427	0.0015 586 083	60
31	0.0015 487 286	0.0014 443 419	0.0013 470 967	0.0012 564 973	62
32	0.0012 569 829	0.0011 696 245	0.0010 884 256	0.0010 129 456	64
33	0.0010 201 955	0.0009 471 591	0.0008 794 248	0.0008 166 024	66
34	0.0008 280 135	0.0007 670 071	0.0007 105 566	0.0006 583 173	68
35	0.0006 720 344	0.0006 211 204	0.0005 741 146	0.0005 307 131	70
36	0.0005 454 382	0.0005 029 818	0.0004 638 725	0.0004 278 429	72
37	0.0004 426 899	0.0004 073 134	0.0003 747 991	0.0003 449 125	74
38	0.0003 592 970	0.0003 298 414	0.0003 028 297	0.0002 780 568	76
39	0.0002 916 135	0.0002 671 048	0.0002 446 800	0.0002 241 600	78
40	0.0002 366 801	0.0002 163 008	0.0001 976 962	0.0001 807 102	80
41	0.0001 920 949	0.0001 751 598	0.0001 597 344	0.0001 456 824	82
42	0.0001 559 085	0.0001 418 440	0.0001 290 620	0.0001 174 443	84
43	0.0001 265 388	0.0001 148 649	0.0001 042 793	0.0000 946 796	86
44	0.0001 027 018	0.0000 930 173	0.0000 842 555	0.0000 763 275	88
45	0.0000 833 550	0.0000 753 252	0.0000 680 767	0.0000 615 326	90
46	0.0000 676 528	0.0000 609 982	0.0000 550 045	0.0000 496 055	92
47	0.0000 549 086	0.0000 493 962	0.0000 444 425	0.0000 399 903	94
48	0.0000 445 650	0.0000 400 009	0.0000 359 086	0.0000 322 388	96
49	0.0000 361 700	0.0000 323 926	0.0000 290 134	0.0000 259 898	98
50	0.0000 293 564	0.0000 262 315	0.0000 234 422	0.0000 209 521	100
51	0.0000 238 263	0.0000 212 422	0.0000 189 408	0.0000 168 909	102
52	0.0000 193 379	0.0000 172 019	0.0000 153 038	0.0000 136 169	104
53	0.0000 156 951	0.0000 139 300	0.0000 123 651	0.0000 109 775	106
54	0.0000 127 385	0.0000 112 805	0.0000 099 907	0.0000 088 497	108
55	0.0000 103 389	0.0000 091 349	0.0000 080 723	0.0000 071 343	110
56	0.0000 083 912	0.0000 073 974	0.0000 065 223	0.0000 057 514	112
57	0.0000 068 105	0.0000 059 904	0.0000 052 698	0.0000 046 366	114
58	0.0000 055 276	0.0000 048 510	0.0000 042 579	0.0000 037 379	116
59	0.0000 044 863	0.0000 039 284	0.0000 034 403	0.0000 030 133	118
60	0.0000 036 412	0.0000 031 812	0.0000 027 797	0.0000 024 293	120

TABLE 5. PRESENT WORTH OF ONE DOLLAR PER PERIOD
Payable at end of each period

SEMI ANNUAL Compounding

HALF YEARS	5% Nominal Annual Rate	5¼% Nominal Annual Rate	5½% Nominal Annual Rate	5¾% Nominal Annual Rate	HALF YEARS
1	0.9756 097 561	0.9744 214 373	0.9732 360 097	0.9720 534 629	1
YEARS					
1	1.9274 241 523	1.9239 185 747	1.9204 243 404	1.9169 413 978	2
2	3.7619 742 080	3.7506 737 540	3.7394 278 654	3.7282 361 962	4
3	5.5081 253 616	5.4851 725 675	5.4623 667 778	5.4397 067 977	6
4	7.1701 371 675	7.1320 742 257	7.0943 144 100	7.0568 547 199	8
5	8.7520 639 310	8.6958 026 358	8.6400 761 634	8.5848 782 803	10
6	10.2577 645 982	10.1805 582 849	10.1042 036 582	10.0286 893 066	12
7	11.6909 121 696	11.5903 295 235	11.4910 081 358	11.3929 289 256	14
8	13.0550 026 599	12.9289 032 789	12.8045 731 539	12.6819 824 818	16
9	14.3533 636 264	14.1998 752 280	14.0487 666 106	13.8999 936 343	18
10	15.5891 622 856	15.4066 594 553	15.2272 521 338	15.0508 776 768	20
11	16.7654 132 404	16.5524 976 246	16.3434 998 692	16.1383 341 229	22
12	17.8849 858 326	17.6404 676 863	17.4007 966 983	17.1658 585 985	24
13	18.9506 111 434	18.6734 921 455	18.4022 559 168	18.1367 540 782	26
14	19.9648 886 553	19.6543 459 123	19.3508 264 022	19.0541 415 030	28
15	20.9302 925 928	20.5856 637 562	20.2493 012 968	19.9209 698 122	30
16	21.8491 779 586	21.4699 473 830	21.1003 262 323	20.7400 254 231	32
17	22.7237 862 783	22.3095 721 553	21.9064 071 203	21.5139 411 878	34
18	23.5562 510 680	23.1067 934 731	22.6699 175 310	22.2452 048 564	36
19	24.3486 030 391	23.8637 528 322	23.3931 056 823	22.9361 670 740	38
20	25.1027 750 521	24.5824 835 768	24.0781 010 600	23.5890 489 369	40
21	25.8206 068 313	25.2649 163 614	24.7269 206 884	24.2059 491 320	42
22	26.5038 494 527	25.9128 843 369	25.3414 750 691	24.7888 506 833	44
23	27.1541 696 159	26.5281 280 747	25.9235 738 070	25.3396 273 263	46
24	27.7731 537 094	27.1123 002 426	26.4749 309 389	25.8600 495 311	48
25	28.3623 116 805	27.6669 700 437	26.9971 699 802	26.3517 901 934	50
26	28.9230 807 191	28.1936 274 321	27.4918 287 059	26.8164 300 123	52
27	29.4568 287 630	28.6936 871 148	27.9603 636 785	27.2554 625 711	54
28	29.9648 578 351	29.1684 923 521	28.4041 545 371	27.6702 991 390	56
29	30.4484 072 196	29.6193 185 657	28.8245 080 596	28.0622 732 069	58
30	30.9086 564 851	30.0473 767 650	29.2226 620 109	28.4326 447 744	60
31	31.3467 283 617	30.4538 167 998	29.5997 887 873	28.7826 044 000	62
32	31.7636 914 805	30.8397 304 495	29.9569 988 691	29.1132 770 278	64
33	32.1605 629 797	31.2061 543 551	30.2953 440 902	29.4257 256 043	66
34	32.5383 109 860	31.5540 728 046	30.6158 207 353	29.7209 544 944	68
35	32.8978 569 766	31.8844 203 764	30.9193 724 738	29.9999 127 107	70
36	33.2400 780 265	32.1980 844 502	31.2068 931 383	30.2634 969 636	72
37	33.5658 089 485	32.4959 075 904	31.4792 293 565	30.5125 545 439	74
38	33.8758 443 293	32.7786 898 094	31.7371 830 443	30.7478 860 467	76
39	34.1709 404 681	33.0471 907 169	31.9815 137 674	30.9702 479 443	78
40	34.4518 172 213	33.3021 315 600	32.2129 409 770	31.1803 550 186	80
41	34.7191 597 585	33.5441 971 607	32.4321 461 294	31.3788 826 580	82
42	34.9736 202 342	33.7740 377 557	32.6397 746 917	31.5664 690 293	84
43	35.2158 193 781	33.9922 707 426	32.8364 380 431	31.7437 171 282	86
44	35.4463 480 101	34.1994 823 390	33.0227 152 746	31.9111 967 184	88
45	35.6657 684 808	34.3962 291 566	33.1991 548 945	32.0694 461 624	90
46	35.8746 160 436	34.5830 396 968	33.3662 764 435	32.2189 741 528	92
47	36.0734 001 605	34.7604 157 699	33.5245 720 246	32.3602 613 469	94
48	36.2626 057 446	34.9288 338 435	33.6745 077 517	32.4937 619 119	96
49	36.4426 943 435	35.0887 463 223	33.8165 251 229	32.6199 049 850	98
50	36.6141 052 645	35.2405 827 632	33.9510 423 195	32.7390 960 529	100
51	36.7772 566 467	35.3847 510 292	34.0784 554 385	32.8517 182 549	102
52	36.9325 464 811	35.5216 383 850	34.1991 396 579	32.9581 336 147	104
53	37.0803 535 811	35.6516 125 375	34.3134 503 423	33.0586 842 043	106
54	37.2210 385 067	35.7750 226 233	34.4217 240 886	33.1536 932 432	108
55	37.3549 444 442	35.8922 001 464	34.5242 797 176	33.2434 661 378	110
56	37.4823 980 433	36.0034 598 692	34.6214 192 126	33.3282 914 628	112
57	37.6037 102 137	36.1091 006 575	34.7134 286 087	33.4084 418 889	114
58	37.7191 768 839	36.2094 062 836	34.8005 788 351	33.4841 750 596	116
59	37.8290 797 230	36.3046 461 885	34.8831 265 125	33.5557 344 188	118
60	37.9336 868 273	36.3950 762 055	34.9613 147 092	33.6233 499 939	120

SEMI ANNUAL
Compounding

TABLE 5. PRESENT WORTH OF ONE DOLLAR PER PERIOD
Payable at end of each period

HALF YEARS	6% Nominal Annual Rate	6¼% Nominal Annual Rate	6½% Nominal Annual Rate	6¾% Nominal Annual Rate	HALF YEARS
1	0.9708 737 864	0.9696 969 697	0.9685 230 024	0.9673 518 742	1
YEARS					
1	1.9134 696 955	1.9100 091 827	1.9065 598 086	1.9031 215 228	2
2	3.7170 984 028	3.7060 141 443	3.6949 830 824	3.6840 048 815	4
3	5.4171 914 439	5.3948 195 443	5.3725 899 383	5.3505 014 763	6
4	7.0196 921 895	6.9828 238 874	6.9462 469 155	6.9099 584 092	8
5	8.5302 028 368	8.4760 437 656	8.4223 950 804	8.3692 508 753	10
6	9.9540 039 936	9.8801 366 537	9.8070 763 906	9.7348 124 735	12
7	11.2960 731 394	11.2004 223 447	11.1059 584 244	11.0126 635 704	14
8	12.5611 020 260	12.4419 031 047	12.3243 575 791	12.2084 378 423	16
9	13.7535 130 795	13.6092 826 255	13.4672 608 309	13.3274 071 125	18
10	14.8774 748 605	14.7069 838 462	14.5393 461 469	14.3745 045 933	20
11	15.9369 166 372	15.7391 657 103	15.5450 016 328	15.3543 466 350	22
12	16.9355 421 220	16.7097 389 232	16.4883 434 930	16.2712 530 780	24
13	17.8768 424 187	17.6223 807 689	17.3732 328 786	17.1292 662 980	26
14	18.7641 082 277	18.4805 490 426	18.2032 916 918	17.9321 690 274	28
15	19.6004 413 495	19.2874 951 512	18.9819 174 099	18.6835 010 323	30
16	20.3887 655 288	20.0462 764 323	19.7122 969 917	19.3865 747 186	32
17	21.1318 366 752	20.7597 677 380	20.3974 199 220	20.0444 897 349	34
18	21.8322 524 981	21.4306 723 267	21.0400 904 474	20.6601 466 385	36
19	22.4924 615 874	22.0615 321 051	21.6429 390 545	21.2362 596 828	38
20	23.1147 719 742	22.6547 372 596	22.2084 332 365	21.7753 687 839	40
21	23.7013 591 990	23.2125 353 111	22.7388 875 929	22.2798 507 180	42
22	24.2542 739 174	23.7370 396 314	23.2364 733 033	22.7519 296 002	44
23	24.7754 490 691	24.2302 374 495	23.7032 270 139	23.1936 866 899	46
24	25.2667 066 350	24.6939 973 814	24.1410 591 738	23.6070 695 665	48
25	25.7297 640 070	25.1300 765 092	24.5517 618 548	23.9939 007 156	50
26	26.1662 399 915	25.5401 270 390	24.9370 160 860	24.3558 855 641	52
27	26.5776 604 690	25.9257 025 600	25.2983 987 346	24.6946 199 986	54
28	26.9654 637 279	26.2882 639 316	25.6373 889 601	25.0115 974 014	56
29	27.3310 054 934	26.6291 848 172	25.9553 742 685	25.3082 152 342	58
30	27.6755 636 661	26.9497 568 896	26.2536 561 917	25.5857 811 993	60
31	28.0003 427 902	27.2511 947 245	26.5334 556 143	25.8455 190 050	62
32	28.3064 782 639	27.5346 404 021	26.7959 177 710	26.0885 737 601	64
33	28.5950 403 091	27.8011 678 345	27.0421 169 343	26.3160 170 229	66
34	28.8670 377 124	28.0517 868 343	27.2730 608 111	26.5288 515 251	68
35	29.1234 213 521	28.2874 469 406	27.4896 946 677	26.7280 155 923	70
36	29.3650 875 220	28.5090 410 167	27.6929 051 987	26.9143 872 815	72
37	29.5928 810 651	28.7174 086 328	27.8835 241 561	27.0887 882 517	74
38	29.8075 983 270	28.9133 392 470	28.0623 317 542	27.2519 873 862	76
39	30.0099 899 397	29.0975 751 964	28.2300 598 624	27.4047 041 830	78
40	30.2007 634 458	29.2708 145 098	28.3873 950 014	27.5476 119 263	80
41	30.3805 857 723	29.4337 135 519	28.5349 811 526	27.6813 406 550	82
42	30.5500 855 616	29.5868 895 107	28.6734 223 945	27.8064 799 404	84
43	30.7098 553 696	29.7309 227 355	28.8032 853 750	27.9235 814 856	86
44	30.8604 537 370	29.8663 589 358	28.9251 016 304	28.0331 615 574	88
45	31.0024 071 421	29.9937 112 491	29.0393 697 616	28.1357 032 627	90
46	31.1362 118 409	30.1134 621 847	29.1465 574 744	28.2316 586 782	92
47	31.2623 356 027	30.2260 654 519	29.2471 034 942	28.3214 508 437	94
48	31.3812 193 446	30.3319 476 793	29.3414 193 615	28.4054 756 268	96
49	31.4932 786 734	30.4315 100 308	29.4298 911 165	28.4841 034 685	98
50	31.5989 053 383	30.5251 297 260	29.5128 808 789	28.5576 810 164	100
51	31.6984 686 006	30.6131 614 687	29.5907 283 306	28.6265 326 525	102
52	31.7923 165 242	30.6959 387 915	29.6637 521 056	28.6909 619 238	104
53	31.8807 771 932	30.7737 753 191	29.7322 510 943	28.7512 528 804	106
54	31.9641 598 578	30.8469 659 566	29.7965 056 668	28.8076 713 277	108
55	32.0427 560 164	30.9157 880 069	29.8567 788 208	28.8604 659 982	110
56	32.1168 404 340	30.9805 022 214	29.9133 172 577	28.9098 696 486	112
57	32.1866 721 029	31.0413 537 876	29.9663 523 925	28.9561 000 851	114
58	32.2524 951 484	31.0985 732 585	30.0161 013 009	28.9993 611 244	116
59	32.3145 396 818	31.1523 774 258	30.0627 676 081	29.0398 434 920	118
60	32.3730 226 051	31.2029 701 414	30.1065 423 219	29.0777 256 628	120

TABLE 5. PRESENT WORTH OF ONE DOLLAR PER PERIOD
Payable at end of each period

SEMI ANNUAL Compounding

HALF YEARS	7% Nominal Annual Rate	7¼% Nominal Annual Rate	7½% Nominal Annual Rate	7¾% Nominal Annual Rate	HALF YEARS
1	0.9661 835 749	0.9650 180 941	0.9638 554 217	0.9626 955 475	1
YEARS					
1	1.8996 942 752	1.8962 780 160	1.8928 726 956	1.8894 782 648	2
2	3.6730 792 086	3.6622 057 331	3.6513 841 271	3.6406 140 652	4
3	5.3285 530 198	5.3067 434 411	5.2850 716 234	5.2635 364 605	6
4	6.8739 555 367	6.8382 354 986	6.8027 955 276	6.7676 328 879	8
5	8.3166 053 226	8.2644 526 725	8.2127 872 517	8.1616 034 619	10
6	9.6633 343 346	9.5926 315 665	9.5226 939 194	9.4535 112 983	12
7	10.9205 202 778	10.8295 113 397	10.7396 198 409	10.6508 291 532	14
8	12.0941 168 081	11.9813 679 006	11.8701 650 431	11.7604 826 483	16
9	13.1896 817 271	13.0540 457 516	12.9204 610 649	12.7888 903 296	18
10	14.2124 033 020	14.0529 876 434	13.8962 042 118	13.7420 007 949	20
11	15.1671 248 355	14.9832 621 915	14.8026 864 502	14.6253 271 018	22
12	16.0583 676 030	15.8495 895 946	15.6448 241 082	15.4439 786 567	24
13	16.8903 522 631	16.6563 655 843	16.4271 845 395	16.2026 907 692	26
14	17.6670 188 458	17.4076 837 295	17.1540 108 946	16.9058 520 425	28
15	18.3920 454 114	18.1073 562 068	17.8292 451 336	17.5575 297 580	30
16	19.0688 654 684	18.7589 331 433	18.4565 494 056	18.1614 934 019	32
17	19.7006 842 338	19.3657 206 303	19.0393 259 102	18.7212 364 689	34
18	20.2904 938 121	19.9307 974 981	19.5807 353 499	19.2399 966 695	36
19	20.8410 873 645	20.4570 309 379	20.0837 140 716	19.7207 746 578	38
20	21.3550 723 373	20.9470 910 500	20.5509 899 925	20.1663 513 882	40
21	21.8348 828 092	21.4034 643 917	20.9850 973 947	20.5793 042 012	42
22	22.2827 910 189	21.8284 665 942	21.3883 906 701	20.9620 217 313	44
23	22.7009 181 254	22.2242 541 121	21.7630 570 893	21.3167 177 237	46
24	23.0912 442 535	22.5928 351 652	22.1111 286 648	21.6454 438 394	48
25	23.4556 178 706	22.9360 799 279	22.4344 931 709	21.9501 015 221	50
26	23.7957 645 412	23.2557 300 188	22.7349 043 829	22.2324 529 971	52
27	24.1132 950 978	23.5534 073 375	23.0139 915 882	22.4941 314 644	54
28	24.4097 132 702	23.8306 222 941	23.2732 684 227	22.7366 505 453	56
29	24.6864 228 058	24.0887 814 729	23.5141 410 808	22.9614 130 381	58
30	24.9447 341 182	24.3291 947 696	23.7379 159 409	23.1697 190 319	60
31	25.1858 704 924	24.5530 820 375	23.9458 066 515	23.3627 734 268	62
32	25.4109 738 780	24.7615 792 771	24.1389 407 126	23.5416 929 035	64
33	25.6211 102 971	24.9557 444 003	24.3183 655 916	23.7075 123 823	66
34	25.8172 748 928	25.1365 625 976	24.4850 544 036	23.8611 910 095	68
35	26.0003 966 420	25.3049 513 380	24.6399 111 893	24.0036 177 051	70
36	26.1713 427 543	25.4617 650 232	24.7837 758 182	24.1356 163 051	72
37	26.3309 227 794	25.6077 993 235	24.9174 285 435	24.2579 503 263	74
38	26.4798 924 403	25.7437 952 145	25.0415 942 341	24.3713 273 828	76
39	26.6189 572 128	25.8704 427 374	25.1569 463 054	24.4764 032 794	78
40	26.7487 756 660	25.9883 844 997	25.2641 103 723	24.5737 858 043	80
41	26.8699 625 812	26.0982 189 360	25.3636 676 416	24.6640 382 454	82
42	26.9830 918 632	26.2005 033 446	25.4561 580 645	24.7476 826 479	84
43	27.0886 992 585	26.2957 567 149	25.5420 832 650	24.8252 028 346	86
44	27.1872 848 921	26.3844 623 612	25.6219 092 606	24.8970 472 039	88
45	27.2793 156 359	26.4670 703 744	25.6960 689 893	24.9636 313 236	90
46	27.3652 273 200	26.5439 999 063	25.7649 646 584	25.0253 403 351	92
47	27.4454 267 965	26.6156 412 962	25.8289 699 251	25.0825 311 804	94
48	27.5202 938 659	26.6823 580 513	25.8884 319 234	25.1355 346 674	96
49	27.5901 830 763	26.7444 886 915	25.9436 731 470	25.1846 573 831	98
50	27.6554 254 020	26.8023 484 667	25.9949 931 980	25.2301 834 670	100
51	27.7163 298 112	26.8562 309 563	26.0426 704 118	25.2723 762 548	102
52	27.7731 847 289	26.9064 095 595	26.0869 633 671	25.3114 798 013	104
53	27.8262 594 029	26.9531 388 815	26.1281 122 876	25.3477 202 924	106
54	27.8758 051 790	26.9966 560 263	26.1663 403 456	25.3813 073 532	108
55	27.9220 566 912	27.0371 817 991	26.2018 548 718	25.4124 352 607	110
56	27.9652 329 727	27.0749 218 272	26.2348 484 801	25.4412 840 674	112
57	28.0055 384 935	27.1100 676 028	26.2655 001 121	25.4680 206 428	114
58	28.0431 641 285	27.1427 974 550	26.2939 760 078	25.4927 996 388	116
59	28.0782 880 613	27.1732 774 546	26.3204 306 068	25.5157 643 841	118
60	28.1110 766 284	27.2016 622 567	26.3450 073 862	25.5370 477 131	120

SEMI ANNUAL
Compounding

TABLE 5. PRESENT WORTH OF ONE DOLLAR PER PERIOD
Payable at end of each period

HALF YEARS	8% Nominal Annual Rate	8¼% Nominal Annual Rate	8½% Nominal Annual Rate	8¾% Nominal Annual Rate	HALF YEARS
1	0.9615 384 615	0.9603 841 537	0.9592 326 139	0.9580 838 323	1
YEARS					
1	1.8860 946 746	1.8827 218 763	1.8793 598 215	1.8760 084 621	2
2	3.6298 952 243	3.6192 272 839	3.6086 099 261	3.5980 428 352	4
3	5.2421 368 567	5.2208 717 269	5.1997 399 961	5.1787 405 995	6
4	6.7327 448 750	6.6981 288 149	6.6637 820 642	6.6297 020 097	8
5	8.1108 957 794	8.0606 587 531	8.0108 870 042	7.9615 752 249	10
6	9.3850 737 605	9.3173 715 133	9.2503 949 110	9.1841 344 529	12
7	10.5631 229 295	10.4764 850 985	10.3908 998 600	10.3063 516 797	14
8	11.6522 956 079	11.5455 792 829	11.4403 094 940	11.3364 625 121	16
9	12.6592 969 747	12.5316 451 782	12.4058 998 501	12.2820 266 166	18
10	13.5903 263 450	13.4411 309 504	13.2943 658 082	13.1499 831 971	20
11	14.4511 153 337	14.2799 839 863	14.1118 675 092	13.9467 019 200	22
12	15.2469 631 414	15.0536 897 850	14.8640 730 666	14.6780 296 587	24
13	15.9827 691 766	15.7673 078 293	15.5561 978 656	15.3493 334 025	26
14	16.6630 632 180	16.4255 046 712	16.1930 407 243	15.9655 396 430	28
15	17.2920 333 007	17.0325 844 473	16.7790 171 654	16.5311 705 282	30
16	17.8735 514 984	17.5925 170 254	17.3181 900 320	17.0503 770 491	32
17	18.4111 977 611	18.1089 639 644	17.8142 976 561	17.5269 695 026	34
18	18.9082 819 537	18.5853 024 579	18.2707 797 789	17.9644 454 540	36
19	19.3678 642 323	19.0246 474 192	18.6908 013 999	18.3660 154 047	38
20	19.7927 738 834	19.4298 718 502	19.0772 747 211	18.7346 263 531	40
21	20.1856 267 413	19.8036 256 291	19.4328 793 390	19.0729 834 214	42
22	20.5488 412 919	20.1483 528 383	19.7600 808 230	19.3835 697 080	44
23	20.8846 535 613	20.4663 077 474	20.0611 478 109	19.6686 645 102	46
24	21.1951 308 814	20.7595 695 541	20.3381 677 377	19.9303 600 510	48
25	21.4821 846 167	21.0300 559 810	20.5930 613 094	20.1705 768 333	50
26	21.7475 819 311	21.2795 358 160	20.8275 958 198	20.3910 777 343	52
27	21.9929 566 671	21.5096 404 789	21.0433 974 039	20.5934 809 423	54
28	22.2198 194 037	21.7218 746 896	21.2419 623 129	20.7792 718 320	56
29	22.4295 667 564	21.9176 263 082	21.4246 672 881	20.9498 138 656	58
30	22.6234 899 745	22.0981 754 102	21.5927 791 068	21.1063 585 987	60
31	22.8027 828 906	22.2647 026 578	21.7474 633 650	21.2500 548 649	62
32	22.9685 492 702	22.4182 970 202	21.8897 925 596	21.3819 572 069	64
33	23.1218 096 063	22.5599 628 945	22.0207 535 240	21.5030 336 152	66
34	23.2635 074 023	22.6906 266 744	22.1412 542 705	21.6141 726 326	68
35	23.3945 149 799	22.8111 428 076	22.2521 302 859	21.7161 898 739	70
36	23.5156 388 498	22.9222 993 834	22.3541 503 243	21.8098 340 124	72
37	23.6276 246 762	23.0248 232 864	22.4480 217 374	21.8957 922 736	74
38	23.7311 618 678	23.1193 849 496	22.5343 953 785	21.9746 954 787	76
39	23.8268 878 215	23.2066 027 387	22.6138 701 158	22.0471 226 739	78
40	23.9153 918 468	23.2870 469 957	22.6869 969 839	22.1136 053 804	80
41	23.9972 187 933	23.3612 437 684	22.7542 830 048	22.1746 314 940	82
42	24.0728 724 050	23.4296 782 508	22.8161 947 033	22.2306 488 668	84
43	24.1428 184 218	23.4927 979 555	22.8731 613 416	22.2820 685 930	86
44	24.2074 874 462	23.5510 156 401	22.9255 778 954	22.3292 680 262	88
45	24.2672 775 945	23.6047 120 068	22.9738 077 927	22.3725 935 483	90
46	24.3225 569 476	23.6542 381 913	23.0181 854 334	22.4123 631 123	92
47	24.3736 658 169	23.6999 180 596	23.0590 185 081	22.4488 685 745	94
48	24.4209 188 396	23.7420 503 252	23.0965 901 310	22.4823 778 374	96
49	24.4646 069 153	23.7809 105 032	23.1311 608 035	22.5131 368 151	98
50	24.5049 989 972	23.8167 527 112	23.1629 702 199	22.5413 712 384	100
51	24.5423 437 474	23.8498 113 318	23.1922 389 293	22.5672 883 109	102
52	24.5768 710 682	23.8803 025 446	23.2191 698 652	22.5910 782 301	104
53	24.6087 935 172	23.9084 257 403	23.2439 497 520	22.6129 155 829	106
54	24.6383 076 158	23.9343 648 246	23.2667 504 001	22.6329 606 268	108
55	24.6655 950 589	23.9582 894 206	23.2877 298 968	22.6513 604 664	110
56	24.6908 238 341	23.9803 559 779	23.3070 337 024	22.6682 501 323	112
57	24.7141 492 549	24.0007 087 962	23.3247 956 592	22.6837 535 726	114
58	24.7357 149 176	24.0194 809 682	23.3411 389 190	22.6979 845 623	116
59	24.7556 535 851	24.0367 952 506	23.3561 767 969	22.7110 475 383	118
60	24.7740 880 039	24.0527 648 664	23.3700 135 575	22.7230 383 657	120

TABLE 5. PRESENT WORTH OF ONE DOLLAR PER PERIOD
Payable at end of each period

HALF YEARS	9% Nominal Annual Rate	9¼% Nominal Annual Rate	9½% Nominal Annual Rate	9¾% Nominal Annual Rate	HALF YEARS
1	0.9569 377 990	0.9557 945 042	0.9546 539 379	0.9535 160 906	1
YEARS					
1	1.8726 677 503	1.8693 376 384	1.8660 180 792	1.8627 090 256	2
2	3.5875 256 979	3.5770 582 035	3.5666 400 435	3.5562 709 116	4
3	5.1578 724 827	5.1371 346 009	5.1165 259 195	5.0960 454 134	6
4	6.5958 860 674	6.5623 316 827	6.5290 363 299	6.4959 975 119	8
5	7.9127 181 771	7.8643 106 916	7.8163 476 671	7.7688 240 692	10
6	9.1185 807 808	9.0537 246 761	8.9895 570 585	8.9260 689 826	12
7	10.2228 252 840	10.1403 056 554	10.0587 780 279	9.9782 278 819	14
8	11.2340 150 491	11.1329 442 489	11.0332 276 785	10.9348 433 196	16
9	12.1599 918 034	12.0397 624 207	11.9213 061 475	11.8045 913 172	18
10	13.0079 364 515	12.8681 799 355	12.7306 690 187	12.5953 600 518	20
11	13.7844 247 627	13.6249 750 684	13.4682 933 168	13.3143 213 985	22
12	14.4954 783 660	14.3163 400 661	14.1405 376 518	13.9679 959 754	24
13	15.1466 114 476	14.9479 318 130	14.7531 970 329	14.5623 122 826	26
14	15.7428 735 126	15.5249 181 170	15.3115 528 236	15.1026 604 702	28
15	16.2888 885 443	16.0520 199 936	15.8204 182 693	15.5939 412 248	30
16	16.7888 908 627	16.5335 502 940	16.2841 799 892	16.0406 102 161	32
17	17.2467 579 613	16.9734 489 938	16.7068 357 908	16.4467 185 072	34
18	17.6660 405 772	17.3753 154 308	17.0920 291 325	16.8159 492 963	36
19	18.0499 902 266	17.7424 377 552	17.4430 805 316	17.1516 513 211	38
20	18.4015 844 203	18.0778 198 341	17.7630 161 884	17.4568 692 304	40
21	18.7235 497 542	18.3842 058 295	18.0545 940 735	17.7343 711 971	42
22	19.0183 830 536	18.6641 026 521	18.3203 277 024	17.9866 740 247	44
23	19.2883 707 366	18.9198 004 727	18.5625 078 029	18.2160 659 731	46
24	19.5356 065 444	19.1533 914 611	18.7832 220 622	18.4246 275 118	48
25	19.7620 077 785	19.3667 869 048	18.9843 731 236	18.6142 501 894	50
26	19.9693 301 697	19.5617 328 473	19.1676 949 880	18.7866 537 882	52
27	20.1591 814 928	19.7398 243 746	19.3347 679 614	18.9434 019 221	54
28	20.3330 340 357	19.9025 186 666	19.4870 322 784	19.0859 162 181	56
29	20.4922 360 163	20.0511 469 200	19.6258 005 169	19.2154 892 091	58
30	20.6380 220 382	20.1869 252 405	19.7522 689 134	19.3332 960 571	60
31	20.7715 226 650	20.3109 645 929	19.8675 276 749	19.4404 052 111	62
32	20.8937 731 874	20.4242 798 918	19.9725 703 772	19.5377 880 971	64
33	21.0057 216 523	20.5277 983 050	20.0683 025 293	19.6263 279 290	66
34	21.1082 362 147	20.6223 668 406	20.1555 493 799	19.7068 277 187	68
35	21.2021 118 699	20.7087 592 771	20.2350 630 310	19.7800 175 587	70
36	21.2880 766 190	20.7876 824 943	20.3075 289 214	19.8465 612 442	72
37	21.3667 971 145	20.8597 822 575	20.3735 717 353	19.9070 622 929	74
38	21.4388 838 301	20.9256 485 012	20.4337 607 877	19.9620 694 190	76
39	21.5048 957 946	20.9858 201 558	20.4886 149 317	20.0120 815 094	78
40	21.5653 449 276	21.0407 895 578	20.5386 070 316	20.0575 521 486	80
41	21.6207 000 093	21.0910 064 776	20.5841 680 388	20.0988 937 325	82
42	21.6713 903 155	21.1368 817 999	20.6256 907 070	20.1364 812 086	84
43	21.7178 089 471	21.1787 908 856	20.6635 329 778	20.1706 554 762	86
44	21.7603 158 784	21.2170 766 431	20.6980 210 664	20.2017 264 790	88
45	21.7992 407 485	21.2520 523 340	20.7294 522 737	20.2299 760 151	90
46	21.8348 854 179	21.2840 041 363	20.7580 975 490	20.2556 602 938	92
47	21.8675 263 093	21.3131 934 859	20.7842 038 257	20.2790 122 585	94
48	21.8974 165 512	21.3398 592 158	20.8079 961 501	20.3002 436 999	96
49	21.9247 879 409	21.3642 195 103	20.8296 796 214	20.3195 471 763	98
50	21.9498 527 423	21.3864 736 901	20.8494 411 596	20.3370 977 608	100
51	21.9728 053 317	21.4068 038 433	20.8674 511 169	20.3530 546 281	102
52	21.9938 237 052	21.4253 763 151	20.8838 647 462	20.3675 624 992	104
53	22.0130 708 594	21.4423 430 692	20.8988 235 394	20.3807 529 531	106
54	22.0306 960 549	21.4578 429 310	20.9124 564 470	20.3927 456 206	108
55	22.0468 359 744	21.4720 027 232	20.9248 809 902	20.4036 492 691	110
56	22.0616 157 820	21.4849 383 043	20.9362 042 734	20.4135 627 893	112
57	22.0751 500 946	21.4967 555 155	20.9465 239 076	20.4225 760 919	114
58	22.0875 438 699	21.5075 510 477	20.9559 288 522	20.4307 709 229	116
59	22.0988 932 213	21.5174 132 320	20.9645 001 814	20.4382 216 053	118
60	22.1092 861 622	21.5264 227 627	20.9723 117 835	20.4449 957 132	120

TABLE 5. PRESENT WORTH OF ONE DOLLAR PER PERIOD
Payable at end of each period

HALF YEARS	10% Nominal Annual Rate	10¼% Nominal Annual Rate	10½% Nominal Annual Rate	10¾% Nominal Annual Rate	HALF YEARS
1	0.9523 809 524	0.9512 485 137	0.9501 187 648	0.9489 916 963	1
YEARS					
1	1.8594 104 308	1.8561 222 484	1.8528 444 322	1.8495 769 360	2
2	3.5459 505 042	3.5356 785 196	3.5254 546 586	3.5152 786 243	4
3	5.0756 920 673	5.0554 648 754	5.0353 628 414	5.0153 849 784	6
4	6.4632 127 594	6.4306 796 312	6.3983 957 133	6.3663 586 189	8
5	7.7217 349 292	7.6750 753 434	7.6288 404 722	7.5830 255 388	10
6	8.8632 516 364	8.8010 963 391	8.7395 945 382	8.6787 378 084	12
7	9.8986 409 401	9.8200 031 628	9.7423 007 437	9.6655 201 054	14
8	10.8377 695 602	10.7419 851 858	10.6474 693 722	10.5542 016 769	16
9	11.6895 869 027	11.5762 625 023	11.4645 883 263	11.3545 351 829	18
10	12.4622 103 425	12.3311 781 336	12.2022 225 795	12.0753 037 253	20
11	13.1630 025 783	13.0142 814 603	12.8681 039 529	12.7244 172 358	22
12	13.7986 417 943	13.6324 037 187	13.4692 121 601	13.3089 992 822	24
13	14.3751 853 010	14.1917 263 152	14.0118 479 676	13.8354 652 446	26
14	14.8981 272 571	14.6978 426 421	14.5016 992 389	14.3095 927 195	28
15	15.3724 510 269	15.1558 140 130	14.9439 005 548	14.7365 849 252	30
16	15.8026 766 684	15.5702 202 779	15.3430 870 327	15.1211 278 031	32
17	16.1929 040 076	15.9452 056 224	15.7034 429 124	15.4674 414 429	34
18	16.5468 517 076	16.2845 200 116	16.0287 454 143	15.7793 263 952	36
19	16.8678 927 053	16.5915 566 903	16.3224 043 325	16.0602 053 798	38
20	17.1590 863 540	16.8693 861 164	16.5874 977 753	16.3131 608 475	40
21	17.4232 075 773	17.1207 866 668	16.8268 044 304	16.5409 688 079	42
22	17.6627 733 128	17.3482 724 218	17.0428 326 903	16.7461 292 946	44
23	17.8800 664 968	17.5541 183 065	17.2378 469 454	16.9308 938 006	46
24	18.0771 578 203	17.7403 828 410	17.4138 913 190	17.0972 899 876	48
25	18.2559 254 606	17.9089 287 260	17.5728 110 936	17.2471 439 375	50
26	18.4180 729 801	18.0614 414 704	17.7162 720 532	17.3821 001 930	52
27	18.5651 455 602	18.1994 462 470	17.8457 779 436	17.5036 398 046	54
28	18.6985 447 258	18.3243 231 447	17.9626 862 350	17.6130 965 849	56
29	18.8195 417 014	18.4373 209 695	18.0682 223 504	17.7116 717 456	58
30	18.9292 895 251	18.5395 697 332	18.1634 925 105	17.8004 470 803	60
31	19.0288 340 363	18.6320 919 539	18.2494 953 294	17.8803 968 364	62
32	19.1191 238 425	18.7158 128 813	18.3271 322 815	17.9523 984 067	64
33	19.2010 193 583	18.7915 697 495	18.3972 171 509	18.0172 419 581	66
34	19.2753 010 052	18.8601 201 498	18.4604 845 614	18.0756 391 034	68
35	19.3426 766 487	18.9221 496 066	18.5175 976 767	18.1282 307 105	70
36	19.4037 883 435	18.9782 784 328	18.5691 551 519	18.1755 939 355	72
37	19.4592 184 522	19.0290 679 334	18.6156 974 081	18.2182 485 569	74
38	19.5094 951 947	19.0750 260 185	18.6577 122 973	18.2566 626 794	76
39	19.5550 976 823	19.1166 122 825	18.6956 402 163	18.2912 578 710	78
40	19.5964 604 828	19.1542 426 006	18.7298 787 222	18.3224 137 900	80
41	19.6339 777 622	19.1882 932 871	18.7607 867 003	18.3504 723 508	82
42	19.6680 070 405	19.2191 048 590	18.7886 881 255	18.3757 414 765	84
43	19.6988 725 991	19.2469 854 411	18.8138 754 582	18.3984 984 781	86
44	19.7268 685 706	19.2722 138 475	18.8366 127 099	18.4189 930 978	88
45	19.7522 617 421	19.2950 423 699	18.8571 382 106	18.4374 502 498	90
46	19.7752 940 971	19.3156 993 002	18.8756 671 069	18.4540 724 885	92
47	19.7961 851 221	19.3343 912 138	18.8923 936 172	18.4690 422 313	94
48	19.8151 338 976	19.3513 050 356	18.9074 930 673	18.4825 237 607	96
49	19.8323 209 955	19.3666 099 086	18.9211 237 286	18.4946 650 271	98
50	19.8479 102 000	19.3804 588 862	18.9334 284 763	18.5055 992 725	100
51	19.8620 500 681	19.3929 904 623	18.9445 362 879	18.5154 464 924	102
52	19.8748 753 452	19.4043 299 564	18.9545 635 946	18.5243 147 533	104
53	19.8865 082 496	19.4145 907 667	18.9636 155 017	18.5323 013 782	106
54	19.8970 596 368	19.4238 755 045	18.9717 868 906	18.5394 940 147	108
55	19.9066 300 561	19.4322 770 199	18.9791 634 130	18.5459 715 970	110
56	19.9153 107 085	19.4398 793 304	18.9858 223 892	18.5518 052 119	112
57	19.9231 843 161	19.4467 584 616	18.9918 336 179	18.5570 588 795	114
58	19.9303 259 103	19.4529 832 067	18.9972 601 084	18.5617 902 549	116
59	19.9368 035 467	19.4586 158 151	19.0021 587 406	18.5660 512 618	118
60	19.9426 789 539	19.4637 126 144	19.0065 808 616	18.5698 886 617	120

TABLE 5. PRESENT WORTH OF ONE DOLLAR PER PERIOD
Payable at end of each period

HALF YEARS	11% Nominal Annual Rate	11¼% Nominal Annual Rate	11½% Nominal Annual Rate	11¾% Nominal Annual Rate	HALF YEARS
1	0.9478 672 986	0.9467 455 621	0.9456 264 775	0.9445 100 354	1
YEARS					
1	1.8463 197 143	1.8430 727 215	1.8398 359 126	1.8366 092 424	2
2	3.5051 501 218	3.4950 688 586	3.4850 345 445	3.4750 468 912	4
3	4.9955 303 086	4.9757 978 636	4.9561 866 836	4.9366 958 184	6
4	6.3345 659 879	6.3030 154 864	6.2717 048 068	6.2406 316 672	8
5	7.5376 258 286	7.4926 366 882	7.4480 535 246	7.4038 718 040	10
6	8.6185 178 487	8.5589 264 808	8.4999 556 468	8.4415 974 075	12
7	9.5896 478 954	9.5146 709 817	9.4405 764 493	9.3673 515 956	14
8	10.4621 620 317	10.3713 307 353	10.2816 884 456	10.1932 161 726	16
9	11.2460 744 653	11.1391 781 389	11.0338 187 286	10.9299 693 069	18
10	11.9503 824 849	11.8274 206 210	11.7063 807 241	11.5872 261 937	20
11	12.5831 697 266	12.4443 110 499	12.3077 920 061	12.1735 645 412	22
12	13.1516 989 525	12.9972 466 958	12.8455 796 488	12.6966 365 161	24
13	13.6624 954 089	13.4928 579 325	13.3264 744 329	13.1632 686 101	26
14	14.1214 217 191	13.9370 877 446	13.7564 950 861	13.5795 507 311	28
15	14.5337 451 711	14.3352 629 901	14.1410 236 115	13.9509 156 812	30
16	14.9041 981 727	14.6921 582 769	14.4848 726 469	14.2822 100 586	32
17	15.2370 325 668	15.0120 532 156	14.7923 456 986	14.5777 575 101	34
18	15.5360 684 322	15.2987 837 372	15.0672 910 024	14.8414 151 571	36
19	15.8047 379 279	15.5557 880 912	15.3131 496 872	15.0766 239 349	38
20	16.0461 246 854	15.7861 480 738	15.5329 988 429	15.2864 534 991	40
21	16.2629 992 007	15.9926 259 826	15.7295 900 321	15.4736 422 870	42
22	16.4578 506 329	16.1776 977 401	15.9053 837 284	15.6406 332 561	44
23	16.6329 153 729	16.3435 825 827	16.0625 801 103	15.7896 057 673	46
24	16.7902 027 114	16.4922 696 726	16.2031 465 980	15.9225 040 264	48
25	16.9315 179 007	16.6255 419 494	16.3288 424 777	16.0410 624 580	50
26	17.0584 828 739	16.7449 975 108	16.4412 409 192	16.1468 283 407	52
27	17.1725 548 608	16.8520 687 748	16.5417 486 660	16.2411 820 009	54
28	17.2750 431 129	16.9480 396 567	16.6316 236 416	16.3253 548 263	56
29	17.3671 239 307	17.0340 609 646	16.7119 906 927	16.4004 453 371	58
30	17.4498 541 638	17.1111 641 992	16.7838 556 681	16.4674 335 222	60
31	17.5241 833 416	17.1802 739 225	16.8481 180 071	16.5271 936 290	62
32	17.5909 645 710	17.2422 188 444	16.9055 819 970	16.5805 055 729	64
33	17.6509 643 278	17.2977 417 604	16.9569 668 389	16.6280 651 158	66
34	17.7048 712 543	17.3475 084 579	17.0029 156 493	16.6704 929 463	68
35	17.7533 040 626	17.3921 157 005	17.0440 035 092	16.7083 427 803	70
36	17.7968 186 363	17.4320 983 835	17.0807 446 611	16.7421 085 871	72
37	17.8359 144 101	17.4679 359 483	17.1135 989 458	16.7722 310 366	74
38	17.8710 401 025	17.5000 581 309	17.1429 775 572	16.7991 032 499	76
39	17.9025 988 657	17.5288 501 155	17.1692 481 887	16.8230 759 301	78
40	17.9309 529 127	17.5546 571 534	17.1927 396 352	16.8444 619 391	80
41	17.9564 276 748	17.5777 887 023	17.2137 459 083	16.8635 403 808	82
42	17.9793 155 363	17.5985 221 379	17.2325 299 160	16.8805 602 435	84
43	17.9998 791 908	17.6171 060 792	17.2493 267 528	16.8957 436 495	86
44	18.0183 546 558	17.6337 633 706	17.2643 466 428	16.9092 887 539	88
45	18.0349 539 820	17.6486 937 533	17.2777 775 702	16.9213 723 309	90
46	18.0498 676 867	17.6620 762 608	17.2897 876 321	16.9321 520 803	92
47	18.0632 669 407	17.6740 713 657	17.3005 271 428	16.9417 686 862	94
48	18.0753 055 329	17.6848 229 040	17.3101 305 146	16.9503 476 526	96
49	18.0861 216 351	17.6944 597 999	17.3187 179 403	16.9580 009 419	98
50	18.0958 393 882	17.7030 976 113	17.3263 968 974	16.9648 284 351	100
51	18.1045 703 270	17.7108 399 163	17.3332 634 932	16.9709 192 364	102
52	18.1124 146 600	17.7177 795 545	17.3394 036 680	16.9763 528 354	104
53	18.1194 624 200	17.7239 997 408	17.3448 942 703	16.9812 001 448	106
54	18.1257 944 970	17.7295 750 626	17.3498 040 186	16.9855 244 256	108
55	18.1314 835 669	17.7345 723 750	17.3541 943 619	16.9893 821 131	110
56	18.1365 949 254	17.7390 516 019	17.3581 202 482	16.9928 235 531	112
57	18.1411 872 379	17.7430 664 545	17.3616 308 129	16.9958 936 589	114
58	18.1453 132 121	17.7466 650 760	17.3647 699 929	16.9986 324 980	116
59	18.1490 202 036	17.7498 906 182	17.3675 770 773	17.0010 758 141	118
60	18.1523 507 590	17.7527 817 592	17.3700 871 987	17.0032 554 944	120

TABLE 5. PRESENT WORTH OF ONE DOLLAR PER PERIOD
Payable at end of each period

HALF YEARS	12% Nominal Annual Rate	12¼% Nominal Annual Rate	12½% Nominal Annual Rate	12¾% Nominal Annual Rate	HALF YEARS
1	0.9433 962 264	0.9422 850 412	0.9411 764 706	0.9400 705 053	1
YEARS					
1	1.8333 926 664	1.8301 861 401	1.8269 896 194	1.8238 030 602	2
2	3.4651 056 127	3.4552 104 252	3.4453 610 469	3.4355 571 982	4
3	4.9173 243 260	4.8980 712 737	4.8789 357 371	4.8599 168 006	6
4	6.2097 938 110	6.1791 890 066	6.1488 150 474	6.1186 697 510	8
5	7.3600 870 514	7.3166 948 495	7.2736 908 378	7.2310 707 119	10
6	8.3838 439 404	8.3266 875 375	8.2701 206 037	8.2141 356 552	12
7	9.2949 839 270	9.2234 611 550	9.1527 711 922	9.0829 021 492	14
8	10.1058 952 715	10.0197 074 355	9.9346 346 893	9.8506 593 825	16
9	10.8276 034 812	10.7266 953 829	10.6272 196 556	10.5291 514 439	18
10	11.4699 212 186	11.3544 307 584	11.2407 205 254	11.1287 569 667	20
11	12.0415 817 182	11.9117 976 881	11.7841 676 626	11.6586 478 874	22
12	12.5503 575 278	12.4066 843 974	12.2655 602 824	12.1269 297 446	24
13	13.0031 661 870	12.8460 948 505	12.6919 841 948	12.5407 656 666	26
14	13.4061 642 818	13.2362 478 747	13.0697 161 034	12.9064 859 433	28
15	13.7648 311 515	13.5826 651 736	13.4043 159 947	13.2296 848 578	30
16	14.0840 433 887	13.8902 494 740	13.7007 089 780	13.5153 062 603	32
17	14.3681 411 433	14.1633 539 123	13.9632 577 798	13.7677 191 920	34
18	14.6209 871 336	14.4058 436 433	14.1958 269 607	13.9907 847 171	36
19	14.8460 191 648	14.6211 505 418	14.4018 397 991	14.1879 149 835	38
20	15.0462 968 715	14.8123 217 736	14.5843 286 801	14.3621 254 174	40
21	15.2245 433 175	14.9820 629 205	14.7459 797 305	14.5160 808 493	42
22	15.3831 820 198	15.1327 762 712	14.8891 723 564	14.6521 362 765	44
23	15.5243 699 002	15.2665 948 210	15.0160 142 673	14.7723 728 867	46
24	15.6500 266 110	15.3854 124 584	15.1283 724 997	14.8786 298 935	48
25	15.7618 606 364	15.4909 107 693	15.2279 008 994	14.9725 326 696	50
26	15.8613 925 208	15.5845 828 354	15.3160 644 645	15.0555 176 098	52
27	15.9499 755 436	15.6677 543 658	15.3941 609 098	15.1288 541 030	54
28	16.0288 141 186	15.7416 024 591	15.4633 397 678	15.1936 639 496	56
29	16.0989 801 696	15.8071 722 623	15.5246 193 099	15.2509 385 208	58
30	16.1614 277 052	15.8653 917 626	15.5789 015 340	15.3015 539 240	60
31	16.2170 057 896	15.9170 849 209	15.6269 854 419	15.3462 844 036	62
32	16.2664 700 869	15.9629 833 329	15.6695 787 998	15.3858 141 846	64
33	16.3104 931 354	16.0037 365 834	15.7073 085 562	15.4207 479 390	66
34	16.3496 734 918	16.0399 214 394	15.7407 300 705	15.4516 200 350	68
35	16.3845 438 695	16.0720 500 127	15.7703 352 874	15.4789 027 112	70
36	16.4155 783 816	16.1005 770 082	15.7965 599 778	15.5030 133 004	72
37	16.4431 989 868	16.1259 061 589	15.8197 901 533	15.5243 206 130	74
38	16.4677 812 271	16.1483 959 397	15.8403 677 483	15.5431 505 788	76
39	16.4896 593 335	16.1683 646 407	15.8585 956 524	15.5597 912 326	78
40	16.5091 307 703	16.1860 948 723	15.8747 421 696	15.5744 971 201	80
41	16.5264 602 797	16.2018 375 644	15.8890 449 669	15.5874 931 916	82
42	16.5418 834 814	16.2158 155 181	15.9017 145 727	15.5989 782 431	84
43	16.5556 100 760	16.2282 265 585	15.9129 374 762	15.6091 279 570	86
44	16.5678 266 963	16.2392 463 349	15.9228 788 716	15.6180 975 896	88
45	16.5786 994 450	16.2490 308 064	15.9316 850 905	15.6260 243 459	90
46	16.5883 761 525	16.2577 184 495	15.9394 857 549	15.6330 294 785	92
47	16.5969 883 878	16.2654 322 173	15.9463 956 860	15.6392 201 423	94
48	16.6046 532 465	16.2722 812 803	15.9525 165 938	15.6446 910 334	96
49	16.6114 749 435	16.2783 625 708	15.9579 385 744	15.6495 258 379	98
50	16.6175 462 295	16.2837 621 553	15.9627 414 362	15.6537 985 121	100
51	16.6229 496 525	16.2885 564 523	15.9669 958 743	15.6575 744 134	102
52	16.6277 586 797	16.2928 133 139	15.9707 645 115	15.6609 113 003	104
53	16.6320 386 967	16.2965 929 860	15.9741 028 198	15.6638 602 159	106
54	16.6358 478 967	16.2999 489 610	15.9770 599 373	15.6664 662 685	108
55	16.6392 380 711	16.3029 287 349	15.9796 793 908	15.6687 693 222	110
56	16.6422 553 143	16.3055 744 794	15.9819 997 372	15.6708 046 056	112
57	16.6449 406 499	16.3079 236 389	15.9840 551 305	15.6726 032 518	114
58	16.6473 305 891	16.3100 094 601	15.9858 758 250	15.6741 927 741	116
59	16.6494 576 265	16.3118 614 631	15.9874 886 200	15.6755 974 866	118
60	16.6513 506 822	16.3135 058 586	15.9889 172 551	15.6768 388 768	120

TABLE 5. PRESENT WORTH OF ONE DOLLAR PER PERIOD
Payable at end of each period

SEMI ANNUAL Compounding

HALF YEARS	13% Nominal Annual Rate	13¼% Nominal Annual Rate	13½% Nominal Annual Rate	13¾% Nominal Annual Rate	HALF YEARS
1	0.9389 671 362	0.9378 663 540	0.9367 681 499	0.9356 725 146	1
YEARS					
1	1.8206 264 189	1.8174 596 521	1.8143 027 165	1.8111 555 692	2
2	3.4257 986 016	3.4160 849 815	3.4064 160 646	3.3967 915 794	4
3	4.8410 135 569	4.8222 251 074	4.8035 505 615	4.7849 890 370	6
4	6.0887 509 594	6.0590 565 383	6.0295 843 769	6.0003 323 877	8
5	7.1888 302 228	7.1469 651 757	7.1054 714 297	7.0643 448 967	10
6	8.1587 253 171	8.1038 823 220	8.0495 995 083	7.9958 698 183	12
7	9.0138 423 303	8.9455 802 307	8.8781 045 326	8.8114 041 020	14
8	9.7677 641 828	9.6859 320 702	9.6051 463 301	9.5253 905 479	16
9	10.4324 663 826	10.3371 405 864	10.2431 506 387	10.1504 735 825	18
10	11.0185 072 474	10.9099 392 329	10.8030 214 733	10.6977 231 871	20
11	11.5351 956 158	11.4137 690 834	11.2943 274 834	11.1768 309 425	22
12	11.9907 387 122	11.8569 344 434	11.7254 654 901	11.5962 816 637	24
13	12.3923 725 118	12.2467 397 239	12.1038 039 940	11.9635 036 623	26
14	12.7464 766 795	12.5896 098 362	12.4358 091 090	12.2850 002 994	28
15	13.0586 759 060	12.8911 960 890	12.7271 550 737	12.5664 651 573	30
16	13.3339 292 521	13.1564 693 358	12.9828 212 287	12.8128 828 709	32
17	13.5766 089 199	13.3898 019 059	13.2071 771 171	13.0286 174 035	34
18	13.7905 697 017	13.5950 396 707	13.4040 571 644	13.2174 893 310	36
19	13.9792 102 111	13.7755 654 332	13.5768 262 115	13.3828 435 031	38
20	14.1455 268 673	13.9343 546 839	13.7284 370 223	13.5276 082 788	40
21	14.2921 614 912	14.0740 246 447	13.8614 807 494	13.6543 473 868	42
22	14.4214 432 685	14.1968 774 062	13.9782 312 189	13.7653 053 282	44
23	14.5354 257 475	14.3049 378 718	14.0806 837 915	13.8624 471 257	46
24	14.6359 194 582	14.3999 871 331	14.1705 894 654	13.9474 931 232	48
25	14.7245 206 711	14.4835 918 264	14.2494 848 020	14.0219 494 530	50
26	14.8026 367 530	14.5571 299 542	14.3187 181 870	14.0871 347 080	52
27	14.8715 085 216	14.6218 135 987	14.3794 728 756	14.1442 032 942	54
28	14.9322 299 558	14.6787 088 988	14.4327 872 148	14.1941 658 743	56
29	14.9857 655 719	14.7287 536 235	14.4795 723 904	14.2379 072 666	58
30	15.0329 657 448	14.7727 726 279	14.5206 279 992	14.2762 021 143	60
31	15.0745 802 154	14.8114 914 492	14.5566 557 151	14.3097 286 046	62
32	15.1112 699 997	14.8455 482 649	14.5882 712 811	14.3390 804 787	64
33	15.1436 178 886	14.8755 044 118	14.6160 150 331	14.3647 775 471	66
34	15.1721 377 051	14.9018 536 378	14.6403 611 345	14.3872 748 950	68
35	15.1972 824 661	14.9250 302 404	14.6617 256 801	14.4069 709 419	70
36	15.2194 515 781	14.9454 162 247	14.6804 738 073	14.4242 144 972	72
37	15.2389 971 814	14.9633 475 999	14.6969 259 370	14.4393 109 377	74
38	15.2562 297 440	14.9791 199 174	14.7113 632 495	14.4525 276 155	76
39	15.2714 229 928	14.9929 931 421	14.7240 324 903	14.4640 985 930	78
40	15.2848 182 616	15.0051 959 375	14.7351 501 870	14.4742 287 877	80
41	15.2966 283 247	15.0159 294 347	14.7449 063 502	14.4830 976 014	82
42	15.3070 407 765	15.0253 705 468	14.7534 677 206	14.4908 620 976	84
43	15.3162 210 113	15.0336 748 858	14.7609 806 191	14.4976 597 825	86
44	15.3243 148 505	15.0409 793 267	14.7675 734 472	14.5036 110 404	88
45	15.3314 508 589	15.0474 042 639	14.7733 588 817	14.5088 212 658	90
46	15.3377 423 870	15.0530 555 957	14.7784 358 006	14.5133 827 299	92
47	15.3432 893 712	15.0580 264 692	14.7828 909 723	14.5173 762 144	94
48	15.3481 799 213	15.0623 988 162	14.7868 005 395	14.5208 724 424	96
49	15.3524 917 201	15.0662 447 034	14.7902 313 199	14.5239 333 308	98
50	15.3562 932 576	15.0696 275 200	14.7932 419 482	14.5266 130 867	100
51	15.3596 449 184	15.0726 030 227	14.7958 838 787	14.5289 591 676	102
52	15.3625 999 413	15.0752 202 550	14.7982 022 640	14.5310 131 217	104
53	15.3652 052 647	15.0775 223 550	14.8002 367 272	14.5328 113 236	106
54	15.3675 022 722	15.0795 472 668	14.8020 220 390	14.5343 856 190	108
55	15.3695 274 502	15.0813 283 656	14.8035 887 119	14.5357 638 879	110
56	15.3713 129 672	15.0828 950 081	14.8049 635 214	14.5369 705 390	112
57	15.3728 871 848	15.0842 730 164	14.8061 699 643	14.5380 269 416	114
58	15.3742 751 084	15.0854 851 033	14.8072 286 597	14.5389 518 041	116
59	15.3754 987 841	15.0865 512 467	14.8081 577 015	14.5397 615 056	118
60	15.3765 776 491	15.0874 890 194	14.8089 729 677	14.5404 703 855	120

TABLE 5. PRESENT WORTH OF ONE DOLLAR PER PERIOD
Payable at end of each period

HALF YEARS	14% Nominal Annual Rate	14¼% Nominal Annual Rate	14½% Nominal Annual Rate	14¾% Nominal Annual Rate	HALF YEARS
1	0.9345 794 393	0.9334 889 148	0.9324 009 324	0.9313 154 831	1
YEARS					
1	1.8080 181 675	1.8048 904 689	1.8017 724 311	1.7986 640 122	2
2	3.3872 112 565	3.3776 748 285	3.3681 820 300	3.3587 325 976	4
3	4.7665 396 598	4.7482 015 637	4.7299 738 906	4.7118 557 903	6
4	5.9712 985 062	5.9424 806 906	5.9138 769 214	5.8854 852 013	8
5	7.0235 815 409	6.9831 773 779	6.9431 284 737	6.9034 309 446	10
6	7.9426 862 966	7.8900 420 885	7.8379 304 383	7.7863 446 878	12
7	8.7454 679 855	8.6802 854 066	8.6158 457 633	8.5521 386 242	14
8	9.4466 486 029	9.3689 046 622	9.2921 431 753	9.2163 488 686	16
9	10.0590 869 097	9.9689 685 517	9.8800 968 700	9.7924 506 470	18
10	10.5940 142 455	10.4918 651 575	10.3912 470 547	10.2921 316 772	20
11	11.0612 404 974	10.9475 180 725	10.8356 264 569	10.7255 292 837	22
12	11.4693 340 007	11.3445 747 307	11.2219 572 438	11.1014 360 603	24
13	11.8257 786 713	11.6905 705 197	11.5578 222 190	11.4274 782 500	26
14	12.1371 112 510	11.9920 717 880	11.8498 136 559	11.7102 704 636	28
15	12.4090 411 835	12.2548 004 617	12.1036 626 890	11.9555 498 742	30
16	12.6465 553 179	12.4837 426 363	12.3243 518 033	12.1682 926 102	32
17	12.8540 093 615	12.6832 432 031	12.5162 126 294	12.3528 147 093	34
18	13.0352 077 574	12.8570 883 070	12.6830 109 634	12.5128 596 806	36
19	13.1934 734 539	13.0085 772 007	12.8280 206 809	12.6516 744 510	38
20	13.3317 088 426	13.1405 848 581	12.9540 879 964	12.7720 752 379	40
21	13.4524 489 847	13.2556 165 359	13.0636 873 274	12.8765 046 834	42
22	13.5579 081 009	13.3558 553 187	13.1589 698 621	12.9670 814 093	44
23	13.6500 201 772	13.4432 035 498	13.2418 057 820	13.0456 429 993	46
24	13.7304 744 320	13.5193 189 342	13.3138 209 699	13.1137 832 788	48
25	13.8007 462 940	13.5856 459 984	13.3764 289 218	13.1728 846 500	50
26	13.8621 244 598	13.6434 435 052	13.4308 584 907	13.2241 461 374	52
27	13.9157 345 269	13.6938 083 425	13.4781 780 066	13.2686 077 131	54
28	13.9625 596 357	13.7376 963 400	13.5193 162 450	13.3071 713 953	56
29	14.0034 584 991	13.7759 404 092	13.5550 806 570	13.3406 195 484	58
30	14.0391 811 504	13.8092 663 505	13.5861 732 175	13.3696 307 548	60
31	14.0703 826 976	13.8383 066 276	13.6132 042 034	13.3947 935 820	62
32	14.0976 353 372	13.8636 123 702	13.6367 041 722	13.4166 185 231	64
33	14.1214 388 481	13.8856 638 336	13.6571 343 752	13.4355 483 538	66
34	14.1422 297 564	13.9048 795 131	13.6748 958 114	13.4519 671 145	68
35	14.1603 893 409	13.9216 240 860	13.6903 370 979	13.4662 079 025	70
36	14.1762 506 253	13.9362 153 329	13.7037 613 122	13.4785 596 289	72
37	14.1901 044 854	13.9489 301 682	13.7154 319 415	13.4892 728 808	74
38	14.2022 049 833	13.9600 098 954	13.7255 780 541	13.4985 650 040	76
39	14.2127 740 268	13.9696 647 868	13.7343 987 951	13.5066 245 133	78
40	14.2220 054 387	13.9780 780 743	13.7420 672 960	13.5136 149 170	80
41	14.2300 685 114	13.9854 094 260	13.7487 340 720	13.5196 780 333	82
42	14.2371 111 114	13.9917 979 773	13.7545 299 772	13.5249 368 683	84
43	14.2432 623 909	13.9973 649 709	13.7595 687 719	13.5294 981 111	86
44	14.2486 351 567	14.0022 160 577	13.7639 493 564	13.5334 542 983	88
45	14.2533 279 384	14.0064 433 023	13.7677 577 117	13.5368 856 915	90
46	14.2574 267 957	14.0101 269 298	13.7710 685 873	13.5398 619 053	92
47	14.2610 068 965	14.0133 368 485	13.7739 469 682	13.5424 433 200	94
48	14.2641 338 951	14.0161 339 767	13.7764 493 505	13.5446 823 062	96
49	14.2668 651 367	14.0185 713 986	13.7786 248 503	13.5466 242 876	98
50	14.2692 507 090	14.0206 953 717	13.7805 161 678	13.5483 086 623	100
51	14.2713 343 602	14.0225 462 053	13.7821 604 254	13.5497 696 023	102
52	14.2731 543 019	14.0241 590 245	13.7835 898 961	13.5510 367 464	104
53	14.2747 439 094	14.0255 644 377	13.7848 326 372	13.5521 358 020	106
54	14.2761 323 342	14.0267 891 169	13.7859 130 408	13.5530 890 662	108
55	14.2773 450 381	14.0278 563 042	13.7868 523 130	13.5539 158 785	110
56	14.2784 042 608	14.0287 862 530	13.7876 688 894	13.5546 330 130	112
57	14.2793 294 268	14.0295 966 118	13.7883 787 977	13.5552 550 185	114
58	14.2801 375 027	14.0303 027 597	13.7889 959 717	13.5557 945 141	116
59	14.2808 433 074	14.0309 180 980	13.7895 325 252	13.5562 624 448	118
60	14.2814 597 846	14.0314 543 048	13.7899 989 895	13.5566 683 038	120

TABLE 5. PRESENT WORTH OF ONE DOLLAR PER PERIOD
Payable at end of each period

HALF YEARS	15% Nominal Annual Rate	15¼% Nominal Annual Rate	15½% Nominal Annual Rate	15¾% Nominal Annual Rate	HALF YEARS
1	0.9302 325 581	0.9291 521 487	0.9280 742 459	0.9269 988 413	1
YEARS					
1	1.7955 651 704	1.7924 758 640	1.7893 960 519	1.7863 256 929	2
2	3.3493 262 696	3.3399 627 867	3.3306 418 910	3.3213 633 267	4
3	4.6938 464 205	4.6759 449 462	4.6581 505 405	4.6404 623 838	6
4	5.8573 035 548	5.8293 300 279	5.8015 626 880	5.7739 996 235	8
5	6.8640 809 560	6.8250 747 218	6.7864 085 038	6.7480 786 110	10
6	7.7352 782 745	7.6847 247 305	7.6346 776 805	7.5851 308 406	12
7	8.4891 537 259	8.4268 809 699	8.3653 104 197	8.3044 322 978	14
8	9.1415 067 396	9.0676 020 520	8.9946 203 302	8.9225 473 544	16
9	9.7060 090 770	9.6207 517 570	9.5366 586 788	9.4537 102 200	18
10	10.1944 913 592	10.0982 990 155	10.0035 281 281	9.9101 527 330	20
11	10.6171 910 085	10.5105 768 890	10.4056 529 654	10.3023 860 407	22
12	10.9829 668 002	10.8665 061 545	10.7520 118 564	10.6394 426 541	24
13	11.2994 845 215	11.1737 883 304	11.0503 383 220	10.9290 844 525	26
14	11.5733 776 282	11.4390 723 202	11.3072 934 120	11.1779 814 272	28
15	11.8103 862 656	11.6680 982 798	11.5286 144 343	11.3918 652 810	30
16	12.0154 775 689	11.8658 218 223	11.7192 430 569	11.5756 614 196	32
17	12.1929 497 622	12.0365 212 455	11.8834 356 463	11.7336 023 768	34
18	12.3465 222 388	12.1838 901 058	12.0248 583 040	11.8693 252 822	36
19	12.4794 135 111	12.3111 171 378	12.1466 687 229	11.9859 556 193	38
20	12.5944 086 629	12.4209 552 518	12.2515 866 930	12.0861 791 997	40
21	12.6939 177 181	12.5157 811 004	12.3419 548 284	12.1723 040 134	42
22	12.7800 261 487	12.5976 465 044	12.4197 908 740	12.2463 133 785	44
23	12.8545 385 819	12.6683 228 491	12.4868 327 573	12.3099 116 132	46
24	12.9190 166 203	12.7293 394 136	12.5445 773 934	12.3645 632 840	48
25	12.9748 115 698	12.7820 164 607	12.5943 141 076	12.4115 269 322	50
26	13.0230 927 591	12.8274 938 048	12.6371 534 241	12.4518 840 561	52
27	13.0648 720 469	12.8667 554 744	12.6740 518 616	12.4865 640 164	54
28	13.1010 250 270	12.9006 510 050	12.7058 332 904	12.5163 654 374	56
29	13.1323 093 798	12.9299 138 203	12.7332 073 280	12.5419 745 988	58
30	13.1593 807 505	12.9551 771 027	12.7567 851 836	12.5639 812 388	60
31	13.1828 064 904	12.9769 874 936	12.7770 933 047	12.5828 921 354	62
32	13.2030 775 471	12.9958 169 213	12.7945 851 322	12.5991 427 767	64
33	13.2206 187 536	13.0120 728 128	12.8096 512 247	12.6131 073 891	66
34	13.2357 977 316	13.0261 069 094	12.8226 279 787	12.6251 075 556	68
35	13.2489 325 963	13.0382 228 778	12.8338 051 399	12.6354 196 208	70
36	13.2602 986 231	13.0486 828 807	12.8434 322 726	12.6442 810 554	72
37	13.2701 340 168	13.0577 132 492	12.8517 243 319	12.6518 959 240	74
38	13.2786 449 036	13.0655 093 806	12.8588 664 634	12.6584 395 851	76
39	13.2860 096 516	13.0722 399 656	12.8650 181 369	12.6640 627 288	78
40	13.2923 826 082	13.0780 506 393	12.8703 167 075	12.6688 948 472	80
41	13.2978 973 354	13.0830 671 318	12.8748 804 820	12.6730 472 162	82
42	13.3026 694 087	13.0873 979 886	12.8788 113 604	12.6766 154 585	84
43	13.3067 988 393	13.0911 369 201	12.8821 971 117	12.6796 817 448	86
44	13.3103 721 703	13.0943 648 282	12.8851 133 331	12.6823 166 871	88
45	13.3134 642 901	13.0971 515 579	12.8876 251 382	12.6845 809 636	90
46	13.3161 400 023	13.0995 574 078	12.8897 886 107	12.6865 267 173	92
47	13.3184 553 833	13.1016 344 350	12.8916 520 567	12.6881 987 557	94
48	13.3204 589 579	13.1034 275 818	12.8932 570 834	12.6896 355 832	96
49	13.3221 927 164	13.1049 756 480	12.8946 395 279	12.6908 702 876	98
50	13.3236 929 942	13.1063 121 303	12.8958 302 575	12.6919 313 023	100
51	13.3249 912 335	13.1074 659 471	12.8968 558 589	12.6928 430 607	102
52	13.3261 146 423	13.1084 620 645	12.8977 392 317	12.6936 265 592	104
53	13.3270 867 646	13.1093 220 364	12.8985 001 000	12.6942 998 404	106
54	13.3279 279 737	13.1100 644 704	12.8991 554 524	12.6948 784 091	108
55	13.3286 558 993	13.1107 054 313	12.8997 199 218	12.6953 755 887	110
56	13.3292 857 971	13.1112 587 881	12.9002 061 115	12.6958 028 285	112
57	13.3298 308 683	13.1117 365 141	12.9006 248 774	12.6961 699 671	114
58	13.3303 025 361	13.1121 489 463	12.9009 855 695	12.6964 854 592	116
59	13.3307 106 856	13.1125 050 088	12.9012 962 415	12.6967 565 700	118
60	13.3310 638 708	13.1128 124 060	12.9015 638 301	12.6969 895 428	120

TABLE 5. PRESENT WORTH OF ONE DOLLAR PER PERIOD
Payable at end of each period

HALF YEARS	16% Nominal Annual Rate	16¼% Nominal Annual Rate	16½% Nominal Annual Rate	16¾% Nominal Annual Rate	HALF YEARS
1	0.9259 259 259	0.9248 554 913	0.9237 875 289	0.9227 220 300	1
YEARS					
1	1.7832 647 462	1.7802 131 712	1.7771 709 274	1.7741 379 746	2
2	3.3121 268 400	3.3029 321 789	3.2937 790 931	3.2846 673 342	4
3	4.6228 796 640	4.6054 015 764	4.5880 273 237	4.5707 561 157	6
4	5.7466 389 437	5.7194 787 783	5.6925 172 772	5.6657 526 105	8
5	6.7100 813 989	6.6724 132 689	6.6350 706 674	6.5980 500 855	10
6	7.5360 780 169	7.4875 131 038	7.4394 300 827	7.3918 230 209	12
7	8.2442 369 830	8.1847 150 074	8.1258 570 542	8.0676 539 544	14
8	8.8513 691 555	8.7810 720 101	8.7116 424 359	8.6430 671 872	16
9	9.3718 871 360	9.2911 705 522	9.2115 419 558	9.1329 831 882	18
10	9.8181 474 074	9.7274 872 578	9.6381 479 070	9.5501 054 831	20
11	10.2007 436 621	10.1006 941 027	10.0022 063 434	9.9052 500 558	22
12	10.5287 582 837	10.4199 194 436	10.3128 877 691	10.2076 258 076	24
13	10.8099 779 524	10.6929 712 906	10.5780 181 400	10.4650 733 440	26
14	11.0510 784 914	10.9265 282 849	10.8042 759 970	10.6842 682 814	28
15	11.2577 833 431	11.1263 030 537	10.9973 606 959	10.8708 943 460	30
16	11.4349 994 368	11.2971 819 364	11.1621 359 725	11.0297 907 532	32
17	11.5869 336 736	11.4433 445 011	11.3027 524 580	11.1650 776 878	34
18	11.7171 927 928	11.5683 657 732	11.4227 522 323	11.2802 631 410	36
19	11.8288 689 925	11.6753 036 785	11.5251 580 475	11.3783 338 724	38
20	11.9246 133 337	11.7667 738 371	11.6125 494 701	11.4618 328 569	40
21	12.0066 986 743	11.8450 135 397	11.6871 278 593	11.5329 252 236	42
22	12.0770 736 234	11.9119 364 702	11.7507 718 186	11.5934 543 981	44
23	12.1374 087 992	11.9691 795 127	11.8050 845 168	11.6449 899 025	46
24	12.1891 364 877	12.0181 427 888	11.8514 340 718	11.6888 680 526	48
25	12.2334 846 431	12.0600 239 030	11.8909 880 126	11.7262 266 092	50
26	12.2715 060 383	12.0958 472 357	11.9247 426 890	11.7580 342 800	52
27	12.3041 032 564	12.1264 889 984	11.9535 483 694	11.7851 158 381	54
28	12.3320 501 170	12.1526 986 655	11.9781 306 589	11.8081 735 084	56
29	12.3560 100 454	12.1751 173 055	11.9991 087 766	11.8278 051 766	58
30	12.3765 518 222	12.1942 932 614	12.0170 111 541	11.8445 198 919	60
31	12.3941 630 849	12.2106 955 626	12.0322 887 457	11.8587 510 670	62
32	12.4092 619 040	12.2247 253 968	12.0453 263 888	11.8708 677 164	64
33	12.4222 067 079	12.2367 259 233	12.0564 524 970	11.8811 840 249	66
34	12.4333 047 907	12.2469 906 658	12.0659 473 330	11.8899 674 945	68
35	12.4428 196 079	12.2557 706 921	12.0740 500 685	11.8974 458 805	70
36	12.4509 770 301	12.2632 807 551	12.0809 648 084	11.9038 130 976	72
37	12.4579 707 048	12.2697 045 451	12.0868 657 326	11.9092 342 478	74
38	12.4639 666 537	12.2751 991 832	12.0919 014 834	11.9138 499 014	76
39	12.4691 072 134	12.2798 990 641	12.0961 989 095	11.9177 797 426	78
40	12.4735 144 147	12.2839 191 434	12.0998 662 616	11.9211 256 720	80
41	12.4772 928 796	12.2873 577 490	12.1029 959 190	11.9239 744 496	82
42	12.4805 323 042	12.2902 989 868	12.1056 667 166	11.9263 999 443	84
43	12.4833 095 886	12.2928 147 970	12.1079 459 310	11.9284 650 492	86
44	12.4856 906 624	12.2949 667 147	12.1098 909 747	11.9302 233 124	88
45	12.4877 320 494	12.2968 073 740	12.1115 508 428	11.9317 203 258	90
46	12.4894 822 097	12.2983 817 961	12.1129 673 466	11.9329 949 068	92
47	12.4909 826 901	12.2997 284 901	12.1141 761 674	11.9340 801 054	94
48	12.4922 691 101	12.3008 803 951	12.1152 077 550	11.9350 040 608	96
49	12.4933 720 080	12.3018 656 860	12.1160 880 948	11.9357 907 312	98
50	12.4943 175 652	12.3027 084 621	12.1168 393 621	11.9364 605 148	100
51	12.4951 282 280	12.3034 293 370	12.1174 804 812	11.9370 307 793	102
52	12.4958 232 408	12.3040 459 430	12.1180 276 016	11.9375 163 116	104
53	12.4964 191 022	12.3045 733 617	12.1184 945 050	11.9379 297 016	106
54	12.4969 299 573	12.3050 244 933	12.1188 929 527	11.9382 816 684	108
55	12.4973 679 332	12.3054 103 721	12.1192 329 813	11.9385 813 385	110
56	12.4977 434 269	12.3057 404 366	12.1195 231 561	11.9388 364 824	112
57	12.4980 653 523	12.3060 227 597	12.1197 707 864	11.9390 537 160	114
58	12.4983 413 514	12.3062 642 470	12.1199 821 100	11.9392 386 722	116
59	12.4985 779 762	12.3064 708 050	12.1201 624 501	11.9393 961 468	118
60	12.4987 808 438	12.3066 474 860	12.1203 163 493	11.9395 302 232	120

TABLE 5. PRESENT WORTH OF ONE DOLLAR PER PERIOD
Payable at end of each period

SEMI ANNUAL Compounding

HALF YEARS	17% Nominal Annual Rate	17¼% Nominal Annual Rate	17½% Nominal Annual Rate	17¾% Nominal Annual Rate	HALF YEARS
1	0.9216 589 862	0.9205 983 890	0.9195 402 299	0.9184 845 006	1
YEARS					
1	1.7711 142 730	1.7680 997 827	1.7650 944 643	1.7620 982 784	2
2	3.2755 966 557	3.2665 668 128	3.2575 775 626	3.2486 286 638	4
3	4.5535 871 695	4.5365 197 093	4.5195 529 661	4.5026 861 781	6
4	5.6391 829 680	5.6128 065 591	5.5866 216 123	5.5606 263 753	8
5	6.5613 480 584	6.5249 611 643	6.4888 860 244	6.4531 193 018	10
6	7.3446 860 697	7.2980 134 636	7.2517 995 186	7.2060 386 311	12
7	8.0100 966 847	7.9531 763 646	7.8968 842 540	7.8412 117 509	14
8	8.5753 332 496	8.5084 278 364	8.4423 383 836	8.3770 525 460	16
9	9.0554 764 379	8.9790 042 326	8.9035 494 326	8.8290 952 235	18
10	9.4633 366 076	9.3778 183 842	9.2935 283 880	9.2104 446 544	20
11	9.8097 955 850	9.7158 139 336	9.6232 767 450	9.5321 562 884	22
12	10.1040 969 951	10.0022 656 328	9.9020 968 646	9.8035 566 554	24
13	10.3540 928 838	10.2450 338 470	10.1378 543 973	10.0325 137 442	26
14	10.5664 532 131	10.4507 802 470	10.3372 001 774	10.2256 650 989	28
15	10.7468 438 175	10.6251 506 077	10.5057 578 459	10.3886 102 429	30
16	10.9000 775 701	10.7729 297 315	10.6482 824 962	10.5260 730 114	32
17	11.0302 427 914	10.8981 727 448	10.7687 948 178	10.6420 384 969	34
18	11.1408 123 268	11.0043 163 732	10.8706 945 216	10.7398 685 782	36
19	11.2347 362 032	11.0942 732 461	10.9568 562 476	10.8223 993 826	38
20	11.3145 203 366	11.1705 118 214	11.0297 106 599	10.8920 235 063	40
21	11.3822 933 904	11.2351 241 201	11.0913 130 167	10.9507 593 764	42
22	11.4398 635 694	11.2898 831 334	11.1434 011 503	11.0003 097 656	44
23	11.4887 668 622	11.3362 914 734	11.1874 444 923	11.0421 111 566	46
24	11.5303 080 229	11.3756 226 063	11.2246 855 266	11.0773 753 861	48
25	11.5655 953 814	11.4089 557 962	11.2561 748 408	11.1071 247 758	50
26	11.5955 704 146	11.4372 057 211	11.2828 007 638	11.1322 217 710	52
27	11.6210 328 651	11.4611 475 719	11.3053 144 257	11.1533 939 418	54
28	11.6426 620 783	11.4814 383 237	11.3243 509 479	11.1712 550 769	56
29	11.6610 351 278	11.4986 347 642	11.3404 473 598	11.1863 229 765	58
30	11.6766 422 118	11.5132 087 715	11.3540 577 491	11.1990 344 642	60
31	11.6898 997 318	11.5255 602 630	11.3655 660 714	11.2097 580 503	62
32	11.7011 614 023	11.5360 281 693	11.3752 969 820	11.2188 046 154	64
33	11.7107 276 878	11.5448 997 344	11.3835 249 947	11.2264 364 223	66
34	11.7188 538 196	11.5524 183 982	11.3904 822 257	11.2328 747 198	68
35	11.7257 566 053	11.5587 904 763	11.3963 649 418	11.2383 061 562	70
36	11.7316 202 130	11.5641 908 213	11.4013 390 973	11.2428 881 908	72
37	11.7366 010 856	11.5687 676 213	11.4055 450 155	11.2467 536 583	74
38	11.7408 321 142	11.5726 464 656	11.4091 013 475	11.2500 146 200	76
39	11.7444 261 838	11.5759 337 916	11.4121 084 191	11.2527 656 122	78
40	11.7474 791 852	11.5787 198 049	11.4146 510 612	11.2550 863 871	80
41	11.7500 725 734	11.5810 809 551	11.4168 010 030	11.2570 442 248	82
42	11.7522 755 407	11.5830 820 332	11.4186 188 954	11.2586 958 837	84
43	11.7541 468 629	11.5847 779 497	11.4201 560 220	11.2600 892 458	86
44	11.7557 364 674	11.5862 152 412	11.4214 557 459	11.2612 647 054	88
45	11.7570 867 654	11.5874 333 479	11.4225 547 330	11.2622 563 392	90
46	11.7582 337 832	11.5884 656 949	11.4234 839 861	11.2630 928 952	92
47	11.7592 081 235	11.5893 406 105	11.4242 697 201	11.2637 986 253	94
48	11.7600 357 820	11.5900 821 026	11.4249 341 007	11.2643 939 890	96
49	11.7607 388 410	11.5907 105 183	11.4254 958 706	11.2648 962 460	98
50	11.7613 360 581	11.5912 431 014	11.4259 708 775	11.2653 199 569	100
51	11.7618 433 673	11.5916 944 663	11.4263 725 216	11.2656 774 053	102
52	11.7622 743 038	11.5920 769 987	11.4267 121 335	11.2659 789 537	104
53	11.7626 403 651	11.5924 011 955	11.4269 992 937	11.2662 333 440	106
54	11.7629 513 178	11.5926 759 527	11.4272 421 033	11.2664 479 512	108
55	11.7632 154 582	11.5929 088 098	11.4274 474 120	11.2666 289 968	110
56	11.7634 398 337	11.5931 061 565	11.4276 210 116	11.2667 817 294	112
57	11.7636 304 306	11.5932 734 082	11.4277 677 995	11.2669 105 767	114
58	11.7637 923 342	11.5934 151 542	11.4278 919 166	11.2670 192 741	116
59	11.7639 298 640	11.5935 352 841	11.4279 968 643	11.2671 109 726	118
60	11.7640 466 895	11.5936 370 944	11.4280 856 033	11.2671 883 308	120

TABLE 5. PRESENT WORTH OF ONE DOLLAR PER PERIOD
Payable at end of each period

HALF YEARS	18% Nominal Annual Rate	18¼% Nominal Annual Rate	18½% Nominal Annual Rate	18¾% Nominal Annual Rate	HALF YEARS
1	0.9174 311 927	0.9163 802 978	0.9153 318 078	0.9142 857 143	1
YEARS					
1	1.7591 111 859	1.7561 331 481	1.7531 641 261	1.7502 040 816	2
2	3.2397 198 771	3.2308 509 645	3.2220 216 903	3.2132 318 201	4
3	4.4859 185 902	4.4692 494 542	4.4526 780 286	4.4362 035 786	6
4	5.5348 191 147	5.5091 981 157	5.4837 616 816	5.4585 081 343	8
5	6.4176 577 012	6.3824 979 682	6.3476 368 890	6.3130 712 894	10
6	7.1607 252 766	7.1158 540 085	7.0714 194 568	7.0274 163 268	12
7	7.7861 503 885	7.7316 918 336	7.6778 278 835	7.6245 504 642	14
8	8.3125 581 925	8.2488 434 025	8.1858 964 615	8.1237 058 574	16
9	8.7556 251 094	8.6831 229 065	8.6115 727 361	8.5409 590 188	18
10	9.1285 456 691	9.0478 103 578	8.9682 180 761	8.8897 486 002	20
11	9.4424 254 432	9.3540 576 844	9.2670 270 682	9.1813 082 176	22
12	9.7066 117 694	9.6112 297 499	9.5173 788 987	9.4250 282 570	24
13	9.9289 721 146	9.8271 907 248	9.7271 317 533	9.6287 583 144	26
14	10.1161 283 685	10.0085 445 691	9.9028 694 737	9.7990 600 114	28
15	10.2736 540 430	10.1608 369 767	10.0501 082 154	9.9414 183 279	30
16	10.4062 402 517	10.2887 249 601	10.1734 695 918	10.0604 182 594	32
17	10.5178 354 109	10.3961 192 586	10.2768 257 397	10.1598 924 879	34
18	10.6117 628 237	10.4863 039 269	10.3634 208 607	10.2430 448 225	36
19	10.6908 196 480	10.5620 367 591	10.4359 730 517	10.3125 533 863	38
20	10.7573 601 952	10.6256 336 209	10.4967 596 221	10.3706 568 715	40
21	10.8133 660 426	10.6790 392 668	10.5476 885 753	10.4192 266 420	42
22	10.8605 050 439	10.7238 868 102	10.5903 584 982	10.4598 270 052	44
23	10.9001 809 981	10.7615 476 626	10.6261 087 387	10.4937 655 946	46
24	10.9335 754 550	10.7931 734 707	10.6560 614 455	10.5221 354 848	48
25	10.9616 829 013	10.8197 313 332	10.6811 567 913	10.5458 503 971	50
26	10.9853 403 765	10.8420 333 739	10.7021 824 831	10.5656 741 278	52
27	11.0052 524 000	10.8607 615 762	10.7197 984 872	10.5822 451 485	54
28	11.0220 119 519	10.8764 886 375	10.7345 577 447	10.5960 971 690	56
29	11.0361 181 314	10.8896 954 820	10.7469 235 276	10.6076 763 274	58
30	11.0479 910 204	10.9007 859 673	10.7572 839 802	10.6173 555 586	60
31	11.0579 841 936	10.9100 992 339	10.7659 643 023	10.6254 466 057	62
32	11.0663 952 475	10.9179 200 762	10.7732 369 566	10.6322 100 606	64
33	11.0734 746 634	10.9244 876 507	10.7793 302 214	10.6378 637 568	66
34	11.0794 332 660	10.9300 027 901	10.7844 353 556	10.6425 897 853	68
35	11.0844 485 027	10.9346 341 442	10.7887 126 020	10.6465 403 593	70
36	11.0886 697 270	10.9385 233 370	10.7922 962 173	10.6498 427 166	72
37	11.0922 226 471	10.9417 892 977	10.7952 986 860	10.6526 032 178	74
38	11.0952 130 689	10.9445 318 975	10.7978 142 513	10.6549 107 715	76
39	11.0977 300 470	10.9468 350 035	10.7999 218 733	10.6568 396 980	78
40	11.0998 485 372	10.9487 690 434	10.8016 877 070	10.6584 521 230	80
41	11.1016 316 280	10.9503 931 589	10.8031 671 796	10.6597 999 788	82
42	11.1031 324 198	10.9517 570 145	10.8044 067 296	10.6609 266 761	84
43	11.1043 956 063	10.9529 023 161	10.8054 452 646	10.6618 685 031	86
44	11.1054 588 050	10.9538 640 864	10.8063 153 828	10.6626 557 936	88
45	11.1063 536 782	10.9546 717 357	10.8070 443 959	10.6633 139 042	90
46	11.1071 068 750	10.9553 499 616	10.8076 551 867	10.6638 640 310	92
47	11.1077 408 257	10.9559 195 037	10.8081 669 269	10.6643 238 920	94
48	11.1082 744 093	10.9563 977 783	10.8085 956 795	10.6647 082 983	96
49	11.1087 235 159	10.9567 994 107	10.8089 549 022	10.6650 296 306	98
50	11.1091 015 200	10.9571 366 827	10.8092 558 706	10.6652 982 381	100
51	11.1094 196 785	10.9574 199 078	10.8095 080 316	10.6655 227 721	102
52	11.1096 874 661	10.9576 577 469	10.8097 193 003	10.6657 104 642	104
53	11.1099 128 576	10.9578 574 730	10.8098 963 080	10.6658 673 595	106
54	11.1101 025 651	10.9580 251 935	10.8100 446 108	10.6659 985 111	108
55	11.1102 622 381	10.9581 660 373	10.8101 688 637	10.6661 081 432	110
56	11.1103 966 317	10.9582 843 113	10.8102 729 668	10.6661 997 866	112
57	11.1105 097 481	10.9583 836 322	10.8103 601 877	10.6662 763 930	114
58	11.1106 049 559	10.9584 670 372	10.8104 332 642	10.6663 404 298	116
59	11.1106 850 904	10.9585 370 768	10.8104 944 901	10.6663 939 593	118
60	11.1107 525 380	10.9585 958 928	10.8105 457 871	10.6664 387 055	120

TABLE 5. PRESENT WORTH OF ONE DOLLAR PER PERIOD
Payable at end of each period

SEMI ANNUAL Compounding

HALF YEARS	19% Nominal Annual Rate	19¼% Nominal Annual Rate	19½% Nominal Annual Rate	19¾% Nominal Annual Rate	HALF YEARS
1	0.9132 420 091	0.9122 006 842	0.9111 617 312	0.9101 251 422	1
YEARS					
1	1.7472 529 764	1.7443 107 723	1.7413 774 316	1.7384 529 167	2
2	3.2044 811 212	3.1957 693 629	3.1870 963 157	3.1784 617 522	4
3	4.4198 253 758	4.4035 426 986	4.3873 548 317	4.3712 610 661	6
4	5.4334 358 131	5.4085 430 755	5.3838 282 962	5.3592 898 673	8
5	6.2787 980 343	6.2448 140 277	6.2111 162 115	6.1777 015 652	10
6	6.9838 393 981	6.9406 835 235	6.8979 436 275	6.8556 147 056	12
7	7.5718 516 279	7.5197 235 510	7.4681 585 318	7.4171 489 884	14
8	8.0622 602 764	8.0015 485 993	7.9415 598 979	7.8822 834 312	16
9	8.4712 664 676	8.4024 800 827	8.3345 851 446	8.2675 672 091	18
10	8.8123 821 168	8.7360 992 147	8.6608 808 752	8.5867 084 633	20
11	9.0968 763 094	9.0137 070 601	8.9317 767 136	8.8510 620 282	22
12	9.3341 475 861	9.2447 073 488	9.1566 786 919	9.0700 334 283	24
13	9.5320 344 330	9.4369 250 194	9.3433 958 453	9.2514 135 208	26
14	9.6970 742 337	9.5968 712 822	9.4984 113 576	9.4016 556 891	28
15	9.8347 192 374	9.7299 641 810	9.6271 076 697	9.5261 054 500	30
16	9.9495 166 802	9.8407 121 248	9.7339 533 686	9.6291 906 436	32
17	10.0452 590 064	9.9328 666 061	9.8226 583 454	9.7145 789 725	34
18	10.1251 091 565	10.0095 492 797	9.8963 026 098	9.7853 084 969	36
19	10.1917 050 575	10.0733 577 059	9.9574 432 343	9.8438 957 265	38
20	10.2472 467 692	10.1264 533 411	10.0082 031 408	9.8924 251 560	40
21	10.2935 691 660	10.1706 347 548	10.0503 448 121	9.9326 234 304	42
22	10.3322 025 529	10.2073 985 548	10.0853 314 892	9.9659 207 775	44
23	10.3644 232 213	10.2379 900 837	10.1143 779 779	9.9935 018 949	46
24	10.3912 956 121	10.2634 456 035	10.1384 928 288	10.0163 481 005	48
25	10.4137 074 807	10.2846 273 983	10.1585 133 567	10.0352 722 472	50
26	10.4323 992 250	10.3022 529 834	10.1751 347 132	10.0509 476 435	52
27	10.4479 883 447	10.3169 194 107	10.1889 340 244	10.0639 320 096	54
28	10.4609 898 415	10.3291 234 927	10.2003 904 292	10.0746 873 207	56
29	10.4718 332 324	10.3392 786 325	10.2099 017 163	10.0835 962 436	58
30	10.4808 767 393	10.3477 288 268	10.2177 981 362	10.0909 757 519	60
31	10.4884 191 233	10.3547 603 187	10.2243 538 680	10.0970 884 035	62
32	10.4947 095 543	10.3606 112 940	10.2297 965 395	10.1021 516 827	64
33	10.4999 558 427	10.3654 799 496	10.2343 151 307	10.1063 457 374	66
34	10.5043 313 048	10.3695 312 070	10.2380 665 362	10.1098 197 895	68
35	10.5079 804 881	10.3729 022 992	10.2411 810 119	10.1126 974 433	70
36	10.5110 239 471	10.3757 074 191	10.2437 666 985	10.1150 810 838	72
37	10.5135 622 252	10.3780 415 876	10.2459 133 761	10.1170 555 195	74
38	10.5156 791 770	10.3799 838 727	10.2476 955 816	10.1186 909 994	76
39	10.5174 447 380	10.3816 000 678	10.2491 751 965	10.1200 457 129	78
40	10.5189 172 353	10.3829 449 200	10.2504 035 961	10.1211 678 596	80
41	10.5201 453 141	10.3840 639 851	10.2514 234 327	10.1220 973 650	82
42	10.5211 695 454	10.3849 951 705	10.2522 701 171	10.1228 673 000	84
43	10.5220 237 654	10.3857 700 192	10.2529 730 477	10.1235 050 587	86
44	10.5227 361 944	10.3864 147 787	10.2535 566 318	10.1240 333 318	88
45	10.5233 303 679	10.3869 512 895	10.2540 411 325	10.1244 709 152	90
46	10.5238 259 151	10.3873 977 256	10.2544 433 725	10.1248 333 776	92
47	10.5242 392 070	10.3877 692 096	10.2547 773 185	10.1251 336 153	94
48	10.5245 838 969	10.3880 783 251	10.2550 545 657	10.1253 823 105	96
49	10.5248 713 721	10.3883 355 433	10.2552 847 407	10.1255 883 117	98
50	10.5251 111 295	10.3885 495 771	10.2554 758 356	10.1257 589 482	100
51	10.5253 110 899	10.3887 276 768	10.2556 344 856	10.1259 002 911	102
52	10.5254 778 590	10.3888 758 754	10.2557 661 993	10.1260 173 694	104
53	10.5256 169 462	10.3889 991 929	10.2558 755 501	10.1261 143 486	106
54	10.5257 329 466	10.3891 018 067	10.2559 663 348	10.1261 946 792	108
55	10.5258 296 921	10.3891 871 926	10.2560 417 057	10.1262 612 192	110
56	10.5259 103 789	10.3892 582 431	10.2561 042 799	10.1263 163 362	112
57	10.5259 776 726	10.3893 173 650	10.2561 562 299	10.1263 619 911	114
58	10.5260 337 963	10.3893 665 609	10.2561 993 596	10.1263 998 083	116
59	10.5260 806 041	10.3894 074 972	10.2562 351 666	10.1264 311 334	118
60	10.5261 196 423	10.3894 415 608	10.2562 648 941	10.1264 570 808	120

SEMI ANNUAL
Compounding

TABLE 5. PRESENT WORTH OF ONE DOLLAR PER PERIOD
Payable at end of each period

HALF YEARS	20% Nominal Annual Rate	20¼% Nominal Annual Rate	20½% Nominal Annual Rate	20¾% Nominal Annual Rate	HALF YEARS
1	0.9090 909 091	0.9080 590 238	0.9070 294 785	0.9060 022 650	1
YEARS					
1	1.7355 371 901	1.7326 302 146	1.7297 319 532	1.7268 423 692	2
2	3.1698 654 463	3.1613 071 738	3.1527 867 119	3.1443 038 395	4
3	4.3552 606 995	4.3393 530 353	4.3235 373 836	4.3078 130 604	6
4	5.3349 261 979	5.3107 357 141	5.2867 168 586	5.2628 680 906	8
5	6.1445 671 057	6.1117 098 863	6.0791 269 964	6.0468 155 610	10
6	6.8136 918 229	6.7721 701 132	6.7310 447 777	6.6903 110 844	12
7	7.3666 874 569	7.3167 665 889	7.2673 791 498	7.2185 180 168	14
8	7.8237 086 421	7.7658 251 534	7.7086 227 651	7.6520 914 502	16
9	8.2014 121 009	8.1361 059 087	8.0716 349 793	8.0079 859 125	18
10	8.5135 637 198	8.4414 287 520	8.3702 860 263	8.3001 183 600	20
11	8.7715 402 643	8.6931 891 724	8.6159 869 818	8.5399 123 887	22
12	8.9847 440 201	8.9007 835 621	8.8181 257 660	8.7367 449 441	24
13	9.1609 454 711	9.0719 599 152	8.9844 258 439	8.8983 129 995	26
14	9.3065 665 051	9.2131 070 045	9.1212 413 296	9.0309 345 389	28
15	9.4269 144 670	9.3294 928 280	9.2337 997 683	9.1397 956 171	30
16	9.5263 755 926	9.4254 612 251	9.3264 018 744	9.2291 531 558	32
17	9.6085 748 699	9.5045 940 006	9.4025 858 562	9.3025 014 073	34
18	9.6765 081 569	9.5698 446 074	9.4652 626 066	9.3627 085 936	36
19	9.7326 513 694	9.6236 483 781	9.5168 269 243	9.4121 290 667	38
20	9.7790 507 185	9.6680 134 173	9.5592 490 160	9.4526 953 730	40
21	9.8173 972 880	9.7045 955 505	9.5941 497 759	9.4859 938 241	42
22	9.8490 886 678	9.7347 601 236	9.6228 627 174	9.5133 265 282	44
23	9.8752 798 907	9.7596 329 616	9.6464 849 254	9.5357 623 079	46
24	9.8969 255 295	9.7801 423 872	9.6659 189 744	9.5541 784 956	48
25	9.9148 144 872	9.7970 538 688	9.6819 074 147	9.5692 952 410	50
26	9.9295 987 498	9.8109 985 892	9.6950 611 440	9.5817 036 719	52
27	9.9418 171 486	9.8224 970 040	9.7058 827 497	9.5918 890 096	54
28	9.9519 149 988	9.8319 782 655	9.7147 857 114	9.6002 495 433	56
29	9.9602 603 296	9.8397 962 406	9.7221 102 001	9.6071 122 046	58
30	9.9671 572 972	9.8462 427 177	9.7281 360 751	9.6127 453 523	60
31	9.9728 572 704	9.8515 582 970	9.7330 935 773	9.6173 692 657	62
32	9.9775 679 921	9.8559 413 705	9.7371 721 267	9.6211 647 594	64
33	9.9814 611 505	9.8595 555 266	9.7405 275 594	9.6242 802 528	66
34	9.9846 786 368	9.8625 356 557	9.7432 880 821	9.6268 375 747	68
35	9.9873 377 163	9.8649 929 842	9.7455 591 710	9.6289 367 271	70
36	9.9895 353 027	9.8670 192 266	9.7474 276 015	9.6306 597 956	72
37	9.9913 514 899	9.8686 900 076	9.7489 647 638	9.6320 741 593	74
38	9.9928 524 710	9.8700 676 855	9.7502 293 911	9.6332 351 257	76
39	9.9940 929 512	9.8712 036 791	9.7512 698 031	9.6341 880 935	78
40	9.9951 181 415	9.8721 403 866	9.7521 257 526	9.6349 703 277	80
41	9.9959 654 062	9.8729 127 686	9.7528 299 444	9.6356 124 169	82
42	9.9966 656 250	9.8735 496 526	9.7534 092 848	9.6361 394 695	84
43	9.9972 443 181	9.8740 748 088	9.7538 859 095	9.6365 720 954	86
44	9.9977 225 770	9.8745 078 375	9.7542 780 298	9.6369 272 121	88
45	9.9981 178 322	9.8748 649 004	9.7546 006 282	9.6372 187 061	90
46	9.9984 444 894	9.8751 593 243	9.7548 660 307	9.6374 579 760	92
47	9.9987 144 541	9.8754 020 977	9.7550 843 779	9.6376 543 784	94
48	9.9989 375 654	9.8756 022 816	9.7552 640 128	9.6378 155 934	96
49	9.9991 219 548	9.8757 673 475	9.7554 117 988	9.6379 479 251	98
50	9.9992 743 428	9.8759 034 561	9.7555 333 827	9.6380 565 483	100
51	9.9994 002 833	9.8760 156 874	9.7556 334 102	9.6381 457 105	102
52	9.9995 043 664	9.8761 082 300	9.7557 157 029	9.6382 188 985	104
53	9.9995 903 855	9.8761 845 380	9.7557 834 054	9.6382 789 741	106
54	9.9996 614 756	9.8762 474 594	9.7558 391 044	9.6383 282 866	108
55	9.9997 202 278	9.8762 993 426	9.7558 849 281	9.6383 687 642	110
56	9.9997 687 833	9.8763 421 239	9.7559 226 274	9.6384 019 899	112
57	9.9998 089 118	9.8763 774 002	9.7559 536 427	9.6384 292 629	114
58	9.9998 420 759	9.8764 064 880	9.7559 791 591	9.6384 516 496	116
59	9.9998 694 842	9.8764 304 729	9.7560 001 514	9.6384 700 255	118
60	9.9998 921 357	9.8764 502 502	9.7560 174 219	9.6384 851 093	120

TABLE 5. PRESENT WORTH OF ONE DOLLAR PER PERIOD
Payable at end of each period

HALF YEARS	21% Nominal Annual Rate	21¼% Nominal Annual Rate	21½% Nominal Annual Rate	21¾% Nominal Annual Rate	HALF YEARS
1	0.9049 773 756	0.9039 548 023	0.9029 345 372	0.9019 165 727	1
YEARS					
1	1.7239 614 259	1.7210 890 868	1.7182 253 158	1.7153 700 769	2
2	3.1358 583 369	3.1274 499 863	3.1190 785 712	3.1107 438 768	4
3	4.2921 793 878	4.2766 356 938	4.2611 813 125	4.2458 155 839	6
4	5.2391 878 854	5.2156 747 346	5.1923 271 456	5.1691 436 415	8
5	6.0147 727 404	5.9829 957 294	5.9514 817 568	5.9202 280 855	10
6	6.6499 643 664	6.6100 000 215	6.5704 135 109	6.5312 003 583	12
7	7.1701 761 769	7.1223 467 251	7.0750 228 625	7.0281 978 946	14
8	7.5962 213 524	7.5410 027 821	7.4864 262 136	7.4324 822 820	16
9	7.9451 455 559	7.8831 009 998	7.8218 395 721	7.7613 488 336	18
10	8.2309 089 134	8.1626 411 821	8.0952 989 902	8.0288 664 824	20
11	8.4649 445 453	8.3910 630 490	8.3182 479 321	8.2464 796 513	22
12	8.6566 159 950	8.5777 143 878	8.5000 161 486	8.4234 978 460	24
13	8.8135 918 552	8.7302 335 959	8.6482 100 993	8.5674 939 168	26
14	8.9421 525 810	8.8548 622 700	8.7690 312 607	8.6846 280 252	28
15	9.0474 417 649	8.9567 006 324	8.8675 356 395	8.7799 111 761	30
16	9.1336 719 272	9.0399 162 498	8.9478 453 512	8.8574 195 891	32
17	9.2042 930 548	9.1079 145 837	9.0133 211 185	8.9204 690 793	34
18	9.2621 306 318	9.1634 783 537	9.0667 029 078	8.9717 569 080	36
19	9.3094 986 850	9.2088 814 151	9.1102 245 884	9.0134 771 720	38
20	9.3482 923 650	9.2459 818 133	9.1457 074 133	9.0474 146 669	40
21	9.3800 637 702	9.2762 978 205	9.1746 362 332	9.0750 212 411	42
22	9.4060 840 443	9.3010 700 694	9.1982 216 333	9.0974 779 056	44
23	9.4273 942 338	9.3213 123 233	9.2174 505 925	9.1157 453 580	46
24	9.4448 469 391	9.3378 529 630	9.2331 277 856	9.1306 050 812	48
25	9.4591 404 263	9.3513 688 867	9.2459 092 566	9.1426 927 751	50
26	9.4708 465 644	9.3624 132 114	9.2563 298 720	9.1525 255 520	52
27	9.4804 337 048	9.3714 379 078	9.2648 257 037	9.1605 240 589	54
28	9.4882 854 199	9.3788 122 966	9.2717 522 769	9.1670 304 724	56
29	9.4947 158 493	9.3848 381 625	9.2773 994 482	9.1723 231 372	58
30	9.4999 822 684	9.3897 621 041	9.2820 035 348	9.1766 284 739	60
31	9.5042 953 817	9.3937 856 256	9.2857 572 042	9.1801 306 652	62
32	9.5078 277 527	9.3970 733 830	9.2888 175 363	9.1829 795 349	64
33	9.5107 207 081	9.3997 599 223	9.2913 125 968	9.1852 969 580	66
34	9.5130 899 925	9.4019 551 856	9.2933 467 966	9.1871 820 739	68
35	9.5150 303 987	9.4037 490 105	9.2950 052 609	9.1887 155 281	70
36	9.5166 195 603	9.4052 148 064	9.2963 573 916	9.1899 629 217	72
37	9.5179 210 584	9.4064 125 585	9.2974 597 713	9.1909 776 185	74
38	9.5189 869 646	9.4073 912 827	9.2983 585 313	9.1918 030 271	76
39	9.5198 599 247	9.4081 910 319	9.2990 912 820	9.1924 744 586	78
40	9.5205 748 651	9.4088 445 343	9.2996 886 870	9.1930 206 370	80
41	9.5211 603 900	9.4093 785 336	9.3001 757 457	9.1934 649 276	82
42	9.5216 399 254	9.4098 148 827	9.3005 728 402	9.1938 263 375	84
43	9.5220 326 573	9.4101 714 385	9.3008 965 876	9.1941 203 275	86
44	9.5223 542 985	9.4104 627 925	9.3011 605 360	9.1943 594 748	88
45	9.5226 177 175	9.4107 008 678	9.3013 757 306	9.1945 540 100	90
46	9.5228 334 535	9.4108 954 073	9.3015 511 768	9.1947 122 553	92
47	9.5230 101 378	9.4110 543 722	9.3016 942 165	9.1948 409 805	94
48	9.5231 548 394	9.4111 842 679	9.3018 108 354	9.1949 456 925	96
49	9.5232 733 477	9.4112 904 101	9.3019 059 137	9.1950 308 708	98
50	9.5233 704 041	9.4113 771 425	9.3019 834 302	9.1951 001 594	100
51	9.5234 498 918	9.4114 480 146	9.3020 466 287	9.1951 565 224	102
52	9.5235 149 909	9.4115 059 266	9.3020 981 538	9.1952 023 712	104
53	9.5235 683 061	9.4115 532 484	9.3021 401 618	9.1952 396 670	106
54	9.5236 119 703	9.4115 919 168	9.3021 744 105	9.1952 700 054	108
55	9.5236 477 307	9.4116 235 140	9.3022 023 332	9.1952 946 843	110
56	9.5236 770 178	9.4116 493 331	9.3022 250 982	9.1953 147 594	112
57	9.5237 010 035	9.4116 704 308	9.3022 436 584	9.1953 310 896	114
58	9.5237 206 474	9.4116 876 705	9.3022 587 903	9.1953 443 734	116
59	9.5237 367 355	9.4117 017 576	9.3022 711 273	9.1953 551 792	118
60	9.5237 499 113	9.4117 132 687	9.3022 811 854	9.1953 639 692	120

SEMI ANNUAL
Compounding

TABLE 5. PRESENT WORTH OF ONE DOLLAR PER PERIOD
Payable at end of each period

HALF YEARS	22% Nominal Annual Rate	22¼% Nominal Annual Rate	22½% Nominal Annual Rate	22¾% Nominal Annual Rate	HALF YEARS
1	0.9009 009 009	0.8998 875 141	0.8988 764 045	0.8978 675 645	1
YEARS					
1	1.7125 233 341	1.7096 850 520	1.7068 551 951	1.7040 337 280	2
2	3.1024 456 896	3.0941 837 978	3.0859 579 912	3.0777 680 608	4
3	4.2305 378 537	4.2153 474 735	4.2002 438 005	4.1852 261 975	6
4	5.1461 227 609	5.1232 630 577	5.1005 631 010	5.0780 214 748	8
5	5.8892 320 111	5.8584 908 625	5.8280 020 006	5.7977 628 182	10
6	6.4923 561 490	6.4538 765 287	6.4157 572 028	6.3779 939 357	12
7	6.9818 652 293	6.9360 183 752	6.8906 509 403	6.8457 566 296	14
8	7.3791 617 801	7.3264 556 556	7.2743 550 079	7.2228 510 859	16
9	7.7016 165 734	7.6426 308 039	7.5843 797 565	7.5268 518 770	18
10	7.9633 281 174	7.8986 686 606	7.8348 731 778	7.7719 270 285	20
11	8.1757 390 775	8.1060 074 865	8.0372 665 494	7.9694 983 231	22
12	8.3481 365 778	8.2739 099 573	8.2007 961 010	8.1287 736 156	24
13	8.4880 582 565	8.4098 769 648	8.3329 245 104	8.2571 759 672	26
14	8.6016 218 298	8.5199 827 127	8.4396 814 627	8.3606 895 983	28
15	8.6937 925 735	8.6091 460 762	8.5259 388 160	8.4441 387 852	30
16	8.7686 004 167	8.6813 503 485	8.5956 329 280	8.5114 126 960	32
17	8.8293 161 405	8.7398 211 904	8.6519 442 923	8.5656 466 466	34
18	8.8785 943 840	8.7871 707 343	8.6974 426 803	8.6093 682 225	36
19	8.9185 897 119	8.8255 142 783	8.7342 044 128	8.6446 150 776	38
20	8.9510 508 172	8.8565 647 858	8.7639 071 130	8.6730 298 995	40
21	8.9773 969 785	8.8817 094 104	8.7879 062 647	8.6959 369 675	42
22	8.9987 801 140	8.9020 714 655	8.8072 970 704	8.7144 038 706	44
23	9.0161 351 465	8.9185 606 075	8.8229 644 300	8.7292 912 630	46
24	9.0302 208 802	8.9319 134 742	8.8356 233 244	8.7412 929 751	48
25	9.0416 531 777	8.9427 265 927	8.8458 514 425	8.7509 683 492	50
26	9.0509 318 868	8.9514 830 295	8.8541 155 450	8.7587 683 085	52
27	9.0584 626 952	8.9585 739 704	8.8607 927 645	8.7650 563 717	54
28	9.0645 748 683	8.9643 161 969	8.8661 878 163	8.7701 255 955	56
29	9.0695 356 451	8.9689 662 378	8.8705 469 037	8.7742 122 322	58
30	9.0735 619 228	8.9727 318 295	8.8740 689 539	8.7775 067 405	60
31	9.0768 297 401	8.9757 811 963	8.8769 146 957	8.7801 626 615	62
32	9.0794 819 740	8.9782 505 661	8.8792 139 948	8.7823 037 752	64
33	9.0816 345 864	8.9802 502 556	8.8810 717 797	8.7840 298 686	66
34	9.0833 816 950	8.9818 695 993	8.8825 728 304	8.7854 213 867	68
35	9.0847 996 875	8.9831 809 399	8.8837 856 476	8.7865 431 815	70
36	9.0859 505 621	8.9842 428 602	8.8847 655 782	8.7874 475 346	72
37	9.0868 846 377	8.9851 028 007	8.8855 573 413	8.7881 765 934	74
38	9.0876 427 544	8.9857 991 783	8.8861 970 691	8.7887 643 359	76
39	9.0882 580 589	8.9863 631 033	8.8867 139 556	8.7892 381 541	78
40	9.0887 574 539	8.9868 197 683	8.8871 315 889	8.7896 201 302	80
41	9.0891 627 740	8.9871 895 745	8.8874 690 278	8.7899 280 665	82
42	9.0894 917 409	8.9874 890 426	8.8877 416 712	8.7901 763 143	84
43	9.0897 587 379	8.9877 315 512	8.8879 619 613	8.7903 764 432	86
44	9.0899 754 386	8.9879 279 341	8.8881 399 511	8.7905 377 804	88
45	9.0901 513 177	8.9880 869 644	8.8882 837 630	8.7906 678 450	90
46	9.0902 940 652	8.9882 157 468	8.8883 999 600	8.7907 726 987	92
47	9.0904 099 223	8.9883 200 345	8.8884 938 447	8.7908 572 282	94
48	9.0905 039 544	8.9884 044 863	8.8885 697 016	8.7909 253 730	96
49	9.0905 802 731	8.9884 728 753	8.8886 309 923	8.7909 803 090	98
50	9.0906 422 150	8.9885 282 565	8.8886 805 139	8.7910 245 966	100
51	9.0906 924 884	8.9885 731 040	8.8887 205 263	8.7910 602 998	102
52	9.0907 332 915	8.9886 094 214	8.8887 528 555	8.7910 890 824	104
53	9.0907 664 081	8.9886 388 312	8.8887 789 768	8.7911 122 860	106
54	9.0907 932 864	8.9886 626 472	8.8888 000 823	8.7911 309 920	108
55	9.0908 151 013	8.9886 819 333	8.8888 171 350	8.7911 460 721	110
56	9.0908 328 069	8.9886 975 511	8.8888 309 133	8.7911 582 292	112
57	9.0908 471 771	8.9887 101 984	8.8888 420 458	8.7911 680 298	114
58	9.0908 588 402	8.9887 204 402	8.8888 510 407	8.7911 759 308	116
59	9.0908 683 063	8.9887 287 339	8.8888 583 083	8.7911 823 002	118
60	9.0908 759 892	8.9887 354 501	8.8888 641 805	8.7911 874 351	120

TABLE 6. PARTIAL PAYMENT TO AMORTIZE ONE
Payable at end of each period

SEMI ANNUAL Compounding

HALF YEARS	5% Nominal Annual Rate	5¼% Nominal Annual Rate	5½% Nominal Annual Rate	5¾% Nominal Annual Rate	HALF YEARS
1	1.0250 000 000	1.0262 500 000	1.0275 000 000	1.0287 500 000	1
YEARS					
1	0.5188 271 605	0.5197 725 170	0.5207 182 491	0.5216 643 561	2
2	0.2658 178 777	0.2666 187 639	0.2674 205 884	0.2682 233 494	4
3	0.1815 499 711	0.1823 096 699	0.1830 708 264	0.1838 334 376	6
4	0.1394 673 458	0.1402 116 647	0.1409 579 478	0.1417 061 906	8
5	0.1142 587 632	0.1149 980 102	0.1157 397 205	0.1164 838 880	10
6	0.0974 871 270	0.0982 264 402	0.0989 687 098	0.0997 139 277	12
7	0.0855 365 249	0.0862 788 239	0.0870 245 664	0.0877 737 416	14
8	0.0765 989 886	0.0773 460 810	0.0780 970 977	0.0788 520 250	16
9	0.0696 700 805	0.0704 231 540	0.0711 806 259	0.0719 424 790	18
10	0.0641 471 287	0.0649 069 971	0.0656 717 306	0.0664 413 080	20
11	0.0596 466 061	0.0604 138 434	0.0611 864 049	0.0619 642 642	22
12	0.0559 128 204	0.0566 878 394	0.0574 686 330	0.0582 551 694	24
13	0.0527 687 467	0.0535 518 473	0.0543 411 636	0.0551 366 576	26
14	0.0500 879 327	0.0508 793 325	0.0516 773 795	0.0524 820 286	28
15	0.0477 776 407	0.0485 774 961	0.0493 844 200	0.0501 983 593	30
16	0.0457 683 123	0.0465 767 327	0.0473 926 322	0.0482 159 486	32
17	0.0440 067 508	0.0448 238 089	0.0456 487 453	0.0464 814 880	34
18	0.0424 515 767	0.0432 773 159	0.0441 113 206	0.0449 535 082	36
19	0.0410 701 180	0.0419 045 574	0.0427 476 374	0.0435 992 639	38
20	0.0398 362 332	0.0406 793 722	0.0415 315 144	0.0423 925 527	40
21	0.0387 287 567	0.0395 805 783	0.0404 417 522	0.0413 121 582	42
22	0.0377 303 683	0.0385 908 410	0.0394 610 021	0.0403 407 166	44
23	0.0368 267 568	0.0376 958 373	0.0385 749 283	0.0394 638 795	46
24	0.0360 059 938	0.0368 836 281	0.0377 715 811	0.0386 696 862	48
25	0.0352 580 569	0.0361 441 820	0.0370 409 195	0.0379 480 860	50
26	0.0345 744 635	0.0354 690 081	0.0363 744 446	0.0372 905 715	52
27	0.0339 479 856	0.0348 508 714	0.0357 649 139	0.0366 898 928	54
28	0.0333 724 260	0.0342 835 683	0.0352 061 174	0.0361 398 334	56
29	0.0328 424 404	0.0337 617 490	0.0346 926 996	0.0356 350 319	58
30	0.0323 533 959	0.0332 807 755	0.0342 200 173	0.0351 708 400	60
31	0.0319 012 558	0.0328 366 065	0.0337 840 249	0.0347 432 076	62
32	0.0314 824 869	0.0324 257 049	0.0333 811 810	0.0343 485 894	64
33	0.0310 939 830	0.0320 449 610	0.0330 083 724	0.0339 838 689	66
34	0.0307 330 027	0.0316 916 300	0.0326 628 513	0.0336 462 949	68
35	0.0303 971 168	0.0313 632 799	0.0323 421 829	0.0333 334 303	70
36	0.0300 841 652	0.0310 577 482	0.0320 442 024	0.0330 431 080	72
37	0.0297 922 211	0.0307 731 057	0.0317 669 784	0.0327 733 949	74
38	0.0295 195 594	0.0305 076 257	0.0315 087 826	0.0325 225 610	76
39	0.0292 646 321	0.0302 597 582	0.0312 680 634	0.0322 890 537	78
40	0.0290 260 451	0.0300 281 079	0.0310 434 245	0.0320 714 758	80
41	0.0288 025 404	0.0298 114 155	0.0308 336 055	0.0318 685 662	82
42	0.0285 929 793	0.0296 085 415	0.0306 374 664	0.0316 791 846	84
43	0.0283 963 292	0.0294 184 524	0.0304 539 731	0.0315 022 968	86
44	0.0282 116 510	0.0292 402 087	0.0302 821 858	0.0313 369 633	88
45	0.0280 380 893	0.0290 729 543	0.0301 212 487	0.0311 823 283	90
46	0.0278 748 628	0.0289 159 082	0.0299 703 805	0.0310 376 114	92
47	0.0277 212 571	0.0287 683 556	0.0298 288 670	0.0309 020 990	94
48	0.0275 766 173	0.0286 296 418	0.0296 960 540	0.0307 751 378	96
49	0.0274 403 421	0.0284 991 658	0.0295 713 411	0.0306 561 285	98
50	0.0273 118 787	0.0283 763 752	0.0294 541 767	0.0305 445 208	100
51	0.0271 907 176	0.0282 607 612	0.0293 440 529	0.0304 398 081	102
52	0.0270 763 891	0.0281 518 546	0.0292 405 017	0.0303 415 239	104
53	0.0269 684 591	0.0280 492 221	0.0291 430 908	0.0302 492 378	106
54	0.0268 665 260	0.0279 524 631	0.0290 514 211	0.0301 625 521	108
55	0.0267 702 178	0.0278 612 065	0.0289 651 228	0.0300 810 991	110
56	0.0266 791 895	0.0277 751 084	0.0288 838 535	0.0300 045 384	112
57	0.0265 931 206	0.0276 938 495	0.0288 072 956	0.0299 325 543	114
58	0.0265 117 132	0.0276 171 333	0.0287 351 542	0.0298 648 540	116
59	0.0264 346 901	0.0275 446 838	0.0286 671 552	0.0298 011 657	118
60	0.0263 617 930	0.0274 762 442	0.0286 030 433	0.0297 412 364	120

TABLE 6. PARTIAL PAYMENT TO AMORTIZE ONE
Payable at end of each period

HALF YEARS	6% Nominal Annual Rate	6¼% Nominal Annual Rate	6½% Nominal Annual Rate	6¾% Nominal Annual Rate	HALF YEARS
1	1.0300 000 000	1.0312 500 000	1.0325 000 000	1.0337 500 000	1
YEARS					
1	0.5226 108 374	0.5235 576 923	0.5245 049 200	0.5254 525 200	2
2	0.2690 270 452	0.2698 316 739	0.2706 372 337	0.2714 437 228	4
3	0.1845 975 005	0.1853 630 120	0.1861 299 692	0.1868 983 691	6
4	0.1424 563 888	0.1432 085 380	0.1439 626 337	0.1447 186 713	8
5	0.1172 305 066	0.1179 795 701	0.1187 310 724	0.1194 850 071	10
6	0.1004 620 855	0.1012 131 750	0.1019 671 878	0.1027 241 154	12
7	0.0885 263 390	0.0892 823 475	0.0900 417 561	0.0908 045 536	14
8	0.0796 108 493	0.0803 735 563	0.0811 401 319	0.0819 105 616	16
9	0.0727 086 959	0.0734 792 588	0.0742 541 496	0.0750 333 498	18
10	0.0672 157 076	0.0679 949 071	0.0687 788 839	0.0695 676 149	20
11	0.0627 473 948	0.0635 357 692	0.0643 293 596	0.0651 281 376	22
12	0.0590 474 159	0.0598 453 396	0.0606 489 063	0.0614 580 816	24
13	0.0559 382 903	0.0567 460 216	0.0575 598 109	0.0583 796 167	26
14	0.0532 932 334	0.0541 109 465	0.0549 351 193	0.0557 657 023	28
15	0.0510 192 593	0.0518 470 642	0.0526 817 169	0.0535 231 592	30
16	0.0490 466 183	0.0498 845 760	0.0507 297 552	0.0515 820 878	32
17	0.0473 219 633	0.0481 700 958	0.0490 258 084	0.0498 890 225	34
18	0.0458 037 942	0.0466 620 918	0.0475 283 128	0.0484 023 670	36
19	0.0444 593 401	0.0453 277 676	0.0462 044 456	0.0470 892 716	38
20	0.0432 623 779	0.0441 408 783	0.0450 279 400	0.0459 234 473	40
21	0.0421 916 731	0.0430 801 714	0.0439 775 251	0.0448 836 041	42
22	0.0412 298 469	0.0421 282 525	0.0430 357 906	0.0439 523 160	44
23	0.0403 625 378	0.0412 707 470	0.0421 883 484	0.0431 151 810	46
24	0.0395 777 738	0.0404 956 713	0.0414 232 032	0.0423 601 920	48
25	0.0388 654 944	0.0397 929 549	0.0407 302 745	0.0416 772 584	50
26	0.0382 171 837	0.0391 540 731	0.0401 010 288	0.0410 578 378	52
27	0.0376 255 841	0.0385 717 609	0.0395 281 935	0.0404 946 503	54
28	0.0370 844 726	0.0380 397 885	0.0390 055 322	0.0399 814 528	56
29	0.0365 884 819	0.0375 527 830	0.0385 276 664	0.0395 128 614	58
30	0.0361 329 587	0.0371 060 861	0.0380 899 328	0.0390 842 082	60
31	0.0357 138 485	0.0366 956 389	0.0376 882 685	0.0386 914 265	62
32	0.0353 276 021	0.0363 178 885	0.0373 191 174	0.0383 309 570	64
33	0.0349 710 995	0.0359 697 120	0.0369 793 534	0.0379 996 714	66
34	0.0346 415 871	0.0356 483 530	0.0366 662 182	0.0376 948 093	68
35	0.0343 366 251	0.0353 513 699	0.0363 772 684	0.0374 139 261	70
36	0.0340 540 446	0.0350 765 920	0.0361 103 320	0.0371 548 492	72
37	0.0337 919 109	0.0348 220 835	0.0358 634 724	0.0369 156 417	74
38	0.0335 484 929	0.0345 861 124	0.0356 349 575	0.0366 945 715	76
39	0.0333 222 371	0.0343 671 249	0.0354 232 334	0.0364 900 855	78
40	0.0331 117 457	0.0341 637 230	0.0352 269 026	0.0363 007 873	80
41	0.0329 157 577	0.0339 746 461	0.0350 447 051	0.0361 254 179	82
42	0.0327 331 325	0.0337 987 540	0.0348 755 020	0.0359 628 404	84
43	0.0325 628 365	0.0336 350 139	0.0347 182 617	0.0358 120 251	86
44	0.0324 039 306	0.0334 824 878	0.0345 720 479	0.0356 720 378	88
45	0.0322 555 599	0.0333 403 223	0.0344 360 091	0.0355 420 297	90
46	0.0321 169 449	0.0332 077 392	0.0343 093 692	0.0354 212 273	92
47	0.0319 873 733	0.0330 840 281	0.0341 914 200	0.0353 089 256	94
48	0.0318 661 932	0.0329 685 390	0.0340 815 142	0.0352 044 800	96
49	0.0317 528 070	0.0328 606 763	0.0339 790 588	0.0351 073 012	98
50	0.0316 466 659	0.0327 598 935	0.0338 835 102	0.0350 168 489	100
51	0.0315 472 653	0.0326 656 886	0.0337 943 693	0.0349 326 274	102
52	0.0314 541 408	0.0325 775 995	0.0337 111 771	0.0348 541 817	104
53	0.0313 668 639	0.0324 952 005	0.0336 335 112	0.0347 810 930	106
54	0.0312 850 394	0.0324 180 991	0.0335 609 823	0.0347 129 759	108
55	0.0312 083 018	0.0323 459 328	0.0334 932 313	0.0346 494 752	110
56	0.0311 363 131	0.0322 783 663	0.0334 299 266	0.0345 902 632	112
57	0.0310 687 603	0.0322 150 898	0.0333 707 615	0.0345 350 374	114
58	0.0310 053 531	0.0321 558 160	0.0333 154 526	0.0344 835 183	116
59	0.0309 458 222	0.0321 002 788	0.0332 637 372	0.0344 354 473	118
60	0.0308 899 176	0.0320 482 312	0.0332 153 719	0.0343 905 851	120

TABLE 6. PARTIAL PAYMENT TO AMORTIZE ONE
Payable at end of each period

SEMI ANNUAL Compounding

HALF YEARS	7% Nominal Annual Rate	7¼% Nominal Annual Rate	7½% Nominal Annual Rate	7¾% Nominal Annual Rate	HALF YEARS
1	1.0350 000 000	1.0362 500 000	1.0375 000 000	1.0387 500 000	1
YEARS					
1	0.5264 004 914	0.5273 488 336	0.5282 975 460	0.5292 466 278	2
2	0.2722 511 395	0.2730 594 819	0.2738 687 482	0.2746 789 366	4
3	0.1876 682 087	0.1884 394 848	0.1892 121 945	0.1899 863 348	6
4	0.1454 766 465	0.1462 365 548	0.1469 983 915	0.1477 621 521	8
5	0.1202 413 679	0.1210 001 484	0.1217 613 423	0.1225 249 431	10
6	0.1034 839 493	0.1042 466 807	0.1050 123 010	0.1057 808 013	12
7	0.0915 707 287	0.0923 402 699	0.0931 131 655	0.0938 894 039	14
8	0.0826 848 306	0.0834 629 241	0.0842 448 270	0.0850 305 238	16
9	0.0758 168 408	0.0766 046 036	0.0773 966 188	0.0781 928 670	18
10	0.0703 610 768	0.0711 592 457	0.0719 620 973	0.0727 696 072	20
11	0.0659 320 742	0.0667 411 400	0.0675 553 051	0.0683 745 391	22
12	0.0622 728 303	0.0630 931 163	0.0639 189 033	0.0647 501 542	24
13	0.0592 053 963	0.0600 371 068	0.0608 747 042	0.0617 181 439	26
14	0.0566 026 452	0.0574 458 966	0.0582 954 043	0.0591 511 151	28
15	0.0543 713 316	0.0552 261 737	0.0560 876 242	0.0569 556 204	30
16	0.0524 415 048	0.0533 079 356	0.0541 813 087	0.0550 615 513	32
17	0.0507 596 583	0.0516 376 343	0.0525 228 679	0.0534 152 753	34
18	0.0492 841 628	0.0501 736 070	0.0510 706 050	0.0519 750 610	36
19	0.0479 821 414	0.0488 829 490	0.0497 915 872	0.0507 079 472	38
20	0.0468 272 823	0.0477 393 256	0.0486 594 563	0.0495 875 521	40
21	0.0457 982 765	0.0467 214 084	0.0476 528 644	0.0485 925 078	42
22	0.0448 776 816	0.0458 117 383	0.0467 543 358	0.0477 053 222	44
23	0.0440 510 817	0.0449 958 858	0.0459 494 269	0.0469 115 374	46
24	0.0433 064 580	0.0442 618 199	0.0452 260 947	0.0461 990 989	48
25	0.0426 337 096	0.0435 994 295	0.0445 742 185	0.0455 578 758	50
26	0.0420 242 854	0.0430 001 552	0.0439 852 301	0.0449 792 922	52
27	0.0414 708 979	0.0424 567 022	0.0434 518 278	0.0444 560 396	54
28	0.0409 672 981	0.0419 628 152	0.0429 677 509	0.0439 818 520	56
29	0.0405 080 966	0.0415 131 002	0.0425 276 006	0.0435 513 267	58
30	0.0400 886 213	0.0411 028 811	0.0421 266 973	0.0431 597 810	60
31	0.0397 048 020	0.0407 280 845	0.0417 609 653	0.0428 031 374	62
32	0.0393 530 765	0.0403 851 462	0.0414 268 386	0.0424 778 288	64
33	0.0390 303 148	0.0400 709 345	0.0411 211 846	0.0421 807 225	66
34	0.0387 337 550	0.0397 826 869	0.0408 412 407	0.0419 090 564	68
35	0.0384 609 517	0.0395 179 578	0.0405 845 619	0.0416 603 869	70
36	0.0382 097 323	0.0392 745 750	0.0403 489 770	0.0414 325 446	72
37	0.0379 781 601	0.0390 506 028	0.0401 325 521	0.0412 235 983	74
38	0.0377 645 038	0.0388 443 115	0.0399 335 598	0.0410 318 234	76
39	0.0375 672 117	0.0386 541 510	0.0397 504 525	0.0408 556 759	78
40	0.0373 848 887	0.0384 787 288	0.0395 818 410	0.0406 937 705	80
41	0.0372 162 781	0.0383 167 910	0.0394 264 747	0.0405 448 609	82
42	0.0370 602 452	0.0381 672 057	0.0392 832 256	0.0404 078 238	84
43	0.0369 157 629	0.0380 289 493	0.0391 510 743	0.0402 816 447	86
44	0.0367 819 002	0.0379 010 945	0.0390 290 977	0.0401 654 056	88
45	0.0366 578 111	0.0377 827 990	0.0389 164 584	0.0400 582 747	90
46	0.0365 427 259	0.0376 732 973	0.0388 123 956	0.0399 594 965	92
47	0.0364 359 428	0.0375 718 920	0.0387 162 168	0.0398 683 846	94
48	0.0363 368 213	0.0374 779 470	0.0386 272 913	0.0397 843 139	96
49	0.0362 447 758	0.0373 908 812	0.0385 450 431	0.0397 067 145	98
50	0.0361 592 702	0.0373 101 634	0.0384 689 464	0.0396 350 665	100
51	0.0360 798 131	0.0372 353 068	0.0383 985 200	0.0395 688 949	102
52	0.0360 059 536	0.0371 658 655	0.0383 333 233	0.0395 077 652	104
53	0.0359 372 773	0.0371 014 302	0.0382 729 525	0.0394 512 796	106
54	0.0358 734 032	0.0370 416 247	0.0382 170 371	0.0393 990 737	108
55	0.0358 139 807	0.0369 861 033	0.0381 652 370	0.0393 508 135	110
56	0.0357 586 865	0.0369 345 480	0.0381 172 394	0.0393 061 921	112
57	0.0357 072 227	0.0368 866 657	0.0380 727 569	0.0392 649 281	114
58	0.0356 593 142	0.0368 421 863	0.0380 315 248	0.0392 267 626	116
59	0.0356 147 069	0.0368 008 608	0.0379 932 994	0.0391 914 577	118
60	0.0355 731 662	0.0367 624 592	0.0379 578 561	0.0391 587 944	120

TABLE 6. PARTIAL PAYMENT TO AMORTIZE ONE
Payable at end of each period

HALF YEARS	8% Nominal Annual Rate	8¼% Nominal Annual Rate	8½% Nominal Annual Rate	8¾% Nominal Annual Rate	HALF YEARS
1	1.0400 000 000	1.0412 500 000	1.0425 000 000	1.0437 500 000	1
YEARS					
1	0.5301 960 784	0.5311 458 971	0.5320 960 832	0.5330 466 361	2
2	0.2754 900 454	0.2763 020 727	0.2771 150 167	0.2779 288 757	4
3	0.1907 619 025	0.1915 388 947	0.1923 173 083	0.1930 971 403	6
4	0.1485 278 320	0.1492 954 268	0.1500 649 316	0.1508 363 420	8
5	0.1232 909 443	0.1240 593 394	0.1248 301 217	0.1256 032 847	10
6	0.1065 521 727	0.1073 264 062	0.1081 034 928	0.1088 834 234	12
7	0.0946 689 731	0.0954 518 611	0.0962 380 557	0.0970 275 449	14
8	0.0858 199 992	0.0866 132 375	0.0874 102 226	0.0882 109 387	16
9	0.0789 933 281	0.0797 979 823	0.0806 068 090	0.0814 197 877	18
10	0.0735 817 503	0.0743 985 014	0.0752 198 348	0.0760 457 245	20
11	0.0691 988 111	0.0700 280 897	0.0708 623 433	0.0717 015 396	22
12	0.0655 868 313	0.0664 288 965	0.0672 763 108	0.0681 290 352	24
13	0.0625 673 805	0.0634 223 680	0.0642 830 600	0.0651 494 090	26
14	0.0600 129 752	0.0608 809 300	0.0617 549 240	0.0626 349 013	28
15	0.0578 300 991	0.0587 109 962	0.0595 982 464	0.0604 917 842	30
16	0.0559 485 897	0.0568 423 494	0.0577 427 548	0.0586 497 294	32
17	0.0543 147 715	0.0552 212 706	0.0561 346 857	0.0570 549 290	34
18	0.0528 868 780	0.0538 059 578	0.0547 322 015	0.0556 655 090	36
19	0.0516 319 191	0.0525 633 920	0.0535 022 538	0.0544 483 917	38
20	0.0505 234 893	0.0514 671 434	0.0524 183 886	0.0533 770 987	40
21	0.0495 402 007	0.0504 958 041	0.0514 591 782	0.0524 301 824	42
22	0.0486 645 444	0.0496 318 487	0.0506 070 805	0.0515 900 845	44
23	0.0478 820 488	0.0488 607 917	0.0498 475 964	0.0508 422 928	46
24	0.0471 806 476	0.0481 705 556	0.0491 686 377	0.0501 747 082	48
25	0.0465 502 004	0.0475 509 909	0.0485 600 458	0.0495 771 642	50
26	0.0459 821 236	0.0469 935 063	0.0480 132 229	0.0490 410 567	52
27	0.0454 691 025	0.0464 907 817	0.0475 208 438	0.0485 590 563	54
28	0.0450 048 662	0.0460 365 422	0.0470 766 300	0.0481 248 818	56
29	0.0445 840 087	0.0456 253 787	0.0466 751 706	0.0477 331 210	58
30	0.0442 018 451	0.0452 526 049	0.0463 117 784	0.0473 790 870	60
31	0.0438 542 964	0.0449 141 412	0.0459 823 743	0.0470 587 020	62
32	0.0435 377 955	0.0446 064 212	0.0456 833 932	0.0467 684 034	64
33	0.0432 492 100	0.0443 263 140	0.0454 117 067	0.0465 050 661	66
34	0.0429 857 795	0.0440 710 613	0.0451 645 597	0.0462 659 393	68
35	0.0427 450 623	0.0438 382 245	0.0449 395 176	0.0460 485 935	70
36	0.0425 248 919	0.0436 256 408	0.0447 344 223	0.0458 508 762	72
37	0.0423 233 403	0.0434 313 865	0.0445 473 553	0.0456 708 754	74
38	0.0421 386 869	0.0432 537 458	0.0443 766 067	0.0455 068 877	76
39	0.0419 693 922	0.0430 911 845	0.0442 206 484	0.0453 573 927	78
40	0.0418 140 755	0.0429 423 276	0.0440 781 123	0.0452 210 294	80
41	0.0416 714 957	0.0428 059 400	0.0439 477 702	0.0450 965 781	82
42	0.0415 405 351	0.0426 809 105	0.0438 285 180	0.0449 829 425	84
43	0.0414 201 848	0.0425 662 368	0.0437 193 611	0.0448 791 366	86
44	0.0413 095 329	0.0424 610 138	0.0436 194 021	0.0447 842 714	88
45	0.0412 077 538	0.0423 644 228	0.0435 278 300	0.0446 975 447	90
46	0.0411 140 984	0.0422 757 221	0.0434 439 110	0.0446 182 312	92
47	0.0410 278 867	0.0421 942 387	0.0433 669 802	0.0445 456 748	94
48	0.0409 485 002	0.0421 193 615	0.0432 964 344	0.0444 792 809	96
49	0.0408 753 757	0.0420 505 346	0.0432 317 257	0.0444 185 103	98
50	0.0408 080 000	0.0419 872 521	0.0431 723 562	0.0443 628 735	100
51	0.0407 459 047	0.0419 290 529	0.0431 178 725	0.0443 119 256	102
52	0.0406 886 620	0.0418 755 164	0.0430 678 618	0.0442 652 621	104
53	0.0406 358 808	0.0418 262 587	0.0430 219 481	0.0442 225 151	106
54	0.0405 872 033	0.0417 809 291	0.0429 797 880	0.0441 833 491	108
55	0.0405 423 018	0.0417 392 069	0.0429 410 683	0.0441 474 587	110
56	0.0405 008 762	0.0417 007 988	0.0429 055 028	0.0441 145 653	112
57	0.0404 626 512	0.0416 654 362	0.0428 728 300	0.0440 844 147	114
58	0.0404 273 741	0.0416 328 730	0.0428 428 109	0.0440 567 751	116
59	0.0403 948 131	0.0416 028 838	0.0428 152 265	0.0440 314 344	118
60	0.0403 647 553	0.0415 752 620	0.0427 898 768	0.0440 081 993	120

TABLE 6. PARTIAL PAYMENT TO AMORTIZE ONE
Payable at end of each period

HALF YEARS	9% Nominal Annual Rate	9¼% Nominal Annual Rate	9½% Nominal Annual Rate	9¾% Nominal Annual Rate	HALF YEARS
1	1.0450 000 000	1.0462 500 000	1.0475 000 000	1.0487 500 000	1
YEARS					
1	0.5339 975 550	0.5349 488 393	0.5359 004 884	0.5368 525 015	2
2	0.2787 436 479	0.2795 593 315	0.2803 759 246	0.2811 934 256	4
3	0.1938 783 875	0.1946 610 470	0.1954 451 156	0.1962 305 904	6
4	0.1516 096 533	0.1523 848 608	0.1531 619 598	0.1539 409 457	8
5	0.1263 788 217	0.1271 567 260	0.1279 369 909	0.1287 196 094	10
6	0.1096 661 886	0.1104 517 793	0.1112 401 861	0.1120 313 995	12
7	0.0978 203 160	0.0986 163 567	0.0994 156 544	0.1002 181 962	14
8	0.0890 153 694	0.0898 234 984	0.0906 353 090	0.0914 507 845	16
9	0.0822 368 975	0.0830 581 173	0.0838 834 258	0.0847 128 014	18
10	0.0768 761 443	0.0777 110 675	0.0785 504 673	0.0793 943 163	20
11	0.0725 456 461	0.0733 946 297	0.0742 484 572	0.0751 070 948	22
12	0.0689 870 299	0.0698 502 547	0.0707 186 689	0.0715 922 314	24
13	0.0660 213 674	0.0668 988 869	0.0677 819 186	0.0686 704 131	26
14	0.0635 208 051	0.0644 125 781	0.0653 101 623	0.0662 134 994	28
15	0.0613 915 429	0.0622 974 554	0.0632 094 539	0.0641 274 701	30
16	0.0595 631 962	0.0604 830 773	0.0614 092 942	0.0623 417 680	32
17	0.0579 819 119	0.0589 155 451	0.0598 557 388	0.0608 024 026	34
18	0.0566 057 796	0.0575 529 120	0.0585 068 041	0.0594 673 534	36
19	0.0554 016 920	0.0563 620 408	0.0573 293 231	0.0583 034 240	38
20	0.0543 431 466	0.0553 164 048	0.0562 967 454	0.0572 840 403	40
21	0.0534 086 759	0.0543 945 172	0.0553 875 648	0.0563 876 773	42
22	0.0525 807 056	0.0535 787 880	0.0545 841 765	0.0555 967 156	44
23	0.0518 447 107	0.0528 546 800	0.0538 720 312	0.0548 965 952	46
24	0.0511 885 821	0.0522 100 748	0.0532 390 022	0.0542 751 814	48
25	0.0506 021 459	0.0516 347 913	0.0526 749 023	0.0537 222 821	50
26	0.0500 767 923	0.0511 202 156	0.0521 711 140	0.0532 292 771	52
27	0.0496 051 886	0.0506 590 120	0.0517 203 000	0.0527 888 287	54
28	0.0491 810 518	0.0502 448 970	0.0513 161 771	0.0523 946 552	56
29	0.0487 989 695	0.0498 724 589	0.0509 533 356	0.0520 413 500	58
30	0.0484 542 558	0.0495 370 141	0.0506 270 953	0.0517 242 377	60
31	0.0481 428 356	0.0492 344 908	0.0503 333 891	0.0514 392 570	62
32	0.0478 611 494	0.0489 613 345	0.0500 686 682	0.0511 828 665	64
33	0.0476 060 769	0.0487 144 303	0.0498 298 248	0.0509 519 663	66
34	0.0473 748 725	0.0484 910 393	0.0496 141 277	0.0507 438 343	68
35	0.0471 651 129	0.0482 887 452	0.0494 191 690	0.0505 560 724	70
36	0.0469 746 524	0.0481 054 105	0.0492 428 204	0.0503 865 626	72
37	0.0468 015 863	0.0479 391 389	0.0490 831 953	0.0502 334 290	74
38	0.0466 442 194	0.0477 882 442	0.0489 386 173	0.0500 950 066	76
39	0.0465 010 391	0.0476 512 232	0.0488 075 940	0.0499 698 145	78
40	0.0463 706 935	0.0475 267 336	0.0486 887 937	0.0498 565 325	80
41	0.0462 519 715	0.0474 135 742	0.0485 810 259	0.0497 539 821	82
42	0.0461 437 861	0.0473 106 681	0.0484 832 248	0.0496 611 096	84
43	0.0460 451 606	0.0472 170 487	0.0483 944 348	0.0495 769 709	86
44	0.0459 552 152	0.0471 318 465	0.0483 137 976	0.0495 007 197	88
45	0.0458 731 573	0.0470 542 790	0.0482 405 414	0.0494 315 959	90
46	0.0457 982 710	0.0469 836 406	0.0481 739 715	0.0493 689 164	92
47	0.0457 299 095	0.0469 192 944	0.0481 134 620	0.0493 120 664	94
48	0.0456 674 877	0.0468 606 653	0.0480 584 480	0.0492 604 924	96
49	0.0456 104 754	0.0468 072 330	0.0480 084 196	0.0492 136 951	98
50	0.0455 583 922	0.0467 585 267	0.0479 629 162	0.0491 712 245	100
51	0.0455 108 023	0.0467 141 198	0.0479 215 211	0.0491 326 741	102
52	0.0454 673 100	0.0466 736 260	0.0478 838 573	0.0490 976 768	104
53	0.0454 275 556	0.0466 366 944	0.0478 495 834	0.0490 659 007	106
54	0.0453 912 122	0.0466 030 068	0.0478 183 901	0.0490 370 458	108
55	0.0453 579 825	0.0465 722 743	0.0477 899 970	0.0490 108 405	110
56	0.0453 275 957	0.0465 442 342	0.0477 641 499	0.0489 870 392	112
57	0.0452 998 052	0.0465 186 479	0.0477 406 182	0.0489 654 192	114
58	0.0452 743 866	0.0464 952 982	0.0477 191 924	0.0489 457 791	116
59	0.0452 511 350	0.0464 739 878	0.0476 996 824	0.0489 279 361	118
60	0.0452 298 637	0.0464 545 369	0.0476 819 156	0.0489 117 246	120

SEMI ANNUAL
Compounding

TABLE 6. PARTIAL PAYMENT TO AMORTIZE ONE
Payable at end of each period

HALF YEARS	10% Nominal Annual Rate	10¼% Nominal Annual Rate	10½% Nominal Annual Rate	10¾% Nominal Annual Rate	HALF YEARS
1	1.0500 000 000	1.0512 500 000	1.0525 000 000	1.0537 500 000	1
YEARS					
1	0.5378 048 780	0.5387 576 173	0.5397 107 186	0.5406 641 814	2
2	0.2820 118 326	0.2828 311 439	0.2836 513 576	0.2844 724 720	4
3	0.1970 174 681	0.1978 057 458	0.1985 954 203	0.1993 864 886	6
4	0.1547 218 136	0.1555 045 590	0.1562 891 770	0.1570 756 628	8
5	0.1295 045 750	0.1302 918 806	0.1310 815 194	0.1318 734 844	10
6	0.1128 254 100	0.1136 222 081	0.1144 217 842	0.1152 241 284	12
7	0.1010 239 695	0.1018 329 611	0.1026 451 581	0.1034 605 473	14
8	0.0922 699 080	0.0930 926 624	0.0939 190 304	0.0947 489 948	16
9	0.0855 462 223	0.0863 836 666	0.0872 251 119	0.0880 705 360	18
10	0.0802 425 872	0.0810 952 521	0.0819 522 832	0.0828 136 520	20
11	0.0759 705 086	0.0768 386 640	0.0777 115 264	0.0785 890 608	22
12	0.0724 709 008	0.0733 546 351	0.0742 433 921	0.0751 371 293	24
13	0.0695 643 207	0.0704 635 911	0.0713 681 737	0.0722 780 176	26
14	0.0671 225 304	0.0680 371 960	0.0689 574 362	0.0698 831 909	28
15	0.0650 514 351	0.0659 812 795	0.0669 169 335	0.0678 583 271	30
16	0.0632 804 189	0.0642 251 672	0.0651 759 322	0.0661 326 333	32
17	0.0617 554 454	0.0627 147 761	0.0636 803 028	0.0646 519 338	34
18	0.0604 344 571	0.0614 080 120	0.0623 879 146	0.0633 740 614	36
19	0.0592 842 282	0.0602 716 200	0.0612 654 839	0.0622 657 044	38
20	0.0582 781 612	0.0592 789 799	0.0602 863 683	0.0613 001 986	40
21	0.0573 947 131	0.0584 085 311	0.0594 289 905	0.0604 559 510	42
22	0.0566 162 506	0.0576 426 272	0.0586 756 919	0.0597 152 920	44
23	0.0559 282 036	0.0569 666 891	0.0580 118 853	0.0590 636 272	46
24	0.0553 184 306	0.0563 685 693	0.0574 254 187	0.0584 888 015	48
25	0.0547 767 355	0.0558 380 691	0.0569 060 917	0.0579 806 143	50
26	0.0542 944 966	0.0553 665 665	0.0564 452 836	0.0575 304 474	52
27	0.0538 643 770	0.0549 467 268	0.0560 356 631	0.0571 309 745	54
28	0.0534 800 978	0.0545 722 749	0.0556 709 607	0.0567 759 335	56
29	0.0531 362 568	0.0542 378 148	0.0553 457 878	0.0564 599 443	58
30	0.0528 281 845	0.0539 386 844	0.0550 554 911	0.0561 783 643	60
31	0.0525 518 273	0.0536 708 386	0.0547 960 358	0.0559 271 704	62
32	0.0523 036 520	0.0534 307 543	0.0545 639 102	0.0557 028 636	64
33	0.0520 805 683	0.0532 153 521	0.0543 560 470	0.0555 023 906	66
34	0.0518 798 643	0.0530 219 316	0.0541 697 590	0.0553 230 784	68
35	0.0516 991 530	0.0528 481 183	0.0540 026 853	0.0551 625 813	70
36	0.0515 363 280	0.0526 918 184	0.0538 527 462	0.0550 188 348	72
37	0.0513 895 254	0.0525 511 814	0.0537 181 056	0.0548 900 185	74
38	0.0512 570 925	0.0524 245 681	0.0535 971 390	0.0547 745 236	76
39	0.0511 375 610	0.0523 105 237	0.0534 884 063	0.0546 709 257	78
40	0.0510 296 235	0.0522 077 547	0.0533 906 287	0.0545 779 618	80
41	0.0509 321 143	0.0521 151 092	0.0533 026 688	0.0544 945 101	82
42	0.0508 439 924	0.0520 315 596	0.0532 235 137	0.0544 195 727	84
43	0.0507 643 265	0.0519 561 883	0.0531 522 600	0.0543 522 615	86
44	0.0506 922 828	0.0518 881 748	0.0530 881 011	0.0542 917 843	88
45	0.0506 271 136	0.0518 267 844	0.0530 303 161	0.0542 374 345	90
46	0.0505 681 481	0.0517 713 589	0.0529 782 600	0.0541 885 809	92
47	0.0505 147 832	0.0517 213 078	0.0529 313 554	0.0541 446 593	94
48	0.0504 664 770	0.0516 761 013	0.0528 890 846	0.0541 051 651	96
49	0.0504 227 418	0.0516 352 632	0.0528 509 836	0.0540 696 465	98
50	0.0503 831 381	0.0515 983 654	0.0528 166 360	0.0540 376 988	100
51	0.0503 472 701	0.0515 650 230	0.0527 856 678	0.0540 089 595	102
52	0.0503 147 810	0.0515 348 895	0.0527 577 433	0.0539 831 035	104
53	0.0502 853 486	0.0515 076 528	0.0527 325 604	0.0539 598 391	106
54	0.0502 586 824	0.0514 830 318	0.0527 098 478	0.0539 389 047	108
55	0.0502 345 197	0.0514 607 732	0.0526 893 614	0.0539 200 653	110
56	0.0502 126 236	0.0514 406 485	0.0526 708 814	0.0539 031 102	112
57	0.0501 927 796	0.0514 224 518	0.0526 542 102	0.0538 878 497	114
58	0.0501 747 942	0.0514 059 972	0.0526 391 698	0.0538 741 138	116
59	0.0501 584 919	0.0513 911 169	0.0526 255 997	0.0538 617 494	118
60	0.0501 437 145	0.0513 776 595	0.0526 133 557	0.0538 506 190	120

TABLE 6. PARTIAL PAYMENT TO AMORTIZE ONE
Payable at end of each period

HALF YEARS	11% Nominal Annual Rate	11¼% Nominal Annual Rate	11½% Nominal Annual Rate	11¾% Nominal Annual Rate	HALF YEARS
1	1.0550 000 000	1.0562 500 000	1.0575 000 000	1.0587 500 000	1
YEARS					
1	0.5416 180 049	0.5425 721 884	0.5435 267 315	0.5444 816 333	2
2	0.2852 944 853	0.2861 173 958	0.2869 412 017	0.2877 659 011	4
3	0.2001 789 476	0.2009 727 942	0.2017 680 253	0.2025 646 377	6
4	0.1578 640 118	0.1586 542 191	0.1594 462 799	0.1602 401 893	8
5	0.1326 677 687	0.1334 643 653	0.1342 632 671	0.1350 644 671	10
6	0.1160 292 312	0.1168 370 826	0.1176 476 727	0.1184 609 916	12
7	0.1042 791 154	0.1051 008 492	0.1059 257 351	0.1067 537 596	14
8	0.0955 825 380	0.0964 196 423	0.0972 602 900	0.0981 044 631	16
9	0.0889 199 163	0.0897 732 299	0.0906 304 539	0.0914 915 652	18
10	0.0836 793 300	0.0845 492 886	0.0854 234 988	0.0863 019 314	20
11	0.0794 712 319	0.0803 580 042	0.0812 493 418	0.0821 452 087	22
12	0.0760 358 037	0.0769 393 721	0.0778 477 910	0.0787 610 166	24
13	0.0731 930 713	0.0741 132 831	0.0750 386 012	0.0759 689 732	26
14	0.0708 143 996	0.0717 510 012	0.0726 929 348	0.0736 401 387	28
15	0.0688 053 897	0.0697 580 505	0.0707 162 386	0.0716 798 827	30
16	0.0670 951 895	0.0680 635 194	0.0690 375 417	0.0700 171 749	32
17	0.0656 295 769	0.0666 131 398	0.0676 025 304	0.0685 976 563	34
18	0.0643 663 488	0.0653 646 732	0.0663 689 312	0.0673 790 194	36
19	0.0632 721 659	0.0642 847 533	0.0653 033 517	0.0663 278 466	38
20	0.0623 203 434	0.0633 466 755	0.0643 790 687	0.0654 173 972	40
21	0.0614 892 731	0.0625 288 180	0.0635 744 478	0.0646 260 254	42
22	0.0607 612 757	0.0618 134 926	0.0628 717 934	0.0639 360 302	44
23	0.0601 217 512	0.0611 860 952	0.0622 564 988	0.0633 328 035	46
24	0.0595 585 424	0.0606 344 681	0.0617 164 076	0.0628 041 920	48
25	0.0590 614 501	0.0601 484 152	0.0612 413 281	0.0623 400 104	50
26	0.0586 218 603	0.0597 193 281	0.0608 226 596	0.0619 316 673	52
27	0.0582 324 534	0.0593 398 955	0.0604 531 008	0.0615 718 733	54
28	0.0578 869 756	0.0590 038 742	0.0601 264 207	0.0612 544 114	56
29	0.0575 800 578	0.0587 059 071	0.0598 372 760	0.0609 739 540	58
30	0.0573 070 692	0.0584 413 771	0.0595 810 653	0.0607 259 169	60
31	0.0570 640 001	0.0582 062 896	0.0593 538 103	0.0605 063 402	62
32	0.0568 473 659	0.0579 971 759	0.0591 520 600	0.0603 117 918	64
33	0.0566 541 284	0.0578 110 145	0.0589 728 110	0.0601 392 882	66
34	0.0564 816 307	0.0576 451 657	0.0588 134 424	0.0599 862 286	68
35	0.0563 275 431	0.0574 973 176	0.0586 716 612	0.0598 503 402	70
36	0.0561 898 180	0.0573 654 404	0.0585 454 569	0.0597 296 329	72
37	0.0560 666 516	0.0572 477 483	0.0584 330 627	0.0596 223 602	74
38	0.0559 564 521	0.0571 426 673	0.0583 329 236	0.0595 269 870	76
39	0.0558 578 119	0.0570 488 077	0.0582 436 685	0.0594 421 617	78
40	0.0557 694 845	0.0569 649 405	0.0581 640 868	0.0593 666 930	80
41	0.0556 903 644	0.0568 899 773	0.0580 931 080	0.0592 995 289	82
42	0.0556 194 699	0.0568 229 532	0.0580 297 847	0.0592 397 400	84
43	0.0555 559 284	0.0567 630 118	0.0579 732 771	0.0591 865 041	86
44	0.0554 989 631	0.0567 093 920	0.0579 228 407	0.0591 390 930	88
45	0.0554 478 820	0.0566 614 172	0.0578 778 142	0.0590 968 617	90
46	0.0554 020 682	0.0566 184 850	0.0578 376 103	0.0590 592 380	92
47	0.0553 609 712	0.0565 800 590	0.0578 017 070	0.0590 257 144	94
48	0.0553 240 994	0.0565 456 610	0.0577 696 395	0.0589 958 401	96
49	0.0552 910 137	0.0565 148 646	0.0577 409 947	0.0589 692 148	98
50	0.0552 613 216	0.0564 872 895	0.0577 154 042	0.0589 454 826	100
51	0.0552 346 718	0.0564 625 961	0.0576 925 401	0.0589 243 273	102
52	0.0552 107 501	0.0564 404 810	0.0576 721 102	0.0589 054 675	104
53	0.0551 892 753	0.0564 206 734	0.0576 538 539	0.0588 886 528	106
54	0.0551 699 955	0.0564 029 311	0.0576 375 387	0.0588 736 606	108
55	0.0551 526 849	0.0563 870 376	0.0576 229 573	0.0588 602 925	110
56	0.0551 371 415	0.0563 727 995	0.0576 099 247	0.0588 483 719	112
57	0.0551 231 839	0.0563 600 437	0.0575 982 758	0.0588 377 416	114
58	0.0551 106 497	0.0563 486 151	0.0575 878 633	0.0588 282 616	116
59	0.0550 993 932	0.0563 383 753	0.0575 785 555	0.0588 198 071	118
60	0.0550 892 837	0.0563 292 003	0.0575 702 349	0.0588 122 669	120

TABLE 6. PARTIAL PAYMENT TO AMORTIZE ONE
Payable at end of each period

HALF YEARS	12% Nominal Annual Rate	12¼% Nominal Annual Rate	12½% Nominal Annual Rate	12¾% Nominal Annual Rate	HALF YEARS
1	1.0600 000 000	1.0612 500 000	1.0625 000 000	1.0637 500 000	1
YEARS					
1	0.5454 368 932	0.5463 925 106	0.5473 484 848	0.5483 048 153	2
2	0.2885 914 924	0.2894 179 737	0.2902 453 433	0.2910 735 995	4
3	0.2033 626 285	0.2041 619 944	0.2049 627 324	0.2057 648 394	6
4	0.1610 359 426	0.1618 335 349	0.1626 329 614	0.1634 342 170	8
5	0.1358 679 582	0.1366 737 332	0.1374 817 850	0.1382 921 064	10
6	0.1192 770 294	0.1200 957 758	0.1209 172 209	0.1217 413 544	12
7	0.1075 849 090	0.1084 191 697	0.1092 565 278	0.1100 969 694	14
8	0.0989 521 436	0.0998 033 133	0.1006 579 538	0.1015 160 469	16
9	0.0923 565 406	0.0932 253 564	0.0940 979 892	0.0949 744 151	18
10	0.0871 845 570	0.0880 713 460	0.0889 622 687	0.0898 572 952	20
11	0.0830 455 685	0.0839 503 848	0.0848 596 209	0.0857 732 397	22
12	0.0796 790 050	0.0806 017 118	0.0815 290 926	0.0824 611 028	24
13	0.0769 043 467	0.0778 446 689	0.0787 898 870	0.0797 399 478	26
14	0.0745 925 515	0.0755 501 113	0.0765 127 561	0.0774 804 237	28
15	0.0726 489 115	0.0736 232 534	0.0746 028 369	0.0755 875 904	30
16	0.0710 023 374	0.0719 929 474	0.0729 889 235	0.0739 901 842	32
17	0.0695 984 254	0.0706 047 456	0.0716 165 250	0.0726 336 720	34
18	0.0683 948 348	0.0694 162 747	0.0704 432 368	0.0714 756 191	36
19	0.0673 581 240	0.0683 940 704	0.0694 355 731	0.0704 825 199	38
20	0.0664 615 359	0.0675 113 608	0.0685 667 487	0.0696 275 775	40
21	0.0656 834 152	0.0667 464 825	0.0678 150 939	0.0688 891 176	42
22	0.0650 060 565	0.0660 817 276	0.0671 629 004	0.0682 494 335	44
23	0.0644 148 527	0.0655 024 917	0.0665 955 681	0.0676 939 316	46
24	0.0638 976 549	0.0649 966 325	0.0661 009 636	0.0672 104 896	48
25	0.0634 442 864	0.0645 539 836	0.0656 689 327	0.0667 889 676	50
26	0.0630 461 669	0.0641 659 780	0.0652 909 239	0.0664 208 316	52
27	0.0626 960 209	0.0638 253 560	0.0649 596 952	0.0660 988 594	54
28	0.0623 876 472	0.0635 259 341	0.0646 690 828	0.0658 169 092	56
29	0.0621 157 359	0.0632 624 219	0.0644 138 178	0.0655 697 352	58
30	0.0618 757 215	0.0630 302 746	0.0641 893 780	0.0653 528 397	60
31	0.0616 636 642	0.0628 255 742	0.0639 918 687	0.0651 623 529	62
32	0.0614 761 528	0.0626 449 317	0.0638 179 247	0.0649 949 355	64
33	0.0613 102 248	0.0624 854 074	0.0636 646 308	0.0648 476 977	66
34	0.0611 633 009	0.0623 444 450	0.0635 294 548	0.0647 181 330	68
35	0.0610 331 302	0.0622 198 163	0.0634 101 927	0.0646 040 626	70
36	0.0609 177 439	0.0621 095 753	0.0633 049 222	0.0645 035 891	72
37	0.0608 154 168	0.0620 120 191	0.0632 119 636	0.0644 150 572	74
38	0.0607 246 347	0.0619 256 553	0.0631 298 475	0.0643 370 207	76
39	0.0606 440 667	0.0618 491 741	0.0630 572 859	0.0642 682 145	78
40	0.0605 725 410	0.0617 814 246	0.0629 931 491	0.0642 075 306	80
41	0.0605 090 251	0.0617 213 940	0.0629 364 447	0.0641 539 975	82
42	0.0604 526 081	0.0616 681 905	0.0628 863 004	0.0641 067 629	84
43	0.0604 024 856	0.0616 210 278	0.0628 419 487	0.0640 650 780	86
44	0.0603 579 467	0.0615 792 124	0.0628 027 135	0.0640 282 848	88
45	0.0603 183 623	0.0615 421 321	0.0627 679 994	0.0639 958 046	90
46	0.0602 831 761	0.0615 092 458	0.0627 372 812	0.0639 671 281	92
47	0.0602 518 949	0.0614 800 755	0.0627 100 957	0.0639 418 073	94
48	0.0602 240 821	0.0614 541 983	0.0626 860 342	0.0639 194 470	96
49	0.0601 993 504	0.0614 312 401	0.0626 647 355	0.0638 996 996	98
50	0.0601 773 563	0.0614 108 699	0.0626 458 810	0.0638 822 583	100
51	0.0601 577 952	0.0613 927 946	0.0626 291 889	0.0638 668 528	102
52	0.0601 403 965	0.0613 767 543	0.0626 144 102	0.0638 532 446	104
53	0.0601 249 202	0.0613 625 192	0.0626 013 249	0.0638 412 234	106
54	0.0601 111 531	0.0613 498 854	0.0625 897 383	0.0638 306 037	108
55	0.0600 989 057	0.0613 386 721	0.0625 794 783	0.0638 212 217	110
56	0.0600 880 098	0.0613 287 193	0.0625 703 927	0.0638 129 327	112
57	0.0600 783 157	0.0613 198 849	0.0625 623 468	0.0638 056 093	114
58	0.0600 696 907	0.0613 120 429	0.0625 552 213	0.0637 991 388	116
59	0.0600 620 166	0.0613 050 817	0.0625 489 108	0.0637 934 216	118
60	0.0600 551 883	0.0612 989 022	0.0625 433 220	0.0637 883 701	120

TABLE 6. PARTIAL PAYMENT TO AMORTIZE ONE
Payable at end of each period

HALF YEARS	13% Nominal Annual Rate	13¼% Nominal Annual Rate	13½% Nominal Annual Rate	13¾% Nominal Annual Rate	HALF YEARS
1	1.0650 000 000	1.0662 500 000	1.0675 000 000	1.0687 500 000	1
YEARS					
1	0.5492 615 012	0.5502 185 420	0.5511 759 371	0.5521 336 858	2
2	0.2919 027 404	0.2927 327 644	0.2935 636 696	0.2943 954 542	4
3	0.2065 683 122	0.2073 731 478	0.2081 793 430	0.2089 868 947	6
4	0.1642 372 971	0.1650 421 965	0.1658 489 106	0.1666 574 342	8
5	0.1391 046 901	0.1399 195 288	0.1407 366 154	0.1415 559 425	10
6	0.1225 681 661	0.1233 976 458	0.1242 297 830	0.1250 645 674	12
7	0.1109 404 806	0.1117 870 473	0.1126 366 553	0.1134 892 905	14
8	0.1023 775 740	0.1032 425 163	0.1041 108 553	0.1049 825 721	16
9	0.0958 546 103	0.0967 385 508	0.0976 262 124	0.0985 175 708	18
10	0.0907 563 954	0.0916 595 389	0.0925 666 956	0.0934 778 347	20
11	0.0866 912 043	0.0876 134 774	0.0885 400 217	0.0894 707 995	22
12	0.0833 976 975	0.0843 388 318	0.0852 844 606	0.0862 345 387	24
13	0.0806 947 983	0.0816 543 850	0.0826 186 545	0.0835 875 533	26
14	0.0784 530 522	0.0794 305 791	0.0804 129 423	0.0814 000 794	28
15	0.0765 774 422	0.0775 723 209	0.0785 721 549	0.0795 768 729	30
16	0.0749 966 481	0.0760 082 340	0.0770 248 610	0.0780 464 483	32
17	0.0736 560 953	0.0746 837 038	0.0757 164 072	0.0767 541 151	34
18	0.0725 133 205	0.0735 562 399	0.0746 042 775	0.0756 573 336	36
19	0.0715 347 995	0.0725 923 016	0.0736 549 164	0.0747 225 356	38
20	0.0706 937 260	0.0717 650 744	0.0728 415 040	0.0739 228 975	40
21	0.0699 684 229	0.0710 528 811	0.0721 423 647	0.0732 367 481	42
22	0.0693 411 874	0.0704 380 246	0.0715 398 096	0.0726 464 089	44
23	0.0687 974 344	0.0699 059 310	0.0710 192 782	0.0721 373 356	46
24	0.0683 250 549	0.0694 445 065	0.0705 686 946	0.0716 974 722	48
25	0.0679 139 255	0.0690 436 469	0.0701 779 758	0.0713 167 597	50
26	0.0675 555 319	0.0686 948 597	0.0698 386 536	0.0709 867 564	52
27	0.0672 426 740	0.0683 909 690	0.0695 435 785	0.0707 003 413	54
28	0.0669 692 339	0.0681 258 827	0.0692 866 863	0.0704 514 805	56
29	0.0667 299 909	0.0678 944 075	0.0690 628 130	0.0702 350 410	58
30	0.0665 204 735	0.0676 920 999	0.0688 675 449	0.0700 466 407	60
31	0.0663 368 390	0.0675 151 455	0.0686 970 977	0.0698 825 273	62
32	0.0661 757 748	0.0673 602 606	0.0685 482 180	0.0697 394 789	64
33	0.0660 344 184	0.0672 246 112	0.0684 181 015	0.0696 147 223	66
34	0.0659 102 903	0.0671 057 457	0.0683 043 260	0.0695 058 659	68
35	0.0658 012 380	0.0670 015 393	0.0682 047 954	0.0694 108 431	70
36	0.0657 053 899	0.0669 101 472	0.0681 176 925	0.0693 278 653	72
37	0.0656 211 159	0.0668 299 652	0.0680 414 397	0.0692 553 824	74
38	0.0655 469 940	0.0667 595 964	0.0679 746 658	0.0691 920 491	76
39	0.0654 817 826	0.0666 978 228	0.0679 161 772	0.0691 366 969	78
40	0.0654 243 958	0.0666 435 816	0.0678 649 343	0.0690 883 096	80
41	0.0653 738 836	0.0665 959 443	0.0678 200 306	0.0690 460 030	82
42	0.0653 294 137	0.0665 540 991	0.0677 806 750	0.0690 090 067	84
43	0.0652 902 566	0.0665 173 358	0.0677 461 766	0.0689 766 497	86
44	0.0652 557 723	0.0664 850 325	0.0677 159 320	0.0689 483 465	88
45	0.0652 253 990	0.0664 566 448	0.0676 894 136	0.0689 235 867	90
46	0.0651 986 436	0.0664 316 951	0.0676 661 599	0.0689 019 244	92
47	0.0651 750 727	0.0664 097 651	0.0676 457 671	0.0688 829 707	94
48	0.0651 543 053	0.0663 904 875	0.0676 278 819	0.0688 663 855	96
49	0.0651 360 065	0.0663 735 403	0.0676 121 947	0.0688 518 721	98
50	0.0651 198 817	0.0663 586 408	0.0675 984 347	0.0688 391 708	100
51	0.0651 056 717	0.0663 455 409	0.0675 863 644	0.0688 280 550	102
52	0.0650 931 485	0.0663 340 225	0.0675 757 759	0.0688 183 261	104
53	0.0650 821 114	0.0663 238 944	0.0675 664 868	0.0688 098 110	106
54	0.0650 723 834	0.0663 149 883	0.0675 583 375	0.0688 023 578	108
55	0.0650 638 091	0.0663 071 565	0.0675 511 877	0.0687 958 340	110
56	0.0650 562 514	0.0663 002 692	0.0675 449 148	0.0687 901 236	112
57	0.0650 495 894	0.0662 942 124	0.0675 394 111	0.0687 851 250	114
58	0.0650 437 171	0.0662 888 858	0.0675 345 821	0.0687 807 494	116
59	0.0650 385 405	0.0662 842 013	0.0675 303 451	0.0687 769 190	118
60	0.0650 339 772	0.0662 800 814	0.0675 266 274	0.0687 735 660	120

TABLE 6. PARTIAL PAYMENT TO AMORTIZE ONE
Payable at end of each period

HALF YEARS	14% Nominal Annual Rate	14¼% Nominal Annual Rate	14½% Nominal Annual Rate	14¾% Nominal Annual Rate	HALF YEARS
1	1.0700 000 000	1.0712 500 000	1.0725 000 000	1.0737 500 000	1
YEARS					
1	0.5530 917 874	0.5540 502 414	0.5550 090 470	0.5559 682 037	2
2	0.2952 281 167	0.2960 616 551	0.2968 960 677	0.2977 313 528	4
3	0.2097 957 998	0.2106 060 551	0.2114 176 575	0.2122 306 039	6
4	0.1674 677 625	0.1682 798 905	0.1690 938 133	0.1699 095 259	8
5	0.1423 775 027	0.1432 012 887	0.1440 272 931	0.1448 555 085	10
6	0.1259 019 887	0.1267 420 362	0.1275 846 995	0.1284 299 681	12
7	0.1143 449 386	0.1152 035 853	0.1160 652 161	0.1169 298 165	14
8	0.1058 576 477	0.1067 360 632	0.1076 177 994	0.1085 028 371	16
9	0.0994 126 017	0.1003 112 804	0.1012 135 825	0.1021 194 833	18
10	0.0943 929 257	0.0953 119 379	0.0962 348 402	0.0971 616 018	20
11	0.0904 057 732	0.0913 449 052	0.0922 881 574	0.0932 354 920	22
12	0.0871 890 207	0.0881 478 613	0.0891 110 150	0.0900 784 362	24
13	0.0845 610 279	0.0855 390 247	0.0865 214 900	0.0875 083 704	26
14	0.0823 919 283	0.0833 884 268	0.0843 895 127	0.0853 951 241	28
15	0.0805 864 035	0.0816 006 758	0.0826 196 190	0.0836 431 624	30
16	0.0790 729 155	0.0801 041 826	0.0811 401 700	0.0821 807 982	32
17	0.0777 967 381	0.0788 441 871	0.0798 963 736	0.0809 532 097	34
18	0.0767 153 097	0.0777 781 078	0.0788 456 308	0.0799 177 826	36
19	0.0757 950 515	0.0768 723 577	0.0779 543 489	0.0790 409 209	38
20	0.0750 091 389	0.0761 001 136	0.0771 957 084	0.0782 958 119	40
21	0.0743 359 072	0.0754 397 200	0.0765 480 660	0.0776 608 268	42
22	0.0737 576 913	0.0748 735 275	0.0759 937 906	0.0771 183 560	44
23	0.0732 599 650	0.0743 870 311	0.0755 184 011	0.0766 539 449	46
24	0.0728 306 953	0.0739 682 232	0.0751 099 179	0.0762 556 448	48
25	0.0724 598 495	0.0736 070 997	0.0747 583 683	0.0759 135 168	50
26	0.0721 390 147	0.0732 952 791	0.0744 554 044	0.0756 192 490	52
27	0.0718 611 007	0.0730 257 044	0.0741 940 045	0.0753 658 576	54
28	0.0716 201 059	0.0727 924 082	0.0739 682 379	0.0751 474 502	56
29	0.0714 109 304	0.0725 903 256	0.0737 730 763	0.0749 590 374	58
30	0.0712 292 255	0.0724 151 432	0.0736 042 434	0.0747 963 813	60
31	0.0710 712 723	0.0722 631 769	0.0734 580 915	0.0746 558 724	62
32	0.0709 338 819	0.0721 312 724	0.0733 315 021	0.0745 344 289	64
33	0.0708 143 137	0.0720 167 226	0.0732 218 028	0.0744 294 147	66
34	0.0707 102 075	0.0719 171 999	0.0731 266 997	0.0743 385 701	68
35	0.0706 195 272	0.0718 306 998	0.0730 442 204	0.0742 599 555	70
36	0.0705 405 136	0.0717 554 929	0.0729 726 662	0.0741 919 038	72
37	0.0704 716 446	0.0716 900 858	0.0729 105 729	0.0741 329 802	74
38	0.0704 116 017	0.0716 331 870	0.0728 566 765	0.0740 819 487	76
39	0.0703 592 415	0.0715 836 790	0.0728 098 852	0.0740 377 434	78
40	0.0703 135 718	0.0715 405 934	0.0727 692 551	0.0739 994 447	80
41	0.0702 737 305	0.0715 030 908	0.0727 339 692	0.0739 662 585	82
42	0.0702 389 686	0.0714 704 430	0.0727 033 204	0.0739 374 985	84
43	0.0702 086 343	0.0714 420 180	0.0726 766 962	0.0739 125 718	86
44	0.0701 821 605	0.0714 172 668	0.0726 535 658	0.0738 909 652	88
45	0.0701 590 537	0.0713 957 126	0.0726 334 688	0.0738 722 349	90
46	0.0701 388 837	0.0713 769 408	0.0726 160 061	0.0738 559 970	92
47	0.0701 212 760	0.0713 605 910	0.0726 008 313	0.0738 419 188	94
48	0.0701 059 039	0.0713 463 500	0.0725 876 439	0.0738 297 125	96
49	0.0700 924 829	0.0713 339 449	0.0725 761 831	0.0738 191 286	98
50	0.0700 807 646	0.0713 231 387	0.0725 662 223	0.0738 099 511	100
51	0.0700 705 326	0.0713 137 247	0.0725 575 649	0.0738 019 929	102
52	0.0700 615 981	0.0713 055 234	0.0725 500 401	0.0737 950 917	104
53	0.0700 537 962	0.0712 983 784	0.0725 434 995	0.0737 891 071	106
54	0.0700 469 831	0.0712 921 533	0.0725 378 143	0.0737 839 171	108
55	0.0700 410 334	0.0712 867 297	0.0725 328 724	0.0737 794 161	110
56	0.0700 358 375	0.0712 820 042	0.0725 285 767	0.0737 755 127	112
57	0.0700 312 998	0.0712 778 869	0.0725 248 425	0.0737 721 274	114
58	0.0700 273 369	0.0712 742 994	0.0725 215 964	0.0737 691 914	116
59	0.0700 238 759	0.0712 711 736	0.0725 187 745	0.0737 666 451	118
60	0.0700 208 533	0.0712 684 500	0.0725 163 215	0.0737 644 366	120

TABLE 6. PARTIAL PAYMENT TO AMORTIZE ONE
Payable at end of each period

HALF YEARS	15% Nominal Annual Rate	15¼% Nominal Annual Rate	15½% Nominal Annual Rate	15¾% Nominal Annual Rate	HALF YEARS
1	1.0750 000 000	1.0762 500 000	1.0775 000 000	1.0787 500 000	1
YEARS					
1	0.5569 277 108	0.5578 875 677	0.5588 477 738	0.5598 083 283	2
2	0.2985 675 087	0.2994 045 335	0.3002 424 256	0.3010 811 831	4
3	0.2130 448 912	0.2138 605 162	0.2146 774 758	0.2154 957 669	6
4	0.1707 270 232	0.1715 463 004	0.1723 673 523	0.1731 901 741	8
5	0.1456 859 274	0.1465 185 424	0.1473 533 459	0.1481 903 306	10
6	0.1292 778 313	0.1301 282 785	0.1309 812 990	0.1318 368 821	12
7	0.1177 973 721	0.1186 678 682	0.1195 412 901	0.1204 176 233	14
8	0.1093 911 571	0.1102 827 401	0.1111 775 665	0.1120 756 170	16
9	0.1030 289 578	0.1039 419 814	0.1048 585 289	0.1057 785 755	18
10	0.0980 921 916	0.0990 265 785	0.0999 647 312	0.1009 066 184	20
11	0.0941 868 710	0.0951 422 563	0.0961 016 097	0.0970 648 931	22
12	0.0910 500 795	0.0920 258 992	0.0930 058 498	0.0939 898 858	24
13	0.0884 996 124	0.0894 951 623	0.0904 949 668	0.0914 989 727	26
14	0.0864 051 993	0.0874 196 764	0.0884 384 939	0.0894 615 908	28
15	0.0846 712 358	0.0857 037 690	0.0867 406 925	0.0877 819 370	30
16	0.0832 259 887	0.0842 756 629	0.0853 297 432	0.0863 881 522	32
17	0.0820 146 084	0.0830 804 831	0.0841 507 481	0.0852 253 185	34
18	0.0809 944 680	0.0820 755 926	0.0831 610 631	0.0842 507 873	36
19	0.0801 319 709	0.0812 273 971	0.0823 270 991	0.0834 309 780	38
20	0.0794 003 138	0.0805 091 058	0.0816 220 809	0.0827 391 340	40
21	0.0787 778 858	0.0798 991 283	0.0810 244 417	0.0821 537 154	42
22	0.0782 471 012	0.0793 799 064	0.0805 166 536	0.0816 572 277	44
23	0.0777 935 352	0.0789 370 473	0.0800 843 592	0.0812 353 518	46
24	0.0774 052 724	0.0785 586 720	0.0797 157 185	0.0808 762 895	48
25	0.0770 724 102	0.0782 349 172	0.0794 009 099	0.0805 702 639	50
26	0.0767 866 757	0.0779 575 508	0.0791 317 448	0.0803 091 320	52
27	0.0765 411 247	0.0777 196 708	0.0789 013 656	0.0800 860 828	54
28	0.0763 299 053	0.0775 154 680	0.0787 040 076	0.0798 953 981	56
29	0.0761 480 689	0.0773 400 360	0.0785 348 086	0.0797 322 616	58
30	0.0759 914 178	0.0771 892 188	0.0783 896 558	0.0795 926 053	60
31	0.0758 563 816	0.0770 594 871	0.0782 650 620	0.0794 729 852	62
32	0.0757 399 172	0.0769 478 368	0.0781 580 637	0.0793 704 792	64
33	0.0756 394 249	0.0768 517 064	0.0780 661 380	0.0792 826 041	66
34	0.0755 526 807	0.0767 689 078	0.0779 871 335	0.0792 072 460	68
35	0.0754 777 785	0.0766 975 691	0.0779 192 133	0.0791 426 031	70
36	0.0754 130 829	0.0766 360 873	0.0778 608 069	0.0790 871 379	72
37	0.0753 571 892	0.0765 830 878	0.0778 105 703	0.0790 395 373	74
38	0.0753 088 894	0.0765 373 910	0.0777 673 524	0.0789 986 786	76
39	0.0752 671 439	0.0764 979 837	0.0777 301 664	0.0789 636 013	78
40	0.0752 310 575	0.0764 639 951	0.0776 981 657	0.0789 334 833	80
41	0.0751 998 587	0.0764 346 762	0.0776 706 239	0.0789 076 205	82
42	0.0751 728 822	0.0764 093 826	0.0776 469 173	0.0788 854 094	84
43	0.0751 495 542	0.0763 875 595	0.0776 265 098	0.0788 663 328	86
44	0.0751 293 793	0.0763 687 291	0.0776 089 410	0.0788 499 471	88
45	0.0751 119 302	0.0763 524 798	0.0775 938 149	0.0788 358 719	90
46	0.0750 968 374	0.0763 384 570	0.0775 807 913	0.0788 237 807	92
47	0.0750 837 820	0.0763 263 549	0.0775 695 772	0.0788 133 934	94
48	0.0750 724 884	0.0763 159 100	0.0775 599 209	0.0788 044 695	96
49	0.0750 627 184	0.0763 068 949	0.0775 516 057	0.0787 968 025	98
50	0.0750 542 661	0.0762 991 137	0.0775 444 450	0.0787 902 153	100
51	0.0750 469 537	0.0762 923 973	0.0775 382 784	0.0787 845 556	102
52	0.0750 406 271	0.0762 865 998	0.0775 329 678	0.0787 796 927	104
53	0.0750 351 534	0.0762 815 954	0.0775 283 942	0.0787 755 144	106
54	0.0750 304 175	0.0762 772 755	0.0775 244 553	0.0787 719 242	108
55	0.0750 263 198	0.0762 735 465	0.0775 210 629	0.0787 688 393	110
56	0.0750 227 743	0.0762 703 274	0.0775 181 413	0.0787 661 886	112
57	0.0750 197 065	0.0762 675 485	0.0775 156 250	0.0787 639 109	114
58	0.0750 170 521	0.0762 651 495	0.0775 134 578	0.0787 619 537	116
59	0.0750 147 553	0.0762 630 786	0.0775 115 912	0.0787 602 719	118
60	0.0750 127 679	0.0762 612 908	0.0775 099 835	0.0787 588 268	120

TABLE 6. PARTIAL PAYMENT TO AMORTIZE ONE
Payable at end of each period

	16% Nominal Annual Rate	16¼% Nominal Annual Rate	16½% Nominal Annual Rate	16¾% Nominal Annual Rate	
HALF YEARS					HALF YEARS
1	1.0800 000 000	1.0812 500 000	1.0825 000 000	1.0837 500 000	1
YEARS					
1	0.5607 692 308	0.5617 304 805	0.5626 920 768	0.5636 540 192	2
2	0.3019 208 045	0.3027 612 878	0.3036 026 314	0.3044 448 336	4
3	0.2163 153 862	0.2171 363 308	0.2179 585 973	0.2187 821 828	6
4	0.1740 147 606	0.1748 411 068	0.1756 692 077	0.1764 990 582	8
5	0.1490 294 887	0.1498 708 128	0.1507 142 953	0.1515 599 286	10
6	0.1326 950 169	0.1335 556 928	0.1344 188 989	0.1352 846 243	12
7	0.1212 968 528	0.1221 789 640	0.1230 639 419	0.1239 517 716	14
8	0.1129 768 720	0.1138 813 119	0.1147 889 169	0.1156 996 675	16
9	0.1067 020 959	0.1076 290 651	0.1085 594 578	0.1094 932 487	18
10	0.1018 522 088	0.1028 014 711	0.1037 543 737	0.1047 108 853	20
11	0.0980 320 684	0.0990 030 972	0.0999 779 414	0.1009 565 629	22
12	0.0949 779 616	0.0959 700 318	0.0969 660 509	0.0979 659 736	24
13	0.0925 071 267	0.0935 193 757	0.0945 356 670	0.0955 559 476	26
14	0.0904 889 057	0.0915 203 781	0.0925 559 473	0.0935 955 532	28
15	0.0888 274 334	0.0898 771 133	0.0909 309 086	0.0919 887 516	30
16	0.0874 508 132	0.0885 176 503	0.0895 885 879	0.0906 635 513	32
17	0.0863 041 101	0.0873 870 397	0.0884 740 247	0.0895 649 836	34
18	0.0853 446 741	0.0864 426 333	0.0875 445 759	0.0886 504 142	36
19	0.0845 389 361	0.0856 508 771	0.0867 667 060	0.0878 863 295	38
20	0.0838 601 615	0.0849 850 617	0.0861 137 343	0.0872 460 812	40
21	0.0832 868 407	0.0844 237 110	0.0855 642 218	0.0867 082 705	42
22	0.0828 015 156	0.0839 494 068	0.0851 007 930	0.0862 555 685	44
23	0.0823 899 085	0.0835 479 156	0.0847 092 622	0.0858 738 400	46
24	0.0820 402 660	0.0832 075 319	0.0843 779 743	0.0855 514 833	48
25	0.0817 428 582	0.0829 185 753	0.0840 973 012	0.0852 789 250	50
26	0.0814 895 903	0.0826 730 018	0.0838 592 518	0.0850 482 297	52
27	0.0812 737 003	0.0824 640 999	0.0836 571 677	0.0848 527 935	54
28	0.0810 895 180	0.0822 862 500	0.0834 854 810	0.0846 871 025	56
29	0.0809 322 748	0.0821 347 322	0.0833 395 228	0.0845 465 397	58
30	0.0807 979 488	0.0820 055 725	0.0832 153 675	0.0844 272 296	60
31	0.0806 831 404	0.0818 954 166	0.0831 097 076	0.0843 259 121	62
32	0.0805 849 701	0.0818 014 285	0.0830 197 512	0.0842 398 402	64
33	0.0805 009 950	0.0817 212 060	0.0829 431 377	0.0841 666 957	66
34	0.0804 291 391	0.0816 527 119	0.0828 778 688	0.0841 045 192	68
35	0.0803 676 362	0.0815 942 159	0.0828 222 506	0.0840 516 536	70
36	0.0803 149 823	0.0815 442 474	0.0827 748 459	0.0840 066 953	72
37	0.0802 698 950	0.0815 015 550	0.0827 344 344	0.0839 684 550	74
38	0.0802 312 801	0.0814 650 732	0.0826 999 791	0.0839 359 240	76
39	0.0801 982 037	0.0814 338 941	0.0826 705 982	0.0839 082 465	78
40	0.0801 698 677	0.0814 072 438	0.0826 455 416	0.0838 846 958	80
41	0.0801 455 900	0.0813 844 620	0.0826 241 706	0.0838 646 547	82
42	0.0801 247 876	0.0813 649 856	0.0826 059 418	0.0838 475 990	84
43	0.0801 069 615	0.0813 483 337	0.0825 903 919	0.0838 330 830	86
44	0.0800 916 847	0.0813 340 957	0.0825 771 266	0.0838 207 277	88
45	0.0800 785 920	0.0813 219 212	0.0825 658 095	0.0838 102 112	90
46	0.0800 673 705	0.0813 115 105	0.0825 561 542	0.0838 012 593	92
47	0.0800 577 524	0.0813 026 077	0.0825 479 163	0.0837 936 390	94
48	0.0800 495 083	0.0812 949 942	0.0825 408 875	0.0837 871 521	96
49	0.0800 424 417	0.0812 884 830	0.0825 348 902	0.0837 816 298	98
50	0.0800 363 841	0.0812 829 145	0.0825 297 728	0.0837 769 286	100
51	0.0800 311 915	0.0812 781 520	0.0825 254 063	0.0837 729 263	102
52	0.0800 267 402	0.0812 740 788	0.0825 216 803	0.0837 695 190	104
53	0.0800 229 243	0.0812 705 951	0.0825 185 009	0.0837 666 182	106
54	0.0800 196 531	0.0812 676 156	0.0825 157 879	0.0837 641 486	108
55	0.0800 168 488	0.0812 650 671	0.0825 134 727	0.0837 620 461	110
56	0.0800 144 447	0.0812 628 874	0.0825 114 971	0.0837 602 560	112
57	0.0800 123 837	0.0812 610 231	0.0825 098 113	0.0837 587 320	114
58	0.0800 106 168	0.0812 594 285	0.0825 083 726	0.0837 574 344	116
59	0.0800 091 020	0.0812 580 646	0.0825 071 449	0.0837 563 297	118
60	0.0800 078 034	0.0812 568 980	0.0825 060 973	0.0837 553 891	120

TABLE 6. PARTIAL PAYMENT TO AMORTIZE ONE
Payable at end of each period

HALF YEARS	17% Nominal Annual Rate	17¼% Nominal Annual Rate	17½% Nominal Annual Rate	17¾% Nominal Annual Rate	HALF YEARS
1	1.0850 000 000	1.0862 500 000	1.0875 000 000	1.0887 500 000	1
YEARS					
1	0.5646 163 070	0.5655 789 395	0.5665 419 162	0.5675 052 364	2
2	0.3052 878 926	0.3061 318 067	0.3069 765 741	0.3078 221 931	4
3	0.2196 070 840	0.2204 332 978	0.2212 608 210	0.2220 896 506	6
4	0.1773 306 533	0.1781 639 879	0.1789 990 569	0.1798 358 553	8
5	0.1524 077 051	0.1532 576 171	0.1541 096 571	0.1549 638 172	10
6	0.1361 528 581	0.1370 235 894	0.1378 968 072	0.1387 725 006	12
7	0.1248 424 382	0.1257 359 266	0.1266 322 220	0.1275 313 092	14
8	0.1166 135 439	0.1175 305 261	0.1184 505 944	0.1193 737 289	16
9	0.1104 304 127	0.1113 709 242	0.1123 147 580	0.1132 618 886	18
10	0.1056 709 744	0.1066 346 094	0.1076 017 588	0.1085 723 912	20
11	0.1019 389 233	0.1029 249 847	0.1039 147 087	0.1049 080 575	22
12	0.0989 697 546	0.0999 773 488	0.1009 887 111	0.1020 037 967	24
13	0.0965 801 651	0.0976 082 671	0.0986 402 014	0.0996 759 163	26
14	0.0946 391 357	0.0956 866 355	0.0967 379 932	0.0977 931 499	28
15	0.0930 505 753	0.0941 163 130	0.0951 858 985	0.0962 592 663	30
16	0.0917 424 664	0.0928 252 597	0.0939 118 586	0.0950 021 911	32
17	0.0906 598 358	0.0917 585 015	0.0928 609 020	0.0939 669 595	34
18	0.0897 600 615	0.0908 734 324	0.0919 904 426	0.0931 110 090	36
19	0.0890 096 556	0.0901 365 937	0.0912 670 548	0.0924 009 515	38
20	0.0883 820 056	0.0895 214 128	0.0906 642 097	0.0918 103 050	40
21	0.0878 557 568	0.0890 065 823	0.0901 606 508	0.0913 178 681	42
22	0.0874 136 299	0.0885 748 761	0.0897 392 086	0.0909 065 309	44
23	0.0870 415 434	0.0882 122 696	0.0893 859 184	0.0905 623 921	46
24	0.0867 279 519	0.0879 072 763	0.0890 893 556	0.0902 740 916	48
25	0.0864 633 395	0.0876 504 404	0.0888 401 268	0.0900 323 009	50
26	0.0862 398 282	0.0874 339 436	0.0886 304 758	0.0898 293 279	52
27	0.0860 508 710	0.0872 512 978	0.0884 539 750	0.0896 588 075	54
28	0.0858 910 096	0.0870 971 016	0.0883 052 817	0.0895 154 567	56
29	0.0857 556 803	0.0869 668 461	0.0881 799 428	0.0893 948 800	58
30	0.0856 410 586	0.0868 567 590	0.0880 742 394	0.0892 934 121	60
31	0.0855 439 330	0.0867 636 780	0.0879 850 589	0.0892 079 914	62
32	0.0854 616 021	0.0866 849 478	0.0879 097 927	0.0891 360 563	64
33	0.0853 917 900	0.0866 183 356	0.0878 462 515	0.0890 754 610	66
34	0.0853 325 773	0.0865 619 618	0.0877 925 956	0.0890 244 060	68
35	0.0852 823 433	0.0865 142 423	0.0877 472 778	0.0889 813 808	70
36	0.0852 397 181	0.0864 738 411	0.0877 089 955	0.0889 451 165	72
37	0.0852 035 434	0.0864 396 306	0.0876 766 519	0.0889 145 464	74
38	0.0851 728 387	0.0864 106 584	0.0876 493 222	0.0888 887 734	76
39	0.0851 467 738	0.0863 861 195	0.0876 262 267	0.0888 670 425	78
40	0.0851 246 454	0.0863 653 337	0.0876 067 078	0.0888 487 183	80
41	0.0851 058 573	0.0863 477 256	0.0875 902 102	0.0888 332 656	82
42	0.0850 899 042	0.0863 328 082	0.0875 762 655	0.0888 202 337	84
43	0.0850 763 574	0.0863 201 698	0.0875 644 779	0.0888 092 428	86
44	0.0850 648 535	0.0863 094 616	0.0875 545 134	0.0887 999 728	88
45	0.0850 550 838	0.0863 003 885	0.0875 460 896	0.0887 921 541	90
46	0.0850 467 867	0.0862 927 005	0.0875 389 681	0.0887 855 591	92
47	0.0850 397 399	0.0862 861 860	0.0875 329 474	0.0887 799 963	94
48	0.0850 337 549	0.0862 806 658	0.0875 278 572	0.0887 753 039	96
49	0.0850 286 715	0.0862 759 879	0.0875 235 536	0.0887 713 458	98
50	0.0850 243 540	0.0862 720 237	0.0875 199 150	0.0887 680 069	100
51	0.0850 206 867	0.0862 686 644	0.0875 168 386	0.0887 651 904	102
52	0.0850 175 718	0.0862 658 176	0.0875 142 375	0.0887 628 145	104
53	0.0850 149 260	0.0862 634 051	0.0875 120 383	0.0887 608 102	106
54	0.0850 126 786	0.0862 613 605	0.0875 101 788	0.0887 591 195	108
55	0.0850 107 697	0.0862 596 279	0.0875 086 066	0.0887 576 932	110
56	0.0850 091 482	0.0862 581 595	0.0875 072 772	0.0887 564 900	112
57	0.0850 077 708	0.0862 569 151	0.0875 061 532	0.0887 554 750	114
58	0.0850 066 009	0.0862 558 605	0.0875 052 028	0.0887 546 187	116
59	0.0850 056 071	0.0862 549 667	0.0875 043 992	0.0887 538 964	118
60	0.0850 047 629	0.0862 542 093	0.0875 037 198	0.0887 532 870	120

TABLE 6. PARTIAL PAYMENT TO AMORTIZE ONE
Payable at end of each period

HALF YEARS	18% Nominal Annual Rate	18¼% Nominal Annual Rate	18½% Nominal Annual Rate	18¾% Nominal Annual Rate	HALF YEARS
1	1.0900 000 000	1.0912 500 000	1.0925 000 000	1.0937 500 000	1
YEARS					
1	0.5684 688 995	0.5694 329 050	0.5703 972 521	0.5713 619 403	2
2	0.3086 686 621	0.3095 159 792	0.3103 641 428	0.3112 131 511	4
3	0.2229 197 833	0.2237 512 160	0.2245 839 456	0.2254 179 688	6
4	0.1806 743 778	0.1815 146 196	0.1823 565 753	0.1832 002 400	8
5	0.1558 200 899	0.1566 784 674	0.1575 389 420	0.1584 015 060	10
6	0.1396 506 585	0.1405 312 699	0.1414 143 237	0.1422 998 088	12
7	0.1284 331 730	0.1293 377 984	0.1302 451 703	0.1311 552 733	14
8	0.1202 999 097	0.1212 291 168	0.1221 613 301	0.1230 965 298	16
9	0.1142 122 907	0.1151 659 387	0.1161 228 071	0.1170 828 706	18
10	0.1095 464 750	0.1105 239 788	0.1115 048 710	0.1124 891 203	20
11	0.1059 049 930	0.1069 054 771	0.1079 094 722	0.1089 169 404	22
12	0.1030 225 607	0.1040 449 585	0.1050 709 455	0.1061 004 777	24
13	0.1007 153 599	0.1017 584 809	0.1028 052 282	0.1038 555 510	26
14	0.0988 520 473	0.0999 146 273	0.1009 808 321	0.1020 506 047	28
15	0.0973 363 514	0.0984 170 893	0.0995 014 162	0.1005 892 688	30
16	0.0960 961 861	0.0971 937 732	0.0982 948 827	0.0993 994 458	32
17	0.0950 765 971	0.0961 897 392	0.0973 063 109	0.0984 262 384	34
18	0.0942 350 500	0.0953 624 849	0.0964 932 346	0.0976 272 209	36
19	0.0935 381 975	0.0946 787 085	0.0958 224 015	0.0969 691 950	38
20	0.0929 596 092	0.0941 120 347	0.0952 674 955	0.0964 259 075	40
21	0.0924 781 420	0.0936 413 824	0.0948 075 015	0.0959 764 131	42
22	0.0920 767 493	0.0932 497 720	0.0944 255 098	0.0956 038 756	44
23	0.0917 415 959	0.0929 234 373	0.0941 078 267	0.0952 946 767	46
24	0.0914 613 892	0.0926 511 561	0.0938 433 027	0.0950 377 422	48
25	0.0912 268 681	0.0924 237 367	0.0936 228 182	0.0948 240 267	50
26	0.0910 304 065	0.0922 336 213	0.0934 388 852	0.0946 461 142	52
27	0.0908 657 034	0.0920 745 744	0.0932 853 357	0.0944 979 053	54
28	0.0907 275 373	0.0919 414 375	0.0931 570 749	0.0943 743 705	56
29	0.0906 115 709	0.0918 299 324	0.0930 498 852	0.0942 713 530	58
30	0.0905 141 938	0.0917 365 044	0.0929 602 678	0.0941 854 113	60
31	0.0904 323 955	0.0916 581 947	0.0928 853 163	0.0941 136 911	62
32	0.0903 636 620	0.0915 925 371	0.0928 226 126	0.0940 538 227	64
33	0.0903 058 914	0.0915 374 736	0.0927 701 424	0.0940 038 360	66
34	0.0902 573 242	0.0914 912 850	0.0927 262 269	0.0939 620 920	68
35	0.0902 164 866	0.0914 525 339	0.0926 894 651	0.0939 272 258	70
36	0.0901 821 431	0.0914 200 180	0.0926 586 873	0.0938 981 003	72
37	0.0901 532 571	0.0913 927 305	0.0926 329 163	0.0938 737 677	74
38	0.0901 289 587	0.0913 698 283	0.0926 113 357	0.0938 534 373	76
39	0.0901 085 173	0.0913 506 050	0.0925 932 624	0.0938 364 495	78
40	0.0900 913 194	0.0913 344 684	0.0925 781 255	0.0938 222 538	80
41	0.0900 768 494	0.0913 209 220	0.0925 654 471	0.0938 103 906	82
42	0.0900 646 738	0.0913 095 496	0.0925 548 274	0.0938 004 763	84
43	0.0900 544 285	0.0913 000 017	0.0925 459 318	0.0937 921 903	86
44	0.0900 458 070	0.0912 919 854	0.0925 384 800	0.0937 852 651	88
45	0.0900 385 517	0.0912 852 547	0.0925 322 376	0.0937 794 769	90
46	0.0900 324 460	0.0912 796 034	0.0925 270 082	0.0937 746 390	92
47	0.0900 273 076	0.0912 748 583	0.0925 226 273	0.0937 705 953	94
48	0.0900 229 832	0.0912 708 739	0.0925 189 571	0.0937 672 154	96
49	0.0900 193 437	0.0912 675 283	0.0925 158 823	0.0937 643 902	98
50	0.0900 162 806	0.0912 647 190	0.0925 133 064	0.0937 620 287	100
51	0.0900 137 027	0.0912 623 600	0.0925 111 482	0.0937 600 548	102
52	0.0900 115 330	0.0912 603 791	0.0925 093 402	0.0937 584 049	104
53	0.0900 097 069	0.0912 587 157	0.0925 078 254	0.0937 570 257	106
54	0.0900 081 700	0.0912 573 189	0.0925 065 563	0.0937 558 728	108
55	0.0900 068 764	0.0912 561 460	0.0925 054 930	0.0937 549 092	110
56	0.0900 057 877	0.0912 551 611	0.0925 046 022	0.0937 541 036	112
57	0.0900 048 713	0.0912 543 340	0.0925 038 558	0.0937 534 303	114
58	0.0900 041 000	0.0912 536 395	0.0925 032 305	0.0937 528 674	116
59	0.0900 034 509	0.0912 530 562	0.0925 027 066	0.0937 523 969	118
60	0.0900 029 045	0.0912 525 665	0.0925 022 677	0.0937 520 036	120

TABLE 6. PARTIAL PAYMENT TO AMORTIZE ONE
Payable at end of each period

SEMI ANNUAL Compounding

HALF YEARS	19% Nominal Annual Rate	19¼% Nominal Annual Rate	19½% Nominal Annual Rate	19¾% Nominal Annual Rate	HALF YEARS
1	1.0950 000 000	1.0962 500 000	1.0975 000 000	1.0987 500 000	1
YEARS					
1	0.5723 269 690	0.5732 923 375	0.5742 580 453	0.5752 240 917	2
2	0.3120 630 025	0.3129 136 951	0.3137 652 273	0.3146 175 974	4
3	0.2262 532 826	0.2270 898 839	0.2279 277 693	0.2287 669 359	6
4	0.1840 456 084	0.1848 926 755	0.1857 414 362	0.1865 918 853	8
5	0.1592 661 517	0.1601 328 711	0.1610 016 567	0.1618 725 005	10
6	0.1431 877 142	0.1440 780 287	0.1449 707 411	0.1458 658 403	12
7	0.1320 680 923	0.1329 836 121	0.1339 018 174	0.1348 226 929	14
8	0.1240 346 957	0.1249 758 078	0.1259 198 461	0.1268 667 904	16
9	0.1180 461 037	0.1190 124 809	0.1199 819 766	0.1209 545 656	18
10	0.1134 766 953	0.1144 675 645	0.1154 616 966	0.1164 590 605	20
11	0.1099 278 440	0.1109 421 455	0.1119 598 073	0.1129 807 922	22
12	0.1071 335 107	0.1081 700 007	0.1092 099 039	0.1102 531 769	24
13	0.1049 093 986	0.1059 667 209	0.1070 274 680	0.1080 915 903	26
14	0.1031 238 883	0.1042 006 265	0.1052 807 635	0.1063 642 440	28
15	0.1016 805 845	0.1027 753 013	0.1038 733 578	0.1049 746 935	30
16	0.1005 073 947	0.1016 186 621	0.1027 331 817	0.1038 508 881	32
17	0.0995 494 491	0.1006 758 713	0.1018 054 344	0.1029 380 689	34
18	0.0987 643 673	0.0999 045 983	0.1010 478 397	0.1021 940 187	36
19	0.0981 190 090	0.0992 717 651	0.1004 273 865	0.1015 857 977	38
20	0.0975 871 883	0.0987 512 574	0.0999 180 358	0.1010 874 466	40
21	0.0971 480 333	0.0983 222 802	0.0994 990 738	0.1006 783 361	42
22	0.0967 847 847	0.0979 681 546	0.0991 539 050	0.1003 419 576	44
23	0.0964 839 025	0.0976 754 218	0.0988 691 546	0.1000 650 233	46
24	0.0962 343 905	0.0974 331 661	0.0986 339 900	0.0998 367 858	48
25	0.0960 272 796	0.0972 324 967	0.0984 396 008	0.0996 485 173	50
26	0.0958 552 274	0.0970 661 468	0.0982 787 971	0.0994 931 061	52
27	0.0957 122 048	0.0969 281 585	0.0981 456 939	0.0993 647 412	54
28	0.0955 932 484	0.0968 136 358	0.0980 354 631	0.0992 586 636	56
29	0.0954 942 633	0.0967 185 464	0.0979 441 358	0.0991 709 680	58
30	0.0954 118 653	0.0966 395 638	0.0978 684 435	0.0990 984 445	60
31	0.0953 432 532	0.0965 739 398	0.0978 056 915	0.0990 384 515	62
32	0.0952 861 053	0.0965 194 014	0.0977 536 548	0.0989 888 126	64
33	0.0952 384 958	0.0964 740 663	0.0977 104 953	0.0989 477 330	66
34	0.0951 988 252	0.0964 363 750	0.0976 746 924	0.0989 137 315	68
35	0.0951 657 648	0.0964 050 341	0.0976 449 883	0.0988 855 847	70
36	0.0951 382 097	0.0963 789 706	0.0976 203 412	0.0988 622 821	72
37	0.0951 152 405	0.0963 572 936	0.0975 998 882	0.0988 429 883	74
38	0.0950 960 925	0.0963 392 634	0.0975 829 143	0.0988 270 123	76
39	0.0950 801 288	0.0963 242 654	0.0975 688 268	0.0988 137 829	78
40	0.0950 668 189	0.0963 117 890	0.0975 571 343	0.0988 028 273	80
41	0.0950 557 212	0.0963 014 097	0.0975 474 291	0.0987 937 543	82
42	0.0950 464 676	0.0962 927 747	0.0975 393 731	0.0987 862 401	84
43	0.0950 387 513	0.0962 855 906	0.0975 326 859	0.0987 800 168	86
44	0.0950 323 168	0.0962 796 134	0.0975 271 348	0.0987 748 625	88
45	0.0950 269 511	0.0962 746 404	0.0975 225 267	0.0987 705 934	90
46	0.0950 224 764	0.0962 705 026	0.0975 187 013	0.0987 670 575	92
47	0.0950 187 449	0.0962 670 598	0.0975 155 256	0.0987 641 288	94
48	0.0950 156 329	0.0962 641 952	0.0975 128 892	0.0987 617 029	96
49	0.0950 130 377	0.0962 618 117	0.0975 107 006	0.0987 596 937	98
50	0.0950 108 733	0.0962 598 284	0.0975 088 836	0.0987 580 294	100
51	0.0950 090 683	0.0962 581 782	0.0975 073 752	0.0987 566 509	102
52	0.0950 075 629	0.0962 568 051	0.0975 061 230	0.0987 555 091	104
53	0.0950 063 075	0.0962 556 625	0.0975 050 833	0.0987 545 633	106
54	0.0950 052 604	0.0962 547 118	0.0975 042 202	0.0987 537 798	108
55	0.0950 043 872	0.0962 539 207	0.0975 035 037	0.0987 531 309	110
56	0.0950 036 590	0.0962 532 624	0.0975 029 088	0.0987 525 934	112
57	0.0950 030 516	0.0962 527 147	0.0975 024 149	0.0987 521 482	114
58	0.0950 025 451	0.0962 522 589	0.0975 020 049	0.0987 517 794	116
59	0.0950 021 226	0.0962 518 796	0.0975 016 645	0.0987 514 739	118
60	0.0950 017 703	0.0962 515 641	0.0975 013 819	0.0987 512 209	120

SEMI ANNUAL
Compounding

TABLE 6. PARTIAL PAYMENT TO AMORTIZE ONE
Payable at end of each period

	20% Nominal Annual Rate	20¼% Nominal Annual Rate	20½% Nominal Annual Rate	20¾% Nominal Annual Rate	
HALF YEARS					HALF YEARS
1	1.1000 000 000	1.1012 500 000	1.1025 000 000	1.1037 500 000	1
YEARS					
1	0.5761 904 762	0.5771 571 981	0.5781 242 568	0.5790 916 518	2
2	0.3154 708 037	0.3163 248 444	0.3171 797 179	0.3180 354 225	4
3	0.2296 073 804	0.2304 490 996	0.2312 920 905	0.2321 363 499	6
4	0.1874 440 176	0.1882 978 280	0.1891 533 114	0.1900 104 625	8
5	0.1627 453 949	0.1636 203 319	0.1644 973 037	0.1653 763 026	10
6	0.1467 633 151	0.1476 631 542	0.1485 653 465	0.1494 698 808	12
7	0.1357 462 232	0.1366 723 932	0.1376 011 874	0.1385 325 904	14
8	0.1278 166 207	0.1287 693 169	0.1297 248 588	0.1306 832 265	16
9	0.1219 302 222	0.1229 089 212	0.1238 906 371	0.1248 753 446	18
10	0.1174 596 248	0.1184 633 584	0.1194 702 304	0.1204 802 096	20
11	0.1140 050 630	0.1150 325 824	0.1160 633 137	0.1170 972 200	22
12	0.1112 997 764	0.1123 496 592	0.1134 027 827	0.1144 591 042	24
13	0.1091 590 386	0.1102 297 639	0.1113 037 179	0.1123 808 524	26
14	0.1074 510 132	0.1085 410 166	0.1096 342 004	0.1107 305 114	28
15	0.1060 792 483	0.1071 869 627	0.1082 977 783	0.1094 116 370	30
16	0.1049 717 167	0.1060 956 038	0.1072 224 866	0.1083 523 031	32
17	0.1040 737 064	0.1052 122 794	0.1063 537 218	0.1074 979 682	34
18	0.1033 430 638	0.1044 949 047	0.1056 494 723	0.1068 066 992	36
19	0.1027 469 250	0.1039 106 959	0.1050 770 396	0.1062 458 869	38
20	0.1022 594 144	0.1034 338 656	0.1046 107 281	0.1057 899 319	40
21	0.1018 599 911	0.1030 439 646	0.1042 301 844	0.1054 185 801	42
22	0.1015 322 365	0.1027 246 678	0.1039 191 797	0.1051 157 024	44
23	0.1012 629 527	0.1024 628 697	0.1036 647 035	0.1048 683 857	46
24	0.1010 414 797	0.1022 480 001	0.1034 562 779	0.1046 662 463	48
25	0.1008 591 740	0.1020 715 016	0.1032 854 330	0.1045 009 037	50
26	0.1007 090 040	0.1019 264 238	0.1031 453 010	0.1043 655 736	52
27	0.1005 852 336	0.1018 071 066	0.1030 302 988	0.1042 547 510	54
28	0.1004 831 734	0.1017 089 311	0.1029 358 783	0.1041 639 590	56
29	0.1003 989 822	0.1016 281 207	0.1028 583 280	0.1040 895 514	58
30	0.1003 295 092	0.1015 615 833	0.1027 946 147	0.1040 285 541	60
31	0.1002 721 660	0.1015 067 840	0.1027 422 568	0.1039 785 385	62
32	0.1002 248 244	0.1014 616 425	0.1026 992 218	0.1039 375 195	64
33	0.1001 857 328	0.1014 244 504	0.1026 638 438	0.1039 038 737	66
34	0.1001 534 487	0.1013 938 033	0.1026 347 565	0.1038 762 722	68
35	0.1001 267 834	0.1013 685 465	0.1026 108 387	0.1038 536 267	70
36	0.1001 047 566	0.1013 477 300	0.1025 911 698	0.1038 350 457	72
37	0.1000 865 600	0.1013 305 717	0.1025 749 938	0.1038 197 987	74
38	0.1000 715 264	0.1013 164 278	0.1025 616 896	0.1038 072 866	76
39	0.1000 591 054	0.1013 047 681	0.1025 507 467	0.1037 970 185	78
40	0.1000 488 424	0.1012 951 559	0.1025 417 458	0.1037 885 916	80
41	0.1000 403 622	0.1012 872 314	0.1025 343 419	0.1037 816 754	82
42	0.1000 333 549	0.1012 806 979	0.1025 282 515	0.1037 759 990	84
43	0.1000 275 644	0.1012 753 113	0.1025 232 414	0.1037 713 401	86
44	0.1000 227 794	0.1012 708 700	0.1025 191 200	0.1037 675 161	88
45	0.1000 188 252	0.1012 672 082	0.1025 157 296	0.1037 643 775	90
46	0.1000 155 575	0.1012 641 890	0.1025 129 404	0.1037 618 013	92
47	0.1000 128 571	0.1012 616 995	0.1025 106 459	0.1037 596 868	94
48	0.1000 106 255	0.1012 596 469	0.1025 087 582	0.1037 579 512	96
49	0.1000 087 812	0.1012 579 544	0.1025 072 053	0.1037 565 266	98
50	0.1000 072 571	0.1012 565 589	0.1025 059 277	0.1037 553 572	100
51	0.1000 059 975	0.1012 554 082	0.1025 048 767	0.1037 543 974	102
52	0.1000 049 566	0.1012 544 594	0.1025 040 121	0.1037 536 095	104
53	0.1000 040 963	0.1012 536 771	0.1025 033 007	0.1037 529 628	106
54	0.1000 033 854	0.1012 530 320	0.1025 027 155	0.1037 524 320	108
55	0.1000 027 978	0.1012 525 001	0.1025 022 340	0.1037 519 963	110
56	0.1000 023 122	0.1012 520 615	0.1025 018 379	0.1037 516 386	112
57	0.1000 019 109	0.1012 516 998	0.1025 015 121	0.1037 513 450	114
58	0.1000 015 793	0.1012 514 016	0.1025 012 440	0.1037 511 041	116
59	0.1000 013 052	0.1012 511 557	0.1025 010 234	0.1037 509 062	118
60	0.1000 010 787	0.1012 509 530	0.1025 008 420	0.1037 507 439	120

TABLE 6. PARTIAL PAYMENT TO AMORTIZE ONE
Payable at end of each period

HALF YEARS	21% Nominal Annual Rate	21¼% Nominal Annual Rate	21½% Nominal Annual Rate	21¾% Nominal Annual Rate	HALF YEARS
1	1.1050 000 000	1.1062 500 000	1.1075 000 000	1.1087 500 000	1
YEARS					
1	0.5800 593 824	0.5810 274 481	0.5819 958 482	0.5829 645 821	2
2	0.3188 919 564	0.3197 493 179	0.3206 075 054	0.3214 665 172	4
3	0.2329 818 746	0.2338 286 615	0.2346 767 074	0.2355 260 091	6
4	0.1908 692 763	0.1917 297 475	0.1925 918 710	0.1934 556 417	8
5	0.1662 573 206	0.1671 403 500	0.1680 253 827	0.1689 124 111	10
6	0.1503 767 456	0.1512 859 299	0.1521 974 223	0.1531 112 116	12
7	0.1394 665 871	0.1404 031 619	0.1413 422 994	0.1422 839 845	14
8	0.1316 443 997	0.1326 083 584	0.1335 750 826	0.1345 445 522	16
9	0.1258 630 182	0.1268 536 329	0.1278 471 632	0.1288 435 839	18
10	0.1214 932 653	0.1225 093 665	0.1235 284 825	0.1245 505 828	20
11	0.1181 342 647	0.1191 744 114	0.1202 176 237	0.1212 638 656	22
12	0.1155 185 815	0.1165 811 724	0.1176 468 353	0.1187 155 287	24
13	0.1134 611 196	0.1145 444 723	0.1156 308 633	0.1167 202 463	26
14	0.1118 298 968	0.1129 323 043	0.1140 376 822	0.1151 459 794	28
15	0.1105 284 815	0.1116 482 554	0.1127 709 028	0.1138 963 686	30
16	0.1094 849 922	0.1106 204 939	0.1117 587 487	0.1128 996 984	32
17	0.1086 449 545	0.1097 946 177	0.1109 468 959	0.1121 017 282	34
18	0.1079 665 187	0.1091 288 659	0.1102 936 768	0.1114 608 889	36
19	0.1074 171 697	0.1085 908 217	0.1097 667 780	0.1109 449 751	38
20	0.1069 714 084	0.1081 550 905	0.1093 409 132	0.1105 288 126	40
21	0.1066 090 833	0.1078 016 273	0.1089 961 470	0.1101 925 795	42
22	0.1063 141 681	0.1075 145 110	0.1087 166 672	0.1099 205 747	44
23	0.1060 738 498	0.1072 810 314	0.1084 898 682	0.1097 002 999	46
24	0.1058 778 407	0.1070 909 988	0.1083 056 601	0.1095 217 668	48
25	0.1057 178 512	0.1069 362 157	0.1081 559 393	0.1093 769 663	50
26	0.1055 871 820	0.1068 100 689	0.1080 341 792	0.1092 594 601	52
27	0.1054 804 064	0.1067 072 108	0.1079 351 120	0.1091 640 602	54
28	0.1053 931 196	0.1066 233 088	0.1078 544 778	0.1090 865 797	56
29	0.1053 217 406	0.1065 548 476	0.1077 888 266	0.1090 236 339	58
30	0.1052 633 544	0.1064 989 708	0.1077 353 608	0.1089 724 840	60
31	0.1052 155 851	0.1064 533 554	0.1076 918 099	0.1089 309 114	62
32	0.1051 764 952	0.1064 161 106	0.1076 563 294	0.1088 971 173	64
33	0.1051 445 028	0.1063 856 958	0.1076 274 197	0.1088 696 429	66
34	0.1051 183 160	0.1063 608 558	0.1076 038 613	0.1088 473 040	68
35	0.1050 968 792	0.1063 405 668	0.1075 846 621	0.1088 291 391	70
36	0.1050 793 292	0.1063 239 937	0.1075 690 142	0.1088 143 672	72
37	0.1050 649 605	0.1063 104 551	0.1075 562 599	0.1088 023 540	74
38	0.1050 531 957	0.1062 993 948	0.1075 458 638	0.1087 925 837	76
39	0.1050 435 624	0.1062 903 588	0.1075 373 894	0.1087 846 373	78
40	0.1050 356 742	0.1062 829 762	0.1075 304 813	0.1087 781 742	80
41	0.1050 292 148	0.1062 769 445	0.1075 248 498	0.1087 729 173	82
42	0.1050 239 253	0.1062 720 162	0.1075 202 589	0.1087 686 414	84
43	0.1050 195 936	0.1062 679 895	0.1075 165 163	0.1087 651 634	86
44	0.1050 160 463	0.1062 646 994	0.1075 134 652	0.1087 623 344	88
45	0.1050 131 413	0.1062 620 111	0.1075 109 778	0.1087 600 333	90
46	0.1050 107 623	0.1062 598 145	0.1075 089 500	0.1087 581 615	92
47	0.1050 088 140	0.1062 580 196	0.1075 072 967	0.1087 566 389	94
48	0.1050 072 184	0.1062 565 530	0.1075 059 489	0.1087 554 004	96
49	0.1050 059 117	0.1062 553 546	0.1075 048 500	0.1087 543 929	98
50	0.1050 048 415	0.1062 543 754	0.1075 039 541	0.1087 535 734	100
51	0.1050 039 651	0.1062 535 753	0.1075 032 237	0.1087 529 068	102
52	0.1050 032 473	0.1062 529 215	0.1075 026 283	0.1087 523 645	104
53	0.1050 026 595	0.1062 523 872	0.1075 021 428	0.1087 519 234	106
54	0.1050 021 781	0.1062 519 507	0.1075 017 470	0.1087 515 646	108
55	0.1050 017 838	0.1062 515 939	0.1075 014 243	0.1087 512 727	110
56	0.1050 014 609	0.1062 513 025	0.1075 011 612	0.1087 510 353	112
57	0.1050 011 964	0.1062 510 643	0.1075 009 467	0.1087 508 422	114
58	0.1050 009 799	0.1062 508 697	0.1075 007 719	0.1087 506 851	116
59	0.1050 008 025	0.1062 507 106	0.1075 006 293	0.1087 505 573	118
60	0.1050 006 572	0.1062 505 807	0.1075 005 131	0.1087 504 533	120

TABLE 6. PARTIAL PAYMENT TO AMORTIZE ONE
Payable at end of each period

HALF YEARS	22% Nominal Annual Rate	22¼% Nominal Annual Rate	22½% Nominal Annual Rate	22¾% Nominal Annual Rate	HALF YEARS
1	1.1100 000 000	1.1112 500 000	1.1125 000 000	1.1137 500 000	1
YEARS					
1	0.5839 336 493	0.5849 030 491	0.5858 727 811	0.5868 428 445	2
2	0.3223 263 515	0.3231 870 068	0.3240 484 812	0.3249 107 731	4
3	0.2363 765 636	0.2372 283 676	0.2380 814 180	0.2389 357 117	6
4	0.1943 210 542	0.1951 881 035	0.1960 567 844	0.1969 270 916	8
5	0.1698 014 271	0.1706 924 229	0.1715 853 907	0.1724 803 224	10
6	0.1540 272 864	0.1549 456 355	0.1558 662 475	0.1567 891 111	12
7	0.1432 282 015	0.1441 749 352	0.1451 241 702	0.1460 758 911	14
8	0.1355 167 470	0.1364 916 471	0.1374 692 325	0.1384 494 832	16
9	0.1298 428 701	0.1308 449 964	0.1318 499 379	0.1328 576 696	18
10	0.1255 756 369	0.1266 036 142	0.1276 344 846	0.1286 682 178	20
11	0.1223 131 011	0.1233 652 944	0.1244 204 101	0.1254 784 128	22
12	0.1197 872 113	0.1208 618 422	0.1219 393 810	0.1230 197 872	24
13	0.1178 125 750	0.1189 078 038	0.1200 058 873	0.1211 067 808	26
14	0.1162 571 454	0.1173 711 302	0.1184 878 842	0.1196 073 587	28
15	0.1150 245 985	0.1161 555 387	0.1172 891 363	0.1184 253 392	30
16	0.1140 432 854	0.1151 894 532	0.1163 381 462	0.1174 893 094	32
17	0.1132 590 547	0.1144 188 168	0.1155 809 569	0.1167 454 182	34
18	0.1126 304 409	0.1138 022 727	0.1149 763 254	0.1161 525 415	36
19	0.1121 253 508	0.1133 078 446	0.1144 923 971	0.1156 789 505	38
20	0.1117 187 267	0.1129 105 950	0.1141 043 586	0.1152 999 599	40
21	0.1113 908 633	0.1125 909 387	0.1137 927 477	0.1149 962 337	42
22	0.1111 261 735	0.1123 334 051	0.1135 422 130	0.1147 525 424	44
23	0.1109 122 683	0.1121 257 167	0.1133 405 907	0.1145 568 374	46
24	0.1107 392 624	0.1119 580 931	0.1131 782 064	0.1143 995 520	48
25	0.1105 992 433	0.1118 227 187	0.1130 473 428	0.1142 730 679	50
26	0.1104 858 607	0.1117 133 325	0.1129 418 286	0.1141 713 041	52
27	0.1103 940 076	0.1116 249 085	0.1128 567 191	0.1140 893 974	54
28	0.1103 195 698	0.1115 534 055	0.1127 880 461	0.1140 234 526	56
29	0.1102 592 282	0.1114 955 697	0.1127 326 208	0.1139 703 455	58
30	0.1102 103 020	0.1114 487 783	0.1126 878 780	0.1139 275 685	60
31	0.1101 706 244	0.1114 109 155	0.1126 517 528	0.1138 931 064	62
32	0.1101 384 421	0.1113 802 731	0.1126 225 813	0.1138 653 394	64
33	0.1101 123 361	0.1113 554 713	0.1125 990 224	0.1138 429 644	66
34	0.1100 911 570	0.1113 353 950	0.1125 799 945	0.1138 249 329	68
35	0.1100 739 735	0.1113 191 426	0.1125 646 250	0.1138 104 007	70
36	0.1100 600 309	0.1113 059 849	0.1125 522 099	0.1137 986 880	72
37	0.1100 487 175	0.1112 953 321	0.1125 421 807	0.1137 892 473	74
38	0.1100 395 369	0.1112 867 070	0.1125 340 787	0.1137 816 378	76
39	0.1100 320 868	0.1112 797 233	0.1125 275 332	0.1137 755 039	78
40	0.1100 260 410	0.1112 740 687	0.1125 222 452	0.1137 705 595	80
41	0.1100 211 345	0.1112 694 899	0.1125 179 730	0.1137 665 738	82
42	0.1100 171 526	0.1112 657 824	0.1125 145 213	0.1137 633 609	84
43	0.1100 139 210	0.1112 627 802	0.1125 117 327	0.1137 607 708	86
44	0.1100 112 984	0.1112 603 491	0.1125 094 795	0.1137 586 829	88
45	0.1100 091 698	0.1112 583 806	0.1125 076 591	0.1137 569 998	90
46	0.1100 074 423	0.1112 567 865	0.1125 061 883	0.1137 556 429	92
47	0.1100 060 403	0.1112 554 956	0.1125 050 000	0.1137 545 491	94
48	0.1100 049 024	0.1112 544 503	0.1125 040 399	0.1137 536 673	96
49	0.1100 039 788	0.1112 536 038	0.1125 032 641	0.1137 529 564	98
50	0.1100 032 293	0.1112 529 183	0.1125 026 373	0.1137 523 834	100
51	0.1100 026 210	0.1112 523 632	0.1125 021 309	0.1137 519 214	102
52	0.1100 021 272	0.1112 519 137	0.1125 017 217	0.1137 515 489	104
53	0.1100 017 265	0.1112 515 497	0.1125 013 911	0.1137 512 487	106
54	0.1100 014 013	0.1112 512 550	0.1125 011 240	0.1137 510 067	108
55	0.1100 011 373	0.1112 510 163	0.1125 009 081	0.1137 508 115	110
56	0.1100 009 230	0.1112 508 230	0.1125 007 338	0.1137 506 542	112
57	0.1100 007 492	0.1112 506 664	0.1125 005 929	0.1137 505 274	114
58	0.1100 006 080	0.1112 505 397	0.1125 004 790	0.1137 504 252	116
59	0.1100 004 935	0.1112 504 370	0.1125 003 870	0.1137 503 428	118
60	0.1100 004 005	0.1112 503 539	0.1125 003 127	0.1137 502 763	120

TABLE 1. FUTURE WORTH OF ONE DOLLAR WITH INTEREST
Payable at beginning of each period

YEARLY Compounding

YEARS	5% Nominal Annual Rate	5¼% Nominal Annual Rate	5½% Nominal Annual Rate	5¾% Nominal Annual Rate	YEARS
1	1.0500 000 000	1.0525 000 000	1.0550 000 000	1.0575 000 000	1
2	1.1025 000 000	1.1077 562 500	1.1130 250 000	1.1183 062 500	2
3	1.1576 250 000	1.1659 134 531	1.1742 413 750	1.1826 088 594	3
4	1.2155 062 500	1.2271 239 094	1.2388 246 506	1.2506 088 688	4
5	1.2762 815 625	1.2915 479 147	1.3069 600 064	1.3225 188 787	5
6	1.3400 956 406	1.3593 541 802	1.3788 428 068	1.3985 637 143	6
7	1.4071 004 227	1.4307 202 746	1.4546 791 611	1.4789 811 278	7
8	1.4774 554 438	1.5058 330 891	1.5346 865 150	1.5640 225 427	8
9	1.5513 282 160	1.5848 893 262	1.6190 942 733	1.6539 538 389	9
10	1.6288 946 268	1.6680 960 159	1.7081 444 584	1.7490 561 846	10
11	1.7103 393 581	1.7556 710 567	1.8020 924 036	1.8496 269 153	11
12	1.7958 563 260	1.8478 437 872	1.9012 074 858	1.9559 804 629	12
13	1.8856 491 423	1.9448 555 860	2.0057 738 975	2.0684 493 395	13
14	1.9799 315 994	2.0469 605 043	2.1160 914 618	2.1873 851 765	14
15	2.0789 281 794	2.1544 259 307	2.2324 764 922	2.3131 598 242	15
16	2.1828 745 884	2.2675 332 921	2.3552 626 993	2.4461 665 141	16
17	2.2920 183 178	2.3865 787 899	2.4848 021 478	2.5868 210 886	17
18	2.4066 192 337	2.5118 741 764	2.6214 662 659	2.7355 633 012	18
19	2.5269 501 954	2.6437 475 707	2.7656 469 105	2.8928 581 910	19
20	2.6532 977 051	2.7825 443 181	2.9177 574 906	3.0591 975 370	20
21	2.7859 625 904	2.9286 278 948	3.0782 341 526	3.2351 013 954	21
22	2.9252 607 199	3.0823 808 593	3.2475 370 310	3.4211 197 256	22
23	3.0715 237 559	3.2442 058 544	3.4261 515 677	3.6178 341 098	23
24	3.2250 999 437	3.4145 266 618	3.6145 899 039	3.8258 595 712	24
25	3.3863 549 409	3.5937 893 115	3.8133 923 486	4.0458 464 965	25
26	3.5556 726 879	3.7824 632 504	4.0231 289 278	4.2784 826 701	26
27	3.7334 563 223	3.9810 425 710	4.2444 010 188	4.5244 954 236	27
28	3.9201 291 385	4.1900 473 060	4.4778 430 749	4.7846 539 104	28
29	4.1161 355 954	4.4100 247 896	4.7241 244 440	5.0597 715 103	29
30	4.3219 423 752	4.6415 510 910	4.9839 512 884	5.3507 083 721	30
31	4.5380 394 939	4.8852 325 233	5.2580 686 093	5.6583 741 035	31
32	4.7649 414 686	5.1417 072 308	5.5472 623 828	5.9837 306 145	32
33	5.0031 885 420	5.4116 468 604	5.8523 618 138	6.3277 951 248	33
34	5.2533 479 691	5.6957 583 205	6.1742 417 136	6.6916 433 445	34
35	5.5160 153 676	5.9947 856 324	6.5138 250 078	7.0764 128 368	35
36	5.7918 161 360	6.3095 118 781	6.8720 853 833	7.4833 065 749	36
37	6.0814 069 428	6.6407 612 517	7.2500 500 793	7.9135 967 030	37
38	6.3854 772 899	6.9894 012 174	7.6488 028 337	8.3686 285 134	38
39	6.7047 511 544	7.3563 447 813	8.0694 869 896	8.8498 246 529	39
40	7.0399 887 121	7.7425 528 823	8.5133 087 740	9.3586 895 705	40
41	7.3919 881 477	8.1490 369 086	8.9815 407 565	9.8968 142 208	41
42	7.7615 875 551	8.5768 613 463	9.4755 254 982	10.4658 810 385	42
43	8.1496 669 329	9.0271 465 670	9.9966 794 006	11.0676 691 982	43
44	8.5571 502 795	9.5010 717 618	10.5464 967 676	11.7040 601 771	44
45	8.9850 077 935	9.9998 780 293	11.1265 540 898	12.3770 436 372	45
46	9.4342 581 832	10.5248 716 258	11.7385 145 647	13.0887 236 464	46
47	9.9059 710 923	11.0774 273 862	12.3841 328 658	13.8413 252 560	47
48	10.4012 696 469	11.6589 923 240	13.0652 601 734	14.6372 014 583	48
49	10.9213 331 293	12.2710 894 210	13.7838 494 830	15.4788 405 421	49
50	11.4673 997 858	12.9153 216 156	14.5419 612 045	16.3688 738 733	50
51	12.0407 697 750	13.5933 760 004	15.3417 690 708	17.3100 841 210	51
52	12.6428 082 638	14.3070 282 404	16.1855 663 697	18.3054 139 580	52
53	13.2749 486 770	15.0581 472 230	17.0757 725 200	19.3579 752 605	53
54	13.9386 961 108	15.8486 999 522	18.0149 400 086	20.4710 588 380	54
55	14.6356 309 164	16.6807 566 997	19.0057 617 091	21.6481 447 212	55
56	15.3674 124 622	17.5564 964 265	20.0510 786 031	22.8929 130 427	56
57	16.1357 830 853	18.4782 124 888	21.1538 879 262	24.2092 555 426	57
58	16.9425 722 396	19.4483 186 445	22.3173 517 622	25.6012 877 363	58
59	17.7897 008 515	20.4693 553 733	23.5448 061 091	27.0733 617 812	59
60	18.6791 858 941	21.5439 965 304	24.8397 704 451	28.6300 800 836	60

YEARLY
Compounding

TABLE 1. FUTURE WORTH OF ONE DOLLAR WITH INTEREST
Payable at beginning of each period

YEARS	6% Nominal Annual Rate	6¼% Nominal Annual Rate	6½% Nominal Annual Rate	6¾% Nominal Annual Rate	YEARS
1	1.0600 000 000	1.0625 000 000	1.0650 000 000	1.0675 000 000	1
2	1.1236 000 000	1.1289 062 500	1.1342 250 000	1.1395 562 500	2
3	1.1910 160 000	1.1994 628 906	1.2079 496 250	1.2164 762 969	3
4	1.2624 769 600	1.2744 293 213	1.2864 663 506	1.2985 884 469	4
5	1.3382 255 776	1.3540 811 539	1.3700 866 634	1.3862 431 671	5
6	1.4185 191 123	1.4387 112 260	1.4591 422 965	1.4798 145 809	6
7	1.5036 302 590	1.5286 306 776	1.5539 865 458	1.5797 020 651	7
8	1.5938 480 745	1.6241 700 950	1.6549 956 713	1.6863 319 545	8
9	1.6894 789 590	1.7256 807 259	1.7625 703 899	1.8001 593 614	9
10	1.7908 476 965	1.8335 357 713	1.8771 374 653	1.9216 701 183	10
11	1.8982 985 583	1.9481 317 570	1.9991 514 005	2.0513 828 513	11
12	2.0121 964 718	2.0698 899 918	2.1290 962 415	2.1898 511 937	12
13	2.1329 282 601	2.1992 581 163	2.2674 874 972	2.3376 661 493	13
14	2.2609 039 558	2.3367 117 485	2.4148 741 846	2.4954 586 144	14
15	2.3965 581 931	2.4827 562 328	2.5718 410 066	2.6639 020 708	15
16	2.5403 516 847	2.6379 284 974	2.7390 106 720	2.8437 154 606	16
17	2.6927 727 858	2.8027 990 285	2.9170 463 657	3.0356 662 542	17
18	2.8543 391 529	2.9779 739 677	3.1066 543 794	3.2405 737 264	18
19	3.0255 995 021	3.1640 973 407	3.3085 869 141	3.4593 124 529	19
20	3.2071 354 722	3.3618 534 245	3.5236 450 635	3.6928 160 435	20
21	3.3995 636 005	3.5719 692 635	3.7526 819 926	3.9420 811 264	21
22	3.6035 374 166	3.7952 173 425	3.9966 063 222	4.2081 716 025	22
23	3.8197 496 616	4.0324 184 264	4.2563 857 331	4.4922 231 856	23
24	4.0489 346 413	4.2844 445 781	4.5330 508 058	4.7954 482 506	24
25	4.2918 707 197	4.5522 223 642	4.8276 991 081	5.1191 410 076	25
26	4.5493 829 629	4.8367 362 620	5.1414 995 502	5.4646 830 256	26
27	4.8223 459 407	5.1390 322 783	5.4756 970 209	5.8335 491 298	27
28	5.1116 866 971	5.4602 217 957	5.8316 173 273	6.2273 136 961	28
29	5.4183 878 990	5.8014 856 580	6.2106 724 536	6.6476 573 705	29
30	5.7434 911 729	6.1640 785 116	6.6143 661 630	7.0963 742 431	30
31	6.0881 006 433	6.5493 334 186	7.0442 999 636	7.5753 795 045	31
32	6.4533 866 819	6.9586 667 572	7.5021 794 613	8.0867 176 210	32
33	6.8405 898 828	7.3935 834 295	7.9898 211 263	8.6325 710 604	33
34	7.2510 252 758	7.8556 823 939	8.5091 594 995	9.2152 696 070	34
35	7.6860 867 923	8.3466 625 435	9.0622 548 669	9.8373 003 055	35
36	8.1472 519 999	8.8683 289 525	9.6513 014 333	10.5013 180 761	36
37	8.6360 871 198	9.4225 995 120	10.2786 360 264	11.2101 570 462	37
38	9.1542 523 470	10.0115 119 815	10.9467 473 682	11.9668 426 469	38
39	9.7035 074 879	10.6372 314 804	11.6582 859 471	12.7746 045 255	39
40	10.2857 179 371	11.3020 584 479	12.4160 745 337	13.6368 903 310	40
41	10.9028 610 134	12.0084 371 009	13.2231 193 783	14.5573 804 283	41
42	11.5570 326 742	12.7589 644 197	14.0826 221 379	15.5400 036 073	42
43	12.2504 546 346	13.5563 996 959	14.9979 925 769	16.5889 538 508	43
44	12.9854 819 127	14.4036 746 769	15.9728 620 944	17.7087 082 357	44
45	13.7646 108 274	15.3039 043 442	17.0110 981 305	18.9040 460 416	45
46	14.5904 874 771	16.2603 983 657	18.1168 195 090	20.1800 691 494	46
47	15.4659 167 257	17.2766 732 636	19.2944 127 771	21.5422 238 170	47
48	16.3938 717 293	18.3564 653 425	20.5485 496 076	22.9963 239 246	48
49	17.3775 040 330	19.5037 444 265	21.8842 053 321	24.5485 757 895	49
50	18.4201 542 750	20.7227 284 531	23.3066 786 787	26.2056 046 553	50
51	19.5253 635 315	22.0178 989 814	24.8216 127 928	27.9744 829 696	51
52	20.6968 853 434	23.3940 176 678	26.4350 176 243	29.8627 605 700	52
53	21.9386 984 640	24.8561 437 720	28.1532 937 699	31.8784 969 085	53
54	23.2550 203 718	26.4096 527 578	29.9832 578 650	34.0302 954 498	54
55	24.6503 215 941	28.0602 560 551	31.9321 696 262	36.3273 403 927	55
56	26.1293 408 898	29.8140 220 586	34.0077 606 519	38.7794 358 692	56
57	27.6971 013 432	31.6773 984 372	36.2182 650 943	41.3970 477 903	57
58	29.3589 274 238	33.6572 358 395	38.5724 523 254	44.1913 485 162	58
59	31.1204 630 692	35.7608 130 795	41.0796 617 266	47.1742 645 410	59
60	32.9876 908 533	37.9958 638 970	43.7498 397 388	50.3585 273 976	60

TABLE 1. FUTURE WORTH OF ONE DOLLAR WITH INTEREST
Payable at beginning of each period

YEARLY Compounding

YEARS	7% Nominal Annual Rate	7¼% Nominal Annual Rate	7½% Nominal Annual Rate	7¾% Nominal Annual Rate	YEARS
1	1.0700 000 000	1.0725 000 000	1.0750 000 000	1.0775 000 000	1
2	1.1449 000 000	1.1502 562 500	1.1556 250 000	1.1610 062 500	2
3	1.2250 430 000	1.2336 498 281	1.2422 968 750	1.2509 842 344	3
4	1.3107 960 100	1.3230 894 407	1.3354 691 406	1.3479 355 125	4
5	1.4025 517 307	1.4190 134 251	1.4356 293 262	1.4524 005 148	5
6	1.5007 303 518	1.5218 918 984	1.5433 015 256	1.5649 615 547	6
7	1.6057 814 765	1.6322 290 611	1.6590 491 401	1.6862 460 751	7
8	1.7181 861 798	1.7505 656 680	1.7834 778 256	1.8169 301 460	8
9	1.8384 592 124	1.8774 816 789	1.9172 386 625	1.9577 422 323	9
10	1.9671 513 573	2.0135 991 006	2.0610 315 622	2.1094 672 553	10
11	2.1048 519 523	2.1595 850 354	2.2156 089 293	2.2729 509 676	11
12	2.2521 915 890	2.3161 549 505	2.3817 795 990	2.4491 046 675	12
13	2.4098 450 002	2.4840 761 844	2.5604 130 690	2.6389 102 793	13
14	2.5785 341 502	2.6641 717 078	2.7524 440 491	2.8434 258 259	14
15	2.7590 315 407	2.8573 241 566	2.9588 773 528	3.0637 913 274	15
16	2.9521 637 486	3.0644 801 580	3.1807 931 543	3.3012 351 553	16
17	3.1588 152 110	3.2866 549 694	3.4193 526 408	3.5570 808 798	17
18	3.3799 322 757	3.5249 374 547	3.6758 040 889	3.8327 546 480	18
19	3.6165 275 350	3.7804 954 202	3.9514 893 956	4.1297 931 333	19
20	3.8696 844 625	4.0545 813 381	4.2478 511 002	4.4498 521 011	20
21	4.1405 623 749	4.3485 384 851	4.5664 399 328	4.7947 156 389	21
22	4.4304 017 411	4.6638 075 253	4.9089 229 277	5.1663 061 009	22
23	4.7405 298 630	5.0019 335 709	5.2770 921 473	5.5666 948 238	23
24	5.0723 669 534	5.3645 737 548	5.6728 740 583	5.9981 136 726	24
25	5.4274 326 401	5.7535 053 520	6.0983 396 127	6.4629 674 822	25
26	5.8073 529 249	6.1706 344 900	6.5557 150 837	6.9638 474 621	26
27	6.2138 676 297	6.6180 054 906	7.0473 937 149	7.5035 456 404	27
28	6.6488 383 638	7.0978 108 886	7.5759 482 436	8.0850 704 275	28
29	7.1142 570 492	7.6124 021 781	8.1441 443 618	8.7116 633 857	29
30	7.6122 550 427	8.1643 013 360	8.7549 551 890	9.3868 172 981	30
31	8.1451 128 956	8.7562 131 828	9.4115 768 281	10.1142 956 387	31
32	8.7152 707 983	9.3910 386 386	10.1174 450 903	10.8981 535 507	32
33	9.3253 397 542	10.0718 889 399	10.8762 534 720	11.7427 604 508	33
34	9.9781 135 370	10.8021 008 880	11.6919 724 824	12.6528 243 858	34
35	10.6765 814 846	11.5852 532 024	12.5688 704 186	13.6334 182 757	35
36	11.4239 421 885	12.4251 840 596	13.5115 357 000	14.6900 081 921	36
37	12.2236 181 417	13.3260 099 039	14.5249 008 775	15.8284 838 269	37
38	13.0792 714 117	14.2921 456 219	15.6142 684 433	17.0551 913 235	38
39	13.9948 204 105	15.3283 261 795	16.7853 385 766	18.3769 686 511	39
40	14.9744 578 392	16.4396 298 275	18.0442 389 698	19.8011 837 216	40
41	16.0226 698 880	17.6315 029 900	19.3975 568 925	21.3357 754 600	41
42	17.1442 567 801	18.9097 869 568	20.8523 736 595	22.9892 980 581	42
43	18.3443 547 547	20.2807 465 112	22.4163 016 839	24.7709 686 576	43
44	19.6284 595 875	21.7511 006 332	24.0975 243 102	26.6907 187 286	44
45	21.0024 517 587	23.3280 554 292	25.9048 386 335	28.7592 494 301	45
46	22.4726 233 818	25.0193 394 478	27.8477 015 310	30.9880 912 609	46
47	24.0457 070 185	26.8332 415 577	29.9362 791 458	33.3896 683 336	47
48	25.7289 065 098	28.7786 515 707	32.1815 000 818	35.9773 676 295	48
49	27.5299 299 655	30.8651 038 095	34.5951 125 879	38.7656 136 208	49
50	29.4570 250 631	33.1028 238 357	37.1897 460 320	41.7699 486 764	50
51	31.5190 168 175	35.5027 785 638	39.9789 769 844	45.0071 196 988	51
52	33.7253 479 947	38.0767 300 097	42.9774 002 582	48.4951 714 754	52
53	36.0861 223 543	40.8372 929 354	46.2007 052 776	52.2535 472 648	53
54	38.6121 509 191	43.7979 966 732	49.6657 581 734	56.3031 971 778	54
55	41.3150 014 835	46.9733 514 320	53.3906 900 364	60.6666 949 591	55
56	44.2070 515 873	50.3789 194 108	57.3949 917 892	65.3683 638 184	56
57	47.3015 451 984	54.0313 910 681	61.6996 161 734	70.4344 120 143	57
58	50.6126 533 623	57.9486 669 206	66.3270 873 864	75.8930 789 455	58
59	54.1555 390 977	62.1499 452 723	71.3016 189 403	81.7747 925 637	59
60	57.9464 268 345	66.6558 163 046	76.6492 403 609	88.1123 389 874	60

YEARLY
Compounding

TABLE 1. FUTURE WORTH OF ONE DOLLAR WITH INTEREST
Payable at beginning of each period

YEARS	8% Nominal Annual Rate	8¼% Nominal Annual Rate	8½% Nominal Annual Rate	8¾% Nominal Annual Rate	YEARS
1	1.0800 000 000	1.0825 000 000	1.0850 000 000	1.0875 000 000	1
2	1.1664 000 000	1.1718 062 500	1.1772 250 000	1.1826 562 500	2
3	1.2597 120 000	1.2684 802 656	1.2772 891 250	1.2861 386 719	3
4	1.3604 889 600	1.3731 298 875	1.3858 587 006	1.3986 758 057	4
5	1.4693 280 768	1.4864 131 033	1.5036 566 902	1.5210 599 387	5
6	1.5868 743 229	1.6090 421 843	1.6314 675 088	1.6541 526 833	6
7	1.7138 242 688	1.7417 881 645	1.7701 422 471	1.7988 910 431	7
8	1.8509 302 103	1.8854 856 881	1.9206 043 381	1.9562 940 094	8
9	1.9990 046 271	2.0410 382 573	2.0838 557 068	2.1274 697 352	9
10	2.1589 249 973	2.2094 239 135	2.2609 834 419	2.3136 233 370	10
11	2.3316 389 971	2.3917 013 864	2.4531 670 345	2.5160 653 790	11
12	2.5181 701 168	2.5890 167 508	2.6616 862 324	2.7362 210 996	12
13	2.7196 237 262	2.8026 106 327	2.8879 295 622	2.9756 404 459	13
14	2.9371 936 243	3.0338 260 099	3.1334 035 750	3.2360 089 849	14
15	3.1721 691 142	3.2841 166 558	3.3997 428 788	3.5191 597 711	15
16	3.4259 426 433	3.5550 562 799	3.6887 210 235	3.8270 862 510	16
17	3.7000 180 548	3.8483 484 229	4.0022 623 105	4.1619 562 980	17
18	3.9960 194 992	4.1658 371 678	4.3424 546 069	4.5261 274 741	18
19	4.3157 010 591	4.5095 187 342	4.7115 632 485	4.9221 636 280	19
20	4.6609 571 438	4.8815 540 297	5.1120 461 246	5.3528 529 455	20
21	5.0338 337 154	5.2842 822 372	5.5465 700 452	5.8212 275 782	21
22	5.4365 404 126	5.7202 355 218	6.0180 284 991	6.3305 849 913	22
23	5.8714 636 456	6.1921 549 523	6.5295 609 215	6.8845 111 781	23
24	6.3411 807 372	6.7030 077 359	7.0845 735 998	7.4869 059 061	24
25	6.8484 751 962	7.2560 058 741	7.6867 623 558	8.1420 101 729	25
26	7.3963 532 119	7.8546 263 587	8.3401 371 560	8.8544 360 631	26
27	7.9880 614 689	8.5026 330 333	9.0490 488 143	9.6291 992 186	27
28	8.6271 063 864	9.2041 002 586	9.8182 179 635	10.4717 541 502	28
29	9.3172 748 973	9.9634 385 299	10.6527 664 904	11.3880 326 383	29
30	10.0626 568 891	10.7854 222 086	11.5582 516 421	12.3844 854 942	30
31	10.8676 694 402	11.6752 195 408	12.5407 030 317	13.4681 279 749	31
32	11.7370 829 954	12.6384 251 529	13.6066 627 894	14.6465 891 727	32
33	12.6760 496 350	13.6810 952 280	14.7632 291 265	15.9281 657 254	33
34	13.6901 336 059	14.8097 855 844	16.0181 036 022	17.3218 802 263	34
35	14.7853 442 943	16.0315 928 951	17.3796 424 084	18.8375 447 461	35
36	15.9681 718 379	17.3541 993 089	18.8569 120 131	20.4858 299 114	36
37	17.2456 255 849	18.7859 207 519	20.4597 495 342	22.2783 400 287	37
38	18.6252 756 317	20.3357 592 139	22.1988 282 446	24.2276 947 812	38
39	20.1152 976 822	22.0134 593 491	24.0857 286 454	26.3476 180 745	39
40	21.7245 214 968	23.8295 697 454	26.1330 155 803	28.6530 346 560	40
41	23.4624 832 165	25.7955 092 494	28.3543 219 046	31.1601 751 884	41
42	25.3394 818 739	27.9236 387 624	30.7644 392 665	33.8866 905 174	42
43	27.3666 404 238	30.2273 389 603	33.3794 166 042	36.8517 759 377	43
44	29.5559 716 577	32.7210 944 246	36.2166 670 155	40.0763 063 323	44
45	31.9204 493 903	35.4205 847 146	39.2950 837 118	43.5829 831 363	45
46	34.4740 853 415	38.3427 829 535	42.6351 658 273	47.3964 941 608	46
47	37.2320 121 688	41.5060 625 472	46.2591 549 227	51.5436 873 998	47
48	40.2105 731 423	44.9303 127 073	50.1911 830 911	56.0537 600 473	48
49	43.4274 189 937	48.6370 635 057	54.4574 336 538	60.9584 640 514	49
50	46.9016 125 132	52.6496 212 449	59.0863 155 144	66.2923 296 559	50
51	50.6537 415 143	56.9932 149 976	64.1086 523 331	72.0929 085 008	51
52	54.7060 408 354	61.6951 552 349	69.5578 877 815	78.4010 379 947	52
53	59.0825 241 023	66.7850 055 418	75.4703 082 429	85.2611 288 192	53
54	63.8091 260 304	72.2947 684 990	81.8852 844 435	92.7214 775 909	54
55	68.9138 561 129	78.2590 869 002	88.8455 336 212	100.8346 068 801	55
56	74.4269 646 019	84.7154 615 694	96.3974 039 790	109.6576 349 821	56
57	80.3811 217 701	91.7044 871 489	104.5911 833 172	119.2526 780 430	57
58	86.8116 115 117	99.2701 073 387	113.4814 338 992	129.6872 873 718	58
59	93.7565 404 326	107.4598 911 941	123.1273 557 806	141.0349 250 168	59
60	101.2570 636 672	116.3253 322 177	133.5931 810 220	153.3754 809 558	60

TABLE 1. FUTURE WORTH OF ONE DOLLAR WITH INTEREST
Payable at beginning of each period

YEARLY Compounding

YEARS	9% Nominal Annual Rate	9¼% Nominal Annual Rate	9½% Nominal Annual Rate	9¾% Nominal Annual Rate	YEARS
1	1.0900 000 000	1.0925 000 000	1.0950 000 000	1.0975 000 000	1
2	1.1881 000 000	1.1935 562 500	1.1990 250 000	1.2045 062 500	2
3	1.2950 290 000	1.3039 602 031	1.3129 323 750	1.3219 456 094	3
4	1.4115 816 100	1.4245 765 219	1.4376 609 506	1.4508 353 063	4
5	1.5386 239 549	1.5563 498 502	1.5742 387 409	1.5922 917 487	5
6	1.6771 001 108	1.7003 122 113	1.7237 914 213	1.7475 401 941	6
7	1.8280 391 208	1.8575 910 909	1.8875 516 063	1.9179 253 631	7
8	1.9925 626 417	2.0294 182 668	2.0668 690 090	2.1049 230 860	8
9	2.1718 932 794	2.2171 394 565	2.2632 215 648	2.3101 530 869	9
10	2.3673 636 746	2.4222 248 562	2.4782 276 135	2.5353 930 128	10
11	2.5804 264 053	2.6462 806 554	2.7136 592 367	2.7825 938 316	11
12	2.8126 647 818	2.8910 616 160	2.9714 568 642	3.0538 967 302	12
13	3.0658 046 121	3.1584 848 155	3.2537 452 663	3.3516 516 613	13
14	3.3417 270 272	3.4506 446 609	3.5628 510 666	3.6784 376 983	14
15	3.6424 824 597	3.7698 292 921	3.9013 219 180	4.0370 853 739	15
16	3.9703 058 811	4.1185 385 016	4.2719 475 002	4.4307 011 979	16
17	4.3276 334 104	4.4995 033 130	4.6777 825 127	4.8626 945 647	17
18	4.7171 204 173	4.9157 073 694	5.1221 718 514	5.3368 072 847	18
19	5.1416 612 548	5.3704 103 011	5.6087 781 773	5.8571 459 950	19
20	5.6044 107 678	5.8671 732 539	6.1416 121 041	6.4282 177 295	20
21	6.1088 077 369	6.4098 867 799	6.7250 652 540	7.0549 689 581	21
22	6.6586 004 332	7.0028 013 071	7.3639 464 531	7.7428 284 315	22
23	7.2578 744 722	7.6505 604 280	8.0635 213 662	8.4977 542 036	23
24	7.9110 831 747	8.3582 372 676	8.8295 558 960	9.3262 852 385	24
25	8.6230 806 604	9.1313 742 148	9.6683 637 061	10.2355 980 492	25
26	9.3991 579 198	9.9760 263 297	10.5868 582 582	11.2335 688 590	26
27	10.2450 821 326	10.8988 087 652	11.5926 097 927	12.3288 418 228	27
28	11.1671 395 246	11.9069 485 760	12.6939 077 230	13.5309 039 005	28
29	12.1721 820 818	13.0083 413 192	13.8998 289 567	14.8501 670 308	29
30	13.2676 784 691	14.2116 128 913	15.2203 127 076	16.2980 583 163	30
31	14.4617 695 314	15.5261 870 837	16.6662 424 148	17.8871 190 021	31
32	15.7633 287 892	16.9623 593 890	18.2495 354 442	19.6311 131 048	32
33	17.1820 283 802	18.5313 776 324	19.9832 413 114	21.5451 466 325	33
34	18.7284 109 344	20.2455 300 634	21.8816 492 360	23.6457 984 292	34
35	20.4139 679 185	22.1182 415 943	23.9604 059 134	25.9512 637 760	35
36	22.2512 250 312	24.1641 789 418	26.2366 444 751	28.4815 119 942	36
37	24.2538 352 840	26.3993 654 939	28.7291 257 003	31.2584 594 136	37
38	26.4366 804 595	28.8413 068 021	31.4583 926 418	34.3061 592 065	38
39	28.8159 817 009	31.5091 276 813	34.4469 399 428	37.6510 097 291	39
40	31.4094 200 540	34.4237 219 918	37.7193 992 373	41.3219 831 777	40
41	34.2362 678 588	37.6079 162 760	41.3027 421 649	45.3508 765 375	41
42	37.3175 319 661	41.0866 485 316	45.2265 026 705	49.7725 869 999	42
43	40.6761 098 431	44.8871 635 207	49.5230 204 243	54.6254 142 324	43
44	44.3369 597 290	49.0392 261 464	54.2277 073 646	59.9513 921 201	44
45	48.3272 861 046	53.5753 545 650	59.3793 395 642	65.7966 528 518	45
46	52.6767 418 540	58.5310 748 622	65.0203 768 228	72.2118 265 048	46
47	57.4176 486 209	63.9451 992 870	71.1973 126 209	79.2524 795 891	47
48	62.5852 369 967	69.8601 302 210	77.9610 573 199	86.9795 963 490	48
49	68.2179 083 264	76.3221 922 665	85.3673 577 653	95.4601 069 930	49
50	74.3575 200 758	83.3819 950 511	93.4772 567 530	104.7674 674 248	50
51	81.0496 968 826	91.0948 295 933	102.3575 961 446	114.9822 954 988	51
52	88.3441 696 021	99.5211 013 307	112.0815 677 783	126.1930 693 099	52
53	96.2951 448 663	108.7268 032 038	122.7293 167 173	138.4968 935 676	53
54	104.9617 079 042	118.7840 325 002	134.3886 018 054	152.0003 406 904	54
55	114.4082 616 156	129.7715 555 064	147.1555 189 769	166.8203 739 078	55
56	124.7050 051 610	141.7754 243 908	161.1352 932 797	183.0853 603 638	56
57	135.9284 556 255	154.8896 511 469	176.4431 461 413	200.9361 829 992	57
58	148.1620 166 318	169.2169 438 780	193.2052 450 247	220.5274 608 417	58
59	161.4965 981 287	184.8695 111 867	211.5597 433 021	242.0288 882 737	59
60	176.0312 919 602	201.9699 409 715	231.6579 189 157	265.6267 048 804	60

YEARLY
Compounding

TABLE 1. FUTURE WORTH OF ONE DOLLAR WITH INTEREST
Payable at beginning of each period

YEARS	10% Nominal Annual Rate	10¼% Nominal Annual Rate	10½% Nominal Annual Rate	10¾% Nominal Annual Rate	YEARS
1	1.1000 000 000	1.1025 000 000	1.1050 000 000	1.1075 000 000	1
2	1.2100 000 000	1.2155 062 500	1.2210 250 000	1.2265 562 500	2
3	1.3310 000 000	1.3400 956 406	1.3492 326 250	1.3584 110 469	3
4	1.4641 000 000	1.4774 554 438	1.4909 020 506	1.5044 402 344	4
5	1.6105 100 000	1.6288 946 268	1.6474 467 659	1.6661 675 596	5
6	1.7715 610 000	1.7958 563 260	1.8204 286 764	1.8452 805 723	6
7	1.9487 171 000	1.9799 315 994	2.0115 736 874	2.0436 482 338	7
8	2.1435 888 100	2.1828 745 884	2.2227 889 246	2.2633 404 189	8
9	2.3579 476 910	2.4066 192 337	2.4561 817 616	2.5066 495 140	9
10	2.5937 424 601	2.6532 977 051	2.7140 808 466	2.7761 143 367	10
11	2.8531 167 061	2.9252 607 199	2.9990 593 355	3.0745 466 279	11
12	3.1384 283 767	3.2250 999 437	3.3139 605 657	3.4050 603 904	12
13	3.4522 712 144	3.5556 726 879	3.6619 264 251	3.7711 043 824	13
14	3.7974 983 358	3.9201 291 385	4.0464 286 998	4.1764 981 035	14
15	4.1772 481 694	4.3219 423 752	4.4713 037 132	4.6254 716 496	15
16	4.5949 729 864	4.7649 414 686	4.9407 906 031	5.1227 098 519	16
17	5.0544 702 850	5.2533 479 691	5.4595 736 165	5.6734 011 610	17
18	5.5599 173 135	5.7918 161 360	6.0328 288 462	6.2832 917 858	18
19	6.1159 090 448	6.3854 772 899	6.6662 758 750	6.9587 456 528	19
20	6.7274 999 493	7.0399 887 121	7.3662 348 419	7.7068 108 105	20
21	7.4002 499 443	7.7615 875 551	8.1396 895 003	8.5352 929 726	21
22	8.1402 749 387	8.5571 502 795	8.9943 568 979	9.4528 369 672	22
23	8.9543 024 326	9.4342 581 832	9.9387 643 721	10.4690 169 411	23
24	9.8497 326 758	10.4012 696 469	10.9823 346 312	11.5944 362 623	24
25	10.8347 059 434	11.4673 997 858	12.1354 797 675	12.8408 381 605	25
26	11.9181 765 377	12.6428 082 638	13.4097 051 431	14.2212 282 628	26
27	13.1099 941 915	13.9386 961 108	14.8177 241 831	15.7500 103 010	27
28	14.4209 936 106	15.3674 124 622	16.3735 852 223	17.4431 364 084	28
29	15.8630 929 717	16.9425 722 396	18.0928 116 707	19.3182 735 723	29
30	17.4494 022 689	18.6791 858 941	19.9925 568 961	21.3949 879 813	30
31	19.1943 424 958	20.5938 024 483	22.0917 753 702	23.6949 491 893	31
32	21.1137 767 454	22.7046 671 992	24.4114 117 840	26.2421 562 271	32
33	23.2251 544 199	25.0318 955 871	26.9746 100 214	29.0631 880 215	33
34	25.5476 698 619	27.5976 648 848	29.8069 440 736	32.1874 807 338	34
35	28.1024 368 481	30.4264 255 355	32.9366 732 013	35.6476 349 127	35
36	30.9126 805 329	33.5451 341 529	36.3950 238 875	39.4797 556 658	36
37	34.0039 485 862	36.9835 104 036	40.2165 013 957	43.7238 293 999	37
38	37.4043 434 448	40.7743 202 199	44.4392 340 422	48.4241 410 604	38
39	41.1447 777 893	44.9536 880 425	49.1053 536 167	53.6297 362 244	39
40	45.2592 555 682	49.5614 410 668	54.2614 157 464	59.3949 328 685	40
41	49.7851 811 250	54.6414 887 762	59.9588 643 998	65.7798 881 519	41
42	54.7636 992 375	60.2422 413 758	66.2545 451 617	72.8512 261 282	42
43	60.2400 691 612	66.4170 711 168	73.2112 724 037	80.6827 329 370	43
44	66.2640 760 774	73.2248 209 062	80.8984 560 061	89.3561 267 277	44
45	72.8904 836 851	80.7303 650 491	89.3927 938 868	98.9619 103 510	45
46	80.1795 320 536	89.0052 274 667	98.7790 372 449	109.6003 157 137	46
47	88.1974 852 590	98.1282 632 820	109.1508 361 556	121.3823 496 529	47
48	97.0172 337 849	108.1864 102 684	120.6116 739 519	134.4309 522 406	48
49	106.7189 571 634	119.2755 173 209	133.2758 997 169	148.8822 796 065	49
50	117.3908 528 797	131.5012 578 463	147.2698 691 871	164.8871 246 641	50
51	129.1299 381 677	144.9801 367 755	162.7332 054 518	182.6124 905 655	51
52	142.0429 319 844	159.8406 007 950	179.8201 920 242	202.2433 333 013	52
53	156.2472 251 829	176.2242 623 765	198.7013 121 868	223.9844 916 312	53
54	171.8719 477 012	194.2872 492 701	219.5649 499 664	248.0628 244 816	54
55	189.0591 424 713	214.2016 923 203	242.6192 697 129	274.7295 781 134	55
56	207.9650 567 184	236.1573 657 832	268.0942 930 327	304.2630 077 606	56
57	228.7615 623 902	260.3634 957 759	296.2441 938 012	336.9712 810 948	57
58	251.6377 186 293	287.0507 540 930	327.3498 341 503	373.1956 938 125	58
59	276.8014 904 922	316.4734 563 875	361.7215 667 360	413.3142 308 973	59
60	304.4816 395 414	348.9119 856 672	399.7023 312 433	457.7455 107 188	60

TABLE 1. FUTURE WORTH OF ONE DOLLAR WITH INTEREST

Payable at beginning of each period

YEARLY Compounding

YEARS	11% Nominal Annual Rate	11¼% Nominal Annual Rate	11½% Nominal Annual Rate	11¾% Nominal Annual Rate	YEARS
1	1.1100 000 000	1.1125 000 000	1.1150 000 000	1.1175 000 000	1
2	1.2321 000 000	1.2376 562 500	1.2432 250 000	1.2488 062 500	2
3	1.3676 310 000	1.3768 925 781	1.3861 958 750	1.3955 409 844	3
4	1.5180 704 100	1.5317 929 932	1.5456 084 006	1.5595 170 500	4
5	1.6850 581 551	1.7041 197 049	1.7233 533 667	1.7427 603 034	5
6	1.8704 145 522	1.8958 331 717	1.9215 390 039	1.9475 346 391	6
7	2.0761 601 529	2.1091 144 035	2.1425 159 893	2.1763 699 592	7
8	2.3045 377 697	2.3463 897 739	2.3889 053 281	2.4320 934 294	8
9	2.5580 369 244	2.6103 586 235	2.6636 294 408	2.7178 644 073	9
10	2.8394 209 861	2.9040 239 686	2.9699 468 265	3.0372 134 752	10
11	3.1517 572 945	3.2307 266 651	3.3114 907 116	3.3940 860 585	11
12	3.4984 505 969	3.5941 834 149	3.6923 121 434	3.7928 911 704	12
13	3.8832 801 626	3.9985 290 491	4.1169 280 399	4.2385 558 829	13
14	4.3104 409 805	4.4483 635 671	4.5903 747 645	4.7365 861 991	14
15	4.7845 894 883	4.9488 044 684	5.1182 678 624	5.2931 350 775	15
16	5.3108 943 321	5.5055 449 711	5.7068 686 665	5.9150 784 491	16
17	5.8950 927 086	6.1249 187 803	6.3631 585 632	6.6101 001 669	17
18	6.5435 529 065	6.8139 721 431	7.0949 217 980	7.3867 869 365	18
19	7.2633 437 262	7.5805 440 092	7.9108 378 047	8.2547 344 016	19
20	8.0623 115 361	8.4333 552 103	8.8205 841 523	9.2246 656 938	20
21	8.9491 658 051	9.3821 076 714	9.8349 513 298	10.3085 639 128	21
22	9.9335 740 437	10.4375 947 845	10.9659 707 327	11.5198 201 725	22
23	11.0262 671 885	11.6118 241 977	12.2270 573 670	12.8733 990 428	23
24	12.2391 565 792	12.9181 544 200	13.6331 689 642	14.3860 234 303	24
25	13.5854 638 029	14.3714 467 922	15.2009 833 950	16.0763 811 834	25
26	15.0798 648 212	15.9882 345 563	16.9490 964 855	17.9653 559 725	26
27	16.7386 499 516	17.7869 109 439	18.8982 425 813	20.0762 852 992	27
28	18.5799 014 462	19.7879 384 251	21.0715 404 782	22.4352 488 219	28
29	20.6236 906 053	22.0140 814 979	23.4947 676 331	25.0713 905 584	29
30	22.8922 965 719	24.4906 656 664	26.1966 659 110	28.0172 789 491	30
31	25.4104 491 948	27.2458 655 539	29.2092 824 907	31.3093 092 256	31
32	28.2055 986 063	30.3110 254 287	32.5683 499 772	34.9881 530 596	32
33	31.3082 144 529	33.7210 157 895	36.3137 102 245	39.0992 610 441	33
34	34.7521 180 428	37.5146 300 658	40.4897 869 003	43.6934 242 168	34
35	38.5748 510 275	41.7350 259 482	45.1461 123 939	48.8274 015 622	35
36	42.8180 846 405	46.4302 163 673	50.3379 153 192	54.5646 212 458	36
37	47.5280 739 509	51.6536 157 087	56.1267 755 809	60.9759 642 422	37
38	52.7561 620 855	57.4646 474 759	62.5813 547 727	68.1406 400 406	38
39	58.5593 399 150	63.9294 203 169	69.7782 105 715	76.1471 652 454	39
40	65.0008 673 056	71.1214 801 026	77.8027 047 873	85.0944 571 617	40
41	72.1509 627 092	79.1226 466 141	86.7500 158 378	95.0930 558 782	41
42	80.0875 686 072	88.0239 443 582	96.7262 676 592	106.2664 899 439	42
43	88.8972 011 540	97.9266 380 985	107.8497 884 400	118.7528 025 123	43
44	98.6758 932 810	108.9433 848 846	120.2525 141 106	132.7062 568 075	44
45	109.5302 415 419	121.1995 156 841	134.0815 532 333	148.2992 419 824	45
46	121.5785 681 115	134.8344 611 986	149.5009 318 551	165.7244 029 154	46
47	134.9522 106 037	150.0033 380 834	166.6935 390 184	185.1970 202 579	47
48	149.7969 537 702	166.8787 136 178	185.8632 960 056	206.9576 701 382	48
49	166.2746 186 849	185.6525 688 998	207.2375 750 462	231.2751 963 795	49
50	184.5648 267 402	206.5384 829 010	231.0698 961 765	258.4500 319 541	50
51	204.8669 576 816	229.7740 622 274	257.6429 342 368	288.8179 107 087	51
52	227.4023 230 266	255.6236 442 280	287.2718 716 740	322.7540 152 169	52
53	252.4165 785 595	284.3813 042 036	320.3081 369 165	360.6776 120 049	53
54	280.1824 022 011	316.3742 009 266	357.1435 726 620	403.0572 314 155	54
55	311.0024 664 432	351.9662 985 308	398.2150 835 181	450.4164 561 068	55
56	345.2127 377 520	391.5625 071 155	444.0098 181 227	503.3403 896 994	56
57	383.1861 389 047	435.6132 891 660	495.0709 472 068	562.4828 854 890	57
58	425.3366 141 842	484.6197 841 972	552.0041 061 355	628.5746 245 340	58
59	472.1236 417 445	539.1395 099 194	615.4845 783 411	702.4321 429 168	59
60	524.0572 423 363	599.7927 047 853	686.2653 048 504	784.9679 197 095	60

YEARLY Compounding

TABLE 1. FUTURE WORTH OF ONE DOLLAR WITH INTEREST
Payable at beginning of each period

YEARS	12% Nominal Annual Rate	12¼% Nominal Annual Rate	12½% Nominal Annual Rate	12¾% Nominal Annual Rate	YEARS
1	1.1200 000 000	1.1225 000 000	1.1250 000 000	1.1275 000 000	1
2	1.2544 000 000	1.2600 062 500	1.2656 250 000	1.2712 562 500	2
3	1.4049 280 000	1.4143 570 156	1.4238 281 250	1.4333 414 219	3
4	1.5735 193 600	1.5876 157 500	1.6018 066 406	1.6160 924 532	4
5	1.7623 416 832	1.7820 986 794	1.8020 324 707	1.8221 442 409	5
6	1.9738 226 852	2.0004 057 676	2.0272 865 295	2.0544 676 317	6
7	2.2106 814 074	2.2454 554 742	2.2806 973 457	2.3164 122 547	7
8	2.4759 631 763	2.5205 237 698	2.5657 845 140	2.6117 548 172	8
9	2.7730 787 575	2.8292 879 316	2.8865 075 782	2.9447 535 564	9
10	3.1058 482 083	3.1758 757 032	3.2473 210 255	3.3202 096 348	10
11	3.4785 499 933	3.5649 204 768	3.6532 361 537	3.7435 363 632	11
12	3.8959 759 925	4.0016 232 352	4.1098 906 729	4.2208 372 495	12
13	4.3634 931 117	4.4918 220 816	4.6236 270 070	4.7589 939 989	13
14	4.8871 122 851	5.0420 702 865	5.2015 803 828	5.3657 657 337	14
15	5.4735 657 593	5.6597 238 966	5.8517 779 307	6.0499 008 648	15
16	6.1303 936 504	6.3530 400 740	6.5832 501 720	6.8212 632 250	16
17	6.8660 408 884	7.1312 874 830	7.4061 564 435	7.6909 742 862	17
18	7.6899 657 950	8.0048 701 997	8.3319 259 990	8.6715 735 077	18
19	8.6127 616 904	8.9854 667 992	9.3734 167 488	9.7771 991 299	19
20	9.6462 930 933	10.0861 864 821	10.5450 938 424	11.0237 920 190	20
21	10.8038 482 645	11.3217 443 261	11.8632 305 728	12.4293 255 014	21
22	12.1003 100 562	12.7086 580 061	13.3461 343 943	14.0140 645 029	22
23	13.5523 472 629	14.2654 686 118	15.0144 011 936	15.8008 577 270	23
24	15.1786 289 345	16.0129 885 168	16.8912 013 428	17.8154 670 872	24
25	17.0000 644 066	17.9745 796 101	19.0026 015 107	20.0869 391 408	25
26	19.0400 721 354	20.1764 656 123	21.3779 266 995	22.6480 238 813	26
27	21.3248 807 917	22.6480 826 499	24.0501 675 370	25.5356 469 261	27
28	23.8838 664 867	25.4224 727 745	27.0564 384 791	28.7914 419 092	28
29	26.7499 304 651	28.5367 256 893	30.4384 932 890	32.4623 507 526	29
30	29.9599 221 209	32.0324 745 863	34.2433 049 501	36.6013 004 736	30
31	33.5551 127 754	35.9564 527 231	38.5237 180 689	41.2679 662 840	31
32	37.5817 263 085	40.3611 181 817	43.3391 828 275	46.5296 319 852	32
33	42.0915 334 655	45.3053 551 589	48.7565 806 809	52.4621 600 633	33
34	47.1425 174 813	50.8552 611 659	54.8511 532 661	59.1510 854 713	34
35	52.7996 195 791	57.0850 306 587	61.7075 474 243	66.6928 488 689	35
36	59.1355 739 286	64.0779 469 144	69.4209 908 523	75.1961 870 997	36
37	66.2318 428 000	71.9274 954 114	78.0986 147 089	84.7837 009 549	37
38	74.1796 639 360	80.7386 135 993	87.8609 415 475	95.5936 228 267	38
39	83.0812 236 084	90.6290 937 652	98.8435 592 409	107.7818 097 371	39
40	93.0509 704 414	101.7311 577 515	111.1990 041 461	121.5239 904 786	40
41	104.2170 868 943	114.1932 245 760	125.0988 796 643	137.0182 992 646	41
42	116.7231 373 216	128.1818 945 866	140.7362 396 224	154.4881 324 208	42
43	130.7299 138 002	143.8841 766 735	158.3282 695 752	174.1853 693 045	43
44	146.4175 034 563	161.5099 883 160	178.1193 032 720	196.3940 038 908	44
45	163.9876 038 710	181.2949 618 847	200.3842 161 811	221.4342 393 869	45
46	183.6661 163 355	203.5035 947 156	225.4322 432 037	249.6671 049 087	46
47	205.7060 502 958	228.4327 850 682	253.6112 736 041	281.4996 607 845	47
48	230.3907 763 313	256.4158 012 391	285.3126 828 047	317.3908 675 346	48
49	258.0376 694 911	287.8267 368 908	320.9767 681 552	357.8582 031 452	49
50	289.0021 898 300	323.0855 121 600	361.0988 641 746	403.4851 240 462	50
51	323.6824 526 096	362.6634 873 996	406.2362 221 965	454.9294 773 621	51
52	362.5243 469 228	407.0897 646 060	457.0157 499 710	512.9329 857 258	52
53	406.0272 685 535	456.9582 607 703	514.1427 187 174	578.3319 414 058	53
54	454.7505 407 799	512.9356 477 146	578.4105 585 571	652.0692 639 351	54
55	509.3206 056 735	575.7702 645 597	650.7118 783 767	735.2080 950 868	55
56	570.4390 783 543	646.3021 219 682	732.0508 631 738	828.9471 272 104	56
57	638.8917 677 568	725.4741 319 093	823.5572 210 706	934.6378 859 297	57
58	715.5587 798 876	814.3447 130 682	926.5018 737 044	1053.8042 163 857	58
59	801.4258 334 742	914.1019 404 191	1042.3146 079 174	1188.1642 539 749	59
60	897.5969 334 911	1026.0794 281 204	1172.6039 339 071	1339.6551 963 567	60

TABLE 1. FUTURE WORTH OF ONE DOLLAR WITH INTEREST
Payable at beginning of each period

YEARLY Compounding

YEARS	13% Nominal Annual Rate	13¼% Nominal Annual Rate	13½% Nominal Annual Rate	13¾% Nominal Annual Rate	YEARS
1	1.1300 000 000	1.1325 000 000	1.1350 000 000	1.1375 000 000	1
2	1.2769 000 000	1.2825 562 500	1.2882 250 000	1.2939 062 500	2
3	1.4428 970 000	1.4524 949 531	1.4621 353 750	1.4718 183 594	3
4	1.6304 736 100	1.6449 505 344	1.6595 236 506	1.6741 933 838	4
5	1.8424 351 793	1.8629 064 802	1.8835 593 435	1.9043 949 741	5
6	2.0819 517 526	2.1097 415 889	2.1378 398 548	2.1662 492 830	6
7	2.3526 054 804	2.3892 823 494	2.4264 482 352	2.4641 085 594	7
8	2.6584 441 929	2.7058 622 607	2.7540 187 470	2.8029 234 863	8
9	3.0040 419 380	3.0643 890 102	3.1258 112 778	3.1883 254 657	9
10	3.3945 673 899	3.4704 205 541	3.5477 958 003	3.6267 202 172	10
11	3.8358 611 506	3.9302 512 775	4.0267 482 334	4.1253 942 471	11
12	4.3345 231 002	4.4510 095 717	4.5703 592 449	4.6926 359 561	12
13	4.8980 111 032	5.0407 683 400	5.1873 577 429	5.3378 734 000	13
14	5.5347 525 466	5.7086 701 450	5.8876 510 382	6.0718 309 925	14
15	6.2542 703 777	6.4650 689 393	6.6824 839 284	6.9067 077 540	15
16	7.0673 255 268	7.3216 905 737	7.5846 192 587	7.8563 800 702	16
17	7.9860 778 453	8.2918 145 747	8.6085 428 587	8.9366 323 298	17
18	9.0242 679 652	9.3904 800 059	9.7706 961 446	10.1654 192 752	18
19	10.1974 228 006	10.6347 186 067	11.0897 401 241	11.5631 644 255	19
20	11.5230 877 647	12.0438 188 220	12.5868 550 409	13.1530 995 340	20
21	13.0210 891 741	13.6396 248 160	14.2860 804 714	14.9616 507 200	21
22	14.7138 307 668	15.4468 751 041	16.2147 013 350	17.0188 776 940	22
23	16.6266 287 665	17.4935 860 554	18.4036 860 152	19.3589 733 769	23
24	18.7880 905 061	19.8114 862 077	20.8881 836 273	22.0208 322 162	24
25	21.2305 422 719	22.4365 081 302	23.7080 884 170	25.0486 966 459	25
26	23.9905 127 672	25.4093 454 575	26.9086 803 533	28.4928 924 347	26
27	27.1092 794 270	28.7760 837 306	30.5413 522 010	32.4106 651 445	27
28	30.6334 857 525	32.5889 148 249	34.6644 347 481	36.8671 316 019	28
29	34.6158 389 003	36.9069 460 392	39.3441 334 391	41.9363 621 971	29
30	39.1158 979 573	41.7971 163 894	44.6555 914 534	47.7026 119 992	30
31	44.2009 646 918	47.3352 343 110	50.6840 962 996	54.2617 211 491	31
32	49.9470 901 017	53.6071 528 572	57.5264 493 000	61.7227 078 071	32
33	56.4402 118 150	60.7101 006 108	65.2925 199 555	70.2095 801 306	33
34	63.7774 393 509	68.7541 889 417	74.1070 101 495	79.8633 973 986	34
35	72.0685 064 665	77.8641 189 765	84.1114 565 197	90.8446 145 409	35
36	81.4374 123 072	88.1811 147 409	95.4665 031 499	103.3357 490 403	36
37	92.0242 759 071	99.8651 124 440	108.3544 810 751	117.5444 145 333	37
38	103.9874 317 750	113.0972 398 429	122.9823 360 202	133.7067 715 316	38
39	117.5057 979 058	128.0826 241 221	139.5849 513 830	152.0914 526 172	39
40	132.7815 516 335	145.0535 718 182	158.4289 198 197	173.0040 273 521	40
41	150.0431 533 459	164.2731 700 841	179.8168 239 953	196.7920 811 130	41
42	169.5487 632 808	186.0393 651 203	204.0920 952 347	223.8509 922 661	42
43	191.5901 025 073	210.6895 809 987	231.6445 280 914	254.6305 037 026	43
44	216.4968 158 333	238.6059 504 811	262.9165 393 837	289.6421 979 618	44
45	244.6414 018 916	270.2212 389 198	298.4102 722 005	329.4680 001 815	45
46	276.4447 841 375	306.0255 530 767	338.6956 589 476	374.7698 502 064	46
47	312.3826 060 754	346.5739 388 593	384.4195 729 055	426.3007 046 098	47
48	352.9923 448 652	392.4949 857 582	436.3162 152 477	484.9170 514 937	48
49	398.8813 496 977	444.5005 713 712	495.2189 043 062	551.5931 460 741	49
50	450.7359 251 584	503.3968 970 778	562.0734 563 875	627.4372 036 593	50
51	509.3315 954 290	570.0969 859 406	637.9533 729 998	713.7098 191 624	51
52	575.5447 028 348	645.6348 365 778	724.0770 783 548	811.8449 192 972	52
53	650.3655 142 033	731.1814 524 243	821.8274 839 327	923.4735 957 006	53
54	734.9130 310 497	828.0629 948 706	932.7741 942 636	1050.4512 151 094	54
55	830.4517 250 862	937.7813 416 909	1058.6987 104 891	1194.8882 571 870	55
56	938.4104 493 474	1062.0373 694 650	1201.6230 364 052	1359.1853 925 502	56
57	1060.4038 077 626	1202.7573 209 191	1363.8421 463 199	1546.0733 840 258	57
58	1198.2563 027 717	1362.1226 659 408	1547.9608 360 731	1758.6584 743 294	58
59	1354.0296 221 320	1542.6039 191 780	1756.9355 489 429	2000.4740 145 497	59
60	1530.0534 730 092	1746.9989 384 691	1994.1218 480 502	2275.5391 915 503	60

YEARLY
Compounding

TABLE 1. FUTURE WORTH OF ONE DOLLAR WITH INTEREST
Payable at beginning of each period

YEARS	14% Nominal Annual Rate	14¼% Nominal Annual Rate	14½% Nominal Annual Rate	14¾% Nominal Annual Rate	YEARS
1	1.1400 000 000	1.1425 000 000	1.1450 000 000	1.1475 000 000	1
2	1.2996 000 000	1.3053 062 500	1.3110 250 000	1.3167 562 500	2
3	1.4815 440 000	1.4913 123 906	1.5011 236 250	1.5109 777 969	3
4	1.6889 601 600	1.7038 244 063	1.7187 865 506	1.7338 470 219	4
5	1.9254 145 824	1.9466 193 842	1.9680 106 005	1.9895 894 576	5
6	2.1949 726 239	2.2240 126 464	2.2533 721 375	2.2830 539 026	6
7	2.5022 687 913	2.5409 344 485	2.5801 110 975	2.6198 043 533	7
8	2.8525 864 221	2.9030 176 075	2.9542 272 066	3.0062 254 954	8
9	3.2519 485 212	3.3166 976 165	3.3825 901 516	3.4496 437 560	9
10	3.7072 213 141	3.7893 270 269	3.8730 657 235	3.9584 662 100	10
11	4.2262 322 981	4.3293 061 282	4.4346 602 535	4.5423 399 759	11
12	4.8179 048 198	4.9462 322 515	5.0776 859 902	5.2123 351 224	12
13	5.4924 114 946	5.6510 703 473	5.8139 504 588	5.9811 545 530	13
14	6.2613 491 038	6.4563 478 718	6.6569 732 753	6.8633 748 495	14
15	7.1379 379 784	7.3763 774 436	7.6222 344 002	7.8757 226 398	15
16	8.1372 492 954	8.4275 112 293	8.7274 583 883	9.0373 917 292	16
17	9.2764 641 967	9.6284 315 794	9.9929 398 546	10.3704 070 093	17
18	10.5751 691 843	11.0004 830 795	11.4419 161 335	11.9000 420 431	18
19	12.0556 928 700	12.5680 519 183	13.1009 939 728	13.6552 982 445	19
20	13.7434 898 719	14.3589 993 167	15.0006 380 989	15.6694 547 355	20
21	15.6675 784 539	16.4051 567 193	17.1757 306 232	17.9806 993 090	21
22	17.8610 394 375	18.7428 915 518	19.6662 115 636	20.6328 524 571	22
23	20.3615 849 587	21.4137 535 980	22.5178 122 403	23.6761 981 945	23
24	23.2122 068 529	24.4652 134 857	25.7828 950 152	27.1684 374 282	24
25	26.4619 158 123	27.9515 064 074	29.5214 147 924	31.1757 819 489	25
26	30.1665 840 261	31.9345 960 704	33.8020 199 373	35.7742 097 863	26
27	34.3899 057 897	36.4852 760 104	38.7033 128 282	41.0509 057 298	27
28	39.2044 926 003	41.6844 278 419	44.3152 931 883	47.1059 143 250	28
29	44.6931 215 643	47.6244 588 094	50.7410 107 006	54.0540 366 879	29
30	50.9501 585 833	54.4109 441 898	58.0984 572 522	62.0270 070 994	30
31	58.0831 807 850	62.1645 037 368	66.5227 335 537	71.1759 906 465	31
32	66.2148 260 949	71.0229 455 193	76.1685 299 190	81.6744 492 669	32
33	75.4849 017 482	81.1437 152 558	87.2129 667 573	93.7214 305 338	33
34	86.0527 879 929	92.7066 946 797	99.8588 469 371	107.5453 415 375	34
35	98.1001 783 119	105.9173 986 716	114.3383 797 429	123.4082 794 143	35
36	111.8342 032 756	121.0106 279 823	130.9174 448 057	141.6110 006 279	36
37	127.4909 917 342	138.2546 424 698	149.9004 743 025	162.4986 232 205	37
38	145.3397 305 769	157.9559 290 217	171.6360 430 763	186.4671 701 456	38
39	165.6872 928 577	180.4646 489 073	196.5232 693 224	213.9710 777 420	39
40	188.8835 138 578	206.1808 613 766	225.0191 433 742	245.5318 117 090	40
41	215.3272 057 979	235.5616 341 228	257.6469 191 634	281.7477 539 360	41
42	245.4730 146 096	269.1291 669 853	295.0057 224 421	323.3055 476 416	42
43	279.8392 366 549	307.4800 732 807	337.7815 521 962	370.9931 159 188	43
44	319.0167 297 866	351.2959 837 232	386.7598 772 647	425.7146 005 168	44
45	363.6790 719 567	401.3556 614 037	442.8400 594 680	488.5075 040 930	45
46	414.5941 420 307	458.5488 431 538	507.0518 680 909	560.5623 609 467	46
47	472.6373 219 150	523.8920 533 032	580.5743 889 641	643.2453 091 863	47
48	538.8065 469 831	598.5466 708 989	664.7576 753 639	738.1239 922 913	48
49	614.2394 635 607	683.8395 715 020	761.1475 382 916	846.9972 811 543	49
50	700.2329 884 592	781.2867 104 410	871.5139 313 439	971.9293 801 246	50
51	798.2656 068 435	892.6200 666 789	997.8834 513 888	1115.2889 636 929	51
52	910.0227 918 015	1019.8184 261 806	1142.5765 518 402	1279.7940 858 376	52
53	1037.4259 826 538	1165.1425 519 113	1308.2501 518 570	1468.5637 134 987	53
54	1182.6656 202 253	1331.1753 655 587	1497.9464 238 763	1685.1768 612 398	54
55	1348.2388 070 568	1520.8678 551 508	1715.1486 553 383	1933.7404 482 726	55
56	1536.9922 400 448	1737.5915 245 098	1963.8452 103 624	2218.9671 643 928	56
57	1752.1711 536 510	1985.1983 167 524	2248.6027 658 649	2546.2648 211 408	57
58	1997.4751 151 622	2268.0890 768 897	2574.6501 669 154	2921.8388 822 590	58
59	2277.1216 312 849	2591.2917 703 464	2947.9744 411 181	3352.8101 173 922	59
60	2595.9186 596 648	2960.5508 476 208	3375.4307 350 802	3847.3496 097 076	60

TABLE 1. FUTURE WORTH OF ONE DOLLAR WITH INTEREST

Payable at beginning of each period

YEARLY Compounding

YEARS	15% Nominal Annual Rate	15¼% Nominal Annual Rate	15½% Nominal Annual Rate	15¾% Nominal Annual Rate	YEARS
1	1.1500 000 000	1.1525 000 000	1.1550 000 000	1.1575 000 000	1
2	1.3225 000 000	1.3282 562 500	1.3340 250 000	1.3398 062 500	2
3	1.5208 750 000	1.5308 153 281	1.5407 988 750	1.5508 257 344	3
4	1.7490 062 500	1.7642 646 657	1.7796 227 006	1.7950 807 875	4
5	2.0113 571 875	2.0333 150 272	2.0554 642 192	2.0778 060 116	5
6	2.3130 607 656	2.3433 955 688	2.3740 611 732	2.4050 604 584	6
7	2.6600 198 805	2.7007 633 931	2.7420 406 550	2.7838 574 806	7
8	3.0590 228 625	3.1126 298 105	3.1670 569 566	3.2223 150 338	8
9	3.5178 762 919	3.5873 058 566	3.6579 507 848	3.7298 296 516	9
10	4.0455 577 357	4.1343 699 997	4.2249 331 565	4.3172 778 217	10
11	4.6523 913 961	4.7648 614 247	4.8797 977 958	4.9972 490 787	11
12	5.3502 501 055	5.4915 027 920	5.6361 664 541	5.7843 158 086	12
13	6.1527 876 213	6.3289 569 678	6.5097 722 545	6.6953 455 484	13
14	7.0757 057 645	7.2941 229 053	7.5187 869 539	7.7498 624 723	14
15	8.1370 616 292	8.4064 766 484	8.6841 989 318	8.9704 658 117	15
16	9.3576 208 735	9.6884 643 373	10.0302 497 662	10.3833 141 770	16
17	10.7612 640 046	11.1659 551 487	11.5849 384 800	12.0186 861 599	17
18	12.3754 536 053	12.8687 633 089	13.3806 039 444	13.9116 292 301	18
19	14.2317 716 460	14.8312 497 135	15.4545 975 558	16.1027 108 338	19
20	16.3665 373 929	17.0930 152 948	17.8500 601 769	18.6388 877 901	20
21	18.8215 180 019	19.6997 001 273	20.6168 195 043	21.5745 126 171	21
22	21.6447 457 022	22.7039 043 967	23.8124 265 275	24.9724 983 542	22
23	24.8914 575 575	26.1662 498 172	27.5033 526 393	28.9056 668 450	23
24	28.6251 761 911	30.1566 029 143	31.7663 722 983	33.4583 093 731	24
25	32.9189 526 198	34.7554 848 587	36.6901 600 046	38.7279 930 994	25
26	37.8567 955 128	40.0556 962 997	42.3771 348 053	44.8276 520 126	26
27	43.5353 148 397	46.1641 899 854	48.9455 907 001	51.8880 072 045	27
28	50.0656 120 656	53.2042 289 581	56.5321 572 586	60.0603 683 393	28
29	57.5754 538 755	61.3178 738 743	65.2946 416 337	69.5198 763 527	29
30	66.2117 719 568	70.6688 496 401	75.4153 110 870	80.4692 568 782	30
31	76.1435 377 503	81.4458 492 102	87.1046 843 054	93.1431 648 366	31
32	87.5650 684 128	93.8663 412 147	100.6059 103 728	107.8132 132 983	32
33	100.6998 286 748	108.1809 582 500	116.1998 264 805	124.7937 943 928	33
34	115.8048 029 760	124.6785 543 831	134.2107 995 850	144.4488 170 097	34
35	133.1755 234 224	143.6920 339 265	155.0134 735 207	167.1995 056 887	35
36	153.1518 519 358	165.6050 691 003	179.0405 619 164	193.5334 278 346	36
37	176.1246 297 261	190.8598 421 381	206.7918 490 135	224.0149 427 186	37
38	202.5433 241 850	219.9659 680 642	238.8445 856 106	259.2972 961 968	38
39	232.9248 228 128	253.5107 781 940	275.8654 963 802	300.1366 203 478	39
40	267.8635 462 347	292.1711 718 686	318.6246 483 191	347.4081 380 526	40
41	308.0430 781 699	336.7272 755 786	368.0114 688 086	402.1249 197 958	41
42	354.2495 398 954	388.0781 851 043	425.0532 464 739	465.4595 946 637	42
43	407.3869 708 797	447.2601 083 327	490.9364 996 774	538.7694 808 232	43
44	468.4950 165 117	515.4672 748 534	567.0316 571 274	623.6256 740 529	44
45	538.7692 689 884	594.0760 342 686	654.9215 639 821	721.8467 177 162	45
46	619.5846 593 367	684.6726 294 945	756.4344 063 993	835.5375 757 565	46
47	712.5223 582 372	789.0852 054 924	873.6817 393 912	967.1347 439 381	47
48	819.4007 119 727	909.4206 993 300	1009.1024 089 969	1119.4584 661 084	48
49	942.3108 187 687	1048.1073 559 779	1165.5132 823 914	1295.7731 745 205	49
50	1083.6574 415 840	1207.9437 277 645	1346.1678 411 621	1499.8574 495 074	50
51	1246.2060 578 216	1392.1551 462 486	1554.8238 565 422	1736.0849 978 049	51
52	1433.1369 664 948	1604.4588 060 515	1795.8215 543 062	2009.5183 849 591	52
53	1648.1075 114 690	1849.1387 739 743	2074.1738 952 237	2326.0175 305 902	53
54	1895.3236 381 894	2131.1324 370 054	2395.6708 489 833	2692.3652 916 581	54
55	2179.6221 839 178	2456.1301 336 488	2766.9998 305 758	3116.4128 250 943	55
56	2506.5655 115 054	2830.6899 790 302	3195.8848 043 150	3607.2478 450 466	56
57	2882.5503 382 312	3262.3702 008 323	3691.2469 489 838	4175.3893 806 415	57
58	3314.9328 889 659	3759.8816 564 592	4263.3902 260 763	4833.0132 080 925	58
59	3812.1728 223 108	4333.2636 090 692	4924.2157 111 182	5594.2127 883 671	59
60	4383.9987 456 574	4994.0863 094 523	5687.4691 463 415	6475.3013 025 349	60

YEARLY
Compounding

TABLE 1. FUTURE WORTH OF ONE DOLLAR WITH INTEREST
Payable at beginning of each period

YEARS	16% Nominal Annual Rate	16¼% Nominal Annual Rate	16½% Nominal Annual Rate	16¾% Nominal Annual Rate	YEARS
1	1.1600 000 000	1.1625 000 000	1.1650 000 000	1.1675 000 000	1
2	1.3456 000 000	1.3514 062 500	1.3572 250 000	1.3630 562 500	2
3	1.5608 960 000	1.5710 097 656	1.5811 671 250	1.5913 681 719	3
4	1.8106 393 600	1.8262 988 525	1.8420 597 006	1.8579 223 407	4
5	2.1003 416 576	2.1230 724 161	2.1459 995 512	2.1691 243 327	5
6	2.4363 963 228	2.4680 716 837	2.5000 894 772	2.5324 526 585	6
7	2.8262 197 345	2.8691 333 323	2.9126 042 409	2.9566 384 787	7
8	3.2784 148 920	3.3353 674 988	3.3931 839 407	3.4518 754 239	8
9	3.8029 612 747	3.8773 647 173	3.9530 592 909	4.0300 645 574	9
10	4.4114 350 786	4.5074 364 839	4.6053 140 739	4.7051 003 708	10
11	5.1172 646 912	5.2398 949 125	5.3651 908 961	5.4932 046 829	11
12	5.9360 270 418	6.0913 778 358	6.2504 473 939	6.4133 164 673	12
13	6.8857 913 685	7.0812 267 342	7.2817 712 139	7.4875 469 756	13
14	7.9875 179 875	8.2319 260 784	8.4832 634 642	8.7417 110 940	14
15	9.2655 208 655	9.5696 140 662	9.8830 019 358	10.2059 477 023	15
16	10.7480 042 040	11.1246 763 520	11.5136 972 552	11.9154 439 424	16
17	12.4676 848 766	12.9324 362 591	13.4134 573 023	13.9112 808 027	17
18	14.4625 144 569	15.0339 571 513	15.6266 777 572	16.2414 203 372	18
19	16.7765 167 700	17.4769 751 883	18.2050 795 871	18.9618 582 437	19
20	19.4607 594 531	20.3169 836 564	21.2089 177 190	22.1379 694 995	20
21	22.5744 809 656	23.6184 935 006	24.7083 891 426	25.8460 793 907	21
22	26.1863 979 201	27.4564 986 945	28.7852 733 512	30.1752 976 886	22
23	30.3762 215 874	31.9181 797 323	33.5348 434 541	35.2296 600 514	23
24	35.2364 170 414	37.1048 839 388	39.0680 926 240	41.1306 281 101	24
25	40.8742 437 680	43.1344 275 789	45.5143 279 070	48.0200 083 185	25
26	47.4141 227 708	50.1437 720 604	53.0241 920 117	56.0633 597 118	26
27	55.0003 824 142	58.2921 350 203	61.7731 836 936	65.4539 724 636	27
28	63.8004 436 004	67.7646 069 611	71.9657 590 030	76.4175 128 512	28
29	74.0085 145 765	78.7763 555 922	83.8401 092 385	89.2174 462 538	29
30	85.8498 769 088	91.5775 133 760	97.6737 272 629	104.1613 685 013	30
31	99.5858 572 142	106.4588 592 996	113.7898 922 613	121.6083 977 253	31
32	115.5195 943 684	123.7584 239 357	132.5652 244 844	141.9778 043 443	32
33	134.0027 294 674	143.8691 678 253	154.4384 865 243	165.7590 865 719	33
34	155.4431 661 822	167.2479 075 969	179.9208 368 008	193.5237 335 727	34
35	180.3140 727 713	194.4256 925 814	209.6077 748 729	225.9389 589 462	35
36	209.1643 244 147	226.0198 676 259	244.1930 577 269	263.7837 345 697	36
37	242.6306 163 211	262.7480 961 151	284.4849 122 519	307.9675 101 101	37
38	281.4515 149 324	305.4446 617 338	331.4249 227 734	359.5520 680 535	38
39	326.4837 573 216	355.0794 192 655	386.1100 350 311	419.7770 394 525	39
40	378.7211 584 931	412.7798 248 962	449.8181 908 112	490.0896 935 608	40
41	439.3165 438 520	479.8565 464 418	524.0381 922 950	572.1797 172 322	41
42	509.6071 908 683	557.8332 352 386	610.5044 940 237	668.0198 198 686	42
43	591.1443 414 072	648.4811 359 649	711.2377 355 376	779.9131 396 966	43
44	685.7274 360 324	753.8593 205 592	828.5919 619 013	910.5485 905 958	44
45	795.4438 257 976	876.3614 601 500	965.3096 356 151	1063.0654 795 205	45
46	922.7148 379 252	1018.7701 974 244	1124.5857 254 916	1241.1289 473 402	46
47	1070.3492 119 932	1184.3203 545 059	1310.1423 701 977	1449.0180 460 197	47
48	1241.6050 859 121	1376.7724 121 131	1526.3158 612 803	1691.7285 687 280	48
49	1440.2618 996 581	1600.4979 290 815	1778.1579 783 915	1975.0931 039 900	49
50	1670.7038 036 034	1860.5788 425 572	2071.5540 448 261	2305.9211 989 083	50
51	1938.0164 121 799	2162.9229 044 727	2413.3604 622 224	2692.1629 997 254	51
52	2248.0990 381 287	2514.3978 764 496	2811.5649 384 891	3143.1003 021 794	52
53	2607.7948 842 293	2922.9875 313 726	3275.4731 533 398	3669.5696 027 945	53
54	3025.0420 657 060	3397.9730 052 207	3815.9262 236 409	4284.2225 112 626	54
55	3509.0487 962 189	3950.1436 185 690	4445.5540 505 417	5001.8297 818 990	55
56	4070.4966 036 140	4592.0419 565 865	5179.0704 688 810	5839.6362 703 671	56
57	4721.7760 601 922	5338.2487 745 318	6033.6170 962 464	6817.7753 456 536	57
58	5477.2602 298 229	6205.7142 003 932	7029.1639 171 271	7959.7527 160 506	58
59	6353.6218 665 946	7214.1427 579 571	8188.9759 634 530	9293.0112 959 891	59
60	7370.2013 652 497	8386.4409 561 251	9540.1569 974 228	10849.5906 880 673	60

TABLE 1. FUTURE WORTH OF ONE DOLLAR WITH INTEREST
Payable at beginning of each period

YEARS	17% Nominal Annual Rate	17¼% Nominal Annual Rate	17½% Nominal Annual Rate	17¾% Nominal Annual Rate	YEARS
1	1.1700 000 000	1.1725 000 000	1.1750 000 000	1.1775 000 000	1
2	1.3689 000 000	1.3747 562 500	1.3806 250 000	1.3865 062 500	2
3	1.6016 130 000	1.6119 017 031	1.6222 343 750	1.6326 111 094	3
4	1.8738 872 100	1.8899 547 469	1.9061 253 906	1.9223 995 813	4
5	2.1924 480 357	2.2159 719 408	2.2396 973 340	2.2636 255 070	5
6	2.5651 642 018	2.5982 271 005	2.6316 443 674	2.6654 190 345	6
7	3.0012 421 161	3.0464 212 754	3.0921 821 317	3.1385 309 131	7
8	3.5114 532 758	3.5719 289 454	3.6333 140 048	3.6956 201 501	8
9	4.1084 003 327	4.1880 866 885	4.2691 439 556	4.3515 927 268	9
10	4.8068 283 892	4.9105 316 422	5.0162 441 479	5.1240 004 358	10
11	5.6239 892 154	5.7575 983 505	5.8940 868 737	6.0335 105 131	11
12	6.5800 673 820	6.7507 840 660	6.9255 520 766	7.1044 586 292	12
13	7.6986 788 370	7.9152 943 173	8.1375 236 900	8.3655 000 359	13
14	9.0074 542 393	9.2806 825 871	9.5615 903 358	9.8503 762 923	14
15	10.5387 214 599	10.8816 003 334	11.2348 686 446	11.5988 180 842	15
16	12.3303 041 081	12.7586 763 909	13.2009 706 574	13.6576 082 941	16
17	14.4264 558 065	14.9595 480 683	15.5111 405 224	16.0818 337 663	17
18	16.8789 532 936	17.5400 701 101	18.2255 901 138	18.9363 592 599	18
19	19.7483 753 535	20.5657 322 041	21.4150 683 838	22.2975 630 285	19
20	23.1055 991 636	24.1133 210 093	25.1627 053 509	26.2553 804 660	20
21	27.0335 510 215	28.2728 688 834	29.5661 787 873	30.9157 104 988	21
22	31.6292 546 951	33.1499 387 657	34.7402 600 751	36.4032 491 123	22
23	37.0062 279 933	38.8683 032 028	40.8198 055 882	42.8648 258 297	23
24	43.2972 867 521	45.5730 855 053	47.9632 715 662	50.4733 324 145	24
25	50.6578 255 000	53.4344 427 550	56.3568 440 903	59.4323 489 181	25
26	59.2696 558 350	62.6518 841 302	66.2192 918 061	69.9815 908 510	26
27	69.3454 973 270	73.4593 341 427	77.8076 678 721	82.4033 232 271	27
28	81.1342 318 726	86.1310 692 823	91.4240 097 497	97.0299 130 999	28
29	94.9270 512 909	100.9886 787 335	107.4232 114 559	114.2527 226 751	29
30	111.0646 500 103	118.4092 258 150	126.2222 734 607	134.5325 809 499	30
31	129.9456 405 121	138.8348 172 681	148.3111 713 164	158.4121 140 685	31
32	152.0363 993 992	162.7838 232 468	174.2656 262 967	186.5302 643 157	32
33	177.8825 872 970	190.8640 327 569	204.7621 108 986	219.6393 862 317	33
34	208.1226 271 375	223.7880 784 075	240.5954 803 059	258.6253 772 879	34
35	243.5034 737 509	262.3915 219 327	282.6996 893 594	304.5313 817 565	35
36	284.8990 642 885	307.6540 594 661	332.1721 349 973	358.5857 020 183	36
37	333.3319 052 176	360.7243 847 240	390.3022 586 219	422.2346 641 265	37
38	389.9983 291 046	422.9493 410 889	458.6051 538 807	497.1813 170 090	38
39	456.2980 450 523	495.9081 024 268	538.8610 558 098	585.4310 007 780	39
40	533.8687 127 112	581.4522 500 954	633.1617 405 766	689.3450 034 161	40
41	624.6263 938 722	681.7527 632 369	743.9650 451 774	811.7037 415 225	41
42	730.8128 808 304	799.3551 148 952	874.1589 280 835	955.7811 556 428	42
43	855.0510 705 716	937.2438 722 146	1027.1367 404 981	1125.4323 107 693	43
44	1000.4097 525 688	1098.9184 401 717	1206.8856 700 853	1325.1965 459 309	44
45	1170.4794 105 055	1288.4818 711 013	1418.0906 623 502	1560.4189 328 336	45
46	1369.4609 102 914	1510.7449 938 663	1666.2565 282 615	1837.3932 934 116	46
47	1602.2692 650 409	1771.3485 053 082	1957.8514 207 073	2163.5306 029 922	47
48	1874.6550 400 979	2076.9061 224 738	2300.4754 193 310	2547.5572 850 233	48
49	2193.3463 969 145	2435.1724 286 006	2703.0586 177 140	2999.7487 031 149	49
50	2566.2152 843 900	2855.2396 725 342	3176.0938 758 139	3532.2040 979 178	50
51	3002.4718 827 363	3347.7685 160 463	3731.9103 040 813	4159.1703 252 982	51
52	3512.8921 028 015	3925.2585 850 643	4384.9946 072 956	4897.4230 580 387	52
53	4110.0837 602 777	4602.3656 909 879	5152.3686 635 723	5766.7156 508 405	53
54	4808.7979 995 249	5396.2737 726 833	6054.0331 796 974	6790.3076 788 647	54
55	5626.2936 594 442	6327.1309 984 712	7113.4889 861 445	7995.5872 918 632	55
56	6582.7635 815 497	7418.5610 957 075	8358.3495 587 198	9414.8040 361 689	56
57	7701.8333 904 131	8698.2628 847 170	9821.0607 314 957	11085.9317 525 889	57
58	9011.1450 667 833	10198.7132 323 307	11539.7463 595 075	13053.6846 386 735	58
59	10543.0397 281 365	11957.9912 649 077	13559.2019 724 213	15370.7136 620 380	59
60	12335.3564 819 197	14020.7447 581 043	15932.0623 175 950	18099.0153 370 498	60

YEARLY
Compounding

TABLE 1. FUTURE WORTH OF ONE DOLLAR WITH INTEREST

Payable at beginning of each period

YEARS	18% Nominal Annual Rate	18¼% Nominal Annual Rate	18½% Nominal Annual Rate	18¾% Nominal Annual Rate	YEARS
1	1.1800 000 000	1.1825 000 000	1.1850 000 000	1.1875 000 000	1
2	1.3924 000 000	1.3983 062 500	1.4042 250 000	1.4101 562 500	2
3	1.6430 320 000	1.6534 971 406	1.6640 066 250	1.6745 605 469	3
4	1.9387 777 600	1.9552 603 688	1.9718 478 506	1.9885 406 494	4
5	2.2877 577 568	2.3120 953 861	2.3366 397 030	2.3613 920 212	5
6	2.6995 541 530	2.7340 527 941	2.7689 180 480	2.8041 530 252	6
7	3.1854 739 006	3.2330 174 290	3.2811 678 869	3.3299 317 174	7
8	3.7588 592 027	3.8230 431 098	3.8881 839 460	3.9542 939 144	8
9	4.4354 538 592	4.5207 484 773	4.6074 979 760	4.6957 240 233	9
10	5.2338 355 538	5.3457 850 744	5.4598 851 016	5.5761 722 777	10
11	6.1759 259 535	6.3213 908 505	6.4699 638 454	6.6217 045 798	11
12	7.2875 926 251	7.4750 446 807	7.6669 071 568	7.8632 741 885	12
13	8.5993 592 976	8.8392 403 349	9.0852 849 808	9.3376 380 988	13
14	10.1472 439 712	10.4524 016 960	10.7660 627 022	11.0884 452 423	14
15	11.9737 478 860	12.3599 650 055	12.7577 843 021	13.1675 287 253	15
16	14.1290 225 055	14.6156 586 191	15.1179 743 980	15.6364 403 612	16
17	16.6722 465 565	17.2830 163 170	17.9147 996 617	18.5682 729 290	17
18	19.6732 509 367	20.4371 667 949	21.2290 375 991	22.0498 241 032	18
19	23.2144 361 053	24.1669 497 350	25.1564 095 549	26.1841 661 225	19
20	27.3930 346 042	28.5774 180 616	29.8103 453 226	31.0936 972 705	20
21	32.3237 808 330	33.7927 968 578	35.3252 592 073	36.9237 655 087	21
22	38.1420 613 829	39.9599 822 844	41.8604 321 606	43.8469 715 416	22
23	45.0076 324 318	47.2526 790 513	49.6046 121 103	52.0682 787 056	23
24	53.1090 062 695	55.8762 929 782	58.7814 653 507	61.8310 809 629	24
25	62.6686 273 981	66.0737 164 467	69.6560 364 406	73.4244 086 434	25
26	73.9489 803 297	78.1321 696 982	82.5424 031 821	87.1914 852 641	26
27	87.2597 967 891	92.3912 906 681	97.8127 477 708	103.5398 887 511	27
28	102.9665 602 111	109.2527 012 151	115.9081 061 084	122.9536 178 919	28
29	121.5005 410 491	129.1913 191 868	137.3511 057 385	146.0074 212 467	29
30	143.3706 384 379	152.7687 349 384	162.7610 603 001	173.3838 127 304	30
31	169.1773 533 568	180.6490 290 646	192.8718 564 556	205.8932 776 174	31
32	199.6292 769 610	213.6174 768 689	228.5531 498 999	244.4982 671 706	32
33	235.5625 468 139	252.6026 663 975	270.8354 826 314	290.3416 922 651	33
34	277.9638 052 405	298.7026 530 151	320.9400 469 182	344.7807 595 648	34
35	327.9972 901 837	353.2158 871 903	380.3139 555 981	409.4271 519 832	35
36	387.0368 024 168	417.6777 866 026	450.6720 373 837	486.1947 429 801	36
37	456.7034 268 518	493.9039 826 575	534.0463 642 997	577.3562 572 888	37
38	538.9100 436 852	584.0414 594 925	632.8449 416 952	685.6105 555 305	38
39	635.9138 515 485	690.6290 258 499	749.9212 559 088	814.1625 346 925	39
40	750.3783 448 272	816.6688 230 675	888.6566 882 519	966.8180 099 473	40
41	885.4464 468 961	965.7108 832 774	1053.0581 755 785	1148.0963 868 124	41
42	1044.8268 073 374	1141.9531 194 755	1247.8739 380 605	1363.3644 593 398	42
43	1232.8956 326 582	1350.3595 637 798	1478.7306 166 018	1618.9952 954 660	43
44	1454.8168 465 366	1596.8001 841 696	1752.2957 806 731	1922.5569 133 658	44
45	1716.6838 789 132	1888.2162 177 805	2076.4705 000 976	2283.0363 346 219	45
46	2025.6869 771 176	2232.8156 775 255	2460.6175 426 156	2711.1056 473 636	46
47	2390.3106 329 988	2640.3045 386 738	2915.8317 879 995	3219.4379 562 442	47
48	2820.5665 469 386	3122.1601 169 818	3455.2606 687 795	3823.0825 730 400	48
49	3328.2685 253 875	3691.9543 383 310	4094.4838 925 037	4539.9105 554 850	49
50	3927.3568 599 573	4365.7360 050 764	4851.9634 126 168	5391.1437 846 385	50
51	4634.2810 947 496	5162.4828 260 029	5749.5766 439 509	6401.9832 442 582	51
52	5468.4516 918 045	6104.6359 417 484	6813.2483 230 819	7602.3551 025 566	52
53	6452.7729 963 293	7218.7320 011 175	8073.6992 628 520	9027.7966 842 860	53
54	7614.2721 356 686	8536.1505 913 214	9567.3336 264 796	10720.5085 625 896	54
55	8984.8411 200 889	10093.9980 742 376	11337.2903 473 784	12730.6039 180 751	55
56	10602.1125 217 049	11936.1527 227 859	13434.6890 616 434	15117.5921 527 142	56
57	12510.4927 756 118	14114.5005 946 943	15920.1065 380 474	17952.1406 813 481	57
58	14762.3814 752 219	16690.3969 532 260	18865.3262 475 862	21318.1670 591 009	58
59	17419.6101 407 618	19736.3943 971 898	22355.4116 033 896	25315.3233 826 823	59
60	20555.1399 660 990	23338.2863 746 769	26491.1627 500 167	30061.9465 169 352	60

TABLE 1. FUTURE WORTH OF ONE DOLLAR WITH INTEREST
Payable at beginning of each period

YEARLY Compounding

YEARS	19% Nominal Annual Rate	19¼% Nominal Annual Rate	19½% Nominal Annual Rate	19¾% Nominal Annual Rate	YEARS
1	1.1900 000 000	1.1925 000 000	1.1950 000 000	1.1975 000 000	1
2	1.4161 000 000	1.4220 562 500	1.4280 250 000	1.4340 062 500	2
3	1.6851 590 000	1.6958 020 781	1.7064 898 750	1.7172 224 844	3
4	2.0053 392 100	2.0222 439 782	2.0392 554 006	2.0563 739 250	4
5	2.3863 536 599	2.4115 259 440	2.4369 102 037	2.4625 077 752	5
6	2.8397 608 553	2.8757 446 882	2.9121 076 935	2.9488 530 608	6
7	3.3793 154 178	3.4293 255 406	3.4799 686 937	3.5312 515 404	7
8	4.0213 853 472	4.0894 707 072	4.1585 625 890	4.2286 737 196	8
9	4.7854 485 631	4.8766 938 184	4.9694 822 938	5.0638 367 792	9
10	5.6946 837 901	5.8154 573 784	5.9385 313 411	6.0639 445 431	10
11	6.7766 737 102	6.9349 329 237	7.0965 449 526	7.2615 735 903	11
12	8.0642 417 152	8.2699 075 116	8.4803 712 184	8.6957 343 744	12
13	9.5964 476 411	9.8618 647 075	10.1340 436 060	10.4131 419 134	13
14	11.4197 726 929	11.7602 736 637	12.1101 821 092	12.4697 374 413	14
15	13.5895 295 045	14.0241 263 440	14.4716 676 205	14.9325 105 859	15
16	16.1715 401 104	16.7237 706 652	17.2936 428 064	17.8816 814 267	16
17	19.2441 327 314	19.9430 965 183	20.6659 031 537	21.4133 135 084	17
18	22.9005 179 503	23.7821 425 980	24.6957 542 687	25.6424 429 264	18
19	27.2516 163 609	28.3602 050 482	29.5114 263 511	30.7068 254 043	19
20	32.4294 234 694	33.8195 445 199	35.2661 544 895	36.7714 234 217	20
21	38.5910 139 286	40.3298 068 400	42.1430 546 150	44.0337 795 474	21
22	45.9233 065 751	48.0932 946 567	50.3609 502 649	52.7304 510 081	22
23	54.6487 348 243	57.3512 538 781	60.1813 355 666	63.1447 150 822	23
24	65.0319 944 410	68.3913 702 497	71.9166 960 021	75.6157 963 109	24
25	77.3880 733 847	81.5567 090 227	85.9404 517 225	90.5499 160 823	25
26	92.0918 073 278	97.2563 755 096	102.6988 398 083	108.4335 245 085	26
27	109.5892 507 201	115.9782 277 952	122.7251 135 710	129.8491 455 990	27
28	130.4112 083 569	138.3040 366 458	146.6565 107 173	155.4943 518 548	28
29	155.1893 379 448	164.9275 637 001	175.2545 303 072	186.2044 863 461	29
30	184.6753 121 543	196.6761 197 124	209.4291 637 171	222.9798 723 994	30
31	219.7636 214 636	234.5362 727 570	250.2678 506 419	267.0183 971 983	31
32	261.5187 095 417	279.6845 052 628	299.0700 815 171	319.7545 306 450	32
33	311.2072 643 546	333.5237 725 259	357.3887 474 129	382.9060 504 473	33
34	370.3366 445 819	397.7270 987 371	427.0795 531 584	458.5299 954 107	34
35	440.7006 070 525	474.2895 652 440	510.3600 660 243	549.0896 695 043	35
36	524.4337 223 925	565.5903 065 534	609.8802 788 990	657.5348 792 314	36
37	624.0761 296 470	674.4664 405 650	728.8069 332 843	787.3980 178 796	37
38	742.6505 942 800	804.3012 303 737	870.9242 852 748	942.9091 264 108	38
39	883.7542 071 932	959.1292 172 207	1040.7545 209 033	1129.1336 788 770	39
40	1051.6675 065 599	1143.7615 915 357	1243.7016 524 795	1352.1375 804 552	40
41	1251.4843 328 063	1363.9356 979 063	1486.2234 747 130	1619.1847 525 951	41
42	1489.2663 560 395	1626.4933 197 532	1776.0370 522 820	1938.9737 412 326	42
43	1772.2269 636 869	1939.5932 838 057	2122.3642 774 770	2321.9210 551 260	43
44	2108.9500 867 875	2312.9649 909 383	2536.2253 115 851	2780.5004 635 134	44
45	2509.6506 032 771	2758.2107 516 940	3030.7892 473 441	3329.6493 050 573	45
46	2986.4842 178 997	3289.1663 213 951	3621.7931 505 762	3987.2550 428 061	46
47	3553.9162 193 007	3922.3308 382 636	4328.0428 149 386	4774.7379 137 603	47
48	4229.1603 009 678	4677.3795 246 294	5172.0111 638 516	5717.7486 517 280	48
49	5032.7007 581 517	5577.7750 831 205	6180.5533 408 027	6847.0040 104 443	49
50	5988.9139 022 005	6651.4967 866 212	7385.7612 422 592	8199.2873 025 070	50
51	7126.8075 436 186	7931.9099 180 458	8825.9846 844 998	9818.6465 447 521	51
52	8480.9009 769 062	9458.8025 772 696	10547.0516 979 773	11757.8292 373 407	52
53	10092.2721 625 183	11279.6220 733 940	12603.7267 790 828	14080.0005 117 155	53
54	12009.8038 733 968	13450.9493 225 224	15061.4535 010 040	16860.8006 127 793	54
55	14291.6666 093 422	16040.2570 671 079	17998.4369 336 997	20190.8087 338 032	55
56	17007.0832 651 172	19128.0065 525 262	21508.1321 357 712	24178.4934 587 293	56
57	20238.4290 854 895	22810.1478 138 875	25702.2179 022 466	28953.7459 168 284	57
58	24083.7306 117 325	27201.1012 680 609	30714.1503 931 847	34672.1107 354 020	58
59	28659.6394 279 617	32437.3132 621 626	36703.4097 198 557	41519.8526 056 439	59
60	34104.9709 192 744	38681.4960 651 289	43860.5746 152 275	49720.0234 952 585	60

YEARLY
Compounding

TABLE 1. FUTURE WORTH OF ONE DOLLAR WITH INTEREST
Payable at beginning of each period

YEARS	20% Nominal Annual Rate	20¼% Nominal Annual Rate	20½% Nominal Annual Rate	20¾% Nominal Annual Rate	YEARS
1	1.2000 000 000	1.2025 000 000	1.2050 000 000	1.2075 000 000	1
2	1.4400 000 000	1.4460 062 500	1.4520 250 000	1.4580 562 500	2
3	1.7280 000 000	1.7388 225 156	1.7496 901 250	1.7606 029 219	3
4	2.0736 000 000	2.0909 340 750	2.1083 766 006	2.1259 280 282	4
5	2.4883 200 000	2.5143 482 252	2.5405 938 038	2.5670 580 940	5
6	2.9859 840 000	3.0235 037 408	3.0614 155 335	3.0997 226 485	6
7	3.5831 808 000	3.6357 632 484	3.6890 057 179	3.7429 150 981	7
8	4.2998 169 600	4.3720 053 062	4.4452 518 901	4.5195 699 809	8
9	5.1597 803 520	5.2573 363 807	5.3565 285 275	5.4573 807 520	9
10	6.1917 364 224	6.3219 469 977	6.4546 168 757	6.5897 872 580	10
11	7.4300 837 069	7.6021 412 648	7.7778 133 352	7.9571 681 141	11
12	8.9161 004 483	9.1415 748 709	9.3722 650 689	9.6082 804 977	12
13	10.6993 205 379	10.9927 437 823	11.2935 794 080	11.6019 987 010	13
14	12.8391 846 455	13.2187 743 982	13.6087 631 867	14.0094 134 314	14
15	15.4070 215 746	15.8955 762 138	16.3985 596 399	16.9163 667 185	15
16	18.4884 258 895	19.1144 303 971	19.7602 643 661	20.4265 128 126	16
17	22.1861 110 674	22.9851 025 525	23.8111 185 612	24.6650 142 212	17
18	26.6233 332 809	27.6395 858 194	28.6923 978 662	29.7830 046 721	18
19	31.9479 999 371	33.2366 019 478	34.5743 394 288	35.9629 781 415	19
20	38.3375 999 245	39.9670 138 422	41.6620 790 117	43.4252 961 059	20
21	46.0051 199 094	48.0603 341 453	50.2028 052 091	52.4360 450 478	21
22	55.2061 438 912	57.7925 518 097	60.4943 802 769	63.3165 243 953	22
23	66.2473 726 695	69.4955 435 512	72.8957 282 337	76.4547 032 073	23
24	79.4968 472 034	83.5683 911 203	87.8393 525 216	92.3190 541 228	24
25	95.3962 166 441	100.4909 903 221	105.8464 197 885	111.4752 578 533	25
26	114.4754 599 729	120.8404 158 624	127.5449 358 452	134.6063 738 578	26
27	137.3705 519 675	145.3106 000 745	153.6916 476 934	162.5371 964 333	27
28	164.8446 623 610	174.7359 965 896	185.1984 354 706	196.2636 646 932	28
29	197.8135 948 331	210.1200 358 990	223.1641 147 420	236.9883 751 171	29
30	237.3763 137 998	252.6693 431 685	268.9127 582 642	286.1634 629 538	30
31	284.8515 765 597	303.8348 851 601	324.0398 737 083	345.5423 815 168	31
32	341.8218 918 717	365.3614 494 051	390.4680 478 185	417.2424 256 815	32
33	410.1862 702 460	439.3471 429 096	470.5139 976 213	503.8202 290 104	33
34	492.2235 242 952	528.3149 393 488	566.9693 671 337	608.3629 265 301	34
35	590.6682 291 542	635.2987 145 669	683.1980 873 961	734.5982 337 851	35
36	708.8018 749 851	763.9467 042 667	823.2536 953 123	887.0273 672 955	36
37	850.5622 499 821	918.6459 118 807	992.0207 028 513	1071.0855 460 093	37
38	1020.6746 999 785	1104.6717 090 366	1195.3849 469 358	1293.3357 968 062	38
39	1224.8096 399 742	1328.3677 301 165	1440.4388 610 577	1561.7029 746 435	39
40	1469.7715 679 691	1597.3621 954 650	1735.7288 275 745	1885.7563 418 820	40
41	1763.7258 815 629	1920.8280 400 467	2091.5532 372 272	2277.0507 828 225	41
42	2116.4710 578 755	2309.7957 181 562	2520.3216 508 588	2749.5388 202 582	42
43	2539.7652 694 506	2777.5293 510 828	3036.9875 892 849	3320.0681 254 617	43
44	3047.7183 233 407	3339.9790 446 771	3659.5700 450 883	4008.9822 614 951	44
45	3657.2619 880 088	4016.3248 012 242	4409.7819 043 314	4840.8460 807 553	45
46	4388.7143 856 106	4829.6305 734 721	5313.7871 947 193	5845.3216 425 120	46
47	5266.4572 627 327	5807.6307 646 002	6403.1135 696 368	7058.2258 833 332	47
48	6319.7487 152 793	6983.6759 944 317	7715.7518 514 123	8522.8077 541 249	48
49	7583.6984 583 351	8397.8703 833 041	9297.4809 809 519	10291.2903 631 058	49
50	9100.4381 500 021	10098.4391 359 232	11203.4645 820 470	12426.7331 134 502	50
51	10920.5257 800 026	12143.3730 609 477	13500.1748 213 666	15005.2802 344 912	51
52	13104.6309 360 031	14602.4061 057 896	16267.7106 597 468	18118.8758 831 481	52
53	15725.5571 232 037	17559.3933 422 120	19602.5913 449 949	21878.5426 289 013	53
54	18870.6685 478 445	21115.1704 940 099	23621.1225 707 188	26418.3402 243 983	54
55	22644.8022 574 133	25390.9925 190 469	28463.4526 977 162	31900.1458 209 610	55
56	27173.7627 088 960	30532.6685 041 539	34298.4605 007 480	38519.4260 788 104	56
57	32608.5152 506 752	36715.5338 762 450	41329.6449 034 013	46512.2069 901 636	57
58	39130.2183 008 103	44150.4294 861 847	49802.2221 085 986	56163.4899 406 225	58
59	46956.2619 609 723	53090.8914 571 371	60011.6776 408 613	67817.4141 033 017	59
60	56347.5143 531 668	63841.7969 772 073	72314.0715 572 378	81889.5275 297 368	60

TABLE 1. FUTURE WORTH OF ONE DOLLAR WITH INTEREST
Payable at beginning of each period

YEARLY Compounding

YEARS	21% Nominal Annual Rate	21¼% Nominal Annual Rate	21½% Nominal Annual Rate	21¾% Nominal Annual Rate	YEARS
1	1.2100 000 000	1.2125 000 000	1.2150 000 000	1.2175 000 000	1
2	1.4641 000 000	1.4701 562 500	1.4762 250 000	1.4823 062 500	2
3	1.7715 610 000	1.7825 644 531	1.7936 133 750	1.8047 078 594	3
4	2.1435 888 100	2.1613 593 994	2.1792 402 506	2.1972 318 188	4
5	2.5937 424 601	2.6206 482 718	2.6477 769 045	2.6751 297 394	5
6	3.1384 283 767	3.1775 360 295	3.2170 489 390	3.2569 704 577	6
7	3.7974 983 358	3.8527 624 358	3.9087 144 609	3.9653 615 322	7
8	4.5949 729 864	4.6714 744 534	4.7490 880 699	4.8278 276 655	8
9	5.5599 173 135	5.6641 627 748	5.7701 420 050	5.8778 801 827	9
10	6.7274 999 493	6.8677 973 644	7.0107 225 361	7.1563 191 225	10
11	8.1402 749 387	8.3272 043 044	8.5180 278 813	8.7128 185 316	11
12	9.8497 326 758	10.0967 352 191	10.3494 038 758	10.6078 565 623	12
13	11.9181 765 377	12.2422 914 531	12.5745 257 091	12.9150 653 646	13
14	14.4209 936 106	14.8437 783 869	15.2780 487 365	15.7240 920 813	14
15	17.4494 022 689	17.9980 812 941	18.5628 292 149	19.1440 821 090	15
16	21.1137 767 454	21.8226 735 691	22.5538 374 961	23.3079 199 678	16
17	25.5476 698 619	26.4599 917 025	27.4029 125 577	28.3773 925 607	17
18	30.9126 805 329	32.0827 399 393	33.2945 387 577	34.5494 754 427	18
19	37.4043 434 448	38.9003 221 764	40.4528 645 906	42.0639 863 515	19
20	45.2592 555 682	47.1666 406 389	49.1502 304 775	51.2129 033 829	20
21	54.7636 992 375	57.1895 517 747	59.7175 300 302	62.3517 098 687	21
22	66.2640 760 774	69.3423 315 268	72.5567 989 867	75.9132 067 652	22
23	80.1795 320 536	84.0775 769 763	88.1565 107 688	92.4243 292 366	23
24	97.0172 337 849	101.9440 620 837	107.1101 605 841	112.5266 208 456	24
25	117.3908 528 797	123.6071 752 765	130.1388 451 097	137.0011 608 795	25
26	142.0429 319 844	149.8737 000 228	158.1186 968 083	166.7989 133 708	26
27	171.8719 477 012	181.7218 612 776	192.1142 166 221	203.0776 770 289	27
28	207.9650 567 184	220.3377 567 991	233.4187 731 958	247.2470 717 827	28
29	251.6377 186 293	267.1595 301 189	283.6038 094 329	301.0233 098 955	29
30	304.4816 395 414	323.9309 302 692	344.5786 284 610	366.4958 797 977	30
31	368.4227 838 451	392.7662 529 514	418.6630 335 801	446.2087 336 537	31
32	445.7915 684 526	476.2290 817 035	508.6755 857 998	543.2591 332 234	32
33	539.4077 978 276	577.4277 615 655	618.0408 367 468	661.4179 946 995	33
34	652.6834 353 714	700.1311 608 982	750.9196 166 474	805.2764 085 467	34
35	789.7469 567 994	848.9090 325 891	912.3673 342 265	980.4240 274 056	35
36	955.5938 177 273	1029.3022 020 142	1108.5263 110 852	1193.6662 533 663	36
37	1156.2685 194 501	1248.0289 199 423	1346.8594 679 686	1453.2886 634 735	37
38	1399.0849 085 346	1513.2350 654 300	1636.4342 535 818	1769.3789 477 789	38
39	1692.8927 393 268	1834.7975 168 339	1988.2676 181 019	2154.2188 689 209	39
40	2048.4002 145 855	2224.6919 891 611	2415.7451 559 938	2622.7614 729 111	40
41	2478.5642 596 484	2697.4390 368 578	2935.1303 645 325	3193.2120 932 693	41
42	2999.0627 541 746	3270.6448 321 901	3566.1833 929 070	3887.7357 235 554	42
43	3628.8659 325 512	3965.6568 590 305	4332.9128 223 820	4733.3182 434 287	43
44	4390.9277 783 870	4808.3589 415 744	5264.4890 791 941	5762.8149 613 744	44
45	5313.0226 118 483	5830.1352 166 590	6396.3542 312 208	7016.2272 154 734	45
46	6428.7573 603 364	7069.0389 501 991	7771.5703 909 333	8542.2566 348 388	46
47	7778.7964 060 071	8571.2097 271 164	9442.4580 249 840	10400.1974 529 162	47
48	9412.3436 512 685	10392.5917 941 286	11472.5865 003 555	12662.2403 989 255	48
49	11388.9358 180 349	12601.0175 503 809	13939.1925 979 319	15416.2776 856 918	49
50	13780.6123 398 223	15278.7337 798 368	16936.1190 064 873	18769.3180 823 298	50
51	16674.5409 311 849	18525.4647 080 522	20577.3845 928 821	22851.6447 652 365	51
52	20176.1945 267 338	22462.1259 585 133	25001.5222 803 517	27821.8775 016 755	52
53	24413.1953 773 479	27235.3277 246 973	30376.8495 706 273	33873.1358 582 899	53
54	29539.9664 065 909	33022.8348 661 955	36907.8722 283 122	41240.5429 074 680	54
55	35743.3593 519 750	40040.1872 752 621	44843.0647 573 994	50210.3609 898 422	55
56	43249.4648 158 898	48548.7270 712 553	54484.3236 802 402	61131.1145 051 329	56
57	52331.8524 272 266	58865.3315 738 970	66198.4532 714 919	74427.1319 099 993	57
58	63321.5414 369 442	71374.2145 333 501	80431.1207 248 626	90615.0331 004 242	58
59	76619.0651 387 025	86541.2351 216 870	97723.8116 807 081	110323.8027 997 665	59
60	92709.0688 178 300	104931.2475 850 455	118734.4311 920 603	134319.2299 087 157	60

YEARLY
Compounding

TABLE 1. FUTURE WORTH OF ONE DOLLAR WITH INTEREST
Payable at beginning of each period

YEARS	22% Nominal Annual Rate	22¼% Nominal Annual Rate	22½% Nominal Annual Rate	22¾% Nominal Annual Rate	YEARS
1	1.2200 000 000	1.2225 000 000	1.2250 000 000	1.2275 000 000	1
2	1.4884 000 000	1.4945 062 500	1.5006 250 000	1.5067 562 500	2
3	1.8158 480 000	1.8270 338 906	1.8382 656 250	1.8495 432 969	3
4	2.2153 345 600	2.2335 489 313	2.2518 753 906	2.2703 143 969	4
5	2.7027 081 632	2.7305 135 685	2.7585 473 535	2.7868 109 222	5
6	3.2973 039 591	3.3380 528 375	3.3792 205 081	3.4208 104 070	6
7	4.0227 108 301	4.0807 695 938	4.1395 451 224	4.1990 447 746	7
8	4.9077 072 127	4.9887 408 285	5.0709 427 749	5.1543 274 608	8
9	5.9874 027 995	6.0987 356 628	6.2119 048 993	6.3269 369 582	9
10	7.3046 314 154	7.4557 043 478	7.6095 835 016	7.7663 151 162	10
11	8.9116 503 268	9.1145 985 651	9.3217 397 894	9.5331 518 051	11
12	10.8722 133 987	11.1425 967 459	11.4191 312 421	11.7019 438 407	12
13	13.2641 003 464	13.6218 245 219	13.9884 357 715	14.3641 360 645	13
14	16.1822 024 227	16.6526 804 780	17.1358 338 201	17.6319 770 192	14
15	19.7422 869 556	20.3579 018 843	20.9913 964 297	21.6432 517 911	15
16	24.0855 900 859	24.8875 350 536	25.7144 606 263	26.5670 915 735	16
17	29.3844 199 048	30.4250 116 030	31.5002 142 673	32.6111 049 065	17
18	35.8489 922 838	37.1945 766 847	38.5877 624 774	40.0301 312 727	18
19	43.7357 705 863	45.4703 699 970	47.2700 090 348	49.1369 861 373	19
20	53.3576 401 153	55.5875 273 213	57.9057 610 676	60.3156 504 835	20
21	65.0963 209 406	67.9557 521 503	70.9345 573 079	74.0374 609 685	21
22	79.4175 115 475	83.0759 070 038	86.8948 327 021	90.8809 833 388	22
23	96.8893 640 880	101.5602 963 121	106.4461 700 601	111.5564 070 484	23
24	118.2050 241 874	124.1574 622 415	130.3965 583 236	136.9354 896 519	24
25	144.2101 295 086	151.7824 975 903	159.7357 839 464	168.0883 135 477	25
26	175.9363 580 005	185.5541 033 041	195.6763 353 344	206.3284 048 798	26
27	214.6423 567 606	226.8398 912 893	239.7035 107 846	253.2681 169 900	27
28	261.8636 752 479	277.3117 671 011	293.6368 007 112	310.8866 136 052	28
29	319.4736 838 025	339.0136 352 811	359.7050 808 712	381.6133 182 004	29
30	389.7578 942 390	414.4441 691 312	440.6387 240 672	468.4303 480 910	30
31	475.5046 309 716	506.6579 967 629	539.7824 369 823	574.9982 522 817	31
32	580.1156 497 853	619.3894 010 426	661.2334 853 034	705.8103 546 758	32
33	707.7410 927 381	757.2035 427 746	810.0110 194 966	866.3822 103 646	33
34	863.4441 331 405	925.6813 310 419	992.2634 988 834	1063.4841 632 225	34
35	1053.4018 424 314	1131.6454 271 988	1215.5227 861 321	1305.4268 103 556	35
36	1285.1502 477 663	1383.4365 347 505	1489.0154 130 119	1602.4114 097 115	36
37	1567.8833 022 749	1691.2511 637 325	1824.0438 809 395	1966.9600 054 209	37
38	1912.8176 287 753	2067.5545 476 630	2234.4537 541 509	2414.4434 066 542	38
39	2333.6375 071 059	2527.5854 345 180	2737.2058 488 349	2963.7292 816 680	39
40	2847.0377 586 692	3089.9731 936 982	3353.0771 648 227	3637.9776 932 475	40
41	3473.3860 655 765	3777.4922 292 961	4107.5195 269 079	4465.6176 184 613	41
42	4237.5310 000 033	4617.9842 503 145	5031.7114 204 621	5481.5456 266 612	42
43	5169.7878 200 040	5645.4857 460 095	6163.8464 900 661	6728.5972 567 266	43
44	6307.1411 404 049	6901.6063 244 966	7550.7119 503 310	8259.3531 326 319	44
45	7694.7121 912 939	8437.2137 316 971	9249.6221 391 555	10138.3559 703 057	45
46	9387.5488 733 786	10314.4937 869 997	11330.7871 204 654	12444.8319 535 503	46
47	11452.8096 255 219	12609.4686 546 071	13880.2142 225 702	15276.0312 229 830	47
48	13972.4277 431 367	15415.0754 302 572	17003.2624 226 485	18751.3283 262 116	48
49	17046.3618 466 268	18844.9297 134 894	20828.9964 677 444	23017.2555 204 247	49
50	20796.5614 528 847	23037.9265 747 408	25515.5206 729 868	28253.6811 513 213	50
51	25371.8049 725 193	28163.8652 376 206	31256.5128 244 089	34681.3936 132 469	51
52	30953.6020 664 736	34430.3252 529 912	38289.2282 099 009	42571.4106 602 606	52
53	37763.3945 210 978	42091.0726 217 817	46904.3045 571 286	52256.4065 854 699	53
54	46071.3413 157 393	51456.3362 801 281	57457.7730 824 825	64144.7390 836 643	54
55	56207.0364 052 020	62905.3711 024 566	70385.7720 260 411	78737.6672 251 979	55
56	68572.5844 143 464	76901.8161 727 532	86222.5707 319 003	96650.4865 189 305	56
57	83658.5529 855 026	94012.4702 711 908	105622.6491 465 779	118638.4722 019 871	57
58	102063.4346 423 132	114930.2449 065 308	129387.7452 045 579	145628.7246 279 392	58
59	124517.3902 636 220	140502.2243 982 339	158499.9878 755 834	178759.2594 807 954	59
60	151911.2161 216 189	171763.9693 268 409	194162.4851 475 897	219426.9910 126 763	60

TABLE 1. FUTURE WORTH OF ONE DOLLAR WITH INTEREST
Payable at beginning of each period

YEARLY Compounding

YEARS	23% Nominal Annual Rate	24% Nominal Annual Rate	25% Nominal Annual Rate	26% Nominal Annual Rate	YEARS
1	1.2300 000 000	1.2400 000 000	1.2500 000 000	1.2600 000 000	1
2	1.5129 000 000	1.5376 000 000	1.5625 000 000	1.5876 000 000	2
3	1.8608 670 000	1.9066 240 000	1.9531 250 000	2.0003 760 000	3
4	2.2888 664 100	2.3642 137 600	2.4414 062 500	2.5204 737 600	4
5	2.8153 056 843	2.9316 250 624	3.0517 578 125	3.1757 969 376	5
6	3.4628 259 917	3.6352 150 774	3.8146 972 656	4.0015 041 414	6
7	4.2592 759 698	4.5076 666 959	4.7683 715 820	5.0418 952 181	7
8	5.2389 094 428	5.5895 067 030	5.9604 644 775	6.3527 879 748	8
9	6.4438 586 147	6.9309 883 117	7.4505 805 969	8.0045 128 483	9
10	7.9259 460 961	8.5944 255 065	9.3132 257 462	10.0856 861 889	10
11	9.7489 136 981	10.6570 876 280	11.6415 321 827	12.7079 645 980	11
12	11.9911 638 487	13.2147 886 588	14.5519 152 284	16.0120 353 934	12
13	14.7491 315 339	16.3863 379 369	18.1898 940 355	20.1751 645 957	13
14	18.1414 317 867	20.3190 590 417	22.7373 675 443	25.4207 073 906	14
15	22.3139 610 977	25.1956 332 118	28.4217 094 304	32.0300 913 122	15
16	27.4461 721 501	31.2425 851 826	35.5271 367 880	40.3579 150 534	16
17	33.7587 917 447	38.7408 056 264	44.4089 209 850	50.8509 729 673	17
18	41.5233 138 459	48.0385 989 767	55.5111 512 313	64.0722 259 387	18
19	51.0736 760 305	59.5678 627 312	69.3889 390 391	80.7310 046 828	19
20	62.8206 215 175	73.8641 497 866	86.7361 737 988	101.7210 659 004	20
21	77.2693 644 665	91.5915 457 354	108.4202 172 486	128.1685 430 344	21
22	95.0413 182 939	113.5735 167 119	135.5252 715 607	161.4923 642 234	22
23	116.9008 215 014	140.8311 607 228	169.4065 894 509	203.4803 789 215	23
24	143.7880 104 468	174.6306 392 963	211.7582 368 136	256.3852 774 411	24
25	176.8592 528 495	216.5419 927 274	264.6977 960 170	323.0454 495 758	25
26	217.5368 810 049	268.5120 709 819	330.8722 450 212	407.0372 664 654	26
27	267.5703 636 361	332.9549 680 176	413.5903 062 765	512.8669 557 465	27
28	329.1115 472 724	412.8641 603 418	516.9878 828 456	646.2123 642 405	28
29	404.8072 031 450	511.9515 588 239	646.2348 535 571	814.2275 789 431	29
30	497.9128 598 683	634.8199 329 416	807.7935 669 463	1025.9267 494 683	30
31	612.4328 176 381	787.1767 168 476	1009.7419 586 829	1292.6677 043 300	31
32	753.2923 656 948	976.0991 288 910	1262.1774 483 536	1628.7613 074 559	32
33	926.5496 098 046	1210.3629 198 249	1577.7218 104 420	2052.2392 473 944	33
34	1139.6560 200 597	1500.8500 205 828	1972.1522 630 525	2585.8214 517 169	34
35	1401.7769 046 734	1861.0540 255 227	2465.1903 288 157	3258.1350 291 633	35
36	1724.1855 927 483	2307.7069 916 481	3081.4879 110 196	4105.2501 367 458	36
37	2120.7482 790 804	2861.5566 696 437	3851.8598 887 745	5172.6151 722 997	37
38	2608.5203 832 689	3548.3302 703 582	4814.8248 609 681	6517.4951 170 976	38
39	3208.4800 714 208	4399.9295 352 441	6018.5310 762 101	8212.0438 475 429	39
40	3946.4304 878 475	5455.9126 237 027	7523.1638 452 626	10347.1752 479 041	40
41	4854.1095 000 525	6765.3316 533 914	9403.9548 065 783	13037.4408 123 592	41
42	5970.5546 850 645	8389.0112 502 053	11754.9435 082 229	16427.1754 235 726	42
43	7343.7822 626 294	10402.3739 502 546	14693.6793 852 786	20698.2410 337 014	43
44	9032.8521 830 341	12898.9436 983 157	18367.0992 315 982	26079.7837 024 638	44
45	11110.4081 851 320	15994.6901 859 115	22958.8740 394 978	32860.5274 651 044	45
46	13665.8020 677 123	19833.4158 305 302	28698.5925 493 723	41404.2646 060 315	46
47	16808.9365 432 861	24593.4356 298 575	35873.2406 867 153	52169.3734 035 997	47
48	20674.9919 482 419	30495.8601 810 233	44841.5508 583 941	65733.4104 885 357	48
49	25430.2400 963 376	37814.8666 244 689	56051.9385 729 927	82824.0972 155 549	49
50	31279.1953 184 952	46890.4346 143 414	70064.9232 162 408	104358.3624 915 992	50
51	38473.4102 417 491	58144.1389 217 833	87581.1540 203 011	131491.5367 394 150	51
52	47322.2945 973 515	72098.7322 630 113	109476.4425 253 763	165679.3362 916 629	52
53	58206.4223 547 423	89402.4280 061 340	136845.5531 567 204	208755.9637 274 953	53
54	71593.8994 963 330	110859.0107 276 062	171056.9414 459 005	263032.5142 966 441	54
55	88060.4963 804 896	137465.1733 022 317	213821.1768 073 756	331420.9680 137 715	55
56	108314.4105 480 022	170456.8148 947 673	267276.4710 092 195	417590.4196 973 521	56
57	133226.7249 740 427	211366.4504 695 114	334095.5887 615 244	526163.9288 186 637	57
58	163868.8717 180 725	262094.3985 821 941	417619.4859 519 055	662966.5503 115 162	58
59	201558.7122 132 292	324997.0542 419 207	522024.3574 398 819	835337.8533 925 104	59
60	247917.2160 222 720	402996.3472 599 817	652530.4467 998 524	1052525.6952 745 631	60

TABLE 1. FUTURE WORTH OF ONE DOLLAR WITH INTEREST
Payable at beginning of each period

YEARS	27% Nominal Annual Rate	28% Nominal Annual Rate	29% Nominal Annual Rate	30% Nominal Annual Rate	YEARS
1	1.2700 000 000	1.2800 000 000	1.2900 000 000	1.3000 000 000	1
2	1.6129 000 000	1.6384 000 000	1.6641 000 000	1.6900 000 000	2
3	2.0483 830 000	2.0971 520 000	2.1466 890 000	2.1970 000 000	3
4	2.6014 464 100	2.6843 545 600	2.7692 288 100	2.8561 000 000	4
5	3.3038 369 407	3.4359 738 368	3.5723 051 649	3.7129 300 000	5
6	4.1958 729 147	4.3980 465 111	4.6082 736 627	4.8268 090 000	6
7	5.3287 586 017	5.6294 995 342	5.9446 730 249	6.2748 517 000	7
8	6.7675 234 241	7.2057 594 038	7.6686 282 021	8.1573 072 100	8
9	8.5947 547 486	9.2233 720 369	9.8925 303 808	10.6044 993 730	9
10	10.9153 385 307	11.8059 162 072	12.7613 641 912	13.7858 491 849	10
11	13.8624 799 340	15.1115 727 452	16.4621 598 066	17.9216 039 404	11
12	17.6053 495 162	19.3428 131 138	21.2361 861 505	23.2980 851 225	12
13	22.3587 938 856	24.7588 007 857	27.3946 801 342	30.2875 106 592	13
14	28.3956 682 347	31.6912 650 057	35.3391 373 731	39.3737 638 570	14
15	36.0624 986 581	40.5648 192 073	45.5874 872 113	51.1858 930 141	15
16	45.7993 732 958	51.9229 685 853	58.8078 585 026	66.5416 609 183	16
17	58.1652 040 856	66.4613 997 892	75.8621 374 683	86.5041 591 938	17
18	73.8698 091 887	85.0705 917 302	97.8621 573 341	112.4554 069 520	18
19	93.8146 576 697	108.8903 574 147	126.2421 829 610	146.1920 290 375	19
20	119.1446 152 405	139.3796 574 908	162.8524 160 197	190.0496 377 488	20
21	151.3136 613 555	178.4059 615 882	210.0796 166 654	247.0645 290 735	21
22	192.1683 499 214	228.3596 308 330	271.0027 054 984	321.1838 877 955	22
23	244.0538 044 002	292.3003 274 662	349.5934 900 929	417.5390 541 341	23
24	309.9483 315 883	374.1444 191 567	450.9756 022 199	542.8007 703 744	24
25	393.6343 811 171	478.9048 565 206	581.7585 268 636	705.6410 014 867	25
26	499.9156 640 188	612.9982 163 464	750.4684 996 541	917.3333 019 327	26
27	634.8928 933 038	784.6377 169 233	968.1043 645 538	1192.5332 925 125	27
28	806.3139 744 959	1004.3362 776 619	1248.8546 302 744	1550.2932 802 662	28
29	1024.0187 476 097	1285.5504 354 072	1611.0224 730 540	2015.3812 643 461	29
30	1300.5038 094 644	1645.5045 573 212	2078.2189 902 396	2619.9956 436 499	30
31	1651.6398 380 198	2106.2458 333 711	2680.9024 974 091	3405.9943 367 449	31
32	2097.5825 942 851	2695.9946 667 151	3458.3642 216 577	4427.7926 377 684	32
33	2663.9298 947 421	3450.8731 733 953	4461.2898 459 385	5756.1304 290 989	33
34	3383.1909 663 224	4417.1176 619 460	5755.0639 012 606	7482.9695 578 286	34
35	4296.6525 272 295	5653.9106 072 908	7424.0324 326 262	9727.8604 251 772	35
36	5456.7487 095 814	7237.0055 773 323	9577.0018 380 878	12646.2185 527 303	36
37	6930.0708 611 684	9263.3671 389 853	12354.3323 711 333	16440.0841 185 494	37
38	8801.1899 936 839	11857.1099 379 012	15937.0887 587 619	21372.1093 541 143	38
39	11177.5112 919 785	15177.1007 205 135	20558.8444 988 029	27783.7421 603 486	39
40	14195.4393 408 127	19426.6889 222 573	26520.9094 034 557	36118.8648 084 531	40
41	18028.2079 628 321	24866.1618 204 893	34211.9731 304 579	46954.5242 509 891	41
42	22895.8241 127 968	31828.6871 302 263	44133.4453 382 907	61040.8815 262 858	42
43	29077.6966 232 520	40740.7195 266 897	56932.1444 863 949	79353.1459 841 716	43
44	36928.6747 115 300	52148.1209 941 628	73442.4663 874 495	103159.0897 794 230	44
45	46899.4168 836 431	66749.5948 725 284	94740.7816 398 098	134106.8167 132 499	45
46	59562.2594 422 267	85439.4814 368 364	122215.6083 153 547	174338.8617 272 249	46
47	75644.0694 916 279	109362.5362 391 506	157658.1347 268 075	226640.5202 453 924	47
48	96067.9682 543 675	139984.0463 861 128	203378.9937 975 817	294632.6763 190 101	48
49	122006.3196 830 467	179179.5793 742 243	262358.9019 988 804	383022.4792 147 131	49
50	154948.0259 974 693	229349.8615 990 071	338442.9835 785 558	497929.2229 791 270	50
51	196783.9930 167 860	293567.8228 467 291	436591.4488 163 369	647307.9898 728 651	51
52	249915.6711 313 182	375766.8132 438 133	563202.9689 730 746	841500.3868 347 246	52
53	317392.9023 367 741	480981.5209 520 810	726531.8299 752 663	1093950.5028 851 420	53
54	403088.9859 677 032	615656.3468 186 637	937226.0606 680 935	1422135.6537 506 846	54
55	511923.0121 789 830	788040.1239 278 895	1209021.6182 618 406	1848776.3498 758 900	55
56	650142.2254 673 084	1008691.3586 276 986	1559637.8875 577 744	2403409.2548 386 570	56
57	825680.6263 434 817	1291124.9390 434 542	2011932.8749 495 289	3124432.0312 902 541	57
58	1048614.3954 562 218	1652639.9219 756 213	2595393.4086 848 923	4061761.6406 773 304	58
59	1331740.2822 294 016	2115379.1001 287 953	3348057.4972 035 110	5280290.1328 805 295	59
60	1691310.1584 313 401	2707685.2481 648 580	4318994.1713 925 293	6864377.1727 446 883	60

TABLE 2. FUTURE WORTH OF ONE DOLLAR PER PERIOD WITH INTEREST
Payable at end of each period

YEARLY Compounding

YEARS	5% Nominal Annual Rate	5¼% Nominal Annual Rate	5½% Nominal Annual Rate	5¾% Nominal Annual Rate	YEARS
1	1.0000 000 000	1.0000 000 000	1.0000 000 000	1.0000 000 000	1
2	2.0500 000 000	2.0525 000 000	2.0550 000 000	2.0575 000 000	2
3	3.1525 000 000	3.1602 562 500	3.1680 250 000	3.1758 062 500	3
4	4.3101 250 000	4.3261 697 031	4.3422 663 750	4.3584 151 094	4
5	5.5256 312 500	5.5532 936 125	5.5810 910 256	5.6090 239 782	5
6	6.8019 128 125	6.8448 415 272	6.8880 510 320	6.9315 428 569	6
7	8.1420 084 531	8.2041 957 074	8.2668 938 388	8.3301 065 712	7
8	9.5491 088 758	9.6349 159 820	9.7215 729 999	9.8090 876 990	8
9	11.0265 643 196	11.1407 490 711	11.2562 595 149	11.3731 102 417	9
10	12.5778 925 355	12.7256 383 973	12.8753 537 882	13.0270 640 806	10
11	14.2067 871 623	14.3937 344 132	14.5834 982 466	14.7761 202 653	11
12	15.9171 265 204	16.1494 054 698	16.3855 906 502	16.6257 471 805	12
13	17.7129 828 465	17.9972 492 570	18.2867 981 359	18.5817 276 434	13
14	19.5986 319 888	19.9421 048 430	20.2925 720 334	20.6501 769 829	14
15	21.5785 635 882	21.9890 653 473	22.4086 634 952	22.8375 621 594	15
16	23.6574 917 676	24.1434 912 780	24.6411 399 875	25.1507 219 836	16
17	25.8403 663 560	26.4110 245 701	26.9964 026 868	27.5968 884 976	17
18	28.1323 846 738	28.7976 033 600	29.4812 048 346	30.1837 095 862	18
19	30.5390 039 075	31.3094 775 364	32.1026 711 005	32.9192 728 874	19
20	33.0659 541 029	33.9532 251 071	34.8683 180 110	35.8121 310 785	20
21	35.7192 518 080	36.7357 694 252	37.7860 755 016	38.8713 286 155	21
22	38.5052 143 984	39.6643 973 200	40.8643 096 542	42.1064 300 109	22
23	41.4304 751 184	42.7467 781 793	44.1118 466 852	45.5275 497 365	23
24	44.5019 988 743	45.9909 840 337	47.5379 982 528	49.1453 838 463	24
25	47.7270 988 180	49.4055 106 955	51.1525 881 567	52.9712 434 175	25
26	51.1134 537 589	52.9993 000 070	54.9659 805 054	57.0170 899 140	26
27	54.6691 264 468	56.7817 632 574	58.9891 094 332	61.2955 725 841	27
28	58.4025 827 692	60.7628 058 284	63.2335 104 520	65.8200 680 076	28
29	62.3227 119 076	64.9528 531 344	67.7113 535 268	70.6047 219 181	29
30	66.4388 475 030	69.3628 779 240	72.4354 779 708	75.6644 934 284	30
31	70.7607 898 782	74.0044 290 150	77.4194 292 592	81.0152 018 005	31
32	75.2988 293 721	78.8896 615 383	82.6774 978 685	86.6735 759 040	32
33	80.0637 708 407	84.0313 687 690	88.2247 602 512	92.6573 065 185	33
34	85.0669 593 827	89.4430 156 294	94.0771 220 651	98.9851 016 433	34
35	90.3203 073 518	95.1387 739 499	100.2513 637 786	105.6767 449 878	35
36	95.8363 227 194	101.1335 595 823	106.7651 887 865	112.7531 578 246	36
37	101.6281 388 554	107.4430 714 604	113.6372 741 697	120.2364 643 995	37
38	107.7095 457 982	114.0838 327 120	120.8873 242 490	128.1500 611 025	38
39	114.0950 230 881	121.0732 339 294	128.5361 270 827	136.5186 896 159	39
40	120.7997 742 425	128.4295 787 107	136.6056 140 723	145.3685 142 688	40
41	127.8397 629 546	136.1721 315 930	145.1189 228 463	154.7272 038 393	41
42	135.2317 511 023	144.3211 685 017	154.1004 636 028	164.6240 180 600	42
43	142.9933 386 575	152.8980 298 480	163.5759 891 010	175.0898 990 985	43
44	151.1430 055 903	161.9251 764 150	173.5726 685 015	186.1575 682 966	44
45	159.7001 558 699	171.4262 481 768	184.1191 652 691	197.8616 284 737	45
46	168.6851 636 633	181.4261 262 061	195.2457 193 589	210.2386 721 109	46
47	178.1194 218 465	191.9509 978 319	206.9842 339 237	223.3273 957 573	47
48	188.0253 929 388	203.0284 252 181	219.3683 667 895	237.1687 210 134	48
49	198.4266 625 858	214.6874 175 421	232.4336 269 629	251.8059 224 716	49
50	209.3479 957 151	226.9585 069 630	246.2174 764 458	267.2847 630 138	50
51	220.8153 955 008	239.8738 285 786	260.7594 376 503	283.6536 368 870	51
52	232.8561 652 759	253.4672 045 789	276.1012 067 211	300.9637 210 081	52
53	245.4989 735 397	267.7742 328 193	292.2867 730 908	319.2691 349 660	53
54	258.7739 222 166	282.8323 800 424	309.3625 456 108	338.6271 102 266	54
55	272.7126 183 275	298.6810 799 946	327.3774 856 194	359.0981 690 646	55
56	287.3482 492 439	315.3618 366 943	346.3832 473 284	380.7463 137 858	56
57	302.7156 617 060	332.9183 331 207	366.4343 259 315	403.6392 268 285	57
58	318.8514 447 913	351.3965 456 096	387.5882 138 577	427.8484 823 711	58
59	335.7940 170 309	370.8448 642 541	409.9055 656 199	453.4497 701 075	59
60	353.5837 178 825	391.3142 196 274	433.4503 717 290	480.5231 318 886	60

TABLE 2. FUTURE WORTH OF ONE DOLLAR PER PERIOD WITH INTEREST
Payable at end of each period

YEARS	6% Nominal Annual Rate	6¼% Nominal Annual Rate	6½% Nominal Annual Rate	6¾% Nominal Annual Rate	YEARS
1	1.0000 000 000	1.0000 000 000	1.0000 000 000	1.0000 000 000	1
2	2.0600 000 000	2.0625 000 000	2.0650 000 000	2.0675 000 000	2
3	3.1836 000 000	3.1914 062 500	3.1992 250 000	3.2070 562 500	3
4	4.3746 160 000	4.3908 691 406	4.4071 746 250	4.4235 325 469	4
5	5.6370 929 600	5.6652 984 619	5.6936 409 756	5.7221 209 938	5
6	6.9753 185 376	7.0193 796 158	7.0637 276 390	7.1083 641 609	6
7	8.3938 376 499	8.4580 908 418	8.5228 699 356	8.5881 787 417	7
8	9.8974 679 088	9.9867 215 194	10.0768 564 814	10.1678 808 068	8
9	11.4913 159 834	11.6108 916 143	11.7318 521 527	11.8542 127 613	9
10	13.1807 949 424	13.3365 723 402	13.4944 225 426	13.6543 721 226	10
11	14.9716 426 389	15.1701 081 115	15.3715 600 079	15.5760 422 409	11
12	16.8699 411 973	17.1182 398 685	17.3707 114 084	17.6274 250 922	12
13	18.8821 376 691	19.1881 298 603	19.4998 076 499	19.8172 762 859	13
14	21.0150 659 292	21.3873 879 765	21.7672 951 472	22.1549 424 352	14
15	23.2759 698 850	23.7240 997 250	24.1821 693 317	24.6504 010 496	15
16	25.6725 280 781	26.2068 559 579	26.7540 103 383	27.3143 031 204	16
17	28.2128 797 628	28.8447 844 552	29.4930 210 103	30.1580 185 810	17
18	30.9056 525 485	31.6475 834 837	32.4100 673 760	33.1936 848 353	18
19	33.7599 917 015	34.6255 574 514	35.5167 217 554	36.4342 585 617	19
20	36.7855 912 035	37.7896 547 921	38.8253 086 695	39.8935 710 146	20
21	39.9927 266 758	41.1515 082 166	42.3489 537 330	43.5863 870 580	21
22	43.3922 902 763	44.7234 774 802	46.1016 357 257	47.5284 681 845	22
23	46.9958 276 929	48.5186 948 227	50.0982 420 478	51.7366 397 869	23
24	50.8155 773 545	52.5511 132 491	54.3546 277 809	56.2288 629 725	24
25	54.8645 119 957	56.8355 578 272	58.8876 785 867	61.0243 112 232	25
26	59.1563 827 155	61.3877 801 914	63.7153 776 948	66.1434 522 307	26
27	63.7057 656 784	66.2245 164 533	68.8568 772 450	71.6081 352 563	27
28	68.5281 116 191	71.3635 487 317	74.3325 742 659	77.4416 843 861	28
29	73.6397 983 162	76.8237 705 274	80.1641 915 932	83.6689 980 822	29
30	79.0581 862 152	82.6252 561 854	86.3748 640 468	90.3166 554 527	30
31	84.8016 773 881	88.7893 346 969	92.9892 302 098	97.4130 296 958	31
32	90.8897 780 314	95.3386 681 155	100.0335 301 735	104.9884 092 003	32
33	97.3431 647 133	102.2973 348 727	107.5357 096 347	113.0751 268 213	33
34	104.1837 545 961	109.6909 183 023	115.5255 307 610	121.7076 978 817	34
35	111.4347 798 719	117.5466 006 962	124.0346 902 605	130.9229 674 887	35
36	119.1208 666 642	125.8932 632 397	133.0969 451 274	140.7602 677 942	36
37	127.2681 186 640	134.7615 921 921	142.7482 465 607	151.2615 858 703	37
38	135.9042 057 839	144.1841 917 042	153.0268 825 871	162.4717 429 166	38
39	145.0584 581 309	154.1957 036 857	163.9736 299 553	174.4385 855 634	39
40	154.7619 656 188	164.8329 351 660	175.6319 159 024	187.2131 900 890	40
41	165.0476 835 559	176.1349 936 139	188.0479 904 360	200.8500 804 200	41
42	175.9505 445 692	188.1434 307 148	201.2711 098 144	215.4074 608 483	42
43	187.5075 772 434	200.9023 951 344	215.3537 319 523	230.9474 644 556	43
44	199.7580 318 780	214.4587 948 303	230.3517 245 292	247.5364 183 063	44
45	212.7435 137 907	228.8624 695 072	246.3245 866 236	265.2451 265 420	45
46	226.5081 246 181	244.1663 738 514	263.3356 847 541	284.1491 725 836	46
47	241.0986 120 952	260.4267 722 171	281.4525 042 631	304.3292 417 330	47
48	256.5645 288 209	277.7034 454 807	300.7469 170 403	325.8714 655 500	48
49	272.9584 005 502	296.0599 108 233	321.2954 666 479	348.8677 894 746	49
50	290.3359 045 832	315.5636 552 497	343.1796 719 800	373.4163 652 641	50
51	308.7560 588 582	336.2863 837 028	366.4863 506 587	399.6219 699 195	51
52	328.2814 223 897	358.3042 826 843	391.3079 634 515	427.5964 528 890	52
53	348.9783 077 331	381.6983 003 520	417.7429 810 758	457.4592 134 590	53
54	370.9170 061 970	406.5544 441 240	445.8962 748 458	489.3377 103 675	54
55	394.1720 265 689	432.9640 968 818	475.8795 327 107	523.3680 058 173	55
56	418.8223 481 630	461.0243 529 369	507.8117 023 369	559.6953 462 100	56
57	444.9516 890 528	490.8383 749 954	541.8194 629 888	598.4747 820 792	57
58	472.6487 903 959	522.5157 734 327	578.0377 280 831	639.8718 298 695	58
59	502.0077 178 197	556.1730 092 722	616.6101 804 085	684.0631 783 857	59
60	533.1281 808 889	591.9338 223 517	657.6898 421 351	731.2374 429 267	60

TABLE 2. FUTURE WORTH OF ONE DOLLAR PER PERIOD WITH INTEREST

Payable at end of each period

YEARLY Compounding

YEARS	7% Nominal Annual Rate	7¼% Nominal Annual Rate	7½% Nominal Annual Rate	7¾% Nominal Annual Rate	YEARS
1	1.0000 000 000	1.0000 000 000	1.0000 000 000	1.0000 000 000	1
2	2.0700 000 000	2.0725 000 000	2.0750 000 000	2.0775 000 000	2
3	3.2149 000 000	3.2227 562 500	3.2306 250 000	3.2385 062 500	3
4	4.4399 430 000	4.4564 060 781	4.4729 218 750	4.4894 904 844	4
5	5.7507 390 100	5.7794 955 188	5.8083 910 156	5.8374 259 969	5
6	7.1532 907 407	7.1985 089 439	7.2440 203 418	7.2898 265 117	6
7	8.6540 210 925	8.7204 008 423	8.7873 218 674	8.8547 880 663	7
8	10.2598 025 690	10.3526 299 034	10.4463 710 075	10.5410 341 415	8
9	11.9779 887 489	12.1031 955 714	12.2298 488 331	12.3579 642 874	9
10	13.8164 479 613	13.9806 772 503	14.1470 874 955	14.3157 065 197	10
11	15.7835 993 186	15.9942 763 510	16.2081 190 577	16.4251 737 750	11
12	17.8884 512 709	18.1538 613 864	18.4237 279 870	18.6981 247 425	12
13	20.1406 428 598	20.4700 163 369	20.8055 075 860	21.1472 294 101	13
14	22.5504 878 600	22.9540 925 214	23.3659 206 550	23.7861 396 894	14
15	25.1290 220 102	25.6182 642 292	26.1183 647 041	26.6295 655 153	15
16	27.8880 535 509	28.4755 883 858	29.0772 420 569	29.6933 568 427	16
17	30.8402 172 995	31.5400 685 437	32.2580 352 112	32.9945 919 981	17
18	33.9990 325 105	34.8267 235 132	35.6773 878 520	36.5516 728 779	18
19	37.3789 647 862	38.3516 609 679	39.3531 919 410	40.3844 275 259	19
20	40.9954 923 212	42.1321 563 880	43.3046 813 365	44.5142 206 592	20
21	44.8651 767 837	46.1867 377 262	47.5525 324 368	48.9640 727 603	21
22	49.0057 391 586	50.5352 762 113	52.1189 723 695	53.7587 883 992	22
23	53.4361 408 997	55.1990 837 366	57.0278 952 972	58.9250 945 002	23
24	58.1766 707 627	60.2010 173 076	62.3049 874 445	64.4917 893 239	24
25	63.2490 377 160	65.5655 910 623	67.9778 615 029	70.4899 029 965	25
26	68.6764 703 562	71.3190 964 144	74.0762 011 156	76.9528 704 787	26
27	74.4838 232 811	77.4897 309 044	80.6319 161 992	83.9167 179 409	27
28	80.6976 909 108	84.1077 363 950	87.6793 099 142	91.4202 635 813	28
29	87.3465 292 745	91.2055 472 836	95.2552 581 578	99.5053 340 088	29
30	94.4607 863 237	98.8179 494 617	103.3994 025 196	108.2169 973 945	30
31	102.0730 413 664	106.9822 507 977	112.1543 577 086	117.6038 146 926	31
32	110.2181 542 621	115.7384 639 805	121.5659 345 367	127.7181 103 312	32
33	118.9334 250 604	125.1295 026 191	131.6833 796 269	138.6162 638 819	33
34	128.2587 648 146	135.2013 915 589	142.5596 330 990	150.3590 243 328	34
35	138.2368 783 516	146.0034 924 470	154.2516 055 814	163.0118 487 186	35
36	148.9134 598 363	157.5887 456 494	166.8204 760 000	176.6452 669 942	36
37	160.3374 020 248	170.0139 297 090	180.3320 117 000	191.3352 751 863	37
38	172.5610 201 665	183.3399 396 129	194.8569 125 775	207.1637 590 132	38
39	185.6402 915 782	197.6320 852 348	210.4711 810 208	224.2189 503 368	39
40	199.6351 119 887	212.9604 114 143	227.2565 195 974	242.5959 189 879	40
41	214.6095 698 279	229.4000 412 419	245.3007 585 672	262.3971 027 094	41
42	230.6322 397 158	247.0315 442 319	264.6983 154 597	283.7328 781 694	42
43	247.7764 964 959	265.9413 311 887	285.5506 891 192	306.7221 762 275	43
44	266.1208 512 507	286.2220 776 999	307.9669 908 031	331.4931 448 852	44
45	285.7493 108 382	307.9731 783 331	332.0645 151 134	358.1838 636 138	45
46	306.7517 625 969	331.3012 337 623	357.9693 537 469	386.9431 130 438	46
47	329.2243 859 787	356.3205 732 100	385.8170 552 779	417.9312 043 047	47
48	353.2700 929 972	383.1538 147 678	415.7533 344 237	451.3208 726 383	48
49	378.9989 995 070	411.9324 663 384	447.9348 345 055	487.2982 402 678	49
50	406.5289 294 724	442.7975 701 480	482.5299 470 934	526.0638 538 886	50
51	435.9859 545 355	475.9003 939 837	519.7196 931 254	567.8338 025 649	51
52	467.5049 713 530	511.4031 725 475	559.6986 701 098	612.8409 222 637	52
53	501.2303 193 477	549.4799 025 572	602.6760 703 681	661.3360 937 392	53
54	537.3164 417 021	590.3171 954 926	648.8767 756 457	713.5896 410 039	54
55	575.9285 926 212	634.1151 921 658	698.5425 338 191	769.8928 381 817	55
56	617.2435 941 047	681.0885 435 978	751.9332 238 555	830.5595 331 408	56
57	661.4506 456 920	731.4674 630 087	809.3282 156 447	895.9278 969 592	57
58	708.7521 908 905	785.4988 540 768	871.0278 318 180	966.3623 089 736	58
59	759.3648 442 528	843.4475 209 974	937.3549 192 044	1042.2553 879 190	59
60	813.5203 833 505	905.5974 662 697	1008.6565 381 447	1124.0301 804 828	60

YEARLY Compounding

TABLE 2. FUTURE WORTH OF ONE DOLLAR PER PERIOD WITH INTEREST
Payable at end of each period

YEARS	8% Nominal Annual Rate	8¼% Nominal Annual Rate	8½% Nominal Annual Rate	8¾% Nominal Annual Rate	YEARS
1	1.0000 000 000	1.0000 000 000	1.0000 000 000	1.0000 000 000	1
2	2.0800 000 000	2.0825 000 000	2.0850 000 000	2.0875 000 000	2
3	3.2464 000 000	3.2543 062 500	3.2622 250 000	3.2701 562 500	3
4	4.5061 120 000	4.5227 865 156	4.5395 141 250	4.5562 949 219	4
5	5.8666 009 600	5.8959 164 032	5.9253 728 256	5.9549 707 275	5
6	7.3359 290 368	7.3823 295 064	7.4290 295 158	7.4760 306 662	6
7	8.9228 033 597	8.9913 716 907	9.0604 970 246	9.1301 833 495	7
8	10.6366 276 285	10.7331 598 552	10.8306 392 717	10.9290 743 926	8
9	12.4875 578 388	12.6186 455 432	12.7512 436 098	12.8853 684 019	9
10	14.4865 624 659	14.6596 838 006	14.8350 993 167	15.0128 381 371	10
11	16.6454 874 632	16.8691 077 141	17.0960 827 586	17.3264 614 741	11
12	18.9771 264 602	19.2608 091 005	19.5492 497 931	19.8425 268 531	12
13	21.4952 965 771	21.8498 258 513	22.2109 360 255	22.5787 479 527	13
14	24.2149 203 032	24.6524 364 840	25.0988 655 877	25.5543 883 986	14
15	27.1521 139 275	27.6862 624 940	28.2322 691 626	28.7903 973 834	15
16	30.3242 830 417	30.9703 791 497	31.6320 120 414	32.3095 571 545	16
17	33.7502 256 850	34.5254 354 296	35.3207 330 649	36.1366 434 055	17
18	37.4502 437 398	38.3737 838 525	39.3229 953 755	40.2985 997 035	18
19	41.4462 632 390	42.5396 210 204	43.6654 499 824	44.8247 271 776	19
20	45.7619 642 981	47.0491 397 545	48.3770 132 309	49.7468 908 056	20
21	50.4229 214 420	51.9306 937 843	53.4890 593 555	55.0997 437 511	21
22	55.4567 551 573	57.2149 760 215	59.0356 294 007	60.9209 713 293	22
23	60.8932 955 699	62.9352 115 433	65.0536 578 998	67.2515 563 206	23
24	66.7647 592 155	69.1273 664 956	71.5832 188 213	74.1360 674 987	24
25	73.1059 399 527	75.8303 742 315	78.6677 924 211	81.6229 734 048	25
26	79.9544 151 490	83.0863 801 056	86.3545 547 769	89.7649 835 777	26
27	87.3507 683 609	90.9410 064 643	94.6946 919 329	98.6194 196 408	27
28	95.3388 298 297	99.4436 394 976	103.7437 407 472	108.2486 188 593	28
29	103.9659 362 161	108.6477 397 561	113.5619 587 107	118.7203 730 095	29
30	113.2832 111 134	118.6111 782 860	124.2147 252 011	130.1084 056 479	30
31	123.3458 680 025	129.3966 004 946	135.7729 768 432	142.4928 911 421	31
32	134.2135 374 427	141.0718 200 354	148.3136 798 749	155.9610 191 170	32
33	145.9506 204 381	153.7102 451 883	161.9203 426 642	170.6076 082 897	33
34	158.6266 700 732	167.3913 404 164	176.6835 717 907	186.5357 740 151	34
35	172.3168 036 790	182.2011 260 007	192.7016 753 929	203.8576 542 414	35
36	187.1021 479 733	198.2327 188 958	210.0813 178 013	222.6951 989 875	36
37	203.0703 198 112	215.5869 182 047	228.9382 298 144	243.1810 288 989	37
38	220.3159 453 961	234.3728 389 566	249.3979 793 487	265.4593 689 276	38
39	238.9412 210 278	254.7085 981 705	271.5968 075 933	289.6870 637 088	39
40	259.0565 187 100	276.7220 575 195	295.6825 362 387	316.0346 817 833	40
41	280.7810 402 068	300.5516 272 649	321.8155 518 190	344.6877 164 393	41
42	304.2435 234 233	326.3471 365 143	350.1698 737 236	375.8478 916 277	42
43	329.5830 052 972	354.2707 752 767	380.9343 129 901	409.7345 821 452	43
44	356.9496 457 210	384.4981 142 370	414.3137 295 943	446.5863 580 829	44
45	386.5056 173 787	417.2192 086 616	450.5303 966 098	486.6626 644 151	45
46	418.4260 667 690	452.6397 933 761	489.8254 803 217	530.2456 475 514	46
47	452.9001 521 105	490.9825 763 297	532.4606 461 490	577.6421 417 122	47
48	490.1321 642 793	532.4886 388 769	578.7198 010 717	629.1858 291 120	48
49	530.3427 374 217	577.4189 515 842	628.9109 841 627	685.2395 891 593	49
50	573.7701 564 154	626.0560 150 899	683.3684 178 166	746.1980 532 108	50
51	620.6717 689 286	678.7056 363 348	742.4547 333 310	812.4903 828 667	51
52	671.3255 104 429	735.6988 513 325	806.5633 856 641	884.5832 913 675	52
53	726.0315 512 783	797.3940 065 674	876.1212 734 456	962.9843 293 622	53
54	785.1140 753 806	864.1790 121 092	951.5915 816 884	1048.2454 581 814	54
55	848.9232 014 111	936.4737 806 082	1033.4768 661 320	1140.9669 357 723	55
56	917.8370 575 239	1014.7328 675 084	1122.3223 997 532	1241.8015 426 523	56
57	992.2640 221 259	1099.4483 290 778	1218.7198 037 322	1351.4591 776 344	57
58	1072.6451 438 959	1191.1528 162 267	1323.3109 870 494	1470.7118 556 774	58
59	1159.4567 554 076	1290.4229 235 654	1436.7924 209 486	1600.3991 430 492	59
60	1253.2132 958 402	1397.8828 147 596	1559.9197 767 293	1741.4340 680 660	60

TABLE 2. FUTURE WORTH OF ONE DOLLAR PER PERIOD WITH INTEREST
Payable at end of each period

YEARS	9% Nominal Annual Rate	9¼% Nominal Annual Rate	9½% Nominal Annual Rate	9¾% Nominal Annual Rate	YEARS
1	1.0000 000 000	1.0000 000 000	1.0000 000 000	1.0000 000 000	1
2	2.0900 000 000	2.0925 000 000	2.0950 000 000	2.0975 000 000	2
3	3.2781 000 000	3.2860 562 500	3.2940 250 000	3.3020 062 500	3
4	4.5731 290 000	4.5900 164 531	4.6069 573 750	4.6239 518 594	4
5	5.9847 106 100	6.0145 929 750	6.0446 183 256	6.0747 871 657	5
6	7.5233 345 649	7.5709 428 252	7.6188 570 666	7.6670 789 143	6
7	9.2004 346 757	9.2712 550 366	9.3426 484 879	9.4146 191 085	7
8	11.0284 737 966	11.1288 461 274	11.2302 000 942	11.3325 444 715	8
9	13.0210 364 382	13.1582 643 942	13.2970 691 032	13.4374 675 575	9
10	15.1929 297 177	15.3754 038 507	15.5602 906 680	15.7476 206 444	10
11	17.5602 933 923	17.7976 287 069	18.0385 182 814	18.2830 136 572	11
12	20.1407 197 976	20.4439 093 623	20.7521 775 182	21.0656 074 888	12
13	22.9533 845 794	23.3349 709 783	23.7236 343 824	24.1195 042 189	13
14	26.0191 891 915	26.4934 557 938	26.9773 796 487	27.4711 558 803	14
15	29.3609 162 188	29.9441 004 547	30.5402 307 154	31.1495 935 786	15
16	33.0033 986 784	33.7139 297 468	34.4415 526 333	35.1866 789 525	16
17	36.9737 045 595	37.8324 682 483	38.7135 001 335	39.6173 801 504	17
18	41.3013 379 699	42.3319 715 613	43.3912 826 462	44.4800 747 150	18
19	46.0184 583 871	47.2476 789 307	48.5134 544 976	49.8168 819 998	19
20	51.1601 196 420	52.6180 892 318	54.1222 326 748	55.6740 279 947	20
21	56.7645 304 098	58.4852 624 858	60.2638 447 789	62.1022 457 242	21
22	62.8733 381 466	64.8951 492 657	66.9889 100 329	69.1572 146 823	22
23	69.5319 385 798	71.8979 505 728	74.3528 564 861	76.9000 431 139	23
24	76.7898 130 520	79.5485 110 008	82.4163 778 522	85.3977 973 175	24
25	84.7008 962 267	87.9067 482 683	91.2459 337 482	94.7240 825 559	25
26	93.3239 768 871	97.0381 224 832	100.9142 974 543	104.9596 806 051	26
27	102.7231 348 069	107.0141 488 129	111.5011 557 124	116.1932 494 641	27
28	112.9682 169 396	117.9129 575 780	123.0937 655 051	128.5220 912 869	28
29	124.1353 564 641	129.8199 061 540	135.7876 732 281	142.0529 951 873	29
30	136.3075 385 459	142.8282 474 733	149.6875 021 848	156.9031 622 181	30
31	149.5752 170 150	157.0398 603 645	164.9078 148 923	173.2012 205 344	31
32	164.0369 865 464	172.5660 474 483	181.5740 573 071	191.0883 395 365	32
33	179.8003 153 356	189.5284 068 372	199.8235 927 513	210.7194 526 413	33
34	196.9823 437 158	208.0597 844 697	219.8068 340 627	232.2645 992 738	34
35	215.7107 546 502	228.3053 145 331	241.6884 832 986	255.9103 977 030	35
36	236.1247 225 687	250.4235 561 274	265.6488 892 120	281.8616 614 791	36
37	258.3759 475 999	274.5877 350 692	291.8855 336 871	310.3431 734 733	37
38	282.6297 828 839	300.9871 005 631	320.6146 593 874	341.6016 328 869	38
39	309.0664 633 434	329.8284 073 652	352.0730 520 292	375.9077 920 934	39
40	337.8824 450 443	361.3375 350 465	386.5199 919 720	413.5588 018 225	40
41	369.2918 650 983	395.7612 570 383	424.2393 912 093	454.8807 850 002	41
42	403.5281 329 572	433.3691 733 143	465.5421 333 742	500.2316 615 377	42
43	440.8456 649 233	474.4558 218 459	510.7686 360 447	550.0042 485 376	43
44	481.5217 747 664	519.3429 853 666	560.2916 564 690	604.6296 627 700	44
45	525.8587 344 954	568.3822 115 130	614.5193 638 335	664.5810 548 901	45
46	574.1860 206 000	621.9575 660 780	673.8987 033 977	730.3777 077 419	46
47	626.8627 624 540	680.4886 409 402	738.9190 802 205	802.5895 342 467	47
48	684.2804 110 748	744.4338 402 272	810.1163 928 415	881.8420 138 358	48
49	746.8656 480 716	814.2939 704 482	888.0774 501 614	968.8216 101 848	49
50	815.0835 563 980	890.6161 627 146	973.4448 079 267	1064.2817 171 778	50
51	889.4410 764 738	973.9981 577 657	1066.9220 646 798	1169.0491 846 026	51
52	970.4907 733 565	1065.0929 873 591	1169.2796 608 244	1284.0314 801 014	52
53	1058.8349 429 585	1164.6140 886 898	1281.3612 286 027	1410.2245 494 113	53
54	1155.1300 878 248	1273.3408 918 936	1404.0905 453 199	1548.7214 429 789	54
55	1260.0917 957 290	1392.1249 243 938	1538.4791 471 253	1700.7217 836 693	55
56	1374.5000 573 447	1521.8964 799 002	1685.6346 661 022	1867.5421 575 770	56
57	1499.2050 625 057	1663.6719 042 909	1846.7699 593 819	2050.6275 179 408	57
58	1635.1335 181 312	1818.5615 554 378	2023.2131 055 232	2251.5637 009 400	58
59	1783.2955 347 630	1987.7784 993 159	2216.4183 505 479	2472.0911 617 817	59
60	1944.7921 328 917	2172.6480 105 026	2427.9780 938 500	2714.1200 500 554	60

YEARLY
Compounding

TABLE 2. FUTURE WORTH OF ONE DOLLAR PER PERIOD WITH INTEREST
Payable at end of each period

YEARS	10% Nominal Annual Rate	10¼% Nominal Annual Rate	10½% Nominal Annual Rate	10¾% Nominal Annual Rate	YEARS
1	1.0000 000 000	1.0000 000 000	1.0000 000 000	1.0000 000 000	1
2	2.1000 000 000	2.1025 000 000	2.1050 000 000	2.1075 000 000	2
3	3.3100 000 000	3.3180 062 500	3.3260 250 000	3.3340 562 500	3
4	4.6410 000 000	4.6581 018 906	4.6752 576 250	4.6924 672 969	4
5	6.1051 000 000	6.1355 573 344	6.1661 596 756	6.1969 075 313	5
6	7.7156 100 000	7.7644 519 612	7.8136 064 416	7.8630 750 909	6
7	9.4871 710 000	9.5603 082 872	9.6340 351 179	9.7083 556 632	7
8	11.4358 881 000	11.5402 398 867	11.6456 088 053	11.7520 038 970	8
9	13.5794 769 100	13.7231 144 750	13.8683 977 299	14.0153 443 159	9
10	15.9374 246 010	16.1297 337 087	16.3245 794 915	16.5219 938 298	10
11	18.5311 670 611	18.7830 314 139	19.0386 603 381	19.2981 081 666	11
12	21.3842 837 672	21.7082 921 338	22.0377 196 736	22.3726 547 945	12
13	24.5227 121 439	24.9333 920 775	25.3516 802 393	25.7777 151 849	13
14	27.9749 833 583	28.4890 647 655	29.0136 066 645	29.5488 195 672	14
15	31.7724 816 942	32.4091 939 039	33.0600 353 642	33.7253 176 707	15
16	35.9497 298 636	36.7311 362 791	37.5313 390 775	38.3507 893 203	16
17	40.5447 028 499	41.4960 777 477	42.4721 296 806	43.4734 991 723	17
18	45.5991 731 349	46.7494 257 168	47.9317 032 971	49.1469 003 333	18
19	51.1590 904 484	52.5412 418 528	53.9645 321 433	55.4301 921 191	19
20	57.2749 994 933	58.9267 191 427	60.6308 080 183	62.3889 377 719	20
21	64.0024 994 426	65.9667 078 548	67.9970 428 603	70.0957 485 824	21
22	71.4027 493 868	73.7282 954 099	76.1367 323 606	78.6310 415 550	22
23	79.5430 243 255	82.2854 456 894	85.1310 892 585	88.0838 785 221	23
24	88.4973 267 581	91.7197 038 726	95.0698 536 306	98.5528 954 633	24
25	98.3470 594 339	102.1209 735 195	106.0521 882 618	110.1473 317 256	25
26	109.1817 653 773	113.5883 733 053	118.1876 680 293	122.9881 698 861	26
27	121.0999 419 150	126.2311 815 691	131.5973 731 724	137.2093 981 488	27
28	134.2099 361 065	140.1698 776 799	146.4150 973 555	152.9594 084 498	28
29	148.6309 297 171	155.5372 901 421	162.7886 825 778	170.4025 448 582	29
30	164.4940 226 889	172.4798 623 817	180.8814 942 485	189.7208 184 304	30
31	181.9434 249 578	191.1590 482 758	200.8740 511 446	211.1158 064 117	31
32	201.1377 674 535	211.7528 507 241	222.9658 265 147	234.8107 556 010	32
33	222.2515 441 989	234.4575 179 233	247.3772 382 988	261.0529 118 281	33
34	245.4766 986 188	259.4894 135 104	274.3518 483 201	290.1160 998 496	34
35	271.0243 684 806	287.0870 783 953	304.1587 923 938	322.3035 805 834	35
36	299.1268 053 287	317.5135 039 308	337.0954 655 951	357.9512 154 962	36
37	330.0394 858 616	351.0586 380 837	373.4904 894 826	397.4309 711 620	37
38	364.0434 344 477	388.0421 484 873	413.7069 908 783	441.1548 005 619	38
39	401.4477 778 925	428.8164 687 072	458.1462 249 205	489.5789 416 223	39
40	442.5925 556 818	473.7701 567 497	507.2515 785 371	543.2086 778 467	40
41	487.8518 112 499	523.3315 978 165	561.5129 942 835	602.6036 107 152	41
42	537.6369 923 749	577.9730 865 927	621.4718 586 833	668.3834 988 671	42
43	592.4006 916 124	638.2153 279 685	687.7264 038 450	741.2347 249 953	43
44	652.6407 607 737	704.6323 990 852	760.9376 762 488	821.9174 579 323	44
45	718.9048 368 510	777.8572 199 915	841.8361 322 549	911.2735 846 601	45
46	791.7953 205 361	858.5875 850 406	931.2289 261 417	1010.2354 950 110	46
47	871.9748 525 897	947.5928 125 073	1030.0079 633 865	1119.8358 107 247	47
48	960.1723 378 487	1045.7210 757 893	1139.1587 995 421	1241.2181 603 776	48
49	1057.1895 716 336	1153.9074 860 577	1259.7704 734 941	1375.6491 126 182	49
50	1163.9085 287 970	1273.1830 033 786	1393.0463 732 109	1524.5313 922 246	50
51	1281.2993 816 766	1404.6842 612 249	1540.3162 423 981	1689.4185 168 888	51
52	1410.4293 198 443	1549.6643 980 004	1703.0494 478 499	1872.0310 074 543	52
53	1552.4722 518 287	1709.5049 987 955	1882.8696 398 741	2074.2743 407 557	53
54	1708.7194 770 116	1885.7292 611 720	2081.5709 520 609	2298.2588 323 869	54
55	1880.5914 247 128	2080.0165 104 421	2301.1359 020 273	2546.3216 568 685	55
56	2069.6505 671 841	2294.2182 027 625	2543.7551 717 401	2821.0512 349 819	56
57	2277.6156 239 025	2530.3755 685 456	2811.8494 647 729	3125.3142 427 424	57
58	2506.3771 862 927	2790.7390 643 215	3108.0936 585 740	3462.2855 238 372	58
59	2758.0149 049 220	3077.7898 184 145	3435.4434 927 243	3835.4812 176 497	59
60	3034.8163 954 142	3394.2632 748 020	3797.1650 594 603	4248.7954 485 471	60

TABLE 2. FUTURE WORTH OF ONE DOLLAR PER PERIOD WITH INTEREST
Payable at end of each period

YEARLY Compounding

YEARS	11% Nominal Annual Rate	11¼% Nominal Annual Rate	11½% Nominal Annual Rate	11¾% Nominal Annual Rate	YEARS
1	1.0000 000 000	1.0000 000 000	1.0000 000 000	1.0000 000 000	1
2	2.1100 000 000	2.1125 000 000	2.1150 000 000	2.1175 000 000	2
3	3.3421 000 000	3.3501 562 500	3.3582 250 000	3.3663 062 500	3
4	4.7097 310 000	4.7270 488 281	4.7444 208 750	4.7618 472 344	4
5	6.2278 014 100	6.2588 418 213	6.2900 292 756	6.3213 642 844	5
6	7.9128 595 651	7.9629 615 262	8.0133 826 423	8.0641 245 878	6
7	9.7832 741 173	9.8587 946 979	9.9349 216 462	10.0116 592 269	7
8	11.8594 342 702	11.9679 091 014	12.0774 376 355	12.1880 291 861	8
9	14.1639 720 399	14.3142 988 753	14.4663 429 636	14.6201 226 154	9
10	16.7220 089 643	16.9246 574 988	17.1299 724 044	17.3379 870 227	10
11	19.5614 299 503	19.8286 814 674	20.0999 192 309	20.3752 004 979	11
12	22.7131 872 449	23.0594 081 325	23.4114 099 425	23.7692 865 564	12
13	26.2116 378 418	26.6535 915 474	27.1037 220 858	27.5621 777 268	13
14	30.0949 180 044	30.6521 205 964	31.2206 501 257	31.8007 336 097	14
15	34.4053 589 849	35.1004 841 635	35.8110 248 902	36.5373 198 088	15
16	39.1899 484 732	40.0492 886 319	40.9292 927 525	41.8304 548 864	16
17	44.5008 428 053	45.5548 336 030	46.6361 614 191	47.7455 333 355	17
18	50.3959 355 139	51.6797 523 834	52.9993 199 823	54.3556 335 024	18
19	56.9394 884 204	58.4937 245 265	60.0942 417 802	61.7424 204 390	19
20	64.2028 321 466	66.0742 685 357	68.0050 795 850	69.9971 548 406	20
21	72.2651 436 828	74.5076 237 460	76.8256 637 372	79.2218 205 343	21
22	81.2143 094 879	83.8897 314 174	86.6606 150 670	89.5303 844 471	22
23	91.1478 835 315	94.3273 262 019	97.6265 857 997	101.0502 046 196	23
24	102.1741 507 200	105.9391 503 996	109.8536 431 667	113.9236 036 625	24
25	114.4133 072 992	118.8573 048 196	123.4868 121 308	128.3096 270 928	25
26	127.9987 711 021	133.2287 516 118	138.6877 955 259	144.3860 082 762	26
27	143.0786 359 233	149.2169 861 681	155.6368 920 114	162.3513 642 486	27
28	159.8172 858 749	167.0038 971 120	174.5351 345 927	182.4276 495 479	28
29	178.3971 873 211	186.7918 355 371	195.6066 750 708	204.8628 983 697	29
30	199.0208 779 265	208.8059 170 350	219.1014 427 040	229.9342 889 282	30
31	221.9131 744 984	233.2965 827 014	245.2981 086 149	257.9515 678 772	31
32	247.3236 236 932	260.5424 482 554	274.5073 911 057	289.2608 771 028	32
33	275.5292 222 995	290.8534 736 841	307.0757 410 828	324.2490 301 624	33
34	306.8374 367 524	324.5744 894 736	343.3894 513 073	363.3482 912 065	34
35	341.5895 547 952	362.0891 195 393	383.8792 382 077	407.0417 154 232	35
36	380.1644 058 226	403.8241 454 875	429.0253 506 016	455.8691 169 855	36
37	422.9824 904 631	450.2543 618 548	479.3632 659 207	510.4337 382 313	37
38	470.5105 644 141	501.9079 775 635	535.4900 415 016	571.4097 024 734	38
39	523.2667 264 996	559.3726 250 394	598.0713 962 743	639.5503 425 141	39
40	581.8260 664 146	623.3020 453 563	667.8496 068 459	715.6975 077 595	40
41	646.8269 337 202	694.4235 254 589	745.6523 116 331	800.7919 649 212	41
42	718.9778 964 294	773.5461 720 731	832.4023 274 709	895.8850 207 994	42
43	799.0654 650 366	861.5701 164 313	929.1285 951 301	1002.1515 107 434	43
44	887.9626 661 906	959.4967 545 298	1036.9783 835 701	1120.9043 132 557	44
45	986.6385 594 716	1068.4401 394 144	1157.2308 976 806	1253.6105 700 633	45
46	1096.1688 010 135	1189.6396 550 985	1291.3124 509 139	1401.9098 120 457	46
47	1217.7473 691 250	1324.4741 162 971	1440.8133 827 690	1567.6342 149 611	47
48	1352.6995 797 287	1474.4774 543 805	1607.5069 217 874	1752.8312 352 190	48
49	1502.4965 334 989	1641.3561 679 983	1793.3702 177 930	1959.7889 053 572	49
50	1668.7711 521 837	1827.0087 368 982	2000.6077 928 392	2191.0641 017 367	50
51	1853.3359 789 239	2033.5472 197 992	2231.6776 890 157	2449.5141 336 907	51
52	2058.2029 366 056	2263.3212 820 266	2489.3206 232 525	2738.3320 443 994	52
53	2285.6052 596 322	2518.9449 262 546	2776.5924 949 265	3061.0860 596 163	53
54	2538.0218 381 917	2803.3262 304 582	3096.9006 318 430	3421.7636 716 213	54
55	2818.2042 403 928	3119.7004 313 848	3454.0442 045 050	3824.8209 030 368	55
56	3129.2067 068 360	3471.6667 299 156	3852.2592 880 231	4275.2373 591 436	56
57	3474.4194 445 880	3863.2292 370 311	4296.2691 061 457	4778.5777 488 429	57
58	3857.6055 834 927	4298.8425 261 971	4791.3400 533 525	5341.0606 343 320	58
59	4282.9421 976 769	4783.4623 103 942	5343.3441 594 880	5969.6352 588 660	59
60	4755.0658 394 213	5322.6018 203 136	5958.8287 378 291	6672.0674 017 828	60

YEARLY
Compounding

TABLE 2. FUTURE WORTH OF ONE DOLLAR PER PERIOD WITH INTEREST
Payable at end of each period

YEARS	12% Nominal Annual Rate	12¼% Nominal Annual Rate	12½% Nominal Annual Rate	12¾% Nominal Annual Rate	YEARS
1	1.0000 000 000	1.0000 000 000	1.0000 000 000	1.0000 000 000	1
2	2.1200 000 000	2.1225 000 000	2.1250 000 000	2.1275 000 000	2
3	3.3744 000 000	3.3825 062 500	3.3906 250 000	3.3987 562 500	3
4	4.7793 280 000	4.7968 632 656	4.8144 531 250	4.8320 976 719	4
5	6.3528 473 600	6.3844 790 157	6.4162 597 656	6.4481 901 250	5
6	8.1151 890 432	8.1665 776 951	8.2182 922 363	8.2703 343 660	6
7	10.0890 117 284	10.1669 834 627	10.2455 787 659	10.3248 019 976	7
8	12.2996 931 358	12.4124 389 369	12.5262 761 116	12.6412 142 523	8
9	14.7756 563 121	14.9329 627 067	15.0920 606 256	15.2529 690 695	9
10	17.5487 350 695	17.7622 506 383	17.9785 682 037	18.1977 226 259	10
11	20.6545 832 779	20.9381 263 414	21.2258 892 292	21.5179 322 607	11
12	24.1331 332 712	24.5030 468 183	24.8791 253 829	25.2614 686 239	12
13	28.0291 092 638	28.5046 700 535	28.9890 160 557	29.4823 058 735	13
14	32.3926 023 754	32.9964 921 351	33.6126 430 627	34.2412 998 723	14
15	37.2797 146 605	38.0385 624 216	38.8142 234 455	39.6070 656 061	15
16	42.7532 804 197	43.6982 863 183	44.6660 013 762	45.6569 664 708	16
17	48.8836 740 701	50.0513 263 922	51.2492 515 482	52.4782 296 959	17
18	55.7497 149 585	57.1826 138 753	58.6554 079 918	60.1692 039 821	18
19	63.4396 807 535	65.1874 840 750	66.9873 339 907	68.8407 774 898	19
20	72.0524 424 440	74.1729 508 742	76.3607 507 396	78.6179 766 197	20
21	81.6987 355 372	84.2591 373 563	86.9058 445 820	89.6417 686 388	21
22	92.5025 838 017	95.5808 816 824	98.7690 751 548	102.0710 941 402	22
23	104.6028 938 579	108.2895 396 885	112.1152 095 491	116.0851 586 431	23
24	118.1552 411 209	122.5550 083 004	127.1296 107 428	131.8860 163 701	24
25	133.3338 700 554	138.5679 968 172	144.0208 120 856	149.7014 834 573	25
26	150.3339 344 620	156.5425 764 273	163.0234 135 963	169.7884 225 981	26
27	169.3740 065 974	176.7190 420 396	184.4013 402 959	192.4364 464 793	27
28	190.6988 873 891	199.3671 246 895	208.4515 078 329	217.9720 934 054	28
29	214.5827 538 758	224.7895 974 639	235.5079 463 120	246.7635 353 146	29
30	241.3326 843 409	253.3263 231 533	265.9464 396 010	279.2258 860 672	30
31	271.2926 064 618	285.3587 977 395	300.1897 445 511	315.8271 865 408	31
32	304.8477 192 373	321.3152 504 626	338.7134 626 200	357.0951 528 248	32
33	342.4294 455 457	361.6763 686 443	382.0526 454 475	403.6247 848 099	33
34	384.5209 790 112	406.9817 238 032	430.8092 261 284	456.0869 448 732	34
35	431.6634 964 926	457.8369 849 691	485.6603 793 945	515.2380 303 445	35
36	484.4631 160 717	514.9220 156 279	547.3679 268 188	581.9308 792 134	36
37	543.5986 900 003	578.9999 625 423	616.7889 176 711	657.1270 663 131	37
38	609.8305 328 003	650.9274 579 537	694.8875 323 800	741.9107 672 681	38
39	684.0101 967 363	731.6660 715 530	782.7484 739 275	837.5043 900 948	39
40	767.0914 203 447	822.2951 653 183	881.5920 331 685	945.2861 998 318	40
41	860.1423 907 861	924.0263 230 698	992.7910 373 145	1066.8101 903 104	41
42	964.3594 776 804	1038.2195 476 458	1117.8899 169 789	1203.8284 895 750	42
43	1081.0826 150 020	1166.4014 422 324	1258.6261 566 012	1358.3166 219 958	43
44	1211.8125 288 023	1310.2856 189 059	1416.9544 261 764	1532.5019 913 002	44
45	1358.2300 322 586	1471.7956 072 219	1595.0737 294 484	1728.8959 951 910	45
46	1522.2176 361 296	1653.0905 691 066	1795.4579 456 295	1950.3302 345 779	46
47	1705.8837 524 651	1856.5941 638 221	2020.8901 888 331	2199.9973 394 866	47
48	1911.5898 027 609	2085.0269 488 903	2274.5014 624 373	2481.4970 002 711	48
49	2141.9805 790 923	2341.4427 501 294	2559.8141 452 420	2798.8878 678 057	49
50	2400.0182 485 833	2629.2694 870 202	2880.7909 133 972	3156.7460 709 509	50
51	2689.0204 384 133	2952.3549 991 802	3241.8897 775 718	3560.2311 949 971	51
52	3012.7028 910 229	3315.0184 865 798	3648.1259 997 683	4015.1606 723 593	52
53	3375.2272 379 457	3722.1082 511 858	4105.1417 497 394	4528.0936 580 851	53
54	3781.2545 064 992	4179.0665 119 561	4619.2844 684 568	5106.4255 994 909	54
55	4236.0050 472 791	4692.0021 596 707	5197.6950 270 139	5758.4948 634 260	55
56	4745.3256 529 525	5267.7724 242 303	5848.4069 053 906	6493.7029 585 128	56
57	5315.7647 313 069	5914.0745 461 986	6580.4577 685 644	7322.6500 857 232	57
58	5954.6564 990 637	6639.5486 781 079	7404.0149 896 350	8257.2879 716 529	58
59	6670.2152 789 513	7453.8933 911 761	8330.5168 633 394	9311.0921 880 386	59
60	7471.6411 124 255	8367.9953 315 952	9372.8314 712 568	10499.2564 420 136	60

TABLE 2. FUTURE WORTH OF ONE DOLLAR PER PERIOD WITH INTEREST
Payable at end of each period

YEARLY Compounding

YEARS	13% Nominal Annual Rate	13¼% Nominal Annual Rate	13½% Nominal Annual Rate	13¾% Nominal Annual Rate	YEARS
1	1.0000 000 000	1.0000 000 000	1.0000 000 000	1.0000 000 000	1
2	2.1300 000 000	2.1325 000 000	2.1350 000 000	2.1375 000 000	2
3	3.4069 000 000	3.4150 562 500	3.4232 250 000	3.4314 062 500	3
4	4.8497 970 000	4.8675 512 031	4.8853 603 750	4.9032 246 094	4
5	6.4802 706 100	6.5125 017 375	6.5448 840 256	6.5774 179 932	5
6	8.3227 057 893	8.3754 082 178	8.4284 433 691	8.4818 129 672	6
7	10.4046 575 419	10.4851 498 066	10.5662 832 239	10.6480 622 502	7
8	12.7572 630 224	12.8744 321 560	12.9927 314 591	13.1121 708 096	8
9	15.4157 072 153	15.5802 944 167	15.7467 502 061	15.9150 942 959	9
10	18.4197 491 532	18.6446 834 269	18.8725 614 839	19.1034 197 616	10
11	21.8143 165 432	22.1151 039 809	22.4203 572 843	22.7301 399 789	11
12	25.6501 776 938	26.0453 552 584	26.4471 055 177	26.8555 342 260	12
13	29.9847 007 940	30.4963 648 301	31.0174 647 625	31.5481 701 820	13
14	34.8827 118 972	35.5371 331 701	36.2048 225 055	36.8860 435 821	14
15	40.4174 644 438	41.2458 033 152	42.0924 735 437	42.9578 745 746	15
16	46.6717 348 215	47.7108 722 544	48.7749 574 721	49.8645 823 286	16
17	53.7390 603 483	55.0325 628 282	56.3595 767 309	57.7209 623 988	17
18	61.7251 381 936	63.3243 774 029	64.9681 195 895	66.6575 947 286	18
19	70.7494 061 588	72.7148 574 088	74.7388 157 341	76.8230 140 038	19
20	80.9468 289 594	83.3495 760 154	85.8285 558 582	88.3861 784 293	20
21	92.4699 167 241	95.3933 948 375	98.4154 108 991	101.5392 779 633	21
22	105.4910 058 983	109.0330 196 534	112.7014 913 705	116.5009 286 833	22
23	120.2048 366 650	124.4798 947 575	128.9161 927 055	133.5198 063 773	23
24	136.8314 654 315	141.9734 808 129	147.3198 787 207	152.8787 797 541	24
25	155.6195 559 376	161.7849 670 206	168.2080 623 480	174.8996 119 703	25
26	176.8500 982 095	184.2214 751 508	191.9161 507 650	199.9483 086 162	26
27	200.8406 109 767	209.6308 206 083	218.8248 311 183	228.4412 010 510	27
28	227.9498 904 037	238.4069 043 389	249.3661 833 192	260.8518 661 955	28
29	258.5833 761 562	270.9958 191 638	284.0306 180 673	297.7189 977 974	29
30	293.1992 150 565	307.9027 652 030	323.3747 515 064	339.6553 599 945	30
31	332.3151 130 138	349.6998 815 924	368.0303 429 598	387.3579 719 937	31
32	376.5160 777 056	397.0351 159 034	418.7144 392 594	441.6196 931 429	32
33	426.4631 678 073	450.6422 687 606	476.2408 885 594	503.3424 009 500	33
34	482.9033 796 223	511.3523 693 714	541.5334 085 149	573.5519 810 806	34
35	546.6808 189 732	580.1065 583 131	615.6404 186 644	653.4153 784 792	35
36	618.7493 254 397	657.9706 772 896	699.7518 751 841	744.2599 930 201	36
37	700.1867 377 469	746.1517 920 305	795.2183 783 340	847.5957 420 604	37
38	792.2110 136 540	846.0169 044 745	903.5728 594 091	965.1401 565 937	38
39	896.1984 454 290	959.1141 443 174	1026.5551 954 293	1098.8469 281 253	39
40	1013.7042 433 348	1087.1967 684 394	1166.1401 468 123	1250.9383 807 426	40
41	1146.4857 949 683	1232.2503 402 577	1324.5690 666 319	1423.9424 080 947	41
42	1296.5289 483 141	1396.5235 103 418	1504.3858 906 272	1620.7344 892 077	42
43	1466.0777 115 950	1582.5628 754 621	1708.4779 858 619	1844.5854 814 737	43
44	1657.6678 141 023	1793.2524 564 608	1940.1225 139 532	2099.2159 851 764	44
45	1874.1646 299 356	2031.8584 069 419	2203.0390 533 369	2388.8581 831 381	45
46	2118.8060 318 273	2302.0796 458 617	2501.4493 255 374	2718.3261 833 196	46
47	2395.2508 159 648	2608.1051 989 383	2840.1449 844 850	3093.0960 335 261	47
48	2707.6334 220 402	2954.6791 377 977	3224.5645 573 904	3519.3967 381 359	48
49	3060.6257 669 055	3347.1741 235 559	3660.8807 726 382	4004.3137 896 296	49
50	3459.5071 166 032	3791.6746 949 270	4156.0996 769 443	4555.9069 357 037	50
51	3910.2430 417 616	4295.0715 920 049	4718.1731 333 318	5183.3441 393 629	51
52	4419.5746 371 906	4865.1685 779 455	5356.1265 063 316	5897.0539 585 253	52
53	4995.1193 400 254	5510.8034 145 233	6080.2035 846 863	6708.8988 778 225	53
54	5645.4848 542 287	6241.9848 669 476	6902.0310 686 190	7632.3724 735 231	54
55	6380.3978 852 784	7070.0478 618 182	7834.8052 628 826	8682.8236 886 326	55
56	7210.8496 103 646	8007.8292 035 091	8893.5039 733 717	9877.7119 458 196	56
57	8149.2600 597 120	9069.8665 729 740	10095.1270 097 769	11236.8973 383 697	57
58	9209.6638 674 745	10272.6238 938 931	11458.9691 560 968	12782.9707 223 956	58
59	10407.9201 702 462	11634.7465 598 339	13006.9299 921 698	14541.6291 967 250	59
60	11761.9497 923 782	13177.3504 790 119	14763.8655 411 128	16542.1032 112 747	60

YEARLY Compounding

TABLE 2. FUTURE WORTH OF ONE DOLLAR PER PERIOD WITH INTEREST
Payable at end of each period

YEARS	14% Nominal Annual Rate	14¼% Nominal Annual Rate	14½% Nominal Annual Rate	14¾% Nominal Annual Rate	YEARS
1	1.0000 000 000	1.0000 000 000	1.0000 000 000	1.0000 000 000	1
2	2.1400 000 000	2.1425 000 000	2.1450 000 000	2.1475 000 000	2
3	3.4396 000 000	3.4478 062 500	3.4560 250 000	3.4642 562 500	3
4	4.9211 440 000	4.9391 186 406	4.9571 486 250	4.9752 340 469	4
5	6.6101 041 600	6.6429 430 469	6.6759 351 756	6.7090 810 688	5
6	8.5355 187 424	8.5895 624 311	8.6439 457 761	8.6986 705 264	6
7	10.7304 913 663	10.8135 750 775	10.8973 179 136	10.9817 244 291	7
8	13.2327 601 576	13.3545 095 261	13.4774 290 111	13.6015 287 824	8
9	16.0853 465 797	16.2575 271 335	16.4316 562 177	16.6077 542 778	9
10	19.3372 951 008	19.5742 247 501	19.8142 463 693	20.0573 980 337	10
11	23.0445 164 150	23.3635 517 770	23.6873 120 928	24.0158 642 437	11
12	27.2707 487 131	27.6928 579 052	28.1219 723 463	28.5582 042 197	12
13	32.0886 535 329	32.6390 901 567	33.1996 583 365	33.7705 393 421	13
14	37.5810 650 275	38.2901 605 040	39.0136 087 953	39.7516 938 950	14
15	43.8424 141 313	44.7465 083 758	45.6705 820 706	46.6150 687 445	15
16	50.9803 521 097	52.1228 858 194	53.2928 164 708	54.4907 913 844	16
17	59.1176 014 051	60.5503 970 486	62.0202 748 591	63.5281 831 136	17
18	68.3940 656 018	70.1788 286 281	72.0132 147 137	73.8985 901 228	18
19	78.9692 347 861	81.1793 117 075	83.4551 308 472	85.7986 321 659	19
20	91.0249 276 561	93.7473 636 259	96.5561 248 200	99.4539 304 104	20
21	104.7684 175 280	108.1063 629 426	111.5567 629 189	115.1233 851 459	21
22	120.4359 959 819	124.5115 196 619	128.7324 935 421	133.1040 844 550	22
23	138.2970 354 193	143.2544 112 137	148.3987 051 057	153.7369 369 121	23
24	158.6586 203 780	164.6681 648 116	170.9165 173 461	177.4131 351 066	24
25	181.8708 272 310	189.1333 782 973	196.6994 123 613	204.5815 725 348	25
26	208.3327 430 433	217.0848 847 047	226.2208 271 536	235.7573 544 837	26
27	238.4993 270 694	249.0194 807 751	260.0228 470 909	271.5315 642 701	27
28	272.8892 328 591	285.5047 567 855	298.7261 599 191	312.5824 699 999	28
29	312.0937 254 594	327.1891 846 275	343.0414 531 074	359.6883 843 249	29
30	356.7868 470 237	374.8136 434 369	393.7824 638 079	413.7424 210 128	30
31	407.7370 056 070	429.2245 876 266	451.8809 210 601	475.7694 281 122	31
32	465.8201 863 920	491.3890 913 634	518.4036 546 138	546.9454 187 587	32
33	532.0350 124 868	562.4120 368 827	594.5721 845 328	628.6198 680 257	33
34	607.5199 142 350	643.5557 521 385	681.7851 512 901	722.3412 985 594	34
35	693.5727 022 279	736.2624 468 183	781.6439 982 271	829.8866 400 970	35
36	791.6728 805 398	842.1798 454 899	895.9823 779 701	953.2949 195 113	36
37	903.5070 838 154	963.1904 734 722	1026.8998 227 757	1094.9059 201 392	37
38	1030.9980 755 495	1101.4451 159 420	1176.8002 970 782	1257.4045 433 597	38
39	1176.3378 061 264	1259.4010 449 637	1348.4363 401 546	1443.8717 135 052	39
40	1342.0250 989 841	1439.8656 938 710	1544.9596 094 770	1657.8427 912 473	40
41	1530.9086 128 419	1646.0465 552 476	1769.9787 528 511	1903.3746 029 562	41
42	1746.2358 186 398	1881.6081 893 704	2027.6256 720 145	2185.1223 568 923	42
43	1991.7088 332 494	2150.7373 563 557	2322.6313 944 567	2508.4279 045 339	43
44	2271.5480 699 043	2458.2174 296 364	2660.4129 466 529	2879.4210 204 527	44
45	2590.5647 996 909	2809.5134 133 596	3047.1728 239 175	3305.1356 209 694	45
46	2954.2438 716 476	3210.8690 747 633	3490.0128 833 856	3793.6431 250 624	46
47	3368.8380 136 783	3669.4179 179 171	3997.0647 514 765	4354.2054 860 091	47
48	3841.4753 355 932	4193.3099 712 202	4577.6391 404 406	4997.4507 951 955	48
49	4380.2818 825 763	4791.8566 421 191	5242.3968 158 045	5735.5747 874 868	49
50	4994.5213 461 370	5475.6962 136 211	6003.5443 540 961	6582.5720 686 411	50
51	5694.7543 345 961	6256.9829 240 621	6875.0582 854 401	7554.5014 487 657	51
52	6493.0199 414 396	7149.6029 907 410	7872.9417 368 289	8669.7904 124 586	52
53	7403.0427 332 411	8169.4214 169 216	9015.5182 886 690	9949.5844 982 962	53
54	8440.4687 158 949	9334.5639 688 329	10323.7684 405 261	11418.1482 117 949	54
55	9623.1343 361 202	10665.7393 343 916	11821.7148 644 023	13103.3250 730 347	55
56	10971.3731 431 770	12186.6071 895 424	13536.8635 197 407	15037.0655 213 073	56
57	12508.3653 832 218	13924.1987 140 521	15500.7087 301 031	17256.0326 857 001	57
58	14260.5365 368 728	15909.3970 308 046	17749.3114 959 680	19802.2975 068 409	58
59	16258.0116 520 350	18177.4861 076 942	20323.9616 628 834	22724.1363 890 999	59
60	18535.1332 833 199	20768.7778 780 406	23271.9361 040 015	26076.9465 064 922	60

TABLE 2. FUTURE WORTH OF ONE DOLLAR PER PERIOD WITH INTEREST
Payable at end of each period

YEARLY Compounding

YEARS	15% Nominal Annual Rate	15¼% Nominal Annual Rate	15½% Nominal Annual Rate	15¾% Nominal Annual Rate	YEARS
1	1.0000 000 000	1.0000 000 000	1.0000 000 000	1.0000 000 000	1
2	2.1500 000 000	2.1525 000 000	2.1550 000 000	2.1575 000 000	2
3	3.4725 000 000	3.4807 562 500	3.4890 250 000	3.4973 062 500	3
4	4.9933 750 000	5.0115 715 781	5.0298 238 750	5.0481 319 844	4
5	6.7423 812 500	6.7758 362 438	6.8094 465 756	6.8432 127 719	5
6	8.7537 384 375	8.8091 512 710	8.8649 107 948	8.9210 187 835	6
7	11.0667 992 031	11.1525 468 398	11.2389 719 680	11.3260 792 419	7
8	13.7268 190 836	13.8533 102 329	13.9810 126 231	14.1099 367 225	8
9	16.7858 419 461	16.9659 400 434	17.1480 695 797	17.3322 517 563	9
10	20.3037 182 381	20.5532 459 000	20.8060 203 645	21.0620 814 079	10
11	24.3492 759 738	24.6876 158 997	25.0309 535 210	25.3793 592 296	11
12	29.0016 673 698	29.4524 773 244	29.9107 513 168	30.3766 083 083	12
13	34.3519 174 753	34.9439 801 164	35.5469 177 709	36.1609 241 169	13
14	40.5047 050 966	41.2729 370 842	42.0566 900 254	42.8562 696 653	14
15	47.5804 108 611	48.5670 599 895	49.5754 769 793	50.6061 321 375	15
16	55.7174 724 902	56.9735 366 379	58.2596 759 111	59.5765 979 492	16
17	65.0750 933 638	66.6620 009 752	68.2899 256 773	69.9599 121 262	17
18	75.8363 573 683	77.8279 561 239	79.8748 641 573	81.9785 982 861	18
19	88.2118 109 736	90.6967 194 328	93.2554 681 017	95.8902 275 162	19
20	102.4435 826 196	105.5279 691 463	108.7100 656 575	111.9929 383 499	20
21	118.8101 200 126	122.6209 844 411	126.5601 258 344	130.6318 261 401	21
22	137.6316 380 145	142.3206 845 684	147.1769 453 387	152.2063 387 571	22
23	159.2763 837 166	165.0245 889 650	170.9893 718 662	177.1788 371 114	23
24	184.1678 412 741	191.1908 387 822	198.4927 245 054	206.0845 039 564	24
25	212.7930 174 653	221.3474 416 965	230.2590 968 038	239.5428 133 295	25
26	245.7119 700 851	256.1029 265 552	266.9492 568 084	278.2708 064 289	26
27	283.5687 655 978	296.1586 228 549	309.3263 916 137	323.0984 584 415	27
28	327.1040 804 375	342.3228 128 403	358.2719 823 138	374.9864 656 460	28
29	377.1696 925 031	395.5270 417 984	414.8041 395 724	435.0468 339 853	29
30	434.7451 463 786	456.8449 156 727	480.0987 812 061	504.5667 103 380	30
31	500.9569 183 354	527.5137 653 127	555.5140 922 931	585.0359 672 162	31
32	577.1004 560 857	608.9596 145 229	642.6187 765 985	678.1791 320 528	32
33	664.6655 244 985	702.8259 557 377	743.2246 869 713	785.9923 453 511	33
34	765.3653 531 733	811.0069 139 877	859.4245 134 518	910.7861 397 439	34
35	881.1701 561 493	935.6854 683 708	993.6353 130 369	1055.2349 567 535	35
36	1014.3456 795 717	1079.3775 022 973	1148.6487 865 576	1222.4344 624 422	36
37	1167.4975 315 074	1244.9825 713 977	1327.6893 484 740	1415.9678 902 769	37
38	1343.6221 612 335	1435.8424 135 358	1534.4811 974 875	1639.9828 329 955	38
39	1546.1654 854 186	1655.8083 816 000	1773.3257 830 980	1899.2801 291 923	39
40	1779.0903 082 314	1909.3191 597 941	2049.1912 794 782	2199.4167 495 400	40
41	2046.9538 544 661	2201.4903 316 626	2367.8159 277 973	2546.8248 875 926	41
42	2354.9969 326 360	2538.2176 072 412	2735.8273 966 059	2948.9498 073 884	42
43	2709.2464 725 314	2926.2957 923 455	3160.8806 430 798	3414.4094 020 521	43
44	3116.6334 434 111	3373.5559 006 782	3651.8171 427 572	3953.1788 828 753	44
45	3585.1284 599 227	3889.0231 755 316	4218.8487 998 846	4576.8045 569 282	45
46	4123.8977 289 111	4483.0992 098 002	4873.7703 638 667	5298.6512 746 444	46
47	4743.4823 882 478	5167.7718 392 947	5630.2047 702 660	6134.1888 504 008	47
48	5456.0047 464 850	5956.8570 447 871	6503.8865 096 573	7101.3235 943 390	48
49	6275.4054 584 577	6866.2777 441 172	7512.9889 186 541	8220.7820 604 474	49
50	7217.7162 772 264	7914.3851 000 950	8678.5022 010 455	9516.5552 349 678	50
51	8301.3737 188 103	9122.3288 278 595	10024.6700 422 076	11016.4126 844 752	51
52	9547.5797 766 319	10514.4839 741 081	11579.4938 987 498	12752.4976 822 801	52
53	10980.7167 431 267	12118.9427 801 596	13375.3154 530 560	14762.0160 672 392	53
54	12628.8242 545 957	13968.0815 541 339	15449.4893 482 797	17088.0335 978 294	54
55	14524.1478 927 850	16099.2139 911 394	17845.1601 972 630	19780.3988 894 875	55
56	16703.7700 767 028	18555.3441 247 881	20612.1600 278 388	22896.8117 145 818	56
57	19210.3355 882 082	21386.0341 038 183	23808.0448 321 538	26504.0595 596 284	57
58	22092.8859 264 394	24648.4043 046 506	27499.2917 811 376	30679.4489 402 699	58
59	25407.8188 154 053	28408.2859 611 098	31762.6820 072 140	35512.4621 483 624	59
60	29219.9916 377 161	32741.5495 701 790	36686.8977 183 321	41106.6749 367 295	60

TABLE 2. FUTURE WORTH OF ONE DOLLAR PER PERIOD WITH INTEREST
Payable at end of each period

YEARS	16% Nominal Annual Rate	16¼% Nominal Annual Rate	16½% Nominal Annual Rate	16¾% Nominal Annual Rate	YEARS
1	1.0000 000 000	1.0000 000 000	1.0000 000 000	1.0000 000 000	1
2	2.1600 000 000	2.1625 000 000	2.1650 000 000	2.1675 000 000	2
3	3.5056 000 000	3.5139 062 500	3.5222 250 000	3.5305 562 500	3
4	5.0664 960 000	5.0849 160 156	5.1033 921 250	5.1219 244 219	4
5	6.8771 353 600	6.9112 148 682	6.9454 518 256	6.9798 467 625	5
6	8.9774 770 176	9.0342 872 842	9.0914 513 769	9.1489 710 953	6
7	11.4138 733 404	11.5023 589 679	11.5915 408 540	11.6814 237 537	7
8	14.2400 930 749	14.3714 923 002	14.5041 450 949	14.6380 622 325	8
9	17.5185 079 669	17.7068 597 990	17.8973 290 356	18.0899 376 564	9
10	21.3214 692 416	21.5842 245 163	21.8503 883 265	22.1200 022 139	10
11	25.7329 043 202	26.0916 610 002	26.4557 024 004	26.8251 025 847	11
12	30.8501 690 114	31.3315 559 128	31.8208 932 964	32.3183 072 676	12
13	36.7861 960 533	37.4229 337 486	38.0713 406 903	38.7316 237 349	13
14	43.6719 874 218	44.5041 604 828	45.3531 119 042	46.2191 707 105	14
15	51.6595 054 093	52.7360 865 612	53.8363 753 684	54.9608 818 046	15
16	60.9250 262 748	62.3057 006 274	63.7193 773 042	65.1668 295 068	16
17	71.6730 304 787	73.4303 769 794	75.2330 745 594	77.0822 734 492	17
18	84.1407 153 553	86.3628 132 385	88.6465 318 617	90.9935 542 519	18
19	98.6032 298 122	101.3967 703 898	104.2732 096 189	107.2349 745 891	19
20	115.3797 465 821	118.8737 455 781	122.4782 892 060	126.1968 328 328	20
21	134.8405 060 353	139.1907 292 346	143.6872 069 250	148.3348 023 323	21
22	157.4149 870 009	162.8092 227 352	168.3955 960 677	174.1808 817 230	22
23	183.6013 849 211	190.2657 214 296	197.1808 694 188	204.3561 794 116	23
24	213.9776 065 085	222.1839 011 620	230.7157 128 729	239.5858 394 630	24
25	249.2140 235 498	259.2887 851 008	269.7838 054 970	280.7164 675 731	25
26	290.0882 673 178	302.4232 126 796	315.2981 334 040	328.7364 758 916	26
27	337.5023 900 886	352.5669 847 401	368.3223 254 156	384.7998 356 034	27
28	392.5027 725 028	410.8591 197 603	430.0955 091 092	450.2538 080 670	28
29	456.3032 161 032	478.6237 267 214	502.0612 681 122	526.6713 209 182	29
30	530.3117 306 798	557.4000 823 136	585.9013 773 508	615.8887 671 720	30
31	616.1616 075 885	648.9775 956 896	683.5751 046 136	720.0501 356 734	31
32	715.7474 648 027	755.4364 549 892	797.3649 968 749	841.6585 333 987	32
33	831.2670 591 711	879.1948 789 249	929.9302 213 593	983.6363 377 429	33
34	965.2697 886 385	1023.0640 467 502	1084.3687 078 835	1149.3954 243 149	34
35	1120.7129 548 207	1190.3119 543 471	1264.2895 446 843	1342.9191 578 876	35
36	1301.0270 275 920	1384.7376 469 285	1473.8973 195 572	1568.8581 168 338	36
37	1510.1913 520 067	1610.7575 145 544	1718.0903 772 842	1832.6418 514 034	37
38	1752.8219 683 278	1873.5056 106 695	2002.5752 895 360	2140.6093 615 135	38
39	2034.2734 832 602	2178.9502 724 033	2334.0002 123 095	2500.1614 295 670	39
40	2360.7572 405 818	2534.0296 916 688	2720.1102 473 406	2919.9384 690 195	40
41	2739.4783 990 749	2946.8095 165 650	3169.9284 381 518	3410.0281 625 803	41
42	3178.7949 429 269	3426.6660 630 068	3693.9666 304 468	3982.2078 798 125	42
43	3688.4021 337 952	3984.4992 982 454	4304.4711 244 705	4650.2276 996 810	43
44	4279.5464 752 025	4632.9804 342 103	5015.7088 600 082	5430.1408 393 776	44
45	4965.2739 112 349	5386.8397 547 694	5844.3008 219 095	6340.6894 299 734	45
46	5760.7177 370 324	6263.2012 149 194	6809.6104 575 246	7403.7549 094 939	46
47	6683.4325 749 576	7281.9714 123 439	7934.1961 830 161	8644.8838 568 341	47
48	7753.7817 869 508	8466.2917 668 497	9244.3385 532 138	10093.9019 028 539	48
49	8995.3868 728 630	9843.0641 789 628	10770.6544 144 941	11785.6304 715 819	49
50	10435.6487 725 211	11443.5621 080 443	12548.8123 928 856	13760.7235 755 719	50
51	12106.3525 761 244	13304.1409 506 015	14620.3664 377 117	16066.6447 744 801	51
52	14044.3689 883 043	15467.0638 550 742	17033.7268 999 341	18758.8077 742 056	52
53	16292.4680 264 330	17981.4617 315 238	19845.2918 384 233	21901.9080 763 850	53
54	18900.2629 106 623	20904.4492 628 964	23120.7649 917 631	25571.4776 791 795	54
55	21925.3049 763 683	24302.4222 681 170	26936.6912 154 040	29855.7001 904 421	55
56	25434.3537 725 872	28252.5658 866 861	31382.2452 659 457	34857.5299 723 411	56
57	29504.8503 762 012	32844.6078 432 725	36561.3157 348 267	40697.1662 427 082	57
58	34226.6264 363 934	38182.8566 178 043	42594.9328 310 731	47514.9415 883 619	58
59	39703.8866 662 163	44388.5708 181 975	49624.0967 482 002	55474.6943 044 125	59
60	46057.5085 328 109	51602.7135 761 546	57813.0727 116 532	64767.7056 004 016	60

TABLE 2. FUTURE WORTH OF ONE DOLLAR PER PERIOD WITH INTEREST
Payable at end of each period

YEARS	17% Nominal Annual Rate	17¼% Nominal Annual Rate	17½% Nominal Annual Rate	17¾% Nominal Annual Rate	YEARS
1	1.0000 000 000	1.0000 000 000	1.0000 000 000	1.0000 000 000	1
2	2.1700 000 000	2.1725 000 000	2.1750 000 000	2.1775 000 000	2
3	3.5389 000 000	3.5472 562 500	3.5556 250 000	3.5640 062 500	3
4	5.1405 130 000	5.1591 579 531	5.1778 593 750	5.1966 173 594	4
5	7.0144 002 100	7.0491 127 000	7.0839 847 656	7.1190 169 407	5
6	9.2068 482 457	9.2650 846 408	9.3236 820 996	9.3826 424 476	6
7	11.7720 124 475	11.8633 117 413	11.9553 264 670	12.0480 614 821	7
8	14.7732 545 635	14.9097 330 167	15.0475 085 988	15.1865 923 952	8
9	18.2847 078 393	18.4816 619 621	18.6808 226 036	18.8822 125 453	9
10	22.3931 081 720	22.6697 486 506	22.9499 665 592	23.2338 052 721	10
11	27.1999 365 613	27.5802 802 928	27.9662 107 070	28.3578 057 079	11
12	32.8239 257 767	33.3378 786 433	33.8602 975 808	34.3913 162 210	12
13	39.4039 931 587	40.0886 627 092	40.7858 496 574	41.4957 748 503	13
14	47.1026 719 957	48.0039 570 266	48.9233 733 475	49.8612 748 862	14
15	56.1101 262 350	57.2846 396 137	58.4849 636 833	59.7116 511 785	15
16	66.6488 476 949	68.1662 399 470	69.7198 323 278	71.3104 692 627	16
17	78.9791 518 031	80.9249 163 379	82.9208 029 852	84.9680 775 568	17
18	93.4056 076 096	95.8844 644 062	98.4319 435 076	101.0499 113 231	18
19	110.2845 609 032	113.4245 345 163	116.6575 336 214	119.9862 705 830	19
20	130.0329 362 568	133.9902 667 203	138.0726 020 052	142.2838 336 115	20
21	153.1385 354 204	158.1035 877 296	163.2353 073 561	168.5392 140 775	21
22	180.1720 864 419	186.3764 566 129	192.8014 861 434	199.4549 245 762	22
23	211.8013 411 370	219.5263 953 787	227.5417 462 185	235.8581 736 885	23
24	248.8075 691 303	258.3946 985 815	268.3615 518 067	278.7229 995 182	24
25	292.1048 558 824	303.9677 840 868	316.3248 233 729	329.1963 319 327	25
26	342.7626 813 825	357.4022 268 418	372.6816 674 632	388.6286 808 508	26
27	402.0323 372 175	420.0541 109 720	438.9009 592 692	458.6102 717 018	27
28	471.3778 345 444	493.5134 451 146	516.7086 271 413	541.0135 949 289	28
29	552.5120 664 170	579.6445 143 969	608.1326 368 911	638.0435 080 287	29
30	647.4391 177 079	680.6331 931 304	715.5558 483 470	752.2962 307 038	30
31	758.5037 677 182	799.0424 189 453	841.7781 218 078	886.8288 116 538	31
32	888.4494 082 303	937.8772 362 134	990.0892 931 241	1045.2409 257 223	32
33	1040.4858 076 295	1100.6610 594 602	1164.3549 194 208	1231.7711 900 380	33
34	1218.3683 949 265	1291.5250 922 171	1369.1170 303 195	1451.4105 762 698	34
35	1426.4910 220 640	1515.3131 706 246	1609.7125 106 254	1710.0359 535 577	35
36	1669.9944 958 149	1777.7046 925 573	1892.4121 999 848	2014.5673 353 141	36
37	1954.8935 601 034	2085.3587 520 234	2224.5843 349 822	2373.1530 373 324	37
38	2288.2254 653 210	2446.0831 367 475	2614.8865 936 040	2795.3877 014 589	38
39	2678.2237 944 256	2869.0324 778 364	3073.4917 474 847	3292.5690 184 679	39
40	3134.5218 394 779	3364.9405 802 632	3612.3528 032 946	3878.0000 192 459	40
41	3668.3905 521 892	3946.3928 303 586	4245.5145 438 711	4567.3450 226 620	41
42	4293.0169 460 613	4628.1455 935 955	4989.4795 890 486	5379.0487 641 846	42
43	5023.8298 268 918	5427.5007 084 907	5863.6385 171 321	6334.8299 198 273	43
44	5878.8808 974 634	6364.7445 807 053	6890.7752 576 302	7460.2622 305 967	44
45	6879.2906 500 321	7463.6630 208 770	8097.6609 277 155	8785.4587 765 276	45
46	8049.7700 605 376	8752.1448 919 783	9515.7515 900 657	10345.8777 093 612	46
47	9419.2309 708 290	10262.8898 858 445	11182.0081 183 272	12183.2710 027 728	47
48	11021.5002 358 699	12034.2383 911 527	13139.8595 390 344	14346.8016 057 650	48
49	12896.1552 759 678	14111.1445 136 265	15440.3349 583 655	16894.3588 907 883	49
50	15089.5016 728 823	16546.3169 422 271	18143.3935 760 794	19894.1075 939 032	50
51	17655.7169 572 723	19401.5566 147 613	21319.4874 518 933	23426.3116 918 211	51
52	20658.1888 400 086	22749.3251 308 076	25051.3977 559 747	27585.4820 171 193	52
53	24171.0809 428 101	26674.5837 158 719	29436.3923 632 702	32482.9050 751 580	53
54	28281.1647 030 878	31276.9494 068 598	34588.7610 268 425	38249.6207 259 985	54
55	33089.9627 026 127	36673.2231 795 432	40642.7942 065 400	45039.9284 048 632	55
56	38716.2563 620 568	43000.3541 780 144	47756.2831 926 844	53035.5156 967 265	56
57	45299.0199 436 065	50418.9152 737 218	56114.6327 514 042	62450.3197 328 954	57
58	53000.8533 340 196	59117.1781 584 389	65935.6934 829 000	73536.2514 854 844	58
59	62011.9984 008 029	69315.8913 907 696	77475.4398 424 075	86589.9361 241 578	59
60	72555.0381 289 394	81273.8826 556 773	91034.6418 148 288	101960.6497 861 958	60

YEARLY
Compounding

TABLE 2. FUTURE WORTH OF ONE DOLLAR PER PERIOD WITH INTEREST
Payable at end of each period

YEARS	18% Nominal Annual Rate	18¼% Nominal Annual Rate	18½% Nominal Annual Rate	18¾% Nominal Annual Rate	YEARS
1	1.0000 000 000	1.0000 000 000	1.0000 000 000	1.0000 000 000	1
2	2.1800 000 000	2.1825 000 000	2.1850 000 000	2.1875 000 000	2
3	3.5724 000 000	3.5808 062 500	3.5892 250 000	3.5976 562 500	3
4	5.2154 320 000	5.2343 033 906	5.2532 316 250	5.2722 167 969	4
5	7.1542 097 600	7.1895 637 594	7.2250 794 756	7.2607 574 463	5
6	9.4419 675 168	9.5016 591 455	9.5617 191 786	9.6221 494 675	6
7	12.1415 216 698	12.2357 119 396	12.3306 372 267	12.4263 024 926	7
8	15.3269 955 704	15.4687 293 685	15.6118 051 136	15.7562 342 100	8
9	19.0858 547 731	19.2917 724 783	19.4999 890 596	19.7105 281 244	9
10	23.5213 086 322	23.8125 209 556	24.1074 870 356	24.4062 521 477	10
11	28.7551 441 860	29.1583 060 300	29.5673 721 372	29.9824 244 254	11
12	34.9310 701 395	35.4796 968 804	36.0373 359 826	36.6041 290 051	12
13	42.2186 627 646	42.9547 415 611	43.7042 431 394	44.4674 031 936	13
14	50.8180 220 622	51.7939 818 960	52.7895 281 202	53.8050 412 924	14
15	60.9652 660 334	62.2463 835 920	63.5555 908 224	64.8934 865 347	15
16	72.9390 139 195	74.6063 485 976	76.3133 751 246	78.0610 152 599	16
17	87.0680 364 250	89.2220 072 167	91.4313 495 226	93.6974 556 212	17
18	103.7402 829 814	106.5050 235 337	109.3461 491 843	112.2657 285 502	18
19	123.4135 339 181	126.9421 903 286	130.5751 867 834	134.3155 526 533	19
20	146.6279 700 234	151.1091 400 636	155.7315 963 383	160.4997 187 758	20
21	174.0210 046 276	179.6865 581 252	185.5419 416 609	191.5934 160 463	21
22	206.3447 854 605	213.4793 549 830	220.8672 008 682	228.5171 815 550	22
23	244.4868 468 434	253.4393 372 674	262.7276 330 288	272.3641 530 965	23
24	289.4944 792 752	300.6920 163 187	312.3322 451 391	324.4324 318 021	24
25	342.6034 855 448	356.5683 092 969	371.1137 104 898	386.2635 127 650	25
26	405.2721 129 429	422.6420 257 436	440.7697 469 305	459.6879 214 084	26
27	479.2210 932 726	500.7741 954 418	523.3121 501 126	546.8794 066 725	27
28	566.4808 900 616	593.1654 861 099	621.1248 978 834	650.4192 954 236	28
29	669.4474 502 727	702.4181 873 249	737.0330 039 918	773.3729 133 155	29
30	790.9479 913 218	831.6095 065 117	874.3841 097 303	919.3803 345 622	30
31	934.3186 297 597	984.3782 414 501	1037.1451 700 304	1092.7641 472 926	31
32	1103.4959 831 165	1165.0272 705 148	1230.0170 264 861	1298.6574 249 100	32
33	1303.1252 600 775	1378.6447 473 837	1458.5701 763 860	1543.1556 920 806	33
34	1538.6878 068 914	1631.2474 137 813	1729.4056 590 174	1833.4973 843 457	34
35	1816.6516 121 319	1929.9500 667 963	2050.3457 059 356	2178.2781 439 105	35
36	2144.6489 023 156	2283.1659 539 867	2430.6596 615 337	2587.7052 958 938	36
37	2531.6857 047 324	2700.8437 405 892	2881.3316 989 175	3073.9000 388 739	37
38	2988.3891 315 843	3194.7477 232 468	3415.3780 632 172	3651.2562 961 627	38
39	3527.2991 752 694	3778.7891 827 393	4048.2230 049 124	4336.8668 516 932	39
40	4163.2130 268 179	4469.4182 085 892	4798.1442 608 212	5151.0293 863 857	40
41	4913.5913 716 451	5286.0870 316 568	5686.8009 490 731	6117.8473 963 330	41
42	5799.0378 185 413	6251.7979 149 341	6739.8591 246 516	7265.9437 831 454	42
43	6843.8646 258 787	7393.7510 344 096	7987.7330 627 122	8629.3082 424 852	43
44	8076.7602 585 369	8744.1105 981 894	9466.4636 793 139	10248.3035 379 512	44
45	9531.5771 050 735	10340.9107 823 589	11218.7594 599 870	12170.8604 513 170	45
46	11248.2609 839 867	12229.1270 001 395	13295.2299 600 846	14453.8967 859 390	46
47	13273.9479 611 043	14461.9426 776 649	15755.8475 027 002	17165.0024 333 026	47
48	15664.2585 941 031	17102.2472 163 388	18671.6792 906 998	20384.4403 895 468	48
49	18484.8251 410 417	20224.4073 333 206	22126.9399 594 792	24207.5229 625 868	49
50	21813.0936 664 292	23916.3616 716 516	26221.4238 519 829	28747.4335 180 718	50
51	25740.4505 263 864	28282.0976 767 280	31073.3872 645 997	34138.5773 027 103	51
52	30374.7316 211 360	33444.5805 027 308	36822.9639 085 507	40540.5605 469 685	52
53	35843.1833 129 405	39549.2164 444 792	43636.2122 316 325	48142.9156 495 251	53
54	42295.9563 092 698	46767.9484 455 967	51709.9114 944 846	57170.7123 338 110	54
55	49910.2284 449 383	55304.0990 369 181	61277.2451 209 642	67891.2208 964 006	55
56	58895.0695 650 272	65398.0971 111 556	72614.5354 683 426	80621.8248 144 757	56
57	69497.1820 867 321	77334.2498 339 415	86049.2245 299 860	95739.4169 671 899	57
58	82007.6748 623 439	91448.7504 286 359	101969.3310 680 334	113691.5576 485 380	58
59	96770.0563 375 658	108139.1473 818 619	120834.6573 156 195	135009.7247 076 389	59
60	114189.6664 783 276	127875.5417 790 517	143190.0689 190 091	160325.0480 903 212	60

TABLE 2. FUTURE WORTH OF ONE DOLLAR PER PERIOD WITH INTEREST
Payable at end of each period

YEARLY Compounding

YEARS	19% Nominal Annual Rate	19¼% Nominal Annual Rate	19½% Nominal Annual Rate	19¾% Nominal Annual Rate	YEARS
1	1.0000 000 000	1.0000 000 000	1.0000 000 000	1.0000 000 000	1
2	2.1900 000 000	2.1925 000 000	2.1950 000 000	2.1975 000 000	2
3	3.6061 000 000	3.6145 562 500	3.6230 250 000	3.6315 062 500	3
4	5.2912 590 000	5.3103 583 281	5.3295 148 750	5.3487 287 344	4
5	7.2965 982 100	7.3326 023 063	7.3687 702 756	7.4051 026 594	5
6	9.6829 518 699	9.7441 282 502	9.8056 804 794	9.8676 104 346	6
7	12.5227 127 252	12.6198 729 384	12.7177 881 728	12.8164 634 955	7
8	15.9020 281 430	16.0491 984 791	16.1977 568 666	16.3477 150 359	8
9	19.9234 134 901	20.1386 691 863	20.3563 194 555	20.5763 887 554	9
10	24.7088 620 533	25.0153 630 047	25.3258 017 494	25.6402 255 346	10
11	30.4035 458 434	30.8308 203 830	31.2643 330 905	31.7041 700 777	11
12	37.1802 195 536	37.7657 533 068	38.3608 780 431	38.9657 436 681	12
13	45.2444 612 688	46.0356 608 183	46.8412 492 615	47.6614 780 425	13
14	54.8409 089 099	55.8975 255 259	56.9752 928 675	58.0746 199 559	14
15	66.2606 816 027	67.6577 991 896	69.0854 749 767	70.5443 573 972	15
16	79.8502 111 073	81.6819 255 336	83.5571 425 972	85.4768 679 831	16
17	96.0217 512 176	98.4056 961 988	100.8507 854 036	103.3585 494 098	17
18	115.2658 839 490	118.3487 927 171	121.5166 885 573	124.7718 629 183	18
19	138.1664 018 993	142.1309 353 151	146.2124 428 260	150.4143 058 446	19
20	165.4180 182 602	170.4911 403 633	175.7238 691 771	181.1211 312 489	20
21	197.8474 417 296	204.3106 848 832	210.9900 236 666	217.8925 546 706	21
22	236.4384 556 582	244.6404 917 232	253.1330 782 816	261.9263 342 180	22
23	282.3617 622 333	292.7337 863 800	303.4940 285 465	314.6567 852 261	23
24	337.0104 970 576	350.0850 402 581	363.6753 641 131	377.8015 003 082	24
25	402.0424 914 986	418.4764 105 078	435.5920 601 151	453.4172 966 191	25
26	479.4305 648 833	500.0331 195 305	521.5325 118 376	543.9672 127 014	26
27	571.5223 722 111	597.2894 950 402	624.2313 516 459	652.4007 372 099	27
28	681.1116 229 313	713.2677 228 354	746.9564 652 169	782.2498 828 089	28
29	811.5228 312 882	851.5717 594 812	893.6129 759 342	937.7442 346 636	29
30	966.7121 692 330	1016.4993 231 813	1068.8675 062 413	1123.9487 210 097	30
31	1151.3874 813 872	1213.1754 428 937	1278.2966 699 584	1346.9285 934 091	31
32	1371.1511 028 508	1447.7117 156 508	1528.5645 206 003	1613.9469 906 074	32
33	1632.6698 123 924	1727.3962 209 136	1827.6346 021 173	1933.7015 212 524	33
34	1943.8770 767 470	2060.9199 934 394	2185.0233 495 302	2316.6075 716 997	34
35	2314.2137 213 289	2458.6470 921 765	2612.1029 026 886	2775.1375 671 104	35
36	2754.9143 283 814	2932.9366 574 205	3122.4629 687 129	3324.2272 366 147	36
37	3279.3480 507 739	3498.5269 639 739	3732.3432 476 119	3981.7621 158 461	37
38	3903.4241 804 210	4172.9934 045 389	4461.1501 808 962	4769.1601 337 257	38
39	4646.0747 747 010	4977.2946 349 127	5332.0744 661 710	5712.0692 601 365	39
40	5529.8289 818 941	5936.4238 521 333	6372.8289 870 744	6841.2029 390 135	40
41	6581.4964 884 540	7080.1854 436 690	7616.5306 395 538	8193.3405 194 686	41
42	7832.9808 212 603	8444.1211 415 753	9102.7541 142 668	9812.5252 720 637	42
43	9322.2471 772 997	10070.6144 613 285	10878.7911 665 489	11751.4990 132 963	43
44	11094.4741 409 867	12010.2077 451 343	13001.1554 440 259	14073.4200 684 223	44
45	13203.4242 277 742	14323.1727 360 726	15537.3807 556 110	16853.9205 319 357	45
46	15713.0748 310 512	17081.3834 877 666	18568.1700 029 551	20183.5698 369 930	46
47	18699.5590 489 510	20370.5498 091 617	22189.9631 535 314	24170.8248 797 991	47
48	22253.4752 682 517	24292.8806 474 253	26518.0059 684 700	28945.5627 935 594	48
49	26482.6355 692 195	28970.2601 720 547	31690.0171 323 216	34663.3114 452 874	49
50	31515.3363 273 712	34548.0352 551 752	37870.5704 731 243	41510.3154 557 317	50
51	37504.2502 295 717	41199.5320 417 964	45256.3317 153 836	49709.6027 582 387	51
52	44631.0577 731 903	49131.4419 598 422	54082.3163 998 834	59528.2493 029 909	52
53	53111.9587 500 965	58590.2445 371 118	64629.3680 978 606	71286.0785 403 316	53
54	63204.2309 126 148	69869.8666 105 059	77233.0948 769 435	85366.0790 520 470	54
55	75214.0347 860 116	83320.8159 330 282	92294.5483 779 474	102226.8796 648 263	55
56	89505.7013 953 538	99361.0730 001 362	110292.9853 116 472	122417.6883 986 295	56
57	106512.7846 604 711	118489.0795 526 624	131801.1174 474 184	146596.1818 573 589	57
58	126751.2137 459 606	141299.2273 665 499	157503.3353 496 650	175549.9277 741 872	58
59	150834.9443 576 931	168500.3286 346 108	188217.4857 428 496	210222.0385 095 892	59
60	179494.5837 856 548	200937.6418 967 733	224920.8954 627 053	251741.8911 152 331	60

YEARLY Compounding

TABLE 2. FUTURE WORTH OF ONE DOLLAR PER PERIOD WITH INTEREST
Payable at end of each period

YEARS	20% Nominal Annual Rate	20¼% Nominal Annual Rate	20½% Nominal Annual Rate	20¾% Nominal Annual Rate	YEARS
1	1.0000 000 000	1.0000 000 000	1.0000 000 000	1.0000 000 000	1
2	2.2000 000 000	2.2025 000 000	2.2050 000 000	2.2075 000 000	2
3	3.6400 000 000	3.6485 062 500	3.6570 250 000	3.6655 562 500	3
4	5.3680 000 000	5.3873 287 656	5.4067 151 250	5.4261 591 719	4
5	7.4416 000 000	7.4782 628 407	7.5150 917 256	7.5520 872 000	5
6	9.9299 200 000	9.9926 110 659	10.0556 855 294	10.1191 452 940	6
7	12.9159 040 000	13.0161 148 067	13.1171 010 629	13.2188 679 426	7
8	16.4990 848 000	16.6518 780 551	16.8061 067 808	16.9617 830 406	8
9	20.7989 017 600	21.0238 833 613	21.2513 586 709	21.4813 530 216	9
10	25.9586 821 120	26.2812 197 419	26.6078 871 984	26.9387 337 736	10
11	32.1504 185 344	32.6031 667 397	33.0625 040 741	33.5285 210 316	11
12	39.5805 022 413	40.2053 080 044	40.8403 174 092	41.4856 891 456	12
13	48.4966 026 895	49.3468 828 753	50.2125 824 781	51.0939 696 433	13
14	59.1959 232 274	60.3396 266 576	61.5061 618 861	62.6959 683 443	14
15	72.0351 078 729	73.5584 010 558	75.1149 250 728	76.7053 817 758	15
16	87.4421 294 475	89.4539 772 696	91.5134 847 127	93.6217 484 942	16
17	105.9305 553 370	108.5684 076 666	111.2737 490 788	114.0482 613 068	17
18	128.1166 664 044	131.5535 102 191	135.0848 676 400	138.7132 755 280	18
19	154.7399 996 853	159.1930 960 385	163.7772 655 062	168.4962 802 000	19
20	186.6879 996 224	192.4296 979 863	198.3516 049 350	204.4592 583 415	20
21	225.0255 995 468	232.3967 118 286	240.0136 839 466	247.8845 544 474	21
22	271.0307 194 562	280.4570 459 738	290.2164 891 557	300.3205 994 952	22
23	326.2368 633 475	338.2495 977 835	350.7108 694 326	363.6371 238 905	23
24	392.4842 360 170	407.7451 413 347	423.6065 976 663	440.0918 270 977	24
25	471.9810 832 203	491.3135 324 550	511.4459 501 879	532.4108 812 205	25
26	567.3772 998 644	591.8045 227 771	617.2923 699 764	643.8861 390 738	26
27	681.8527 598 373	712.6449 386 395	744.8373 058 216	778.4925 129 316	27
28	819.2233 118 048	857.9555 387 140	898.5289 535 150	941.0297 093 649	28
29	984.0679 741 657	1032.6915 353 036	1083.7273 889 856	1137.2933 740 581	29
30	1181.8815 689 988	1242.8115 712 025	1306.8915 037 276	1374.2817 491 752	30
31	1419.2578 827 986	1495.4809 143 710	1575.8042 619 918	1660.4452 121 290	31
32	1704.1094 593 583	1799.3157 995 312	1899.8441 357 001	2005.9875 936 458	32
33	2045.9313 512 300	2164.6772 489 362	2290.3121 835 186	2423.2300 193 273	33
34	2456.1176 214 760	2604.0243 918 458	2760.8261 811 399	2927.0502 483 377	34
35	2948.3411 457 712	3132.3393 311 946	3327.7955 482 736	3535.4131 748 677	35
36	3539.0093 749 255	3767.6380 457 615	4010.9936 356 697	4270.0114 086 528	36
37	4247.8112 499 106	4531.5847 500 282	4834.2473 309 819	5157.0387 759 483	37
38	5098.3734 998 927	5450.2306 619 089	5826.2680 338 332	6228.1243 219 575	38
39	6119.0481 998 712	6554.9023 709 455	7021.6529 807 691	7521.4601 187 637	39
40	7343.8578 398 454	7883.2701 010 620	8462.0918 418 267	9083.1630 934 072	40
41	8813.6294 078 145	9480.6322 965 270	10197.8206 694 012	10968.9194 352 892	41
42	10577.3552 893 774	11401.4603 365 737	12289.3739 066 284	13245.9702 181 117	42
43	12693.8263 472 529	13711.2560 547 299	14809.6955 574 873	15995.5090 383 698	43
44	15233.5916 167 035	16488.7854 058 127	17846.6831 467 721	19315.5771 638 316	44
45	18281.3099 400 442	19828.7644 504 898	21506.2531 918 604	23324.5594 253 266	45
46	21938.5719 280 530	23845.0892 517 140	25916.0350 961 918	28165.4055 060 819	46
47	26327.2863 136 636	28674.7198 251 861	31229.8222 909 111	34010.7271 485 939	47
48	31593.7435 763 963	34482.3505 897 862	37632.9358 605 479	41068.9530 319 271	48
49	37913.4922 916 756	41466.0265 842 179	45348.6877 119 603	49591.7607 860 520	49
50	45497.1907 500 107	49863.8969 675 221	54646.1686 929 121	59883.0511 491 578	50
51	54597.6289 000 129	59962.3361 034 453	65849.6332 749 591	72309.7842 626 081	51
52	65518.1546 800 155	72105.7091 643 930	79349.8080 963 257	87315.0644 970 992	52
53	78622.7856 160 186	86708.1152 701 825	95617.5187 560 725	105433.9403 802 473	53
54	94348.3427 392 223	104267.5086 123 945	115220.1101 010 673	127312.4830 091 487	54
55	113219.0112 870 667	125382.6791 064 044	138841.2326 717 861	153730.8232 335 470	55
56	135863.8135 444 801	150773.6716 254 613	167304.6853 695 023	185630.9690 545 080	56
57	163037.5762 533 761	181306.3401 296 052	201603.1458 702 502	224150.3951 333 184	57
58	195646.0915 040 513	218021.8740 058 502	242932.7907 736 515	270662.6021 234 820	58
59	234776.3098 048 615	262172.3034 920 349	292735.0128 822 501	326826.0920 641 045	59
60	281732.5717 658 338	315263.1949 491 719	352746.6905 231 114	394643.5061 674 062	60

TABLE 2. FUTURE WORTH OF ONE DOLLAR PER PERIOD WITH INTEREST
Payable at end of each period

YEARLY Compounding

YEARS	21% Nominal Annual Rate	21¼% Nominal Annual Rate	21½% Nominal Annual Rate	21¾% Nominal Annual Rate	YEARS
1	1.0000 000 000	1.0000 000 000	1.0000 000 000	1.0000 000 000	1
2	2.2100 000 000	2.2125 000 000	2.2150 000 000	2.2175 000 000	2
3	3.6741 000 000	3.6826 562 500	3.6912 250 000	3.6998 062 500	3
4	5.4456 610 000	5.4652 207 031	5.4848 383 750	5.5045 141 094	4
5	7.5892 498 100	7.6265 801 025	7.6640 786 256	7.7017 459 282	5
6	10.1829 922 701	10.2472 283 743	10.3118 555 301	10.3768 756 675	6
7	13.3214 206 468	13.4247 644 039	13.5289 044 691	13.6338 461 252	7
8	17.1189 189 827	17.2775 268 397	17.4376 189 300	17.5992 076 575	8
9	21.7138 919 690	21.9490 012 931	22.1867 069 999	22.4270 353 230	9
10	27.2738 092 825	27.6131 640 679	27.9568 490 049	28.3049 155 057	10
11	34.0013 092 318	34.4809 614 324	34.9675 715 410	35.4612 346 282	11
12	42.1415 841 705	42.8081 657 367	43.4855 994 223	44.1740 531 598	12
13	51.9913 168 463	52.9049 009 558	53.8350 032 980	54.7819 097 221	13
14	63.9094 933 840	65.1471 924 089	66.4095 290 071	67.6969 750 867	14
15	78.3304 869 947	79.9909 707 958	81.6875 777 437	83.4210 671 680	15
16	95.7798 892 636	97.9890 520 899	100.2504 069 585	102.5651 492 771	16
17	116.8936 660 089	119.8117 256 590	122.8042 444 546	125.8730 692 448	17
18	142.4413 358 708	146.2717 173 615	150.2071 570 124	154.2504 618 056	18
19	173.3540 164 037	178.3544 573 008	183.5016 957 700	188.7999 372 483	19
20	210.7583 598 485	217.2547 794 773	223.9545 603 606	230.8639 235 998	20
21	256.0176 154 166	264.4214 201 162	273.1047 908 381	282.0768 269 827	21
22	310.7813 146 541	321.6109 718 909	332.8223 208 683	344.4285 368 514	22
23	377.0453 907 315	390.9533 034 177	405.3791 198 550	420.3417 436 166	23
24	457.2249 227 851	475.0308 803 940	493.5356 306 238	512.7660 728 533	24
25	554.2421 565 700	576.9749 424 777	600.6457 912 079	625.2926 936 988	25
26	671.6330 094 497	700.5821 177 542	730.7846 363 176	762.2938 545 783	26
27	813.6759 414 341	850.4558 177 769	888.9033 331 259	929.0927 679 491	27
28	985.5478 891 353	1032.1776 790 545	1081.0175 497 480	1132.1704 449 781	28
29	1193.5129 458 537	1252.5154 358 536	1314.4363 229 438	1379.4175 167 608	29
30	1445.1506 644 829	1519.6749 659 725	1598.0401 323 767	1680.4408 266 563	30
31	1749.6323 040 244	1843.6058 962 417	1942.6187 608 377	2046.9367 064 540	31
32	2118.0550 878 695	2236.3721 491 931	2361.2817 944 178	2493.1454 401 077	32
33	2563.8466 563 221	2712.6012 308 966	2869.9573 802 177	3036.4045 733 312	33
34	3103.2544 541 497	3290.0289 924 621	3487.9982 169 645	3697.8225 680 307	34
35	3755.9378 895 211	3990.1601 533 603	4238.9178 336 118	4503.0989 765 774	35
36	4545.6848 463 206	4839.0691 859 494	5151.2851 678 383	5483.5230 039 829	36
37	5501.2786 640 479	5868.3713 879 636	6259.8114 789 236	6677.1892 573 492	37
38	6657.5471 834 980	7116.4003 079 059	7606.6709 468 922	8130.4779 208 227	38
39	8056.6320 920 325	8629.6353 733 359	9243.1052 004 740	9899.8568 686 016	39
40	9749.5248 313 594	10464.4328 901 697	11231.3728 185 759	12054.0757 375 225	40
41	11797.9250 459 448	12689.1248 793 308	13647.1179 745 697	14676.8372 104 336	41
42	14276.4893 055 932	15386.5639 161 886	16582.2483 391 022	17870.0493 037 029	42
43	17275.5520 597 678	18657.2087 483 787	20148.4317 320 092	21757.7850 272 583	43
44	20904.4179 923 191	22622.8656 074 092	24481.3445 543 911	26491.1032 706 870	44
45	25295.3457 707 061	27431.2245 489 836	29745.8336 335 852	32253.9182 320 614	45
46	30608.3683 825 543	33261.3597 656 426	36142.1878 648 060	39270.1454 475 347	46
47	37037.1257 428 907	40330.3987 158 417	43913.7582 557 393	47812.4020 823 736	47
48	44815.9221 488 978	48901.6084 429 580	53356.2162 807 233	58212.5995 352 898	48
49	54228.2658 001 663	59294.2002 370 866	64828.8027 810 788	70874.8399 342 153	49
50	65617.2016 182 013	71895.2177 874 675	78767.9953 790 107	86291.1176 199 072	50
51	79397.8139 580 235	87173.9515 673 044	95704.1143 854 980	105060.4357 022 370	51
52	96072.3548 892 085	105699.4162 753 566	116281.4989 783 801	127912.0804 674 735	52
53	116248.5494 159 422	128161.5422 338 698	141283.0212 587 319	155733.9579 691 490	53
54	140661.7447 932 901	155396.8699 585 672	171659.8708 293 592	189607.0938 274 389	54
55	170201.7111 998 810	188419.7048 247 627	208567.7430 576 714	230847.6367 349 069	55
56	205945.0705 518 561	228459.8921 000 248	253410.8078 150 708	281057.9977 247 491	56
57	249194.5353 677 458	277008.6191 712 800	307895.1314 953 110	342189.1122 298 821	57
58	301526.3877 949 725	335873.9507 451 770	374093.5847 668 029	416616.2441 398 814	58
59	364847.9292 319 167	407248.1652 785 271	454524.7054 916 655	507231.2772 403 056	59
60	441466.9943 706 192	493789.4004 002 141	552248.5171 723 735	617555.0800 400 721	60

TABLE 2. FUTURE WORTH OF ONE DOLLAR PER PERIOD WITH INTEREST
Payable at end of each period

YEARS	22% Nominal Annual Rate	22¼% Nominal Annual Rate	22½% Nominal Annual Rate	22¾% Nominal Annual Rate	YEARS
1	1.0000 000 000	1.0000 000 000	1.0000 000 000	1.0000 000 000	1
2	2.2200 000 000	2.2225 000 000	2.2250 000 000	2.2275 000 000	2
3	3.7084 000 000	3.7170 062 500	3.7256 250 000	3.7342 562 500	3
4	5.5242 480 000	5.5440 401 406	5.5638 906 250	5.5837 995 469	4
5	7.7395 825 600	7.7775 890 719	7.8157 660 156	7.8541 139 438	5
6	10.4422 907 232	10.5081 026 404	10.5743 133 691	10.6409 248 660	6
7	13.7395 946 823	13.8461 554 779	13.9535 338 772	14.0617 352 730	7
8	17.7623 055 124	17.9269 250 717	18.0930 789 996	18.2607 800 476	8
9	22.6700 127 251	22.9156 659 002	23.1640 217 745	23.4151 075 085	9
10	28.6574 155 247	29.0144 015 630	29.3759 266 737	29.7420 444 666	10
11	35.9620 469 401	36.4701 059 108	36.9855 101 753	37.5083 595 828	11
12	44.8736 972 669	45.5847 044 759	46.3072 499 648	47.0415 113 879	12
13	55.7459 106 656	56.7273 012 218	57.7263 812 068	58.7434 552 286	13
14	69.0100 110 121	70.3491 257 437	71.7148 169 784	73.1075 912 931	14
15	85.1922 134 347	87.0018 062 216	88.8506 507 985	90.7395 683 123	15
16	104.9345 003 904	107.3597 081 059	109.8420 472 282	112.3828 201 034	16
17	129.0200 904 763	132.2472 431 595	135.5565 078 545	138.9499 116 769	17
18	158.4045 103 811	162.6722 547 625	167.0567 221 218	171.5610 165 834	18
19	194.2535 026 649	199.8668 314 471	205.6444 845 992	211.5911 478 561	19
20	237.9892 732 512	245.3372 014 441	252.9144 936 340	260.7281 339 934	20
21	291.3469 133 664	300.9247 287 654	310.8202 547 016	321.0437 844 769	21
22	356.4432 343 070	368.8804 809 158	381.7548 120 095	395.0812 454 454	22
23	435.8607 458 546	451.9563 879 195	468.6496 447 116	485.9622 287 842	23
24	532.7501 099 426	553.5166 842 316	575.0958 147 717	597.5186 358 326	24
25	650.9551 341 300	677.6741 464 731	705.4923 730 953	734.4541 254 845	25
26	795.1652 636 386	829.4566 440 634	865.2281 570 418	902.5424 390 323	26
27	971.1016 216 390	1015.0107 473 675	1060.9044 923 762	1108.8708 439 121	27
28	1185.7439 783 996	1241.8506 386 568	1300.6080 031 608	1362.1389 609 021	28
29	1447.6076 536 475	1519.1624 057 579	1594.2448 038 720	1673.0255 745 074	29
30	1767.0813 374 500	1858.1760 410 390	1953.9498 847 432	2054.6388 927 078	30
31	2156.8392 316 890	2272.6202 101 702	2394.5886 088 104	2523.0692 407 988	31
32	2632.3438 626 606	2779.2782 069 331	2934.3710 457 928	3098.0674 930 805	32
33	3212.4595 124 459	3398.6676 079 757	3595.6045 310 962	3803.8778 477 564	33
34	3920.2006 051 840	4155.8711 507 503	4405.6155 505 928	4670.2600 581 209	34
35	4783.6447 383 245	5081.5524 817 923	5397.8790 494 762	5733.7442 213 435	35
36	5837.0465 807 559	6213.1979 089 911	6613.4018 356 083	7039.1710 316 991	36
37	7122.1968 285 222	7596.6344 437 416	8102.4172 486 202	8641.5824 414 106	37
38	8690.0801 307 970	9287.8856 074 741	9926.4611 295 597	10608.5424 468 315	38
39	10602.8977 595 724	11355.4401 551 371	12160.9148 837 107	13022.9858 534 857	39
40	12936.5352 666 783	13883.0255 896 550	14898.1207 325 455	15986.7151 351 537	40
41	15783.5730 253 475	16972.9987 833 533	18251.1978 973 683	19624.6928 284 012	41
42	19256.9590 909 240	20750.4910 126 494	22358.7174 242 762	24090.3104 468 625	42
43	23494.4900 909 273	25368.4752 629 639	27390.4288 447 383	29571.8560 735 237	43
44	28664.2779 109 312	31013.9610 089 734	33554.2753 348 044	36300.4533 302 503	44
45	34971.4190 513 361	37915.5673 334 699	41104.9872 851 354	44559.8064 628 823	45
46	42666.1312 426 301	46352.7810 651 670	50354.6094 242 909	54698.1624 331 880	46
47	52053.6801 160 087	56667.2748 521 667	61685.3965 447 563	67142.9943 867 383	47
48	63506.4897 415 306	69276.7435 067 737	75565.6107 673 265	82419.0256 097 212	48
49	77478.9174 846 673	84691.8189 370 309	92568.8731 899 749	101170.3539 359 328	49
50	94525.2793 312 941	103536.7486 505 203	113397.8696 577 193	124187.6094 563 575	50
51	115321.8407 841 788	126574.6752 252 610	138913.3903 307 062	152441.2906 076 788	51
52	140693.6457 566 982	154738.5404 628 816	170169.9031 551 150	187122.6842 209 258	52
53	171647.2478 231 718	189168.8657 158 728	208459.1313 650 159	229694.0948 811 864	53
54	209410.6423 442 696	231259.9383 376 545	255363.4359 221 445	281950.5014 666 563	54
55	255481.9836 600 089	282716.2746 177 826	312821.2090 046 270	346095.2405 503 206	55
56	311689.0200 652 108	345621.6457 202 392	383206.9810 306 681	424832.9077 755 185	56
57	380261.6044 795 572	422523.4618 929 924	469429.5517 625 684	521483.3942 944 489	57
58	463920.1574 650 598	516535.9321 641 832	575052.2009 091 463	640121.8664 964 361	58
59	565983.5921 073 730	631466.1770 707 140	704439.9461 137 042	785750.5911 243 753	59
60	690500.9823 709 950	771968.4014 689 479	862939.9339 892 876	964509.8506 051 706	60

TABLE 2. FUTURE WORTH OF ONE DOLLAR PER PERIOD WITH INTEREST
Payable at end of each period

YEARLY Compounding

YEARS	23% Nominal Annual Rate	24% Nominal Annual Rate	25% Nominal Annual Rate	26% Nominal Annual Rate	YEARS
1	1.0000 000 000	1.0000 000 000	1.0000 000 000	1.0000 000 000	1
2	2.2300 000 000	2.2400 000 000	2.2500 000 000	2.2600 000 000	2
3	3.7429 000 000	3.7776 000 000	3.8125 000 000	3.8476 000 000	3
4	5.6037 670 000	5.6842 240 000	5.7656 250 000	5.8479 760 000	4
5	7.8926 334 100	8.0484 377 600	8.2070 312 500	8.3684 497 600	5
6	10.7079 390 943	10.9800 628 224	11.2587 890 625	11.5442 466 976	6
7	14.1707 650 860	14.6152 778 998	15.0734 863 281	15.5457 508 390	7
8	18.4300 410 558	19.1229 445 957	19.8418 579 102	20.5876 460 571	8
9	23.6689 504 986	24.7124 512 987	25.8023 223 877	26.9404 340 320	9
10	30.1128 091 133	31.6434 396 104	33.2529 029 846	34.9449 468 803	10
11	38.0387 552 093	40.2378 651 169	42.5661 287 308	45.0306 330 691	11
12	47.7876 689 075	50.8949 527 449	54.2076 609 135	57.7385 976 671	12
13	59.7788 327 562	64.1097 414 037	68.7595 761 418	73.7506 330 606	13
14	74.5279 642 901	80.4960 793 406	86.9494 701 773	93.9257 976 563	14
15	92.6693 960 768	100.8151 383 823	109.6868 377 216	119.3465 050 469	15
16	114.9833 571 745	126.0107 715 941	138.1085 471 520	151.3765 963 592	16
17	142.4295 293 246	157.2533 567 767	173.6356 839 400	191.7345 114 125	17
18	176.1883 210 693	195.9941 624 031	218.0446 049 250	242.5854 843 798	18
19	217.7116 349 152	244.0327 613 798	273.5557 561 563	306.6577 103 185	19
20	268.7853 109 457	303.6006 241 110	342.9446 951 954	387.3887 150 014	20
21	331.6059 324 633	377.4647 738 976	429.6808 689 942	489.1097 809 017	21
22	408.8752 969 298	469.0563 196 331	538.1010 862 428	617.2783 239 362	22
23	503.9166 152 237	582.6298 363 450	673.6263 578 034	778.7706 881 596	23
24	620.8174 367 251	723.4609 970 678	843.0329 472 543	982.2510 670 810	24
25	764.6054 471 719	898.0916 363 641	1054.7911 840 679	1238.6363 445 221	25
26	941.4647 000 214	1114.6336 290 914	1319.4889 800 848	1561.6817 940 979	26
27	1159.0015 810 263	1383.1457 000 734	1650.3612 251 061	1968.7190 605 633	27
28	1426.5719 446 624	1716.1006 680 910	2063.9515 313 826	2481.5860 163 098	28
29	1755.6834 919 348	2128.9648 284 328	2580.9394 142 282	3127.7983 805 503	29
30	2160.4906 950 798	2640.9163 872 567	3227.1742 677 853	3942.0259 594 934	30
31	2658.4035 549 481	3275.7363 201 983	4034.9678 347 316	4967.9527 089 617	31
32	3270.8363 725 862	4062.9130 370 459	5044.7097 934 145	6260.6204 132 917	32
33	4024.1287 382 810	5039.0121 659 369	6306.8872 417 681	7889.3817 207 476	33
34	4950.6783 480 856	6249.3750 857 617	7884.6090 522 101	9941.6209 681 420	34
35	6090.3343 681 453	7750.2251 063 445	9856.7613 152 626	12527.4424 198 589	35
36	7492.1112 728 187	9611.2791 318 672	12321.9516 440 783	15785.5774 490 222	36
37	9216.2968 655 670	11918.9861 235 154	15403.4395 550 979	19890.8275 857 679	37
38	11337.0451 446 474	14780.5427 931 591	19255.2994 438 724	25063.4427 580 676	38
39	13945.5655 279 163	18328.8730 635 172	24070.1243 048 404	31580.9378 751 652	39
40	17154.0455 993 371	22728.8025 987 614	30088.6553 810 506	39792.9817 227 081	40
41	21100.4760 871 846	28184.7152 224 641	37611.8192 263 132	50140.1569 706 122	41
42	25954.5855 872 370	34950.0468 758 555	47015.7740 328 915	63177.5977 829 714	42
43	31925.1402 723 016	43339.0581 260 608	58770.7175 411 144	79604.7732 065 440	43
44	39268.9225 349 309	53741.4320 763 154	73464.3969 263 930	100303.0142 402 454	44
45	48301.7747 179 650	66640.3757 746 311	91831.4961 579 912	126382.7979 427 092	45
46	59412.1829 030 970	82635.0659 605 426	114790.3701 974 890	159243.3254 078 136	46
47	73077.9849 708 093	102468.4817 910 728	143488.9627 468 613	200647.5900 138 451	47
48	89886.9215 140 954	127061.9174 209 303	179362.2034 335 766	252816.9634 174 449	48
49	110561.9134 623 374	157557.7776 019 536	224203.7542 919 707	318550.3739 059 805	49
50	135992.1535 586 750	195372.6442 264 224	280255.6928 649 634	401374.4711 215 355	50
51	167271.3488 771 702	242263.0788 407 638	350320.6160 812 042	505732.8336 131 347	51
52	205744.7591 189 194	300407.2177 625 471	437901.7701 015 053	637224.3703 525 497	52
53	253067.0537 162 708	372505.9500 255 584	547378.2126 268 816	802903.7066 442 126	53
54	311273.4760 710 131	461908.3780 316 924	684223.7657 836 020	1011659.6703 717 079	54
55	382867.3755 673 461	572767.3887 592 986	855280.7072 295 025	1274692.1846 683 520	55
56	470927.8719 478 357	710232.5620 615 302	1069101.8840 368 781	1606113.1526 821 235	56
57	579242.2824 958 379	880689.3769 562 975	1336378.3550 460 977	2023703.5723 794 756	57
58	712469.0074 698 806	1092055.8274 258 089	1670473.9438 076 221	2549867.5011 981 392	58
59	876337.8791 879 532	1354150.2260 080 030	2088093.4297 595 276	3212834.0515 096 554	59
60	1077896.5914 011 824	1679147.2802 499 237	2610117.7871 994 095	4048171.9049 021 658	60

TABLE 2. FUTURE WORTH OF ONE DOLLAR PER PERIOD WITH INTEREST
Payable at end of each period

YEARS	27% Nominal Annual Rate	28% Nominal Annual Rate	29% Nominal Annual Rate	30% Nominal Annual Rate	YEARS
1	1.0000 000 000	1.0000 000 000	1.0000 000 000	1.0000 000 000	1
2	2.2700 000 000	2.2800 000 000	2.2900 000 000	2.3000 000 000	2
3	3.8829 000 000	3.9184 000 000	3.9541 000 000	3.9900 000 000	3
4	5.9312 830 000	6.0155 520 000	6.1007 890 000	6.1870 000 000	4
5	8.5327 294 100	8.6999 065 600	8.8700 178 100	9.0431 000 000	5
6	11.8365 663 507	12.1358 803 968	12.4423 229 749	12.7560 300 000	6
7	16.0324 392 654	16.5339 269 079	17.0505 966 376	17.5828 390 000	7
8	21.3611 978 670	22.1634 264 421	22.9952 696 625	23.8576 907 000	8
9	28.1287 212 911	29.3691 858 459	30.6638 978 647	32.0149 979 100	9
10	36.7234 760 398	38.5925 578 828	40.5564 282 454	42.6194 972 830	10
11	47.6388 145 705	50.3984 740 899	53.3177 924 366	56.4053 464 679	11
12	61.5012 945 045	65.5100 468 351	69.7799 522 432	74.3269 504 083	12
13	79.1066 440 207	84.8528 599 490	91.0161 383 937	97.6250 355 308	13
14	101.4654 379 063	109.6116 607 347	118.4108 185 279	127.9125 461 900	14
15	129.8611 061 411	141.3029 257 404	153.7499 559 010	167.2863 100 470	15
16	165.9236 047 991	181.8677 449 477	199.3374 431 123	218.4722 030 611	16
17	211.7229 780 949	233.7907 135 330	258.1453 016 149	285.0138 639 794	17
18	269.8881 821 805	300.2521 133 223	334.0074 390 832	371.5180 231 732	18
19	343.7579 913 693	385.3227 050 525	431.8695 964 173	483.9734 301 251	19
20	437.5726 490 390	494.2130 624 672	558.1117 793 783	630.1654 591 627	20
21	556.7172 642 795	633.5927 199 580	720.9641 953 980	820.2150 969 115	21
22	708.0309 256 350	811.9986 815 463	931.0438 120 634	1067.2796 259 850	22
23	900.1992 755 564	1040.3583 123 792	1202.0465 175 618	1388.4635 137 804	23
24	1144.2530 799 566	1332.6586 398 454	1551.6400 076 548	1806.0025 679 146	24
25	1454.2014 115 449	1706.8030 590 021	2002.6156 098 746	2348.8033 382 889	25
26	1847.8357 926 621	2185.7079 155 227	2584.3741 367 383	3054.4443 397 756	26
27	2347.7514 566 808	2798.7061 318 691	3334.8426 363 924	3971.7776 417 083	27
28	2982.6443 499 847	3583.3438 487 924	4302.9470 009 462	5164.3109 342 208	28
29	3788.9583 244 805	4587.6801 264 543	5551.8016 312 205	6714.6042 144 870	29
30	4812.9770 720 903	5873.2305 618 614	7162.8241 042 745	8729.9854 788 331	30
31	6113.4808 815 546	7518.7351 191 827	9241.0430 945 141	11349.9811 224 831	31
32	7765.1207 195 744	9624.9809 525 538	11921.9455 919 232	14755.9754 592 280	32
33	9862.7033 138 595	12320.9756 192 689	15380.3098 135 809	19183.7680 969 964	33
34	12526.6332 086 015	15771.8487 926 641	19841.5996 595 194	24939.8985 260 954	34
35	15909.8241 749 239	20188.9664 546 101	25596.6635 607 800	32422.8680 839 240	35
36	20206.4767 021 534	25842.8770 619 009	33020.6959 934 062	42150.7285 091 012	36
37	25663.2254 117 348	33079.8826 392 332	42597.6978 314 940	54796.9470 618 315	37
38	32593.2962 729 032	42343.2497 782 185	54952.0302 026 273	71237.0311 803 809	38
39	41394.4862 665 871	54200.3597 161 197	70889.1189 613 892	92609.1405 344 952	39
40	52571.9975 585 656	69377.4604 366 332	91447.9634 601 921	120392.8826 948 438	40
41	66767.4368 993 783	88804.1493 588 905	117968.8728 636 478	156511.7475 032 969	41
42	84795.6448 622 104	113670.3111 793 798	152180.8459 941 057	203466.2717 542 860	42
43	107691.4689 750 073	145498.9983 096 061	196314.2913 323 964	264507.1532 805 718	43
44	136769.1655 982 592	186239.7178 362 959	253246.4358 187 913	343860.2992 647 434	44
45	173697.8403 097 892	238387.8388 304 587	326688.9022 062 408	447019.3890 441 664	45
46	220597.2571 934 323	305137.4337 029 871	421429.6838 460 506	581126.2057 574 163	46
47	280159.5166 356 590	390576.9151 398 235	543645.2921 614 053	755465.0674 846 412	47
48	355803.5861 272 869	499939.4513 789 741	701303.4268 882 129	982105.5877 300 336	48
49	451871.5543 816 544	639923.4977 650 869	904682.4206 857 946	1276738.2640 490 436	49
50	573877.8740 647 011	819103.0771 393 112	1167041.3226 846 750	1659760.7432 637 567	50
51	728825.9000 621 704	1048452.9387 383 183	1505484.3062 632 308	2157689.9662 428 837	51
52	925609.8930 789 564	1342020.7615 850 475	1942075.7550 795 677	2804997.9561 157 488	52
53	1175525.5642 102 746	1717787.5748 288 607	2505278.7240 526 423	3646498.3429 504 735	53
54	1492918.4665 470 488	2198769.0957 809 417	3231810.5540 279 086	4740448.8458 356 155	54
55	1896007.4525 147 519	2814425.4425 996 054	4169036.6146 960 020	6162584.4995 863 001	55
56	2407930.4646 937 349	3602465.5665 274 949	5378058.2329 578 426	8011360.8494 621 901	56
57	3058072.6901 610 433	4611156.9251 551 935	6937696.1205 156 169	10414770.1043 008 472	57
58	3883753.3165 045 250	5902281.8641 986 476	8949628.9954 651 458	13539202.1355 911 012	58
59	4932367.7119 607 468	7554921.7861 742 690	11545022.4041 500 381	17600963.7762 684 316	59
60	6264107.9941 901 484	9670300.8863 030 643	14893079.9013 535 492	22881253.9091 489 610	60

TABLE 3. SINKING FUND FACTORS
Payable at end of each period

YEARS	5% Nominal Annual Rate	5¼% Nominal Annual Rate	5½% Nominal Annual Rate	5¾% Nominal Annual Rate	YEARS
1	1.0000 000 000	1.0000 000 000	1.0000 000 000	1.0000 000 000	1
2	0.4878 048 780	0.4872 107 186	0.4866 180 049	0.4860 267 315	2
3	0.3172 085 646	0.3164 300 363	0.3156 540 747	0.3148 806 701	3
4	0.2320 118 326	0.2311 513 576	0.2302 944 853	0.2294 412 017	4
5	0.1809 747 981	0.1800 733 168	0.1791 764 362	0.1782 841 371	5
6	0.1470 174 681	0.1460 954 203	0.1451 789 476	0.1442 680 253	6
7	0.1228 198 184	0.1218 888 524	0.1209 644 178	0.1200 464 834	7
8	0.1047 218 136	0.1037 891 770	0.1028 640 118	0.1019 462 799	8
9	0.0906 900 800	0.0897 605 712	0.0888 394 585	0.0879 266 954	9
10	0.0795 045 750	0.0785 815 194	0.0776 677 687	0.0767 632 671	10
11	0.0703 888 915	0.0694 746 736	0.0685 706 532	0.0676 767 637	11
12	0.0628 254 100	0.0619 217 842	0.0610 292 312	0.0601 476 727	12
13	0.0564 557 652	0.0555 640 468	0.0546 842 587	0.0538 163 092	13
14	0.0510 239 695	0.0501 451 581	0.0492 791 154	0.0484 257 351	14
15	0.0463 422 876	0.0454 771 489	0.0446 255 976	0.0437 875 108	15
16	0.0422 699 080	0.0414 190 304	0.0405 825 380	0.0397 602 900	16
17	0.0386 991 417	0.0378 629 764	0.0370 419 723	0.0362 359 691	17
18	0.0355 462 223	0.0347 251 119	0.0339 199 163	0.0331 304 539	18
19	0.0327 450 104	0.0319 392 107	0.0311 500 559	0.0303 773 417	19
20	0.0302 425 872	0.0294 522 832	0.0286 793 300	0.0279 234 988	20
21	0.0279 961 071	0.0272 214 252	0.0264 647 754	0.0257 259 022	21
22	0.0259 705 086	0.0252 115 264	0.0244 712 319	0.0237 493 418	22
23	0.0241 368 219	0.0233 935 759	0.0226 696 472	0.0219 647 226	23
24	0.0224 709 008	0.0217 433 921	0.0210 358 037	0.0203 477 910	24
25	0.0209 524 573	0.0202 406 571	0.0195 493 529	0.0188 781 674	25
26	0.0195 643 207	0.0188 681 737	0.0181 930 713	0.0175 386 012	26
27	0.0182 918 599	0.0176 112 882	0.0169 522 817	0.0163 143 920	27
28	0.0171 225 304	0.0164 574 362	0.0158 143 996	0.0151 929 348	28
29	0.0160 455 149	0.0153 957 825	0.0147 685 720	0.0141 633 587	29
30	0.0150 514 351	0.0144 169 335	0.0138 053 897	0.0132 162 386	30
31	0.0141 321 204	0.0135 127 048	0.0129 166 543	0.0123 433 625	31
32	0.0132 804 189	0.0126 759 322	0.0120 951 895	0.0115 375 417	32
33	0.0124 900 437	0.0119 003 179	0.0113 346 865	0.0107 924 570	33
34	0.0117 554 454	0.0111 803 028	0.0106 295 769	0.0101 025 304	34
35	0.0110 717 072	0.0105 109 616	0.0099 749 266	0.0094 628 198	35
36	0.0104 344 571	0.0098 879 146	0.0093 663 488	0.0088 689 312	36
37	0.0098 397 945	0.0093 072 544	0.0087 999 295	0.0083 169 445	37
38	0.0092 842 282	0.0087 654 839	0.0082 721 659	0.0078 033 517	38
39	0.0087 646 242	0.0082 594 639	0.0077 799 139	0.0073 250 044	39
40	0.0082 781 612	0.0077 863 683	0.0073 203 434	0.0068 790 687	40
41	0.0078 222 924	0.0073 436 465	0.0068 909 001	0.0064 629 876	41
42	0.0073 947 131	0.0069 289 905	0.0064 892 731	0.0060 744 478	42
43	0.0069 933 328	0.0065 403 066	0.0061 133 667	0.0057 113 517	43
44	0.0066 162 506	0.0061 756 919	0.0057 612 757	0.0053 717 934	44
45	0.0062 617 347	0.0058 334 124	0.0054 312 651	0.0050 540 370	45
46	0.0059 282 036	0.0055 118 853	0.0051 217 512	0.0047 564 988	46
47	0.0056 142 109	0.0052 096 629	0.0048 312 858	0.0044 777 310	47
48	0.0053 184 306	0.0049 254 187	0.0045 585 424	0.0042 164 076	48
49	0.0050 396 453	0.0046 579 348	0.0043 023 035	0.0039 713 125	49
50	0.0047 767 355	0.0044 060 917	0.0040 614 501	0.0037 413 281	50
51	0.0045 286 697	0.0041 688 583	0.0038 349 523	0.0035 254 263	51
52	0.0042 944 966	0.0039 452 836	0.0036 218 603	0.0033 226 596	52
53	0.0040 733 368	0.0037 344 893	0.0034 212 975	0.0031 321 537	53
54	0.0038 643 770	0.0035 356 631	0.0032 324 534	0.0029 531 008	54
55	0.0036 668 637	0.0033 480 527	0.0030 545 778	0.0027 847 538	55
56	0.0034 800 978	0.0031 709 607	0.0028 869 756	0.0026 264 207	56
57	0.0033 034 300	0.0030 037 397	0.0027 290 020	0.0024 774 599	57
58	0.0031 362 568	0.0028 457 878	0.0025 800 578	0.0023 372 760	58
59	0.0029 780 161	0.0026 965 454	0.0024 395 863	0.0022 053 159	59
60	0.0028 281 845	0.0025 554 911	0.0023 070 692	0.0020 810 653	60

TABLE 3. SINKING FUND FACTORS
Payable at end of each period

YEARS	6% Nominal Annual Rate	6¼% Nominal Annual Rate	6½% Nominal Annual Rate	6¾% Nominal Annual Rate	YEARS
1	1.0000 000 000	1.0000 000 000	1.0000 000 000	1.0000 000 000	1
2	0.4854 368 932	0.4848 484 848	0.4842 615 012	0.4836 759 371	2
3	0.3141 098 128	0.3133 414 933	0.3125 757 019	0.3118 124 292	3
4	0.2285 914 924	0.2277 453 433	0.2269 027 404	0.2260 636 696	4
5	0.1773 964 004	0.1765 132 070	0.1756 345 376	0.1747 603 731	5
6	0.1433 626 285	0.1424 627 324	0.1415 683 122	0.1406 793 430	6
7	0.1191 350 181	0.1182 299 905	0.1173 313 693	0.1164 391 229	7
8	0.1010 359 426	0.1001 329 614	0.0992 372 971	0.0983 489 106	8
9	0.0870 222 350	0.0861 260 300	0.0852 380 329	0.0843 581 957	9
10	0.0758 679 582	0.0749 817 850	0.0741 046 901	0.0732 366 154	10
11	0.0667 929 381	0.0659 191 083	0.0650 552 058	0.0642 011 613	11
12	0.0592 770 294	0.0584 172 209	0.0575 681 661	0.0567 297 830	12
13	0.0529 601 053	0.0521 155 531	0.0512 825 571	0.0504 610 213	13
14	0.0475 849 090	0.0467 565 278	0.0459 404 806	0.0451 366 553	14
15	0.0429 627 640	0.0421 512 307	0.0413 527 830	0.0405 672 913	15
16	0.0389 521 436	0.0381 579 538	0.0373 775 740	0.0366 108 553	16
17	0.0354 448 042	0.0346 683 124	0.0339 063 265	0.0331 586 771	17
18	0.0323 565 406	0.0315 979 892	0.0308 546 103	0.0301 262 124	18
19	0.0296 208 604	0.0288 804 015	0.0281 557 517	0.0274 466 955	19
20	0.0271 845 570	0.0264 622 687	0.0257 563 954	0.0250 666 956	20
21	0.0250 045 467	0.0243 004 459	0.0236 133 343	0.0229 429 431	21
22	0.0230 455 685	0.0223 596 209	0.0216 912 043	0.0210 400 217	22
23	0.0212 784 847	0.0206 106 121	0.0199 607 802	0.0193 286 615	23
24	0.0196 790 050	0.0190 290 926	0.0183 976 975	0.0177 844 606	24
25	0.0182 267 182	0.0175 946 193	0.0169 814 811	0.0163 869 117	25
26	0.0169 043 467	0.0162 898 870	0.0156 947 983	0.0151 186 545	26
27	0.0156 971 663	0.0151 001 480	0.0145 228 776	0.0139 648 937	27
28	0.0145 925 515	0.0140 127 561	0.0134 530 522	0.0129 129 423	28
29	0.0135 796 135	0.0130 168 045	0.0124 743 976	0.0119 518 582	29
30	0.0126 489 115	0.0121 028 369	0.0115 774 422	0.0110 721 549	30
31	0.0117 922 196	0.0112 626 140	0.0107 539 335	0.0102 655 672	31
32	0.0110 023 374	0.0104 889 235	0.0099 966 481	0.0095 248 610	32
33	0.0102 729 350	0.0097 754 257	0.0092 992 365	0.0088 436 779	33
34	0.0095 984 254	0.0091 165 250	0.0086 560 953	0.0082 164 072	34
35	0.0089 738 590	0.0085 072 643	0.0080 622 606	0.0076 380 792	35
36	0.0083 948 348	0.0079 432 368	0.0075 133 205	0.0071 042 775	36
37	0.0078 574 274	0.0074 205 119	0.0070 053 400	0.0066 110 638	37
38	0.0073 581 240	0.0069 355 731	0.0065 347 995	0.0061 549 164	38
39	0.0068 937 724	0.0064 852 650	0.0060 985 416	0.0057 326 766	39
40	0.0064 615 359	0.0060 667 487	0.0056 937 260	0.0053 415 040	40
41	0.0060 588 551	0.0056 774 635	0.0053 177 915	0.0049 788 379	41
42	0.0056 834 152	0.0053 150 939	0.0049 684 229	0.0046 423 647	42
43	0.0053 331 178	0.0049 775 415	0.0046 435 230	0.0043 299 891	43
44	0.0050 060 565	0.0046 629 004	0.0043 411 874	0.0040 398 096	44
45	0.0047 004 958	0.0043 694 364	0.0040 596 841	0.0037 700 975	45
46	0.0044 148 527	0.0040 955 681	0.0037 974 344	0.0035 192 782	46
47	0.0041 476 805	0.0038 398 510	0.0035 529 973	0.0032 859 149	47
48	0.0038 976 549	0.0036 009 636	0.0033 250 549	0.0030 686 946	48
49	0.0036 635 619	0.0033 776 947	0.0031 124 000	0.0028 664 154	49
50	0.0034 442 864	0.0031 689 327	0.0029 139 255	0.0026 779 758	50
51	0.0032 388 028	0.0029 736 559	0.0027 286 146	0.0025 023 649	51
52	0.0030 461 669	0.0027 909 239	0.0025 555 319	0.0023 386 536	52
53	0.0028 655 076	0.0026 198 702	0.0023 938 164	0.0021 859 872	53
54	0.0026 960 209	0.0024 596 952	0.0022 426 740	0.0020 435 785	54
55	0.0025 369 634	0.0023 096 603	0.0021 013 722	0.0019 107 014	55
56	0.0023 876 472	0.0021 690 828	0.0019 692 339	0.0017 866 863	56
57	0.0022 474 350	0.0020 373 305	0.0018 456 332	0.0016 709 142	57
58	0.0021 157 359	0.0019 138 178	0.0017 299 909	0.0015 628 130	58
59	0.0019 920 012	0.0017 980 017	0.0016 217 702	0.0014 618 533	59
60	0.0018 757 215	0.0016 893 780	0.0015 204 735	0.0013 675 449	60

TABLE 3. SINKING FUND FACTORS
Payable at end of each period

YEARLY Compounding

YEARS	7% Nominal Annual Rate	7¼% Nominal Annual Rate	7½% Nominal Annual Rate	7¾% Nominal Annual Rate	YEARS
1	1.0000 000 000	1.0000 000 000	1.0000 000 000	1.0000 000 000	1
2	0.4830 917 874	0.4825 090 470	0.4819 277 108	0.4813 477 738	2
3	0.3110 516 657	0.3102 934 018	0.3095 376 282	0.3087 843 354	3
4	0.2252 281 167	0.2243 960 677	0.2235 675 087	0.2227 424 256	4
5	0.1738 906 944	0.1730 254 824	0.1721 647 178	0.1713 083 816	5
6	0.1397 957 998	0.1389 176 575	0.1380 448 912	0.1371 774 758	6
7	0.1155 532 196	0.1146 736 277	0.1138 003 154	0.1129 332 506	7
8	0.0974 677 625	0.0965 938 133	0.0957 270 232	0.0948 673 523	8
9	0.0834 864 701	0.0826 228 077	0.0817 671 595	0.0809 194 764	9
10	0.0723 775 027	0.0715 272 931	0.0706 859 274	0.0698 533 459	10
11	0.0633 569 048	0.0625 223 660	0.0616 974 737	0.0608 821 565	11
12	0.0559 019 887	0.0550 846 995	0.0542 778 313	0.0534 812 990	12
13	0.0496 508 481	0.0488 519 395	0.0480 641 963	0.0472 875 184	13
14	0.0443 449 386	0.0435 652 161	0.0427 973 721	0.0420 412 901	14
15	0.0397 946 247	0.0390 346 509	0.0382 872 363	0.0375 522 462	15
16	0.0358 576 477	0.0351 177 994	0.0343 911 571	0.0336 775 665	16
17	0.0324 251 931	0.0317 057 015	0.0310 000 282	0.0303 079 971	17
18	0.0294 126 017	0.0287 135 825	0.0280 289 578	0.0273 585 289	18
19	0.0267 530 148	0.0260 744 900	0.0254 108 994	0.0247 620 199	19
20	0.0243 929 257	0.0237 348 402	0.0230 921 916	0.0224 647 312	20
21	0.0222 890 017	0.0216 512 369	0.0210 293 742	0.0204 231 377	21
22	0.0204 057 732	0.0197 881 574	0.0191 868 710	0.0186 016 097	22
23	0.0187 139 263	0.0181 162 427	0.0175 352 780	0.0169 706 983	23
24	0.0171 890 207	0.0166 110 150	0.0160 500 795	0.0155 058 498	24
25	0.0158 105 172	0.0152 519 025	0.0147 106 716	0.0141 864 289	25
26	0.0145 610 279	0.0140 214 900	0.0134 996 124	0.0129 949 668	26
27	0.0134 257 340	0.0129 049 358	0.0124 020 369	0.0119 165 766	27
28	0.0123 919 283	0.0118 895 127	0.0114 051 993	0.0109 384 939	28
29	0.0114 486 518	0.0109 642 454	0.0104 981 081	0.0100 497 125	29
30	0.0105 864 035	0.0101 196 190	0.0096 712 358	0.0092 406 925	30
31	0.0097 969 061	0.0093 473 449	0.0089 162 831	0.0085 031 255	31
32	0.0090 729 155	0.0086 401 700	0.0082 259 887	0.0078 297 432	32
33	0.0084 080 653	0.0079 917 204	0.0075 939 728	0.0072 141 607	33
34	0.0077 967 381	0.0073 963 736	0.0070 146 084	0.0066 507 481	34
35	0.0072 339 596	0.0068 491 512	0.0064 829 147	0.0061 345 234	35
36	0.0067 153 097	0.0063 456 308	0.0059 944 680	0.0056 610 631	36
37	0.0062 368 480	0.0058 818 710	0.0055 453 271	0.0052 264 278	37
38	0.0057 950 515	0.0054 543 489	0.0051 319 709	0.0048 270 991	38
39	0.0053 867 616	0.0050 599 071	0.0047 512 443	0.0044 599 263	39
40	0.0050 091 389	0.0046 957 084	0.0044 003 138	0.0041 220 809	40
41	0.0046 596 245	0.0043 591 971	0.0040 766 282	0.0038 110 177	41
42	0.0043 359 072	0.0040 480 660	0.0037 778 858	0.0035 244 417	42
43	0.0040 358 953	0.0037 602 278	0.0035 020 052	0.0032 602 794	43
44	0.0037 576 913	0.0034 937 906	0.0032 471 012	0.0030 166 536	44
45	0.0034 995 710	0.0032 470 360	0.0030 114 630	0.0027 918 622	45
46	0.0032 599 650	0.0030 184 011	0.0027 935 352	0.0025 843 592	46
47	0.0030 374 421	0.0028 064 616	0.0025 919 020	0.0023 927 383	47
48	0.0028 306 953	0.0026 099 179	0.0024 052 724	0.0022 157 185	48
49	0.0026 385 294	0.0024 275 824	0.0022 324 676	0.0020 521 314	49
50	0.0024 598 495	0.0022 583 683	0.0020 724 102	0.0019 009 099	50
51	0.0022 936 519	0.0021 012 800	0.0019 241 141	0.0017 610 787	51
52	0.0021 390 147	0.0019 554 044	0.0017 866 757	0.0016 317 448	52
53	0.0019 950 908	0.0018 199 028	0.0016 592 661	0.0015 120 905	53
54	0.0018 611 007	0.0016 940 045	0.0015 411 247	0.0014 013 656	54
55	0.0017 363 264	0.0015 770 005	0.0014 315 521	0.0012 988 821	55
56	0.0016 201 059	0.0014 682 379	0.0013 299 053	0.0012 040 076	56
57	0.0015 118 286	0.0013 671 148	0.0012 355 927	0.0011 161 612	57
58	0.0014 109 304	0.0012 730 763	0.0011 480 689	0.0010 348 086	58
59	0.0013 168 900	0.0011 856 102	0.0010 668 318	0.0009 594 577	59
60	0.0012 292 255	0.0011 042 434	0.0009 914 178	0.0008 896 558	60

YEARLY
Compounding

TABLE 3. SINKING FUND FACTORS
Payable at end of each period

YEARS	8% Nominal Annual Rate	8¼% Nominal Annual Rate	8½% Nominal Annual Rate	8¾% Nominal Annual Rate	YEARS
1	1.0000 000 000	1.0000 000 000	1.0000 000 000	1.0000 000 000	1
2	0.4807 692 308	0.4801 920 768	0.4796 163 070	0.4790 419 162	2
3	0.3080 335 140	0.3072 851 549	0.3065 392 485	0.3057 957 858	3
4	0.2219 208 045	0.2211 026 314	0.2202 878 926	0.2194 765 741	4
5	0.1704 564 546	0.1696 089 177	0.1687 657 519	0.1679 269 380	5
6	0.1363 153 862	0.1354 585 973	0.1346 070 840	0.1337 608 210	6
7	0.1120 724 014	0.1112 177 357	0.1103 692 212	0.1095 268 257	7
8	0.0940 147 606	0.0931 692 077	0.0923 306 533	0.0914 990 569	8
9	0.0800 797 092	0.0792 478 081	0.0784 237 233	0.0776 074 047	9
10	0.0690 294 887	0.0682 142 953	0.0674 077 051	0.0666 096 571	10
11	0.0600 763 421	0.0592 799 582	0.0584 929 316	0.0577 151 891	11
12	0.0526 950 169	0.0519 188 989	0.0511 528 581	0.0503 968 072	12
13	0.0465 218 052	0.0457 669 552	0.0450 228 662	0.0442 894 355	13
14	0.0412 968 528	0.0405 639 419	0.0398 424 382	0.0391 322 220	14
15	0.0368 295 449	0.0361 189 958	0.0354 204 614	0.0347 338 033	15
16	0.0329 768 720	0.0322 889 169	0.0316 135 439	0.0309 505 944	16
17	0.0296 294 315	0.0289 641 532	0.0283 119 832	0.0276 727 417	17
18	0.0267 020 959	0.0260 594 578	0.0254 304 127	0.0248 147 580	18
19	0.0241 276 275	0.0235 074 967	0.0229 014 015	0.0223 091 151	19
20	0.0218 522 088	0.0212 543 737	0.0206 709 744	0.0201 017 588	20
21	0.0198 322 503	0.0192 564 344	0.0186 954 120	0.0181 489 047	21
22	0.0180 320 684	0.0174 779 414	0.0169 389 233	0.0164 147 087	22
23	0.0164 221 692	0.0158 893 563	0.0153 719 258	0.0148 695 444	23
24	0.0149 779 616	0.0144 660 509	0.0139 697 546	0.0134 887 111	24
25	0.0136 787 791	0.0131 873 278	0.0127 116 825	0.0122 514 527	25
26	0.0125 071 267	0.0120 356 670	0.0115 801 651	0.0111 402 014	26
27	0.0114 480 962	0.0109 961 396	0.0105 602 540	0.0101 399 907	27
28	0.0104 889 057	0.0100 559 473	0.0096 391 357	0.0092 379 932	28
29	0.0096 185 350	0.0092 040 571	0.0088 057 657	0.0084 231 541	29
30	0.0088 274 334	0.0084 309 086	0.0080 505 753	0.0076 858 985	30
31	0.0081 072 841	0.0077 281 783	0.0073 652 359	0.0070 178 940	31
32	0.0074 508 132	0.0070 885 879	0.0067 424 664	0.0064 118 586	32
33	0.0068 516 324	0.0065 057 472	0.0061 758 763	0.0058 614 033	33
34	0.0063 041 101	0.0059 740 247	0.0056 598 358	0.0053 609 020	34
35	0.0058 032 646	0.0054 884 403	0.0051 893 685	0.0049 053 836	35
36	0.0053 446 741	0.0050 445 759	0.0047 600 615	0.0044 904 426	36
37	0.0049 244 025	0.0046 385 004	0.0043 679 904	0.0041 121 629	37
38	0.0045 389 361	0.0042 667 060	0.0040 096 556	0.0037 670 548	38
39	0.0041 851 297	0.0039 260 551	0.0036 819 284	0.0034 520 009	39
40	0.0038 601 615	0.0036 137 343	0.0033 820 056	0.0031 642 097	40
41	0.0035 614 940	0.0033 272 154	0.0031 073 700	0.0029 011 768	41
42	0.0032 868 407	0.0030 642 218	0.0028 557 568	0.0026 606 508	42
43	0.0030 341 370	0.0028 226 997	0.0026 251 245	0.0024 406 043	43
44	0.0028 015 156	0.0026 007 930	0.0024 136 299	0.0022 392 086	44
45	0.0025 872 845	0.0023 968 216	0.0022 196 061	0.0020 548 114	45
46	0.0023 899 085	0.0022 092 622	0.0020 415 434	0.0018 859 184	46
47	0.0022 079 922	0.0020 367 322	0.0018 780 731	0.0017 311 756	47
48	0.0020 402 660	0.0018 779 743	0.0017 279 519	0.0015 893 556	48
49	0.0018 855 731	0.0017 318 448	0.0015 900 501	0.0014 593 436	49
50	0.0017 428 582	0.0015 973 012	0.0014 633 395	0.0013 401 268	50
51	0.0016 111 575	0.0014 733 928	0.0013 468 835	0.0012 307 838	51
52	0.0014 895 903	0.0013 592 518	0.0012 398 282	0.0011 304 758	52
53	0.0013 773 506	0.0012 540 852	0.0011 413 945	0.0010 384 385	53
54	0.0012 737 003	0.0011 571 677	0.0010 508 710	0.0009 539 750	54
55	0.0011 779 629	0.0010 678 356	0.0009 676 075	0.0008 764 496	55
56	0.0010 895 180	0.0009 854 810	0.0008 910 096	0.0008 052 817	56
57	0.0010 077 963	0.0009 095 471	0.0008 205 332	0.0007 399 410	57
58	0.0009 322 748	0.0000 395 228	0.0007 556 803	0.0006 799 428	58
59	0.0008 624 729	0.0007 749 397	0.0006 959 948	0.0006 248 441	59
60	0.0007 979 488	0.0007 153 675	0.0006 410 586	0.0005 742 394	60

TABLE 3. SINKING FUND FACTORS
Payable at end of each period

YEARLY
Compounding

YEARS	9% Nominal Annual Rate	9¼% Nominal Annual Rate	9½% Nominal Annual Rate	9¾% Nominal Annual Rate	YEARS
1	1.0000 000 000	1.0000 000 000	1.0000 000 000	1.0000 000 000	1
2	0.4784 688 995	0.4778 972 521	0.4773 269 690	0.4767 580 453	2
3	0.3050 547 573	0.3043 161 541	0.3035 799 668	0.3028 461 863	3
4	0.2186 686 621	0.2178 641 428	0.2170 630 025	0.2162 652 273	4
5	0.1670 924 570	0.1662 622 898	0.1654 364 173	0.1646 148 207	5
6	0.1329 197 833	0.1320 839 456	0.1312 532 826	0.1304 277 693	6
7	0.1086 905 168	0.1078 602 623	0.1070 360 296	0.1062 177 862	7
8	0.0906 743 778	0.0898 565 753	0.0890 456 084	0.0882 414 362	8
9	0.0767 988 021	0.0759 978 649	0.0752 045 426	0.0744 187 843	9
10	0.0658 200 899	0.0650 389 420	0.0642 661 517	0.0635 016 567	10
11	0.0569 466 567	0.0561 872 605	0.0554 369 258	0.0546 955 780	11
12	0.0496 506 585	0.0489 143 237	0.0481 877 142	0.0474 707 411	12
13	0.0435 665 597	0.0428 541 351	0.0421 520 575	0.0414 602 220	13
14	0.0384 331 730	0.0377 451 703	0.0370 680 923	0.0364 018 174	14
15	0.0340 588 827	0.0333 955 599	0.0327 436 950	0.0321 031 476	15
16	0.0302 999 097	0.0296 613 301	0.0290 346 957	0.0284 198 461	16
17	0.0270 462 485	0.0264 323 225	0.0258 307 825	0.0252 414 470	17
18	0.0242 122 907	0.0236 228 071	0.0230 461 037	0.0224 819 766	18
19	0.0217 304 107	0.0211 650 609	0.0206 128 384	0.0200 735 164	19
20	0.0195 464 750	0.0190 048 710	0.0184 766 953	0.0179 616 966	20
21	0.0176 166 348	0.0170 983 246	0.0165 936 973	0.0161 024 773	21
22	0.0159 049 930	0.0154 094 722	0.0149 278 440	0.0144 598 073	22
23	0.0143 818 800	0.0139 086 023	0.0134 493 824	0.0130 038 939	23
24	0.0130 225 607	0.0125 709 455	0.0121 335 107	0.0117 099 039	24
25	0.0118 062 505	0.0113 756 909	0.0109 593 925	0.0105 569 774	25
26	0.0107 153 599	0.0103 052 282	0.0099 093 986	0.0095 274 680	26
27	0.0097 349 054	0.0093 445 587	0.0089 685 169	0.0086 063 520	27
28	0.0088 520 473	0.0084 808 321	0.0081 238 883	0.0077 807 635	28
29	0.0080 557 226	0.0077 029 789	0.0073 644 387	0.0070 396 263	29
30	0.0073 363 514	0.0070 014 162	0.0066 805 845	0.0063 733 578	30
31	0.0066 855 995	0.0063 678 100	0.0060 639 940	0.0057 736 314	31
32	0.0060 961 861	0.0057 948 827	0.0055 073 947	0.0052 331 817	32
33	0.0055 617 255	0.0052 762 539	0.0050 044 141	0.0047 456 463	33
34	0.0050 765 971	0.0048 063 109	0.0045 494 491	0.0043 054 344	34
35	0.0046 358 375	0.0043 800 995	0.0041 375 575	0.0039 076 177	35
36	0.0042 350 500	0.0039 932 346	0.0037 643 673	0.0035 478 397	36
37	0.0038 703 293	0.0036 418 233	0.0034 260 006	0.0032 222 394	37
38	0.0035 381 975	0.0033 224 015	0.0031 190 090	0.0029 273 865	38
39	0.0032 355 500	0.0030 318 795	0.0028 403 196	0.0026 602 268	39
40	0.0029 596 092	0.0027 674 955	0.0025 871 883	0.0024 180 358	40
41	0.0027 078 853	0.0025 267 759	0.0023 571 597	0.0021 983 782	41
42	0.0024 781 420	0.0023 075 015	0.0021 480 333	0.0019 990 738	42
43	0.0022 683 675	0.0021 076 778	0.0019 578 336	0.0018 181 678	43
44	0.0020 767 493	0.0019 255 098	0.0017 847 847	0.0016 539 050	44
45	0.0019 016 514	0.0017 593 795	0.0016 272 880	0.0015 047 074	45
46	0.0017 415 959	0.0016 078 267	0.0014 839 025	0.0013 691 546	46
47	0.0015 952 455	0.0014 695 322	0.0013 533 282	0.0012 459 669	47
48	0.0014 613 892	0.0013 433 027	0.0012 343 905	0.0011 339 900	48
49	0.0013 389 289	0.0012 280 577	0.0011 260 279	0.0010 321 818	49
50	0.0012 268 681	0.0011 228 182	0.0010 272 796	0.0009 396 008	50
51	0.0011 243 016	0.0010 266 960	0.0009 372 756	0.0008 553 960	51
52	0.0010 304 065	0.0009 388 852	0.0008 552 274	0.0007 787 971	52
53	0.0009 444 343	0.0008 586 535	0.0007 804 201	0.0007 091 069	53
54	0.0008 657 034	0.0007 853 357	0.0007 122 048	0.0006 456 939	54
55	0.0007 935 930	0.0007 183 263	0.0006 499 926	0.0005 879 856	55
56	0.0007 275 373	0.0006 570 749	0.0005 932 484	0.0005 354 631	56
57	0.0006 670 202	0.0006 010 801	0.0005 414 860	0.0004 876 556	57
58	0.0006 115 709	0.0005 498 852	0.0004 942 633	0.0004 441 358	58
59	0.0005 607 595	0.0005 030 742	0.0004 511 784	0.0004 045 158	59
60	0.0005 141 938	0.0004 602 678	0.0004 118 653	0.0003 684 435	60

YEARLY
Compounding

TABLE 3. SINKING FUND FACTORS
Payable at end of each period

YEARS	10% Nominal Annual Rate	10¼% Nominal Annual Rate	10½% Nominal Annual Rate	10¾% Nominal Annual Rate	YEARS
1	1.0000 000 000	1.0000 000 000	1.0000 000 000	1.0000 000 000	1
2	0.4761 904 762	0.4756 242 568	0.4750 593 824	0.4744 958 482	2
3	0.3021 148 036	0.3013 858 096	0.3006 591 953	0.2999 349 516	3
4	0.2154 708 037	0.2146 797 179	0.2138 919 564	0.2131 075 054	4
5	0.1637 974 808	0.1629 843 787	0.1621 754 954	0.1613 708 120	5
6	0.1296 073 804	0.1287 920 905	0.1279 818 746	0.1271 767 074	6
7	0.1054 054 997	0.1045 991 374	0.1037 986 667	0.1030 040 549	7
8	0.0874 440 176	0.0866 533 114	0.0858 692 763	0.0850 918 710	8
9	0.0736 405 391	0.0728 697 558	0.0721 063 831	0.0713 503 698	9
10	0.0627 453 949	0.0619 973 037	0.0612 573 206	0.0605 253 827	10
11	0.0539 631 420	0.0532 395 425	0.0525 247 041	0.0518 185 509	11
12	0.0467 633 151	0.0460 653 465	0.0453 767 456	0.0446 974 223	12
13	0.0407 785 238	0.0401 068 574	0.0394 451 173	0.0387 931 976	13
14	0.0357 462 232	0.0351 011 874	0.0344 665 871	0.0338 422 994	14
15	0.0314 737 769	0.0308 554 419	0.0302 480 015	0.0296 513 145	15
16	0.0278 166 207	0.0272 248 588	0.0266 443 997	0.0260 750 826	16
17	0.0246 641 344	0.0240 986 632	0.0235 448 518	0.0230 025 192	17
18	0.0219 302 222	0.0213 906 371	0.0208 630 182	0.0203 471 632	18
19	0.0195 468 682	0.0190 326 678	0.0185 306 897	0.0180 407 096	19
20	0.0174 596 248	0.0169 702 304	0.0164 932 653	0.0160 284 825	20
21	0.0156 243 898	0.0151 591 618	0.0147 065 219	0.0142 662 005	21
22	0.0140 050 630	0.0135 633 137	0.0131 342 647	0.0127 176 237	22
23	0.0125 718 127	0.0121 528 174	0.0117 465 900	0.0113 528 153	23
24	0.0112 997 764	0.0109 027 827	0.0105 185 815	0.0101 468 353	24
25	0.0101 680 722	0.0097 923 077	0.0094 293 198	0.0090 787 492	25
26	0.0091 590 386	0.0088 037 179	0.0084 611 196	0.0081 308 633	26
27	0.0082 576 423	0.0079 219 729	0.0075 989 359	0.0072 881 305	27
28	0.0074 510 132	0.0071 342 004	0.0068 298 968	0.0065 376 822	28
29	0.0067 280 747	0.0064 293 264	0.0061 429 332	0.0058 684 570	29
30	0.0060 792 483	0.0057 977 783	0.0055 284 815	0.0052 709 028	30
31	0.0054 962 140	0.0052 312 460	0.0049 782 438	0.0047 367 368	31
32	0.0049 717 167	0.0047 224 866	0.0044 849 922	0.0042 587 487	32
33	0.0044 994 063	0.0042 651 650	0.0040 424 091	0.0038 306 410	33
34	0.0040 737 064	0.0038 537 218	0.0036 449 545	0.0034 468 959	34
35	0.0036 897 051	0.0034 832 637	0.0032 877 563	0.0031 026 649	35
36	0.0033 430 638	0.0031 494 723	0.0029 665 187	0.0027 936 768	36
37	0.0030 299 405	0.0028 485 270	0.0026 774 443	0.0025 161 602	37
38	0.0027 469 250	0.0025 770 396	0.0024 171 697	0.0022 667 780	38
39	0.0024 909 840	0.0023 320 000	0.0021 827 092	0.0020 425 715	39
40	0.0022 594 144	0.0021 107 281	0.0019 714 084	0.0018 409 132	40
41	0.0020 498 028	0.0019 108 344	0.0017 809 027	0.0016 594 657	41
42	0.0018 599 911	0.0017 301 844	0.0016 090 833	0.0014 961 470	42
43	0.0016 880 466	0.0015 668 693	0.0014 540 666	0.0013 491 003	43
44	0.0015 322 365	0.0014 191 797	0.0013 141 681	0.0012 166 672	44
45	0.0013 910 047	0.0012 855 830	0.0011 878 796	0.0010 973 653	45
46	0.0012 629 527	0.0011 647 035	0.0010 738 498	0.0009 898 682	46
47	0.0011 468 221	0.0010 553 056	0.0009 708 663	0.0008 929 881	47
48	0.0010 414 797	0.0009 562 779	0.0008 778 407	0.0008 056 601	48
49	0.0009 459 041	0.0008 666 206	0.0007 937 954	0.0007 269 296	49
50	0.0008 591 740	0.0007 854 330	0.0007 178 512	0.0006 559 393	50
51	0.0007 804 577	0.0007 119 038	0.0006 492 173	0.0005 919 196	51
52	0.0007 090 040	0.0006 453 010	0.0005 871 820	0.0005 341 792	52
53	0.0006 441 339	0.0005 849 647	0.0005 311 042	0.0004 820 963	53
54	0.0005 852 336	0.0005 302 988	0.0004 804 064	0.0004 351 120	54
55	0.0005 317 476	0.0004 807 654	0.0004 345 680	0.0003 927 234	55
56	0.0004 831 734	0.0004 358 783	0.0003 931 196	0.0003 544 778	56
57	0.0004 390 556	0.0003 951 983	0.0003 556 378	0.0003 199 670	57
58	0.0003 985 822	0.0003 583 280	0.0003 217 406	0.0002 888 266	58
59	0.0003 625 796	0.0003 249 085	0.0002 910 832	0.0002 607 235	59
60	0.0003 295 092	0.0002 946 147	0.0002 633 544	0.0002 353 608	60

TABLE 3. SINKING FUND FACTORS
Payable at end of each period

YEARLY Compounding

YEARS	11% Nominal Annual Rate	11¼% Nominal Annual Rate	11½% Nominal Annual Rate	11¾% Nominal Annual Rate	YEARS
1	1.0000 000 000	1.0000 000 000	1.0000 000 000	1.0000 000 000	1
2	0.4739 336 493	0.4733 727 811	0.4728 132 388	0.4722 550 177	2
3	0.2992 130 696	0.2984 935 404	0.2977 763 551	0.2970 615 047	3
4	0.2123 263 515	0.2115 484 812	0.2107 738 808	0.2100 025 370	4
5	0.1605 703 095	0.1597 739 691	0.1589 817 720	0.1581 936 992	5
6	0.1263 765 636	0.1255 814 180	0.1247 912 454	0.1240 060 206	6
7	0.1022 152 695	0.1014 322 775	0.1006 550 465	0.0998 835 435	7
8	0.0843 210 542	0.0835 567 844	0.0827 990 200	0.0820 477 195	8
9	0.0706 016 644	0.0698 602 152	0.0691 259 707	0.0683 988 792	9
10	0.0598 014 271	0.0590 853 907	0.0583 772 102	0.0576 768 225	10
11	0.0511 210 071	0.0504 319 968	0.0497 514 437	0.0490 792 716	11
12	0.0440 272 864	0.0433 662 475	0.0427 142 151	0.0420 710 987	12
13	0.0381 509 925	0.0375 183 959	0.0368 953 016	0.0362 816 034	13
14	0.0332 282 015	0.0326 241 702	0.0320 300 825	0.0314 458 154	14
15	0.0290 652 395	0.0284 896 355	0.0279 243 614	0.0273 692 763	15
16	0.0255 167 470	0.0249 692 325	0.0244 323 792	0.0239 060 274	16
17	0.0224 714 845	0.0219 515 674	0.0214 425 881	0.0209 443 676	17
18	0.0198 428 701	0.0193 499 379	0.0188 681 666	0.0183 973 571	18
19	0.0175 625 041	0.0170 958 510	0.0166 405 294	0.0161 963 200	19
20	0.0155 756 369	0.0151 344 846	0.0147 047 839	0.0142 862 950	20
21	0.0138 379 300	0.0134 214 453	0.0130 164 837	0.0126 227 849	21
22	0.0123 131 011	0.0119 204 101	0.0115 392 673	0.0111 693 924	22
23	0.0109 711 818	0.0106 013 818	0.0102 431 115	0.0098 960 710	23
24	0.0097 872 113	0.0094 393 810	0.0091 030 208	0.0087 778 122	24
25	0.0087 402 421	0.0084 134 501	0.0080 980 307	0.0077 936 475	25
26	0.0078 125 750	0.0075 058 873	0.0072 104 398	0.0069 258 788	26
27	0.0069 891 636	0.0067 016 499	0.0064 252 118	0.0061 594 801	27
28	0.0062 571 454	0.0059 878 842	0.0057 295 054	0.0054 816 252	28
29	0.0056 054 695	0.0053 535 530	0.0051 123 000	0.0048 813 133	29
30	0.0050 245 985	0.0047 891 363	0.0045 640 959	0.0043 490 686	30
31	0.0045 062 669	0.0042 863 894	0.0040 766 723	0.0038 766 967	31
32	0.0040 432 854	0.0038 381 462	0.0036 428 892	0.0034 570 869	32
33	0.0036 293 791	0.0034 381 573	0.0032 565 256	0.0030 840 493	33
34	0.0032 590 547	0.0030 809 569	0.0029 121 454	0.0027 521 803	34
35	0.0029 274 900	0.0027 617 510	0.0026 049 859	0.0024 567 507	35
36	0.0026 304 409	0.0024 763 254	0.0023 308 646	0.0021 936 121	36
37	0.0023 641 641	0.0022 209 668	0.0020 861 006	0.0019 591 181	37
38	0.0021 253 508	0.0019 923 971	0.0018 674 484	0.0017 500 578	38
39	0.0019 110 713	0.0017 877 171	0.0016 720 412	0.0015 635 986	39
40	0.0017 187 267	0.0016 043 586	0.0014 973 431	0.0013 972 383	40
41	0.0015 460 086	0.0014 400 434	0.0013 411 076	0.0012 487 638	41
42	0.0013 908 633	0.0012 927 477	0.0012 013 421	0.0011 162 147	42
43	0.0012 514 619	0.0011 606 716	0.0010 762 773	0.0009 978 531	43
44	0.0011 261 735	0.0010 422 130	0.0009 643 403	0.0008 921 368	44
45	0.0010 135 424	0.0009 359 439	0.0008 641 318	0.0007 976 959	45
46	0.0009 122 683	0.0008 405 907	0.0007 744 059	0.0007 133 126	46
47	0.0008 211 884	0.0007 550 166	0.0006 940 524	0.0006 379 039	47
48	0.0007 392 624	0.0006 782 064	0.0006 220 813	0.0005 705 056	48
49	0.0006 655 589	0.0006 092 523	0.0005 576 093	0.0005 102 590	49
50	0.0005 992 433	0.0005 473 428	0.0004 998 481	0.0004 563 992	50
51	0.0005 395 676	0.0004 917 516	0.0004 480 934	0.0004 082 442	51
52	0.0004 858 607	0.0004 418 286	0.0004 017 160	0.0003 651 858	52
53	0.0004 375 209	0.0003 969 916	0.0003 601 537	0.0003 266 814	53
54	0.0003 940 076	0.0003 567 191	0.0003 229 035	0.0002 922 470	54
55	0.0003 548 359	0.0003 205 436	0.0002 895 157	0.0002 614 502	55
56	0.0003 195 698	0.0002 880 461	0.0002 595 879	0.0002 339 051	56
57	0.0002 878 179	0.0002 588 508	0.0002 327 601	0.0002 092 673	57
58	0.0002 592 282	0.0002 326 208	0.0002 087 099	0.0001 872 287	58
59	0.0002 334 844	0.0002 090 536	0.0001 871 487	0.0001 675 144	59
60	0.0002 103 020	0.0001 878 780	0.0001 678 182	0.0001 498 786	60

TABLE 3. SINKING FUND FACTORS
Payable at end of each period

YEARS	12% Nominal Annual Rate	12¼% Nominal Annual Rate	12½% Nominal Annual Rate	12¾% Nominal Annual Rate	YEARS
1	1.0000 000 000	1.0000 000 000	1.0000 000 000	1.0000 000 000	1
2	0.4716 981 132	0.4711 425 206	0.4705 882 353	0.4700 352 526	2
3	0.2963 489 806	0.2956 387 738	0.2949 308 756	0.2942 252 773	3
4	0.2092 344 363	0.2084 695 653	0.2077 079 108	0.2069 494 592	4
5	0.1574 097 319	0.1566 298 515	0.1558 540 390	0.1550 822 759	5
6	0.1232 257 184	0.1224 503 136	0.1216 797 811	0.1209 140 956	6
7	0.0991 177 359	0.0983 575 909	0.0976 030 757	0.0968 541 576	7
8	0.0813 028 414	0.0805 643 440	0.0798 321 856	0.0791 063 248	8
9	0.0676 788 888	0.0669 659 477	0.0662 600 042	0.0655 610 062	9
10	0.0569 841 642	0.0562 991 718	0.0556 217 819	0.0549 519 311	10
11	0.0484 154 043	0.0477 597 653	0.0471 122 783	0.0464 728 668	11
12	0.0414 368 076	0.0408 112 512	0.0401 943 390	0.0395 859 803	12
13	0.0356 771 951	0.0350 819 707	0.0344 958 241	0.0339 186 495	13
14	0.0308 712 461	0.0303 062 518	0.0297 507 101	0.0292 044 988	14
15	0.0268 242 396	0.0262 891 113	0.0257 637 513	0.0252 480 204	15
16	0.0233 900 180	0.0228 841 926	0.0223 883 932	0.0219 024 626	16
17	0.0204 567 275	0.0199 794 905	0.0195 124 801	0.0190 555 208	17
18	0.0179 373 114	0.0174 878 330	0.0170 487 264	0.0166 197 977	18
19	0.0157 630 049	0.0153 403 681	0.0149 281 952	0.0145 262 741	19
20	0.0138 787 800	0.0134 820 037	0.0130 957 330	0.0127 197 372	20
21	0.0122 400 915	0.0118 681 490	0.0115 067 060	0.0111 555 139	21
22	0.0108 105 088	0.0104 623 433	0.0101 246 265	0.0097 970 930	22
23	0.0095 599 650	0.0092 345 023	0.0089 193 964	0.0086 143 656	23
24	0.0084 634 417	0.0081 596 013	0.0078 659 881	0.0075 823 050	24
25	0.0074 999 698	0.0072 166 736	0.0069 434 409	0.0066 799 605	25
26	0.0066 518 581	0.0063 880 385	0.0061 340 882	0.0058 896 831	26
27	0.0059 040 937	0.0056 586 998	0.0054 229 541	0.0051 965 208	27
28	0.0052 438 691	0.0050 158 721	0.0047 972 788	0.0045 877 432	28
29	0.0046 602 068	0.0044 486 044	0.0042 461 412	0.0040 524 626	29
30	0.0041 436 576	0.0039 474 777	0.0037 601 556	0.0035 813 298	30
31	0.0036 860 570	0.0035 043 602	0.0033 312 264	0.0031 662 885	31
32	0.0032 803 263	0.0031 122 083	0.0029 523 480	0.0028 003 741	32
33	0.0029 203 096	0.0027 649 028	0.0026 174 403	0.0024 775 485	33
34	0.0026 006 383	0.0024 571 128	0.0023 212 131	0.0021 925 644	34
35	0.0023 166 193	0.0021 841 835	0.0020 590 521	0.0019 408 505	35
36	0.0020 641 406	0.0019 420 416	0.0018 269 247	0.0017 184 171	36
37	0.0018 395 924	0.0017 271 158	0.0016 213 002	0.0015 217 757	37
38	0.0016 397 998	0.0015 362 695	0.0014 390 818	0.0013 478 710	38
39	0.0014 619 665	0.0013 667 437	0.0012 775 496	0.0011 940 236	39
40	0.0013 036 256	0.0012 161 083	0.0011 343 115	0.0010 578 807	40
41	0.0011 625 982	0.0010 822 203	0.0010 072 613	0.0009 373 739	41
42	0.0010 369 577	0.0009 631 874	0.0008 945 425	0.0008 306 831	42
43	0.0009 249 987	0.0008 573 378	0.0007 945 171	0.0007 362 054	43
44	0.0008 252 102	0.0007 631 924	0.0007 057 390	0.0006 525 277	44
45	0.0007 362 523	0.0006 794 422	0.0006 269 303	0.0005 784 038	45
46	0.0006 569 363	0.0006 049 275	0.0005 569 610	0.0005 127 337	46
47	0.0005 862 064	0.0005 386 207	0.0004 948 314	0.0004 545 460	47
48	0.0005 231 248	0.0004 796 101	0.0004 396 568	0.0004 029 826	48
49	0.0004 668 576	0.0004 270 871	0.0003 906 534	0.0003 572 848	49
50	0.0004 166 635	0.0003 803 338	0.0003 471 269	0.0003 167 819	50
51	0.0003 718 826	0.0003 387 127	0.0003 084 621	0.0002 808 806	51
52	0.0003 319 279	0.0003 016 574	0.0002 741 133	0.0002 490 560	52
53	0.0002 962 763	0.0002 686 649	0.0002 435 969	0.0002 208 435	53
54	0.0002 644 625	0.0002 392 879	0.0002 164 837	0.0001 958 317	54
55	0.0002 360 715	0.0002 131 286	0.0001 923 930	0.0001 736 565	55
56	0.0002 107 337	0.0001 898 336	0.0001 709 867	0.0001 539 953	56
57	0.0001 881 197	0.0001 690 882	0.0001 519 651	0.0001 365 626	57
58	0.0001 679 358	0.0001 506 126	0.0001 350 619	0.0001 211 051	58
59	0.0001 499 202	0.0001 341 581	0.0001 200 406	0.0001 073 988	59
60	0.0001 338 394	0.0001 195 029	0.0001 066 913	0.0000 952 448	60

TABLE 3. SINKING FUND FACTORS
Payable at end of each period

YEARLY Compounding

YEARS	13% Nominal Annual Rate	13¼% Nominal Annual Rate	13½% Nominal Annual Rate	13¾% Nominal Annual Rate	YEARS
1	1.0000 000 000	1.0000 000 000	1.0000 000 000	1.0000 000 000	1
2	0.4694 835 681	0.4689 331 770	0.4683 840 749	0.4678 362 573	2
3	0.2935 219 701	0.2928 209 455	0.2921 221 947	0.2914 257 092	3
4	0.2061 941 974	0.2054 421 121	0.2046 931 901	0.2039 474 182	4
5	0.1543 145 434	0.1535 508 228	0.1527 910 955	0.1520 353 429	5
6	0.1201 532 321	0.1193 971 654	0.1186 458 704	0.1178 993 222	6
7	0.0961 108 038	0.0953 729 816	0.0946 406 583	0.0939 138 011	7
8	0.0783 867 196	0.0776 733 286	0.0769 661 101	0.0762 650 224	8
9	0.0648 689 020	0.0641 836 395	0.0635 051 669	0.0628 334 323	9
10	0.0542 895 558	0.0536 345 926	0.0529 869 780	0.0523 466 485	10
11	0.0458 414 545	0.0452 179 651	0.0446 023 222	0.0439 944 497	11
12	0.0389 860 847	0.0383 945 617	0.0378 113 211	0.0372 362 729	12
13	0.0333 503 411	0.0327 907 934	0.0322 399 012	0.0316 975 595	13
14	0.0286 674 959	0.0281 395 799	0.0276 206 298	0.0271 105 248	14
15	0.0247 417 797	0.0242 448 909	0.0237 572 163	0.0232 786 191	15
16	0.0214 262 445	0.0209 595 833	0.0205 023 244	0.0200 543 142	16
17	0.0186 084 385	0.0181 710 600	0.0177 432 135	0.0173 247 285	17
18	0.0162 008 548	0.0157 917 068	0.0153 921 647	0.0150 020 415	18
19	0.0141 343 943	0.0137 523 477	0.0133 799 284	0.0130 169 327	19
20	0.0123 537 884	0.0119 976 615	0.0116 511 339	0.0113 139 862	20
21	0.0108 143 279	0.0104 829 061	0.0101 610 103	0.0098 484 057	21
22	0.0094 794 811	0.0091 715 336	0.0088 729 970	0.0085 836 226	22
23	0.0083 191 328	0.0080 334 258	0.0077 569 775	0.0074 895 255	23
24	0.0073 082 605	0.0070 435 689	0.0067 879 502	0.0065 411 302	24
25	0.0064 259 276	0.0061 810 440	0.0059 450 182	0.0057 175 656	25
26	0.0056 545 063	0.0054 282 488	0.0052 106 089	0.0050 012 926	26
27	0.0049 790 727	0.0047 702 909	0.0045 698 653	0.0043 774 941	27
28	0.0043 869 291	0.0041 945 094	0.0040 101 668	0.0038 335 934	28
29	0.0038 672 246	0.0036 900 938	0.0035 207 472	0.0033 588 720	29
30	0.0034 106 503	0.0032 477 786	0.0030 923 874	0.0029 441 608	30
31	0.0030 091 921	0.0028 595 949	0.0027 171 673	0.0025 815 914	31
32	0.0026 559 291	0.0025 186 689	0.0023 882 625	0.0022 643 918	32
33	0.0023 448 684	0.0022 190 550	0.0020 997 777	0.0019 867 192	33
34	0.0020 708 076	0.0019 555 986	0.0018 466 081	0.0017 435 211	34
35	0.0018 292 209	0.0017 238 212	0.0016 243 248	0.0015 304 201	35
36	0.0016 161 634	0.0015 198 246	0.0014 290 780	0.0013 436 165	36
37	0.0014 281 904	0.0013 402 099	0.0012 575 162	0.0011 798 077	37
38	0.0012 622 899	0.0011 820 095	0.0011 067 176	0.0010 361 189	38
39	0.0011 158 243	0.0010 426 288	0.0009 741 317	0.0009 100 449	39
40	0.0009 864 810	0.0009 197 967	0.0008 575 299	0.0007 993 999	40
41	0.0008 722 306	0.0008 115 234	0.0007 549 625	0.0007 022 756	41
42	0.0007 712 901	0.0007 160 638	0.0006 647 231	0.0006 170 042	42
43	0.0006 820 921	0.0006 318 864	0.0005 853 163	0.0005 421 272	43
44	0.0006 032 572	0.0005 576 460	0.0005 154 314	0.0004 763 683	44
45	0.0005 335 711	0.0004 921 603	0.0004 539 184	0.0004 186 100	45
46	0.0004 719 639	0.0004 343 898	0.0003 997 682	0.0003 678 734	46
47	0.0004 174 928	0.0003 834 201	0.0003 520 947	0.0003 233 007	47
48	0.0003 693 262	0.0003 384 462	0.0003 101 194	0.0002 841 396	48
49	0.0003 267 306	0.0002 987 595	0.0002 731 583	0.0002 497 307	49
50	0.0002 890 585	0.0002 637 357	0.0002 406 102	0.0002 194 953	50
51	0.0002 557 386	0.0002 328 250	0.0002 119 464	0.0001 929 256	51
52	0.0002 262 661	0.0002 055 427	0.0001 867 021	0.0001 695 762	52
53	0.0002 001 954	0.0001 814 617	0.0001 644 682	0.0001 490 558	53
54	0.0001 771 327	0.0001 602 055	0.0001 448 849	0.0001 310 209	54
55	0.0001 567 300	0.0001 414 418	0.0001 276 356	0.0001 151 699	55
56	0.0001 386 799	0.0001 248 778	0.0001 124 416	0.0001 012 380	56
57	0.0001 227 105	0.0001 102 552	0.0000 990 577	0.0000 889 925	57
58	0.0001 085 816	0.0000 973 461	0.0000 872 679	0.0000 782 291	58
59	0.0000 960 807	0.0000 859 494	0.0000 768 821	0.0000 687 681	59
60	0.0000 850 199	0.0000 758 878	0.0000 677 329	0.0000 604 518	60

YEARLY
Compounding

TABLE 3. SINKING FUND FACTORS
Payable at end of each period

YEARS	14% Nominal Annual Rate	14¼% Nominal Annual Rate	14½% Nominal Annual Rate	14¾% Nominal Annual Rate	YEARS
1	1.0000 000 000	1.0000 000 000	1.0000 000 000	1.0000 000 000	1
2	0.4672 897 196	0.4667 444 574	0.4662 004 662	0.4656 577 416	2
3	0.2907 314 804	0.2900 394 998	0.2893 497 588	0.2886 622 489	3
4	0.2032 047 833	0.2024 652 722	0.2017 288 719	0.2009 955 694	4
5	0.1512 835 465	0.1505 356 877	0.1497 917 481	0.1490 517 091	5
6	0.1171 574 957	0.1164 203 658	0.1156 879 076	0.1149 600 961	6
7	0.0931 923 773	0.0924 763 543	0.0917 656 994	0.0910 603 800	7
8	0.0755 700 238	0.0748 810 728	0.0741 981 278	0.0735 211 472	8
9	0.0621 683 838	0.0615 099 696	0.0608 581 379	0.0602 128 369	9
10	0.0517 135 408	0.0510 875 916	0.0504 687 376	0.0498 569 156	10
11	0.0433 942 714	0.0428 017 114	0.0422 166 937	0.0416 391 428	11
12	0.0366 693 269	0.0361 103 936	0.0355 593 835	0.0350 162 073	12
13	0.0311 636 635	0.0306 381 089	0.0301 207 919	0.0296 116 088	13
14	0.0266 091 448	0.0261 163 700	0.0256 320 815	0.0251 561 607	14
15	0.0228 089 630	0.0223 481 124	0.0218 959 329	0.0214 522 906	15
16	0.0196 154 000	0.0191 854 304	0.0187 642 550	0.0183 517 247	16
17	0.0169 154 359	0.0165 151 683	0.0161 237 596	0.0157 410 452	17
18	0.0146 211 516	0.0142 493 116	0.0138 863 402	0.0135 320 579	18
19	0.0126 631 593	0.0123 184 094	0.0119 824 868	0.0116 551 975	19
20	0.0109 860 016	0.0106 669 666	0.0103 566 708	0.0100 549 068	20
21	0.0095 448 612	0.0092 501 493	0.0089 640 464	0.0086 863 325	21
22	0.0083 031 654	0.0080 313 854	0.0077 680 465	0.0075 129 175	22
23	0.0072 308 130	0.0069 805 878	0.0067 386 033	0.0065 046 177	23
24	0.0063 028 406	0.0060 728 192	0.0058 508 096	0.0056 365 612	24
25	0.0054 984 079	0.0052 872 740	0.0050 838 993	0.0048 880 258	25
26	0.0048 000 136	0.0046 064 930	0.0044 204 595	0.0042 416 492	26
27	0.0041 928 839	0.0040 157 501	0.0038 458 159	0.0036 828 131	27
28	0.0036 644 905	0.0035 025 686	0.0033 475 475	0.0031 991 557	28
29	0.0032 041 657	0.0030 563 357	0.0029 150 996	0.0027 801 843	29
30	0.0028 027 939	0.0026 679 925	0.0025 394 732	0.0024 169 627	30
31	0.0024 525 613	0.0023 297 827	0.0022 129 724	0.0021 018 585	31
32	0.0021 467 511	0.0020 350 472	0.0019 289 987	0.0018 283 360	32
33	0.0018 795 755	0.0017 780 558	0.0016 818 816	0.0015 907 865	33
34	0.0016 460 366	0.0015 538 669	0.0014 667 377	0.0013 843 871	34
35	0.0014 418 099	0.0013 582 113	0.0012 793 548	0.0012 049 839	35
36	0.0012 631 480	0.0011 873 948	0.0011 160 934	0.0010 489 933	36
37	0.0011 067 982	0.0010 382 162	0.0009 738 048	0.0009 133 205	37
38	0.0009 699 339	0.0009 078 982	0.0008 497 619	0.0007 952 890	38
39	0.0008 500 959	0.0007 940 282	0.0007 415 997	0.0006 925 823	39
40	0.0007 451 425	0.0006 945 092	0.0006 472 661	0.0006 031 935	40
41	0.0006 532 069	0.0006 075 162	0.0005 649 785	0.0005 253 827	41
42	0.0005 726 603	0.0005 314 603	0.0004 931 877	0.0004 576 403	42
43	0.0005 020 814	0.0004 649 568	0.0004 305 461	0.0003 986 561	43
44	0.0004 402 284	0.0004 067 988	0.0003 758 815	0.0003 472 920	44
45	0.0003 860 162	0.0003 559 335	0.0003 281 731	0.0003 025 594	45
46	0.0003 384 961	0.0003 114 422	0.0002 865 319	0.0002 635 989	46
47	0.0002 968 383	0.0002 725 228	0.0002 501 836	0.0002 296 630	47
48	0.0002 603 167	0.0002 384 751	0.0002 184 532	0.0002 001 020	48
49	0.0002 282 958	0.0002 086 874	0.0001 907 524	0.0001 743 504	49
50	0.0002 002 194	0.0001 826 252	0.0001 665 683	0.0001 519 163	50
51	0.0001 756 002	0.0001 598 214	0.0001 454 533	0.0001 323 714	51
52	0.0001 540 115	0.0001 398 679	0.0001 270 173	0.0001 153 430	52
53	0.0001 350 796	0.0001 224 077	0.0001 109 199	0.0001 005 067	53
54	0.0001 184 768	0.0001 071 287	0.0000 968 639	0.0000 875 799	54
55	0.0001 039 162	0.0000 937 582	0.0000 845 901	0.0000 763 165	55
56	0.0000 911 463	0.0000 820 573	0.0000 738 724	0.0000 665 023	56
57	0.0000 799 465	0.0000 718 174	0.0000 645 132	0.0000 579 507	57
58	0.0000 701 236	0.0000 628 559	0.0000 563 402	0.0000 504 992	58
59	0.0000 615 081	0.0000 550 131	0.0000 492 030	0.0000 440 061	59
60	0.0000 539 516	0.0000 481 492	0.0000 429 702	0.0000 383 480	60

TABLE 3. SINKING FUND FACTORS
Payable at end of each period

YEARLY Compounding

YEARS	15% Nominal Annual Rate	15¼% Nominal Annual Rate	15½% Nominal Annual Rate	15¾% Nominal Annual Rate	YEARS
1	1.0000 000 000	1.0000 000 000	1.0000 000 000	1.0000 000 000	1
2	0.4651 162 791	0.4645 760 743	0.4640 371 230	0.4634 994 206	2
3	0.2879 769 618	0.2872 938 891	0.2866 130 223	0.2859 343 530	3
4	0.2002 653 516	0.1995 382 056	0.1988 141 185	0.1980 930 774	4
5	0.1483 155 525	0.1475 832 597	0.1468 548 125	0.1461 301 925	5
6	0.1142 369 066	0.1135 183 140	0.1128 042 936	0.1120 948 206	6
7	0.0903 603 636	0.0896 656 176	0.0889 761 095	0.0882 918 068	7
8	0.0728 500 896	0.0721 849 134	0.0715 255 774	0.0708 720 400	8
9	0.0595 740 150	0.0589 416 205	0.0583 156 020	0.0576 959 078	9
10	0.0492 520 625	0.0486 541 155	0.0480 630 117	0.0474 786 884	10
11	0.0410 689 830	0.0405 061 390	0.0399 505 356	0.0394 020 980	11
12	0.0344 807 761	0.0339 530 013	0.0334 327 944	0.0329 200 676	12
13	0.0291 104 565	0.0286 172 324	0.0281 318 343	0.0276 541 605	13
14	0.0246 884 898	0.0242 289 517	0.0237 774 299	0.0233 338 087	14
15	0.0210 170 526	0.0205 900 872	0.0201 712 633	0.0197 604 511	15
16	0.0179 476 914	0.0175 520 085	0.0171 645 308	0.0167 851 142	16
17	0.0153 668 623	0.0150 010 499	0.0146 434 484	0.0142 939 002	17
18	0.0131 862 874	0.0128 488 534	0.0125 195 831	0.0121 983 057	18
19	0.0113 363 504	0.0110 257 571	0.0107 232 318	0.0104 285 914	19
20	0.0097 614 704	0.0094 761 608	0.0091 987 802	0.0089 291 344	20
21	0.0084 167 914	0.0081 552 110	0.0079 013 828	0.0076 551 024	21
22	0.0072 657 713	0.0070 263 855	0.0067 945 424	0.0065 700 286	22
23	0.0062 783 947	0.0060 597 030	0.0058 483 167	0.0056 440 149	23
24	0.0054 298 296	0.0052 303 761	0.0050 379 680	0.0048 523 784	24
25	0.0046 994 023	0.0045 177 843	0.0043 429 337	0.0041 746 191	25
26	0.0040 698 058	0.0039 046 801	0.0037 460 303	0.0035 936 217	26
27	0.0035 264 815	0.0033 765 689	0.0032 328 312	0.0030 950 318	27
28	0.0030 571 309	0.0029 212 193	0.0027 911 756	0.0026 667 629	28
29	0.0026 513 265	0.0025 282 721	0.0024 107 763	0.0022 986 031	29
30	0.0023 001 982	0.0021 889 266	0.0020 829 047	0.0019 818 985	30
31	0.0019 961 796	0.0018 956 851	0.0018 001 344	0.0017 092 966	31
32	0.0017 328 006	0.0016 421 450	0.0015 561 326	0.0014 745 367	32
33	0.0015 045 161	0.0014 228 274	0.0013 454 881	0.0012 722 770	33
34	0.0013 065 655	0.0012 330 351	0.0011 635 693	0.0010 979 526	34
35	0.0011 348 546	0.0010 687 352	0.0010 064 055	0.0009 476 562	35
36	0.0009 858 572	0.0009 264 599	0.0008 705 881	0.0008 180 398	36
37	0.0008 565 329	0.0008 032 241	0.0007 531 882	0.0007 062 307	37
38	0.0007 442 569	0.0006 964 553	0.0006 516 861	0.0006 097 625	38
39	0.0006 467 613	0.0006 039 346	0.0005 639 122	0.0005 265 153	39
40	0.0005 620 850	0.0005 237 469	0.0004 879 974	0.0004 546 660	40
41	0.0004 885 308	0.0004 542 377	0.0004 223 301	0.0003 926 458	41
42	0.0004 246 290	0.0003 939 773	0.0003 655 201	0.0003 391 038	42
43	0.0003 691 063	0.0003 417 290	0.0003 163 675	0.0002 928 764	43
44	0.0003 208 590	0.0002 964 231	0.0002 738 363	0.0002 529 610	44
45	0.0002 789 300	0.0002 571 340	0.0002 370 315	0.0002 184 931	45
46	0.0002 424 890	0.0002 230 600	0.0002 051 800	0.0001 887 273	46
47	0.0002 108 156	0.0001 935 070	0.0001 776 134	0.0001 630 207	47
48	0.0001 832 843	0.0001 678 738	0.0001 537 542	0.0001 408 188	48
49	0.0001 593 523	0.0001 456 393	0.0001 331 028	0.0001 216 429	49
50	0.0001 385 480	0.0001 263 522	0.0001 152 273	0.0001 050 800	50
51	0.0001 204 620	0.0001 096 211	0.0000 997 539	0.0000 907 737	51
52	0.0001 047 386	0.0000 951 069	0.0000 863 596	0.0000 784 160	52
53	0.0000 910 687	0.0000 825 154	0.0000 747 646	0.0000 677 414	53
54	0.0000 791 839	0.0000 715 918	0.0000 647 271	0.0000 585 205	54
55	0.0000 688 509	0.0000 621 148	0.0000 560 376	0.0000 505 551	55
56	0.0000 598 667	0.0000 538 928	0.0000 485 151	0.0000 436 742	56
57	0.0000 520 553	0.0000 467 595	0.0000 420 026	0.0000 377 301	57
58	0.0000 452 634	0.0000 405 706	0.0000 363 646	0.0000 325 951	58
59	0.0000 393 580	0.0000 352 010	0.0000 314 835	0.0000 281 591	59
60	0.0000 342 231	0.0000 305 422	0.0000 272 577	0.0000 243 269	60

YEARLY Compounding

TABLE 3. SINKING FUND FACTORS
Payable at end of each period

YEARS	16% Nominal Annual Rate	16¼% Nominal Annual Rate	16½% Nominal Annual Rate	16¾% Nominal Annual Rate	YEARS
1	1.0000 000 000	1.0000 000 000	1.0000 000 000	1.0000 000 000	1
2	0.4629 629 630	0.4624 277 457	0.4618 937 644	0.4613 610 150	2
3	0.2852 578 731	0.2845 835 742	0.2839 114 480	0.2832 414 864	3
4	0.1973 750 695	0.1966 600 819	0.1959 481 019	0.1952 391 167	4
5	0.1454 093 816	0.1446 923 615	0.1439 791 140	0.1432 696 210	5
6	0.1113 898 702	0.1106 894 178	0.1099 934 387	0.1093 019 083	6
7	0.0876 126 771	0.0869 386 882	0.0862 698 077	0.0856 060 033	7
8	0.0702 242 601	0.0695 821 964	0.0689 458 078	0.0683 150 532	8
9	0.0570 824 868	0.0564 752 876	0.0558 742 591	0.0552 793 503	9
10	0.0469 010 831	0.0463 301 333	0.0457 657 770	0.0452 079 521	10
11	0.0388 607 515	0.0383 264 216	0.0377 990 342	0.0372 785 154	11
12	0.0324 147 333	0.0319 167 041	0.0314 258 934	0.0309 422 146	12
13	0.0271 841 100	0.0267 215 822	0.0262 664 771	0.0258 186 955	13
14	0.0228 979 733	0.0224 698 093	0.0220 492 036	0.0216 360 438	14
15	0.0193 575 218	0.0189 623 475	0.0185 748 018	0.0181 947 590	15
16	0.0164 136 162	0.0160 498 958	0.0156 938 131	0.0153 452 302	16
17	0.0139 522 494	0.0136 183 422	0.0132 920 262	0.0129 731 514	17
18	0.0118 848 526	0.0115 790 577	0.0112 807 572	0.0109 897 894	18
19	0.0101 416 556	0.0098 622 471	0.0095 901 910	0.0093 253 158	19
20	0.0086 670 324	0.0084 122 865	0.0081 647 123	0.0079 241 291	20
21	0.0074 161 691	0.0071 843 865	0.0069 595 618	0.0067 415 063	21
22	0.0063 526 353	0.0061 421 582	0.0059 383 976	0.0057 411 582	22
23	0.0054 465 820	0.0052 558 075	0.0050 714 859	0.0048 934 170	23
24	0.0046 733 862	0.0045 007 761	0.0043 343 385	0.0041 738 694	24
25	0.0040 126 153	0.0038 567 036	0.0037 066 717	0.0035 623 133	25
26	0.0034 472 266	0.0033 066 245	0.0031 716 014	0.0030 419 502	26
27	0.0029 629 420	0.0028 363 404	0.0027 150 133	0.0025 987 537	27
28	0.0025 477 527	0.0024 339 243	0.0023 250 650	0.0022 209 696	28
29	0.0021 915 252	0.0020 893 239	0.0019 917 888	0.0018 987 174	29
30	0.0018 856 833	0.0017 940 435	0.0017 067 719	0.0016 236 698	30
31	0.0016 229 508	0.0015 408 852	0.0014 628 970	0.0013 887 922	31
32	0.0013 971 408	0.0013 237 381	0.0012 541 308	0.0011 881 303	32
33	0.0012 029 828	0.0011 374 043	0.0010 753 495	0.0010 166 359	33
34	0.0010 359 798	0.0009 774 559	0.0009 221 956	0.0008 700 226	34
35	0.0008 922 891	0.0008 401 159	0.0007 909 581	0.0007 446 465	35
36	0.0007 686 235	0.0007 221 585	0.0006 784 733	0.0006 374 063	36
37	0.0006 621 677	0.0006 208 259	0.0005 820 416	0.0005 456 604	37
38	0.0005 705 086	0.0005 337 587	0.0004 993 570	0.0004 671 567	38
39	0.0004 915 760	0.0004 589 366	0.0004 284 490	0.0003 999 742	39
40	0.0004 235 929	0.0003 946 284	0.0003 676 322	0.0003 424 730	40
41	0.0003 650 330	0.0003 393 501	0.0003 154 645	0.0002 932 527	41
42	0.0003 145 846	0.0002 918 288	0.0002 707 117	0.0002 511 170	42
43	0.0002 711 201	0.0002 509 726	0.0002 323 166	0.0002 150 432	43
44	0.0002 336 696	0.0002 158 438	0.0001 993 736	0.0001 841 573	44
45	0.0002 013 988	0.0001 856 376	0.0001 711 069	0.0001 577 116	45
46	0.0001 735 895	0.0001 596 628	0.0001 468 513	0.0001 350 666	46
47	0.0001 496 237	0.0001 373 254	0.0001 260 367	0.0001 156 754	47
48	0.0001 289 693	0.0001 181 155	0.0001 081 743	0.0000 990 697	48
49	0.0001 111 681	0.0001 015 944	0.0000 928 449	0.0000 848 491	49
50	0.0000 958 254	0.0000 873 854	0.0000 796 888	0.0000 726 706	50
51	0.0000 826 013	0.0000 751 646	0.0000 683 977	0.0000 622 407	51
52	0.0000 712 029	0.0000 646 535	0.0000 587 071	0.0000 533 083	52
53	0.0000 613 781	0.0000 556 128	0.0000 503 898	0.0000 456 581	53
54	0.0000 529 093	0.0000 478 367	0.0000 432 512	0.0000 391 061	54
55	0.0000 456 094	0.0000 411 482	0.0000 371 241	0.0000 334 944	55
56	0.0000 393 169	0.0000 353 950	0.0000 318 652	0.0000 286 882	56
57	0.0000 338 927	0.0000 304 464	0.0000 273 513	0.0000 245 717	57
58	0.0000 292 170	0.0000 261 898	0.0000 234 770	0.0000 210 460	58
59	0.0000 251 865	0.0000 225 283	0.0000 201 515	0.0000 180 262	59
60	0.0000 217 120	0.0000 193 788	0.0000 172 971	0.0000 154 398	60

TABLE 3. SINKING FUND FACTORS
Payable at end of each period

YEARS	17% Nominal Annual Rate	17¼% Nominal Annual Rate	17½% Nominal Annual Rate	17¾% Nominal Annual Rate	YEARS
1	1.0000 000 000	1.0000 000 000	1.0000 000 000	1.0000 000 000	1
2	0.4608 294 931	0.4602 991 945	0.4597 701 149	0.4592 422 503	2
3	0.2825 736 811	0.2819 080 240	0.2812 445 069	0.2805 831 219	3
4	0.1945 331 137	0.1938 300 802	0.1931 300 037	0.1924 328 714	4
5	0.1425 638 643	0.1418 618 261	0.1411 634 882	0.1404 688 328	5
6	0.1086 148 021	0.1079 320 955	0.1072 537 641	0.1065 797 834	6
7	0.0849 472 428	0.0842 934 942	0.0836 447 254	0.0830 009 045	7
8	0.0676 898 916	0.0670 702 821	0.0664 561 840	0.0658 475 564	8
9	0.0546 905 102	0.0541 076 880	0.0535 308 333	0.0529 598 953	9
10	0.0446 565 967	0.0441 116 492	0.0435 730 482	0.0430 407 326	10
11	0.0367 647 916	0.0362 577 896	0.0357 574 364	0.0352 636 593	11
12	0.0304 655 819	0.0299 959 098	0.0295 331 132	0.0290 771 075	12
13	0.0253 781 386	0.0249 447 084	0.0245 183 074	0.0240 988 391	13
14	0.0212 302 181	0.0208 316 160	0.0204 401 277	0.0200 556 444	14
15	0.0178 220 950	0.0174 566 866	0.0170 984 119	0.0167 471 504	15
16	0.0150 040 103	0.0146 700 185	0.0143 431 211	0.0140 231 864	16
17	0.0126 615 693	0.0123 571 336	0.0120 596 999	0.0117 691 259	17
18	0.0107 059 953	0.0104 292 182	0.0101 593 036	0.0098 960 997	18
19	0.0090 674 523	0.0088 164 347	0.0085 720 996	0.0083 342 869	19
20	0.0076 903 593	0.0074 632 287	0.0072 425 665	0.0070 282 053	20
21	0.0065 300 350	0.0063 249 672	0.0061 261 256	0.0059 333 373	21
22	0.0055 502 493	0.0053 654 846	0.0051 866 820	0.0050 136 641	22
23	0.0047 214 054	0.0045 552 609	0.0043 947 980	0.0042 398 361	23
24	0.0040 191 703	0.0038 700 484	0.0037 263 162	0.0035 877 915	24
25	0.0034 234 282	0.0032 898 223	0.0031 613 074	0.0030 377 009	25
26	0.0029 174 705	0.0027 979 680	0.0026 832 551	0.0025 731 503	26
27	0.0024 873 621	0.0023 806 457	0.0022 784 184	0.0021 805 007	27
28	0.0021 214 404	0.0020 262 872	0.0019 353 267	0.0018 483 824	28
29	0.0018 099 152	0.0017 251 953	0.0016 443 781	0.0015 672 912	29
30	0.0015 445 468	0.0014 692 201	0.0013 975 150	0.0013 292 636	30
31	0.0013 183 850	0.0012 514 980	0.0011 879 615	0.0011 276 133	31
32	0.0011 255 565	0.0010 662 376	0.0010 100 099	0.0009 567 172	32
33	0.0009 610 895	0.0009 085 449	0.0008 588 447	0.0008 118 391	33
34	0.0008 207 698	0.0007 742 784	0.0007 303 978	0.0006 889 849	34
35	0.0007 010 209	0.0006 599 296	0.0006 212 289	0.0005 847 830	35
36	0.0005 988 044	0.0005 625 231	0.0005 284 261	0.0004 963 845	36
37	0.0005 115 368	0.0004 795 338	0.0004 495 222	0.0004 213 803	37
38	0.0004 370 199	0.0004 088 168	0.0003 824 258	0.0003 577 321	38
39	0.0003 733 818	0.0003 485 496	0.0003 253 628	0.0003 037 142	39
40	0.0003 190 279	0.0002 971 821	0.0002 768 279	0.0002 578 649	40
41	0.0002 725 991	0.0002 533 960	0.0002 355 427	0.0002 189 456	41
42	0.0002 329 364	0.0002 160 693	0.0002 004 217	0.0001 859 065	42
43	0.0001 990 513	0.0001 842 469	0.0001 705 426	0.0001 578 574	43
44	0.0001 701 004	0.0001 571 155	0.0001 451 216	0.0001 340 435	44
45	0.0001 453 638	0.0001 339 825	0.0001 234 925	0.0001 138 244	45
46	0.0001 242 272	0.0001 142 577	0.0001 050 889	0.0000 966 569	46
47	0.0001 061 658	0.0000 974 384	0.0000 894 294	0.0000 820 798	47
48	0.0000 907 317	0.0000 830 962	0.0000 761 043	0.0000 697 019	48
49	0.0000 775 425	0.0000 708 660	0.0000 647 654	0.0000 591 914	49
50	0.0000 662 712	0.0000 604 364	0.0000 551 165	0.0000 502 661	50
51	0.0000 566 389	0.0000 515 423	0.0000 469 054	0.0000 426 870	51
52	0.0000 484 070	0.0000 439 573	0.0000 399 179	0.0000 362 510	52
53	0.0000 413 718	0.0000 374 889	0.0000 339 716	0.0000 307 854	53
54	0.0000 353 592	0.0000 319 724	0.0000 289 111	0.0000 261 441	54
55	0.0000 302 206	0.0000 272 679	0.0000 246 046	0.0000 222 025	55
56	0.0000 258 289	0.0000 232 556	0.0000 209 397	0.0000 188 553	56
57	0.0000 220 755	0.0000 198 338	0.0000 178 207	0.0000 160 127	57
58	0.0000 188 676	0.0000 169 156	0.0000 151 663	0.0000 135 987	58
59	0.0000 161 259	0.0000 144 267	0.0000 129 073	0.0000 115 487	59
60	0.0000 137 826	0.0000 123 041	0.0000 109 848	0.0000 098 077	60

YEARLY
Compounding

TABLE 3. SINKING FUND FACTORS
Payable at end of each period

YEARS	18% Nominal Annual Rate	18¼% Nominal Annual Rate	18½% Nominal Annual Rate	18¾% Nominal Annual Rate	YEARS
1	1.0000 000 000	1.0000 000 000	1.0000 000 000	1.0000 000 000	1
2	0.4587 155 963	0.4581 901 489	0.4576 659 039	0.4571 428 571	2
3	0.2799 238 607	0.2792 667 154	0.2786 116 780	0.2779 587 405	3
4	0.1917 386 709	0.1910 473 898	0.1903 590 154	0.1896 735 355	4
5	0.1397 778 418	0.1390 904 975	0.1384 067 820	0.1377 266 776	5
6	0.1059 101 292	0.1052 447 772	0.1045 837 031	0.1039 268 828	6
7	0.0823 619 994	0.0817 279 783	0.0810 988 095	0.0804 744 614	7
8	0.0652 443 589	0.0646 465 509	0.0640 540 919	0.0634 669 418	8
9	0.0523 948 239	0.0518 355 688	0.0512 820 801	0.0507 343 078	9
10	0.0425 146 413	0.0419 947 137	0.0414 808 893	0.0409 731 078	10
11	0.0347 763 862	0.0342 955 451	0.0338 210 645	0.0333 528 732	11
12	0.0286 278 089	0.0281 851 337	0.0277 489 990	0.0273 193 224	12
13	0.0236 862 073	0.0232 803 170	0.0228 810 735	0.0224 883 831	13
14	0.0196 780 583	0.0193 072 624	0.0189 431 510	0.0185 856 190	14
15	0.0164 027 825	0.0160 651 903	0.0157 342 570	0.0154 098 671	15
16	0.0137 100 839	0.0134 036 851	0.0131 038 628	0.0128 104 919	16
17	0.0114 852 711	0.0112 079 971	0.0109 371 677	0.0106 726 484	17
18	0.0096 394 570	0.0093 892 285	0.0091 452 695	0.0089 074 379	18
19	0.0081 028 390	0.0078 776 016	0.0076 584 229	0.0074 451 542	19
20	0.0068 199 812	0.0066 177 334	0.0064 213 045	0.0062 305 405	20
21	0.0057 464 327	0.0055 652 466	0.0053 896 170	0.0052 193 860	21
22	0.0048 462 577	0.0046 842 937	0.0045 276 075	0.0043 760 386	22
23	0.0040 901 996	0.0039 457 174	0.0038 062 232	0.0036 715 551	23
24	0.0034 542 973	0.0033 256 620	0.0032 017 187	0.0030 823 059	24
25	0.0029 188 261	0.0028 045 117	0.0026 945 919	0.0025 889 062	25
26	0.0024 674 779	0.0023 660 685	0.0022 687 583	0.0021 753 889	26
27	0.0020 867 195	0.0019 969 080	0.0019 109 054	0.0018 285 567	27
28	0.0017 652 846	0.0016 858 702	0.0016 099 822	0.0015 374 698	28
29	0.0014 937 692	0.0014 236 533	0.0013 567 913	0.0012 930 373	29
30	0.0012 643 056	0.0012 024 875	0.0011 436 621	0.0010 876 891	30
31	0.0010 702 987	0.0010 158 697	0.0009 641 852	0.0009 151 106	31
32	0.0009 062 108	0.0008 583 490	0.0008 129 969	0.0007 700 260	32
33	0.0007 673 859	0.0007 253 500	0.0006 856 029	0.0006 480 228	33
34	0.0006 499 044	0.0006 130 278	0.0005 782 333	0.0005 454 057	34
35	0.0005 504 633	0.0005 181 481	0.0004 877 226	0.0004 590 782	35
36	0.0004 662 768	0.0004 379 883	0.0004 114 109	0.0003 864 428	36
37	0.0003 949 937	0.0003 702 547	0.0003 470 617	0.0003 253 196	37
38	0.0003 346 284	0.0003 130 138	0.0002 927 934	0.0002 738 783	38
39	0.0002 835 030	0.0002 646 350	0.0002 470 220	0.0002 305 812	39
40	0.0002 401 991	0.0002 237 428	0.0002 084 139	0.0001 941 360	40
41	0.0002 035 171	0.0001 891 758	0.0001 758 458	0.0001 634 562	41
42	0.0001 724 424	0.0001 599 540	0.0001 483 711	0.0001 376 284	42
43	0.0001 461 163	0.0001 352 493	0.0001 251 920	0.0001 158 841	43
44	0.0001 238 120	0.0001 143 627	0.0001 056 361	0.0000 975 771	44
45	0.0001 049 144	0.0000 967 033	0.0000 891 364	0.0000 821 635	45
46	0.0000 889 026	0.0000 817 720	0.0000 752 149	0.0000 691 855	46
47	0.0000 753 355	0.0000 691 470	0.0000 634 685	0.0000 582 581	47
48	0.0000 638 396	0.0000 584 718	0.0000 535 570	0.0000 490 570	48
49	0.0000 540 984	0.0000 494 452	0.0000 451 938	0.0000 413 095	49
50	0.0000 458 440	0.0000 418 124	0.0000 381 368	0.0000 347 857	50
51	0.0000 388 494	0.0000 353 581	0.0000 321 819	0.0000 292 924	51
52	0.0000 329 221	0.0000 299 002	0.0000 271 570	0.0000 246 667	52
53	0.0000 278 993	0.0000 252 850	0.0000 229 167	0.0000 207 715	53
54	0.0000 236 429	0.0000 213 822	0.0000 193 387	0.0000 174 915	54
55	0.0000 200 360	0.0000 180 818	0.0000 163 193	0.0000 147 294	55
56	0.0000 169 794	0.0000 152 910	0.0000 137 713	0.0000 124 036	56
57	0.0000 143 891	0.0000 129 309	0.0000 116 213	0.0000 104 450	57
58	0.0000 121 940	0.0000 109 351	0.0000 098 069	0.0000 087 957	58
59	0.0000 103 338	0.0000 092 473	0.0000 082 758	0.0000 074 069	59
60	0.0000 087 574	0.0000 078 201	0.0000 069 837	0.0000 062 373	60

TABLE 3. SINKING FUND FACTORS
Payable at end of each period

YEARLY Compounding

YEARS	19% Nominal Annual Rate	19¼% Nominal Annual Rate	19½% Nominal Annual Rate	19¾% Nominal Annual Rate	YEARS
1	1.0000 000 000	1.0000 000 000	1.0000 000 000	1.0000 000 000	1
2	0.4566 210 046	0.4561 003 421	0.4555 808 656	0.4550 625 711	2
3	0.2773 078 950	0.2766 591 335	0.2760 124 482	0.2753 678 312	3
4	0.1889 909 377	0.1883 112 096	0.1876 343 389	0.1869 603 133	4
5	0.1370 501 666	0.1363 772 312	0.1357 078 539	0.1350 420 171	5
6	0.1032 742 921	0.1026 259 070	0.1019 817 036	0.1013 416 578	6
7	0.0798 549 022	0.0792 401 005	0.0786 300 248	0.0780 246 439	7
8	0.0628 850 604	0.0623 084 076	0.0617 369 435	0.0611 706 283	8
9	0.0501 922 023	0.0496 557 141	0.0491 247 940	0.0485 993 928	9
10	0.0404 713 094	0.0399 754 343	0.0394 854 232	0.0390 012 170	10
11	0.0328 909 005	0.0324 350 759	0.0319 853 296	0.0315 415 921	11
12	0.0268 960 219	0.0264 790 164	0.0260 682 250	0.0256 635 677	12
13	0.0221 021 529	0.0217 222 906	0.0213 487 047	0.0209 813 048	13
14	0.0182 345 628	0.0178 898 796	0.0175 514 675	0.0172 192 259	14
15	0.0150 919 063	0.0147 802 620	0.0144 748 227	0.0141 754 782	15
16	0.0125 234 484	0.0122 426 105	0.0119 678 578	0.0116 990 716	16
17	0.0104 143 070	0.0101 620 134	0.0099 156 392	0.0096 750 584	17
18	0.0086 755 939	0.0084 496 003	0.0082 293 223	0.0080 146 275	18
19	0.0072 376 496	0.0070 357 660	0.0068 393 632	0.0066 483 038	19
20	0.0060 452 907	0.0058 654 074	0.0056 907 465	0.0055 211 669	20
21	0.0050 543 994	0.0048 945 066	0.0047 395 606	0.0045 894 179	21
22	0.0042 294 304	0.0040 876 308	0.0039 504 912	0.0038 178 674	22
23	0.0035 415 560	0.0034 160 731	0.0032 949 577	0.0031 780 659	23
24	0.0029 672 666	0.0028 564 488	0.0027 497 051	0.0026 468 926	24
25	0.0024 872 993	0.0023 896 210	0.0022 957 260	0.0022 054 739	25
26	0.0020 858 078	0.0019 998 675	0.0019 174 260	0.0018 383 461	26
27	0.0017 497 128	0.0016 742 300	0.0016 019 702	0.0015 328 002	27
28	0.0014 681 881	0.0014 019 981	0.0013 387 661	0.0012 783 639	28
29	0.0012 322 512	0.0011 742 992	0.0011 190 527	0.0010 663 889	29
30	0.0010 344 341	0.0009 837 685	0.0009 355 697	0.0008 897 203	30
31	0.0008 685 173	0.0008 242 831	0.0007 822 910	0.0007 424 299	31
32	0.0007 293 142	0.0006 907 453	0.0006 542 086	0.0006 195 990	32
33	0.0006 124 937	0.0005 789 060	0.0005 471 553	0.0005 171 429	33
34	0.0005 144 358	0.0004 852 202	0.0004 576 610	0.0004 316 657	34
35	0.0004 321 122	0.0004 067 278	0.0003 828 333	0.0003 603 425	35
36	0.0003 629 877	0.0003 409 552	0.0003 202 600	0.0003 008 218	36
37	0.0003 049 387	0.0002 858 346	0.0002 679 282	0.0002 511 451	37
38	0.0002 561 853	0.0002 396 361	0.0002 241 574	0.0002 096 805	38
39	0.0002 152 355	0.0002 009 124	0.0001 875 443	0.0001 750 679	39
40	0.0001 808 374	0.0001 684 516	0.0001 569 162	0.0001 461 731	40
41	0.0001 519 411	0.0001 412 392	0.0001 312 934	0.0001 220 503	41
42	0.0001 276 653	0.0001 184 256	0.0001 098 569	0.0001 019 106	42
43	0.0001 072 703	0.0000 992 988	0.0000 919 220	0.0000 850 955	43
44	0.0000 901 350	0.0000 832 625	0.0000 769 162	0.0000 710 559	44
45	0.0000 757 379	0.0000 698 169	0.0000 643 609	0.0000 593 334	45
46	0.0000 636 413	0.0000 585 433	0.0000 538 556	0.0000 495 452	46
47	0.0000 534 772	0.0000 490 905	0.0000 450 654	0.0000 413 722	47
48	0.0000 449 368	0.0000 411 643	0.0000 377 102	0.0000 345 476	48
49	0.0000 377 606	0.0000 345 182	0.0000 315 557	0.0000 288 489	49
50	0.0000 317 306	0.0000 289 452	0.0000 264 057	0.0000 240 904	50
51	0.0000 266 636	0.0000 242 721	0.0000 220 964	0.0000 201 168	51
52	0.0000 224 059	0.0000 203 536	0.0000 184 903	0.0000 167 987	52
53	0.0000 188 282	0.0000 170 677	0.0000 154 728	0.0000 140 280	53
54	0.0000 158 217	0.0000 143 123	0.0000 129 478	0.0000 117 143	54
55	0.0000 132 954	0.0000 120 018	0.0000 108 349	0.0000 097 822	55
56	0.0000 111 725	0.0000 100 643	0.0000 090 668	0.0000 081 688	56
57	0.0000 093 885	0.0000 084 396	0.0000 075 872	0.0000 068 215	57
58	0.0000 078 895	0.0000 070 772	0.0000 063 491	0.0000 056 964	58
59	0.0000 066 298	0.0000 059 347	0.0000 053 130	0.0000 047 569	59
60	0.0000 055 712	0.0000 049 767	0.0000 044 460	0.0000 039 723	60

YEARLY Compounding

TABLE 3. SINKING FUND FACTORS
Payable at end of each period

YEARS	20% Nominal Annual Rate	20¼% Nominal Annual Rate	20½% Nominal Annual Rate	20¾% Nominal Annual Rate	YEARS
1	1.0000 000 000	1.0000 000 000	1.0000 000 000	1.0000 000 000	1
2	0.4545 454 545	0.4540 295 119	0.4535 147 392	0.4530 011 325	2
3	0.2747 252 747	0.2740 847 710	0.2734 463 122	0.2728 098 907	3
4	0.1862 891 207	0.1856 207 489	0.1849 551 857	0.1842 924 191	4
5	0.1343 797 033	0.1337 208 950	0.1330 655 748	0.1324 137 253	5
6	0.1007 057 459	0.1000 739 440	0.0994 462 284	0.0988 225 755	6
7	0.0774 239 263	0.0768 278 411	0.0762 363 570	0.0756 494 432	7
8	0.0606 094 224	0.0600 532 863	0.0595 021 805	0.0589 560 660	8
9	0.0480 794 617	0.0475 649 519	0.0470 558 149	0.0465 520 025	9
10	0.0385 227 569	0.0380 499 844	0.0375 828 412	0.0371 212 696	10
11	0.0311 037 942	0.0306 718 672	0.0302 457 430	0.0298 253 537	11
12	0.0252 649 649	0.0248 723 377	0.0244 856 079	0.0241 046 978	12
13	0.0206 200 011	0.0202 647 045	0.0199 153 270	0.0195 717 813	13
14	0.0168 930 552	0.0165 728 569	0.0162 585 336	0.0159 499 889	14
15	0.0138 821 198	0.0135 946 403	0.0133 129 335	0.0130 368 949	15
16	0.0114 361 350	0.0111 789 328	0.0109 273 513	0.0106 812 788	16
17	0.0094 401 469	0.0092 107 826	0.0089 868 456	0.0087 682 178	17
18	0.0078 053 857	0.0076 014 695	0.0074 027 537	0.0072 091 153	18
19	0.0064 624 532	0.0062 816 795	0.0061 058 536	0.0059 348 491	19
20	0.0053 565 307	0.0051 967 031	0.0050 415 524	0.0048 909 500	20
21	0.0044 439 388	0.0043 029 869	0.0041 664 291	0.0040 341 360	21
22	0.0036 896 187	0.0035 656 084	0.0034 457 036	0.0033 297 749	22
23	0.0030 652 575	0.0029 563 967	0.0028 513 516	0.0027 499 943	23
24	0.0025 478 730	0.0024 525 124	0.0023 606 809	0.0022 722 531	24
25	0.0021 187 290	0.0020 353 602	0.0019 552 408	0.0018 782 486	25
26	0.0017 624 956	0.0016 897 471	0.0016 199 779	0.0015 530 696	26
27	0.0014 665 923	0.0014 032 233	0.0013 425 751	0.0012 845 339	27
28	0.0012 206 684	0.0011 655 616	0.0011 129 302	0.0010 626 657	28
29	0.0010 161 900	0.0009 683 434	0.0009 227 413	0.0008 792 806	29
30	0.0008 461 085	0.0008 046 272	0.0007 651 745	0.0007 276 528	30
31	0.0007 045 936	0.0006 686 812	0.0006 345 966	0.0006 022 481	31
32	0.0005 868 168	0.0005 557 668	0.0005 263 590	0.0004 985 076	32
33	0.0004 887 750	0.0004 619 626	0.0004 366 217	0.0004 126 723	33
34	0.0004 071 466	0.0003 840 210	0.0003 622 104	0.0003 416 409	34
35	0.0003 391 738	0.0003 192 502	0.0003 004 992	0.0002 828 524	35
36	0.0002 825 649	0.0002 654 183	0.0002 493 148	0.0002 341 914	36
37	0.0002 354 154	0.0002 206 734	0.0002 068 574	0.0001 939 097	37
38	0.0001 961 410	0.0001 834 785	0.0001 716 365	0.0001 605 620	38
39	0.0001 634 241	0.0001 525 576	0.0001 424 166	0.0001 329 529	39
40	0.0001 361 682	0.0001 268 509	0.0001 181 741	0.0001 100 938	40
41	0.0001 134 606	0.0001 054 782	0.0000 980 602	0.0000 911 667	41
42	0.0000 945 416	0.0000 877 081	0.0000 813 711	0.0000 754 947	42
43	0.0000 787 785	0.0000 729 328	0.0000 675 233	0.0000 625 175	43
44	0.0000 656 444	0.0000 606 473	0.0000 560 328	0.0000 517 717	44
45	0.0000 547 007	0.0000 504 318	0.0000 464 981	0.0000 428 733	45
46	0.0000 455 818	0.0000 419 374	0.0000 385 861	0.0000 355 045	46
47	0.0000 379 834	0.0000 348 739	0.0000 320 207	0.0000 294 025	47
48	0.0000 316 518	0.0000 290 003	0.0000 265 725	0.0000 243 493	48
49	0.0000 263 758	0.0000 241 161	0.0000 220 514	0.0000 201 646	49
50	0.0000 219 794	0.0000 200 546	0.0000 182 995	0.0000 166 992	50
51	0.0000 183 158	0.0000 166 771	0.0000 151 861	0.0000 138 294	51
52	0.0000 152 629	0.0000 138 685	0.0000 126 024	0.0000 114 528	52
53	0.0000 127 190	0.0000 115 329	0.0000 104 583	0.0000 094 846	53
54	0.0000 105 990	0.0000 095 907	0.0000 086 790	0.0000 078 547	54
55	0.0000 088 324	0.0000 079 756	0.0000 072 025	0.0000 065 049	55
56	0.0000 073 603	0.0000 066 325	0.0000 059 771	0.0000 053 870	56
57	0.0000 061 336	0.0000 055 155	0.0000 049 602	0.0000 044 613	57
58	0.0000 051 113	0.0000 045 867	0.0000 041 164	0.0000 036 946	58
59	0.0000 042 594	0.0000 038 143	0.0000 034 161	0.0000 030 597	59
60	0.0000 035 495	0.0000 031 720	0.0000 028 349	0.0000 025 339	60

TABLE 3. SINKING FUND FACTORS
Payable at end of each period

YEARLY Compounding

YEARS	21% Nominal Annual Rate	21¼% Nominal Annual Rate	21½% Nominal Annual Rate	21¾% Nominal Annual Rate	YEARS
1	1.0000 000 000	1.0000 000 000	1.0000 000 000	1.0000 000 000	1
2	0.4524 886 878	0.4519 774 011	0.4514 672 686	0.4509 582 864	2
3	0.2721 754 988	0.2715 431 287	0.2709 127 729	0.2702 844 237	3
4	0.1836 324 369	0.1829 752 272	0.1823 207 780	0.1816 690 774	4
5	0.1317 653 293	0.1311 203 694	0.1304 788 284	0.1298 406 893	5
6	0.0982 029 617	0.0975 873 635	0.0969 757 574	0.0963 681 200	6
7	0.0750 670 688	0.0744 892 029	0.0739 158 150	0.0733 468 744	7
8	0.0584 149 035	0.0578 786 541	0.0573 472 791	0.0568 207 399	8
9	0.0460 534 667	0.0455 601 595	0.0450 720 334	0.0445 890 411	9
10	0.0366 652 120	0.0362 146 112	0.0357 694 102	0.0353 295 526	10
11	0.0294 106 322	0.0290 015 115	0.0285 979 253	0.0281 998 078	11
12	0.0237 295 303	0.0233 600 292	0.0229 961 186	0.0226 377 235	12
13	0.0192 339 810	0.0189 018 405	0.0185 752 752	0.0182 542 012	13
14	0.0156 471 276	0.0153 498 557	0.0150 580 800	0.0147 717 088	14
15	0.0127 664 213	0.0125 014 110	0.0122 417 634	0.0119 873 796	15
16	0.0104 406 051	0.0102 052 217	0.0099 750 219	0.0097 499 005	16
17	0.0085 547 835	0.0083 464 285	0.0081 430 410	0.0079 445 111	17
18	0.0070 204 340	0.0068 365 916	0.0066 574 724	0.0064 829 628	18
19	0.0057 685 424	0.0056 068 125	0.0054 495 409	0.0052 966 119	19
20	0.0047 447 703	0.0046 028 907	0.0044 651 915	0.0043 315 559	20
21	0.0039 059 812	0.0037 818 419	0.0036 615 982	0.0035 451 335	21
22	0.0032 176 967	0.0031 093 467	0.0030 046 062	0.0029 033 599	22
23	0.0026 522 006	0.0025 578 502	0.0024 668 266	0.0023 790 166	23
24	0.0021 871 074	0.0021 051 263	0.0020 261 962	0.0019 502 070	24
25	0.0018 042 655	0.0017 331 775	0.0016 648 747	0.0015 992 511	25
26	0.0014 889 084	0.0014 273 844	0.0013 683 922	0.0013 118 301	26
27	0.0012 289 905	0.0011 758 400	0.0011 249 817	0.0010 763 188	27
28	0.0010 146 640	0.0009 688 254	0.0009 250 544	0.0008 832 592	28
29	0.0008 378 627	0.0007 983 934	0.0007 607 824	0.0007 249 437	29
30	0.0006 919 694	0.0006 580 354	0.0006 257 665	0.0005 950 819	30
31	0.0005 715 487	0.0005 424 153	0.0005 147 690	0.0004 885 349	31
32	0.0004 721 313	0.0004 471 528	0.0004 234 988	0.0004 010 997	32
33	0.0003 900 389	0.0003 686 498	0.0003 484 372	0.0003 293 369	33
34	0.0003 222 423	0.0003 039 487	0.0002 866 974	0.0002 704 294	34
35	0.0002 662 451	0.0002 506 165	0.0002 359 093	0.0002 220 693	35
36	0.0002 199 889	0.0002 066 513	0.0001 941 263	0.0001 823 645	36
37	0.0001 817 759	0.0001 704 050	0.0001 597 492	0.0001 497 636	37
38	0.0001 502 055	0.0001 405 205	0.0001 314 636	0.0001 229 940	38
39	0.0001 241 213	0.0001 158 798	0.0001 081 888	0.0001 010 116	39
40	0.0001 025 691	0.0000 955 618	0.0000 890 363	0.0000 829 595	40
41	0.0000 847 607	0.0000 788 076	0.0000 732 755	0.0000 681 346	41
42	0.0000 700 452	0.0000 649 918	0.0000 603 055	0.0000 559 596	42
43	0.0000 578 853	0.0000 535 986	0.0000 496 317	0.0000 459 606	43
44	0.0000 478 368	0.0000 442 031	0.0000 408 474	0.0000 377 485	44
45	0.0000 395 330	0.0000 364 548	0.0000 336 182	0.0000 310 040	45
46	0.0000 326 708	0.0000 300 649	0.0000 276 685	0.0000 254 646	46
47	0.0000 269 999	0.0000 247 952	0.0000 227 719	0.0000 209 151	47
48	0.0000 223 135	0.0000 204 492	0.0000 187 420	0.0000 171 784	48
49	0.0000 184 406	0.0000 168 651	0.0000 154 252	0.0000 141 094	49
50	0.0000 152 399	0.0000 139 091	0.0000 126 955	0.0000 115 887	50
51	0.0000 125 948	0.0000 114 713	0.0000 104 489	0.0000 095 183	51
52	0.0000 104 088	0.0000 094 608	0.0000 085 998	0.0000 078 179	52
53	0.0000 086 023	0.0000 078 027	0.0000 070 780	0.0000 064 212	53
54	0.0000 071 093	0.0000 064 351	0.0000 058 255	0.0000 052 741	54
55	0.0000 058 754	0.0000 053 073	0.0000 047 946	0.0000 043 319	55
56	0.0000 048 557	0.0000 043 771	0.0000 039 462	0.0000 035 580	56
57	0.0000 040 129	0.0000 036 100	0.0000 032 479	0.0000 029 224	57
58	0.0000 033 165	0.0000 029 773	0.0000 026 731	0.0000 024 003	58
59	0.0000 027 409	0.0000 024 555	0.0000 022 001	0.0000 019 715	59
60	0.0000 022 652	0.0000 020 252	0.0000 018 108	0.0000 016 193	60

YEARLY
Compounding

TABLE 3. SINKING FUND FACTORS
Payable at end of each period

YEARS	22% Nominal Annual Rate	22¼% Nominal Annual Rate	22½% Nominal Annual Rate	22¾% Nominal Annual Rate	YEARS
1	1.0000 000 000	1.0000 000 000	1.0000 000 000	1.0000 000 000	1
2	0.4504 504 505	0.4499 437 570	0.4494 382 022	0.4489 337 823	2
3	0.2696 580 736	0.2690 337 150	0.2684 113 404	0.2677 909 423	3
4	0.1810 201 135	0.1803 738 744	0.1797 303 483	0.1790 895 235	4
5	0.1292 059 348	0.1285 745 481	0.1279 465 120	0.1273 218 096	5
6	0.0957 644 282	0.0951 646 586	0.0945 687 881	0.0939 767 936	6
7	0.0727 823 508	0.0722 222 137	0.0716 664 329	0.0711 149 784	7
8	0.0562 989 979	0.0557 820 148	0.0552 697 526	0.0547 621 732	8
9	0.0441 111 354	0.0436 382 693	0.0431 703 963	0.0427 074 699	9
10	0.0348 949 820	0.0344 656 428	0.0340 414 793	0.0336 224 365	10
11	0.0278 070 935	0.0274 197 175	0.0270 376 154	0.0266 607 234	11
12	0.0222 847 695	0.0219 371 829	0.0215 948 907	0.0212 578 204	12
13	0.0179 385 355	0.0176 281 963	0.0173 231 022	0.0170 231 730	13
14	0.0144 906 512	0.0142 148 177	0.0139 441 198	0.0136 784 701	14
15	0.0117 381 620	0.0114 940 142	0.0112 548 416	0.0110 205 506	15
16	0.0095 297 542	0.0093 144 814	0.0091 039 818	0.0088 981 572	16
17	0.0077 507 309	0.0075 615 943	0.0073 769 974	0.0071 968 380	17
18	0.0063 129 516	0.0061 473 298	0.0059 859 908	0.0058 288 300	18
19	0.0051 479 123	0.0050 033 314	0.0048 627 611	0.0047 260 956	19
20	0.0042 018 701	0.0040 760 227	0.0039 539 055	0.0038 354 127	20
21	0.0034 323 343	0.0033 230 901	0.0032 172 935	0.0031 148 399	21
22	0.0028 054 958	0.0027 109 052	0.0026 194 824	0.0025 311 250	22
23	0.0022 943 108	0.0022 126 029	0.0021 337 902	0.0020 577 731	23
24	0.0018 770 526	0.0018 066 303	0.0017 388 407	0.0016 735 880	24
25	0.0015 362 042	0.0014 756 355	0.0014 174 498	0.0013 615 554	25
26	0.0012 576 002	0.0012 056 085	0.0011 557 645	0.0011 079 811	26
27	0.0010 297 583	0.0009 852 112	0.0009 425 919	0.0009 018 183	27
28	0.0008 433 524	0.0008 052 498	0.0007 688 712	0.0007 341 395	28
29	0.0006 907 949	0.0006 582 575	0.0006 272 562	0.0005 977 195	29
30	0.0005 659 049	0.0005 381 621	0.0005 117 839	0.0004 867 035	30
31	0.0004 636 414	0.0004 400 207	0.0004 176 083	0.0003 963 427	31
32	0.0003 798 896	0.0003 598 056	0.0003 407 885	0.0003 227 819	32
33	0.0003 112 880	0.0002 942 330	0.0002 781 173	0.0002 628 896	33
34	0.0002 550 890	0.0002 406 234	0.0002 269 830	0.0002 141 208	34
35	0.0002 090 456	0.0001 967 903	0.0001 852 579	0.0001 744 061	35
36	0.0001 713 195	0.0001 609 477	0.0001 512 081	0.0001 420 622	36
37	0.0001 404 061	0.0001 316 372	0.0001 234 200	0.0001 157 195	37
38	0.0001 150 737	0.0001 076 671	0.0001 007 408	0.0000 942 637	38
39	0.0000 943 138	0.0000 880 635	0.0000 822 307	0.0000 767 873	39
40	0.0000 773 005	0.0000 720 304	0.0000 671 226	0.0000 625 519	40
41	0.0000 633 570	0.0000 589 171	0.0000 547 909	0.0000 509 562	41
42	0.0000 519 293	0.0000 481 916	0.0000 447 253	0.0000 415 105	42
43	0.0000 425 632	0.0000 394 190	0.0000 365 091	0.0000 338 159	43
44	0.0000 348 866	0.0000 322 435	0.0000 298 025	0.0000 275 479	44
45	0.0000 285 948	0.0000 263 744	0.0000 243 279	0.0000 224 417	45
46	0.0000 234 378	0.0000 215 737	0.0000 198 592	0.0000 182 821	46
47	0.0000 192 109	0.0000 176 469	0.0000 162 113	0.0000 148 936	47
48	0.0000 157 464	0.0000 144 349	0.0000 132 335	0.0000 121 331	48
49	0.0000 129 067	0.0000 118 075	0.0000 108 028	0.0000 098 843	49
50	0.0000 105 792	0.0000 096 584	0.0000 088 185	0.0000 080 523	50
51	0.0000 086 714	0.0000 079 005	0.0000 071 987	0.0000 065 599	51
52	0.0000 071 076	0.0000 064 625	0.0000 058 765	0.0000 053 441	52
53	0.0000 058 259	0.0000 052 863	0.0000 047 971	0.0000 043 536	53
54	0.0000 047 753	0.0000 043 241	0.0000 039 160	0.0000 035 467	54
55	0.0000 039 142	0.0000 035 371	0.0000 031 967	0.0000 028 894	55
56	0.0000 032 083	0.0000 028 933	0.0000 026 096	0.0000 023 539	56
57	0.0000 026 298	0.0000 023 667	0.0000 021 302	0.0000 019 176	57
58	0.0000 021 555	0.0000 019 360	0.0000 017 390	0.0000 015 622	58
59	0.0000 017 668	0.0000 015 836	0.0000 014 196	0.0000 012 727	59
60	0.0000 014 482	0.0000 012 954	0.0000 011 588	0.0000 010 368	60

TABLE 3. SINKING FUND FACTORS
Payable at end of each period

YEARLY Compounding

YEARS	23% Nominal Annual Rate	24% Nominal Annual Rate	25% Nominal Annual Rate	26% Nominal Annual Rate	YEARS
1	1.0000 000 000	1.0000 000 000	1.0000 000 000	1.0000 000 000	1
2	0.4484 304 933	0.4464 285 714	0.4444 444 444	0.4424 778 761	2
3	0.2671 725 133	0.2647 183 397	0.2622 950 820	0.2599 022 767	3
4	0.1784 513 881	0.1759 255 089	0.1734 417 344	0.1709 993 338	4
5	0.1267 004 241	0.1242 477 149	0.1218 467 396	0.1194 964 454	5
6	0.0933 886 522	0.0910 741 602	0.0888 194 987	0.0866 232 355	6
7	0.0705 678 200	0.0684 215 522	0.0663 416 530	0.0643 262 593	7
8	0.0542 592 389	0.0522 932 018	0.0503 985 063	0.0485 728 187	8
9	0.0422 494 441	0.0404 654 313	0.0387 562 013	0.0371 189 268	9
10	0.0332 084 594	0.0316 021 271	0.0300 725 624	0.0286 164 407	10
11	0.0262 889 780	0.0248 522 131	0.0234 928 576	0.0222 071 051	11
12	0.0209 259 004	0.0196 483 138	0.0184 475 770	0.0173 194 369	12
13	0.0167 283 293	0.0155 982 535	0.0145 434 288	0.0135 592 056	13
14	0.0134 177 823	0.0124 229 653	0.0115 009 326	0.0106 467 022	14
15	0.0107 910 491	0.0099 191 452	0.0091 168 642	0.0083 789 634	15
16	0.0086 969 108	0.0079 358 295	0.0072 406 815	0.0066 060 410	16
17	0.0070 210 160	0.0063 591 647	0.0057 591 848	0.0052 155 451	17
18	0.0056 757 451	0.0051 021 928	0.0045 862 176	0.0041 222 582	18
19	0.0045 932 318	0.0040 978 105	0.0036 555 619	0.0032 609 648	19
20	0.0037 204 414	0.0032 938 009	0.0029 159 221	0.0025 813 865	20
21	0.0030 156 276	0.0026 492 538	0.0023 273 086	0.0020 445 308	21
22	0.0024 457 335	0.0021 319 401	0.0018 583 869	0.0016 200 148	22
23	0.0019 844 553	0.0017 163 556	0.0014 845 025	0.0012 840 750	23
24	0.0016 107 795	0.0013 822 445	0.0011 861 933	0.0010 180 696	24
25	0.0013 078 641	0.0011 134 721	0.0009 480 549	0.0008 073 395	25
26	0.0010 621 747	0.0008 971 558	0.0007 578 692	0.0006 403 353	26
27	0.0008 628 116	0.0007 229 896	0.0006 059 280	0.0005 079 445	27
28	0.0007 009 811	0.0005 827 164	0.0004 845 075	0.0004 029 681	28
29	0.0005 695 787	0.0004 697 118	0.0003 874 558	0.0003 197 137	29
30	0.0004 628 578	0.0003 786 564	0.0003 098 686	0.0002 536 767	30
31	0.0003 761 656	0.0003 052 749	0.0002 478 335	0.0002 012 902	31
32	0.0003 057 322	0.0002 461 288	0.0001 982 275	0.0001 597 286	32
33	0.0002 485 010	0.0001 984 516	0.0001 585 568	0.0001 267 526	33
34	0.0002 019 925	0.0001 600 160	0.0001 268 294	0.0001 005 872	34
35	0.0001 641 946	0.0001 290 285	0.0001 014 532	0.0000 798 248	35
36	0.0001 334 737	0.0001 040 444	0.0000 811 560	0.0000 633 490	36
37	0.0001 085 034	0.0000 838 998	0.0000 649 206	0.0000 502 744	37
38	0.0000 882 064	0.0000 676 565	0.0000 519 338	0.0000 398 987	38
39	0.0000 717 074	0.0000 545 587	0.0000 415 453	0.0000 316 647	39
40	0.0000 582 953	0.0000 439 970	0.0000 332 351	0.0000 251 301	40
41	0.0000 473 923	0.0000 354 802	0.0000 265 874	0.0000 199 441	41
42	0.0000 385 288	0.0000 286 123	0.0000 212 695	0.0000 158 284	42
43	0.0000 313 233	0.0000 230 739	0.0000 170 153	0.0000 125 621	43
44	0.0000 254 654	0.0000 186 076	0.0000 136 120	0.0000 099 698	44
45	0.0000 207 032	0.0000 150 059	0.0000 108 895	0.0000 079 125	45
46	0.0000 168 316	0.0000 121 014	0.0000 087 115	0.0000 062 797	46
47	0.0000 136 840	0.0000 097 591	0.0000 069 692	0.0000 049 839	47
48	0.0000 111 251	0.0000 078 702	0.0000 055 753	0.0000 039 554	48
49	0.0000 090 447	0.0000 063 469	0.0000 044 602	0.0000 031 392	49
50	0.0000 073 534	0.0000 051 184	0.0000 035 682	0.0000 024 914	50
51	0.0000 059 783	0.0000 041 277	0.0000 028 545	0.0000 019 773	51
52	0.0000 048 604	0.0000 033 288	0.0000 022 836	0.0000 015 693	52
53	0.0000 039 515	0.0000 026 845	0.0000 018 269	0.0000 012 455	53
54	0.0000 032 126	0.0000 021 649	0.0000 014 615	0.0000 009 885	54
55	0.0000 026 119	0.0000 017 459	0.0000 011 692	0.0000 007 845	55
56	0.0000 021 235	0.0000 014 080	0.0000 009 354	0.0000 006 226	56
57	0.0000 017 264	0.0000 011 355	0.0000 007 483	0.0000 004 941	57
58	0.0000 014 036	0.0000 009 157	0.0000 005 986	0.0000 003 922	58
59	0.0000 011 411	0.0000 007 385	0.0000 004 789	0.0000 003 113	59
60	0.0000 009 277	0.0000 005 955	0.0000 003 831	0.0000 002 470	60

YEARLY
Compounding

TABLE 3. SINKING FUND FACTORS
Payable at end of each period

YEARS	27% Nominal Annual Rate	28% Nominal Annual Rate	29% Nominal Annual Rate	30% Nominal Annual Rate	YEARS
1	1.0000 000 000	1.0000 000 000	1.0000 000 000	1.0000 000 000	1
2	0.4405 286 344	0.4385 964 912	0.4366 812 227	0.4347 826 087	2
3	0.2575 394 679	0.2552 062 066	0.2529 020 510	0.2506 265 664	3
4	0.1685 975 867	0.1662 357 835	0.1639 132 250	0.1616 292 226	4
5	0.1171 957 942	0.1149 437 633	0.1127 393 452	0.1105 815 484	5
6	0.0844 839 602	0.0824 002 847	0.0803 708 441	0.0783 942 967	6
7	0.0623 735 405	0.0604 816 996	0.0586 489 741	0.0568 736 368	7
8	0.0468 138 541	0.0451 193 773	0.0434 872 047	0.0419 152 051	8
9	0.0355 508 517	0.0340 492 925	0.0326 116 401	0.0312 353 605	9
10	0.0272 305 377	0.0259 117 316	0.0246 570 037	0.0234 634 396	10
11	0.0209 912 864	0.0198 418 706	0.0187 554 652	0.0177 288 158	11
12	0.0162 598 204	0.0152 648 341	0.0143 307 636	0.0134 540 701	12
13	0.0126 411 632	0.0117 851 066	0.0109 870 625	0.0102 432 741	13
14	0.0098 555 727	0.0091 231 170	0.0084 451 743	0.0078 178 414	14
15	0.0077 005 351	0.0070 769 943	0.0065 040 669	0.0059 777 755	15
16	0.0060 268 700	0.0054 985 011	0.0050 166 190	0.0045 772 413	16
17	0.0047 231 529	0.0042 773 299	0.0038 737 873	0.0035 086 013	17
18	0.0037 052 382	0.0033 305 344	0.0029 939 453	0.0026 916 595	18
19	0.0029 090 233	0.0025 952 273	0.0023 155 138	0.0020 662 291	19
20	0.0022 853 348	0.0020 234 188	0.0017 917 558	0.0015 868 848	20
21	0.0017 962 439	0.0015 783 010	0.0013 870 314	0.0012 191 924	21
22	0.0014 123 677	0.0012 315 291	0.0010 740 633	0.0009 369 616	22
23	0.0011 108 651	0.0009 612 073	0.0008 319 146	0.0007 202 206	23
24	0.0008 739 325	0.0007 503 797	0.0006 444 794	0.0005 537 091	24
25	0.0006 876 627	0.0005 858 907	0.0004 993 470	0.0004 257 487	25
26	0.0005 411 736	0.0004 575 177	0.0003 869 409	0.0003 273 918	26
27	0.0004 259 395	0.0003 573 080	0.0002 998 642	0.0002 517 764	27
28	0.0003 352 730	0.0002 790 689	0.0002 323 989	0.0001 936 367	28
29	0.0002 639 248	0.0002 179 751	0.0001 801 217	0.0001 489 291	29
30	0.0002 077 716	0.0001 702 640	0.0001 396 097	0.0001 145 477	30
31	0.0001 635 729	0.0001 330 011	0.0001 082 129	0.0000 881 059	31
32	0.0001 287 810	0.0001 038 963	0.0000 838 789	0.0000 677 692	32
33	0.0001 013 921	0.0000 811 624	0.0000 650 182	0.0000 521 274	33
34	0.0000 798 299	0.0000 634 041	0.0000 503 992	0.0000 400 964	34
35	0.0000 628 542	0.0000 495 320	0.0000 390 676	0.0000 308 424	35
36	0.0000 494 891	0.0000 386 954	0.0000 302 840	0.0000 237 244	36
37	0.0000 389 663	0.0000 302 299	0.0000 234 754	0.0000 182 492	37
38	0.0000 306 812	0.0000 236 165	0.0000 181 977	0.0000 140 376	38
39	0.0000 241 578	0.0000 184 501	0.0000 141 065	0.0000 107 981	39
40	0.0000 190 215	0.0000 144 139	0.0000 109 352	0.0000 083 061	40
41	0.0000 149 774	0.0000 112 607	0.0000 084 768	0.0000 063 893	41
42	0.0000 117 931	0.0000 087 974	0.0000 065 711	0.0000 049 148	42
43	0.0000 092 858	0.0000 068 729	0.0000 050 939	0.0000 037 806	43
44	0.0000 073 116	0.0000 053 694	0.0000 039 487	0.0000 029 082	44
45	0.0000 057 571	0.0000 041 948	0.0000 030 610	0.0000 022 370	45
46	0.0000 045 331	0.0000 032 772	0.0000 023 729	0.0000 017 208	46
47	0.0000 035 694	0.0000 025 603	0.0000 018 394	0.0000 013 237	47
48	0.0000 028 105	0.0000 020 002	0.0000 014 259	0.0000 010 182	48
49	0.0000 022 130	0.0000 015 627	0.0000 011 054	0.0000 007 832	49
50	0.0000 017 425	0.0000 012 208	0.0000 008 569	0.0000 006 025	50
51	0.0000 013 721	0.0000 009 538	0.0000 006 642	0.0000 004 635	51
52	0.0000 010 804	0.0000 007 451	0.0000 005 149	0.0000 003 565	52
53	0.0000 008 507	0.0000 005 821	0.0000 003 992	0.0000 002 742	53
54	0.0000 006 698	0.0000 004 548	0.0000 003 094	0.0000 002 110	54
55	0.0000 005 274	0.0000 003 553	0.0000 002 399	0.0000 001 623	55
56	0.0000 004 153	0.0000 002 776	0.0000 001 859	0.0000 001 248	56
57	0.0000 003 270	0.0000 002 169	0.0000 001 441	0.0000 000 960	57
58	0.0000 002 575	0.0000 001 694	0.0000 001 117	0.0000 000 739	58
59	0.0000 002 027	0.0000 001 324	0.0000 000 866	0.0000 000 568	59
60	0.0000 001 596	0.0000 001 034	0.0000 000 671	0.0000 000 437	60

TABLE 4. PRESENT WORTH OF ONE DOLLAR
Payable at end of each period

YEARLY Compounding

YEARS	5% Nominal Annual Rate	5¼% Nominal Annual Rate	5½% Nominal Annual Rate	5¾% Nominal Annual Rate	YEARS
1	0.9523 809 524	0.9501 187 648	0.9478 672 986	0.9456 264 775	1
2	0.9070 294 785	0.9027 256 673	0.8984 524 157	0.8942 094 350	2
3	0.8638 375 985	0.8576 965 960	0.8516 136 642	0.8455 881 182	3
4	0.8227 024 748	0.8149 136 304	0.8072 167 433	0.7996 105 137	4
5	0.7835 261 665	0.7742 647 320	0.7651 343 538	0.7561 328 735	5
6	0.7462 153 966	0.7356 434 508	0.7252 458 330	0.7150 192 657	6
7	0.7106 813 301	0.6989 486 469	0.6874 368 086	0.6761 411 496	7
8	0.6768 393 620	0.6640 842 250	0.6515 988 707	0.6393 769 736	8
9	0.6446 089 162	0.6309 588 837	0.6176 292 613	0.6046 117 954	9
10	0.6139 132 535	0.5994 858 752	0.5854 305 794	0.5717 369 223	10
11	0.5846 792 891	0.5695 827 793	0.5549 105 018	0.5406 495 720	11
12	0.5568 374 182	0.5411 712 867	0.5259 815 183	0.5112 525 503	12
13	0.5303 213 506	0.5141 769 945	0.4985 606 809	0.4834 539 483	13
14	0.5050 679 530	0.4885 292 110	0.4725 693 658	0.4571 668 542	14
15	0.4810 170 981	0.4641 607 705	0.4479 330 481	0.4323 090 820	15
16	0.4581 115 220	0.4410 078 580	0.4245 810 883	0.4088 029 144	16
17	0.4362 966 876	0.4190 098 413	0.4024 465 292	0.3865 748 599	17
18	0.4155 206 549	0.3981 091 129	0.3814 659 044	0.3655 554 231	18
19	0.3957 339 570	0.3782 509 386	0.3615 790 563	0.3456 788 871	19
20	0.3768 894 829	0.3593 833 146	0.3427 289 633	0.3268 831 084	20
21	0.3589 423 646	0.3414 568 310	0.3248 615 766	0.3091 093 223	21
22	0.3418 498 711	0.3244 245 425	0.3079 256 650	0.2923 019 597	22
23	0.3255 713 058	0.3082 418 456	0.2918 726 683	0.2764 084 725	23
24	0.3100 679 103	0.2928 663 616	0.2766 565 576	0.2613 791 702	24
25	0.2953 027 717	0.2782 578 257	0.2622 337 039	0.2471 670 640	25
26	0.2812 407 350	0.2643 779 817	0.2485 627 525	0.2337 277 201	26
27	0.2678 483 190	0.2511 904 814	0.2356 045 047	0.2210 191 207	27
28	0.2550 936 371	0.2386 607 900	0.2233 218 055	0.2090 015 325	28
29	0.2429 463 211	0.2267 560 950	0.2116 794 364	0.1976 373 830	29
30	0.2313 774 487	0.2154 452 209	0.2006 440 156	0.1868 911 423	30
31	0.2203 594 749	0.2046 985 471	0.1901 839 010	0.1767 292 126	31
32	0.2098 661 666	0.1944 879 308	0.1802 691 005	0.1671 198 228	32
33	0.1998 725 396	0.1847 866 326	0.1708 711 853	0.1580 329 294	33
34	0.1903 547 996	0.1755 692 471	0.1619 632 088	0.1494 401 223	34
35	0.1812 902 854	0.1668 116 362	0.1535 196 292	0.1413 145 365	35
36	0.1726 574 146	0.1584 908 657	0.1455 162 362	0.1336 307 674	36
37	0.1644 356 330	0.1505 851 456	0.1379 300 817	0.1263 647 918	37
38	0.1566 053 647	0.1430 737 725	0.1307 394 140	0.1194 938 930	38
39	0.1491 479 664	0.1359 370 761	0.1239 236 151	0.1129 965 891	39
40	0.1420 456 823	0.1291 563 668	0.1174 631 423	0.1068 525 665	40
41	0.1352 816 022	0.1227 138 877	0.1113 394 714	0.1010 426 161	41
42	0.1288 396 211	0.1165 927 674	0.1055 350 440	0.0955 485 732	42
43	0.1227 044 011	0.1107 769 762	0.1000 332 170	0.0903 532 607	43
44	0.1168 613 344	0.1052 512 838	0.0948 182 152	0.0854 404 356	44
45	0.1112 965 089	0.1000 012 197	0.0898 750 855	0.0807 947 382	45
46	0.1059 966 752	0.0950 130 354	0.0851 896 545	0.0764 016 437	46
47	0.1009 492 144	0.0902 736 678	0.0807 484 877	0.0722 474 172	47
48	0.0961 421 090	0.0857 707 058	0.0765 388 509	0.0683 190 706	48
49	0.0915 639 133	0.0814 923 570	0.0725 486 738	0.0646 043 221	49
50	0.0872 037 270	0.0774 274 176	0.0687 665 155	0.0610 915 575	50
51	0.0830 511 685	0.0735 652 424	0.0651 815 312	0.0577 697 944	51
52	0.0790 963 510	0.0698 957 172	0.0617 834 419	0.0546 286 471	52
53	0.0753 298 581	0.0664 092 325	0.0585 625 042	0.0516 582 952	53
54	0.0717 427 220	0.0630 966 580	0.0555 094 827	0.0488 494 517	54
55	0.0683 264 019	0.0599 493 187	0.0526 156 234	0.0461 933 349	55
56	0.0650 727 637	0.0569 589 727	0.0498 726 288	0.0436 816 406	56
57	0.0619 740 607	0.0541 177 888	0.0472 726 339	0.0413 065 159	57
58	0.0590 229 149	0.0514 183 266	0.0448 081 838	0.0390 605 352	58
59	0.0562 122 999	0.0488 535 170	0.0424 722 121	0.0369 366 763	59
60	0.0535 355 237	0.0464 166 432	0.0402 580 210	0.0349 282 991	60

YEARLY Compounding

TABLE 4. PRESENT WORTH OF ONE DOLLAR
Payable at end of each period

YEARS	6% Nominal Annual Rate	6¼% Nominal Annual Rate	6½% Nominal Annual Rate	6¾% Nominal Annual Rate	YEARS
1	0.9433 962 264	0.9411 764 706	0.9389 671 362	0.9367 681 499	1
2	0.8899 964 400	0.8858 131 488	0.8816 592 828	0.8775 345 666	2
3	0.8396 192 830	0.8337 064 930	0.8278 490 918	0.8220 464 324	3
4	0.7920 936 632	0.7846 649 346	0.7773 230 909	0.7700 669 156	4
5	0.7472 581 729	0.7385 081 737	0.7298 808 365	0.7213 741 598	5
6	0.7049 605 404	0.6950 665 164	0.6853 341 188	0.6757 603 371	6
7	0.6650 571 136	0.6541 802 508	0.6435 062 148	0.6330 307 607	7
8	0.6274 123 713	0.6156 990 595	0.6042 311 876	0.5930 030 546	8
9	0.5918 984 635	0.5794 814 678	0.5673 532 278	0.5555 063 743	9
10	0.5583 947 769	0.5453 943 226	0.5327 260 355	0.5203 806 785	10
11	0.5267 875 254	0.5133 123 037	0.5002 122 399	0.4874 760 454	11
12	0.4969 693 636	0.4831 174 623	0.4696 828 544	0.4566 520 332	12
13	0.4688 390 222	0.4546 987 880	0.4410 167 647	0.4277 770 803	13
14	0.4423 009 644	0.4279 518 005	0.4141 002 485	0.4007 279 440	14
15	0.4172 650 607	0.4027 781 652	0.3888 265 244	0.3753 891 748	15
16	0.3936 462 837	0.3790 853 319	0.3650 953 281	0.3516 526 227	16
17	0.3713 644 186	0.3567 861 947	0.3428 125 147	0.3294 169 768	17
18	0.3503 437 911	0.3357 987 715	0.3218 896 851	0.3085 873 319	18
19	0.3305 130 105	0.3160 459 026	0.3022 438 358	0.2890 747 840	19
20	0.3118 047 269	0.2974 549 672	0.2837 970 289	0.2707 960 506	20
21	0.2941 554 027	0.2799 576 162	0.2664 760 835	0.2536 731 153	21
22	0.2775 050 969	0.2634 895 211	0.2502 122 850	0.2376 328 949	22
23	0.2617 972 612	0.2479 901 375	0.2349 411 126	0.2226 069 273	23
24	0.2469 785 483	0.2334 024 823	0.2206 019 837	0.2085 310 794	24
25	0.2329 986 305	0.2196 729 246	0.2071 380 129	0.1953 452 735	25
26	0.2198 100 288	0.2067 509 878	0.1944 957 867	0.1829 932 304	26
27	0.2073 679 517	0.1945 891 650	0.1826 251 519	0.1714 222 299	27
28	0.1956 301 431	0.1831 427 435	0.1714 790 158	0.1605 828 851	28
29	0.1845 567 388	0.1723 696 410	0.1610 131 604	0.1504 289 322	29
30	0.1741 101 309	0.1622 302 503	0.1511 860 661	0.1409 170 325	30
31	0.1642 548 405	0.1526 872 944	0.1419 587 475	0.1320 065 878	31
32	0.1549 573 967	0.1437 056 889	0.1332 945 986	0.1236 595 671	32
33	0.1461 862 233	0.1352 524 131	0.1251 592 475	0.1158 403 439	33
34	0.1379 115 314	0.1272 963 888	0.1175 204 202	0.1085 155 446	34
35	0.1301 052 183	0.1198 083 659	0.1103 478 124	0.1016 539 059	35
36	0.1227 407 720	0.1127 608 150	0.1036 129 694	0.0952 261 414	36
37	0.1157 931 811	0.1061 278 258	0.0972 891 731	0.0892 048 163	37
38	0.1092 388 501	0.0998 850 126	0.0913 513 363	0.0835 642 307	38
39	0.1030 555 190	0.0940 094 236	0.0857 759 026	0.0782 803 098	39
40	0.0972 221 877	0.0884 794 575	0.0805 407 536	0.0733 305 010	40
41	0.0917 190 450	0.0832 747 835	0.0756 251 208	0.0686 936 777	41
42	0.0865 274 010	0.0783 762 668	0.0710 095 031	0.0643 500 494	42
43	0.0816 296 235	0.0737 658 982	0.0666 755 897	0.0602 810 767	43
44	0.0770 090 788	0.0694 267 277	0.0626 061 876	0.0564 693 927	44
45	0.0726 500 743	0.0653 428 026	0.0587 851 526	0.0528 987 285	45
46	0.0685 378 060	0.0614 991 083	0.0551 973 264	0.0495 538 441	46
47	0.0646 583 075	0.0578 815 137	0.0518 284 755	0.0464 204 628	47
48	0.0609 984 033	0.0544 767 188	0.0486 652 352	0.0434 852 111	48
49	0.0575 456 635	0.0512 722 059	0.0456 950 565	0.0407 355 607	49
50	0.0542 883 618	0.0482 561 938	0.0429 061 564	0.0381 597 759	50
51	0.0512 154 357	0.0454 175 942	0.0402 874 708	0.0357 468 626	51
52	0.0483 164 488	0.0427 459 710	0.0378 286 111	0.0334 865 224	52
53	0.0455 815 554	0.0402 315 021	0.0355 198 226	0.0313 691 076	53
54	0.0430 014 674	0.0378 649 431	0.0333 519 461	0.0293 855 809	54
55	0.0405 674 221	0.0356 375 935	0.0313 163 813	0.0275 274 763	55
56	0.0382 711 529	0.0335 412 645	0.0294 050 529	0.0257 868 630	56
57	0.0361 048 612	0.0315 682 490	0.0276 103 783	0.0241 563 119	57
58	0.0340 611 898	0.0297 112 931	0.0259 252 378	0.0226 288 636	58
59	0.0321 331 979	0.0279 635 700	0.0243 429 463	0.0211 979 987	59
60	0.0303 143 377	0.0263 186 541	0.0228 572 266	0.0198 576 101	60

TABLE 4. PRESENT WORTH OF ONE DOLLAR
Payable at end of each period

YEARS	7% Nominal Annual Rate	7¼% Nominal Annual Rate	7½% Nominal Annual Rate	7¾% Nominal Annual Rate	YEARS
1	0.9345 794 393	0.9324 009 324	0.9302 325 581	0.9280 742 459	1
2	0.8734 387 283	0.8693 714 987	0.8653 326 122	0.8613 218 060	2
3	0.8162 978 769	0.8106 027 960	0.8049 605 695	0.7993 705 856	3
4	0.7628 952 120	0.7558 068 028	0.7488 005 298	0.7418 752 535	4
5	0.7129 861 795	0.7047 149 677	0.6965 586 324	0.6885 153 164	5
6	0.6663 422 238	0.6570 768 929	0.6479 615 185	0.6389 933 331	6
7	0.6227 497 419	0.6126 591 076	0.6027 549 009	0.5930 332 558	7
8	0.5820 091 046	0.5712 439 232	0.5607 022 334	0.5503 788 917	8
9	0.5439 337 426	0.5326 283 666	0.5215 834 729	0.5107 924 749	9
10	0.5083 492 921	0.4966 231 857	0.4851 939 283	0.4740 533 410	10
11	0.4750 927 964	0.4630 519 214	0.4513 431 891	0.4399 566 969	11
12	0.4440 119 592	0.4317 500 432	0.4198 541 294	0.4083 124 798	12
13	0.4149 644 479	0.4025 641 429	0.3905 619 808	0.3789 442 968	13
14	0.3878 172 410	0.3753 511 822	0.3633 134 706	0.3516 884 425	14
15	0.3624 460 196	0.3499 777 922	0.3379 660 191	0.3263 929 861	15
16	0.3387 345 978	0.3263 196 198	0.3143 869 945	0.3029 169 244	16
17	0.3165 743 905	0.3042 607 178	0.2924 530 182	0.2811 293 962	17
18	0.2958 639 163	0.2836 929 769	0.2720 493 192	0.2609 089 524	18
19	0.2765 083 330	0.2645 155 962	0.2530 691 342	0.2421 428 793	19
20	0.2584 190 028	0.2466 345 885	0.2354 131 481	0.2247 265 701	20
21	0.2415 130 867	0.2299 623 203	0.2189 889 749	0.2085 629 421	21
22	0.2257 131 652	0.2144 170 819	0.2037 106 744	0.1935 618 952	22
23	0.2109 468 833	0.1999 226 871	0.1894 983 017	0.1796 398 099	23
24	0.1971 466 199	0.1864 080 998	0.1762 774 900	0.1667 190 811	24
25	0.1842 491 775	0.1738 070 861	0.1639 790 605	0.1547 276 855	25
26	0.1721 954 930	0.1620 578 891	0.1525 386 609	0.1435 987 800	26
27	0.1609 303 673	0.1511 029 269	0.1418 964 287	0.1332 703 295	27
28	0.1504 022 124	0.1408 885 099	0.1319 966 779	0.1236 847 606	28
29	0.1405 628 154	0.1313 645 780	0.1227 876 073	0.1147 886 409	29
30	0.1313 671 172	0.1224 844 550	0.1142 210 301	0.1065 323 813	30
31	0.1227 730 067	0.1142 046 201	0.1062 521 210	0.0988 699 595	31
32	0.1147 411 277	0.1064 844 943	0.0988 391 823	0.0917 586 631	32
33	0.1072 346 988	0.0992 862 417	0.0919 434 254	0.0851 588 521	33
34	0.1002 193 447	0.0925 745 844	0.0855 287 678	0.0790 337 374	34
35	0.0936 629 390	0.0863 166 288	0.0795 616 445	0.0733 491 763	35
36	0.0875 354 570	0.0804 817 052	0.0740 108 321	0.0680 734 814	36
37	0.0818 088 383	0.0750 412 169	0.0688 472 857	0.0631 772 450	37
38	0.0764 568 582	0.0699 685 006	0.0640 439 867	0.0586 331 740	38
39	0.0714 550 077	0.0652 386 952	0.0595 758 016	0.0544 159 387	39
40	0.0667 803 810	0.0608 286 203	0.0554 193 503	0.0505 020 313	40
41	0.0624 115 710	0.0567 166 622	0.0515 528 840	0.0468 696 346	41
42	0.0583 285 711	0.0528 826 688	0.0479 561 711	0.0434 985 008	42
43	0.0545 126 832	0.0493 078 497	0.0446 103 918	0.0403 698 383	43
44	0.0509 464 329	0.0459 746 850	0.0414 980 388	0.0374 662 073	44
45	0.0476 134 887	0.0428 668 392	0.0386 028 268	0.0347 714 221	45
46	0.0444 985 876	0.0399 690 808	0.0359 096 064	0.0322 704 613	46
47	0.0415 874 650	0.0372 672 082	0.0334 042 850	0.0299 493 840	47
48	0.0388 667 898	0.0347 479 797	0.0310 737 535	0.0277 952 520	48
49	0.0363 241 026	0.0323 990 487	0.0289 058 172	0.0257 960 576	49
50	0.0339 477 594	0.0302 089 032	0.0268 891 323	0.0239 406 567	50
51	0.0317 268 780	0.0281 668 095	0.0250 131 463	0.0222 187 069	51
52	0.0296 512 878	0.0262 627 594	0.0232 680 431	0.0206 206 096	52
53	0.0277 114 839	0.0244 874 214	0.0216 446 912	0.0191 374 567	53
54	0.0258 985 831	0.0228 320 945	0.0201 345 965	0.0177 609 807	54
55	0.0242 042 833	0.0212 886 662	0.0187 298 572	0.0164 835 088	55
56	0.0226 208 255	0.0198 495 722	0.0174 231 230	0.0152 979 200	56
57	0.0211 409 584	0.0185 077 597	0.0162 075 563	0.0141 976 056	57
58	0.0197 579 051	0.0172 566 524	0.0150 767 965	0.0131 764 321	58
59	0.0184 653 318	0.0160 901 188	0.0140 249 270	0.0122 287 073	59
60	0.0172 573 195	0.0150 024 417	0.0130 464 437	0.0113 491 483	60

TABLE 4. PRESENT WORTH OF ONE DOLLAR
Payable at end of each period

YEARS	8% Nominal Annual Rate	8¼% Nominal Annual Rate	8½% Nominal Annual Rate	8¾% Nominal Annual Rate	YEARS
1	0.9259 259 259	0.9237 875 289	0.9216 589 862	0.9195 402 299	1
2	0.8573 388 203	0.8533 833 985	0.8494 552 868	0.8455 542 344	2
3	0.7938 322 410	0.7883 449 409	0.7829 080 984	0.7775 211 351	3
4	0.7350 298 528	0.7282 632 248	0.7215 742 843	0.7149 619 633	4
5	0.6805 831 970	0.6727 604 848	0.6650 454 233	0.6574 362 881	5
6	0.6301 696 269	0.6214 877 458	0.6129 450 906	0.6045 391 155	6
7	0.5834 903 953	0.5741 226 289	0.5649 263 508	0.5558 980 372	7
8	0.5402 688 845	0.5303 673 246	0.5206 694 477	0.5111 706 089	8
9	0.5002 489 671	0.4899 467 202	0.4798 796 753	0.4700 419 392	9
10	0.4631 934 881	0.4526 066 699	0.4422 854 150	0.4322 224 729	10
11	0.4288 828 593	0.4181 123 972	0.4076 363 272	0.3974 459 521	11
12	0.3971 137 586	0.3862 470 182	0.3757 016 841	0.3654 675 421	12
13	0.3676 979 247	0.3568 101 785	0.3462 688 333	0.3360 621 077	13
14	0.3404 610 414	0.3296 167 930	0.3191 417 818	0.3090 226 278	14
15	0.3152 417 050	0.3044 958 827	0.2941 398 911	0.2841 587 382	15
16	0.2918 904 676	0.2812 894 990	0.2710 966 738	0.2612 953 914	16
17	0.2702 689 514	0.2598 517 312	0.2498 586 855	0.2402 716 243	17
18	0.2502 490 291	0.2400 477 886	0.2302 845 028	0.2209 394 246	18
19	0.2317 120 640	0.2217 531 535	0.2122 437 814	0.2031 626 893	19
20	0.2145 482 074	0.2048 527 977	0.1956 163 884	0.1868 162 661	20
21	0.1986 557 476	0.1892 404 597	0.1802 916 022	0.1717 850 722	21
22	0.1839 405 070	0.1748 179 767	0.1661 673 753	0.1579 632 848	22
23	0.1703 152 843	0.1614 946 667	0.1531 496 546	0.1452 535 952	23
24	0.1576 993 373	0.1491 867 590	0.1411 517 554	0.1335 665 243	24
25	0.1460 179 049	0.1378 168 675	0.1300 937 838	0.1228 197 925	25
26	0.1352 017 638	0.1273 135 034	0.1199 021 049	0.1129 377 402	26
27	0.1251 868 183	0.1176 106 267	0.1105 088 524	0.1038 507 956	27
28	0.1159 137 207	0.1086 472 302	0.1018 514 769	0.0954 949 845	28
29	0.1073 275 192	0.1003 669 563	0.0938 723 289	0.0878 114 800	29
30	0.0993 773 325	0.0927 177 426	0.0865 182 755	0.0807 461 885	30
31	0.0920 160 487	0.0856 514 943	0.0797 403 461	0.0742 493 687	31
32	0.0852 000 451	0.0791 237 823	0.0734 934 065	0.0682 752 816	32
33	0.0788 889 306	0.0730 935 633	0.0677 358 586	0.0627 818 681	33
34	0.0730 453 061	0.0675 229 222	0.0624 293 627	0.0577 304 534	34
35	0.0676 345 427	0.0623 768 335	0.0575 385 832	0.0530 854 744	35
36	0.0626 245 766	0.0576 229 408	0.0530 309 522	0.0488 142 294	36
37	0.0579 857 190	0.0532 313 541	0.0488 764 537	0.0448 866 477	37
38	0.0536 904 806	0.0491 744 611	0.0450 474 227	0.0412 750 783	38
39	0.0497 134 080	0.0454 267 539	0.0415 183 620	0.0379 540 950	39
40	0.0460 309 333	0.0419 646 687	0.0382 657 714	0.0349 003 173	40
41	0.0426 212 345	0.0387 664 376	0.0352 679 921	0.0320 922 458	41
42	0.0394 641 061	0.0358 119 516	0.0325 050 618	0.0295 101 110	42
43	0.0365 408 389	0.0330 826 343	0.0299 585 823	0.0271 357 343	43
44	0.0338 341 101	0.0305 613 250	0.0276 115 966	0.0249 523 993	44
45	0.0313 278 797	0.0282 321 709	0.0254 484 761	0.0229 447 350	45
46	0.0290 072 961	0.0260 805 274	0.0234 548 167	0.0210 986 069	46
47	0.0268 586 075	0.0240 928 659	0.0216 173 426	0.0194 010 179	47
48	0.0248 690 810	0.0222 566 891	0.0199 238 181	0.0178 400 164	48
49	0.0230 269 268	0.0205 604 518	0.0183 629 660	0.0164 046 128	49
50	0.0213 212 286	0.0189 934 890	0.0169 243 926	0.0150 847 014	50
51	0.0197 418 783	0.0175 459 482	0.0155 985 185	0.0138 709 898	51
52	0.0182 795 169	0.0162 087 282	0.0143 765 148	0.0127 549 332	52
53	0.0169 254 786	0.0149 734 209	0.0132 502 440	0.0117 286 742	53
54	0.0156 717 395	0.0138 322 595	0.0122 122 065	0.0107 849 878	54
55	0.0145 108 699	0.0127 780 688	0.0112 554 898	0.0099 172 301	55
56	0.0134 359 906	0.0118 042 206	0.0103 737 233	0.0091 192 921	56
57	0.0124 407 321	0.0109 045 918	0.0095 610 353	0.0083 855 559	57
58	0.0115 191 964	0.0100 735 259	0.0088 120 141	0.0077 108 560	58
59	0.0106 659 226	0.0093 057 976	0.0081 216 720	0.0070 904 423	59
60	0.0098 758 542	0.0085 965 798	0.0074 854 120	0.0065 199 470	60

TABLE 4. PRESENT WORTH OF ONE DOLLAR
Payable at end of each period

YEARLY Compounding

YEARS	9% Nominal Annual Rate	9¼% Nominal Annual Rate	9½% Nominal Annual Rate	9¾% Nominal Annual Rate	YEARS
1	0.9174 311 927	0.9153 318 078	0.9132 420 091	0.9111 617 312	1
2	0.8416 799 933	0.8378 323 183	0.8340 109 672	0.8302 157 004	2
3	0.7721 834 801	0.7668 945 706	0.7616 538 514	0.7564 607 749	3
4	0.7084 252 111	0.7019 629 936	0.6955 742 935	0.6892 581 092	4
5	0.6499 313 863	0.6425 290 560	0.6352 276 653	0.6280 256 120	5
6	0.5962 673 269	0.5881 272 824	0.5801 165 893	0.5722 329 039	6
7	0.5470 342 448	0.5383 316 086	0.5297 868 395	0.5213 967 234	7
8	0.5018 662 797	0.4927 520 444	0.4838 235 978	0.4750 767 411	8
9	0.4604 277 795	0.4510 316 196	0.4418 480 345	0.4328 717 459	9
10	0.4224 108 069	0.4128 435 878	0.4035 141 867	0.3944 161 694	10
11	0.3875 328 504	0.3778 888 675	0.3685 061 066	0.3593 769 197	11
12	0.3555 347 251	0.3458 937 002	0.3365 352 572	0.3274 504 963	12
13	0.3261 786 469	0.3166 075 059	0.3073 381 344	0.2983 603 611	13
14	0.2992 464 650	0.2898 009 208	0.2806 740 954	0.2718 545 432	14
15	0.2745 380 413	0.2652 640 007	0.2563 233 748	0.2477 034 562	15
16	0.2518 697 627	0.2428 045 773	0.2340 852 737	0.2256 979 100	16
17	0.2310 731 768	0.2222 467 527	0.2137 765 057	0.2056 472 984	17
18	0.2119 937 402	0.2034 295 219	0.1952 296 856	0.1873 779 484	18
19	0.1944 896 699	0.1862 055 120	0.1782 919 503	0.1707 316 159	19
20	0.1784 308 898	0.1704 398 280	0.1628 236 989	0.1555 641 147	20
21	0.1636 980 640	0.1560 089 958	0.1486 974 419	0.1417 440 680	21
22	0.1501 817 101	0.1427 999 962	0.1357 967 506	0.1291 517 704	22
23	0.1377 813 854	0.1307 093 787	0.1240 152 974	0.1176 781 507	23
24	0.1264 049 408	0.1196 424 519	0.1132 559 793	0.1072 238 275	24
25	0.1159 678 356	0.1095 125 418	0.1034 301 181	0.0976 982 483	25
26	0.1063 925 097	0.1002 403 128	0.0944 567 289	0.0890 189 051	26
27	0.0976 078 070	0.0917 531 467	0.0862 618 528	0.0811 106 197	27
28	0.0895 484 468	0.0839 845 737	0.0787 779 478	0.0739 048 926	28
29	0.0821 545 384	0.0768 737 517	0.0719 433 313	0.0673 393 099	29
30	0.0753 711 361	0.0703 649 901	0.0657 016 724	0.0613 570 022	30
31	0.0691 478 313	0.0644 073 136	0.0600 015 273	0.0559 061 523	31
32	0.0634 383 773	0.0589 540 628	0.0547 959 154	0.0509 395 466	32
33	0.0582 003 462	0.0539 625 288	0.0500 419 319	0.0464 141 654	33
34	0.0533 948 130	0.0493 936 191	0.0457 003 944	0.0422 908 113	34
35	0.0489 860 670	0.0452 115 506	0.0417 355 200	0.0385 337 689	35
36	0.0449 413 459	0.0413 835 704	0.0381 146 301	0.0351 104 955	36
37	0.0412 305 925	0.0378 796 983	0.0348 078 814	0.0319 913 399	37
38	0.0378 262 317	0.0346 724 927	0.0317 880 195	0.0291 492 847	38
39	0.0347 029 648	0.0317 368 354	0.0290 301 548	0.0265 597 127	39
40	0.0318 375 824	0.0290 497 350	0.0265 115 569	0.0242 001 938	40
41	0.0292 087 912	0.0265 901 464	0.0242 114 675	0.0220 502 905	41
42	0.0267 970 562	0.0243 388 068	0.0221 109 292	0.0200 913 808	42
43	0.0245 844 552	0.0222 780 840	0.0201 926 294	0.0183 064 973	43
44	0.0225 545 461	0.0203 918 389	0.0184 407 575	0.0166 801 798	44
45	0.0206 922 441	0.0186 652 988	0.0168 408 744	0.0151 983 415	45
46	0.0189 837 102	0.0170 849 417	0.0153 797 940	0.0138 481 472	46
47	0.0174 162 479	0.0156 383 905	0.0140 454 740	0.0126 179 017	47
48	0.0159 782 090	0.0143 143 163	0.0128 269 169	0.0114 969 492	48
49	0.0146 589 074	0.0131 023 490	0.0117 140 793	0.0104 755 801	49
50	0.0134 485 389	0.0119 929 968	0.0106 977 893	0.0095 449 477	50
51	0.0123 381 091	0.0109 775 714	0.0097 696 706	0.0086 969 911	51
52	0.0113 193 661	0.0100 481 203	0.0089 220 736	0.0079 243 655	52
53	0.0103 847 396	0.0091 973 641	0.0081 480 124	0.0072 203 786	53
54	0.0095 272 840	0.0084 186 399	0.0074 411 073	0.0065 789 326	54
55	0.0087 406 275	0.0077 058 489	0.0067 955 317	0.0059 944 716	55
56	0.0080 189 243	0.0070 534 086	0.0062 059 651	0.0054 619 332	56
57	0.0073 568 113	0.0064 562 093	0.0056 675 480	0.0049 767 045	57
58	0.0067 493 682	0.0059 095 737	0.0051 758 429	0.0045 345 827	58
59	0.0061 920 809	0.0054 092 208	0.0047 267 972	0.0041 317 382	59
60	0.0056 808 082	0.0049 512 318	0.0043 167 098	0.0037 646 817	60

TABLE 4. PRESENT WORTH OF ONE DOLLAR
Payable at end of each period

YEARS	10% Nominal Annual Rate	10¼% Nominal Annual Rate	10½% Nominal Annual Rate	10¾% Nominal Annual Rate	YEARS
1	0.9090 909 091	0.9070 294 785	0.9049 773 756	0.9029 345 372	1
2	0.8264 462 810	0.8227 024 748	0.8189 840 503	0.8152 907 786	2
3	0.7513 148 009	0.7462 153 966	0.7411 620 365	0.7361 542 019	3
4	0.6830 134 554	0.6768 393 620	0.6707 348 746	0.6646 990 536	4
5	0.6209 213 231	0.6139 132 535	0.6069 998 865	0.6001 797 324	5
6	0.5644 739 301	0.5568 374 182	0.5493 211 643	0.5419 230 089	6
7	0.5131 581 182	0.5050 679 530	0.4971 232 256	0.4893 210 013	7
8	0.4665 073 802	0.4581 115 220	0.4498 852 720	0.4418 248 318	8
9	0.4240 976 184	0.4155 206 549	0.4071 359 928	0.3989 389 001	9
10	0.3855 432 894	0.3768 894 829	0.3684 488 623	0.3602 157 111	10
11	0.3504 938 995	0.3418 498 711	0.3334 378 844	0.3252 512 064	11
12	0.3186 308 177	0.3100 679 103	0.3017 537 415	0.2936 805 476	12
13	0.2896 643 797	0.2812 407 350	0.2730 803 091	0.2651 743 093	13
14	0.2633 312 543	0.2550 936 371	0.2471 315 014	0.2394 350 423	14
15	0.2393 920 494	0.2313 774 487	0.2236 484 176	0.2161 941 691	15
16	0.2176 291 358	0.2098 661 666	0.2023 967 580	0.1952 091 820	16
17	0.1978 446 689	0.1903 547 996	0.1831 644 869	0.1762 611 124	17
18	0.1798 587 899	0.1726 574 146	0.1657 597 166	0.1591 522 460	18
19	0.1635 079 908	0.1566 053 647	0.1500 087 933	0.1437 040 596	19
20	0.1486 436 280	0.1420 456 823	0.1357 545 641	0.1297 553 586	20
21	0.1351 305 709	0.1288 396 211	0.1228 548 091	0.1171 605 946	21
22	0.1228 459 736	0.1168 613 344	0.1111 808 227	0.1057 883 473	22
23	0.1116 781 578	0.1059 966 752	0.1006 161 292	0.0955 199 524	23
24	0.1015 255 980	0.0961 421 090	0.0910 553 205	0.0862 482 640	24
25	0.0922 959 982	0.0872 037 270	0.0824 030 050	0.0778 765 364	25
26	0.0839 054 529	0.0790 963 510	0.0745 728 552	0.0703 174 143	26
27	0.0762 776 844	0.0717 427 220	0.0674 867 468	0.0634 920 220	27
28	0.0693 433 495	0.0650 727 637	0.0610 739 790	0.0573 291 395	28
29	0.0630 394 086	0.0590 229 149	0.0552 705 692	0.0517 644 600	29
30	0.0573 085 533	0.0535 355 237	0.0500 186 147	0.0467 399 188	30
31	0.0520 986 848	0.0485 582 982	0.0452 657 146	0.0422 030 869	31
32	0.0473 624 407	0.0440 438 079	0.0409 644 476	0.0381 066 248	32
33	0.0430 567 643	0.0399 490 321	0.0370 718 983	0.0344 077 876	33
34	0.0391 425 130	0.0362 349 497	0.0335 492 293	0.0310 679 798	34
35	0.0355 841 027	0.0328 661 676	0.0303 612 934	0.0280 523 519	35
36	0.0323 491 843	0.0298 105 828	0.0274 762 837	0.0253 294 374	36
37	0.0294 083 494	0.0270 390 774	0.0248 654 151	0.0228 708 238	37
38	0.0267 348 631	0.0245 252 403	0.0225 026 381	0.0206 508 567	38
39	0.0243 044 210	0.0222 451 159	0.0203 643 783	0.0186 463 718	39
40	0.0220 949 282	0.0201 769 759	0.0184 293 017	0.0168 364 531	40
41	0.0200 862 983	0.0183 011 119	0.0166 781 011	0.0152 022 150	41
42	0.0182 602 712	0.0165 996 480	0.0150 933 041	0.0137 266 049	42
43	0.0166 002 465	0.0150 563 700	0.0136 590 988	0.0123 942 257	43
44	0.0150 911 332	0.0136 565 715	0.0123 611 753	0.0111 911 744	44
45	0.0137 192 120	0.0123 869 129	0.0111 865 840	0.0101 048 979	45
46	0.0124 720 109	0.0112 352 951	0.0101 236 055	0.0091 240 613	46
47	0.0113 381 918	0.0101 907 439	0.0091 616 339	0.0082 384 301	47
48	0.0103 074 470	0.0092 433 051	0.0082 910 714	0.0074 387 630	48
49	0.0093 704 064	0.0083 839 502	0.0075 032 320	0.0067 167 161	49
50	0.0085 185 513	0.0076 044 900	0.0067 902 552	0.0060 647 549	50
51	0.0077 441 375	0.0068 974 966	0.0061 450 274	0.0054 760 767	51
52	0.0070 401 250	0.0062 562 327	0.0055 611 107	0.0049 445 388	52
53	0.0064 001 137	0.0056 745 875	0.0050 326 794	0.0044 645 948	53
54	0.0058 182 851	0.0051 470 182	0.0045 544 610	0.0040 312 369	54
55	0.0052 893 501	0.0046 684 972	0.0041 216 842	0.0036 399 430	55
56	0.0048 085 001	0.0042 344 646	0.0037 300 309	0.0032 866 302	56
57	0.0043 713 637	0.0038 407 842	0.0033 755 936	0.0029 676 119	57
58	0.0039 739 670	0.0034 837 045	0.0030 548 358	0.0026 795 593	58
59	0.0036 126 973	0.0031 598 227	0.0027 645 573	0.0024 194 667	59
60	0.0032 842 703	0.0028 660 523	0.0025 018 618	0.0021 846 200	60

TABLE 4. PRESENT WORTH OF ONE DOLLAR
Payable at end of each period

YEARLY Compounding

YEARS	11% Nominal Annual Rate	11¼% Nominal Annual Rate	11½% Nominal Annual Rate	11¾% Nominal Annual Rate	YEARS
1	0.9009 009 009	0.8988 764 045	0.8968 609 865	0.8948 545 861	1
2	0.8116 224 332	0.8079 787 906	0.8043 596 292	0.8007 647 303	2
3	0.7311 913 813	0.7262 730 702	0.7213 987 706	0.7165 679 913	3
4	0.6587 309 741	0.6528 297 260	0.6469 944 131	0.6412 241 533	4
5	0.5934 513 281	0.5868 132 368	0.5802 640 476	0.5738 023 743	5
6	0.5346 408 361	0.5274 725 724	0.5204 161 862	0.5134 696 862	6
7	0.4816 584 109	0.4741 326 494	0.4667 409 742	0.4594 807 035	7
8	0.4339 264 963	0.4261 866 511	0.4186 017 705	0.4111 684 148	8
9	0.3909 247 714	0.3830 891 246	0.3754 275 969	0.3679 359 417	9
10	0.3521 844 788	0.3443 497 749	0.3367 063 649	0.3292 491 648	10
11	0.3172 833 142	0.3095 278 876	0.3019 788 026	0.2946 301 251	11
12	0.2858 408 236	0.2782 273 147	0.2708 330 068	0.2636 511 187	12
13	0.2575 142 555	0.2500 919 683	0.2428 995 577	0.2359 294 127	13
14	0.2319 948 248	0.2248 017 692	0.2178 471 370	0.2111 225 169	14
15	0.2090 043 467	0.2020 690 060	0.1953 785 982	0.1889 239 525	15
16	0.1882 922 042	0.1816 350 616	0.1752 274 423	0.1690 594 653	16
17	0.1696 326 164	0.1632 674 711	0.1571 546 568	0.1512 836 379	17
18	0.1528 221 769	0.1467 572 774	0.1409 458 805	0.1353 768 572	18
19	0.1376 776 369	0.1319 166 538	0.1264 088 614	0.1211 426 015	19
20	0.1240 339 071	0.1185 767 675	0.1133 711 762	0.1084 050 125	20
21	0.1117 422 586	0.1065 858 584	0.1016 781 849	0.0970 067 226	21
22	0.1006 687 015	0.0958 075 132	0.0911 911 972	0.0868 069 106	22
23	0.0906 925 239	0.0861 191 130	0.0817 858 271	0.0776 795 621	23
24	0.0817 049 764	0.0774 104 386	0.0733 505 176	0.0695 119 124	24
25	0.0736 080 869	0.0695 824 168	0.0657 852 176	0.0622 030 536	25
26	0.0663 135 918	0.0625 459 926	0.0590 001 951	0.0556 626 878	26
27	0.0597 419 746	0.0562 211 169	0.0529 149 732	0.0498 100 114	27
28	0.0538 215 987	0.0505 358 354	0.0474 573 751	0.0445 727 172	28
29	0.0484 879 268	0.0454 254 701	0.0425 626 682	0.0398 861 004	29
30	0.0436 828 169	0.0408 318 832	0.0381 727 966	0.0356 922 598	30
31	0.0393 538 891	0.0367 028 164	0.0342 356 920	0.0319 393 824	31
32	0.0354 539 542	0.0329 912 956	0.0307 046 565	0.0285 811 028	32
33	0.0319 404 992	0.0296 550 972	0.0275 378 086	0.0255 759 309	33
34	0.0287 752 245	0.0266 562 671	0.0246 975 861	0.0228 867 391	34
35	0.0259 236 257	0.0239 606 895	0.0221 503 015	0.0204 803 034	35
36	0.0233 546 178	0.0215 376 985	0.0198 657 412	0.0183 268 935	36
37	0.0210 401 962	0.0193 597 290	0.0178 168 083	0.0163 999 047	37
38	0.0189 551 317	0.0174 020 036	0.0159 792 003	0.0146 755 299	38
39	0.0170 766 952	0.0156 422 504	0.0143 311 213	0.0131 324 652	39
40	0.0153 844 101	0.0140 604 498	0.0128 530 236	0.0117 516 467	40
41	0.0138 598 289	0.0126 386 066	0.0115 273 754	0.0105 160 150	41
42	0.0124 863 324	0.0113 605 452	0.0103 384 533	0.0094 103 042	42
43	0.0112 489 481	0.0102 117 260	0.0092 721 554	0.0084 208 539	43
44	0.0101 341 875	0.0091 790 796	0.0083 158 345	0.0075 354 397	44
45	0.0091 298 986	0.0082 508 581	0.0074 581 475	0.0067 431 228	45
46	0.0082 251 339	0.0074 165 016	0.0066 889 215	0.0060 341 144	46
47	0.0074 100 305	0.0066 665 183	0.0059 990 328	0.0053 996 549	47
48	0.0066 757 032	0.0059 923 760	0.0053 802 984	0.0048 319 060	48
49	0.0060 141 470	0.0053 864 054	0.0048 253 798	0.0043 238 532	49
50	0.0054 181 505	0.0048 417 127	0.0043 276 949	0.0038 692 199	50
51	0.0048 812 166	0.0043 521 013	0.0038 813 407	0.0034 623 891	51
52	0.0043 974 925	0.0039 120 012	0.0034 810 230	0.0030 983 348	52
53	0.0039 617 049	0.0035 164 056	0.0031 219 937	0.0027 725 591	53
54	0.0035 691 035	0.0031 608 140	0.0027 999 944	0.0024 810 372	54
55	0.0032 154 086	0.0028 411 811	0.0025 112 057	0.0022 201 676	55
56	0.0028 967 645	0.0025 538 707	0.0022 522 024	0.0019 867 271	56
57	0.0026 096 977	0.0022 956 141	0.0020 199 125	0.0017 778 319	57
58	0.0023 510 790	0.0020 634 733	0.0018 115 807	0.0015 909 010	58
59	0.0021 180 892	0.0018 548 075	0.0016 247 361	0.0014 236 251	59
60	0.0019 081 885	0.0016 672 427	0.0014 571 624	0.0012 739 374	60

YEARLY
Compounding

TABLE 4. PRESENT WORTH OF ONE DOLLAR
Payable at end of each period

YEARS	12% Nominal Annual Rate	12¼% Nominal Annual Rate	12½% Nominal Annual Rate	12¾% Nominal Annual Rate	YEARS
1	0.8928 571 429	0.8908 685 969	0.8888 888 889	0.8869 179 601	1
2	0.7971 938 776	0.7936 468 569	0.7901 234 568	0.7866 234 679	2
3	0.7117 802 478	0.7070 350 618	0.7023 319 616	0.6976 704 815	3
4	0.6355 180 784	0.6298 753 335	0.6242 950 770	0.6187 764 803	4
5	0.5674 268 557	0.5611 361 546	0.5549 289 573	0.5488 039 737	5
6	0.5066 311 212	0.4998 985 787	0.4932 701 843	0.4867 441 008	6
7	0.4523 492 153	0.4453 439 454	0.4384 623 860	0.4317 020 850	7
8	0.4038 832 280	0.3967 429 357	0.3897 443 431	0.3828 843 326	8
9	0.3606 100 250	0.3534 458 225	0.3464 394 161	0.3395 869 912	9
10	0.3219 732 366	0.3148 737 839	0.3079 461 477	0.3011 858 015	10
11	0.2874 761 041	0.2805 111 661	0.2737 299 090	0.2671 270 967	11
12	0.2566 750 929	0.2498 985 890	0.2433 154 747	0.2369 198 197	12
13	0.2291 741 901	0.2226 268 053	0.2162 804 219	0.2101 284 432	13
14	0.2046 198 126	0.1983 312 297	0.1922 492 640	0.1863 666 902	14
15	0.1826 962 613	0.1766 870 643	0.1708 882 346	0.1652 919 647	15
16	0.1631 216 618	0.1574 049 571	0.1519 006 530	0.1466 004 121	16
17	0.1456 443 409	0.1402 271 332	0.1350 228 027	0.1300 225 385	17
18	0.1300 395 901	0.1249 239 494	0.1200 202 690	0.1153 193 246	18
19	0.1161 067 769	0.1112 908 235	0.1066 846 836	0.1022 787 801	19
20	0.1036 667 651	0.0991 454 998	0.0948 308 299	0.0907 128 870	20
21	0.0925 596 117	0.0883 256 123	0.0842 940 710	0.0804 548 887	21
22	0.0826 425 104	0.0786 865 143	0.0749 280 631	0.0713 568 858	22
23	0.0737 879 557	0.0700 993 446	0.0666 027 228	0.0632 877 036	23
24	0.0658 821 033	0.0624 493 048	0.0592 024 202	0.0561 310 010	24
25	0.0588 233 066	0.0556 341 245	0.0526 243 735	0.0497 835 929	25
26	0.0525 208 094	0.0495 626 944	0.0467 772 209	0.0441 539 626	26
27	0.0468 935 798	0.0441 538 481	0.0415 797 519	0.0391 609 425	27
28	0.0418 692 677	0.0393 352 767	0.0369 597 795	0.0347 325 432	28
29	0.0373 832 747	0.0350 425 627	0.0328 531 373	0.0308 049 164	29
30	0.0333 779 239	0.0312 183 187	0.0292 027 887	0.0273 214 336	30
31	0.0298 017 177	0.0278 114 198	0.0259 580 344	0.0242 318 701	31
32	0.0266 086 766	0.0247 763 205	0.0230 738 084	0.0214 916 808	32
33	0.0237 577 469	0.0220 724 459	0.0205 100 519	0.0190 613 577	33
34	0.0212 122 740	0.0196 636 489	0.0182 311 572	0.0169 058 605	34
35	0.0189 395 304	0.0175 177 273	0.0162 054 731	0.0149 941 113	35
36	0.0169 102 950	0.0156 059 931	0.0144 048 650	0.0132 985 466	36
37	0.0150 984 777	0.0139 028 892	0.0128 043 244	0.0117 947 198	37
38	0.0134 807 836	0.0123 856 474	0.0113 816 217	0.0104 609 489	38
39	0.0120 364 140	0.0110 339 843	0.0101 169 971	0.0092 780 034	39
40	0.0107 467 982	0.0098 298 301	0.0089 928 863	0.0082 288 279	40
41	0.0095 953 555	0.0087 570 870	0.0079 936 767	0.0072 982 952	41
42	0.0085 672 817	0.0078 014 138	0.0071 054 904	0.0064 729 891	42
43	0.0076 493 587	0.0069 500 346	0.0063 159 915	0.0057 410 103	43
44	0.0068 297 845	0.0061 915 675	0.0056 142 146	0.0050 918 051	44
45	0.0060 980 219	0.0055 158 731	0.0049 904 130	0.0045 160 134	45
46	0.0054 446 624	0.0049 139 181	0.0044 359 227	0.0040 053 334	46
47	0.0048 613 057	0.0043 776 553	0.0039 430 424	0.0035 524 021	47
48	0.0043 404 515	0.0038 999 157	0.0035 049 266	0.0031 506 893	48
49	0.0038 754 032	0.0034 743 124	0.0031 154 903	0.0027 944 029	49
50	0.0034 601 814	0.0030 951 558	0.0027 693 247	0.0024 784 061	50
51	0.0030 894 477	0.0027 573 771	0.0024 616 219	0.0021 981 429	51
52	0.0027 584 354	0.0024 564 607	0.0021 881 084	0.0019 495 724	52
53	0.0024 628 888	0.0021 883 837	0.0019 449 852	0.0017 291 108	53
54	0.0021 990 078	0.0019 495 623	0.0017 288 758	0.0015 335 794	54
55	0.0019 633 998	0.0017 368 038	0.0015 367 785	0.0013 601 591	55
56	0.0017 530 356	0.0015 472 640	0.0013 660 253	0.0012 063 496	56
57	0.0015 652 103	0.0013 784 089	0.0012 142 447	0.0010 699 331	57
58	0.0013 975 092	0.0012 279 812	0.0010 793 286	0.0009 489 429	58
59	0.0012 477 761	0.0010 939 699	0.0009 594 032	0.0008 416 345	59
60	0.0011 140 858	0.0009 745 834	0.0008 528 029	0.0007 464 607	60

TABLE 4. PRESENT WORTH OF ONE DOLLAR
Payable at end of each period

YEARLY Compounding

YEARS	13% Nominal Annual Rate	13¼% Nominal Annual Rate	13½% Nominal Annual Rate	13¾% Nominal Annual Rate	YEARS
1	0.8849 557 522	0.8830 022 075	0.8810 572 687	0.8791 208 791	1
2	0.7831 466 834	0.7796 928 985	0.7762 619 108	0.7728 535 201	2
3	0.6930 501 623	0.6884 705 505	0.6839 311 989	0.6794 316 660	3
4	0.6133 187 277	0.6079 210 159	0.6025 825 541	0.5973 025 635	4
5	0.5427 599 360	0.5367 955 990	0.5309 097 393	0.5251 011 548	5
6	0.4803 185 274	0.4739 916 989	0.4677 618 848	0.4616 273 888	6
7	0.4250 606 437	0.4185 357 165	0.4121 250 087	0.4058 262 759	7
8	0.3761 598 617	0.3695 679 616	0.3631 057 345	0.3567 703 524	8
9	0.3328 848 334	0.3263 293 259	0.3199 169 467	0.3136 442 659	9
10	0.2945 883 481	0.2881 495 151	0.2818 651 513	0.2757 312 227	10
11	0.2606 976 532	0.2544 366 580	0.2483 393 403	0.2424 010 749	11
12	0.2307 058 878	0.2246 681 307	0.2188 011 809	0.2130 998 461	12
13	0.2041 645 025	0.1983 824 553	0.1927 763 709	0.1873 405 240	13
14	0.1806 765 509	0.1751 721 460	0.1698 470 228	0.1646 949 662	14
15	0.1598 907 530	0.1546 773 916	0.1496 449 540	0.1447 867 835	15
16	0.1414 962 416	0.1365 804 782	0.1318 457 744	0.1272 850 844	16
17	0.1252 179 129	0.1206 008 638	0.1161 636 779	0.1118 989 753	17
18	0.1108 123 123	0.1064 908 289	0.1023 468 528	0.0983 727 255	18
19	0.0980 639 932	0.0940 316 370	0.0901 734 386	0.0864 815 169	19
20	0.0867 822 949	0.0830 301 431	0.0794 479 635	0.0760 277 072	20
21	0.0767 984 910	0.0733 157 996	0.0699 982 057	0.0668 375 448	21
22	0.0679 632 664	0.0647 380 129	0.0616 724 280	0.0587 582 811	22
23	0.0601 444 835	0.0571 638 083	0.0543 369 409	0.0516 556 318	23
24	0.0532 252 067	0.0504 757 689	0.0478 739 568	0.0454 115 444	24
25	0.0471 019 528	0.0445 702 154	0.0421 796 976	0.0399 222 368	25
26	0.0416 831 441	0.0393 555 986	0.0371 627 292	0.0350 964 719	26
27	0.0368 877 381	0.0347 510 804	0.0327 424 927	0.0308 540 413	27
28	0.0326 440 160	0.0306 852 807	0.0288 480 111	0.0271 244 319	28
29	0.0288 885 098	0.0270 951 706	0.0254 167 499	0.0238 456 544	29
30	0.0255 650 529	0.0239 250 955	0.0223 936 123	0.0209 632 127	30
31	0.0226 239 406	0.0211 259 121	0.0197 300 548	0.0184 291 979	31
32	0.0200 211 864	0.0186 542 270	0.0173 833 082	0.0162 014 927	32
33	0.0177 178 641	0.0164 717 236	0.0153 156 901	0.0142 430 705	33
34	0.0156 795 257	0.0145 445 683	0.0134 940 001	0.0125 213 807	34
35	0.0138 756 865	0.0128 428 860	0.0118 889 868	0.0110 078 072	35
36	0.0122 793 686	0.0113 402 966	0.0104 748 783	0.0096 771 931	36
37	0.0108 666 978	0.0100 135 070	0.0092 289 676	0.0085 074 225	37
38	0.0096 165 468	0.0088 419 488	0.0081 312 490	0.0074 790 528	38
39	0.0085 102 184	0.0078 074 603	0.0071 640 961	0.0065 749 914	39
40	0.0075 311 667	0.0068 940 047	0.0063 119 789	0.0057 802 123	40
41	0.0066 647 493	0.0060 874 213	0.0055 612 149	0.0050 815 053	41
42	0.0058 980 082	0.0053 752 065	0.0048 997 488	0.0044 672 574	42
43	0.0052 194 763	0.0047 463 192	0.0043 169 593	0.0039 272 592	43
44	0.0046 190 056	0.0041 910 103	0.0038 034 884	0.0034 525 356	44
45	0.0040 876 156	0.0037 006 714	0.0033 510 911	0.0030 351 961	45
46	0.0036 173 589	0.0032 677 010	0.0029 525 032	0.0026 683 043	46
47	0.0032 012 026	0.0028 853 872	0.0026 013 244	0.0023 457 620	47
48	0.0028 329 226	0.0025 478 032	0.0022 919 157	0.0020 622 084	48
49	0.0025 070 112	0.0022 497 159	0.0020 193 090	0.0018 129 304	49
50	0.0022 185 940	0.0019 865 041	0.0017 791 269	0.0015 937 850	50
51	0.0019 633 575	0.0017 540 875	0.0015 675 127	0.0014 011 297	51
52	0.0017 374 845	0.0015 488 631	0.0013 810 684	0.0012 317 623	52
53	0.0015 375 969	0.0013 676 496	0.0012 168 004	0.0010 828 680	53
54	0.0013 607 052	0.0012 076 376	0.0010 720 708	0.0009 519 719	54
55	0.0012 041 639	0.0010 663 467	0.0009 445 558	0.0008 368 983	55
56	0.0010 656 318	0.0009 415 865	0.0008 322 077	0.0007 357 348	56
57	0.0009 430 370	0.0008 314 229	0.0007 332 227	0.0006 467 998	57
58	0.0008 345 460	0.0007 341 483	0.0006 460 112	0.0005 686 152	58
59	0.0007 385 363	0.0006 482 545	0.0005 691 728	0.0004 998 815	59
60	0.0006 535 719	0.0005 724 102	0.0005 014 739	0.0004 394 563	60

YEARLY Compounding

TABLE 4. PRESENT WORTH OF ONE DOLLAR
Payable at end of each period

YEARS	14% Nominal Annual Rate	14¼% Nominal Annual Rate	14½% Nominal Annual Rate	14¾% Nominal Annual Rate	YEARS
1	0.8771 929 825	0.8752 735 230	0.8733 624 454	0.8714 596 950	1
2	0.7694 675 285	0.7661 037 400	0.7627 619 611	0.7594 420 000	2
3	0.6749 715 162	0.6705 503 195	0.6661 676 516	0.6618 230 937	3
4	0.5920 802 774	0.5869 149 405	0.5818 058 092	0.5767 521 513	4
5	0.5193 686 644	0.5137 111 076	0.5081 273 443	0.5026 162 539	5
6	0.4555 865 477	0.4496 377 310	0.4437 793 400	0.4380 098 073	6
7	0.3996 373 225	0.3935 560 009	0.3875 802 096	0.3817 078 931	7
8	0.3505 590 549	0.3444 691 474	0.3384 979 997	0.3326 430 441	8
9	0.3075 079 429	0.3015 047 242	0.2956 314 408	0.2898 850 057	9
10	0.2697 438 095	0.2638 991 021	0.2581 933 980	0.2526 230 987	10
11	0.2366 173 768	0.2309 838 968	0.2254 964 175	0.2201 508 485	11
12	0.2075 591 024	0.2021 740 891	0.1969 401 026	0.1918 525 913	12
13	0.1820 693 881	0.1769 576 272	0.1720 000 896	0.1671 918 007	13
14	0.1597 099 896	0.1548 863 258	0.1502 184 189	0.1457 009 156	14
15	0.1400 964 821	0.1355 679 001	0.1311 951 257	0.1269 724 755	15
16	0.1228 916 509	0.1186 589 935	0.1145 808 958	0.1106 513 948	16
17	0.1077 996 938	0.1038 590 753	0.1000 706 513	0.0964 282 307	17
18	0.0945 611 349	0.0909 050 987	0.0873 979 488	0.0840 333 166	18
19	0.0829 483 640	0.0795 668 260	0.0763 300 863	0.0732 316 484	19
20	0.0727 617 228	0.0696 427 361	0.0666 638 308	0.0638 184 300	20
21	0.0638 260 726	0.0609 564 430	0.0582 216 863	0.0556 151 895	21
22	0.0559 877 830	0.0533 535 606	0.0508 486 343	0.0484 663 961	22
23	0.0491 120 903	0.0466 989 589	0.0444 092 876	0.0422 365 108	23
24	0.0430 807 810	0.0408 743 623	0.0387 854 040	0.0368 074 168	24
25	0.0377 901 588	0.0357 762 471	0.0338 737 153	0.0320 761 802	25
26	0.0331 492 621	0.0313 140 018	0.0295 840 308	0.0279 530 982	26
27	0.0290 783 001	0.0274 083 167	0.0258 375 815	0.0243 599 985	27
28	0.0255 072 808	0.0239 897 739	0.0225 655 734	0.0212 287 568	28
29	0.0223 748 077	0.0209 976 139	0.0197 079 243	0.0185 000 059	29
30	0.0196 270 243	0.0183 786 555	0.0172 121 610	0.0161 220 095	30
31	0.0172 166 880	0.0160 863 506	0.0150 324 550	0.0140 496 815	31
32	0.0151 023 579	0.0140 799 567	0.0131 287 817	0.0122 437 312	32
33	0.0132 476 823	0.0123 238 133	0.0114 661 849	0.0106 699 182	33
34	0.0116 207 740	0.0107 867 075	0.0100 141 353	0.0092 984 037	34
35	0.0101 936 614	0.0094 413 195	0.0087 459 697	0.0081 031 840	35
36	0.0089 418 082	0.0082 637 370	0.0076 384 014	0.0070 615 983	36
37	0.0078 436 914	0.0072 330 302	0.0066 710 930	0.0061 538 983	37
38	0.0068 804 311	0.0063 308 798	0.0058 262 821	0.0053 628 743	38
39	0.0060 354 659	0.0055 412 515	0.0050 884 560	0.0046 735 288	39
40	0.0052 942 683	0.0048 501 107	0.0044 440 663	0.0040 727 920	40
41	0.0046 440 950	0.0042 451 735	0.0038 812 806	0.0035 492 741	41
42	0.0040 737 675	0.0037 156 879	0.0033 897 648	0.0030 930 493	42
43	0.0035 734 803	0.0032 522 433	0.0029 604 932	0.0026 954 678	43
44	0.0031 346 318	0.0028 466 024	0.0025 855 836	0.0023 489 916	44
45	0.0027 496 771	0.0024 915 557	0.0022 581 516	0.0020 470 515	45
46	0.0024 119 974	0.0021 807 928	0.0019 721 848	0.0017 839 228	46
47	0.0021 157 872	0.0019 087 902	0.0017 224 322	0.0015 546 169	47
48	0.0018 559 537	0.0016 707 135	0.0015 043 076	0.0013 547 859	48
49	0.0016 280 296	0.0014 623 313	0.0013 138 057	0.0011 806 413	49
50	0.0014 280 961	0.0012 799 399	0.0011 474 286	0.0010 288 813	50
51	0.0012 527 159	0.0011 202 975	0.0010 021 210	0.0008 966 286	51
52	0.0010 988 736	0.0009 805 667	0.0008 752 149	0.0007 813 757	52
53	0.0009 639 242	0.0008 582 641	0.0007 643 798	0.0006 809 374	53
54	0.0008 455 475	0.0007 512 158	0.0006 675 806	0.0005 934 095	54
55	0.0007 417 084	0.0006 575 193	0.0005 830 398	0.0005 171 325	55
56	0.0006 506 214	0.0005 755 093	0.0005 092 051	0.0004 506 601	56
57	0.0005 707 205	0.0005 037 280	0.0004 447 206	0.0003 927 321	57
58	0.0005 006 320	0.0004 408 998	0.0003 884 023	0.0003 422 502	58
59	0.0004 391 509	0.0003 859 079	0.0003 392 160	0.0002 982 573	59
60	0.0003 852 201	0.0003 377 750	0.0002 962 585	0.0002 599 192	60

TABLE 4. PRESENT WORTH OF ONE DOLLAR
Payable at end of each period

YEARLY Compounding

YEARS	15% Nominal Annual Rate	15¼% Nominal Annual Rate	15½% Nominal Annual Rate	15¾% Nominal Annual Rate	YEARS
1	0.8695 652 174	0.8676 789 588	0.8658 008 658	0.8639 308 855	1
2	0.7561 436 673	0.7528 667 755	0.7496 111 392	0.7463 765 750	2
3	0.6575 162 324	0.6532 466 599	0.6490 139 734	0.6448 177 754	3
4	0.5717 532 456	0.5668 083 817	0.5619 168 600	0.5570 779 917	4
5	0.4971 767 353	0.4918 077 064	0.4865 081 039	0.4812 768 826	5
6	0.4323 275 959	0.4267 311 987	0.4212 191 376	0.4157 899 634	6
7	0.3759 370 399	0.3702 656 821	0.3646 918 940	0.3592 137 913	7
8	0.3269 017 738	0.3212 717 415	0.3157 505 576	0.3103 358 888	8
9	0.2842 624 120	0.2787 607 302	0.2733 771 061	0.2681 087 592	9
10	0.2471 847 061	0.2418 748 201	0.2366 901 352	0.2316 274 378	10
11	0.2149 432 227	0.2098 696 921	0.2049 265 240	0.2001 100 974	11
12	0.1869 071 502	0.1820 995 159	0.1774 255 619	0.1728 812 937	12
13	0.1625 279 567	0.1580 039 184	0.1536 152 051	0.1493 574 891	13
14	0.1413 286 580	0.1370 966 754	0.1330 001 776	0.1290 345 478	14
15	0.1228 944 852	0.1189 559 005	0.1151 516 689	0.1114 769 312	15
16	0.1068 647 697	0.1032 155 319	0.0996 984 146	0.0963 083 639	16
17	0.0929 258 867	0.0895 579 453	0.0863 189 737	0.0832 037 701	17
18	0.0808 051 189	0.0777 075 447	0.0747 350 422	0.0718 823 068	18
19	0.0702 653 208	0.0674 252 015	0.0647 056 642	0.0621 013 449	19
20	0.0611 002 789	0.0585 034 286	0.0560 222 201	0.0536 512 699	20
21	0.0531 306 773	0.0507 621 940	0.0485 040 867	0.0463 509 891	21
22	0.0462 005 890	0.0440 452 877	0.0419 948 802	0.0400 440 511	22
23	0.0401 744 252	0.0382 171 693	0.0363 592 037	0.0345 952 925	23
24	0.0349 342 828	0.0331 602 337	0.0314 798 300	0.0298 879 417	24
25	0.0303 776 372	0.0287 724 370	0.0272 552 641	0.0258 211 159	25
26	0.0264 153 367	0.0249 652 382	0.0235 976 312	0.0223 076 596	26
27	0.0229 698 580	0.0216 618 119	0.0204 308 496	0.0192 722 761	27
28	0.0199 737 896	0.0187 954 984	0.0176 890 472	0.0166 499 145	28
29	0.0173 685 127	0.0163 084 585	0.0153 151 924	0.0143 843 754	29
30	0.0151 030 545	0.0141 505 063	0.0132 599 068	0.0124 271 062	30
31	0.0131 330 909	0.0122 780 965	0.0114 804 388	0.0107 361 609	31
32	0.0114 200 790	0.0106 534 460	0.0099 397 739	0.0092 753 010	32
33	0.0099 305 035	0.0092 437 710	0.0086 058 648	0.0080 132 190	33
34	0.0086 352 204	0.0080 206 256	0.0074 509 652	0.0069 228 674	34
35	0.0075 088 873	0.0069 593 280	0.0064 510 521	0.0059 808 789	35
36	0.0065 294 672	0.0060 384 625	0.0055 853 265	0.0051 670 660	36
37	0.0056 777 976	0.0052 394 469	0.0048 357 805	0.0044 639 879	37
38	0.0049 372 153	0.0045 461 578	0.0041 868 230	0.0038 565 770	38
39	0.0042 932 307	0.0039 446 055	0.0036 249 550	0.0033 318 160	39
40	0.0037 332 441	0.0034 226 512	0.0031 384 891	0.0028 784 588	40
41	0.0032 462 992	0.0029 697 624	0.0027 173 066	0.0024 867 894	41
42	0.0028 228 689	0.0025 768 003	0.0023 526 464	0.0021 484 142	42
43	0.0024 546 686	0.0022 358 354	0.0020 369 233	0.0018 560 814	43
44	0.0021 344 944	0.0019 399 874	0.0017 635 700	0.0016 035 260	44
45	0.0018 560 821	0.0016 832 862	0.0015 269 004	0.0013 853 357	45
46	0.0016 139 844	0.0014 605 520	0.0013 219 917	0.0011 968 343	46
47	0.0014 034 647	0.0012 672 903	0.0011 445 816	0.0010 339 821	47
48	0.0012 204 041	0.0010 996 011	0.0009 909 797	0.0008 932 891	48
49	0.0010 612 210	0.0009 541 007	0.0008 579 911	0.0007 717 400	49
50	0.0009 228 008	0.0008 278 531	0.0007 428 494	0.0006 667 300	50
51	0.0008 024 355	0.0007 183 107	0.0006 431 597	0.0005 760 087	51
52	0.0006 977 700	0.0006 232 631	0.0005 568 482	0.0004 976 317	52
53	0.0006 067 565	0.0005 407 923	0.0004 821 197	0.0004 299 194	53
54	0.0005 276 144	0.0004 692 341	0.0004 174 196	0.0003 714 206	54
55	0.0004 587 951	0.0004 071 446	0.0003 614 023	0.0003 208 817	55
56	0.0003 989 523	0.0003 532 708	0.0003 129 024	0.0002 772 197	56
57	0.0003 469 150	0.0003 065 256	0.0002 709 112	0.0002 394 986	57
58	0.0003 016 652	0.0002 659 658	0.0002 345 551	0.0002 069 103	58
59	0.0002 623 176	0.0002 307 729	0.0002 030 780	0.0001 787 562	59
60	0.0002 281 023	0.0002 002 368	0.0001 758 251	0.0001 544 330	60

YEARLY
Compounding

TABLE 4. PRESENT WORTH OF ONE DOLLAR
Payable at end of each period

YEARS	16% Nominal Annual Rate	16¼% Nominal Annual Rate	16½% Nominal Annual Rate	16¾% Nominal Annual Rate	YEARS
1	0.8620 689 655	0.8602 150 538	0.8583 690 987	0.8565 310 493	1
2	0.7431 629 013	0.7399 699 387	0.7367 975 096	0.7336 454 383	2
3	0.6406 576 735	0.6365 332 806	0.6324 442 143	0.6283 900 971	3
4	0.5522 910 979	0.5475 555 102	0.5428 705 702	0.5382 356 292	4
5	0.4761 130 154	0.4710 154 927	0.4659 833 221	0.4610 155 282	5
6	0.4104 422 547	0.4051 746 173	0.3999 856 842	0.3948 741 141	6
7	0.3538 295 299	0.3485 373 052	0.3433 353 512	0.3382 219 393	7
8	0.3050 254 568	0.2998 170 368	0.2947 084 560	0.2896 975 925	8
9	0.2629 529 800	0.2579 071 284	0.2529 686 317	0.2481 349 829	9
10	0.2266 836 034	0.2218 555 943	0.2171 404 564	0.2125 353 172	10
11	0.1954 168 995	0.1908 435 220	0.1863 866 579	0.1820 430 983	11
12	0.1684 628 444	0.1641 664 705	0.1599 885 475	0.1559 255 660	12
13	0.1452 265 900	0.1412 184 693	0.1373 292 254	0.1335 550 886	13
14	0.1251 953 362	0.1214 782 531	0.1178 791 634	0.1143 940 802	14
15	0.1079 270 140	0.1044 974 221	0.1011 838 312	0.0979 820 815	15
16	0.0930 405 293	0.0898 902 555	0.0868 530 740	0.0839 246 951	16
17	0.0802 073 528	0.0773 249 510	0.0745 519 949	0.0718 841 072	17
18	0.0691 442 697	0.0665 160 869	0.0639 931 286	0.0615 709 697	18
19	0.0596 071 290	0.0572 181 393	0.0549 297 242	0.0527 374 473	19
20	0.0513 854 561	0.0492 199 047	0.0471 499 778	0.0451 712 611	20
21	0.0442 978 070	0.0423 397 030	0.0404 720 840	0.0386 905 876	21
22	0.0381 877 646	0.0364 212 499	0.0347 399 862	0.0331 396 896	22
23	0.0329 204 867	0.0313 301 074	0.0298 197 307	0.0283 851 731	23
24	0.0283 797 299	0.0269 506 300	0.0255 963 353	0.0243 127 821	24
25	0.0244 652 844	0.0231 833 377	0.0219 711 033	0.0208 246 528	25
26	0.0210 907 624	0.0199 426 561	0.0188 593 161	0.0178 369 617	26
27	0.0181 816 918	0.0171 549 730	0.0161 882 542	0.0152 779 115	27
28	0.0156 738 722	0.0147 569 660	0.0138 954 972	0.0130 860 056	28
29	0.0135 119 588	0.0126 941 643	0.0119 274 654	0.0112 085 701	29
30	0.0116 482 403	0.0109 197 112	0.0102 381 677	0.0096 004 883	30
31	0.0100 415 865	0.0093 933 000	0.0087 881 268	0.0082 231 163	31
32	0.0086 565 401	0.0080 802 580	0.0075 434 565	0.0070 433 544	32
33	0.0074 625 346	0.0069 507 596	0.0064 750 699	0.0060 328 518	33
34	0.0064 332 194	0.0059 791 480	0.0055 579 999	0.0051 673 249	34
35	0.0055 458 788	0.0051 433 532	0.0047 708 154	0.0044 259 742	35
36	0.0047 809 300	0.0044 243 898	0.0040 951 205	0.0037 909 843	36
37	0.0041 214 914	0.0038 059 267	0.0035 151 249	0.0032 470 958	37
38	0.0035 530 098	0.0032 739 155	0.0030 172 746	0.0027 812 383	38
39	0.0030 629 395	0.0028 162 714	0.0025 899 353	0.0023 822 170	39
40	0.0026 404 651	0.0024 225 990	0.0022 231 204	0.0020 404 428	40
41	0.0022 762 630	0.0020 839 561	0.0019 082 579	0.0017 477 026	41
42	0.0019 622 957	0.0017 926 504	0.0016 379 896	0.0014 969 616	42
43	0.0016 916 342	0.0015 420 649	0.0014 059 996	0.0012 821 941	43
44	0.0014 583 054	0.0013 265 074	0.0012 068 666	0.0010 982 390	44
45	0.0012 571 598	0.0011 410 817	0.0010 359 370	0.0009 406 758	45
46	0.0010 837 584	0.0009 815 756	0.0008 892 163	0.0008 057 181	46
47	0.0009 342 745	0.0008 443 661	0.0007 632 758	0.0006 901 225	47
48	0.0008 054 091	0.0007 263 365	0.0006 551 724	0.0005 911 114	48
49	0.0006 943 182	0.0006 248 056	0.0005 623 797	0.0005 063 052	49
50	0.0005 985 501	0.0005 374 671	0.0004 827 294	0.0004 336 662	50
51	0.0005 159 915	0.0004 623 373	0.0004 143 600	0.0003 714 485	51
52	0.0004 448 203	0.0003 977 095	0.0003 556 738	0.0003 181 572	52
53	0.0003 834 657	0.0003 421 157	0.0003 052 994	0.0002 725 115	53
54	0.0003 305 739	0.0002 942 931	0.0002 620 596	0.0002 334 146	54
55	0.0002 849 775	0.0002 531 554	0.0002 249 438	0.0001 999 268	55
56	0.0002 456 703	0.0002 177 680	0.0001 930 848	0.0001 712 435	56
57	0.0002 117 847	0.0001 873 274	0.0001 657 381	0.0001 466 754	57
58	0.0001 825 730	0.0001 611 418	0.0001 422 644	0.0001 256 320	58
59	0.0001 573 905	0.0001 386 166	0.0001 221 154	0.0001 076 077	59
60	0.0001 356 815	0.0001 192 401	0.0001 048 201	0.0000 921 694	60

TABLE 4. PRESENT WORTH OF ONE DOLLAR
Payable at end of each period

YEARLY Compounding

YEARS	17% Nominal Annual Rate	17¼% Nominal Annual Rate	17½% Nominal Annual Rate	17¾% Nominal Annual Rate	YEARS
1	0.8547 008 547	0.8528 784 648	0.8510 638 298	0.8492 569 002	1
2	0.7305 135 510	0.7274 016 758	0.7243 096 424	0.7212 372 826	2
3	0.6243 705 564	0.6203 852 245	0.6164 337 382	0.6125 157 389	3
4	0.5336 500 482	0.5291 131 979	0.5246 244 580	0.5201 832 178	4
5	0.4561 111 523	0.4512 692 519	0.4464 889 005	0.4417 691 871	5
6	0.3898 385 917	0.3848 778 268	0.3799 905 536	0.3751 755 304	6
7	0.3331 953 776	0.3282 540 101	0.3233 962 158	0.3186 204 080	7
8	0.2847 823 740	0.2799 607 762	0.2752 308 220	0.2705 905 800	8
9	0.2434 037 384	0.2387 725 170	0.2342 389 974	0.2298 009 172	9
10	0.2080 373 833	0.2036 439 377	0.1993 523 382	0.1951 600 146	10
11	0.1778 097 293	0.1736 835 290	0.1696 615 644	0.1657 409 891	11
12	0.1519 741 276	0.1481 309 416	0.1443 928 208	0.1407 566 786	12
13	0.1298 924 168	0.1263 376 900	0.1228 875 071	0.1195 385 806	13
14	0.1110 191 596	0.1077 506 951	0.1045 851 124	0.1015 189 644	14
15	0.0948 881 706	0.0918 982 474	0.0890 086 063	0.0862 156 810	15
16	0.0811 010 005	0.0783 780 362	0.0757 520 054	0.0732 192 620	16
17	0.0693 170 945	0.0668 469 392	0.0644 697 918	0.0621 819 635	17
18	0.0592 453 799	0.0570 123 149	0.0548 679 079	0.0528 084 616	18
19	0.0506 370 768	0.0486 245 756	0.0466 960 918	0.0448 479 504	19
20	0.0432 795 528	0.0414 708 534	0.0397 413 548	0.0380 874 313	20
21	0.0369 910 708	0.0353 695 978	0.0338 224 296	0.0323 460 139	21
22	0.0316 162 998	0.0301 659 682	0.0287 850 465	0.0274 700 755	22
23	0.0270 224 785	0.0257 279 047	0.0244 979 119	0.0233 291 511	23
24	0.0230 961 355	0.0219 427 758	0.0208 492 867	0.0198 124 426	24
25	0.0197 402 867	0.0187 145 210	0.0177 440 738	0.0168 258 536	25
26	0.0168 720 399	0.0159 612 119	0.0151 013 394	0.0142 894 722	26
27	0.0144 205 470	0.0136 129 739	0.0128 522 037	0.0121 354 329	27
28	0.0123 252 538	0.0116 102 123	0.0109 380 457	0.0103 061 001	28
29	0.0105 344 050	0.0099 021 000	0.0093 089 751	0.0087 525 266	29
30	0.0090 037 649	0.0084 452 879	0.0079 225 320	0.0074 331 437	30
31	0.0076 955 256	0.0072 028 042	0.0067 425 804	0.0063 126 485	31
32	0.0065 773 723	0.0061 431 166	0.0057 383 663	0.0053 610 603	32
33	0.0056 216 857	0.0052 393 318	0.0048 837 160	0.0045 529 175	33
34	0.0048 048 596	0.0044 685 133	0.0041 563 541	0.0038 665 966	34
35	0.0041 067 176	0.0038 110 987	0.0035 373 226	0.0032 837 338	35
36	0.0035 100 150	0.0032 504 040	0.0030 104 873	0.0027 887 336	36
37	0.0030 000 129	0.0027 721 996	0.0025 621 169	0.0023 683 513	37
38	0.0025 641 135	0.0023 643 494	0.0021 805 250	0.0020 113 387	38
39	0.0021 915 500	0.0020 165 026	0.0018 557 660	0.0017 081 432	39
40	0.0018 731 197	0.0017 198 317	0.0015 793 753	0.0014 506 524	40
41	0.0016 009 570	0.0014 668 074	0.0013 441 492	0.0012 319 766	41
42	0.0013 683 393	0.0012 510 084	0.0011 439 567	0.0010 462 646	42
43	0.0011 695 208	0.0010 669 582	0.0009 735 802	0.0008 885 474	43
44	0.0009 995 904	0.0009 099 856	0.0008 285 789	0.0007 546 050	44
45	0.0008 543 508	0.0007 761 072	0.0007 051 735	0.0006 408 535	45
46	0.0007 302 143	0.0006 619 251	0.0006 001 477	0.0005 442 493	46
47	0.0006 241 148	0.0005 645 416	0.0005 107 640	0.0004 622 075	47
48	0.0005 334 315	0.0004 814 854	0.0004 346 928	0.0003 925 329	48
49	0.0004 559 243	0.0004 106 485	0.0003 699 513	0.0003 333 613	49
50	0.0003 896 789	0.0003 502 333	0.0003 148 522	0.0002 831 093	50
51	0.0003 330 589	0.0002 987 064	0.0002 679 593	0.0002 404 326	51
52	0.0002 846 657	0.0002 547 603	0.0002 280 505	0.0002 041 890	52
53	0.0002 433 040	0.0002 172 796	0.0001 940 855	0.0001 734 089	53
54	0.0002 079 522	0.0001 853 131	0.0001 651 791	0.0001 472 687	54
55	0.0001 777 369	0.0001 580 495	0.0001 405 780	0.0001 250 690	55
56	0.0001 519 119	0.0001 347 970	0.0001 196 408	0.0001 062 157	56
57	0.0001 298 392	0.0001 149 655	0.0001 018 220	0.0000 902 044	57
58	0.0001 109 737	0.0000 980 516	0.0000 866 570	0.0000 766 067	58
59	0.0000 948 493	0.0000 836 261	0.0000 737 507	0.0000 650 588	59
60	0.0000 810 678	0.0000 713 229	0.0000 627 665	0.0000 552 516	60

YEARLY
Compounding

TABLE 4. PRESENT WORTH OF ONE DOLLAR
Payable at end of each period

YEARS	18% Nominal Annual Rate	18¼% Nominal Annual Rate	18½% Nominal Annual Rate	18¾% Nominal Annual Rate	YEARS
1	0.8474 576 271	0.8456 659 619	0.8438 818 565	0.8421 052 632	1
2	0.7181 844 298	0.7151 509 192	0.7121 365 878	0.7091 412 742	2
3	0.6086 308 727	0.6047 787 900	0.6009 591 458	0.5971 715 994	3
4	0.5157 888 752	0.5114 408 372	0.5071 385 197	0.5028 813 468	4
5	0.4371 092 162	0.4325 081 076	0.4279 649 955	0.4234 790 289	5
6	0.3704 315 392	0.3657 573 849	0.3611 518 949	0.3566 139 191	6
7	0.3139 250 332	0.3093 085 707	0.3047 695 316	0.3003 064 582	7
8	0.2660 381 637	0.2615 717 300	0.2571 894 781	0.2528 896 490	8
9	0.2254 560 710	0.2212 023 086	0.2170 375 343	0.2129 597 044	9
10	0.1910 644 669	0.1870 632 631	0.1831 540 374	0.1793 344 879	10
11	0.1619 190 398	0.1581 930 344	0.1545 603 691	0.1510 185 161	11
12	0.1372 195 252	0.1337 784 646	0.1304 306 912	0.1271 734 873	12
13	0.1162 877 332	0.1131 318 939	0.1100 680 939	0.1070 934 630	13
14	0.0985 489 265	0.0956 717 919	0.0928 844 674	0.0901 839 688	14
15	0.0835 160 394	0.0809 063 779	0.0783 835 168	0.0759 443 948	15
16	0.0707 763 046	0.0684 197 699	0.0661 464 277	0.0639 531 746	16
17	0.0599 799 191	0.0578 602 705	0.0558 197 702	0.0538 553 049	17
18	0.0508 304 399	0.0489 304 614	0.0471 052 913	0.0453 518 357	18
19	0.0430 766 440	0.0413 788 257	0.0397 513 007	0.0381 910 195	19
20	0.0365 056 305	0.0349 926 644	0.0335 454 014	0.0321 608 586	20
21	0.0309 369 750	0.0295 921 052	0.0283 083 556	0.0270 828 283	21
22	0.0262 177 754	0.0250 250 361	0.0238 889 077	0.0228 065 922	22
23	0.0222 184 538	0.0211 628 212	0.0201 594 158	0.0192 055 513	23
24	0.0188 291 981	0.0178 966 776	0.0170 121 652	0.0161 730 959	24
25	0.0159 569 475	0.0151 346 111	0.0143 562 576	0.0136 194 492	25
26	0.0135 228 369	0.0127 988 254	0.0121 149 853	0.0114 690 098	26
27	0.0114 600 313	0.0108 235 310	0.0102 236 163	0.0096 581 135	27
28	0.0097 118 909	0.0091 530 918	0.0086 275 243	0.0081 331 482	28
29	0.0082 304 160	0.0077 404 582	0.0072 806 112	0.0068 489 669	29
30	0.0069 749 288	0.0065 458 420	0.0061 439 757	0.0057 675 511	30
31	0.0059 109 566	0.0055 355 958	0.0051 847 896	0.0048 568 851	31
32	0.0050 092 853	0.0046 812 649	0.0043 753 499	0.0040 900 085	32
33	0.0042 451 570	0.0039 587 864	0.0036 922 784	0.0034 442 177	33
34	0.0035 975 907	0.0033 478 109	0.0031 158 467	0.0029 003 939	34
35	0.0030 488 057	0.0028 311 297	0.0026 294 065	0.0024 424 369	35
36	0.0025 837 336	0.0023 941 900	0.0022 189 085	0.0020 567 890	36
37	0.0021 896 048	0.0020 246 850	0.0018 724 966	0.0017 320 328	37
38	0.0018 555 973	0.0017 122 072	0.0015 801 659	0.0014 585 540	38
39	0.0015 725 401	0.0014 479 554	0.0013 334 733	0.0012 282 560	39
40	0.0013 326 611	0.0012 244 866	0.0011 252 940	0.0010 343 208	40
41	0.0011 293 738	0.0010 355 066	0.0009 496 152	0.0008 710 070	41
42	0.0009 570 964	0.0008 756 927	0.0008 013 630	0.0007 334 796	42
43	0.0008 110 987	0.0007 405 435	0.0006 762 557	0.0006 176 670	43
44	0.0006 873 717	0.0006 262 524	0.0005 706 799	0.0005 201 406	44
45	0.0005 825 184	0.0005 296 004	0.0004 815 864	0.0004 380 132	45
46	0.0004 936 597	0.0004 478 650	0.0004 064 020	0.0003 688 532	46
47	0.0004 183 557	0.0003 787 442	0.0003 429 553	0.0003 106 132	47
48	0.0003 545 387	0.0003 202 911	0.0002 894 138	0.0002 615 690	48
49	0.0003 004 565	0.0002 708 593	0.0002 442 310	0.0002 202 687	49
50	0.0002 546 242	0.0002 290 565	0.0002 061 021	0.0001 854 894	50
51	0.0002 157 832	0.0001 937 052	0.0001 739 258	0.0001 562 016	51
52	0.0001 828 671	0.0001 638 099	0.0001 467 729	0.0001 315 382	52
53	0.0001 549 721	0.0001 385 285	0.0001 238 590	0.0001 107 690	53
54	0.0001 313 323	0.0001 171 488	0.0001 045 223	0.0000 932 792	54
55	0.0001 112 986	0.0000 990 688	0.0000 882 045	0.0000 785 509	55
56	0.0000 943 208	0.0000 837 791	0.0000 744 342	0.0000 661 481	56
57	0.0000 799 329	0.0000 708 491	0.0000 628 136	0.0000 557 037	57
58	0.0000 677 397	0.0000 599 147	0.0000 530 073	0.0000 469 083	58
59	0.0000 574 066	0.0000 506 678	0.0000 447 319	0.0000 395 018	59
60	0.0000 486 496	0.0000 428 480	0.0000 377 484	0.0000 332 646	60

TABLE 4. PRESENT WORTH OF ONE DOLLAR
Payable at end of each period

YEARLY Compounding

YEARS	19% Nominal Annual Rate	19¼% Nominal Annual Rate	19½% Nominal Annual Rate	19¾% Nominal Annual Rate	YEARS
1	0.8403 361 345	0.8385 744 235	0.8368 200 837	0.8350 730 689	1
2	0.7061 648 189	0.7032 070 637	0.7002 678 525	0.6973 470 304	2
3	0.5934 158 142	0.5896 914 580	0.5859 982 029	0.5823 357 248	3
4	0.4986 687 514	0.4945 001 745	0.4903 750 652	0.4862 928 808	4
5	0.4190 493 709	0.4146 751 987	0.4103 557 031	0.4060 900 883	5
6	0.3521 423 285	0.3477 360 157	0.3433 938 938	0.3391 148 963	6
7	0.2959 179 231	0.2916 025 289	0.2873 589 069	0.2831 857 172	7
8	0.2486 705 236	0.2445 304 225	0.2404 677 046	0.2364 807 659	8
9	0.2089 668 266	0.2050 569 581	0.2012 282 046	0.1974 787 189	9
10	0.1756 023 753	0.1719 555 204	0.1683 918 030	0.1649 091 599	10
11	0.1475 650 212	0.1441 975 014	0.1409 136 427	0.1377 111 982	11
12	0.1240 042 195	0.1209 203 366	0.1179 193 663	0.1149 989 129	12
13	0.1042 052 265	0.1014 007 016	0.0986 772 940	0.0960 324 951	13
14	0.0875 674 172	0.0850 320 348	0.0825 751 414	0.0801 941 504	14
15	0.0735 860 649	0.0713 056 896	0.0691 005 367	0.0669 679 753	15
16	0.0618 370 293	0.0597 951 275	0.0578 247 169	0.0559 231 526	16
17	0.0519 638 902	0.0501 426 646	0.0483 888 845	0.0466 999 187	17
18	0.0436 671 346	0.0420 483 561	0.0404 927 903	0.0389 978 444	18
19	0.0366 950 711	0.0352 606 759	0.0338 851 802	0.0325 660 496	19
20	0.0308 361 942	0.0295 687 010	0.0283 557 993	0.0271 950 310	20
21	0.0259 127 682	0.0247 955 564	0.0237 287 024	0.0227 098 380	21
22	0.0217 754 355	0.0207 929 194	0.0198 566 547	0.0189 643 741	22
23	0.0182 986 853	0.0174 364 104	0.0166 164 475	0.0158 366 381	23
24	0.0153 770 465	0.0146 217 278	0.0139 049 769	0.0132 247 500	24
25	0.0129 218 878	0.0122 614 070	0.0116 359 640	0.0110 436 325	25
26	0.0108 587 292	0.0102 821 023	0.0097 372 083	0.0092 222 401	26
27	0.0091 249 825	0.0086 223 080	0.0081 482 915	0.0077 012 444	27
28	0.0076 680 526	0.0072 304 470	0.0068 186 540	0.0064 311 018	28
29	0.0064 437 416	0.0060 632 679	0.0057 059 866	0.0053 704 399	29
30	0.0054 149 089	0.0050 845 014	0.0047 748 842	0.0044 847 097	30
31	0.0045 503 437	0.0042 637 328	0.0039 957 190	0.0037 450 603	31
32	0.0038 238 182	0.0035 754 573	0.0033 436 979	0.0031 273 990	32
33	0.0032 132 926	0.0029 982 870	0.0027 980 735	0.0026 116 067	33
34	0.0027 002 459	0.0025 142 868	0.0023 414 841	0.0021 808 824	34
35	0.0022 691 142	0.0021 084 166	0.0019 594 010	0.0018 211 962	35
36	0.0019 068 186	0.0017 680 642	0.0016 396 661	0.0015 208 319	36
37	0.0016 023 686	0.0014 826 535	0.0013 721 055	0.0012 700 057	37
38	0.0013 465 282	0.0012 433 153	0.0011 482 054	0.0010 605 476	38
39	0.0011 315 363	0.0010 426 124	0.0009 608 414	0.0008 856 347	39
40	0.0009 508 709	0.0008 743 081	0.0008 040 514	0.0007 395 697	40
41	0.0007 990 512	0.0007 331 724	0.0006 728 463	0.0006 175 947	41
42	0.0006 714 716	0.0006 148 196	0.0005 630 513	0.0005 157 367	42
43	0.0005 642 618	0.0005 155 720	0.0004 711 726	0.0004 306 779	43
44	0.0004 741 696	0.0004 323 455	0.0003 942 867	0.0003 596 475	44
45	0.0003 984 618	0.0003 625 539	0.0003 299 471	0.0003 003 319	45
46	0.0003 348 419	0.0003 040 284	0.0002 761 063	0.0002 507 991	46
47	0.0002 813 797	0.0002 549 504	0.0002 310 513	0.0002 094 356	47
48	0.0002 364 536	0.0002 137 949	0.0001 933 484	0.0001 748 940	48
49	0.0001 987 005	0.0001 792 830	0.0001 617 978	0.0001 460 493	49
50	0.0001 669 752	0.0001 503 421	0.0001 353 957	0.0001 219 618	50
51	0.0001 403 153	0.0001 260 730	0.0001 133 018	0.0001 018 470	51
52	0.0001 179 120	0.0001 057 216	0.0000 948 132	0.0000 850 497	52
53	0.0000 990 857	0.0000 886 555	0.0000 793 416	0.0000 710 227	53
54	0.0000 832 653	0.0000 743 442	0.0000 663 947	0.0000 593 092	54
55	0.0000 699 708	0.0000 623 431	0.0000 555 604	0.0000 495 275	55
56	0.0000 587 990	0.0000 522 794	0.0000 464 940	0.0000 413 591	56
57	0.0000 494 109	0.0000 438 401	0.0000 389 071	0.0000 345 378	57
58	0.0000 415 218	0.0000 367 632	0.0000 325 583	0.0000 288 416	58
59	0.0000 348 923	0.0000 308 287	0.0000 272 454	0.0000 240 849	59
60	0.0000 293 212	0.0000 258 522	0.0000 227 995	0.0000 201 126	60

TABLE 4. PRESENT WORTH OF ONE DOLLAR
Payable at end of each period

YEARS	20% Nominal Annual Rate	20¼% Nominal Annual Rate	20½% Nominal Annual Rate	20¾% Nominal Annual Rate	YEARS
1	0.8333 333 333	0.8316 008 316	0.8298 755 187	0.8281 573 499	1
2	0.6944 444 444	0.6915 599 431	0.6886 933 765	0.6858 445 962	2
3	0.5787 037 037	0.5751 018 238	0.5715 297 730	0.5679 872 432	3
4	0.4822 530 864	0.4782 551 549	0.4742 985 668	0.4703 828 101	4
5	0.4018 775 720	0.3977 173 846	0.3936 087 691	0.3895 509 815	5
6	0.3348 979 767	0.3307 421 077	0.3266 462 815	0.3226 095 085	6
7	0.2790 816 472	0.2750 454 118	0.2710 757 522	0.2671 714 356	7
8	0.2325 680 394	0.2287 279 932	0.2249 591 305	0.2212 599 881	8
9	0.1938 066 995	0.1902 103 894	0.1866 880 751	0.1832 380 853	9
10	0.1615 055 829	0.1581 791 180	0.1549 278 632	0.1517 499 672	10
11	0.1345 879 857	0.1315 418 861	0.1285 708 408	0.1256 728 507	11
12	0.1121 566 548	0.1093 903 418	0.1066 977 932	0.1040 768 949	12
13	0.0934 638 790	0.0909 690 992	0.0885 458 865	0.0861 920 455	13
14	0.0778 865 658	0.0756 499 786	0.0734 820 635	0.0713 805 760	14
15	0.0649 054 715	0.0629 105 851	0.0609 809 655	0.0591 143 486	15
16	0.0540 878 929	0.0523 164 949	0.0506 066 104	0.0489 559 823	16
17	0.0450 732 441	0.0435 064 406	0.0419 971 870	0.0405 432 566	17
18	0.0375 610 368	0.0361 799 922	0.0348 524 374	0.0335 761 959	18
19	0.0313 008 640	0.0300 873 116	0.0289 231 846	0.0278 063 734	19
20	0.0260 840 533	0.0250 206 334	0.0240 026 428	0.0230 280 525	20
21	0.0217 367 111	0.0208 071 795	0.0199 192 056	0.0190 708 510	21
22	0.0181 139 259	0.0173 032 678	0.0165 304 611	0.0157 936 654	22
23	0.0150 949 383	0.0143 894 119	0.0137 182 250	0.0130 796 401	23
24	0.0125 791 152	0.0119 662 469	0.0113 844 191	0.0108 320 001	24
25	0.0104 825 960	0.0099 511 409	0.0094 476 507	0.0089 706 005	25
26	0.0087 354 967	0.0082 753 770	0.0078 403 740	0.0074 290 687	26
27	0.0072 795 806	0.0068 818 104	0.0065 065 344	0.0061 524 379	27
28	0.0060 663 171	0.0057 229 193	0.0053 996 136	0.0050 951 866	28
29	0.0050 552 643	0.0047 591 844	0.0044 810 072	0.0042 196 163	29
30	0.0042 127 202	0.0039 577 417	0.0037 186 782	0.0034 945 062	30
31	0.0035 106 002	0.0032 912 613	0.0030 860 400	0.0028 940 010	31
32	0.0029 255 002	0.0027 370 156	0.0025 610 290	0.0023 966 882	32
33	0.0024 379 168	0.0022 761 045	0.0021 253 353	0.0019 848 350	33
34	0.0020 315 973	0.0018 928 104	0.0017 637 637	0.0016 437 557	34
35	0.0016 929 978	0.0015 740 627	0.0014 637 043	0.0013 612 883	35
36	0.0014 108 315	0.0013 089 918	0.0012 146 924	0.0011 273 609	36
37	0.0011 756 929	0.0010 885 587	0.0010 080 435	0.0009 336 322	37
38	0.0009 797 441	0.0009 052 463	0.0008 365 506	0.0007 731 944	38
39	0.0008 164 534	0.0007 528 036	0.0006 942 329	0.0006 403 266	39
40	0.0006 803 778	0.0006 260 321	0.0005 761 269	0.0005 302 912	40
41	0.0005 669 815	0.0005 206 088	0.0004 781 136	0.0004 391 646	41
42	0.0004 724 846	0.0004 329 387	0.0003 967 748	0.0003 636 974	42
43	0.0003 937 372	0.0003 600 322	0.0003 292 737	0.0003 011 986	43
44	0.0003 281 143	0.0002 994 031	0.0002 732 561	0.0002 494 399	44
45	0.0002 734 286	0.0002 489 838	0.0002 267 686	0.0002 065 755	45
46	0.0002 278 572	0.0002 070 552	0.0001 881 897	0.0001 710 770	46
47	0.0001 898 810	0.0001 721 873	0.0001 561 740	0.0001 416 787	47
48	0.0001 582 341	0.0001 431 911	0.0001 296 050	0.0001 173 322	48
49	0.0001 318 618	0.0001 190 778	0.0001 075 560	0.0000 971 695	49
50	0.0001 098 848	0.0000 990 252	0.0000 892 581	0.0000 804 717	50
51	0.0000 915 707	0.0000 823 494	0.0000 740 731	0.0000 666 432	51
52	0.0000 763 089	0.0000 684 819	0.0000 614 715	0.0000 551 911	52
53	0.0000 635 908	0.0000 569 496	0.0000 510 137	0.0000 457 069	53
54	0.0000 529 923	0.0000 473 593	0.0000 423 350	0.0000 378 525	54
55	0.0000 441 602	0.0000 393 840	0.0000 351 328	0.0000 313 478	55
56	0.0000 368 002	0.0000 327 518	0.0000 291 558	0.0000 259 609	56
57	0.0000 306 668	0.0000 272 364	0.0000 241 957	0.0000 214 997	57
58	0.0000 255 557	0.0000 226 498	0.0000 200 794	0.0000 178 052	58
59	0.0000 212 964	0.0000 188 356	0.0000 166 634	0.0000 147 455	59
60	0.0000 177 470	0.0000 156 637	0.0000 138 286	0.0000 122 116	60

TABLE 4. PRESENT WORTH OF ONE DOLLAR
Payable at end of each period

YEARLY Compounding

YEARS	21% Nominal Annual Rate	21¼% Nominal Annual Rate	21½% Nominal Annual Rate	21¾% Nominal Annual Rate	YEARS
1	0.8264 462 810	0.8247 422 680	0.8230 452 675	0.8213 552 361	1
2	0.6830 134 554	0.6801 998 087	0.6774 035 123	0.6746 244 239	2
3	0.5644 739 301	0.5609 895 329	0.5575 337 550	0.5541 063 030	3
4	0.4665 073 802	0.4626 717 797	0.4588 755 185	0.4551 181 134	4
5	0.3855 432 894	0.3815 849 730	0.3776 753 239	0.3738 136 455	5
6	0.3186 308 177	0.3147 092 561	0.3108 438 880	0.3070 337 951	6
7	0.2633 312 543	0.2595 540 256	0.2558 385 909	0.2521 838 152	7
8	0.2176 291 358	0.2140 651 758	0.2105 667 415	0.2071 324 971	8
9	0.1798 587 899	0.1765 485 986	0.1733 059 601	0.1701 293 611	9
10	0.1486 436 280	0.1456 070 916	0.1426 386 503	0.1397 366 415	10
11	0.1228 459 736	0.1200 883 230	0.1173 980 661	0.1147 734 222	11
12	0.1015 255 980	0.0990 419 159	0.0966 239 227	0.0942 697 513	12
13	0.0839 054 529	0.0816 840 543	0.0795 258 623	0.0774 289 538	13
14	0.0693 433 495	0.0673 682 922	0.0654 533 846	0.0635 966 767	14
15	0.0573 085 533	0.0555 614 781	0.0538 710 984	0.0522 354 634	15
16	0.0473 624 407	0.0458 238 995	0.0443 383 526	0.0429 038 714	16
17	0.0391 425 130	0.0377 929 068	0.0364 924 713	0.0352 393 194	17
18	0.0323 491 843	0.0311 694 077	0.0300 349 558	0.0289 439 995	18
19	0.0267 348 631	0.0257 067 280	0.0247 201 282	0.0237 733 055	19
20	0.0220 949 282	0.0212 014 251	0.0203 457 846	0.0195 263 290	20
21	0.0182 602 712	0.0174 857 114	0.0167 455 017	0.0160 380 526	21
22	0.0150 911 332	0.0144 212 053	0.0137 823 059	0.0131 729 384	22
23	0.0124 720 109	0.0118 937 776	0.0113 434 617	0.0108 196 620	23
24	0.0103 074 470	0.0098 093 011	0.0093 361 824	0.0088 867 860	24
25	0.0085 185 513	0.0080 901 452	0.0076 841 008	0.0072 992 082	25
26	0.0070 401 250	0.0066 722 847	0.0063 243 628	0.0059 952 429	26
27	0.0058 182 851	0.0055 029 152	0.0052 052 369	0.0049 242 241	27
28	0.0048 085 001	0.0045 384 868	0.0042 841 456	0.0040 445 373	28
29	0.0039 739 670	0.0037 430 819	0.0035 260 457	0.0033 220 019	29
30	0.0032 842 703	0.0030 870 779	0.0029 020 952	0.0027 285 436	30
31	0.0027 142 730	0.0025 460 436	0.0023 885 558	0.0022 411 036	31
32	0.0022 432 008	0.0020 998 298	0.0019 658 895	0.0018 407 422	32
33	0.0018 538 850	0.0017 318 184	0.0016 180 161	0.0015 119 032	33
34	0.0015 321 363	0.0014 283 038	0.0013 317 005	0.0012 418 096	34
35	0.0012 662 284	0.0011 779 825	0.0010 960 498	0.0010 199 668	35
36	0.0010 464 697	0.0009 715 320	0.0009 020 986	0.0008 377 551	36
37	0.0008 648 510	0.0008 012 635	0.0007 424 680	0.0006 880 945	37
38	0.0007 147 529	0.0006 608 359	0.0006 110 847	0.0005 651 701	38
39	0.0005 907 049	0.0005 450 193	0.0005 029 504	0.0004 642 054	39
40	0.0004 881 859	0.0004 495 004	0.0004 139 509	0.0003 812 775	40
41	0.0004 034 594	0.0003 707 220	0.0003 407 004	0.0003 131 643	41
42	0.0003 334 375	0.0003 057 501	0.0002 804 118	0.0002 572 191	42
43	0.0002 755 682	0.0002 521 650	0.0002 307 916	0.0002 112 683	43
44	0.0002 277 423	0.0002 079 712	0.0001 899 520	0.0001 735 263	44
45	0.0001 882 168	0.0001 715 226	0.0001 563 391	0.0001 425 267	45
46	0.0001 555 511	0.0001 414 619	0.0001 286 741	0.0001 170 651	46
47	0.0001 285 546	0.0001 166 696	0.0001 059 046	0.0000 961 520	47
48	0.0001 062 435	0.0000 962 224	0.0000 871 643	0.0000 789 750	48
49	0.0000 878 045	0.0000 793 587	0.0000 717 402	0.0000 648 665	49
50	0.0000 725 657	0.0000 654 504	0.0000 590 454	0.0000 532 784	50
51	0.0000 599 717	0.0000 539 798	0.0000 485 970	0.0000 437 605	51
52	0.0000 495 634	0.0000 445 194	0.0000 399 976	0.0000 359 429	52
53	0.0000 409 615	0.0000 367 170	0.0000 329 198	0.0000 295 219	53
54	0.0000 338 524	0.0000 302 821	0.0000 270 945	0.0000 242 480	54
55	0.0000 279 772	0.0000 249 749	0.0000 223 000	0.0000 199 162	55
56	0.0000 231 217	0.0000 205 979	0.0000 183 539	0.0000 163 583	56
57	0.0000 191 088	0.0000 169 879	0.0000 151 061	0.0000 134 360	57
58	0.0000 157 924	0.0000 140 107	0.0000 124 330	0.0000 110 357	58
59	0.0000 130 516	0.0000 115 552	0.0000 102 329	0.0000 090 642	59
60	0.0000 107 864	0.0000 095 300	0.0000 084 222	0.0000 074 450	60

YEARLY
Compounding

TABLE 4. PRESENT WORTH OF ONE DOLLAR
Payable at end of each period

YEARS	22% Nominal Annual Rate	22¼% Nominal Annual Rate	22½% Nominal Annual Rate	22¾% Nominal Annual Rate	YEARS
1	0.8196 721 311	0.8179 959 100	0.8163 265 306	0.8146 639 511	1
2	0.6718 624 026	0.6691 173 088	0.6663 890 046	0.6636 773 533	2
3	0.5507 068 874	0.5473 352 219	0.5439 910 241	0.5406 740 149	3
4	0.4513 990 880	0.4477 179 729	0.4440 743 054	0.4404 676 292	4
5	0.3699 992 525	0.3662 314 707	0.3625 096 371	0.3588 330 992	5
6	0.3032 780 758	0.2995 758 452	0.2959 262 344	0.2923 283 904	6
7	0.2485 885 867	0.2450 518 161	0.2415 724 362	0.2381 494 015	7
8	0.2037 611 366	0.2004 513 833	0.1972 019 887	0.1940 117 324	8
9	0.1670 173 251	0.1639 684 117	0.1609 812 153	0.1580 543 645	9
10	0.1368 994 468	0.1341 254 901	0.1314 132 370	0.1287 611 931	10
11	0.1122 126 613	0.1097 141 024	0.1072 761 118	0.1048 971 023	11
12	0.0919 775 913	0.0897 456 870	0.0875 723 362	0.0854 558 878	12
13	0.0753 914 682	0.0734 116 049	0.0714 876 214	0.0696 178 312	13
14	0.0617 962 854	0.0600 503 926	0.0583 572 419	0.0567 151 374	14
15	0.0506 526 930	0.0491 209 755	0.0476 385 648	0.0462 037 780	15
16	0.0415 186 008	0.0401 807 571	0.0388 886 244	0.0376 405 523	16
17	0.0340 316 400	0.0328 676 949	0.0317 458 158	0.0306 644 011	17
18	0.0278 947 869	0.0268 856 400	0.0259 149 517	0.0249 811 821	18
19	0.0228 645 794	0.0219 923 436	0.0211 550 626	0.0203 512 685	19
20	0.0187 414 585	0.0179 896 471	0.0172 694 389	0.0165 794 448	20
21	0.0153 618 513	0.0147 154 578	0.0140 975 011	0.0135 066 760	21
22	0.0125 916 814	0.0120 371 843	0.0115 081 642	0.0110 034 021	22
23	0.0103 210 503	0.0098 463 675	0.0093 944 197	0.0089 640 750	23
24	0.0084 598 773	0.0080 542 883	0.0076 689 141	0.0073 027 088	24
25	0.0069 343 256	0.0065 883 749	0.0062 603 380	0.0059 492 536	25
26	0.0056 838 735	0.0053 892 637	0.0051 104 800	0.0048 466 424	26
27	0.0046 589 127	0.0044 083 957	0.0041 718 204	0.0039 483 849	27
28	0.0038 187 809	0.0036 060 496	0.0034 055 677	0.0032 166 068	28
29	0.0031 301 483	0.0029 497 339	0.0027 800 553	0.0026 204 536	29
30	0.0025 656 953	0.0024 128 702	0.0022 694 329	0.0021 347 891	30
31	0.0021 030 289	0.0019 737 180	0.0018 525 983	0.0017 391 357	31
32	0.0017 237 942	0.0016 144 932	0.0015 123 251	0.0014 168 112	32
33	0.0014 129 461	0.0013 206 489	0.0012 345 511	0.0011 542 250	33
34	0.0011 581 525	0.0010 802 854	0.0010 077 968	0.0009 403 055	34
35	0.0009 493 053	0.0008 836 690	0.0008 226 913	0.0007 660 330	35
36	0.0007 781 191	0.0007 228 376	0.0006 715 847	0.0006 240 595	36
37	0.0006 378 026	0.0005 912 782	0.0005 482 324	0.0005 083 987	37
38	0.0005 227 890	0.0004 836 632	0.0004 475 367	0.0004 141 741	38
39	0.0004 285 156	0.0003 956 345	0.0003 653 361	0.0003 374 127	39
40	0.0003 512 423	0.0003 236 274	0.0002 982 335	0.0002 748 780	40
41	0.0002 879 035	0.0002 647 259	0.0002 434 559	0.0002 239 332	41
42	0.0002 359 865	0.0002 165 447	0.0001 987 395	0.0001 824 303	42
43	0.0001 934 315	0.0001 771 327	0.0001 622 364	0.0001 486 194	43
44	0.0001 585 504	0.0001 448 938	0.0001 324 378	0.0001 210 749	44
45	0.0001 299 594	0.0001 185 225	0.0001 081 125	0.0000 986 353	45
46	0.0001 065 241	0.0000 969 510	0.0000 882 551	0.0000 803 546	46
47	0.0000 873 148	0.0000 793 055	0.0000 720 450	0.0000 654 620	47
48	0.0000 715 695	0.0000 648 716	0.0000 588 122	0.0000 533 296	48
49	0.0000 586 635	0.0000 530 647	0.0000 480 100	0.0000 434 457	49
50	0.0000 480 849	0.0000 434 067	0.0000 391 918	0.0000 353 936	50
51	0.0000 394 138	0.0000 355 065	0.0000 319 933	0.0000 288 339	51
52	0.0000 323 064	0.0000 290 442	0.0000 261 170	0.0000 234 899	52
53	0.0000 264 807	0.0000 237 580	0.0000 213 200	0.0000 191 364	53
54	0.0000 217 055	0.0000 194 340	0.0000 174 041	0.0000 155 897	54
55	0.0000 177 914	0.0000 158 969	0.0000 142 074	0.0000 127 004	55
56	0.0000 145 831	0.0000 130 036	0.0000 115 979	0.0000 103 466	56
57	0.0000 119 534	0.0000 106 369	0.0000 094 677	0.0000 084 290	57
58	0.0000 097 978	0.0000 087 009	0.0000 077 287	0.0000 068 668	58
59	0.0000 080 310	0.0000 071 173	0.0000 063 091	0.0000 055 941	59
60	0.0000 065 828	0.0000 058 219	0.0000 051 503	0.0000 045 573	60

TABLE 4. PRESENT WORTH OF ONE DOLLAR
Payable at end of each period

YEARLY Compounding

YEARS	23% Nominal Annual Rate	24% Nominal Annual Rate	25% Nominal Annual Rate	26% Nominal Annual Rate	YEARS
1	0.8130 081 301	0.8064 516 129	0.8000 000 000	0.7936 507 937	1
2	0.6609 822 196	0.6503 642 040	0.6400 000 000	0.6298 815 823	2
3	0.5373 839 184	0.5244 872 613	0.5120 000 000	0.4999 060 177	3
4	0.4368 974 946	0.4229 735 978	0.4096 000 000	0.3967 508 077	4
5	0.3552 012 151	0.3411 077 401	0.3276 800 000	0.3148 815 934	5
6	0.2887 814 757	0.2750 868 872	0.2621 440 000	0.2499 060 265	6
7	0.2347 816 876	0.2218 442 639	0.2097 152 000	0.1983 381 163	7
8	0.1908 794 208	0.1789 066 644	0.1677 721 600	0.1574 112 034	8
9	0.1551 865 210	0.1442 795 681	0.1342 177 280	0.1249 295 265	9
10	0.1261 679 032	0.1163 544 904	0.1073 741 824	0.0991 504 179	10
11	0.1025 755 311	0.0938 342 664	0.0858 993 459	0.0786 908 078	11
12	0.0833 947 407	0.0756 727 955	0.0687 194 767	0.0624 530 221	12
13	0.0678 006 022	0.0610 264 480	0.0549 755 814	0.0495 658 905	13
14	0.0551 224 408	0.0492 148 774	0.0439 804 651	0.0393 380 084	14
15	0.0448 149 925	0.0396 894 173	0.0351 843 721	0.0312 206 416	15
16	0.0364 349 533	0.0320 075 946	0.0281 474 977	0.0247 782 870	16
17	0.0296 219 132	0.0258 125 763	0.0225 179 981	0.0196 653 071	17
18	0.0240 828 563	0.0208 165 938	0.0180 143 985	0.0156 073 866	18
19	0.0195 795 580	0.0167 875 756	0.0144 115 188	0.0123 868 148	19
20	0.0159 183 398	0.0135 383 674	0.0115 292 150	0.0098 308 054	20
21	0.0129 417 397	0.0109 180 383	0.0092 233 720	0.0078 022 265	21
22	0.0105 217 396	0.0088 048 696	0.0073 786 976	0.0061 922 432	22
23	0.0085 542 598	0.0071 007 013	0.0059 029 581	0.0049 144 788	23
24	0.0069 546 828	0.0057 263 720	0.0047 223 665	0.0039 003 800	24
25	0.0056 542 136	0.0046 180 419	0.0037 778 932	0.0030 955 397	25
26	0.0045 969 217	0.0037 242 274	0.0030 223 145	0.0024 567 775	26
27	0.0037 373 347	0.0030 034 092	0.0024 178 516	0.0019 498 234	27
28	0.0030 384 835	0.0024 221 042	0.0019 342 813	0.0015 474 789	28
29	0.0024 703 118	0.0019 533 098	0.0015 474 250	0.0012 281 579	29
30	0.0020 083 836	0.0015 752 498	0.0012 379 400	0.0009 747 285	30
31	0.0016 328 322	0.0012 703 628	0.0009 903 520	0.0007 735 940	31
32	0.0013 275 058	0.0010 244 861	0.0007 922 816	0.0006 139 635	32
33	0.0010 792 730	0.0008 261 985	0.0006 338 253	0.0004 872 726	33
34	0.0008 774 577	0.0006 662 891	0.0005 070 602	0.0003 867 243	34
35	0.0007 133 803	0.0005 373 299	0.0004 056 482	0.0003 069 241	35
36	0.0005 799 840	0.0004 333 306	0.0003 245 186	0.0002 435 905	36
37	0.0004 715 317	0.0003 494 601	0.0002 596 148	0.0001 933 258	37
38	0.0003 833 591	0.0002 818 227	0.0002 076 919	0.0001 534 332	38
39	0.0003 116 741	0.0002 272 764	0.0001 661 535	0.0001 217 724	39
40	0.0002 533 935	0.0001 832 874	0.0001 329 228	0.0000 966 447	40
41	0.0002 060 110	0.0001 478 124	0.0001 063 382	0.0000 767 022	41
42	0.0001 674 886	0.0001 192 036	0.0000 850 706	0.0000 608 747	42
43	0.0001 361 696	0.0000 961 319	0.0000 680 565	0.0000 483 133	43
44	0.0001 107 070	0.0000 775 257	0.0000 544 452	0.0000 383 439	44
45	0.0000 900 057	0.0000 625 207	0.0000 435 561	0.0000 304 316	45
46	0.0000 731 754	0.0000 504 200	0.0000 348 449	0.0000 241 521	46
47	0.0000 594 922	0.0000 406 613	0.0000 278 759	0.0000 191 683	47
48	0.0000 483 676	0.0000 327 913	0.0000 223 007	0.0000 152 130	48
49	0.0000 393 233	0.0000 264 446	0.0000 178 406	0.0000 120 738	49
50	0.0000 319 701	0.0000 213 263	0.0000 142 725	0.0000 095 824	50
51	0.0000 259 920	0.0000 171 986	0.0000 114 180	0.0000 076 051	51
52	0.0000 211 317	0.0000 138 699	0.0000 091 344	0.0000 060 358	52
53	0.0000 171 802	0.0000 111 854	0.0000 073 075	0.0000 047 903	53
54	0.0000 139 677	0.0000 090 205	0.0000 058 460	0.0000 038 018	54
55	0.0000 113 558	0.0000 072 746	0.0000 046 768	0.0000 030 173	55
56	0.0000 092 324	0.0000 058 666	0.0000 037 414	0.0000 023 947	56
57	0.0000 075 060	0.0000 047 311	0.0000 029 932	0.0000 019 005	57
58	0.0000 061 024	0.0000 038 154	0.0000 023 945	0.0000 015 084	58
59	0.0000 049 613	0.0000 030 770	0.0000 019 156	0.0000 011 971	59
60	0.0000 040 336	0.0000 024 814	0.0000 015 325	0.0000 009 501	60

YEARLY
Compounding

TABLE 4. PRESENT WORTH OF ONE DOLLAR
Payable at end of each period

YEARS	27% Nominal Annual Rate	28% Nominal Annual Rate	29% Nominal Annual Rate	30% Nominal Annual Rate	YEARS
1	0.7874 015 748	0.7812 500 000	0.7751 937 984	0.7692 307 692	1
2	0.6200 012 400	0.6103 515 625	0.6009 254 252	0.5917 159 763	2
3	0.4881 899 528	0.4768 371 582	0.4658 336 629	0.4551 661 356	3
4	0.3844 015 376	0.3725 290 298	0.3611 113 666	0.3501 277 966	4
5	0.3026 783 761	0.2910 383 046	0.2799 312 919	0.2693 290 743	5
6	0.2383 294 300	0.2273 736 754	0.2170 010 015	0.2071 762 110	6
7	0.1876 609 685	0.1776 356 839	0.1682 178 306	0.1593 663 162	7
8	0.1477 645 421	0.1387 778 781	0.1304 014 191	0.1225 894 740	8
9	0.1163 500 332	0.1084 202 172	0.1010 863 714	0.0942 995 954	9
10	0.0916 141 993	0.0847 032 947	0.0783 615 282	0.0725 381 503	10
11	0.0721 371 648	0.0661 744 490	0.0607 453 707	0.0557 985 771	11
12	0.0568 009 172	0.0516 987 883	0.0470 894 347	0.0429 219 824	12
13	0.0447 251 316	0.0403 896 783	0.0365 034 377	0.0330 169 096	13
14	0.0352 166 391	0.0315 544 362	0.0282 972 385	0.0253 976 227	14
15	0.0277 296 371	0.0246 519 033	0.0219 358 438	0.0195 366 329	15
16	0.0218 343 599	0.0192 592 994	0.0170 045 301	0.0150 281 791	16
17	0.0171 924 094	0.0150 463 277	0.0131 818 063	0.0115 601 378	17
18	0.0135 373 302	0.0117 549 435	0.0102 184 545	0.0088 924 137	18
19	0.0106 593 151	0.0091 835 496	0.0079 212 825	0.0068 403 182	19
20	0.0083 931 615	0.0071 746 481	0.0061 405 291	0.0052 617 832	20
21	0.0066 087 886	0.0056 051 939	0.0047 601 001	0.0040 475 256	21
22	0.0052 037 706	0.0043 790 577	0.0036 900 001	0.0031 134 812	22
23	0.0040 974 571	0.0034 211 388	0.0028 604 652	0.0023 949 855	23
24	0.0032 263 442	0.0026 727 647	0.0022 174 149	0.0018 422 966	24
25	0.0025 404 285	0.0020 880 974	0.0017 189 262	0.0014 171 512	25
26	0.0020 003 374	0.0016 313 261	0.0013 325 010	0.0010 901 163	26
27	0.0015 750 688	0.0012 744 735	0.0010 329 465	0.0008 385 510	27
28	0.0012 402 117	0.0009 956 824	0.0008 007 337	0.0006 450 392	28
29	0.0009 765 446	0.0007 778 769	0.0006 207 238	0.0004 961 840	29
30	0.0007 689 328	0.0006 077 163	0.0004 811 812	0.0003 816 800	30
31	0.0006 054 589	0.0004 747 784	0.0003 730 087	0.0002 936 000	31
32	0.0004 767 393	0.0003 709 206	0.0002 891 540	0.0002 258 462	32
33	0.0003 753 853	0.0002 897 817	0.0002 241 504	0.0001 737 278	33
34	0.0002 955 789	0.0002 263 920	0.0001 737 600	0.0001 336 368	34
35	0.0002 327 393	0.0001 768 687	0.0001 346 977	0.0001 027 975	35
36	0.0001 832 593	0.0001 381 787	0.0001 044 168	0.0000 790 750	36
37	0.0001 442 987	0.0001 079 521	0.0000 809 433	0.0000 608 269	37
38	0.0001 136 210	0.0000 843 376	0.0000 627 467	0.0000 467 900	38
39	0.0000 894 654	0.0000 658 887	0.0000 486 409	0.0000 359 923	39
40	0.0000 704 452	0.0000 514 756	0.0000 377 061	0.0000 276 864	40
41	0.0000 554 686	0.0000 402 153	0.0000 292 295	0.0000 212 972	41
42	0.0000 436 761	0.0000 314 182	0.0000 226 586	0.0000 163 825	42
43	0.0000 343 906	0.0000 245 455	0.0000 175 648	0.0000 126 019	43
44	0.0000 270 792	0.0000 191 761	0.0000 136 161	0.0000 096 938	44
45	0.0000 213 222	0.0000 149 814	0.0000 105 551	0.0000 074 567	45
46	0.0000 167 892	0.0000 117 042	0.0000 081 823	0.0000 057 360	46
47	0.0000 132 198	0.0000 091 439	0.0000 063 428	0.0000 044 123	47
48	0.0000 104 093	0.0000 071 437	0.0000 049 169	0.0000 033 941	48
49	0.0000 081 963	0.0000 055 810	0.0000 038 116	0.0000 026 108	49
50	0.0000 064 538	0.0000 043 602	0.0000 029 547	0.0000 020 083	50
51	0.0000 050 817	0.0000 034 064	0.0000 022 905	0.0000 015 449	51
52	0.0000 040 013	0.0000 026 612	0.0000 017 756	0.0000 011 884	52
53	0.0000 031 507	0.0000 020 791	0.0000 013 764	0.0000 009 141	53
54	0.0000 024 808	0.0000 016 243	0.0000 010 670	0.0000 007 032	54
55	0.0000 019 534	0.0000 012 690	0.0000 008 271	0.0000 005 409	55
56	0.0000 015 381	0.0000 009 914	0.0000 006 412	0.0000 004 161	56
57	0.0000 012 111	0.0000 007 745	0.0000 004 970	0.0000 003 201	57
58	0.0000 009 536	0.0000 006 051	0.0000 003 853	0.0000 002 462	58
59	0.0000 007 509	0.0000 004 727	0.0000 002 987	0.0000 001 894	59
60	0.0000 005 913	0.0000 003 693	0.0000 002 315	0.0000 001 457	60

TABLE 5. PRESENT WORTH OF ONE DOLLAR PER PERIOD
Payable at end of each period

YEARLY Compounding

YEARS	5% Nominal Annual Rate	5¼% Nominal Annual Rate	5½% Nominal Annual Rate	5¾% Nominal Annual Rate	YEARS
1	0.9523 809 524	0.9501 187 648	0.9478 672 986	0.9456 264 775	1
2	1.8594 104 308	1.8528 444 322	1.8463 197 143	1.8398 359 126	2
3	2.7232 480 294	2.7105 410 282	2.6979 333 785	2.6854 240 308	3
4	3.5459 505 042	3.5254 546 586	3.5051 501 218	3.4850 345 445	4
5	4.3294 766 706	4.2997 193 906	4.2702 844 756	4.2411 674 180	5
6	5.0756 920 673	5.0353 628 414	4.9955 303 086	4.9561 866 836	6
7	5.7863 733 974	5.7343 114 883	5.6829 671 172	5.6323 278 332	7
8	6.4632 127 594	6.3983 957 133	6.3345 659 879	6.2717 048 068	8
9	7.1078 216 756	7.0293 545 970	6.9521 952 492	6.8763 166 022	9
10	7.7217 349 292	7.6288 404 722	7.5376 258 286	7.4480 535 246	10
11	8.3064 142 183	8.1984 232 515	8.0925 363 304	7.9887 030 965	11
12	8.8632 516 364	8.7395 945 382	8.6185 178 487	8.4999 556 468	12
13	9.3935 729 871	9.2537 715 328	9.1170 785 296	8.9834 095 951	13
14	9.8986 409 401	9.7423 007 437	9.5896 478 954	9.4405 764 493	14
15	10.3796 580 382	10.2064 615 142	10.0375 809 435	9.8728 855 312	15
16	10.8377 695 602	10.6474 693 722	10.4621 620 317	10.2816 884 456	16
17	11.2740 662 478	11.0664 792 135	10.8646 085 609	10.6682 633 055	17
18	11.6895 869 027	11.4645 883 263	11.2460 744 653	11.0338 187 286	18
19	12.0853 208 597	11.8428 392 649	11.6076 535 216	11.3794 976 157	19
20	12.4622 103 425	12.2022 225 795	11.9503 824 849	11.7063 807 241	20
21	12.8211 527 072	12.5436 794 105	12.2752 440 615	12.0154 900 464	21
22	13.1630 025 783	12.8681 039 529	12.5831 697 266	12.3077 920 061	22
23	13.4885 738 841	13.1763 457 985	12.8750 423 949	12.5842 004 786	23
24	13.7986 417 943	13.4692 121 601	13.1516 989 525	12.8455 796 488	24
25	14.0939 445 660	13.7474 699 859	13.4139 326 564	13.0927 467 128	25
26	14.3751 853 010	14.0118 479 676	13.6624 954 089	13.3264 744 329	26
27	14.6430 336 200	14.2630 384 490	13.8980 999 136	13.5474 935 535	27
28	14.8981 272 571	14.5016 992 389	14.1214 217 191	13.7564 950 861	28
29	15.1410 735 782	14.7284 553 339	14.3331 011 555	13.9541 324 691	29
30	15.3724 510 269	14.9439 005 548	14.5337 451 711	14.1410 236 115	30
31	15.5928 105 018	15.1485 991 019	14.7239 290 722	14.3177 528 241	31
32	15.8026 766 684	15.3430 870 327	14.9041 981 727	14.4848 726 469	32
33	16.0025 492 080	15.5278 736 653	15.0750 693 580	14.6429 055 762	33
34	16.1929 040 076	15.7034 429 124	15.2370 325 668	14.7923 456 986	34
35	16.3741 942 929	15.8702 545 486	15.3905 521 960	14.9336 602 351	35
36	16.5468 517 076	16.0287 454 143	15.5360 684 322	15.0672 910 024	36
37	16.7112 873 405	16.1793 305 599	15.6739 985 140	15.1936 557 943	37
38	16.8678 927 053	16.3224 043 325	15.8047 379 279	15.3131 496 872	38
39	17.0170 406 717	16.4583 414 085	15.9286 615 431	15.4261 462 763	39
40	17.1590 863 540	16.5874 977 753	16.0461 246 854	15.5329 988 429	40
41	17.2943 679 562	16.7102 116 630	16.1574 641 568	15.6340 414 590	41
42	17.4232 075 773	16.8268 044 304	16.2629 992 007	15.7295 900 321	42
43	17.5459 119 784	16.9375 814 066	16.3630 324 177	15.8199 432 928	43
44	17.6627 733 128	17.0428 326 903	16.4578 506 329	15.9053 837 284	44
45	17.7740 698 217	17.1428 339 101	16.5477 257 184	15.9861 784 666	45
46	17.8800 664 968	17.2378 469 454	16.6329 153 729	16.0625 801 103	46
47	17.9810 157 113	17.3281 206 132	16.7136 638 606	16.1348 275 274	47
48	18.0771 578 203	17.4138 913 190	16.7902 027 114	16.2031 465 980	48
49	18.1687 217 336	17.4953 836 760	16.8627 513 853	16.2677 509 201	49
50	18.2559 254 606	17.5728 110 936	16.9315 179 007	16.3288 424 777	50
51	18.3389 766 291	17.6463 763 359	16.9966 994 320	16.3866 122 720	51
52	18.4180 729 801	17.7162 720 532	17.0584 828 739	16.4412 409 192	52
53	18.4934 028 382	17.7826 812 857	17.1170 453 781	16.4928 992 143	53
54	18.5651 455 602	17.8457 779 436	17.1725 548 608	16.5417 486 660	54
55	18.6334 719 621	17.9057 272 623	17.2251 704 841	16.5879 420 010	55
56	18.6985 447 258	17.9626 862 350	17.2750 431 129	16.6316 236 416	56
57	18.7605 187 865	18.0168 040 238	17.3223 157 468	16.6729 301 575	57
58	18.8195 417 014	18.0682 223 504	17.3671 239 307	16.7119 906 927	58
59	18.8757 540 013	18.1170 758 673	17.4095 961 428	16.7489 273 690	59
60	18.9292 895 251	18.1634 925 105	17.4498 541 638	16.7838 556 681	60

YEARLY
Compounding

TABLE 5. PRESENT WORTH OF ONE DOLLAR PER PERIOD
Payable at end of each period

YEARS	6% Nominal Annual Rate	6¼% Nominal Annual Rate	6½% Nominal Annual Rate	6¾% Nominal Annual Rate	YEARS
1	0.9433 962 264	0.9411 764 706	0.9389 671 362	0.9367 681 499	1
2	1.8333 926 664	1.8269 896 194	1.8206 264 189	1.8143 027 165	2
3	2.6730 119 495	2.6606 961 124	2.6484 755 107	2.6363 491 490	3
4	3.4651 056 127	3.4453 610 469	3.4257 986 016	3.4064 160 646	4
5	4.2123 637 856	4.1838 692 206	4.1556 794 381	4.1277 902 245	5
6	4.9173 243 260	4.8789 357 371	4.8410 135 569	4.8035 505 615	6
7	5.5823 814 396	5.5331 159 878	5.4845 197 718	5.4365 813 223	7
8	6.2097 938 110	6.1488 150 474	6.0887 509 594	6.0295 843 769	8
9	6.8016 922 745	6.7282 965 152	6.6561 041 872	6.5850 907 512	9
10	7.3600 870 514	7.2736 908 378	7.1888 302 228	7.1054 714 297	10
11	7.8868 745 768	7.7870 031 415	7.6890 424 627	7.5929 474 751	11
12	8.3838 439 404	8.2701 206 037	8.1587 253 171	8.0495 995 083	12
13	8.8526 829 626	8.7248 193 917	8.5997 420 818	8.4773 765 885	13
14	9.2949 839 270	9.1527 711 922	9.0138 423 303	8.8781 045 326	14
15	9.7122 489 877	9.5555 493 574	9.4026 688 547	9.2534 937 074	15
16	10.1058 952 715	9.9346 346 893	9.7677 641 828	9.6051 463 301	16
17	10.4772 596 901	10.2914 208 841	10.1105 766 975	9.9345 633 069	17
18	10.8276 034 812	10.6272 196 556	10.4324 663 826	10.2431 506 387	18
19	11.1581 164 917	10.9432 655 582	10.7347 102 184	10.5322 254 227	19
20	11.4699 212 186	11.2407 205 254	11.0185 072 474	10.8030 214 733	20
21	11.7640 766 213	11.5206 781 415	11.2849 833 309	11.0566 945 885	21
22	12.0415 817 182	11.7841 676 626	11.5351 956 158	11.2943 274 834	22
23	12.3033 789 794	12.0321 578 001	11.7701 367 285	11.5169 344 107	23
24	12.5503 575 278	12.2655 602 824	11.9907 387 122	11.7254 654 901	24
25	12.7833 561 583	12.4852 332 070	12.1978 767 251	11.9208 107 636	25
26	13.0031 661 870	12.6919 841 948	12.3923 725 118	12.1038 039 940	26
27	13.2105 341 387	12.8865 733 598	12.5749 976 637	12.2752 262 239	27
28	13.4061 642 818	13.0697 161 034	12.7464 766 795	12.4358 091 090	28
29	13.5907 210 206	13.2420 857 444	12.9074 898 399	12.5862 380 412	29
30	13.7648 311 515	13.4043 159 947	13.0586 759 060	12.7271 550 737	30
31	13.9290 859 920	13.5570 032 891	13.2006 346 535	12.8591 616 616	31
32	14.0840 433 887	13.7007 089 780	13.3339 292 521	12.9828 212 287	32
33	14.2302 296 119	13.8359 613 911	13.4590 884 997	13.0986 615 725	33
34	14.3681 411 433	13.9632 577 798	13.5766 089 199	13.2071 771 171	34
35	14.4982 463 616	14.0830 661 457	13.6869 567 323	13.3088 310 230	35
36	14.6209 871 336	14.1958 269 607	13.7905 697 017	13.4040 571 644	36
37	14.7367 803 147	14.3019 547 865	13.8878 588 748	13.4932 619 807	37
38	14.8460 191 648	14.4018 397 991	13.9792 102 111	13.5768 262 115	38
39	14.9490 746 838	14.4958 492 227	14.0649 861 137	13.6551 065 213	39
40	15.0462 968 715	14.5843 286 801	14.1455 268 673	13.7284 370 223	40
41	15.1380 159 165	14.6676 034 637	14.2211 519 881	13.7971 307 000	41
42	15.2245 433 175	14.7459 797 305	14.2921 614 912	13.8614 807 494	42
43	15.3061 729 410	14.8197 456 287	14.3588 370 809	13.9217 618 262	43
44	15.3831 820 198	14.8891 723 564	14.4214 432 685	13.9782 312 189	44
45	15.4558 320 942	14.9545 151 590	14.4802 284 211	14.0311 299 474	45
46	15.5243 699 002	15.0160 142 673	14.5354 257 475	14.0806 837 915	46
47	15.5890 282 077	15.0738 957 810	14.5872 542 230	14.1271 042 544	47
48	15.6500 266 110	15.1283 724 997	14.6359 194 582	14.1705 894 654	48
49	15.7075 722 746	15.1796 447 056	14.6816 145 148	14.2113 250 262	49
50	15.7618 606 364	15.2279 008 994	14.7245 206 711	14.2494 848 020	50
51	15.8130 760 721	15.2733 184 936	14.7648 081 419	14.2852 316 647	51
52	15.8613 925 208	15.3160 644 645	14.8026 367 530	14.3187 181 870	52
53	15.9069 740 762	15.3562 959 666	14.8381 565 756	14.3500 872 947	53
54	15.9499 755 436	15.3941 609 098	14.8715 085 216	14.3794 728 756	54
55	15.9905 429 657	15.4297 985 033	14.9028 249 030	14.4070 003 518	55
56	16.0288 141 186	15.4633 397 678	14.9322 299 558	14.4327 872 148	56
57	16.0649 189 798	15.4949 080 168	14.9598 403 341	14.4569 435 267	57
58	16.0989 801 696	15.5246 193 099	14.9857 655 719	14.4795 723 904	58
59	16.1311 133 676	15.5525 828 799	15.0101 085 182	14.5007 703 891	59
60	16.1614 277 052	15.5789 015 340	15.0329 657 448	14.5206 279 992	60

TABLE 5. PRESENT WORTH OF ONE DOLLAR PER PERIOD
Payable at end of each period

YEARLY Compounding

YEARS	7% Nominal Annual Rate	7¼% Nominal Annual Rate	7½% Nominal Annual Rate	7¾% Nominal Annual Rate	YEARS
1	0.9345 794 393	0.9324 009 324	0.9302 325 581	0.9280 742 459	1
2	1.8080 181 675	1.8017 724 311	1.7955 651 704	1.7893 960 519	2
3	2.6243 160 444	2.6123 752 272	2.6005 257 399	2.5887 666 375	3
4	3.3872 112 565	3.3681 820 300	3.3493 262 696	3.3306 418 910	4
5	4.1001 974 359	4.0728 969 977	4.0458 849 020	4.0191 572 074	5
6	4.7665 396 598	4.7299 738 906	4.6938 464 205	4.6581 505 405	6
7	5.3892 894 016	5.3426 329 982	5.2966 013 214	5.2511 837 963	7
8	5.9712 985 062	5.9138 769 214	5.8573 035 548	5.8015 626 880	8
9	6.5152 322 488	6.4465 052 880	6.3788 870 277	6.3123 551 628	9
10	7.0235 815 409	6.9431 284 737	6.8640 809 560	6.7864 085 038	10
11	7.4986 743 373	7.4061 803 951	7.3154 241 451	7.2263 652 007	11
12	7.9426 862 966	7.8379 304 383	7.7352 782 745	7.6346 776 805	12
13	8.3576 507 444	8.2404 945 811	8.1258 402 554	8.0136 219 773	13
14	8.7454 679 855	8.6158 457 633	8.4891 537 259	8.3653 104 197	14
15	9.1079 140 051	8.9658 235 555	8.8271 197 450	8.6917 034 058	15
16	9.4466 486 029	9.2921 431 753	9.1415 067 396	8.9946 203 302	16
17	9.7632 229 934	9.5964 038 931	9.4339 597 577	9.2757 497 264	17
18	10.0590 869 097	9.8800 968 700	9.7060 090 770	9.5366 586 788	18
19	10.3355 952 427	10.1446 124 662	9.9590 782 111	9.7788 015 580	19
20	10.5940 142 455	10.3912 470 547	10.1944 913 592	10.0035 281 281	20
21	10.8355 273 323	10.6212 093 750	10.4134 803 341	10.2120 910 702	21
22	11.0612 404 974	10.8356 264 569	10.6171 910 085	10.4056 529 654	22
23	11.2721 873 808	11.0355 491 440	10.8066 893 102	10.5852 927 753	23
24	11.4693 340 007	11.2219 572 438	10.9829 668 002	10.7520 118 564	24
25	11.6535 831 783	11.3957 643 299	11.1469 458 607	10.9067 395 419	25
26	11.8257 786 713	11.5578 222 190	11.2994 845 215	11.0503 383 220	26
27	11.9867 090 386	11.7089 251 459	11.4413 809 503	11.1836 086 515	27
28	12.1371 112 510	11.8498 136 559	11.5733 776 282	11.3072 934 120	28
29	12.2776 740 664	11.9811 782 339	11.6961 652 355	11.4220 820 529	29
30	12.4090 411 835	12.1036 626 890	11.8103 862 656	11.5286 144 343	30
31	12.5318 141 902	12.2178 673 091	11.9166 383 866	11.6274 843 938	31
32	12.6465 553 179	12.3243 518 033	12.0154 775 689	11.7192 430 569	32
33	12.7537 900 168	12.4236 380 451	12.1074 209 943	11.8044 019 089	33
34	12.8540 093 615	12.5162 126 294	12.1929 497 622	11.8834 356 463	34
35	12.9476 723 004	12.6025 292 582	12.2725 114 067	11.9567 848 226	35
36	13.0352 077 574	12.6830 109 634	12.3465 222 388	12.0248 583 040	36
37	13.1170 165 957	12.7580 521 803	12.4153 695 244	12.0880 355 490	37
38	13.1934 734 539	12.8280 206 809	12.4794 135 111	12.1466 687 229	38
39	13.2649 284 616	12.8932 593 761	12.5389 893 127	12.2010 846 617	39
40	13.3317 088 426	12.9540 879 964	12.5944 086 629	12.2515 866 930	40
41	13.3941 204 137	13.0108 046 587	12.6459 615 469	12.2984 563 276	41
42	13.4524 489 847	13.0636 873 274	12.6939 177 181	12.3419 548 284	42
43	13.5069 616 680	13.1129 951 771	12.7385 281 098	12.3823 246 667	43
44	13.5579 081 009	13.1589 698 621	12.7800 261 487	12.4197 908 740	44
45	13.6055 215 896	13.2018 367 012	12.8186 289 755	12.4545 622 960	45
46	13.6500 201 772	13.2418 057 820	12.8545 385 819	12.4868 327 573	46
47	13.6916 076 423	13.2790 729 902	12.8879 428 669	12.5167 821 414	47
48	13.7304 744 320	13.3138 209 699	12.9190 166 203	12.5445 773 934	48
49	13.7667 985 346	13.3462 200 186	12.9479 224 375	12.5703 734 509	49
50	13.8007 462 940	13.3764 289 218	12.9748 115 698	12.5943 141 076	50
51	13.8324 731 720	13.4045 957 312	12.9998 247 161	12.6165 328 145	51
52	13.8621 244 598	13.4308 584 907	13.0230 927 591	12.6371 534 241	52
53	13.8898 359 437	13.4553 459 120	13.0447 374 504	12.6562 908 808	53
54	13.9157 345 269	13.4781 780 066	13.0648 720 469	12.6740 518 616	54
55	13.9399 388 102	13.4994 666 728	13.0836 019 040	12.6905 353 704	55
56	13.9625 596 357	13.5193 162 450	13.1010 250 270	12.7058 332 904	56
57	13.9837 005 941	13.5378 240 047	13.1172 325 833	12.7200 308 959	57
58	14.0034 584 991	13.5550 806 570	13.1323 093 798	12.7332 073 280	58
59	14.0219 238 310	13.5711 707 758	13.1463 343 068	12.7454 360 353	59
60	14.0391 811 504	13.5861 732 175	13.1593 807 505	12.7567 851 836	60

TABLE 5. PRESENT WORTH OF ONE DOLLAR PER PERIOD
Payable at end of each period

YEARS	8% Nominal Annual Rate	8¼% Nominal Annual Rate	8½% Nominal Annual Rate	8¾% Nominal Annual Rate	YEARS
1	0.9259 259 259	0.9237 875 289	0.9216 589 862	0.9195 402 299	1
2	1.7832 647 462	1.7771 709 274	1.7711 142 730	1.7650 944 643	2
3	2.5770 969 872	2.5655 158 682	2.5540 223 714	2.5426 155 993	3
4	3.3121 268 400	3.2937 790 931	3.2755 966 557	3.2575 775 626	4
5	3.9927 100 371	3.9665 395 779	3.9406 420 790	3.9150 138 507	5
6	4.6228 796 640	4.5880 273 237	4.5535 871 695	4.5195 529 661	6
7	5.2063 700 592	5.1621 499 526	5.1185 135 203	5.0754 510 033	7
8	5.7466 389 437	5.6925 172 772	5.6391 829 680	5.5866 216 123	8
9	6.2468 879 109	6.1824 639 974	6.1190 626 434	6.0566 635 515	9
10	6.7100 813 989	6.6350 706 674	6.5613 480 584	6.4888 860 244	10
11	7.1389 642 583	7.0531 830 645	6.9689 843 856	6.8863 319 764	11
12	7.5360 780 169	7.4394 300 827	7.3446 860 697	7.2517 995 186	12
13	7.9037 759 416	7.7962 402 612	7.6909 549 029	7.5878 616 263	13
14	8.2442 369 830	8.1258 570 542	8.0100 966 847	7.8968 842 540	14
15	8.5594 786 879	8.4303 529 369	8.3042 365 758	8.1810 429 922	15
16	8.8513 691 555	8.7116 424 359	8.5753 332 496	8.4423 383 836	16
17	9.1216 381 069	8.9714 941 672	8.8251 919 351	8.6826 100 080	17
18	9.3718 871 360	9.2115 419 558	9.0554 764 379	8.9035 494 326	18
19	9.6035 992 000	9.4332 951 093	9.2677 202 192	9.1067 121 219	19
20	9.8181 474 074	9.6381 479 070	9.4633 366 076	9.2935 283 880	20
21	10.0168 031 550	9.8273 883 667	9.6436 282 098	9.4653 134 602	21
22	10.2007 436 621	10.0022 063 434	9.8097 955 850	9.6232 767 450	22
23	10.3710 589 464	10.1637 010 100	9.9629 452 397	9.7685 303 403	23
24	10.5287 582 837	10.3128 877 691	10.1040 969 951	9.9020 968 646	24
25	10.6747 761 886	10.4507 046 366	10.2341 907 789	10.0249 166 571	25
26	10.8099 779 524	10.5780 181 400	10.3540 928 838	10.1378 543 973	26
27	10.9351 647 707	10.6956 287 668	10.4646 017 362	10.2417 051 930	27
28	11.0510 784 914	10.8042 759 970	10.5664 532 131	10.3372 001 774	28
29	11.1584 060 106	10.9046 429 534	10.6603 255 420	10.4250 116 574	29
30	11.2577 833 431	10.9973 606 959	10.7468 438 175	10.5057 578 459	30
31	11.3497 993 918	11.0830 121 903	10.8265 841 636	10.5800 072 146	31
32	11.4349 994 368	11.1621 359 725	10.9000 775 701	10.6482 824 962	32
33	11.5138 883 674	11.2352 295 358	10.9678 134 287	10.7110 643 643	33
34	11.5869 336 736	11.3027 524 580	11.0302 427 914	10.7687 948 178	34
35	11.6545 682 163	11.3651 292 915	11.0877 813 746	10.8218 802 922	35
36	11.7171 927 928	11.4227 522 323	11.1408 123 268	10.8706 945 216	36
37	11.7751 785 119	11.4759 835 864	11.1896 887 805	10.9155 811 692	37
38	11.8288 689 925	11.5251 580 475	11.2347 362 032	10.9568 562 476	38
39	11.8785 824 004	11.5705 848 014	11.2762 545 652	10.9948 103 426	39
40	11.9246 133 337	11.6125 494 701	11.3145 203 366	11.0297 106 599	40
41	11.9672 345 683	11.6513 159 077	11.3497 883 286	11.0618 029 056	41
42	12.0066 986 743	11.6871 278 593	11.3822 933 904	11.0913 130 167	42
43	12.0432 395 133	11.7202 104 936	11.4122 519 728	11.1184 487 510	43
44	12.0770 736 234	11.7507 718 186	11.4398 635 694	11.1434 011 503	44
45	12.1084 015 032	11.7790 039 894	11.4653 120 455	11.1663 458 853	45
46	12.1374 087 992	11.8050 845 168	11.4887 668 622	11.1874 444 923	46
47	12.1642 674 067	11.8291 773 827	11.5103 842 048	11.2068 455 101	47
48	12.1891 364 877	11.8514 340 718	11.5303 080 229	11.2246 855 266	48
49	12.2121 634 145	11.8719 945 236	11.5486 709 888	11.2410 901 394	49
50	12.2334 846 431	11.8909 880 126	11.5655 953 814	11.2561 748 408	50
51	12.2532 265 214	11.9085 339 608	11.5811 938 999	11.2700 458 306	51
52	12.2715 060 383	11.9247 426 890	11.5955 704 146	11.2828 007 638	52
53	12.2884 315 169	11.9397 161 099	11.6088 206 587	11.2945 294 380	53
54	12.3041 032 564	11.9535 483 694	11.6210 328 651	11.3053 144 257	54
55	12.3186 141 263	11.9663 264 383	11.6322 883 550	11.3152 316 558	55
56	12.3320 501 170	11.9781 306 589	11.6426 620 783	11.3243 509 479	56
57	12.3444 908 490	11.9890 352 507	11.6522 231 136	11.3327 365 038	57
58	12.3560 100 454	11.9991 087 766	11.6610 351 278	11.3404 473 598	58
59	12.3666 759 680	12.0084 145 743	11.6691 567 998	11.3475 378 021	59
60	12.3765 518 222	12.0170 111 541	11.6766 422 118	11.3540 577 491	60

TABLE 5. PRESENT WORTH OF ONE DOLLAR PER PERIOD
Payable at end of each period

YEARLY Compounding

YEARS	9% Nominal Annual Rate	9¼% Nominal Annual Rate	9½% Nominal Annual Rate	9¾% Nominal Annual Rate	YEARS
1	0.9174 311 927	0.9153 318 078	0.9132 420 091	0.9111 617 312	1
2	1.7591 111 859	1.7531 641 261	1.7472 529 764	1.7413 774 316	2
3	2.5312 946 660	2.5200 586 967	2.5089 068 277	2.4978 382 065	3
4	3.2397 198 771	3.2220 216 903	3.2044 811 212	3.1870 963 157	4
5	3.8896 512 634	3.8645 507 463	3.8397 087 865	3.8151 219 278	5
6	4.4859 185 902	4.4526 780 286	4.4198 253 758	4.3873 548 317	6
7	5.0329 528 351	4.9910 096 372	4.9496 122 153	4.9087 515 550	7
8	5.5348 191 147	5.4837 616 816	5.4334 358 131	5.3838 282 962	8
9	5.9952 468 943	5.9347 933 013	5.8752 838 476	5.8167 000 421	9
10	6.4176 577 012	6.3476 368 890	6.2787 980 343	6.2111 162 115	10
11	6.8051 905 515	6.7255 257 566	6.6473 041 409	6.5704 931 312	11
12	7.1607 252 766	7.0714 194 568	6.9838 393 981	6.8979 436 275	12
13	7.4869 039 235	7.3880 269 627	7.2911 775 325	7.1963 039 886	13
14	7.7861 503 885	7.6778 278 835	7.5718 516 279	7.4681 585 318	14
15	8.0606 884 299	7.9430 918 842	7.8281 750 026	7.7158 619 879	15
16	8.3125 581 925	8.1858 964 615	8.0622 602 764	7.9415 598 979	16
17	8.5436 313 693	8.4081 432 142	8.2760 367 821	8.1472 071 963	17
18	8.7556 251 094	8.6115 727 361	8.4712 664 676	8.3345 851 446	18
19	8.9501 147 793	8.7977 782 482	8.6495 584 179	8.5053 167 605	19
20	9.1285 456 691	8.9682 180 761	8.8123 821 168	8.6608 808 752	20
21	9.2922 437 331	9.1242 270 720	8.9610 795 588	8.8026 249 432	21
22	9.4424 254 432	9.2670 270 682	9.0968 763 094	8.9317 767 136	22
23	9.5802 068 286	9.3977 364 468	9.2208 916 067	9.0494 548 644	23
24	9.7066 117 694	9.5173 788 987	9.3341 475 861	9.1566 786 919	24
25	9.8225 796 049	9.6268 914 405	9.4375 777 042	9.2543 769 402	25
26	9.9289 721 146	9.7271 317 533	9.5320 344 330	9.3433 958 453	26
27	10.0265 799 217	9.8188 849 000	9.6182 962 859	9.4245 064 650	27
28	10.1161 283 685	9.9028 694 737	9.6970 742 337	9.4984 113 576	28
29	10.1982 829 069	9.9797 432 254	9.7690 175 650	9.5657 506 675	29
30	10.2736 540 430	10.0501 082 154	9.8347 192 374	9.6271 076 697	30
31	10.3428 018 743	10.1145 155 290	9.8947 207 648	9.6830 138 221	31
32	10.4062 402 517	10.1734 695 918	9.9495 166 802	9.7339 533 686	32
33	10.4644 405 979	10.2274 321 206	9.9995 586 120	9.7803 675 341	33
34	10.5178 354 109	10.2768 257 397	10.0452 590 064	9.8226 583 454	34
35	10.5668 214 779	10.3220 372 903	10.0869 945 264	9.8611 921 142	35
36	10.6117 628 237	10.3634 208 607	10.1251 091 565	9.8963 026 098	36
37	10.6529 934 163	10.4013 005 590	10.1599 170 379	9.9282 939 497	37
38	10.6908 196 480	10.4359 730 517	10.1917 050 575	9.9574 432 343	38
39	10.7255 226 128	10.4677 098 872	10.2207 352 123	9.9840 029 470	39
40	10.7573 601 952	10.4967 596 221	10.2472 467 692	10.0082 031 408	40
41	10.7865 689 865	10.5233 497 685	10.2714 582 367	10.0302 534 312	41
42	10.8133 660 426	10.5476 885 753	10.2935 691 660	10.0503 448 121	42
43	10.8379 504 978	10.5699 666 593	10.3137 617 954	10.0686 513 094	43
44	10.8605 050 439	10.5903 584 982	10.3322 025 529	10.0853 314 892	44
45	10.8811 972 880	10.6090 237 970	10.3490 434 273	10.1005 298 307	45
46	10.9001 809 981	10.6261 087 387	10.3644 232 213	10.1143 779 779	46
47	10.9175 972 460	10.6417 471 292	10.3784 686 952	10.1269 958 796	47
48	10.9335 754 550	10.6560 614 455	10.3912 956 121	10.1384 928 288	48
49	10.9482 343 624	10.6691 637 945	10.4030 096 914	10.1489 684 089	49
50	10.9616 829 013	10.6811 567 913	10.4137 074 807	10.1585 133 567	50
51	10.9740 210 104	10.6921 343 628	10.4234 771 513	10.1672 103 477	51
52	10.9853 403 765	10.7021 824 831	10.4323 992 250	10.1751 347 132	52
53	10.9957 251 160	10.7113 798 472	10.4405 472 374	10.1823 550 918	53
54	11.0052 524 000	10.7197 984 872	10.4479 883 447	10.1889 340 244	54
55	11.0139 930 276	10.7275 043 361	10.4547 838 764	10.1949 284 960	55
56	11.0220 119 519	10.7345 577 447	10.4609 898 415	10.2003 904 292	56
57	11.0293 687 632	10.7410 139 539	10.4666 573 895	10.2053 671 336	57
58	11.0361 181 314	10.7469 235 276	10.4718 332 324	10.2099 017 163	58
59	11.0423 102 123	10.7523 327 484	10.4765 600 296	10.2140 334 545	59
60	11.0479 910 204	10.7572 839 802	10.4808 767 393	10.2177 981 362	60

YEARLY Compounding

TABLE 5. PRESENT WORTH OF ONE DOLLAR PER PERIOD
Payable at end of each period

YEARS	10% Nominal Annual Rate	10¼% Nominal Annual Rate	10½% Nominal Annual Rate	10¾% Nominal Annual Rate	YEARS
1	0.9090 909 091	0.9070 294 785	0.9049 773 756	0.9029 345 372	1
2	1.7355 371 901	1.7297 319 532	1.7239 614 259	1.7182 253 158	2
3	2.4868 519 910	2.4759 473 499	2.4651 234 623	2.4543 795 177	3
4	3.1698 654 463	3.1527 867 119	3.1358 583 369	3.1190 785 712	4
5	3.7907 867 694	3.7666 999 655	3.7428 582 235	3.7192 583 036	5
6	4.3552 606 995	4.3235 373 836	4.2921 793 878	4.2611 813 125	6
7	4.8684 188 177	4.8286 053 366	4.7893 026 134	4.7505 023 138	7
8	5.3349 261 979	5.2867 168 586	5.2391 878 854	5.1923 271 456	8
9	5.7590 238 163	5.7022 375 135	5.6463 238 782	5.5912 660 457	9
10	6.1445 671 057	6.0791 269 964	6.0147 727 404	5.9514 817 568	10
11	6.4950 610 052	6.4209 768 674	6.3482 106 248	6.2767 329 633	11
12	6.8136 918 229	6.7310 447 777	6.6499 643 664	6.5704 135 109	12
13	7.1033 562 026	7.0122 855 127	6.9230 446 754	6.8355 878 202	13
14	7.3666 874 569	7.2673 791 498	7.1701 761 769	7.0750 228 625	14
15	7.6060 795 063	7.4987 565 985	7.3938 245 944	7.2912 170 316	15
16	7.8237 086 421	7.7086 227 651	7.5962 213 524	7.4864 262 136	16
17	8.0215 533 110	7.8989 775 647	7.7793 858 393	7.6626 873 261	17
18	8.2014 121 009	8.0716 349 793	7.9451 455 559	7.8218 395 721	18
19	8.3649 200 917	8.2282 403 440	8.0951 543 493	7.9655 436 317	19
20	8.5135 637 198	8.3702 860 263	8.2309 089 134	8.0952 989 902	20
21	8.6486 942 907	8.4991 256 475	8.3537 637 225	8.2124 595 849	21
22	8.7715 402 643	8.6159 869 818	8.4649 445 453	8.3182 479 321	22
23	8.8832 184 221	8.7219 836 570	8.5655 606 744	8.4137 678 846	23
24	8.9847 440 201	8.8181 257 660	8.6566 159 950	8.5000 161 486	24
25	9.0770 400 182	8.9053 294 930	8.7390 190 000	8.5778 926 850	25
26	9.1609 454 711	8.9844 258 439	8.8135 918 552	8.6482 100 993	26
27	9.2372 231 556	9.0561 685 659	8.8810 786 020	8.7117 021 212	27
28	9.3065 665 051	9.1212 413 296	8.9421 525 810	8.7690 312 607	28
29	9.3696 059 137	9.1802 642 446	8.9974 231 502	8.8207 957 207	29
30	9.4269 144 670	9.2337 997 683	9.0474 417 649	8.8675 356 395	30
31	9.4790 131 518	9.2823 580 665	9.0927 074 795	8.9097 387 264	31
32	9.5263 755 926	9.3264 018 744	9.1336 719 272	8.9478 453 512	32
33	9.5694 323 569	9.3663 509 065	9.1707 438 255	8.9822 531 387	33
34	9.6085 748 699	9.4025 858 562	9.2042 930 548	9.0133 211 185	34
35	9.6441 589 726	9.4354 520 238	9.2346 543 482	9.0413 734 704	35
36	9.6765 081 569	9.4652 626 066	9.2621 306 318	9.0667 029 078	36
37	9.7059 165 063	9.4923 016 840	9.2869 960 469	9.0895 737 317	37
38	9.7326 513 694	9.5168 269 243	9.3094 986 850	9.1102 245 884	38
39	9.7569 557 903	9.5390 720 401	9.3298 630 633	9.1288 709 602	39
40	9.7790 507 185	9.5592 490 160	9.3482 923 650	9.1457 074 133	40
41	9.7991 370 168	9.5775 501 279	9.3649 704 661	9.1609 096 282	41
42	9.8173 972 880	9.5941 497 759	9.3800 637 702	9.1746 362 332	42
43	9.8339 975 345	9.6092 061 459	9.3937 228 690	9.1870 304 588	43
44	9.8490 886 678	9.6228 627 174	9.4060 840 443	9.1982 216 333	44
45	9.8628 078 798	9.6352 496 303	9.4172 706 283	9.2083 265 312	45
46	9.8752 798 907	9.6464 849 254	9.4273 942 338	9.2174 505 925	46
47	9.8866 180 825	9.6566 756 693	9.4365 558 677	9.2256 890 226	47
48	9.8969 255 295	9.6659 189 744	9.4448 469 391	9.2331 277 856	48
49	9.9062 959 359	9.6743 029 247	9.4523 501 711	9.2398 445 017	49
50	9.9148 144 872	9.6819 074 147	9.4591 404 263	9.2459 092 566	50
51	9.9225 586 247	9.6888 049 113	9.4652 854 537	9.2513 853 333	51
52	9.9295 987 498	9.6950 611 440	9.4708 465 644	9.2563 298 720	52
53	9.9359 988 634	9.7007 357 315	9.4758 792 438	9.2607 944 668	53
54	9.9418 171 486	9.7058 827 497	9.4804 337 048	9.2648 257 037	54
55	9.9471 064 987	9.7105 512 469	9.4845 553 890	9.2684 656 467	55
56	9.9519 149 988	9.7147 857 114	9.4882 854 199	9.2717 522 769	56
57	9.9562 863 626	9.7186 264 956	9.4916 610 135	9.2747 198 889	57
58	9.9602 603 296	9.7221 102 001	9.4947 158 493	9.2773 994 402	58
59	9.9638 730 269	9.7252 700 228	9.4974 804 066	9.2798 189 148	59
60	9.9671 572 972	9.7281 360 751	9.4999 822 684	9.2820 035 348	60

TABLE 5. PRESENT WORTH OF ONE DOLLAR PER PERIOD
Payable at end of each period

YEARLY Compounding

YEARS	11% Nominal Annual Rate	11¼% Nominal Annual Rate	11½% Nominal Annual Rate	11¾% Nominal Annual Rate	YEARS
1	0.9009 009 009	0.8988 764 045	0.8968 609 865	0.8948 545 861	1
2	1.7125 233 341	1.7068 551 951	1.7012 206 157	1.6956 193 164	2
3	2.4437 147 154	2.4331 282 652	2.4226 193 863	2.4121 873 078	3
4	3.1024 456 896	3.0859 579 912	3.0696 137 994	3.0534 114 611	4
5	3.6958 970 176	3.6727 712 280	3.6498 778 470	3.6272 138 354	5
6	4.2305 378 537	4.2002 438 005	4.1702 940 332	4.1406 835 216	6
7	4.7121 962 646	4.6743 764 499	4.6370 350 073	4.6001 642 252	7
8	5.1461 227 609	5.1005 631 010	5.0556 367 779	5.0113 326 400	8
9	5.5370 475 324	5.4836 522 256	5.4310 643 748	5.3792 685 816	9
10	5.8892 320 111	5.8280 020 006	5.7677 707 397	5.7085 177 464	10
11	6.2065 153 254	6.1375 298 882	6.0697 495 423	6.0031 478 715	11
12	6.4923 561 490	6.4157 572 028	6.3405 825 492	6.2667 989 902	12
13	6.7498 704 045	6.6658 491 711	6.5834 821 069	6.5027 284 029	13
14	6.9818 652 293	6.8906 509 403	6.8013 292 438	6.7138 509 198	14
15	7.1908 695 759	7.0927 199 463	6.9967 078 420	6.9027 748 723	15
16	7.3791 617 801	7.2743 550 079	7.1719 352 843	7.0718 343 376	16
17	7.5487 943 965	7.4376 224 791	7.3290 899 411	7.2231 179 755	17
18	7.7016 165 734	7.5843 797 565	7.4700 358 216	7.3584 948 327	18
19	7.8392 942 103	7.7162 964 103	7.5964 446 831	7.4796 374 341	19
20	7.9633 281 174	7.8348 731 778	7.7098 158 592	7.5880 424 467	20
21	8.0750 703 760	7.9414 590 362	7.8114 940 442	7.6850 491 693	21
22	8.1757 390 775	8.0372 665 494	7.9026 852 414	7.7718 560 799	22
23	8.2664 316 013	8.1233 856 624	7.9844 710 685	7.8495 356 420	23
24	8.3481 365 778	8.2007 961 010	8.0578 215 861	7.9190 475 543	24
25	8.4217 446 647	8.2703 785 178	8.1236 068 037	7.9812 506 079	25
26	8.4880 582 565	8.3329 245 104	8.1826 069 988	8.0369 132 957	26
27	8.5478 002 310	8.3891 456 273	8.2355 219 720	8.0867 233 071	27
28	8.6016 218 298	8.4396 814 627	8.2829 793 471	8.1312 960 242	28
29	8.6501 097 565	8.4851 069 328	8.3255 420 154	8.1711 821 246	29
30	8.6937 925 735	8.5259 388 160	8.3637 148 120	8.2068 743 844	30
31	8.7331 464 626	8.5626 416 324	8.3979 505 040	8.2388 137 668	31
32	8.7686 004 167	8.5956 329 280	8.4286 551 606	8.2673 948 696	32
33	8.8005 409 160	8.6252 880 251	8.4561 929 691	8.2929 708 006	33
34	8.8293 161 405	8.6519 442 923	8.4808 905 553	8.3158 575 397	34
35	8.8552 397 662	8.6759 049 818	8.5030 408 567	8.3363 378 431	35
36	8.8785 943 840	8.6974 426 803	8.5229 065 980	8.3546 647 366	36
37	8.8996 345 802	8.7168 024 092	8.5407 234 062	8.3710 646 412	37
38	8.9185 897 119	8.7342 044 128	8.5567 026 065	8.3857 401 711	38
39	8.9356 664 071	8.7498 466 632	8.5710 337 278	8.3988 726 363	39
40	8.9510 508 172	8.7639 071 130	8.5838 867 514	8.4106 242 831	40
41	8.9649 106 461	8.7765 457 195	8.5954 141 268	8.4211 402 981	41
42	8.9773 969 785	8.7879 062 647	8.6057 525 801	8.4305 506 023	42
43	8.9886 459 266	8.7981 179 908	8.6150 247 355	8.4389 714 562	43
44	8.9987 801 140	8.8072 970 704	8.6233 405 700	8.4465 068 959	44
45	9.0079 100 126	8.8155 479 284	8.6307 987 175	8.4532 500 187	45
46	9.0161 351 465	8.8229 644 300	8.6374 876 390	8.4592 841 331	46
47	9.0235 451 770	8.8296 309 483	8.6434 866 717	8.4646 837 880	47
48	9.0302 208 802	8.8356 233 244	8.6488 669 702	8.4695 156 939	48
49	9.0362 350 272	8.8410 097 298	8.6536 923 499	8.4738 395 472	49
50	9.0416 531 777	8.8458 514 425	8.6580 200 448	8.4777 087 670	50
51	9.0465 343 943	8.8502 035 438	8.6619 013 854	8.4811 711 562	51
52	9.0509 318 868	8.8541 155 450	8.6653 824 085	8.4842 694 910	52
53	9.0548 935 917	8.8576 319 506	8.6685 044 022	8.4870 420 501	53
54	9.0584 626 952	8.8607 927 645	8.6713 043 966	8.4895 230 873	54
55	9.0616 781 038	8.8636 339 457	8.6738 156 023	8.4917 432 549	55
56	9.0645 748 683	8.8661 878 163	8.6760 678 048	8.4937 299 820	56
57	9.0671 845 660	8.8684 834 304	8.6780 877 173	8.4955 078 139	57
58	9.0695 356 451	8.8705 469 037	8.6798 992 980	8.4970 987 149	58
59	9.0716 537 343	8.8724 017 112	8.6815 240 341	8.4985 223 390	59
60	9.0735 619 228	8.8740 689 539	8.6829 811 965	8.4997 962 773	60

TABLE 5. PRESENT WORTH OF ONE DOLLAR PER PERIOD
Payable at end of each period

YEARS	12% Nominal Annual Rate	12¼% Nominal Annual Rate	12½% Nominal Annual Rate	12¾% Nominal Annual Rate	YEARS
1	0.8928 571 429	0.8908 685 969	0.8888 888 889	0.8869 179 601	1
2	1.6900 510 204	1.6845 154 538	1.6790 123 457	1.6735 414 280	2
3	2.4018 312 682	2.3915 505 156	2.3813 443 073	2.3712 119 095	3
4	3.0373 493 466	3.0214 258 491	3.0056 393 842	2.9899 883 898	4
5	3.6047 762 023	3.5825 620 037	3.5605 683 415	3.5387 923 635	5
6	4.1114 073 235	4.0824 605 823	4.0538 385 258	4.0255 364 643	6
7	4.5637 565 389	4.5278 045 277	4.4923 009 118	4.4572 385 493	7
8	4.9676 397 668	4.9245 474 634	4.8820 452 550	4.8401 228 818	8
9	5.3282 497 918	5.2779 932 859	5.2284 846 711	5.1797 098 730	9
10	5.6502 230 284	5.5928 670 698	5.5364 308 187	5.4808 956 745	10
11	5.9376 991 325	5.8733 782 359	5.8101 607 278	5.7480 227 712	11
12	6.1943 742 255	6.1232 768 249	6.0534 762 025	5.9849 425 909	12
13	6.4235 484 156	6.3459 036 302	6.2697 566 244	6.1950 710 340	13
14	6.6281 682 282	6.5442 348 599	6.4620 058 884	6.3814 377 242	14
15	6.8108 644 895	6.7209 219 241	6.6328 941 230	6.5467 296 889	15
16	6.9739 861 513	6.8783 268 812	6.7847 947 760	6.6933 301 010	16
17	7.1196 304 922	7.0185 540 144	6.9198 175 787	6.8233 526 395	17
18	7.2496 700 824	7.1434 779 639	7.0398 378 477	6.9386 719 640	18
19	7.3657 768 592	7.2547 687 874	7.1465 225 313	7.0409 507 442	19
20	7.4694 436 243	7.3539 142 872	7.2413 533 611	7.1316 636 312	20
21	7.5620 032 360	7.4422 398 995	7.3256 474 321	7.2121 185 199	21
22	7.6446 457 464	7.5209 264 138	7.4005 754 952	7.2834 754 057	22
23	7.7184 337 022	7.5910 257 584	7.4671 782 180	7.3467 631 092	23
24	7.7843 158 055	7.6534 750 632	7.5263 806 382	7.4028 941 102	24
25	7.8431 391 121	7.7091 091 877	7.5790 050 117	7.4526 777 031	25
26	7.8956 599 215	7.7586 718 821	7.6257 822 327	7.4968 316 657	26
27	7.9425 535 013	7.8028 257 302	7.6673 619 846	7.5359 926 081	27
28	7.9844 227 690	7.8421 610 068	7.7043 217 641	7.5707 251 513	28
29	8.0218 060 438	7.8772 035 696	7.7371 749 014	7.6015 300 677	29
30	8.0551 839 677	7.9084 218 883	7.7663 776 901	7.6288 515 013	30
31	8.0849 856 854	7.9362 333 080	7.7923 357 246	7.6530 833 714	31
32	8.1115 943 620	7.9610 096 285	7.8154 095 329	7.6745 750 523	32
33	8.1353 521 089	7.9830 820 744	7.8359 195 848	7.6936 364 100	33
34	8.1565 643 830	8.0027 457 233	7.8541 507 421	7.7105 422 705	34
35	8.1755 039 134	8.0202 634 506	7.8703 562 152	7.7255 363 818	35
36	8.1924 142 084	8.0358 694 438	7.8847 610 802	7.7388 349 284	36
37	8.2075 126 860	8.0497 723 330	7.8975 654 046	7.7506 296 483	37
38	8.2209 934 697	8.0621 579 804	7.9089 470 263	7.7610 905 972	38
39	8.2330 298 836	8.0731 919 647	7.9190 640 234	7.7703 686 006	39
40	8.2437 766 818	8.0830 217 948	7.9280 569 097	7.7785 974 285	40
41	8.2533 720 373	8.0917 788 818	7.9360 505 864	7.7858 957 237	41
42	8.2619 393 190	8.0995 802 956	7.9431 560 768	7.7923 687 128	42
43	8.2695 886 777	8.1065 303 302	7.9494 720 682	7.7981 097 231	43
44	8.2764 184 623	8.1127 218 977	7.9550 862 829	7.8032 015 283	44
45	8.2825 164 842	8.1182 377 708	7.9600 766 959	7.8077 175 417	45
46	8.2879 611 466	8.1231 516 889	7.9645 126 186	7.8117 228 751	46
47	8.2928 224 523	8.1275 293 442	7.9684 556 610	7.8152 752 773	47
48	8.2971 629 038	8.1314 292 599	7.9719 605 875	7.8184 259 665	48
49	8.3010 383 070	8.1349 035 723	7.9750 760 778	7.8212 203 694	49
50	8.3044 984 884	8.1379 987 281	7.9778 454 025	7.8236 987 755	50
51	8.3075 879 361	8.1407 561 052	7.9803 070 244	7.8258 969 184	51
52	8.3103 463 715	8.1432 125 659	7.9824 951 328	7.8278 464 909	52
53	8.3128 092 603	8.1454 009 496	7.9844 401 181	7.8295 756 016	53
54	8.3150 082 681	8.1473 505 119	7.9861 689 938	7.8311 091 811	54
55	8.3169 716 679	8.1490 873 157	7.9877 057 723	7.8324 693 402	55
56	8.3187 247 035	8.1506 345 797	7.9890 717 976	7.8336 756 897	56
57	8.3202 899 138	8.1520 129 886	7.9902 860 423	7.8347 456 228	57
58	8.3216 874 231	8.1532 409 698	7.9913 653 709	7.8356 945 657	58
59	8.3229 351 992	8.1543 349 397	7.9923 247 742	7.8365 362 002	59
60	8.3240 492 850	8.1553 095 231	7.9931 775 770	7.8372 826 609	60

TABLE 5. PRESENT WORTH OF ONE DOLLAR PER PERIOD
Payable at end of each period

YEARLY Compounding

YEARS	13% Nominal Annual Rate	13¼% Nominal Annual Rate	13½% Nominal Annual Rate	13¾% Nominal Annual Rate	YEARS
1	0.8849 557 522	0.8830 022 075	0.8810 572 687	0.8791 208 791	1
2	1.6681 024 356	1.6626 951 060	1.6573 191 795	1.6519 743 992	2
3	2.3611 525 979	2.3511 656 565	2.3412 503 784	2.3314 060 653	3
4	2.9744 713 255	2.9590 866 724	2.9438 329 325	2.9287 086 288	4
5	3.5172 312 615	3.4958 822 714	3.4747 426 718	3.4538 097 836	5
6	3.9975 497 890	3.9698 739 704	3.9425 045 567	3.9154 371 724	6
7	4.4226 104 327	4.3884 096 868	4.3546 295 653	4.3212 634 482	7
8	4.7987 702 944	4.7579 776 484	4.7177 352 999	4.6780 338 006	8
9	5.1316 551 278	5.0843 069 743	5.0376 522 466	4.9916 780 665	9
10	5.4262 434 760	5.3724 564 895	5.3195 173 979	5.2674 092 892	10
11	5.6869 411 292	5.6268 931 474	5.5678 567 382	5.5098 103 642	11
12	5.9176 470 170	5.8515 612 781	5.7866 579 191	5.7229 102 102	12
13	6.1218 115 194	6.0499 437 334	5.9794 342 900	5.9102 507 343	13
14	6.3024 880 703	6.2251 158 794	6.1492 813 128	6.0749 457 005	14
15	6.4623 788 233	6.3797 932 710	6.2989 262 667	6.2197 324 839	15
16	6.6038 750 648	6.5163 737 492	6.4307 720 412	6.3470 175 683	16
17	6.7290 929 777	6.6369 746 130	6.5469 357 191	6.4589 165 436	17
18	6.8399 052 900	6.7434 654 419	6.6492 825 719	6.5572 892 691	18
19	6.9379 692 832	6.8374 970 790	6.7394 560 105	6.6437 707 860	19
20	7.0247 515 781	6.9205 272 221	6.8189 039 740	6.7197 984 932	20
21	7.1015 500 691	6.9938 430 217	6.8889 021 797	6.7866 360 380	21
22	7.1695 133 355	7.0585 810 346	6.9505 746 077	6.8453 943 191	22
23	7.2296 578 190	7.1157 448 429	7.0049 115 486	6.8970 499 508	23
24	7.2828 830 257	7.1662 206 118	7.0527 855 054	6.9424 614 952	24
25	7.3299 849 785	7.2107 908 272	7.0949 652 030	6.9823 837 321	25
26	7.3716 681 225	7.2501 464 258	7.1321 279 322	7.0174 802 040	26
27	7.4085 558 607	7.2848 975 062	7.1648 704 248	7.0483 342 453	27
28	7.4411 998 767	7.3155 827 870	7.1937 184 360	7.0754 586 772	28
29	7.4700 883 864	7.3426 779 576	7.2191 351 859	7.0993 043 316	29
30	7.4956 534 393	7.3666 030 531	7.2415 287 981	7.1202 675 443	30
31	7.5182 773 799	7.3877 289 652	7.2612 588 530	7.1386 967 422	31
32	7.5382 985 663	7.4063 831 922	7.2786 421 612	7.1548 982 349	32
33	7.5560 164 304	7.4228 549 159	7.2939 578 513	7.1691 413 054	33
34	7.5716 959 561	7.4373 994 842	7.3074 518 513	7.1816 626 861	34
35	7.5855 716 425	7.4502 423 702	7.3193 408 382	7.1926 704 933	35
36	7.5978 510 111	7.4615 826 668	7.3298 157 165	7.2023 476 864	36
37	7.6087 177 089	7.4715 961 738	7.3390 446 841	7.2108 551 089	37
38	7.6183 342 557	7.4804 381 225	7.3471 759 331	7.2183 341 617	38
39	7.6268 444 741	7.4882 455 828	7.3543 400 292	7.2249 091 531	39
40	7.6343 756 408	7.4951 395 875	7.3606 520 081	7.2306 893 654	40
41	7.6410 403 901	7.5012 270 088	7.3662 132 230	7.2357 708 707	41
42	7.6469 383 983	7.5066 022 153	7.3711 129 718	7.2402 381 281	42
43	7.6521 578 746	7.5113 485 345	7.3754 299 311	7.2441 653 873	43
44	7.6567 768 802	7.5155 395 448	7.3792 334 195	7.2476 179 229	44
45	7.6608 644 957	7.5192 402 161	7.3825 845 106	7.2506 531 190	45
46	7.6644 818 546	7.5225 079 171	7.3855 370 137	7.2533 214 233	46
47	7.6676 830 572	7.5253 933 043	7.3881 383 381	7.2556 671 853	47
48	7.6705 159 798	7.5279 411 076	7.3904 302 538	7.2577 293 937	48
49	7.6730 229 910	7.5301 908 234	7.3924 495 628	7.2595 423 241	49
50	7.6752 415 849	7.5321 773 275	7.3942 286 897	7.2611 361 091	50
51	7.6772 049 424	7.5339 314 151	7.3957 962 024	7.2625 372 388	51
52	7.6789 424 269	7.5354 802 782	7.3971 772 708	7.2637 690 011	52
53	7.6804 800 238	7.5368 479 278	7.3983 940 712	7.2648 518 691	53
54	7.6818 407 291	7.5380 555 654	7.3994 661 420	7.2658 038 410	54
55	7.6830 448 930	7.5391 219 120	7.4004 106 978	7.2666 407 393	55
56	7.6841 105 247	7.5400 634 985	7.4012 429 056	7.2673 764 741	56
57	7.6850 535 617	7.5408 949 214	7.4019 761 283	7.2680 232 740	57
58	7.6858 881 077	7.5416 290 697	7.4026 221 394	7.2685 918 892	58
59	7.6866 266 440	7.5422 773 242	7.4031 913 123	7.2690 917 707	59
60	7.6872 802 159	7.5428 497 344	7.4036 927 861	7.2695 312 270	60

YEARLY
Compounding

TABLE 5. PRESENT WORTH OF ONE DOLLAR PER PERIOD
Payable at end of each period

YEARS	14% Nominal Annual Rate	14¼% Nominal Annual Rate	14½% Nominal Annual Rate	14¾% Nominal Annual Rate	YEARS
1	0.8771 929 825	0.8752 735 230	0.8733 624 454	0.8714 596 950	1
2	1.6466 605 109	1.6413 772 630	1.6361 244 065	1.6309 016 950	2
3	2.3216 320 271	2.3119 275 825	2.3022 920 581	2.2927 247 887	3
4	2.9137 123 045	2.8988 425 230	2.8840 978 673	2.8694 769 400	4
5	3.4330 809 689	3.4125 536 306	3.3922 252 116	3.3720 931 939	5
6	3.8886 675 165	3.8621 913 616	3.8360 045 516	3.8101 030 012	6
7	4.2883 048 391	4.2557 473 624	4.2235 847 612	4.1918 108 943	7
8	4.6388 638 939	4.6002 165 098	4.5620 827 609	4.5244 539 384	8
9	4.9463 718 368	4.9017 212 340	4.8577 142 017	4.8143 389 441	9
10	5.2161 156 463	5.1656 203 361	5.1159 075 997	5.0669 620 428	10
11	5.4527 330 231	5.3966 042 329	5.3414 040 172	5.2871 128 913	11
12	5.6602 921 255	5.5987 783 220	5.5383 441 198	5.4789 654 827	12
13	5.8423 615 136	5.7757 359 492	5.7103 442 095	5.6461 572 834	13
14	6.0020 715 032	5.9306 222 750	5.8605 626 284	5.7918 581 990	14
15	6.1421 679 852	6.0661 901 751	5.9917 577 540	5.9188 306 745	15
16	6.2650 596 362	6.1848 491 686	6.1063 386 498	6.0294 820 693	16
17	6.3728 593 300	6.2887 082 438	6.2064 093 011	6.1259 103 000	17
18	6.4674 204 649	6.3796 133 425	6.2938 072 499	6.2099 436 166	18
19	6.5503 688 288	6.4591 801 685	6.3701 373 362	6.2831 752 650	19
20	6.6231 305 516	6.5288 229 046	6.4368 011 670	6.3469 936 950	20
21	6.6869 566 242	6.5897 793 476	6.4950 228 532	6.4026 088 845	21
22	6.7429 444 072	6.6431 329 082	6.5458 714 875	6.4510 752 806	22
23	6.7920 564 976	6.6898 318 671	6.5902 807 751	6.4933 117 914	23
24	6.8351 372 786	6.7307 062 294	6.6290 661 792	6.5301 192 082	24
25	6.8729 274 373	6.7664 824 765	6.6629 398 945	6.5621 953 884	25
26	6.9060 766 994	6.7977 964 783	6.6925 239 253	6.5901 484 866	26
27	6.9351 549 995	6.8252 047 950	6.7183 615 068	6.6145 084 851	27
28	6.9606 622 803	6.8491 945 690	6.7409 270 802	6.6357 372 419	28
29	6.9830 370 879	6.8701 921 829	6.7606 350 045	6.6542 372 478	29
30	7.0026 641 122	6.8885 708 384	6.7778 471 655	6.6703 592 574	30
31	7.0198 808 002	6.9046 571 890	6.7928 796 205	6.6844 089 389	31
32	7.0349 831 581	6.9187 371 457	6.8060 084 022	6.6966 526 701	32
33	7.0482 308 404	6.9310 609 591	6.8174 745 871	6.7073 225 883	33
34	7.0598 516 144	6.9418 476 666	6.8274 887 224	6.7166 209 920	34
35	7.0700 452 758	6.9512 889 861	6.8362 346 920	6.7247 241 760	35
36	7.0789 870 840	6.9595 527 230	6.8438 730 935	6.7317 857 743	36
37	7.0868 307 755	6.9667 857 532	6.8505 441 864	6.7379 396 726	37
38	7.0937 112 065	6.9731 166 330	6.8563 704 685	6.7433 025 469	38
39	7.0997 466 724	6.9786 578 845	6.8614 589 245	6.7479 760 757	39
40	7.1050 409 407	6.9835 079 952	6.8659 029 908	6.7520 488 678	40
41	7.1096 850 357	6.9877 531 686	6.8697 842 714	6.7555 981 418	41
42	7.1137 588 033	6.9914 688 566	6.8731 740 362	6.7586 911 911	42
43	7.1173 322 836	6.9947 210 998	6.8761 345 294	6.7613 866 589	43
44	7.1204 669 154	6.9975 677 023	6.8787 201 130	6.7637 356 505	44
45	7.1232 165 925	7.0000 592 580	6.8809 782 647	6.7657 827 020	45
46	7.1256 285 899	7.0022 400 508	6.8829 504 495	6.7675 666 248	46
47	7.1277 443 771	7.0041 488 409	6.8846 728 816	6.7691 212 417	47
48	7.1296 003 308	7.0058 195 544	6.8861 771 892	6.7704 760 276	48
49	7.1312 283 603	7.0072 818 857	6.8874 909 949	6.7716 566 689	49
50	7.1326 564 564	7.0085 618 256	6.8886 384 235	6.7726 855 503	50
51	7.1339 091 723	7.0096 821 230	6.8896 405 446	6.7735 821 789	51
52	7.1350 080 459	7.0106 626 897	6.8905 157 594	6.7743 635 546	52
53	7.1359 719 701	7.0115 209 538	6.8912 801 393	6.7750 444 920	53
54	7.1368 175 176	7.0122 721 697	6.8919 477 199	6.7756 379 015	54
55	7.1375 592 260	7.0129 296 890	6.8925 307 597	6.7761 550 340	55
56	7.1382 098 473	7.0135 051 982	6.8930 399 648	6.7766 056 941	56
57	7.1387 805 678	7.0140 089 262	6.8934 846 854	6.7769 984 263	57
58	7.1392 811 999	7.0144 498 260	6.8938 730 877	6.7773 406 765	58
59	7.1397 203 508	7.0148 357 339	6.8942 123 037	6.7776 389 337	59
60	7.1401 055 708	7.0151 735 089	6.8945 085 622	6.7778 988 529	60

TABLE 5. PRESENT WORTH OF ONE DOLLAR PER PERIOD
Payable at end of each period

YEARLY Compounding

YEARS	15% Nominal Annual Rate	15¼% Nominal Annual Rate	15½% Nominal Annual Rate	15¾% Nominal Annual Rate	YEARS
1	0.8695 652 174	0.8676 789 588	0.8658 008 658	0.8639 308 855	1
2	1.6257 088 847	1.6205 457 343	1.6154 120 050	1.6103 074 605	2
3	2.2832 251 171	2.2737 923 942	2.2644 259 784	2.2551 252 359	3
4	2.8549 783 627	2.8406 007 759	2.8263 428 384	2.8122 032 275	4
5	3.3521 550 980	3.3324 084 823	3.3128 509 424	3.2934 801 102	5
6	3.7844 826 939	3.7591 396 810	3.7340 700 800	3.7092 700 736	6
7	4.1604 197 338	4.1294 053 631	4.0987 619 740	4.0684 838 649	7
8	4.4873 215 077	4.4506 771 046	4.4145 125 316	4.3788 197 537	8
9	4.7715 839 197	4.7294 378 348	4.6878 896 377	4.6469 285 129	9
10	5.0187 686 259	4.9713 126 549	4.9245 797 729	4.8785 559 507	10
11	5.2337 118 486	5.1811 823 470	5.1295 062 969	5.0786 660 481	11
12	5.4206 189 988	5.3632 818 629	5.3069 318 588	5.2515 473 418	12
13	5.5831 469 554	5.5212 857 813	5.4605 470 639	5.4009 048 309	13
14	5.7244 756 134	5.6583 824 566	5.5935 472 415	5.5299 393 787	14
15	5.8473 700 986	5.7773 383 572	5.7086 989 104	5.6414 163 099	15
16	5.9542 348 684	5.8805 538 891	5.8083 973 250	5.7377 246 738	16
17	6.0471 607 551	5.9701 118 344	5.8947 162 987	5.8209 284 439	17
18	6.1279 658 740	6.0478 193 790	5.9694 513 409	5.8928 107 507	18
19	6.1982 311 948	6.1152 445 805	6.0341 570 051	5.9549 120 956	19
20	6.2593 314 737	6.1737 480 091	6.0901 792 252	6.0085 633 655	20
21	6.3124 621 511	6.2245 102 031	6.1386 833 118	6.0549 143 547	21
22	6.3586 627 401	6.2685 554 908	6.1806 781 921	6.0949 584 058	22
23	6.3988 371 653	6.3067 726 601	6.2170 373 957	6.1295 536 983	23
24	6.4337 714 481	6.3399 328 938	6.2485 172 257	6.1594 416 400	24
25	6.4641 490 853	6.3687 053 309	6.2757 724 898	6.1852 627 559	25
26	6.4905 644 220	6.3936 705 691	6.2993 701 211	6.2075 704 155	26
27	6.5135 342 800	6.4153 323 810	6.3198 009 706	6.2268 426 916	27
28	6.5335 080 695	6.4341 278 794	6.3374 900 178	6.2434 926 061	28
29	6.5508 765 822	6.4504 363 379	6.3528 052 103	6.2578 769 815	29
30	6.5659 796 367	6.4645 868 441	6.3660 651 171	6.2703 040 877	30
31	6.5791 127 276	6.4768 649 407	6.3775 455 559	6.2810 402 486	31
32	6.5905 328 066	6.4875 183 867	6.3874 853 298	6.2903 155 495	32
33	6.6004 633 101	6.4967 621 577	6.3960 911 946	6.2983 287 685	33
34	6.6090 985 305	6.5047 827 832	6.4035 421 599	6.3052 516 358	34
35	6.6166 074 178	6.5117 421 113	6.4099 932 120	6.3112 325 148	35
36	6.6231 368 851	6.5177 805 738	6.4155 785 385	6.3163 995 808	36
37	6.6288 146 827	6.5230 200 206	6.4204 143 191	6.3208 635 687	37
38	6.6337 518 980	6.5275 661 784	6.4246 011 421	6.3247 201 458	38
39	6.6380 451 287	6.5315 107 839	6.4282 260 970	6.3280 519 618	39
40	6.6417 783 728	6.5349 334 350	6.4313 645 862	6.3309 304 205	40
41	6.6450 246 720	6.5379 031 974	6.4340 818 928	6.3334 172 100	41
42	6.6478 475 408	6.5404 799 978	6.4364 345 392	6.3355 656 242	42
43	6.6503 022 094	6.5427 158 332	6.4384 714 625	6.3374 217 055	43
44	6.6524 367 038	6.5446 558 206	6.4402 350 325	6.3390 252 316	44
45	6.6542 927 860	6.5463 391 068	6.4417 619 329	6.3404 105 672	45
46	6.6559 067 704	6.5477 996 588	6.4430 839 246	6.3416 074 015	46
47	6.6573 102 351	6.5490 669 491	6.4442 285 061	6.3426 413 836	47
48	6.6585 306 392	6.5501 665 502	6.4452 194 858	6.3435 346 726	48
49	6.6595 918 602	6.5511 206 509	6.4460 774 769	6.3443 064 126	49
50	6.6605 146 611	6.5519 485 040	6.4468 203 263	6.3449 731 427	50
51	6.6613 170 966	6.5526 668 148	6.4474 634 860	6.3455 491 513	51
52	6.6620 148 666	6.5532 900 779	6.4480 203 342	6.3460 467 830	52
53	6.6626 216 231	6.5538 308 702	6.4485 024 538	6.3464 767 024	53
54	6.6631 492 375	6.5543 001 043	6.4489 198 735	6.3468 481 230	54
55	6.6636 080 326	6.5547 072 488	6.4492 812 757	6.3471 690 048	55
56	6.6640 069 849	6.5550 605 196	6.4495 941 781	6.3474 462 244	56
57	6.6643 538 999	6.5553 670 452	6.4498 650 893	6.3476 857 230	57
58	6.6646 555 651	6.5556 330 110	6.4500 996 444	6.3478 926 333	58
59	6.6649 178 827	6.5558 637 840	6.4503 027 224	6.3480 713 895	59
60	6.6651 459 850	6.5560 640 208	6.4504 785 476	6.3482 258 224	60

TABLE 5. PRESENT WORTH OF ONE DOLLAR PER PERIOD
Payable at end of each period

YEARS	16% Nominal Annual Rate	16¼% Nominal Annual Rate	16½% Nominal Annual Rate	16¾% Nominal Annual Rate	YEARS
1	0.8620 689 655	0.8602 150 538	0.8583 690 987	0.8565 310 493	1
2	1.6052 318 668	1.6001 849 925	1.5951 666 083	1.5901 764 876	2
3	2.2458 895 404	2.2367 182 731	2.2276 108 226	2.2185 665 847	3
4	2.7981 806 382	2.7842 737 833	2.7704 813 928	2.7568 022 138	4
5	3.2742 936 537	3.2552 892 760	3.2364 647 148	3.2178 177 420	5
6	3.6847 359 083	3.6604 638 933	3.6364 503 990	3.6126 918 561	6
7	4.0385 654 382	4.0090 011 985	3.9797 857 502	3.9509 137 954	7
8	4.3435 908 950	4.3088 182 353	4.2744 942 062	4.2406 113 879	8
9	4.6065 438 750	4.5667 253 637	4.5274 628 379	4.4887 463 708	9
10	4.8332 274 785	4.7885 809 580	4.7446 032 944	4.7012 816 881	10
11	5.0286 443 780	4.9794 244 800	4.9309 899 522	4.8833 247 864	11
12	5.1971 072 224	5.1435 909 506	5.0909 784 998	5.0392 503 523	12
13	5.3423 338 124	5.2848 094 198	5.2283 077 251	5.1728 054 410	13
14	5.4675 291 486	5.4062 876 730	5.3461 868 885	5.2871 995 212	14
15	5.5754 561 626	5.5107 850 950	5.4473 707 198	5.3851 816 027	15
16	5.6684 966 919	5.6006 753 506	5.5342 237 938	5.4691 062 978	16
17	5.7487 040 447	5.6780 003 016	5.6087 757 887	5.5409 904 050	17
18	5.8178 483 144	5.7445 163 884	5.6727 689 173	5.6025 613 747	18
19	5.8774 554 435	5.8017 345 277	5.7276 986 415	5.6552 988 220	19
20	5.9288 408 996	5.8509 544 324	5.7748 486 193	5.7004 700 831	20
21	5.9731 387 065	5.8932 941 354	5.8153 207 032	5.7391 606 708	21
22	6.0113 264 711	5.9297 153 853	5.8500 606 895	5.7723 003 604	22
23	6.0442 469 579	5.9610 454 927	5.8798 804 202	5.8006 855 335	23
24	6.0726 266 878	5.9879 961 228	5.9054 767 555	5.8249 983 157	24
25	6.0970 919 723	6.0111 794 605	5.9274 478 588	5.8458 229 684	25
26	6.1181 827 347	6.0311 221 165	5.9463 071 749	5.8636 599 301	26
27	6.1363 644 265	6.0482 770 895	5.9624 954 291	5.8789 378 417	27
28	6.1520 382 987	6.0630 340 555	5.9763 909 263	5.8920 238 473	28
29	6.1655 502 575	6.0757 282 198	5.9883 183 917	5.9032 324 173	29
30	6.1771 984 978	6.0866 479 310	5.9985 565 594	5.9128 329 056	30
31	6.1872 400 843	6.0960 412 309	6.0073 446 862	5.9210 560 220	31
32	6.1958 966 244	6.1041 214 890	6.0148 881 426	5.9280 993 764	32
33	6.2033 591 590	6.1110 722 486	6.0213 632 126	5.9341 322 282	33
34	6.2097 923 784	6.1170 513 966	6.0269 212 125	5.9392 995 531	34
35	6.2153 382 573	6.1221 947 498	6.0316 920 279	5.9437 255 272	35
36	6.2201 191 873	6.1266 191 396	6.0357 871 484	5.9475 165 116	36
37	6.2242 406 787	6.1304 250 663	6.0393 022 733	5.9507 636 073	37
38	6.2277 936 885	6.1336 989 818	6.0423 195 479	5.9535 448 457	38
39	6.2308 566 281	6.1365 152 532	6.0449 094 832	5.9559 270 627	39
40	6.2334 970 932	6.1389 378 522	6.0471 326 036	5.9579 675 055	40
41	6.2357 733 562	6.1410 218 083	6.0490 408 614	5.9597 152 081	41
42	6.2377 356 519	6.1428 144 588	6.0506 788 510	5.9612 121 697	42
43	6.2394 272 861	6.1443 565 237	6.0520 848 507	5.9624 943 638	43
44	6.2408 855 915	6.1456 830 311	6.0532 917 173	5.9635 926 028	44
45	6.2421 427 513	6.1468 241 128	6.0543 276 543	5.9645 332 786	45
46	6.2432 265 097	6.1478 056 884	6.0552 168 707	5.9653 389 967	46
47	6.2441 607 842	6.1486 500 546	6.0559 801 465	5.9660 291 192	47
48	6.2449 661 933	6.1493 763 910	6.0566 353 189	5.9666 202 306	48
49	6.2456 605 115	6.1500 011 966	6.0571 976 986	5.9671 265 358	49
50	6.2462 590 616	6.1505 386 637	6.0576 804 280	5.9675 602 020	50
51	6.2467 750 531	6.1510 010 010	6.0580 947 880	5.9679 316 505	51
52	6.2472 198 734	6.1513 987 106	6.0584 504 618	5.9682 498 077	52
53	6.2476 033 391	6.1517 408 263	6.0587 557 612	5.9685 223 193	53
54	6.2479 339 130	6.1520 351 194	6.0590 178 208	5.9687 557 338	54
55	6.2482 188 905	6.1522 882 748	6.0592 427 646	5.9689 556 607	55
56	6.2484 645 608	6.1525 060 428	6.0594 358 494	5.9691 269 042	56
57	6.2486 763 455	6.1526 933 701	6.0596 015 875	5.9692 735 796	57
58	6.2488 589 186	6.1528 545 120	6.0597 438 519	5.9693 992 117	58
59	6.2490 163 091	6.1529 931 286	6.0598 659 673	5.9695 068 194	59
60	6.2491 519 906	6.1531 123 687	6.0599 707 874	5.9695 989 888	60

TABLE 5. PRESENT WORTH OF ONE DOLLAR PER PERIOD
Payable at end of each period

YEARLY Compounding

YEARS	17% Nominal Annual Rate	17¼% Nominal Annual Rate	17½% Nominal Annual Rate	17¾% Nominal Annual Rate	YEARS
1	0.8547 008 547	0.8528 784 648	0.8510 638 298	0.8492 569 002	1
2	1.5852 144 057	1.5802 801 406	1.5753 734 722	1.5704 941 828	2
3	2.2095 849 622	2.2006 653 651	2.1918 072 103	2.1830 099 217	3
4	2.7432 350 104	2.7297 785 630	2.7164 316 684	2.7031 931 394	4
5	3.1993 461 627	3.1810 478 149	3.1629 205 688	3.1449 623 265	5
6	3.5891 847 545	3.5659 256 417	3.5429 111 224	3.5201 378 569	6
7	3.9223 801 320	3.8941 796 518	3.8663 073 382	3.8387 582 649	7
8	4.2071 625 060	4.1741 404 280	4.1415 381 602	4.1093 488 449	8
9	4.4505 662 444	4.4129 129 450	4.3757 771 576	4.3391 497 621	9
10	4.6586 036 277	4.6165 568 827	4.5751 294 958	4.5343 097 767	10
11	4.8364 133 570	4.7902 404 117	4.7447 910 603	4.7000 507 658	11
12	4.9883 874 846	4.9383 713 532	4.8891 838 811	4.8408 074 444	12
13	5.1182 799 014	5.0647 090 433	5.0120 713 882	4.9603 460 250	13
14	5.2292 990 610	5.1724 597 384	5.1166 565 006	5.0618 649 894	14
15	5.3241 872 317	5.2643 579 858	5.2056 651 069	5.1480 806 704	15
16	5.4052 882 322	5.3427 360 220	5.2814 171 122	5.2212 999 324	16
17	5.4746 053 267	5.4095 829 612	5.3458 869 040	5.2834 818 959	17
18	5.5338 507 065	5.4665 952 761	5.4007 548 119	5.3362 903 574	18
19	5.5844 877 834	5.5152 198 517	5.4474 509 038	5.3811 383 078	19
20	5.6277 673 362	5.5566 907 051	5.4871 922 585	5.4192 257 391	20
21	5.6647 584 070	5.5920 603 028	5.5210 146 881	5.4515 717 530	21
22	5.6963 747 069	5.6222 262 711	5.5497 997 346	5.4790 418 284	22
23	5.7233 971 853	5.6479 541 757	5.5742 976 464	5.5023 709 795	23
24	5.7464 933 208	5.6698 969 516	5.5951 469 331	5.5221 834 221	24
25	5.7662 336 075	5.6886 114 726	5.6128 910 069	5.5390 092 757	25
26	5.7831 056 475	5.7045 726 845	5.6279 923 463	5.5532 987 479	26
27	5.7975 261 944	5.7181 856 584	5.6408 445 501	5.5654 341 808	27
28	5.8098 514 482	5.7297 958 707	5.6517 825 958	5.5757 402 810	28
29	5.8203 858 532	5.7396 979 708	5.6610 915 709	5.5844 928 076	29
30	5.8293 896 181	5.7481 432 586	5.6690 141 029	5.5919 259 513	30
31	5.8370 851 437	5.7553 460 628	5.6757 566 833	5.5982 385 998	31
32	5.8436 625 160	5.7614 891 794	5.6814 950 496	5.6035 996 601	32
33	5.8492 842 017	5.7667 285 112	5.6863 787 656	5.6081 525 776	33
34	5.8540 890 613	5.7711 970 245	5.6905 351 197	5.6120 191 742	34
35	5.8581 957 789	5.7750 081 232	5.6940 724 423	5.6153 029 080	35
36	5.8617 057 939	5.7782 585 273	5.6970 829 296	5.6180 916 416	36
37	5.8647 058 067	5.7810 307 269	5.6996 450 465	5.6204 599 929	37
38	5.8672 699 203	5.7833 950 762	5.7018 255 715	5.6224 713 315	38
39	5.8694 614 703	5.7854 115 789	5.7036 813 374	5.6241 794 748	39
40	5.8713 345 900	5.7871 314 106	5.7052 607 127	5.6256 301 272	40
41	5.8729 355 470	5.7885 982 180	5.7066 048 619	5.6268 621 038	41
42	5.8743 038 864	5.7898 492 264	5.7077 488 186	5.6279 083 684	42
43	5.8754 734 071	5.7909 161 846	5.7087 223 988	5.6287 969 158	43
44	5.8764 729 976	5.7918 261 702	5.7095 509 777	5.6295 515 209	44
45	5.8773 273 483	5.7926 022 774	5.7102 561 513	5.6301 923 744	45
46	5.8780 575 627	5.7932 642 024	5.7108 562 989	5.6307 366 237	46
47	5.8786 816 775	5.7938 287 441	5.7113 670 629	5.6311 988 312	47
48	5.8792 151 090	5.7943 102 295	5.7118 017 557	5.6315 913 641	48
49	5.8796 710 333	5.7947 208 780	5.7121 717 070	5.6319 247 253	49
50	5.8800 607 122	5.7950 711 113	5.7124 865 591	5.6322 078 347	50
51	5.8803 937 711	5.7953 698 178	5.7127 545 184	5.6324 482 672	51
52	5.8806 784 369	5.7956 245 781	5.7129 825 688	5.6326 524 562	52
53	5.8809 217 409	5.7958 418 576	5.7131 766 543	5.6328 258 652	53
54	5.8811 296 931	5.7960 271 707	5.7133 418 335	5.6329 731 339	54
55	5.8813 074 300	5.7961 852 202	5.7134 824 115	5.6330 982 029	55
56	5.8814 593 419	5.7963 200 172	5.7136 020 523	5.6332 044 186	56
57	5.8815 891 811	5.7964 349 827	5.7137 038 743	5.6332 946 230	57
58	5.8817 001 548	5.7965 330 343	5.7137 905 313	5.6333 712 297	58
59	5.8817 950 041	5.7966 166 604	5.7138 642 820	5.6334 362 885	59
60	5.8818 760 719	5.7966 879 833	5.7139 270 485	5.6334 915 401	60

TABLE 5. PRESENT WORTH OF ONE DOLLAR PER PERIOD
Payable at end of each period

YEARS	18% Nominal Annual Rate	18¼% Nominal Annual Rate	18½% Nominal Annual Rate	18¾% Nominal Annual Rate	YEARS
1	0.8474 576 271	0.8456 659 619	0.8438 818 565	0.8421 052 632	1
2	1.5656 420 569	1.5608 168 811	1.5560 184 443	1.5512 465 374	2
3	2.1742 729 296	2.1655 956 712	2.1569 775 902	2.1484 181 368	3
4	2.6900 618 047	2.6770 365 084	2.6641 161 098	2.6512 994 836	4
5	3.1271 710 209	3.1095 446 160	3.0920 811 053	3.0747 785 125	5
6	3.4976 025 601	3.4753 020 008	3.4532 330 003	3.4313 924 316	6
7	3.8115 275 933	3.7846 105 715	3.7580 025 319	3.7316 988 897	7
8	4.0775 657 571	4.0461 823 015	4.0151 920 100	3.9845 885 387	8
9	4.3030 218 280	4.2673 846 101	4.2322 295 443	4.1975 482 431	9
10	4.4940 862 949	4.4544 478 733	4.4153 835 817	4.3768 827 311	10
11	4.6560 053 347	4.6126 409 076	4.5699 439 508	4.5279 012 472	11
12	4.7932 248 599	4.7464 193 722	4.7003 746 420	4.6550 747 345	12
13	4.9095 125 931	4.8595 512 661	4.8104 427 359	4.7621 681 975	13
14	5.0080 615 196	4.9552 230 580	4.9033 272 033	4.8523 521 663	14
15	5.0915 775 590	5.0361 294 360	4.9817 107 201	4.9282 965 611	15
16	5.1623 538 635	5.1045 492 059	5.0478 571 477	4.9922 497 357	16
17	5.2223 337 827	5.1624 094 764	5.1036 769 179	5.0461 050 405	17
18	5.2731 642 226	5.2113 399 378	5.1507 822 092	5.0914 568 763	18
19	5.3162 408 666	5.2527 187 635	5.1905 335 099	5.1296 478 958	19
20	5.3527 464 971	5.2877 114 279	5.2240 789 113	5.1618 087 544	20
21	5.3836 834 721	5.3173 035 331	5.2523 872 669	5.1888 915 826	21
22	5.4099 012 476	5.3423 285 692	5.2762 761 746	5.2116 981 748	22
23	5.4321 197 013	5.3634 913 905	5.2964 355 904	5.2309 037 262	23
24	5.4509 488 994	5.3813 880 680	5.3134 477 556	5.2470 768 220	24
25	5.4669 058 470	5.3965 226 791	5.3278 040 132	5.2606 962 712	25
26	5.4804 286 839	5.4093 215 045	5.3399 189 985	5.2721 652 810	26
27	5.4918 887 152	5.4201 450 355	5.3501 426 147	5.2818 233 945	27
28	5.5016 006 061	5.4292 981 273	5.3587 701 390	5.2899 565 428	28
29	5.5098 310 221	5.4370 385 855	5.3660 507 502	5.2968 055 097	29
30	5.5168 059 509	5.4435 844 274	5.3721 947 259	5.3025 730 608	30
31	5.5227 169 076	5.4491 200 232	5.3773 795 155	5.3074 299 459	31
32	5.5277 261 928	5.4538 012 881	5.3817 548 654	5.3115 199 545	32
33	5.5319 713 499	5.4577 600 745	5.3854 471 438	5.3149 641 722	33
34	5.5355 689 406	5.4611 078 854	5.3885 629 906	5.3178 645 661	34
35	5.5386 177 462	5.4639 390 152	5.3911 923 971	5.3203 070 030	35
36	5.5412 014 799	5.4663 332 052	5.3934 113 056	5.3223 637 920	36
37	5.5433 910 846	5.4683 578 902	5.3952 838 022	5.3240 958 248	37
38	5.5452 466 819	5.4700 700 975	5.3968 639 681	5.3255 543 788	38
39	5.5468 192 219	5.4715 180 528	5.3981 974 414	5.3267 826 348	39
40	5.5481 518 830	5.4727 425 394	5.3993 227 354	5.3278 169 556	40
41	5.5492 812 568	5.4737 780 460	5.4002 723 505	5.3286 879 626	41
42	5.5502 383 532	5.4746 537 387	5.4010 737 135	5.3294 214 422	42
43	5.5510 494 519	5.4753 942 822	5.4017 499 692	5.3300 391 092	43
44	5.5517 368 236	5.4760 205 346	5.4023 206 491	5.3305 592 499	44
45	5.5523 193 420	5.4765 501 350	5.4028 022 356	5.3309 972 631	45
46	5.5528 130 017	5.4769 980 000	5.4032 086 376	5.3313 661 163	46
47	5.5532 313 574	5.4773 767 442	5.4035 515 929	5.3316 767 295	47
48	5.5535 858 961	5.4776 970 352	5.4038 410 067	5.3319 382 985	48
49	5.5538 863 526	5.4779 678 945	5.4040 852 377	5.3321 585 672	49
50	5.5541 409 768	5.4781 969 509	5.4042 913 398	5.3323 440 566	50
51	5.5543 567 600	5.4783 906 562	5.4044 652 657	5.3325 002 582	51
52	5.5545 396 271	5.4785 544 661	5.4046 120 385	5.3326 317 963	52
53	5.5546 945 993	5.4786 929 946	5.4047 358 975	5.3327 425 653	53
54	5.5548 259 316	5.4788 101 434	5.4048 404 198	5.3328 358 445	54
55	5.5549 372 301	5.4789 092 122	5.4049 286 243	5.3329 143 954	55
56	5.5550 315 510	5.4789 929 913	5.4050 030 585	5.3329 805 435	56
57	5.5551 114 839	5.4790 638 404	5.4050 658 722	5.3330 362 471	57
58	5.5551 792 236	5.4791 237 551	5.4051 188 795	5.3330 831 555	58
59	5.5552 366 302	5.4791 744 229	5.4051 636 114	5.3331 226 572	59
60	5.5552 852 798	5.4792 172 710	5.4052 013 598	5.3331 559 219	60

TABLE 5. PRESENT WORTH OF ONE DOLLAR PER PERIOD
Payable at end of each period

YEARLY Compounding

YEARS	19% Nominal Annual Rate	19¼% Nominal Annual Rate	19½% Nominal Annual Rate	19¾% Nominal Annual Rate	YEARS
1	0.8403 361 345	0.8385 744 235	0.8368 200 837	0.8350 730 689	1
2	1.5465 009 533	1.5417 814 872	1.5370 879 361	1.5324 200 993	2
3	2.1399 167 675	2.1314 729 452	2.1230 861 390	2.1147 558 240	3
4	2.6385 855 189	2.6259 731 197	2.6134 612 042	2.6010 487 048	4
5	3.0576 348 898	3.0406 483 184	3.0238 169 073	3.0071 387 932	5
6	3.4097 772 184	3.3883 843 341	3.3672 108 011	3.3462 536 895	6
7	3.7056 951 415	3.6799 868 630	3.6545 697 080	3.6294 394 067	7
8	3.9543 656 651	3.9245 172 855	3.8950 374 126	3.8659 201 726	8
9	4.1633 324 917	4.1295 742 436	4.0962 656 172	4.0633 988 915	9
10	4.3389 348 670	4.3015 297 640	4.2646 574 203	4.2283 080 514	10
11	4.4864 998 882	4.4457 272 654	4.4055 710 630	4.3660 192 496	11
12	4.6105 041 077	4.5666 476 020	4.5234 904 293	4.4810 181 625	12
13	4.7147 093 342	4.6680 483 036	4.6221 677 232	4.5770 506 576	13
14	4.8022 767 515	4.7530 803 385	4.7047 428 646	4.6572 448 080	14
15	4.8758 628 163	4.8243 860 281	4.7738 434 014	4.7242 127 833	15
16	4.9376 998 457	4.8841 811 556	4.8316 681 183	4.7801 359 360	16
17	4.9896 637 359	4.9343 238 202	4.8800 570 028	4.8268 358 547	17
18	5.0333 308 705	4.9763 721 763	4.9205 497 931	4.8658 336 991	18
19	5.0700 259 416	5.0116 328 522	4.9544 349 733	4.8983 997 487	19
20	5.1008 621 358	5.0412 015 532	4.9827 907 726	4.9255 947 797	20
21	5.1267 749 040	5.0659 971 096	5.0065 194 750	4.9483 046 177	21
22	5.1485 503 395	5.0867 900 290	5.0263 761 297	4.9672 689 918	22
23	5.1668 490 248	5.1042 264 394	5.0429 925 772	4.9831 056 299	23
24	5.1822 260 713	5.1188 481 672	5.0568 975 541	4.9963 303 799	24
25	5.1951 479 590	5.1311 095 742	5.0685 335 181	5.0073 740 124	25
26	5.2060 066 883	5.1413 916 765	5.0782 707 264	5.0165 962 526	26
27	5.2151 316 708	5.1500 139 845	5.0864 190 179	5.0242 974 969	27
28	5.2227 997 234	5.1572 444 314	5.0932 376 719	5.0307 285 987	28
29	5.2292 434 650	5.1633 076 993	5.0989 436 585	5.0360 990 386	29
30	5.2346 583 740	5.1683 922 007	5.1037 185 427	5.0405 837 483	30
31	5.2392 087 176	5.1726 559 335	5.1077 142 617	5.0443 288 086	31
32	5.2430 325 358	5.1762 313 908	5.1110 579 595	5.0474 562 076	32
33	5.2462 458 284	5.1792 296 778	5.1138 560 331	5.0500 678 143	33
34	5.2489 460 743	5.1817 439 646	5.1161 975 172	5.0522 486 967	34
35	5.2512 151 885	5.1838 523 812	5.1181 569 182	5.0540 698 928	35
36	5.2531 220 071	5.1856 204 455	5.1197 965 843	5.0555 907 247	36
37	5.2547 243 757	5.1871 030 989	5.1211 686 898	5.0568 607 304	37
38	5.2560 709 040	5.1883 464 142	5.1223 168 952	5.0579 212 780	38
39	5.2572 024 403	5.1893 890 266	5.1232 777 366	5.0588 069 128	39
40	5.2581 533 112	5.1902 633 347	5.1240 817 879	5.0595 464 825	40
41	5.2589 523 623	5.1909 965 070	5.1247 546 342	5.0601 640 772	41
42	5.2596 238 339	5.1916 113 267	5.1253 176 856	5.0606 798 140	42
43	5.2601 880 957	5.1921 268 987	5.1257 888 582	5.0611 104 918	43
44	5.2606 622 653	5.1925 592 442	5.1261 831 449	5.0614 701 393	44
45	5.2610 607 272	5.1929 217 980	5.1265 130 920	5.0617 704 712	45
46	5.2613 955 690	5.1932 258 265	5.1267 891 983	5.0620 212 703	46
47	5.2616 769 488	5.1934 807 769	5.1270 202 496	5.0622 307 059	47
48	5.2619 134 023	5.1936 945 718	5.1272 135 980	5.0624 055 999	48
49	5.2621 121 028	5.1938 738 548	5.1273 753 958	5.0625 516 492	49
50	5.2622 790 780	5.1940 241 969	5.1275 107 915	5.0626 736 110	50
51	5.2624 193 933	5.1941 502 699	5.1276 240 933	5.0627 754 581	51
52	5.2625 373 053	5.1942 559 915	5.1277 189 065	5.0628 605 078	52
53	5.2626 363 910	5.1943 446 470	5.1277 982 481	5.0629 315 305	53
54	5.2627 196 563	5.1944 189 912	5.1278 646 428	5.0629 908 397	54
55	5.2627 896 271	5.1944 813 343	5.1279 202 032	5.0630 403 672	55
56	5.2628 484 262	5.1945 336 137	5.1279 666 972	5.0630 817 262	56
57	5.2628 978 371	5.1945 774 538	5.1280 056 044	5.0631 162 641	57
58	5.2629 393 589	5.1946 142 171	5.1280 381 627	5.0631 451 057	58
59	5.2629 742 512	5.1946 450 457	5.1280 654 081	5.0631 691 906	59
60	5.2630 035 724	5.1946 708 979	5.1280 882 076	5.0631 893 032	60

TABLE 5. PRESENT WORTH OF ONE DOLLAR PER PERIOD
Payable at end of each period

YEARS	20% Nominal Annual Rate	20¼% Nominal Annual Rate	20½% Nominal Annual Rate	20¾% Nominal Annual Rate	YEARS
1	0.8333 333 333	0.8316 008 316	0.8298 755 187	0.8281 573 499	1
2	1.5277 777 778	1.5231 607 747	1.5185 688 952	1.5140 019 461	2
3	2.1064 814 815	2.0982 625 985	2.0900 986 682	2.0819 891 893	3
4	2.5887 345 679	2.5765 177 534	2.5643 972 350	2.5523 719 994	4
5	2.9906 121 399	2.9742 351 380	2.9580 060 042	2.9419 229 809	5
6	3.3255 101 166	3.3049 772 457	3.2846 522 856	3.2645 324 893	6
7	3.6045 917 638	3.5800 226 576	3.5557 280 378	3.5317 039 249	7
8	3.8371 598 032	3.8087 506 508	3.7806 871 683	3.7529 639 130	8
9	4.0309 665 027	3.9989 610 402	3.9673 752 434	3.9362 019 983	9
10	4.1924 720 856	4.1571 401 581	4.1223 031 066	4.0879 519 655	10
11	4.3270 600 713	4.2886 820 442	4.2508 739 474	4.2136 248 161	11
12	4.4392 167 261	4.3980 723 860	4.3575 717 406	4.3177 017 111	12
13	4.5326 806 051	4.4890 414 853	4.4461 176 270	4.4038 937 566	13
14	4.6105 671 709	4.5646 914 638	4.5195 996 905	4.4752 743 326	14
15	4.6754 726 424	4.6276 020 489	4.5805 806 560	4.5343 886 812	15
16	4.7295 605 353	4.6799 185 438	4.6311 872 664	4.5833 446 635	16
17	4.7746 337 794	4.7234 249 845	4.6731 844 534	4.6238 879 201	17
18	4.8121 948 162	4.7596 049 767	4.7080 368 908	4.6574 641 160	18
19	4.8434 956 802	4.7896 922 883	4.7369 600 754	4.6852 704 895	19
20	4.8695 797 335	4.8147 129 217	4.7609 627 181	4.7082 985 420	20
21	4.8913 164 446	4.8355 201 012	4.7808 819 238	4.7273 693 930	21
22	4.9094 303 705	4.8528 233 690	4.7974 123 849	4.7431 630 584	22
23	4.9245 253 087	4.8672 127 808	4.8111 306 099	4.7562 426 984	23
24	4.9371 044 239	4.8791 790 277	4.8225 150 289	4.7670 746 985	24
25	4.9475 870 199	4.8891 301 686	4.8319 626 796	4.7760 452 990	25
26	4.9563 225 166	4.8974 055 456	4.8398 030 536	4.7834 743 677	26
27	4.9636 020 972	4.9042 873 560	4.8463 095 881	4.7896 268 055	27
28	4.9696 684 143	4.9100 102 753	4.8517 092 017	4.7947 219 922	28
29	4.9747 236 786	4.9147 694 597	4.8561 902 089	4.7989 416 084	29
30	4.9789 363 988	4.9187 272 014	4.8599 088 870	4.8024 361 146	30
31	4.9824 469 990	4.9220 184 627	4.8629 949 270	4.8053 301 156	31
32	4.9853 724 992	4.9247 554 783	4.8655 559 560	4.8077 268 038	32
33	4.9878 104 160	4.9270 315 828	4.8676 812 913	4.8097 116 388	33
34	4.9898 420 133	4.9289 243 932	4.8694 450 550	4.8113 553 944	34
35	4.9915 350 111	4.9304 984 559	4.8709 087 594	4.8127 166 828	35
36	4.9929 458 426	4.9318 074 477	4.8721 234 517	4.8138 440 437	36
37	4.9941 215 355	4.9328 960 064	4.8731 314 952	4.8147 776 759	37
38	4.9951 012 796	4.9338 012 527	4.8739 680 458	4.8155 508 703	38
39	4.9959 177 330	4.9345 540 563	4.8746 622 787	4.8161 911 970	39
40	4.9965 981 108	4.9351 800 884	4.8752 384 056	4.8167 214 882	40
41	4.9971 650 923	4.9357 006 972	4.8757 165 191	4.8171 606 527	41
42	4.9976 375 770	4.9361 336 360	4.8761 132 939	4.8175 243 501	42
43	4.9980 313 141	4.9364 936 682	4.8764 425 675	4.8178 255 487	43
44	4.9983 594 284	4.9367 930 712	4.8767 158 237	4.8180 749 886	44
45	4.9986 328 570	4.9370 420 551	4.8769 425 923	4.8182 815 641	45
46	4.9988 607 142	4.9372 491 103	4.8771 307 820	4.8184 526 410	46
47	4.9990 505 952	4.9374 212 975	4.8772 869 560	4.8185 943 197	47
48	4.9992 088 293	4.9375 644 886	4.8774 165 610	4.8187 116 519	48
49	4.9993 406 911	4.9376 835 664	4.8775 241 170	4.8188 088 215	49
50	4.9994 505 759	4.9377 825 916	4.8776 133 751	4.8188 892 931	50
51	4.9995 421 466	4.9378 649 410	4.8776 874 482	4.8189 559 364	51
52	4.9996 184 555	4.9379 334 229	4.8777 489 197	4.8190 111 274	52
53	4.9996 820 462	4.9379 903 725	4.8777 999 333	4.8190 568 343	53
54	4.9997 350 385	4.9380 377 318	4.8778 422 683	4.8190 946 868	54
55	4.9997 791 988	4.9380 771 158	4.8778 774 011	4.8191 260 346	55
56	4.9998 159 990	4.9381 098 676	4.8779 065 569	4.8191 519 955	56
57	4.9998 466 658	4.9381 371 041	4.8779 307 526	4.8191 734 953	57
58	4.9998 722 215	4.9381 597 539	4.8779 508 321	4.8191 913 004	58
59	4.9998 935 179	4.9381 785 895	4.8779 674 955	4.8192 060 459	59
60	4.9999 112 649	4.9381 942 532	4.8779 813 241	4.8192 182 575	60

TABLE 5. PRESENT WORTH OF ONE DOLLAR PER PERIOD
Payable at end of each period

YEARLY Compounding

YEARS	21% Nominal Annual Rate	21¼% Nominal Annual Rate	21½% Nominal Annual Rate	21¾% Nominal Annual Rate	YEARS
1	0.8264 462 810	0.8247 422 680	0.8230 452 675	0.8213 552 361	1
2	1.5094 597 364	1.5049 420 767	1.5004 487 798	1.4959 796 601	2
3	2.0739 336 664	2.0659 316 097	2.0579 825 348	2.0500 859 631	3
4	2.5404 410 466	2.5286 033 894	2.5168 580 534	2.5052 040 765	4
5	2.9259 843 360	2.9101 883 624	2.8945 333 773	2.8790 177 219	5
6	3.2446 151 538	3.2248 976 185	3.2053 772 652	3.1860 515 170	6
7	3.5079 464 081	3.4844 516 441	3.4612 158 562	3.4382 353 322	7
8	3.7255 755 439	3.6985 168 199	3.6717 825 977	3.6453 678 294	8
9	3.9054 343 338	3.8750 654 185	3.8450 885 577	3.8154 971 904	9
10	4.0540 779 618	4.0206 725 101	3.9877 272 080	3.9552 338 320	10
11	4.1769 239 354	4.1407 608 330	4.1051 252 741	4.0700 072 542	11
12	4.2784 495 334	4.2398 027 489	4.2017 491 968	4.1642 770 055	12
13	4.3623 549 862	4.3214 868 032	4.2812 750 591	4.2417 059 593	13
14	4.4316 983 357	4.3888 550 954	4.3467 284 437	4.3053 026 360	14
15	4.4890 068 890	4.4444 165 736	4.4005 995 421	4.3575 380 994	15
16	4.5363 693 298	4.4902 404 730	4.4449 378 948	4.4004 419 708	16
17	4.5755 118 428	4.5280 333 798	4.4814 303 661	4.4356 812 901	17
18	4.6078 610 271	4.5592 027 875	4.5114 653 219	4.4646 252 896	18
19	4.6345 958 902	4.5849 095 155	4.5361 854 501	4.4883 985 952	19
20	4.6566 908 183	4.6061 109 406	4.5565 312 346	4.5079 249 242	20
21	4.6749 510 895	4.6235 966 520	4.5732 767 363	4.5239 629 767	21
22	4.6900 422 227	4.6380 178 573	4.5870 590 422	4.5371 359 152	22
23	4.7025 142 337	4.6499 116 349	4.5984 025 039	4.5479 555 772	23
24	4.7128 216 807	4.6597 209 360	4.6077 386 863	4.5568 423 632	24
25	4.7213 402 320	4.6678 110 812	4.6154 227 871	4.5641 415 714	25
26	4.7283 803 570	4.6744 833 660	4.6217 471 499	4.5701 368 143	26
27	4.7341 986 422	4.6799 862 812	4.6269 523 867	4.5750 610 384	27
28	4.7390 071 423	4.6845 247 680	4.6312 365 323	4.5791 055 757	28
29	4.7429 811 093	4.6882 678 499	4.6347 625 780	4.5824 275 776	29
30	4.7462 653 796	4.6913 549 278	4.6376 646 733	4.5851 561 212	30
31	4.7489 796 526	4.6939 009 713	4.6400 532 290	4.5873 972 248	31
32	4.7512 228 534	4.6960 008 011	4.6420 191 185	4.5892 379 670	32
33	4.7530 767 383	4.6977 326 195	4.6436 371 346	4.5907 498 702	33
34	4.7546 088 746	4.6991 609 233	4.6449 688 351	4.5919 916 799	34
35	4.7558 751 030	4.7003 389 058	4.6460 648 848	4.5930 116 467	35
36	4.7569 215 727	4.7013 104 378	4.6469 669 834	4.5938 494 018	36
37	4.7577 864 237	4.7021 117 013	4.6477 094 514	4.5945 374 964	37
38	4.7585 011 767	4.7027 725 371	4.6483 205 361	4.5951 026 664	38
39	4.7590 918 815	4.7033 175 564	4.6488 234 865	4.5955 668 718	39
40	4.7595 800 674	4.7037 670 568	4.6492 374 374	4.5959 481 493	40
41	4.7599 835 268	4.7041 377 788	4.6495 781 378	4.5962 613 136	41
42	4.7603 169 643	4.7044 435 289	4.6498 585 496	4.5965 185 327	42
43	4.7605 925 325	4.7046 956 940	4.6500 893 413	4.5967 298 010	43
44	4.7608 202 748	4.7049 036 651	4.6502 792 932	4.5969 033 273	44
45	4.7610 084 915	4.7050 751 877	4.6504 356 323	4.5970 458 541	45
46	4.7611 640 426	4.7052 166 497	4.6505 643 064	4.5971 629 191	46
47	4.7612 925 972	4.7053 333 193	4.6506 702 110	4.5972 590 712	47
48	4.7613 988 406	4.7054 295 417	4.6507 573 753	4.5973 380 461	48
49	4.7614 866 452	4.7055 089 004	4.6508 291 155	4.5974 029 126	49
50	4.7615 592 109	4.7055 743 508	4.6508 881 609	4.5974 561 911	50
51	4.7616 191 825	4.7056 283 306	4.6509 367 579	4.5974 999 516	51
52	4.7616 687 459	4.7056 728 500	4.6509 767 555	4.5975 358 945	52
53	4.7617 097 074	4.7057 095 670	4.6510 096 753	4.5975 654 165	53
54	4.7617 435 598	4.7057 398 491	4.6510 367 698	4.5975 896 644	54
55	4.7617 715 370	4.7057 648 240	4.6510 590 698	4.5976 095 807	55
56	4.7617 946 587	4.7057 854 218	4.6510 774 237	4.5976 259 389	56
57	4.7618 137 675	4.7058 024 098	4.6510 925 298	4.5976 393 749	57
58	4.7618 295 599	4.7058 164 204	4.6511 049 628	4.5976 504 106	58
59	4.7618 426 115	4.7058 279 756	4.6511 151 957	4.5976 594 748	59
60	4.7618 533 979	4.7058 375 056	4.6511 236 179	4.5976 669 198	60

TABLE 5. PRESENT WORTH OF ONE DOLLAR PER PERIOD
Payable at end of each period

YEARS	22% Nominal Annual Rate	22¼% Nominal Annual Rate	22½% Nominal Annual Rate	22¾% Nominal Annual Rate	YEARS
1	0.8196 721 311	0.8179 959 100	0.8163 265 306	0.8146 639 511	1
2	1.4915 345 337	1.4871 132 188	1.4827 155 352	1.4783 413 044	2
3	2.0422 414 211	2.0344 484 408	2.0267 065 593	2.0190 153 192	3
4	2.4936 405 091	2.4821 664 137	2.4707 808 648	2.4594 829 485	4
5	2.8636 397 615	2.8483 978 844	2.8332 905 019	2.8183 160 476	5
6	3.1669 178 373	3.1479 737 296	3.1292 167 362	3.1106 444 380	6
7	3.4155 064 240	3.3930 255 457	3.3707 891 724	3.3487 938 395	7
8	3.6192 675 607	3.5934 769 290	3.5679 911 612	3.5428 055 719	8
9	3.7862 848 858	3.7574 453 407	3.7289 723 765	3.7008 599 364	9
10	3.9231 843 326	3.8915 708 308	3.8603 856 134	3.8296 211 294	10
11	4.0353 969 940	4.0012 849 332	3.9676 617 252	3.9345 182 317	11
12	4.1273 745 852	4.0910 306 202	4.0552 340 614	4.0199 741 195	12
13	4.2027 660 535	4.1644 422 251	4.1267 216 828	4.0895 919 507	13
14	4.2645 623 389	4.2244 926 177	4.1850 789 247	4.1463 070 882	14
15	4.3152 150 319	4.2736 135 932	4.2327 174 896	4.1925 108 661	15
16	4.3567 336 327	4.3137 943 503	4.2716 061 139	4.2301 514 184	16
17	4.3907 652 727	4.3466 620 452	4.3033 519 297	4.2608 158 195	17
18	4.4186 600 596	4.3735 476 852	4.3292 668 814	4.2857 970 016	18
19	4.4415 246 390	4.3955 400 288	4.3504 219 440	4.3061 482 702	19
20	4.4602 660 975	4.4135 296 759	4.3676 913 829	4.3227 277 150	20
21	4.4756 279 488	4.4282 451 337	4.3817 888 840	4.3362 343 910	21
22	4.4882 196 302	4.4402 823 179	4.3932 970 481	4.3472 377 931	22
23	4.4985 406 805	4.4501 286 854	4.4026 914 679	4.3562 018 681	23
24	4.5070 005 578	4.4581 829 738	4.4103 603 819	4.3635 045 769	24
25	4.5139 348 834	4.4647 713 487	4.4166 207 199	4.3694 538 304	25
26	4.5196 187 569	4.4701 606 124	4.4217 312 000	4.3743 004 729	26
27	4.5242 776 696	4.4745 690 081	4.4259 030 204	4.3782 488 577	27
28	4.5280 964 505	4.4781 750 578	4.4293 085 881	4.3814 654 645	28
29	4.5312 265 988	4.4811 247 916	4.4320 886 433	4.3840 859 182	29
30	4.5337 922 941	4.4835 376 619	4.4343 580 762	4.3862 207 073	30
31	4.5358 953 230	4.4855 113 798	4.4362 106 744	4.3879 598 430	31
32	4.5376 191 172	4.4871 258 731	4.4377 229 995	4.3893 766 542	32
33	4.5390 320 633	4.4884 465 220	4.4389 575 506	4.3905 308 792	33
34	4.5401 902 158	4.4895 268 073	4.4399 653 475	4.3914 711 846	34
35	4.5411 395 212	4.4904 104 763	4.4407 880 387	4.3922 372 176	35
36	4.5419 176 403	4.4911 333 140	4.4414 596 235	4.3928 612 771	36
37	4.5425 554 429	4.4917 245 922	4.4420 078 559	4.3933 696 758	37
38	4.5430 782 319	4.4922 082 554	4.4424 553 926	4.3937 838 500	38
39	4.5435 067 474	4.4926 038 899	4.4428 207 286	4.3941 212 627	39
40	4.5438 579 897	4.4929 275 173	4.4431 189 621	4.3943 961 407	40
41	4.5441 458 932	4.4931 922 432	4.4433 624 181	4.3946 200 739	41
42	4.5443 818 797	4.4934 087 879	4.4435 611 576	4.3948 025 042	42
43	4.5445 753 112	4.4935 859 206	4.4437 233 940	4.3949 511 236	43
44	4.5447 338 616	4.4937 308 144	4.4438 558 318	4.3950 721 984	44
45	4.5448 638 210	4.4938 493 369	4.4439 639 443	4.3951 708 338	45
46	4.5449 703 451	4.4939 462 879	4.4440 521 995	4.3952 511 884	46
47	4.5450 576 599	4.4940 255 933	4.4441 242 445	4.3953 166 504	47
48	4.5451 292 294	4.4940 904 649	4.4441 830 567	4.3953 699 800	48
49	4.5451 878 930	4.4941 435 296	4.4442 310 667	4.3954 134 256	49
50	4.5452 359 779	4.4941 869 363	4.4442 702 585	4.3954 488 193	50
51	4.5452 753 917	4.4942 224 427	4.4443 022 519	4.3954 776 532	51
52	4.5453 076 981	4.4942 514 869	4.4443 283 689	4.3955 011 431	52
53	4.5453 341 788	4.4942 752 449	4.4443 496 889	4.3955 202 795	53
54	4.5453 558 842	4.4942 946 789	4.4443 670 930	4.3955 358 693	54
55	4.5453 736 756	4.4943 105 758	4.4443 813 004	4.3955 485 697	55
56	4.5453 882 587	4.4943 235 794	4.4443 928 983	4.3955 589 162	56
57	4.5454 002 120	4.4943 342 162	4.4444 023 659	4.3955 673 452	57
58	4.5454 100 099	4.4943 429 172	4.4444 100 946	4.3955 742 120	58
59	4.5454 180 409	4.4943 500 345	4.4444 164 038	4.3955 798 061	59
60	4.5454 246 237	4.4943 558 564	4.4444 215 541	4.3955 843 634	60

TABLE 5. PRESENT WORTH OF ONE DOLLAR PER PERIOD
Payable at end of each period

YEARLY Compounding

YEARS	23% Nominal Annual Rate	24% Nominal Annual Rate	25% Nominal Annual Rate	26% Nominal Annual Rate	YEARS
1	0.8130 081 301	0.8064 516 129	0.8000 000 000	0.7936 507 937	1
2	1.4739 903 497	1.4568 158 169	1.4400 000 000	1.4235 323 759	2
3	2.0113 742 680	1.9813 030 781	1.9520 000 000	1.9234 383 936	3
4	2.4482 717 626	2.4042 766 759	2.3616 000 000	2.3201 892 013	4
5	2.8034 729 777	2.7453 844 160	2.6892 800 000	2.6350 707 946	5
6	3.0922 544 534	3.0204 713 033	2.9514 240 000	2.8849 768 211	6
7	3.3270 361 410	3.2423 155 671	3.1611 392 000	3.0833 149 374	7
8	3.5179 155 618	3.4212 222 316	3.3289 113 600	3.2407 261 408	8
9	3.6731 020 828	3.5655 017 997	3.4631 290 880	3.3656 556 673	9
10	3.7992 699 860	3.6818 562 900	3.5705 032 704	3.4648 060 852	10
11	3.9018 455 171	3.7756 905 565	3.6564 026 163	3.5434 968 930	11
12	3.9852 402 578	3.8513 633 520	3.7251 220 931	3.6059 499 151	12
13	4.0530 408 600	3.9123 898 000	3.7800 976 744	3.6555 158 056	13
14	4.1081 633 008	3.9616 046 774	3.8240 781 396	3.6948 538 140	14
15	4.1529 782 933	4.0012 940 947	3.8592 625 116	3.7260 744 555	15
16	4.1894 132 466	4.0333 016 893	3.8874 100 093	3.7508 527 425	16
17	4.2190 351 598	4.0591 142 655	3.9099 280 075	3.7705 180 496	17
18	4.2431 180 161	4.0799 308 593	3.9279 424 060	3.7861 254 362	18
19	4.2626 975 741	4.0967 184 349	3.9423 539 248	3.7985 122 509	19
20	4.2786 159 139	4.1102 568 024	3.9538 831 398	3.8083 430 563	20
21	4.2915 576 536	4.1211 748 406	3.9631 065 119	3.8161 452 828	21
22	4.3020 793 932	4.1299 797 102	3.9704 852 095	3.8223 375 260	22
23	4.3106 336 530	4.1370 804 114	3.9763 881 676	3.8272 520 048	23
24	4.3175 883 357	4.1428 067 834	3.9811 105 341	3.8311 523 847	24
25	4.3232 425 494	4.1474 248 253	3.9848 884 273	3.8342 479 244	25
26	4.3278 394 710	4.1511 490 527	3.9879 107 418	3.8367 047 019	26
27	4.3315 768 057	4.1541 524 618	3.9903 285 934	3.8386 545 253	27
28	4.3346 152 892	4.1565 745 660	3.9922 628 748	3.8402 020 042	28
29	4.3370 856 010	4.1585 278 758	3.9938 102 998	3.8414 301 621	29
30	4.3390 939 845	4.1601 031 257	3.9950 482 398	3.8424 048 905	30
31	4.3407 268 167	4.1613 734 884	3.9960 385 919	3.8431 784 846	31
32	4.3420 543 225	4.1623 979 745	3.9968 308 735	3.8437 924 481	32
33	4.3431 335 955	4.1632 241 730	3.9974 646 988	3.8442 797 207	33
34	4.3440 110 533	4.1638 904 621	3.9979 717 590	3.8446 664 450	34
35	4.3447 244 336	4.1644 277 920	3.9983 774 072	3.8449 733 690	35
36	4.3453 044 175	4.1648 611 226	3.9987 019 258	3.8452 169 596	36
37	4.3457 759 492	4.1652 105 827	3.9989 615 406	3.8454 102 854	37
38	4.3461 593 083	4.1654 924 054	3.9991 692 325	3.8455 637 185	38
39	4.3464 709 824	4.1657 196 818	3.9993 353 860	3.8456 854 909	39
40	4.3467 243 759	4.1659 029 692	3.9994 683 088	3.8457 821 356	40
41	4.3469 303 869	4.1660 507 816	3.9995 746 470	3.8458 588 378	41
42	4.3470 978 755	4.1661 699 852	3.9996 597 176	3.8459 197 125	42
43	4.3472 340 452	4.1662 661 171	3.9997 277 741	3.8459 680 258	43
44	4.3473 447 522	4.1663 436 428	3.9997 822 193	3.8460 063 697	44
45	4.3474 347 579	4.1664 061 635	3.9998 257 754	3.8460 368 014	45
46	4.3475 079 332	4.1664 565 835	3.9998 606 203	3.8460 609 535	46
47	4.3475 674 254	4.1664 972 448	3.9998 884 963	3.8460 801 218	47
48	4.3476 157 930	4.1665 300 361	3.9999 107 970	3.8460 953 348	48
49	4.3476 551 163	4.1665 564 807	3.9999 286 376	3.8461 074 085	49
50	4.3476 870 864	4.1665 778 070	3.9999 429 101	3.8461 169 909	50
51	4.3477 130 784	4.1665 950 057	3.9999 543 281	3.8461 245 960	51
52	4.3477 342 100	4.1666 088 755	3.9999 634 625	3.8461 306 317	52
53	4.3477 513 903	4.1666 200 609	3.9999 707 700	3.8461 354 220	53
54	4.3477 653 580	4.1666 290 814	3.9999 766 160	3.8461 392 238	54
55	4.3477 767 138	4.1666 363 560	3.9999 812 928	3.8461 422 411	55
56	4.3477 859 462	4.1666 422 225	3.9999 850 342	3.8461 446 358	56
57	4.3477 934 522	4.1666 469 537	3.9999 880 274	3.8461 465 364	57
58	4.3477 995 546	4.1666 507 691	3.9999 904 219	3.8461 480 447	58
59	4.3478 045 159	4.1666 538 460	3.9999 923 375	3.8461 492 418	59
60	4.3478 085 495	4.1666 563 274	3.9999 938 700	3.8461 501 919	60

YEARLY
Compounding

TABLE 5. PRESENT WORTH OF ONE DOLLAR PER PERIOD
Payable at end of each period

YEARS	27% Nominal Annual Rate	28% Nominal Annual Rate	29% Nominal Annual Rate	30% Nominal Annual Rate	YEARS
1	0.7874 015 748	0.7812 500 000	0.7751 937 984	0.7692 307 692	1
2	1.4074 028 148	1.3916 015 625	1.3761 192 236	1.3609 467 456	2
3	1.8955 927 676	1.8684 387 207	1.8419 528 865	1.8161 128 812	3
4	2.2799 943 052	2.2409 677 505	2.2030 642 531	2.1662 406 778	4
5	2.5826 726 812	2.5320 060 551	2.4829 955 450	2.4355 697 522	5
6	2.8210 021 112	2.7593 797 306	2.6999 965 465	2.6427 459 632	6
7	3.0086 630 797	2.9370 154 145	2.8682 143 772	2.8021 122 794	7
8	3.1564 276 218	3.0757 932 926	2.9986 157 963	2.9247 017 534	8
9	3.2727 776 550	3.1842 135 098	3.0997 021 676	3.0190 013 488	9
10	3.3643 918 543	3.2689 168 046	3.1780 636 958	3.0915 394 990	10
11	3.4365 290 191	3.3350 912 536	3.2388 090 665	3.1473 380 762	11
12	3.4933 299 363	3.3867 900 418	3.2858 985 012	3.1902 600 586	12
13	3.5380 550 680	3.4271 797 202	3.3224 019 389	3.2232 769 682	13
14	3.5732 717 071	3.4587 341 564	3.3506 991 775	3.2486 745 909	14
15	3.6010 013 441	3.4833 860 597	3.3726 350 213	3.2682 112 238	15
16	3.6228 357 041	3.5026 453 591	3.3896 395 514	3.2832 394 029	16
17	3.6400 281 134	3.5176 916 868	3.4028 213 577	3.2947 995 407	17
18	3.6535 654 436	3.5294 466 303	3.4130 398 121	3.3036 919 544	18
19	3.6642 247 588	3.5386 301 799	3.4209 610 947	3.3105 322 726	19
20	3.6726 179 203	3.5458 048 281	3.4271 016 238	3.3157 940 558	20
21	3.6792 267 089	3.5514 100 219	3.4318 617 239	3.3198 415 814	21
22	3.6844 304 794	3.5557 890 796	3.4355 517 239	3.3229 550 626	22
23	3.6885 279 366	3.5592 102 185	3.4384 121 891	3.3253 500 482	23
24	3.6917 542 808	3.5618 829 832	3.4406 296 039	3.3271 923 448	24
25	3.6942 947 093	3.5639 710 806	3.4423 485 302	3.3286 094 960	25
26	3.6962 950 467	3.5656 024 067	3.4436 810 312	3.3296 996 123	26
27	3.6978 701 155	3.5668 768 803	3.4447 139 776	3.3305 381 633	27
28	3.6991 103 272	3.5678 725 627	3.4455 147 113	3.3311 832 025	28
29	3.7000 868 718	3.5686 504 396	3.4461 354 352	3.3316 793 866	29
30	3.7008 558 045	3.5692 581 559	3.4466 166 164	3.3320 610 666	30
31	3.7014 612 634	3.5697 329 343	3.4469 896 251	3.3323 546 666	31
32	3.7019 380 027	3.5701 038 549	3.4472 787 792	3.3325 805 128	32
33	3.7023 133 879	3.5703 936 367	3.4475 029 296	3.3327 542 406	33
34	3.7026 089 669	3.5706 200 287	3.4476 766 896	3.3328 878 774	34
35	3.7028 417 062	3.5707 968 974	3.4478 113 873	3.3329 906 749	35
36	3.7030 249 655	3.5709 350 761	3.4479 158 041	3.3330 697 499	36
37	3.7031 692 642	3.5710 430 282	3.4479 967 474	3.3331 305 769	37
38	3.7032 828 852	3.5711 273 658	3.4480 594 941	3.3331 773 668	38
39	3.7033 723 505	3.5711 932 545	3.4481 081 349	3.3332 133 591	39
40	3.7034 427 957	3.5712 447 301	3.4481 458 410	3.3332 410 455	40
41	3.7034 982 643	3.5712 849 454	3.4481 750 706	3.3332 623 427	41
42	3.7035 419 404	3.5713 163 636	3.4481 977 291	3.3332 787 251	42
43	3.7035 763 310	3.5713 409 090	3.4482 152 939	3.3332 913 270	43
44	3.7036 034 103	3.5713 600 852	3.4482 289 100	3.3333 010 208	44
45	3.7036 247 325	3.5713 750 666	3.4482 394 651	3.3333 084 775	45
46	3.7036 415 216	3.5713 867 707	3.4482 476 474	3.3333 142 135	46
47	3.7036 547 415	3.5713 959 146	3.4482 539 902	3.3333 186 258	47
48	3.7036 651 508	3.5714 030 583	3.4482 589 071	3.3333 220 198	48
49	3.7036 733 470	3.5714 086 393	3.4482 627 187	3.3333 246 306	49
50	3.7036 798 008	3.5714 129 995	3.4482 656 734	3.3333 266 389	50
51	3.7036 848 825	3.5714 164 058	3.4482 679 639	3.3333 281 838	51
52	3.7036 888 839	3.5714 190 671	3.4482 697 395	3.3333 293 722	52
53	3.7036 920 346	3.5714 211 461	3.4482 711 159	3.3333 302 863	53
54	3.7036 945 154	3.5714 227 704	3.4482 721 828	3.3333 309 894	54
55	3.7036 964 688	3.5714 240 394	3.4482 730 099	3.3333 315 303	55
56	3.7036 980 069	3.5714 250 308	3.4482 736 511	3.3333 319 464	56
57	3.7036 992 181	3.5714 258 053	3.4482 741 482	3.3333 322 665	57
58	3.7037 001 717	3.5714 264 104	3.4482 745 335	3.3333 325 127	58
59	3.7037 009 226	3.5714 268 831	3.4482 748 321	3.3333 327 021	59
60	3.7037 015 139	3.5714 272 524	3.4482 750 637	3.3333 328 477	60

TABLE 6. PARTIAL PAYMENT TO AMORTIZE ONE
Payable at end of each period

YEARS	5% Nominal Annual Rate	5¼% Nominal Annual Rate	5½% Nominal Annual Rate	5¾% Nominal Annual Rate	YEARS
1	1.0500 000 000	1.0525 000 000	1.0550 000 000	1.0575 000 000	1
2	0.5378 048 780	0.5397 107 186	0.5416 180 049	0.5435 267 315	2
3	0.3672 085 646	0.3689 300 363	0.3706 540 747	0.3723 806 701	3
4	0.2820 118 326	0.2836 513 576	0.2852 944 853	0.2869 412 017	4
5	0.2309 747 981	0.2325 733 168	0.2341 764 362	0.2357 841 371	5
6	0.1970 174 681	0.1985 954 203	0.2001 789 476	0.2017 680 253	6
7	0.1728 198 184	0.1743 888 524	0.1759 644 178	0.1775 464 834	7
8	0.1547 218 136	0.1562 891 770	0.1578 640 118	0.1594 462 799	8
9	0.1406 900 800	0.1422 605 712	0.1438 394 585	0.1454 266 954	9
10	0.1295 045 750	0.1310 815 194	0.1326 677 687	0.1342 632 671	10
11	0.1203 888 915	0.1219 746 736	0.1235 706 532	0.1251 767 637	11
12	0.1128 254 100	0.1144 217 842	0.1160 292 312	0.1176 476 727	12
13	0.1064 557 652	0.1080 640 468	0.1096 842 587	0.1113 163 092	13
14	0.1010 239 695	0.1026 451 581	0.1042 791 154	0.1059 257 351	14
15	0.0963 422 876	0.0979 771 489	0.0996 255 976	0.1012 875 108	15
16	0.0922 699 080	0.0939 190 304	0.0955 825 380	0.0972 602 900	16
17	0.0886 991 417	0.0903 629 764	0.0920 419 723	0.0937 359 691	17
18	0.0855 462 223	0.0872 251 119	0.0889 199 163	0.0906 304 539	18
19	0.0827 450 104	0.0844 392 107	0.0861 500 559	0.0878 773 417	19
20	0.0802 425 872	0.0819 522 832	0.0836 793 300	0.0854 234 988	20
21	0.0779 961 071	0.0797 214 252	0.0814 647 754	0.0832 259 022	21
22	0.0759 705 086	0.0777 115 264	0.0794 712 319	0.0812 493 418	22
23	0.0741 368 219	0.0758 935 759	0.0776 696 472	0.0794 647 226	23
24	0.0724 709 008	0.0742 433 921	0.0760 358 037	0.0778 477 910	24
25	0.0709 524 573	0.0727 406 571	0.0745 493 529	0.0763 781 674	25
26	0.0695 643 207	0.0713 681 737	0.0731 930 713	0.0750 386 012	26
27	0.0682 918 599	0.0701 112 882	0.0719 522 817	0.0738 143 920	27
28	0.0671 225 304	0.0689 574 362	0.0708 143 996	0.0726 929 348	28
29	0.0660 455 149	0.0678 957 825	0.0697 685 720	0.0716 633 587	29
30	0.0650 514 351	0.0669 169 335	0.0688 053 897	0.0707 162 386	30
31	0.0641 321 204	0.0660 127 048	0.0679 166 543	0.0698 433 625	31
32	0.0632 804 189	0.0651 759 322	0.0670 951 895	0.0690 375 417	32
33	0.0624 900 437	0.0644 003 179	0.0663 346 865	0.0682 924 570	33
34	0.0617 554 454	0.0636 803 028	0.0656 295 769	0.0676 025 304	34
35	0.0610 717 072	0.0630 109 616	0.0649 749 266	0.0669 628 198	35
36	0.0604 344 571	0.0623 879 146	0.0643 663 488	0.0663 689 312	36
37	0.0598 397 945	0.0618 072 544	0.0637 999 295	0.0658 169 445	37
38	0.0592 842 282	0.0612 654 839	0.0632 721 659	0.0653 033 517	38
39	0.0587 646 242	0.0607 594 639	0.0627 799 139	0.0648 250 044	39
40	0.0582 781 612	0.0602 863 683	0.0623 203 434	0.0643 790 687	40
41	0.0578 222 924	0.0598 436 465	0.0618 909 001	0.0639 629 876	41
42	0.0573 947 131	0.0594 289 905	0.0614 892 731	0.0635 744 478	42
43	0.0569 933 328	0.0590 403 066	0.0611 133 667	0.0632 113 517	43
44	0.0566 162 506	0.0586 756 919	0.0607 612 757	0.0628 717 934	44
45	0.0562 617 347	0.0583 334 124	0.0604 312 651	0.0625 540 370	45
46	0.0559 282 036	0.0580 118 853	0.0601 217 512	0.0622 564 988	46
47	0.0556 142 109	0.0577 096 629	0.0598 312 858	0.0619 777 310	47
48	0.0553 184 306	0.0574 254 187	0.0595 585 424	0.0617 164 076	48
49	0.0550 396 453	0.0571 579 348	0.0593 023 035	0.0614 713 125	49
50	0.0547 767 355	0.0569 060 917	0.0590 614 501	0.0612 413 281	50
51	0.0545 286 697	0.0566 688 583	0.0588 349 523	0.0610 254 263	51
52	0.0542 944 966	0.0564 452 836	0.0586 218 603	0.0608 226 596	52
53	0.0540 733 368	0.0562 344 893	0.0584 212 975	0.0606 321 537	53
54	0.0538 643 770	0.0560 356 631	0.0582 324 534	0.0604 531 008	54
55	0.0536 668 637	0.0558 480 527	0.0580 545 778	0.0602 847 538	55
56	0.0534 800 978	0.0556 709 607	0.0578 869 756	0.0601 264 207	56
57	0.0533 034 300	0.0555 037 397	0.0577 290 020	0.0599 774 599	57
58	0.0531 362 568	0.0553 457 878	0.0575 800 578	0.0598 372 760	58
59	0.0529 780 161	0.0551 965 454	0.0574 395 863	0.0597 053 159	59
60	0.0528 281 845	0.0550 554 911	0.0573 070 692	0.0595 810 653	60

TABLE 6. PARTIAL PAYMENT TO AMORTIZE ONE
Payable at end of each period

YEARS	6% Nominal Annual Rate	6¼% Nominal Annual Rate	6½% Nominal Annual Rate	6¾% Nominal Annual Rate	YEARS
1	1.0600 000 000	1.0625 000 000	1.0650 000 000	1.0675 000 000	1
2	0.5454 368 932	0.5473 484 848	0.5492 615 012	0.5511 759 371	2
3	0.3741 098 128	0.3758 414 933	0.3775 757 019	0.3793 124 292	3
4	0.2885 914 924	0.2902 453 433	0.2919 027 404	0.2935 636 696	4
5	0.2373 964 004	0.2390 132 070	0.2406 345 376	0.2422 603 731	5
6	0.2033 626 285	0.2049 627 324	0.2065 683 122	0.2081 793 430	6
7	0.1791 350 181	0.1807 299 905	0.1823 313 693	0.1839 391 229	7
8	0.1610 359 426	0.1626 329 614	0.1642 372 971	0.1658 489 106	8
9	0.1470 222 350	0.1486 260 300	0.1502 380 329	0.1518 581 957	9
10	0.1358 679 582	0.1374 817 850	0.1391 046 901	0.1407 366 154	10
11	0.1267 929 381	0.1284 191 083	0.1300 552 058	0.1317 011 613	11
12	0.1192 770 294	0.1209 172 209	0.1225 681 661	0.1242 297 830	12
13	0.1129 601 053	0.1146 155 531	0.1162 825 571	0.1179 610 213	13
14	0.1075 849 090	0.1092 565 278	0.1109 404 806	0.1126 366 553	14
15	0.1029 627 640	0.1046 512 307	0.1063 527 830	0.1080 672 913	15
16	0.0989 521 436	0.1006 579 538	0.1023 775 740	0.1041 108 553	16
17	0.0954 448 042	0.0971 683 124	0.0989 063 265	0.1006 586 771	17
18	0.0923 565 406	0.0940 979 892	0.0958 546 103	0.0976 262 124	18
19	0.0896 208 604	0.0913 804 015	0.0931 557 517	0.0949 466 955	19
20	0.0871 845 570	0.0889 622 687	0.0907 563 954	0.0925 666 956	20
21	0.0850 045 467	0.0868 004 459	0.0886 133 343	0.0904 429 431	21
22	0.0830 455 685	0.0848 596 209	0.0866 912 043	0.0885 400 217	22
23	0.0812 784 847	0.0831 106 121	0.0849 607 802	0.0868 286 615	23
24	0.0796 790 050	0.0815 290 926	0.0833 976 975	0.0852 844 606	24
25	0.0782 267 182	0.0800 946 193	0.0819 814 811	0.0838 869 117	25
26	0.0769 043 467	0.0787 898 870	0.0806 947 983	0.0826 186 545	26
27	0.0756 971 663	0.0776 001 480	0.0795 228 776	0.0814 648 937	27
28	0.0745 925 515	0.0765 127 561	0.0784 530 522	0.0804 129 423	28
29	0.0735 796 135	0.0755 168 045	0.0774 743 976	0.0794 518 582	29
30	0.0726 489 115	0.0746 028 369	0.0765 774 422	0.0785 721 549	30
31	0.0717 922 196	0.0737 626 140	0.0757 539 335	0.0777 655 672	31
32	0.0710 023 374	0.0729 889 235	0.0749 966 481	0.0770 248 610	32
33	0.0702 729 350	0.0722 754 257	0.0742 992 365	0.0763 436 779	33
34	0.0695 984 254	0.0716 165 250	0.0736 560 953	0.0757 164 072	34
35	0.0689 738 590	0.0710 072 643	0.0730 622 606	0.0751 380 792	35
36	0.0683 948 348	0.0704 432 368	0.0725 133 205	0.0746 042 775	36
37	0.0678 574 274	0.0699 205 119	0.0720 053 400	0.0741 110 638	37
38	0.0673 581 240	0.0694 355 731	0.0715 347 995	0.0736 549 164	38
39	0.0668 937 724	0.0689 852 650	0.0710 985 416	0.0732 326 766	39
40	0.0664 615 359	0.0685 667 487	0.0706 937 260	0.0728 415 040	40
41	0.0660 588 551	0.0681 774 635	0.0703 177 915	0.0724 788 379	41
42	0.0656 834 152	0.0678 150 939	0.0699 684 229	0.0721 423 647	42
43	0.0653 331 178	0.0674 775 415	0.0696 435 230	0.0718 299 891	43
44	0.0650 060 565	0.0671 629 004	0.0693 411 874	0.0715 398 096	44
45	0.0647 004 958	0.0668 694 364	0.0690 596 841	0.0712 700 975	45
46	0.0644 148 527	0.0665 955 681	0.0687 974 344	0.0710 192 782	46
47	0.0641 476 805	0.0663 398 510	0.0685 529 973	0.0707 859 149	47
48	0.0638 976 549	0.0661 009 636	0.0683 250 549	0.0705 686 946	48
49	0.0636 635 619	0.0658 776 947	0.0681 124 000	0.0703 664 154	49
50	0.0634 442 864	0.0656 689 327	0.0679 139 255	0.0701 779 758	50
51	0.0632 388 028	0.0654 736 559	0.0677 286 146	0.0700 023 649	51
52	0.0630 461 669	0.0652 909 239	0.0675 555 319	0.0698 386 536	52
53	0.0628 655 076	0.0651 198 702	0.0673 938 164	0.0696 859 872	53
54	0.0626 960 209	0.0649 596 952	0.0672 426 740	0.0695 435 785	54
55	0.0625 369 634	0.0648 096 603	0.0671 013 722	0.0694 107 014	55
56	0.0623 876 472	0.0646 690 828	0.0669 692 339	0.0692 866 863	56
57	0.0622 474 350	0.0645 373 305	0.0668 456 332	0.0691 709 142	57
58	0.0621 157 359	0.0644 138 178	0.0667 299 909	0.0690 628 130	58
59	0.0619 920 012	0.0642 980 017	0.0666 217 702	0.0689 618 533	59
60	0.0618 757 215	0.0641 893 780	0.0665 204 735	0.0688 675 449	60

TABLE 6. PARTIAL PAYMENT TO AMORTIZE ONE
Payable at end of each period

YEARS	7% Nominal Annual Rate	7¼% Nominal Annual Rate	7½% Nominal Annual Rate	7¾% Nominal Annual Rate	YEARS
1	1.0700 000 000	1.0725 000 000	1.0750 000 000	1.0775 000 000	1
2	0.5530 917 874	0.5550 090 470	0.5569 277 108	0.5588 477 738	2
3	0.3810 516 657	0.3827 934 018	0.3845 376 282	0.3862 843 354	3
4	0.2952 281 167	0.2968 960 677	0.2985 675 087	0.3002 424 256	4
5	0.2438 906 944	0.2455 254 824	0.2471 647 178	0.2488 083 816	5
6	0.2097 957 998	0.2114 176 575	0.2130 448 912	0.2146 774 758	6
7	0.1855 532 196	0.1871 736 277	0.1888 003 154	0.1904 332 506	7
8	0.1674 677 625	0.1690 938 133	0.1707 270 232	0.1723 673 523	8
9	0.1534 864 701	0.1551 228 077	0.1567 671 595	0.1584 194 764	9
10	0.1423 775 027	0.1440 272 931	0.1456 859 274	0.1473 533 459	10
11	0.1333 569 048	0.1350 223 660	0.1366 974 737	0.1383 821 565	11
12	0.1259 019 887	0.1275 846 995	0.1292 778 313	0.1309 812 990	12
13	0.1196 508 481	0.1213 519 395	0.1230 641 963	0.1247 875 184	13
14	0.1143 449 386	0.1160 652 161	0.1177 973 721	0.1195 412 901	14
15	0.1097 946 247	0.1115 346 509	0.1132 872 363	0.1150 522 462	15
16	0.1058 576 477	0.1076 177 994	0.1093 911 571	0.1111 775 665	16
17	0.1024 251 931	0.1042 057 015	0.1060 000 282	0.1078 079 971	17
18	0.0994 126 017	0.1012 135 825	0.1030 289 578	0.1048 585 289	18
19	0.0967 530 148	0.0985 744 900	0.1004 108 994	0.1022 620 199	19
20	0.0943 929 257	0.0962 348 402	0.0980 921 916	0.0999 647 312	20
21	0.0922 890 017	0.0941 512 369	0.0960 293 742	0.0979 231 377	21
22	0.0904 057 732	0.0922 881 574	0.0941 868 710	0.0961 016 097	22
23	0.0887 139 263	0.0906 162 427	0.0925 352 780	0.0944 706 983	23
24	0.0871 890 207	0.0891 110 150	0.0910 500 795	0.0930 058 498	24
25	0.0858 105 172	0.0877 519 025	0.0897 106 716	0.0916 864 289	25
26	0.0845 610 279	0.0865 214 900	0.0884 996 124	0.0904 949 668	26
27	0.0834 257 340	0.0854 049 358	0.0874 020 369	0.0894 165 766	27
28	0.0823 919 283	0.0843 895 127	0.0864 051 993	0.0884 384 939	28
29	0.0814 486 518	0.0834 642 454	0.0854 981 081	0.0875 497 125	29
30	0.0805 864 035	0.0826 196 190	0.0846 712 358	0.0867 406 925	30
31	0.0797 969 061	0.0818 473 449	0.0839 162 831	0.0860 031 255	31
32	0.0790 729 155	0.0811 401 700	0.0832 259 887	0.0853 297 432	32
33	0.0784 080 653	0.0804 917 204	0.0825 939 728	0.0847 141 607	33
34	0.0777 967 381	0.0798 963 736	0.0820 146 084	0.0841 507 481	34
35	0.0772 339 596	0.0793 491 512	0.0814 829 147	0.0836 345 234	35
36	0.0767 153 097	0.0788 456 308	0.0809 944 680	0.0831 610 631	36
37	0.0762 368 480	0.0783 818 710	0.0805 453 271	0.0827 264 278	37
38	0.0757 950 515	0.0779 543 489	0.0801 319 709	0.0823 270 991	38
39	0.0753 867 616	0.0775 599 071	0.0797 512 443	0.0819 599 263	39
40	0.0750 091 389	0.0771 957 084	0.0794 003 138	0.0816 220 809	40
41	0.0746 596 245	0.0768 591 971	0.0790 766 282	0.0813 110 177	41
42	0.0743 359 072	0.0765 480 660	0.0787 778 858	0.0810 244 417	42
43	0.0740 358 953	0.0762 602 278	0.0785 020 052	0.0807 602 794	43
44	0.0737 576 913	0.0759 937 906	0.0782 471 012	0.0805 166 536	44
45	0.0734 995 710	0.0757 470 360	0.0780 114 630	0.0802 918 622	45
46	0.0732 599 650	0.0755 184 011	0.0777 935 352	0.0800 843 592	46
47	0.0730 374 421	0.0753 064 616	0.0775 919 020	0.0798 927 383	47
48	0.0728 306 953	0.0751 099 179	0.0774 052 724	0.0797 157 185	48
49	0.0726 385 294	0.0749 275 824	0.0772 324 676	0.0795 521 314	49
50	0.0724 598 495	0.0747 583 683	0.0770 724 102	0.0794 009 099	50
51	0.0722 936 519	0.0746 012 800	0.0769 241 141	0.0792 610 787	51
52	0.0721 390 147	0.0744 554 044	0.0767 866 757	0.0791 317 448	52
53	0.0719 950 908	0.0743 199 028	0.0766 592 661	0.0790 120 905	53
54	0.0718 611 007	0.0741 940 045	0.0765 411 247	0.0789 013 656	54
55	0.0717 363 264	0.0740 770 005	0.0764 315 521	0.0787 988 821	55
56	0.0716 201 059	0.0739 682 379	0.0763 299 053	0.0787 040 076	56
57	0.0715 118 286	0.0738 671 148	0.0762 355 927	0.0786 161 612	57
58	0.0714 109 304	0.0737 730 763	0.0761 480 689	0.0785 348 086	58
59	0.0713 168 900	0.0736 856 102	0.0760 668 318	0.0784 594 577	59
60	0.0712 292 255	0.0736 042 434	0.0759 914 178	0.0783 896 558	60

TABLE 6. PARTIAL PAYMENT TO AMORTIZE ONE
Payable at end of each period

YEARS	8% Nominal Annual Rate	8¼% Nominal Annual Rate	8½% Nominal Annual Rate	8¾% Nominal Annual Rate	YEARS
1	1.0800 000 000	1.0825 000 000	1.0850 000 000	1.0875 000 000	1
2	0.5607 692 308	0.5626 920 768	0.5646 163 070	0.5665 419 162	2
3	0.3880 335 140	0.3897 851 549	0.3915 392 485	0.3932 957 858	3
4	0.3019 208 045	0.3036 026 314	0.3052 878 926	0.3069 765 741	4
5	0.2504 564 546	0.2521 089 177	0.2537 657 519	0.2554 269 380	5
6	0.2163 153 862	0.2179 585 973	0.2196 070 840	0.2212 608 210	6
7	0.1920 724 014	0.1937 177 357	0.1953 692 212	0.1970 268 257	7
8	0.1740 147 606	0.1756 692 077	0.1773 306 533	0.1789 990 569	8
9	0.1600 797 092	0.1617 478 081	0.1634 237 233	0.1651 074 047	9
10	0.1490 294 887	0.1507 142 953	0.1524 077 051	0.1541 096 571	10
11	0.1400 763 421	0.1417 799 582	0.1434 929 316	0.1452 151 891	11
12	0.1326 950 169	0.1344 188 989	0.1361 528 581	0.1378 968 072	12
13	0.1265 218 052	0.1282 669 552	0.1300 228 662	0.1317 894 355	13
14	0.1212 968 528	0.1230 639 419	0.1248 424 382	0.1266 322 220	14
15	0.1168 295 449	0.1186 189 958	0.1204 204 614	0.1222 338 033	15
16	0.1129 768 720	0.1147 889 169	0.1166 135 439	0.1184 505 944	16
17	0.1096 294 315	0.1114 641 532	0.1133 119 832	0.1151 727 417	17
18	0.1067 020 959	0.1085 594 578	0.1104 304 127	0.1123 147 580	18
19	0.1041 276 275	0.1060 074 967	0.1079 014 015	0.1098 091 151	19
20	0.1018 522 088	0.1037 543 737	0.1056 709 744	0.1076 017 588	20
21	0.0998 322 503	0.1017 564 344	0.1036 954 120	0.1056 489 047	21
22	0.0980 320 684	0.0999 779 414	0.1019 389 233	0.1039 147 087	22
23	0.0964 221 692	0.0983 893 563	0.1003 719 258	0.1023 695 444	23
24	0.0949 779 616	0.0969 660 509	0.0989 697 546	0.1009 887 111	24
25	0.0936 787 791	0.0956 873 278	0.0977 116 825	0.0997 514 527	25
26	0.0925 071 267	0.0945 356 670	0.0965 801 651	0.0986 402 014	26
27	0.0914 480 962	0.0934 961 396	0.0955 602 540	0.0976 399 907	27
28	0.0904 889 057	0.0925 559 473	0.0946 391 357	0.0967 379 932	28
29	0.0896 185 350	0.0917 040 571	0.0938 057 657	0.0959 231 541	29
30	0.0888 274 334	0.0909 309 086	0.0930 505 753	0.0951 858 985	30
31	0.0881 072 841	0.0902 281 783	0.0923 652 359	0.0945 178 940	31
32	0.0874 508 132	0.0895 885 879	0.0917 424 664	0.0939 118 586	32
33	0.0868 516 324	0.0890 057 472	0.0911 758 763	0.0933 614 033	33
34	0.0863 041 101	0.0884 740 247	0.0906 598 358	0.0928 609 020	34
35	0.0858 032 646	0.0879 884 403	0.0901 893 685	0.0924 053 836	35
36	0.0853 446 741	0.0875 445 759	0.0897 600 615	0.0919 904 426	36
37	0.0849 244 025	0.0871 385 004	0.0893 679 904	0.0916 121 629	37
38	0.0845 389 361	0.0867 667 060	0.0890 096 556	0.0912 670 548	38
39	0.0841 851 297	0.0864 260 551	0.0886 819 284	0.0909 520 009	39
40	0.0838 601 615	0.0861 137 343	0.0883 820 056	0.0906 642 097	40
41	0.0835 614 940	0.0858 272 154	0.0881 073 700	0.0904 011 768	41
42	0.0832 868 407	0.0855 642 218	0.0878 557 568	0.0901 606 508	42
43	0.0830 341 370	0.0853 226 997	0.0876 251 245	0.0899 406 043	43
44	0.0828 015 156	0.0851 007 930	0.0874 136 299	0.0897 392 086	44
45	0.0825 872 845	0.0848 968 216	0.0872 196 061	0.0895 548 114	45
46	0.0823 899 085	0.0847 092 622	0.0870 415 434	0.0893 859 184	46
47	0.0822 079 922	0.0845 367 322	0.0868 780 731	0.0892 311 756	47
48	0.0820 402 660	0.0843 779 743	0.0867 279 519	0.0890 893 556	48
49	0.0818 855 731	0.0842 318 448	0.0865 900 501	0.0889 593 436	49
50	0.0817 428 582	0.0840 973 012	0.0864 633 395	0.0888 401 268	50
51	0.0816 111 575	0.0839 733 928	0.0863 468 835	0.0887 307 838	51
52	0.0814 895 903	0.0838 592 518	0.0862 398 282	0.0886 304 758	52
53	0.0813 773 506	0.0837 540 852	0.0861 413 945	0.0885 384 385	53
54	0.0812 737 003	0.0836 571 677	0.0860 508 710	0.0884 539 750	54
55	0.0811 779 629	0.0835 678 356	0.0859 676 075	0.0883 764 496	55
56	0.0810 895 180	0.0834 854 810	0.0858 910 096	0.0883 052 817	56
57	0.0810 077 963	0.0834 095 471	0.0858 205 332	0.0882 399 410	57
58	0.0809 322 748	0.0833 395 228	0.0857 556 803	0.0881 799 428	58
59	0.0808 624 729	0.0832 749 397	0.0856 959 948	0.0881 248 441	59
60	0.0807 979 488	0.0832 153 675	0.0856 410 586	0.0880 742 394	60

TABLE 6. PARTIAL PAYMENT TO AMORTIZE ONE
Payable at end of each period

YEARLY Compounding

YEARS	9% Nominal Annual Rate	9¼% Nominal Annual Rate	9½% Nominal Annual Rate	9¾% Nominal Annual Rate	YEARS
1	1.0900 000 000	1.0925 000 000	1.0950 000 000	1.0975 000 000	1
2	0.5684 688 995	0.5703 972 521	0.5723 269 690	0.5742 580 453	2
3	0.3950 547 573	0.3968 161 541	0.3985 799 668	0.4003 461 863	3
4	0.3086 686 621	0.3103 641 428	0.3120 630 025	0.3137 652 273	4
5	0.2570 924 570	0.2587 622 898	0.2604 364 173	0.2621 148 207	5
6	0.2229 197 833	0.2245 839 456	0.2262 532 826	0.2279 277 693	6
7	0.1986 905 168	0.2003 602 623	0.2020 360 296	0.2037 177 862	7
8	0.1806 743 778	0.1823 565 753	0.1840 456 084	0.1857 414 362	8
9	0.1667 988 021	0.1684 978 649	0.1702 045 426	0.1719 187 843	9
10	0.1558 200 899	0.1575 389 420	0.1592 661 517	0.1610 016 567	10
11	0.1469 466 567	0.1486 872 605	0.1504 369 258	0.1521 955 780	11
12	0.1396 506 585	0.1414 143 237	0.1431 877 142	0.1449 707 411	12
13	0.1335 665 597	0.1353 541 351	0.1371 520 575	0.1389 602 220	13
14	0.1284 331 730	0.1302 451 703	0.1320 680 923	0.1339 018 174	14
15	0.1240 588 827	0.1258 955 599	0.1277 436 950	0.1296 031 476	15
16	0.1202 999 097	0.1221 613 301	0.1240 346 957	0.1259 198 461	16
17	0.1170 462 485	0.1189 323 225	0.1208 307 825	0.1227 414 470	17
18	0.1142 122 907	0.1161 228 071	0.1180 461 037	0.1199 819 766	18
19	0.1117 304 107	0.1136 650 609	0.1156 128 384	0.1175 735 164	19
20	0.1095 464 750	0.1115 048 710	0.1134 766 953	0.1154 616 966	20
21	0.1076 166 348	0.1095 983 246	0.1115 936 973	0.1136 024 773	21
22	0.1059 049 930	0.1079 094 722	0.1099 278 440	0.1119 598 073	22
23	0.1043 818 800	0.1064 086 023	0.1084 493 824	0.1105 038 939	23
24	0.1030 225 607	0.1050 709 455	0.1071 335 107	0.1092 099 039	24
25	0.1018 062 505	0.1038 756 909	0.1059 593 925	0.1080 569 774	25
26	0.1007 153 599	0.1028 052 282	0.1049 093 986	0.1070 274 680	26
27	0.0997 349 054	0.1018 445 587	0.1039 685 169	0.1061 063 520	27
28	0.0988 520 473	0.1009 808 321	0.1031 238 883	0.1052 807 635	28
29	0.0980 557 226	0.1002 029 789	0.1023 644 387	0.1045 396 263	29
30	0.0973 363 514	0.0995 014 162	0.1016 805 845	0.1038 733 578	30
31	0.0966 855 995	0.0988 678 100	0.1010 639 940	0.1032 736 314	31
32	0.0960 961 861	0.0982 948 827	0.1005 073 947	0.1027 331 817	32
33	0.0955 617 255	0.0977 762 539	0.1000 044 141	0.1022 456 463	33
34	0.0950 765 971	0.0973 063 109	0.0995 494 491	0.1018 054 344	34
35	0.0946 358 375	0.0968 800 995	0.0991 375 575	0.1014 076 177	35
36	0.0942 350 500	0.0964 932 346	0.0987 643 673	0.1010 478 397	36
37	0.0938 703 293	0.0961 418 233	0.0984 260 006	0.1007 222 394	37
38	0.0935 381 975	0.0958 224 015	0.0981 190 090	0.1004 273 865	38
39	0.0932 355 500	0.0955 318 795	0.0978 403 196	0.1001 602 268	39
40	0.0929 596 092	0.0952 674 955	0.0975 871 883	0.0999 180 358	40
41	0.0927 078 853	0.0950 267 759	0.0973 571 597	0.0996 983 782	41
42	0.0924 781 420	0.0948 075 015	0.0971 480 333	0.0994 990 738	42
43	0.0922 683 675	0.0946 076 778	0.0969 578 336	0.0993 181 678	43
44	0.0920 767 493	0.0944 255 098	0.0967 847 847	0.0991 539 050	44
45	0.0919 016 514	0.0942 593 795	0.0966 272 880	0.0990 047 074	45
46	0.0917 415 959	0.0941 078 267	0.0964 839 025	0.0988 691 546	46
47	0.0915 952 455	0.0939 695 322	0.0963 533 282	0.0987 459 669	47
48	0.0914 613 892	0.0938 433 027	0.0962 343 905	0.0986 339 900	48
49	0.0913 389 289	0.0937 280 577	0.0961 260 279	0.0985 321 818	49
50	0.0912 268 681	0.0936 228 182	0.0960 272 796	0.0984 396 008	50
51	0.0911 243 016	0.0935 266 960	0.0959 372 756	0.0983 553 960	51
52	0.0910 304 065	0.0934 388 852	0.0958 552 274	0.0982 787 971	52
53	0.0909 444 343	0.0933 586 535	0.0957 804 201	0.0982 091 069	53
54	0.0908 657 034	0.0932 853 357	0.0957 122 048	0.0981 456 939	54
55	0.0907 935 930	0.0932 183 263	0.0956 499 926	0.0980 879 856	55
56	0.0907 275 373	0.0931 570 749	0.0955 932 484	0.0980 354 631	56
57	0.0906 670 202	0.0931 010 801	0.0955 414 860	0.0979 876 556	57
58	0.0906 115 709	0.0930 498 852	0.0954 942 633	0.0979 441 358	58
59	0.0905 607 595	0.0930 030 742	0.0954 511 784	0.0979 045 158	59
60	0.0905 141 938	0.0929 602 678	0.0954 118 653	0.0978 684 435	60

TABLE 6. PARTIAL PAYMENT TO AMORTIZE ONE
Payable at end of each period

YEARS	10% Nominal Annual Rate	10¼% Nominal Annual Rate	10½% Nominal Annual Rate	10¾% Nominal Annual Rate	YEARS
1	1.1000 000 000	1.1025 000 000	1.1050 000 000	1.1075 000 000	1
2	0.5761 904 762	0.5781 242 568	0.5800 593 824	0.5819 958 482	2
3	0.4021 148 036	0.4038 858 096	0.4056 591 953	0.4074 349 516	3
4	0.3154 708 037	0.3171 797 179	0.3188 919 564	0.3206 075 054	4
5	0.2637 974 808	0.2654 843 787	0.2671 754 954	0.2688 708 120	5
6	0.2296 073 804	0.2312 920 905	0.2329 818 746	0.2346 767 074	6
7	0.2054 054 997	0.2070 991 374	0.2087 986 667	0.2105 040 549	7
8	0.1874 440 176	0.1891 533 114	0.1908 692 763	0.1925 918 710	8
9	0.1736 405 391	0.1753 697 558	0.1771 063 831	0.1788 503 698	9
10	0.1627 453 949	0.1644 973 037	0.1662 573 206	0.1680 253 827	10
11	0.1539 631 420	0.1557 395 425	0.1575 247 041	0.1593 185 509	11
12	0.1467 633 151	0.1485 653 465	0.1503 767 456	0.1521 974 223	12
13	0.1407 785 238	0.1426 068 574	0.1444 451 173	0.1462 931 976	13
14	0.1357 462 232	0.1376 011 874	0.1394 665 871	0.1413 422 994	14
15	0.1314 737 769	0.1333 554 419	0.1352 480 015	0.1371 513 145	15
16	0.1278 166 207	0.1297 248 588	0.1316 443 997	0.1335 750 826	16
17	0.1246 641 344	0.1265 986 632	0.1285 448 518	0.1305 025 192	17
18	0.1219 302 222	0.1238 906 371	0.1258 630 182	0.1278 471 632	18
19	0.1195 468 682	0.1215 326 678	0.1235 306 897	0.1255 407 096	19
20	0.1174 596 248	0.1194 702 304	0.1214 932 653	0.1235 284 825	20
21	0.1156 243 898	0.1176 591 618	0.1197 065 219	0.1217 662 005	21
22	0.1140 050 630	0.1160 633 137	0.1181 342 647	0.1202 176 237	22
23	0.1125 718 127	0.1146 528 174	0.1167 465 900	0.1188 528 153	23
24	0.1112 997 764	0.1134 027 827	0.1155 185 815	0.1176 468 353	24
25	0.1101 680 722	0.1122 923 077	0.1144 293 198	0.1165 787 492	25
26	0.1091 590 386	0.1113 037 179	0.1134 611 196	0.1156 308 633	26
27	0.1082 576 423	0.1104 219 729	0.1125 989 359	0.1147 881 305	27
28	0.1074 510 132	0.1096 342 004	0.1118 298 968	0.1140 376 822	28
29	0.1067 280 747	0.1089 293 264	0.1111 429 332	0.1133 684 570	29
30	0.1060 792 483	0.1082 977 783	0.1105 284 815	0.1127 709 028	30
31	0.1054 962 140	0.1077 312 460	0.1099 782 438	0.1122 367 368	31
32	0.1049 717 167	0.1072 224 866	0.1094 849 922	0.1117 587 487	32
33	0.1044 994 063	0.1067 651 650	0.1090 424 091	0.1113 306 410	33
34	0.1040 737 064	0.1063 537 218	0.1086 449 545	0.1109 468 959	34
35	0.1036 897 051	0.1059 832 637	0.1082 877 563	0.1106 026 649	35
36	0.1033 430 638	0.1056 494 723	0.1079 665 187	0.1102 936 768	36
37	0.1030 299 405	0.1053 485 270	0.1076 774 443	0.1100 161 602	37
38	0.1027 469 250	0.1050 770 396	0.1074 171 697	0.1097 667 780	38
39	0.1024 909 840	0.1048 320 000	0.1071 827 092	0.1095 425 715	39
40	0.1022 594 144	0.1046 107 281	0.1069 714 084	0.1093 409 132	40
41	0.1020 498 028	0.1044 108 344	0.1067 809 027	0.1091 594 657	41
42	0.1018 599 911	0.1042 301 844	0.1066 090 833	0.1089 961 470	42
43	0.1016 880 466	0.1040 668 693	0.1064 540 666	0.1088 491 003	43
44	0.1015 322 365	0.1039 191 797	0.1063 141 681	0.1087 166 672	44
45	0.1013 910 047	0.1037 855 830	0.1061 878 796	0.1085 973 653	45
46	0.1012 629 527	0.1036 647 035	0.1060 738 498	0.1084 898 682	46
47	0.1011 468 221	0.1035 553 056	0.1059 708 663	0.1083 929 881	47
48	0.1010 414 797	0.1034 562 779	0.1058 778 407	0.1083 056 601	48
49	0.1009 459 041	0.1033 666 206	0.1057 937 954	0.1082 269 296	49
50	0.1008 591 740	0.1032 854 330	0.1057 178 512	0.1081 559 393	50
51	0.1007 804 577	0.1032 119 038	0.1056 492 173	0.1080 919 196	51
52	0.1007 090 040	0.1031 453 010	0.1055 871 820	0.1080 341 792	52
53	0.1006 441 339	0.1030 849 647	0.1055 311 042	0.1079 820 963	53
54	0.1005 852 336	0.1030 302 988	0.1054 804 064	0.1079 351 120	54
55	0.1005 317 476	0.1029 807 654	0.1054 345 680	0.1078 927 234	55
56	0.1004 831 734	0.1029 358 783	0.1053 931 196	0.1078 544 778	56
57	0.1004 390 556	0.1028 951 983	0.1053 556 378	0.1078 199 678	57
58	0.1003 989 822	0.1028 583 280	0.1053 217 406	0.1077 888 266	58
59	0.1003 625 796	0.1028 249 085	0.1052 910 832	0.1077 607 235	59
60	0.1003 295 092	0.1027 946 147	0.1052 633 544	0.1077 353 608	60

TABLE 6. PARTIAL PAYMENT TO AMORTIZE ONE
Payable at end of each period

YEARLY Compounding

YEARS	11% Nominal Annual Rate	11¼% Nominal Annual Rate	11½% Nominal Annual Rate	11¾% Nominal Annual Rate	YEARS
1	1.1100 000 000	1.1125 000 000	1.1150 000 000	1.1175 000 000	1
2	0.5839 336 493	0.5858 727 811	0.5878 132 388	0.5897 550 177	2
3	0.4092 130 696	0.4109 935 404	0.4127 763 551	0.4145 615 047	3
4	0.3223 263 515	0.3240 484 812	0.3257 738 808	0.3275 025 370	4
5	0.2705 703 095	0.2722 739 691	0.2739 817 720	0.2756 936 992	5
6	0.2363 765 636	0.2380 814 180	0.2397 912 454	0.2415 060 206	6
7	0.2122 152 695	0.2139 322 775	0.2156 550 465	0.2173 835 435	7
8	0.1943 210 542	0.1960 567 844	0.1977 990 200	0.1995 477 195	8
9	0.1806 016 644	0.1823 602 152	0.1841 259 707	0.1858 988 792	9
10	0.1698 014 271	0.1715 853 907	0.1733 772 102	0.1751 768 225	10
11	0.1611 210 071	0.1629 319 968	0.1647 514 437	0.1665 792 716	11
12	0.1540 272 864	0.1558 662 475	0.1577 142 151	0.1595 710 987	12
13	0.1481 509 925	0.1500 183 959	0.1518 953 016	0.1537 816 034	13
14	0.1432 282 015	0.1451 241 702	0.1470 300 825	0.1489 458 154	14
15	0.1390 652 395	0.1409 896 355	0.1429 243 614	0.1448 692 763	15
16	0.1355 167 470	0.1374 692 325	0.1394 323 792	0.1414 060 274	16
17	0.1324 714 845	0.1344 515 674	0.1364 425 881	0.1384 443 676	17
18	0.1298 428 701	0.1318 499 379	0.1338 681 666	0.1358 973 571	18
19	0.1275 625 041	0.1295 958 510	0.1316 405 294	0.1336 963 200	19
20	0.1255 756 369	0.1276 344 846	0.1297 047 839	0.1317 862 950	20
21	0.1238 379 300	0.1259 214 453	0.1280 164 837	0.1301 227 849	21
22	0.1223 131 011	0.1244 204 101	0.1265 392 673	0.1286 693 924	22
23	0.1209 711 818	0.1231 013 818	0.1252 431 115	0.1273 960 710	23
24	0.1197 872 113	0.1219 393 810	0.1241 030 208	0.1262 778 122	24
25	0.1187 402 421	0.1209 134 501	0.1230 980 307	0.1252 936 475	25
26	0.1178 125 750	0.1200 058 873	0.1222 104 398	0.1244 258 788	26
27	0.1169 891 636	0.1192 016 499	0.1214 252 118	0.1236 594 801	27
28	0.1162 571 454	0.1184 878 842	0.1207 295 054	0.1229 816 252	28
29	0.1156 054 695	0.1178 535 530	0.1201 123 000	0.1223 813 133	29
30	0.1150 245 985	0.1172 891 363	0.1195 640 959	0.1218 490 686	30
31	0.1145 062 669	0.1167 863 894	0.1190 766 723	0.1213 766 967	31
32	0.1140 432 854	0.1163 381 462	0.1186 428 892	0.1209 570 869	32
33	0.1136 293 791	0.1159 381 573	0.1182 565 256	0.1205 840 493	33
34	0.1132 590 547	0.1155 809 569	0.1179 121 454	0.1202 521 803	34
35	0.1129 274 900	0.1152 617 510	0.1176 049 859	0.1199 567 507	35
36	0.1126 304 409	0.1149 763 254	0.1173 308 646	0.1196 936 121	36
37	0.1123 641 641	0.1147 209 668	0.1170 861 006	0.1194 591 181	37
38	0.1121 253 508	0.1144 923 971	0.1168 674 484	0.1192 500 578	38
39	0.1119 110 713	0.1142 877 171	0.1166 720 412	0.1190 635 986	39
40	0.1117 187 267	0.1141 043 586	0.1164 973 431	0.1188 972 383	40
41	0.1115 460 086	0.1139 400 434	0.1163 411 076	0.1187 487 638	41
42	0.1113 908 633	0.1137 927 477	0.1162 013 421	0.1186 162 147	42
43	0.1112 514 619	0.1136 606 716	0.1160 762 773	0.1184 978 531	43
44	0.1111 261 735	0.1135 422 130	0.1159 643 403	0.1183 921 368	44
45	0.1110 135 424	0.1134 359 439	0.1158 641 318	0.1182 976 959	45
46	0.1109 122 683	0.1133 405 907	0.1157 744 059	0.1182 133 126	46
47	0.1108 211 884	0.1132 550 166	0.1156 940 524	0.1181 379 039	47
48	0.1107 392 624	0.1131 782 064	0.1156 220 813	0.1180 705 056	48
49	0.1106 655 589	0.1131 092 523	0.1155 576 093	0.1180 102 590	49
50	0.1105 992 433	0.1130 473 428	0.1154 998 481	0.1179 563 992	50
51	0.1105 395 676	0.1129 917 516	0.1154 480 934	0.1179 082 442	51
52	0.1104 858 607	0.1129 418 286	0.1154 017 160	0.1178 651 858	52
53	0.1104 375 209	0.1128 969 916	0.1153 601 537	0.1178 266 814	53
54	0.1103 940 076	0.1128 567 191	0.1153 229 035	0.1177 922 470	54
55	0.1103 548 359	0.1128 205 436	0.1152 895 157	0.1177 614 502	55
56	0.1103 195 698	0.1127 880 461	0.1152 595 879	0.1177 339 051	56
57	0.1102 878 179	0.1127 588 508	0.1152 327 601	0.1177 092 673	57
58	0.1102 592 282	0.1127 326 208	0.1152 087 099	0.1176 872 287	58
59	0.1102 334 844	0.1127 090 536	0.1151 871 487	0.1176 675 144	59
60	0.1102 103 020	0.1126 878 780	0.1151 678 182	0.1176 498 786	60

TABLE 6. PARTIAL PAYMENT TO AMORTIZE ONE
Payable at end of each period

YEARS	12% Nominal Annual Rate	12¼% Nominal Annual Rate	12½% Nominal Annual Rate	12¾% Nominal Annual Rate	YEARS
1	1.1200 000 000	1.1225 000 000	1.1250 000 000	1.1275 000 000	1
2	0.5916 981 132	0.5936 425 206	0.5955 882 353	0.5975 352 526	2
3	0.4163 489 806	0.4181 387 738	0.4199 308 756	0.4217 252 773	3
4	0.3292 344 363	0.3309 695 653	0.3327 079 108	0.3344 494 592	4
5	0.2774 097 319	0.2791 298 515	0.2808 540 390	0.2825 822 759	5
6	0.2432 257 184	0.2449 503 136	0.2466 797 811	0.2484 140 956	6
7	0.2191 177 359	0.2208 575 909	0.2226 030 757	0.2243 541 576	7
8	0.2013 028 414	0.2030 643 440	0.2048 321 856	0.2066 063 248	8
9	0.1876 788 888	0.1894 659 477	0.1912 600 042	0.1930 610 062	9
10	0.1769 841 642	0.1787 991 718	0.1806 217 819	0.1824 519 311	10
11	0.1684 154 043	0.1702 597 653	0.1721 122 783	0.1739 728 668	11
12	0.1614 368 076	0.1633 112 512	0.1651 943 390	0.1670 859 803	12
13	0.1556 771 951	0.1575 819 707	0.1594 958 241	0.1614 186 495	13
14	0.1508 712 461	0.1528 062 518	0.1547 507 101	0.1567 044 988	14
15	0.1468 242 396	0.1487 891 113	0.1507 637 513	0.1527 480 204	15
16	0.1433 900 180	0.1453 841 926	0.1473 883 932	0.1494 024 626	16
17	0.1404 567 275	0.1424 794 905	0.1445 124 801	0.1465 555 208	17
18	0.1379 373 114	0.1399 878 330	0.1420 487 264	0.1441 197 977	18
19	0.1357 630 049	0.1378 403 681	0.1399 281 952	0.1420 262 741	19
20	0.1338 787 800	0.1359 820 037	0.1380 957 330	0.1402 197 372	20
21	0.1322 400 915	0.1343 681 490	0.1365 067 060	0.1386 555 139	21
22	0.1308 105 088	0.1329 623 433	0.1351 246 265	0.1372 970 930	22
23	0.1295 599 650	0.1317 345 023	0.1339 193 964	0.1361 143 656	23
24	0.1284 634 417	0.1306 596 013	0.1328 659 881	0.1350 823 050	24
25	0.1274 999 698	0.1297 166 736	0.1319 434 409	0.1341 799 605	25
26	0.1266 518 581	0.1288 880 385	0.1311 340 882	0.1333 896 831	26
27	0.1259 040 937	0.1281 586 998	0.1304 229 541	0.1326 965 208	27
28	0.1252 438 691	0.1275 158 721	0.1297 972 788	0.1320 877 432	28
29	0.1246 602 068	0.1269 486 044	0.1292 461 412	0.1315 524 626	29
30	0.1241 436 576	0.1264 474 777	0.1287 601 556	0.1310 813 298	30
31	0.1236 860 570	0.1260 043 602	0.1283 312 264	0.1306 662 885	31
32	0.1232 803 263	0.1256 122 083	0.1279 523 480	0.1303 003 741	32
33	0.1229 203 096	0.1252 649 028	0.1276 174 403	0.1299 775 485	33
34	0.1226 006 383	0.1249 571 128	0.1273 212 131	0.1296 925 644	34
35	0.1223 166 193	0.1246 841 835	0.1270 590 521	0.1294 408 505	35
36	0.1220 641 406	0.1244 420 416	0.1268 269 247	0.1292 184 171	36
37	0.1218 395 924	0.1242 271 158	0.1266 213 002	0.1290 217 757	37
38	0.1216 397 998	0.1240 362 695	0.1264 390 818	0.1288 478 710	38
39	0.1214 619 665	0.1238 667 437	0.1262 775 496	0.1286 940 236	39
40	0.1213 036 256	0.1237 161 083	0.1261 343 115	0.1285 578 807	40
41	0.1211 625 982	0.1235 822 203	0.1260 072 613	0.1284 373 739	41
42	0.1210 369 577	0.1234 631 874	0.1258 945 425	0.1283 306 831	42
43	0.1209 249 987	0.1233 573 378	0.1257 945 171	0.1282 362 054	43
44	0.1208 252 102	0.1232 631 924	0.1257 057 390	0.1281 525 277	44
45	0.1207 362 523	0.1231 794 422	0.1256 269 303	0.1280 784 038	45
46	0.1206 569 363	0.1231 049 275	0.1255 569 610	0.1280 127 337	46
47	0.1205 862 064	0.1230 386 207	0.1254 948 314	0.1279 545 460	47
48	0.1205 231 248	0.1229 796 101	0.1254 396 568	0.1279 029 826	48
49	0.1204 668 576	0.1229 270 871	0.1253 906 534	0.1278 572 848	49
50	0.1204 166 635	0.1228 803 338	0.1253 471 269	0.1278 167 819	50
51	0.1203 718 826	0.1228 387 127	0.1253 084 621	0.1277 808 806	51
52	0.1203 319 279	0.1228 016 574	0.1252 741 133	0.1277 490 560	52
53	0.1202 962 763	0.1227 686 649	0.1252 435 969	0.1277 208 435	53
54	0.1202 644 625	0.1227 392 879	0.1252 164 837	0.1276 958 317	54
55	0.1202 360 715	0.1227 131 286	0.1251 923 930	0.1276 736 565	55
56	0.1202 107 337	0.1226 898 336	0.1251 709 867	0.1276 539 953	56
57	0.1201 881 197	0.1226 690 882	0.1251 519 651	0.1276 365 626	57
58	0.1201 679 358	0.1226 506 126	0.1251 350 619	0.1276 211 051	58
59	0.1201 499 202	0.1226 341 581	0.1251 200 406	0.1276 073 988	59
60	0.1201 338 394	0.1226 195 029	0.1251 066 913	0.1275 952 448	60

TABLE 6. PARTIAL PAYMENT TO AMORTIZE ONE
Payable at end of each period

YEARLY Compounding

YEARS	13% Nominal Annual Rate	13¼% Nominal Annual Rate	13½% Nominal Annual Rate	13¾% Nominal Annual Rate	YEARS
1	1.1300 000 000	1.1325 000 000	1.1350 000 000	1.1375 000 000	1
2	0.5994 835 681	0.6014 331 770	0.6033 840 749	0.6053 362 573	2
3	0.4235 219 701	0.4253 209 455	0.4271 221 947	0.4289 257 092	3
4	0.3361 941 974	0.3379 421 121	0.3396 931 901	0.3414 474 182	4
5	0.2843 145 434	0.2860 508 228	0.2877 910 955	0.2895 353 429	5
6	0.2501 532 321	0.2518 971 654	0.2536 458 704	0.2553 993 222	6
7	0.2261 108 038	0.2278 729 816	0.2296 406 583	0.2314 138 011	7
8	0.2083 867 196	0.2101 733 286	0.2119 661 101	0.2137 650 224	8
9	0.1948 689 020	0.1966 836 395	0.1985 051 669	0.2003 334 323	9
10	0.1842 895 558	0.1861 345 926	0.1879 869 780	0.1898 466 485	10
11	0.1758 414 545	0.1777 179 651	0.1796 023 222	0.1814 944 497	11
12	0.1689 860 847	0.1708 945 617	0.1728 113 211	0.1747 362 729	12
13	0.1633 503 411	0.1652 907 934	0.1672 399 012	0.1691 975 595	13
14	0.1586 674 959	0.1606 395 799	0.1626 206 298	0.1646 105 248	14
15	0.1547 417 797	0.1567 448 909	0.1587 572 163	0.1607 786 191	15
16	0.1514 262 445	0.1534 595 833	0.1555 023 244	0.1575 543 142	16
17	0.1486 084 385	0.1506 710 600	0.1527 432 135	0.1548 247 285	17
18	0.1462 008 548	0.1482 917 068	0.1503 921 647	0.1525 020 415	18
19	0.1441 343 943	0.1462 523 477	0.1483 799 284	0.1505 169 327	19
20	0.1423 537 884	0.1444 976 615	0.1466 511 339	0.1488 139 862	20
21	0.1408 143 279	0.1429 829 061	0.1451 610 103	0.1473 484 057	21
22	0.1394 794 811	0.1416 715 336	0.1438 729 970	0.1460 836 226	22
23	0.1383 191 328	0.1405 334 258	0.1427 569 775	0.1449 895 255	23
24	0.1373 082 605	0.1395 435 689	0.1417 879 502	0.1440 411 302	24
25	0.1364 259 276	0.1386 810 440	0.1409 450 182	0.1432 175 656	25
26	0.1356 545 063	0.1379 282 488	0.1402 106 089	0.1425 012 926	26
27	0.1349 790 727	0.1372 702 909	0.1395 698 653	0.1418 774 941	27
28	0.1343 869 291	0.1366 945 094	0.1390 101 668	0.1413 335 934	28
29	0.1338 672 246	0.1361 900 938	0.1385 207 472	0.1408 588 720	29
30	0.1334 106 503	0.1357 477 786	0.1380 923 874	0.1404 441 608	30
31	0.1330 091 921	0.1353 595 949	0.1377 171 673	0.1400 815 914	31
32	0.1326 559 291	0.1350 186 689	0.1373 882 625	0.1397 643 918	32
33	0.1323 448 684	0.1347 190 550	0.1370 997 777	0.1394 867 192	33
34	0.1320 708 076	0.1344 555 986	0.1368 466 081	0.1392 435 211	34
35	0.1318 292 209	0.1342 238 212	0.1366 243 248	0.1390 304 201	35
36	0.1316 161 634	0.1340 198 246	0.1364 290 780	0.1388 436 165	36
37	0.1314 281 904	0.1338 402 099	0.1362 575 162	0.1386 798 077	37
38	0.1312 622 899	0.1336 820 095	0.1361 067 176	0.1385 361 189	38
39	0.1311 158 243	0.1335 426 288	0.1359 741 317	0.1384 100 449	39
40	0.1309 864 810	0.1334 197 967	0.1358 575 299	0.1382 993 999	40
41	0.1308 722 306	0.1333 115 234	0.1357 549 625	0.1382 022 756	41
42	0.1307 712 901	0.1332 160 638	0.1356 647 231	0.1381 170 042	42
43	0.1306 820 921	0.1331 318 864	0.1355 853 163	0.1380 421 272	43
44	0.1306 032 572	0.1330 576 460	0.1355 154 314	0.1379 763 683	44
45	0.1305 335 711	0.1329 921 603	0.1354 539 184	0.1379 186 100	45
46	0.1304 719 639	0.1329 343 898	0.1353 997 682	0.1378 678 734	46
47	0.1304 174 928	0.1328 834 201	0.1353 520 947	0.1378 233 007	47
48	0.1303 693 262	0.1328 384 462	0.1353 101 194	0.1377 841 396	48
49	0.1303 267 306	0.1327 987 595	0.1352 731 583	0.1377 497 307	49
50	0.1302 890 585	0.1327 637 357	0.1352 406 102	0.1377 194 953	50
51	0.1302 557 386	0.1327 328 250	0.1352 119 464	0.1376 929 256	51
52	0.1302 262 661	0.1327 055 427	0.1351 867 021	0.1376 695 762	52
53	0.1302 001 954	0.1326 814 617	0.1351 644 682	0.1376 490 558	53
54	0.1301 771 327	0.1326 602 055	0.1351 448 849	0.1376 310 209	54
55	0.1301 567 300	0.1326 414 418	0.1351 276 356	0.1376 151 699	55
56	0.1301 386 799	0.1326 248 778	0.1351 124 416	0.1376 012 380	56
57	0.1301 227 105	0.1326 102 552	0.1350 990 577	0.1375 889 925	57
58	0.1301 085 816	0.1325 973 461	0.1350 872 679	0.1375 782 291	58
59	0.1300 960 807	0.1325 859 494	0.1350 768 821	0.1375 687 681	59
60	0.1300 850 199	0.1325 758 878	0.1350 677 329	0.1375 604 518	60

YEARLY
Compounding

TABLE 6. PARTIAL PAYMENT TO AMORTIZE ONE
Payable at end of each period

YEARS	14% Nominal Annual Rate	14¼% Nominal Annual Rate	14½% Nominal Annual Rate	14¾% Nominal Annual Rate	YEARS
1	1.1400 000 000	1.1425 000 000	1.1450 000 000	1.1475 000 000	1
2	0.6072 897 196	0.6092 444 574	0.6112 004 662	0.6131 577 416	2
3	0.4307 314 804	0.4325 394 998	0.4343 497 588	0.4361 622 489	3
4	0.3432 047 833	0.3449 652 722	0.3467 288 719	0.3484 955 694	4
5	0.2912 835 465	0.2930 356 877	0.2947 917 481	0.2965 517 091	5
6	0.2571 574 957	0.2589 203 658	0.2606 879 076	0.2624 600 961	6
7	0.2331 923 773	0.2349 763 543	0.2367 656 994	0.2385 603 800	7
8	0.2155 700 238	0.2173 810 728	0.2191 981 278	0.2210 211 472	8
9	0.2021 683 838	0.2040 099 696	0.2058 581 379	0.2077 128 369	9
10	0.1917 135 408	0.1935 875 916	0.1954 687 376	0.1973 569 156	10
11	0.1833 942 714	0.1853 017 114	0.1872 166 937	0.1891 391 428	11
12	0.1766 693 269	0.1786 103 936	0.1805 593 835	0.1825 162 073	12
13	0.1711 636 635	0.1731 381 089	0.1751 207 919	0.1771 116 088	13
14	0.1666 091 448	0.1686 163 700	0.1706 320 815	0.1726 561 607	14
15	0.1628 089 630	0.1648 481 124	0.1668 959 329	0.1689 522 906	15
16	0.1596 154 000	0.1616 854 304	0.1637 642 550	0.1658 517 247	16
17	0.1569 154 359	0.1590 151 683	0.1611 237 596	0.1632 410 452	17
18	0.1546 211 516	0.1567 493 116	0.1588 863 402	0.1610 320 579	18
19	0.1526 631 593	0.1548 184 094	0.1569 824 868	0.1591 551 975	19
20	0.1509 860 016	0.1531 669 666	0.1553 566 708	0.1575 549 068	20
21	0.1495 448 612	0.1517 501 493	0.1539 640 464	0.1561 863 325	21
22	0.1483 031 654	0.1505 313 854	0.1527 680 465	0.1550 129 175	22
23	0.1472 308 130	0.1494 805 878	0.1517 386 033	0.1540 046 177	23
24	0.1463 028 406	0.1485 728 192	0.1508 508 096	0.1531 365 612	24
25	0.1454 984 079	0.1477 872 740	0.1500 838 993	0.1523 880 258	25
26	0.1448 000 136	0.1471 064 930	0.1494 204 595	0.1517 416 492	26
27	0.1441 928 839	0.1465 157 501	0.1488 458 159	0.1511 828 131	27
28	0.1436 644 905	0.1460 025 686	0.1483 475 475	0.1506 991 557	28
29	0.1432 041 657	0.1455 563 357	0.1479 150 996	0.1502 801 843	29
30	0.1428 027 939	0.1451 679 925	0.1475 394 732	0.1499 169 627	30
31	0.1424 525 613	0.1448 297 827	0.1472 129 724	0.1496 018 585	31
32	0.1421 467 511	0.1445 350 472	0.1469 289 987	0.1493 283 360	32
33	0.1418 795 755	0.1442 780 558	0.1466 818 816	0.1490 907 865	33
34	0.1416 460 366	0.1440 538 669	0.1464 667 377	0.1488 843 871	34
35	0.1414 418 099	0.1438 582 113	0.1462 793 548	0.1487 049 839	35
36	0.1412 631 480	0.1436 873 948	0.1461 160 934	0.1485 489 933	36
37	0.1411 067 982	0.1435 382 162	0.1459 738 048	0.1484 133 205	37
38	0.1409 699 339	0.1434 078 982	0.1458 497 619	0.1482 952 890	38
39	0.1408 500 959	0.1432 940 282	0.1457 415 997	0.1481 925 823	39
40	0.1407 451 425	0.1431 945 092	0.1456 472 661	0.1481 031 935	40
41	0.1406 532 069	0.1431 075 162	0.1455 649 785	0.1480 253 827	41
42	0.1405 726 603	0.1430 314 603	0.1454 931 877	0.1479 576 403	42
43	0.1405 020 814	0.1429 649 568	0.1454 305 461	0.1478 986 561	43
44	0.1404 402 284	0.1429 067 988	0.1453 758 815	0.1478 472 920	44
45	0.1403 860 162	0.1428 559 335	0.1453 281 731	0.1478 025 594	45
46	0.1403 384 961	0.1428 114 422	0.1452 865 319	0.1477 635 989	46
47	0.1402 968 383	0.1427 725 228	0.1452 501 836	0.1477 296 630	47
48	0.1402 603 167	0.1427 384 751	0.1452 184 532	0.1477 001 020	48
49	0.1402 282 958	0.1427 086 874	0.1451 907 524	0.1476 743 504	49
50	0.1402 002 194	0.1426 826 252	0.1451 665 683	0.1476 519 163	50
51	0.1401 756 002	0.1426 598 214	0.1451 454 533	0.1476 323 714	51
52	0.1401 540 115	0.1426 398 679	0.1451 270 173	0.1476 153 430	52
53	0.1401 350 796	0.1426 224 077	0.1451 109 199	0.1476 005 067	53
54	0.1401 184 768	0.1426 071 287	0.1450 968 639	0.1475 875 799	54
55	0.1401 039 162	0.1425 937 582	0.1450 845 901	0.1475 763 165	55
56	0.1400 911 463	0.1425 820 573	0.1450 738 724	0.1475 665 023	56
57	0.1400 799 465	0.1425 718 174	0.1450 645 132	0.1475 579 507	57
58	0.1400 701 236	0.1425 628 559	0.1450 563 402	0.1475 504 992	58
59	0.1400 615 081	0.1425 550 131	0.1450 492 030	0.1475 440 061	59
60	0.1400 539 516	0.1425 481 492	0.1450 429 702	0.1475 383 480	60

TABLE 6. PARTIAL PAYMENT TO AMORTIZE ONE
Payable at end of each period

YEARLY Compounding

YEARS	15% Nominal Annual Rate	15¼% Nominal Annual Rate	15½% Nominal Annual Rate	15¾% Nominal Annual Rate	YEARS
1	1.1500 000 000	1.1525 000 000	1.1550 000 000	1.1575 000 000	1
2	0.6151 162 791	0.6170 760 743	0.6190 371 230	0.6209 994 206	2
3	0.4379 769 618	0.4397 938 891	0.4416 130 223	0.4434 343 530	3
4	0.3502 653 516	0.3520 382 056	0.3538 141 185	0.3555 930 774	4
5	0.2983 155 525	0.3000 832 597	0.3018 548 125	0.3036 301 925	5
6	0.2642 369 066	0.2660 183 140	0.2678 042 936	0.2695 948 206	6
7	0.2403 603 636	0.2421 656 176	0.2439 761 095	0.2457 918 068	7
8	0.2228 500 896	0.2246 849 134	0.2265 255 774	0.2283 720 400	8
9	0.2095 740 150	0.2114 416 205	0.2133 156 020	0.2151 959 078	9
10	0.1992 520 625	0.2011 541 155	0.2030 630 117	0.2049 786 884	10
11	0.1910 689 830	0.1930 061 390	0.1949 505 356	0.1969 020 980	11
12	0.1844 807 761	0.1864 530 013	0.1884 327 944	0.1904 200 676	12
13	0.1791 104 565	0.1811 172 324	0.1831 318 343	0.1851 541 605	13
14	0.1746 884 898	0.1767 289 517	0.1787 774 299	0.1808 338 087	14
15	0.1710 170 526	0.1730 900 872	0.1751 712 633	0.1772 604 511	15
16	0.1679 476 914	0.1700 520 085	0.1721 645 308	0.1742 851 142	16
17	0.1653 668 623	0.1675 010 499	0.1696 434 484	0.1717 939 002	17
18	0.1631 862 874	0.1653 488 534	0.1675 195 831	0.1696 983 057	18
19	0.1613 363 504	0.1635 257 571	0.1657 232 318	0.1679 285 914	19
20	0.1597 614 704	0.1619 761 608	0.1641 987 802	0.1664 291 344	20
21	0.1584 167 914	0.1606 552 110	0.1629 013 828	0.1651 551 024	21
22	0.1572 657 713	0.1595 263 855	0.1617 945 424	0.1640 700 286	22
23	0.1562 783 947	0.1585 597 030	0.1608 483 167	0.1631 440 149	23
24	0.1554 298 296	0.1577 303 761	0.1600 379 680	0.1623 523 784	24
25	0.1546 994 023	0.1570 177 843	0.1593 429 337	0.1616 746 191	25
26	0.1540 698 058	0.1564 046 801	0.1587 460 303	0.1610 936 217	26
27	0.1535 264 815	0.1558 765 689	0.1582 328 312	0.1605 950 318	27
28	0.1530 571 309	0.1554 212 193	0.1577 911 756	0.1601 667 629	28
29	0.1526 513 265	0.1550 282 721	0.1574 107 763	0.1597 986 031	29
30	0.1523 001 982	0.1546 889 266	0.1570 829 047	0.1594 818 985	30
31	0.1519 961 796	0.1543 956 851	0.1568 001 344	0.1592 092 966	31
32	0.1517 328 006	0.1541 421 450	0.1565 561 326	0.1589 745 367	32
33	0.1515 045 161	0.1539 228 274	0.1563 454 881	0.1587 722 770	33
34	0.1513 065 655	0.1537 330 351	0.1561 635 693	0.1585 979 526	34
35	0.1511 348 546	0.1535 687 352	0.1560 064 055	0.1584 476 562	35
36	0.1509 858 572	0.1534 264 599	0.1558 705 881	0.1583 180 398	36
37	0.1508 565 329	0.1533 032 241	0.1557 531 882	0.1582 062 307	37
38	0.1507 442 569	0.1531 964 553	0.1556 516 861	0.1581 097 625	38
39	0.1506 467 613	0.1531 039 346	0.1555 639 122	0.1580 265 153	39
40	0.1505 620 850	0.1530 237 469	0.1554 879 974	0.1579 546 660	40
41	0.1504 885 308	0.1529 542 377	0.1554 223 301	0.1578 926 458	41
42	0.1504 246 290	0.1528 939 773	0.1553 655 201	0.1578 391 038	42
43	0.1503 691 063	0.1528 417 290	0.1553 163 675	0.1577 928 764	43
44	0.1503 208 590	0.1527 964 231	0.1552 738 363	0.1577 529 610	44
45	0.1502 789 300	0.1527 571 340	0.1552 370 315	0.1577 184 931	45
46	0.1502 424 890	0.1527 230 600	0.1552 051 800	0.1576 887 273	46
47	0.1502 108 156	0.1526 935 070	0.1551 776 134	0.1576 630 207	47
48	0.1501 832 843	0.1526 678 738	0.1551 537 542	0.1576 408 188	48
49	0.1501 593 523	0.1526 456 393	0.1551 331 028	0.1576 216 429	49
50	0.1501 385 480	0.1526 263 522	0.1551 152 273	0.1576 050 800	50
51	0.1501 204 620	0.1526 096 211	0.1550 997 539	0.1575 907 737	51
52	0.1501 047 386	0.1525 951 069	0.1550 863 596	0.1575 784 160	52
53	0.1500 910 687	0.1525 825 154	0.1550 747 646	0.1575 677 414	53
54	0.1500 791 839	0.1525 715 918	0.1550 647 271	0.1575 585 205	54
55	0.1500 688 509	0.1525 621 148	0.1550 560 376	0.1575 505 551	55
56	0.1500 598 667	0.1525 538 928	0.1550 485 151	0.1575 436 742	56
57	0.1500 520 553	0.1525 467 595	0.1550 420 026	0.1575 377 301	57
58	0.1500 452 634	0.1525 405 706	0.1550 363 646	0.1575 325 951	58
59	0.1500 393 580	0.1525 352 010	0.1550 314 835	0.1575 281 591	59
60	0.1500 342 231	0.1525 305 422	0.1550 272 577	0.1575 243 269	60

YEARLY
Compounding

TABLE 6. PARTIAL PAYMENT TO AMORTIZE ONE
Payable at end of each period

YEARS	16% Nominal Annual Rate	16¼% Nominal Annual Rate	16½% Nominal Annual Rate	16¾% Nominal Annual Rate	YEARS
1	1.1600 000 000	1.1625 000 000	1.1650 000 000	1.1675 000 000	1
2	0.6229 629 630	0.6249 277 457	0.6268 937 644	0.6288 610 150	2
3	0.4452 578 731	0.4470 835 742	0.4489 114 480	0.4507 414 864	3
4	0.3573 750 695	0.3591 600 819	0.3609 481 019	0.3627 391 167	4
5	0.3054 093 816	0.3071 923 615	0.3089 791 140	0.3107 696 210	5
6	0.2713 898 702	0.2731 894 178	0.2749 934 387	0.2768 019 083	6
7	0.2476 126 771	0.2494 386 882	0.2512 698 077	0.2531 060 033	7
8	0.2302 242 601	0.2320 821 964	0.2339 458 078	0.2358 150 532	8
9	0.2170 824 868	0.2189 752 876	0.2208 742 591	0.2227 793 503	9
10	0.2069 010 831	0.2088 301 333	0.2107 657 770	0.2127 079 521	10
11	0.1988 607 515	0.2008 264 216	0.2027 990 342	0.2047 785 154	11
12	0.1924 147 333	0.1944 167 041	0.1964 258 934	0.1984 422 146	12
13	0.1871 841 100	0.1892 215 822	0.1912 664 771	0.1933 186 955	13
14	0.1828 979 733	0.1849 698 093	0.1870 492 036	0.1891 360 438	14
15	0.1793 575 218	0.1814 623 475	0.1835 748 018	0.1856 947 590	15
16	0.1764 136 162	0.1785 498 958	0.1806 938 131	0.1828 452 302	16
17	0.1739 522 494	0.1761 183 422	0.1782 920 262	0.1804 731 514	17
18	0.1718 848 526	0.1740 790 577	0.1762 807 572	0.1784 897 894	18
19	0.1701 416 556	0.1723 622 471	0.1745 901 910	0.1768 253 158	19
20	0.1686 670 324	0.1709 122 865	0.1731 647 123	0.1754 241 291	20
21	0.1674 161 691	0.1696 843 865	0.1719 595 618	0.1742 415 063	21
22	0.1663 526 353	0.1686 421 582	0.1709 383 976	0.1732 411 582	22
23	0.1654 465 820	0.1677 558 075	0.1700 714 859	0.1723 934 170	23
24	0.1646 733 862	0.1670 007 761	0.1693 343 385	0.1716 738 694	24
25	0.1640 126 153	0.1663 567 036	0.1687 066 717	0.1710 623 133	25
26	0.1634 472 266	0.1658 066 245	0.1681 716 014	0.1705 419 502	26
27	0.1629 629 420	0.1653 363 404	0.1677 150 133	0.1700 987 537	27
28	0.1625 477 527	0.1649 339 243	0.1673 250 650	0.1697 209 696	28
29	0.1621 915 252	0.1645 893 239	0.1669 917 888	0.1693 987 174	29
30	0.1618 856 833	0.1642 940 435	0.1667 067 719	0.1691 236 698	30
31	0.1616 229 508	0.1640 408 852	0.1664 628 970	0.1688 887 922	31
32	0.1613 971 408	0.1638 237 381	0.1662 541 308	0.1686 881 303	32
33	0.1612 029 828	0.1636 374 043	0.1660 753 495	0.1685 166 359	33
34	0.1610 359 798	0.1634 774 559	0.1659 221 956	0.1683 700 226	34
35	0.1608 922 891	0.1633 401 159	0.1657 909 581	0.1682 446 465	35
36	0.1607 686 235	0.1632 221 585	0.1656 784 733	0.1681 374 063	36
37	0.1606 621 677	0.1631 208 259	0.1655 820 416	0.1680 456 604	37
38	0.1605 705 086	0.1630 337 587	0.1654 993 570	0.1679 671 567	38
39	0.1604 915 760	0.1629 589 366	0.1654 284 490	0.1678 999 742	39
40	0.1604 235 929	0.1628 946 284	0.1653 676 322	0.1678 424 730	40
41	0.1603 650 330	0.1628 393 501	0.1653 154 645	0.1677 932 527	41
42	0.1603 145 846	0.1627 918 288	0.1652 707 117	0.1677 511 170	42
43	0.1602 711 201	0.1627 509 726	0.1652 323 166	0.1677 150 432	43
44	0.1602 336 696	0.1627 158 438	0.1651 993 736	0.1676 841 573	44
45	0.1602 013 988	0.1626 856 376	0.1651 711 069	0.1676 577 116	45
46	0.1601 735 895	0.1626 596 628	0.1651 468 513	0.1676 350 666	46
47	0.1601 496 237	0.1626 373 254	0.1651 260 367	0.1676 156 754	47
48	0.1601 289 693	0.1626 181 155	0.1651 081 743	0.1675 990 697	48
49	0.1601 111 681	0.1626 015 944	0.1650 928 449	0.1675 848 491	49
50	0.1600 958 254	0.1625 873 854	0.1650 796 888	0.1675 726 706	50
51	0.1600 826 013	0.1625 751 646	0.1650 683 977	0.1675 622 407	51
52	0.1600 712 029	0.1625 646 535	0.1650 587 071	0.1675 533 083	52
53	0.1600 613 781	0.1625 556 128	0.1650 503 898	0.1675 456 581	53
54	0.1600 529 093	0.1625 478 367	0.1650 432 512	0.1675 391 061	54
55	0.1600 456 094	0.1625 411 482	0.1650 371 241	0.1675 334 944	55
56	0.1600 393 169	0.1625 353 950	0.1650 318 652	0.1675 286 882	56
57	0.1600 338 927	0.1625 304 464	0.1650 273 513	0.1675 245 717	57
58	0.1600 292 170	0.1625 261 898	0.1650 234 770	0.1675 210 460	58
59	0.1600 251 865	0.1625 225 283	0.1650 201 515	0.1675 180 262	59
60	0.1600 217 120	0.1625 193 788	0.1650 172 971	0.1675 154 398	60

TABLE 6. PARTIAL PAYMENT TO AMORTIZE ONE
Payable at end of each period

YEARS	17% Nominal Annual Rate	17¼% Nominal Annual Rate	17½% Nominal Annual Rate	17¾% Nominal Annual Rate	YEARS
1	1.1700 000 000	1.1725 000 000	1.1750 000 000	1.1775 000 000	1
2	0.6308 294 931	0.6327 991 945	0.6347 701 149	0.6367 422 503	2
3	0.4525 736 811	0.4544 080 240	0.4562 445 069	0.4580 831 219	3
4	0.3645 331 137	0.3663 300 802	0.3681 300 037	0.3699 328 714	4
5	0.3125 638 643	0.3143 618 261	0.3161 634 882	0.3179 688 328	5
6	0.2786 148 021	0.2804 320 955	0.2822 537 641	0.2840 797 834	6
7	0.2549 472 428	0.2567 934 942	0.2586 447 254	0.2605 009 045	7
8	0.2376 898 916	0.2395 702 821	0.2414 561 840	0.2433 475 564	8
9	0.2246 905 102	0.2266 076 880	0.2285 308 333	0.2304 598 953	9
10	0.2146 565 967	0.2166 116 492	0.2185 730 482	0.2205 407 326	10
11	0.2067 647 916	0.2087 577 896	0.2107 574 364	0.2127 636 593	11
12	0.2004 655 819	0.2024 959 098	0.2045 331 132	0.2065 771 075	12
13	0.1953 781 386	0.1974 447 084	0.1995 183 074	0.2015 988 391	13
14	0.1912 302 181	0.1933 316 160	0.1954 401 277	0.1975 556 444	14
15	0.1878 220 950	0.1899 566 866	0.1920 984 119	0.1942 471 504	15
16	0.1850 040 103	0.1871 700 185	0.1893 431 211	0.1915 231 864	16
17	0.1826 615 693	0.1848 571 336	0.1870 596 999	0.1892 691 259	17
18	0.1807 059 953	0.1829 292 182	0.1851 593 036	0.1873 960 997	18
19	0.1790 674 523	0.1813 164 347	0.1835 720 996	0.1858 342 869	19
20	0.1776 903 593	0.1799 632 287	0.1822 425 665	0.1845 282 053	20
21	0.1765 300 350	0.1788 249 672	0.1811 261 256	0.1834 333 373	21
22	0.1755 502 493	0.1778 654 846	0.1801 866 820	0.1825 136 641	22
23	0.1747 214 054	0.1770 552 609	0.1793 947 980	0.1817 398 361	23
24	0.1740 191 703	0.1763 700 484	0.1787 263 162	0.1810 877 915	24
25	0.1734 234 282	0.1757 898 223	0.1781 613 074	0.1805 377 009	25
26	0.1729 174 705	0.1752 979 680	0.1776 832 551	0.1800 731 503	26
27	0.1724 873 621	0.1748 806 457	0.1772 784 184	0.1796 805 007	27
28	0.1721 214 404	0.1745 262 872	0.1769 353 267	0.1793 483 824	28
29	0.1718 099 152	0.1742 251 953	0.1766 443 781	0.1790 672 912	29
30	0.1715 445 468	0.1739 692 201	0.1763 975 150	0.1788 292 636	30
31	0.1713 183 850	0.1737 514 980	0.1761 879 615	0.1786 276 133	31
32	0.1711 255 565	0.1735 662 376	0.1760 100 099	0.1784 567 172	32
33	0.1709 610 895	0.1734 085 449	0.1758 588 447	0.1783 118 391	33
34	0.1708 207 698	0.1732 742 784	0.1757 303 978	0.1781 889 849	34
35	0.1707 010 209	0.1731 599 296	0.1756 212 289	0.1780 847 830	35
36	0.1705 988 044	0.1730 625 231	0.1755 284 261	0.1779 963 845	36
37	0.1705 115 368	0.1729 795 338	0.1754 495 222	0.1779 213 803	37
38	0.1704 370 199	0.1729 088 168	0.1753 824 258	0.1778 577 321	38
39	0.1703 733 818	0.1728 485 496	0.1753 253 628	0.1778 037 142	39
40	0.1703 190 279	0.1727 971 821	0.1752 768 279	0.1777 578 649	40
41	0.1702 725 991	0.1727 533 960	0.1752 355 427	0.1777 189 456	41
42	0.1702 329 364	0.1727 160 693	0.1752 004 217	0.1776 859 065	42
43	0.1701 990 513	0.1726 842 469	0.1751 705 426	0.1776 578 574	43
44	0.1701 701 004	0.1726 571 155	0.1751 451 216	0.1776 340 435	44
45	0.1701 453 638	0.1726 339 825	0.1751 234 925	0.1776 138 244	45
46	0.1701 242 272	0.1726 142 577	0.1751 050 889	0.1775 966 569	46
47	0.1701 061 658	0.1725 974 384	0.1750 894 294	0.1775 820 798	47
48	0.1700 907 317	0.1725 830 962	0.1750 761 043	0.1775 697 019	48
49	0.1700 775 425	0.1725 708 660	0.1750 647 654	0.1775 591 914	49
50	0.1700 662 712	0.1725 604 364	0.1750 551 165	0.1775 502 661	50
51	0.1700 566 389	0.1725 515 423	0.1750 469 054	0.1775 426 870	51
52	0.1700 484 070	0.1725 439 573	0.1750 399 179	0.1775 362 510	52
53	0.1700 413 718	0.1725 374 889	0.1750 339 716	0.1775 307 854	53
54	0.1700 353 592	0.1725 319 724	0.1750 289 111	0.1775 261 441	54
55	0.1700 302 206	0.1725 272 679	0.1750 246 046	0.1775 222 025	55
56	0.1700 258 289	0.1725 232 556	0.1750 209 397	0.1775 188 553	56
57	0.1700 220 755	0.1725 198 338	0.1750 178 207	0.1775 160 127	57
58	0.1700 188 676	0.1725 169 156	0.1750 151 663	0.1775 135 987	58
59	0.1700 161 259	0.1725 144 267	0.1750 129 073	0.1775 115 487	59
60	0.1700 137 826	0.1725 123 041	0.1750 109 848	0.1775 098 077	60

YEARLY
Compounding

TABLE 6. PARTIAL PAYMENT TO AMORTIZE ONE
Payable at end of each period

YEARS	18% Nominal Annual Rate	18¼% Nominal Annual Rate	18½% Nominal Annual Rate	18¾% Nominal Annual Rate	YEARS
1	1.1800 000 000	1.1825 000 000	1.1850 000 000	1.1875 000 000	1
2	0.6387 155 963	0.6406 901 489	0.6426 659 039	0.6446 428 571	2
3	0.4599 238 607	0.4617 667 154	0.4636 116 780	0.4654 587 405	3
4	0.3717 386 709	0.3735 473 898	0.3753 590 154	0.3771 735 355	4
5	0.3197 778 418	0.3215 904 975	0.3234 067 820	0.3252 266 776	5
6	0.2859 101 292	0.2877 447 772	0.2895 837 031	0.2914 268 828	6
7	0.2623 619 994	0.2642 279 783	0.2660 988 095	0.2679 744 614	7
8	0.2452 443 589	0.2471 465 509	0.2490 540 919	0.2509 669 418	8
9	0.2323 948 239	0.2343 355 688	0.2362 820 801	0.2382 343 078	9
10	0.2225 146 413	0.2244 947 137	0.2264 808 893	0.2284 731 078	10
11	0.2147 763 862	0.2167 955 451	0.2188 210 645	0.2208 528 732	11
12	0.2086 278 089	0.2106 851 337	0.2127 489 990	0.2148 193 224	12
13	0.2036 862 073	0.2057 803 170	0.2078 810 735	0.2099 883 831	13
14	0.1996 780 583	0.2018 072 624	0.2039 431 510	0.2060 856 190	14
15	0.1964 027 825	0.1985 651 903	0.2007 342 570	0.2029 098 671	15
16	0.1937 100 839	0.1959 036 851	0.1981 038 628	0.2003 104 919	16
17	0.1914 852 711	0.1937 079 971	0.1959 371 677	0.1981 726 484	17
18	0.1896 394 570	0.1918 892 285	0.1941 452 695	0.1964 074 379	18
19	0.1881 028 390	0.1903 776 016	0.1926 584 229	0.1949 451 542	19
20	0.1868 199 812	0.1891 177 334	0.1914 213 045	0.1937 305 405	20
21	0.1857 464 327	0.1880 652 466	0.1903 896 170	0.1927 193 860	21
22	0.1848 462 577	0.1871 842 937	0.1895 276 075	0.1918 760 386	22
23	0.1840 901 996	0.1864 457 174	0.1888 062 232	0.1911 715 551	23
24	0.1834 542 973	0.1858 256 620	0.1882 017 187	0.1905 823 059	24
25	0.1829 188 261	0.1853 045 117	0.1876 945 919	0.1900 889 062	25
26	0.1824 674 779	0.1848 660 685	0.1872 687 583	0.1896 753 889	26
27	0.1820 867 195	0.1844 969 080	0.1869 109 054	0.1893 285 567	27
28	0.1817 652 846	0.1841 858 702	0.1866 099 822	0.1890 374 698	28
29	0.1814 937 692	0.1839 236 533	0.1863 567 913	0.1887 930 373	29
30	0.1812 643 056	0.1837 024 875	0.1861 436 621	0.1885 876 891	30
31	0.1810 702 987	0.1835 158 697	0.1859 641 852	0.1884 151 106	31
32	0.1809 062 108	0.1833 583 490	0.1858 129 969	0.1882 700 260	32
33	0.1807 673 859	0.1832 253 500	0.1856 856 029	0.1881 480 228	33
34	0.1806 499 044	0.1831 130 278	0.1855 782 333	0.1880 454 057	34
35	0.1805 504 633	0.1830 181 481	0.1854 877 226	0.1879 590 782	35
36	0.1804 662 768	0.1829 379 883	0.1854 114 109	0.1878 864 428	36
37	0.1803 949 937	0.1828 702 547	0.1853 470 617	0.1878 253 196	37
38	0.1803 346 284	0.1828 130 138	0.1852 927 934	0.1877 738 783	38
39	0.1802 835 030	0.1827 646 350	0.1852 470 220	0.1877 305 812	39
40	0.1802 401 991	0.1827 237 428	0.1852 084 139	0.1876 941 360	40
41	0.1802 035 171	0.1826 891 758	0.1851 758 458	0.1876 634 562	41
42	0.1801 724 424	0.1826 599 540	0.1851 483 711	0.1876 376 284	42
43	0.1801 461 163	0.1826 352 493	0.1851 251 920	0.1876 158 841	43
44	0.1801 238 120	0.1826 143 627	0.1851 056 361	0.1875 975 771	44
45	0.1801 049 144	0.1825 967 033	0.1850 891 364	0.1875 821 635	45
46	0.1800 889 026	0.1825 817 720	0.1850 752 149	0.1875 691 855	46
47	0.1800 753 355	0.1825 691 470	0.1850 634 685	0.1875 582 581	47
48	0.1800 638 396	0.1825 584 718	0.1850 535 570	0.1875 490 570	48
49	0.1800 540 984	0.1825 494 452	0.1850 451 938	0.1875 413 095	49
50	0.1800 458 440	0.1825 418 124	0.1850 381 368	0.1875 347 857	50
51	0.1800 388 494	0.1825 353 581	0.1850 321 819	0.1875 292 924	51
52	0.1800 329 221	0.1825 299 002	0.1850 271 570	0.1875 246 667	52
53	0.1800 278 993	0.1825 252 850	0.1850 229 167	0.1875 207 715	53
54	0.1800 236 429	0.1825 213 822	0.1850 193 387	0.1875 174 915	54
55	0.1800 200 360	0.1825 180 818	0.1850 163 193	0.1875 147 294	55
56	0.1800 169 794	0.1825 152 910	0.1850 137 713	0.1875 124 036	56
57	0.1800 143 891	0.1825 129 309	0.1850 116 213	0.1875 104 450	57
58	0.1800 121 940	0.1825 109 351	0.1850 098 069	0.1875 087 957	58
59	0.1800 103 338	0.1825 092 473	0.1850 082 758	0.1875 074 069	59
60	0.1800 087 574	0.1825 078 201	0.1850 069 837	0.1875 062 373	60

TABLE 6. PARTIAL PAYMENT TO AMORTIZE ONE
Payable at end of each period

YEARS	19% Nominal Annual Rate	19¼% Nominal Annual Rate	19½% Nominal Annual Rate	19¾% Nominal Annual Rate	YEARS
1	1.1900 000 000	1.1925 000 000	1.1950 000 000	1.1975 000 000	1
2	0.6466 210 046	0.6486 003 421	0.6505 808 656	0.6525 625 711	2
3	0.4673 078 950	0.4691 591 335	0.4710 124 482	0.4728 678 312	3
4	0.3789 909 377	0.3808 112 096	0.3826 343 389	0.3844 603 133	4
5	0.3270 501 666	0.3288 772 312	0.3307 078 539	0.3325 420 171	5
6	0.2932 742 921	0.2951 259 070	0.2969 817 036	0.2988 416 578	6
7	0.2698 549 022	0.2717 401 005	0.2736 300 248	0.2755 246 439	7
8	0.2528 850 604	0.2548 084 076	0.2567 369 435	0.2586 706 283	8
9	0.2401 922 023	0.2421 557 141	0.2441 247 940	0.2460 993 928	9
10	0.2304 713 094	0.2324 754 343	0.2344 854 232	0.2365 012 170	10
11	0.2228 909 005	0.2249 350 759	0.2269 853 296	0.2290 415 921	11
12	0.2168 960 219	0.2189 790 164	0.2210 682 250	0.2231 635 677	12
13	0.2121 021 529	0.2142 222 906	0.2163 487 047	0.2184 813 048	13
14	0.2082 345 628	0.2103 898 796	0.2125 514 675	0.2147 192 259	14
15	0.2050 919 063	0.2072 802 620	0.2094 748 227	0.2116 754 782	15
16	0.2025 234 484	0.2047 426 105	0.2069 678 578	0.2091 990 716	16
17	0.2004 143 070	0.2026 620 134	0.2049 156 392	0.2071 750 584	17
18	0.1986 755 939	0.2009 496 003	0.2032 293 223	0.2055 146 275	18
19	0.1972 376 496	0.1995 357 660	0.2018 393 632	0.2041 483 038	19
20	0.1960 452 907	0.1983 654 074	0.2006 907 465	0.2030 211 669	20
21	0.1950 543 994	0.1973 945 066	0.1997 395 606	0.2020 894 179	21
22	0.1942 294 304	0.1965 876 308	0.1989 504 912	0.2013 178 674	22
23	0.1935 415 560	0.1959 160 731	0.1982 949 577	0.2006 780 659	23
24	0.1929 672 666	0.1953 564 488	0.1977 497 051	0.2001 468 926	24
25	0.1924 872 993	0.1948 896 210	0.1972 957 260	0.1997 054 739	25
26	0.1920 858 078	0.1944 998 675	0.1969 174 260	0.1993 383 461	26
27	0.1917 497 128	0.1941 742 300	0.1966 019 702	0.1990 328 002	27
28	0.1914 681 881	0.1939 019 981	0.1963 387 661	0.1987 783 639	28
29	0.1912 322 512	0.1936 742 992	0.1961 190 527	0.1985 663 889	29
30	0.1910 344 341	0.1934 837 685	0.1959 355 697	0.1983 897 203	30
31	0.1908 685 173	0.1933 242 831	0.1957 822 910	0.1982 424 299	31
32	0.1907 293 142	0.1931 907 453	0.1956 542 086	0.1981 195 990	32
33	0.1906 124 937	0.1930 789 060	0.1955 471 553	0.1980 171 429	33
34	0.1905 144 358	0.1929 852 202	0.1954 576 610	0.1979 316 657	34
35	0.1904 321 122	0.1929 067 278	0.1953 828 333	0.1978 603 425	35
36	0.1903 629 877	0.1928 409 552	0.1953 202 600	0.1978 008 218	36
37	0.1903 049 387	0.1927 858 346	0.1952 679 282	0.1977 511 451	37
38	0.1902 561 853	0.1927 396 361	0.1952 241 574	0.1977 096 805	38
39	0.1902 152 355	0.1927 009 124	0.1951 875 443	0.1976 750 679	39
40	0.1901 808 374	0.1926 684 516	0.1951 569 162	0.1976 461 731	40
41	0.1901 519 411	0.1926 412 392	0.1951 312 934	0.1976 220 503	41
42	0.1901 276 653	0.1926 184 256	0.1951 098 569	0.1976 019 106	42
43	0.1901 072 703	0.1925 992 988	0.1950 919 220	0.1975 850 955	43
44	0.1900 901 350	0.1925 832 625	0.1950 769 162	0.1975 710 559	44
45	0.1900 757 379	0.1925 698 169	0.1950 643 609	0.1975 593 334	45
46	0.1900 636 413	0.1925 585 433	0.1950 538 556	0.1975 495 452	46
47	0.1900 534 772	0.1925 490 905	0.1950 450 654	0.1975 413 722	47
48	0.1900 449 368	0.1925 411 643	0.1950 377 102	0.1975 345 476	48
49	0.1900 377 606	0.1925 345 182	0.1950 315 557	0.1975 288 489	49
50	0.1900 317 306	0.1925 289 452	0.1950 264 057	0.1975 240 904	50
51	0.1900 266 636	0.1925 242 721	0.1950 220 964	0.1975 201 168	51
52	0.1900 224 059	0.1925 203 536	0.1950 184 903	0.1975 167 987	52
53	0.1900 188 282	0.1925 170 677	0.1950 154 728	0.1975 140 280	53
54	0.1900 158 217	0.1925 143 123	0.1950 129 478	0.1975 117 143	54
55	0.1900 132 954	0.1925 120 018	0.1950 108 349	0.1975 097 822	55
56	0.1900 111 725	0.1925 100 643	0.1950 090 668	0.1975 081 688	56
57	0.1900 093 885	0.1925 084 396	0.1950 075 872	0.1975 068 215	57
58	0.1900 078 895	0.1925 070 772	0.1950 063 491	0.1975 056 964	58
59	0.1900 066 298	0.1925 059 347	0.1950 053 130	0.1975 047 569	59
60	0.1900 055 712	0.1925 049 767	0.1950 044 460	0.1975 039 723	60

YEARLY
Compounding

TABLE 6. PARTIAL PAYMENT TO AMORTIZE ONE
Payable at end of each period

YEARS	20% Nominal Annual Rate	20¼% Nominal Annual Rate	20½% Nominal Annual Rate	20¾% Nominal Annual Rate	YEARS
1	1.2000 000 000	1.2025 000 000	1.2050 000 000	1.2075 000 000	1
2	0.6545 454 545	0.6565 295 119	0.6585 147 392	0.6605 011 325	2
3	0.4747 252 747	0.4765 847 710	0.4784 463 122	0.4803 098 907	3
4	0.3862 891 207	0.3881 207 489	0.3899 551 857	0.3917 924 191	4
5	0.3343 797 033	0.3362 208 950	0.3380 655 748	0.3399 137 253	5
6	0.3007 057 459	0.3025 739 440	0.3044 462 284	0.3063 225 755	6
7	0.2774 239 263	0.2793 278 411	0.2812 363 570	0.2831 494 432	7
8	0.2606 094 224	0.2625 532 863	0.2645 021 805	0.2664 560 660	8
9	0.2480 794 617	0.2500 649 519	0.2520 558 149	0.2540 520 025	9
10	0.2385 227 569	0.2405 499 844	0.2425 828 412	0.2446 212 696	10
11	0.2311 037 942	0.2331 718 672	0.2352 457 430	0.2373 253 537	11
12	0.2252 649 649	0.2273 723 377	0.2294 856 079	0.2316 046 978	12
13	0.2206 200 011	0.2227 647 045	0.2249 153 270	0.2270 717 813	13
14	0.2168 930 552	0.2190 728 569	0.2212 585 336	0.2234 499 889	14
15	0.2138 821 198	0.2160 946 403	0.2183 129 335	0.2205 368 949	15
16	0.2114 361 350	0.2136 789 328	0.2159 273 513	0.2181 812 788	16
17	0.2094 401 469	0.2117 107 826	0.2139 868 456	0.2162 682 178	17
18	0.2078 053 857	0.2101 014 695	0.2124 027 537	0.2147 091 153	18
19	0.2064 624 532	0.2087 816 795	0.2111 058 536	0.2134 348 491	19
20	0.2053 565 307	0.2076 967 031	0.2100 415 524	0.2123 909 500	20
21	0.2044 439 388	0.2068 029 869	0.2091 664 291	0.2115 341 360	21
22	0.2036 896 187	0.2060 656 084	0.2084 457 036	0.2108 297 749	22
23	0.2030 652 575	0.2054 563 967	0.2078 513 516	0.2102 499 943	23
24	0.2025 478 730	0.2049 525 124	0.2073 606 809	0.2097 722 531	24
25	0.2021 187 290	0.2045 353 602	0.2069 552 408	0.2093 782 486	25
26	0.2017 624 956	0.2041 897 471	0.2066 199 779	0.2090 530 696	26
27	0.2014 665 923	0.2039 032 233	0.2063 425 751	0.2087 845 339	27
28	0.2012 206 684	0.2036 655 616	0.2061 129 302	0.2085 626 657	28
29	0.2010 161 900	0.2034 683 434	0.2059 227 413	0.2083 792 806	29
30	0.2008 461 085	0.2033 046 272	0.2057 651 745	0.2082 276 528	30
31	0.2007 045 936	0.2031 686 812	0.2056 345 966	0.2081 022 481	31
32	0.2005 868 168	0.2030 557 668	0.2055 263 590	0.2079 985 076	32
33	0.2004 887 750	0.2029 619 626	0.2054 366 217	0.2079 126 723	33
34	0.2004 071 466	0.2028 840 210	0.2053 622 104	0.2078 416 409	34
35	0.2003 391 738	0.2028 192 502	0.2053 004 992	0.2077 828 524	35
36	0.2002 825 649	0.2027 654 183	0.2052 493 148	0.2077 341 914	36
37	0.2002 354 154	0.2027 206 734	0.2052 068 574	0.2076 939 097	37
38	0.2001 961 410	0.2026 834 785	0.2051 716 365	0.2076 605 620	38
39	0.2001 634 241	0.2026 525 576	0.2051 424 166	0.2076 329 529	39
40	0.2001 361 682	0.2026 268 509	0.2051 181 741	0.2076 100 938	40
41	0.2001 134 606	0.2026 054 782	0.2050 980 602	0.2075 911 667	41
42	0.2000 945 416	0.2025 877 081	0.2050 813 711	0.2075 754 947	42
43	0.2000 787 785	0.2025 729 328	0.2050 675 233	0.2075 625 175	43
44	0.2000 656 444	0.2025 606 473	0.2050 560 328	0.2075 517 717	44
45	0.2000 547 007	0.2025 504 318	0.2050 464 981	0.2075 428 733	45
46	0.2000 455 818	0.2025 419 374	0.2050 385 861	0.2075 355 045	46
47	0.2000 379 834	0.2025 348 739	0.2050 320 207	0.2075 294 025	47
48	0.2000 316 518	0.2025 290 003	0.2050 265 725	0.2075 243 493	48
49	0.2000 263 758	0.2025 241 161	0.2050 220 514	0.2075 201 646	49
50	0.2000 219 794	0.2025 200 546	0.2050 182 995	0.2075 166 992	50
51	0.2000 183 158	0.2025 166 771	0.2050 151 861	0.2075 138 294	51
52	0.2000 152 629	0.2025 138 685	0.2050 126 024	0.2075 114 528	52
53	0.2000 127 190	0.2025 115 329	0.2050 104 583	0.2075 094 846	53
54	0.2000 105 990	0.2025 095 907	0.2050 086 790	0.2075 078 547	54
55	0.2000 088 324	0.2025 079 756	0.2050 072 025	0.2075 065 049	55
56	0.2000 073 603	0.2025 066 325	0.2050 059 771	0.2075 053 870	56
57	0.2000 061 336	0.2025 055 155	0.2050 049 602	0.2075 044 613	57
58	0.2000 051 113	0.2025 045 867	0.2050 041 164	0.2075 036 946	58
59	0.2000 042 594	0.2025 038 143	0.2050 034 161	0.2075 030 597	59
60	0.2000 035 495	0.2025 031 720	0.2050 028 349	0.2075 025 339	60

TABLE 6. PARTIAL PAYMENT TO AMORTIZE ONE

Payable at end of each period

YEARLY Compounding

YEARS	21% Nominal Annual Rate	21¼% Nominal Annual Rate	21½% Nominal Annual Rate	21¾% Nominal Annual Rate	YEARS
1	1.2100 000 000	1.2125 000 000	1.2150 000 000	1.2175 000 000	1
2	0.6624 886 878	0.6644 774 011	0.6664 672 686	0.6684 582 864	2
3	0.4821 754 988	0.4840 431 287	0.4859 127 729	0.4877 844 237	3
4	0.3936 324 369	0.3954 752 272	0.3973 207 780	0.3991 690 774	4
5	0.3417 653 293	0.3436 203 694	0.3454 788 284	0.3473 406 893	5
6	0.3082 029 617	0.3100 873 635	0.3119 757 574	0.3138 681 200	6
7	0.2850 670 688	0.2869 892 029	0.2889 158 150	0.2908 468 744	7
8	0.2684 149 035	0.2703 786 541	0.2723 472 791	0.2743 207 399	8
9	0.2560 534 667	0.2580 601 595	0.2600 720 334	0.2620 890 411	9
10	0.2466 652 120	0.2487 146 112	0.2507 694 102	0.2528 295 526	10
11	0.2394 106 322	0.2415 015 115	0.2435 979 253	0.2456 998 078	11
12	0.2337 295 303	0.2358 600 292	0.2379 961 186	0.2401 377 235	12
13	0.2292 339 810	0.2314 018 405	0.2335 752 752	0.2357 542 012	13
14	0.2256 471 276	0.2278 498 557	0.2300 580 800	0.2322 717 088	14
15	0.2227 664 213	0.2250 014 110	0.2272 417 634	0.2294 873 796	15
16	0.2204 406 051	0.2227 052 217	0.2249 750 219	0.2272 499 005	16
17	0.2185 547 835	0.2208 464 285	0.2231 430 410	0.2254 445 111	17
18	0.2170 204 340	0.2193 365 916	0.2216 574 724	0.2239 829 628	18
19	0.2157 685 424	0.2181 068 125	0.2204 495 409	0.2227 966 119	19
20	0.2147 447 703	0.2171 028 907	0.2194 651 915	0.2218 315 559	20
21	0.2139 059 812	0.2162 818 419	0.2186 615 982	0.2210 451 335	21
22	0.2132 176 967	0.2156 093 467	0.2180 046 062	0.2204 033 599	22
23	0.2126 522 006	0.2150 578 502	0.2174 668 266	0.2198 790 166	23
24	0.2121 871 074	0.2146 051 263	0.2170 261 962	0.2194 502 070	24
25	0.2118 042 655	0.2142 331 775	0.2166 648 747	0.2190 992 511	25
26	0.2114 889 084	0.2139 273 844	0.2163 683 922	0.2188 118 301	26
27	0.2112 289 905	0.2136 758 400	0.2161 249 817	0.2185 763 188	27
28	0.2110 146 640	0.2134 688 254	0.2159 250 544	0.2183 832 592	28
29	0.2108 378 627	0.2132 983 934	0.2157 607 824	0.2182 249 437	29
30	0.2106 919 694	0.2131 580 354	0.2156 257 665	0.2180 950 819	30
31	0.2105 715 487	0.2130 424 153	0.2155 147 690	0.2179 885 349	31
32	0.2104 721 313	0.2129 471 528	0.2154 234 988	0.2179 010 997	32
33	0.2103 900 389	0.2128 686 498	0.2153 484 372	0.2178 293 369	33
34	0.2103 222 423	0.2128 039 487	0.2152 866 974	0.2177 704 294	34
35	0.2102 662 451	0.2127 506 165	0.2152 359 093	0.2177 220 693	35
36	0.2102 199 889	0.2127 066 513	0.2151 941 263	0.2176 823 645	36
37	0.2101 817 759	0.2126 704 050	0.2151 597 492	0.2176 497 636	37
38	0.2101 502 055	0.2126 405 205	0.2151 314 636	0.2176 229 940	38
39	0.2101 241 213	0.2126 158 798	0.2151 081 888	0.2176 010 116	39
40	0.2101 025 691	0.2125 955 618	0.2150 890 363	0.2175 829 595	40
41	0.2100 847 607	0.2125 788 076	0.2150 732 755	0.2175 681 346	41
42	0.2100 700 452	0.2125 649 918	0.2150 603 055	0.2175 559 596	42
43	0.2100 578 853	0.2125 535 986	0.2150 496 317	0.2175 459 606	43
44	0.2100 478 368	0.2125 442 031	0.2150 408 474	0.2175 377 485	44
45	0.2100 395 330	0.2125 364 548	0.2150 336 182	0.2175 310 040	45
46	0.2100 326 708	0.2125 300 649	0.2150 276 685	0.2175 254 646	46
47	0.2100 269 999	0.2125 247 952	0.2150 227 719	0.2175 209 151	47
48	0.2100 223 135	0.2125 204 492	0.2150 187 420	0.2175 171 784	48
49	0.2100 184 406	0.2125 168 651	0.2150 154 252	0.2175 141 094	49
50	0.2100 152 399	0.2125 139 091	0.2150 126 955	0.2175 115 887	50
51	0.2100 125 948	0.2125 114 713	0.2150 104 489	0.2175 095 183	51
52	0.2100 104 088	0.2125 094 608	0.2150 085 998	0.2175 078 179	52
53	0.2100 086 023	0.2125 078 027	0.2150 070 780	0.2175 064 212	53
54	0.2100 071 093	0.2125 064 351	0.2150 058 255	0.2175 052 741	54
55	0.2100 058 754	0.2125 053 073	0.2150 047 946	0.2175 043 319	55
56	0.2100 048 557	0.2125 043 771	0.2150 039 462	0.2175 035 580	56
57	0.2100 040 129	0.2125 036 100	0.2150 032 479	0.2175 029 224	57
58	0.2100 033 165	0.2125 029 773	0.2150 026 731	0.2175 024 003	58
59	0.2100 027 409	0.2125 024 555	0.2150 022 001	0.2175 019 715	59
60	0.2100 022 652	0.2125 020 252	0.2150 018 108	0.2175 016 193	60

TABLE 6. PARTIAL PAYMENT TO AMORTIZE ONE
Payable at end of each period

YEARS	22% Nominal Annual Rate	22¼% Nominal Annual Rate	22½% Nominal Annual Rate	22¾% Nominal Annual Rate	YEARS
1	1.2200 000 000	1.2225 000 000	1.2250 000 000	1.2275 000 000	1
2	0.6704 504 505	0.6724 437 570	0.6744 382 022	0.6764 337 823	2
3	0.4896 580 736	0.4915 337 150	0.4934 113 404	0.4952 909 423	3
4	0.4010 201 135	0.4028 738 744	0.4047 303 483	0.4065 895 235	4
5	0.3492 059 348	0.3510 745 481	0.3529 465 120	0.3548 218 096	5
6	0.3157 644 282	0.3176 646 586	0.3195 687 881	0.3214 767 936	6
7	0.2927 823 508	0.2947 222 137	0.2966 664 329	0.2986 149 784	7
8	0.2762 989 979	0.2782 820 148	0.2802 697 526	0.2822 621 732	8
9	0.2641 111 354	0.2661 382 693	0.2681 703 963	0.2702 074 699	9
10	0.2548 949 820	0.2569 656 428	0.2590 414 793	0.2611 224 365	10
11	0.2478 070 935	0.2499 197 175	0.2520 376 154	0.2541 607 234	11
12	0.2422 847 695	0.2444 371 829	0.2465 948 907	0.2487 578 204	12
13	0.2379 385 355	0.2401 281 963	0.2423 231 022	0.2445 231 730	13
14	0.2344 906 512	0.2367 148 177	0.2389 441 198	0.2411 784 701	14
15	0.2317 381 620	0.2339 940 142	0.2362 548 416	0.2385 205 506	15
16	0.2295 297 542	0.2318 144 814	0.2341 039 818	0.2363 981 572	16
17	0.2277 507 309	0.2300 615 943	0.2323 769 974	0.2346 968 380	17
18	0.2263 129 516	0.2286 473 298	0.2309 859 908	0.2333 288 300	18
19	0.2251 479 123	0.2275 033 314	0.2298 627 611	0.2322 260 956	19
20	0.2242 018 701	0.2265 760 227	0.2289 539 055	0.2313 354 127	20
21	0.2234 323 343	0.2258 230 901	0.2282 172 935	0.2306 148 399	21
22	0.2228 054 958	0.2252 109 052	0.2276 194 824	0.2300 311 250	22
23	0.2222 943 108	0.2247 126 029	0.2271 337 902	0.2295 577 731	23
24	0.2218 770 526	0.2243 066 303	0.2267 388 407	0.2291 735 880	24
25	0.2215 362 042	0.2239 756 355	0.2264 174 498	0.2288 615 554	25
26	0.2212 576 002	0.2237 056 085	0.2261 557 645	0.2286 079 811	26
27	0.2210 297 583	0.2234 852 112	0.2259 425 919	0.2284 018 183	27
28	0.2208 433 524	0.2233 052 498	0.2257 688 712	0.2282 341 395	28
29	0.2206 907 949	0.2231 582 575	0.2256 272 562	0.2280 977 195	29
30	0.2205 659 049	0.2230 381 621	0.2255 117 839	0.2279 867 035	30
31	0.2204 636 414	0.2229 400 207	0.2254 176 083	0.2278 963 427	31
32	0.2203 798 896	0.2228 598 056	0.2253 407 885	0.2278 227 819	32
33	0.2203 112 880	0.2227 942 330	0.2252 781 173	0.2277 628 896	33
34	0.2202 550 890	0.2227 406 234	0.2252 269 830	0.2277 141 208	34
35	0.2202 090 456	0.2226 967 903	0.2251 852 579	0.2276 744 061	35
36	0.2201 713 195	0.2226 609 477	0.2251 512 081	0.2276 420 622	36
37	0.2201 404 061	0.2226 316 372	0.2251 234 200	0.2276 157 195	37
38	0.2201 150 737	0.2226 076 671	0.2251 007 408	0.2275 942 637	38
39	0.2200 943 138	0.2225 880 635	0.2250 822 307	0.2275 767 873	39
40	0.2200 773 005	0.2225 720 304	0.2250 671 226	0.2275 625 519	40
41	0.2200 633 570	0.2225 589 171	0.2250 547 909	0.2275 509 562	41
42	0.2200 519 293	0.2225 481 916	0.2250 447 253	0.2275 415 105	42
43	0.2200 425 632	0.2225 394 190	0.2250 365 091	0.2275 338 159	43
44	0.2200 348 866	0.2225 322 435	0.2250 298 025	0.2275 275 479	44
45	0.2200 285 948	0.2225 263 744	0.2250 243 279	0.2275 224 417	45
46	0.2200 234 378	0.2225 215 737	0.2250 198 592	0.2275 182 821	46
47	0.2200 192 109	0.2225 176 469	0.2250 162 113	0.2275 148 936	47
48	0.2200 157 464	0.2225 144 349	0.2250 132 335	0.2275 121 331	48
49	0.2200 129 067	0.2225 118 075	0.2250 108 028	0.2275 098 843	49
50	0.2200 105 792	0.2225 096 584	0.2250 088 185	0.2275 080 523	50
51	0.2200 086 714	0.2225 079 005	0.2250 071 987	0.2275 065 599	51
52	0.2200 071 076	0.2225 064 625	0.2250 058 765	0.2275 053 441	52
53	0.2200 058 259	0.2225 052 863	0.2250 047 971	0.2275 043 536	53
54	0.2200 047 753	0.2225 043 241	0.2250 039 160	0.2275 035 467	54
55	0.2200 039 142	0.2225 035 371	0.2250 031 967	0.2275 028 894	55
56	0.2200 032 083	0.2225 028 933	0.2250 026 096	0.2275 023 539	56
57	0.2200 026 298	0.2225 023 667	0.2250 021 302	0.2275 019 176	57
58	0.2200 021 555	0.2225 019 360	0.2250 017 390	0.2275 015 622	58
59	0.2200 017 668	0.2225 015 836	0.2250 014 196	0.2275 012 727	59
60	0.2200 014 482	0.2225 012 954	0.2250 011 588	0.2275 010 368	60

TABLE 6. PARTIAL PAYMENT TO AMORTIZE ONE
Payable at end of each period

YEARLY Compounding

YEARS	23% Nominal Annual Rate	24% Nominal Annual Rate	25% Nominal Annual Rate	26% Nominal Annual Rate	YEARS
1	1.2300 000 000	1.2400 000 000	1.2500 000 000	1.2600 000 000	1
2	0.6784 304 933	0.6864 285 714	0.6944 444 444	0.7024 778 761	2
3	0.4971 725 133	0.5047 183 397	0.5122 950 820	0.5199 022 767	3
4	0.4084 513 881	0.4159 255 089	0.4234 417 344	0.4309 993 338	4
5	0.3567 004 241	0.3642 477 149	0.3718 467 396	0.3794 964 454	5
6	0.3233 886 522	0.3310 741 602	0.3388 194 987	0.3466 232 355	6
7	0.3005 678 200	0.3084 215 522	0.3163 416 530	0.3243 262 593	7
8	0.2842 592 389	0.2922 932 018	0.3003 985 063	0.3085 728 187	8
9	0.2722 494 441	0.2804 654 313	0.2887 562 013	0.2971 189 268	9
10	0.2632 084 594	0.2716 021 271	0.2800 725 624	0.2886 164 407	10
11	0.2562 889 780	0.2648 522 131	0.2734 928 576	0.2822 071 051	11
12	0.2509 259 004	0.2596 483 138	0.2684 475 770	0.2773 194 369	12
13	0.2467 283 293	0.2555 982 535	0.2645 434 288	0.2735 592 056	13
14	0.2434 177 823	0.2524 229 653	0.2615 009 326	0.2706 467 022	14
15	0.2407 910 491	0.2499 191 452	0.2591 168 642	0.2683 789 634	15
16	0.2386 969 108	0.2479 358 295	0.2572 406 815	0.2666 060 410	16
17	0.2370 210 160	0.2463 591 647	0.2557 591 848	0.2652 155 451	17
18	0.2356 757 451	0.2451 021 928	0.2545 862 176	0.2641 222 582	18
19	0.2345 932 318	0.2440 978 105	0.2536 555 619	0.2632 609 648	19
20	0.2337 204 414	0.2432 938 009	0.2529 159 221	0.2625 813 865	20
21	0.2330 156 276	0.2426 492 538	0.2523 273 086	0.2620 445 308	21
22	0.2324 457 335	0.2421 319 401	0.2518 583 869	0.2616 200 148	22
23	0.2319 844 553	0.2417 163 556	0.2514 845 025	0.2612 840 750	23
24	0.2316 107 795	0.2413 822 445	0.2511 861 933	0.2610 180 696	24
25	0.2313 078 641	0.2411 134 721	0.2509 480 549	0.2608 073 395	25
26	0.2310 621 747	0.2408 971 558	0.2507 578 692	0.2606 403 353	26
27	0.2308 628 116	0.2407 229 896	0.2506 059 280	0.2605 079 445	27
28	0.2307 009 811	0.2405 827 164	0.2504 845 075	0.2604 029 681	28
29	0.2305 695 787	0.2404 697 118	0.2503 874 558	0.2603 197 137	29
30	0.2304 628 578	0.2403 786 564	0.2503 098 686	0.2602 536 767	30
31	0.2303 761 656	0.2403 052 749	0.2502 478 335	0.2602 012 902	31
32	0.2303 057 322	0.2402 461 288	0.2501 982 275	0.2601 597 286	32
33	0.2302 485 010	0.2401 984 516	0.2501 585 568	0.2601 267 526	33
34	0.2302 019 925	0.2401 600 160	0.2501 268 294	0.2601 005 872	34
35	0.2301 641 946	0.2401 290 285	0.2501 014 532	0.2600 798 248	35
36	0.2301 334 737	0.2401 040 444	0.2500 811 560	0.2600 633 490	36
37	0.2301 085 034	0.2400 838 998	0.2500 649 206	0.2600 502 744	37
38	0.2300 882 064	0.2400 676 565	0.2500 519 338	0.2600 398 987	38
39	0.2300 717 074	0.2400 545 587	0.2500 415 453	0.2600 316 647	39
40	0.2300 582 953	0.2400 439 970	0.2500 332 351	0.2600 251 301	40
41	0.2300 473 923	0.2400 354 802	0.2500 265 874	0.2600 199 441	41
42	0.2300 385 288	0.2400 286 123	0.2500 212 695	0.2600 158 284	42
43	0.2300 313 233	0.2400 230 739	0.2500 170 153	0.2600 125 621	43
44	0.2300 254 654	0.2400 186 076	0.2500 136 120	0.2600 099 698	44
45	0.2300 207 032	0.2400 150 059	0.2500 108 895	0.2600 079 125	45
46	0.2300 168 316	0.2400 121 014	0.2500 087 115	0.2600 062 797	46
47	0.2300 136 840	0.2400 097 591	0.2500 069 692	0.2600 049 839	47
48	0.2300 111 251	0.2400 078 702	0.2500 055 753	0.2600 039 554	48
49	0.2300 090 447	0.2400 063 469	0.2500 044 602	0.2600 031 392	49
50	0.2300 073 534	0.2400 051 184	0.2500 035 682	0.2600 024 914	50
51	0.2300 059 783	0.2400 041 277	0.2500 028 545	0.2600 019 773	51
52	0.2300 048 604	0.2400 033 288	0.2500 022 836	0.2600 015 693	52
53	0.2300 039 515	0.2400 026 845	0.2500 018 269	0.2600 012 455	53
54	0.2300 032 126	0.2400 021 649	0.2500 014 615	0.2600 009 885	54
55	0.2300 026 119	0.2400 017 459	0.2500 011 692	0.2600 007 845	55
56	0.2300 021 235	0.2400 014 080	0.2500 009 354	0.2600 006 226	56
57	0.2300 017 264	0.2400 011 355	0.2500 007 483	0.2600 004 941	57
58	0.2300 014 036	0.2400 009 157	0.2500 005 986	0.2600 003 922	58
59	0.2300 011 411	0.2400 007 385	0.2500 004 789	0.2600 003 113	59
60	0.2300 009 277	0.2400 005 955	0.2500 003 831	0.2600 002 470	60

TABLE 6. PARTIAL PAYMENT TO AMORTIZE ONE
Payable at end of each period

YEARS	27% Nominal Annual Rate	28% Nominal Annual Rate	29% Nominal Annual Rate	30% Nominal Annual Rate	YEARS
1	1.2700 000 000	1.2800 000 000	1.2900 000 000	1.3000 000 000	1
2	0.7105 286 344	0.7185 964 912	0.7266 812 227	0.7347 826 087	2
3	0.5275 394 679	0.5352 062 066	0.5429 020 510	0.5506 265 664	3
4	0.4385 975 867	0.4462 357 835	0.4539 132 250	0.4616 292 226	4
5	0.3871 957 942	0.3949 437 633	0.4027 393 452	0.4105 815 484	5
6	0.3544 839 602	0.3624 002 847	0.3703 708 441	0.3783 942 967	6
7	0.3323 735 405	0.3404 816 996	0.3486 489 741	0.3568 736 368	7
8	0.3168 138 541	0.3251 193 773	0.3334 872 047	0.3419 152 051	8
9	0.3055 508 517	0.3140 492 925	0.3226 116 401	0.3312 353 605	9
10	0.2972 305 377	0.3059 117 316	0.3146 570 037	0.3234 634 396	10
11	0.2909 912 864	0.2998 418 706	0.3087 554 652	0.3177 288 158	11
12	0.2862 598 204	0.2952 648 341	0.3043 307 636	0.3134 540 701	12
13	0.2826 411 632	0.2917 851 066	0.3009 870 625	0.3102 432 741	13
14	0.2798 555 727	0.2891 231 170	0.2984 451 743	0.3078 178 414	14
15	0.2777 005 351	0.2870 769 943	0.2965 040 669	0.3059 777 755	15
16	0.2760 268 700	0.2854 985 011	0.2950 166 190	0.3045 772 413	16
17	0.2747 231 529	0.2842 773 299	0.2938 737 873	0.3035 086 013	17
18	0.2737 052 382	0.2833 305 344	0.2929 939 453	0.3026 916 595	18
19	0.2729 090 233	0.2825 952 273	0.2923 155 138	0.3020 662 291	19
20	0.2722 853 348	0.2820 234 188	0.2917 917 558	0.3015 868 848	20
21	0.2717 962 439	0.2815 783 010	0.2913 870 314	0.3012 191 924	21
22	0.2714 123 677	0.2812 315 291	0.2910 740 633	0.3009 369 616	22
23	0.2711 108 651	0.2809 612 073	0.2908 319 146	0.3007 202 206	23
24	0.2708 739 325	0.2807 503 797	0.2906 444 794	0.3005 537 091	24
25	0.2706 876 627	0.2805 858 907	0.2904 993 470	0.3004 257 487	25
26	0.2705 411 736	0.2804 575 177	0.2903 869 409	0.3003 273 918	26
27	0.2704 259 395	0.2803 573 080	0.2902 998 642	0.3002 517 764	27
28	0.2703 352 730	0.2802 790 689	0.2902 323 989	0.3001 936 367	28
29	0.2702 639 248	0.2802 179 751	0.2901 801 217	0.3001 489 291	29
30	0.2702 077 716	0.2801 702 640	0.2901 396 097	0.3001 145 477	30
31	0.2701 635 729	0.2801 330 011	0.2901 082 129	0.3000 881 059	31
32	0.2701 287 810	0.2801 038 963	0.2900 838 789	0.3000 677 692	32
33	0.2701 013 921	0.2800 811 624	0.2900 650 182	0.3000 521 274	33
34	0.2700 798 299	0.2800 634 041	0.2900 503 992	0.3000 400 964	34
35	0.2700 628 542	0.2800 495 320	0.2900 390 676	0.3000 308 424	35
36	0.2700 494 891	0.2800 386 954	0.2900 302 840	0.3000 237 244	36
37	0.2700 389 663	0.2800 302 299	0.2900 234 754	0.3000 182 492	37
38	0.2700 306 812	0.2800 236 165	0.2900 181 977	0.3000 140 376	38
39	0.2700 241 578	0.2800 184 501	0.2900 141 065	0.3000 107 981	39
40	0.2700 190 215	0.2800 144 139	0.2900 109 352	0.3000 083 061	40
41	0.2700 149 774	0.2800 112 607	0.2900 084 768	0.3000 063 893	41
42	0.2700 117 931	0.2800 087 974	0.2900 065 711	0.3000 049 148	42
43	0.2700 092 858	0.2800 068 729	0.2900 050 939	0.3000 037 806	43
44	0.2700 073 116	0.2800 053 694	0.2900 039 487	0.3000 029 082	44
45	0.2700 057 571	0.2800 041 948	0.2900 030 610	0.3000 022 370	45
46	0.2700 045 331	0.2800 032 772	0.2900 023 729	0.3000 017 208	46
47	0.2700 035 694	0.2800 025 603	0.2900 018 394	0.3000 013 237	47
48	0.2700 028 105	0.2800 020 002	0.2900 014 259	0.3000 010 182	48
49	0.2700 022 130	0.2800 015 627	0.2900 011 054	0.3000 007 832	49
50	0.2700 017 425	0.2800 012 208	0.2900 008 569	0.3000 006 025	50
51	0.2700 013 721	0.2800 009 538	0.2900 006 642	0.3000 004 635	51
52	0.2700 010 804	0.2800 007 451	0.2900 005 149	0.3000 003 565	52
53	0.2700 008 507	0.2800 005 821	0.2900 003 992	0.3000 002 742	53
54	0.2700 006 698	0.2800 004 548	0.2900 003 094	0.3000 002 110	54
55	0.2700 005 274	0.2800 003 553	0.2900 002 399	0.3000 001 623	55
56	0.2700 004 153	0.2800 002 776	0.2900 001 859	0.3000 001 248	56
57	0.2700 003 270	0.2800 002 169	0.2900 001 441	0.3000 000 960	57
58	0.2700 002 575	0.2800 001 694	0.2900 001 117	0.3000 000 739	58
59	0.2700 002 027	0.2800 001 324	0.2900 000 866	0.3000 000 568	59
60	0.2700 001 596	0.2800 001 034	0.2900 000 671	0.3000 000 437	60